Worlds Together Worlds Apart

SEVENTH EDITION

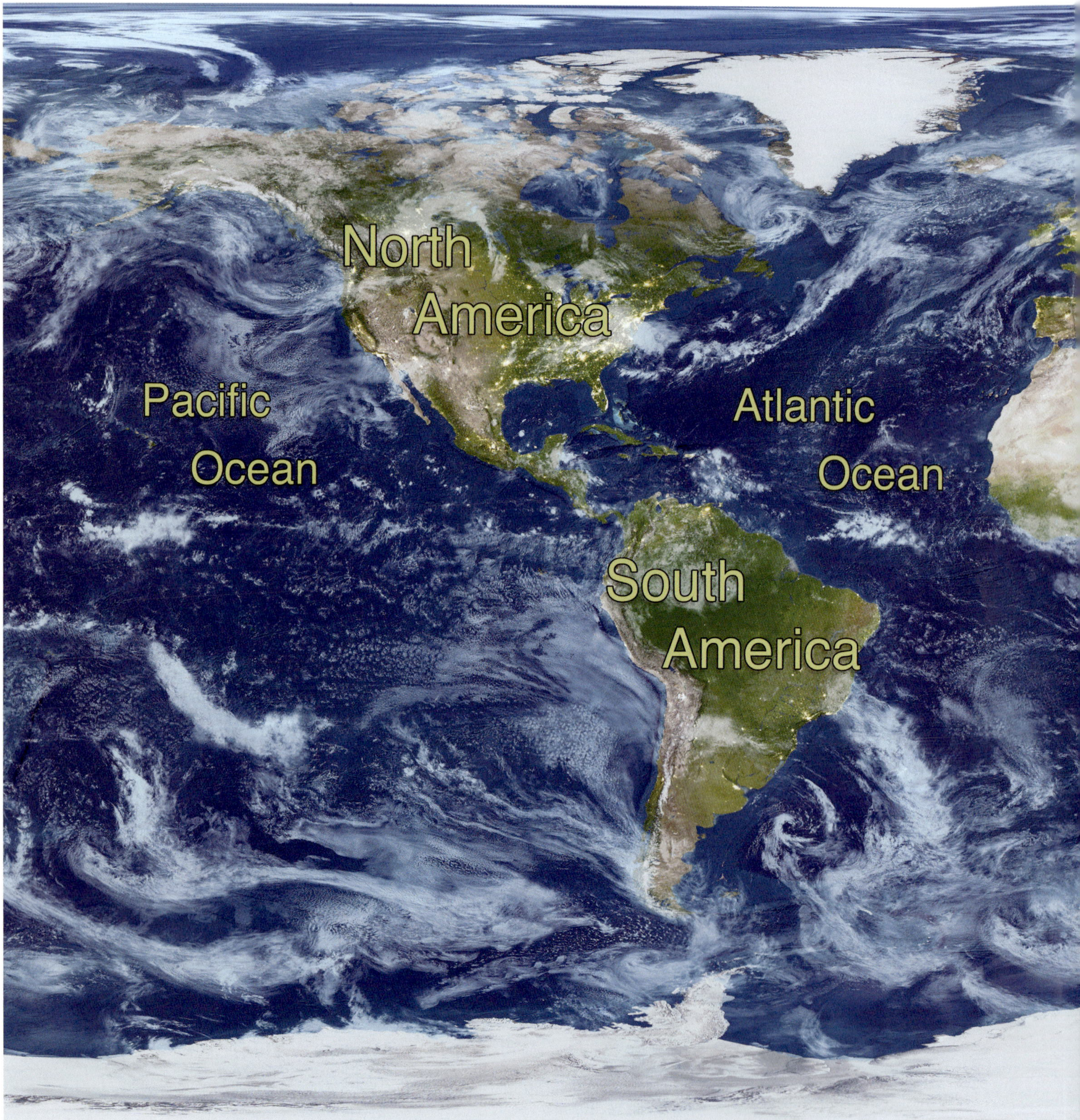
North
America
Pacific
Ocean
Atlantic
Ocean
South
America

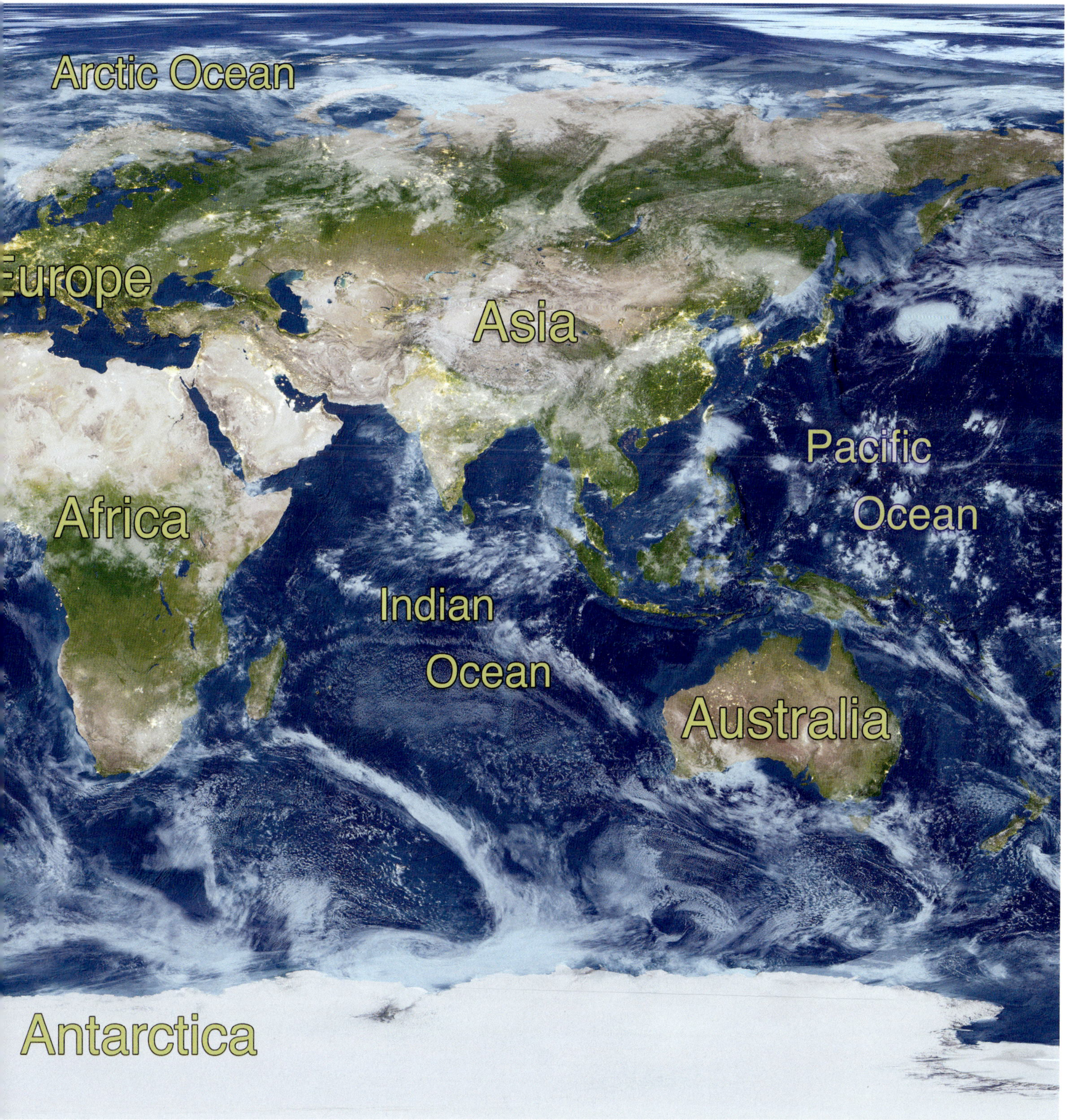
Arctic Ocean
Europe
Asia
Pacific Ocean
Africa
Indian Ocean
Australia
Antarctica

SEVENTH EDITION

Worlds Together Worlds Apart

Volume 2: From 1000 CE to the Present

JEREMY ADELMAN
ELIZABETH POLLARD
ROBERT TIGNOR

W. W. NORTON & COMPANY
Independent Publishers Since 1923

W. W. Norton & Company has been independent since its founding in 1923, when William Warder Norton and Mary D. Herter Norton first published lectures delivered at the People's Institute, the adult education division of New York City's Cooper Union. The firm soon expanded its program beyond the Institute, publishing books by celebrated academics from America and abroad. By midcentury, the two major pillars of Norton's publishing program—trade books and college texts—were firmly established. In the 1950s, the Norton family transferred control of the company to its employees, and today—with a staff of five hundred and hundreds of trade, college, and professional titles published each year—W. W. Norton & Company stands as the largest and oldest publishing house owned wholly by its employees.

Printed in Canada.

Editor: Jon Durbin
Project Editor: David Bradley
Editorial Assistant: Emma Freund
Senior Managing Editor, College: Marian Johnson
Managing Editor, College: Carla Talmadge
Managing Editor, College Digital Media: Kim Yi
Senior Production Manager: Richard Bretan
Media Editor: Carson Russell
Associate Media Editor: Jennifer Jussel
Assistant Media Editor: Clara Drimmer
Media Project Editor: Rachel Mayer
Senior Ebook Producer: Sophia Purut
Marketing Manager, History: Sarah England Bartley
Design Director: Rubina Yeh
Book Design: Marisa Nakasone and Jillian Burr
Photo Editor: Mike Cullen
Director of College Permissions: Megan Schindel
Permissions Specialist: Elizabeth Trammell
Composition: KnowledgeWorks Global, Ltd.
Illustrations: Mapping Specialists, Ltd.
Manufacturing: Transcontinental–Beauceville

Permission to use copyrighted material is included on page C-1.

ISBN: **978-1-324-06399-5**

W. W. Norton & Company, Inc., 500 Fifth Avenue, New York, NY 10110-0017
wwnorton.com

W. W. Norton & Company Ltd., 15 Carlisle Street, London W1D 3BS

1 2 3 4 5 6 7 8 9 0

This edition is dedicated to Robert L. Tignor, a pioneer in world history and founding author and general editor of *Worlds Together, Worlds Apart*.

Contents in Brief

Contents

16 Alternative Visions of the Nineteenth Century 687

Storyline: Global Challenges to Western Expansion

17 Nations and Empires, 1850–1914 731

Storyline: How Nation-States Became Global Empires

20 The Three-World Order, 1940–1975 871

Storyline: World War II and the Emergence of the First, Second, and Third Worlds during the Cold War

22 Twenty-First-Century Global Challenges, 2001–the Present 971

Storyline: The Impact of Modern Globalization Today

Current Trends in World History

Analyzing Global Developments

Global Themes and Sources

CHAPTER 20

CHAPTER 21

CHAPTER 22

Interpreting Visual Evidence

Maps

Preface

Worlds Together, Worlds Apart has set the standard for six editions for those who want to teach a globally integrated and comparative world history survey course. Just as the dynamic field of world history has evolved, so, too, has *Worlds Together, Worlds Apart*. Building on the success of the first six editions, the Seventh Edition continues to offer a coherent, chronological, cutting-edge survey of the field built around world history themes of significance, which we call "Global Storylines." These thematic Global Storylines have the dual benefit of making the material more focused and more manageable for students. They also provide a strong chronological structure to our approach in that each Global Storyline represents a major period in world history. Just as importantly, they allow students to more readily make connections and comparisons across time and place since most, if not all, regions of the world are discussed in many of the chapters. Some of our favorite examples of these thematic Global Storylines include comparing the world's first cities, the creation of the Silk Roads, comparing the Han dynasty and the Roman Empire, the rise and spread of universalizing religions, the destruction and recovery of Afro-Eurasia from the Black Death, the impact of New World silver and the Little Ice Age on global trade, the global impact of the Atlantic and industrial revolutions, alternative visions of societies during the rise of nineteenth-century capitalism, how nation-states became global empires, and the impact of modern globalization today.

NEW TO THE SEVENTH EDITION

Diverse Classroom Experiences

As authors, we are passionate about the global, chronological approach to teaching world history because we have seen it work in our own classrooms. Elizabeth Pollard (author of Volume 1 in the Full and Concise Editions) researches women in the ancient world, is Distinguished Professor for Teaching Excellence at San Diego State University, and has served as both the assessment coordinator for the Arts and Science Division at San Diego State and a consultant to the College Board. Jeremy Adelman (author of Volume 2 in the Full Edition) is an Atlantic World historian, who after many years at Princeton University has moved to Cambridge University, which also will be the new home of his innovative Global History Lab course, a highly popular and well-respected online history of the modern world that he teaches to students around the globe. Each of us has brought our innovative teaching approaches and a cohesive single-author voice to our respective volumes.

From teaching a diverse array of students, we have learned about the challenge of teaching complex global processes—how societies converge, connect, and come together and how global orders fall apart. In addition to teaching a varied set of students, we have also taught world history in multiple formats and settings, including hybrid, fully online, and large lecture classes. In each of these modalities, we have developed extensive experience teaching with primary sources, which the Seventh Edition of *Worlds Together, Worlds Apart* reflects in its unique built-in reader. The Global Themes and Sources and Interpreting Visual Evidence features that appear at the end of each chapter bring a global comparative approach, highlighting the Global Storyline in each chapter to help students learn how to analyze and interpret both textual and visual sources.

New Scholarship on Compelling Topics for Students

Our diverse teaching experience has also made us fully aware that most students taking world history survey courses come from majors across the undergraduate curriculum. As a result, we have purposefully highlighted cutting-edge world history research on a wide range of topics that appeal to students, such as gender, race, migrations, the environment, trade, and technological changes.

In the new Seventh Edition, Chapter 1 discusses the new aDNA research that addresses migration and mixing of populations (rather than arguments over the earliest humans); incorporates new material on a fascinating subspecies of archaic humans known as the Denisovans, who interbred with modern humans; and highlights the newest evidence for earliest humans in the Americas. Chapter 6 now focuses more on the idea of Hellenistic culture and its limits across Afro-Eurasia than on Hellenism. Chapter 8 explores new research that reveals that Sassanian women had more extensive rights than long thought, including freely exercising their civil and legal agency, originating lawsuits, owning property, and conducting business in their name. Chapter 9 has a substantially revised treatment of the history of the rise and early centuries of Islam to create a stronger foundation for understanding the later history of Afro-Eurasia. The new material clarifies the distinction between Islam as a religion and the history of Muslim empires, highlights Islam's continuities with older forms of monotheism and its mechanisms for living productively with large non-Muslim minority populations, and features carefully revised discussions on women and gender in Islamic history to contextualize their experiences. The chapter also includes a fascinating new discussion on the role of elite women in European Christendom, focusing on the social and political role that Charlemagne's daughters played in courtly life. Chapter 10 offers a new heightened focus on how technological innovation and the expansion of major societies led to a dramatic increase in trade and trade networks, making the spread of the bubonic plague even more catastrophic. Chapter 11 has expanded discussions on the impact of the printing press, showing how its use increased literacy rates and how the dissemination of knowledge led people to form collective identities and see themselves in new ways, and it has an updated vignette on Joan of Arc, based on recent research, that explains why she was tried and executed for heresy. Chapter 13 has new discussions on the Little Ice Age and explains how the collapse of Indigenous populations in the Americas cleared the way for a return of trees and bushes to what was once densely tilled land, creating a "carbon sink" that pulled vast quantities of carbon dioxide from the atmosphere and added to the global cooling effect. Chapter 14 offers new coverage on the growth of global knowledge during this major period of cultural flourishing, which benefited elites around the world, while also becoming a business that Europeans began to dominate. New examples focus on the role that European naturalists, both men and women, played in the field of bioprospecting as they acquired knowledge of plants from local herbalists and apothecaries who studied them for their healing powers. Chapter 19 includes a new primary source on the Japanese invasion of Manchuria as part of a larger comparative discussion on global totalitarianism. Chapter 20 offers new and expanded discussions on internationalism in the middle of the twentieth century, with a focus on the creation and impact of the Atlantic Charter, the United Nations, the International Monetary Fund, and the World Bank. Chapter 22 is framed by a new theme of contested globalization and explores the dislocation of millions of people, racial justice protests, and the role of social media in the deepening divides within the world. Further new discussions include Russia's invasion of Ukraine, the ethnic cleansing in Myanmar, and the intense struggles between left- and right-wing regimes in Latin America.

The Seventh Edition looks at world history through the lens of the history of Indigenous peoples and considers what the concept of indigeneity means in world history. These timely new discussions will help instructors and students see history from multiple perspectives and explore a wide range of important current and historical issues, such as group and individual identity, self-determination, sovereignty, race, ethnicity, colonialism, human rights, and reparations.

New discussions in the Seventh Edition include Chapter 3's expanded and up-to-date coverage of migration and settlement in the island chains of early Oceania/Pacific Rim basin, featuring a new section on Aboriginal Australians. Chapter 4 has a new section, "The First Empires and Indigenous Peoples," that explores in depth how the Neo-Assyrian and Persian Empires dealt with Indigenous peoples and how those peoples responded. Chapter 5 offers a new section, "Indigenous Peoples and Colonization," that discusses how Greek and Phoenician colonization and the wealth generated by the colonized cities drew more Indigenous peoples into the processes of violence, conquest, and trade in the Axial Age. Chapter 6 has a new section, "Indigenous Peoples and Hellenistic Culture," that compares the methods and impacts of Alexander the Great and the Macedonians' rule over conquered lands, and the responses of Indigenous peoples. A new section in Chapter 7 explores the different ways that the Roman Empire tried to manage Indigenous peoples, from ethnocide to acculturation to allowing them to maintain their independence. Chapter 10 offers new discussions on borderlands and Indigenous peoples between eastern Europe and the Eurasian steppe, with a focus on the East Slavic peoples and the rise of Kyiv. Chapter 12 has new discussions on Indigenous peoples' powerful religious, medical, and intellectual responses to the massive death rates caused by the biological encounter of the Columbian Exchange. Chapter 13 explores the impact that the rise of global trade built around New World silver had on Indigenous populations around the globe; it includes new vignettes on the Portuguese efforts to subjugate Indigenous peoples in Southeast Asia and the efforts of the Qin dynasty to do the same to the Junghars of central Asia. Chapter 15 compares different types of Indigenous rebellions in the eighteenth century, with a focus on the Haitian and the Andean Indigenous rebellions. Chapter 16 includes a new chapter opener on the Hui Revolt in China, which was notable because it involved a large amount of ethnic cleansing over a long period of time and because it would cause China's ruling dynasties to have special anxiety about religious and ethnic minorities in the territorial fringes of their empire. Chapter 17 has extensive new material on anticolonial resistance throughout the chapter. For example, it explores how the territorial expansions of the United States and Canada affected relations with and the lives of Indigenous peoples in both countries, including the creation of Indigenous empires like the Lakota, an increase in warfare due to the failure of governments to honor treaties, and the rise of the reservation system. Further comparisons are made with Indigenous experiences in Latin America and Africa. Chapter 18 offers new discussions on the effort to modernize immigration policies and laws in western countries to "whiten" the population and the effort to implement new frontier governance policies as a way to segregate races, with South Africa and the Anglo-Boer War serving as a prime example. Similarly, the Maji Maji Revolt serves as an example of European colonizers' efforts to take away land and water rights from Indigenous peoples. Chapter 20 has new Indigenous coverage on the Siberian Chukchi people and the Soviet Union's efforts to assimilate them during its heavy industrialization period. Chapter 21 offers new discussions on the Fourth World and the rise of global Indigenous movements, examining their new use of the language of rights to challenge Eurocentric notions of sovereignty and to demand their own systems of representation. It also features new global examples, with a focus on Indigenous nations in North America, including a vignette on George Manuel, the National Indian Brotherhood, and the World Council of Indigenous Peoples. Chapter 22 discusses the mobilization of Indigenous peoples in the Americas to increase economic development in their sovereign nations and to protect their land and water rights, highlighting the efforts of the Standing Rock Sioux Tribe in North Dakota and the Wet'suwet'en defenders in British Columbia to stop the building of natural gas pipelines through their lands.

New Resources for In-Person, Hybrid, and Remote Learning Experiences

The Seventh Edition is the most innovative to date. Lead media author Alan Karras (University of California, Berkeley) has brought together an outstanding team of media authors to develop a comprehensive support package for the Seventh Edition, substantially increasing the learning and teaching support available to students and instructors for in-person, hybrid, remote, and "flipped classroom" learning modalities.

- NEW: In the **Norton Illumine Ebook**, Norton's high-quality content shines brighter through engaging and motivational features that illuminate core concepts for all students in a supportive, accessible, and low-stakes environment. Embedded "Global View" interactive map features convert the popular two-page map from each chapter into a dynamic, animated tour of the world, walking students through a step-by-step analysis of the map. Check Your Understanding questions with rich answer-specific feedback motivate students and build confidence in their learning. Author videos help students better grasp the key developments in each chapter.
- **Primary Source Exercises** and **Map Exercises** reengage students with important content from the chapter reading that they may have skipped. These exercises exist for each chapter in the book and draw directly from the book's maps and built-in text reader, which includes Global Themes and Sources and Interpreting Visual Evidence features at the end of the chapter. These assignable, interactive learning tools provide the opportunity for critical analysis practice every week of the semester. **InQuizitive**, Norton's award-winning adaptive learning tool, is constructed around the Focus Questions and global comparisons in each chapter. InQuizitive offers an interactive game-like platform that strengthens student comprehension, allowing students to arrive at class better prepared to engage in meaningful discussion.
- **History Skills Tutorials** give students the necessary framework to analyze primary source documents, images, and maps. Guided by videos with author Elizabeth Pollard and supported by interactive assessments, these tutorials help students learn and practice the ways historians think.

OUR GUIDING PRINCIPLES

Five principles inform this book, guiding its framework and the organization of its individual chapters. The first is that **world history is global history**. There are many fine world histories (of which we have endeavored to make good use) that take a more in-depth look at the history of the individual regions of the world in each period. But we have chosen not to deal with the great regions and cultures of the world as separate units—we have not devoted individual chapters to East Asia, South Asia, Southwest Asia, Europe, Africa, and the Americas. Instead, our goal is to place each of these regions in its largest geographical context. Accordingly, we have written chapters that are truly global in that most major regions of the world are discussed in each chapter. We achieved these globally integrated chapters by building each around a significant world history story—a "Global Storyline." It would be misleading, of course, to assert that the context is always "the world," because none of these regions, even the most highly developed commercially, enjoyed prolonged commercial or cultural contact with peoples all over the globe before Columbus's voyage to the Americas and the later expeditions of the sixteenth century. Yet, surprisingly, a "global" story can be told even from the earliest history of humanity. Humans were on the move more than 100,000 years ago and migrated across the planet more than 10,000 years ago. Long after these initial large-scale migrations, the peoples living on the Afro-Eurasian landmass, an important building block for our study, deeply influenced one another, as did the more scattered peoples living in the Americas and in Africa below the Sahara. Products, ideas, and persons traveled widely across the large land units of Eurasia, Africa, and the Americas. Our Global Storylines—sometimes traced across connected regions and sometimes told as comparative narratives—give meaning to these exchanges of goods and ideas and movements of people.

The second principle informing this work is **the importance of chronology in framing world history**. Rather than telling the story of world history by analyzing separate geographical areas, we have framed the chapters around significant world history stories and periods that transcended regional and cultural boundaries—moments or periods of meaningful change in the way that human beings organized their lives. Some of these changes were dramatic and affected many people. The earth became drier and warmer; humans learned to domesticate plants and animals; relationships between men and women changed; innovations in technology, warfare, political organization, and commercial activities occurred; new distributions and accumulations of wealth came about; diseases crossed political and cultural borders; and new religious and cultural beliefs spread far and wide. These changes swept across large landmasses, paying scant heed to preexisting cultural and geographical unity. They affected peoples living in widely dispersed societies, and they often led to radically varied cultural responses in different regions of the world. In other cases, changes occurred in only one locality while other places retained their traditions or took alternative routes. Chronology helps us understand the ways in which the world has, and has not, shared a common history. It also provides a continual forward momentum toward the present for the student, compared to the approach of more regional-based world histories that move forward and then go back within each period as they progress from one regional chapter to another, making it more challenging to make connections and comparisons.

The third principle is **historical and geographical balance**. Ours is not a history focused on the rise of the west. We pay attention to the histories of all peoples and take care not to privilege the developments that led directly into European history, as if the history of the rest of the world were but a prelude to the rise of the west. We engage peoples living outside Europe on their own terms and try to see world history from their perspectives. While we describe societies that obviously influenced Europe's historical development, we do so in a context very different from the one that western historians have stressed. Rather than simply viewing these cultures in terms of their role in western development, we seek to understand them in their own right and to illuminate the ways they influenced other parts of the world. Our presentation of Europe in the period leading up to and including the founding of the Roman Empire is different from many of the standard treatments. The Europeans we describe are rather rough, wild-living, warring peoples living on the fringes of the settled parts of the world and looked down on by more politically stable communities. They hardly seem to be the ilk that will catapult Europeans to world leadership a millennium later—indeed, they were very different people from those who, as the result of myriad intervening and contingent events, founded the nineteenth- and twentieth-century empires whose ruins are still all around us.

Our fourth principle is **an emphasis on connections and disconnections across societal and cultural boundaries**. World history is the history of the connections among peoples often living at great distances from one another, and it is also the history of the resistance of peoples living within and outside societies to connections that threatened to rob them of their independence. A stress on connections inevitably foregrounds the elements within societies that promoted long-distance ties. Merchants are important, as are military men and political potentates seeking to expand their polities. So are scholars and religious leaders, particularly those who believed that they had universalizing messages with which to convert others to their visions. Nomadic pastoral peoples take center stage as agents for the transmission of products, peoples, and ideas across long and harsh distances. They exploded onto the scene of settled societies at critical junctures, erasing old cultural and geographical barriers and producing new unities, as the Arabs did in the seventh century CE and the Mongols did in the thirteenth century. *Worlds Together, Worlds Apart,* as a title, is not intended to convey the message that the history of the world is a story of increasing integration. What for one ruling group brought benefits in the form of increased workforces, material prosperity, and political stability often meant enslavement, political subordination, and loss of territory for other groups. The historian's task, then, is not only to represent the different experiences of increased connectedness, describing worlds that came together, but also to trace the opposite trends, describing peoples and communities that remained, or intentionally grew, apart.

The fifth and final principle is that **world history is a narrative of big stories and broad comparisons**. *Worlds Together, Worlds Apart* is not a book of record or a history of the world. Indeed, in a work that traces global storylines from the beginnings to the present, the notion that no event or individual worthy of attention would be excluded is folly. We have sought to offer clear stories and interpretations that synthesize the vast body of data that often overwhelms histories of the world. Our aspiration is to identify the main historical forces that have shaped human experience and to highlight the monumental innovations that have changed the way humans lived. Cross-cultural comparisons of developments, institutions, and even founding figures receive attention to make students aware that some common institutions, such as family or the economy, did not have the same features in every society. But conversely, the seemingly diverse terms that were used, say, to describe learned and religious people in different parts of the world—monastics in Europe, *ulama* in the Islamic world, Brahmans in India, and scholar-gentries in China—often meant much the same thing in very different settings. We have constructed *Worlds Together, Worlds Apart* around big ideas and stories rather than filling the book with names and dates that encourage students to memorize rather than understand world history concepts.

OVERVIEW OF VOLUME ONE

Volume One of *Worlds Together, Worlds Apart* deals with the period from the beginnings of human history through the development of new political structures like cities, territorial states, and empires and the rise of the world's universalizing religions, all leading toward the emergence of the regions of the world that we recognize today, which then immediately face the major disruptions of the Mongol invasions of the thirteenth century and the spread and destruction of the Black Death across Afro-Eurasia in the fourteenth century. It is divided into eleven chapters, each of which marks a distinct global historical period.

CHAPTER 1 Becoming Human
Global Storyline: Prehistory and the Peopling of the Earth

CHAPTER 2 Rivers, Cities, and First States, 3500–2000 BCE
Global Storyline: Comparing First Cities

CHAPTER 3 Nomads, Territorial States, and Microsocieties, 2000–1200 BCE
Global Storyline: Comparing First States

CHAPTER 4 First Empires and Common Cultures in Afro-Eurasia, 1250–325 BCE
Global Storyline: Comparing First Empires and the Beginnings of Judaism

CHAPTER 5 Worlds Turned Inside Out, 1000–350 BCE
Global Storyline: The Axial Age

CHAPTER 6 Shrinking the Afro-Eurasian World, 350 BCE–100 BCE
Global Storyline: The Creation of the Silk Roads and the Beginnings of Buddhism

CHAPTER 7 Han Dynasty China and Imperial Rome, 300 BCE–300 CE
Global Storyline: Comparing the Han and Roman Empires

CHAPTER 8 The Rise of Universalizing Religions, 300–600 CE
Global Storyline: The Rise of Christianity, the Spread of Buddhism, and the Beginnings of Common Cultures

CHAPTER 9 New Empires and Common Cultures, 600–1000 CE
Global Storyline: Religion and Empire: The Islamic Caliphate, the Tang Dynasty, and Christendom

CHAPTER 10 Becoming "The World," 1000–1300 CE
Global Storyline: The Emergence of the World We Know Today

CHAPTER 11 Crises and Recovery in Eurasia, 1300–1500
Global Storyline: The Black Death, Recovery, and Conquest

OVERVIEW OF VOLUME TWO

The organizational structure for Volume Two reaffirms the commitment to write a decentered, global history of the world that is not moving inevitably toward a "rise of the west" story. Christopher Columbus is not the starting point, as he is in so many modern world histories. Rather, we begin in the eleventh and twelfth centuries with two major developments in world history: the Mongol invasions and the destruction and recovery from the Black Death. From there we describe how major historical processes changed the modern world in significant ways, including the rise of global exploration, the creation of global cultures, the expansion of global trade, alternative visions in the nineteenth century of western expansions, the transformation of nation-states into global empires, the uncertainty and disruption of modernism, World War I and the growth of mass societies, World War II and the emergence of a three-world order during the Cold War, and the emergence and impact of modern globalism today.

CHAPTER 10 Becoming "The World," 1000–1300 CE
Global Storyline: The Emergence of the World We Know Today

CHAPTER 11 Crises and Recovery in Eurasia, 1300–1500
Global Storyline: The Black Death, Recovery, and Conquest

CHAPTER 12 Contact, Commerce, and Colonization, 1450–1600

Global Storyline: The Age of Global Exploration and Colonization

CHAPTER 13 Worlds Entangled, 1600–1750

Global Storyline: The Emergence of Global Trade

CHAPTER 14 Cultures of Splendor and Power, 1500–1780

Global Storyline: The Creation of Global Cultures

CHAPTER 15 Reordering the World, 1750–1850

Global Storyline: The Global Impact of the Atlantic and Industrial Revolutions

CHAPTER 16 Alternative Visions of the Nineteenth Century

Global Storyline: Global Challenges to Western Expansion

CHAPTER 17 Nations and Empires, 1850–1914

Global Storyline: How Nation-States Became Global Empires

CHAPTER 18 An Unsettled World, 1890–1914

Global Storyline: The Global Impact of Modernity

CHAPTER 19 Global Crisis, 1910–1939

Global Storyline: World War I and the Growth of Mass Societies

CHAPTER 20 The Three-World Order, 1940–1975

Global Storyline: World War II and the Emergence of the First, Second, and Third Worlds during the Cold War

CHAPTER 21 Globalization, 1970–2000

Global Storyline: The Emergence of Modern Globalization

CHAPTER 22 Twenty-First-Century Global Challenges, 2001–the Present

Global Storyline: The Impact of Modern Globalization Today

RESOURCES & COURSEWARE

The Seventh Edition of *Worlds Together, Worlds Apart* is supported by a collection of digital resources proven to help faculty meet their course goals—in the classroom and online—and activities for students to develop core skills in reading comprehension, critical thinking, and historical analysis.

For Students

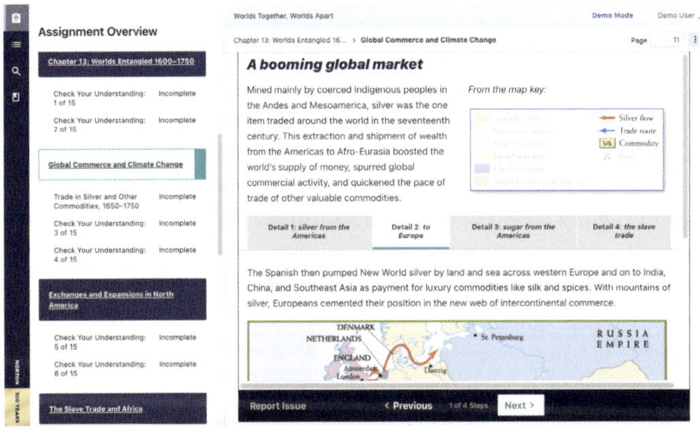

- In the NEW **Norton Illumine Ebook**, Norton's high-quality content shines brighter through engaging and motivational features that illuminate core concepts for all students in a supportive, accessible, and low-stakes environment:
  - CHECK YOUR UNDERSTANDING QUESTIONS are low-stakes questions with rich answer-specific feedback that motivate students and build confidence in their learning.
  - GLOBAL VIEW MAP INTERACTIVES walk students through a step-by-step analysis of Global View maps, breaking down complex keys, geographical features, and chronological processes into their important elements. Animations and embedded questions help students understand the key ideas communicated by the map and allow students to practice map-reading skills.
  - EMBEDDED AUTHOR VIDEOS give students a closer look at the dominant themes in each chapter. All videos are available with transcripts and closed captioning.
  - Key terms include POP-UP DEFINITIONS.
  - IMAGES AND MAPS ARE EXPANDABLE for easy viewing.
  - The active reading experience also includes the ABILITY TO HIGHLIGHT, TAKE NOTES, SEARCH, READ OFFLINE, AND MORE.

Students' progress is tracked as they work toward completion, fostering metacognitive thinking and offering encouragement to keep learning. Instructors can embed their own content into the text and promote student accountability through easy-to-use assignment tools in their campus learning management system.

- To support the continued growth of students' historical skills, *Worlds Together, Worlds Apart* offers a series of brief, assignable **Primary Source Exercises** to accompany every chapter of the book. These exercises give students practice analyzing the primary source documents from the Global Themes and Sources section of the chapter and the primary source images from the Interpreting Visual Evidence section of the chapter, plus a few additional sources from outside the text. Students are asked a series of interactive questions through which they practice analyzing the building blocks of the world history course.

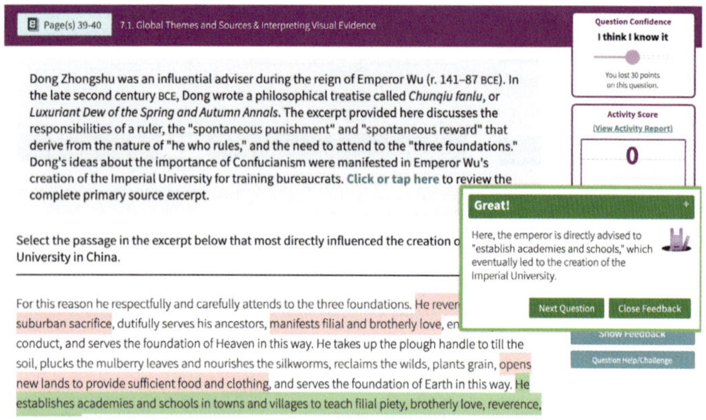

- To provide the opportunity for map-reading practice each week of the semester, *Worlds Together, Worlds Apart* offers stand-alone **Map Exercises** for every chapter of the book. Each exercise extracts the key maps from the chapter and presents students with interactive questions designed to assess their ability to read, dissect, interpret, and draw historical conclusions from the information depicted. Answer-specific feedback helps guide students through the maps and connect the information back to the chapter reading.

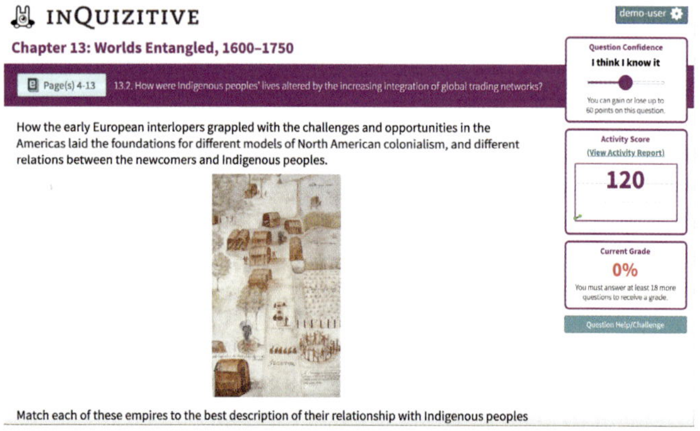

- **InQuizitive** is Norton's award-winning, easy-to-use adaptive learning tool that personalizes the learning experience for students, helping them master—and retain—key learning objectives. Through a variety of question types, answer-specific feedback, and game-like elements such as the ability to wager points, students are motivated to keep working until they've mastered the concepts.

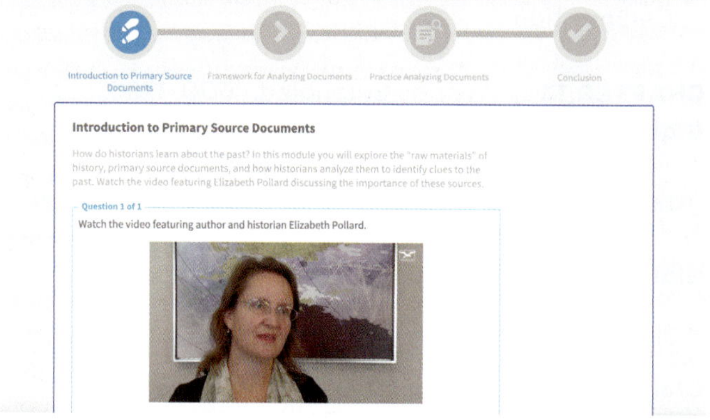

- The **History Skills Tutorials** feature three online modules—"Analyzing Images," "Analyzing Primary Source Documents," and "Analyzing Maps"—to support students' development of the key skills needed for the history course. Each module features author videos modeling the analysis process, followed by interactive questions that will challenge students to apply what they have learned. The tutorials can be integrated directly into an existing LMS, making for easy assignability and easy student access.
- Instructors and students using *Worlds Together, Worlds Apart* receive additional study and review materials to use in or outside class. These resources are available directly to students or via the instructor's LMS. The resources include an **Online Reader** featuring primary source documents and images with support materials such as brief headnotes and discussion prompts; **Flashcards** inviting students to review the key terms from the textbook; and **Chapter Outlines** giving students a detailed snapshot of the key topics of each chapter.

For Instructors

- Easily add high-quality **Norton LMS digital resources** to your online, hybrid, or lecture courses. Get started building your course with our easy-to-use integrated resources; all activities can be accessed right within your existing LMS. The downloadable file includes integration links to the following resources, organized by chapter: the Norton Illumine Ebook, InQuizitive, History Skills Tutorials, Primary Source Exercises, Map Exercises, and Additional Content.
- The **Instructor's Manual** has everything instructors need to prepare lectures and classroom activities: lecture outlines; lecture ideas; classroom activities; image activities; lists of recommended books, films, and websites; and more—great source material for instructors embarking on their first world history course.

- The **Test Bank** contains well over 1,000 multiple-choice, true/false, and short-answer questions. Questions are classified according to level of difficulty and Bloom's Taxonomy, providing multiple avenues for comprehension and skill assessment, and making it easy to construct tests that are meaningful and diagnostic. The Test Bank is available through the new **Norton Testmaker**, which allows you to create assessments for your course from anywhere with an Internet connection, without downloading files or installing specialized software.
- **Lecture PowerPoints and Art PowerPoints**, available for each chapter covered in the text, are fully customizable and feature images, bulleted chapter outlines for in-class presentation, and robust lecture scripts in the Notes section of each slide. Images in the PowerPoints include alt-text, and the slides are designed to be accessible for all students, including students who use screen readers.
- **For the First Day of Class** introductory PowerPoint slides, designed to be shared with students or shown in the classroom early in the semester, help support instructors in delivering transparent assignments, an approach that has been shown to lead to more equitable outcomes. The slides focus on how each Norton product works, what is expected of students, the purpose and relevance of each resource, and strategies for student success.

ACKNOWLEDGMENTS

Worlds Together, Worlds Apart got its start with financial support from Princeton University's 250th Anniversary Fund for undergraduate teaching and, as such, it drew heavily on the expertise of the Princeton history department, in particular, Mariana Candido, Robert Darnton, Natalie Z. Davis, Sheldon Garon, Anthony Grafton, Molly Greene, David Howell, Harold James, William Jordan, Emmanuel Kreike, Elizabeth Lunbeck, Michael Mahoney, Arno Mayer, Kenneth Mills, John Murrin, Susan Naquin, Willard Peterson, Theodore Rabb, Bhavani Raman, Stanley Stein, and Richard Turits. When necessary, the authors of the initial iterations of the book reached outside the history department, getting help from Michael L. Bender, L. Carl Brown, Michael Cook, Norman Itzkowitz, Martin Kern, Thomas Leisten, Heath Lowry, and Peter Schaefer. David Gordon and Shamil Jeppie, graduates of the Princeton history department, offered input as the early editions developed.

The early iterations of *Worlds Together, Worlds Apart* relied on the above-and-beyond administrative support of Judith Hanson, Pamela Long, and Eileen Kane, all at Princeton University. More recent editions owe a debt of gratitude to Emily Pace and Leah Gregory, graduate students at San Diego State University who helped track down sources, images, and permissions.

Reviewers

The quality and range of reviews on this project were truly exceptional. The final versions of the manuscript and the media package were greatly influenced by the thoughts and ideas of numerous instructors, including

Current Edition Reviewers

Emma Alexander, University of Winnipeg
Tannishtha Bhattacharjee, University of California, Santa Barbara
Neilesh Bose, University of Victoria
Shane Carter, University of California, Berkeley
Annette Chamberlin, Virginia West Community College
Brian Cowan, McGill University
Matthew Crawford, Kent State University
Andrew Gallia, University of Minnesota
Emily Gottreich, University of California, Berkeley
Nile Green, University of California, Los Angeles
Jeannie Harding, James Madison University
Andrew Hardy, University of California, Berkeley
Stephen Harp, University of Akron
Matthew T. Herbst, University of California, San Diego
Mark Janda, The Harker School, San Jose, California
Alan Karras, University of California, Berkeley
Eric Kondratieff, Western Kentucky University
Stephen Lazer, Arizona State University
John W. I. Lee, University of California, Santa Barbara
Sheila McManus, University of Lethbridge
Jeffrey Miner, Western Kentucky University
J. N. J. Nammensma, Windesheim University of Applied Sciences
Dana Rabin, University of Illinois, Urbana-Champaign
Babak Rahimi, University of California, San Diego
Charles Scruggs, Genesee Community College (SUNY)
Sarah Stein, University of California, Los Angeles
Erik Vincent, Holy Innocents' Episcopal School
Jan Evert Volders, Windesheim University of Applied Sciences
Jason M. Wolfe, Louisiana State University
Philip Zachernuk, Dalhousie University

Previous Edition Reviewers

Saad Abi-Hamad, Florida International University
Hugh Agnew, Columbian College of Arts and Sciences
Andreas Agocs, University of the Pacific
Stewart Anderson, Brigham Young University
Anthony Barbieri-Low, University of California, Santa Barbara
Michelle Benson-Saxton, University at Buffalo
Brett Berliner, Morgan State University
Carolyn Noelle Biltoft, Georgia State University
Edward Bond, Alabama A&M University
Liam Brockey, Michigan State University

Spencer Brown, Sierra College
Gayle Brunelle, California State University, Fullerton
Kate Burlingham, California State University, Fullerton
Daniel Burton-Rose, Northern Arizona University
Grace Chee, West Los Angeles College
Stephen Colston, San Diego State University
Matthew Conn, Michigan State University
John Corbally, Diablo Valley College
Christian Davis, James Madison University
Paula Devos, San Diego State University
Robert Dietle, Western Kentucky University
Eric Dursteler, Brigham Young University
Beth Fickling, Coastal Carolina Community College
David Gerleman, George Mason University
Norah Gharala, University of Houston
Julie Gibbings, University of Edinburgh
Laura Hilton, Muskingum University
Paul Hudson, Georgia Perimeter College
Holly Hulburt, Southern Illinois University
Bonny Ibhawoh, McMaster University
Stefan Kamola, Eastern Connecticut State University
Alan Karras, University of California, Berkeley
David Kiracofe, Tidewater Community College
Jeremy LaBuff, Northern Arizona University
Senya Lubisich, Citrus College
Elaine MacKinnon, University of West Georgia
Anthony Makowski, Delaware County Community College
Harold Marcuse, University of California, Santa Barbara
Lindsey B. Maxwell, Gulliver Preparatory School
Jamie McCandless, Kennesaw State University
Anthonette McDaniel, Pellissippi State Community College
Jeff McEwen, Chattanooga State Community College
Thomas McKenna, Concord University
Eva Moe, Modesto Junior College
April Najjaj, Texas A&M University
Alice Pate, Kennesaw State University
Chandrika Paul, Shippensburg University
Sandra Peterson, Durham Technical Community College
David Pigott, BYU–Idaho
Jared Poley, Georgia State University
Sara Pulliam, United States Naval Academy
Dana Rabin, University of Illinois, Urbana-Champaign
Masako Racel, Kennesaw State University
Charles Reed, Elizabeth City State University
Alice Roberti, Santa Rosa Junior College
Steven Rowe, Chicago State University
Ariel Salzmann, Queen's University
Lynn Sargeant, California State University, Fullerton
Robert Saunders, Farmingdale State College
Sharlene Sayegh-Canada, California State University, Long Beach
Claire Schen, University at Buffalo
Ethan Segal, Michigan State University
Jason Sharples, Florida Atlantic University
Jeffrey Shumway, Brigham Young University
Greg Smay, University of California, Berkeley
Kristin Stapleton, University at Buffalo
Margaret Stevens, Essex County College
Pamela Stewart, Arizona State University
David Terry, Grand Valley State University
Lisa Tran, California State University, Fullerton
Michael Vann, California State University, Sacramento
Theodore Weeks, Southern Illinois University
Jason Wolfe, Louisiana State University
Reza Yeganehshakib, Saddleback College
Krzysztof Ziarek, University at Buffalo

Publishing a unique book like *Worlds Together, Worlds Apart* involves many talented people. For the Seventh Edition, we would like to thank the following individuals for their substantial contributions to the main text, in particular, the chapters in the early volume: Brent Shaw (Princeton University and an original author of *Worlds Together, Worlds Apart*), Alan Karras (University of California, Berkeley, and lead media author and AP Edition author of *Worlds Together, Worlds Apart*), and Emily Gottreich (University of California, Berkeley). We feel the *Worlds Together, Worlds Apart* media package is the best in the marketplace. We'd particularly like to thank our team of media authors for their extraordinary efforts, including, again, Alan Karras, the lead media author, and his terrific team of media authors—Ryba Epstein, Andrew Hardy, Emily Gottreich, Derek O'Leary, Olivia Benowitz, and Devin Thomas.

And an equally big thanks to our extraordinary book and media team partners at W. W. Norton: Jon Durbin, our print editor for all seven editions; Carson Russell, our media editor; David Bradley, our project editor; Emma Freund, our editorial assistant; Jennifer Jussel and Clara Drimmer, our media team members; Sarah England Bartley, Carrie Polvino, Susan Hood, Cynthia Anderson, and Julie Sindel, our marketing and sales specialist team; Jennifer Greenstein, Rosy Lum, Lynne Cannon Menges, and John Gould, our copy editors; Richard Bretan, our production manager; Rachel Mayer, our media project editor; Marissa Nakasone and Jillian Burr, the book's extraordinary designers; Mike Cullen, our terrific photo editor; and Elizabeth Trammell, our diligent permissions manager.

We dedicate this edition of *Worlds Together, Worlds Apart* to our late colleague and co-author Bob Tignor. Bob passed away late last year after an extraordinary career as an African and world historian. As chair of the History Department at Princeton University for many years, he played a visionary role in internationalizing the focus of the department. The creation of Princeton's first-ever modern world history survey class over thirty years ago with Gyan Prakash was an important part of his global vision and set us on the voyage that has been this book. *Worlds Together, Worlds Apart* grew out of that course and was created to meet the growing demand for a more global approach to world history, one that explained connections as well as divides across societies and regions. He was the founding author and general editor of the book for its first five editions, working tirelessly with all of us to bring the book out in new editions. While we miss Bob greatly as a friend and colleague, his commitment to world history will live on for all of us in *Worlds Together, Worlds Apart*.

Finally, we are grateful for the support and understanding of our family members.

About the Authors

JEREMY ADELMAN (*D.Phil. Oxford University*) has lived and worked in seven countries and on four continents. A graduate of the University of Toronto, he earned a master's degree in economic history at the London School of Economics (1985) and a doctorate in modern history at Oxford University (1989). He is the author or editor of ten books, including *Sovereignty and Revolution in the Iberian Atlantic* (2006) and *Worldly Philosopher: The Odyssey of Albert O. Hirschman* (2013), a chronicle of one of the twentieth century's most original thinkers. He has been awarded fellowships by the British Council, the Social Science and Humanities Research Council of Canada, the Guggenheim Memorial Foundation, and the American Council of Learned Societies (the Frederick Burkhardt Fellowship). For three decades, he conducted his research and taught at Princeton University. He now has joined the faculty at Cambridge University, where he will continue to teach and direct his highly regarded online modern world history survey, The Global History Lab. His next books will be *Latin America: A Global History* and *Earth Hunger: Global Integration and the Need for Strangers*.

ELIZABETH POLLARD (*Ph.D. University of Pennsylvania*) is Distinguished Professor for Teaching Excellence at San Diego State University, where she has been teaching courses in Roman history, world history, and witchcraft studies since 2002. Pollard is the codirector of the Center for Comics Studies and the co-champion of the Comics and Social Justice project for the SDSU president's Big Ideas initiative (2020–present). Her research investigates women accused of witchcraft in the Roman world and explores the exchange of goods and ideas between the Mediterranean and the Indian Ocean in the early centuries of the Common Era. Pollard is currently working on two comics-related projects: an analysis of comics about ancient Rome over the last century and a graphic history exploring the influence of classical understandings of witchcraft on its representations in modern comics. She has also published on various pedagogical and digital history topics, including writing about witchcraft on Wikipedia, tweeting on the back channel of the large lecture, and reporting on digital humanities approaches to visualizing Roman history. Pollard is also deeply immersed in assessment; she served as both the assessment coordinator for the Arts and Science Division at San Diego State University and a consultant to the College Board. She is also the co-editor of *Worlds Together, Worlds Apart: A Companion Reader*, Fourth Edition.

ROBERT TIGNOR (*Ph.D. Yale University*) was professor emeritus and the Rosengarten Professor of Modern and Contemporary History at Princeton University and the four-time chair of the history department. With Gyan Prakash, he introduced Princeton's first course in world history thirty years ago. Professor Tignor taught graduate and undergraduate courses in African history and world history and wrote extensively on the history of twentieth-century Egypt, Nigeria, and Kenya. Besides his many research trips to Africa, Professor Tignor taught at the University of Ibadan in Nigeria and the University of Nairobi in Kenya. Professor Tignor was the founding author and general editor of *Worlds Together, Worlds Apart*.

ALAN KARRAS (*Ph.D. University of Pennsylvania*) is special assistant to the dean of Social Sciences and associate director of Political Economy at the University of California, Berkeley. Professor Karras has previously served as chair of the College Board's test development committee for world history and as co-chair of the College Board's commission on AP history course revisions. The author and editor of several books, he has written about the eighteenth-century Atlantic world and, more broadly, global interactions that focus on illicit activities like smuggling and corruption. An advocate of linking the past to the present, he is now working on a history of corruption in empires, focusing on the East India Company. Professor Karras serves as the lead media author and author of the AP Edition of *Worlds Together, Worlds Apart*.

GEOGRAPHY IN THE ANCIENT AND MODERN WORLDS

Today, geographers usually identify six inhabited continents: Africa, Asia, Australia, Europe, North America, and South America. Inside these continents they locate a vast number of subcontinental units, such as East Asia, South Asia, Southeast Asia, the Middle East, North Africa, and sub-Saharan Africa. Yet this geographic understanding would have been alien to premodern people, who did not think of themselves as inhabiting continents bounded by large bodies of water. Lacking a firm command of the seas, they saw themselves as living on contiguous landmasses. Hence, in this textbook, we have chosen to use a set of geographic terms that more accurately reflect the world of the premoderns.

The most interconnected and populous landmass of premodern times was Afro-Eurasia. The term *Eurasia* is widely used in general histories, but we find it inadequate. The preferred term, from our perspective, must be *Afro-Eurasia*, for the interconnected landmass of premodern—and, indeed, much of modern—times included large parts of Europe and

Asia and significant regions in Africa, particularly Egypt, North Africa, and even parts of sub-Saharan Africa.

It was only in the period from 1000 to 1300 CE that the divisions of the world that we take for granted today began to take shape. The peoples of the northwestern part of Afro-Eurasia did not see themselves as European Christians, and hence as a distinct cultural entity, until the end of the Middle Ages. Islam did not arise and extend its influence throughout the middle zone of Afro-Eurasia until the eighth and ninth centuries CE. Nor did the peoples living in what we today term the Indian subcontinent feel a strong sense of their own cultural and political unity until the Delhi Sultanate and the Mughal Empire brought political unity to that vast region. As a result, we use the terms *South Asia*, *Vedic society*, and *India* in place of *Indian subcontinent* for the premodern part of our narrative, and we use *Southwest Asia* and *North Africa* to refer to what today is designated as the *Middle East*.

Worlds Together Worlds Apart

SEVENTH EDITION

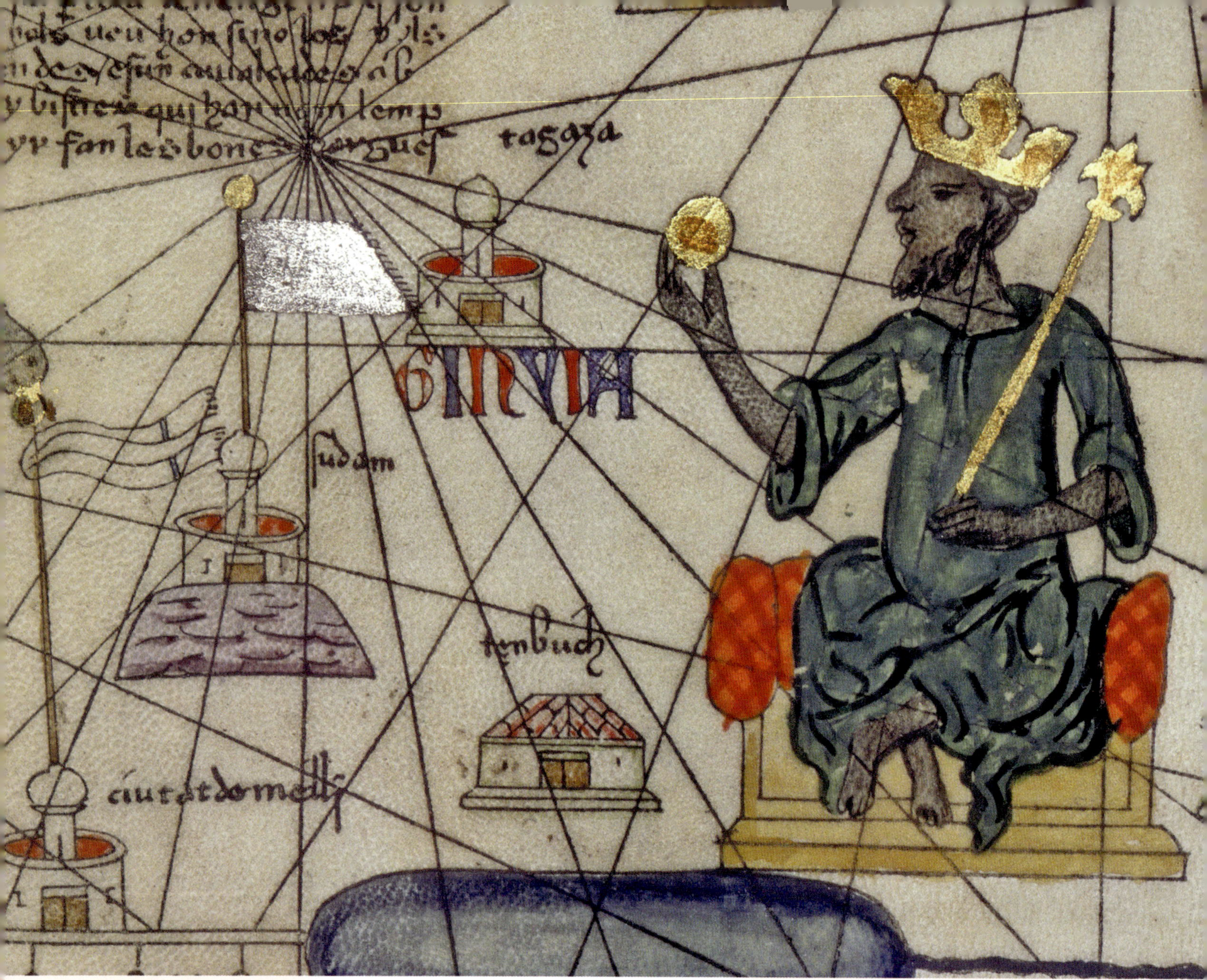

Before You Read This Chapter

GLOBAL STORYLINES

The Emergence of the World We Know Today

- Advances in maritime technology lead to increased sea trade, thereby transforming coastal cities into global trading hubs and deepening the connections across Afro-Eurasia.
- Intensified contact through trade and religion help consolidate four major cultural "spheres": the Islamic world, India, China, and Christian Europe.
- Sub-Saharan African states are integrated into Eurasian exchange networks, resulting in a true Afro-Eurasia-wide network; over the same time period, some states and societies in the Americas experience limited political, economic, and cultural integration.
- The Mongol Empire helps integrate many of Afro-Eurasia's major cultural spheres.

CHAPTER OUTLINE

10

Becoming "The World"

1000–1300 CE

FOCUS QUESTIONS

- What technological advances occurred during this period, especially in ship design and navigation, and how did they facilitate the expansion of Afro-Eurasian trade?
- What social and political forces shaped the Islamic world, India, China, and Christian Europe at this time? To what degree did these forces integrate cultural and geographical areas?
- How did sub-Saharan Africa and the Americas compare with each other, and with the connected Eurasian world, in terms of external interactions and internal consolidation and integration?
- In what ways did the Mongol Empire influence peoples and places across Afro-Eurasia?

Two Nestorian Christian monks, Bar Sāwmā and Markōs, voyaged in the late 1270s from the court of the Mongol leader Kublai Khan in what is now Beijing westward into the heart of the Islamic world and beyond. The monks were not Europeans; rather, they were Uighurs, a Turkish people of central Asia, many of whom had converted centuries earlier to Christianity. The monks hoped to make a pilgrimage to Jerusalem to visit the tombs of martyrs enshrined there and along the way. On their journey, Bar Sāwmā and Markōs traversed a world that had been bound together through economic and cultural exchange. The two monks lingered at the magnificent trading hub of Kashgar in what is now western China, where caravan routes converged at a market for jade, exotic spices, and precious silks. The monks parted ways at Baghdad, unable to continue on to Jerusalem, a result of the route's dangers (including murderous robbers). (See Global Themes and Sources: Primary Source 10.1.) Later, in 1287, Bar Sāwmā was appointed ambassador by the Buddhist Mongol il-Khan of Persia, Arghūn. Bar Sāwmā was assigned to drum up support among

European leaders for an attack on Jerusalem, in order to wrest it from Muslim control. He visited Constantinople (where the Byzantine emperor gave him gold and silver), Rome (where he met with the pope at the shrine of Saint Peter), Paris (where he saw that city's vibrant university), and Bordeaux (where he was welcomed by the English king, Edward I). In the end, neither monk reached Jerusalem nor did they return to China. Bar Sāwmā ended his days in Baghdad, and Markōs became patriarch of the Nestorian branch of Christianity, centered in modern-day Iran. Yet their voyages exemplified the crisscrossing of people, money, goods, and ideas along the trade routes and sea-lanes that increasingly connected the continents of Europe, Asia, and Africa. Collectively known as Afro-Eurasia, places across the region experienced increased interaction after about 1000 CE. As a result of these interactions, disparate locations became to a degree parts of a single entity, which connected locations across the globe's Eastern Hemisphere.

Three related themes dominate the period from 1000 to 1300 CE, at the end of which a monk like Bar Sāwmā could make such a lengthy journey. First, increased trade along sea-based routes caused the dramatic expansion of coastal trading cities. Second, greater trade and religious interaction generated the Afro-Eurasian world's four major cultural "spheres": the Islamic world, India, China, and Christian Europe. The inhabitants within each sphere were connected through shared institutions and beliefs. Societies and states in Sub-Saharan Africa and the Americas also thrived during this period; they remained more fragmented, however, experiencing more limited political and economic integration than in Afro-Eurasia. Third, the Mongol Empire, stretching from China to Persia and even as far as eastern Europe, ruled over huge swaths of land in the world's major cultural spheres. Each of these three themes contributes to an understanding of how places in Afro-Eurasia connected themselves through migration, trade, and religion (including religious conflict) in order to became a "world."

Expansion of Maritime Trade

Even in a single landmass like Afro-Eurasia, sea routes were becoming more important than land networks for long-distance trade by the tenth century CE. Improved navigational aids, better mapmaking, refinements in shipbuilding, and new political support for shipping made seaborne trade easier and slashed its cost. These developments also fostered the growth of maritime commercial hubs (called anchorages), which further facilitated the expansion of maritime trade.

Technological Innovations at Sea

A new navigational instrument spurred this maritime boom: the needle compass. This Chinese invention initially identified promising locations for houses and tombs, but eleventh-century sailors from Guangzhou (Canton) used it to

Belitung Dhow. This museum display in Singapore cleverly depicts a reconstruction of the Belitung dhow (albeit without the signature triangular sail) rising on a wave of Changsha bowls excavated from the actual wreck on the floor of the Java Sea.

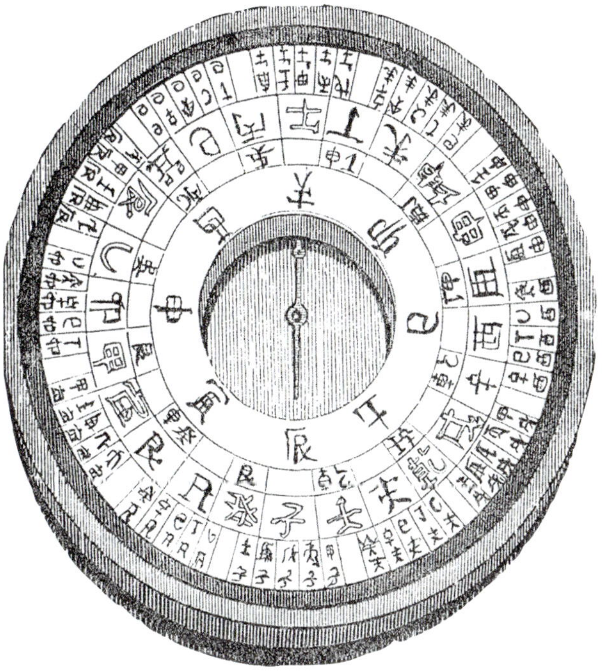

Antique Chinese Compass. Chinese sailors from Guangzhou (Canton) started to use magnetic needle compasses in the eleventh century. By the thirteenth century, magnetic needle compasses were widely used on ships in the Indian Ocean and were starting to appear in the Mediterranean.

find their way on the high seas. The use of this device among sea travelers spread rapidly. The compass not only allowed sailing under cloudy skies but also improved mapmaking.

An array of new ship types—dhows, junks, and cogs—allowed for more impressive mastery of the seas. Dhows, which were ships with triangular sails called lateens, maximized the power of the monsoon trade winds on the Arabian Sea and the wider Indian Ocean. Sailing the South China Sea were junks—large, flat-bottomed ships with internal sealed bulkheads, stern-mounted rudders, as many as four decks, six masts with a dozen sails, and the space to carry as many as 500 men. And, at the other end of Afro-Eurasia, in the Atlantic, cogs, with their single mast and square sail, linked Genoa to distant locations like the Azores and Iceland. The numbers testify to the power of the maritime expansion: while a porter on land could carry about 10 pounds over long distances, and animal-drawn wagons could move 100 pounds of goods over small distances, the Arab dhows could transport up to 5 tons of cargo, Atlantic cogs as much as 200 tons, and Chinese junks more than 500 tons. In short, more transported cargo meant more products in places that were farther and farther away from the cargo's place of origin.

One particularly fascinating archaeological discovery that demonstrates the connections that these ships facilitated is the Belitung dhow. Shipwrecked in the Java Sea off the coast of the Indonesian island of Belitung in the early ninth century CE, this 50-foot ship likely hailed from the southern coast of the Arabian Peninsula (modern-day Oman or Yemen), based on analysis of the wood out of which it was constructed. The ship was filled with more than 60,000 artifacts from Tang dynasty China. Packed with tens of thousands of Changsha bowls (a kind of ceramic from Hunan Province), jars of star anise (a spice from East and Southeast Asia, valued for its medicinal properties), twenty-nine Chinese bronze mirrors, Chinese coins, and many other items, the ship had clearly been loaded in China. Based on some cargo that would have appealed to an Abbasid market, scholars think the Belitung dhow may have been sailing to Basra, in modern-day Iraq. Although the shipwreck dates to a bit earlier than the time frame emphasized in this chapter (to c. 830 CE, based on the writing on a pot and the date of the coins in the wreckage), it nevertheless offers physical evidence for the kind of direct, long-distance maritime trade between China and the Abbasids that increasingly brought the world closer together.

Global Commercial Hubs

After invoking a shipwreck as evidence of increased long-distance trade, it might seem ironic to assert that the business of shipping, on the whole, became less dangerous in the period from 1000 to 1300 CE. This is true not only because of improvements to navigation and innovations in shipbuilding but also because of local political support for expanding commercial connections. Maritime traders enjoyed the protection of political authorities such as the Song rulers in China, who maintained a standing navy that protected traders, as well as lighthouses that guided trading fleets in and out of harbors. The Fatimid caliphate in Egypt profited from maritime trade and defended merchant fleets from pirates, using armed convoys of ships to escort commercial fleets and regulate the ocean traffic. This system of state protection soon spread to North Africa and southern Spain.

In regions with supportive political structures, long-distance trade spawned the growth of commercial cities. (See Map 10.1.) These cosmopolitan **entrepôts** served as transshipment centers located on land between borders or in ports where ships could drop anchor. In these cities, traders exchanged commodities and replenished supplies. Beginning in the late tenth century CE, several regional centers became major anchorages of the maritime trade: in the west, the Egyptian port city of Alexandria on the Mediterranean (and Cairo, just up the Nile); near the tip of the Indian subcontinent, the port of Quilon (now Kollam); in the Malaysian Archipelago, the city of Melaka; and in the east, the Chinese city of Quanzhou. These hubs thrived under the political stability of powerful rulers who recognized that trade would generate wealth for their regimes.

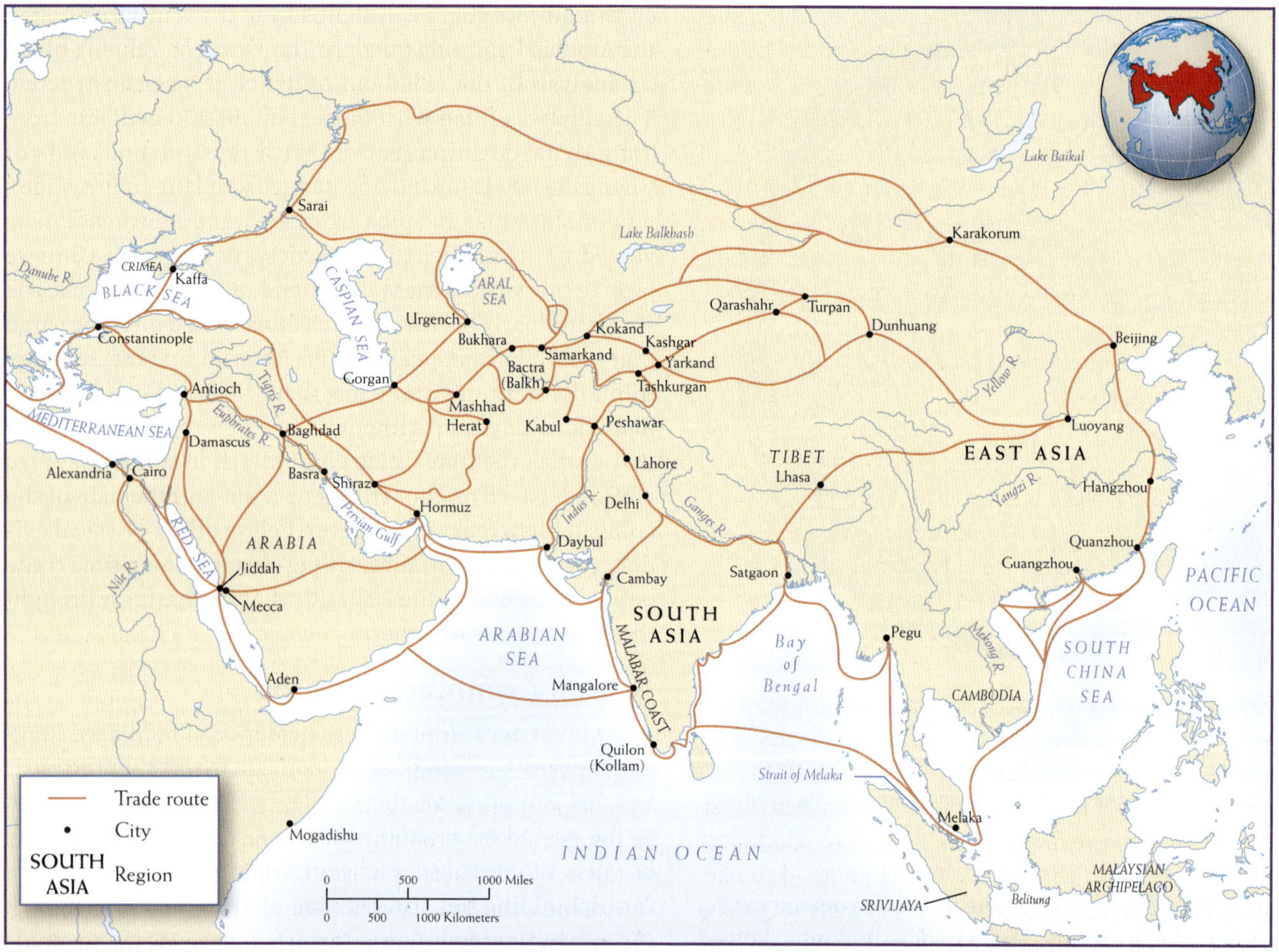

MAP 10.1 | Afro-Eurasian Trade, 1000–1300 CE

During the early second millennium, Afro-Eurasian merchants increasingly turned to the Indian Ocean to transport their goods. Locate the global hubs of Quilon, Alexandria, Cairo, Melaka, and Quanzhou on this map.

- What regions do each of these global hubs represent?
- Based on the map, why would sea travel have been preferable to overland travel?
- According to the text, what innovations in maritime travel facilitated this development?

Cairo and Alexandria were the Mediterranean's main maritime commercial centers. Cairo was home to numerous Muslim and Jewish trading firms, and Alexandria was their lookout post on the Mediterranean. It was through Alexandria that Europeans acquired silks from China, especially the coveted *zaytuni* (satin) fabric from Quanzhou. But many more goods passed through the Egyptian anchorage: from the Mediterranean, olive oil, glassware, flax, corals, and metals; from India, gemstones and aromatic perfumes; and from elsewhere, minerals and chemicals for dyeing or tanning and raw materials such as timber and bamboo. Paper and books (including hand-copied Bibles, Talmuds, and Qurans) traveled across this network as well.

The Islamic legal system prevalent in Egypt promoted a favorable business environment. Legal specialists found a way around the rule that might have brought commerce to a halt—the *sharia*'s (see Chapter 9) prohibition against earning interest on loans. With the clerics' blessing, Muslim traders formed partnerships between those who had capital to lend and those who needed money to expand their businesses: owners of capital entrusted their money or commodities to agents who, after completing their work, returned the investment and a share of the profits to the owners—and kept the rest as their reward. The English word *risk* derives from the Arabic *rizq*, the extra allowance paid to merchants in lieu of interest. As we saw with the Belitung shipwreck possibly bound for Basra (a Persian Gulf port city of the Islamic Abbasid caliphate), shipping was indeed a risky business.

The Cairo Geniza—a cache of documents dating from around 800 CE through the nineteenth century that was preserved by the Jewish community because the documents had the name of God written on them—contains a series of correspondence among a network of Jewish traders from Egypt, the southern Arabian Peninsula, and the west coast of India. For example, Joseph Ben Abraham, a Jewish merchant living in Aden, wrote multiple letters to Abraham Ben Yiju, who lived on the southwest coast of India around 1130. Joseph's letters to Abraham mention shipwrecks and cargo loss, giving insight into the risks of Indian Ocean trade: goods (like betel nuts and spices) received for trading, raw materials sent for manufacturing, and gift packages to be distributed by Abraham to Joseph's connections in India. Abraham, Joseph's Indian point of contact, was a Jewish merchant who had moved from North Africa (Tunisia) to Mangalore on the southwest coast of India and married a local maidservant named Ashu, whom he freed and with whom he had children, and whom he used to establish local connections. The correspondence between Joseph, Abraham, and others in their network demonstrates the personal connections that undergirded Indian Ocean trading in the early twelfth century.

During the tenth century CE, about two centuries before Abraham Ben Yiju was operating out of Mangalore, the Chola dynasty in South India began supporting the port of Quilon, which was the nerve center of maritime trade between China and the Red Sea and the Mediterranean. Trade through Quilon continued to flourish long after the Chola golden age had passed away. Personal connections were key to trade at Quilon, as elsewhere, and as we saw with Abraham Ben Yiju. When striking a deal with a local merchant, a Chinese trader might mention his Indian neighbor in Quanzhou and that family's residence in Quilon. Dhows arrived in Quilon laden not only with goods from the Red Sea and Africa, but also with traders, sojourners, and fugitives. Chinese junks unloaded silks and porcelain, and picked up passengers and commodities bound for East Asian markets. Muslims, the largest foreign community in Quilon, lived in their own neighborhoods and shipped horses from Arab countries to India and its southeastern islands, where kings viewed them as symbols of royalty. There was even trade through Quilon's global marketplace in elephants and cattle from tropical countries, though the most common goods were spices, perfumes, and textiles.

East of Quilon, across the Bay of Bengal, Melaka became a key cosmopolitan entrepôt because of its strategic location and proximity to Malayan tropical produce. Indian, Javanese, and Chinese merchants and sailors spent months in such ports selling their goods, purchasing return cargo, and waiting for the winds to change direction so they could reach their onward destinations. During peak season, Southeast Asian ports were crowded with colorfully dressed foreign sailors, local Javanese artisans who produced finely textured batik handicrafts, and traders eager for profit. The traders converged from all over Asia to flood the markets with their merchandise and to search for pungent herbs, aromatic spices, and agrarian staples such as quick-ripening strains of rice to ship out.

In China, the Song government set up offices of seafaring affairs in its three major ports: Quanzhou, Guangzhou (Canton),

Mazu. As much as sailors used compasses, they could still appeal for divine help at shrines devoted to Mazu, the goddess of seafarers. While many Mazu temples of varying size dotted the shorelines of the East and South China Seas, the shrine at Guangzhou now includes a 48-foot-tall statue of Mazu gazing out into the harbor. Mazu's origin story is rooted in the life of a young girl named Lin Mo (living in the late 900s CE) who miraculously saved her family from stormy seas.

and a third near present-day Shanghai. In return for a portion of the taxes on the goods passing through these entrepôts, these offices registered cargoes, sailors, and traders, while guards kept a keen eye on the traffic. All foreign traders in Song China were guests of the governor, who doubled as the chief of seafaring affairs. Every year, the governor conducted a wind-calling ritual. Traders of every regional origin—Arabs, Persians, Jews, Indians, and Chinese—witnessed the ceremony, then joined together for a sumptuous banquet. Although most foreign merchants did not reside apart from the rest of the city, they did maintain buildings for religious worship according to their faiths. A mosque from this period still stands on a busy street in Quanzhou. Hindu traders living in Quanzhou worshipped in a Buddhist shrine where statues of Hindu deities stood alongside those of the Buddhists. Each of these bustling ports increasingly teemed with a cosmopolitan mix of peoples, goods, and ideas that flowed through growing maritime networks thanks to improved ships and better navigational tools.

The Islamic World in a Time of Political Fragmentation

While the number of Muslim traders began to increase in commercial hubs from the Mediterranean to the South China Sea, it was not until the ninth and tenth centuries CE that Muslims became a majority within their own Abbasid Empire (see Chapter 9), and even then rulers struggled to unite the culturally diverse Islamic world. From the outset, Muslim rulers and clerics dealt with large non-Muslim populations, even as some in these groups were converting to Islam. Rulers accorded non-Muslims religious toleration as long as the non-Muslims accepted Islam's political dominion. Jewish, Christian, and Zoroastrian communities within Muslim lands were free to choose their own religious leaders and to settle internal disputes in their own religious courts. They did, however, have to pay a special tax, the ***jizya***, and defer to their Muslim rulers' political decisions. While tolerant, Islam was an expansionist, universalizing faith. Intense proselytizing—especially by Sufi missionaries (whose ideas are discussed later in the chapter)—carried the sacred word to new frontiers and, in the process, reinforced the spread of Islamic institutions that supported commercial and cultural exchange.

Environmental Challenges and Political Divisions

Severe environmental conditions—freezing temperatures and lack of rainfall—afflicted the eastern Mediterranean and the Islamic lands of Mesopotamia, the Iranian plateau, and the steppe region of central Asia in the late eleventh and early twelfth centuries. The Nile's low water levels devastated Egypt, the breadbasket for much of the area. No less than one-quarter of the summer floods that normally brought sediment-enriching deposits to Egypt's soils and guaranteed abundant harvests failed in this period. Driven in part by drought, Turkish nomadic pastoralists poured out of the steppe lands of central Asia in search of better lands, wreaking political and economic havoc everywhere they invaded.

At the same time that climate-driven Turkish pastoralists were migrating in search of better lands and the Islamic faith was spreading across Afro-Eurasia, the *political* institutions of Islam were fragmenting. (See Map 10.2.) From 950 to 1050 CE, it appeared that Shiism would be the vehicle for uniting the Islamic world. The Fatimid Shiites had established their authority over Egypt and much of North Africa (see Chapter 9), and the Abbasid state in Baghdad was controlled by a Shiite family, the Buyids. Each group created universities, in Cairo and Baghdad respectively, ensuring that leading centers of higher learning were Shiite. But divisions also sapped Shiism, and Sunni Muslims began to challenge Shiite power and establish their own strongholds. In Baghdad, the Shiite Buyid family surrendered to the invading Seljuk Turks, a Sunni group, in 1055. A century later, the last of the Shiite Fatimid rulers gave way to a new Sunni regime in Egypt.

The Seljuk Turks who took Baghdad had been migrating into the Islamic heartland from the Asian steppes as early as the eighth century CE, bringing with them superior military skills and an intense devotion to Sunni Islam. When they flooded into the Iranian plateau in 1029, they contributed to the end of the magnificent cultural flourishing of the early eleventh century. When Seljuk warriors ultimately took Baghdad in 1055, they established a nomadic state in Mesopotamia in place of the once powerful Abbasid state that now lacked the resources to defend its lands and its peoples, weakened by famines and pestilence. The Seljuk invaders destroyed institutions of learning and public libraries and looted the region's antiquities. Once established in Baghdad, they founded outposts in Syria and Palestine, then moved into Anatolia after defeating Byzantine forces in 1071.

The Spread of Sufism

Even in the face of political splintering, Islam's spread was facilitated by a popular, highly mystical, and communal form of the religion, called **Sufism**. The term *Sufi* comes from the Arabic word for wool (*suf*), which many of the early mystics wrapped themselves in to mark their penitence. Seeking closer union with God, Sufis performed ecstatic rituals, such as repeating over and over again the name of God. In time, groups of devotees gathered to read aloud the Quran and other religious tracts. Sufi mystics' desire to experience God's love found ready expression in poetry. Most admired of Islam's mystic

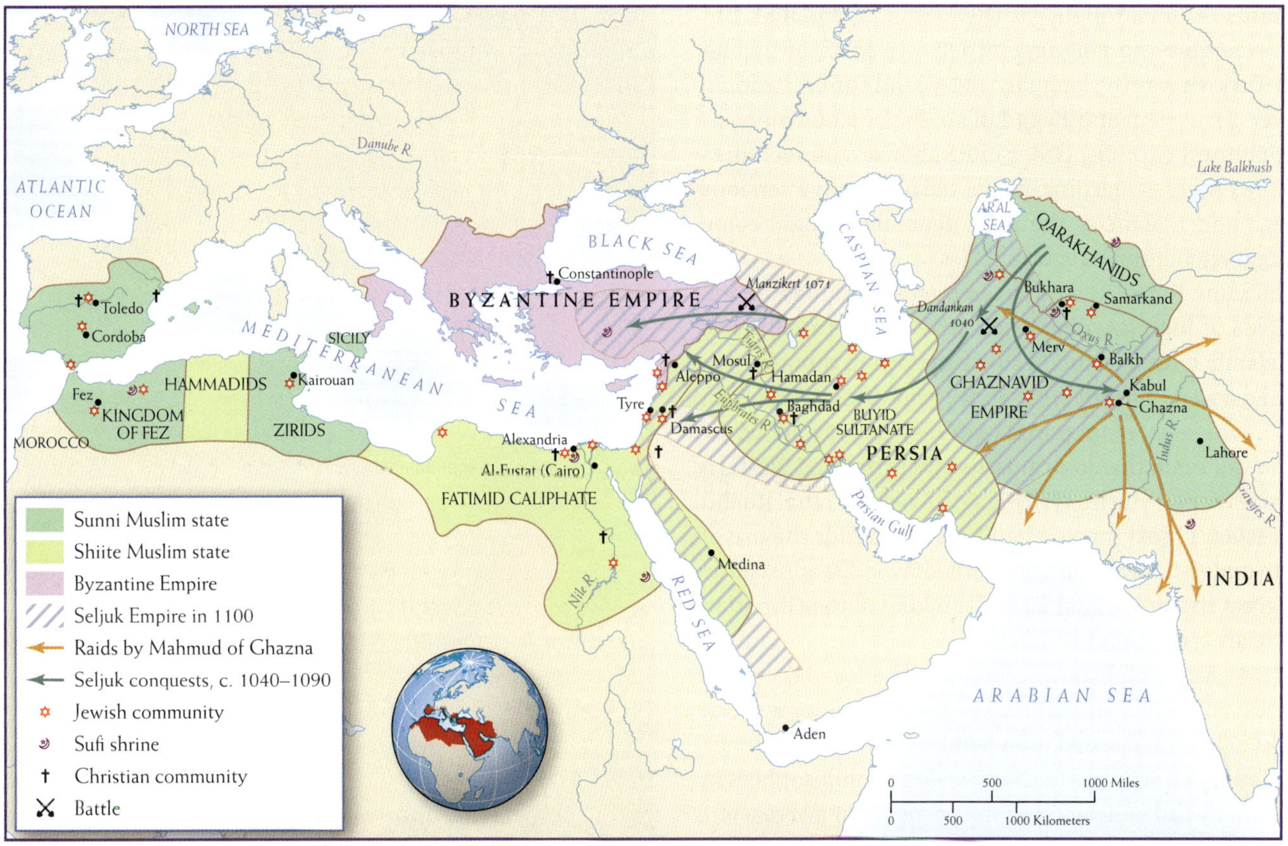

MAP 10.2 | The Islamic World, 900–1200 CE

The Islamic world experienced political fragmentation in the first centuries of the second millennium.

- According to the map key, what were the two major types of Islamic states in this period? What were some of the major political entities?
- What were the sources of instability in this period according to the map?
- What do you note about the locations of Jewish and Christian communities, as well as Sufi shrines, across the Islamic world?

poets was Jalal al-Din Rumi (1207–1273), spiritual founder of the Mevlevi Sufi order that became famous for the ceremonial dancing of its whirling devotees, known as dervishes.

Although many *ulama* (scholars) despised the Sufis and loathed their seeming lack of theological rigor, the movement spread with astonishing speed and offered a unifying force within Islam. Sufism's emotional content and strong social bonds, sustained in Sufi brotherhoods, added to its appeal for many. Sufi missionaries from these brotherhoods carried the universalizing faith to India, to Southeast Asia, across the Sahara Desert, and to other distant locations. It was through these brotherhoods that Islam became truly a religion of the people. As trade increased and more converts appeared in the Islamic lands, urban and peasant populations came to understand the faith practiced by the political, commercial, and scholarly upper classes even while they remained attached to the ways of their Sufi brotherhood. Islam became even more accommodating over time, embracing Persian literature, Turkish ruling skills, and Arabic-language contributions in law, religion, literature, and science.

Expanding the Islamic World

Buoyed by Arab dhows on the high seas and carried on the backs of camels following commercial networks, Islam had been transformed from Muhammad's original goal of creating a religion for Arab peoples (see Chapter 9). By 1300, its influence spanned Afro-Eurasia and it enjoyed multitudes of non-Arab converts. It attracted urbanites and rural peasants alike, as well as its original audience of desert nomads. Its extraordinary universal appeal generated an intense Islamic cultural flowering around 1000 CE.

Some people worried about the preservation of Islam's true nature, as Arabic ceased to be the language of many Muslims. It is true that the devout continued to read and recite the

Quran in its original tongue, as the religion mandated. But Persian was now the language of Islamic philosophy and art, and Turkish was the language of law and administration. Moreover, Jerusalem and Baghdad no longer stood alone as Islamic cultural capitals. Other cities, housing universities and other centers of learning, promoted alternative versions of Islam. In fact, some of the most dynamic thought came from Islam's geographical peripheries.

At the same time, cultural diversity fostered blossoming in all fields of high learning. Indicative of the prominence of the Islamic faith and the Arabic language in thought was the legendary Ibn Rushd (1126–1198). Known as Averroës in the west, where scholars pored over his writings, he wrestled with the same theological issues that troubled western scholars. Steeped in the writings of Aristotle, Ibn Rushd became Islam's most thoroughgoing advocate for the use of reason to understand the universe. His knowledge of Aristotle was so great that it influenced the thinking of the Christian world's leading philosopher and theologian, Thomas Aquinas (1225–1274). Most importantly, Ibn Rushd believed that faith and reason could be compatible. He also argued for a social hierarchy in which learned men would command influence akin to Confucian scholars in China or Greek philosophers in Athens. Ibn Rushd believed that the proper forms of reasoning had to be entrusted to the educated class—in the case of Islam, the *ulama*—who would then serve the common people.

Equally powerful works appeared in Persian, which by now was expressing the most sophisticated ideas of culture and religion. Best representing the new Persian ethnic pride was Abu al-Qasim Firdawsi (920–1020 CE), a devout Muslim who believed in the importance of pre-Islamic Sasanian traditions. In the epic poem *Shah Namah*, or *The Book of Kings*, he celebrated the origins of Persian culture and narrated the history of the Iranian highland peoples from the dawn of time to the Muslim conquest. As part of his effort to extol a pure Persian culture, Firdawsi attempted to compose his entire poem in Persian, unblemished by other languages and even avoiding Arabic words.

The Islamic world's achievements in science were truly remarkable. Its scholars were at the pinnacle of scientific knowledge throughout Afro-Eurasia in this era. The study of the Quran, Islamic law, traditions of the Prophet (*hadith*), theology, poetry, and the Arabic language held primacy among the learned classes. Even so, Ibn al-Shatir (1304–1375), working on his own in Damascus, produced non-Ptolemaic models of the universe that later researchers noted were mathematically equivalent to those of Copernicus. Even earlier, the Maragha school of astronomers (1259 and later) in western Iran had produced a non-Ptolemaic model of the planets. Some historians of science believe that Copernicus must have seen an Arabic manuscript written by a thirteenth-century Persian astronomer that contained a table of the movements of the planets. In addition, scholars in the Islamic world produced works in medicine, optics, and mathematics as well as astronomy that were more advanced than the achievements of Greek and Roman scholars.

Dervishes. The dance of Sufi mystics was an important means of reaching union with God. This illustration from a fifteenth-century publication of Firdawsi's *Shah Namah* depicts whirling dervishes with one hand stretching toward heaven and the other reaching toward the earth. Their richly colored robes and long streaming hair differ from the white garb and tall hats of modern dervishes.

By the fourteenth century, Islam had achieved what early converts would have considered unthinkable. No longer a religion of a minority of peoples living among Christian, Zoroastrian, and Jewish communities, Islam had become the people's faith. The agents of conversion were mainly Sufi saints and Sufi brotherhoods—not the *ulama*, whose exhortations had little impact on common people. The Sufis had carried their faith far and wide to North African Berbers, to Anatolian villagers, and to West African animists who believed that things in nature have souls. Ibn Rushd worried about the growing appeal of what he considered an "irrational" piety. But his message failed, because he did not appreciate that Islam's expansionist powers rested on its appeal to common folk. While the *sharia* was the core of Islam for the educated and scholarly classes, Sufism spoke to ordinary men and women.

During this period, the Islamic world became one of the four cultural spheres that would play a major role in world history, laying the foundation for what would become known as the Middle East. Islam became the majority religion of most of the inhabitants of Southwest Asia and North Africa, Arabic language use became widespread, and the Turks began to establish themselves as a dominant force, ultimately creating the Ottoman Empire, which would last into the twentieth century. The Islamic world thus became integral in transregional trade and in the creation and transmission of knowledge.

India as a Cultural Mosaic

With its pivotal location along land- and sea-based trade routes, India became an intersection for the trade, migration, and culture of Afro-Eurasian peoples. With 80 million inhabitants in 1000 CE, it had the second-largest population in the region, just behind China's 120 million. Turks ultimately spilled into India as they had into the Islamic heartlands, bringing their newfound Islamic beliefs. But the Turkish newcomers encountered an ethnic and religious mix of which they composed only one part. (See Map 10.3.)

Before the Turks arrived, India had been splintered among rival chiefs called *rajas*. These leaders gained support from Brahmans by doling out land grants to them. Since much of the land was uncultivated, the Brahmans first built temples, then converted the indigenous hunting and gathering peoples to the Hindu traditions, and finally taught the converts how to

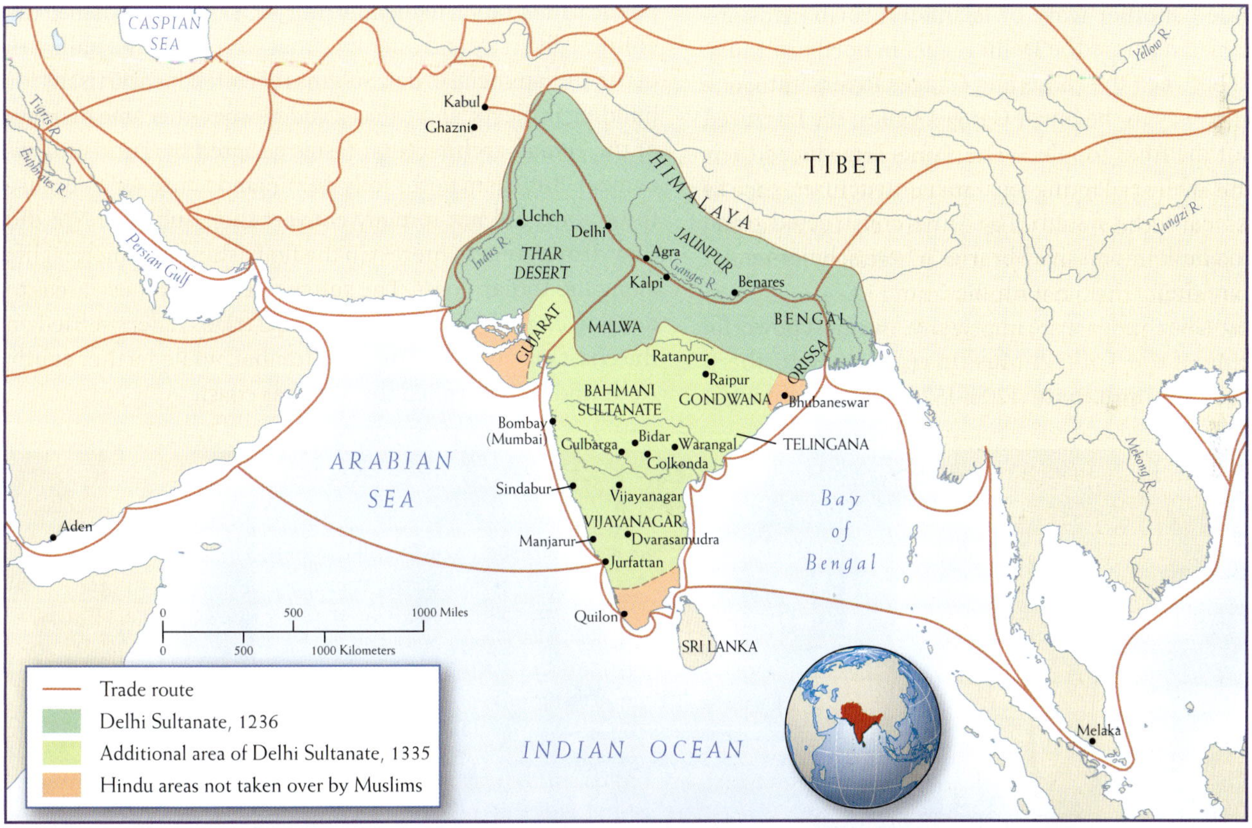

MAP 10.3 | South Asia in 1300

As the fourteenth century began, India was a blend of many cultures. Politically, the Turkish Muslim regime of the Delhi Sultanate dominated the region.

- What region was controlled by the Delhi Sultanate in 1236? How did the area controlled by the Delhi Sultanate change in 100 years?
- How does the map suggest that trade routes helped spread the Muslims' influence in India?
- Where on the map do Hindu areas resist Muslim political control? Based on your reading, what factors may have accounted for Hinduism's continued appeal despite the Muslims' political power?

cultivate the land. In this way the Brahmans simultaneously spread their faith and expanded the agrarian tax base for themselves and the *rajas*. They also repaid the *rajas'* support by compiling elaborate genealogies for them and endowing them with legitimizing ancestries. In return, the *rajas* demonstrated that they, too, were well versed in Sanskrit culture, including equestrian skills and courtly etiquette, and were prepared to patronize artists and poets.

Hindu Temple. When Buddhism started to decline in India, Hinduism was on the rise. Numerous Hindu temples were built, many of them adorned with ornate carvings like this small tenth-century CE temple in Bhubaneshwar in East India.

Invasions and Consolidations

When the Turkish warlords began entering India, the *rajas* had neither the will nor the resources to resist them after centuries of fighting off invaders. For example, Mahmud of Ghazna (r. 998–1030 CE) launched many expeditions from the Afghan heartland into northern India and, eager to win status within Islam, made his capital, Ghazna, a center of Islamic learning. Mahmud's expansion in the early eleventh century marked the height of what came to be known as the Ghaznavid Empire (977–1186 CE). Later, in the 1180s, Muhammad Ghuri led another wave of Islamic Turkish invasions from Afghanistan across the Delhi region in northern India. Wars raged between the Indus and Ganges Rivers until, one by one, all the way to the lower Ganges Valley, the fractured kingdoms of the *rajas* toppled. The Turks introduced their own customs while accepting local social structures, such as the hierarchical *varna* system. The Turks constructed grand mosques and built impressive libraries where scholars could toil and share their wisdom with the court.

While the Ghaznavids were impressive, the most powerful and enduring of the Turkish Muslim regimes of northern India was the **Delhi Sultanate** (1206–1526). Its rulers brought political integration to their territory but also strengthened the cultural diversity and tolerance that were already a hallmark of the Indian social order. Sultans recruited local artisans for building projects, and palaces and mosques became displays of the Indian architectural tastes adopted by Turkish newcomers. But Islam never fully dominated South Asia because the sultans did not forcibly convert their subjects. Nor did they display much interest in the flourishing commercial life along the Indian coast. The sultans permitted these areas to develop on their own: Persian Zoroastrian traders settled on the coast around modern-day Mumbai, while farther south, Arab traders controlled the Malabar coast.

Lodi Gardens. The Lodi dynasty (1451–1526) was the last dynasty of the Delhi Sultanate (1206–1526). Lodi Gardens, the cemetery of Lodi sultans, placed central Asian Islamic architecture in an Indian landscape, thereby creating a scene of "heaven on the earth."

Expanding India

During the eleventh, twelfth, and thirteenth centuries, India became the most diverse and, in some respects, most tolerant region in Afro-Eurasia. India in this era arose as an impressive but fragile mosaic of cultures, religions, and ethnicities.

When the Turks arrived, the local Hindu population, having had much experience with foreign invaders and immigrants, assimilated these intruders as they had done earlier peoples. Before long, the newcomers thought of themselves as Indians who, however, retained their Islamic beliefs and steppe ways. They continued to wear their distinctive trousers and robes and flaunted their horse-riding skills. At the same time, the local population embraced some of their conquerors' ways, donning the tunics and trousers that characterized central Asian peoples.

Diversity and cultural mixing became most discernible in the multiple languages that flourished in India. Although the sultans spoke Turkish languages, they regarded Persian literature as a high cultural achievement and made Persian their courtly and administrative language. Meanwhile, most of their Hindu subjects spoke local languages, adhered to the regulations of the *varna* system of hierarchies, and practiced diverse forms of Hindu worship. The rulers in India did what Muslim rulers in Southwest Asia and the Mediterranean did with Christian and Jewish communities living in their midst: they collected the *jizya* tax and permitted communities to worship as they saw fit and to administer their own communal law.

Vishnu. In addition to the Buddha, the four-armed Vishnu has nine other avatars, some of whom are portrayed at his feet in this tenth-century CE sandstone sculpture.

Ultimately, Islam proved in India that it did not have to be an intolerant conquering religion to prosper. Although Buddhism had been in decline there for centuries, it, too, became part of the cultural intermixing of these centuries. As Vedic Brahmanism evolved into Hinduism (see Chapter 8), it absorbed many Buddhist doctrines and practices, such as nonviolence (*ahimsa*) and vegetarianism. The two religions became so similar in India that Hindus simply considered the Buddha to be one of their deities—an incarnation of the great god Vishnu. Many Buddhist moral teachings mixed with and became Hindu stories. Artistic motifs reflected a similar process of adoption and adaptation. Goddesses, some beautiful and others fierce, appeared alongside Buddhas, Vishnus, and Shivas as their consorts. The Turkish invaders' destruction of major monasteries in the thirteenth century deprived Buddhism of local spiritual leaders. Lacking a political regime to support them, Buddhists in India were more easily assimilated into the Hindu population or converted to Islam.

Once the initial disruptive effects of the Turkish invasions were absorbed, India remained a highly diverse and tolerant region during this period. Most importantly, India emerged as one of the world's four major cultural spheres, enjoying tremendous levels of integration as Turkish-Muslim rulers, and their traditions and practices, successfully mixed with native Hindu society, leading to a more integrated and peaceful India.

Song China: Insiders versus Outsiders

The preeminent world power in 1000 CE was still China, despite its recent turmoil. In 907 CE, the Tang dynasty splintered into regional kingdoms, mostly led by military generals. In 960 CE one of these generals, Zhao Kuangyin, ended the fragmentation, reunified China, and assumed the mandate of heaven for the Song dynasty (960–1279 CE). The following three centuries witnessed many economic and political successes, but northern nomadic tribes kept the Song dynasty from completely securing its reign. (See Map 10.4 and Map 10.5.) Ultimately, one of those nomadic groups, the Mongols, would bring the Song dynasty to an end, but not until after Song influence had fanned out into Southeast Asia, helping to create new identities in the polities that developed there.

Economic Progress

Chinese merchants, like those from India and the Islamic world, participated in Afro-Eurasia's powerful long-distance

MAP 10.4 | East Asia in 1000 CE

Several states emerged in East Asia between 1000 and 1300 CE, but none were as strong as the Song dynasty in China. Using the key to the map, try to identify the factors that contributed to the Song state's economic dynamism.

- What do you note about the location of the major trading centers?
- What do you note about the distribution of the other trading centers?
- According to the map, what external factors kept the Song dynasty from completely securing its reign?

trade. Yet China's commercial successes could not have occurred without the country's strong agrarian base—especially its vast wheat, millet, and rice fields, which fed a population that reached 120 million. Crop cultivation benefited from breakthroughs in metalworking that produced stronger iron plows, which Song farmers harnessed to sturdy water buffalo to extend the agricultural frontier.

Manufacturing also flourished. With the use of piston-driven bellows to force air into furnaces, Song iron production in the eleventh century equaled that of Europe in the early eighteenth century. In the early tenth century CE, Chinese alchemists mixed saltpeter with sulfur and charcoal to produce a product that would burn and could be deployed on the battlefield: gunpowder. Song entrepreneurs were soon inventing a remarkable array of incendiary devices that flowed from their mastery of techniques for controlling explosions and high heat. At the same time, artisans were producing increasingly light, durable, and exquisitely beautiful porcelains. Chinese pottery had long been exported to the west (recall the tens of thousands of early ninth-century CE mass-produced Changsha pieces found in the Belitung shipwreck described earlier in this chapter), but Song pottery was much finer and more delicate. Before long, Song porcelain was the envy of all Afro-Eurasia (hence the modern term *china* for fine dishes). Also flowing from the artisans' skillful hands were vast amounts of clothing and handicrafts, made from the fibers cultivated by Song farmers. In effect, the Song Chinese oversaw the world's first manufacturing

MAP 10.5 | East Asia in 1200

The Song dynasty regularly dealt with "barbarian" neighbors with a balance of military response and outright bribery.

- What were the major "barbarian" tribes on the borders of Song China during this period?
- Approximately what percentage of Song China was lost to the Jin in 1126?
- Apart from so-called barbarians, what other polities existed on the borders of Song China?

revolution, producing finished goods on a large scale for consumption far and wide.

MONEY AND INFLATION Expanding commerce transformed the role of money and its wide circulation. By now the Song government was annually minting nearly 2 million strings of currency, each containing 1,000 copper coins. As the economy grew, the supply of metal currency could not match the demand, which fueled East Asia's desire for gold from East Africa. At the same time, merchant guilds in northwestern Shanxi developed the first letters of exchange, called **flying cash**. These letters linked northern traders with their colleagues in the south. Before long, printed money became more common than minted coins for trading purposes. Even the government collected more than half its tax revenues in cash rather than grain and cloth. The government also issued more notes to pay its bills—a practice that ultimately contributed to runaway inflation.

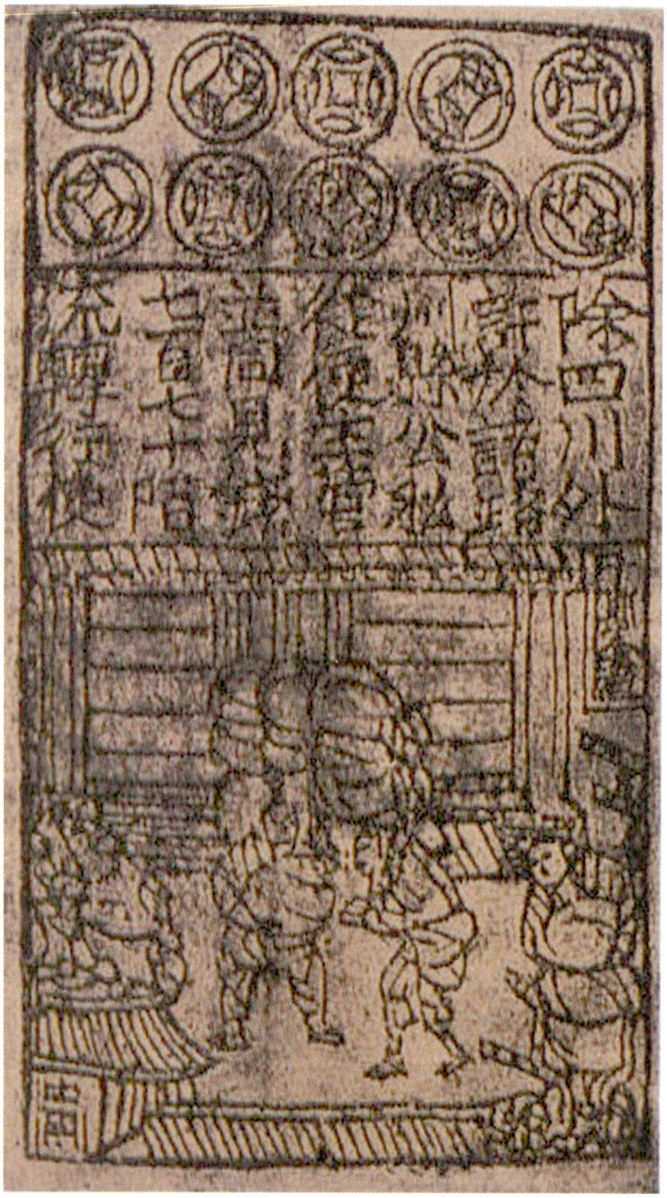

Flying Cash. Among the many innovations fueling the economic boom of the Song dynasty was paper money, called flying cash. Produced with woodblock printing technology that was relatively new at the time, the images printed on this example include, from top to bottom, coins, an inscription, and laborers at a warehouse. The inscription describes how much the bill was worth and in what regions it could be used as payment.

New Elites

Song emperors built on Tang political institutions by expanding a central bureaucracy of scholar-officials chosen even more extensively through competitive civil service examinations. Zhao Kuangyin, or Emperor Taizu (r. 960–976 CE), himself administered the final test for all who had passed the highest-level palace examination. In subsequent dynasties, the emperor was the nation's premier examiner, symbolically demanding oaths of allegiance from successful candidates. By 1100, these ranks of learned men had accumulated sufficient power to become China's new ruling elite.

Expansion of the civil service examination system was crucial to a shift in power from the still-powerful hereditary aristocracy to a less wealthy but more highly schooled class of scholar-officials. Consider the career of the Northern Song reformer Wang Anshi (1021–1086), who ascended to power from a commoner family outside of Hangzhou in the east. He owed his success to gaining high marks in Song state examinations—a not insignificant achievement, for in nearby Fujian Province alone, of the roughly 18,000 candidates who gathered triennially to take the provincial examination, over 90 percent failed! After gaining the emperor's ear, Wang eventually used his position to challenge the political and cultural influence of the old Tang dynasty elites from the northwest.

China's Neighbors: Nomads, Japan, and Southeast Asia

China's prosperity influenced its neighbors and its interactions with them. As the Song flourished, nomads on the outskirts closely eyed the Chinese successes. To the north, nomadic societies formed their own dynasties and adopted Chinese institutions. These non-Chinese nomads sought both to copy China proper and to conquer it.

Despite its sophisticated weapons, the Song army could not match its enemies on the steppe when the latter united against it. Steel tips improved the arrows that the Song soldiers shot from their crossbows, and flamethrowers and "crouching tiger catapults" sent incendiary bombs streaking into their enemies' ranks. But none of these breakthroughs were unique. Warrior neighbors on the steppe mastered the new arts of war more fully than did the Song military.

As a result, China drew on its economic success (and the innovation of paper money) to "buy off" the borderlanders. For example, after losing North China to the Khitan Liao dynasty, the Song agreed to make annual payments of 100,000 ounces of silver and 200,000 bolts of silk. The treaty allowed them to live in relative peace for more than a century. Securing peace meant emptying the state coffers and then printing more paper money. This short-term solution, however, led to economic instability (particularly inflation) and military weakness, especially as the Song forces were cut off, via the steppe nomads, from their supply of horses for warfare purposes.

Feeling the pull of China's economic and political gravity, cultures around China consolidated their own internal political authority and redefined their own identities in order to keep China from swallowing them up. At the same time, they increased their commercial transactions with China. In Japan, for instance, leaders distanced themselves from

Heiji Rebellion. This illustration from the Kamakura shogunate (1185–1333) depicts a battle during the Heiji Rebellion, which was fought between rival subjects of the cloistered emperor Go-Shirakawa in 1159. Riding in full armor on horseback, the fighters on both sides are armed with devastating long bows.

Chinese influences, but they also developed a strong sense of their islands' distinctive identity. Even so, the long-standing dominance of Chinese ways remained apparent at virtually every level of Japanese society and was most pronounced at the imperial court in the capital city of Heian (present-day Kyoto), which was modeled after the Chinese capital city of Chang'an. Outside Kyoto, however, a less China-centered way of life existed and began to impose itself on the center. Here, local notables, mainly military leaders and large landowners, began to challenge the imperial court for dominance. This challenge was accompanied by the arrival of an important new social group in Japanese society—samurai warriors. By the beginning of the fourteenth century, Japan had multiple sources of political and cultural power: an imperial family with prestige but little authority; an endangered and declining aristocracy; powerful landowning notables based in the provinces; and a rising and increasingly ambitious class of samurai.

During the Song period, Southeast Asia became a crossroads of Afro-Eurasian influences. The Malay Peninsula became home to many entrepôts for traders shuttling between India and China, because it connected the Bay of Bengal and the Indian Ocean with the South China Sea. (See Map 10.6.) Consequently, Southeast Asia was characterized by a fusion of religions and cultural influences: Vedic Brahmanism in Bali and other islands, Islam in Java and Sumatra, and Mahayana Buddhism in Vietnam and other parts of mainland Southeast Asia. Important Vedic and Buddhist kingdoms emerged in Southeast Asia. The most powerful and wealthy of these kingdoms was the Khmer

Angkor Wat. Mistaken by later European explorers for a remnant of Alexander the Great's conquests, the enormous temple complexes built by the Khmer people in Angkor borrowed their intricate architecture and stupas (moundlike structures containing religious relics) from the Brahmanic Indian temples of the time. As their capital, Angkor was a microcosm of the world for the Khmer, who aspired to represent the macrocosm of the universe in the magnificence of Angkor's buildings and their geometric layout.

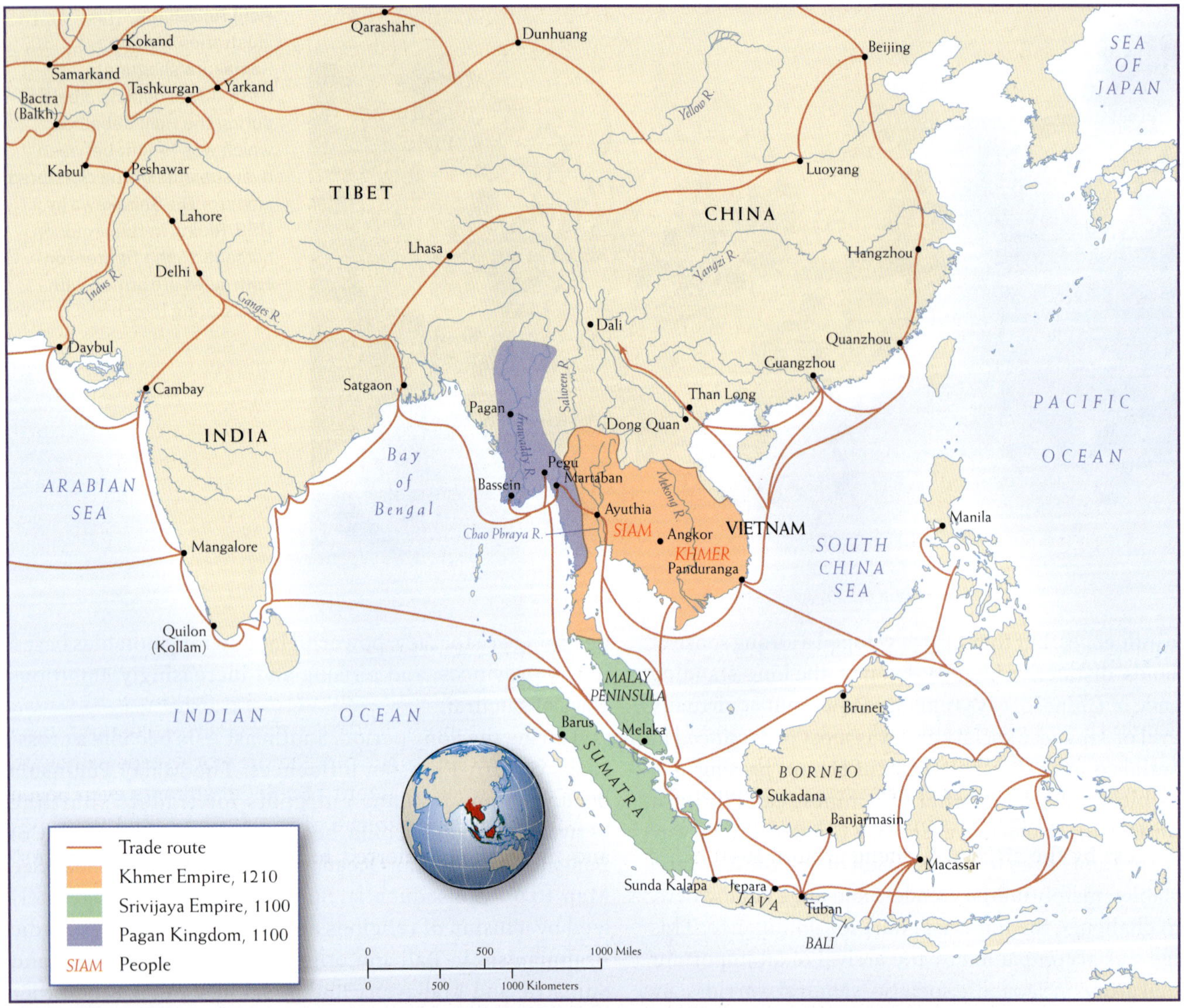

MAP 10.6 | Southeast Asia, 1000–1300 CE

Cross-cultural influences affected Southeast Asian societies during this period.

- What geographic features (rivers, mountains, islands, straits, etc.) shape Southeast Asia?
- What makes Southeast Asia unique geographically compared to other regions of the world?
- Based on the map, why were the kingdoms of Southeast Asia exposed to so many cross-cultural influences?

Empire (889–1431 CE), with its capital at Angkor, in present-day Cambodia. Public works and magnificent temples dedicated to the revived Vedic gods from India went hand in hand with the earlier influence of Indian Buddhism. One of the greatest temple complexes in Angkor—Angkor Wat—exemplified the Khmers' heavy borrowing from Vedic Indian architecture and the revival of the Hindu pantheon within the Khmer royal state. Kingdoms like the Khmer Empire functioned as political buffers between the strong states of China and India and brought stability and further commercial prosperity to the region.

Expanding China

Paradoxically, the increasing exchange between outsiders and insiders within China hardened the lines that divided them and gave residents of China's interior a highly developed sense of themselves as a distinctive people possessing a superior culture. Exchanges with outsiders nurtured a "Chinese" identity among those who considered themselves true insiders and referred to themselves as Han. Song Chinese grew increasingly suspicious and resentful toward the outsiders living in their midst. They called these outsiders "barbarians" and treated them accordingly.

Chinese and Barbarian. After losing the north, the Chinese grew resentful of outsiders. They drew a dividing line between their own agrarian society and the nomadic warriors, calling them "barbarians." Such identities were not fixed, however. Chinese and so-called barbarians were mutually dependent on each other.

Print culture crystallized the distinct Chinese identity. Of all Afro-Eurasian societies in 1300, the Chinese were the most advanced in their use of printing, book publishing, and circulation, a result of the invention of a movable type printing press by the artisan Bi Sheng around 1040. Song dynasty printed books established classical Chinese as the common language of educated classes in East Asia. The Song government used its plentiful supply of paper to print books, especially medical texts, and to distribute calendars. The private publishing industry expanded, and printing houses throughout the country produced Confucian classics, works on history, philosophical treatises, and literature—all of which figured in the civil examinations. Buddhist publications, too, were available everywhere.

In many respects, the Song period represented China's greatest age. China's resources, its huge population base coupled with a strong agrarian economy, and its strong foreign trade and diplomatic relations made China the wealthiest of the four major cultural spheres. And its common language and Confucian civil service system, which enabled a transfer of power from hereditary aristocrats to Confucian scholars, made it the most unified. As a result, China's influence on the surrounding region was tremendous.

Christian Europe

Europe from 1000 to 1300 CE was a continent of strong contrasts. Intensely localized power was balanced by a shared sense of Europe's place in the world, especially with respect to Christian identity. Some inhabitants even began to believe in the existence of something called "Europe" and increasingly referred to themselves as "Europeans"

The Bayeux Tapestry. This tapestry was allegedly prepared by Queen Matilda, wife of William the Conqueror, and her ladies to celebrate the successful invasion of England in 1066. These embroidering women captured the intense brutality of the invasion not only in the central narrative thread showing spears flying, long shields studded with arrows, and cavalry galloping in on great horses, but also in the margins where chain mail is being ripped off corpses.

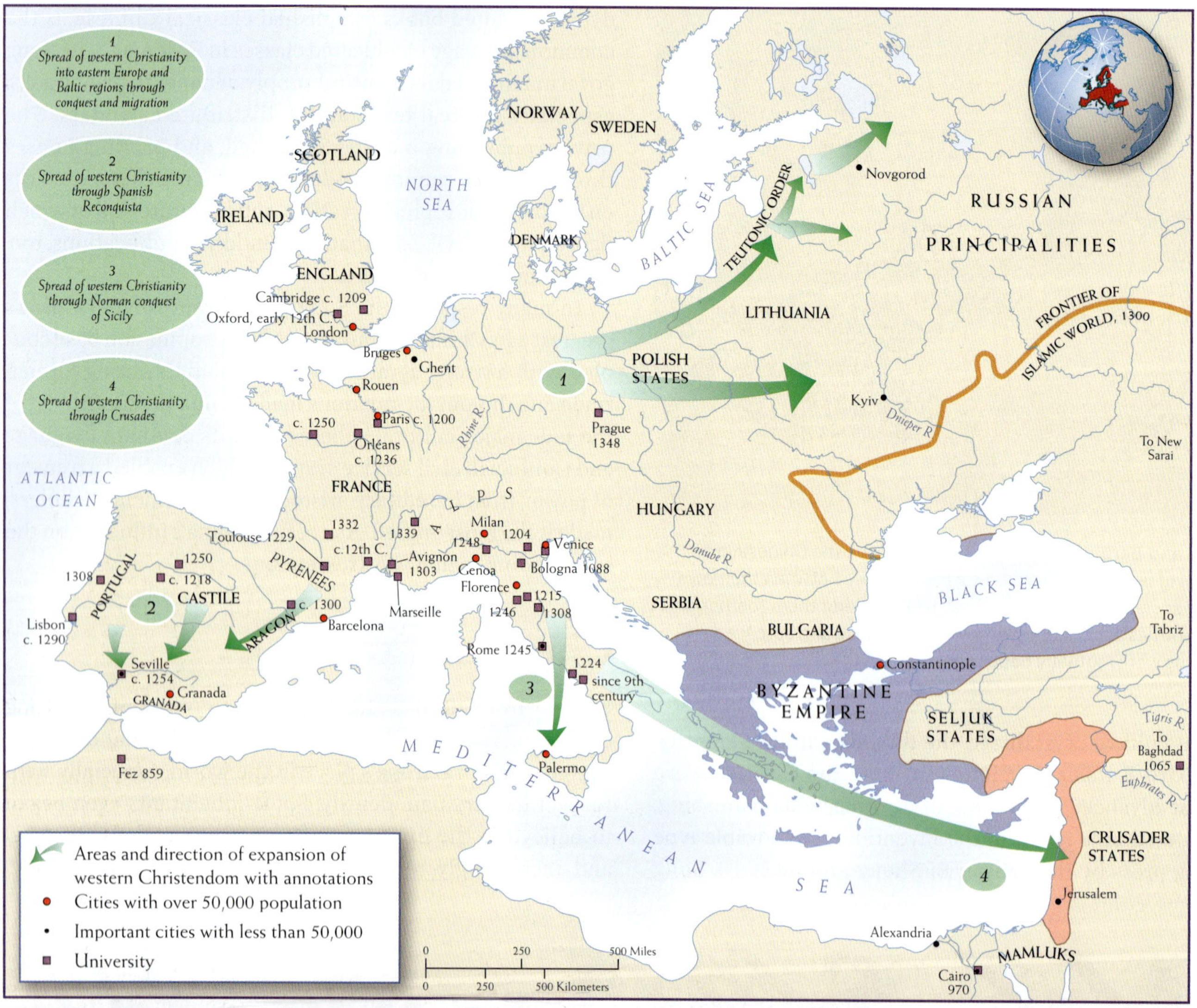

MAP 10.7 | European Christendom in 1300

Catholic Europe expanded geographically and integrated culturally during this era.

- According to this map, into what areas did western Christendom successfully expand?
- What were the different means by which western Christianity expanded?
- Which are the earliest universities on the map? What might account for the flourishing of universities where they were located?

(see Map 10.7), especially in contrast to the world of Islam to the east and south.

Western and Northern Europe

The collapse of Charlemagne's empire had exposed much of northern Europe to invasion, principally from the Vikings, and left the peasantry there with no central authority to protect themselves from local warlords. Armed with deadly weapons, these strongmen collected taxes, imposed forced labor, and became the unchallenged rulers of society. Peasants toiled under the authority of these landholding lords, who controlled every detail of their subjects' lives. The Franks (in northern France) were the trendsetters for this development in eleventh- and twelfth-century Europe.

The peasantry's subjugation to this warlord or knightly class was at the heart of a system scholars have called feudalism (emphasizing the power of the local lords over the peasantry), but a more accurate term for the system is **manorialism**, which emphasizes instead the manor's role as the basic unit of economic power. The manor comprised the lord's fortified home (or castle), the surrounding fields controlled by the lord but worked by peasants (as free tenants or as serfs tied to the

Turku Castle, Finland. Turku Castle, located in western Finland, is one of five remaining medieval castles created for defensive purposes along the Gulf of Finland. A Slavic word by origin, *turku* means "marketplace," demonstrating the connection between trade and the need to protect it. This castle served as a defense when invaders from Novgorod attacked it in 1318.

land), and the village where those peasants lived. Although manorialism was driven by agriculture, limited manufacturing and trade augmented the manor economy. Assured of control of the peasantry, feudal lords watched over an agrarian breakthrough—which fueled a commercial transformation that drew Europe into the rest of the global trading networks. Lordly protection and more advanced metal tools like axes and plows, combined with heavier livestock to pull plows through the root-infested sods of northern Europe, led to massive deforestation. This system harnessed agrarian energy and helped western Europe leap forward and shed its identity as a somewhat "barbarian" appendage of the Mediterranean; it also had unforeseen environmental impacts that resulted from the deforestation.

East-Central Europe

Nowhere did pioneering peasants develop more land than in the wide-open spaces of east-central Europe, the continent's land of opportunity. Between 1100 and 1200, some 200,000 farmers emigrated from Flanders (in modern western Belgium), Holland, and northern Germany to eastern frontiers. Well-watered landscapes covered with vast forests filled up what are now Poland, the Czech Republic, Slovakia, Hungary, Romania, and the Baltic states. These "Little Europes," whose castles, churches, and towns echoed the landscape of France, now replaced economies that had been based on gathering honey, hunting, and the slave trade. For 1,000 miles along the Baltic Sea, forest clearings dotted with new farmsteads and small towns edged inward from the coast up the river valleys.

The social structure here was a marriage of convenience between migrating peasants and local elites. The area offered the promise of freedom from the arbitrary justice and the imposition of forced labor. Even the harsh landscape of the eastern Baltic (where the sea froze every year and impenetrable forests blocked settlers from the coast) was preferable to life in the west. For their part, the elites of eastern Europe—the nobility of Poland, Bohemia, and Hungary and the princes of the Baltic—wished to live well. But they could do so only if they attracted workers to their lands by offering newcomers a liberty that did not exist in the west.

The East Slavic Lands

In the East Slavic lands, western settlers and knights met an eastern brand of Christian devotion. This world looked toward Byzantium, not Rome or western Europe. These lands

Saint Sophia Cathedral, Novgorod. The cathedral of Novgorod (like that of Kyiv) was called Hagia Sophia. It was a deliberate imitation of Hagia Sophia in Constantinople, showing modern Russia's roots in an eastern-focused Byzantine past disconnected from western Europe.

were a giant borderland between the steppes of Eurasia and the booming centers of Europe. Their cities lay at the crossroads of overland trade and migration, and Kyiv became one of the region's greatest cities. Standing on a bluff above the Dnipro River, it straddled newly opened trade routes. With a population exceeding 20,000, including merchants from eastern and western Europe, Southwest Asia, South Asia, Egypt, and North Africa, Kyiv was larger than Paris—larger even than the much-diminished city of Rome.

Kyiv looked south to the Black Sea and to Constantinople. Christianity arrived in 988 CE, and under Yaroslav the Wise (r. 1019–1054), Kyiv became a small-scale Constantinople on the Dnipro. A stone church called Saint Sophia stood beside the imperial palace (as in Constantinople). With its distinctive "Byzantine" domes, it was a miniature Hagia Sophia (see Chapter 8). Its highest dome towered 100 feet above the floor, and its splendid mosaics depicting Byzantine saints echoed the religious art of Constantinople. The embrace of Orthodoxy spread throughout the East Slavic lands, from the elites to the peasants, although paganism did remain active until the early fifteenth century.

Due to the influence of the Orthodox form of Christianity, Byzantine-style churches were erected all along the great rivers leading to the trading cities of the north and northeast. These were not agrarian centers, but hubs of expanding long-distance trade. Each city became a small-scale Kyiv and a smaller-scale echo of Constantinople. The Orthodox religion thus looked to Byzantium's Hagia Sophia rather than Roman Catholicism and the popes. Orthodox Christianity, however, remained the Christianity of a borderland—vivid oases of high culture that were set against the backdrop of vast forests and widely scattered settlements. Like the agricultural manors of western Europe, this region's cities demonstrated the highly localized nature of power in Europe during this period.

Saint Francis of Assisi. In this scene, Saint Francis of Assisi renounces his earthly wealth and embarks on a life of poverty. Saint Francis founded the order that took his name, the Franciscans, and promoted his principles of a life of poverty, devotion to the teachings of Jesus Christ, and concern for the poor. The artist Giotto (1267–1337) painted several series of frescoes depicting scenes from the life of Saint Francis, including those in the basilica at Assisi (pictured here) and in Santa Croce in Florence.

Expanding Christian Europe

Christianity in this era—primarily the Roman Catholicism of the west, but also the Orthodoxy of the east—was a universalizing faith that transformed the territory that was becoming known as "Europe." The Christianity of post-Roman Europe had been a religion of monks, and its most dynamic centers were great monasteries. Members of the laity were expected to revere and support their monks, nuns, and clergy, but not to imitate them. By 1200, all this had changed. The internal colonization of western Europe—the clearing of woods and founding of villages—ensured that parish churches arose in all but the wildest landscapes. Now the clergy reached more deeply into the private lives of the laity. Marriage and divorce, previously considered family matters, became the domain of the church.

New understandings of religious devotion and innovative institutions for learning developed in the west. For instance, the followers of Francis of Assisi (1182–1226) emerged as an order of preachers who brought a message of repentance. Franciscans encouraged the laity—from the poorest to the elite—to feel remorse for their wrongdoings, to confess their sins to local priests, and to strive to be better Christians. At nearly the same time, intellectuals were beginning to gather in Paris to form one of the first European universities, a sort of trade guild of scholars. These professional thinkers endeavored to prove that Christianity was the only religion that fully addressed the concerns of all rational human beings. Such was the message of Thomas Aquinas, who wrote *Summa contra Gentiles (Summary of Christian Belief against Non-Christians)* in 1264. The growing number of churches, new religious orders, and universities began to change what it meant to live in a "Christian Europe."

Christian Europe's Relations with the Islamic World

By the tenth and eleventh centuries CE, western Christianity was on the move, spreading into Scandinavia, southern Italy, the Baltic, and eastern Europe. Its ambitions to reconquer Spain and Portugal (which had been under Muslim control since the eighth century CE) demonstrated one of the effects of feudal power: the lords' self-confidence, their belief in their military capability, and their pious sense of destiny were all inflated. Besides, the wealth of the east was irresistible to those whose piety entwined with an appetite for plunder. Yet the two Christendoms formed an uneasy alliance to roll back the expanding frontiers of Islam. Europeans zealously took war outside their own borders.

CRUSADES In the late eleventh century, western Europeans launched a wave of attacks against the Islamic world known as the Crusades. The First Crusade began in 1095, when Pope Urban II appealed to the warrior nobility of France to put their violence to good use: they should combine their role as pilgrims to Jerusalem with that of soldiers and free Jerusalem from Muslim rule. Such a "just war," the clergy proposed, was a means for absolution, not a source of sin.

Starting in 1097, an armed host of around 60,000 men moved all the way from northwestern Europe to Jerusalem. The crusading forces included knights in heavy armor as well as people drawn from Europe's impoverished masses, who joined the movement to help besiege cities and construct a network of castles as the Christian knights drove their frontier forward. The fleets of Venice, Genoa, and Pisa helped transport later Crusaders and supplied the kingdoms they created as they moved eastward. Later Crusaders, especially those from the upper class, brought their wives, who found a degree of autonomy away from their homelands and thus their prescribed gender roles. Eleanor of Aquitaine, for example, led her own army. Melisende (r. 1131–1152), born Armenian royalty in the Crusader state of Edessa, ruled as queen of Jerusalem after her father's death, despite occasional attempts by her husband and later her son to challenge her authority. Regarded as wise and experienced in affairs of the state, she was popular with local Christians. As a result, the society of the Crusader states remained more open to women and the lower classes than societies back in Europe. There are even accounts of a children's crusade (1212), inspired by the visions of a boy. Over time, the Crusades brought together a range of peoples from varied walks of life in common purpose. That purpose was one of conflict.

No fewer than nine Crusades were fought in the two centuries that followed Urban II's call, but none ultimately created lasting Christian kingdoms in the lands the Crusaders "reconquered." Most knights returned home, their epic pilgrimages completed. The remaining fragile network of Crusader lordships barely threatened the Islamic heartland. The real prosperity and the capital cities of Muslim kingdoms lay inland, away from the coast—in Cairo, Damascus, and Baghdad. The assaults' long-term effect was to harden Muslim feelings against the millions of Christians who had previously lived peacefully in Egypt and Syria.

Crusader. Kneeling, this Crusader promises to serve God (as he would serve a feudal lord) by going to fight on a Crusade (as he would fight for any lord to whom he had sworn loyalty). The two kinds of loyalty—to God and to one's lord—were deliberately intertwined in promoting the Crusades. Both were about war. But fighting for God was unambiguously good, while fighting for a lord was not always so clear-cut.

Even so, a range of sources offer Muslim and Christian perspectives that show tolerance of, and curiosity about, each other. For example, Usāmah Ibn Munqidh (1095–1188), a learned Syrian leader, described his shock at the European Crusaders' backward medical practices and the freedom they offered their wives, in addition to well-meaning exchanges such as a particular Christian's confusion about the direction in which Muslims pray. Similarly, Jean de Joinville (1224–1317), a French chronicler of Louis X of France who led the Seventh Crusade, marveled at the order within the sultan's camp and the role of musicians in calling the Muslim forces to hear the sultan's orders.

Other campaigns of Christian expansion, like the Iberian efforts to drive out the Muslims, were more successful. Beginning with the capture of Toledo in 1061, the Christian kings of northern Spain slowly pushed back the Muslims. Eventually they reached the heart of Andalusia in southern Iberia and conquered Seville, adding more than 100,000 square miles of territory to Christian Europe. Another force, from northern France, crossed Italy to conquer Muslim-held Sicily, ensuring Christian rule in that strategically located mid-Mediterranean island. Unlike the Crusaders' fragile foothold at the edge of the Middle East, these two conquests were a turning point in relations between Christian and Muslim power in the Mediterranean. Christianity—in particular, the rise of the Roman Catholic Church, the spread of universities, and the fight against the Muslims in their native and spiritual homelands—was a force that helped create a cultural sphere known as Europe, whose peoples would become known as European, at the western end of the Afro-Eurasian landmass during this period.

Worlds Coming Together: Sub-Saharan Africa and the Americas

From 1000 to 1300 CE, sub-Saharan Africa and the Americas became far more internally integrated—culturally, economically, and politically—than before. Islam's spread and the growing trade in gold, enslaved people, and other commodities brought sub-Saharan Africa more fully into the exchange networks of the Eastern Hemisphere, but the Americas remained isolated from Afro-Eurasian networks for several more centuries.

Sub-Saharan Africa Comes Together

During this period, sub-Saharan Africa's interactions with the rest of the world dramatically changed. While sub-Saharan Africa before 1000 CE had never been a world entirely apart, its integration with Eurasia now strengthened. Interior hinterlands increasingly found themselves touched by the commercial and migratory impulses emanating from transformations in the Indian Ocean and Arabian Sea. (See Map 10.8.)

WEST AFRICA AND THE MANDE-SPEAKING PEOPLES Once trade routes bridged the Sahara Desert (see Chapter 9), the flow of commodities and ideas linked sub-Saharan Africa to North Africa and Southwest Asia. As the savanna region increasingly connected to developments in Afro-Eurasia, Mande-speaking peoples emerged as the primary agents for integration within and beyond West Africa. Exploiting their expertise in commerce and political organization, the Mande edged out rivals. The Mande homeland was a vast area, 1,000 miles wide, between the bend in the Senegal River to the west and the bend of the Niger River to the east, stretching more than 2,000 miles from the Senegal River in the north to the Bandama River in the south.

By the eleventh century, the Mande-speaking peoples were spreading their cultural, commercial, and political hegemony from the high savanna grasslands southward into the woodlands and tropical rain forests that stretched to the Atlantic Ocean. Those dwelling in the rain forests organized small-scale societies led by local councils, while those in the savanna developed centralized forms of government under sacred kingships. Mande speakers believed that their kings had descended from the gods and that they enjoyed the gods' blessing.

As the Mande extended their territory to the Atlantic coast, they gained access to tradable items that residents of the interior were eager to have—notably peppers and kola nuts, for which the Mande exchanged iron products and manufactured textiles. Mande-speaking peoples, with their far-flung commercial networks and highly dispersed populations, dominated the trans-Saharan trade in salt from the northern Sahel, gold from the Mande homeland, and enslaved people from across the region. Salt was in demand on both sides of the Sahara. Camel caravans carried gold to the far northern side of the Sahara, where traders exchanged it for various manufactures. Enslaved men and women were shipped to the settled Muslim communities of North Africa and Egypt. By 1300, the Mande-speaking merchants had followed the Senegal River to its outlet on the coast and then pushed their commercial frontiers farther inland and down the coast. Thus, even before European explorers and traders arrived in the mid-fifteenth century, West African peoples had created dynamic networks linking the hinterlands with coastal trading hubs.

THE MALI EMPIRE In the early thirteenth century, the **Mali Empire** became the Mande successor state to the kingdom of Ghana (see Chapter 9), and it exercised its political sway over a vast area for three centuries. The origins of the Mali Empire and its legendary founder are enshrined in *The Epic of Sundiata*. Sundiata's triumph, which occurred in the first half of the thirteenth century, marked the victory of new cavalry forces over traditional foot soldiers. Horses now became prestige objects for the savanna peoples, symbols of state power.

Under the Mali Empire, commerce took off. With Mande trade routes extending to the Atlantic Ocean and spanning the Sahara Desert, West Africa was no longer an isolated periphery

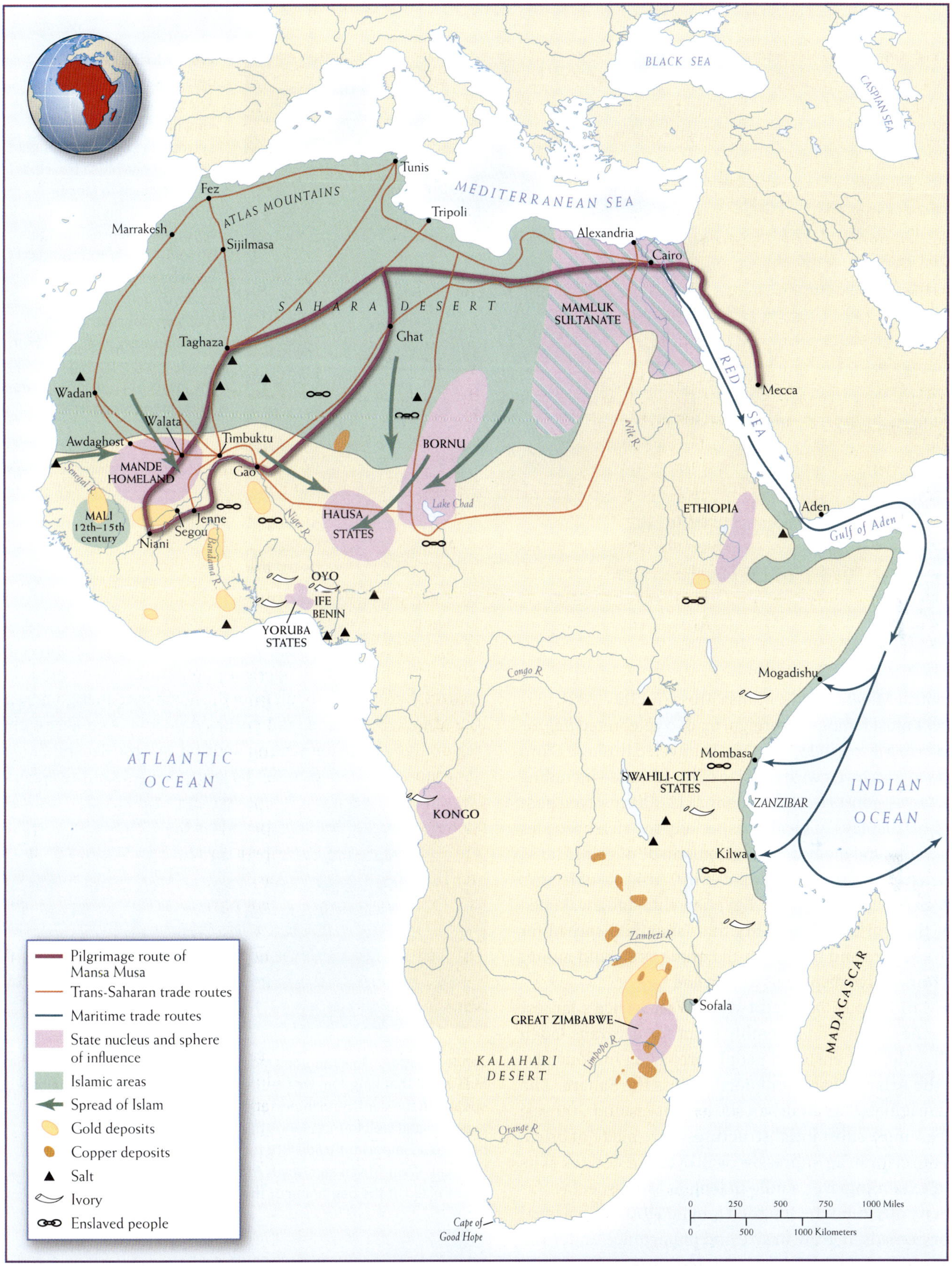

MAP 10.8 | Sub-Saharan Africa, 1300

Increased commercial contacts influenced the religious and political dimensions of sub-Saharan Africa at this time. Compare this map with Map 9.3.

- Where had strong Islamic communities emerged by 1300? By what routes might Islam have spread to those areas?
- According to this map, what types of activity were taking place in sub-Saharan West Africa?
- What goods were traded in sub-Saharan Africa, and along what routes did those exchanges take place?

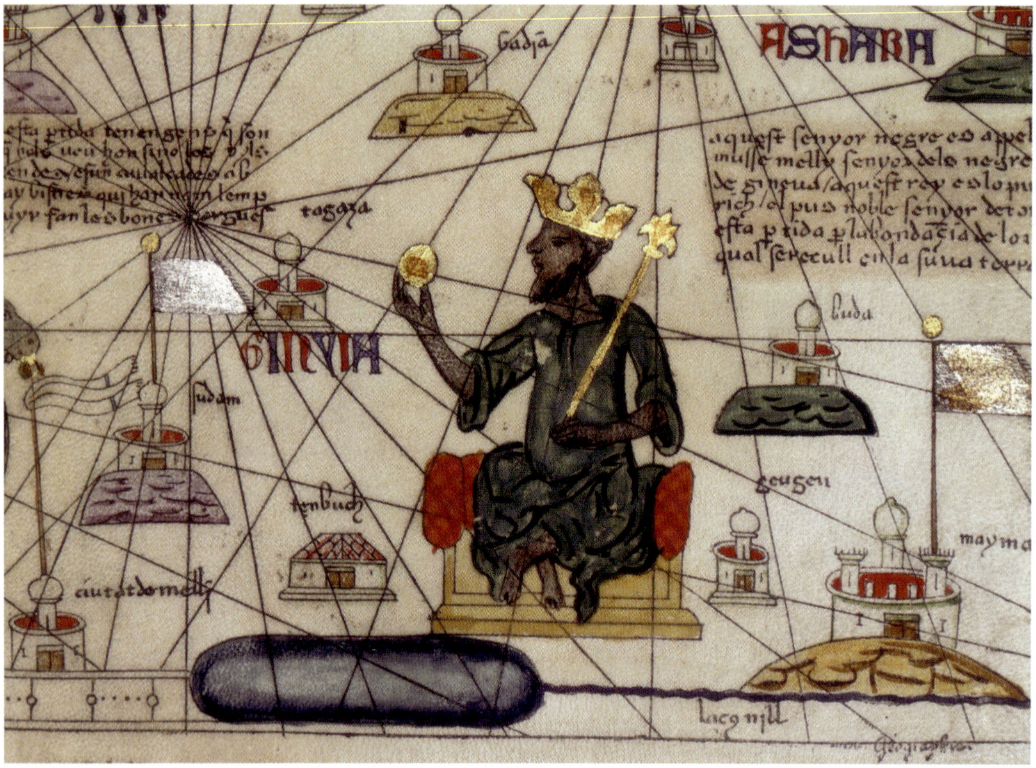

West African Gold. This detail from the 1375 *Catalan Atlas* shows Mansa Musa, the king of Mali, on his throne, surrounded by images of gold. When Mansa Musa traveled on pilgrimage to Mecca (1324–1325), his caravan brought immense quantities of gold—nearly 100 camels each bearing 300-pound sacks of gold—and spent it so generously that the contemporary writer al-Umari (1301–1349) reported that the influx of gold deflated its value in the Mediterranean economy.

of the central Muslim lands. Mansa Musa (r. 1312–1332), perhaps Mali's most famous sovereign, made a celebrated *hajj*, or pilgrimage to Mecca, in 1324–1325. He traveled through Cairo and impressed crowds with the size of his retinue—including soldiers, wives, consorts, and as many as 12,000 enslaved people—and his displays of wealth, especially the rich brocades of Persian silks and many dazzling items made of gold. Mansa Musa's lengthy three-month stopover in Cairo, one of Islam's primary cities, astonished the Egyptian elite and awakened much of the world to the reality that Islam had spread far below the Sahara and that a sub-Saharan state could mount such an impressive display of wealth and power.

The Mali Empire boasted two of West Africa's largest cities. Jenne was a vital assembly point for caravans laden with salt, gold, and enslaved people preparing for journeys west to the Atlantic coast and north across the Sahara. The city had originated as an urban settlement around 200 BCE; by 1000 CE, most substantial structures were made of brick. Around the city ran an impressive wall over 11 feet thick at its base and extending over a mile in length. More spectacular was the city of Timbuktu; founded around 1100 as a seasonal camp for nomads, it grew in size and importance under the patronage of various Mali kings. By the fourteenth century, it was a thriving commercial and religious center famed for its three large mosques, which are still standing. Timbuktu was also renowned for its intellectual vitality. Here, West African Muslim scholars congregated to debate the tenets of Islam and to ensure that the faithful, even when distant from the Muslim heartland, practiced their religion with no taint of local pagan observances. These clerics acquired treatises on Islam from all over the world for their personal libraries, remnants of which remain to this day.

Jenne Mosque. This fabulous mosque arose in the kingdom of Mali when that kingdom was at the height of its power. The mosque speaks to the depth and importance of Islam's roots in the Malian kingdom and well before. Jenne had originated in 200 CE and soon became an important trade city for West Africa, facilitating trade between West Africa and North Africa. The mosque viewed here was modernized at the beginning of the twentieth century.

TRADE BETWEEN EAST AFRICA AND THE INDIAN OCEAN Africa's eastern and southern regions were also integrated into long-distance trading systems. Because of monsoon winds, East Africa was a logical end point for much of the Indian Ocean trade. Swahili peoples living along that coast became brokers for trade from the Arabian Peninsula, the Persian Gulf territories, and the western coast of India. Merchants in the city of Kilwa on the coast of present-day Tanzania brought ivory, enslaved people, gold, and other items from the continent's interior and shipped them to destinations around the Indian Ocean.

The most valued commodity being traded was gold. Shona-speaking peoples grew rich by mining the ore in the highlands between the Limpopo and Zambezi Rivers. By the year 1000 CE, the Shona had founded up to fifty small religious and political centers, each one erected from stone to display its power over the peasant villages surrounding it. Around 1100, one of these centers, Great Zimbabwe, stood supreme among the Shona. Built on the fortunes made from gold, its most impressive landmark was a massive elliptical building made of stone fitted so expertly that it needed no grouting. The buildings of Great Zimbabwe probably housed the king and may also have contained smelters for melting down gold.

THE SLAVE TRADE Enslaved Africans were as valuable as African gold in shipments to the Mediterranean and Indian Ocean markets. There had been a lively trade in enslaved

Enslaved, Bought, and Sold. Enslaved men and women were a common commodity in the marketplaces of the Islamic world. Turkish conquests during the years from 1000 to 1300 CE put many prisoners on the slave market.

Great Zimbabwe. Massive stone walls, at points as high as 36 feet, surrounded the "Great Enclosure" that makes up part of the ruins of Great Zimbabwe. The city, covering almost 3 square miles (almost 8 square kilometers), was a center of the gold trade between the East African coastal peoples and traders sailing on the Indian Ocean. Great Zimbabwe flourished during the thirteenth, fourteenth, and fifteenth centuries.

Africans (mainly from Nubia) into pharaonic Egypt well before the Common Era. After Islam spread into Africa and sailing techniques improved, the slave trade across the Sahara Desert and Indian Ocean boomed. Although the Quran attempted to mitigate the severity of slavery, requiring Muslim owners of enslaved men and women to treat them kindly and praising manumission as an act of piety, the African slave trade nonetheless flourished under Islam.

Africans became enslaved either by being taken as prisoners of war or by being sold into slavery as punishment for committing a crime. Enslaved people might have worked as soldiers, seafarers on dhows, domestic servants, or plantation workers. Still others, mainly women, were domestic servants, and many became concubines of Muslim political figures and businessmen. Yet in this era, enslaved labor on plantations, like that which later became prominent in the Americas, was the exception, not the rule. Enslaved men and women were more prized as additions to family labor or as status symbols for their owners.

The Americas: Worlds Apart

During this period, the Americas were untouched by the connections reverberating across Afro-Eurasia. Other than limited Viking contacts with North America (see Chapter 9), navigators still could not cross the large oceans that separated the Americas from other lands. Yet even here, commercial and expansionist impulses fostered closer contact among the peoples who lived in the Western Hemisphere..

ANDEAN STATES OF SOUTH AMERICA Growth and prosperity in the Andean region gave rise to South America's first empire. The **Chimú Empire** developed early in the second millennium in the fertile Moche Valley, bordering the Pacific Ocean. (See Map 10.9.) Ultimately, the Moche people expanded their influence across numerous valleys and ecological zones, from pastoral highlands to rich valley floodplains to the fecund fishing grounds of the Pacific coast. As their geographical reach expanded, so did their wealth.

The Chimú economy succeeded because it was highly commercialized. Agriculture was its base, and complex irrigation systems turned the arid coast into a string of fertile oases capable of feeding an increasingly dispersed population. Cotton became a lucrative export to distant markets along the Andes. Parades of llamas and porters lugged these commodities up and down the steep mountain chains that form the spine of South America. A well-trained bureaucracy oversaw the construction and maintenance of canals, with a hierarchy of provincial administrators watching over commercial hinterlands.

Andean States. *Above:* This photo shows what remains of Chan Chan. The city covered 15 square miles (about 39 square kilometers) and was divided into neighborhoods for nobles, artisans, and commoners, with the elites living closest to the hub of governmental and spiritual power. *Left:* The buildings of Tiahuanaco were made of giant, hand-hewn stones assembled without mortar. Engineers had not discovered the principle of curved arches and keystones and instead relied on massive slabs atop gateways. Gateways were important symbolic features, for they were places where people acknowledged the importance of sun and moon gods.

MAP 10.9 | Andean States, c. 700–1400 CE

Although the Andes region of South America was isolated from Afro-Eurasian developments before 1500, it was not stagnant. Indeed, political and cultural integration brought the peoples of this region closer together.

- Where are the areas of Chimú Empire and Tiahuanaco influence on the map?
- What was the ecology and geography of each region, and how might that have shaped each region's development?
- From what crops and animals did the Chimú and Tiahuanaco benefit?

The Chimú Empire's biggest city was Chan Chan, which had been growing ever larger since its founding around 900 CE. By the time the Chimú Empire was thriving, Chan Chan's core population had reached 30,000 inhabitants. A sprawling walled metropolis covering nearly 10 square miles, with extensive roads circulating through neighborhoods, Chan Chan boasted ten huge palaces at its center. Protected by thick walls 30 feet high, the opulent residence halls demonstrated the rulers' power. Within the compound, emperors erected burial complexes for storing their accumulated riches: fine cloth, gold and silver objects, splendid *Spondylus* shells, and other luxury goods. Around the compound spread neighborhoods for nobles and artisans; farther out stood rows of commoners' houses. The Chimú regime, centered at Chan Chan, lasted until Inca armies invaded in the 1460s and incorporated the Pacific state into their own immense empire.

AN INVENTIVE HIGHLAND STATE The Andes also saw their first highland empires during this period. On the shores of Lake Titicaca, the people of Tiahuanaco forged a high-altitude state. Though it was neither as large nor as wealthy as the Chimú Empire, its residents converted the inhospitable highlands to an environment where farmers and herders thrived. There is evidence of long-distance trade with neighbors in semitropical valleys and even signs of highlanders migrating to the lowlands to produce agrarian staples for their kin in the mountains. Dried fish and cotton came from the coast; fruits and vegetables came from lowland valleys. Trade sustained an enormous urban population of up to 115,000 people. Looming over the skyline of Tiahuanaco was an imposing pyramid of massive sandstone blocks. Its advanced engineering system conveyed water to the summit, from which an imitation rainfall coursed down the carefully carved sides—an awesome spectacle of engineering prowess in such an arid region.

TOLTECS IN MESOAMERICA Additional hubs of regional trade developed farther north in the Americas. By 1000 CE,

MAP 10.10 | Commercial Hubs in Mesoamerica and North America, 1000 CE

Both Cahokia and Tula were commercial hubs of vibrant regional trade networks.

- What routes linked Tula and the Toltecs with other regions?
- What goods circulated in the regions of Pueblo and Cahokia?
- Based on the map, what appear to be some of the differences between Canyon culture, Mississippian culture, and the Toltecs?

Mesoamerica had seen the rise and fall of several complex societies, including Teotihuacán and the Maya (see Chapter 8). Caravans of porters bound the region together, working the intricate roads that connected the coast of the Gulf of Mexico to the Pacific and the southern lowlands of Central America to the arid regions of modern Texas. (See Map 10.10.) The region's heartland was the rich valley of central Mexico. The **Toltecs** filled the political vacuum left by the decline of Teotihuacán and tapped into the commercial network radiating from the rich valley of central Mexico.

The Toltecs grew to dominate the valley of Mexico between 900 and 1100 CE. They were a combination of migrant groups, farmers from the north and refugees from the south fleeing the strife that followed Teotihuacán's demise. These migrants settled northwest of Teotihuacán as the city waned, making their capital at Tula. They relied on a maize-based economy supplemented by beans and squash, as well as dog, deer, and rabbit meat. Their rulers made sure that enterprising merchants provided them with status goods such as ornamental pottery, rare shells and stones, and precious skins and feathers.

Tula was a commercial hub, political capital, and ceremonial center. While its layout differed from Teotihuacán's, many features revealed borrowings from other Mesoamerican peoples. Temples consisted of giant pyramids topped

Toltec Temple. Tula, the capital of the Toltec Empire, carried on the Mesoamerican tradition of locating ceremonial architecture at the center of the city. The Pyramid of the Morning Star cast its shadow over all other buildings. And above them stood columns of the Atlantes, carved Toltec god-warriors, the figurative pillars of the empire itself. The walls of this pyramid were likely embellished with images of snakes and skulls. The north face of the pyramid has the image of a snake devouring a human.

by colossal stone soldiers; ball courts where subjects and conquered peoples alike played their ritual sport were found everywhere. The architecture and monumental art reflected the mixed and migratory origins of the Toltecs: a combination of Maya and Teotihuacáno influences. At its height, the Toltec capital teemed with 60,000 people, a huge metropolis by contemporary European standards (if small by Song and Abbasid Islamic standards).

THE CAHOKIANS IN NORTH AMERICA As in South America and Mesoamerica, cities took shape at the hubs of trading networks across North America. The largest was **Cahokia**, along the Mississippi River near modern-day East St. Louis, Illinois. A city of about 15,000, it approximated the size of London at the time. Farmers and hunters settled in the region around 600 CE, attracted by its rich soil, its woodlands for fuel and game, and its access to the trading artery of the Mississippi. Eventually, fields of maize and other crops fanned out toward the horizon. The hoe replaced the trusty digging stick, and satellite towns erected granaries to hold the increased yields.

By 1000 CE, Cahokia was an established commercial center for regional and long-distance trade. The hinterlands produced staples for Cahokia's urban consumers, and in return Cahokia's crafts rode inland on the backs of porters and to distant markets in canoes. Woven fabrics and ceramics from Cahokia were exchanged for mica from the Appalachian Mountains, seashells and sharks' teeth from the Gulf of Mexico, and copper from the upper Great Lakes. Cahokia became more than an importer and exporter: it served as the principal exchange hub for an entire regional network trading in salt, tools, pottery, woven stuffs, jewelry, and ceremonial goods.

Dominating Cahokia's urban landscape were enormous mounds (thus the Cahokians' nickname, "mound people"). These earthen monuments reveal a sophisticated design and careful maintenance: their builders applied layers of sand and clay to prevent the foundations from drying and cracking. It was from these artificial hills that the people paid homage to spiritual forces. Building this kind of infrastructure without draft animals, hydraulic tools, or even wheels was labor-intensive, so the Cahokians recruited neighboring people to help. A palisade around the city protected the metropolis from marauders.

Ultimately, Cahokia's success led to its downfall. As woodlands fell to the axe and arable soil lost nutrients, timber and food became scarce. In contrast to the sturdy dhows of the Arabian Sea and the bulky junks of the China seas, Cahokia's river canoes could only carry limited cargoes. Cahokia's commercial networks thus met their technological and environmental limits. When the creeks that fed its water system could not keep up with demand, engineers changed their course, but to no avail. By 1350, the city was practically empty. But Cahokia represented the growing networks of trade and migration in North America and the ability of North Americans to organize vibrant commercial societies.

Two forces contributed to greater integration in sub-Saharan Africa and the Americas from 1000 to 1300 CE: commercial exchange (of salt, gold, ivory, and enslaved people in

Cahokia Mounds. This is all that is left of what was once a large city organized around temple mounds in what today is Illinois. The largest of the temples, known as Monks Mound, was likely a burial site, with four separate terraces for crowds to gather. Centuries of neglect and erosion have taken their toll on what was once the largest human-made earthen mound in North America.

sub-Saharan Africa and of shells, pottery, textiles, and metals in the Americas) and urbanization (at Jenne, Timbuktu, and Great Zimbabwe in sub-Saharan Africa and at Chan Chan, Tula, and Cahokia in the Americas). By 1300, trans-Saharan and Indian Ocean exchange had brought Africa into full-fledged Afro-Eurasian networks of exchange, and, as we will see in Chapter 12, transatlantic exchange would soon connect the Americas into a truly global network.

The Mongol Transformation of Afro-Eurasia

Commercial networks were clearly one way to integrate the world. But just as long-distance trade could connect people, so could conquerors. The Inner Eurasian steppes had already unleashed horse-riding warriors such as the Kushans and Xiongnu (see Chapters 6 and 7). Now, the Mongols created an empire that connected east and west, expanding their reach not only through brutal conquest but also through the intensified trade and cultural exchanges that followed. (See Map 10.11.) The relatively stable connections that emerged across Mongol-controlled areas are sometimes referred to as a *Pax Mongolica*, which makes a reference to the earlier *Pax Romana* (see Chapter 7).

Who Were the Mongols?

The Mongols were a combination of forest and steppe peoples. Residing in circular, felt-covered tents, which they shared with some of their animals, they lived by hunting and livestock herding. They changed campgrounds with the seasons. Life on the steppes was such a constant struggle that only the strong survived. Their food, primarily animal products, provided high levels of protein, which built up their muscle mass and their strength. Always on the march, their society resembled a perpetual standing army with bands of well-disciplined military units led by commanders chosen for their skill.

Wielding heavy compound bows made of sinew, wood, and horn, Mongol archers were deadly accurate at over 200 yards (183 meters)—even at full gallop. Their small but sturdy horses, capable of withstanding extreme cold, bore saddles with high supports in front and back, enabling the warriors to maneuver at high speeds. With their feet secure in iron stirrups, the archers could rise in their saddles to aim their arrows without stopping. These expert horsemen often remained in the saddle all day and night, even sleeping while their horses continued moving forward. Each warrior kept many horses, replacing tired mounts with fresh ones so that the armies could cover up to 70 miles (112 kilometers) per day.

Mongol tribes solidified their conquests by extending kinship networks, building an empire out of an expanding confederation of familial tribes. The tents, or households, were interrelated mostly by marriage: they were alliances sealed by the exchange of daughters. Conquering men married conquered women, and conquered men were selected to marry the conquerors' women. Chinggis Khan (the founder of the Mongol dynasty) may have had more than 500 wives, most of them daughters of tribes that he conquered or that allied with him.

Mongol Warriors. This miniature painting is one of the illustrations for a history by Rashid al-Din, the most outstanding scholar under the Mongol regimes. Note the relatively small horses and strong bows used by the Mongol soldiers.

Elite women could play important political roles. Chinggis Khan's mother, Hoelun, and his first wife, Börte, were instrumental in his rise to power, but even before playing the role of khan maker, women had figured large in Mongol tribal politics. In the generation after Chinggis, Sorghaghtani Beki, a Nestorian Christian and the mother of Kublai Khan (the first official Mongol ruler of China), helped engineer her sons' rule. Illiterate herself, she made sure that each son acquired a second language to aid in administering conquered lands. Despite her own Christian faith, Sorghaghtani gathered Confucian scholars to prepare Kublai Khan to rule China. Chabi, Kublai's senior wife, offered patronage to Tibetan monks who set about converting the Mongol elite in China to Tibetan Buddhism. While some elite Mongol women played a role in fostering religious diversity, others took part in battles. Khutulun, a niece of Kublai Khan, became famous for besting men in wrestling matches and claiming their horses as spoils.

Yet the political influence wielded by these later *khātūns* (Mongol queens) and other elite women of the Mongol ruling class is only one part of the story. Women in Mongol society were responsible for bearing and rearing children, milking and shearing livestock, and processing animal pelts for clothing. They organized camp logistics in times of peace and war. Although women were often bought and sold, Mongol wives had the right to own property and to divorce. More recent studies of Mongol women have emphasized the economic influence they wielded as they acquired wealth and property of their own. Central to making sense of Mongol women is recognizing that theirs was an ever-changing story. Mongol family dynamics and gender roles changed due not only to the dramatic and relatively swift transformation of the Mongols from a pastoral steppe society to a settled empire, but also to the regional differences in ideas about women's roles in the varied regions into which the Mongols spread.

Conquest and Empire

The Mongols' need for grazing lands contributed to their desire to conquer distant fertile belts and rich cities. The Mongols depended on settled peoples for grain and manufactured goods, including iron for tools, wagons, weapons, bridles, and stirrups. Their first expansionist forays followed caravan routes.

The Mongol expansion began in 1206 under a united cluster of tribes. These tribes were unified by a gathering of clan heads who chose one of those present, Temüjin (c. 1162–1227), as khan, or supreme ruler. Taking the name Chinggis (Genghis) Khan, he launched a series of conquests southward across the Great Wall of China and westward to Afghanistan and Persia. The Mongols even invaded Korea in 1231. The armies of Chinggis's sons reached both the Pacific Ocean and the Adriatic Sea. Chinggis's grandsons founded dynasties in Persia, in China, and on the southern Eurasian steppes. Thus, a realm took shape that touched all four of Afro-Eurasia's cultural spheres.

MONGOLS IN ABBASID BAGHDAD In the thirteenth century, Mongol tribes were streaming out of the steppes, crossing the whole of Asia and entering the eastern parts of Europe. Mongke Khan, a grandson of Chinggis, made clear the Mongol aspiration to world domination: he appointed his brother Hulagu to conquer Iran, Syria, Egypt, Byzantium, and

The Global View

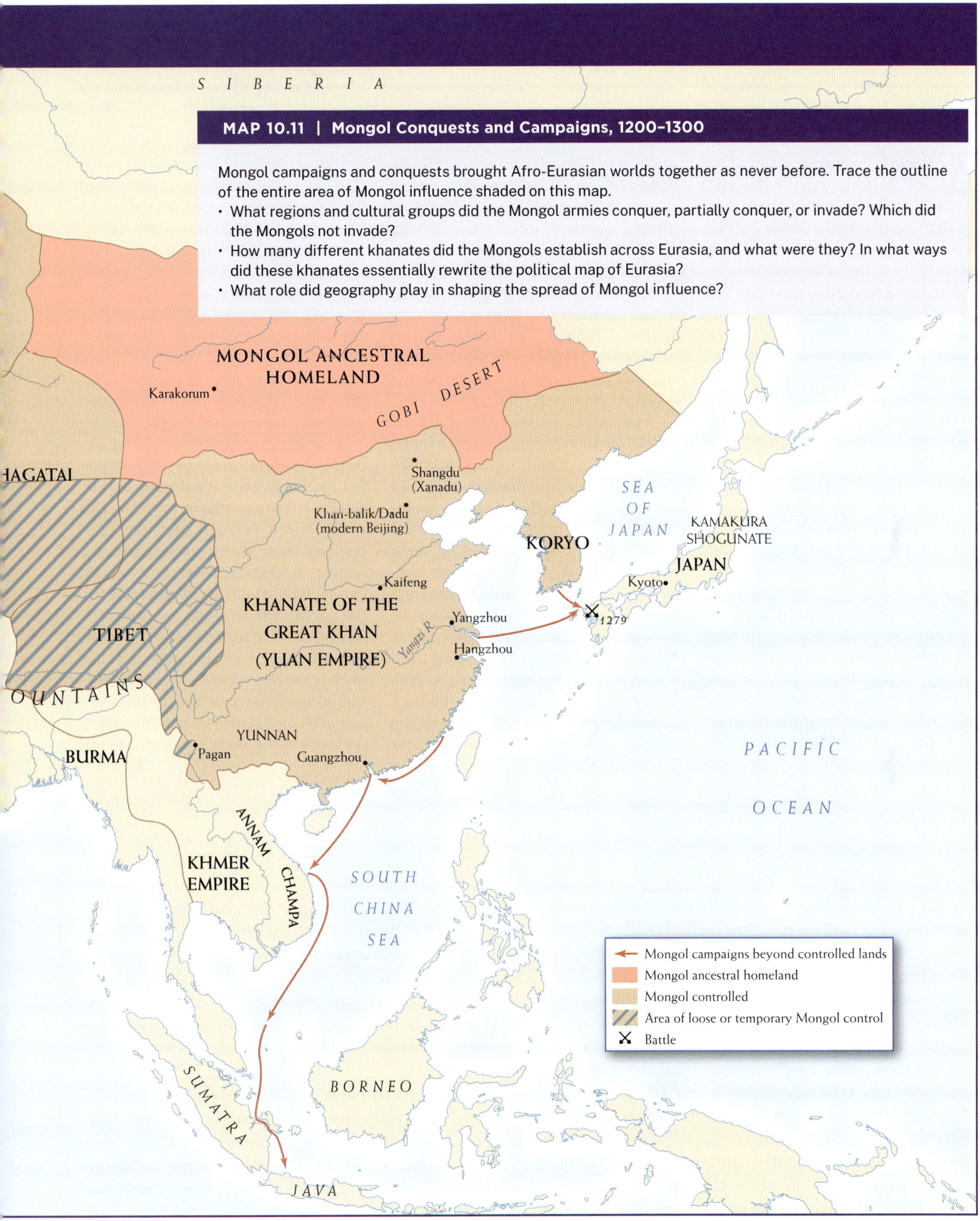

MAP 10.11 | Mongol Conquests and Campaigns, 1200–1300

Mongol campaigns and conquests brought Afro-Eurasian worlds together as never before. Trace the outline of the entire area of Mongol influence shaded on this map.

- What regions and cultural groups did the Mongol armies conquer, partially conquer, or invade? Which did the Mongols not invade?
- How many different khanates did the Mongols establish across Eurasia, and what were they? In what ways did these khanates essentially rewrite the political map of Eurasia?
- What role did geography play in shaping the spread of Mongol influence?

Current Trends in World History

A Most Unusual Nomad Empire

Although nomadic pastoralists and sedentary agriculturalists depended on each other to flourish, their deep commitments to their institutions and ways of life made cooperation difficult. Pastoralists endeavored to be as self-sufficient as possible. They scorned peoples who dug in the soil. On the other hand, as we noted in Chapter 3, sedentary peoples, most notably their literate members, regarded herders as uncivilized barbarians. The Chinese, for instance, saw the steppe peoples who lived to the north of them, and often invaded their state, as greedy, violent raiders from barbarian lands.

The Mongols were the quintessential pastoral nomads. Very little is known of their early history, largely because they were a small, fragmented, and powerless people living along the borderlands of southern Siberia, eastern Mongolia, and northwestern Manchuria. To their east lived the Tatars, and to their west the Uighurs and Khitai, far more powerful pastoral peoples from whom the Mongols learned many of their political and military skills. The Mongols first surface in Chinese sources during the Tang dynasty (618–907 CE). The Chinese, who feared the military capabilities of steppe peoples and were regularly invaded and even conquered by those peoples, had little fear of the Mongols at this time, regarding them as an insignificant community far from the empire's northern frontier. The Mongols were well known, however, for raiding, looting, and violence toward outsiders and among themselves.

Few individuals have had a greater impact on world history than the founder of the Mongol state, Temüjin (c. 1162–1227). His youthful travails hardened him as a warrior and made him a leader. Having lost his father at a young age and being the eldest of his siblings, he, along with his mother, endured a harsh existence. But as an adult, he unified warring Mongol clans and defeated the Mongols' enemies, either assimilating them to the Mongol way of life or exterminating them if they refused his leadership. In 1206, as a result of his spectacular military successes, he took the name Chinggis Khan, meaning "supreme ruler." Not only did he bring most of Inner Asia under his rule, but his armies pushed southward into Manchuria and northern China and west toward central Asia and the Islamic states. At his death in 1227, he divided his vast territorial conquests among the four sons of his first wife, Börte. These men and their successors created four Mongol states, called khanates, loosely linked as an empire: Yuan China; the Khanate of the Golden Horde; the northern steppe (Khanate of the Chagatai); and Persia, known as the Il-Khanate.

The Mongols established and extended their rule over settled societies in China, Iran, central Asia, and part of the East Slavic lands, but then had to decide how to rule over sedentary populations. Specifically, the issue facing Mongol rulers was whether to foster close relations with the ruling classes of the conquered societies or stay apart, relying on military force. In truth, the Mongol Empire was fragmented and each state was ruled in manifestly different ways. Yet one quality underlay all the Mongol territories—the dominant presence of the Mongol military and the

Armenia, and he appointed another brother, Kublai, to rule over China, Tibet, and the northern parts of India.

When Hulagu reached Abbasid Baghdad in 1258, he encountered a feeble foe and a city that was a shadow of its former glorious self. Merely 10,000 horsemen faced his army of 200,000 soldiers, who were eager to acquire the booty of a wealthy city. Even before the battle had begun, Baghdadi poets were composing elegies for their dead and mourning the defeat of Islam. The slaughter was vast. Hulagu claimed to have taken the lives of at least 2 million people (2,000 thousands, to be exact), although given that he was boasting to a French king in an attempt to impress and gain an ally, the exaggerated numbers ought not be taken at face value. The Mongols hunted their adversaries in wells, latrines, and sewers and followed them into the upper floors of buildings, killing them on rooftops until, as an Iraqi Arab historian observed, streets and mosques were filled with blood. In a few weeks of sheer terror, the Abbasid caliphate was demolished. Hulagu's forces showed no mercy to the caliph himself, who was rolled up in a carpet and trampled to death by horses. With Baghdad crushed, the Mongol armies then pushed on to Syria.

MONGOLS IN CHINA In the east, Mongol forces under Chinggis Khan had entered northern China at the beginning of the thirteenth century, defeating the Khitai army, which was no match for the Mongols' superior cavalry on the North China plain. Despite some serious setbacks due to the climate (including malaria for the men and the deaths high prestige that was attached to being a Mongol. Commonly, pastoral nomads who conquered sedentary peoples kept their distance from those settled societies with their cities, bureaucracies, artisans, and priests, instead extracting tribute from them while maintaining their own distinctive way of life. For example, Chinggis forbade his followers to live in towns, and the Golden Horde Mongols lived separately from the peoples they conquered, maintaining their pastoral norms and content to receive tribute payments.

Early on, some of Chinggis's followers wanted to annihilate the northern Chinese population and turn the region into pure pastureland. Ogodei, Chinggis's third son and successor as the Great Khan, was opposed to Chinggis's merciless and destructive practices and ordered his followers not to kill or loot indiscriminately. One of Ogodei's successors, Kublai, became the founder of the Yuan dynasty in China (1279–1368), claiming for himself the Chinese mandate of heaven. Even so, Kublai cherished his Mongol identity, never learned Chinese, and never consulted a book in Chinese. Moreover, the Yuan rulers divided the populations under their rule into four ranked tiers: the first was the Mongols themselves; the second, the non-Han Chinese of the western parts of Inner Asia, mainly nomads like themselves; the third, the northern Chinese, conquered early in the Mongol expansion; and the fourth, the southern Chinese, once ruled by the Song dynasty and the center of Confucian culture. In such a fashion, the Yuan dynasty, although centered in China proper—the heartland of urbanization and high culture—did not allow itself to be swallowed up by the Han population or its culture.

Thus, the Mongol Empire, which lasted for more than two centuries, made an uneasy accommodation with sedentary populations, with its rulers partially embracing the institutions of the sedentary peoples, but never fully renouncing their pastoral, nomadic ways. In this way, they were able to create a *Pax Mongolica*, in which diverse peoples interacted across territory governed by conquerors.

QUESTIONS FOR ANALYSIS

- How did nomads and sedentary peoples view one another?
- Why might one consider the Mongols in general, and Temüjin in particular, to be unlikely conquerors?
- In what ways did different Mongol leaders negotiate the difference between pastoral and sedentary ways?

EXPLORE FURTHER

Di Cosmo, Nicola, Allen J. Frank, and Peter Golden (eds.), *The Cambridge History of Inner Asia: The Chinggisid Age* (2009).

Khazanov, Anatoly M., *Nomads and the Outside World,* 2nd ed., trans. Julia Crookurden, with a foreword by Ernest Gellner (1994).

Mote, Frederick W., *Imperial China, 900–1800* (1999).

Rossabi, Morris, *A History of China* (2014).

Tanner, Harold M., *China: A History* (2009).

Weatherford, Jack, *Genghis Khan and the Making of the Modern World* (2004).

of horses from the heat), Chinggis's grandson Kublai Khan (1215–1294) seized southern China from the Song dynasty beginning in the 1260s. The Song army fell before Mongol warriors brandishing the latest gunpowder-based weapons, technology the Mongols had borrowed from Chinese inventors and now used against them.

Hangzhou, the last Song capital, fell in 1276. Kublai Khan's most able commander, Bayan, led his crack Mongol forces in seizing town after town, moving ever closer to the capital. The Dowager Empress tried to buy them off, proposing substantial tribute payments, but Bayan was uncompromising. Once conquered, the Dowager Empress and Hangzhou were treated well by the Mongols. In fact, Hangzhou was still one of the greatest cities in the world when it was visited by the Venetian traveler Marco Polo in the 1280s and by the Muslim traveler Ibn Battuta in the 1340s. Both men agreed that neither Europe nor the Islamic world had anything like it.

Kublai Khan founded his Yuan dynasty with a capital at Khan-balik (also called Dadu, which became present-day Beijing). The Mongol conquest of both north and south changed China's political and social landscape. But Mongol rule did not impose rough steppe-land ways on the "civilized" urbanite Chinese. While non-Chinese outsiders took political control, they were a conquering elite that ruled over a vast Han majority. The result was a divided ruling system in which incumbent Chinese elites governed locally, while the newcomers managed the unifying central dynasty and collected taxes for the Mongols.

Analyzing Global Developments

Growth in the World Population to 1340

The world experienced considerable human population growth during the first millennium of the Common Era in spite of occasional downturns, such as those resulting from climate change in Asia and Europe between 200 CE and 600 CE and the decline of the Roman and Han Empires. Overall, however, an upward trajectory occurred, though it averaged out to a mere 0.06 percent per year. For the period from 1750 to 1950, that percentage increased to a little more than 0.5 percent per year, and since 1950, the number has risen to 1.75 percent per year. Even so, as we will see in the next chapter, the major populations in the Afro-Eurasian landmass were terrified by the loss of life that accompanied the spread of the Black Death across this immense area.

Since the Afro-Eurasian recovery from the Black Death, the world's population has been on a steady increase, spectacularly so in the twentieth century, the result of more abundant food supplies, more accurate knowledge of the spread of diseases and a resulting control of epidemic diseases, and a general rise in the standards of living. The long-term impact of the pandemic that reached across the globe in 2020 remains to be seen. COVID-19 has tested what scientists thought they knew about the spread of epidemic diseases and has provided firsthand experience of their lopsided demographic impacts (in terms of region, age, and so on), as well as the dramatic social and economic crises such diseases and the responses to them can bring.

	Regional Human Population (in millions)					
Year	Asia	Europe	Africa	Americas	Oceania	World
400 BCE	97	30	17	8	1	**153**
1 CE	172	41	26	12	1	**252**
200	160	55	30	11	1	**257**
600	136	31	24	16	1	**208**
1000	154	41	39	18	1	**253**
1200	260	64	48	26	2	**400**
1340	240	88	80	32	2	**442**

Source: Massimo Livi-Bacci, *A Concise History of World Population* (Malden, MA: Wiley-Blackwell, 2012), p. 25.

QUESTIONS FOR ANALYSIS

- Why was the rate of population growth so limited in premodern times?
- Comparing the population size of the regions in 1340, what do the numbers tell us about where the largest share of wealth and power resided? How does this compare with earlier eras in the chart?
- Why was the population of the Americas in 1340 so small considering its large territorial size?
- Why were the peoples living in the Afro-Eurasian landmass so vulnerable to epidemic diseases in the fourteenth century?
- How do changes in global population relate to the developments tracked in this chapter: a maritime revolution; a more integrally connected Africa; a thriving Abbasid caliphate; and an expanding Mongol Empire?

MONGOL REVERBERATIONS IN SOUTHEAST ASIA Southeast Asia also felt the whiplash of Kublai Khan's conquest. Circling Song defenses in southern China, the Mongols galloped southwest and conquered states in Yunnan and in Burma. From there, in the 1270s, the armies headed directly back east into the soft underbelly of the Song state. In this sweep, portions of mainland Southeast Asia became annexed to China for the first time. Kublai Khan used the conquered Chinese fleets to push his expansionism onto the high seas—meeting with failure during his unsuccessful 1274 and 1281 invasions of Japan from Korea. An ill-fated Javanese expedition to extend Mongol reach beyond the South China Sea in 1293 was Kublai Khan's last.

THE COLLAPSE OF MONGOL RULE In the end, the Mongol Empire reached its outer limits. In the east, as we just saw, the waters of the South China Sea and the Sea of Japan foiled Mongol expansion into Java and Japan. In the west, the Egyptian Mamluks stemmed the advancing Mongol armies and prevented Egypt from falling into their hands. Better at conquering than governing, the Mongols struggled to rule their vast possessions in makeshift states. Bit by bit, they yielded control to local administrators and rulers who governed as their surrogates. There was also frequent feuding among the Mongol rulers themselves. In China and in Persia, Mongol rule collapsed in the fourteenth century. Ultimately, the Mongols would meet a deadly adversary even more brutal than they were: the plague of the fourteenth century (see Chapter 11).

Mongol conquest reshaped Afro-Eurasia's social landscape. Islam would never again have a unifying authority like the caliphate or a powerful center like Baghdad. China, too, was divided and changed by the Mongols' introduction of Persian, Islamic, and Byzantine influences into China's architecture, art, science, and medicine. The Yuan policy of benign tolerance brought elements from Christianity, Judaism, Zoroastrianism, and Islam into the Chinese mix. The Mongol thrust also facilitated the flow of fine goods, traders, and technology from China to the rest of the world. Finally, the Mongol conquests encouraged an unprecedented Afro-Eurasian interconnectedness, surpassing even the Hellenistic connections that Alexander's conquests had brought in the late fourth century BCE (see Chapter 6). Out of Mongol conquest and warfare would come centuries of trade, migration, and increasing contacts among societies in Africa, Europe, and Asia.

Conclusion

Between 1000 and 1300 CE, Afro-Eurasia formed four large cultural spheres. As trade and migration spanned longer distances, each of these spheres expanded, prospered, and became more integrated. In central Afro-Eurasia, Islam was firmly established, and its merchants, scholars, and travelers acted as commercial and cultural intermediaries as they exposed others to their universalizing religion. As seaborne trade expanded, India, too, became a commercial crossroads. Merchants in its port cities welcomed traders arriving from Arab lands to the west, from China to the east, and from Southeast Asia. China itself also boomed, pouring its manufactures into trading networks that reached across Eurasia and North Africa and even into sub-Saharan Africa. Christian Europe had two religious centers at Rome and Constantinople; states supporting each found ways to challenge polities that had adopted Islam as the primary religion. Each of these spheres consolidated internally while also engaging the other spheres through commerce, religion, and even conquest.

Neither the Americas nor sub-Saharan Africa experienced the same degree of integration, but trade and migration in these areas nevertheless had profound effects. Certain African cultures flourished as they encountered the commercial energy of trade on the Indian Ocean. Africans' trade with one another linked coastal and interior regions in an ever more integrated world. American peoples built cities that dominated regional cultural areas and that were also connected through trade of foodstuffs (such as maize), cotton, or even luxury goods.

By 1300, trade, migration, and conflict connected Afro-Eurasian worlds in unprecedented ways. When Mongol armies swept into China, Southeast Asia, and the heart of Islamic territories to the west, they applied a thin coating of political integration to these far-flung regions and built on existing trade links. It is important to note that, at the same time, most people remained focused on local life, driven by the need for subsistence and governed by spiritual and governmental representatives acting at the behest of distant authorities.

Even so, residents noticed the evidence of cross-cultural exchanges everywhere—in the clothing styles of provincial elites, such as Chinese silks in Paris or quetzal plumes in northern Mexico; in enticements to move (and forced removals) to new frontiers; in the news of faraway conquests or advancing armies. Worlds were coming together within themselves and across territorial boundaries, while nevertheless remaining apart as they sought, or struggled, to maintain their own identity and traditions. In Afro-Eurasia especially, as the movement of goods and peoples shifted from ancient land routes to sea-lanes, these contacts were more frequent and far-reaching. Never before had the world seen so much activity connecting its parts to each other. And within each of these spheres, never before had there been so much shared cultural similarity—linguistic, religious, legal, and military. By the time the Mongol Empire arose, the regions composing the globe were well on the way to becoming those that we now recognize as today's cultural spheres.

After You Read This Chapter

TRACING THE GLOBAL STORYLINES

FOCUS ON: The Emergence of the World We Know Today

The Islamic World

- The Islamic world undergoes a burst of expansion, prosperity, and cultural diversification but remains politically fractured.
- Arab merchants and Sufi mystics spread Islam over great distances and make it more appealing to other cultures, helping to transform the religion into the unifying force of a distinct cultural sphere.
- Islam travels across the Sahara Desert; the powerful empire of Mali, supplying gold and enslaved people, arises in West Africa.

China

- The Song dynasty reunites China after three centuries of fragmented rulership, reaching into the past to reestablish a sense of a "true" Han Chinese identity, through a widespread print culture and the denigration of outsiders.
- Agrarian success and advances in manufacturing—including the production of both iron and porcelain—fuel an expanding economy, complete with paper money.

India

- India remains a mosaic under the canopy of Hinduism despite cultural interconnections and increasing prosperity.
- The invasion of Turkish Muslims leads to the creation of the Delhi Sultanate, which rules over India for three centuries, strengthening both cultural diversity and tolerance.

Christian Europe

- Roman Catholicism becomes a "mass" faith and helps create a common European cultural identity, at least in western Europe. A second center continues in Constantinople, providing a focal point for Eastern Orthodox Christianity, which spreads to the north.
- Feudalism organizes the relationship between elites and peasants, while manorialism forms the basis of the economy.
- Europe's growing confidence is manifest in its efforts, including the Crusades and the reconquering of Iberia, to drive Islam out of "Christian" lands.

CHRONOLOGY

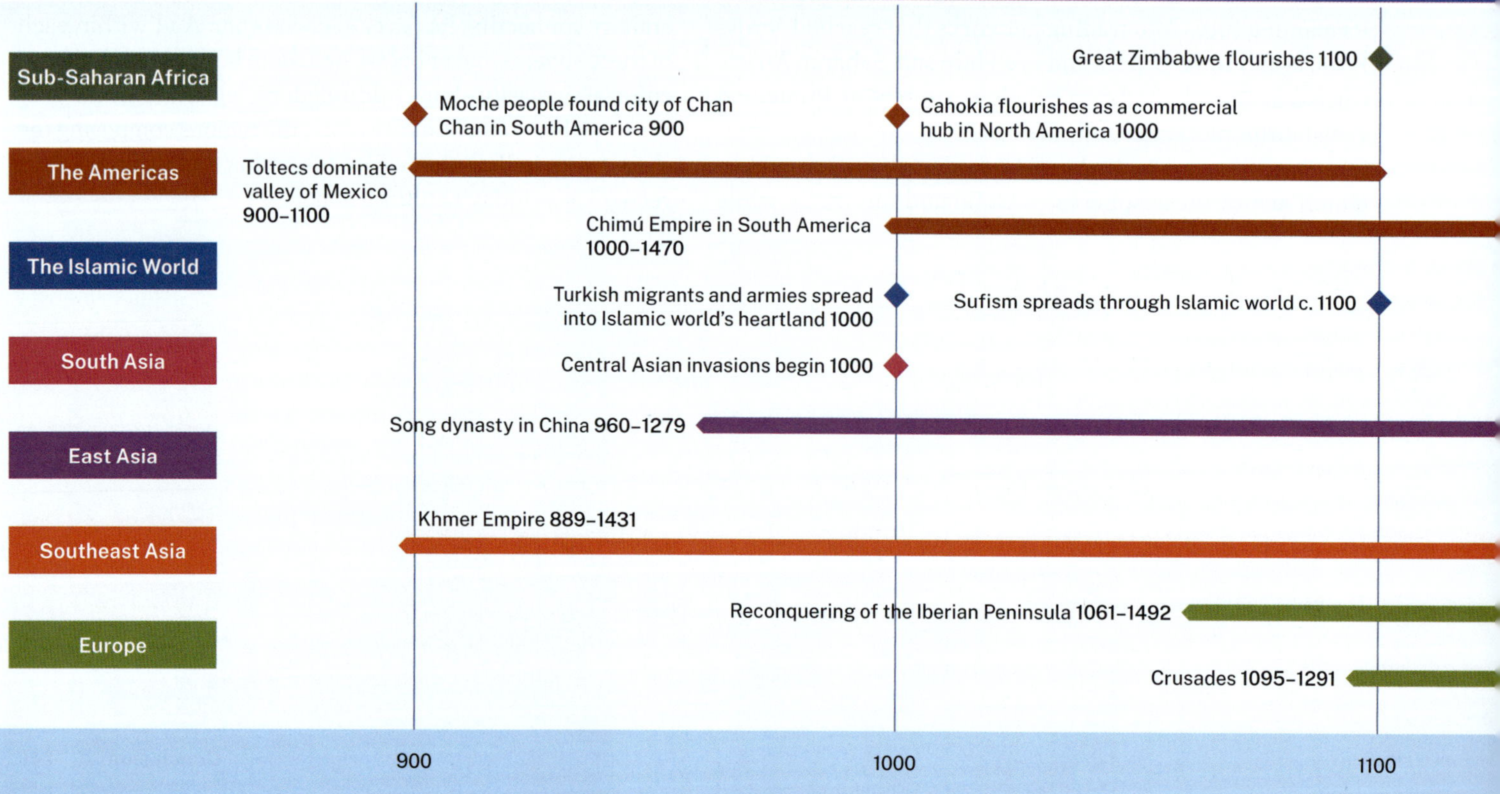

KEY TERMS

Cahokia p. 433
Chimú Empire p. 430
Delhi Sultanate p. 414
entrepôts p. 407
flying cash p. 417
jizya p. 410
Mali Empire p. 426
manorialism p. 422
Sufism p. 410
Toltecs p. 432

THINKING ABOUT GLOBAL CONNECTIONS

Thinking about Worlds Together, Worlds Apart From 1000 to 1300 CE, a range of social and political developments contributed to the consolidation of four cultural spheres that still exist today: Europe, the Islamic world, India, and China. In what ways did these spheres interact with one another? In what ways was each sphere genuinely distinct from the others? To what extent were sub-Saharan Africa and the Americas folded into these spheres, and with what result?

Thinking about Transformation & Conflict and Becoming the World As the four cultural spheres of Afro-Eurasia consolidated, shocking examples of conflict between them began to take place. Whether from Pope Urban II's call in 1095 to reclaim the "holy land" from Muslims or the Mongol Hulagu's brutal sack of Baghdad in 1258, this period was marked by large-scale warfare between rival cultural spheres. To what extent was such conflict inevitable? In what ways did conflict transform the groups involved?

Thinking about Crossing Borders and Becoming the World Major innovations facilitated economic exchange in the Indian Ocean and in Song China. The magnetic needle compass, better ships, and improved maps shrank the Indian Ocean to the benefit of traders. Similarly, paper money in Song China changed the nature of commerce. How did these developments shift the axis of Afro-Eurasian exchange? What evidence suggests that bodies of water and the routes across them became more significant than overland exchange routes in binding together Afro-Eurasia? What were the longer-term implications of these developments?

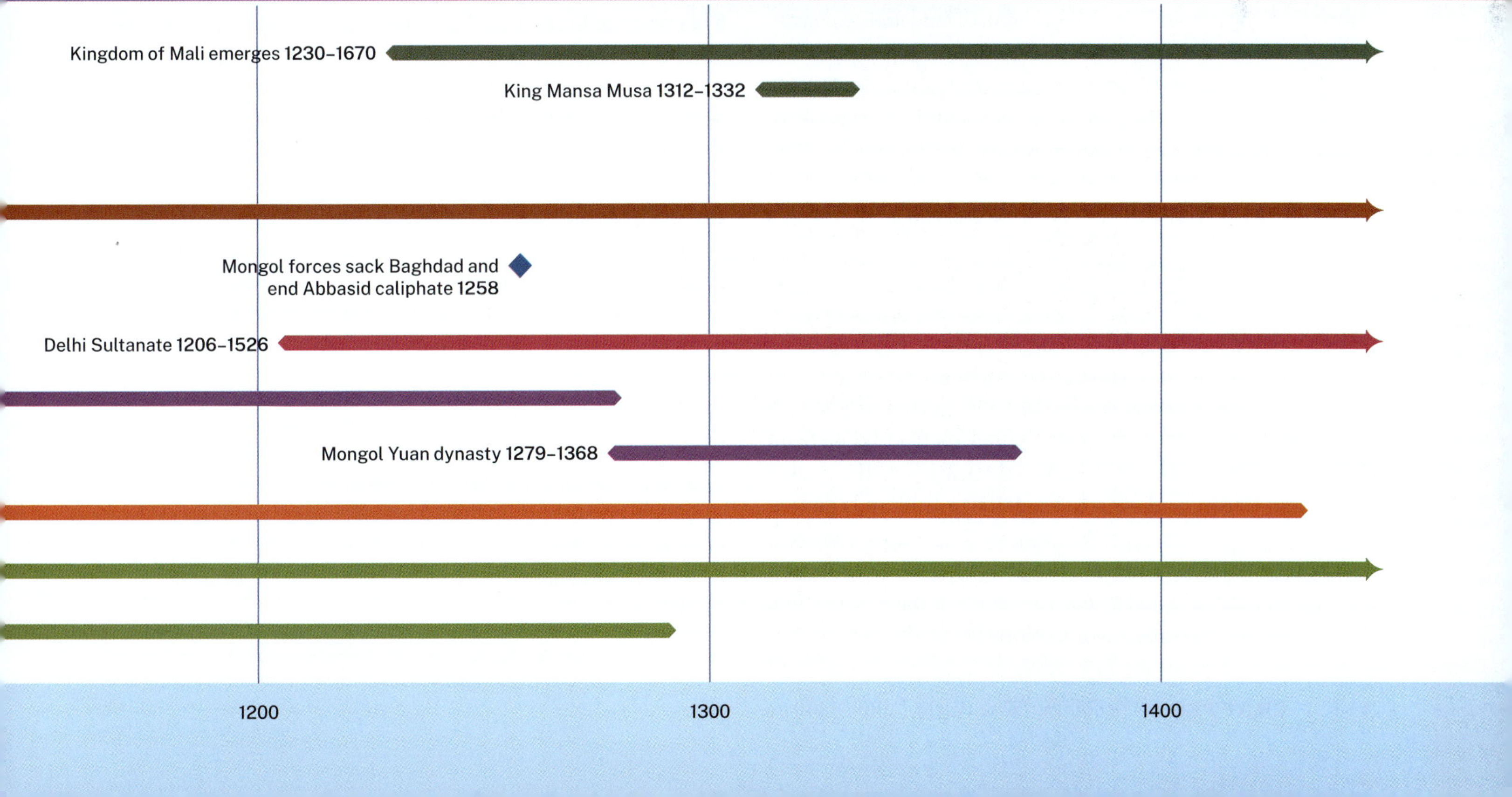

Global Themes and Sources

Comparing "World" Travelers over Time

Changes to maritime practice described in this chapter, along with the Silk Roads across Inner Eurasia, facilitated travel for trade, diplomacy, and religious pilgrimage on a scale previously unseen. While earlier travelers, like the Spanish nun Egeria or the Buddhist monks Faxian and Xuanzang (see Global Themes and Sources in Chapter 8), had covered great distances and for reasons similar to those of some of the travelers whose accounts you'll read here, the sheer distances traveled by Bar Sāwmā or Ibn Battuta eclipse the journeys of their centuries-earlier counterparts. Like the earlier pilgrims, however, several travelers who moved between the worlds of Afro-Eurasia in this period left records of their stunning journeys or were written about by others.

As we saw at the start of this chapter, Bar Sāwmā traveled primarily along land routes from Yuan dynasty China all the way to modern-day France in the late thirteenth century. A Nestorian Christian monk, Bar Sāwmā appears to have made his journeys, which were recorded in a Syriac text shortly after his death in 1294, with both diplomacy and religious pilgrimage in mind. The Venetian merchant Marco Polo was traveling at nearly the same time as Bar Sāwmā, but in the opposite direction. Long after his travels were completed, Marco Polo recounted his twenty-four-year voyage (1271–1295), including his time in the Mongol court of China. About a generation after Bar Sāwmā and Marco Polo completed their journeys, between 1325 and 1354, the North African Muslim scholar Ibn Battuta set out to traverse a combination of land and sea routes through much of Africa, Southwest Asia, Southeast Asia, and East Asia. Writing after his travels were completed, Ibn Battuta offered details about the places he visited and their customs, as well as the hardships of travel. A near contemporary of Ibn Battuta, a Syrian Islamic historian by the name of al-Umari who lived in the first half of the fourteenth century, provides the fourth passage here, a description of the pilgrimage of yet another famous traveler, Mansa Musa, the king of Mali, in 1324–1325. The final "world" traveler represented here is the Chinese naval commander Zheng He, whose voyages came later (1405–1433; see Chapter 11) but can be usefully compared with those of Bar Sāwmā, Marco Polo, Ibn Battuta, and Mansa Musa. In a series of expeditions, Zheng He's fleet sailed from China, through Southeast Asia, to Sri Lanka, into the northern Indian Ocean, and even to the Persian Gulf and the Red Sea, leaving stone inscriptions at many of the sites it visited.

The records of these travelers—Bar Sāwmā, Marco Polo, Ibn Battuta, Mansa Musa, and Zheng He—allow us not only to study the realities of pilgrimage and exploration in this period, but also to analyze how they are similar and how they changed over time. Together with what you've learned in this chapter about the political situations across Afro-Eurasia, you can begin to explain the similarities and differences in patterns of "world" travel over hundreds of years and to think about the historical significance of those journeys.

ANALYZING COMPARISONS OF WORLD TRAVELERS

Based on these excerpts, what sorts of details seem to interest each traveler? How does the form of each text (life of revered holy figure, post-trip travelogue, inscription) influence the reliability of the account?

What sorts of dangers are explicitly mentioned, or implied, in these texts?

What in the texts suggests the exchange of goods and ideas?

Compare these travel accounts with those from the Global Themes and Sources feature of Chapter 8. What are some of the similarities and differences in the "world" travels of these two groups of individuals? What accounts for those changes and continuities over time?

PRIMARY SOURCE 10.1

Pilgrimage to Jerusalem (c. 1300), Bar Sāwmā

This passage illustrates the realities of travel for Bar Sāwmā and his travel companion, Markōs, in the late thirteenth century. Setting out from the Mongol capital Khan-balik, they enter the territory of Mar Denha (or Mar Catholicus), the patriarch of the Nestorian Church, who, after greeting them warmly, sends them on their way to visit holy sites. Just in this one passage, we can see the territory these pilgrims covered, starting in Khan-balik, arriving at Maraghah (in the territory of modern Azerbaijan), continuing on to Baghdad, and then into Armenia and Georgia. (Titles of sites have been set in all capitals as in the original translation.)

What are some of the practical travel issues Bar Sāwmā and his travel companion face?

How do Bar Sāwmā and his companion interact with people and places on their travels?

Why might Bar Sāwmā and his companion have wanted to go to Jerusalem, and why might the road have been blocked?

And having enjoyed the conversation of those brethren they set out to go to ADHÔRBÎJÂN . . . so that they might travel from there to BAGHDÂD, to MÂR DENHÂ, the Catholicus. . . . Now it happened that Mâr Catholicus had come to MÂRÂGHÂH [a town of ADHÔRBÎJÂN, the capital of HÛLÂGÛ KHÂN], and they met him there. And at the sight of him their joy grew great, and their gladness was increased. . . . And when [Mar Catholicus] asked them, "Whence [come] ye?" they replied, "From the countries of the East, from KHÂN BÂLÎK, the city of the King of Kings [KÛBLÂI] KHÂN. We have come to be blessed by you, and by the Fathers (i.e. Bishops), and the monks, and the holy men of this quarter of the world. And if a road [openeth] to us, and God hath mercy upon us, we shall go to JERUSALEM."

. . . [Catholicus] comforted them and said unto them, "Assuredly, O my sons, the Angel of Providence shall protect you on this difficult journey, and he shall be a guide unto you until the completion of your quest." . . .

[After a few days, Bar Sāwmā and his companion] request [of Mar Catholicus]: "If we have found mercy (i.e., favour) in the eyes of Mâr our Father, let him permit us to go to BAGHDÂD, in order that we may receive a blessing from the holy sepulchers (or relics?) of MÂR MÂRÊ, . . . the Apostle, the teacher of the East, and those of the Fathers that are there. And from there we would go to the monasteries that are in the country of BÊTH GARMAI and in NISIBIS that we may be blessed there also, and demand assistance."

And when the Catholicus saw the beauty of their object, and the innocence of their minds, and the honesty of their thoughts, he said unto them, "Go ye, my sons, and may Christ, the Lord of the Universe, grant unto you your petition." . . . And he wrote for them a *pêthîkhâ* (i.e. a letter of introduction) to these countries so that they might be honourably entreated whithersoever they went; and he sent with them a man to show them the way, and to act as a guide along the roads.

And they arrived in Baghdad, and thence they went to the Great Church of KÔKÊ [at Ctesiphon]. . . . And they went to the monastery of MÂR MÂRÎ, the Apostle, and received a blessing from the sepulchers (or relics?) of that country. And from there they turned back and came to the country of BÊTH GARMAI, and they received blessings from the shrine (or tomb) of MÂR EZEKIEL [the prophet, near Dâḳôḳ], which was full of helps and healings. And from there they went to ARBÎL, and thence to MÂWSIL (i.e. Môṣul on the Tigris). And they went [to] SHÎGAR (SINJÂR), and NISIBIS, and MERDÂ (MARDÎN); and were blessed by the shrine [containing] the bones of MÂR AWGÎN, the second CHRIST. And thence they went to GÂZARTÂ of BÊTH ZABHDAI, and they were blessed by all the shrines and monasteries, and the religious houses, and monks, and the Fathers (i.e. Bishops) in their dioceses. . . .

And when they arrived at the city of Animto [i.e. ANÎ, the ancient capital of Christian ARMENIA, situated on an affluent of the river Araxes], and saw the monasteries and the churches therein, they marvelled at the great extent of the buildings and at their magnificence. And thence they went towards BÊTH GÛRGÂYÊ (i.e. the country of Georgia), so that they might travel by a clear (or safe?) road, but when they arrived there they heard from the inhabitants of the country that the road was cut because of the murders and robberies which had taken place along it.

Chapter 4. And the two monks turned back and came to Mâr Catholicus, who rejoiced [at the sight of] them, and said unto them, "This is not the time for a journey to JERUSALEM. The roads are a disturbed state, and the ways are cut. Now behold, ye have received blessings from all the Houses of God, and the shrines (or relics?) which are in them, and it is my opinion that when a man visits them with a pure heart, the service thus paid to them is in no way less than that of a pilgrimage to Jerusalem."

Source: Rabban Bar Sāwmā, *The Monks of Kublai Khan, Emperor of China, or The History of the Life and Travels of Rabban Sāwmā*, translated by E. A. Wallis Budge (London: Religious Tract Society, 1928), pp. 140–43, 145–46.

PRIMARY SOURCE 10.2

The Mongol Capital at Kanbalu (Khan-balik) (c. 1300), Marco Polo

In the last quarter of the thirteenth century, the Venetian merchant Marco Polo, together with his father and uncle, undertook a magnificent trek eastward on the Silk Roads. They ultimately arrived at Khan-balik, the capital of the Mongol Yuan dynasty (and the place from which Bar Sāwmā set out, in the previous passage). There, they encountered Kublai Khan. Long after his journey was completed, Marco Polo offered this thorough description of the city, which would ultimately become Beijing. While some scholars have questioned the veracity of Polo's travels, arguing that he may never have made it all the way to China, the detail offered in this passage suggests firsthand experience.

- What does Marco Polo emphasize in his description of Kanbalu (Khan-balik)?
- What different groups of people live in greater Khan-balik? How are they organized and distributed?
- Why do you think Marco Polo focuses on the issues that he describes?

The city of Kanbalu is situated near a large river in the province of Cathay, and was in ancient times eminently magnificent and royal. The name itself implies "the city of the sovereign"; but his majesty having imbibed an opinion from the astrologers, that it was destined to become rebellious to his authority, resolved upon the measure of building another capital, upon the opposite side of the river, where stand the palaces just described: so that the new and the old cities are separated from each other only by the stream that runs between them. The new-built city received the name of Tai-du, and all the Cathaians, that is, all those of the inhabitants who were natives of the province of Cathay, were compelled to evacuate the ancient city, and to take up their abode in the new. Some of the inhabitants, however, of whose loyalty he did not entertain suspicion, were suffered to remain, especially because the latter, although of the dimensions that shall presently be described, was not capable of containing the same number as the former, which was of vast extent.

This new city is of a form perfectly square, and twenty-four miles in extent, each of its sides being neither more nor less than six miles. It is enclosed with walls of earth, that at the base are about ten paces thick, but gradually diminish to the top, where the thickness is not more than three paces. In all parts the battlements are white. The whole plan of the city was regularly laid out by line, and the streets in general are consequently so straight, that when a person ascends the wall over one of the gates, and looks right forward, he can see the gate opposite to him on the other side of the city. In the public streets there are, on each side, booths and shops of every description. All the allotments of ground upon which the habitations throughout the city were constructed are square, and exactly on a line with each other; each allotment being sufficiently spacious for handsome buildings, with corresponding courts and gardens. One of these was assigned to each head of a family; that is to say, such a person of such a tribe had one square allotted to him, and so of the rest. Afterwards the property passed from hand to hand. In this manner the whole interior of the city is disposed in squares, so as to resemble a chessboard, and planned out with a degree of precision and beauty impossible to describe. The wall of the city has twelve gates, three on each side of the square, and over each gate and compartment of the wall there is a handsome building; so that on each side of the square there are five such buildings, containing large rooms, in which are disposed the arms of those who form the garrison of the city, every gate being guarded by a thousand men. It is not to be understood that such a force is stationed there in consequence of the apprehension of danger from any hostile power whatever, but as a guard suitable to the honour and dignity of the sovereign. Yet it must be allowed that the declaration of the astrologers has excited in his mind a degree of suspicion with regard to the Cathaians. . . .

Outside of each of the gates is a suburb so wide that it reaches to and unites with those of the other nearest gates on both sides, and in length extends to the distance of three or four miles, so that the number of inhabitants in these suburbs exceeds that of the city itself. Within each suburb there are, at intervals, as far perhaps as a mile from the city, many hotels, or caravanserais, in which the merchants arriving from various parts take up their abode; and to each description of people a separate building is assigned, as we should say, one to the Lombards, another to the Germans, and a third to the French. . . .

Guards, in parties of thirty or forty, continually patrol the streets during the course of the night, and make diligent search for persons who may be from their homes at an unseasonable hour, that is, after the third stroke of the great bell. When any are met with under such circumstances, they immediately apprehend and confine them, and take them in the morning for examination before officers appointed for that purpose, who, upon the proof of any delinquency, sentence them, according to the nature of the offence, to a severer or lighter infliction of the bastinade beating with a cudgel, usually on the soles of the feet, which sometimes, however, occasions their death. It is in this manner that crimes are usually punished amongst these people, from a disinclination to the shedding of blood, which their *baksis* or learned astrologers instruct them to avoid.

Source: Marco Polo, *The Travels of Marco Polo, the Venetian*, edited by Thomas Wright (London: George Bell and Sons, 1904), pp. 181–86.

PRIMARY SOURCE 10.3

The Holy Sites of Jerusalem (c. 1360), Ibn Battuta

Ibn Battuta's travels dwarf those of any other world traveler in this period. What began as a *hajj* became a journey of tens of thousands of miles. Traveling for more than a quarter century, Ibn Battuta was particularly interested in the role and practice of Islam in each place he visited. While he was sometimes called into action to serve as a learned Muslim *qadi* (judge) in the places he visited, his travels often took the form of engaged and devoted religious tourism, as when he visited Jerusalem, described in the passage here.

- What do you make of Ibn Battuta's itinerary? What sites does he visit? What, and how, does he learn about the history of each site?
- How does Ibn Battuta describe mosques? Churches? What do you think accounts for the differences in his descriptions?
- How do Ibn Battuta's descriptions of holy sites compare with those in Bar Sāwmā's account?

From Gaza I travelled to the city of Abraham [Hebron], the mosque of which is of elegant, but substantial, construction, imposing and lofty, and built of squared stones. At one angle of it there is a stone, one of whose faces measures twenty-seven spans. It is said that Solomon commanded the *jinn* to build it. Inside it is the sacred cave containing the graves of Abraham, Isaac, and Jacob, opposite which are three graves, which are those of their wives. I questioned the imám, a man of great piety and learning, on the authenticity of these graves, and he replied: "All the scholars whom I have met hold these graves to be the very graves of Abraham, Isaac, Jacob and their wives. No one questions this except introducers of false doctrines; it is a tradition which has passed from father to son for generations and admits of no doubt."...

On the way from Hebron to Jerusalem, I visited Bethlehem, the birthplace of Jesus. The site is covered by a large building; the Christians regard it with intense veneration and hospitably entertain all who alight at it.

We then reached Jerusalem (may God ennoble her!), third in excellence after the two holy shrines of Mecca and Medína, and the place whence the Prophet was caught up into heaven. Its walls were destroyed by the illustrious King Saladin and his successors, for fear lest the Christians should seize it and fortify themselves in it. The sacred mosque is a most beautiful building, and is said to be the largest mosque in the world. Its length from east to west is put at 752 "royal" cubits and its breadth at 435. On three sides it has many entrances, but on the south side I know of one only, which is that by which the imám enters. The entire mosque is an open court and unroofed, except the mosque al-Aqsá, which has a roof of most excellent workmanship, embellished with gold and brilliant colours. Some other parts of the mosque are roofed as well. The Dome of the Rock is a building of extraordinary beauty, solidity, elegance, and singularity of shape. It stands on an elevation in the centre of the mosque and is reached by a flight of marble steps. It has four doors. The space round it is also paved with marble, excellently done, and the interior likewise. Both outside and inside the decoration is so magnificent and the workmanship so surpassing as to defy description. The greater part is covered with gold so that the eyes of one who gazes on its beauties are dazzled by its brilliance, now glowing like a mass of light, now flashing like lightning. In the centre of the Dome is the blessed rock from which the Prophet ascended to heaven, a great rock projecting about a man's height, and underneath it there is a cave the size of a small room, also of a man's height, with steps leading down to it. Encircling the rock are two railings of excellent workmanship, the one nearer the rock being artistically constructed in iron, and the other of wood.

Among the grace-bestowing sanctuaries of Jerusalem is a building, situated on the farther side of the valley called the valley of Jahannam [Gehenna] to the east of the town, on a high hill. This building is said to mark the place whence Jesus ascended to heaven. In the bottom of the same valley is a church venerated by the Christians, who say that it contains the grave of Mary. In the same place there is another church which the Christians venerate and to which they come on pilgrimage. This is the church of which they are falsely persuaded to believe that it contains the grave of Jesus. All who come on pilgrimage to visit it pay a stipulated tax to the Muslims, and suffer very unwillingly various humiliations. Thereabouts also is the place of the cradle of Jesus, which is visited in order to obtain blessing.

Source: Ibn Battúta, *Ibn Battúta: Travels in Asia and Africa, 1325–1354*, translated and edited by H. A. R. Gibb (London: George Routledge & Sons, Ltd., 1929), pp. 55–57.

PRIMARY SOURCE 10.4

The *Hajj* of Mansa Musa (1324–1325), al-Umari

Al-Umari was a historian who lived in the first half of the fourteenth century. While his personal life reflected the vicissitudes of court politics in Mamluk-controlled Syria (complete with a period of imprisonment when he fell out of favor), his well-researched history was much appreciated by his contemporaries. The passage included here, in which al-Umari describes the famed *hajj* of Mansa Musa, shows that al-Umari himself traveled to Cairo to gather information from local informants about Mansa Musa's sojourn in the city.

What are the layers of reporting in this passage? How does the traveling historian al-Umari come by his information on Mansa Musa?

How does Mansa Musa's *hajj* influence the economic lives of the peoples with whom he and his retinue come into contact?

How typical was Mansa Musa's *hajj*? Even if it was atypical, what can you generalize about the role of *hajj* in the Mediterranean and Indian Ocean worlds based on Mansa Musa's and Ibn Battuta's experiences?

The emir Abū'l-Ḥasan 'Alī b. Amīr Ḥājib told me that he was often in the company of sultan Mūsā the king of this country when he came to Egypt on the Pilgrimage. He was staying in [the] Qarāfa [district of Cairo] and Ibn Amīr Ḥājib was governor of Old Cairo and Qarāfa at that time. A friendship grew up between them and this sultan Mūsā told him a great deal about himself and his country and the people of the Sūdān who were his neighbours. One of the things which he told him was that his country was very extensive and contiguous with the Ocean. By his sword and his armies he had conquered 24 cities each with its surrounding district with villages and estates. It is a country rich in livestock—cattle, sheep, goats, horses, mules—and different kinds of poultry—geese, doves, chickens. The inhabitants of his country are numerous, a vast concourse, but compared with the peoples of the Sūdān who are their neighbours and penetrate far to the south they are like a white birth-mark on a black cow. He has a truce with the gold-plant people, who pay him tribute.

Ibn Amīr Ḥājib said that he asked him about the gold-plant, and he said: "It is found in two forms. One is found in the spring and blossoms after the rains in open country (*ṣaḥrā'*). It has leaves like the *najīl* grass and its roots are gold (*tibr*). The other kind is found all the year round at known sites on the banks of the Nīl and is dug up." . . .

Sultan Mūsā told Ibn Amīr Ḥājib that gold was his prerogative and he collected the crop as a tribute except for what the people of that country took by theft.

"This sultan Mūsā, during his stay in Egypt both before and after his journey to the Noble Ḥājib, maintained a uniform attitude of worship and turning towards God. It was as though he were standing before Him because of His continual presence in his mind. He and all those with him behaved in the same manner and were well-dressed, grave, and dignified. He was noble and generous and performed many acts of charity and kindness. He had left his country with 100 loads of gold which he spent during his Pilgrimage on the tribes who lay along his route from his country to Egypt, while he was in Egypt, and again from Egypt to the Noble Hijāz and back."

From the beginning of my coming to stay in Egypt I heard talk of the arrival of this sultan Mūsā on his Pilgrimage and found the Cairenes eager to recount what they had seen of the Africans' prodigal spending. . . .

This man flooded Cairo with his benefactions. He left no court emir (*amīr muqarrab*) nor holder of a royal office without the gift of a load of gold. The Cairenes made incalculable profits out of him and his suite in buying and selling and giving and taking. They exchanged gold until they depressed its value in Egypt and caused its price to fall. . . .

Merchants of Miṣr and Cairo have told me of the profits which they made from the Africans, saying that one of them might buy a shirt or cloak (*thawb*) or robe (*izār*) or other garment for five dinars when it was not worth one. Such was their simplicity and trustfulness that it was possible to practice any deception on them. They greeted anything that was said to them with credulous acceptance. But later they formed the very poorest opinion of the Egyptians because of the obvious falseness of everything they said to them and their outrageous behaviour in fixing the prices of the provisions and other goods which were sold to them. . . .

Muhanna' b. 'Abd al-Bāqī al-'Ujrumī the guide informed me that he accompanied sultan Mūsā when he made the Pilgrimage and that the sultan was very open-handed towards the pilgrims and the inhabitants of the Holy Places. He and his companions maintained great pomp and dressed magnificently during the journey. He gave away much wealth in alms. "About 200 mithqals of gold fell to me," said Muhanna' "and he gave other sums to my companions." Muhanna' waxed eloquent in describing the sultan's generosity, magnanimity, and opulence.

Gold was at a high price in Egypt until they came in that year. The mithqal did not go below 25 *dirhams* and was generally above, but from that time its value fell and it cheapened in price and has remained cheap till now. The mithqal does not exceed 22 *dirhams* or less. This has been the state of affairs for about twelve years until this day by reason of the large amount of gold which they brought into Egypt and spent there.

Source: al-Umari, *Corpus of Early Arabic Sources for West African History*, translated by J. F. P Hopkins (Cambridge: Cambridge University Press, 1981), pp. 267, 269–71.

PRIMARY SOURCE 10.5

The Galle Trilingual Stone Inscription (1411), Zheng He

No discussion of world travelers in this increasingly connected Afro-Eurasian world would be complete without evidence from Zheng He's travels, although he lived in a slightly later period than the other travelers discussed here (namely, during the Ming dynasty, which took the mandate of heaven from the Mongol Yuan dynasty of China in the aftermath of the Black Death; see Chapter 11). The seven far-reaching naval expeditions undertaken by Zheng He from 1405 to 1433 illustrate Ming patronage of voyages of exploration that demonstrated their might. This trilingual inscription (in Chinese, Persian, and Tamil), set up in 1411 by Zheng He and his companions in Sri Lanka (called Ceylon in the source), demonstrates the pragmatic religious devotion of those voyaging for nonreligious aims.

- What range of goods does Zheng He's embassy offer? Why are these specific commodities offered?
- Why do Zheng He, who was born and raised a Muslim, and his companions make offerings to Buddha?
- How do Zheng He's reasons for travel and what he does at this holy site compare with the reasons and actions of the other travelers in this section?

His Majesty, the Emperor of the Great Ming dynasty has despatched the eunuchs Ching-Ho [Zheng He], Wang Ch'ing-Lien, and others to set forth his utterance before Buddha, the World Honoured one, as follows:

"Deeply do we reverence you, Merciful and Honoured One, whose bright perfection is wide-embracing, and whose way of virtue passes all understanding, whose law enters into all human relations, and the years of whose great Kalpa (period) are like the sand of the river in number, you whose controlling influence ennobles and converts, whose kindness quickens, and whose strength discerns, whose mysterious efficacy is beyond compare! Whereas Ceylon's mountainous isle lies in the south of the ocean, and its Buddhist temples are sanctuaries of your gospel, where your miraculous responsive power imbues and enlightens. Of late, we have dispatched missions to announce our mandate to foreign nations, and during their journey over the ocean they have been favoured with the blessing of your beneficent protection. They escaped disaster or misfortune and journeyed in safety to and fro. In everlasting recognition of your supreme virtue, we, therefore, bestow offerings in recompense, and do now reverently present before Buddha, the Honoured One, oblations of gold and silver, gold embroidered jewelled banners of variegated silk, incense burners, and flower vases, silks of many colours in lining and exterior, lamps and candles with other gifts, in order to manifest the high honour of our worship. Do you, Lord Buddha, bestow on them, your regard!"

List of Alms bestowed at the shrine of the Buddhist temple in the Mountain of Ceylon as offerings:

1000 pieces of gold; 5000 pieces of silver; fifty rolls of embroidered silk in many colours; fifty rolls of silk taffeta in many colours; four pairs of jewelled banners, gold embroidered, and of variegated silk; two pairs of the same picked in red; one pair of the same in yellow; one pair in black; five antique brass incense burners; five pairs of antique brass flower vases picked in gold on lacquer, with gold stands; five pairs of yellow brass candle-sticks, picked in gold on lacquer, with gold stand; five yellow brass lamps picked in gold on lacquer, with gold stands; five incense vessels in vermilion red, lacquered gold picked on lacquer, with gold stands; six pairs of golden lotus flowers; 2500 catties of scented oil; ten pairs of wax candles; ten sticks of fragrant incense.

The date being the seventh year of Yung-Lo (1410 a.d.) marked Chi ch'ou in the sixty years' cycle, on the Chia Hsu day of the sixty days cycle in the second moon, being the first day of the month. A reverent oblation.

Source: "Appendix I. Translation of the Chinese Inscription," translated by Edmund Backhouse, in "The Galle Trilingual Stone," *Spolia Zeylanica* 8 (Issued from the Colombo Museum; Ceylon: H. M. Richards, Acting Government Printer, 1913), pp. 125–26. Bracketed notes added by the author.

Interpreting Visual Evidence

Imagining the World

During this period when Afro-Eurasia was "becoming the world," cartographers began producing "world" maps. In 1154, al-Idrisi, a Muslim cartographer sponsored by King Roger II of Sicily, produced his *Tabula Rogeriana*. Al-Idrisi's map was accompanied by a commentary that contained information about the ten regions (numbered west to east; but note that the map was drawn so that the south is at the top) and seven climate zones (numbered south to north and following the scheme set forth by the second-century CE Greco-Roman geographer Ptolemy). In 1375, a Jewish mapmaker named Abraham Cresques, from the island of Majorca off the east coast of Spain, produced the second map included here, which is known as the *Catalan Atlas*. Cresques's map is a mixture of practical information and storytelling. The crisscrossed lines that mark compass bearings, suggestive of a nautical chart, reflect the influence of the compass on European mapmaking beginning around 1300. The ornate depictions of the Mali king Mansa Musa and the caravan of Marco Polo offer historical information. In 1459, a monk named Fra Mauro, from Venice, created his *Mappa Mundi* (Map of the World), the third map pictured here. Fra Mauro's map is striking in its detail and information. Not only does it carefully mark out shorelines, rivers, cities, and other geographic features, but it also includes banners with detailed information and even drawings of the different types of ships (such as the North Atlantic cogs, Chinese junks, and Arabian dhows, discussed in this chapter) that sailed the different seas.

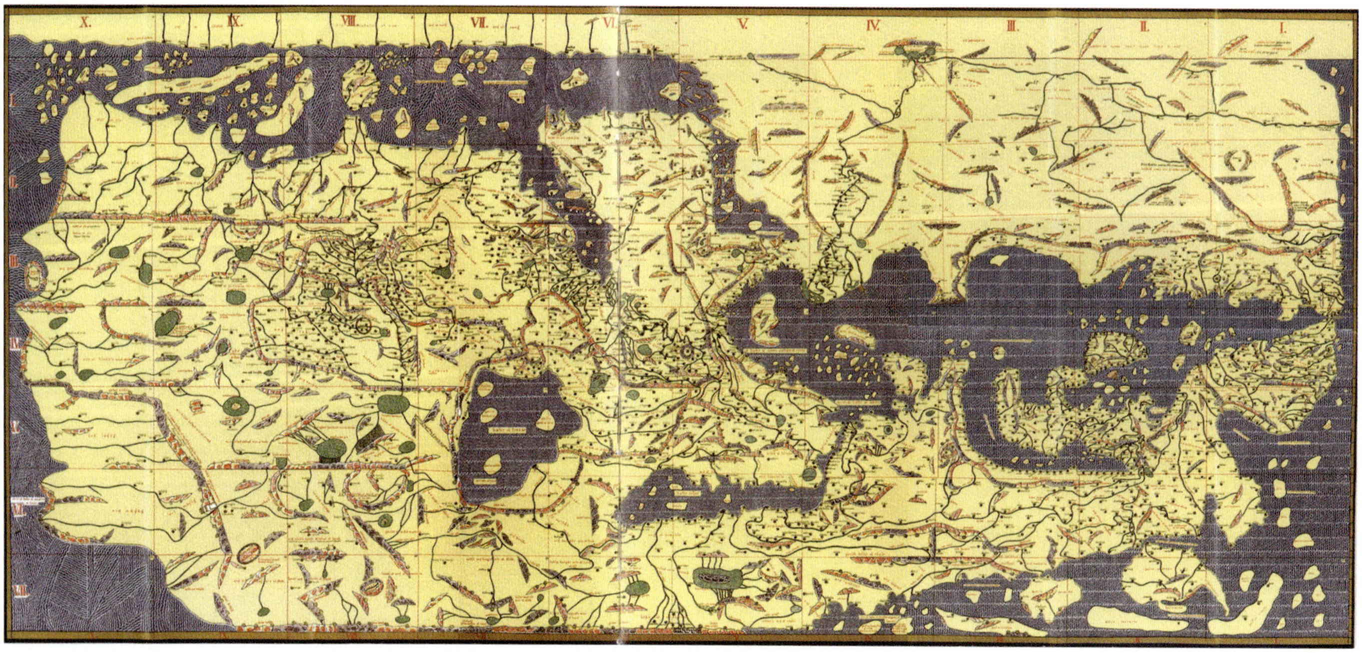

Al-Idrisi's *Tabula Rogeriana*.

QUESTIONS FOR ANALYSIS

1. Compare these maps in terms of their representations of land, water, perspective, and other features. What accounts for the maps' similarities and differences?
2. Based on the features and information on the maps, where did the cartographers get the data to create them? How might these maps have been used, and by whom?
3. What do these maps suggest about how these cartographers and their patrons understood the known world? Why are certain parts of the world emphasized and others left off?

Cresques's *Catalan Atlas* (detail).

Fra Mauro's *Mappa Mundi*.

Before You Read This Chapter

GLOBAL STORYLINES

The Black Death, Recovery, and Conquest

- The spread of the Black Death and the collapse of the Mongol Empire set off crises across Eurasia.
- Continuity in religious beliefs and cultural institutions accompanies changes to political structures in Europe, in an expanding Islamic world, and in China.
- Following the Black Death in central Eurasia, new rulers, using a blend of religion, military expansion, administrative control, and cultural tolerance, replace the Mongols.
- In western Christendom, new monarchies establish political order and the Renaissance brings a cultural rebirth to societies devastated by plague.
- The Ming dynasty replaces the Mongol Yuan dynasty in China, using an elaborate Confucian bureaucracy to oversee infrastructure and long-distance exchange.

CHAPTER OUTLINE

11

Crises and Recovery in Eurasia

1300–1500

FOCUS QUESTIONS

- What were the nature and origins of the crises spanning Eurasia during the fourteenth century? How did the Black Death affect China, the Islamic world, and Europe?
- What role did religious belief systems play in rebuilding the Islamic world, Europe, and Ming China after the plague ended, in the fourteenth and fifteenth centuries?
- How similar and different were the ways in which regional rulers in postplague Eurasia attempted to construct unified states? What were the extent and nature of their successes?
- How did art and architecture reflect the political realities of the Islamic world, Europe, and Ming China after the Black Death?
- What were the similarities and differences between the ways that Islamic dynasties, Iberian rulers, and Ming rulers extended their territories and regional influence?

When Mongol armies besieged the Genoese trading outpost of Caffa on the Black Sea in 1346, they not only damaged trading links between East Asia and the Mediterranean but also unleashed a devastating disease: the bubonic plague. Defeated Genoese merchants and soldiers withdrew, inadvertently taking the germs with them aboard their ships. By the time they arrived in Messina, Sicily, half the passengers were dead. The rest were dying. People waiting on shore for the ships' cargoes were horrified at the sight and turned the ships away. Desperately, the captains went to the next port, only to face the same fate. Despite these efforts at isolation, Europeans could not keep the plague (called the Black Death) from reaching their shores. As the disease spread from port to port, it eventually contaminated all of Europe, killing nearly two-thirds of the population.

This story illustrates the magnitude and complexity of the connected world created by the Mongol invasions. They devastated polities, ravaged trade routes, and unwittingly unleashed the bubonic plague. The invasions left behind a series of khanates ruled by local warlords, rather than a centralized state. But Mongol invasions had also intensified cultural and political contacts. The channels of exchange—the land trails and sea-lanes of human voyagers—accidentally became conduits for deadly microbes. Indeed, these pathogens devastated societies far more decisively than did Mongol warfare. They were the real "murderous hordes" of world history. So staggering was the Black Death's toll that population densities did not recover for 200 years. Most severely affected were regions that the Mongols had brought together: settlements and commercial hubs along the old Silk Roads and around the Mediterranean and South China Sea. While segments of the Indian Ocean trading world experienced death and disruption, South Asian societies, which had escaped the Mongol conquest, also escaped the great loss of life and political disruptions associated with the Black Death.

Out of the rubble of Mongol conquest and disease emerged the green shoots of a new world. This chapter explores the ways in which Eurasian peoples restored what they cherished from pre-pandemic ways while discarding what they felt had failed. In some cases, they embraced radically new institutions and ideas. The recovery had striking parallels across Eurasia. Societies reaffirmed their most deeply held and long-standing beliefs, though with modifications that took into account changed circumstances. Chinese rulers looked to Confucian thought and well-known dynastic institutions to provide guidance going forward. In Muslim-controlled regions, a small band of Turkish-speaking warriors—the Ottomans—channeled the energies of a revived Islam to expand their own territory and spread their wings over the Islamic world. Europeans also invoked their traditions. In the Iberian Peninsula, political elites used a resurgent Catholicism to advance their political power, while driving Muslim communities out of Europe. Europeans also created new dynastic monarchies, while looking to the continent's distant Greek and Roman past for inspiration.

Radically new political institutions and ideas appeared across Eurasia in the aftermath of the Black Death. An outburst of cultural activity in southern Europe was among the most notable. Historians have called this flourishing the Renaissance (rebirth), for during this era Europeans rediscovered their Greek and Roman pasts and used inspiration drawn from classical antiquity to bring about far-reaching innovations in art, architecture, and thought, as well as political and financial institutions. While significant changes reshaped both institutions and ideas in this period, there were also many continuities. Considering how grievously people suffered and how many died, it is perhaps surprising how much of the old—particularly religious beliefs and institutions—survived both the aftermath of Mongol rule and the Black Death.

Collapse and Consolidation

Although the Mongol invasions overturned the political systems that they encountered, the plague devastated society itself. The pandemic killed millions, disrupted economies, and threw communities into chaos. Rulers could explain to their people the assaults of "barbarians," but it was much harder to make sense of an invisible enemy. Many concluded that mass death was God's wish and humankind's punishment. However, the upheaval gave surviving rulers and their regimes the opportunity to consolidate power by making dynastic matches through marriage, establishing new armies and taxes, and creating new systems to administer their states.

The Black Death

The spread of the **Black Death** was the fourteenth century's most significant historical development. (See Map 11.1.) Originating in Inner Asia, the disease combined bubonic, pneumonic, and septicemic plague strains, and it caused a staggering loss of life. Death rates ranged from 25 to 65 percent among infected populations.

How did the Black Death spread so far? One explanation may lie in climate changes. A cooler climate—what scholars refer to as a "Little Ice Age"—may have weakened populations and left them vulnerable to disease. In Europe, for instance, beginning around 1310, harsh winters and rainy summers shortened the growing season and ruined harvests. Exhausted soils could no longer supply the crops that expanding urban and rural populations required; at the same time, nobles squeezed the peasantry in an effort to maintain their luxurious lifestyles. The ensuing European famine lasted from 1315 to 1322, during which time millions died, either of starvation or from diseases against which the malnourished population had little resistance. Climate change and famine had thus crippled populations on the eve of the Black Death. Climate change also spread drought across central Asia, where bubonic plague had lurked for centuries. So when steppe peoples migrated in search of new pastures and herds, they carried the germs with them and into more densely populated agricultural communities. Rats also joined the exodus from the arid lands and transmitted fleas to other rodents, which carried the disease to humans.

The main conduit for the spread of pathogens across Eurasia was its vast trading network. The first outbreak in a heavily populated region occurred in southwestern China during the 1320s. From there, the disease spread through China and then took its death march westward along the major trade routes. The main path of transmission was across central Asia to the Crimea and the Black Sea and from there by ship to the Mediterranean Sea and the Italian city-states.

Plague Victim. The plague was highly contagious and quickly led to death. Here a physician and his helper cover their noses to avoid the unbearable stench emanating from the patient.

Secondary routes were also by sea: one from China to the Red Sea, and another across the Indian Ocean, through the Persian Gulf, and into the Fertile Crescent and what is now Iraq. All routes terminated at the Italian port cities, where ships with dead and dying men aboard arrived in 1347. From there, what Europeans called the Pestilence or the Great Mortality engulfed the western end of the landmass.

The Black Death struck heavily populated and highly integrated societies that were vulnerable to this virulent disease because their members had no immunity to it. Rodents, mainly rats, carried the plague bacilli that caused the disease. Fleas transmitted the bacilli from rodent to rodent, as well as to humans. The epidemic was terrifying, simply because its causes were unknown. Infected victims died quickly—sometimes overnight—and in great agony, coughing up blood and oozing pus and blood from ugly black sores the size of eggs. Some European sages attributed the ravaging of their societies to an unusual alignment of Saturn, Jupiter, and Mars. Many believed that God was angry with humanity. One Florentine historian compared the plague to the biblical flood and believed that the end of humankind was imminent. Everywhere across Eurasia where there was plague, people of all classes had no explanation for the death and disease; in fact, they often acted in ways that would have been considered reprehensible or outrageous in more normal times.

PLAGUE IN CHINA China was ripe for the pandemic. Its population had significantly increased under the Song dynasty (960–1279) and subsequent Mongol rule. But by 1300, hunger and scarcity spread as needed resources stretched thin. This weakened population was especially vulnerable to disease. For seventy years, the Black Death ravaged China, shattering the Mongol rulers' claim to a mandate from heaven. In 1331, plague may have killed 90 percent of the population in Bei Zhili (modern Hebei) Province. From there it spread through other provinces, reaching Fujian and the coast at Shandong. By the 1350s, most of China's large cities had already suffered through severe outbreaks.

The reign of the last Yuan Mongol rulers was thus a time of utter chaos. Even as the Black Death was engulfing large parts of China, bandit groups and dissident religious sects undercut the state's power. As in other areas devastated by the plague, popular religious movements foretold impending doom. Most prominent was the **Red Turban movement**, which took its name from its soldiers' red headbands. This movement blended China's diverse cultural and religious traditions, including Buddhism, Daoism, and other faiths. Its leaders emphasized strict dietary restrictions, penance, and ceremonial rituals in which the sexes freely mixed, while making proclamations that the world was drawing to its end.

PLAGUE IN NORTH AFRICA AND THE EASTERN MEDITERRANEAN The plague also devastated parts of the Muslim world, including places in North Africa. The Black Death reached Baghdad by 1347. By the next year, plague had overtaken Egypt, Syria, and Cyprus; one report from Tunis recorded the death of more than 1,000 people a day in that North African city. (See Global Themes and Sources: Primary Sources 11.1, 11.3, and 11.4.) Animals, too, were afflicted. One Egyptian writer commented: "The country was not far from being ruined. . . . One found in the desert the bodies of savage animals with the bubos under their arms. It was the same with horses, camels, asses, and all the beasts in general, including birds, even the ostriches" (Dols, p. 156). In the eastern Mediterranean, plague left many polities close to political and economic collapse. The great Arab historian Ibn Khaldûn (1332–1406), who lost his mother and father and a number of his teachers to the Black Death in Tunis, underscored the sense of desolation. "Cities and buildings were laid waste, roads and way signs were obliterated, settlements and mansions became empty, dynasties and tribes grew weak," he wrote. "The entire world changed" (Dols, p. 67).

The Global View

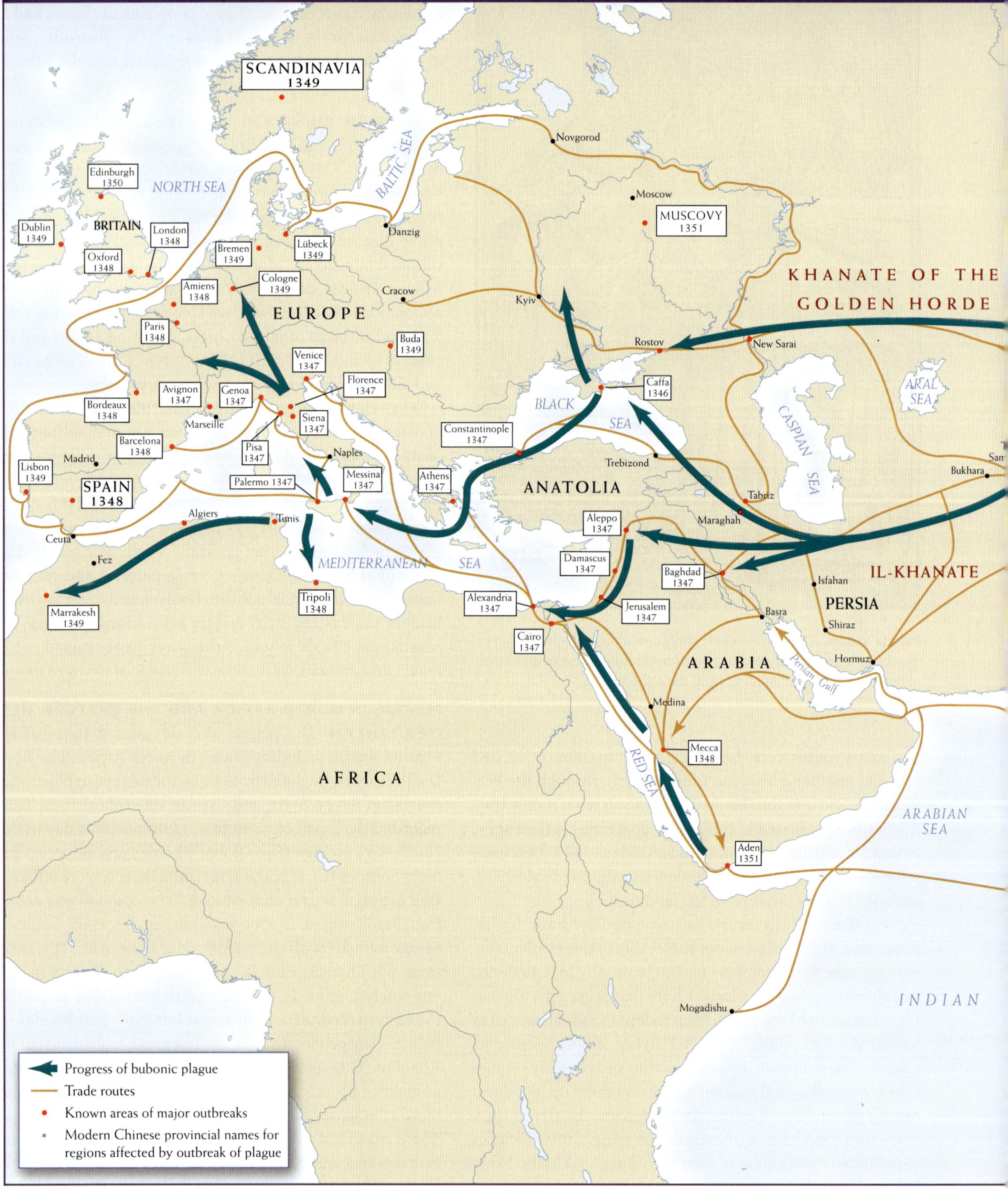

MAP 11.1 | The Spread of the Black Death

The Black Death was largely a Eurasian pandemic of the fourteenth century.

- What was the origin point of the Black Death? How far did it travel?
- Which trade routes did the Black Death follow? Which trade routes did the Black Death not appear to have followed? What do you think accounts for the difference?
- Where was the earliest instance of the Black Death? Where did it occur latest? What hypotheses can you assert about the Black Death based on the dates on the map?

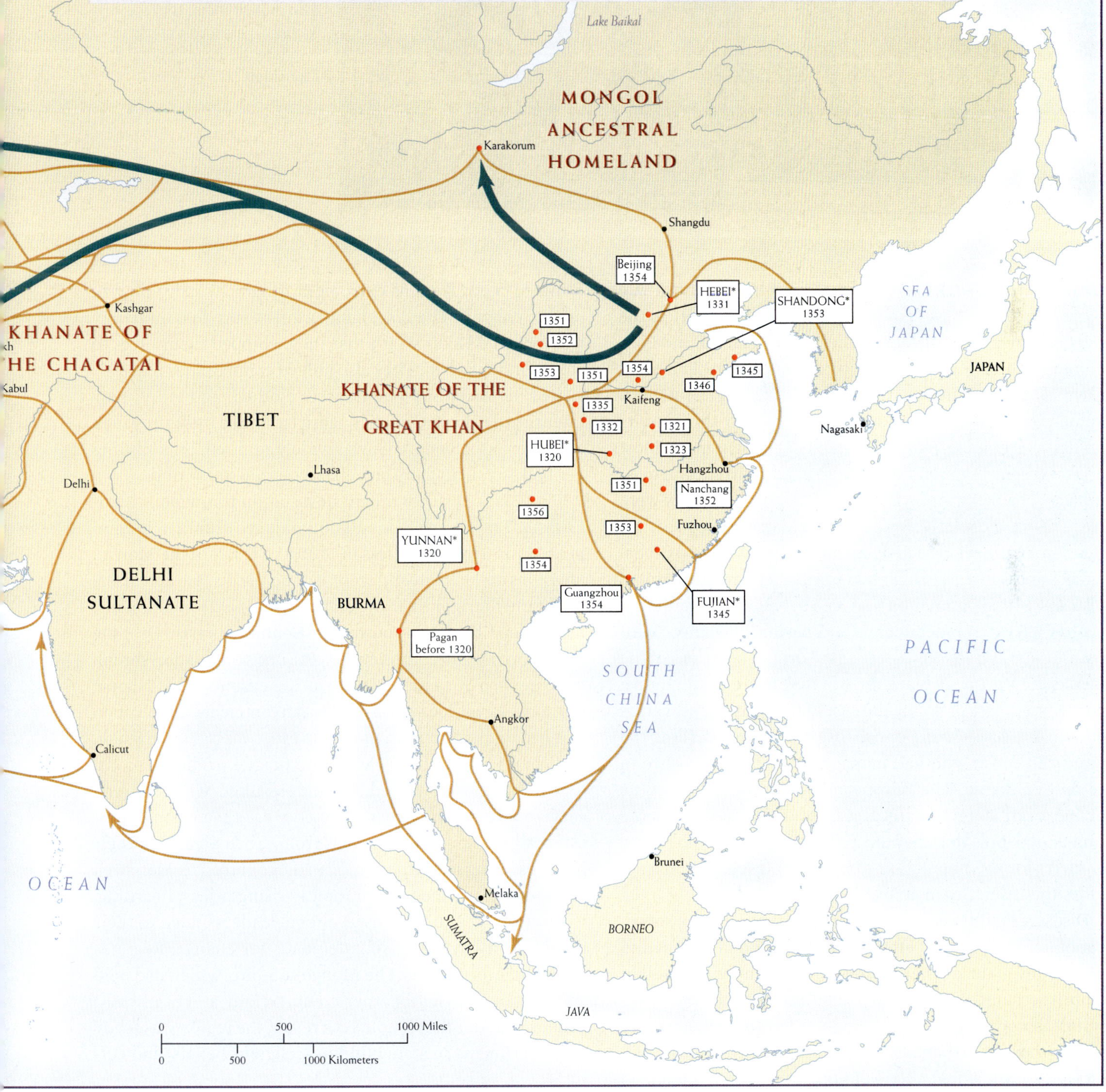

Burning Jews as Scapegoats. Across Europe, local populations blamed Jews for the spread of the plague; false rumors that the Jews had poisoned water wells were sometimes circulated. As a result, mobs gathered Jews together and burned them alive, even though the Catholic Church had official policies in place to protect them. This was a case where locals chose to ignore the church's official position.

PLAGUE IN EUROPE In Europe, the Black Death made landfall on the Italian Peninsula; then it seized France, the Low Countries (present-day Netherlands, Belgium, and Luxembourg), the Holy Roman Empire, and Britain. The overcrowded and unsanitary cities were particularly vulnerable. Bremen lost at least 8,000 souls, perhaps two-thirds of its population; Hamburg, another port city, at least as many. Most at risk were the poor who slept in crowded quarters. But master bakers, bankers, and aristocrats died too, unless they were able to flee to the relatively safer countryside in time to escape infection. No one had seen dying on such a scale. (See Global Themes and Sources: Primary Source 11.2.) Nearly two-thirds of Europe's total population perished between 1346 and 1353.

After 1353, the epidemic subsided, having killed those with no natural immunity and most of the original carriers of the disease, the European black rat. But the plague would return every seven years or so for the rest of the century, as well as sporadically through the entire fifteenth century, killing the young and those who had managed to escape exposure in the first epidemic. The European population continued its decline, until by 1450 many areas had only one-quarter the number of people that they did a century earlier. It took three centuries for the population to return to levels that existed before the Black Death arrived.

Disaster on this scale had enduring psychological, social, economic, and political effects. Many individuals turned to pleasure, even debauchery, determined to enjoy themselves before it became their turn to die. Some incorrectly blamed Jews for unleashing the plague, even though Jews died in numbers equal to those of Christians. Others, believing the church had lost God's favor, sought consolation in more individualized forms of piety, such as extreme fasting or worshipping in private chapels. The Flagellants were so sure that humanity had incurred God's wrath that they whipped themselves to atone for human sin. They also bullied communities that they visited, demanding to be housed, clothed, and fed. A new intensity of private Christian piety, exhibited by figures such as Catherine of Siena, who was widely admired for punishing her body to purify her soul, characterized the period.

The Black Death wrought devastation throughout Afro-Eurasia. The Chinese population plunged from 115 million in 1200 to 75 million or less in 1400, the result of the Mongol invasions of the thirteenth century and the disease and disorder of the fourteenth. (See Analyzing Global Developments: Population Changes in Fourteenth-Century Eurasia.) Over the course of the fourteenth century, Europe's population shrank by more than 50 percent. In the most densely settled Islamic territory—Egypt, located on the African continent—a population that had totaled around 6 million in 1400 was reduced by half.

When farmers fell ill with the plague or died from it, food production collapsed. Famines resulted, which starved survivors to death. Worst afflicted were the coastal cities, especially their ports. Refugees from urban areas fled their homes, seeking security and food in the countryside. Moreover, the shortages of food led to rapidly rising prices, hoarding, work stoppages, and unrest. Political leaders added to their unpopularity by repressing demands for change. Regimes collapsed everywhere. The Mongol Empire, which had held so much of Eurasia together commercially and politically, collapsed under the weight. As a result, the region was ready for experiments in state building, religious beliefs, and cultural achievements.

Analyzing Global Developments

Population Changes in Fourteenth-Century Eurasia

Famine, warfare, and disease led to vast population declines all across fourteenth-century Eurasia. The Mongols were instrumental players in spreading disease across the landmass, starting in China and moving westward along land and sea based trading routes toward the Mediterranean World and ultimately into northern Europe. (See Map 11.1.) While the effects of these destructive forces were felt across the Eurasian landmass, some states and regions were less affected than others. The population data in the table come from the best historical studies of the last forty years and are based on painstaking archival research. They serve as one of the best ways for us to gain historical insight into this tumultuous century.

QUESTIONS FOR ANALYSIS

- In what regions or cities does population loss seem to have been lower? Higher? What might account for those variations in the death rate?
- How do the losses in urban areas compare with the losses in the region where those urban areas are located? What might that comparison suggest about the impact of fourteenth-century disasters on urban versus other populations?
- Why do you think the population decline was more severe and widespread in Europe than in Asia?
- In what ways was the great loss of population in Europe and China a turning point in their histories?

Location	Earlier Population Figures	Later Population Figures	Percent Change
By Region			
Europe	80 m[a] in 1346	30 m in 1353	-60%
Asia	230 m in 1300	235 m in 1400	+2%
By Country			
Spain	6 m in 1346	2.5 m in 1353	-60%
Italy	10 m in 1346	4.5 m in 1363	-55%
France	18 m in 1346	7.2 m in 1353	-60%
England	6 m in 1346	2.25 m in 1353	-62.5%
China	115 m in 1200	75 m in 1400	-35%
Japan	9.75 m in 1300	12.5 m in 1400	+28%
Korea	3 m in 1300	3.5 m in 1400	+17%
India	91 m in 1300	97 m in 1400	+6.5%
By City			
London	100,000 in 1346	37,000 in 1353	-62.5%
Florence	92,000 in 1346	37,250 in 1353	-59.5%
Siena	50,000 in 1346	20,000 in 1353	-60%
Bologna	50,000 in 1346	27,500 in 1353	-45%
Cairo	400,000 in 1300	350,000 in 1350	-12.5%
Damascus	80,000 in 1300	50,000 in 1400	-37%
Constantinople	150,000 in 1300	80,000 in 1350	-47%

[a]m = millions

Sources: Ole J. Benedictow, *The Black Death, 1346–1353: The Complete History* (Woodbridge, England: Boydell Press, 2004); Michael Walter Dols, *The Black Death in the Middle East* (Princeton, NJ: Princeton University Press, 1977); Colin McEvedy and Richard E. Jones, *Atlas of World Population History* (Hammondsworth, England: Penguin, 1978); Ping-ti Ho, *Studies on the Population of China, 1368–1953* (Cambridge, MA: Harvard University Press, 1959).

Rebuilding States

Starting in the late fourteenth century, residents of connected societies in Afro-Eurasia began the task of reconstructing both their political orders and their trading networks. (By then the plague had subsided, though it continued to afflict humans for centuries.) The rebuilding of military and civil administrations—no easy task—also required political legitimacy. Rulers needed to revive confidence in themselves and their political systems, which they did by fostering beliefs and rituals that confirmed their rights to rule, while increasing their control over their subjects.

The form that power took in most places was a political institution well known for centuries: the **dynasty**, a ruling family that passed control from one generation to the next. Like those of the past, new dynasties sought to establish their legitimacy in three ways. First, ruling families insisted that their power derived from a divine calling: Ming emperors in China claimed for themselves what previous dynasts had asserted—the "mandate of heaven"—while European monarchs claimed to rule by "divine right." From their base in Anatolia, Ottoman warrior-princes asserted that they now carried the banner of Islam. In these ways, ruling households affirmed that God or the heavens intended for them to hold power. The new Safavid regime on the Iranian plateau embraced a Shiite form of governance. Second, leaders squelched squabbling among potential heirs by establishing clear rules about succession to the throne. Many European states tried to standardize succession by passing titles to the eldest male heir, but in practice there were countless complications and quarrels. In Islamic states, successors could be designated by the incumbent or elected by the community; here, too, struggles over succession were frequent. Third, ruling families elevated their power through conquest or alliance—by ordering armies to forcibly extend their domains or by marrying their royal offspring to rulers of other states or members of other elite households. Once it established legitimacy, the typical royal family would consolidate power by enacting coercive laws and punishments and sending emissaries to govern far-flung territories. It would also establish standing armies and new administrative structures to collect taxes and to oversee building projects that proclaimed royal power.

As we will see in the remainder of this chapter, the innovative state building that followed the plague's devastating wake would not have been as successful had it not drawn on older traditions. In Europe, a cultural flourishing based largely on ancient Greek and Roman models gave rise to thinkers who proposed novel views of governance. The peoples of the Islamic world held fiercely to their religion as two successor states—the Ottoman Empire and the Safavid state—absorbed numerous Turkish-speaking groups. A third Islamic state—the Mughal Empire—drew on local traditions of religious and cultural tolerance as its rulers built a new regime in the Indian cultural area on top of the foundations of the weakened Delhi Sultanate (see Chapter 10). The Ming, having failed in their attempts to control northern Vietnam and Korea, renounced the expansionist Mongol legacy and emphasized a return to Han rulership, consolidating control of Chinese lands and concentrating on internal markets rather than overseas trade. Many of these regimes lasted for centuries, long enough to set deep roots for political institutions and cultural values that molded societies long after the Black Death.

The Islamic World

The devastation of the Black Death followed hard on the heels of the Mongol destruction of Islam's most important city, Baghdad (see Chapter 10). The double shock of conquest and disease shattered whatever was left of Islamic unity and cleared the way for new Islamic states to emerge. Contrast this fractured recovery with Chinese integrated recovery. Although the Arabic-speaking peoples remained vital in Islam's geographic heartland, they now had to cede authority to Persian and Turkish political leaders as Islamic influences spread outwards. Persians and Turks had embraced Islam and had made their cultural, intellectual, and military influence felt well before the Mongol invasions and the Black Death. The implosion of the Abbasid caliphate in Baghdad made way for powerful, more militarized, expansionist successors capable of extending Islam's reach into Christian heartlands in the west and the Indian cultural area to the east.

The recovery from conquest and disease was slow. Eventually, the Ottomans, the Safavids, and the Mughals would emerge as the dominant states in the Islamic world in the early sixteenth century. They exploited the rich agrarian resources of the Indian Ocean regions and the Mediterranean Sea basin, and they benefited from brisk seaborne and overland trades. By the mid-sixteenth century, the Mughals controlled the northern Indus River valley; the Safavids occupied Persia; and the Ottomans ruled Anatolia, the Arab world, and much of southern and eastern Europe.

Despite sharing core religious beliefs, each empire had unique political features. The most powerful, the **Ottoman Empire**, occupied the pivotal area between Europe and Asia. The Ottomans embraced a Sunni view of Islam, while absorbing and adapting traditional Byzantine ways of governance. One of the signatures of the Ottomans' success was their hybrid approach to ruling diverse peoples and incorporating sprawling territories. By contrast, the Safavids, adherents of the Shiite vision of Islam, were ardently devoted to the pre-Islamic traditions of Persia (present-day Iran). But unlike the Ottoman rulers, the Safavid rulers were less effective at expanding beyond their Persian base. The Mughals ruled over the wealthy but divided realm that is much of today's Indian subcontinent; here they carried even further the region's religious and political traditions of assimilating Islamic and pre-Islamic Indian ways. Their wealth and their domain's lack of centralization made the Mughals constant targets for internal dissent and eventually for external aggression.

The Ottoman Empire

The rise of the Ottoman Empire owed as much to innovative administrative techniques and religious tolerance as it did to military strength. Although the Mongols considered Anatolia to be a borderland region of little economic importance, their military forays against the Anatolian Seljuk Turkish state in the late thirteenth century brought political turmoil, bordering on chaos, but opened up the region to new political forces. The ultimate victors here were the Ottoman Turks. They transformed themselves from warrior bands, roaming the borderlands between Islamic states to the east and Christian worlds to the west, into rulers of a settled state and, eventually, into sovereigns of a far-flung, highly bureaucratic empire. (See Map 11.2.)

Many modern western-trained historians have portrayed the early Ottoman state as a plundering regime, engaged in rape and slaughter and carrying out campaigns of massive devastation by galvanizing its zealous warriors to terrorize local populations. The Ottomans did indeed have stern and disciplined warriors, known as *ghazis*, whose commitment to Islam and its leaders was boundless. Even so, what enabled the Ottoman leaders to triumph in a region of widespread disorder was their ability to form alliances with previously hostile—and divergent—ethnic and religious communities. Their first chief, Osman (r. 1299–1326), and his son Orhan (r. 1326–1362) were Sunni Muslims. But they were adept at working with those who held different religious beliefs, such as Byzantine leaders, Kurds, Sufi dervish orders, and Shiites. By constructing eclectic political institutions possessing enormous elasticity, they succeeded not only in offering toleration to religiously and culturally diverse populations but also in providing opportunities for those populations to exercise

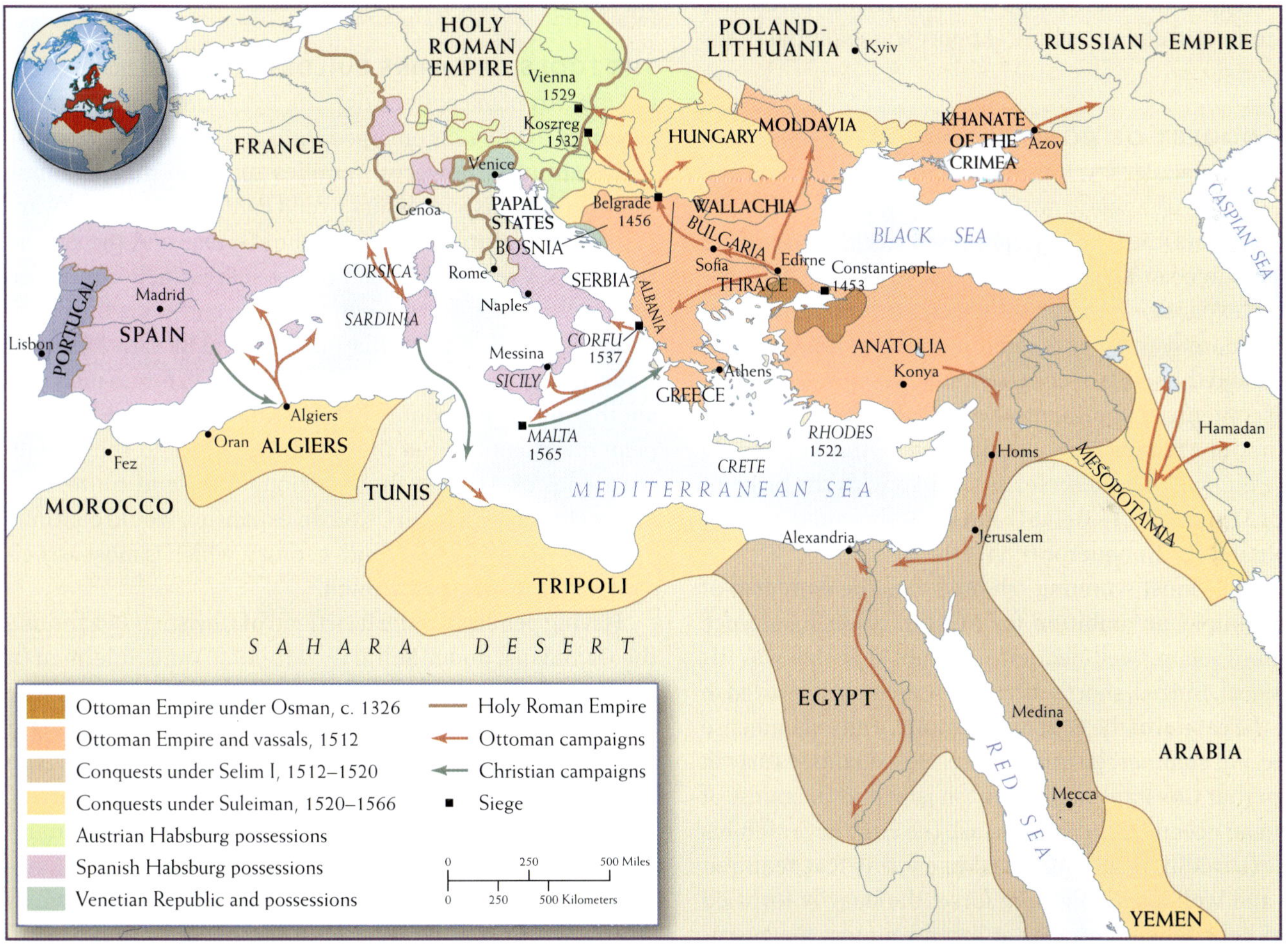

MAP 11.2 | The Ottoman Empire, 1300–1566

This map charts the expansion of the Ottoman state from the time of its founder, Osman, through the reign of Suleiman, the empire's most illustrious ruler.

- Where did the Ottoman Empire originate under Osman? Into what regions did the Ottomans expand between the years 1326 and 1566?
- What were the geographic limits of the Ottoman Empire?
- What governments were able to resist Ottoman expansion?

power and gain wealth. The Ottomans created a hybrid state, which welcomed Christian supporters as fervently as it did Muslims. Hence, the Ottomans prevailed over other Turkic competitors and transformed what was a small principality in northwestern Anatolia during the fourteenth century into the hub of a preeminent state in Anatolia. The principal characteristics of the early Ottoman state were inclusivity, resilience, and syncretism. The Ottomans also took advantage of existing divisions among rivals. As Byzantine leaders feuded, Ottoman forces besieged the city of Bursa, capturing it in 1326. The Ottomans thus achieved a victory that marked their ascendancy in Anatolia. They now threatened the existence of the once powerful, now hobbled Byzantine Empire. Other Turkic warrior bands, which like the Ottomans lived off the land and fought for booty under charismatic military leaders, ultimately failed in their quest for power because they had little regard for other groups such as artisans, merchants, bureaucrats, and clerics, whose support was essential in the Ottoman rise.

THE CONQUEST OF CONSTANTINOPLE The Ottoman Empire's spectacular territorial expansion into Europe and eventually the Arab world was at heart a military affair. To recruit followers, the Ottomans promised wealth and glory to their new subjects. This was an expensive undertaking, but territorial expansion generated financial and administrative rewards. Moreover, by spreading lucrative administrative positions and the spoils of conquest, rulers bought off potentially discontented subordinates who might challenge them. Still, without great military strength, the Ottomans would not have enjoyed the successes associated with the brilliant reigns of Murad II (r. 1421–1451) and his aptly named successor, Mehmed the Conqueror (r. 1451–1481).

Mehmed's most stunning triumph was the conquest of Constantinople, an ambition for Muslim rulers ever since the birth of Islam. Mehmed left no doubt that this was his primary goal. Indeed, shortly after his coronation, he vowed to capture the capital of the Byzantine Empire, a city of immense strategic and commercial importance. He exclaimed early in his reign that Constantinople was "an island in the midst of an Ottoman ocean." His desire to take the city "never left his tongue" (Faroqhi, p. 23). Mehmed knew this feat required a large and well-armed fighting force; the heavily fortified city had kept Muslim attacks at bay for almost a century. First, he built a fortress of his own, on the European bank of the Bosporus Strait, at its narrowest point, to prevent European vessels from reaching the capital. Then, by promising his soldiers free access to booty and portraying the city's conquest as a holy cause, he amassed a huge army that outnumbered the defending force of 7,000 by more than tenfold. For fifty-three days his troops bombarded Constantinople's massive walls with artillery that included enormous cannons built by Hungarian and Italian engineers. On May 29, 1453, Ottoman troops overwhelmed the surviving soldiers and took the ancient Roman and Christian capital of Byzantium—which Mehmed promptly renamed Istanbul.

Although Christians generally portrayed the "fall" of Constantinople as a calamity, in fact the Muslim conquest brought benefits to western Europe. Many Christian survivors fled to ports in the west, bringing with them classical and Arabic manuscripts previously unknown in Europe. The well-educated, Greek-speaking émigrés generally became teachers and translators, thereby helping to revive Europeans' interest in antiquity and spreading knowledge of ancient Greek (which had virtually died out in the Middle Ages). These manuscripts and teachers would play a vital role in Europe's Renaissance. Once the Ottomans consolidated their place in the eastern Mediterranean, sea trading, especially with the Italian city-states, also bounced back.

THE TOOLS OF EMPIRE BUILDING Mehmed made Istanbul the Ottoman capital, adopting Byzantine administrative practices to unify his enlarged state and incorporating many of Byzantium's powerful families into it. From Istanbul, Mehmed and his successors would continue their westward expansion, eventually seizing all of Greece and the Balkan region. As a result, Ottoman navies increasingly controlled sea-lanes in the eastern Mediterranean, curtailing European access to the rich ports that handled the lucrative caravan trade. By the late fifteenth century, Ottoman forces menaced another of Christendom's great capitals, Vienna, and European merchants feared that never again would they obtain the riches of Asia via the traditional overland route, now under Ottoman control. Ottoman expansion would continue apace, even into the sixteenth century, which is most associated with the Empire's growth.

Having penetrated the heartland of Christian Byzantium, the Ottomans, under Selim (r. 1512–1520) and Suleiman (r. 1520–1566), turned their expansionist designs to the Arab world. Under Suleiman, the Ottomans reached the height of their territorial expansion. He personally led thirteen major military campaigns and many minor engagements. An exceptional commander, Suleiman was an equally gifted administrator. His subjects called him "the Lawgiver." In the western part of the realm, he was known as "the Magnificent" in recognition of his attention to civil bureaucratic efficiency and justice for his people. His fame spread to Europe, where he was known as "the Great Turk." The courts of Europe sent envoys and diplomats seeking alliances. The rebel German theologian Martin Luther saw Muslims as kindred in the fight against icons. Though he saw the "Turk" penetration into the heart of Europe as a threat, Luther also recognized that the Ottomans could cripple Habsburg and Catholic power and upend the

The Siege of Constantinople. A depiction of the Turkish siege of Constantinople from Burgundian spy Bertrandon de la Broquière's 1453 book of travels, *Voyage d'Outre-Mer*. The use of heavy artillery in the fifty-three-day siege of Constantinople was instrumental to the Ottoman victory.

papacy in Rome. Indeed, by dragging Catholic armies and navies into a protracted and costly war from Vienna to the Mediterranean, Suleiman later gave Protestant insurgents in Germany some breathing room. For a time, Istanbul was one of the globe's powerhouse capitals. Under Suleiman's administration, the Ottoman state ruled over 20 to 30 million people. By the time Suleiman died, the Ottoman Empire bridged Europe and the Arab world.

Ottoman dynastic power was not only military; it also rested on a firm religious foundation. The sultans combined a warrior ethos with an unwavering devotion to Islam. Describing themselves as the "shadow of God" on earth, they claimed to be caretakers for the welfare of the Islamic faith and assumed the role of protectors of the holy cities on the Arabian Peninsula and in Jerusalem after the conquests in the Arab world. They devoted substantial resources to the construction of elaborate mosques and the support of Islamic schools throughout the empire, and to the extension of the borders of Islam. Thus, the Islamic faith helped unite a diverse and sprawling imperial populace, with the sultan's power fusing the sacred and the secular.

ISTANBUL AND THE TOPKAPI PALACE Istanbul reflected the splendor of this awesome empire. After the Ottoman conquest, the sultans' engineers rebuilt the city's crumbling walls, while their architects redesigned homes, public buildings, baths, inns, and marketplaces to display the majesty of Islam's new imperial center. To crown his achievements, Suleiman ordered the construction of the Süleymaniye Mosque, which sat opposite Hagia Sophia. The latter, a domed Byzantine cathedral, was formerly the most sacred of Christian cathedrals, the largest house of worship in all of Christendom, but Suleiman had it turned into a mosque. Moreover, the Ottoman dynasts welcomed (indeed, forcibly transported) thousands of Muslims and non-Muslims to the city and revived Istanbul as a major trading center. Within twenty-five years of its conquest, its population more than tripled; by the end of the sixteenth century, 400,000 people regularly swarmed through its streets and knelt in its mosques, making it the world's largest city outside China.

Istanbul's **Topkapi Palace** reflected the Ottomans' view of governance, the sultans' emphasis on religion, and the continuing influence of Ottoman familial traditions—even in the administration of a far-flung empire. Laid out by Mehmed II, the palace complex reflected a vision of Istanbul as the center of the world. As a way to exalt the sultan's magnificent power, architects designed the complex so that the buildings containing the imperial household nestled behind layers of outer courtyards in a mosaic of mosques, courts, and special dwellings for the sultan's harem.

The Süleymaniye Mosque. Built by Sultan Suleiman to crown his achievements, the Süleymaniye Mosque was designed by the architect Sinan to dominate the city. Four tall minarets called the faithful to prayer.

Topkapi Palace. In Topkapi Palace's second courtyard, the Imperial Council, or the Divan, met to discuss imperial affairs with the viziers. Note the grand construction of the buildings, which were designed to visually display the power of the Ottoman Empire.

The growing importance of Topkapi Palace as the command post of the empire represented a crucial transition in the history of Ottoman rulers. Not only was the palace the place where future bureaucrats received their training; it was also the place where the chief bureaucrat, the grand vizier, carried out the day-to-day running of the empire. Whereas the early sultans had led their soldiers into battle personally and had met face-to-face with their kinsmen, the later rulers withdrew into the sanctity of the palace, venturing out only occasionally for grand ceremonies. Still, every Friday, subjects queued up outside the palace to introduce their petitions, ask for favors, and seek justice. If they were lucky, the sultans would be there to greet them—but they did so behind grated glass, issuing their decisions by tapping on the window. The palace thus projected a sense of majesty, distant wonder, a home fit for commanders of the faithful.

Topkapi became a home for the increasingly sedentary sultan and his harem. Among his most cherished quarters were those set aside for women. At first, women's influence in the Ottoman polity was slight. But as the realm consolidated, women became a powerful political force. The harem, like the rest of Ottoman society, had its own hierarchy of rank and prestige. At the bottom were enslaved women; at the top were the sultan's mother and his favorite consorts. As many as 10,000 to 12,000 women inhabited the palace, often in cramped quarters. Those who had the ruler's ear conspired to have him favor their own children, which made for widespread intrigue. When a sultan died, the entire retinue of women would be sent to a distant palace poignantly called the Palace of Tears, because the women who occupied it wept at the loss of the sultan and their own banishment from power.

DIVERSITY AND CONTROL The Ottoman Empire's endurance into the twentieth century owed much to the ruling elite's ability to gain the support and employ the talents of exceedingly diverse populations. After all, neither conquest nor conversion eliminated cultural differences in the empire's distant provinces. Thus, for example, the Ottomans' language policy was one of flexibility and tolerance. Although Ottoman Turkish was the official language of administration, Arabic was the primary language of the Arab provinces, the common tongue of street life. Within the empire's European corner, the sounds and cadences of various languages continued to prevail. From the fifteenth century onward, the Ottoman Empire was more multilingual than any of its rivals.

In politics, as in language, the Ottomans showed flexibility and tolerance. The imperial bureaucracy permitted extensive regional and religious autonomy. In fact, Ottoman military cadres perfected a technique for absorbing newly conquered territories into the empire by parceling them out as revenue-producing units among loyal followers and kin. Regional appointees could collect local taxes, part of which they earmarked for Istanbul and part of which they pocketed for themselves. (This was a common administrative device for many world dynasties that controlled extensive domains.)

The *Devshirme*. A miniature painting from 1558 depicts the *devshirme* system of taking non-Muslim children from their families in the Balkan Peninsula as a human tribute in place of cash taxes, which the poor region could not pay. The children were converted to Islam, educated, and prepared for service in the sultan's civil and military bureaucracy.

Like other empires, the Ottoman state was always in danger of losing control over its provincial rulers. Local rulers—the group that the imperial center allowed to be (and remain) in charge—found that great distances enabled them to operate independently from central authority. These local authorities kept larger amounts of tax revenues than Istanbul deemed proper. So, to clip local autonomy, the Ottomans established a corps of infantry soldiers and bureaucrats called janissaries who owed the Sultan direct allegiance. The system at its high point involved a conscription of Christian youths from the empire's European lands. This conscription, called the ***devshirme***, required each village to hand over a certain number of males between the ages of eight and eighteen. Uprooted from their families and villages, these young men—chosen for their fine physiques and good looks—were converted to Islam and sent to farms to build up their bodies and learn Turkish. A select few were moved to Topkapi Palace, where they learned Ottoman military, religious, and administrative techniques. Some of these men—such as the architect Sinan, who designed the Süleymaniye Mosque—later enjoyed exceptional careers. Recipients of the best education available in the Islamic world, trained in Ottoman ways, instructed in the use of modern weaponry, and shorn of all family connections, the *devshirme* recruits were prepared to serve the sultan (and the empire as a whole) rather than the interests of any locality or ethnic group.

The Ottomans thus established their legitimacy via military skills, religious backing, and a loyal bureaucracy. They artfully balanced the decentralizing tendencies of the outlying regions with the centralizing forces of the imperial capital. Relying on a careful mixture of faith, patronage, and tolerance, the sultans curried loyalty and secured political stability. Indeed, so strong and stable was the political system that the Ottoman Empire dominated the coveted and highly contested crossroads between Europe and Asia for many centuries.

The Safavid Empire in Iran

The Ottoman dynasts were not the only rulers of Islamic regimes to spring from the rubble of conquest and disease. In Persia, too, a new empire arose in the aftermath of the Mongols' decline. The legitimacy of the Safavid Empire, like that of the Ottoman Empire, rested on an Islamic foundation. But the Shiism espoused by Safavid rulers was quite different from the Sunni faith of the Ottomans, and these contrasting religious visions shaped distinct political systems.

In the western part of central Asia, the Khanate of the Chagatai, one of four governments created by the Mongols (see again Map 11.1), slipped into decline at the end of the thirteenth century. With no power dominating the area, the region fell into disorder, with warrior chieftains squabbling for preeminence. Adding to the volatility were various populist Islamic movements, some of which urged followers to withdraw from society or to parade around without clothing. Among the more prominent movements was a Sufi brotherhood led by Safi al-Din (1252–1334), which gained the backing of religious adherents and Turkish-speaking warrior bands. His successors, known as Safaviyeh or Safavids, embraced Shiism.

A RELIGIOUS SHIITE STATE The Safavids emerged from Turkic Sufi groups in eastern Anatolia and Azerbaijan. The Ottoman claims over most of Anatolia turned these regions into conflict zones with the Safavids and ultimately pushed Sufis into the Iranian plateau. As so often happens when migrant communities relocate, they had to reckon with the indigenous peoples of the area where they moved. In this case, they merged with tribal groups in devastated parts of Persia. In return for offering good governance, the newcomers were welcome. But as Turkic groups became Persianate, they also gave up some of their Sufi ways and steeped themselves in the sacred traditions of Shiism. As a result, the Safavid state became not just devout but devoted to persecuting those who did not follow its Shiite form of Islam. Of the three successor empires to the old caliphate, the Safavids were the least pluralist and religiously diverse. The most dynamic of Safi al-Din's successors, Ismail (r. 1501–1524), required that the call to prayer announce that there is no God but Allah, that Muhammad is his prophet, and that Ali is the successor of Muhammad. Rejecting his advisers' counsel to tolerate the Sunni creed of the majority of the city's population, Ismail made Shiism the official state religion. He offered the people a choice between conversion to Shiism or death, exclaiming at the moment of conquest that "with God's help, if the people utter one word of protest, I will draw the sword and leave not one of them alive" (Savory, p. 29). In 1502, Ismail proclaimed himself the first shah of the Safavid Empire. (*Shah* is the Persian word for "king" or "leader," a title that many other cultures adopted as well.) Under Ismail and his successors, the Safavid shahs restored Persian sovereignty over the entire region traditionally regarded as the homeland of Persian speakers.

In the hands of the Safavids, Islam assumed an extreme and often militant form. The Safavids revived the traditional Persian idea that rulers were ordained by God, and believed the shahs to be divinely chosen. Some Shiites even went so far as to affirm that there was no God but the shah. Moreover, Persian Shiism fostered an activist clergy who (in contrast to Sunni clerics) saw themselves as political and religious enforcers against any heretical authority. They compelled Safavid leaders to rule with a sacred purpose. Because the Safavids, unlike the Ottomans, did not tolerate diversity, they never had as expansive an empire. Whatever territories they conquered, the Safavids ruled much more directly, based on central—and theocratic—authority. They also succeeded in transforming Iran, once a Sunni area, into a Shiite stronghold, a change that has endured to the present.

An Affirmation of Shiism. Shah Ismail (center right) is depicted at the moment of his declaration of Shiism as the state religion of Iran during the Safavid dynasty.

The Delhi Sultanate and the Early Mughal Empire

A quarter century after the Safavids seized power in Persia, another Islamic dynasty, the Mughals, emerged in South Asia. Like the Ottomans and Safavids, the Mughals created a regime destined to last for many centuries and leave an enduring imprint. But unlike those other empires, the Mughal Empire did not replace a Mongol regime. Instead, the Mughals erected their state on the foundations of the old Delhi Sultanate, in the Indian cultural area (described in the last chapter) which had come into existence in 1206.

Raid on Delhi. Timur's swift raid on Delhi in 1398, depicted in this sixteenth-century miniature, was one of the great battles of world history. Timur outmaneuvered the ranks of chain-mail-clad elephants (shown at left), deposing the sultan of Delhi and capturing the city. The city was then plundered and razed. It took a century for Delhi to recover, and in the meantime Timur laid the groundwork for the Mughal Empire.

The peoples of India, although spared the devastating direct effects of the Mongols and the Black Death, nonetheless had to deal with an invading nomadic force that was directly affected by these earlier dislocations: the warriors of Timur, or Tamerlane. Every bit as disruptive as the Mongols' attacks, Timur's invasions crushed the Delhi Sultanate and opened the way for a new, even more powerful regime.

RIVALRIES, RELIGIOUS REVIVAL, AND THE FIRST MUGHAL EMPEROR As head of the Barlas tribe from Central Asia, Timur was an indirect heir of Chinggis Khan's rule. Timur waged wars that sprawled from the Caspian Sea to India. By the time he reached Delhi, Timur commanded a pillaging war machine. Timur's campaigns were so widespread, relentless, and furious that some historians have estimated that up to 17 million people, 5 percent of the world population, may have perished in the warring and sickness his armies brought. But of all his conquests, Delhi was the prize. Though crippled by infighting, Delhi was rich and enormous, but was also no match for a cunning invader. While the sultan's forces included elephant cavalries wearing chain mail and wielding poisoned tusks, Timur quickly learned that these animals were hard to defeat but easy to panic. He ordered his soldiers to tie flaming bunches of hay to the tails of his camels and drive them into the elephant formations, driving all the animals into hysterics and trampling the paralyzed foot soldiers. Routed, the sultan fled with his remnant forces, leaving Delhi to be sacked and almost demolished.

The Delhi Sultanate lost much of its power after Timur's conquests. Soon, a wave of religious revivals occurred. Bengal broke away from Delhi and soon embraced Sufism, a mystical form of Islam that emphasized personal union with God. Here, too, a special form of Hinduism, called Bhakti Hinduism, put down deep roots. Its devotees preached the doctrine of divine love. In the Punjab, previously a core area of the Delhi Sultanate, a new religion known as **Sikhism** came into being. Sikhism largely followed the teachings of Nanak (1469–1539). Although born a Hindu, he was inspired by Islamic ideals and called on his followers to renounce the caste system and to treat all believers as equal before God.

Following Timur's victory, rival kingdoms and sultanates asserted their independence. The Delhi Sultanate became a mere shadow of its former self, just one of several competing powers in northern India. Out of this political chaos emerged a Turkish prince, Babur (the "Tiger"), invited in 1526 by the governor of the Punjab to restore order. A great-grandson of Timur, Babur traced his lineage to both the Turks and the Mongols (he was said to be a descendant of Chinggis Khan). For years, Babur had longed to conquer India. Massing an army of Turks and Afghans armed with matchlock cannons, he easily breached the wall of elephants put together by the sultan's defenders. Delhi fell, and with it the Delhi Sultanate

Babur Holding Court. Babur founded a Muslim empire in India ruled by conquerors from central Asia. He continued Timur's pattern of military victories over smaller states and laid claim over Hindu peoples. He also relocated his entourage from Afghanistan and began the process of creating a courtly culture in northern India, sponsoring poets, musicians, and painters. Many of these artists adopted the techniques and styles of the Hindu artists that the Mughals governed. In this image, consider the portrait of courtly life and its finery, which echoed the trappings of similar new monarchies across Asia and Europe at the time.

also came to an end. Babur proclaimed himself emperor and spent the next few years snuffing out the remaining resistance to his rule. He thus laid the foundation of the Mughal Empire, the third great Islamic dynasty (discussed in detail in Chapter 12).

By the sixteenth century, three new Islamic empires had emerged across the Asian continent. Their differences were obvious, especially regarding religion. The Ottomans were Sunni Islam's most fervent champions, determined to eradicate the Shiite heresy on their border, where an equally determined Persian Safavid dynasty sought to expand the reach of Shiism. In contrast to these dynasties' sectarian religious commitments, the Mughals, drawing on well-established Indian traditions of religious and cultural tolerance, were open-minded toward non-Muslim believers and sectarian groups within the Muslim community. Yet the political similarities of these imperial dynasties were equally clear-cut. Although these states did not hesitate to go to war against one another, they shared similar styles of rule. All established their legitimacy via military prowess, religious backing, and a loyal bureaucracy. This combination of spiritual and military weaponry enabled emperors, espousing the Prophet Muhammad's teaching, to claim vast domains. Moreover, their religious differences did not prevent the movement of goods, ideas, merchants, and scholars across political and religious boundaries—even across the most divisive boundary of all, that between Sunni Iraq and Shiite Persia.

Western Christendom

No region suffered more from the Black Death than western Christendom, and no region made a more spectacular comeback. From 1100 to 1300, Europe had enjoyed a surge in population, economic growth, and significant technological and intellectual progress, only to see these achievements halted in the fourteenth century by famine and the Black Death. Europeans responded by creating new political and cultural forms. New dynasties arose, and a cultural flourishing called the Renaissance revived Europe's connections with its Greek and Roman past and produced masterpieces in art, architecture, and other forms of thought.

The Catholic Church, Reactions, and Revolts

The Black Death brought with it social and economic disorder that challenged the political order. The massive death toll and the suddenness with which the disease struck also prompted survivors to ask questions about the major institution uniting Christendom, the Catholic Church. Even before the plague arrived, the late medieval western church had found itself divided at the top (at one point there were three popes) and challenged from below, both by individuals critical of the extravagant lifestyles of some clergymen and by increasing demands on the clergy and church administration. Now the Black Death raised questions about God's relationship to humankind and the Catholic Church's role as God's appointed mediator on earth: Could sinful mortals ever find mercy from a vengeful God, and could an already overstretched and self-interested church lead them to salvation? Facing challenges to its right to define religious doctrine and practices, the church responded by demanding strict obedience to the true faith.

This entailed the persecution of Jews, Muslims, "witches," and those who engaged in sexual practices that the church considered deviant, and thus impermissible and heretical. But the church also reacted to society's suffering during this period, expanding its charitable and bureaucratic functions, providing alms to the urban poor, and registering births, deaths, and economic transactions. Its responses reassured many that God—and the church—had not abandoned true Christians, and shored up the power of religious authorities.

Persecution and administration cost money. Indeed, the needs as well as the extravagances of the clergy spurred certain questionable money-making tactics. One was the selling of indulgences (certificates that reduced one's time in purgatory, where souls continued the repentance that would eventually make them fit for heaven). This sort of unconventional fund-raising, and the growing gap between the church's promises and its ability to bring Christianity into people's everyday lives, more than the persecutions, eventually sparked the Protestant Reformation (see Chapter 12).

At the same time, the high death toll of the fourteenth and fifteenth centuries emboldened those who survived to seek higher wages or reductions in their feudal obligations. When landlords resisted or kings tried to impose new taxes, there were uprisings, including a 1358 peasant revolt in France that was dubbed the Jacquerie (the term derived from "Jacques Bonhomme," a name that contemptuous "masters" used for all peasants). Armed with only knives and staves, the peasantry went on a rampage, killing hated nobles and clergy and burning and looting all the property they could get their hands on. At issue was the peasants' insistence that they should no longer be tied to their land or have to pay for the tools they used in farming.

A better-organized uprising took place in England in 1381. Although the English Peasants' Revolt began as a protest against a tax levied to raise money for a war on France, it was also fueled by postplague labor shortages: serfs demanded the freedom to move about, and free farmworkers called for higher wages and lower rents. When landlords balked at these demands, aggrieved peasants assembled at the gates of London. The protesters demanded abolition of the feudal order, but the king ruthlessly suppressed them. Nonetheless, in both France and England a free peasantry gradually emerged as labor shortages made it impossible to keep peasants bound to the soil.

The Imperial Crown. Creating new emblems of authority and a culture of grandeur was important to rising monarchies of Eurasia. In an effort to distance themselves from their often rusting, conquering reputations, they invested heavily in palaces and elaborate courtly cultures. Above all, the crown and the throne became the symbols of imperial regality, as wearing the crown or sitting on the throne conferred supremacy. It was important, therefore, for these emblems to exude wealth and ostentation. This is the crown of the Holy Roman Emperor. Studded with pearls and large sapphires, emeralds, and amethysts, it combined piety (note the cross and the inlaid plaques of biblical scenes) with authority.

State Building and Economic Recovery

Out of the chaos of famine, disease, and warfare, the diverse peoples of Europe found a political way forward. This path involved the formation of centralized monarchies, much as the Ottomans, Safavids, Mughals, and Ming were accomplishing in Asia. (A **monarchy** is a political system in which one individual typically inherits supreme power.) Consolidation of these political systems occurred sometimes through strategic marriages but more often through warfare, both between local princely families and with local aristocratic allies and foreign mercenaries. Many of these dynasties fell as a result of civil war or conquest, but some, like the Tudors in England and the Valois in France, consolidated considerable power.

In central Europe, one family, the Habsburgs, established a powerful and long-lasting dynasty. This family provided continuous emperors for the Holy Roman Empire from 1445 to 1806. The Holy Roman Empire included territory that would later be divided into separate states such as the Netherlands, Germany, Austria, Belgium, and Croatia, and it also incorporated parts of present-day Italy, Poland, and Switzerland. Yet the Habsburg monarchs never succeeded in restoring an integrated empire to western Europe (as Chinese dynasts had done by claiming the mandate of heaven). Indeed, although hereditary monarchy was Europe's dominant form of governance, there were also a number of oligarchic republics in which a handful of wealthy and influential voters selected their leaders, a sprinkling of political systems ruled by archbishops or other clergymen, and many "free" towns, surrounded by walls and protective of their special privileges.

Those who sought to rule the emerging states faced numerous obstacles. For example, rival claimants to the throne financed private armies. Also, the clergy demanded and received privileges and often meddled in politics. The church's huge landholdings and exemptions from taxation made it, too, a formidable economic powerhouse. Towns—many of which had the right to rule themselves—refused to submit to rulers' demands. And once the printing press became available in the 1460s, printers circulated anonymous pamphlets criticizing the court and the clergy. Some states had consultative bodies—such as the Estates-General in France, the Cortes in Spain, and Parliament in England—in which princes formally asked representatives of their people for advice and, in the case of the English Parliament, for consent to new forms of taxation. Such bodies gave no voice to most nonaristocratic men and no representation at all to women. They did, however, allow the collective expression of grievances against policies that the aristocracy found troubling.

If Europe in 1450 had no central government and no prospect of obtaining political unity, it also had no common language. In China, the written literary Chinese script remained a key administrative tool for the dynasts. And in the Islamic world, Arabic was the common language of faith, Persian the language of poetry, and Turkish the language of administration. But in Europe, Latin lost ground as rulers chose various regional dialects to be their official state language. For centuries afterward, Latin continued to be the language of the church and of scholarship. Poets, however, took advantage of the upgrading of vernacular languages such as Italian or English and composed sophisticated poetic masterpieces, such as Dante Alighieri's *The Divine Comedy* or, later, Edmund Spenser's *The Faerie Queen*.

Despite, or perhaps because of, Europe's political fragmentation, new economic initiatives began to take hold, as the English and Flemish competed to expand cloth production and German and Dutch merchants extended their trading networks in the North Sea. Economic recovery was swiftest in southern Europe, where trade with Southwest Asia enriched merchants and subsidized the flourishing of luxury industries, such as glass-making in Venice. Although they remained small compared with other Eurasian cities such as Istanbul or Beijing, Europe's towns rebounded quickly from the Black Death, particularly in Italy, the Netherlands, and along the North Sea coast. (See Map 11.3.) New prosperity and the influx of Christian exiles from Istanbul into Italian city-states such as Venice and Florence led to a cultural flowering known as the Renaissance (discussed shortly). In northern and western Europe, the process took longer. In England and France, in particular, internal feuding, regional warfare, and religious fragmentation delayed recovery for decades (see Chapter 12).

Political Consolidation and Trade in Portugal

Portugal's fortunes demonstrate how political stabilization and the emergence of a stronger state could be useful in the revival of trade. After the chaos of the fourteenth century, Spain, England, and France followed the Portuguese example and established national monarchies. In Spain and Portugal, warfare against Muslims would help unite Christian territories, and Mediterranean trade would add valuable income to state coffers.

Through the fourteenth century, Portuguese Christians devoted themselves to fighting the Moors, who were Muslim occupants of North Africa, the western Sahara, and the Iberian Peninsula. Decisive in this struggle was the Portuguese decision to cross the Strait of Gibraltar and seize the Moorish Moroccan fortresses at Ceuta, in North Africa: their ships could now sail between the Mediterranean and the Atlantic without Muslim interference. With that threat diminished, the Portuguese perceived their neighbor Castile (part of what is now Spain) as their chief foe. Under João I (r. 1385–1433) the Castilians were defeated, and the monarchy could seek new territories and trading opportunities in the North Atlantic and along the West African coast. João's son Prince Henrique, known later as Henry the Navigator, further expanded the family's domain by supporting expeditions down the coast of Africa and offshore to the Atlantic islands of the Madeiras and the Azores. The west and central coasts of Africa and the islands of the North and South Atlantic, including the Cape Verde Islands, São Tomé, Principe, and Fernando Po, soon became Portuguese ports of call.

The Portuguese monarchs granted these largely uninhabited Atlantic islands to nobles as hereditary possessions on condition that the grantees colonize them, and soon the colonizers were establishing lucrative sugar plantations. In gratitude, noble families and merchants threw their political weight behind the king. Subsequent monarchs continued to reduce local elites' authority and to ensure smooth succession for members of the royal family. This political consolidation enabled Portugal to thrive in the wake of the Black Death.

Dynasty Building and Reconquest in Spain

The road to Spanish unity was arduous. Medieval Spain comprised rival kingdoms that quarreled ceaselessly. Spain also lacked religious homogeneity: Muslims, Jews, and Christians lived side by side in relative harmony, and Muslim armies still occupied strategic areas in the south. Over time, however, marriages and the formation of kinship ties among nobles and between royal lineages yielded a new political order. One by one, the major houses of the Spanish kingdoms intermarried, culminating in the fateful wedding of Isabella of Castile

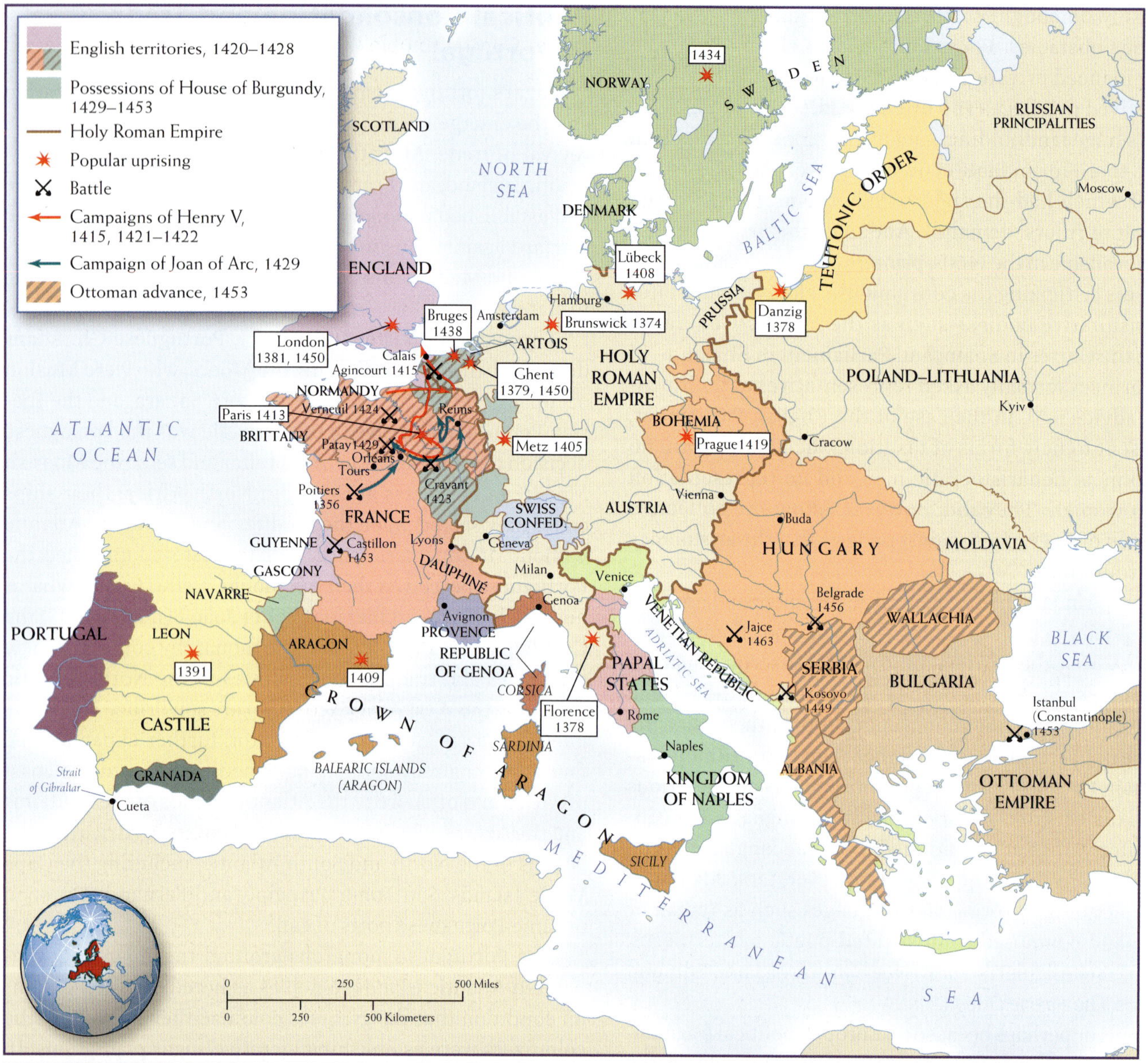

MAP 11.3 | Western Christendom, 1400–1500

Europe was a region divided by dynastic rivalries during the fifteenth century. Locate the most powerful regional dynasties on the map: Portugal, Castile, Aragon, France, Burgundy, England, and the Holy Roman Empire.

- Using the scale, contrast the sizes of political units in this map with those in Maps 11.2 (Ottoman Empire) and 11.4 (Ming China). Explain the significance of the differences.
- Where did popular uprisings take place? Based on your reading, why did those regions experience popular unrest?
- Based on the map, why might the Venetian Republic have been particularly engaged, both in trade and intermittent warfare, with the Ottomans?

and Ferdinand of Aragon. Thus, Spain's two most important provinces were joined, and Spain became a state with which to be reckoned.

THE UNION OF CASTILE AND ARAGON By the time Isabella and Ferdinand married in 1469, Spain was recovering from the miseries of the fourteenth century. This was more than a marriage of convenience. Castile was wealthy and populous; Aragon enjoyed an extended trading network in the Mediterranean. Together, the monarchs brought unruly nobles and distant towns under their domain. They topped off their achievements by marrying their children into other

European royal families—especially the Habsburgs, central Europe's most powerful dynasty.

The new rulers also sent Christian armies south to push Muslim forces out of the Iberian Peninsula. By the mid-fifteenth century, only Granada, a strategic lynchpin overlooking the straits between the Mediterranean and the Atlantic, remained in Muslim hands. After a long and costly siege, Christian forces captured the fortress there in January 1492. This was a victory of enormous symbolic importance, as joyous as the fall of Constantinople was depressing for Christians. Many people in Spain thumped their chests in pride, unaware or unconcerned that at the same time Ottoman armies were conquering large sections of southeastern Europe.

THE INQUISITION AND WESTWARD EXPLORATION Just as the Safavid rulers had tried to stamp out all non-Shiite

Conquest of Granada. This colorized woodcut from the nineteenth century depicts Sultan Muhammad XII (known in Europe as Boabdil), the last Muslim ruler of Granada, surrendering—by handing over his sword and the key to the city—to King Ferdinand and Queen Isabella, who are about to enter the city in triumph.

SURRENDER OF GRANADA TO FERDINAND AND ISABELLA.

forms of Islam within their domains, so Isabella and Ferdinand sought to drive all non-Catholics out of Spain. Terrified by Ottoman incursions into Europe, they launched an **Inquisition** in 1481, taking aim especially against *conversos*—converted Jews and Muslims—whom they suspected were Christians only in name. When Granada fell, the crown ordered the expulsion of all Jews from Spain; after 1499, a more tolerant attempt to convert the Moors by persuasion gave way to forced conversion—or emigration. This lack of religious toleration meant that Spain, like other European states in this era, became increasingly homogenous. With fewer groups vying for influence within their territories, rulers turned their attention outward, fueling rivalries among the various European states.

Confident in the stability of their state, the Spanish monarchs were willing by late 1491 to listen to a Genoese navigator whose pleas for patronage they had previously rejected. Christopher Columbus promised them unimaginable riches that could finance their military campaigns and bankroll a crusade to liberate Jerusalem from Muslim hands. Off he sailed into the Atlantic with a royal patent that guaranteed the monarchs a share of all he discovered. Soon the Spanish economy was reorienting itself toward the Atlantic, and Spain's merchants, missionaries, and soldiers were preparing for conquest and profiteering in what the Spanish had perceived, just a few years before, as a blank space on the map.

Joan of Arc. Joan of Arc became an icon of French identity. Inspired by divine visions of the archangel Michael as well as Saint Margaret and Saint Catherine, she was famous for leading troops to battle in the drive to repel English forces during the Hundred Years' War. But for many French nobles, she was a troublemaker; they captured her and gave her to the English, who burned her at the stake in 1431. She was nineteen years old. It was only later, as the French monarchy consolidated itself and cast about for popular symbols, that she was transformed from a popular rebel to a martyr for the nation.

The Struggles of France and England and the Success of Small States

Warfare and strategic marriages allowed the Portuguese and Spanish monarchies to consolidate state power and to lay the foundations for revived commerce. But by no means were all states immediately successful. In France and England, the great age of European monarchy had yet to dawn, so consolidation often came through warfare.

One striking example of this political turmoil was the Hundred Years' War (1337–1453), in which the French sought to throw off English domination. The Black Death raged in the early years of this intermittent conflict. A central figure toward the end of the war was the peasant girl Joan of Arc, whose visions of various saints inspired her to support the French monarch Charles VII and see him crowned at Reims Cathedral. Dressing as a man in order to wear armor, Joan was a charismatic leader of troops, commanding as many as 8,000 at the decisive battle at Orléans, but eventually the French nobility turned on her, and she was captured by the English. Joan was tried for heresy, in part because she dressed as a man, and burned at the stake in Rouen in 1431. Joan's brief, but remarkable, part in the Hundred Years' War illustrates the role an exceptional woman, even a peasant girl, could play on the predominantly male, elite political stage.

When French forces finally pushed the English back across the English Channel in the Hundred Years' War, the French House of Valois began a slow process of consolidating royal power. Although diplomatic marriages helped the French crown expand its domain, two more centuries of royal initiatives and civil war were required to tame the powerful nobility. In England, even thirty years of civil war between the houses of Lancaster and York did not settle which one would take the throne. Both families in this War of the Roses ultimately lost out to the Tudors, who seized the throne in 1485.

Even where stable states did arise, they were fairly small compared with the Ottoman and Ming Empires. In the mid-sixteenth century, Portugal and Spain, Europe's two most expansionist states, had populations of 1 million and 9 million, respectively. England, excluding Wales, was a mere 3 million in 1550. Only France, with 17 million, had a population close to the Ottoman Empire's 20 to 30 million. And these numbers paled in comparison with Ming China's population of nearly 200 million in 1550 and Mughal India's 110 million in 1600.

But in Europe, small was advantageous. Portugal's relatively small population meant that the crown had fewer groups in which to cultivate loyalty. Also, in the world of finance, the most successful merchants were those inhabiting the smaller Italian city-states and, a bit later, the cities of the northern Netherlands. The Florentines developed sophisticated banking techniques, created extensive networks of agents throughout Europe and the Mediterranean, and served as bankers to the popes. Venetian merchants enjoyed a unique role in the exchange of silks and spices from East Asia. It was in these prosperous city-states that the Renaissance began.

The Renaissance

Just as the Ming harkened back to Han Chinese traditions and the Ottomans looked to Sunni Islam to point the way forward, so European elites looked to their own traditions for guidance as they rebuilt after the plague's devastation. They found inspiration in ancient Greek and Roman ideas. Europe's political and economic revival also included a powerful outpouring of cultural achievements, led by Italian scholars and artists and financed by bankers, churchmen, and nobles. Much later, scholars coined the word **Renaissance** ("rebirth") to characterize the expanded cultural production of the Italian city-states, France, the Low Countries, England, and the Holy Roman Empire in the period 1430–1550. What was being "reborn" was ancient Greek and Roman art and learning—knowledge that could illuminate a world of expanding horizons and support the rights of people other than clergymen or kings to exert power in it. Although the Renaissance was largely funded by popes and Christian monarchs, it broke the medieval church's monopoly on answers to the big questions and opened the way for secular forms of learning and a more human-centered understanding of the cosmos.

THE ITALIAN RENAISSANCE The Renaissance, ironically, was all about the new—new exposure, that is, to the old classical texts and ancient art and architectural forms. Although some Greek and Roman texts were known in Europe and the Islamic world, the fall of Constantinople and the invention of the printing press made others accessible to western scholars for the first time. Scholars now realized that the pre-Christian Greeks and Romans had known more: more about how to represent and care for the human body; more about geography, astronomy, and architecture; more about how to properly govern states and armies. It was no longer enough to understand Christian doctrine and to trust medieval authorities; one had to accurately retranslate the original sources, which required the learning of languages and of history. This dive backward into ancient Greece and Rome became known as **humanism**, the aspiration to know more about the human experience beyond what the Christian scriptures offered. Humanism was a powerful tool in the hands of those who knew how to use it. Several women, including the celebrated Italian humanist Laura Cereta (1469–1499), used their learning and rhetorical skills to defend the equality of male and female intellects at a

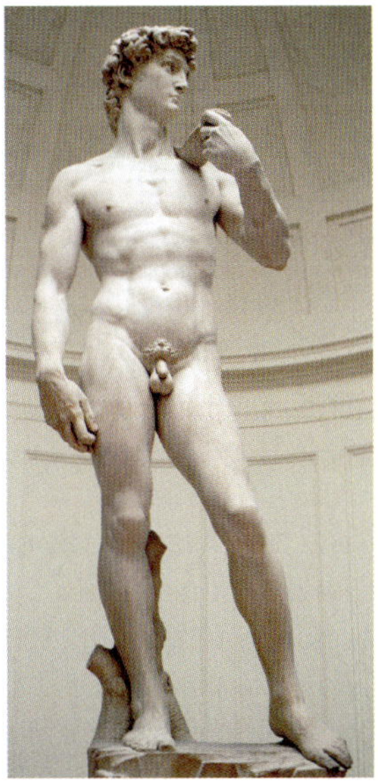

Renaissance Masterpieces. *Left:* Leonardo da Vinci's *The Last Supper* depicts Christ's disciples reacting to his announcement that one of them will betray him. *Right:* Michelangelo's *David* stands over 13 feet high and was conceived as an expression of Florentine civic ideals.

time when both the church and society as a whole believed women scholars to be inappropriately stepping out of their assigned gender roles.

Wealthy families, powerful rulers, and the Catholic Church sponsored much Renaissance achievement. For example, by the 1480s the Medici family had been patronizing art based on ancient models for three generations. The Medicis were bankers but also influential political players in both Florence and Rome. The family greatly contributed to making Florence one of the showplaces of Renaissance art and architecture as well as the center stage for early Renaissance philosophy. Cosimo de' Medici (1389–1464) funded the completion of the sumptuous duomo (cathedral) of Florence, topped by the architect Brunelleschi's masterful dome, the largest built since antiquity. Cosimo's grandson Lorenzo the Magnificent supported many of the great Renaissance artists, including Leonardo da Vinci, Sandro Botticelli, and Michelangelo Buonarroti. The Medici family's wealth was sometimes also associated with religious power: Pope Leo X (r. 1513–1521) was the first of four Medici popes. In addition to Leo (whose name was Giovanni de' Medici), Popes Clement VII (born Giulio de' Medici; r. 1523–1534), Pius IV (born Giovanni Angelo de' Medici, from a Milan branch of the family; r. 1539–1565), and Leo XI (born Alessandro Ottaviano de' Medici; r. April 1605) all served in this highest of offices in Rome.

The artists who flourished in Florence, Rome, and Venice embraced a distinctive form of humanism. For them, the return to ancient sources meant reviving the principles of the Roman architect Vitruvius and the imitation of nude classical sculpture. Their masterpieces, like Leonardo da Vinci's *Last Supper* or Michelangelo's *David*, used the technique of perspective and classical treatments of the body to give vivacity and three-dimensionality to paintings and sculptures—even religious ones. Raphael's Madonnas portrayed the Virgin Mary as a beautiful woman and not just as a symbol of chastity; similarly, Michelangelo's Sistine Chapel ceiling gave Adam the beautiful body of a Greek god so that viewers could appreciate the glory of the Creation. Of course, these artists also hoped to draw attention to their own achievements, and they were not disappointed. Northern European princes soon sought out both ancient artifacts and the modern artists and humanists who could bring this inspiring new style to their courts.

THE RENAISSANCE SPREADS In the sixteenth century, a series of crises on the Italian Peninsula—including the sacking of Rome in 1527 by troops under the control of the Holy Roman Empire—and increasing economic prosperity in other parts of Europe helped spread Renaissance culture throughout Europe. Philip II of Spain, for example, purchased more than 1,000 paintings during his reign; Henry IV of France and his queen, Marie de' Medici, invested a fortune in renovating the Louvre, building a new royal residence at Fontainebleau, and hiring Peter Paul Rubens to paint grand canvases. Courtiers built up-to-date palaces and invited scholars to live on their estates; Dutch, German, and French merchants also patronized the arts. All wanted their sons to be educated in the humanistic manner. Some families and religious institutions offered women access to the new learning, and some men encouraged their sisters, daughters, and wives to expand their horizons. The well-educated nun Caritas Pirckheimer (1467–1532), for example, exchanged learned letters and books with male humanists in the German states. Studying Greek, Latin, and ancient rhetoric did not make the commercial elite equal to the aristocrats, or women equal to men, but this sort of education did enable some non-nobles to obtain social influence and to criticize the ruling elites.

THE REPUBLIC OF LETTERS Since political and religious powers were not united in Europe (as they were in China and the Islamic world), scholars and artists could play one side against the other or, alternatively, could suffer both clerical and political persecution. Michelangelo completed commissions for the Medicis, for the Florentine Wool Guild, and for Pope Julius II. Peter Paul Rubens painted for the courts of France, Spain, England, and the Netherlands, as well as selling paintings on the open market. These two painters, renowned for showing a great deal of flesh, frequently offended conservative church officials, but their secular patrons kept them in oils. The Dutch scholar Desiderius Erasmus was able to ridicule the church because he had the patronage of English, Dutch, and French supporters. Other scholars used their learning to defend the older elites: for example, numerous lawyers and scholars continued to work for the popes, defending the papacy.

The search for patrons and the flight from persecution, especially after the Reformation, made Europe's educated elite increasingly cosmopolitan. Scholars met one another in royal palaces and cultural centers such as Florence, Antwerp, and Amsterdam. Seeking specialized information or rare books, they formed what was known as "the republic of letters"—a network of correspondents who were more interested in individual knowledge or talent than in noble titles or clerical rank. In this way, the Renaissance knitted together the European elite. This did not mean, however, that a consensus emerged about who should rule.

THE PRINTING PRESS Over time one major technological advance, the **printing press**, served to increase the spread of knowledge more than any other phenomenon. The earliest advances in printing were made in China, where woodblock printing first appeared around 220 CE, followed by movable type around 1040 CE, and then the first metal movable

Invention of the Printing Press. By 1450, the German goldsmith Johannes Gutenberg had invented the printing press. It was not a complex or elaborate device. Consider the simplicity of this mechanical device, with few moving parts and the use of a modest screw to push plates together. Nonetheless, its ability to reproduce thousands of pages per day—as opposed to only dozens at the hands of scribes—slashed the cost of printing and made information cheap. Just as important, the device itself was inexpensive and easy to build. Within a few decades, printing presses were in operation throughout western Europe, reading books became commonplace, and religious and secular authorities lost what control was left to them over the creation and flow of information.

type was used in Korea in the 1300s. In the 1450s, Johannes Gutenberg, the son of a German goldsmith, applied a technology to printing that was similar to the technology used to stamp metal coins. The first printed newspapers, leaflets, pamphlets, and books were printed on large wood frame presses that used rows of movable type to stamp the ink on the printed pages. Now hundreds of copies could be made in a few hours, hundreds of hours faster than handwritten and hand-bound copies of books could be produced. A second key factor that made this communication revolution possible was readily available cheap paper, made from old rags turned into pulp at local mills. Rising literacy rates, which increased the demand for books, were a third factor.

Artistic and intellectual experiments, specifications for innovative weapons, and humanist writings were rapidly exported from Renaissance Italy to other parts of Europe. Major news like Columbus's first voyage and the resulting encounters and conquests spread rapidly around Europe, as did major criticisms of this new form of European imperialism. Rulers also used this revolution in communication to expand and centralize their own power through widely distributed printed propaganda and the creation of standardized national languages. The powerful impact of printing was immediate, and the industry would continue to grow and evolve for the centuries ahead both in Europe and globally.

While the technology of the printing press made it easier to disseminate news, it had another—and more profound—impact on society; it directly led to increased literacy. For example, at the time of the printing press's origin, only about 30 percent of Europeans were literate; most could not even write their own names. As more writing was published, the numbers increased slowly and consistently so that nearly 200 years after the invention of the Gutenberg press, literacy had increased in Europe to nearly 50 percent. But even for those who did not learn to read or write, the printing press provided greater opportunities for the dissemination of knowledge. For example, those who were literate could read books, pamphlets, and articles to those who were not literate in places where social and religious gatherings took place, like churches. Knowledge could thus diffuse through populations with exposure to printed material, which was often presented in vernacular languages, which people actually spoke. And as societies expanded outside their borders, knowledge was also translated and thus standardized so that it could be disseminated broadly—and across national frontiers. Even so, there were still many who could neither read nor write, especially girls, who attended school, if at all, far fewer hours than did boys. Over the very long run, however, the printing press proved to be instrumental in creating common cultural, political, and religious identities.

As people gained access to information, either through direct reading of the printed word or through being in a place where words on a page could be read to them, they began to form collective identities, which allowed them to see themselves as part of a group, like residents of a city or subjects of a particular ruler. These commonalities could then be further developed with regular communication from leaders, deepening the attachments. Indeed, such identifications could pass much more easily from one generation to the next, which, in turn, helped people think of themselves in new ways and enabled them to refer to themselves as members of specific groups. The printing press thus helped historians understand how identity was created and how it operated, and helped them make generalizations about states, empires, societies, and subgroups within each.

POWER AND THE RENAISSANCE: THEORIZING ABOUT WAR The Renaissance not only embraced the arts and sciences of this world, but also served as a vehicle that enabled the direct study of worldly power. Close reading of the ancient histories of Sallust, Livy, and Caesar emboldened scholars to address more forthrightly the conditions under which power could be maintained or undermined. New forms of governance were invented—and older forms buttressed. The Florentines pioneered a form of civic humanism under which all citizens were to devote themselves to defending the state against tyrants and foreign invaders; according to this view, the state would reward their civic virtue by ensuring their liberty. Yet it was also a Florentine, Niccolò Machiavelli, who wrote the most famous treatise on authoritarian power, *The Prince* (1513). Machiavelli argued that political leadership was not about obeying God's rules but about mastering the amoral means of modern statecraft. Holding and exercising power were ends in themselves, he claimed; civic virtue was desirable but unnecessary if power was in danger of being lost.

In his own lifetime, Machiavelli was even more renowned for his essay *The Art of War* (1521). Here, the Florentine humanist argued that Roman military tactics, including the deploying of trained, armed citizens, would make for a more trustworthy army than the use of mercenary soldiers. The enrollment of a broadly based citizenry in the defense of the state, he insisted, would also make for political stability. His advice was hardly practicable in a Europe in which monarchs put little trust in their fellow nobles and even less in their subjects, but his ideas circulated widely (see the discussion of the printing press above) and would gradually catch on and inspire military reforms in the Dutch Republic and during the Thirty Years' War (see Chapter 13). And he made little of the use of artillery, although cannons had been used in European siege warfare since at least the 1420s; the Portuguese had already mounted them on oceangoing ships and had begun to use them to blast open South Asian ports. Machiavelli's fellow humanist Niccolò Tartaglia noticed the upsurge in cannon usage and produced an important treatise on ballistics, in which mathematics was first applied to the trajectory of projectiles. But neither of these humanists was as influential as a wave of publications devoted to proper fortification designs, written by specialized military engineers who, for the first time, advocated the construction of defenses not to be pleasing to the eye but to best absorb the force of modern cannons. Thus began a long-lasting battle between military architects seeking to construct invincible defense works and artillery makers seeking to destroy them.

Like artistic and early manufacturing techniques, European military technologies diffused across the continent through conflict between states. Europeans learned much by observing one another at close range, especially during the many wars that marked the fifteenth and sixteenth centuries. As princes began to orient themselves more and more to obtaining and preserving power in this world, they began to value subjects who could build sturdy fortifications or more effectively mix gunpowder (a Chinese invention in widespread use in Europe by 1400). By the sixteenth century, many had also formed what were essentially standing armies and had begun to invest heavily in improved fortifications, not only for their castles but for their cities of residence as well. But like the church's new worldly activities, these princely activities also cost a great deal of money and demanded an expansion of state operations. By orienting the elite toward both ancient ideas and worldly power, the Renaissance revolutionized both European culture and politics—even if it could not unify the states and peoples who cultivated it.

Ming China

Like Europeans, the Chinese saw their stable worldview and political order crumble under the cataclysms of human and bacterial invasions. Moreover, like Europeans, people in China had long regarded outsiders as "barbarians." Together, the Mongols and the Black Death upended the political and intellectual foundations of what had appeared to be the world's most integrated society. The Mongols brought the Yuan dynasty to power; then the plague devastated China and prepared the way for the emergence of the Ming dynasty.

Ruled by ethnically Han Chinese, the **Ming dynasty** defined itself against its foreign predecessors. Ming emperors sought to reinforce everything Chinese. In particular, they supported China's vast internal agricultural markets in an attempt to minimize dependence on merchants and foreign trade.

Restoring Order

In the chaotic fourteenth century, as plague and famine ravaged China and as the Mongol Yuan dynasty collapsed, only a strong military movement capable of overpowering other groups could restore order. That intervention began at the hands of a poor young man who had trained in the Red Turban movement: Zhu Yuanzhang. He was an orphan from a peasant household in an area devastated by disease and famine and a former novice at a Buddhist monastery. At age twenty-four, Zhu joined the Red Turbans, after which he rose quickly to become a distinguished commander. Eventually, his forces defeated the Yuan and drove the Mongols from China.

It soon became clear that Zhu had a much grander design for all of China than the ambitions of most warlords. When he took the important city of Nanjing in 1356, he renamed it Yingtian ("In Response to Heaven"). Buoyed by subsequent successful military campaigns, Zhu (r. 1368–1398) proclaimed the founding of the Ming ("brilliant") dynasty twelve years

The Forbidden City. The Yongle Emperor relocated the capital to Beijing, where he began the construction of the Forbidden City, or imperial palace. Like Topkapi, the palace was designed to inspire awe in all who saw it.

later. Soon thereafter, his troops met little resistance when they seized the Yuan capital of Beijing, causing the Mongol emperor to flee to his homeland in the steppe. It would, however, take Zhu almost another twenty years to reunify the entire country.

Centralization under the Ming

Zhu and successive Ming emperors had to rebuild a devastated society from the ground up. Although China in the past had experienced natural catastrophes, wars, and social dislocation, the plague's legacy was devastation on an unprecedented scale. It left the new rulers with the formidable challenge of rebuilding the great cities, restoring respect for ruling elites, and reconstructing the weakened bureaucracy.

IMPERIAL GRANDEUR AND KINSHIP The rebuilding began under Zhu, the Hongwu ("expansive and martial") Emperor, whose extravagant capital at Nanjing reflected imperial grandeur. When the dynasty's third emperor, the Yongle ("perpetual happiness") Emperor, relocated the capital to Beijing, he flaunted an even more grandiose style. Construction here mobilized around 100,000 artisans and a million laborers. The city had three separate walled enclosures. Inside the outer city walls sprawled the imperial city; within its walls lay the palace city, the Forbidden City. Traffic within the walled sections navigated through boulevards leading to the different gates, above which imposing towers soared. The palace compound, where the imperial family resided, had more than 9,000 rooms. Anyone standing in the front courts, which measured more than 400 yards (366 meters) on a side and boasted marble terraces and carved railings, would gasp at the sense of awesome power. That was precisely the effect the Ming emperors wanted (just as the Ottoman sultans did in building Topkapi Palace).

Marriage and kinship buttressed the power of the Ming imperial household. The dynasty's founder married the adopted daughter of a leading Red Turban rebel (her father, according to legend, was a convicted murderer), thereby consolidating his power and eliminating a threat. Empress Ma, as she was known, became the Hongwu Emperor's principal wife and

Chinese Irrigation. Farmers in imperial China used sophisticated devices to extract water for irrigation, as depicted in this illustration from the Yuan Mongol period.

was praised for her compassion. Emerging as the kinder face of the regime, she tempered the harsh and sometimes cruel disposition of her spouse. He had numerous other consorts as well, including Korean and Mongol women, who bore him twenty-six sons and sixteen daughters. (His household was similar to, although on a smaller scale than, the sultan's harem at Topkapi Palace.)

BUILDING A BUREAUCRACY Faced with the challenge of reestablishing order out of turmoil, the Hongwu Emperor initially sought to rule through his many kinsmen by giving imperial princes generous stipends, command of large garrisons, and significant autonomy in running their domains. However, when the princes' power began to threaten the court, the emperor slashed their stipends, reduced their privileges, and took control of their garrisons. No longer dependent on these men, he established an imperial bureaucracy beholden only to him and to his successors. These officials won appointments through their outstanding performance on a reinstated civil service examination.

In addition, the Hongwu Emperor took other steps to install a centralized system of rule. He assigned bureaucrats to oversee the manufacture of porcelain, cotton, and silk products as well as to collect taxes. He reestablished the Confucian school system as a means of selecting a cadre of loyal officials (not unlike the Ottoman janissaries and administrators). He also set up local networks of villages to rebuild irrigation systems and to supervise reforestation projects to prevent flooding—with the astonishing result that the amount of reclaimed land nearly tripled within eight years. Historians estimate that the Hongwu Emperor's reign oversaw the planting of about a billion trees, including 50 million sterculia, palm, and varnish trees around Nanjing. Their timber served in building a maritime expedition fleet in the early fifteenth century. For water control, 40,987 reservoirs underwent repairs or new construction.

Now the imperial palace not only projected the image of a power center; it *was* the center of power. Every official received his appointment from the emperor through the Ministry of Personnel. The Hongwu Emperor also eliminated the post of prime minister (he executed the man who held the post) and then ruled directly. Ming bureaucrats literally lost their seats and had to kneel before the emperor. In one eight-day period, the Hongwu Emperor reputedly reviewed over 1,600 petitions dealing with 3,392 separate matters. The drawback, of course, was that he had to keep tabs on this immense system, and his bureaucrats were not always up to the task, leading to inconsistent results. Indeed, the Hongwu Emperor constantly juggled personal and impersonal forms of authority, sometimes fortifying the administration, sometimes undermining it lest it become too autonomous. In due course, he nurtured a bureaucracy that was far more extensive

Ming Deities. A pantheon of deities were worshipped during the Ming dynasty, demonstrating the rich religious culture of the period and the elaborate way in which faith reinforced hierarchy.

than those of the Islamic empires. The Ming thus established the most highly centralized system of government of all the monarchies of this period.

Religion under the Ming

Just as the Ottoman sultans projected themselves as Muslim rulers, calling themselves the shadow of God, and European monarchs claimed to rule by divine right, so the Ming emperors enhanced their legitimacy by drawing on ancient Chinese religious traditions. Citing the mandate of heaven, the emperor revised and strengthened the elaborate protocol of rites and ceremonies that had undergirded dynastic power for centuries. As well as underscoring the emperor's centrality, official rituals (such as those related to the gods of soil and grain) reinforced political and social hierarchies.

Under the guise of "community" gatherings, rites and sacrifices solidified the Ming order by portraying the rulers as the moral and spiritual benefactors of their subjects. On at least ninety occasions each year, the emperor engaged in sacrificial rites, providing symbolic communion between the human and the spiritual worlds. These lavish festivities reinforced the ruler's image as mediator between otherworldly affairs of the gods and worldly concerns of the empire's subjects. The message was clear: the gods were on the side of the Ming household.

Because religious rituals supported hierarchies, the emperor sanctioned elaborate official cults. Organized into civil or military domains; tiered into great, middle, or minor rites; and categorized as celestial, terrestrial, or human, official cults were meant to reflect the emperor's glory and reinforce Ming rule. But official cults often conflicted with local faiths. In this regard, they revealed the limits of Ming centralism. Consider Dongyang, a hilly interior region. As was common in Ming China, the people of Dongyang supported Buddhist institutions. Guan Yu, a legendary martial hero killed centuries earlier, was enshrined in a local Buddhist monastery there. But he was also worshipped as part of a state cult. Herein lay the problem: the state cult and the Buddhist monastery were separate entities, and imperial law held that the demands of the state cult prevailed over those of the local monastery. So the state-appointed magistrates in Dongyang kept a watchful eye on local religious leaders, although the magistrates refrained from directly tampering with the monastery's affairs. Although the imperial government insisted that people make payments to the state, Dongyang's residents delivered most of their funds to the Buddhist monks. So strong were local sentiments that even the officials siphoned revenues to the monastery.

Ming Rulership

If conquest established the Ming Empire, bureaucracy kept it functioning. The empire's large scale (see Map 11.4) required a remarkably complex administration. To many outsiders (especially Europeans, whose region was in a state of constant war), Ming stability and centralization appeared to be political wizardry.

Ming rulers worried in particular about maintaining the support of ordinary people in the countryside. The emperor wished to be seen as the special guardian of his subjects. He wanted their allegiance as well as their taxes and labor. But during hard times, poor farmers were reluctant to provide resources—taxes or services—to distant officials. For these

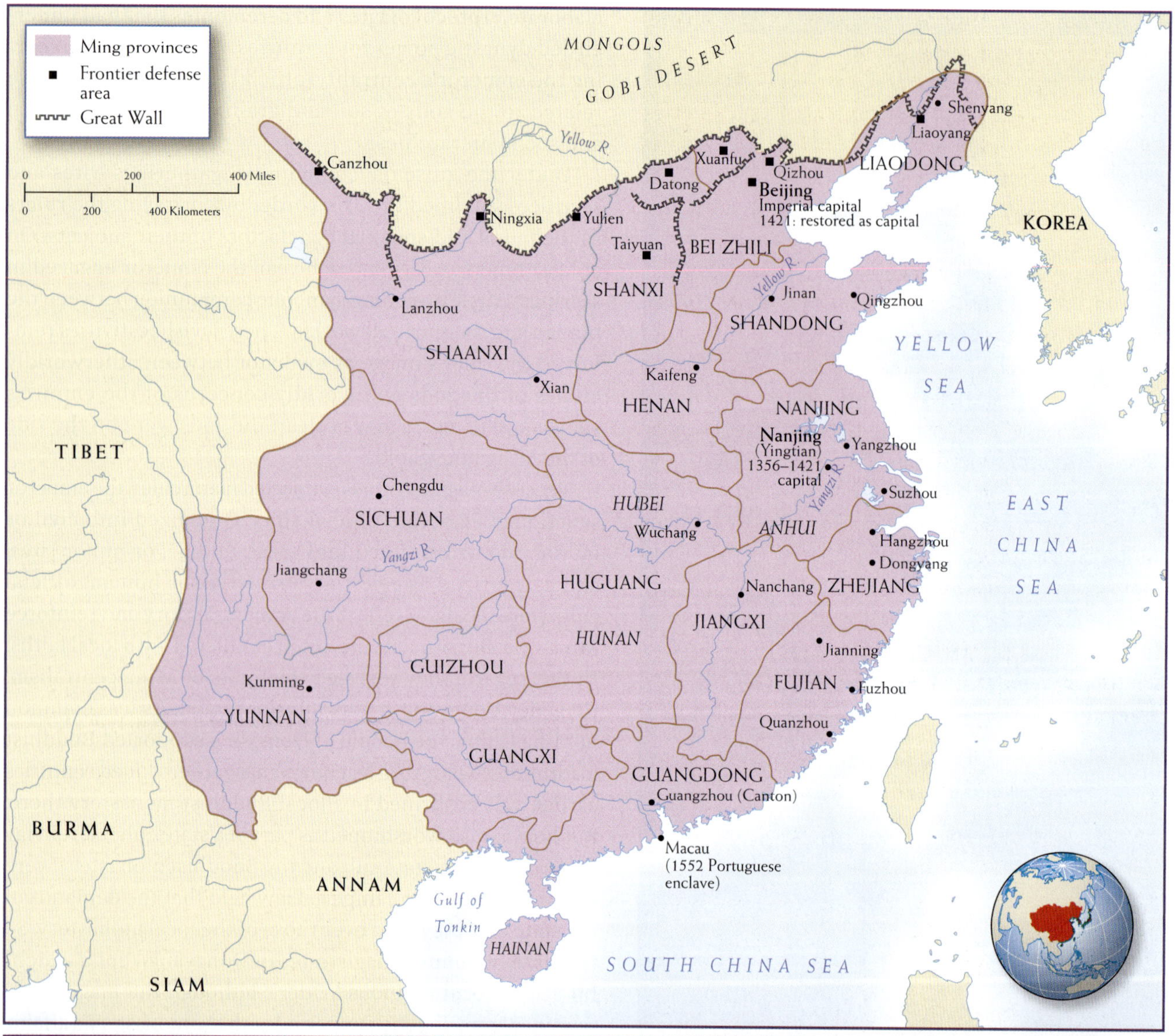

MAP 11.4 | Ming China, 1500s

The Ming state was one of the largest empires at this time—and the most populous. Using the scale, determine the length of its coastline and its internal borders.

- What were the two Ming capitals and the three main seaport trading cities? How far are they from one another?
- According to the map, where did the Ming rulers expect the greatest threat to their security?
- How many provinces are outlined on the map? How far is Beijing from some of the more distant provinces? What sorts of challenges did that create for the centralized style of Ming rule, and how does the chapter suggest those challenges were resolved?

reasons alone, the Hongwu Emperor preferred to entrust management of the rural world to local leaders, whom he appointed as village chiefs, village elders, or tax captains. (In fact, a popular Chinese proverb was "The mountain is high and the emperor is far away.") Within these communities, the dynasty created a social hierarchy based on age, sex, and kinship. While women's labor remained critical for the village economy, the government reinforced a gender hierarchy by promoting women's chastity and constructing commemorative arches for widows who refrained from remarrying. The Ming thus produced a more elaborate system for classifying and controlling its subjects than did the other Eurasian dynasties. But individuals also sought to define themselves by dressing in ways that expressed their own view of their place in the social order. (See Current Trends in World History: Ming Fashion.)

The Ming Empire, like states in Europe and the Islamic world, faced periodic unrest and rebellion. Rebels often proclaimed their own brand of religious beliefs, just as local elites resented central authority. Outright terror helped stymie threats to central authority. In a massive wave of carnage, the Hongwu Emperor slaughtered anyone who posed a threat to his authority, from the highest of ministers to the lowliest of scribes. From 1376 to 1393, four of his purges condemned close to 100,000 subjects to execution.

Yet, despite the emperor's immense power, the Ming Empire was insufficiently governed. Indeed, as the population multiplied, there were too few loyal officials to handle local affairs. By the sixteenth and early seventeenth centuries, for example, some 10,000 to 15,000 officials shouldered the responsibility of managing a population exceeding 200 million people. Nonetheless, the Hongwu Emperor bequeathed to his descendants a set of tools for ruling that drew on subjects' direct loyalty to the emperor and on the intricate workings of an extensive bureaucracy. His legacy enabled his successors to balance local sources of power with the needs of centralized dynastic rulership.

Trade and Exploration

Gradually, consolidation under the Ming allowed for the revival of trade. The new dynasty's merchants reestablished China's preeminence in long-distance commercial exchange. Chinese silk and cotton textiles, as well as fine porcelains, ranked among the world's most coveted luxuries. Wealthy families from across Eurasia loved to wash their hands in delicate Chinese bowls and to flaunt fine wardrobes made from bolts of Chinese dyed linens and smoothly spun silk. When a Chinese merchant ship sailed into port, trading partners and onlookers crowded the docks to watch the unloading of precious cargoes. Although Ming rulers' support for overseas ventures wavered and eventually declined, this period saw important developments in Chinese trade and exploration.

During the Ming period, Chinese traders based in ports such as Hangzhou, Quanzhou, and Guangzhou (Canton) were as energetic as their Muslim counterparts on the Indian Ocean. These ports were home to prosperous merchants and the point of convergence for vast sea-lanes. Leaving the mainland ports, Chinese vessels carried precious wares to offshore islands, the Pescadores, and Taiwan. From there they sailed on to the ports of Kyūshū, the Ryūkyūs, Luzon,

Zheng He's Ships and Exotic Cargo. The largest ship in Zheng He's armada had nine staggered masts and twelve silk sails. This graphic demonstrates just how large and complex Zheng He's ships were, compared with Christopher Columbus's *Santa Maria*. With ships so large, Zheng He's fleet could return to China with magnificent and exotic cargo, like the giraffes brought as tribute from Bengal in 1414 and Malindi in 1415. These tribute giraffes were recorded in several paintings, some inscribed with a poem attributed to his contemporary Shen Du that described the giraffes as *qilin*, mythical creatures that appear during the rule of a great leader.

Current Trends in World History

Ming Fashion

Ming rulers liked to represent themselves as custodians of the "civilized" Han traditions, in contrast to the "barbarian" ways of the previous Mongol Yuan dynasty. However, from governmental practices to clothing fashions, there were visible signs everywhere that the Ming, despite their rhetoric, followed in the Yuan's footsteps and became increasingly linked to an ever-growing, interconnected world. As trade with neighboring and faraway lands continued unabated and merchants and travelers kept moving, it proved to be impossible for the Ming to keep outside influences at arm's length. At the same time, the rhetoric of a return to the Han traditions did generate moves to invoke antiquity in the realm of fashion. Status-conscious elites with newfound wealth eagerly purchased clothes in what they believed to be the ancient Han style, hoping to set themselves apart from the common people. Their flirtation with antiquity, however, often ended up being more reinvention to satisfy the surging demands of the market than a genuine return to earlier conventions.

Founder Zhu Yuanzhang set the tone of the Ming by trying to rid the country of the close-fitting tunics worn by the Mongols. He advocated instead the wearing of the reputedly Tang-style garment of earlier times. While this measure did meet with some success, the vibrant clothing sector was hardly free of its fascination with the "exotic," such as horsehair skirts from Korea for men. These skirts were a rare commodity when they first arrived, probably via trade missions. But by the late fifteenth century, local weavers had become so skilled in making them, and consumers so eager to obtain them, that craftworkers were caught stealing the tails of horses to satisfy the soaring demand for the raw materials. Indeed, undoubtedly to the chagrin of the first Ming emperor and his descendants, much of the Yuan style and even terminology in both male and female clothing persisted during the Ming era.

The retro movement in fashion had more to do with the demands of a changing Ming society than with the official advocacy for restorationism. Nowhere was this more apparent than in the myriad styles of hats for men—a convenient yet highly visible way to make a statement in social standing. Invoking the names of earlier dynasties, styles included the Han cap, the Jin cap, the Tang cap, and so on. The most interesting, however, was the Chunyang hat, which allegedly drew upon both Han and Tang styles in its design but

An example of headwear used by Ming officials, reputedly following the style of earlier dynasties. The beams attached to the crown of the cap indicate the official's rank, so the cap is known as a "beamed cap."

and maritime Southeast Asia. As entrepôts for global goods, East Asian ports flourished. Former fishing villages developed into major urban centers.

The Ming dynasty viewed overseas expansion with suspicion, however. The Hongwu Emperor feared that too much contact with the outside world would cause instability and undermine his rule. In fact, he banned private maritime commerce in 1371. But enforcement was lax, and by the late fifteenth century maritime trade once again surged. Because much of the thriving business took place in defiance of official edicts, constant friction occurred between government officials and maritime traders. Although the Ming government ultimately agreed to issue licenses for overseas trade in the mid-sixteenth century, its policies continued to vacillate. To Ming officials, the sea represented problems of order and control rather than opportunities.

THE EXPEDITIONS OF ZHENG HE One spectacular exception to the Ming's attitude toward maritime trade was a series of officially sponsored expeditions in the early fifteenth century. The ambitious Yongle Emperor took the initiative. One of his loyal followers was a Muslim whom the Ming army had captured as a boy. The youth was castrated and sent to serve at the court (as a eunuch, he could not continue his family line and so theoretically owed sole allegiance to the emperor). Given the name **Zheng He** (1371–1433), he grew up

The "paddy-field gown" for women might have had its origins in Buddhist robes.

had actually become a symbol of the so-called new and strange fashion that so often attracted commentary in Ming writings. In fact, it was favored by the young, who had nothing but disdain for ancient styles!

Nor was the rage for fashion reserved for only men or even for just the privileged. One Ming writer lamented, perhaps with a hint of exaggeration, "Nowadays the very servant girls dress in silk gauze, and the singsong girls look down on brocaded silks and embroidered gowns." Respectable women, we are told, looked to the clothing and style of the courtesans of the prosperous southern region of the country for ideas and inspiration for fashion. Indeed, much of our visual knowledge of Ming women's clothing comes from paintings that likely depicted highly trained courtesans or the female "entertainers" ubiquitous in Ming urban centers. These paintings reveal the different and consistently evolving styles of clothing for Ming women, including the "paddy-field gowns"—which might have owed their origins to Buddhist robes—that were the focus of much criticism from those who frowned on the growing penchant for the exotic, the strange, the outrageous, and the irreverent in the realm of fashion. If nothing else, this debate about clothing certainly tells us that despite the often conservative stance and policies of the Ming regime, the everyday life of many Ming subjects was a constant exercise in negotiating the multiple impacts of both the old and the new, as well as the familiar and the foreign, in different arenas of their rapidly changing society.

QUESTIONS FOR ANALYSIS

- Why did the Ming elite cultivate an "ancient" Han style?
- Can you think of retro styles popular today? What do such styles say about the people who cultivate them?
- How do we know about changes in women's fashion in the Ming era? Are there any dangers in using these sources to understand the dress of all Ming women?

EXPLORE FURTHER

Finnane, Antonia, *Changing Clothes in China: Fashion, History, Nation* (2008).

to be an important military leader. The emperor entrusted him with venturing out to trade, collect tribute, and display China's power to the world.

From 1405 to 1433, Zheng He commanded the world's greatest armada and led seven naval expeditions. His larger ships stretched 400 feet in length (Columbus's *Santa Maria* was 85 feet), carried hundreds of sailors on four tiers of decks, and maneuvered with sophisticated rudders, nine masts, and watertight compartments. The first expedition set sail with a flotilla of 62 large ships and over 200 lesser ones. All 28,000 men aboard pledged to promote Ming glory.

Zheng He and his entourage aimed to establish tributary relations with far-flung territories—from Southeast Asia to the Indian Ocean ports, to the Persian Gulf, and to the east coast of Africa. (See Map 11.5.) These expeditions did not seek territorial expansion but rather expanded control of trade and tribute. Zheng traded for ivory, spices, ointments, exotic woods, and even some wildlife, including giraffes, zebras, and ostriches. He also used his considerable force to intervene in local affairs, exhibiting China's might in the process. If a community refused to pay tribute, Zheng's fleet would attack it. He encouraged rulers or envoys from Southeast Asia, India, Southwest Asia, and Africa to visit his homeland. When local rulers were uncooperative, Zheng might seize them and drag them all the way to China to face the emperor, as he did to the rulers of Sumatra and Ceylon.

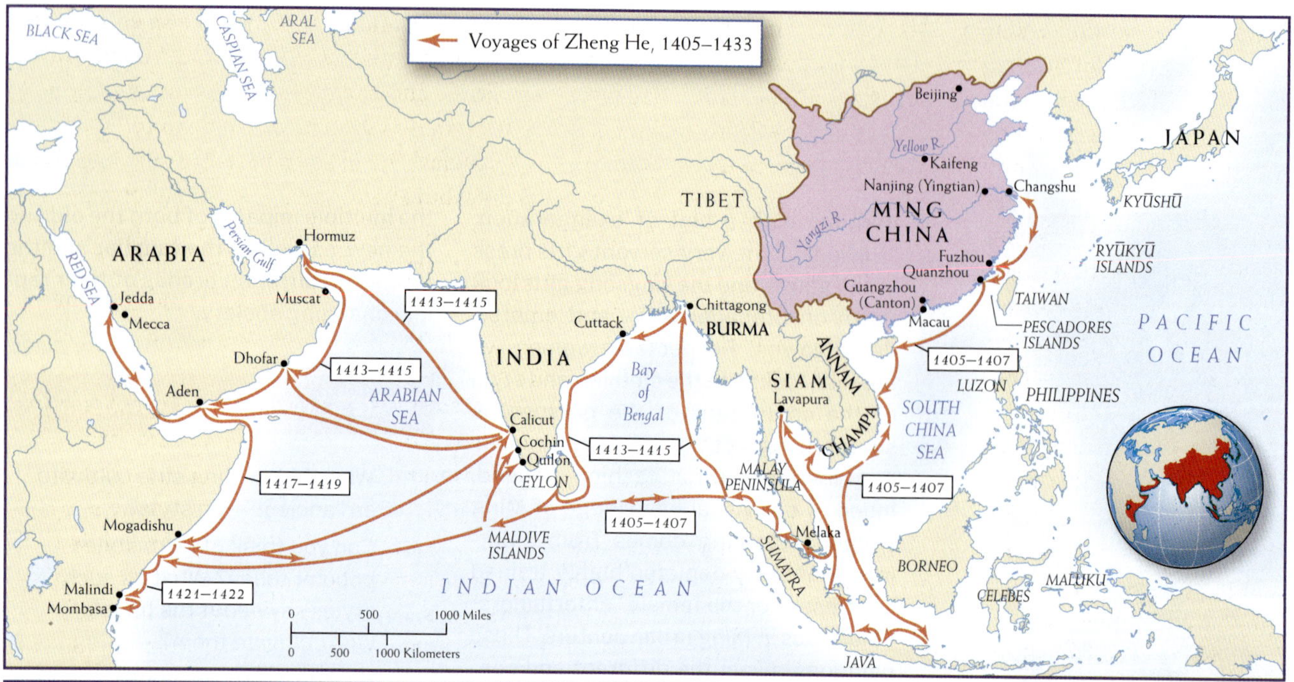

MAP 11.5 | Voyages of Zheng He, 1405–1433

Zheng He's voyages are some of the most famous in world history. Many have speculated about how history might be different if the Chinese emperors had allowed the voyages to continue.

- What routes did Zheng He's armada follow?
- Referring to other maps in this chapter and earlier chapters, with what peoples did Zheng He's armada come into contact?
- Using the scale on the map, estimate how far Zheng He's armada sailed. How does this distance compare with the distances covered by other world travelers you've encountered in this text?

As spectacular as they were, Zheng's accomplishments could not survive the changing tides of events at home. Although many items gathered on his voyages delighted the court, most were not suitable for everyday commerce. The expeditions were glamorous but expensive, and in 1424, when the Yongle Emperor died, they lost their most enthusiastic patron. Moreover, by the mid-fifteenth century there was a revival of military threats from the north. At that time, the Ming court was shocked to discover that during a tour of the frontiers, the emperor had been captured and held hostage by the Mongols. Recalling how the maritime-oriented Song dynasty had been overrun by invaders from the north (see Chapter 10), Ming officials withdrew imperial support for seagoing ventures and instead devoted their energies to overland ventures and defense. Thus, Zheng's expeditions came to a complete halt in 1433. Never again did the Ming undertake such large-scale maritime ventures, although individual merchants returned to their profitable coastal trade routes.

The Chinese decision to forgo overseas ventures after 1433 was momentous. Although China remained the wealthiest, most densely settled region of the world with the most fully developed state structure and thriving market, the empire's wariness of overseas projects deprived merchants and would-be explorers of vital support just at the time that others were beginning to look outward and across the oceans.

Conclusion

How could all the dying and devastation that came with the Black Death not have transformed the peoples of Eurasia? Much did change, but certain underlying ideals and institutions endured. What changed were mainly the political regimes: they took the blame for the catastrophes wrought by disease. The Delhi Sultanate, the Abbasid Empire, and the Yuan dynasty collapsed. Europe's principalities and the papacy took a beating.

And yet, universal religions and wide-ranging cultural systems endured. Indeed, successor regimes reimagined and repurposed older faiths. The Ming dynasty in China set the stage for a long tenure by claiming, as had previous rulers, the mandate of heaven and stressing China's place at the center of the universe. A strict Shiite version of Islam emerged in Iran, while a fervent form of Sunni Islam found its champion in the Ottoman Empire. In Europe, national monarchies appeared in Spain, Portugal, France, and England. Debilitated by death and disorder, the Catholic Church recovered its centrality, though some Europeans, too, began to satisfy their spiritual longings in ways that went beyond established practices.

Despite these parallels, the new states and empires demonstrated notable differences. These were evident in the ambition of a Ming warlord who established a new dynasty, the military expansionism of Turkish households bordering the Byzantine Empire, the unifying vision of Mughal rulers in northern India, and the desire of various European rulers to consolidate power. But interactions among peoples also mattered: an eagerness to reestablish and expand trade networks and a desire to convert unbelievers to "the true faith"—be it a form of Islam, a variant of Hinduism, an exclusive Christianity, or a local type of Buddhism.

The dynasties all faced similar problems. They had to establish legitimacy with their populations, ensure smooth successions into the future, deal with religious groups, and forge working relationships with nobles, townspeople, merchants, and peasants. Yet each state developed distinctive traits as a result of political innovation, traditional ways of ruling, and borrowing from neighbors. European monarchies achieved significant internal unity, often through warfare and in the context of a cultural Renaissance, made possible at least in part with the printing press. Ottoman rulers perfected techniques for ruling an ethnically and religiously diverse empire: they moved military forces swiftly, allowed local communities a degree of political and religious autonomy, and trained a bureaucracy dedicated to the Ottoman and Sunni way of life. The Ming dynasty fashioned an imperial system based on a Confucian-trained bureaucracy and intense subordination to the emperor so that it could manage a mammoth population with some consistency. The rising monarchies of Europe, the Shiite regime of the Safavids in Persia, and the Ottoman state all blazed with religious fervor and sought to eradicate or subordinate the beliefs of other groups.

The new states displayed unprecedented political and economic powers. All demonstrated military prowess, a desire for stable hierarchies and secure borders, and a drive to expand. Each legitimized its rule via dynastic marriage and succession, state-sanctioned religion, and administrative bureaucracies. Each supported vigorous commercial activity. The Islamic regimes, especially, engaged in long-distance commerce and, by conquest and conversion, extended their holdings.

For western Christendom, the Ottoman conquests were decisive. They provoked Europeans to establish commercial connections to the east, south, and west. The consequences of their new toeholds would be momentous—just as the Chinese decision to turn *away* from overseas exploration and commerce marked a turning point in world history. Both decisions were instrumental in determining which worlds would come together and which would remain apart.

After You Read This Chapter

TRACING THE GLOBAL STORYLINES

FOCUS ON: The Black Death, Recovery, and Conquest

Collapse and Consolidation

- Bubonic plague originates in Inner Asia and afflicts people from China to Europe.
- Climate change and famine leave people vulnerable, while commerce facilitates the spread of disease.
- The plague kills 25 to 65 percent of infected populations and leaves societies in turmoil.

The Islamic World

- The Ottoman, Safavid, and Mughal Empires replace the Mongols.
- The Ottomans overrun Constantinople and become the primary Sunni regime in the Islamic world.
- The Ottomans establish their legitimacy with military prowess, religious backing, and a loyal bureaucracy.
- Sultans manage decentralizing tendencies of outlying provinces with flexibility and tolerance, relying on religious faith, patronage, and bureaucracy in order to remain in control.
- Safavid and Mughal regimes arise in Iran and South Asia.

Western Christendom

- New dynastic monarchies that claim to rule by divine right appear in Portugal, Spain, France, and England.
- The Inquisition takes aim against Jews, Muslims, and *conversos*.
- A rebirth of classical learning, known as the Renaissance, originates in Italian city-states and spreads throughout western Europe.
- War making becomes more scientific, expensive, and deadly.

Ming China

- The Ming dynasty replaces the Mongol Yuan dynasty and rebuilds a strong state from the ground up, claiming a mandate from heaven.
- An elaborate, centralized bureaucracy oversees the revival of infrastructure and long-distance trade.
- The emperor and bureaucracy concentrate on developing internal markets and overland trade at the expense of overseas commerce.

CHRONOLOGY

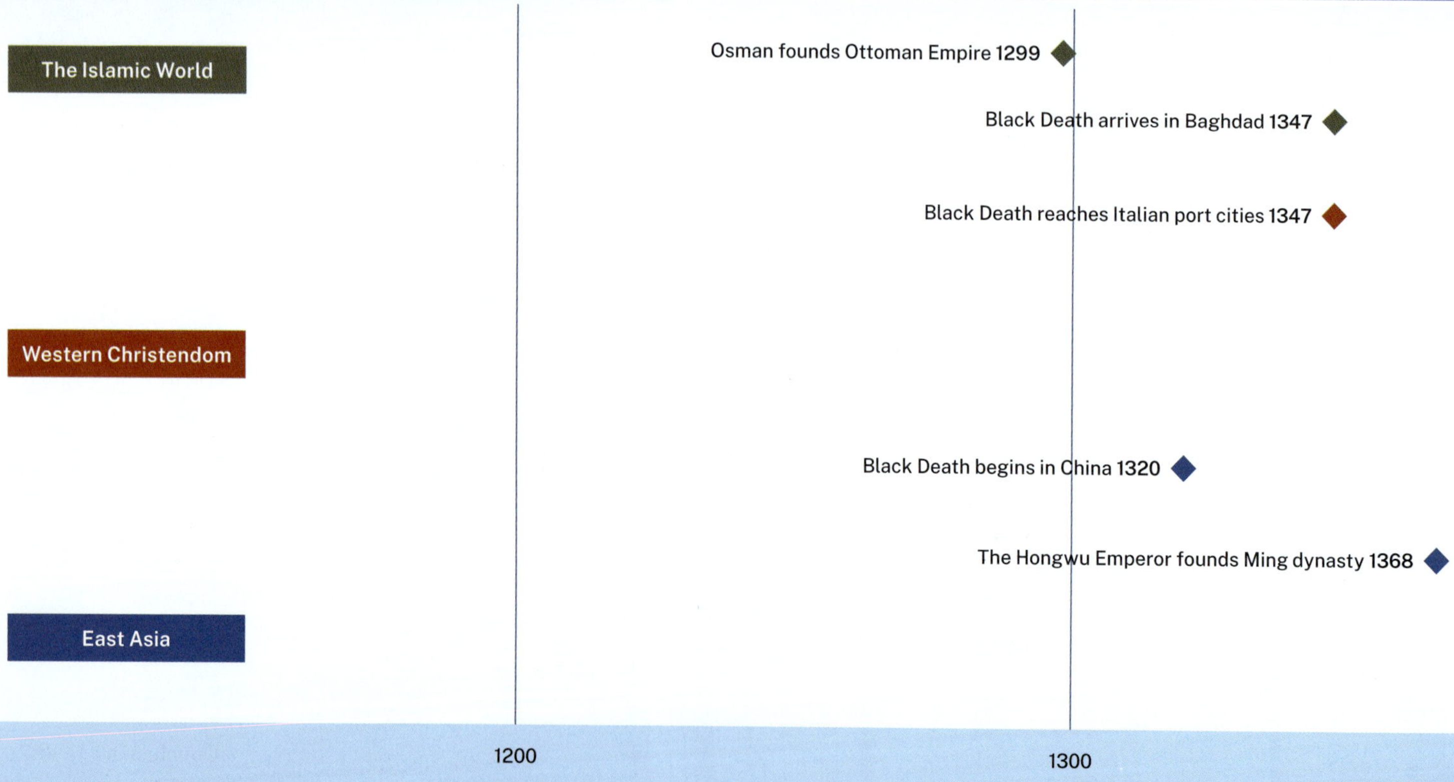

KEY TERMS

Black Death p. 454
devshirme p. 466
dynasty p. 460
humanism p. 475
Inquisition p. 474
Ming dynasty p. 478
monarchy p. 470
Ottoman Empire p. 460
printing press p. 476
Red Turban movement p. 455
Renaissance p. 475
Sikhism p. 468
Topkapi Palace p. 464
Zheng He p. 484

THINKING ABOUT GLOBAL CONNECTIONS

Thinking about Exchange Networks By the fourteenth century, most of the Eurasian landmass was bound together by multiple exchange networks that functioned on many levels—political, cultural, and commercial. How did these exchange networks facilitate the spread of the plague? In what ways did the spread of the Black Death correspond with and diverge from existing political, cultural, and commercial networks?

Thinking about Changing Power Relationships Fourteenth-century famine and plague, and the accompanying political, economic, and natural crises, together triggered powerful, often differing, responses in western Europe, the Ottoman lands, and Ming China. How did men and women at different levels of society respond to the fourteenth-century crises? How did their responses reshape their societies? Pay special attention to the relationships among ordinary men and women, elites, and imperial bureaucracies in all three regions.

Thinking about Environmental Impacts Climate change laid the groundwork for the devastation of the Black Death. What environmental developments in Europe, central Asia, and China set the stage for the Black Death?

Go to INQUIZITIVE to see what you've learned—and learn what you've missed—with personalized feedback along the way.

Ottoman armies conquer Constantinople 1453

Suleiman expands and consolidates Ottoman Empire 1520–1566

The printing press is invented by Johannes Gutenberg and enters commercial use 1450

Castile and Aragon unite to form Spain 1469

Spain conquers Granada 1492

The Inquisition 1481–1826

Zheng He's voyages 1405–1433

1400 | 1500 | 1600

Global Themes and Sources

Causes and Effects of the Black Death

The devastation wrought by the plague in Afro-Eurasia and the upheaval that followed were unprecedented and far-reaching in their impact. Families were broken as parents, spouses, and children deserted one another for fear of contagion. Religious responses varied from hopelessness to ecstatic devotion. The plague affected economic life as well, causing skyrocketing prices, diminished availability of goods and labor, and unmet demand for certain products and services. Dramatic population losses demonstrate its demographic impact: beginning in southwestern China in the 1320s, the Pestilence or Great Mortality, as it came to be known in Europe, wiped out between 25 and 65 percent of the populations it afflicted.

The plague traveled along the trade routes of Inner Eurasia, taking advantage of the connectivity that had bound the Afro-Eurasian world together and facilitated the movement of people, goods, and ideas. The plague also took advantage of an already weakened population that had experienced a "Little Ice Age" and a resulting famine in the early years of the fourteenth century. Modern scholars have scrutinized sources to determine answers to such questions as what the precise death tolls were, why the plague's effects were so much more devastating in some regions than in others, and what kind of disease it was—septicemic (blood-borne and spread by fleas on rats and other animals), pneumonic (airborne, spread by the coughing that accompanied the spewing of blood that so many of the sources report), or a combination of the two. No less fascinating, however, are the attempts by writers of the fourteenth and early fifteenth centuries to understand the plague's causes and immediate effects.

The sources here offer a mix of perspectives. Some come from authors who experienced plague firsthand and others from authors who lived in the plague's aftermath and considered its causes and its effects. There are regional accounts from two different cultural spheres: the Islamic world, particularly Syria and Egypt, and Europe. Ibn al-Wardi, from Aleppo in Syria, recorded his thoughts on what was causing the plague and described immediate responses to, and effects of, the disease. His understanding offers only the most short-term perspective because he died from the plague in 1349 and thus did not live to see the long-term aftermath. The Florentine Baldassarre de Buonaiuti experienced the plague in one of the European cities hit hardest by the disease. There are echoes of Buonaiuti in the introduction to Boccaccio's famed *Decameron*, in which elite youth withdraw from the city and entertain one another with stories, having locked themselves away in a country villa to escape the sickness in the city. In his later years, Buonaiuti recollected the events of 1348 in his *Florentine Chronicle*. The plague offered Ibn Khaldûn an opportunity to ruminate on the patterns of civilization in his *Muqaddimah* (c. 1375). Written in Cairo, his historiographical masterpiece gives a North African perspective on the effects of the plague a full generation after its impact. Finally, a student of Ibn Khaldûn, al-Maqrizi, gives yet another Cairene, Islamic perspective, a generation later.

These sources, with their different perspectives—Christian and Islamic, contemporary and from the plague's aftermath, by chronicler and by philosophical historian, European as well as Southwest Asian and North African—encourage us to think about the complexity of cause and effect. We can see how those who lived in proximity to this catastrophic event described the causes of what they, or their recent relatives, had lived through. The sources allow us to consider the short- and long-term effects of the disease as experienced in the fourteenth and fifteenth centuries. And, together with the material in the chapter, the sources give us an opportunity to reflect both on the complexity of causation, teasing out the primary and secondary causes for how the plague played out, and on the larger historical significance of the plague and its aftermath.

ANALYZING THE CAUSES AND EFFECTS OF THE BLACK DEATH

- How do the responses to, and the effects of, plague in the Muslim world (as reported by al-Wardi, Ibn Khaldûn, and al-Maqrizi) compare with those in Florence (as reported in *The Florentine Chronicle*)?
- What patterns in explaining causes and effects of plague do you detect in these sources? How do the various causes and effects explicitly or implicitly discussed in each text relate to one another?
- Based on your reading of these sources, how would you characterize both the short- and long-term historical significance of the plague's effects?

PRIMARY SOURCE 11.1

Plague in Southwest Asia (1349), Ibn al-Wardi

Al-Wardi wrote two major works, one a natural history of the Islamic world and the other a history, from which this excerpt on the plague's devastation is taken. His is the most thorough extant contemporary Muslim description of the

Black Death. Al-Wardi's discussion is rendered all the more poignant by the fact that he became one of its victims as the plague swept through Aleppo in 1349.

What role does religion and/or God play in al-Wardi's account of the plague? How do the Sunni-Shiite division and other rifts factor into al-Wardi's account?

How does al-Wardi describe the plague's progress across Afro-Eurasia, and what does that description suggest about al-Wardi's understanding of causation?

What are some of the attempted remedies described by al-Wardi, and what do those remedies suggest about the understanding of the plague's causes?

God is my security in every adversity. My sufficiency is in God alone. Is not God sufficient protection for His servant? Oh God, pray for our master, Muḥammad, and give him peace. Save us for his sake from the attacks of the plague and give us shelter.

The plague frightened and killed. It began in the land of darkness. Oh, what a visitor! It has been current for fifteen years. China was not preserved from it nor could the strongest fortress hinder it. The plague afflicted the Indians in India. It weighed upon the Sind. It seized with its hand and ensnared even the lands of the Uzbeks. How many backs did it break in what is Transoxiana! The plague increased and spread further. It attacked the Persians, extended its steps toward the land of Khiṭai, and gnawed away at the Crimea. It pelted Rūm with live coals and led the outrage to Cyprus and the islands. The plague destroyed mankind in Cairo. Its eye was cast upon Egypt, and behold, the people were wide-awake. It stilled all movement in Alexandria. . . .

Then, the plague turned to Upper Egypt. It, also, sent forth its storm to Barqah. The plague attacked Gaza, and it shook Asqalān severely. The plague oppressed Acre. The scourge came to Jerusalem and paid the *zakāt* [with the souls of men]. It overtook those people who fled to the al-'Aqsā Mosque, which stands beside the Dome of the Rock. If the door of mercy had not been opened, the end of the world would have occurred in a moment. It, then, hastened its pace and attacked the entire maritime plain. The plague trapped Sidon and descended unexpectedly upon Beirut, cunningly. Next, it directed the shooting of its arrows to Damascus. There the plague sat like a king on a throne and swayed with power, killing daily one thousand or more and decimating the population. It destroyed mankind with its pustules. May God the Most High spare Damascus to pursue its own path and extinguish the plague's fires so that they do not come close to her fragrant orchards.

Oh God, restore Damascus and protect her from insult.

Its morale has been so lowered that people in the city sell themselves for a grain. . . .

The plague and its poison spread to Sarmīn. It reviled the Sunni and the Shī'ī. It sharpened its spearheads for the Sunni and advanced like an army. The plague was spread in the land of the Shī'ī with a ruinous effect. To Antioch the plague gave its share. Then, it left there quickly with a shyness like a man who has forgotten the memory of his beloved. . . . The plague subjected Dhulūl and went straight through the lowlands and the mountains. It uprooted many people from their homes. Then, the plague sought Aleppo, but it did not succeed. By God's mercy the plague was the lightest oppression. . . . How amazingly does it pursue the people of each house! One of them spits blood, and everyone in the household is certain of death. It brings the entire family to their graves after two or three nights. . . .

Oh God, it is acting by Your command. Lift this from us. It happens where You wish; keep the plague from us. Who will defend us against this horror other than You the Almighty? . . .

Oh, if you could see the nobles of Aleppo studying their inscrutable books of medicine. They multiply its remedies by eating dried and sour foods. The buboes which disturb men's healthy lives are smeared with Armenian clay. Each man treated his humours and made life more comfortable. They perfumed their homes with ambergris and camphor, cyperus and sandal. They wore ruby rings and put onions, vinegar, and sardines together with the daily meal. They ate less broth and fruit but ate the citron and similar things.

If you see many biers and their carriers and hear in every quarter of Aleppo the announcements of death and cries, you run from them and refuse to stay with them. In Aleppo the profits of the undertakers have greatly increased. . . .

We ask God's forgiveness for our souls' bad inclination; the plague is surely part of His punishment. We take refuge from His wrath in His pleasure and from His chastisement in His restoring. . . .

Among the things which exasperated the Muslims and brought suffering is that our enemy, the damned people of Sis, are pleased by our trial. They act as if they are safe from the plague—that there is a treaty so that it will not approach them or that they have triumphed over it. Our Lord does not create us as an enticement for those who disbelieve. . . .

This plague is for the Muslims a martyrdom and a reward, and for the disbelievers a punishment and a rebuke. When the Muslim endures misfortune, then patience is his worship. It has been established by our Prophet, God bless him and give him peace, that the plague-stricken are martyrs. This noble tradition is true and assures martyrdom. And this secret should be pleasing to the true believer. If someone says it causes infection and destruction, say: God creates and recreates.

Source: Michael Dols, "Ibn al-Wardi's Risalah al-Naba an al-Waba, a Translation of a Major Source for the History of the Black Death in the Middle East," in *Near Eastern Numismatics, Iconography, Epigraphy, and History: Studies in Honor of George C. Miles*, edited by Dickran K. Kouymjian (Beirut: American University of Beirut, 1974), pp. 447–54.

PRIMARY SOURCE 11.2

The Florentine Chronicle, Rubric 643 (late fourteenth century), Baldassarre de Buonaiuti

Marchione di Coppo Stefani (the pseudonym for Baldassarre de Buonaiuti) wrote his chronicle in the late fourteenth century after he retired from Florentine business and politics. When Buonaiuti was about twelve years old, in 1348, the Black Death swept through Florence. His later recollection of the plague balances the practical effects of the pestilence, such as inflation, with the pathos of the plague—namely, family members deserting one another and abandoned sick people calling out for help.

- How does Buonaiuti describe the plague and its ferocity? What details does he report to support that description?
- While Buonaiuti may not directly assert an explanation for the causes of the plague, what are some indirect indicators for what those experiencing the plague thought were its causes?
- What were the effects of the plague on family? On religion? On the economy? On the population?

Concerning a Mortality in the City of Florence in Which Many People Died

In the year of the Lord 1348 there was a very great pestilence in the city and district of Florence. It was of such a fury and so tempestuous that in houses in which it took hold previously healthy servants who took care of the ill died of the same illness. Almost none of the ill survived past the fourth day. Neither physicians nor medicines were effective. Whether because these illnesses were previously unknown or because physicians had not previously studied them, there seemed to be no cure. There was such a fear that no one seemed to know what to do. When it took hold in a house it often happened that no one remained who had not died. And it was not just that men and women died, but even sentient animals died. Dogs, cats, chickens, oxen, donkeys, sheep showed the same symptoms and died of the same disease. And almost none, or very few, who showed these symptoms, were cured. The symptoms were the following: a bubo in the groin, where the thigh meets the trunk; or a small swelling under the armpit; sudden fever; spitting blood and saliva (and no one who spit blood survived it). It was such a frightful thing that when it got into a house, as was said, no one remained. Frightened people abandoned the house and fled to another. Those in town fled to villages. Physicians could not be found because they had died like the others. And those who could be found wanted vast sums in hand before they entered the house. And when they did enter, they checked the pulse with face turned away. They inspected the urine from a distance and with something odoriferous under their nose. Child abandoned the father, husband the wife, wife the husband, one brother the other, one sister the other. In all the city there was nothing to do but to carry the dead to a burial. And those who died had neither confessor nor other sacraments. And many died with no one looking after them. And many died of hunger because when someone took to bed sick, another in the house, terrified, said to him: "I'm going for the doctor." Calmly walking out the door, the other left and did not return again. Abandoned by people, without food, but accompanied by fever, they weakened. There were many who pleaded with their relatives not to abandon them when night fell. But [the relatives] said to the sick person, "So that during the night you did not have to awaken those who serve you and who work hard day and night, take some sweetmeats, wine or water. They are here on the bedstead by your head; here are some blankets." And when the sick person had fallen asleep, they left and did not return. . . .

No one, or few, wished to enter a house where anyone was sick, nor did they even want to deal with those healthy people who came out of a sick person's house. And they said to them: "He is stupefied, do not speak to him!" saying further: "He has it because there is a bubo in his house." They call the swelling a bubo. Many died unseen. So they remained in their beds until they stank. And the neighbors, if there were any, having smelled the stench, placed them in a shroud and sent them for burial. . . .

At every church, or at most of them, they dug deep trenches. . . . And those who were responsible for the dead carried them on their backs in the night in which they died and threw them into the ditch, or else they paid a high price to those who would do it for them. The next morning, if there were many [bodies] in the trench, they covered them over with dirt. And then more bodies were put on top of them, with a little more dirt over those; they put layer on layer just like one puts layers of cheese in a lasagna.

The *beccamorti* [literally, vultures] who provided their service, were paid such a high price that many were enriched by it. Many died from [carrying away the dead], some rich, some after earning just a little, but high prices continued. Servants, or those who took care of the ill, charged from one to three florins per day and the cost of things grew. . . .

Some fled to villas, others to villages in order to get a change of air. Where there had been no [pestilence], there they carried it; if it was already there, they caused it to increase. None of the guilds in Florence was working. All the shops were shut, taverns closed; only the apothecaries and the churches remained open. If you went outside, you found almost no one. And many good and rich men were carried from home to church on a pall by four *beccamorti* and one tonsured clerk who carried the cross. Each of them wanted a florin. This mortality enriched apothecaries, doctors, poultry vendors, *beccamorti*, and greengrocers who sold poultices of mallow, nettles, mercury and other herbs necessary to draw off the infirmity. And it was those who made these poultices who made a lot of money. . . .

This pestilence began in March, as was said, and ended in September 1348. And people began to return to look after their houses and possessions. And there were so many houses full of goods without a master that it was stupefying. . . .

Now it was ordered by the bishop and the Lords [of the city government] that they should formally inquire as to how many died in Florence. When it was seen at the beginning of October that no more persons were dying of the pestilence, they found that among males, females, children and adults, 96,000 died between March and October.

Source: Marchione di Coppo Stefani, *Cronaca Fiorentina*, edited by Niccolo Rodolico, vol. 30 of *Rerum Italicarum Scriptores* (Citta di Castello: S. Lapi, 1903–1913). As translated by Duane Osheim.

PRIMARY SOURCE 11.3

Berbers, Arabs, and Plague in the Maghrib, from the *Muqaddimah* (c. 1375), Ibn Khaldûn

Born in Tunis, a North African city on the Mediterranean, Ibn Khaldûn came from a family that had been active in the political development of Spain and the Maghrib (North Africa) in the century before his birth. Ibn Khaldûn followed in his family's tradition of public service. In his forties, however, he stepped back from public life and composed a grand multivolume history, in the introduction to which, the *Muqaddimah*, he outlines a far-reaching analytical philosophy of history. Essential to his analysis is a theory of causation and considerations about the rise and fall of civilizations. (Ibn Khaldûn offers dates according to the Muslim calendar, which marks time beginning with Muhammad's migration from Mecca to Medina in 622 CE. CE equivalents are provided in brackets.)

- What are the causes of population shifts of Berbers and Arabs in the Maghrib, according to Ibn Khaldûn?
- What does Ibn Khaldûn say were the effects of the plague on civilization?
- How does Ibn Khaldûn use earlier writers of history, al-Masûdî and al-Bakrî, to explore the purpose of history? How does the plague fit into Ibn Khaldûn's ideas about history writing?

History refers to events that are peculiar to a particular age or race. Discussion of the general conditions of regions, races, and periods constitutes the historian's foundation. Most of his problems rest upon that foundation, and his historical information derives clarity from it. It forms the topic of special works, such as the *Murúj adh-dhahab* of al-Mas'ūdī. In this work, al-Mas'ūdī commented upon the conditions of nations and regions in the West and in the East during his period (which was) the three hundred and thirties [the nine hundred and forties]. He mentioned their sects and customs. He described the various countries, mountains, oceans, provinces, and dynasties. He distinguished between Arabic and non-Arabic groups. His book, thus, became the basic reference work for historians, their principal source for verifying historical information.

Al-Mas'ūdī was succeeded by al-Bakri who did something similar for routes and provinces, to the exclusion of everything else, because, in his time, not many transformations or great changes had occurred among the nations and races. However, at the present time—that is, at the end of the eighth [fourteenth] century—the situation in the Maghrib, as we can observe, has taken a turn and changed entirely. The Berbers, the original population of the Maghrib, have been replaced by an influx of Arabs, (that began in) the fifth [eleventh] century. The Arabs outnumbered and overpowered the Berbers, stripped them of most of their lands, and (also) obtained a share of those that remained in their possession. This was the situation until, in the middle of the eighth [fourteenth] century, civilization both in the East and the West was visited by a destructive plague which devastated nations and caused populations to vanish. It swallowed up many of the good things of civilization and wiped them out. It overtook the dynasties at the time of their senility, when they had reached the limit of their duration. It lessened their power and curtailed their influence. It weakened their authority. Their situation approached the point of annihilation and dissolution. Civilization decreased with the decrease of mankind. Cities and buildings were laid waste, roads and way signs were obliterated, settlements and mansions became empty, dynasties and tribes grew weak. The entire inhabited world changed. The East, it seems, was similarly visited, though in accordance with and in proportion to (the East's more affluent) civilization. It was as if the voice of existence in the world had called out for oblivion and restriction, and the world had responded to its call. God inherits the earth and whomever is upon it.

When there is a general change of conditions, it is as if the entire creation had changed and the whole world been altered, as if it were a new and repeated creation, a world brought into existence anew. Therefore, there is need at this time that someone should systematically set down the situation of the world among all regions and races, as well as the customs and sectarian beliefs that have changed for their adherents, doing for this age what al-Mas'ūdī did for his. This should be a model for future historians to follow. In this book of mine, I shall discuss as much of that as will be possible for me here in the Maghrib. I shall do so either explicitly or implicitly in connection with the history of the Maghrib, in conformity with my intention to restrict myself in this work to the Maghrib, the circumstances of its races and nations, and its subjects and dynasties, to the exclusion of any other region. (This restriction is necessitated) by my lack of knowledge of conditions in the East and among its nations, and by the fact that secondhand information would not give the essential facts I am after.

Source: Ibn Khaldûn, *The Muqaddimah, an Introduction to History*, vol. 1, translated by Franz Rosenthal (New York: Pantheon Books, 1958), pp. 63–65.

PRIMARY SOURCE 11.4

Plague in Syria and Egypt in 1348–1350 (early fifteenth century), al-Maqrizi

Al-Maqrizi wrote his extensive historical works in the early fifteenth century, while in Cairo. His roots there were deep, but his family also had connections in Damascus, and he lived there for about ten years in his forties. Given that al-Maqrizi was such a prolific historian, it is surprising that much of what is known about him is based on writings about him by his contemporaries and later biographers. Interestingly for our purposes, he was a student of Ibn Khaldûn in Cairo.

- What part of the population seems to have been hardest hit by the plague? Why might the death toll from plague have been higher during Ramadan?
- What was the effect of the plague on religious practices?
- What impact did the plague have on the workforce in terms of wages, available workers, and employment opportunities?

News reached [Cairo from Syria] that the plague in Damascus had been less deadly than in Tripoli, Hama, and Aleppo. From . . . [October 1348] death raged with intensity. 1200 people died daily and, as a result, people stopped requesting permits from the administration to bury the dead and many cadavers were abandoned in gardens and on the roads.

In New and Old Cairo, the plague struck women and children at first, then market people, and the numbers of the dead augmented. . . . The [ravages of the] plague intensified in . . . [November] in [New] Cairo and became extremely grave during *Ramadan* [December], which coincided with the arrival of winter. . . . The plague continued to spread so considerably that it became impossible to count how many died. . . .

In [January 1349], new symptoms developed and people began spitting up blood. One sick person came down with internal fever, followed by an unrestrained need to vomit, then spat blood and died. Those around him in his house fell ill, one after the other and in one or two nights they all perished. Everyone lived with the overwhelming preoccupation that death was near. People prepared themselves for death by distributing alms to the poor, reconciled with one another, and multiplied their acts of devotion.

None had time to consult doctors or drink medicinal syrups or take other medications, so rapidly did they die. By [January 7th,] bodies had piled up in the streets and markets; [town leaders] appointed burial brigades, and some pious people remained permanently at places of prayer in New and Old Cairo to recite funeral orations over the dead. The situation worsened beyond limits, and no solution appeared possible. Almost the entire royal guard disappeared and the barracks in the sultan's citadel contained no more soldiers.

Statistics of the dead from funerals in Cairo during . . . [November and December] attained 900,000. . . . There were 1,400 litters on which they carried the dead and soon even they did not suffice. So they began carrying dead bodies in boxes, on doors taken from stores and on plain boards, on each of which they placed two to three bodies.

People began searching for *Quran* readers for funerals, and many individuals quit their trades to recite prayers at the head of burial procession[s]. A group of people devoted themselves to applying a coat of clay to the inner sides of the graves. Others volunteered to wash corpses, and still others to carry them. Such volunteers received substantial wages. For example, a *Quran* reader earned 10 *dirhams*: the moment he finished with one funeral, he ran off to another. A body carrier demanded six *dirhams* in advance, and still it was hard to find any. A grave digger wanted 50 *dirhams* per grave. But most of them died before they had a chance to spend their earnings.

Family celebrations and marriages no longer took place. . . . No one had held any festivities during the entire duration of the epidemic, and no voice was heard singing. In an attempt to revive these activities, the *wazir* [prime minister] reduced by a third the taxes paid by the woman responsible for collecting dues on singers. The call to prayer was suspended at many locations, and even at the most important ones, there remained only a single *muezzin* [caller to prayer].

The drum batteries before most of the officers' quarters no longer functioned, and the entourage of a commander [who controlled a thousand men] was reduced now from about fifteen to three soldiers.

Most of the mosques and *zawiyas* [*Sufi* lodges] were closed. It was also a known fact that during this epidemic no infant survived more than one or two days after his birth, and his mother usually quickly followed him to the grave.

At [the end of February], all of Upper Egypt was afflicted with the plague. . . . According to information that arrived . . . from . . . other regions, lions, wolves, rabbits, camels, wild asses and boars, and other savage beasts, dropped dead, and were found with scabs on their bodies.

The same thing happened throughout Egypt. When harvest time arrived, many farmers had already perished [and no field hands remained to gather crops]. Soldiers and their young slaves or pages headed for the fields. They tried to recruit workers by promising them half of the proceeds, but they could not find anyone to help them gather the harvest. They threshed the grain with their horses [hoofs], and winnowed the grain themselves, but, unable to carry all the grain back, they had to abandon much of it.

Most craft workshops closed, since artisans devoted themselves to disposing of the dead, while others, not less numerous, auctioned off property and textiles [which the dead left behind]. Even though the prices of fabric and other such commodities sold for a fifth of their original value . . . they remained unsold. . . . Religious texts sold by their weight, and at very low prices.

Workers disappeared. You could not find either water carriers, or launderers or servants. The monthly salary of a horse groom rose from 30 to 80 *dirhams*. . . . This epidemic, they say, continued in several countries for 15 years.

Source: al-Maqrizi, *The Guide to the Knowledge of Dynasties and Kings*, excerpted in *The Middle East and Islamic World Reader*, edited by Marvin Gettleman and Stuart Schaar (New York: Grove Press, 2012), pp. 52–53.

Interpreting Visual Evidence

Marking Boundaries, Inspiring Loyalty

The fourteenth century witnessed the emergence of dynastic states across Eurasia that endured for centuries. The size of these new states and the ethnic and religious diversity of their populations posed formidable challenges to those in power. Rulers had to distinguish those who belonged to the community—and owed taxes or military service—from those who did not. They used a careful mixture of privilege and punishment to create a sense of unity among their subjects while at the same time justifying their own right to rule and reinforcing traditional social hierarchies. The three images featured here show different ways rulers approached this problem.

The first painting, from around 1500, is by the Spanish artist Pedro Berruguete. It portrays a scene from two centuries earlier in which Spanish authorities burned people at the stake for their alleged heretical beliefs. Notice in the

Spanish painting by Berruguete.

The *devshirme* system.

foreground members of the Dominican Order, who were instrumental in the administration of the Inquisition, and soldiers loyal to the crown. The second image, a miniature painting from 1558, depicts the *devshirme* system in the Ottoman Empire. Authorities took non-Muslim children from their families in Europe as a human tribute in place of cash taxes, which poor regions could not pay. The children would then be converted to Islam, educated in Ottoman ways, and prepared for service in the sultan's civil and military bureaucracy. The final image, a painting on silk by Ch'iu Ying, represents a group of Confucian scholars waiting for the results of their civil service examination. Candidates spent three days and two nights taking examinations as they sought to enter the Ming bureaucracy.

Chinese painting by Ch'iu Ying.

QUESTIONS FOR ANALYSIS

1. Assess the combinations of privilege and punishment conveyed by these images. What kinds of assistance or special privileges did leaders grant, to whom did they offer this assistance, and what kinds of punishments did they impose?
2. Consider the original context for these images. Who might have created these images, for whom were they created, and who might have seen them?
3. Interpret the role religion plays in these images. How does each artist present the relationship between religion and social order?
4. Comparing the three paintings, how did Berruguete's painting reframe the relationship between royal authorities and traditional elites?

Before You Read This Chapter

GLOBAL STORYLINES

The Age of Global Exploration and Colonization

- Ottoman expansion and Portuguese overseas ventures begin a complex process that changes the way peoples around the world interact with one another.
- Major world empires become oceanic, overseas empires rather than continental empires.
- Despite the long-term significance of European activity in the Americas, the rest of the world is barely aware of the Americas and what was happening to the Indigenous peoples there or the expansion of long-distance trade.
- Within Europe, dynastic states focus on their own internal rivalries. Religious revolts, especially the Protestant Reformation, intensify those rivalries.
- Asian empires thrive in the sixteenth century, thanks to commercial expansion and political consolidation.

CHAPTER OUTLINE

12

Contact, Commerce, and Colonization

1450–1600

FOCUS QUESTIONS

- What were the broad patterns in world trade after 1450? How were the major features of world trade in Asia, the Americas, Africa, and Europe alike and different?
- What factors enabled Europeans to increase their trade relationships with Asian empires in the fifteenth and sixteenth centuries? How significant was each factor?
- In what ways did European colonization of the Americas affect African and Indigenous peoples? How did those groups respond?
- How similar and different were the practices and the impact of European explorers in Asia and the Americas?
- Within the Afro-Eurasian polities, what types of social and political relationships developed during this period? What were the sources of conflict?

At the time of Christopher Columbus's birth in 1451, the great world power on the rise was neither Spain nor Portugal. It was the Ottoman Empire: the fifteenth and sixteenth centuries brought frenzied territorial expansion in the Mediterranean as well as the Indian Ocean. The Ottomans sought to fulfill what they considered to be Islam's primary mission: to bring the world under Allah's dominion. Sultans Bayezid II (r. 1481–1512), Selim I (r. 1512–1520), and Suleiman the Magnificent (r. 1520–1566) continued the conquests of Mehmed the Conqueror and led the thrust into Arab lands and the Indian Ocean even while pressing ahead in Europe. Selim I proclaimed that "he was the ruler of the east and the west."

Expansion meant exploration; exploration required mobilizing knowledge and technologies. The sultans drew on the talents of two high officials, Ibrahim Pasha, grand vizier and briefly governor of Egypt, and Piri Reis, an Ottoman admiral and arguably the age's most accomplished cartographer. Piri Reis's research into the Indian Ocean, an area previously unknown to the Ottomans, was vital to the Ottoman entry into this region. Not only did he produce a map of the world, but in 1526 he presented to Sultan Suleiman a masterpiece of world geography known as *The Book of the Sea*. It drew upon Arab and European sources, as well as Indian maps obtained from Portuguese expeditions, to create a portrait of the world for its aspiring rulers. Piri Reis pored over Columbus's maps and included a chart outlining Ferdinand Magellan's circumnavigation of the globe, completed in 1522, and information on the travels of Vasco da Gama. On top of their worldly knowledge, the Ottomans were on track to become a world power; their armada dwarfed that of all others at the time. It consisted of seventy-four ships, including twenty-seven large and small galleys and munitions ships, mounted with cannons. The fleet transported 20,000 men, including 6,500 janissaries.

As the Ottomans pivoted from overland to overseas expansion, they fundamentally tilted the global balance of power. By turning their attention to conquest of the Red Sea, the Arabian Peninsula, and North Africa, and sending their flotillas across the Mediterranean and into the Indian Ocean, they asserted control over trade routes. Although commerce had been disrupted by the Mongols and the Black Death, it was bouncing back. Indeed, it was the splendor of economic recovery that induced the Ottomans to expand and seek supremacy. By doing so, the sultans forced others who wanted access to South and East Asian luxuries to seek alternative sea passages. One of these was a small European state known as Portugal. Forced to probe routes around the coast of Africa, the Portuguese entered the Indian Ocean essentially as well-armed pirates. At first, they gave the Ottomans no cause for alarm. The Europeans were, however, a menace to wealthy ports and local kingdoms up and down the rims of Africa and South Asia, which they sometimes plundered, grabbing what they could. Besides, the Ottomans had bigger fish to fry—their eyes were trained on conquering the Balkans and driving into the heart of Europe; they could afford to let the pesky Portuguese behave like petty bandits.

Vasco da Gama's rounding of the Cape of Good Hope in 1498, however, marked a turning point in world history. His entrance into the Indian Ocean and the subsequent Portuguese attempt to establish domination over the region's strategically located port cities gave Europeans their first toeholds in Asia. When the Portuguese pulled off a surprising naval victory against an Ottoman attempt to seize the South Asian Portuguese-controlled port city of Diu in 1538, the Ottomans withdrew, leaving it to the Portuguese—and later the Spanish, Dutch, English, and French—to exploit. No one could have predicted, in 1538, that European toeholds in a few South Asian trading cities were particularly significant—compared with the Ottomans' relentless annexations of large territories, spread into central Europe, and power in the Mediterranean. The Indian Ocean seemed far off.

Even more world changing was how Ottoman expansion compelled Europeans westward, to stumble onto continents unknown to Afro-Eurasia. Seeking to circumvent Ottoman power in the eastern Mediterranean, a Genoese ship captain named Christopher Columbus opened up a "New World." For the first time since the Ice Age, peoples again moved from Afro-Eurasian landmasses to the Americas. So did animals, plants, commercial products, and—most momentously—deadly germs. Two different **biomes** (distinct biological systems, including humans, that have formed in response to shared physical conditions) converged.

Who would have imagined poor, fractured, and feuding Europeans shaking things up? The mighty Ottomans or Chinese might have been the ones to stumble on the Americas. But they had bigger challenges in their own territorial and prosperous empires. The Europeans became empire builders of a different kind, creating overseas commercial empires and, in the process, developing structures that disrupted the cultures and economies of millions. Along the way, they transformed their own cultures and societies.

The encounter of the New and Old Worlds was as if two separate worlds unknown to each other merged into one. It took some time for the full effects on both sides to sink in. Despite the significance of Europeans' activity in the Americas, most Africans and Asians, and even most peoples indigenous to the Americas, remained, for decades or even centuries, barely aware of the importance of Columbus's discovery. As this chapter demonstrates, Asian empires in Ottoman-controlled lands and in India and China continued to flourish after recovering from the Black Death, and the Ottomans continued to focus on their own conquests. Nor did most Europeans pay much immediate attention to events in the Americas; they were grappling with a religious revolt—the Protestant Reformation—and invasions in their own backyards. But this was an age of imperial conquests, whether Ottoman or European, that reshaped all worlds. With time, the effects unleashed productive forces and volatile new cultural syntheses.

The Old Expansionism and the New

Ottoman expansion overland continued as European expansion overseas began. To a large extent, it was Ottoman spread that pushed Europeans to probe west. Increasing Ottoman control in the eastern Mediterranean motivated Portuguese and Spanish explorers to turn toward the Atlantic in hopes of reaching the rich trading posts of China and the Indian Ocean by another route. Ottoman domination of Afro-Eurasian trade routes, which recovered in the wake of the Black Death, buoyed the Islamic empire's expansion and the sultanate's

The Cantino Planisphere. Creating and controlling information from different parts of the world was a source of political power. It was also a recipe for espionage between rival powers. This map conveyed valuable information about early Portuguese explorations and trade routes. It was stolen from an unknown Portuguese cartographer by Alberto Cantino, servant of the duke of Ferrara. The wily Cantino smuggled it back to Italy. It is greatly detailed, and yet is missing entire chunks of the world. Only fragments of the New World appear, like the outsized Caribbean islands and a sliver of Florida. The vast interior of Brazil is vacant.

co-optation of local elites. Imperial growth required a relatively tolerant attitude toward subject peoples and religions. It was so successful that by 1529 the Ottomans had conquered Egypt and were knocking on the doors of Vienna. But expansionism was not endless. Powerful resistance of the Shiite Safavid regime in Persia halted the spread east. And although the Ottomans were now unquestionably *the* great power in Mediterranean shipping and the Afro-Eurasian caravan trades, their trading methods and goods did not change all that much. Older forms of imperial expansion and long-distance trade worked well for them, and they stuck to them.

For the Europeans, in contrast, expansion overseas was quite new and experimental. Born from a position of weakness, Portuguese and Spanish exploration and expansion benefited greatly from unexpected accidents: first, that Columbus found a "New World" rather than the "Old World" he hoped to reach, and second, tragically, that European pathogens killed or greatly weakened Indigenous populations, making conquest and settlement possible. Expansion across the Atlantic entailed, first, the military conquest of the rich empires of the Aztecs and the Incas and the scramble to locate and exploit gold and silver deposits. But the Europeans stayed, co-opting some local elites but also inventing new forms of landholding and resource extraction. The importation of thousands, and then millions, of enslaved Africans to form a new, fully subservient labor force was also a tragic and inhumane innovation that transformed both global commerce and the Atlantic ecosystem.

The creation of loosely connected worlds laid the foundations for a new chapter in world history. It set the stage for making an integrated and increasingly interdependent globe. But we must not forget that even in the midst of this global transformation, the peoples of each continent continued to focus on local, and often religious, struggles closer to their everyday lives.

Ottoman Expansion

Having built the period's most powerful military forces and equipped themselves with the latest maps and scientific instruments, the Ottomans began the sixteenth century in possession of Constantinople and great swaths of southeastern Europe and Anatolia. During the sultanate of Suleiman the Magnificent (r. 1520–1566), Ottoman forces carried the empire southward into Egypt, eastward to the Iranian borderlands, and westward into Europe. By 1550, the Ottoman Empire stretched from Hungary and the Crimea in the north to the Arabian Peninsula in the south, from Morocco in the west to the contested border with Safavid Iran in the east.

The Multiethnic Ottoman Elite

The early sultans' institutions from the fifteenth century—the *devshirme* system involving the seizing of young recruits for service in the Ottoman military and civil bureaucracies, the rise of the janissaries in the military's front ranks, and the replacement of powerful landholding families in Anatolia with individuals of proven loyalty to the state—laid durable foundations for later centuries. They proved effective at accommodating new peoples and territories. As it spread, the Ottoman Empire encountered more and more ethnic and religious groups, incorporating them into the Ottoman hierarchy. Those who were willing to serve could rise high. Of the fifteen grand viziers who held that position between 1453 and 1515, eight were drawn from Byzantine and Balkan nobility, four were from the *devshirme* system, and only three were of Muslim Turkish descent. Other subject peoples were not forced to convert but left largely to govern their own communities, as well as pay hefty taxes to their Turkish overlords.

Ottoman Conquests in Egypt

The conquest of Syria and Egypt in 1516–1517 enabled Ottoman leaders to treat their Sunni state as the preeminent Muslim empire from that moment forward; some sultans called themselves caliphs. Egypt became the Ottomans' most lucrative and important acquisition, the breadbasket of the empire and the province that provided Istanbul with the largest revenue stream. But the conquest was no easy matter. The Mamluk rulers resisted mightily, losing a bloody battle in 1516 at Marj Dabiq, north of Aleppo, after which, according to Ibn Iyas, the Arab chronicler of the age, "the battlefield was strewn with corpses and headless bodies and faces covered with dust and grown hideous." Nor did the conquest of Egypt prove any easier, for the Mamluks were determined to hold on to their most precious possession. Emotions ran high, for both sides prided themselves on being warrior states. Decapitation of enemies was common practice. In revenge for the Mamluk beheading of their fallen soldiers, the Ottoman troops plundered, raped, and killed an estimated 10,000 residents of Cairo. The destruction, wrote Ibn Iyas, was such as "to strike terror into the hearts of man and its horrors to unhinge their reason."

Ottoman Expansionism Stalls in Iran

The conquest of Constantinople and the Arab lands transformed the Ottoman Empire, creating a Muslim majority in an empire once mainly populated by conquered Christians and enabling Ottoman sultans to see themselves as heirs of a long line of empires that had ruled over these regions.

Yet on the eastern front, in conflicts with the Safavid Empire, the Ottomans faced their military match, an enemy state that plagued the Ottoman Empire until its collapse early in the eighteenth century (see Chapter 13). The Safavid state had arisen when Turkic tribesmen migrated from eastern Anatolia and Azerbaijan to the Iranian plateau, where they established a zealous Shiite state (see Chapter 11). Their leaders continued to seek support and to spread their faith among the dispossessed in Ottoman-ruled Syria and Anatolia, stirring discontent against the Ottomans. To defeat the Safavids, Selim II mustered an overwhelming force of up to 200,000 armed with muskets and heavy artillery. They squared off against 80,000 Shiite fighters under the command of a messianic shah called Ismail and thoroughly trounced

The Catalan Atlas. This 1375 map shows the world as it was then known. Not only does it depict the location of continents and islands, but it also includes information on ancient and medieval tales, regional politics, astronomy, and astrology.

him at the Battle of Chaldiran in 1514. Selim's forces sacked the Safavid capital at Tabriz. But triumph was short-lived. After Selim's troops withdrew, the Safavid rulers returned and doubled down in turning the entire Iranian population to Shiism. The Ottomans, even with superior weapons and more troops, could not unseat a politically and religiously antagonistic state with deeper devotional roots.

The result hardened the line between rival Islamic states, Sunni and Shiite. The bitter rivalry between Safavids and Ottomans intensified the religious commitments of both sides. The Ottomans, who relied upon a mixed ethnic and flexible religious state governing relatively autonomous Christian and Jewish communities and heterodox Muslims, became champions of Sunni Islam. By contrast, the Safavids, who had been Sufis and had migrated from eastern Anatolia, doubled down on their Shiite commitments even more firmly, embraced an elaborate hierarchy of clerics, and insisted on doctrinal conformity within their borders.

The Ottomans in Europe

Blocked from further eastward expansion by the Safavids, the Ottomans marched westward, into Europe. Having taken Constantinople in 1453, Sultan Mehmed II took Athens in 1458 and set in motion plans to conquer Italy, though that project lapsed after his death. The Ottomans also added large swaths of Balkan territory, cutting into the Venetians' empire, and coveted commercial and naval regions in the Black Sea. The Turks then turned to North Africa and Egypt, succeeding in bringing coastal areas as well as Egypt under their dominion by 1550. This allowed them to exert more control than ever over commerce in the Mediterranean and to capture many European ships, often enslaving their crews or holding them hostage for ransom, and spreading fear of "the Turk" across Christendom.

The Ottomans' encroachment into central Europe terrified Europeans. Just at the time Martin Luther's reformers were stirring up trouble inside the Holy Roman Empire, the Turks were slicing off large sections of its easternmost territories. In the 1520s, the Ottomans seized chunks of the Balkans. By 1529, they stood at the gates of the Habsburg capital, Vienna, and came close to repeating the victory at Constantinople (1453) in the heart of Europe. Although winter weather forced Suleiman to retreat, he ultimately took Budapest in 1541, and Turkish armies marched on into Transylvania. A series of popes launched futile efforts to unite a Christendom splintered by the Reformation. In 1571, in a moment of rare unity, a coalition of European princes did destroy much of the Ottoman navy in the Battle of Lepanto, near the western coast of Greece. This crippled the Turkish striking force in the Mediterranean, but the Ottomans continued to exert control over most of southeastern Europe. Ottoman control, which lasted for centuries in places like Bosnia, left a multiethnic legacy, including large populations of Muslims in areas reconquered by the Habsburg Empire. Thus, the Ottomans, too, from the eastern end of the Mediterranean, became key players in the transformation of Europe's religious as well as economic and political history in the age of da Gama and Columbus.

Ottoman Attack. In 1480, at the height of the Ottomans' naval strength, a huge Ottoman army besieged the island of Rhodes, one of the most prized territories held by the Venetian Republic. After a brutal battle, the Christian Hospitaller Knights, whose ships are pictured in the foreground, narrowly managed to defeat the Turkish invaders (whose tent camp is pictured here, outside the walls of the port city of Otranto). But the Ottomans would return in 1521–1522, and this time they would conquer the island.

European Exploration and Expansion

The Muslim conquest of Constantinople and the Ottoman expansion into the Mediterranean sent shock waves through Christendom and prompted Europeans to look south and west—and venture across the seas. (See Map 12.1.) Taking

The Global View

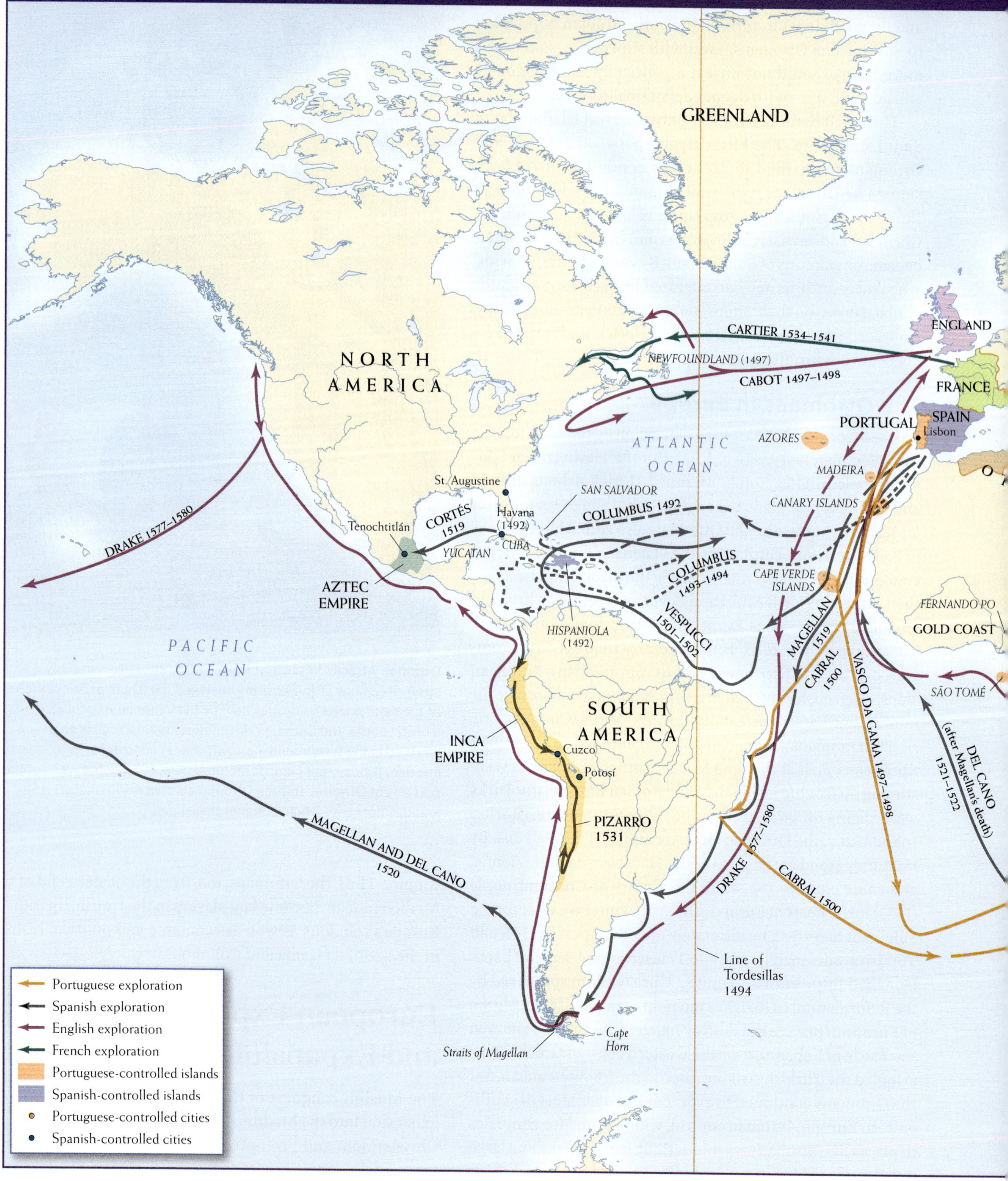

MAP 12.1 | European Exploration of the World, 1420–1580

In the fifteenth and sixteenth centuries, sailors from Portugal, Spain, England, and France explored and mapped the coastline of most of the world's continents. Their activities took place in the shadow of the leading land-based empires of the day, with the Ottomans, Safavids, Mughals, and Ming largely unconcerned by their activity. As a result, European states established contacts and made connections that, over time, became increasingly important.

- Explain why Europeans would have chosen sea routes to reach Asia rather than land routes.
- Examine the voyages that began in Portugal, and then those that originated in Spain. Explain why Portuguese explorers concentrated on traveling to Africa and the Indian Ocean, while their Spanish counterparts focused on voyages to the Americas.
- Compare the different patterns of exploration in the Americas with those in the Indian Ocean and the South China Sea. How might you explain the differences?

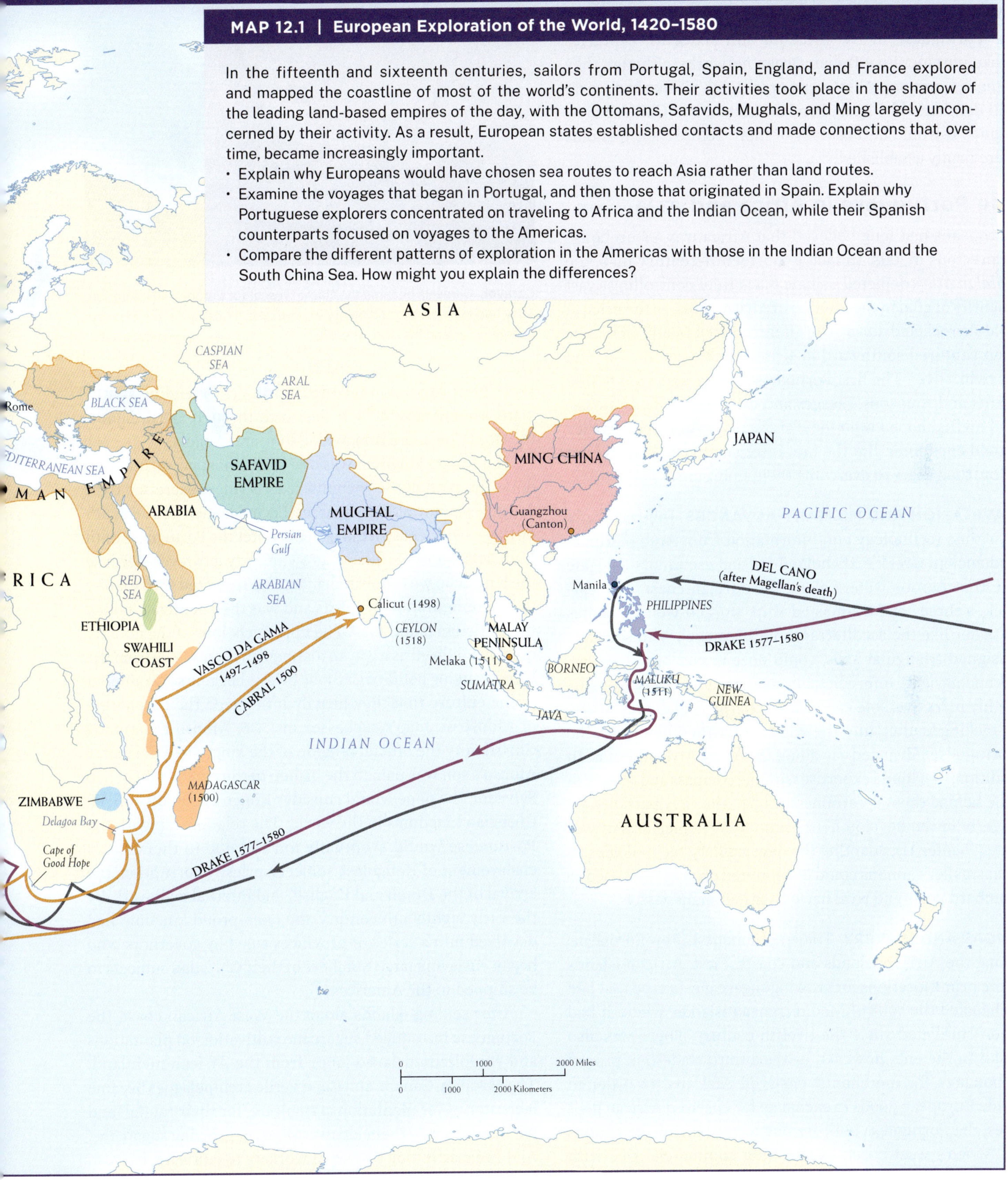

the lead were the Portuguese, whose search for new routes to Asia led them first to Africa, then the Canary Islands, and then into the Indian Ocean. Using New World silver and new military and maritime technology as their tickets to entry, the Portuguese in the fifteenth and sixteenth centuries broke into lucrative Indian Ocean networks, although they remained minor go-betweens or irksome pirates in a world still dominated by Arab, Persian, Indian, and Chinese merchants. It would be a century or more before their toeholds were firmly established.

The Portuguese in Africa and Asia

Europeans had long believed that Africa was a storehouse of precious metals. In fact, a fourteenth-century map, the *Catalan Atlas*, depicted a single Black ruler controlling a vast quantity of gold in the interior of Africa. Thus, as the price of gold skyrocketed during and after the Black Death, ambitious men ventured southward in search of this commodity and its twin, silver. The first Portuguese sailors expected to find giants and Amazons, savages and cannibals. Sailors' stories and myths shaped their view of the places and peoples they would encounter. But the first intrepid adventurers did not allow their fears to overcome their ambitions.

NAVIGATION AND MILITARY ADVANCES Innovations in maritime technology and information from Arab mariners and ancient Greek texts helped Portuguese sailors navigate the treacherous waters along the African coast. The carrack, a three- or four-masted ship, worked well on bodies of water like the Mediterranean; the caravel, with specially designed triangular sails, could nose in and out of estuaries and navigate unpredictable currents and winds. By using highly maneuverable caravels and perfecting the technique of tacking (sailing into the wind rather than before it), the Portuguese advanced far along the West African coast. In addition, newfound expertise with the compass and the astrolabe helped them determine latitude. And they participated eagerly in the development of the Renaissance arts of war (see Chapter 11), adapting the new artillery technologies so that smaller cannons could be mounted on ships and used to bombard ports and rival navies—or merchant vessels.

SUGAR AND SLAVERY Trade, not conquest, drew Europeans along the African islands and coasts. First, African islands were prime locations for growing sugarcane—a crop that had exhausted the soils of Mediterranean islands, where it had been cultivated since the twelfth century. There was also gold. In the end, however, it was a third trade that proved a bonanza for merchants: enslaved Africans. In order to trade European goods in exchange for enslaved African peoples, the Portuguese built trading forts along major regions of Africa's west coast, establishing commercial ties with prominent African kingdoms and rulers extending southward from Senegambia in the north through Sierra Leone, the Gold Coast, the Kongo kingdom, and Angola.

Caravel. Caravels became the classic vessel for European exploration. They had many decks and plenty of portholes for cannons, could house a large crew, and had lots of storage for provisions, cargo, and booty.

The Kongo kingdom was one of the most powerful kingdoms the Portuguese encountered. Its rulers exercised tight control over its trading resources. Located much farther south on the Atlantic coast, it did not encounter the Portuguese until 1482. Portuguese influence grew quickly, however, because the king, who was a spiritual man, eagerly added Christianity to his configuration of spirits and was then baptized, taking the Christian name João. The upper echelons of the nobility quickly followed as a way to distinguish themselves from the lower-ranking nobility. Catholic priests became so prominent in the culture that they heavily influenced the coronation of Afonso as João's successor in 1506; Afonso then made Christianity the official religion of the kingdom. Later, after Afonso's son was named the bishop of the capital city of São Salvador, the pope would consider Kongo one of the official Christian kingdoms in the world. The relationship with the Portuguese would eventually unravel due to their illegal enslavement of Kongolese subjects, priestly corruption, the arrival of the Dutch and English, and internal civil wars. By the early eighteenth century, the once-proud kingdom had devolved into a series of provinces ruled by governors who began enslaving large numbers of their Christian subjects to be shipped to the Americas.

After seizing islands along the West African coast, the Portuguese introduced sugarcane cultivation on plantations and exploited enslaved labor from the African mainland. The Madeira, Canary, and Cape Verde archipelagoes became laboratories for plantation agriculture, for their rainfall and fertile soils made them ideally suited for growing sugarcane. And because it took droves of workers to cultivate, harvest, and process sugarcane, a ready supply of enslaved labor enabled Portugal and Spain to build sizable plantations in their first formal colonies (regions under the political control of another country). In the fifteenth century, these islands saw the beginnings of a system of plantation agriculture built on slavery, a model that would travel across the Atlantic in the following century.

COMMERCE AND CONQUEST IN THE INDIAN OCEAN

Having established plantation colonies on West Africa's outlying islands, Portuguese seafarers ventured into the Indian Ocean and inserted themselves into its thriving commerce. In Asia, Portugal never wanted to rule directly or to establish colonies. Rather, its seaborne empire adapted to local circumstances in order to exploit Asian commercial networks and trading systems.

The first Portuguese mariner to reach the Indian Ocean was Vasco da Gama (1469–1524). Like Columbus, da Gama was relatively unknown before his extraordinary voyage with four ships rounded the Cape of Good Hope at the southern tip of Africa. He explored Africa's eastern coast. Instead of the savages or impoverished lands that he expected to find, the mariner stumbled into a network of commercial ties spanning the Indian Ocean, as well as pools of skilled Muslim mariners who knew the currents, winds, and ports of call. Da Gama took on board a Muslim pilot at Malindi for instruction in navigating the Indian Ocean's winds and currents. He then sailed for the Malabar coast in southern India, one of the region's most important trading areas, arriving in 1498. Da Gama was briefly taken hostage near Calicut but was eventually allowed to leave India with a valuable cargo of spices and silks.

To the Portuguese, who traded in the name of their crown, commercial access was worth fighting for. Although da Gama lost more than half his crew on the difficult voyage back to Lisbon, he had proved the feasibility—and profitability—of trade with the Indian Ocean. When he returned to Calicut in 1502 with a larger crew, he bullied his way into the port, boarding all twenty ships in the harbor and cutting off the noses, ears, and hands of their sailors. Then he burned the ships with the mutilated sailors on board. The Portuguese repeated their predatory ways, especially at the three naval choke points: Aden, at the base of the Red Sea; Hormuz, in the Persian Gulf; and Melaka, at the tip of the Malay Peninsula. These were not just strategic ports—they were also commercial hubs. Although the Portuguese did not hold Aden for long, they seized Sofala, Kilwa, and other important ports on the East African coast, in Goa and Calicut, in India, and in Macau in southern China. This gave them an archipelago of strongholds from which to assert command over the active sea-lanes of the Indian Ocean. (See again Map 12.1.)

It is important to note that the Portuguese did not want to change the system of trade, just to skim profits for themselves. They let the luxuries flow among Asian and African elites in the Indian Ocean while their naval captains gouged a share for themselves. The Portuguese introduced a pass system that required ships to pay for *cartazes*—documents identifying the ship's captain, the size of the ship and crew, and its cargo. The Portuguese were unable to impose this system on major rulers and powerful merchants, however. So the Portuguese focused on minor players and outsiders who calculated that they would rather pay off intruders than risk being plundered by Portuguese gunships. The Portuguese were also active in the spice trade, and Lisbon gradually eclipsed Italian ports, such as Venice, that had previously been prime entrepôts (commercial hubs for long-distance trade) for Asian goods. But they found it even more lucrative to enter the spice trade *within* the Indian Ocean world, where there were wealthier customers to serve. Only with the discovery of the Americas and the conquest of Brazil did Portugal become an empire with large overseas colonies. For this to transpire, mariners would have to traverse the Atlantic Ocean itself.

The Atlantic World

Crossing the Atlantic changed the course of world history. But changing the world was not the original intention. Columbus wanted to voyage into the "Ocean Sea" to open a more direct—and more lucrative—route to Japan and China. For their part, the Spanish monarchs financed his trip hoping for riches to bankroll a triumphal crusade to liberate Jerusalem from Muslim hands. Europeans did not want to create a new world; they wanted to rebalance the old one. Few dreamed of conquest and profiteering in what had been, just a few years before, a blank space on their maps. (Thus, the term *New World*, as applied to the Americas, reflects the Europeans' view that anything previously unknown to them was "new," even if it had supported societies long before European explorers arrived on its shores.)

Columbus's voyages, in opening new sea-lanes in the Atlantic, set the stage for an epochal transformation. As news of his voyages spread through Europe and Asia, ambitious mariners prepared to sail west. Eurasian rivalries, for trade and prestige, sharpened. By 1550, many empires were scrambling, not just for a share of Indian Ocean action but also for spoils from the Atlantic.

But the opening of new trade routes for Europeans was less important for world history than the biological consequences of the first contacts between Europeans and Indigenous people. In Africa and Asia, long-standing patterns of trade had yielded the development of shared immunities. But Indigenous populations, in their world apart, had no immunity for Eurasian diseases such as smallpox, typhus, and cholera; a few decades after their first contact with Europeans, these groups suffered a catastrophic decline. More than any other factor, the spread of "Old World" diseases allowed Europeans to conquer and colonize vast swaths of the Americas. The devastation of the Indigenous population resulted in severe labor shortages, which in turn led to the large-scale introduction of enslaved laborers imported from Africa. After 1500, in fact, most of the people who made the Atlantic voyage were not Europeans but Africans. The global reordering of populations and the exchange of crops, cultures, and microbes that followed from these developments changed world history much more than did any European explorer.

First Encounters

In early 1492, three modest ships set sail from Spain. They stopped in the Canary Islands for supplies and repairs and cast off into the unknown. When the expedition leader stepped onto the beach of San Salvador (in the Bahamas) on October 12, 1492, he must have been disappointed: Where were the rich Asian entrepôts he had sought? This leader, an ambitious but little-known Genoese ship captain in the pay of the Spanish monarchs, would attempt three subsequent voyages in hopes of gaining access to the bonanza of the South China Sea and the Indian Ocean.

It is important to see Christopher Columbus as a man of his time. Skilled in dead reckoning, the ability to navigate without celestial bearings by calculating positions using estimates of speed, elapsed time, and direction, he aimed not to find a "New World" but to break into much older trade routes. He meant not to lay the foundation for the Atlantic system that would so enrich Europeans, but to generate revenues to cover the reconquest of Muslim-ruled Granada and a redemptive crusade to "free" the Holy Land. He was fixated on the Old World. Yet his accidental discoveries did usher in a new era in world history.

When Columbus made landfall in the Caribbean Sea, he unfurled the royal standard of Ferdinand and Isabella and claimed the "many islands filled with people innumerable" for Spain. It is fitting that the first encounter with Caribbean inhabitants, in this case the Tainos, drew blood. Columbus noted, "I showed them swords and they took them by the edge and through ignorance cut themselves." The Tainos had their own weapons but did not forge steel and thus had no knowledge of such sharp edges. What they thought of this encounter is difficult for us to understand, as the Tainos left no written record and we rely on Spanish observers. Moments like this one, so momentous in world history, also reveal the limits of historians' craft.

Columbus. As Columbus made landfall and encountered Indigenous peoples, he planted a cross to indicate the spiritual purpose of the voyage and read aloud a document proclaiming the sovereign authority of the king and queen of Spain. Quickly, he learned that the Spanish could barter for precious stones and metals.

For Columbus, the Tainos' naïveté in grabbing his sword symbolized the childlike primitivism of these people, whom he would mislabel "Indians" because he thought he had arrived off the coast of Asia. In Columbus's view, the Tainos had no religion, but they did have at least some gold (found initially hanging as pendants from their noses). Likewise, Pedro Álvares Cabral, a Portuguese mariner whose trip down the coast of Africa in 1500 was blown off course across the Atlantic, wrote that the people of Brazil had all "the innocence of Adam." He also noted that they were ripe for conversion and that the soils "if rightly cultivated would yield everything." But, as with Africans and Asians, Europeans also developed a contradictory view of the peoples of the Americas. From the Tainos, Columbus learned of another people, the Caribs, who (according to his informants) were savage, warlike cannibals. For centuries, these contrasting images—innocents and savages—shaped European (mis)understandings of the Indigenous Peoples of the Americas.

We know less about what the Indigenous peoples thought of Columbus or other Europeans on their first encounters. Certainly, the Europeans' appearance and technologies inspired awe. The Tainos fled into the forest at the approach of European ships, which they thought were giant monsters; others thought they were floating islands. European metal goods, especially weaponry, struck them as otherworldly. The strangely dressed White men seemed godlike to some; many Indigenous Peoples soon revised this view. They found the newcomers different not for their skin color (only Europeans drew the distinction based on skin pigmentation) but for their hairiness. Indeed, the Europeans' long beards, bad breath, and bad manners repulsed their Indigenous hosts. The newcomers' inability to live off the land also stood out.

In due course, Indigenous people realized that the strange, hairy people bearing metal weapons meant to stay and force the Indigenous population to labor for them. By then it was too late: the explorers had become **conquistadors** (conquerors).

First Conquests

First contacts between peoples gave way to dramatic conquests in the Americas. After his first voyage, Columbus claimed that on Hispaniola (present-day Haiti and the Dominican Republic) "he had found what he was looking for"—gold. That was sufficient to persuade the Spanish crown to invest in larger expeditions and to seek to conquer this promising new territory. Whereas Columbus first sailed with three small ships and 87 men, ten years later the Spanish outfitted an expedition with 2,500 men. Exploration now yielded to warfare and exploitation.

Between 1492 and 1519, the Spanish conquerors of Hispaniola experimented with institutions of colonial rule over local populations. Ultimately, they created a model that the rest of the New World colonies would adopt. But the Spaniards faced Indigenous resistance. As early as 1494, starving Spaniards raided and pillaged Indigenous villages. When Indigenous people revolted, Spanish soldiers replied with punitive expeditions and began enslaving them to work in mines extracting gold. This practice became institutionalized as grants (*encomiendas*) to the conquistadors for control over Indigenous labor. A rich class of ***encomenderos*** arose. Although the placer gold mines in river beds soon ran dry, the model of granting favored settlers the right to coerce Indigenous labor endured. In return, those who received the labor rights paid special taxes on the precious metals that were extracted. Thus, both the crown and the *encomenderos* benefited from the extractive economy. The same cannot be said of the Indigenous laborers, who perished in great numbers from disease, dislocation, malnutrition, and overwork.

Not all Europeans celebrated the pillaging. Dominican friars protested the abuse of the Indigenous, seeing them as potential converts who were equal to the Spaniards in the eyes of God. In 1511, Father Antonio Montesinos accused the settlers of barbarity: "By what right and with what justice do you keep these poor Indians in such cruel and horrible servitude?" Dissent and debate would be a permanent feature of Spanish colonialism in the New World.

The Aztec Empire and the Spanish Conquest

As Spanish colonists saw the bounty of Hispaniola dry up, they set out to discover and conquer new territories. Finding their way to the mainlands of the American landmasses, they encountered larger, more complex, and more militarized societies than those they had overrun in the Caribbean.

On the mainland, great civilizations had arisen centuries before, boasting large cities, monumental buildings, and riches based on wealthy agrarian societies. In both Mesoamerica, starting with the Olmecs (see Chapter 5), and the Andes, starting with the Chimú (see Chapter 10), large polities had laid the foundations for subsequent Aztec and Inca Empires. These empires were powerful. But they also represented the evolution of states and commercial systems untouched by Afro-Eurasian developments; as worlds apart, they were unprepared for the kind of assaults that European invaders had perfected. In pre-Columbian Mesoamerica and then the Andes, warfare was as ceremonial as it was political. Less inclined to wipe out enemies, victors aimed to make the vanquished into tributary subjects, to control them not conquer them. Nonetheless, the Aztec and Inca Empires were exceedingly wealthy, which made them irresistible to outside conquerors, whose habits of war they could never have foreseen.

AZTEC SOCIETY In Mesoamerica, the ascendant Mexica had created an empire known to us as Aztec. Around Lake Texcoco, Mexica cities grew and formed a three-city league in 1430, which then expanded through the valley of central Mexico to incorporate neighboring peoples. Gradually, the **Aztec Empire** united numerous small, independent states under a single monarch who ruled with the help of counselors, military leaders, and priests. By the late fifteenth century, the Aztec realm may have embraced 25 million people. Tenochtitlán, the primary city, situated on an immense island in Lake Texcoco, ranked among the world's largest.

Tenochtitlán spread in concentric circles, with the main religious and political buildings in the center and residences radiating outward. The city's outskirts connected a mosaic of floating gardens producing food for urban markets. As the city grew, clan-like networks evolved, and powerful families married their children to each other or found nuptial partners among the prominent families of other important cities. (Certain ruling houses in Europe were solidifying alliances in much the same way at this time; see Chapter 11.) Not only did this practice concentrate power in the great city, but it also ensured a pool of potential successors to the throne. Soon a lineage emerged to create a corps of "natural" rulers.

Holding this stratified order together was a shared understanding of the cosmos. But unlike adherents of European and most Asian cosmologies, Aztecs saw the natural order as intrinsically unstable. They believed that the universe was prone to recurring cycles of disaster that would eventually end in apocalypse. Such an unstable cosmos exposed mortals to repeated creations and destructions of their world. It was the priesthood's job to balance a belief that history was destined to run in cycles with a faith that mortals could influence the gods, and their own fate, through religious rituals. These rituals also legitimized the Aztec power structure by portraying the emperor and the elite as closer to the gods than the lower orders were.

Ultimately, Aztec power spread through much of Mesoamerica, but the empire's constant wars and conquests deprived it of stability. In successive military campaigns, the Aztecs subjugated their neighbors, feeding off plunder and then forcing subject peoples to pay tribute of crops, gold, silver, textiles, and other goods that financed Aztec grandeur. Such conquests also provided a constant supply of humans for sacrifice, because the Aztecs believed that the great god of the sun required human hearts to keep on burning and blood to replace that given by the gods to moisten the earth through rain. Priests escorted captured warriors up the temple steps and tore out their hearts, offering their lives and blood as a sacrifice to the sun god. Allegedly, between 20,000 and 80,000 men, women, and children were slaughtered in a single ceremony in 1487, with the four-person-wide line of victims stretching for over two miles. In this marathon of bloodletting, knife-wielding priests collapsed from exhaustion and surrendered their places to fresh executioners.

Those whom the Aztecs sought to dominate did not submit peacefully. From 1440, the empire faced constant turmoil as subject peoples resented Aztec domination, and independent peoples—such as the Tlaxcalans to the east and Tarascans

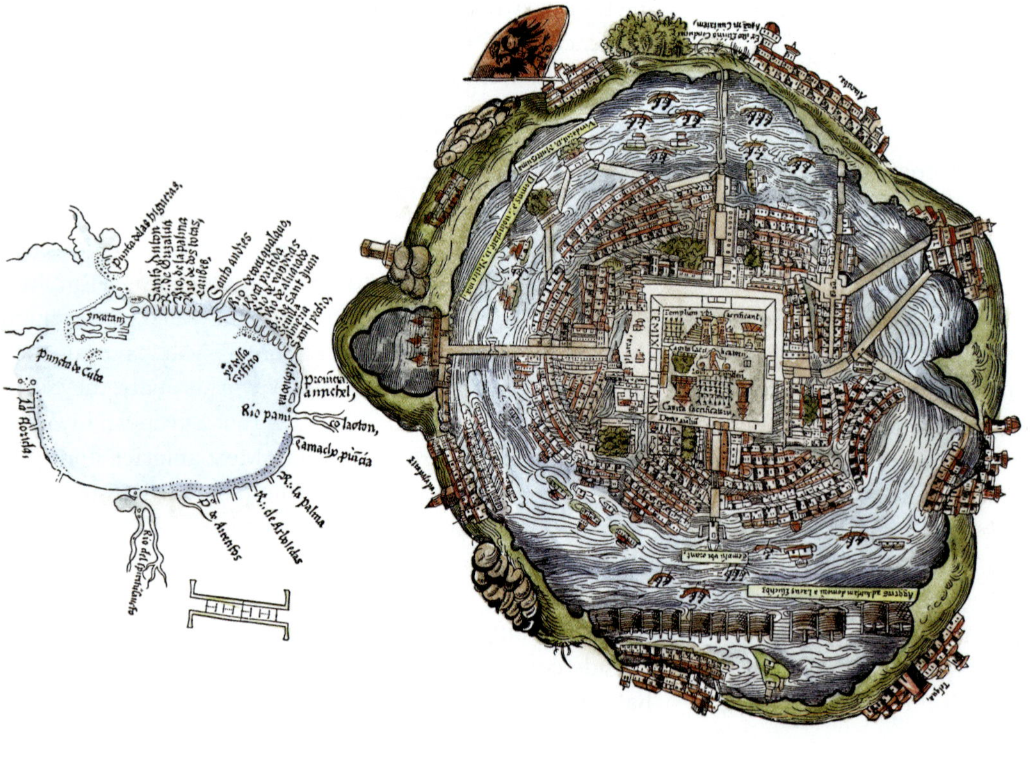

Tenochtitlán. At its height, the Aztec capital, Tenochtitlán, was as populous as Europe's largest city. As can be seen from this map, it spread in concentric circles, with the main religious and political buildings in the center and residences radiating outward.

(or Purépecha) to the west—waged war to preserve their independence and fiercely resisted incorporation into the Aztecs' tributary empire. To pacify the realm, the Aztecs diverted more and more men and money into their armies. By the time the electoral committee chose Moctezuma II as emperor in 1502, divisions among elites and pressures from the periphery had placed the Aztec Empire under extreme stress.

CORTÉS AND CONQUEST Not long after Moctezuma became emperor, news arrived from the coast of strange sightings of floating mountains (ships) bearing pale, bearded men and monsters (horses and dogs). Moctezuma consulted with his ministers and soothsayers, wondering if these men were the god Quetzalcoatl and his entourage. The people of Tenochtitlán saw omens of impending disaster. Moctezuma sank into despair, hesitating over what to do. He sent emissaries bearing jewels and prized feathers; later he sent sorcerers to confuse and bewitch the newcomers. But he did not prepare for any military engagement. After all, Mesoamericans had no idea of the interlopers' destructive potential in weaponry and germs.

Aboard one of the ships was Hernán Cortés (1485–1547), a former law student from one of the Spanish provinces. He would become the conquistador whom all subsequent conquerors tried to emulate, just as Columbus was the model explorer. For a brief time, Cortés was an *encomendero* in Hispaniola, but when news arrived of a potentially wealthier land to the west, he set sail with over 500 men, eleven ships, sixteen horses, and artillery.

When the expedition arrived near present-day Veracruz, Cortés acquired two translators, including the daughter of a local Indigenous noble family. The daughter, who became known as Doña Marina, was a "gift" to the triumphant Spaniards from the ruler of the Tabasco region (a rival to the Aztecs). Fluent in several languages, Doña Marina displayed such linguistic skills and personal charm that she soon became Cortés's lover and ultimately revealed several Aztec plots against the tiny Spanish force. Doña Marina subsequently bore Cortés a son, who is considered one of the first mixed-blooded Mexicans (Mestizos).

With the assistance of Doña Marina and other Indigenous allies, Cortés marched his troops to Tenochtitlán. Upon entering, he gasped in wonder that "this city is so big and so remarkable" that it was "almost unbelievable." In a letter home, one of his soldiers wrote, "It was all so wonderful that I do not know how to describe this first glimpse of things never heard of, seen or dreamed of before."

How was this tiny force to overcome an empire of many millions with an elaborate warring tradition? First, crucial

Cortés Meets Mesoamerican Rulers. *Left:* This colonial image depicts the meeting of Cortés (second from right) and Moctezuma (seated on the left), with Doña Marina serving as an interpreter and informer for the Spanish conquistador. Notice at the bottom what are likely Aztec offerings for the newcomer. *Right:* This detail from a twentieth-century Mexican mural depicts the meeting of Cortés and the king of Tlaxcala (enemy of the Aztecs). As Mexicans began to celebrate their mixed-blood heritage, Doña Marina (in the middle) became the symbolic mother of the first Mestizos. But she remains controversial and has also been viewed in Mexico as a traitor for the help she provided to the Spanish.

to Spanish conquest was their alliance with Moctezuma's enemies—especially the Tlaxcalans. After decades of yearning for release from the Aztec yoke, the Tlaxcalans and other Mesoamerican peoples, with the aid of Indigenous translators, accepted Cortés's promise of help. The Spaniards' second advantage was their method of warfare. The Aztecs were seasoned fighters, but they fought to capture, not to kill. Nor were they familiar with gunpowder or sharp steel swords. Although outnumbered, the Spaniards killed their foe with abandon, using superior weaponry, horses, and war dogs. The Aztecs, still unsure who these strange men were, allowed Cortés to enter their city. With the aid of the thousands of Tlaxcalan warriors and a handful of his own men, in 1519 Cortés captured Moctezuma, who became a puppet of the Spanish conqueror. (See Global Themes and Sources: Primary Source 12.2.)

Aztec Society. Less than two decades after the fall of Tenochtitlán, the Spanish Viceroy commissioned Indigenous artists to compose a history of the Aztec rulers and the conquest of their empire. Conveyed by traditional Aztec pictograms and Nahua writing—with Spanish translations—this image is from the first folio. It tells the story the founding of the Aztec capital. Observe the waterways that separated the city from the mainland and the canals running through it. At the center is an eagle perched on a cactus (which grows, according to legend, out of stone). All around are the ten founding fathers of the city. It is possible that the painter's name was Francisco Gualpuyogualcacal, an Indigenous man who worked for the friars.

Within two years, the Aztecs realized that the newcomers were not gods, and they staged an uprising that forced Cortés to retreat and regroup. This time, with more Tlaxcalan help, he chose to defeat the Aztecs completely. He ordered the building of boats to sail across Lake Texcoco to bombard the capital with artillery. Even more devastating was the spread of smallpox, brought by the Spanish, which ran through the soldiers and commoners like wildfire. The total number of Aztec casualties may have reached 240,000. As Spanish troops retook the capital, they found it in ruins, with a population too weak to resist. The last emperor, Cuauhtémoc, himself faced execution, thereby ending the royal Mexica lineage. The Aztecs lamented their defeat in verse: "We have pounded our hands in despair against the adobe walls, for our inheritance, our city, is lost and dead." Cortés became governor of the new Spanish colony, renamed "New Spain." He promptly allocated *encomiendas* to his loyal followers and dispatched expeditions to conquer the more distant Mesoamerican provinces.

The Mesoamerican experience taught the Spanish an important lesson: an effective conquest had to be swift—exploit local divides and destroy the symbols of older legitimate authority. Their winning advantage, however, was disease. The Spaniards unintentionally introduced germs that made their subsequent efforts at military conquest much easier.

The Incas

The other great Spanish conquest occurred in the Andes, where Quechua-speaking rulers, called Incas, had established an impressive polity. By the mid-fifteenth century, the **Inca Empire** controlled a vast domain incorporating 4 to 6 million people and running from what is now Chile to southern Colombia. At its center was the capital, Cuzco, with the magnificent fortress of Sacsayhuamán as its head. Built of hand-carved huge boulders, the citadel was the nerve center of a complex network of strongholds that held the empire together.

But the Incas were internally split. Lacking a clear inheritance system, the empire suffered repeated convulsions. In the early sixteenth century, the struggle over who would succeed Huayna Capac, the ruler, was especially fierce. Huáscar, his "official" son, took Cuzco (the capital), while Atahualpa, his favored son, governed the province of present-day Ecuador. Open conflict might have been averted were it not for Huayna's premature death. His killer was probably smallpox, which swept down from Mesoamerica via trade and migration routes into the Andes well in advance of the arrival of the Spaniards (much as the bubonic plague had earlier spread through Afro-Eurasian trade routes; see Chapter 11). With the father gone, Atahualpa declared war on his brother, crushed him, forced him to witness the execution of all his supporters, and then killed him and used his skull as a vessel for maize beer.

When the Spaniards arrived in 1532, they wandered into a fractured Andean empire, a situation they exploited. Francisco

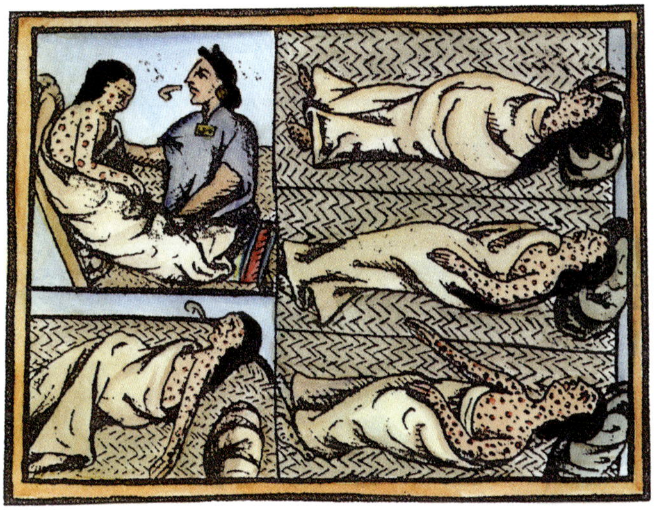

Disease and Decimation of Indigenous Peoples. The real conqueror of Indigenous people was not so much guns as germs. Even before Spanish soldiers seized the Aztec capital, germs had begun decimating the population. The first big killer was smallpox, recorded here by an Indigenous artist.

Pizarro, who led the Spanish campaign, had been inspired by Cortés's victory and yearned for his own glory. Commanding a force of about 600 men, he invited Atahualpa to confer at the town of Cajamarca. There he laid a trap. As columns of Inca warriors and servants covered with colorful plumage and plates of silver and gold marched into the main square, the Spanish soldiers were awed. Writing home, one recalled, "Many of us urinated without noticing it, out of sheer terror." But Pizarro's plan worked. He trained his guns and artillery on the Andean army and its spears and opened fire. The conquistadors' galloping horses added shock. Atahualpa himself fell into Spanish hands, later to be decapitated. Pizarro's conquistadors overran Cuzco in 1533 and then vanquished the rest of the Inca forces, a process that took decades in some areas.

From Conquest to Colonization in the Atlantic World

Spanish conquests led to the merger of two biomes, leading to an exchange of previously unknown plants, people, and products—and pathogens. It was as if two planets that did not know of each other suddenly became one. The Mestizo writer Garcilaso de la Vega (also known as El Inca), raised in Cuzco as the son of a Spanish conquistador and an Inca noblewoman, wrote in the early seventeenth century that many people still wondered "if there was one world or many, if it is flat or round." The time had come, he declared, to put an end to the speculation: "There is only one world." The result of the merger integrated the natural and human ecosystems and transformed them.

Pizarro and the Incas. This illustration is by the Indigenous Andean Guaman Poma, whose circa 1587 epic of the conquest of Peru depicted many of the barbarities of the Spanish. Here we see the conquistador Pizarro and a Catholic priest appealing to Atahualpa—before betraying and then killing him.

Those who came to the Americas carried devastating diseases that killed tens of millions of Indigenous people. The newcomers also brought horses, cattle, pigs, wheat, grapevines, and sugarcane. In exchange, they learned about crops such as potatoes, tomatoes, peanuts, and corn that would fuel a population explosion across Afro-Eurasia. Historians call this hemispheric transfer of animals, plants, people, and pathogens in the wake of Columbus's voyages the **Columbian exchange**. Over time, these transfers would change the demography and the diets of both the New and the Old Worlds.

The Columbian Exchange

The first and most profound effect of the Columbian exchange was a destructive one: the decimation of the Indigenous population by European diseases. (See Analyzing Global Developments: The European Conquest of the Americas and Indigenous Mortality.) For millennia, the populations of the Americas had been cut off from the disease pools in Afro-Eurasia. Africans, Europeans, and Asians had long interacted, sharing pathogens and gaining immunities; in this sense, the Indigenous people of the Americas were indeed "worlds apart."

Sickness spread from the moment the Spaniards arrived. Even Cortés took note. "Their excretions," he wrote to the

Analyzing Global Developments

The European Conquest of the Americas and Indigenous Mortality

If the fourteenth century was an age of dying across Afro-Eurasia, the sixteenth century saw even higher mortality rates in the Americas. As a result of European conquest, the exposure to virulent diseases, and hyper-exploitation of their labor under miserable conditions, the Indigenous populations saw their numbers reduced by 85 percent. The numbers themselves, however, are highly controversial and have sparked intense debates. Some scholars believe that no reliable numbers can be found for the population of the Americas when Europeans first arrived. Others have used a range of methods and data sources to establish population figures, including European firsthand accounts from that period, archaeological and anthropological evidence, estimates of the maximum population size of people the land can contain indefinitely (carrying capacity), and projections built backward from more recent censuses. These estimates vary widely from as low as 8 million to as high as more than 100 million.

Area	Population in 1492	Later Populations	Mortality Rates
The Americas	53.9 m[a]	8.0 m in 1650	85%
The Caribbean			
Hispaniola	1.0 m	extinct by 1600	100%
The other islands	2.0 m	extinct by 1600	100%
Mexico	17.2 m	3.5 m in 1600	80%
The Andes	15.0 m	3.0 m in 1650	80%
Central America	5.63 m	1.12 m in 1700	80%
North America	3.79 m	1.5 m in 1700	60%
		250,000 in 1900	84%

[a]m = millions.

QUESTIONS FOR ANALYSIS

- Imagine yourself as a historical demographer. How would you attempt to estimate the population of the Americas in 1492?
- What effect did European conquest and Indigenous dying have on the polities and religious beliefs of the Indigenous people of the Americas?
- Why do you think Indigenous population growth never recovered from the initial encounter with Europeans whereas Afro-Eurasian population growth eventually recovered from the Black Death?

Sources: Suzanne Austin Alchon, *A Pest in the Land: New World Epidemics in a Global Perspective* (2003); David Noble Cook, *Born to Die: Disease and New World Conquest, 1492 to 1650* (1998); William M. Denevan, *The Native Populations of the Americas in 1492* (1992); David Henige, *Numbers from Nowhere: The Amerindian Contact Population Debate* (1998); "La Catastrophe Demographique," *L'Histoire*, no. 322 (July–August 2007):17; Russell Thornton, *American Indian Holocaust: A Population History since 1492* (1987), p. xvii.

Spanish emperor, "were the sort of filth that thin swine pass which have been fed on nothing but grass." Indigenous accounts of the fall of Tenochtitlán recalled the smallpox epidemic more vividly than the fighting. Even worse, no sooner had smallpox done its work than Indigenous Peoples faced a second pandemic: measles. Then came pneumonic plague and influenza. As each wave retreated, it left a population more emaciated than before, even less prepared for the next wave. The scale of death remains unprecedented: imported pathogens wiped out up to 90 percent of the Indigenous population. A century after smallpox arrived on Hispaniola in 1519, no more than 5 to 10 percent of the island's population was left alive. Diminished and weakened by disease, Indigenous peoples could not resist European settlement and colonization of the Americas. Thus were Europeans the unintended beneficiaries of a horrifying catastrophe.

Mortality rates were so high that death was a meeting ground for Spaniards and Indigenous peoples. Funeral rites, processions, burials, and shrines became rituals for cultural exchange and spiritual conquest. Over the ensuing centuries, death was itself Christianized as missionaries and magistrates used these rituals of everyday life—and death—to colonize funerals and holy sites. They wrote elaborate scripts for how Indigenous people were supposed to venerate the deceased—with pomp and rites that emphasized the centrality of the church and marked the passage of the deceased to the new Christian lord. They also condemned pagan rites, like leaving offerings in tombs or venerating old burial grounds. As long as Indigenous people followed the new rules, they were permitted to create their own hospitals (like Santa Ana in Lima), confraternities, and churches where they could bid farewell to the sick and dying—and learn the new doctrine. Indeed, hospitals became important institutions that allowed new Christians to integrate into a Hispanicized world, become community leaders, and re-create their society in the wake of the calamity of conquest.

It did not take long for Indigenous intellectuals to chronicle the world they were losing to conquest and death. Atahualpa, the murdered Inca emperor, became a "martyr" for some early authors. One Peruvian writer, Guaman Poma, portrayed him as stern and expressionless, as he was being tortured—a symbol of stoical resistance who was sacrificed. It is worth noting that Guaman Poma was a devout Christian, so Atahualpa's sacrifice was likened to that of Jesus Christ for his people. Another example is Don Juan Buenaventura Zapata y Mendoza of Quiahuiztlan in Mexico. Don Juan Zapata sought to preserve his people's history by recording community public performances and turning them into historical annals. He knew death close up: his parents had died in an epidemic in 1641. Because his father had been an officeholder in the local town council, Don Juan rose to prominence. He wrote in text and in pictures of "we the Indigenous people," who needed an epic of trauma, social memories, and expectations of the future.

If the Columbian exchange compelled Indigenous peoples to grapple with the effects of conquest and colonization, it also led to world-making exchanges. As time passed, all sides adopted new forms of agriculture from one another. Indigenous Peoples taught Europeans how to grow potatoes and corn, crops that would become staples all across Afro-Eurasia. The Chinese found that they could grow corn in areas too dry for rice and too wet for wheat, while corn replaced, at first by fits and starts, Africa's major food grains, sorghum, millet, and rice, to become the continent's principal food crop by the twentieth century. (See Current Trends in World History: Corn and the Rise of Kingdoms in West Africa as Suppliers of Enslaved People.) Europeans also took away tomatoes, beans, cacao, peanuts, tobacco, and squash, while exporting livestock such as cattle, swine, and horses to the New World. The environmental effects of the introduction of livestock to the Americas were manifold. In the highland regions north of the valley of central Mexico (where Indigenous people had once maintained irrigated, highly productive agricultural estates), Spanish settlers opened up large herding ranches. An area that had once produced corn and squash now supported herds of sheep and cattle. Without natural predators, these animals reproduced with lightning speed, destroying entire landscapes with their hoofs and their foraging.

As Europeans cleared trees and other vegetation for ranches, mines, or plantations, they undermined the habitats of many indigenous mammals and birds. On the islands of the West Indies, described by Columbus as "roses of the sea," the Spanish chopped down lush tropical and semitropical forests to make way for sugar plantations. Before long, nearly all of the islands' tall trees as well as many shrubs and ground plants were gone, and residents lamented the absence of birdsong. Over ensuing centuries, the flora and fauna of the Americas took on an increasingly European appearance—a process that the historian Alfred Crosby has called ecological imperialism. At the same time, the interactions between Europeans and Indigenous peoples would continue to shape societies on both sides of the Atlantic.

Spain's Tributary Empire

Like the Europeans who sailed into the Indian Ocean to join existing commercial systems, the Spaniards sought to exploit the wealth of Indigenous empires. To do so required leaving much of the Indigenous structures intact. Those Indigenous people who survived the original encounters could be harnessed for tribute payments to the new masters. Spain could thereby extract wealth without extensive settlement. In Mexico and Peru, conquistadors decapitated Indigenous communities but left much of their social and economic structure in place—including networks of tribute. But unlike the European penetration of the Indian Ocean, the occupation of the New World went beyond the control of commercial outposts. Instead, European colonialism in the Americas involved laying claim to large amounts of territory—and ultimately the entire landmass. (See Map 12.2.) We should be careful, however, not to mistake the expansive claims made by European empires in the Americas for actual control of the territory. Through the fifteenth and sixteenth centuries—and as we will see in Chapter 13, through the seventeenth and eighteenth—Indigenous peoples still maintained their dominion over much of the Americas, even as disease continued to diminish their numbers.

Within their colonial heartlands, Spanish masters fused traditional tribute-taking with their own innovations to make villagers deliver goods and services. But because the Spanish authorities also bestowed *encomiendas*, those favored individuals could demand labor from their lands' Indigenous inhabitants—for mines, estates, and public works. Whereas Aztec and Inca rulers had conscripted labor to build up their public wealth, the Spaniards did so for private gain.

Women also played a role in the conquest. Most Spanish migrants were men; very few were women. One, Inés Suárez, reached the Indies only to find her husband, who had arrived earlier, dead. She then became mistress of the conquistador Pedro de Valdivia, and the pair worked as a conquering team. Initially, she joined an expedition to conquer Chile as Valdivia's domestic servant, but she soon became much more—nurse, caretaker, adviser, and guard, having uncovered several plots to assassinate her lover. Suárez even served as a diplomat between warring Indigenous people and Spaniards in an effort to secure the conquest. Later, she helped rule Chile as the wife of Rodrigo de Quiroga, governor of the province. Admittedly, hers was an exceptional story. More typical were

Current Trends in World History

Corn and the Rise of Kingdoms in West Africa as Suppliers of Enslaved People

New World varieties of corn spread rapidly throughout the Afro-Eurasian landmass soon after the arrival of Columbus in the Americas. Its hardiness and fast-ripening qualities made it more desirable than many of the Old World grain products. In communities that consumed large quantities of meat, it became the main product fed to livestock.

Corn's impact on Africa was as substantial as it was on the rest of Afro-Eurasia. Seeds made their way to western regions more quickly than to the south of the Sahara along two routes. One was via European merchants calling into ports along the coast; the other was via West African Muslims returning across the Sahara after participating in the pilgrimage to Mecca. The first evidence of corn cultivation in sub-Saharan Africa comes from a Portuguese navigator who identified the crop being grown on the island of Cape Verde in 1540. By the early seventeenth century, corn was replacing millet and sorghum as the main grain being grown in many West African regions and was destined to transform the work routines and diets of the peoples living in the region's tropical rain forests all the way from present-day Sierra Leone in the east to Nigeria in the west. In many ways this area, which saw the rise of a group of powerful slave-supplying kingdoms in the eighteenth century, notably Asante, Dahomey, Oyo, and Benin, owed its prosperity to the cultivation of this New World crop. (See Chapter 14 for a fuller discussion of these states.)

Corn Plantation. This nineteenth-century engraving by famed Italian explorer Savorgnan de Brazza shows women of the West African Bateke tribe working in corn plantations. Brazza would later serve as the governor-general of the French colony in the Congo.

The tropical rain forests of West and central Africa were thick with trees and ground cover in 1500. Clearing them so that they could support intensive agriculture was exhausting work, requiring enormous outlays of human energy and man-hours. Corn, a crop first domesticated in central Mexico 7,000 years ago, made this task possible. It added much-needed carbohydrates to the carbon-deficient diets of rain forest dwellers. In addition, as a crop that matured more quickly than those that were indigenous to the region (millet, sorghum, and rice) and required less labor, it yielded two harvests in a single year. Farmers also cultivated cassava, another New World native, which in turn provided households with more carbohydrate calories. Yet corn did more than produce more food per unit of land and labor. Households put every part of the plant to use—grain, leaves, stalks, tassels, and roots were made to serve useful purposes.

Thus, at the very time that West African groups were moving southward into the rain forests, European navigators were arriving along the coast with new crops. Corn gave communities of cultivators the caloric energy to change their forest landscapes, expanding the arable areas. In a select few of these regions, enterprising clans emerged to dominate the political scene, creating centralized kingdoms like Asante in present-day Ghana, Dahomey in present-day Benin, and Oyo and Benin in present-day Nigeria. These elites transformed what had once been thinly settled environments into densely populated states, with elaborate bureaucracies, big cities, and large and powerful standing armies.

There was much irony in the rise of these states, which owed so much of their strength to the linking of the Americas with Afro-Eurasia. The armies that they created and the increased populations that the new crops allowed were part and parcel of the Atlantic slave trade. That which the Americas gave with one hand (new crops), it took back with the other in warfare, captives, and New World slavery.

QUESTIONS FOR ANALYSIS

- What were the major effects of growing corn in West Africa?
- How did the growing of corn reshape the history of the Atlantic world during this period?

EXPLORE FURTHER

McCann, James, *Maize and Grace: Africa's Encounter with a New World Crop, 1500–2000* (2005).

MAP 12.2 | The Spanish and Portuguese Empires in the Americas, 1492–1750

This map depicts the growth of the Spanish and Portuguese Empires in the Americas over two and a half centuries. It also shows the extent of the Indigenous Aztec and Inca Empires.

- What did European colonizers find so appealing that it caused them to push further into the Americas? What resistance might they have met?
- Referring back to Map 12.1, explain why you believe Spanish settlement covered so much more area than Portuguese settlement.
- According to your reading, describe and explain how the production and export of American products shaped the labor systems.

women who foraged for food, tended wounded soldiers, and set up European-style settlements.

However, there were too few Spanish women to go around, so Spanish men consorted with local women—despite the crown's disapproval. From the onset of colonization, Spaniards also married into Indigenous families. After conquering the Incas, Pizarro himself wedded an Inca princess, thereby (or so he hoped) inheriting the mantle of local dynastic rule. As a result of intermarriages, Mestizos became the fastest-growing segment of the population of Spanish America.

Spanish migrants and their progeny preferred towns to the countryside. Ports excepted, the major cities of Spanish

America were the former centers of Indigenous empires. Mexico City took shape on the ruins of Tenochtitlán; Cuzco arose from the razed Inca capital. In their architecture, economy, and most intimate aspects, the Spanish colonies adopted as much as they transformed the worlds they encountered.

Portugal's New World Colony

No sooner did Europeans—starting with the Portuguese and Spanish—venture into the seas than they carved them up to prevent a free-for-all. The Treaty of Tordesillas of 1494, drawn up by the pope, had foreseen that the non-European world—the Americas, Africa, and Asia—would be divided into spheres of interest between Spain and Portugal. Yet the treaty was unenforceable. No less interested in immediate riches than the Spanish, the Portuguese were disappointed by the absence of tributary populations and precious metals in the areas set aside for them. What they did find in Brazil, however, was abundant, fertile land on which favored persons received massive royal grants. These estate owners governed their plantations like feudal lords (see Chapter 10).

COASTAL ENCLAVES Hemmed in along the coast, the Portuguese created enclaves. Unlike the Spanish, they rarely intermarried with Indigenous people, most of whom had fled or had died from imported diseases. Failing to find established cities, the colonists remained in more dispersed settlements. By the late seventeenth century, Brazil's White population was 300,000.

The problem was where to find labor to work the rich lands. Lacking a centralized government to deal with the labor shortage, the Portuguese settlers initially tried to enlist the dispersed Indigenous population, but when recruitment became increasingly coercive, Indigenous people turned on the settlers, whom they perceived to be interlopers. Some fought. Others fled to the vast interior. Reluctant to pursue the Indigenous people inland, the Portuguese hugged their beachheads, extracting brazilwood (the source of a beautiful red dye) and sugar from their enclaves.

Enslaved Africans became the solution to this labor problem. What had worked for the Portuguese on sugarcane plantations in the Azores and other Atlantic islands now found application on their Brazilian plantations. Especially in the northeast, in the Bay of All Saints, the Atlantic world's first sugar-producing commercial center appeared.

SUGAR PLANTATIONS Along with silver, sugar emerged as the most valuable export from the Americas. It also was decisive in rearranging relations between peoples around the Atlantic. Cultivation of sugarcane had originated in India, spread to the Mediterranean region, and then reached the coastal islands of West Africa. The Portuguese transported the West African model to Brazil, and other Europeans took it to the Caribbean. (See again Map 12.2.) By the early seventeenth century, sugar had become a major export from the New World. By the eighteenth century, its production required continuous and enormous transfers of labor from Africa, and its value surpassed that of silver as an export from the Americas to Europe.

Mission São Miguel. The Jesuits were avid missionaries in the Spanish and Portuguese Empires and often tried to shelter Indigenous peoples from conquistadors and labor recruiters. Missions, like this one, in the borderlands between Brazil and Spanish colonies were targets of attack from both sides.

At first, most Brazilian sugar plantations were fairly small, employing between 60 and 100 enslaved people. But they were efficient enough to create an alternative model of empire, one that resulted in full-scale colonization and dislocation of the existing population. The enslaved lived in wretched conditions: their barracks were miserable, and their diets were insufficient to keep them alive under backbreaking work routines. Moreover, they were disproportionately men. As they rapidly died off, the only way to ensure replenishment was to import more Africans. This model of settlement relied on the transatlantic flow of enslaved human beings.

Beginnings of the Transatlantic Slave Trade

As European demand for sugar increased, the slave trade expanded. Although enslaved Africans were imported into the Americas starting in the fifteenth century, the first direct voyage carrying them from Africa to the Americas occurred in 1525. The transatlantic slave trade began modestly in support of one commodity, sugar. From the time of Columbus until 1820, more than five times as many Africans as Europeans moved to the Americas: approximately 2 million Europeans (voluntarily) and 12 million Africans (involuntarily) crossed the Atlantic—though the especially high mortality rate for Africans meant that only 10 million survived to reach New World shores.

First to master long-distance seafaring, the Portuguese also led the way in human cargo. Trade in enslaved people grew steadily throughout the sixteenth century, then surged in the seventeenth and eighteenth centuries (see Chapter 13). Initially, all European powers participated—Portuguese, Spanish, Dutch, English, and French. Eventually, New World merchants in both North and South America also established direct trade links with Africa.

Well before European merchants arrived off its western coast, Africa had known long-distance slave trading. In fact, the overall number of Africans sold into captivity in the Muslim world exceeded that of the Atlantic slave trade. Moreover, Africans kept a population of enslaved people locally. African slavery, like its American counterpart, was a response to labor scarcities. In many parts of Africa, however, the enslaved did not face permanent servitude. Instead, they were assimilated into families, gradually losing their servile status and swelling the size and power of their adopted lineage-based groups.

With the additional European demand for enslaved people to work New World plantations alongside the ongoing Muslim slave trade, pressure on the supply of enslaved Africans intensified. Only a narrow band stretching down the spine of the African landmass, from present-day Uganda and the highlands of Kenya to Zambia and Zimbabwe, escaped the impact of Asian and European slave traders.

Within Africa, the social and political consequences were not fully evident until the great age of the slave trade in the eighteenth century, but already some economic consequences were clear. The overwhelming trend was to further limit Africa's population. Indeed, African laborers fetched high enough prices to more than cover the costs of their capture and transportation across the Atlantic.

By the late sixteenth century, important pieces had fallen into place to create a new Atlantic world, one that could not have been imagined a century earlier. This was the three-cornered **Atlantic system**, with Africa supplying labor, the Americas land and minerals, and Europe the technology and military power to hold the system together. If observers at the time counted the Ottomans or the Ming as the greatest world powers, in the longer run the wealth flows to Europe and the slavery-based development of the Americas would tip the world balance of power in Europe's favor.

Silver

For the first Europeans in the Americas, the foremost measure of success was the gold and silver that they could hoard for themselves and their monarchs. In plundering massive amounts of silver, the conquistadors introduced it to the world's commercial systems, an act that electrified them. In the twenty years after the fall of Tenochtitlán, conquistadors took more precious metals from Mexico and the Andes than all the gold accumulated by Europeans over the previous centuries. (See again Map 12.2.)

But once the looting was over, the Spanish entered the business of mining directly, opening the Andean Potosí mines in 1545. Between 1560 and 1685, Spanish America sent 25,000 to 35,000 tons of silver annually to Spain. From 1685 to 1810, this sum doubled. The two mother lodes were Potosí, in present-day Bolivia, and Zacatecas, in northern Mexico. Silver brought bounty not only to the crown but also to privileged families based in Spain's colonial capitals; thus, private wealth funded the formation of local aristocracies.

Colonial mines epitomized the Atlantic world's new extractive economy. They relied on an extensive network of Indigenous labor, at first enslaved, subsequently drafted. Here again, the Spanish adopted Inca and Aztec practices of requiring labor from subjugated villages: each year, village elders selected a stipulated number of men to toil in the shafts, refineries, and smelters. Under the Spanish, the digging, hauling, and smelting taxed human limits to their capacity—and beyond. Those unfortunate enough to be sent underground pounded the rock walls with chisels and hammers, releasing silicon dust. Miners could not help but breathe in the toxic dust, which created lesions and made simply inhaling seem like swallowing broken glass. Mortality rates were appalling. But the miners' sufferings reaped huge profits and significant

Silver. Silver was an important discovery for Spanish conquerors in Mesoamerica and the Andes. Conquerors expanded the custom of Inca and Aztec labor drafts to force the Indigenous peoples to work in mines, often in brutal conditions.

consequences for the Europeans. The Spanish pumped so much New World silver into global commercial networks that they caused painful price inflation in Europe and transformed Europe's relationship to all its trading partners, especially those in China and India.

The defeat of the New World's two great empires gave Europeans the means to suck human and material wealth from the Americas. In time, as Europeans settled in to stay, it also gave Europeans a market for their own products—goods that found little favor in Afro-Eurasia—and opened a new frontier that the Europeans could colonize as staple-producing provinces. Extracting wealth from the new world inflamed religious and political conflicts at the heart of Christendom itself. It gave Old World belligerents the means and money to wage a spiritual civil war that would fracture Europe and stamp the balance of Afro-Eurasian power.

Religious Turmoil in Europe

The conquest of the Americas and enslavement of Africans were a bonanza to Europe. But the wealth destabilized an already fractured Old World and heightened the rivalry between hypercompetitive kingdoms in Europe. In the sixteenth century, most European rulers and their subjects were focused on Europe or on Ottoman threats to the east. Their lives and belief systems were being turned upside down by the religious split within the Catholic Church known as the Reformation and by the wars that followed it. Religious fragmentation exacerbated already-existing dynastic rivalries and encouraged states to further centralize their bureaucracies and build up their military forces. Some of those military forces had to be used to keep the Ottomans at bay, for in this period, as we have seen, the Ottomans were making significant inroads into eastern and southern Europe. Waging war so relentlessly required finances; silver from the Americas was the source. The result splintered Europe into a collection of aggressive, religiously stoked, midsize states locked in a struggle for mastery at home—and scrambling abroad.

The Reformation

Religious divides deepened Europe's splinters. Like the Renaissance, the **Protestant Reformation** in Europe began as a movement devoted to returning to ancient sources—in this case, to biblical scriptures. But it was also provoked by long-simmering dissatisfaction with the Catholic Church that came from below. Long before Martin Luther came on the scene, some scholars and believers had despaired of the church's ability to satisfy their longings for deeper, more individualized religious experience. In the fourteenth and fifteenth centuries, the church hierarchy continued to oppose reforms such as allowing laypersons to read the scriptures for themselves, as it feared heresies and challenges to its authority would arise. The church was right, for when political circumstances and the arrival of the printing press permitted Luther to avoid a heretic's death and to expand the campaign for reform, he paved the way for a "Protestant" Reformation that split Christendom for good.

MARTIN LUTHER CHALLENGES THE CHURCH The opening challenge to the authority of the pope and the Catholic Church originated in the **Holy Roman Empire**, the sprawling, loosely hinged, multiethnic empire that covered much of central and eastern Europe. When the Reformation commenced, the Holy Roman Empire was under the rule of the Habsburg prince Charles V, who inherited three great kingdoms: that of Spanish monarchs Isabella and Ferdinand (including their New World holdings), that of Holy Roman Emperor Maximilian I (in central Europe), and that of Burgundy and the Netherlands. Charles's transatlantic empire, although larger than any before or since, was not destined to last. By the time of his death (1556), it had been shattered, largely by the ideas of a stubborn and rhetorically gifted professor of theology named **Martin Luther** (1483–1546).

Initially a pious Catholic believer, Luther nonetheless believed that mortals were so given to sin that none would ever be worthy of salvation. In 1516, Luther found an answer to his quest for salvation in reading Paul's Letters to the Romans: since no human acts could be sufficient to earn admittance to heaven, individuals could be saved only by their faith in God's grace. This faith, moreover, was something Christians could obtain just from reading the Bible—rather than by having a priest tell them what to believe. Finally, Luther concluded that Christians did not need mediators to speak to God for them; all were, in his eyes, priests, equally bound by God's laws.

Other things motivated Luther as well: corrupt practices in the church, such as the keeping of mistresses by monks, priests, and even popes; and the selling of indulgences, certificates that would supposedly shorten the buyer's time in purgatory. In the 1510s, clerics were hawking indulgences across Europe in an effort to raise money for the sumptuous new Saint Peter's Basilica in Rome.

In 1517, Luther formulated ninety-five statements, or theses, and posted them on the doors to the Wittenberg cathedral, hoping to stir up his colleagues in debate. Before long, his theses made him famous—and bolder in his criticisms. In a widely circulated pamphlet called *On the Freedom of the Christian Man* (1520), he upbraided "the Roman Church, which in past ages was the holiest of all" for having "become a den of murderers beyond all other dens of murderers, a thieves' castle beyond all other thieves' castles, the head and empire of every sin, as well as of death and damnation." As Luther's ideas spread, Pope Leo X and the Habsburg emperor, Charles V, demanded that Luther take back his criticisms and theological claims. When he refused, he was declared a heretic and avoided being burned at the stake only through the intervention of a powerful German prince who let Luther hole up in his castle.

Luther wrote many more pamphlets attacking the church and the pope, whom he now described as the anti-Christ. To stir things up for the Holy Roman Empire, he sent some to the Ottoman sultan, hoping to convince him to bleed Catholic forces in Vienna. Luther also translated the New Testament from Latin into German so that laypersons could have direct access, without priests, to the word of God. This act spurred many other daring scholars across Europe to undertake translations of their own, and it encouraged the Protestant clergy to teach children (and adults) to read their local languages. With the aid of the printing press, cheap, accessible Bibles added to the dissension from what remained of Catholic imperial unity.

OTHER "PROTESTANT" REFORMERS Luther's doctrines won widespread support. The renewed Christian creed appealed to commoners as well as elites, especially in communities that resented rule by Catholic "outsiders" (like the Dutch, who resented being ruled by Philip II, a Habsburg prince who lived in Spain). Thus, the reformed ideas took particularly firm hold in the German states, France, Switzerland, Scandinavia, the Low Countries, and England.

Some zealous reformers, like **Jean Calvin** (1509–1564), in France, modified Luther's ideas. To Luther's emphasis on the individual's relationship to God, Calvin added a focus on preaching and moral discipline, which he believed was best applied by autonomous religious communities. Calvin's belief that morally righteous persons should be free to govern themselves emboldened political and religious dissenters to challenge the church and to seek more religious and political independence for their followers, who were known as Puritans in England, Presbyterians in Scotland, and Huguenots in France, the places where (in addition to Switzerland and the Netherlands) Calvinism was most popular. In contrast, those who remained loyal to the original Protestant cause now described themselves as Lutherans.

In England, Henry VIII (r. 1509–1547) and his daughter Elizabeth (r. 1558–1603) crafted a moderate reformed religion—a "middle way"—called Anglicanism, which retained many Catholic practices and a hierarchy topped by bishops. (American followers later called themselves Episcopalians, from the Latin word for bishop, *episcopus*.) Although Anglican rule was imposed on Ireland, most nonelite Irish remained Catholic. The Scots maintained a fierce devotion to their Presbyterian Church, ensuring a measure of religious diversity within the British Isles. In England, as with the rest of Europe,

Protestant Reformation. Following Luther's lead, many reformers created inexpensive pamphlets to increase the circulation of their message. Pictured here is a woodcut from one such pamphlet, which shows Luther and his followers fending off the corrupt Pope Leo X.

more radical Protestant sects, such as the Anabaptists and Quakers, also developed. While all Protestants were opposed to Catholicism and distrustful of the papal hierarchy, these different communities sometimes developed animosities toward one another as well. (See Map 12.3.)

COUNTER-REFORMATION AND PERSECUTION The Catholic Church responded to Luther and Calvin by embarking on its own renovation, which became known as the **Counter-Reformation**. At the Council of Trent in northern Italy, whose twenty-five sessions stretched from 1545 to 1563, Catholic leaders reaffirmed most church doctrines, including papal supremacy, the holiness of all seven sacraments, the clergy's distinctive role, and the insistence that priests, monks, and nuns remain celibate. But the council also enacted reforms and adopted some of the Protestants' tactics in an effort to win back European believers and to spread the church's message abroad. The reformed Catholics carried their message overseas—especially through an order established by Ignatius Loyola (1491–1556). Loyola founded a brotherhood of priests, the Society of Jesus, or **Jesuits**, dedicated to the revival of the Catholic Church. From bases in Lisbon, Rome, Paris, and elsewhere in Europe, the Jesuits opened missions as far away as South and North America, India, Japan, and China.

Yet the Vatican continued to use repression and persecution to combat what it regarded as heretical beliefs. Priests in Augsburg performed public exorcisms, seeking to free Protestant parishioners from possession by "demons." The Index of Prohibited Books (a list of books and theological treatises banned by the Catholic Church) and the medieval Inquisition (which began around 1184 CE) were weapons against those deemed the church's enemies.

Both Catholics and Protestants persecuted witches. Between about 1500 and 1700, up to 100,000 people, mostly women, were accused of being witches. Many were tried, tortured, burned at the stake, or hanged. Older women, widows, and nurses were vulnerable to charges of cursing or poisoning babies. Other charges included killing livestock, causing hailstorms, and tampering with marriage arrangements. People also believed that weak and susceptible women might have sex with the devil or be tempted to do his bidding. Clearly, neither the Reformation—nor the Catholic response to it—made Europe a more tolerant society. Indeed, the Reformation split European society deeply as both Catholics and Protestants promoted their faiths.

With the aid of the printing press, Europe's empires spread Christianity worldwide. They also spread religious schisms. In Lima, Peru, the Inquisition reached a fever pitch in the 1630s. Almost 100 people were arrested from 1635 to 1639 for committing treason and practicing heresy in a "Great Jewish Conspiracy." The inquisitors held trials for two men and one woman accused of practicing Judaism. Doña Mencia de Luna, Manuel Hernández, and Manuel Bautista Pérez were charged as Judaizers and infidels, which led to a wave of unrest and mass torture. The convicted faced an auto-da-fé: a dramatic public judgment and acts of ritual penance. Inquisitors ordered Manuel Bautista Pérez and ten others lashed to the stake and burned alive. Fifty-two others were publicly whipped, then exiled. Doña Mencia de Luna, Manuel Hernández, and the remaining conspirators wallowed in prison for decades while the inquisitors gathered evidence.

MAP 12.3 | Christian Divisions in Europe after the Reformation, 1590

The Protestant Reformation divided Europe religiously and politically.

- Within the formerly all-Catholic Holy Roman Empire, identify the Protestant groups that emerged. Can you identify any patterns?
- Looking at the entirety of the map, can you identify any geographic patterns in the distribution of Protestant communities? What do you think explains them?
- In which regions would you expect Protestant-Catholic tensions to be the most intense? Explain why you chose those regions.

Religious Warfare in Europe

Religious divides intensified civil war in Europe. Their ultimate effect was to weaken the Holy Roman Empire and strengthen the English, French, and Dutch. Already in the 1520s, the circulation of books presenting Luther's ideas sparked peasant revolts across central Europe. Some peasants, hoping that Luther's assault on the church's authority would help liberate them, rose up against repressive

Inquisition in Lima. The Catholic drive to be rid of heresy spread throughout the Spanish and Portuguese Empires, which were at their zenith. Campaigns to rid the colonies of idols and pre-Columbian symbols were ferocious. Since many Jews and Muslims took flight to the colonies, there was also perpetual fear of infidels. In Lima, the Inquisition staged a spectacular public ceremony to display the power of church authority in the 1630s.

feudal landlords. In contrast to earlier wars, in which one noble's retinue fought a rival's, the defense of the Catholic mass and the Protestant Bible brought crowds of simple folk to arms. Now wars between and within central European states raged for nearly forty years as Holy Roman Emperor Charles V tried to force the Lutheran genie back into the bottle.

In 1555, the exhausted Charles V gave up the fight. He agreed to allow the German princes the right to choose Lutheranism or Catholicism as the official religion within their domains (Calvinism was still outlawed). In 1556, he abdicated and divided his realm between his younger brother Ferdinand and his son Philip. Ferdinand (r. 1556–1564) became Holy Roman Emperor and the head of the Austrian Habsburg dynasty. Philip II (r. Spain 1556–1598) received Spain, Belgium, the Netherlands, southern Italy, and the New World possessions. Philip also inherited the Portuguese throne (from his mother), giving his Spanish Habsburg house a monopoly on Atlantic commerce.

Backed by a world empire and American silver, Catholic allies might have won. Instead, the feuding spread. Religious conflicts led to civil wars in France and a revolt against Spanish rule in the Netherlands, which finally ended, after nearly a hundred years of conflict, with Spain conceding the Calvinist Netherlands its independence. In 1588, the Spanish further embroiled themselves in conflict with Protestant powers by sending a mighty armada of 130 ships and almost 20,000 men into the English Channel in retaliation for English privateers' plundering of Spanish ships. It failed miserably. Spain's entanglement in these conflicts depleted the fortune it had made from New World silver mines. The Dutch and English took advantage of Spanish hemorrhaging to extend their trading networks into Asia and the New World. By the middle of the seventeenth century, the center of power in Europe was shifting to the north—and to the non-European power in the eastern Mediterranean, the Ottoman Empire.

The sprawl of the Spanish and Portuguese Empires did not lead to their own imperial hegemony. If anything, the

St. Bartholomew's Day Massacre. An important wedding between French Catholic and Huguenot families in Paris was scheduled for August 24, 1572, St. Bartholomew's Day. But instead of reconciliation, that day saw a massacre, as Catholics tried to stamp out Protestantism in France's capital city.

wealth from Asian trade, African slave trade, and American colonization and silver fueled Europe's religious civil war and splintered its state system. This would mean that European powers paled in comparison to the cohesive dynasties of Asia, at least for the moment. It also meant that Europeans were competing with one another for access to the spoils and the souls of the worlds they encountered. In the ensuing centuries, European rivalry turned encounters into aggressive expansion.

The Revival of the Asian Economies

By the time the Ottomans were seizing Constantinople, the economies clustered around the Indian Ocean and the China Sea had begun a vigorous revival. This economic renewal would be linked to political developments as Asian empires expanded and consolidated their power. The Mughal ruler, Akbar, and the Ottoman sultan, Suleiman the Magnificent (see Chapter 11), were equally effective and esteemed rulers. The Ming dynasty's elegant manufactures enjoyed worldwide renown, and its ability to govern highly diverse peoples led outsiders to consider China the model imperial state. The Ming, like the Mughals, seemed unconcerned with the increasing appearance of foreigners, including Europeans bearing silver, although both regimes confined European traders to port cities. If anything, the arrival of European sailors and traders in the Indian Ocean strengthened trading ties across the region and enhanced the political power and expansionist interests of Asia's imperial regimes.

The Revival of the Ottoman Caravan Trade

Seaborne commerce eclipsed but did not eliminate overland caravan trading at this time. In fact, along some routes, overland commerce thrived. One well-trafficked route linked the Baltic Sea, Muscovy, the Caspian Sea, the central Asian oases, and China. Other land routes carried goods to the ports of China and the Indian Ocean; from there, they crossed to the Ottoman Empire's heartland and went by land farther into Europe.

Of the many entrepôts that sprang up, none enjoyed more spectacular success than Aleppo, in Syria. Located at the end of caravan routes from India and Baghdad, Aleppo soon overshadowed its Syrian rivals, Damascus and Homs. A vital supply point for Anatolia and the Mediterranean cities, Aleppo by the late sixteenth century was the most important commercial center in Southwest Asia. Here, successful merchants of the type celebrated in the stories of *The Thousand and One Nights* were revered. The caravans gathered on the city's edge, where animals were hired, tents sewn, and saddles and packs arranged. Large caravans involved 600 to 1,000 camels and up to 400 men; smaller parties required no more than a dozen animals. A good leader was essential. Only someone who knew the difficult desert routes and enjoyed the confidence of nomadic Bedouin tribes (which provided safe passage for a fee) could hope to make the journey profitable.

Overland Caravans and Caravanserais. Muslim governments and merchants' associations constructed inns, or caravanserais, along the major trading routes. These areas were capable of accommodating a large number of traders and their animals in great comfort. This illustration of a caravanserai comes from the 1581 travel journal of Venetian envoy Jacopo Soranzo.

Ottoman authorities took a keen interest in this trade, since it generated considerable tax revenue. To facilitate the caravans' movement, the government maintained refreshment and military stations along the route. But gathering so many traders, animals, and cargoes could also attract marauders, especially desert tribesmen. To prevent raids, authorities and merchants offered cash payments to tribal chieftains as "protection money"—a small price to pay to protect the caravan trade, whose revenues ultimately supported imperial expansion.

Prosperity in Ming China

China's economic dynamism was the crucial ingredient in Afro-Eurasia's global economic revival following the devastation wrought by the Black Death. External trade revived and then expanded in the sixteenth century. But China's vast internal economy was also a mainspring of the country's economic expansion. Reconstruction of the Grand Canal opened a major artery that allowed food and riches from the economically vibrant Lower Yangzi area to reach the capital region of Beijing. Cities were hubs of economic activity, but periodic markets also proliferated in many rural areas, as commercialization gathered pace and increasingly shaped the everyday life of the inhabitants of Ming China. Urban manufacturing surged, but even more important was the spread of rural handicraft industries, in which the majority of spinners and weavers were women.

Along China's elaborate trading networks flowed silk and cotton textiles, rice, porcelain ceramics, paper, and many other products. The Ming's initial concern about the potentially disruptive effects of trade did not dampen this activity, and efforts to curb overseas commerce (following Zheng He's voyages; see Chapter 11) were largely unsuccessful. Indeed, the prohibition of maritime trade was officially repealed in 1567, benefiting coastal regions in particular. (See Map 12.4.)

While Chinese silks and porcelain were esteemed across Afro-Eurasia, what did foreign buyers have to trade with the Chinese? The answer is silver, which became an important stimulant to the Ming economy and essential to the Ming monetary system. Whereas their predecessors had used paper money, Ming consumers and traders mistrusted anything other than silver or gold for commercial dealings. However, China did not produce sufficient silver for its growing needs—a situation that foreigners learned to exploit. Indeed, silver and other precious metals were about the only commodities for which the Chinese would trade their precious manufactures. Through most of the sixteenth century, China's main source of silver was Japan. After the 1570s, however, the Philippines, under the control of the Spanish, became a gateway for New World silver. According to one estimate, one-third of all silver mined in the Americas wound up in Chinese hands. This influx fueled China's phenomenal economic expansion, providing further impetus to its maritime trade.

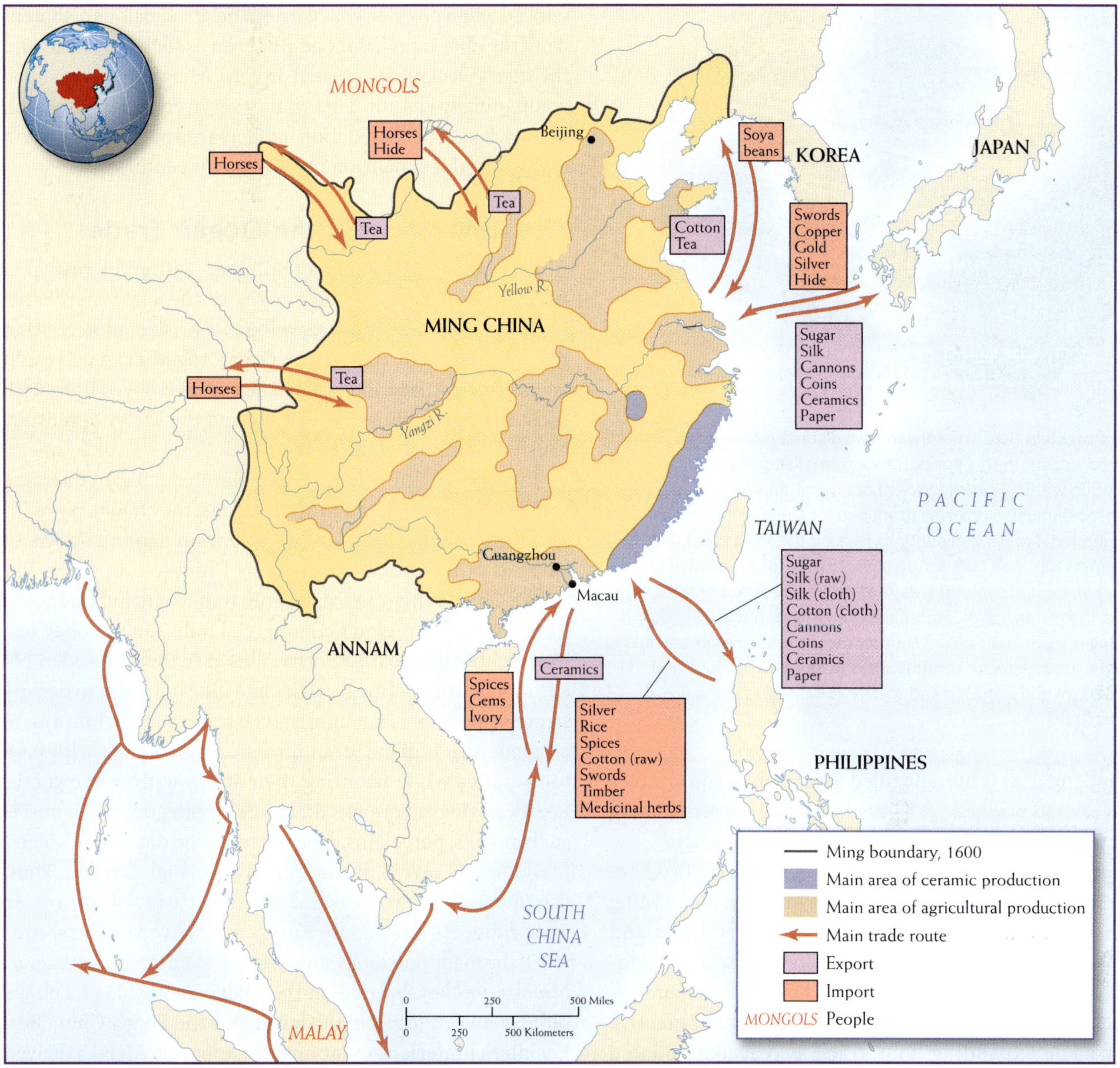

MAP 12.4 | Trade and Production in Ming China, c. 1600

The Ming Empire in the early seventeenth century was the world's most populous state and arguably its wealthiest.

- Referring to the map, identify the main items imported and exported in China's external trade. Then explain where these goods and commodities went, and why they might have been desirable.
- How would you compare China's overland trade with its overseas trade? Can you explain the differences?
- What does this map tell you about the relationship of geography to both agricultural production and porcelain manufacturing?

One measure of greater prosperity under the Ming was its population surge. By the mid-seventeenth century, China's population probably accounted for more than one-third of the total world population. Although 90 percent of Chinese people lived in the countryside, large numbers filled the cities. Beijing, the capital, had perhaps a million inhabitants. Cities offered diversions ranging from literary and theatrical societies to schools of learning, religious societies, urban associations, and manufactures from all over the empire. The elegance and material prosperity of Chinese cities dazzled European visitors. One Jesuit missionary described Nanjing, the secondary capital, as surpassing all other cities "in beauty

Chinese Porcelain Box. There were two distinct markets for Chinese porcelains in this period, one external and one internal, for consumption within China itself. Although it ultimately ended up in a French museum, this box was produced for the vibrant internal Chinese market, for Persian eunuchs serving the Ming court. The inscription on top, in Arabic script, says, "Strive for excellence in penmanship, for it is one of the keys of livelihood"; the inscription on the sides, in Persian, says, "Ignorance is an irremediable evil, [but] knowledge is a priceless elixir." Neither comes from the Quran, but they both express Islamic sentiments in favor of calligraphy and intellectualism glorying God and testify to extensive commercial activity in China.

and grandeur. . . . It is literally filled with palaces and temples and towers and bridges. . . . There is a gaiety of spirit among the people who are well mannered and nicely spoken."

Urban prosperity fostered entertainment districts where people could indulge themselves anonymously. Some Ming women found a place here as refined entertainers and courtesans; others as midwives, poets, sorcerers, and matchmakers. Female painters, mostly from scholar-official families, emulated males who used the home and garden for creative pursuits. The expanding book trade also accommodated women, who were writers as well as readers, not to mention literary characters and archetypes (especially of Confucian virtues). But Chinese women made their greatest fortunes inside the emperor's Forbidden City as healers, consorts, and power brokers.

To be sure, Ming rule faced a variety of problems, from piracy along the coasts to ineptness in the state. Corruption and perceptions of social decay elicited even more criticism. Consider Wang Yangming, a government official and scholar of neo-Confucian thought who urged commitment to social action. Arguing for the unity of knowledge and action, he claimed that one's own thoughts and intuition, rather than observations and external principles (as earlier neo-Confucian thinkers had emphasized), could provide the answers to problems. His more radical followers suggested that women were equal to men intellectually and should receive a full education—a position that earned these radicals banishment from the elite establishment. But even as such new ideas and the state's weaknesses created discord, Ming society remained commercially vibrant. This vitality survived the dynasty's fall in 1644, laying the foundation for increased population growth and territorial expansion in subsequent centuries.

The Revival of Indian Ocean Trade

China's economic expansion occurred within the revival of Indian Ocean trade. In fact, many of the same merchants seeking trade with China developed a brisk commerce that tied the whole of the Indian Ocean together. As a result, ports in East Africa and the Red Sea again enjoyed links with coastal cities of India, South Asia, and the Malay Peninsula. Muslims dominated this trade.

In dealing with China, Indian merchants faced the same problem as Europeans and West Asians: they had to pay with silver. So they became as dependent on gaining access to silver as others who were courting Chinese commerce. But unlike Chinese merchants, Islamic traders, including Indian Muslims, in the region's commercial hubs did not obey one overarching political authority. This gave them considerable autonomy from political affairs and allowed them to occupy strategic positions in long-distance trade. Meanwhile, rulers all along the Indian Ocean enriched themselves with customs duties while flaunting their status with exotic goods. For glorifying sovereigns and worshipping deities, luxuries such as silks, porcelains, ivory, gold, silver, diamonds, spices, frankincense, myrrh, and incense were in high demand. Thus, the Indian Ocean trade connected a vast array of consumers and producers long before Europeans arrived on the scene.

Of the many port cities supporting Indian Ocean commerce, Melaka was key, located on the Malay Peninsula at a choke point between the Indian Ocean and the South China Sea. Lacking a hinterland of farmers to support it, Melaka thrived as an entrepôt for world traders, thousands of whom resided in the city or passed through it. Indeed, Melaka's merchants were a microcosm of the region's diverse commercial community. Arabs, Indians, Armenians, Jews, East Africans, Persians, and eventually western Europeans established themselves there to profit from the commerce that flowed in and out of the port.

India was the geographical and economic hub of the trade routes connected by port cities. With a population expanding as rapidly as China's, it had large cities (such as Agra, Delhi, and Lahore) that each boasted nearly half a million residents. India's manufacturing center, Bengal, exported silk and cotton textiles and rice throughout South and Southeast Asia. Like China, India had a favorable trade balance with Europe and West Asia (it was exporting more than it was importing), exporting textiles and pepper (a spice that Europeans prized) in exchange for silver.

Mughal India and Commerce

The **Mughal Empire** ruled over the hub of the Indian Ocean trade in India. It became one of the world's wealthiest empires just when Europeans were establishing sustained connections with India. These connections, however, touched only the outer layer of Mughal India, one of Islam's greatest regimes. Established in 1526, it was a vigorous, centralized state whose political authority encompassed most of modern-day India. During the sixteenth century, it had a population of between 100 and 150 million.

The Mughals' strength rested on their military power (see Chapter 11). The dynasty's founder, Babur, had introduced horsemanship, artillery, and field cannons from central Asia, and gunpowder had secured his swift military victories over northern India. Under his grandson, Akbar (r. 1556–1605), the empire enjoyed expansion and consolidation. His heirs, notably his grandson, Aurangzeb, continued the trend until the empire covered almost all of India. (See Map 12.5.) Known as the "Great Mughal," Akbar was skilled not only in military tactics but also in the art of alliance making. Deals with Hindu chieftains through favors and intermarriage also undergirded his empire.

The Mughals derived their imperial power not only from military strength but also from their flexible attitude toward the realm's diverse peoples, especially in spiritual affairs. Akbar was a Muslim, but his regime did not rely on an Islamic sectarian ideology for its legitimation. He projected a new image of the emperor that stressed his earthly political and military prowess as much as his role as a guide in divine affairs. He was a philosopher-king. In keeping with this image, the imperial court welcomed advocates of different religions. Brahman, Jain, Zoroastrian, and Muslim scholars, along with Jesuit priests, who traveled from the new Portuguese settlements, gathered in his court for learned discussions. Akbar and his successor, Jahangir, believed that the universal truths of religion existed across traditions. Accordingly, their use of Islam and its symbols in imperial culture and architecture was never exclusionary; they coexisted with the subcontinent's diverse cultural and religious heritage. This tolerant imperial policy stood in stark contrast to the sharp religious conflict in contemporary Europe. But underlying the Mughals' pluralistic attitude was the history of Islam in India. It did not expand and spread as a religion of conquest. Rather, conversions occurred and an Indian Islam took shape gradually over centuries as the people of the subcontinent engaged creatively with the rulers' religion, interpreting it according to their own cultural traditions. In this sense, the erudite discussions on comparative religion in the Mughal court recognized the ground-level reality of India's plural religious and cultural context. This earned it widespread legitimacy.

Akbar's court thrived thanks to the commercial prosperity in the Indian Ocean. Although the Mughals possessed no ocean navy, merchants from Mughal lands used overland routes and rivers to exchange Indian cottons, tobacco, saffron, betel leaf, sugar, and indigo for Iranian melons, dried fruits, nuts, silks, carpets, and precious metals or for Russian pelts, leathers, walrus tusks, saddles, and chain mail armor. Based in the interior, they franchised trading to powerful coastal merchants who reciprocated with tax payments and favors. Every year, Akbar ordered 1,000 new suits stitched of the most exquisite material. His harem preened in fine silks dripping with gold, brocades, and pearls. Carpets, mirrors, and precious metals adorned nobles' households and camps, while perfume and wine flowed freely. Soldiers, servants, and even horses and elephants sported elaborate attire.

During the sixteenth century, expanded trade with Europe brought more wealth to the Mughal polity, while the empire's strength limited European incursions. Although the Portuguese occupied Goa and Bombay on the Indian coast, they had little presence elsewhere and dared not antagonize the Mughal emperor. In 1578, Akbar recognized the credentials of a Portuguese ambassador and allowed a Jesuit missionary to enter his court. Thereafter, commercial ties between Mughals and Portuguese intensified, but merchants were still restricted to a handful of ports. In the 1580s and 1590s, the Mughals ended the Portuguese monopoly on trade with Europe by allowing Dutch and English merchantmen to dock in Indian ports.

Akbar used the commercial boom to overhaul his revenue system. Until the 1560s, the Mughal state relied on a network of decentralized tribute collectors called *zamindars*. These collectors possessed rights to claim a share of the harvest while earmarking part of their earnings for the emperor. But the Mughals did not always receive their agreed share and the peasants resented the high levies, so local populations resisted. As flourishing trade bolstered the money supply, Akbar's officials monetized the tax assessment system and curbed the *zamindars*' power. After other centralizing reforms, increased imperial revenues helped finance military expeditions and the extravagant beautification of Akbar's court.

Centered in northern India, the Mughal Empire used surrounding regions' wealth and resources—military, architectural, and artistic—to glorify the court. Over time, the enhanced wealth caused friction among Indian regions and even between merchants and rulers. Yet as long as merchants relied on rulers for their commercial gains, and as long as rulers balanced local and imperial interests, the realm remained unified and kept Europeans on the outskirts of society.

Asian Relations with Europe

As actors in the world of Asian commerce, Europeans were the newest, and weakest, kids on the block. Europeans' overseas expansion had originally looked toward Asia in hopes of acquiring greater access to luxury goods such

MAP 12.5 | Expansion of the Mughal Empire, 1556–1707

Under Akbar and Aurangzeb, the Mughal Empire expanded and dominated much of South Asia. Look at the trading ports along the subcontinent's coast and consider the growing influence of Portuguese, Dutch, French, and English interests.

- Look at the dates for each port, and identify which traders came first and which came last.
- Compare this map with Map 12.1 (showing a period that begins earlier, 1420–1580). To what extent do the trading posts shown here reflect increased European influence in the region?
- Based on the location of the ports, which commodities do you think European traders most desired?
- Describe the growth of the Mughal Empire and the challenges it faced.

Manila Galleon. For centuries after 1571, there was continual direct trade between the New World and China. The most famous example was the regular "Manila Galleon" that carried precious metals and enslaved human beings from Mexico to the Philippines. From there, the silver was transported to China in return for silks, porcelain, and other fine goods to be shipped back to Mexico, creating a vibrant transpacific trading system.

as silk and spices. It took some time for them to acquire access to these markets. But silver, followed by maritime and military advances and state-backed trading companies, offered Europeans the opportunity to gradually insert themselves into the Eurasian luxury trade. They did not conquer it; before the advent of the industrial revolution, Europeans grafted onto Asian commercial networks and their powerful actors.

The Portuguese blazed the way as collectors of customs duties from Asian traders and, after 1557, as transshippers of Chinese porcelain and silks from the coastal enclave of Macau. (See again Map 12.4.) The Portuguese also dominated the silver trade from Japan. Envying Portuguese profits, the Spanish, English, and Dutch also ventured into Asian waters.

The real breakthrough came when the American silver supply got hitched directly to Asian silver demand—and Europeans could play the intermediaries. With its monopoly on American silver, Spain enjoyed a competitive advantage. In 1565, the first Spanish trading galleon reached the mouth of the Pasig River on one of the islands in the current-day Philippines. Ruled by Rajah Ladyang Matanda, the town of Maynila, later changed to Manila, was a vibrant marketplace in 1570. Merchants from China and Borneo did a swift business there, trading in gold, beeswax, porcelains, and forest products. Maynila was a strategic spot on the sea routes that connected China, Japan, and the Spice Islands—the exclusive source of prized nutmeg and cloves. The Spanish eyed the town not from Europe, but from the other side of the Pacific, in Mexico. Officials and adventurers mortgaged their fortunes in Mexico to fund an expedition to Maynila, taking control of the chieftainship after a series of skirmishes. Thus, in 1571, was born Manila, an administrative dependency of distant Mexico and eventually the capital of the Philippines, the Spanish colony named after the king, Philip II.

Taking Manila opened up a portal to China. Each year, ships from Peru and Mexico crossed the Pacific to Manila bearing cargoes of silver. They returned with a ballast of porcelain and silks. Merchants in Manila also procured silks, tapestries, and feathers from the China seas for shipment to the Americas, where the mining elite eagerly awaited these imports. Cultural sharing and influences were not limited to just trade. Mexican theater groups represented the work of the great writer Sor Juana Inés de la Cruz on a Manila stage. Africans and Filipinos joined the same religious brotherhoods in Mexico

Porcelain Bowl. This Dutch still-life painting features an imported Chinese porcelain bowl, demonstrating Europeans' appreciation for East Asian craftsmanship as well as their dependence on long-distance trade for the acquisition of such coveted luxury goods.

and Manila. Filipino migrants taught Native Mexicans how to produce wine from palm trees. Even Chinese migrants and traders joined the flow from Manila to Mexico. In 1635, Spanish barbers in the Viceroyalty complained that a glut of cheap Chinese hair and beard trimmers was driving them out of business. Not only did the Chinese barbers' stalls around the Plaza Mayor offer discounts, but they also provided acupuncture, bloodletting, and coveted Chinese herbal medicines. Missions as far away as California boasted lavish silk vestments brought back on the galleons from Manila. Spain's conquests of Manila and Mexico created a booming Pacific world system.

The year 1571 was decisive in the history of the modern world. In that year Spain inaugurated a trade circuit that made good on Magellan's earlier achievement of circumnavigating the globe. As Spanish ships circled the globe from the New World to China and from China back to Europe, the world became commercially interconnected. Silver solidified the linkage, as it was the only foreign commodity for which the Chinese had an insatiable demand. From the mother lodes of the Andes and Mesoamerica, silver made the commerce of the world go round. Between 1500 and 1800, the Spanish colonies pumped out 150,000 tons of silver, dwarfing all other supplies combined; much of it sailed east, directly to Asia to monetize and fuel its commercial boom. The silver also coursed through European trading systems and financiers' accounts. Financiers lent money to the Spanish crown to wage the religious wars in Europe; the Catholic monarchs paid their creditors with silver from the colonies. Europe's economy also grew—despite the political and religious mayhem. Though the Dutch were caught in an endless war with Spanish and Portuguese forces, business was lucrative

Macau. This color engraving depicts the Portuguese enclave of Macau, on the southern border of China, in 1598.

enough that blue and white Chinese porcelain became commonplace on dinner tables in Amsterdam. Soon, there were imitation items made in Europe, items later called "chinoiserie." Whether imported or imitation, Chinese styles became all the rage among prosperous European urbanites. Well-to-do aristocratic women had to be seen in the finest—and latest—of Chinese silks.

By creating an interconnected trading system and finding the means for Europeans to trade with Asian suppliers of precious commodities, the Spanish and the Portuguese created the first world market. It was increasingly integrated. But it also set off a scramble and ramped up competition from envious latecomers. Bristling with their Protestant faiths and determined to muscle in on the Iberian empires' terrain and traffic, the English and the Dutch reached the South China Sea late in the sixteenth century. Captain James Lancaster made the first English voyage to the East Indies between 1591 and 1594. Five years later, 101 English subscribers pooled their funds and formed a joint-stock company (an association in which each member owns shares of capital). This English East India Company soon won a royal charter granting it exclusive rights to import East Indian goods. Soon the company displaced the Portuguese in the Arabian Sea and the Persian Gulf. Doing a brisk trade in indigo, saltpeter, pepper, and cotton textiles, the English East India Company eventually acquired control of ports on both coasts of India—Fort St. George (Madras; 1639), Bombay (1661), and Calcutta (1690).

Though they fought among themselves for toeholds and trade, Europeans trading in Asia remained dependent on local power brokers and commercial traders. The number of European settlers was minuscule, their cultural inroads few. Trade in Asia continued, largely in Asian hands, and focused on older routes. Although Europeans came to control some small coastal enclaves, they did not have large colonial lands to rule. This did not mean that Spaniards did not dream of extending their string of conquests to Asia. Taking Manila was—for some dreamers—the first step in the advance from Mexico on to China. The governor of the Philippines, Francisco de Sande, mustered an army in Mexico, backed by religious and secular authorities there, with a plan to invade China. Subordinating China would, in this fantasy, open the back door to Asia and lead to a wave of conversions and commerce that would eventually encircle Islam. It was the ultimate plan to wage the final crusade. But like so many grand schemes, this plan was beset by internal squabbling. Worse, when Sande returned to Manila with his Mexican force, he found his capital charred and plundered by Chinese and Japanese pirates; they too saw the riches from Mexico as booty and were only too pleased to help themselves while authorities concocted wild schemes of global encirclement. In Asia, Europeans were, for all intents and purposes, consigned to the role of intermediaries or predators. This contrasted with the Atlantic world, where Europeans created trading and colonizing systems that placed them increasingly at the center—and buoyed their fledgling empires.

Conclusion

Even as Europeans connected the world's parts, it remained a multicentered world. Europe was a poor cousin, embroiled in religious warfare. It was the Ottoman Empire that was on the rise. The Ottomans, like the Ming in China and the Mughals in India, built wealthy, multiethnic empires and thriving trade networks. But Ottoman inroads in the Mediterranean spurred European merchants and mariners to seek alternative routes to Asia. Breaking into the Indian Ocean trade, the Portuguese had some success; Spanish silver gave more Europeans access to these rich markets. But Asian empires did not lose their autonomy. On the contrary, they absorbed Europeans—and their silver—into their own networks.

But the incorporation into Afro-Eurasian history of a "New World" after Columbus's voyages was an event of monumental significance. In the Americas, Europeans found riches. Mountains of silver and rivers of gold helped them break into Asian markets. Europeans also found opportunities for conquest and colonization, which in turn transformed their own realm as rivals fought over the spoils.

Thus, two conquests characterize this age of increasing world interconnections. Ottoman expansionism drove Europeans to find new links to Asia, demonstrating Islam's pivotal role in shaping modern world history. In turn, the Spanish conquest of the Aztecs and the Incas gave Europeans access to silver, which bought them an increased presence in Asian trading networks. Yet this remained a world whose regions were not yet fully entangled, with many of its peoples still living in ecosystems little touched by these global developments.

Indigenous people also played an important role, as Europeans sought to conquer their lands, exploit their labor, and confiscate their gold and silver. Sometimes local people worked with Europeans, sometimes under Europeans, sometimes against Europeans—and sometimes none were left to work at all. Then Europeans brought in African laborers, compounding the calamity of the encounter with the tragedy of slavery. Out of the catastrophe of contact, a new oceanic system arose to link Africa, America, and Europe. This was the Atlantic system. Unlike the tributary and trading orders of the Indian Ocean and China seas, the system of formal imperial control and long-distance colonization supported in the Atlantic Ocean profoundly transformed economies, agricultural practices, and environments across the globe. These catastrophes and exchanges would be foundational for the ways in which worlds connected and collided in the following centuries.

After You Read This Chapter

TRACING THE GLOBAL STORYLINES

FOCUS ON: The Age of Global Exploration and Colonization

Europe

- Portugal creates a trading empire in the Indian Ocean and the South China Sea.
- Spain and Portugal establish colonies in the Americas, discover silver, and establish export-oriented plantation economies.
- The Protestant Reformation breaks out in northern and western Europe, splitting the Catholic Church.

The Americas

- Millions of Indigenous people, lacking immunity to European diseases, perish across the Americas.
- Spanish conquest and disease destroy the two greatest Indigenous empires in Mexico (the Aztecs) and Peru (the Incas).

Africa

- Trade in African captives fuels the Atlantic slave trade, which furnishes labor for European plantations in the Americas.

Asia

- Asian empires—the Mughals in India, the Ming in China, the Safavids in Iran, and the Ottomans in western Asia and the eastern Mediterranean—barely notice the Americas but profit economically from enhanced global trade.

CHRONOLOGY

Europe

- Luther begins Protestant Reformation 1517
- Religious and dynastic wars (1520 onward)

The Americas

- Columbus discovers the "New World" 1492
- Cortés conquers Aztec Empire 1521
- Pizarro conquers Inca Empire 1533

South Asia

- Da Gama sails to India 1498
- Portuguese establish bases around Indian Ocean 1508–1511

East Asia

1500 | 1510 | 1520 | 1530 | 1540

KEY TERMS

Atlantic system p. 519
Aztec Empire p. 510
biomes p. 500
Calvin, Jean p. 521
Columbian exchange p. 513
conquistadors p. 509
Counter-Reformation p. 522
encomenderos p. 509
Holy Roman Empire p. 521
Inca Empire p. 512
Jesuits p. 522
Luther, Martin p. 521
Mughal Empire p. 529
Protestant Reformation p. 520

THINKING ABOUT GLOBAL CONNECTIONS

Thinking about Exchange Networks and the Age of Exploration In the fifteenth and sixteenth centuries, the densest trade networks and most powerful states remained centered in Asia. How did Columbus's "discovery" of the New World alter the terms on which peoples across Afro-Eurasia interacted with one another? What commodities and trade networks brought peoples together, and on what terms? What new inequalities did those contacts create around the world?

Thinking about Changing Power Relationships and the Age of Exploration The effort to expand empires and trading networks differed substantially across Afro-Eurasia and the Americas in the fifteenth and sixteenth centuries. How did men and women at all levels of society contribute to this expansion? How did that participation shape or reshape their societies? Pay particular attention to the relationship between lower classes and elites.

Thinking about Environmental Impacts and the Age of Exploration The Columbian exchange led to demographic catastrophe and environmental transformation in the New World. Why did the Indigenous populations of the Americas get sick so much more often than Europeans did? Why did the plants and animals of the New World increasingly come to resemble those of Afro-Eurasia?

1520s–1570s

Expansion and consolidation of Mughal Empire
1556–1605

Portuguese establish trading port in Macau
1557

Spanish make Manila their major port in the Pacific Ocean
1571

1550 | 1560 | 1570 | 1580 | 1590 | 1600

Global Themes and Sources

Cultural Contexts in the Age of Exploration

Overseas exploration and commerce brought new contacts between Indigenous peoples, Europeans, Africans, and Asians in the fifteenth and sixteenth centuries. The primary sources brought together here document important examples of cultural contact in this era and allow us to see how people from radically different cultures perceived one another. They also provide clues about conflict within each of the communities.

The first two documents present opposing views of the initial confrontation between the Spaniards, led by Hernán Cortés (1485–1547), and the Mexica. The third document, a selection from *The History and Description of Africa* by Leo Africanus (al-Ḥasan ibn Muḥammad al-Wazzān al-Zayyātī or al-Fāsī, born c. 1485, died c. 1554), recounts the author's travels in Egypt, Morocco, and Mali, especially Timbuktu (Tombuto), a great center of Islamic learning. The final document, from a Ming official named He Ao, complains that Europeans were untrustworthy. Such sentiments were also common among officials in subsequent centuries, even as China thrived in the commercial exchanges of an increasingly connected world.

Making sense of these sources requires careful attention to context. It's important to note how the prior experiences of the different communities shaped their responses to alien cultures, and how prior exposure to outsiders influenced the ways communities marked the boundaries between "us" and "them." You should pay just as much attention to divisions within each cultural group as to those between the groups.

ANALYZING CONTEXTS: THE AGE OF EXPLORATION

How did prior experiences of different cultures shape the encounters in these sources?

All of these documents were produced by elite men. How do you think the authors' gender and status influenced their portrayal of events? How did the authors' gender and status shape their attribution of responsibility for the problems they identified within their societies?

Compare Cortés's description of Tenochtitlán in his letter to Charles V with Leo Africanus's description of Timbuktu.

PRIMARY SOURCE 12.1

Mexica Views of the Spaniards (c. sixteenth century), Florentine Codex

The Florentine Codex compiled accounts of the Spanish conquest from Mexica elites a generation after the fall of Tenochtitlán. The passages about Moctezuma's response to the Spaniards are drawn largely from interviews with elites from Tenochtitlán's junior partner, the city-state of Tlatelolco, in the aftermath of the Mexica defeat.

What about the Spaniards most struck the authors of the Florentine Codex? Identify the factors—appearance, animals, behavior, beliefs—they used to mark the Spaniards as different.

Explain why the Mexica elite (of the 1550s–1560s) might have portrayed Moctezuma as afraid. Pay special attention to local politics before the Spaniards arrived.

Evaluate the claim that Moctezuma believed the Spaniards to be gods. Is it plausible?

During this time Montezuma neither slept nor touched food. Whatever he did, he was abstracted; it seemed as though he was ill at ease, frequently sighing. He tired and felt weak. He no longer found anything tasteful, enjoyable, or amusing.

Therefore he said, "What is to come of us? Who in the world must endure it? Will it not be me [as ruler]? My heart is tormented, as though chile water were poured on it; it greatly burns and smarts. Where in the world [are we to turn], o our lord?"

Then [the messengers] notified those who guarded [Montezuma], who kept watch at the head of his bed, saying to them, "Even if he is asleep, tell him. 'Those whom you sent out on the sea have come back.'"

But when they went to tell him, he replied, "I will not hear it here. I will hear it at the Coacalco; let them go there." And he gave orders, saying, "Let some captives be covered with chalk [for sacrifice]."

Then the messengers went to the Coacalco, and so did Montezuma. Thereupon the captives died in their presence; they cut open their chests and sprinkled blood on the messengers. (The reason they did it was that they had gone to very dangerous places and had seen, gazed on the countenances of, and spoken to the gods.)

Seventh chapter, where is told the account that the messengers who went to see the boat gave to Montezuma.

When this was done, they talked to Montezuma, telling him what they had beheld, and they showed him what [the Spaniards'] food was like.

And when he heard what the messengers reported he was greatly afraid and taken aback, and he was amazed at their food. It especially made him faint when he heard how the guns went off at [the Spaniards'] command, sounding like thunder, causing people actually to swoon, blocking the ears. And when it went off, something like a ball came out from inside, and fire went showering and spitting out. And the smoke that came from it had a very foul stench, striking one in the face. And if they shot at a hill, it seemed to crumble and come apart. And it turned a tree to dust; it seemed to make it vanish, as though someone had conjured it away. Their war gear was all iron. They clothed their bodies in iron, they put iron on their heads, their swords were iron, their bows were iron, and their shields and lances were iron.

And their deer that carried them were as tall as the roof. And they wrapped their bodies all over; only their faces could be seen, very white. Their faces were the color of limestone and their hair yellow-reddish, though some had black hair. They had long beards, also yellow-reddish. [The hair of some] was tightly curled. And their food was like fasting food, very large, white, not heavy, like chaff, like dried maize stalks, as tasty as maize stalk flour, a bit sweet or honeyed, honeyed and sweet to eat.

And their dogs were huge creatures, with their ears folded over and their jowls dragging. They had burning eyes, eyes like coals, yellow and fiery. They had thin, gaunt flanks with the rib lines showing; they were very tall. They did not keep quiet, they went about panting, with their tongues hanging down. They had spots like a jaguar's, they were vari-colored.

When Montezuma heard it, he was greatly afraid; he seemed to faint away, he grew concerned and disturbed.

Eighth chapter, where it is said how Montezuma sent witches, wizards, and sorcerers to do something to the Spaniards.

Then at that time Montezuma sent out emissaries. Those whom he sent were all bad people, soothsayers and witches. He also sent elders, strong warriors, to see to all [the Spaniards] needed as to food: turkey hens, eggs, white tortillas, and whatever they might request, and to look after them well so that they would be satisfied in every way. He sent captives in case [the Spaniards] should drink their blood. And the emissaries did as indicated.

Montezuma did this because he took them for gods, considered them gods, worshiped them as gods. They were called and given the name of gods who have come from heaven, and the blacks were called soiled gods.

They say that Montezuma sent the witches, the rainmakers, to see what [the Spaniards] were like and perhaps be able to enchant them, cast spells on them, to use conjury or the evil eye on them or hurl something else at them, perhaps addressing some words of wizardry to them so that they would take sick, die, or turn back. But when they performed the assignment they had been given concerning the Spaniards, they could do nothing; they had no power at all. Then they quickly returned to tell Montezuma what they were like, how strong they were, [saying,] "We are not their match; we are as nothing."

Source: The Florentine Codex, translated by James Lockhart, in *We People Here: Nahuatl Accounts of the Conquest of Mexico* (University of California Press, 1993), pp. 56–86.

PRIMARY SOURCE 12.2

Approaching Tenochtitlán (1520), Hernán Cortés

Written in the midst of the Spanish invasion of Mexico, Cortés's Second Letter was addressed to Emperor Charles V of Spain. In it, Cortés provides an account of his meeting with Moctezuma. He also describes the capital city of Tenochtitlán and its houses of worship.

- Explain how Tenochtitlán compares to Spanish cities, in Cortés's view.
- Why does Cortés mention mosques in Tenochtitlán when there were no Muslims there?
- Analyze the relationship between respect and contempt in this source. What does Cortés admire about the Mexica, and what does he dismiss?

This great city of Tenochtitlan is built on the salt lake, and from the mainland to the city is a distance of two leagues, from any side from which you enter. It has four approaches by means of artificial causeways, two cavalry lances in width. The city is as large as Seville or Cordoba. Its streets (I speak of the principal ones) are very broad and straight, some of these, and all the others, are one half land, and the other half water on which they go about in canoes. All the streets have openings at regular intervals, to let the water flow from one to the other, and at all of these openings, some of which are very broad, there are bridges, very large, strong, and well constructed, so that, over many, ten horsemen can ride abreast. Perceiving that, if the inhabitants wished to practise any treachery against us, they had plenty of opportunity, because the said city being built as I have described, they might, by raising the bridges at the exits and entrances, starve us without our being able to reach land, as soon as I entered the city, I made great haste to build four brigantines, which I had completed in a short time, capable whenever we might wish, of taking three hundred men and the horses to land.

The city has many squares where markets are held and trading is carried on. There is one square, twice as large as that of Salamanca, all surrounded by arcades, where there are daily more than sixty thousand souls, buying and selling, and where are found all the kinds of merchandise produced in these countries, including food products, jewels of gold and silver, lead, brass, copper, zinc, stone, bones, shells, and feathers. Stones are sold, hewn and unhewn, adobe bricks, wood, both in the rough and manufactured in various ways. There is a street for game, where they sell every sort of bird, such as chickens, partridges, quails, wild ducks, fly-catchers, widgeons, turtle-doves, pigeons, reed-birds, parrots, owls, eaglets, owlets, falcons, sparrow-hawks and kestrels, and they sell the skins of some of these birds of prey with their feathers, heads, beaks, and claws. They sell rabbits, hares, and small dogs which they castrate, and raise for the purpose of eating.

***

This great city contains many mosques, or houses for idols, very beautiful edifices situated in the different precincts of it; in the principal ones of The Aztec which are the religious orders of their sect. Priests for whom, besides the houses in which they keep their idols, there are very good habitations provided. All these priests dress in black, and never cut or comb their hair from the time they enter the religious order until they leave it; and the sons of all the principal families, both of chiefs as well as noble citizens, are in these religious orders and habits from the age of seven or eight years till they are taken away for the purpose of marriage. This happens more frequently with the first-born, who inherit the property, than with the others. They have no access to women, nor are any allowed to enter the religious houses; they abstain from eating certain dishes, and more so at certain times of the year than at others.

Amongst these mosques, there is one principal one, and no human tongue is able to describe its greatness and details, because it is so large that within its circuit, which is surrounded by a high wall, a village of five hundred houses could easily be built. Within, and all around it, are very handsome buildings, in which there are large rooms and galleries, where the religious who live there are lodged. There are as many as forty very high and well-built towers, the largest having fifty steps to reach the top; the principal one is higher than the tower of the chief church in Seville. They are so well built, both in their masonry, and their wood work, that they could not be better made nor constructed anywhere; for all the masonry inside the chapels, where they keep their idols, is carved with figures, and the wood work is all wrought with designs of monsters, and other shapes. All these towers are places of burial for the chiefs, and each one of their chapels is dedicated to the idol to which they have a particular devotion. Within this great mosque, there are three halls wherein stand the principal idols of marvelous grandeur in size, and much decorated with carved figures, both of stone and wood; and within these halls there are other chapels, entered by very small doors, and which have no light, and nobody but the religious are admitted to them. Within these are the images and figures of the idols, although, as I have said, there are many outside.

The principal idols in which they have the most faith and belief I overturned from their seats, and rolled down the stairs, and I had those chapels, where they kept them, cleansed, for they were full of blood from the sacrifices; and I set up images of Our Lady, and other Saints in them, which grieved Montezuma, and the natives not a little. At first they told me not to do it, for, if it became known throughout the town, the people would rise against me, as they believed that these idols gave them all their temporal goods, and, in allowing them to be ill-treated, they would be angered, and give nothing, and would take away all the fruits of the soil, and cause the people to die of want. I made them understand by the interpreters how deceived they were in putting their hope in idols, made of unclean things by their own hands, and I told them that they should know there was but one God, the Universal Lord of all, who had created the heavens, and earth, and all things else, and them, and us, who was without beginning, and immortal; that they should adore, and believe in Him, and not in any creature, or thing.

Source: *Letters of Cortes,* translated and edited by Francis Augustus MacNutt (New York: G. P. Putnam's Sons, 1908), vol. 1, pp. 256–57, 259–61.

PRIMARY SOURCE 12.3

Leo Africanus's Travels in Africa (1550)

Published in Italian in 1550, *The History and Description of Africa* was the first European account of the geography of Africa. The author, Leo Africanus, was a Berber, born in Spanish Grenada. His family moved to Morocco when he was a young child, and he later served as a diplomat. (Archaic spelling from the original translation has been preserved.)

- Leo describes the people of Egypt as savages. Explain how he uses the term.
- Explain how Leo divides up the peoples of Africa he encounters. What groups does he describe? How does he distinguish them?
- Does this document reveal more about Europe or Africa?

Wherein he intreateth of the land of Negros, and of the confines of Egypt.

Our ancient Chroniclers of Africa, to wit, *Bichri* and *Meshudi* knew nothing of the land of Negros but onely the regions of Guechet and Cano: for in their time all other places of the land of Negros were vndiscouered. But in the yeere of the Hegeira 380, by the meanes of a certaine Mahumetan which came into Barbarie, the residue of the said land was found out, being as then inhabited by great numbers of people, which liued a brutish and sauage life, without any king, gouernour, common wealth, or knowledge of husbandrie. Clad they were in skins of beasts, neither had they any peculiar wiues: in the day time they kept their cattell; and when night came they resorted ten or twelue both men and women into one cottage together, using hairie skins instead of beds, and each man choosing his leman which he had most fancy vnto. Warre they wage against no other nation, ne yet are desirous to trauell out of their owne countrie. Some of them performe great adoration vnto the sunne rising: others, namely the people of Gualata, worship the fire: and some others, to wit, the inhabitants of Gaoga, approch (after the Egyptians manner) neerervnto the Christian faith. These Negros were first subject vnto king *Ioseph* the founder of Maroco, and afterward vnto the fiue nations of Libya; of whom they learned the Mahumetan lawe, and diuers needfull handycrafts: a while after when the merchants of Barbarie began to resort vnto them with merchandize, they learned the Barbarian language also. But the foresaid fiue people or nations of Libya diuided this land so among themselues, that euery third part of each nation possessed one region. Howbeit the king of Tombuto that now raigneth, called *Abuacre Izchia*, is a Negro by birth: this *Abuacre* after the decease of the former king, who was a Libyan borne, slue all his sonnes, and so vsurped the kingdome. And hauing by warres for the space of fifteen yeeres conquered many large dominions, he then concluded a league with all nations, and went on pilgrimage to Mecca, in which iournie he so consumed his treasure, that he was constrained to borrow great summes of money of other princes. Moreouer the fifteene kingdomes of Negros knowen to vs, are all situate vpon the riuer of Niger, and vpon other riuers which fall thereinto. And all the land of Negros standeth betweene two vast deserts, for on the one side lieth the maine desert betweene Numidia and it, which extendeth it selfe vnto this very land: and the south side thereof adioineth vpon another desert, which stretcheth from thence to the maine Ocean: in which desert are infinite nations vnknowen to vs, both by reason of the huge distance of place, and also in regarde of the diuersitie of languages and religions. They haue no traffique at all with our people, but we haue heard oftentimes of their traffique with the inhabitants of the Ocean sea shore.

A description of the kingdome of Gualata.

This region in regarde of others is very small: for it containeth onely three great villages, with certaine granges and fields of dates. From Nun it is distant southward about three hundred, from Tombuto northward fiue hundred, and from the Ocean sea about two hundred miles. In this region the people of Libya, while they were lords of the land of Negros, ordained their chiefe princely seate: and then great store of Barbarie-merchants frequented Gualata: but afterward in the raigne of the mighty and rich prince *Heli*, the said merchants leauing Gualata, began to resort vnto Tombuto and Gago, which was the occasion that the region of Gualata grew extreme beggerly. The language of this region is called Sungai, and the inhabitants are blacke people, and most friendly vnto strangers. In my time this region was conquered by the king of Tombuto, and the prince thereof fled into the deserts, whereof the king of Tombuto hauing intelligence, and fearing least the prince would returne with all the people of the deserts, graunted him peace, conditionally that he should pay a great yeerely tribute vnto him, and so the said prince hath remained tributarie to the king of Tombuto vntill this present. The people agree in manners and fashions with the inhabitants of the next desert. Here groweth some quantitie of Mil-seed, and great store of a round & white kind of pulse, the like whereof I neuer saw in Europe; but flesh is extreme scarce among them. Both the men & the women do so couer their heads, that al their countenance is almost hidden. Here is no forme of a common wealth, nor yet any gouernours or iudges, but the people lead a most miserable life.

Source: Leo Africanus, *The History and Description of Africa and of the Notable Things Therein Contained*, edited by Robert Brown (London: Printed for the Hakluyt Society, Lincoln's Inn Fields W.C., 1896), pp. 819–21.

PRIMARY SOURCE 12.4

Commentary on Foreigners (c. 1420), Ming Official He Ao

He Ao was a censor, a high official in the provincial bureaucracy of the Ming Empire. The censorate was part of the central state. Responsible directly to the emperor, it was tasked with rooting out corruption at the local level. This document, in which He describes the threats posed by Europeans (called Feringis), is an official government report to his superiors.

- Identify the factors He used to mark foreigners as different, and evaluate their relative significance. Pay special attention to his language and the terms he used.
- What specific threats resulting from European influence does He identify, and what remedies does he propose?
- Explain the distinction this document draws between the way trade was conducted in the past (in the "time of our ancestors") and in the present. What is He's view of commerce?

The Feringis are most cruel and crafty. Their arms are superior to those of other foreigners. Some years ago they came suddenly to the city of Canton, and the noise of their cannon shook the earth [these were cannon-shots fired as a salute by the fleet of Fernão Peres]. Those who remained at the post-station [places where foreigners were lodged] disobeyed the law and had intercourse with others. Those who came to the Capital were proud and struggled [among themselves?] to become head. Now if we allow them to come and go and to carry on their trade, it will inevitably lead to fighting and bloodshed, and the misfortune of our South may be boundless.

In the time of our ancestors, foreigners came to bring tribute only at fixed periods, and the law provided for precautionary measures, therefore the foreigners who could come were not many. But some time ago the Provincial Treasurer, Wu T'ing-chü, saying that he needed spice to be sent to the Court, took some of their goods no matter when they came. It was due to what he did that foreigner ships have never ceased visiting our shores and that barbarians have lived scattered in our departmental cities. Prohibition and precaution having been neglected, the Feringis became more and more familiar with our fair ways. And thus availing themselves of the situation the Feringis came into our port. I pray that all the foreign junks in our bay and the foreigners who secretly live (in our territory) be driven away, that private intercourse be prohibited and that our strategical defence be close, so that that part of our country will have peace.

Source: T'ien-Tse Chang, *Sino-Portuguese Trade from 1514 to 1644: A Synthesis of Portuguese and Chinese Sources* (Leyden: E. J. Brill, 1934), pp. 51–52.

Interpreting Visual Evidence

Conflict and Consent

In the fifteenth and sixteenth centuries, new contacts led to conflict and, in some cases, consent. The consolidation of existing land empires, especially in Asia, required rulers to manage vast, diverse populations. They often used policies of tolerance to win the consent of their new subjects. European overseas empires, by contrast, almost immediately came into conflict with Indigenous societies, decimating the Indigenous population and drafting enslaved Africans to perform labor the remaining Indigenous peoples refused. This resulted in societies in the Americas that initially had extremely pronounced cultural differences.

Depictions of these encounters show the dynamics between the groups involved, as well as the artist's point of view. The first image below, an anonymous Mexican painting (c. 1520), portrays Spanish soldiers in gleaming body armor with muskets firing on Indigenous people, who are barely visible at the painting's edges and armed only with bows and arrows. The second, *The Conquest of the Aztecs*, was drawn by a converted Indigenous person later in the sixteenth century and relied on Indigenous oral histories and familiar artistic forms. It shows the Aztec (Mexica) warriors in full battle dress and also portrays their battles with other Indigenous people who had sided with the Spanish.

Anonymous Mexican painting of the Spanish conquest.

The Conquest of the Aztecs, drawn by a converted Indigenous person.

In the final image, *Akbar Hears a Petition*, the individuals gathered before Akbar represent the diversity of people who sought the assistance of the Mughal emperor. This miniature reflects the multiethnic and multireligious character of Akbar's empire and the tolerance required to maintain social cohesion.

Akbar Hears a Petition.

QUESTIONS FOR ANALYSIS

1. In the first two images, note the divisions within each camp, Spanish and Aztec. Explain how each portrays the Aztec defeat. What do the images present to explain the defeat, and what factors, emphasized in this chapter, do they both omit?
2. Interpret the artist's portrayal of Akbar's authority in the third image. Describe the audience presented in the painting. What can you tell about the different groups present?
3. Contrast the first two images with the third. Pay special attention to the center of each image. Describe which elements the artists emphasize, in visual terms. What does that say about the social order?
4. Explain who you think was the audience for each image. Were all three produced for rulers, their court, the elite in general, a particular ethno-religious or social group, or the general public?

Before You Read This Chapter

GLOBAL STORYLINES

The Emergence of Global Trade

- Transoceanic trade networks create vast wealth, new kinds of inequality, and fundamentally alter the lives of Indigenous peoples.
- A sharp drop in global temperatures produces the Little Ice Age, which leads to warfare, disease, famine, and dying on a scale comparable in some areas to that of the Black Death.
- New World sugar also accelerates the shift of power in the Atlantic world from the Spanish and Portuguese to the British and French.
- Silver begins to tilt the balance of wealth and power from Asia toward Europe.
- European merchants and African leaders radically increase the volume and violence of the slave trade, destabilizing African societies.
- Rulers in India, China, Japan, and Russia enlarge their empires, while Muslim empires struggle.

CHAPTER OUTLINE

FOCUS QUESTIONS

- What were the major steps in the integration of global trade networks in the seventeenth and eighteenth centuries?
- How were Indigenous peoples' lives altered by the increased integration of global trading networks?
- What effects did the Little Ice Age have on different parts of the world?
- How did the Atlantic slave trade change African societies socially and politically?
- What effect did New World silver and increased trade have on Asian empires?
- How was the impact of trade and religion on state power in various regions alike and different?
- What was the significance of European consumption of goods (like tobacco, textiles, and sugar) for the global economy?

13

Worlds Entangled

1600–1750

The leading Ottoman intellectual of the sixteenth century, Mustafa Ali, was a gloomy man. He lived during difficult times and became convinced that the Ottoman Empire had slipped into an irreversible decline. Islam was approaching its 1,000th year (1000 After Hijra, AH, or 1591–1592 in the Julian calendar). Many *ulama* and high-level bureaucrats warned of a pending apocalypse, a day of judgment that would reward the virtuous and condemn the evil. Although Mustafa Ali regarded doomsayers skeptically, he did think that the time was ripe for assessing all of human history. As far as he was concerned, the fate of humanity was at stake in an era of upheaval and crisis, much of it driven by ecological and economic pressures. He began his magnum opus, *The Essence of History*, in the year when many thought that the world would end (1591). The first half of that century had brought triumphs for the sultans. After that, a slump set in. By century's end, the empire was losing territory to its rivals, the Hapsburgs, the Venetians, and the Russians; soldiers had rioted when they were paid in debased silver coinage imported from New

World mines; and agrarian uprisings had ripped across eastern Anatolia. After the glory days, Ottoman rulers, like many others, had to grapple with the longer-term consequences of fusing two biomes, the New World and Afro-Eurasia, and a wave of environmental shocks to their agrarian systems. Entangling these worlds brought bounty and opportunity, but also competition and disruption. How different parts of the world responded to the upheavals of "the long seventeenth century" (the period running from the 1590s to the early 1700s) would have deep, long-term consequences. It was these transformations that Mustafa Ali was struggling to explain.

As we become more aware of how decisive climate change has been on human evolution, we have learned how it stamped the global seventeenth century. Many of the problems of this period stemmed from a severe cold and arid spell that swept the entire world. Now known as the Little Ice Age, the era saw a plunge in global temperatures lasting from 1620 to 1680 (and in some regions dragged into the next centuries). The decline in precipitation, increase in early frosts, and shortened growing seasons laid waste to agricultural and pastoral lands. Hunger, famine, and misery went global.

The result was a double-edged crisis. Just as world empires ramped up their competition and warfare after the conquest of the Americas and the resurgence of Asian empires, they squeezed their peasants for resources to pay for the fighting. At the same time, global cooling meant that peasants produced less food and surpluses and could ill afford the exactions of their rulers. Across much of Afro-Eurasia, the result was mass suffering and a wave of peasant unrest and political upheaval.

Mustafa Ali captured the sentiments of this age well: "Prosperity had turned to famine, the government careers had become confused, venality was rampant, and the military class was being overrun by *re'aya* [tax-paying subjects]." Even more apocalyptic were his poems. Here his view was that "in the social sphere the world is upside down; the *ulama* are no longer learned or pious; the pillars of the state are fiends and lions; the truly learned are disdained and dismissed and government service now brings pain and poverty rather than pride and wealth. The plague destroying the world is moral as well as physical, for bribery and corruption are the order of the day."

What a paradox! In spite of the turmoil, the period 1600–1750 saw the world's oceans give way to booming sea-lanes for global trading networks. Sugar flowed from Brazil and the Caribbean, spices from Southeast Asia, cotton textiles from India, silks from China, and silver from Mesoamerica and the Andes. New World silver was crucial to these networks: it gave Europeans a commodity to exchange with Asians, and it tilted the balance of wealth and power in a westerly direction across Afro-Eurasia.

Imperial expansion and transoceanic trade, like climate change, spread across the entire globe. Europeans conquered and colonized more of the Americas, the demand for enslaved Africans to work New World plantations leaped upward, and global trade intensified. Conquest, colonization, and commerce created riches for some but also provoked bitter rivalries. In the Americas, Spain and Portugal faced new competitors—primarily England and France. With religious tensions added to the mix, the stage was set for decades of bloody warfare in Europe and the Americas. At the same time, rulers in India, China, and Japan enlarged their empires, while Russia's tsars incorporated Siberian territories into their domain. Meanwhile, the Ottoman, Safavid, and Mughal dynasties, though resisting most European intrusions, faced shocks from an increasingly entangled world.

Global Commerce and Climate Change

In spite of the worldwide trauma brought on by the plunge in temperatures, global trade flourished during this period. Sugar and silver, along with enslaved human beings, were considered the primary items, promoted equally by merchant groups and the rulers and commoners of sponsoring nations. Increasing economic ties brought new products into world markets: furs from French North America, sugar from the Caribbean, tobacco from British colonies on the American mainland, coffee from Southeast and Southwest Asia, and enslaved people from West and central Africa. (See Current Trends in World History: Stimulants, Sociability, and Coffeehouses; see also Map 13.1.)

Closer economic contact bolstered some states and destabilized others. It buoyed the legitimacy of England and France, and it prompted strong local support of new rulers in Japan and parts of sub-Saharan Africa. With rising powers and scrambles to get into the commodities business came competition, friction, and warfare. Governments had to squeeze more resources from trade and agriculture, which spurred protest and open rebellions during the Little Ice Age. Civil wars and social unrest swept through much of the world. England, France, and Japan faced mass peasant uprisings. In the Ottoman state, rebellions almost brought the empire to its knees; the Safavid regime foundered and then collapsed; the Ming dynasty imploded and gave way to the Qing. In India, rivalries among princes and merchants eroded the Mughals' authority, compounding the instability caused by peasant uprisings.

Another result of the plunge in temperatures was a flight from marginal agricultural lands into the cities. The world had never experienced such massive urbanization: 2.5 million Japanese lived in cities, roughly 10 percent of the population, and in Holland over 200,000 lived in ten cities close to Amsterdam. But city officials were ill equipped to deal with the influx. Disease swept through overcrowded houses, and fire ravaged whole districts. London had an excess of 228,000 deaths over births, yet continued to grow through in-migration. Hardly an escape from rural poverty, cities had inordinately high mortality rates, what one scholar has called "the graveyard effect" (Parker, *Global Crisis*, p. 58).

Transformations in global relations began in the Atlantic, where the extraction and shipment of gold and silver siphoned wealth from the Americas to Afro-Eurasia. Mined mainly by coerced Indigenous people and delivered into the hands of merchants and monarchs, silver from the Andes and Mesoamerica boosted the world's supply of money and injected liquidity into the global trading networks. Increasing dependence on silver flows posed risks around the world; during the boom years of the sixteenth century, liquidity poured into the world economy and inflated prices. But there could also be sharp contractions, especially after 1620, which deflated prices and led to shortages. Then, a new boom began after 1690: new silver veins opened in Mexico and a gold rush made Brazil the world's largest producer of that gilded ore. For societies that depended on precious metals for money supply, the ups and downs of mining output, resulting in inflation and deflation, created an economic roller coaster.

But overall, rising money supply and new institutions like stock markets and lending houses spurred global commercial activity. American mining exports were so lucrative for Spain and Portugal that other European powers wanted a share of the bounty, so they, too, launched colonizing ventures and conquests. Although these latecomers found few precious minerals, they devised other ways to extract wealth, for the Americas had fertile lands on which to cultivate sugarcane, cotton, tobacco, indigo, and rice. The Americas also had fur-bearing wildlife, whose pelts were prized in Europe.

If silver quickened the pace of global trade, sugar transformed diets. First domesticated in Polynesia, sugar was not central to European diets before American plantations started exporting it. Previously, Europeans had used honey for sweetener, but they soon became insatiable consumers of sugar. Between 1690 and 1790, Europe imported 12 million tons of sugar—approximately 1 ton for every African enslaved in the Americas. Public tooth pulling became a popular entertainment (for spectators!) in cities like Paris, and tooth decay became a leading cause of death for Europeans.

Extracting wealth from colonies gave rise to a new economic model to govern long-distance relations between societies. No matter what products they supplied, colonies were supposed to provide wealth for their "mother countries"—according to exponents of mercantilism, the economic theory that drove European empire builders. Hitherto, conquests aimed to plunder the defeated or to claim tribute. But the economic integration of the Americas—the peoples and lands—gave rise to policies and concepts that aimed to keep wealth flowing from one society to another in large sums year after year, generation after generation. **Mercantilism** saw the world's wealth as fixed: any one country's wealth came at the expense of other countries. The theory further assumed that overseas possessions existed solely to enrich European motherlands because it measured imperial power according to the hoard of treasure in the crown's coffers. To bulk up the treasury, motherlands were supposed to export more goods than they imported and thereby sustain trade surpluses. Lucrative colonies were like magnets for competitors who wanted in on the action. Empires were therefore in a constant struggle to shut out rivals and interlopers, lest foreign traders drain precious resources from an empire's exclusive domain. The result was a vicious cycle: extraction allowed European states to grow rich while the feud to protect extraction rackets generated unceasing wars between rivals. Ultimately, mercantilists believed, as did the English philosopher Thomas Hobbes (1588–1679), that "wealth is power and power is wealth."

The mercantilist system required an alliance between the state and its merchants. Mercantilists understood economics and politics as interdependent, with the merchant needing the monarch to protect his interests and the monarch relying on the merchant's trade to enrich the state's treasury. **Chartered companies**, such as the Virginia Company (English) and the East India Companies (Dutch and English), were visible examples of the collaboration between the state and the merchant classes. European monarchs awarded these firms monopoly trading rights over vast areas. These policies and institutions of mercantilism augmented the competition among European empires for markets, colonies, and spoils, and this escalated the penetration into colonial interiors and wars between empires. As competition and extraction intensified, this cycle coincided with a global environmental shock. The combination of global war and global climate change was explosive.

The Little Ice Age

While commerce laced the world together, the global climate entered what is known as the **Little Ice Age**, which shocked the planet's survival systems with plunging temperatures and drought. It also happened to coincide with a downturn in New World mining output. The combination

Current Trends in World History

Stimulants, Sociability, and Coffeehouses

While armies, travelers, and missionaries were breaching the world's main political and cultural barriers, it was commodities that had unsung effects on everyday lives. The rise of world commodities transformed production and consumption. Ruling elites struggled to control and to curtail the desire of their populations to dress themselves in fine garments, to possess jewelry, and to consume satisfying food and drink no matter where these products came from. The history of commodities is a central concern for world historical research: to make products for other peoples' consumption meant crossing cultural barriers and connecting peoples over long distances. As the world's trading networks thrived in the seventeenth and eighteenth centuries, merchants in Europe, Asia, Africa, and the Americas served as the brokers of new commodity exchange—at a scale that would have made the Silk Road traders green with envy. By far the most popular commodities were a group of stimulants: coffee, cocoa, sugar, tobacco, and tea. These were not just stimulating—they were addicting. And they were not just addicting—they reinforced the demand for each other. People added sugar to ease the bitterness of coffee and consumed tea while puffing on tobacco; these items functioned like a narcotic cocktail. Previously, many of these products had been grown in isolated parts of the world: the coffee bean in Yemen, tobacco and cocoa in the New World, and sugar in Bengal. Yet, by the seventeenth century, in nearly every corner of the world, the well-to-do began to congregate in coffeehouses, consuming these new products and engaging in sociable activities. While new consumption habits laced the world together, globalized commodity frontiers expanded commercial production across the tropics.

Coffee. Coffee drinkers at an Ottoman banquet (*left*) and in an English coffeehouse (*right*).

was toxic. In some places, the effect of falling temperatures, shorter growing seasons, and irregular precipitation patterns was felt as early as the fourteenth century. But the impact of the Little Ice Age reached farther and deeper in the seventeenth century. What caused this climate change is a matter of debate. Unlike climate change today, it was not caused by human energy needs. Some experts claim that a combination of low sunspot activity and volcanic eruptions choked the atmosphere and changed ocean currents. Others have argued the reverse—that changing currents altered the pressure on continental shelves, which set off earthquakes and volcanoes. Whatever the explanation, the results ravaged an interconnected world. What's more, recent research has revealed that the great dying of Indigenous peoples in the sixteenth and seventeenth centuries, as described in the previous chapter, was a major factor producing the Little Ice Age. The collapse in Indigenous populations cleared the way for a return of trees and bushes to what was once densely tilled land. This created what scientists call a "carbon sink." The return of forests gave the planet the means to pull vast quantities of carbon dioxide from the atmosphere; this meant that the earth trapped less of the sun's heat—which in turn cooled and dried the air. In a sense, this was the reverse of the trend we see today, in

Coffeehouses everywhere served as locations for social exchange, political discussions, and business activities. Yet they also varied from cultural area to cultural area, reflecting the values of the societies in which they arose.

The coffeehouse first appeared in Islamic lands late in the fifteenth century. As coffee consumption caught on among the wealthy and leisured classes in the Arabian Peninsula and the Ottoman Empire, local growers protected their advantage by monopolizing its cultivation and sale and refusing to allow any seeds or cuttings from the coffee tree to be taken abroad.

Despite some religious opposition, coffee spread into Egypt and throughout the Ottoman Empire in the sixteenth century. Ottoman bureaucrats, merchants, and artists assembled in coffeehouses to trade stories, read, listen to poetry, and play chess and backgammon. Indeed, so deeply connected were coffeehouses with literary and artistic pursuits that people referred to them as schools of knowledge.

From the Ottoman territories, the culture of coffee drinking spread to western Europe. The first coffeehouse in London opened in 1652, and within sixty years the city claimed no fewer than 500 such establishments. In fact, the Fleet Street area of London had so many that the English essayist Charles Lamb commented, "The man must have a rare recipe for melancholy who can be dull in Fleet Street." Although coffeehouses attracted people from all levels of society, they especially appealed to the new merchant and professional classes as locations where stimulating beverages like coffee, cocoa, and tea promoted lively conversation without the inebriating effects of alcohol—and spared patrons the reputational toll of bawdy taverns. However, some opponents claimed that excessive coffee drinking destabilized the thinking processes; the narcotic effects of caffeine, it was said, might even promote conversions to Islam. But consumer demand won out: the pleasures of coffee, tea, and cocoa prevailed. These bitter beverages in turn required liberal doses of the sweetener sugar. A smoke of tobacco topped off the experience. In this environment of pleasure, patrons of the coffeehouses indulged their addictions, engaged in gossip, conducted business, and talked politics.

QUESTIONS FOR ANALYSIS

- What factors drove the consumption of stimulants like coffee on a global scale?
- What other commodities from earlier in world history played a similar role? Were there differences in the underlying factors, such as scale of consumption, between the different periods?

EXPLORE FURTHER

Hattox, Ralph S., *Coffee and Coffeehouses: The Origins of a Social Beverage in the Medieval Near East* (1985).

Pendergrast, Mark, *Uncommon Grounds: The History of Coffee and How It Transformed Our World* (2010).

which deforestation reduces the planet's capacity to absorb carbon dioxide, leading to warming.

While the seventeenth century was especially severe, the cold lasted well into the next century and in parts of North America into the nineteenth. One night in 1709, it is said, the king of France's beard froze solid while he slept. The Thames River and Dutch canals iced over, inspiring artists to create now-famous paintings of people skating on Dutch ponds and lakes. So did the waters separating Sweden from Denmark, which allowed Swedish armies to march right across to Copenhagen. In West Africa, colder and drier conditions saw an advance of the Sahara Desert, leading to repeated famines in the Senegambia region. In addition, Timbuktu and the region around the Niger bend suffered their greatest famines in the seventeenth century. It was still so cold in the early nineteenth century that the English novelist Mary Shelley and her husband spent their summer vacation indoors in Switzerland telling each other horror stories, which inspired Shelley to write *Frankenstein*. Climate change brought mass suffering because harvests failed. In China, the orange groves of Jiangxi Province had to be abandoned after constant and widespread freezing; rice fields, which need a wet spring, went dry. Famine spread across Afro-Eurasia.

The Global View

MAP 13.1 | Trade in Silver and Other Commodities, 1650–1750

The seventeenth and eighteenth centuries were the first centuries of true global commerce. Silver was the one item that was traded all over the world.

- Trace the flows of silver from the Americas around the globe (by following the thick orange arrows), and identify the commodities that silver was exchanged for in different parts of the world.
- Explain the relationship between the trade of manufactures and natural resources.
- According to this map, how did increased trade shape European states' territorial ambitions?

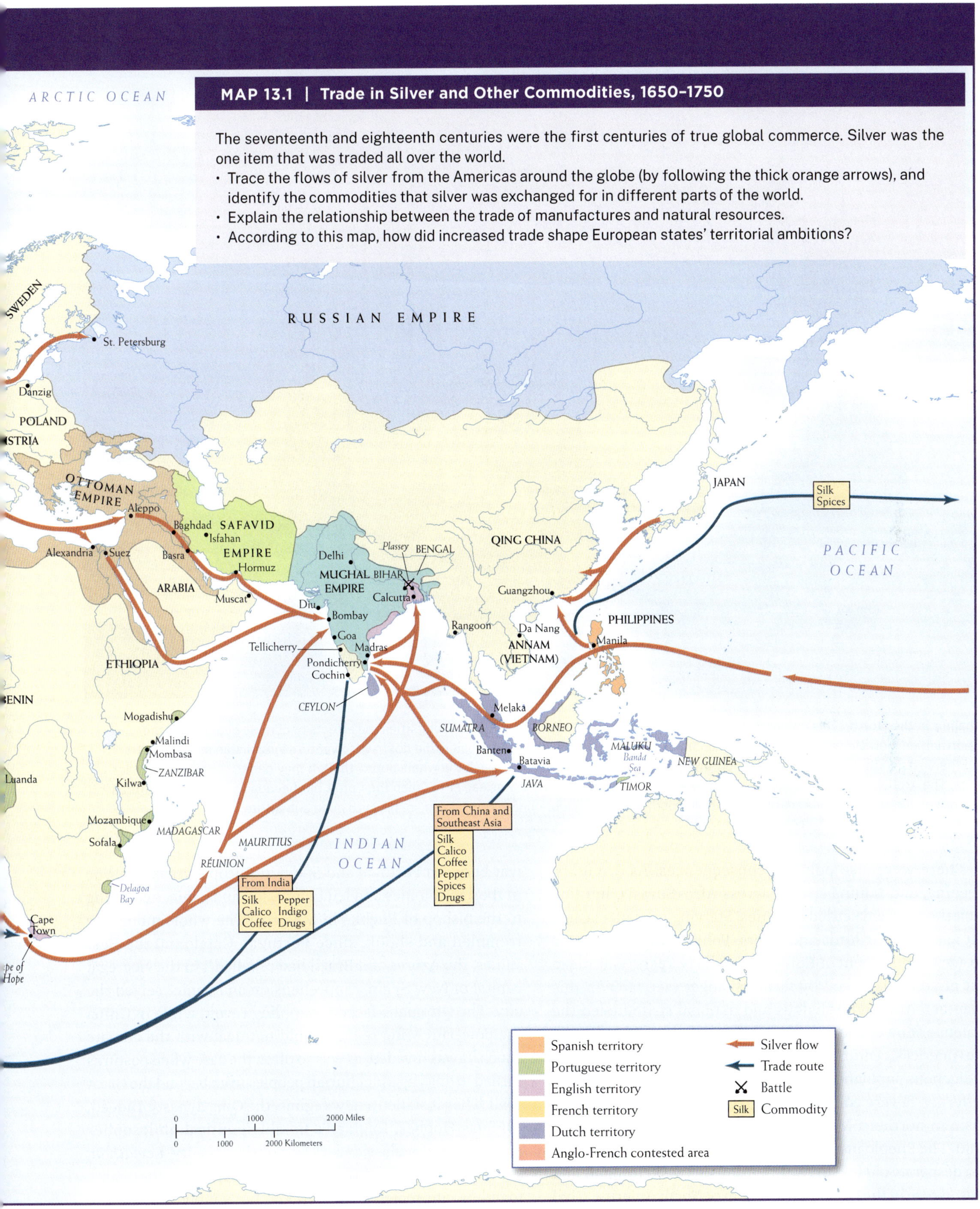

Whaling in the North. This painting by Dutch painter Abraham Storck (1654–1708) exemplifies the effects of climate change and the opportunities it presented for extractive economies. As temperatures dropped, whalers did not have to venture long distances in search of their harvests. In this painting, three Dutch whalers did not have to sail far to reach the whale pods—though they had to contend with polar bears. The Arctic spread was a bonanza for the whalers not just because it was easier to reach their prey, but because colder temperatures sent prices for vegetable oils soaring. Whale oil, good for candles, lubricants, lamp oil and soap, was a good substitute.

There were also political consequences. As droughts, freezing, and famine spread across Afro-Eurasia, herding societies invaded settled societies. Starving peasants lashed out against their lords and rulers. Political divides opened up. On the continent of Europe, the Thirty Years' War raged out of control, stoked by farmers' anger (see later in this chapter). Although religious and national strife fueled the violence, it owed much to the decline of food production. In the Americas, centuries of plagues had already ripped through Indigenous populations. But the long cold snap brought more suffering. Severe cold and drought afflicted the Rio Grande basin in northern Mexico, culminating in a deep freeze in 1680. The Puebloans rose up en masse against Spanish rulers in a desperate bid for survival. Tensions between Iroquois and Huron rose in the Great Lakes region of North America. Civil war between Portugal and Spain in Europe wreaked havoc in Iberian colonies and led to invasion and panic. According to the bishop of Puebla, in Mexico, "The whole monarchy trembled and shook, since Portugal, Catalonia, the East Indies, the Azores and Brazil had rebelled." In the viceregal capital of New Spain, "apprehension and panic" seized the city. The Ottomans faced a crippling revolt, while in China the powerful Ming regime could not deal with the climate shock. It was invaded, as was so often the case when pastures turned to dust, by Manchurian peoples from beyond the Great Wall. They installed a new regime, the Qing dynasty. Indeed, Thomas Hobbes, England's notable political philosopher and author of a classic work of political theory, *Leviathan*, summed up the age: "Man's natural state, before they came together into society, was war; and not simply war, but the

Indigenous Peoples in the Woodlands. This late sixteenth-century drawing by John White, a pioneer settler on Roanoke Island, off the coast of North Carolina, depicts the Indigenous village of Secoton in eastern Virginia. In contrast to the great empires that the Spanish conquered in the Valley of Mexico and in the Andes, the Indigenous Peoples whom English, French, and Dutch colonizers encountered in the woodlands of eastern North America generally lived in villages that were politically autonomous entities.

war of every man against every other man." He went on to add famously that "the life of man [is] solitary, poor, nasty, brutish, and short."

The Little Ice Age had a devastating impact on populations. It is hard, however, to separate the victims of starvation from the victims of war, since warfare aggravated starvation and famine contributed to war. But in continental Europe, the Thirty Years' War carried off an estimated two-thirds of the total population, on par with the impact of the Black Death (see Chapter 11). Elsewhere, estimates were closer to one-third. Not until the twentieth century did the world again witness such extensive warfare. For some Afro-Eurasian regimes, the global crisis led to collapse and decline; for others, it became an opportunity for renewal and reinvention.

Exchanges and Expansions in North America

Freezing temperatures and warfare in Europe did not prevent England, France, and Holland from joining Spain and Portugal in the rush to reap riches from American colonies and to take a greater share of global commerce. As rulers in England, France, and Holland granted monopolies to merchant companies, they began to dominate the settlement and trade of new colonies in the Americas. (See Map 13.2.) Although the search for precious metals or water routes to Asia had initially spurred many of these enterprises, the new colonizers learned that only by exploiting other resources could their claims in the Americas generate profits. Also, differences among New World societies required rethinking the character of colonies within mercantilist regimes.

The Little Ice Age made the repopulating of mainland North America traumatic. Especially hard-hit were the first English, French, and Spanish settlers. Getting a toehold in freezing woodlands or in areas where Indigenous peoples were already scrambling for survival presented the European interlopers with never-ending frustrations. Early settlements ended badly: namely, the Spanish in Florida, the French in the mouth of the St. Lawrence River, and then the English in Jamestown in 1607 on the northern bank of the James River in what would become Virginia. The English arrived in the midst of a severe drought that lasted from 1606 to 1612; 80 percent of the settlers died of starvation and disease. The survivors were desperate to return to England. It was not until June 10, 1610, when a relief fleet arrived, that the struggling base avoided calamity. The first English settlement in North America could sink its roots.

How the interlopers grappled with the challenges and opportunities laid the foundations for different models of North American colonialism. The important determinants were the resources they found and the relations between newcomers and Indigenous peoples. In Indigenous peoples' colonies along the Atlantic seaboard, the English established one model for new colonies in the Americas. Although these territories failed to yield precious metals or a waterway across the continent, they boasted land suitable for growing numerous crops. Within the English domain, different climates and soils made for very different agricultural possibilities: wheat, rye, barley, and oats from the Middle Colonies (Pennsylvania, New York, New Jersey, and Delaware); tobacco from Virginia and North Carolina; and rice and indigo from farther south.

But all the English colonies shared a common feature: population growth led to greater demand for farmlands, which put pressure on Indigenous holdings. The Little Ice Age exacerbated the stress, because shorter growing seasons diminished harvests. Thus, more acreage had to be cultivated to support the colonies' surging population in North America, which meant more lands taken from Indigenous tribes. The result: a souring of relations between Indigenous peoples and colonists. In 1675, which colonists described as a "year without a summer," ferocious wars broke out between Indigenous peoples and English colonists in Virginia and New England. Similar pressures ignited other conflicts throughout the seventeenth and eighteenth centuries and led to the dispossession of Indigenous peoples from lands between the Atlantic Ocean and the Appalachian Mountains.

By contrast, Dutch and French colonies rested not on the expulsion of Indigenous peoples but on dependence on them. Holland's North American venture, however, proved short-lived, as the English took over New Netherland and renamed it New York in 1664. French claims were more enduring and extended across a vast swath of the continent, encompassing eastern Canada, the Great Lakes, and the Mississippi Valley.

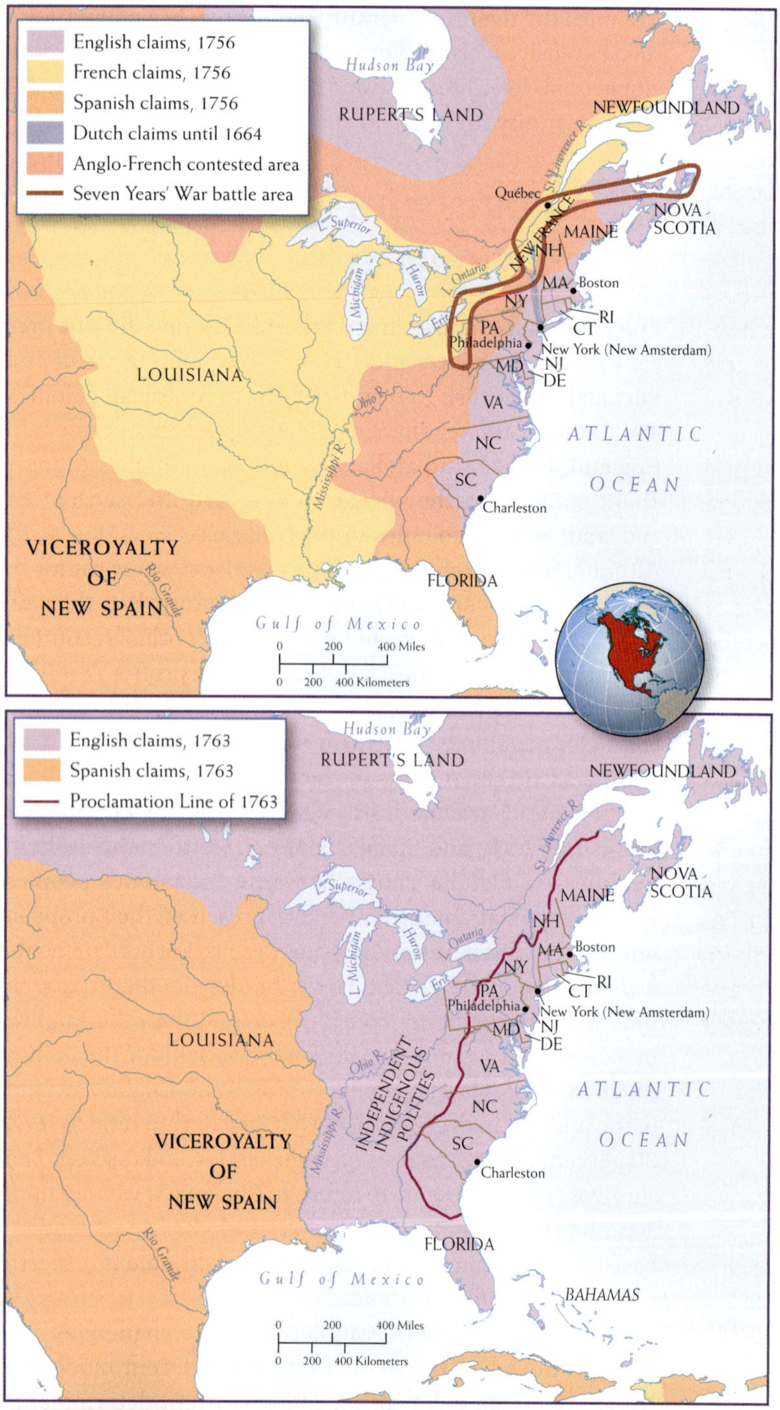

MAP 13.2 | Colonies in North America, 1607–1763

France, England, and Spain laid claim to much of North America at this time.

- Where was each of these colonial powers strongest before the outbreak of the Seven Years' War in 1756? (See p. 582 for a discussion of the Seven Years' War.)
- Which empire gained the most North American territory, and which lost the most at the end of the war in 1763?
- How do you think Indigenous peoples reacted to the territorial arrangements agreed to by Spain, France, and England at the Peace of Paris, which ended the war?

Trade between European and Indigenous Peoples

Crucial to the trade between European and Indigenous peoples in northern North America was the beaver, an animal for which local peoples previously had only minor use. In response to the Europeans' interest, one French Jesuit heard an Innu man explain, "The beaver does everything perfectly well; it makes kettles, hatchets, swords, knives, bread; in short it makes everything." As long as there were beavers to be trapped, trade between the Europeans and their Indigenous partners flourished.

The distinctive aspect of the fur trade was the Europeans' utter dependence on Indigenous know-how. After all, trapping required familiarity with the beaver's habits and habitats, which Europeans lacked. In particular, this reliance forced French traders who ventured farther into the continent's interior to adapt to local ways, especially when living among Huron and Algonquin peoples. Responding to Indigenous peoples' desires to use trade as an instrument to cement familial bonds, the French gave gifts, participated in Indigenous diplomatic rituals, and even married into local families. Women and girls were crucial mediators and brokers in the relationships between newcomers and Indigenous peoples. French-Indigenous offspring, Métis, inherited the mantle in New France as interpreters, traders, and guides. Thus, the French colonization of the Americas—owing to French reliance on Indigenous peoples as trading partners, military allies, and mates—rested more on cooperation than conquest, especially compared with the empires built by their Spanish and English rivals. Intermarriage and the creation of mixed-race peoples became commonplace across the rest of the Americas as well, with the notable exception of the English colonies.

Over the long run, Europeans' trade in guns, alcohol, and trinkets gave them power advantages. It also set off a crippling arms race between Indigenous groups, many of whom competed to extract furs to trade. This led to a depletion of beaver stocks. But through the seventeenth century and into the middle of the eighteenth, the majority of lands in the interior of the North American continent remained firmly in local hands, despite the invaders' expansive claims. On the Great Plains in the center of North America, some locals lost ground to newcomers, but here the winners were other, often-displaced, Indigenous groups. In effect, European penetration turned Indigenous peoples against each other as fugitives from one place became invaders of others. In retrospect, it became more and more difficult to name anyone truly "Indigenous" as populations responded to the great upheaval. On the northern plains, the Lakotas, who had migrated westward onto the grasslands, emerged as the most successful expansionists. Coming eastward, the Comanches reigned across a vast swath of the southern plains. These and other invaders displaced existing Indigenous societies from some lands, added to their ranks by capturing and often enslaving large numbers of people (especially females), and enriched themselves by their raiding and through their control over trading. The control that the Comanches asserted extended not only over other local peoples whom they captured and whose horses they plundered, but also over would-be European colonizers. From the eastern Plains almost to the Pacific Ocean, with the exception of a few enclaves of European settlement, it was Indigenous peoples who largely determined where Europeans could go, stay, and trade. Thus, while early eighteenth-century maps drawn by European empire makers divvied up North America principally among British, French, and Spanish realms, the reality on the ground mocked these imperial pretensions.

There was considerable irony in the fact that Spanish colonizers had empowered the Plains peoples. The Spanish, after all, had brought horses to the Americas, and it was the acquisition of these animals that revolutionized local life and enabled Indigenous expansions on the Great Plains. Recognizing the role that horses played in their conquests, the Spanish had tried to keep them out of local hands. They failed. Raiders targeted horses because they were so valuable. Once introduced into local habitats, the animals dispersed and flourished on the grasses of the Plains. So did the Indigenous peoples who had greatest access to horses and who most decisively adapted to equestrianism. On horseback, incumbents could kill bison much more effectively, which encouraged some groups to forsake farming for hunting. Other groups, like the

The Fur Trade. *Left:* For Europeans in northern North America, no commodity was as important as beaver pelts. For the French especially, the fur trade determined the character of their colonial regime in North America. For Indigenous peoples, it offered access to European goods, but overhunting depleted resources and provoked intertribal conflicts. *Right:* A handcolored woodcut of the seal of New Netherland depicts a beaver surrounded by wampum, a string of beads used by Indigenous peoples in religious ceremonies and as currency.

Lakotas and Comanches, moved onto the Plains in pursuit of buffalo. Astride horses, Indigenous peoples and newcomers also gained military superiority over more sedentary peoples, whose villages and cornfields were vulnerable to mobile forces. By the early nineteenth century, equestrian empires brought vast areas under one roof. This was most significant for the Comanche, who had gone from being a tribal or ethnic group to becoming a powerful confederation capable of subduing and defeating European and Indigenous folk alike.

Not all Indigenous peoples prospered, however, and certainly not all equally. The gains of nomadic equestrians often came at the expense of those who remained wedded to a mixture of horticulture and hunting. Within horse cultures, new inequalities materialized. More successful raiders and hunters not only earned greater honor but also acquired more horses. One effect was to create new divides within Indigenous households between women who remained closer to the villages and worked on their sustenance and men who became more ambulatory and devoted to hunting. For victorious men, capturing more horses usually brought higher status and more wives. At the same time, the status of women generally declined in the transition from horticultural to hunting societies. Their burdens, however, did not, as there were now more buffalo waiting to be turned by women into the products that sustained Plains peoples' life.

The Plantation Complex in the Caribbean

As late as 1670, the most populous English colony was not on the North American mainland. It was the Caribbean island of Barbados. Because sugar was so desirable, from the mid-seventeenth century onward the English- and French-controlled islands of the Caribbean replicated the Portuguese sugarcane plantations of Brazil; sugar became a quintessential mercantilist commodity. All was not sweet here, however. To begin with, the Indigenous peoples were all but wiped out or scattered to the mainland (see Chapter 12). Moreover, because no colonial power held a monopoly over the archipelago of islands, competition to control the region—and sugar production—was fierce. The resulting turbulence did not simply reflect imperial rivalry; it also reflected labor arrangements in the colonies. Competing owners of Caribbean estates looked to Africa to supply workers for their plantations.

Sugar was a killing crop. So deadly was the hot, humid environment in which sugarcane flourished (as fertile for disease as for sugarcane) that many sugar barons spent little time on their plantations. Management fell to overseers, who worked their enslaved laborers to death. Despite having immunity to yellow fever and malaria from their homeland's similar environment, Africans could not withstand the regimen. Inadequate food, atrocious living conditions, and filthy

Tobacco. The cultivation of tobacco saved the Virginia colony from ruin and brought prosperity to increasing numbers of planters. The spread of tobacco plantations also pushed Indigenous peoples off their lands and led planters to turn to Africa for a labor force. Here, enslaved Africans roll dried tobacco into ropes in the background, while in the foreground the leaves are sorted and pressed.

Sugarcane. Sugar was the preeminent agricultural export from the New World for centuries. Owners of sugarcane plantations relied almost exclusively on enslaved Africans to produce the sweetener. This 1640 drawing by Frans Post shows enslaved Africans working in a sugar mill in Brazil.

sanitation added to their miseries. Moreover, plantation managers dehumanized African workers starting on the first day they became property, when they were branded with the enslaver's seal. One English observer commented that the enslaved were like cows, "as near as beasts may be, setting their souls aside."

More than disease and inadequate rations, the work itself was decimating. Average life expectancy was three years. Six days a week, people who were enslaved on a plantation rose before dawn, labored until noon, ate a short lunch, and then worked until dusk. At harvest time, 16-hour days saw hundreds of men, women, and children bent over to cut the sugarcane and transport it to refineries, sometimes seven days per week. Entire households labored in the fields, erasing distinctions of age and gender. Under this brutal schedule, people occasionally dropped dead from exhaustion.

Amid disease and toil, the enslaved coped and resisted as they could. The most dramatic form of resistance was violent revolt. A more common form was flight. Casting around for refuge from overseers, thousands of freedom seekers took to the hills—for example, to the remote highlands of Caribbean islands or to Brazil's vast interior. Those who remained on the plantations resisted via foot-dragging, pilfering, and sabotage.

Caribbean settlements and slaveholdings were not restricted to any single European power. But it was the latecomers—the Dutch, the English, and especially the French—who concentrated on the West Indies and who grew wealthy and powerful. (See Map 13.3.) The English took Jamaica from the Spanish in 1655 and made it the premier site of Caribbean sugar by the 1740s. When the French seized half of Santo Domingo in the 1660s (renaming it Saint-Domingue, which is present-day Haiti), they created one of the wealthiest societies based on slavery of all time. This French colony's exports eclipsed those of all the Spanish and English Antilles combined. The capital, Port-au-Prince, was one of the richest cities in the Atlantic world. The colony's merchants and planters built immense mansions worthy of the highest European nobles. Thus, the Atlantic system benefited elite Europeans, who amassed new fortunes by exploiting the colonies' natural resources and the labor of the Africans they enslaved. The American trade also laid the financial foundations and the heightened consumer demands that were crucial for Europe's late eighteenth- and early nineteenth-century industrial revolution (see Chapter 15).

The Slave Trade and Africa

Wiping out Indigenous populations, or pushing them farther afield, cleared the way for European occupation. But there was a problem: Who was going to work the land? Where Indigenous labor could not be recruited or forced,

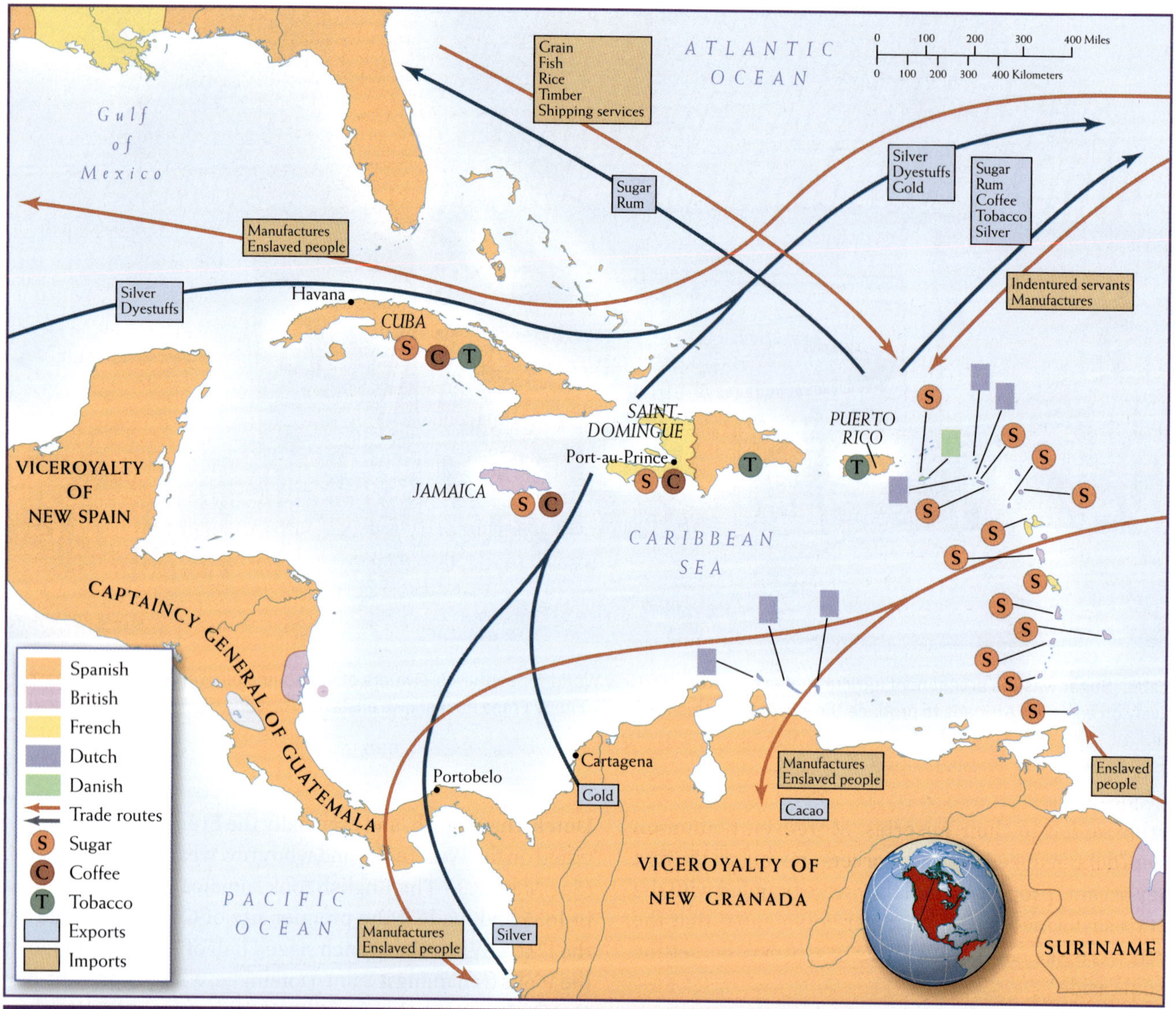

MAP 13.3 | Caribbean Colonies, 1625–1763

The Caribbean was a region of expanding trade in the seventeenth and eighteenth centuries.

- What were its major exports and imports?
- Who were its main colonizers and trading partners?
- According to your reading, how did the transformation of this region shape other societies in the Atlantic world?

Europeans turned to indentured workers and increasingly to imported enslaved African peoples. Although the chattel slave trade began in the mid-fifteenth century, only in the seventeenth and eighteenth centuries did the numbers of human exports from Africa begin to soar and feed mercantilist regimes. (See Map 13.4.) By 1820, four enslaved Africans had crossed the Atlantic for every free European. (See Analyzing Global Developments: The Atlantic Trade in Enslaved African People (1501–1900).) At the same time, the departure of so many inhabitants depopulated and destabilized many parts of Africa.

Capturing and Shipping Enslaved People

Merchants in Europe and the Americas prospered as the slave trade soared, but their fortunes depended on trading and political networks in Africa. Because European slave traders feared African diseases, mainly malaria, they confined themselves to the coast, where they supplied powerful interior states with firearms with which to conquer other indigenous peoples and ship their defeated adversaries to the enslavers.

Before the Europeans' arrival, Africa had long-standing enslaving networks, mainly flowing across the Sahara to North Africa and Egypt and eastward to the Red Sea and the Swahili coast of East Africa. From the Red Sea and Swahili coast destinations, Muslim and Hindu merchants shipped enslaved humans to ports around the Indian Ocean. However, their numbers could not match the chattel volume destined for the Americas once plantation agriculture began to spread. Indeed, 12.5 million Africans departed for forcible enslavement and shipment to Atlantic ports from the early fifteenth century until 1867, when the last voyage took place.

The enslavement ports along the African coast became gruesome entrepôts. Many captives perished before losing sight of Africa. Stuck in vast holding camps where disease and hunger were rampant, the enslaved were then forced aboard vessels in cramped and wretched conditions. These ships waited for weeks to fill their holds while their human cargoes wasted away belowdecks. Crew members tossed dead Africans overboard as they loaded on other Africans from the shore. When the cargo hold was full, the ships set sail. In their wake, crews continued to dump bodies. Most died of gastrointestinal diseases leading to dehydration. Smallpox and dysentery were also scourges. Either way, death was slow and agonizing. Because high mortality led to lost profits, enslavers learned to carry better food and more fresh water as the trade became more sophisticated. Still, when enslaver ships finally reached New World ports, they reeked of disease and excrement. (See Global Themes and Sources: Primary Source 13.1.)

Slavery's Gender Imbalance

In moving so many from Africa to the Americas, the slave trade played havoc with the ratios of men to women in both places because most people shipped to the Americas were men. European slave traders sought "well-formed" and strong men between the ages of ten and twenty-five, even though many plantation owners came to realize that women of the same age worked as hard as men. Although the numbers indicate Europeans' preferences for male laborers, they also reflect African enslavers' desire to keep enslaved women, primarily for household work. The gender imbalance made it difficult for enslaved people to have children in the Americas. So enslavers had to return to Africa to procure more human beings to force into bondage—especially for the Caribbean islands, where death rates were so high.

Enslaved men outnumbered enslaved women in the New World, but in the regions of Africa where captives were seized, women outnumbered men. Female captives were especially prized in Africa because of their traditional role in the production of grains, leathers, and cotton. Indeed, the Atlantic slave trade made the role of those women who remained in Africa even more essential for ensuring the subsistence of children and the aged. Moreover, the slave trade reinforced the traditional practice of polygyny—allowing relatively scarce men to take several wives. But in some states, notably the supplier kingdom of Dahomey, on the West African coast, women managed to assert power because of their large numbers and heightened importance. In fact, Dahomean women became so deeply involved in succession disputes that their intrigues could make the difference between winning and losing political power. Ultimately, though, the fact that some women rose to power in a few societies did not diminish the destabilizing effects of the Atlantic slave trade or the chaos that the raiding and trading wrought on the relations among African states.

Africa's New Slave-Supplying States

Africans did not passively let captives fall into the arms of European buyers; instead, local political leaders and merchants were energetic suppliers. This activity promoted the growth of centralized political systems, particularly in West African rain forest areas. The trade also shifted control of wealth away from households owning large herds or lands to those who profited from the capture and exchange of enslaved people—urban merchants and warrior elites.

Queen Nzinga. The slave trade shifted political alliances and created new politics up and down the African coast. In what is now Angola, the Mbundu people formed a great kingdom. Under Queen Nzinga of Ndongo and Matamba, they flourished. She was adept at managing Portuguese relations and, after her brother died, rose to the throne to rule for thirty-seven years. Under her reign, her state flourished and she deftly played off the Dutch against Portuguese interlopers.

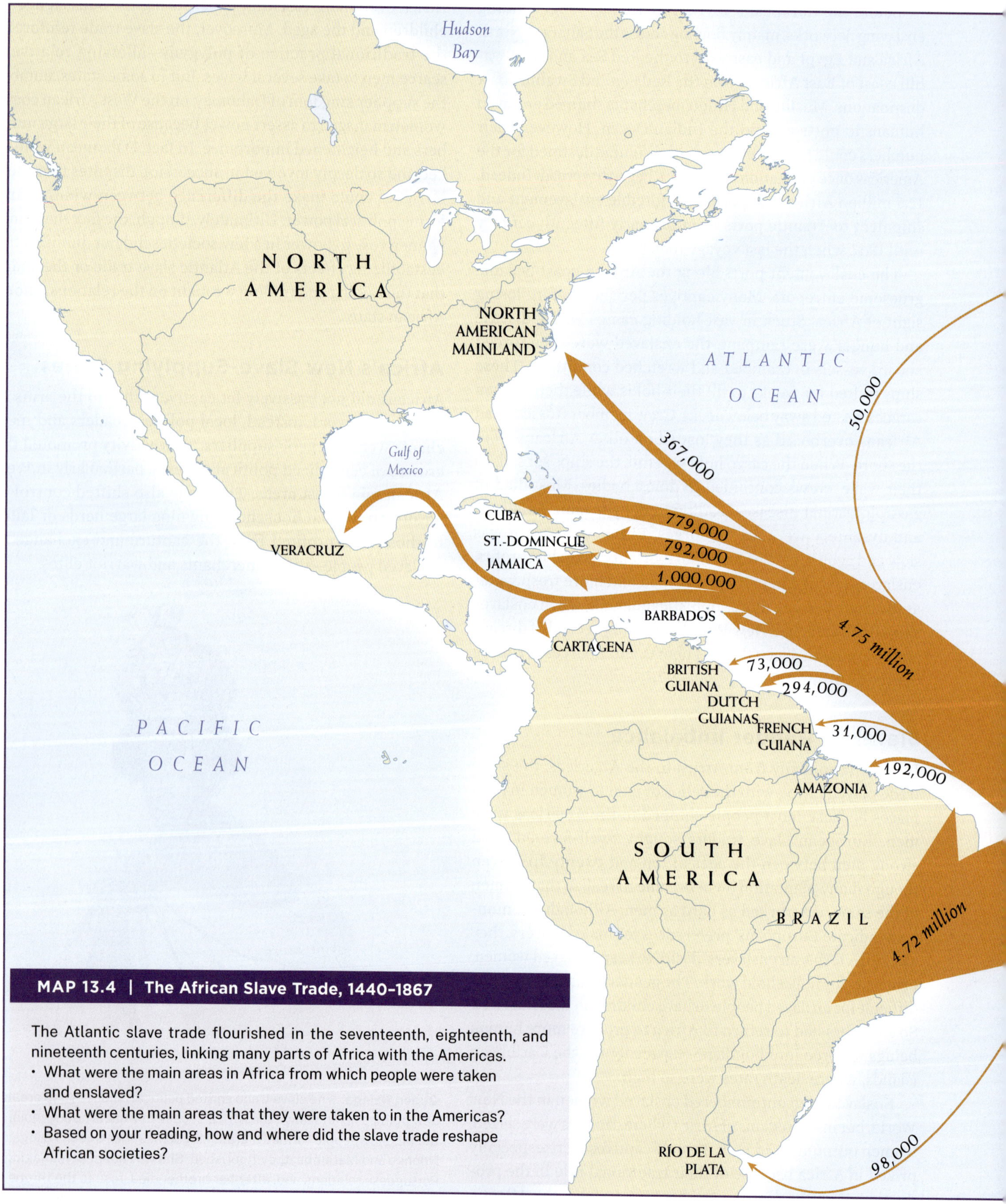

MAP 13.4 | The African Slave Trade, 1440–1867

The Atlantic slave trade flourished in the seventeenth, eighteenth, and nineteenth centuries, linking many parts of Africa with the Americas.

- What were the main areas in Africa from which people were taken and enslaved?
- What were the main areas that they were taken to in the Americas?
- Based on your reading, how and where did the slave trade reshape African societies?

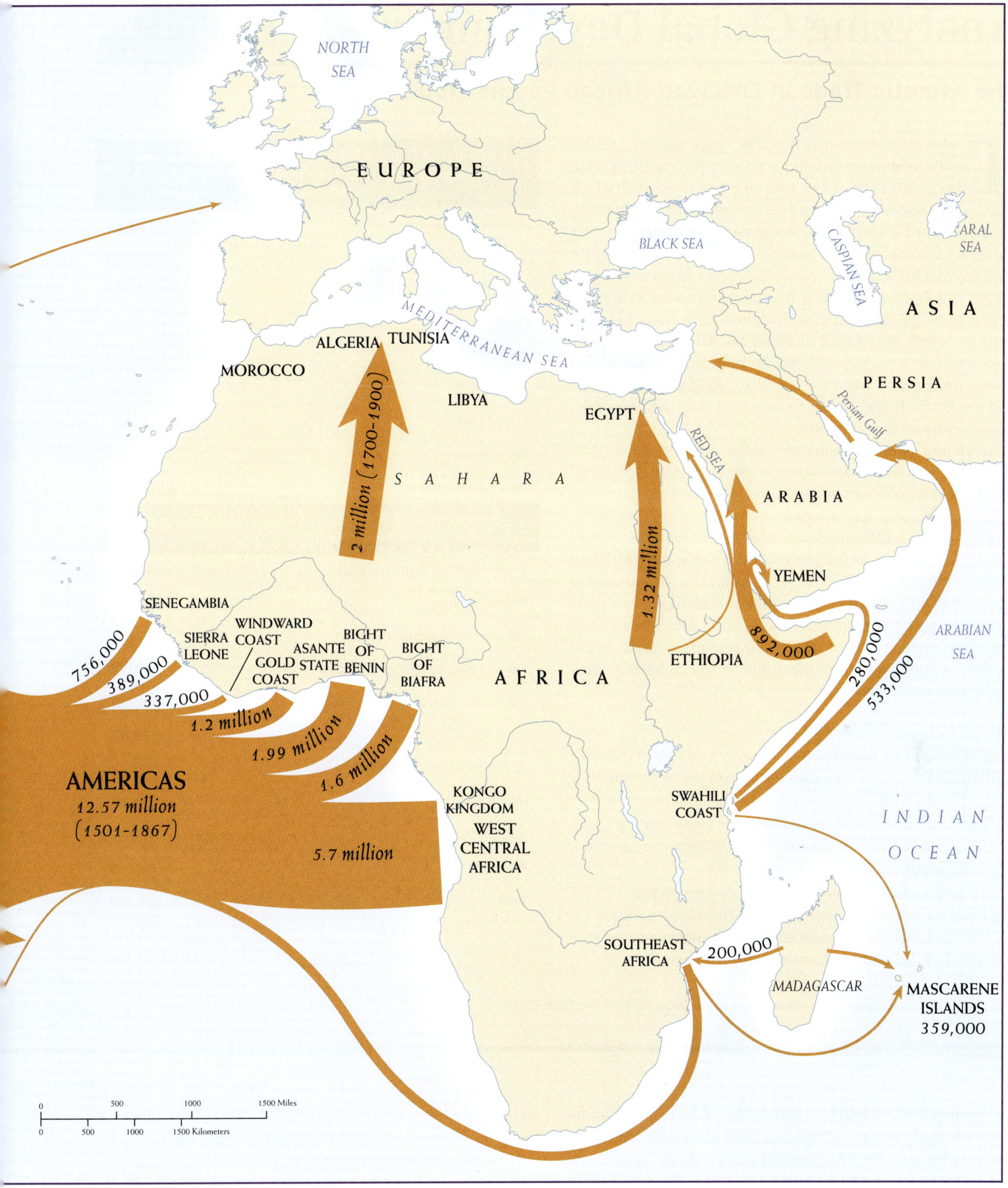
NORTH SEA
EUROPE
BLACK SEA
ARAL SEA
CASPIAN SEA
ASIA
MEDITERRANEAN SEA
ALGERIA
TUNISIA
MOROCCO
LIBYA
EGYPT
PERSIA
Persian Gulf
RED SEA
2 million (1700–1900)
SAHARA
ARABIA
1.32 million
YEMEN
SENEGAMBIA
WINDWARD COAST
SIERRA LEONE
BIGHT OF BENIN
ASANTE STATE
GOLD COAST
BIGHT OF BIAFRA
ETHIOPIA
892,000
280,000
533,000
ARABIAN SEA
AFRICA
756,000
389,000
337,000
1.2 million
1.99 million
1.6 million
AMERICAS
12.57 million
(1501–1867)
5.7 million
KONGO KINGDOM
WEST CENTRAL AFRICA
SWAHILI COAST
INDIAN OCEAN
SOUTHEAST AFRICA
200,000
MADAGASCAR
MASCARENE ISLANDS
359,000
0 500 1000 1500 Miles
0 500 1000 1500 Kilometers

Analyzing Global Developments

The Atlantic Trade in Enslaved African People (1501–1900)

The world's leading slave traders were also the world's most important maritime powers during the period from 1501 to 1900. The following tables focus on which countries transported enslaved human beings and where they ended up. The Spanish and Portuguese established the first European empires in the Americas and created the model for the early slave trade. But northern European powers like Great Britain and France, reflecting their growing strength in maritime commerce, dominated the Atlantic slave trade between 1642 and 1808. In the final phase of the Atlantic slave trade, 1808–1867, the northern European powers and the United States disengaged from the trade, allowing the Portuguese and the Spanish once again to dominate the trade now centered largely on Cuba and Brazil.

In recent decades, scholars of the Atlantic slave trade have created the Trans-Atlantic Slave Trade Database, which can be accessed at the Slave Voyages Web site (www.slavevoyages.org). Constructed from nearly 35,000 documented voyages during this period, this database incorporates roughly 80 percent of the ventures that set out for Africa to obtain enslaved laborers from all around the Atlantic world during this era. Through painstaking research, historians have been able to reconstruct the Atlantic world slave trade and offer a clear insight into the experiences of all those involved and the impact of this trade on the global economy during four centuries.

QUESTIONS FOR ANALYSIS

- Which countries were the most heavily invested in the Atlantic slave trade based on the data in the first table? How do you know?
- What was the relationship between the slave-trading countries and the colonies in the New World based on the entries in both tables?
- Why is the total number of enslaved people traded different from the number of people that disembarked? Did you expect the differences between these two numbers to be greater than they are? If so, why?

Number of Enslaved People Taken from Africa to the Americas by Nationality of Vessels That Carried Them (1501–1867)

Vessel Nationality	Number of People
Portugal/Brazil	5,849,300
Great Britain	3,259,900
France	1,380,970
Spain/Uruguay	1,060,900
Netherlands	555,300
United States	305,800
Baltic States	110,400
Total Atlantic World	**12,522,570**

Disembarkation of Enslaved People from Africa to the Americas (1501–1900)

Disembarking Country/Colony	Number of People
Brazil (Portugal)	4,720,000
Smaller Caribbean islands (mix)	1,750,000
Jamaica (Spain then Great Britain)	1,000,000
Saint-Domingue (Spain then France)	792,000
Cuba (Spain)	779,000
Spanish Caribbean mainland	390,000
United States	389,000
Dutch Guiana	294,000
Amazonia	142,000
Total	**10,256,000**

Source: David Eltis and David Richardson, *Atlas of the Transatlantic Slave Trade* (2010).

THE KONGO KINGDOM In some parts of Africa, the booming slave trade wreaked havoc as local leaders feuded over control of the traffic; mercantilist rivalry along the African coast disrupted old states and produced new ones. In the Kongo kingdom, civil wars raged for over a century after 1665, and captured warriors were sold into slavery. As members of the royal family clashed, entire provinces saw their populations vanish. Most important to the conduct of war and the control of trade were firearms and gunpowder, which made capturing warriors highly efficient. Moreover, kidnapping

The Slave Trade. Left: Africans were captured in the interior and then bound and marched to the coast. Right: After reaching the coast, the captured Africans would be crammed into the holds of enslaving vessels, where they suffered grievously from overcrowding and unsanitary conditions. Long voyages were especially deadly. If the winds failed or ships had to travel longer distances than usual, many of the captive people would die en route to the slave markets across the ocean.

became so prevalent that cultivators worked their fields bearing weapons, leaving their children behind in guarded stockades.

Some leaders of the Kongo kingdom fought back. Consider Queen Nzinga (1583–1663), a masterful diplomat and a shrewd military planner. Having converted to Christianity, she managed to keep Portuguese enslavers at bay during her long reign. Even after Portuguese forces defeated her troops in battle, she conducted effective guerrilla warfare into her sixties.

Consider also the Christian visionary Dona Beatriz Kimpa Vita. Born in Kongo in 1684 and baptized as a Christian, she claimed at age twenty to have received visions from Saint Anthony of Padua. She believed that she died every Friday and was transported to heaven to converse with God, returning to earth on Monday to broadcast God's commands to believers. Her message aimed to end the Kongo civil wars and re-create a unified kingdom. Although she gained a large following, she failed to win the support of leading political figures. In 1706, she was captured and burned at the stake.

OYO, ASANTE, AND OTHER GROUPS As some African merchants and warlords sold other Africans, their commercial success enabled them to consolidate political power and grow wealthy. Their wealth financed additional weapons, with which they subdued neighbors and extended political control. Among the most durable new polities was the Asante state, which arose in the West African tropical rain forest in 1701 and expanded through 1750. This state benefited from its access to gold, which it used to acquire firearms (from European traders) to raid nearby communities for servile workers. From its capital city at Kumasi, the state eventually encompassed almost all of present-day Ghana. Main roads spread out from the capital like spokes of a wheel, each approximately twenty days' travel from the center. Through the Asante trading networks, African traders bought, bartered, and sold enslaved people, who wound up in the hands of European merchants waiting in ports with vessels carrying manufactured products and weaponry.

Also active in the slave trade—and enriched by it—was the Oyo Empire. This territory, which straddled the main trade routes, linked tropical rain forests with interior markets of the northern savanna areas. The empire's strength rested on its impressive army brandishing weapons secured from trade with Europeans. Deploying cavalry units in the savanna and infantry units in the rain forest, the Oyo's military campaigns became annual events, suspended only so that warriors could return home for agricultural duties. Every dry season, Oyo armies marched on their neighbors to capture entire villages.

Slavery and the emergence of new political organizations enriched and empowered some Africans, but they cost Africa dearly. For the princes, warriors, and merchants who organized the slave trade, their business (like that of Indigenous fur suppliers) enabled them to obtain European goods—especially alcohol, tobacco, textiles, and guns. The Atlantic system also tilted wealth away from rural dwellers and village elders and increasingly toward port cities. Across the landmass, the slave trade thinned the population. True, Africa was spared a demographic catastrophe equal to the devastation of Indigenous peoples. The introduction of American food crops—notably maize and cassava, producing many more calories per acre

The Port of Loango. Partly as a result of the profits of the slave trade, African rulers and merchants were able to create large and prosperous port cities such as Loango (pictured here), which was on the western coast of south-central Africa.

than the old staples of millet and sorghum—blunted the trade's depopulating aspects. Yet some areas suffered grievously from three centuries of heavy involvement in the slave trade. The Atlantic trade enhanced the warrior class, who carried out raids for captives; the dislocations, internal power struggles, and economic hardships that followed precipitated the rise and fall of West African kingdoms.

Since the seventeenth century saw the deportation of 2 million African men, women, and children to the Americas, it is worth asking whether the Little Ice Age was a factor in the fate of these peoples. Unfortunately, information on sub-Saharan Africa is not as rich as it is for Europe and Asia. Nonetheless, what we do know, mainly from travelers' accounts, is that many of the areas from which enslaved Africans came—like Kongo, the interior of West Africa, and Senegambia—suffered from severe drought and witnessed a spike in the number of captives sold to enslavers.

Comparative Perspectives on Climate Change: The Ottoman Empire and Ming China

The Little Ice Age ravaged two of Afro-Eurasia's largest and most stable empires—the Ottoman Empire and Ming China. But what destabilized both regimes was not just the scarcity of food but the growing pressure by rulers to extract wealth from their populations to fund endless wars around imperial fringes and to subdue unrest at the core. In other words, while working populations endured with less, their rulers wanted more. The squeeze was explosive. In both empires, peasants and nomads, driven by severe famines, rose in rebellion, asserting that their rulers had failed to look after them. One survived, and the other did not.

The Ottomans Struggle to Maintain Power and Legitimacy

Hardest and earliest hit by climate change was the eastern Mediterranean. Here, fierce cold and endless drought brought famine and high mortality. In 1620, the Bosporus froze over, enabling residents of Istanbul to walk from the European side of the city into the Asian side. In Ottoman territories dependent on floodwaters for their well-being, such as Egypt and Iraq, food was in short supply and mortality rates skyrocketed. In addition, the import of New World silver led to high levels of inflation and a destabilized economy. Yet, in spite of the dire circumstances, the Ottomans continued their military campaigns against the Habsburgs to the west and a prolonged, brutal struggle with the Safavids to the east. Desperate for revenues to pay their armies, the Ottomans imposed soaring taxes. Banditry, nomadic invasions of settled lands, refusal to pay taxes, and ultimately outright revolt were the inevitable result.

THE CELALI REVOLT AND KÖPRÜLÜ REFORMS A revolt, begun in central Anatolia in the early sixteenth century, continued with fits and starts throughout the century and reached a crescendo at the beginning of the seventeenth century. This later full-blown uprising took its name from Shaykh Celali, who had led a rebellion in the early sixteenth century. Later rebels called themselves Celalis, looking to his life for inspiration. With a 30,000-strong army, the rebels turned much of Anatolia into a heartland of pillaging, looting, burning of villages, and killing. Large segments of the Ottoman population, many of whom were Shiites or turned to Shiism to express their opposition to Ottoman rule, joined the rebellion. Poised to assault Istanbul in 1607–1608, the rebels squared off against the sultan's troops outside the capital. It did not go well for the insurgents; they were no match for Ottoman armies. The empire pulled back from the edge of collapse. Still, the human suffering went on.

The Ottomans may have survived, but their regime was crippled. The empire's population, around 35 million in the 1590s, was still below that number when the first official census was carried out in 1830. Meanwhile, the European powers with access to New World colonies leapfrogged over the Ottomans economically, militarily, and culturally.

The Ottomans did, however, experience a period of good governance in the mid to late seventeenth century in spite of Mustafa Ali's pessimistic predictions. New grand viziers from the Köprülü family spearheaded changes to revitalize the government. Known as the Köprülü reforms, the changes in administration reenergized the state and enabled the military to reacquire some of its lost possessions. Revenues again increased, and inflation decreased. Fired by revived expansionist ambitions, Istanbul decided to renew its assault on Christianity (see Chapter 11)—beginning with rekindled plans to seize Vienna. Although the Ottomans amassed an enormous force outside the Habsburg capital in 1683, both sides suffered heavy losses and the Ottoman forces ultimately retreated. Under the treaty that ended the Austro-Ottoman war, the Ottomans lost major European territorial possessions, including Hungary.

Despite failing to take Vienna, the Ottoman state flourished in the first half of the eighteenth century. No event was more resplendent than the two weeks of feasting, parades, and entertainment that accompanied the circumcision of the sultan's sons in 1720. Istanbul also once again became a beehive of political activity, adorned with new palaces and mosques.

THE MAMLUKS IN OTTOMAN EGYPT A weakened Ottoman state prompted outlying provinces to assert their autonomy. Egypt led the way. Here, too, plummeting temperatures and monsoon failures leading to aridity and low Nile waters may have been factors. Egypt experienced extremely low Niles from 1641 to 1643, owing to catastrophic drought, and then such extreme cold that a Turkish traveler in the 1670s reported that everyone who could afford to wore fur-lined clothing.

In 1517, Egypt had become the Ottoman Empire's greatest conquest. The wealthiest Ottoman territory, it was an important source of revenue and initially was well governed by its Ottoman-appointed governors. Its payments to Istanbul exceeded those of any other Ottoman province. Yet, starting in the mid-seventeenth century, households modeled on the sultan's arose and increasingly asserted their independence from Istanbul. By the latter half of the eighteenth century, the dominant households were made up of **Mamluks** (Arabic for "owned" or "possessed"), military men who had ruled Egypt as an independent regime until the Ottoman conquest (see Chapter 10). Although the Ottoman forces had routed the Mamluks on the battlefield in 1517, Ottoman governors in Egypt allowed the Mamluks to reform themselves. By the second half of the eighteenth century, these military men were nearly as powerful as their ancestors had been in the fifteenth century when they ruled Egypt independently. Mamluk leaders also enhanced their power by aligning with Egyptian merchants and catering to the *ulama*. Turning the Ottoman governor in Egypt into a mere figurehead, this provincial elite kept much of the area's fiscal resources for themselves at the expense of the imperial coffers and the local peasantry.

Although the Ottoman Empire survived the impact of the Little Ice Age (in contrast to the Ming dynasty in China),

Siege of Vienna.
This seventeenth-century painting depicts the Ottoman siege of Vienna, which began on July 14, 1683, and ended on September 12. The city might have fallen if the Polish king, John III, had not answered the pope's plea to defend Christendom and sent an army to assist German and Austrian troops in defeating the Ottomans.

it emerged in a severely weakened condition. The Celali revolts resulted in devastating population losses, while the repeated low Nile floods reduced food and tribute payments from Egypt to Istanbul, further weakening the Ottoman state. The decline was not entirely associated with climate change, however. Heterodox and Sufi religious leaders challenged the Sunni orthodoxy of the clerical and bureaucratic classes. In Egypt and the other Arab provinces of the Ottoman Empire, local notables, notably Mamluks in Egypt and warlords and religious leaders in greater Syria, sought autonomy from Istanbul.

Ming China Succumbs to Manchu Rule

The Ming dynasty was less fortunate than the Ottomans. It did not survive the pincers of climate change and war. Drought and freezing temperatures affected food production not only in China proper, where the Ming prevailed, but also throughout Inner China, where by the seventeenth century the Manchus of Manchuria were a rising power. The Ming capital of Beijing suffered grievously. An estimated 300,000 perished within the inner city in 1644, causing many Han Chinese to conclude that the Ming had lost the mandate of heaven.

Silver. This seventeenth-century helmet from the Ming (1368–1644) or Qing (1644–1911) dynasty features steel, gold, silver, and textiles, all of which were vital to the Chinese economy during this century. Silver was especially important, for its large influx from Japan and the Americas led to severe economic problems, political unrest, and the overthrow of the Ming dynasty.

THE MANCHUS FIND A VULNERABLE TARGET Like the Ottoman Empire, China's imperial state always had contentious enemies on its frontier; what the Safavids posed to Istanbul's eastern flank the Manchus posed to Beijing's northern flank. By the early seventeenth century, a rising **Manchu** population, based in Inner China and unable to feed its people in Manchuria, threatened to breach the Great Wall in search of better lands. Food shortages and drought drove the Manchus into China proper, where they found a Chinese government and its population in disarray from famines, civil war, and fiscal crisis. Peasant rebellions crippled central authorities. Outlaw armies swelled under charismatic leaders. The so-called roving bands wreaked havoc across the countryside. The most famous rebel leader, the "dashing prince," Li Zicheng, reached the outskirts of Beijing in 1644. Only a few companies of soldiers and a few thousand eunuchs stood to defend the capital's 21 miles of walls. Li Zicheng seized Beijing easily. Two days later, the emperor hanged himself. On the following day, the triumphant "dashing prince" rode into the capital and claimed the throne.

News of the fall of the Ming capital sent shock waves around the empire and beyond. In the far northeast, where China meets Manchuria, the Ming army's commander received the news within a matter of days. Tasked to defend the Ming against their Manchu neighbors, the commander knew a precarious position when he saw one. Caught between an advancing rebel army on the one side and the Manchus on the other, he made a fateful decision: he struck a pact with the Manchus for their cooperation to fight the "dashing prince." In return, his new allies got the gold and treasure in the capital. Thus, without shedding a drop of blood, the Manchus joined the Ming forces to bring down Ming power. After years of coveting the riches of the south, the Manchus were finally marching on Beijing. (See Map 13.5.)

While the declining Ming state shared some commonalities with the troubled Ottoman Empire, there were specific features of Chinese rule that accounted for the regime's collapse. An important factor was that China was a dynamo in the emerging world economy, which destabilized its inner balance; opening China was disruptive. There was more hunger for Chinese goods from abroad and more thirst for silver from within. As noted in Chapter 12, Europeans used New World silver to pay for their purchases of Chinese goods. The surge of silver from the New World and Japan had heated the Chinese economy. Increasing monetization of the economy, which turned silver into the primary medium of exchange, bolstered market activity and state revenues at the same time. Then, when silver shipments to China declined due to downturns in New World mining output, and more precious metals were swallowed up in European wars, the supply of money contracted in China; inflation suddenly gave way to

MAP 13.5 | From Ming to Qing China, 1644–1760

Qing China under the Manchus expanded its territory significantly during this period. Find the Manchu homeland and then the area of Manchu expansion after 1644, when the Manchus established the Qing dynasty.

- Where did the Qing dynasty expand? Explain what this tells us about the priorities of the ruling elite, in particular with respect to global commerce.
- Explain the significance of the chronology of Chinese expansion. Does this qualify your answer to the first question?
- What does the chronology of Chinese expansion tell us about the evolution of the ruling elite's priorities?
- Consider the scope of Chinese territorial expansion in this period, and, based on your reading, explain the challenges this posed for central authorities.

deflation and shortages. Chinese peasants could not meet their obligations to state officials and merchants. The frustrated masses thus often seethed with resentment, which quickly turned to rebellion. The result was a perfect storm of food shortages, regional defections, and fiscal crisis, which brought down the Ming dynasty in 1644.

THE QING DYNASTY ASSERTS CONTROL Despite their small numbers, the Manchus overcame early resistance to their rule and oversaw an impressive expansion of their realm. Descendants of the Jurchens (see Chapter 10), the Manchus emerged as a force early in the seventeenth century, when their leader claimed the title of khan after securing the allegiance of various Mongol groups in northeastern Asia and paved the way for their eventual conquest of China.

When the Manchus defeated Li Zicheng and seized power in Beijing, they numbered around 1 million. Assuming control of a domain that included perhaps 250 million people, they were keenly aware of their minority status. Taking power was one thing; keeping it was another. But keep it they did. In fact, during the eighteenth century, the Manchu **Qing** ("pure") **dynasty** (1644–1911) incorporated new territories, experienced substantial population growth, and sustained significant economic growth. Despite coming to power at a time of political chaos, the Manchus established a stable and long-lived imperial system in contrast to the political and economic turmoil that rocked the societies of the Atlantic world.

The key to China's relatively stable economic and geographical expansion lay in its rulers' shrewd and flexible policies. The early Manchu emperors were able administrators who knew that to govern a diverse population, they had to adapt to local ways. To promote continuity, they respected Confucian codes and kept the classic texts as the basis of the prestigious civil service examinations (see Chapter 9). Social hierarchies of age, gender, and kin—indeed, the entire image of the family as the bedrock of social organization—endured. In some areas, like Taiwan, the Manchus added new territories to existing provinces. Elsewhere, they gave newly acquired territories, like Mongolia, Tibet, and Xinjiang, their own form of local administration. Imperial envoys in these regions administered through staffs of locals and relied on native institutions. Until the late nineteenth century, the Qing dynasty showed little interest in integrating those regions into "China proper."

At the same time, Qing rulers conveyed a clear sense of their own majesty and legitimacy. Rulers relentlessly promoted patriarchal values. Widows who remained "chaste" enjoyed public praise, and women in general were urged to lead a "virtuous" life serving male kin and family. To the majority Han population, the Manchu emperor represented himself as the worthy upholder of familial values and classical Chinese civilization; to the Tibetan Buddhists, the Manchu state offered imperial patronage. So, too, with Islamic subjects. Although the Islamic Uighurs, as well as other Muslim subjects, might have disliked the Manchus' easygoing religious attitude, they generally endorsed the emperor's claim to rule.

The Manchus also emphasized their authority, their distinctiveness, and the submission of their mostly Han Chinese subjects. For example, the Manchus required all Han males to shave their forehead and braid their hair in a queue and to wear high collars and tight jackets instead of loose Ming-style clothes.

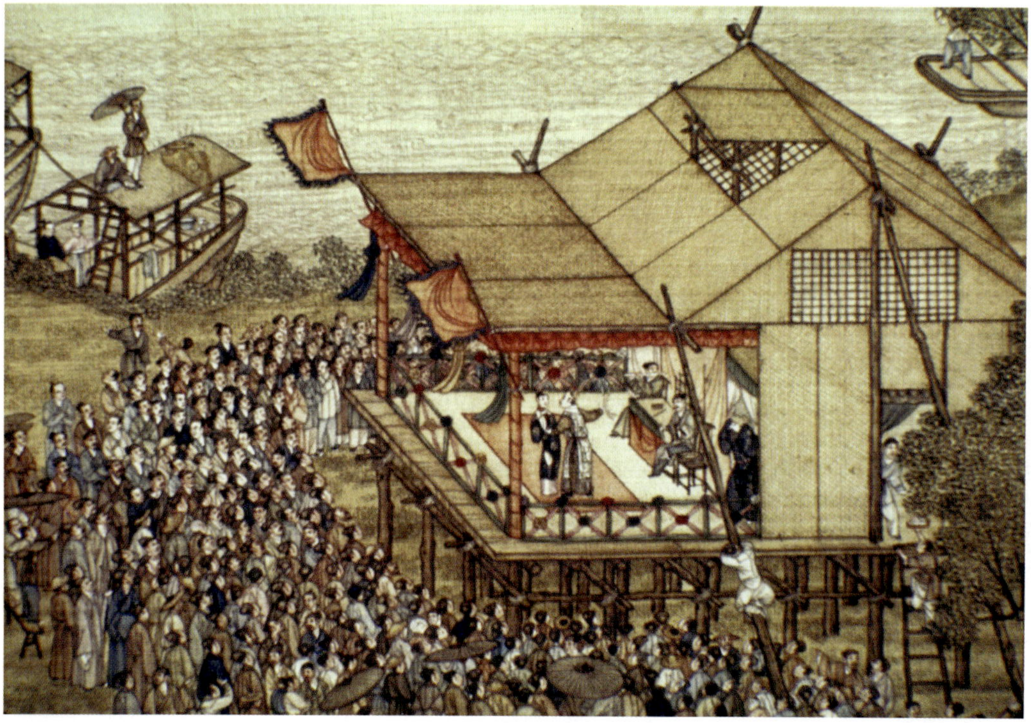

Qing Theater with Female Impersonators. The Qing court banned women from performing in theaters, which led to the practice of using young boys in female roles.

Nothing earned the regime's distrust more than what it regarded as urban elites' sexual norms, especially involving women. The Qing court regarded the "decadence" of the late Ming dynasty, symbolized by its famous actresses, as one of the Ming's principal failings. In 1723, the Qing banned female performers from the court and then from commercial theaters, with young boys taking female roles onstage. The Qing also tried to regulate commercial theater by excluding women from the audience. The popularity of female impersonators onstage, however, brought a new cachet to same-sex relationships. A gulf began to open between the government's aspirations and its ability to police society. For example, the urban public continued to flock to performances by female impersonators in defiance of the Qing's bans.

Manchu impositions fell mostly on the peasantry, for the Qing financed their administrative structure through taxes on peasant households. In response, the peasants sought new lands to cultivate in border areas, having lost much land during the Little Ice Age. On these estates, they planted New World crops that grew well in difficult soils. This move introduced an important change in the Chinese diet: while rice remained the staple diet of the wealthy, peasants increasingly subsisted on corn and sweet potatoes.

EXPANSION AND TRADE UNDER THE QING The Qing dynasty forged tributary relations with Korea, Vietnam, Burma, and Nepal, and its territorial expansion reached far into central Asia, Tibet, and Mongolia. In particular, the Manchus wanted to stabilize their frontiers and check any threat from an expanding Russia. Having brought domestic peace, the Qing accepted, for the first time, the need for diplomacy with expanding overland neighbors. Thanks to Jesuit intermediaries, Russian and Qing envoys negotiated China's first treaty, the Treaty of Nerchinsk, in 1689. By recognizing sovereignty and borders, the pioneering treaty served both empires internally and allowed each to put the squeeze on borderlanders and curb their autonomy.

The treaty gave the Qing the room to crush one group of borderlanders in particular, the Junghars of western Mongolia. Many Junghars had converted to Buddhism from Islam in the seventeenth century and they controlled much of central Asia. Clear of any Junghar-Russian alliance, the Qing launched brutal campaigns against their leader, Eredeniin Galdan. Galdan had studied Buddhist texts with the Dalai Lama in Tibet before subduing other khanate rivals—and then squaring up against the scale and might of Beijing. The conflict took decades, with the Qing's military supply lines stretching across western China and their armies roaming from Mongolia to Tibet. The Junghars played a cat-and-mouse game, with their cavalries escaping and haranguing the heavy artillery dragged by Chinese foot soldiers and tens of thousands of horses. But in the long run, the Junghars could not escape the squeeze and the loss of their pastures for their livestock, and they could not match the scale of the resources the Chinese state was prepared to throw at its frontier. Nor could they overcome internal divides among the Mongolian peoples. Hungry and deserted, Galdan finally took his own life in 1697. But the emperor in Beijing was not done with him. He ordered that Galdan's ashes be brought to the capital and scattered over the parade grounds of his triumphal armies, so his remains could be pulverized into the ground for as long as the Qing would rule. The Junghars finally fell in the mid-eighteenth century. The steppe lands from Mongolia to Tibet became a province of China called Xinjiang, a massive buffer zone between China and other land powers, and the victory made Beijing the ruler of Muslim and Buddhist peoples to the west.

Borderlands. Here is a depiction of the warrior Ayuxi, a Junghar who fought valiantly for nomadic peoples—until he was captured by the Qing. To save his life, he joined the westward expansion of the Manchu forces. His equestrian and fighting skills were so legendary, he was put in charge of a handful of Turkestani horsemen who famously routed a larger Junghar cavalry. For his heroism, the emperor commissioned this portrait.

Canton. A painting by an unknown artist provides a view of the foreign factories in Canton. Not only were foreigners forbidden to trade with the Chinese outside Canton, but they were also required to have Chinese guild members act as guarantors of their good behavior and payment of fees.

While officials redoubled their reliance on an agrarian base, trade and commerce flourished. Chinese merchants continued to ply the waters stretching from Southeast Asia to Japan, exchanging textiles, ceramics, and medicine for spices and rice. Although initially the Qing state vacillated about permitting maritime trade with foreigners, it sought to regulate external commerce more formally as it consolidated its rule. In 1720, in Canton, a group of merchants formed a monopolistic guild to trade with Europeans. Although the guild disbanded in the face of opposition from other merchants, it revived after the Qing restricted European trade to Canton. The **Canton system**, established by imperial decree in 1759, required European traders to have guild merchants act as guarantors for their good behavior and payment of fees.

Though the Qing disrupted some old Ming ways, there was a great deal of continuity, just as there was in the Ottoman Empire. At the heart of this continuity was the peasantry, who continued to practice popular faiths, cultivate crops, and stay close to fields and villages. Trade with the outside world remained marginal and restricted to the coast. Like the Ming, the Qing cared more about the interior agrarian base than the commercial health of the empire, believing the former to be the foundation of prosperity and tranquility. As long as China's peasantry could keep the dynasty's coffers full, the government was content to squeeze the merchants when it needed funds. Some historians view this practice as a failure to adapt to a changing world order, as it ultimately left China vulnerable to outsiders—especially Europeans. But this became only clear in hindsight, after the mid-nineteenth century. Until then, Europe still needed China more than the other way around. For the majority of Chinese, no superior model of belief, politics, or economics was conceivable. Indeed, although the Qing had taken over a fractured dynasty in 1644, it was still a powerful and expanding empire.

In both the Ottoman Empire and China, the Little Ice Age had severe effects. The Ottoman Empire survived, although its population losses were not recouped until well into the nineteenth century and its sense of power and legitimacy were badly shaken. In contrast, while the Ming dynasty lost out to a regime drawn from the much-despised Manchurian region, the new Qing dynasty created a stable political order, a prosperous economy, and a well-functioning social order—though one that favored those of Manchu descent. As noted previously, climate change was not the sole factor in causing these outcomes, but its role was significant.

Other Parts of Asia in the Seventeenth and Eighteenth Centuries

The other regions in Asia also grappled with the Little Ice Age. All faced droughts, high winds, hailstorms, and earthquakes. But some weathered the troubles better than others. The most successful was Japan. The Tokugawa regime, installed early in the sixteenth century, overcame the Little Ice Age adversities. In fact, it experienced a century of increased agricultural productivity, rapid population growth, and impressive urbanization, mostly owing to the shrewd provincial administrators appointed by Tokugawa rulers. At the other end of the spectrum was the Safavid regime in Iran, which crumbled in the seventeenth century, as ethnic diversity and ineffective rulers drained its legitimacy. In the middle was Mughal India, which faced upheavals but endured. In India, four monsoons and a plethora of rebellions led Shah Aurangzeb (r. 1658–1707) to carry out savage persecutions of non-Muslim groups. Nevertheless, Mughal monarchs, even Aurangzeb, dealt promptly and reasonably effectively with the famines, even the most severe one that ravaged the Gujarati region between 1630 and 1632.

Global trading networks boomed in Asia, even as some of the regimes wavered or cracked up. For the most part, however, they kept commercial newcomers to the edges of their prosperous systems. In contrast to the conquests in the Atlantic region, Europeans skirted around the fringes of Asia and had to content themselves as commercial intermediaries in Asia's brisk long-distance trade. They penetrated Asian markets with American silver largely because the Asians, especially the Chinese, scorned European trade goods. Nor could they conquer Asian empires or colonize vast portions of the region or enslave Asian peoples as they had Africans. Still, chipping away at the edges had cumulative effects that became visible by the end of the eighteenth century.

The Dutch in Southeast Asia

In Southeast Asia, the Dutch already enjoyed a dominant position by the seventeenth century. Although the Portuguese had seized the vibrant port city of Melaka in 1511 and the Spaniards had taken Manila in 1571, neither was able to monopolize the lucrative spice trade. To challenge them, the Dutch government persuaded its merchants to charter the Dutch East India Company (abbreviated as VOC) in 1602. Benefiting from Amsterdam's position as the world's most efficient money market, the VOC raised enough capital to build a vast corporate navy. At its peak the company had 257 ships and employed 12,000 persons. Throughout two centuries it sent ships manned by a total of 1 million men to Asia.

The commercial-military drive created a conquering machine in Southeast Asia to develop extractive economies, akin to the labor-plantation camps in the Atlantic. Spices, coffee, tea, and teakwood became key exports. (See again Map 13.1.) The company's objective was to secure a trade monopoly wherever it could, fix prices, and subdue local populations, enslaving them where they could, and where they could not, to import workers from the rest of the region. In 1619, under the leadership of Jan Pieterszoon Coen (who once said that trade could not be conducted without war and war could not be conducted without trade), the Dutch swept into the Javanese port of Jakarta (renamed Batavia by the Dutch) and created a fortress. Two years later, Coen's forces seized a cluster of nutmeg-producing islands known as Banda. Traditional chiefs were killed. Villagers were enslaved. The vibrant local coastal trading systems based on long dugout canoes called

Islander Defense. This image depicts a battle between Dutch invaders and their muskets versus Maluku warriors and their arrows. The Europeans are poised in rows, taking turns firing into the fearless, but falling, defenders.

VOC Coat of Arms. At the center of this image of the VOC's coat of arms is a picture of a Dutch man-of-war ship, equipped with fourteen guns, on a windy sea. The crest has an armillary sphere (a model of the celestial globe) surrounded by a trophy of armory (full three-piece set), nautical instruments, and flags. The central images are supported by Neptune and the self-referring Providentia. The compartment has an arrangement of exotic seashells. Note how important the military was for Dutch commercial iconography.

prahus were forced to accept Dutch monopolies. Salt, indigo, Japanese copper, timber, opium, and anything else that was tradable had to be controlled by Dutch masters. And to buy these goods, islanders had to work on Dutch plantations for miserable wages. To clear the land for commercial spice production and to build fortresses and ships, the Dutch ordered forests to be razed.

Islanders rose up wherever possible, sometimes with the support of Dutch rivals, the English. The people of the Maluku Strait, for instance, objected to the Dutch commercial restrictions and monopoly extraction. One chief, Majira, from the island of Seram, wanted to sell his villagers' cloves directly to Asian merchants and rallied his people to drive the Dutch from their lands. In 1651, he went to war, but his arrows and spears were no match for Dutch muskets.

The islands, once rich with dense forests and ecologically complex, became monocrop (single-crop) plantations. With their monopoly of nutmeg secured, the Dutch went after the market in cloves. Their strategy was to control production in one region and then destroy competitors, which entailed, once again, wars against producers and traders in other areas. Portuguese Melaka soon fell to the Dutch and became a VOC outpost. Although this aggressive expansion met widespread resistance, by 1670 the Dutch controlled all the lucrative spice trade from the Maluku islands.

As a result of the Dutch enterprise, European outposts such as Dutch Batavia and Spanish Manila soon rivaled and in some cases eclipsed old Asian entrepôts and their private merchant networks. Indeed, as Europeans, buoyed by their chartered monopolies, competed for supremacy in the borderlands of Southeast Asia, they made local societies serve their own ambitions and began replacing traditional networks with trade routes that primarily served European interests. The Dutch used Europe's traditional appetite for Southeast Asian spices like nutmeg, pepper, and cloves, to which they added coffee, tea, and teakwood, to integrate the islands of the Dutch East Indies into the global economy.

Transformations in the Islamic Heartland

By the early seventeenth century, the three major Muslim empires of Afro-Eurasia, stretching from the Balkans and North Africa to South Asia, had a combined population of between 130 and 150 million. Yet, compared with Southeast Asia, they did not feel such direct effects of European intrusion. Here, trade was not as crucial as in East Asia. True, the importation of silver was significant and destabilizing. But Islamic regimes were not as dependent on silver as China was. The Islamic heartland did, however, face internal difficulties. While the Ottoman and Mughal Empires muddled along, the Safavid Empire fell into chaos.

THE SAFAVID EMPIRE The Safavid Empire had always required a powerful, religiously inspired ruler to enforce Shiite religious orthodoxy and to hold together the realm's tribal, pastoral, mercantile, and agricultural factions. During its rise, charismatic political leadership and religious messianism had overcome the innate tendencies of the peoples living on the Iranian plateau to resist the authority of state power. The Iranian plateau consisted of vast semidesert and wooded areas surrounded by mountains and was inhabited by diverse, often-hostile ethnic, linguistic, and religious communities. Moreover, a substantial percentage of the Safavid population of 8.5 million comprised nomadic peoples who bristled when confronted with centralized power. Abbas I (r. 1588–1629), the fifth Safavid shah, used the strength of his personality, his commitment to Shiism, and his talent for playing off one group against another to enhance the state's power (see Chapter 14). His successors were weaker and less charismatic, and the state foundered as eunuchs and harem women asserted their authority over that of the shahs and as tribal groups slipped away from control from the center.

By 1722, the state was under assault from within and without, and it collapsed abruptly at the hands of clans from the Afghan borderlands who overran its inept and divided armies and besieged the capital at Isfahan. (See again Map 13.1.) As the city's inhabitants perished from hunger and disease, some desperate survivors ate the corpses of the deceased. After the shah abdicated, the invaders executed thousands of officials and members of the royal household. The empire limped along until 1773, when a revolt toppled the last ruler from the throne.

Even so, the Safavid period left an immense imprint on the peoples of the Iranian plateau. Most importantly, they continued their commitment to Shiism in a predominantly Sunni world and harkened back in admiration to their Persian historical traditions. (For a discussion of Safavid culture at its height, see Chapter 14.)

THE MUGHAL EMPIRE In contrast to the Ottomans' setbacks, the Mughal Empire reached its height in the seventeenth century. The period saw Mughal rulers extend their domain over almost all of India and enjoy increased domestic and international trade. But they eventually had problems governing dispersed and resistant provinces, where many villages retained traditional religions and cultures.

Before the Mughals, India had never had a single political authority. Akbar and his successors had conquered territory in the north (see Chapter 12, Map 12.5), so now the Mughals turned to the south and gained control over most of that region by 1689. As the new provinces provided additional resources, local lords, and warriors, the Mughal bureaucracy grew better at extracting services and taxes. What it did not do was create a degree of centralized authority like the Ming or Qing in China. This made the Mughal Empire less brittle and more adaptive, but vulnerable to decentralizing pressures.

The Mughal Empire did resemble China in one basic aspect: it was an overland, not overseas, power and relied on agrarian rents, not trade, to fund its war-making machinery. Although the Mughals profited from seaborne trade, they never embarked on overseas expansion. The main source of their wealth was land rents, boosted via incentives to bring new land into cultivation. Here peasants planted, in part, New World crops like maize and tobacco. But the imperial economy also benefited from Europeans' increased demand for Indian goods and services—such as a sixfold rise in the English East India Company's textile purchases.

LOCAL AUTONOMY IN MUGHAL INDIA It is important to underscore the differences between European-style conquests, which aimed to dominate and even exterminate the conquered, and Mughal conquests, which aimed to subdue, but not wipe out, local kingdoms. In contrast to European expansion, which was based on the destruction of much Indigenous sovereignty in the Americas or the creation of new states in West Africa to mesh with the new transatlantic slave trade, Mughal expansion relied on confederacies and alliances with neighbors. The result was enormous wealth and resilience, but gradual dissolution. Eventually, Mughals were victims of their own success. More than a century of imperial expansion, commercial prosperity, and agricultural development placed substantial resources in the hands of local and regional authorities. As a result, local warrior elites became more autonomous. By the late seventeenth century, many regional leaders were well positioned to resist Mughal authority.

Aurangzeb. The last powerful Mughal emperor, Aurangzeb continued the conquest of the Indian subcontinent. Pictured in his old age, he is shown here with his courtiers.

Thus, increased prosperity enabled distant provinces to challenge central rulers. When, under Aurangzeb (r. 1658–1707), the Mughals pushed deep into southern India, they encountered fierce opposition from the Marathas in the northwestern Deccan plateau. (See again Map 13.1.) To finance this expansion, Aurangzeb raised taxes on the peasants. As resentment spread, even the elite grew restive at the drain on imperial finances. Seeking support from the *ulama,* the monarch abandoned the toleration of heterodoxy and of non-Muslims that his predecessors had allowed. All this turmoil set the stage for successful peasant revolts.

Now the Indian peasants (like their counterparts in Ming China, Safavid Persia, and the Ottoman Empire) capitalized on weakening central authority to assert their independence. They, too, were feeling the effects of the Little Ice Age on their lands' productivity. Many rose in rebellions; others resorted to banditry. At this point the Mughal emperors had to accept diminished power over a loose unity of provincial "successor states." (For a discussion of Mughal culture at its height, see Chapter 14.) Most of these areas accepted Mughal control in name only; local rulers administered semiautonomous regimes and kept a grip on local resources to prevent Delhi centralization. Yet India still flourished, and landed elites brought new territories into agrarian production. Cotton, for instance, supported a thriving textile industry as peasant households focused on weaving and cloth production. Much of their production was destined for export as the region deepened its integration into world trading systems.

Indian Cotton. European traders were drawn to India by its famed cotton textiles. This image from around 1800 shows a woman separating the cotton from the seeds; it captures the preindustrial technology of cotton production in India.

PRIVATE COMMERCIAL ENTERPRISE The Mughals paid scant attention to commercial matters. Local rulers, however, welcomed Europeans into Indian ports, striking deals with merchants from Portugal, England, and Holland. Some Indian merchants formed trading companies of their own to control the sale of regional produce to competing Europeans; others established intricate trading networks that reached as far north as Russia.

One of these companies built a trading and banking empire that demonstrated how local prosperity could undercut imperial power. This was the House of Jagat Seth, which at first specialized in shipping Bengal cloth through Asian and European merchants. Increasingly, however, most of its business in the provinces of Bengal and Bihar was tax farming, whereby it collected taxes for the imperial coffers. (See again Map 13.1.) The Jagat Seths maintained their own retinue of agents to gather levies from farmers while pocketing substantial profits for themselves. In this way, they and other mercantile houses grew richer and gained greater political influence over financially strapped emperors. Thus, even as global commercial entanglements enriched some in India, the effects undercut the Mughal dynasty.

Tokugawa Japan

Integration with the Asian trading system exposed Japan to new external pressures, even as the islands grappled with internal turmoil. But the Japanese dealt with these pressures more successfully than the mainland Asian empires (Ottoman, Safavid, Mughal, and Ming), which saw political fragmentation and even the overthrow of ruling dynasties. In Japan, a single ruling family emerged. This dynastic state, the **Tokugawa shogunate**, accomplished something that most of the world's other regimes did not: it regulated foreign intrusion. While Japan played a modest role in the expanding global trade, it remained free of outside exploitation.

UNIFICATION OF JAPAN During the sixteenth century, Japan had endured political instability as banditry and civil strife disrupted the countryside. Regional ruling families, called *daimyos,* had commanded private armies of warriors known as samurai. The daimyos sometimes brought order to their domains, but no one family could establish preeminence over the others. Although Japan had an emperor, his authority did not extend beyond the court in Kyoto.

Ultimately, several military leaders attempted to unify Japan. One general, who became the supreme minister, arranged marriages among the children of local authorities to solidify political bonds. Also, to coax cooperation from the daimyos, he ordered that their wives and children be kept as semihostages in the residences they were required to maintain in Edo. After the general died, one of the daimyos, Tokugawa Ieyasu, seized power. This was a decisive moment. In 1603, Ieyasu assumed the title of shogun (military ruler), retaining the emperor in name only while taking the reins of power himself. He also solved the problem of succession, declaring that rulership would be hereditary and that his family would be the ruling household. This hereditary Tokugawa shogunate lasted until 1867.

Now administrative authority shifted from Kyoto to the site of Ieyasu's domain headquarters: the castle town called Edo, later renamed Tokyo. (See Map 13.6.) The Tokugawa built Edo out of a small earthen fortification clinging to a coastal bluff. Behind Edo lay a village in a swampy plain. In a monumental work of engineering, the rulers ordered the swamp drained, the forest cleared, many of the hills leveled, canals dredged, bridges built, the seashore extended by landfill, and a new stone castle completed. By the time Ieyasu died, Edo had a population of 150,000.

The Tokugawa shoguns ensured a flow of resources from the working population to the rulers and from the provinces to the capital. Villages paid taxes to the daimyos, who transferred resources to the seat of shogunate authority. No longer engaged in constant warfare, the samurai became administrators. Peace brought prosperity. Agriculture thrived. Improved farming techniques and land reclamation projects enabled the country's population to triple between 1550 and 1700.

FOREIGN AFFAIRS AND FOREIGNERS Internal peace and prosperity did not insulate Japan from external challenges, especially the intrusion of Christian missionaries and European traders. Initially, Japanese officials welcomed these foreigners out of an eagerness to acquire muskets, gunpowder, and other new technology. But once the ranks of Christian converts swelled, Japanese authorities realized that Christians were intolerant of other faiths, believed Christ to be superior to any authority, and fought among themselves. Trying to stem the tide, the shoguns prohibited conversion to Christianity and attempted to ban its practice. After a rebellion by converted peasants protesting high rents and taxes, the government suppressed Christianity and drove European missionaries from the country.

Even more troublesome was the lure of trade with Europeans. The Tokugawa knew that trading at various Japanese ports would pull the commercial regions in various directions, away from the capital. When it became clear that European traders preferred the ports of Kyūshū (the southernmost island), the shogunate restricted Europeans to trading only in ports under Edo's direct rule in Honshū. Then Japanese authorities expelled all European competitors. Only the Protestant (and nonmissionizing) Dutch won permission to remain in Japan, confined to an island near Nagasaki. The Dutch were allowed to unload just one ship each year, under strict supervision by Japanese authorities.

Edo in the Rain. This facsimile of an ukiyo-e (floating world) print by Hiroshige (1797–1858) depicts one of several bridges in the bustling city of Edo (later Tokyo), with Mount Fuji in the background.

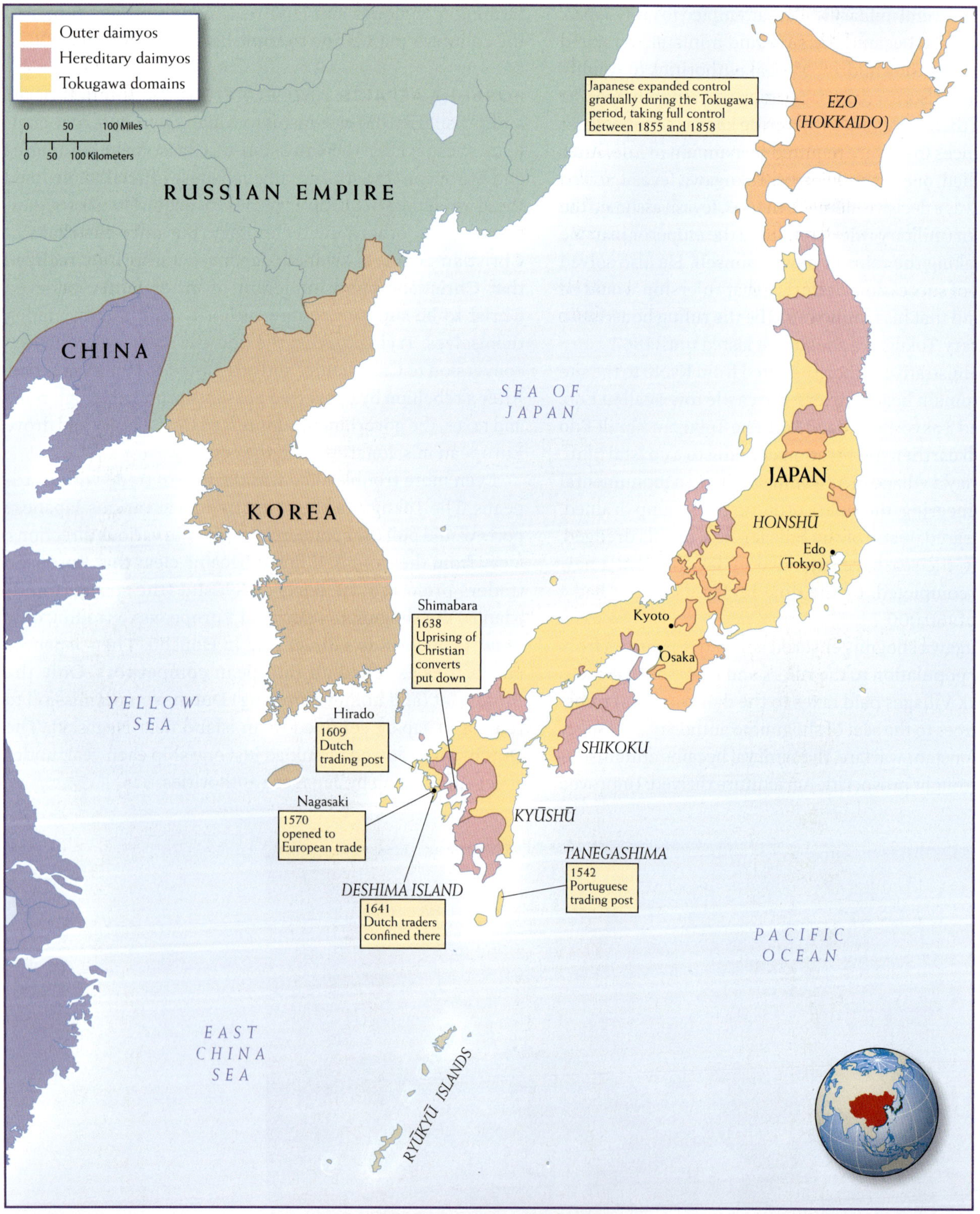

MAP 13.6 | Tokugawa Japan, 1603–1867

The Tokugawa shoguns created a strong central state in Japan at this time.

- According to this map, how extensive was their control?
- Based on your reading, what foreign states were interested in trade with Japan?
- How, according to the chapter, did Tokugawa leaders attempt to control relations with foreign states and other entities?

These measures did not close Tokugawa Japan to the outside world, however. Trade with China and Korea flourished, and the shogun received missions from Korea and the Ryūkyū Islands. Edo also gathered information about the outside world from the resident Dutch and Chinese (who included monks, physicians, and painters). A few Japanese were permitted to learn Dutch and to study European technology, shipbuilding, and medicine (see Chapter 14). By limiting such encounters, the authorities ensured that foreigners would not threaten Japan's security.

New World silver and climate change challenged the major Asian states. Mughal rulers dealt with famines and rebellions while guiding South Asia to its greatest power and influence. China's dynastic change from the Ming to the Qing did not diminish its wealth and power, although irregular supplies of silver (glut followed by scarcity) produced inflation and altered relations between the state and outlying regions. The Ottomans expanded into the Arab world and challenged the Portuguese in the Indian Ocean, but suffered significant military and territorial losses in Europe. The Europeans established commercial footholds in South and East Asia and thrust themselves into the already brisk Indian Ocean trade, while the Dutch created an export-oriented colony in Southeast Asia.

Portuguese Trading in Japan. Namban art specialized in portraits of traders and missionaries from Europe, especially Portuguese. This detail from a folding screen (c. 1568–1600) illustrates the variety of goods imported to Japan starting in the 1540s, many of them not from Europe but from China and Southeast Asia. The Portuguese first worked as intermediaries between Asian buyers and sellers.

Transformations in Europe

Between 1600 and 1750, religious conflict and the consolidation of dynastic power, spurred on by climate change and long-distance trade, transformed Europe. Commercial centers shifted northward, and Spain and Portugal lost ground to England and France. Farther to the north, the state of Muscovy expanded dramatically to become the sprawling Russian Empire.

Expansion and Dynastic Change in Russia

During this period, the Russian Empire became the world's largest-ever state. It gained positions on the Baltic Sea and the Pacific Ocean, and it established political borders with both the Qing Empire and Japan. These momentous shifts involved the elimination of steppe nomads as an independent force. Culturally, Europeans as well as Russians debated whether Russia belonged more to Europe or to Asia. The answer was both.

MUSCOVY BECOMES THE RUSSIAN EMPIRE The principality of Moscow, or **Muscovy**, like Japan and China, used territorial expansion and commercial networks to consolidate a powerful state. Originally a mixture of Slavs, Finnish tribes, Turkic speakers, and many others, Muscovy expanded to become a huge empire that spanned parts of Europe, much of northern Asia, numerous North Pacific islands, and even—for a time—a corner of North America (Alaska).

Like Japan, Russia emerged out of turmoil. Three factors inspired the regime to seize territory: security concerns, the ambitions of private individuals, and religious conviction. Security concerns were foremost, as expansion was inseparable from security. Because the steppe, stretching deep into Asia, remained a highway for nomadic peoples (especially descendants of the powerful Mongols), Muscovy sought to dominate the areas south and east of Moscow. Beginning in the 1590s, Russian authorities built forts and trading posts along Siberian rivers at the same time that privateers, enticed by the fur trade, pushed even farther east. By 1639, the state's borders had reached the Pacific. Now Muscovy claimed an empire straddling Eurasia and incorporating peoples of many languages and religions. (See Map 13.7.)

Much of this expansion occurred during the colorful and violent reign of Ivan IV, known as Ivan the Terrible, a name that could also be translated as "awesome" (r. 1547–1584). A Muscovite grand prince, he restyled himself "tsar of all of the Russias," ruling in the northern reaches of a European-Asian crossroads that lacked natural borders. The many invasions and counterinvasions that had taken place in the past persuaded Ivan that the only way to achieve security against hostile neighbors was to conquer them first and then rule in an autocratic fashion. Ivan's great military victory in 1552 over the powerful Tatar khanate, centered on the Volga River city of Kazan, began a transformation of his largely Orthodox-Christian, Russian-speaking realm through the incorporation of large Muslim, Turkic-speaking populations. Ivan also sponsored expeditions that led to the conquest of even vaster territories in the east, which came to be known as Siberia.

Ivan's paradoxical reign, full of both dynamism and destruction, set Moscow on an expansionist course toward a transcontinental empire, a state of many religions, and a zealous commitment to strongly authoritarian rule. Like the Ottoman and Qing dynasts, the new Romanov tsars who followed Ivan IV and their aristocratic supporters would retain power into the twentieth century.

The next great leap came under Peter the Great (r. 1682–1725), who doubled down on expansion and modernized the Russian state. He founded a new capital at St. Petersburg, revamped agrarian taxes, adopted military reforms to create a more modern army, equipped with artillery and trained for war against other empires, like Sweden's empire. This allowed Peter's successors, including the hard-nosed Catherine the Great, to add even more territory. Catherine carved up the medieval state of Poland. Russia also annexed Ukraine, the grain-growing breadbasket of eastern Europe. By the late eighteenth century, Russia's grasp extended from the Baltic Sea through the heart of Europe, Ukraine, and Crimea on the Black Sea and into the ancient lands of Armenia and Georgia in the Caucasus Mountains.

Expansion brushed this new empire up with older Ottoman (to the south) and Chinese (to the east) empires. By the end of the seventeenth century, Eurasia was being filled in with giant empires—often at the expense of borderland, nomadic communities. It would be a matter of time before the big dynasts turned from warring against borderlanders to fighting with each other over the balance of power in Eurasia.

ABSOLUTIST GOVERNMENT AND SERFDOM In the seventeenth and eighteenth centuries, the Romanovs created an absolutist system of government. Only the tsar had the right to make war, tax, judge, and coin money. The Romanovs also made the nobles serve as state officials. Now Russia became a despotic state that had no political assemblies for nobles or other groups, other than mere consultative bodies like the imperial senate. Indeed, away from Moscow, local aristocrats enjoyed nearly unlimited authority in exchange for loyalty and tribute to the tsar.

During this period, Russia's peasantry bore the burden of maintaining the wealth of the small nobility and the monarchy. Most peasant families gathered into communes, isolated rural worlds where people helped one another deal with plummeting Little Ice Age temperatures, severe landlords, and occasional poor harvests. Communes functioned like

MAP 13.7 | Russian Expansion, 1462–1795

The state of Muscovy incorporated vast territories through overland expansion as it grew and became the Russian Empire.

- Using the map key, identify the different expansions the Russian Empire underwent between 1462 and 1795 and the directions it generally expanded in.
- With what countries and cultures did the Russian Empire come into contact?
- According to the text, what drove such dramatic expansion?

extended kin networks in that members reciprocated favors and chores. The typical peasant hut was a single chamber heated by a wood-burning stove with no chimney. Livestock and humans often shared the same quarters. In 1649, peasants were legally bound as serfs to the nobles and the tsar, meaning they had to perform obligatory services and deliver part of their produce to their lords. The lords essentially controlled all aspects of their serfs' lives.

Economic and Political Fluctuations in Western Europe

During this period, western Europe was a study in contrasts. Its economies adapted to climate change and colonialism with ingenuity and innovation. But it was a political and devotional hodgepodge, feuding over spiritual and dynastic loyalties. The result was the birth of modern capitalism, powered by contending middle-scaled imperial regimes—bigger than the city-states of the Renaissance but puny next to the lumbering agrarian and territorial powerhouses of Asia and now Russia. It was this delicate balance of carnage and competition that set Europe apart. It also explains Europe's outward aggression; once the cycle of war, fueled by the effects of climate change, crested in the middle of the seventeenth century, European rivals set aside their feuding within Europe and turned their eyes, their companies, and their gunships overseas.

Nenets Hunters. Hunters of the Nenets tribe in far northern Asia's treeless tundra show off their warm animal-skin clothing and self-fashioned weapons, as depicted in a 1620 engraving by Theodore de Bry, one of the first Europeans to come into contact with them.

Catherine the Great. Catherine the Great styled herself an enlightened despot, furthering the Russian Empire's adaptation of European high culture.

Would this tilt have happened without the Little Ice age? It's impossible to say for sure. But what we do know is that freezing temperatures shortened agricultural growing seasons by one to two months. The result was escalating prices for essential grain products, famine, death, and widespread peasant unrest that fueled political discord. The cooling had a few benefits, however, among which were the magnificent violins, still prized today, crafted by Antonio Stradivari (1644–1737) from the denser wood that freezing temperatures produced.

THE THIRTY YEARS' WAR For a century after Martin Luther broke with the Catholic Church (see Chapter 12), religious warfare raged in Europe. So did contests over territory, power, and trade. The **Thirty Years' War** (1618–1648)—a war between Protestant princes and the Catholic emperor for religious predominance in central Europe—reflected all of these. At its heart was a civil war within Hapsburg lands, which sucked in Catholic and Protestant neighboring states.

The civil war between Protestants and Catholics within the Habsburg Empire soon became a war for preeminence in Europe. It took the lives of civilians as well as soldiers. In total, fighting, disease, and famine wiped out a third of the German states' urban population and two-fifths of their rural population. The war also depopulated Sweden and Poland. Ultimately, the Treaty of Westphalia (1648) stated, in essence, that as there was a rough balance of power between Protestant and Catholic states, they would simply have to put up with each other. The Dutch won their independence from Spain. But the war's enormous costs provoked severe discontent in Spain, France, and England. Central Europe did not recover in economic or demographic terms for more than a century.

The Thirty Years' War transformed war making. Whereas most medieval struggles had been sieges between nobles leading small armies, centralized states fielding standing armies now waged grand-scale campaigns. The war also changed the ranks of soldiers: as the conflict ground on, local enlisted men defending their king, country, and faith gave way to hired mercenaries or criminals doing forced service. Even officers, who had previously obtained their stripes by purchase or royal decree, now had to earn them. Gunpowder, cannons, and handguns became standardized. By the eighteenth century, Europe's wars featured huge standing armies boasting a professional officer corps, deadly artillery, and long supply lines bringing food and ammunition to the front. The costs—material and human—of war began to soar and put added pressure on empires to expand and compete for overseas spoils.

The Thirty Years' War. The mercenary armies of the Thirty Years' War were renowned for pillaging and tormenting the civilians of central Europe. In this engraving by Jacques Callot, the townsfolk exact revenge on some of these soldiers, hanging many, as an accompanying caption claims, "damned and infamous thieves, like bad fruit, from this tree."

Amsterdam Stock Exchange. The high concentration of merchants in Amsterdam naturally gave way to the world's first stock exchange in the seventeenth century. This diverse gathering of men trading stocks and preparing to participate in auctions, as depicted by renowned painter Emanuel de Witte, was a common sight throughout the Dutch Golden Age.

WESTERN EUROPEAN ECONOMIES In spite of warfare's human toll, it spurred European states' commercial expansion. But not all European states grew equally. Warfare favored the rising powers, like the Netherlands, England (later, Britain), and France, at the expense of Spain and Portugal. As European commercial dynamism shifted northward, the Dutch led the way with innovative commercial practices and a new mercantile elite. They specialized in shipping and in financing regional and long-distance trade. Their famous *fluitschips* carried heavy, bulky cargoes (like Baltic wood) with relatively small crews. Dutch ships transported their own and other countries' goods. Amsterdam's merchants founded an exchange bank, established a rudimentary stock exchange, and pioneered systems of underwriting and insuring cargoes.

England and France also became commercial powerhouses, establishing aggressive policies to promote national business and drive out competitors. Consider the English Navigation Act of 1651. By stipulating that only English ships could carry goods between the mother country and its colonies, it protected English shippers and merchants—especially from the Dutch.

The English subsequently launched several effective trade wars against Holland. The French, too, followed aggressive mercantilist policies and ultimately joined forces with England to invade Holland.

Economic development was not limited to port towns: the countryside, too, enjoyed breakthroughs in production. In northwestern Europe, investments in water drainage, larger livestock herds, and improved cultivation practices generated much greater yields. Also, a four-field crop rotation involving wheat, clover, barley, and turnips kept nutrients in the soil and provided year-round fodder for livestock. As a result (and as we have seen many times throughout history), increased output supported a growing urban population. By contrast, in Spain and Italy, agricultural change and population growth came more slowly.

Production rose most where the organization of rural property changed. In England, for example, in a movement known as **enclosure**, landowners took control of lands that traditionally had been common property serving local needs. Claiming exclusive rights to these lands, the landowners planted new crops or pastured sheep with the aim of selling the products in distant markets. The largest landowners put their farms in the hands of tenants, who hired wage laborers to till, plant, and harvest. Thus, in England, peasant agriculture gave way to farms run by wealthy families who exploited the marketplace to buy what they needed (including labor) and to sell what they produced. In this regard, England led the way in a Europe-wide process of commercializing the countryside.

DYNASTIC MONARCHIES: FRANCE AND ENGLAND If Asian powers wrestled with the balance of centralizing versus decentralizing authority, so did European monarchs. In France, Louis XIII (r. 1610–1643) and especially his chief minister, Cardinal Richelieu, concentrated power in the hands of the king. After 1614, kings refused to convene the Estates-General, a medieval advisory body. Composed of representatives of three groups—the clergy (the First Estate, those who pray), the nobility (the Second Estate, those who fight), and the unprivileged remainder of the population (the Third Estate, those who work)—the Estates-General was an obstacle to the king's full empowerment. Instead of sharing power, the king and his counselors wanted to rule without constraints, to create—in the words of the age—an **absolute monarchy**. The ruler's authority was to be complete and his state free of bloody disorders. His rule would be lawful, but he, not his jurists, would dictate the last legal word. If the king made a mistake, only God could call him to account. Thus, the French, like most Europeans, believed in the "divine right of kings," a political belief akin to that of imperial China, where the emperor was thought to rule with the mandate of heaven.

In absolutist France, privileges and state offices flowed from the king's grace. All patronage networks ultimately linked to the king. The great palace Louis XIV built at Versailles teemed with nobles from all over France seeking favor, dressing according to the king's lavish (and expensive) fashion code, and attending the latest tragedies, comedies, and concerts. Just as the Japanese shogun monitored the daimyos by keeping their families in Edo, Louis XIV kept a watchful eye on the French nobility at Versailles.

In practice, French absolutist government was not as absolute as the king and his ministers wished. Pockets of stalwart Protestants practiced their religion secretly. Peasant disturbances continued. Criticism of court life, wars, and religious policies filled anonymous pamphlets, jurists' notebooks, and courtiers' private journals. Members of the nobility also grumbled about their political misfortunes, but since the king would not call the Estates-General, they had no formal way to express their concerns.

England might also have evolved into an absolutist regime, but there were important differences between England and France. While French Catholic royals consolidated power, England's feud between Catholics and Protestants plunged the country into civil war. Queen Elizabeth (r. 1558–1603) and her successors used many policies similar to those of the French monarchy, such as control of patronage (to grant privileges) and elaborate court festivities. The "Virgin Queen" never married and exerted sole control over the church, military, and aristocracy. However, the English Parliament remained an important force. Whereas the French kings did not need the consent of the Estates-General to enact taxes, the English monarchs had to convene Parliament to raise money.

Under Elizabeth's successors, fierce quarrels broke out over taxation, religion, and royal efforts to rule without parliamentary consent. Tensions ran high between Puritans (who preferred a simpler form of worship and more egalitarian church government) and Anglicans (who supported the state-sponsored, hierarchically organized Church of England headed by the king). Social and economic grievances led to civil war in the 1640s and an ultimate victory for the parliamentary army (largely Puritan)—and the beheading of King Charles I. Twelve years followed of government as a kingless commonwealth, primarily under the leadership of Puritan Oliver Cromwell.

In 1660, the monarchy was restored, but without resolving issues of religious tolerance and the king's relation to Parliament. Charles II and his successor, James II, aroused opposition due to their autocracy and secret efforts to bring England back into the Catholic fold. The conflict between an aspiring absolutist monarch and Parliament's insistence on shared sovereignty and Protestant succession culminated in the Glorious Revolution of 1688–1689. In a bloodless upheaval, James II fled to France and Parliament offered the crown

Versailles. Louis XIV's Versailles, just southwest of Paris, was a hunting lodge that was converted at colossal cost in the 1660s–1670s into a grand royal chateau with expansive grounds. The image presented here was painted by the French artist Pierre Patel in 1688. Much envied and imitated across Europe, the palace became the epicenter of a luxurious court life that included entertainment such as plays and musical offerings, state receptions, royal hunts, boating, and gambling. Thousands of nobles at Versailles vied with each other for closer proximity to the king in the performance of court rituals.

to William of Orange and his wife, Mary (a Protestant). The conflict's outcome established the principle that English monarchs must rule in conjunction with Parliament. Although the Church of England was reaffirmed as the official state church, Presbyterians and Jews were allowed to practice their religions. Catholic worship, still officially forbidden, was tolerated as long as the Catholics kept quiet. By 1700, then, England's nobility and merchant classes had a guaranteed say in public affairs and assurance that state activity would privilege the propertied classes as well as the ruler.

Events in France and England stimulated much political writing. In England, Thomas Hobbes published *Leviathan* (1651), a defense of the state's absolute power over all competing forces. John Locke published *Two Treatises of Civil Government* (1689), which argued not only for the natural rights to liberty and property but also for the rights of peoples to form a government and then to disband and re-form it when it did not live up to its contract. French theorists also proposed new ways of conducting politics and making law and debated the extent to which elites could check the king. As the eighteenth century unfolded, the question of where sovereignty lay grew more pressing.

MERCANTILIST WARS The rise of new powers in Europe intensified rivalries for control of the Atlantic system. As conflicts over colonies and sea-lanes replaced earlier religious and territorial struggles, commercial struggles became worldwide wars. Across the globe, European empires constantly skirmished over control of trade and territory. English and Dutch trading companies took aim at Portuguese outposts in Asia and the Americas and then at each other. Ports in India suffered repeated assaults and counterassaults. In response, European powers built huge navies to protect their colonies and trade routes and to attack their rivals.

Queen Elizabeth of England. This portrait (c. 1600, by the painter Robert Peake, the Elder) depicts an idealized Queen Elizabeth near the end of her long reign. The queen is pictured riding in a procession in the midst of an admiring crowd composed of the most important nobles of the realm.

After 1715, mercantilist wars raged mainly outside Europe, as empires feuded over colonial possessions. Each round of warfare ratcheted up the scale and cost of fighting.

The **Seven Years' War** (known as the French and Indian War in the United States) marked the culmination of this rivalry. Fought from 1756 to 1763, it saw Indigenous peoples, African slaves, Bengali princes, Filipino militiamen, and European foot soldiers dragged into a contest over imperial possessions and control of the seas. Some fleets, like the French at the Battle of Quiberon Bay, were dispatched to the bottom of the ocean. Some fortresses, like Spain's Havana and France's Québec City, fell to invaders. What sparked the war was a skirmish of British colonial troops (featuring a lieutenant colonel named George Washington) allied with Seneca warriors against French soldiers in the Ohio Valley. (See Map 13.2 for North American references.) In India, the war had a decisive outcome, for here the East India Company trader Robert Clive rallied 850 European officers and 2,100 Indian recruits to defeat the French (there were but 40 French artillerymen) and their 50,000 Maratha allies at Plassey. The British seized the upper hand—over everyone—in India. Not only did the British drive off the French from the rich Bengali interior, but they also crippled Indian rulers' resistance against European intruders. (See Map 12.5 for India references.)

The Seven Years' War changed the balance of power around the world. Britain emerged as a foremost colonial empire. Its rivals took a pounding: France lost its North American colonies, and Spain lost Florida (though it gained the Louisiana Territory west of the Mississippi in a secret deal with France). In India, as well, the French were losers and had to acknowledge British supremacy in the wealthy provinces of Bihar and Bengal. But overwhelmingly, the biggest losers were Indigenous peoples everywhere. With the rise of one empire over all others, it was harder for Indigenous peoples to play the Europeans off against each other. Maratha princes faced the same problem. Clearly, as worlds became more entangled, the gaps between winners and losers grew more pronounced.

Wealth from long-distant trade and intense warfare led to the rise of militarily powerful, monarchical states in Europe. In the long run, beginning in the eighteenth century and coming to fulfillment in the nineteenth, the most dynamic of these states, notably Britain and France, ultimately joined by a newly unified Germany, were able to dominate the great states of Afro-Eurasia economically and militarily.

Conclusion

A radical decline in temperatures worldwide made the seventeenth century a time of famine, dying, epidemic disease, and political turmoil that produced regime change in China, Persia, and England and threatened the rulers of the Ottoman and Mughal Empires. Yet by the 1750s, the world's regions were more economically connected than ever. The process of integrating the resources of separated worlds, kicked off by Columbus's voyages, intensified during this period. Traders shipped a wider variety of commodities—from Baltic wood to Indian cotton, from New World silver and sugar to Chinese silks and porcelain—over longer distances. People increasingly wore clothes manufactured elsewhere, consumed beverages made from products cultivated in far-off locations, and used imported guns to settle local conflicts.

Everywhere, this integration and expansion of consumer opportunities came at a heavy price for Indigenous peoples. Nowhere was it more costly than in the Americas, where colonization and exploitation led to the expulsion of Indigenous peoples from their lands and the decimation of their numbers. The cost was also very high for the millions of Africans forced across the Atlantic to work New World plantations and for the millions more who did not survive the journey.

Along with sugar, silver was the product from the Americas that most transformed global trading networks and that showed how greater entanglements could both enrich and destabilize. Although Spanish colonizers mined New World silver and shipped it to western Europe and Asia, it was Spain's main competitors in Europe who gained the upper hand in the seventeenth and eighteenth centuries. Nearly one-third of the silver from the New World ended up in China as payment for products like porcelains and silks that consumers still regarded as the world's finest manufactures. But if China's economy remained vibrant, silver did play a part in the fall of one dynasty and the rise of another. For the Ottoman, Mughal, and Safavid Empires, the influx of silver created rampant inflation and undermined their previous economic autonomy.

Certain societies coped with climate change and increased commercial exchange more successfully than others. The Safavid and Ming dynasties could not withstand the pressures; both collapsed. The Spanish, Ottoman, and Mughal Empires managed to survive but faced increasing pressure from aggressive rivals. More than any other country, England survived the travails of climate change, but witnessed the execution of a monarch (Charles I) and an autocratic Puritan government under Oliver Cromwell. By the end of the eighteenth century, England had a new empire, a strengthened parliament, and an energetic merchant class ready to dominate global markets. For newcomers to the integrating world, the opportunity to trade helped support new dynasties. Japan and Russia emerged on the world stage. But even in these newer regimes, commerce and competition did not erase conflict. To the contrary, while the world was more together economically than ever before, greater prosperity for some hardly translated into peace for most.

After You Read This Chapter

TRACING THE GLOBAL STORYLINE

FOCUS ON: The Emergence of Global Trade

The Americas

- England, France, and Holland join Spain and Portugal as colonial powers in the Americas, fundamentally altering the lives of Indigenous peoples and the relationships among them.
- The English and French colonies in the Caribbean become the world's major exporters of sugar.

Africa

- The Atlantic slave trade increases to record proportions, creating gender imbalances, impoverishing some regions, and elevating the power of the slave-supplying states.

Southeast Asia

- The Dutch East India Company takes over the major islands of Southeast Asia, leading to the enslavement of Indigenous peoples to work on plantations.

The Islamic World

- World trade destabilizes the Safavid, Ottoman, and Mughal Empires.
- The Little Ice Age destabilizes the Ottoman state and leads to a powerful but ultimately unsuccessful rebellion; the Celali revolts.

East Asia

- The Ming dynasty in China, poorly administered and suffering from the effects of climate change, loses the mandate of heaven and is replaced by the Qing.
- The Tokugawa shogunate unifies Japan and limits the influence of Europeans in the country.

Europe

- Tsarist Russia expands toward the Baltic Sea and the Pacific Ocean.
- The Thirty Years' War (1618–1648) is partly the result of a dramatic cooling of the global climate and enmity between Protestant and Catholic countries.
- Europe recovers from the Thirty Years' War, with Holland, England, and France emerging as economic powerhouses.

CHRONOLOGY

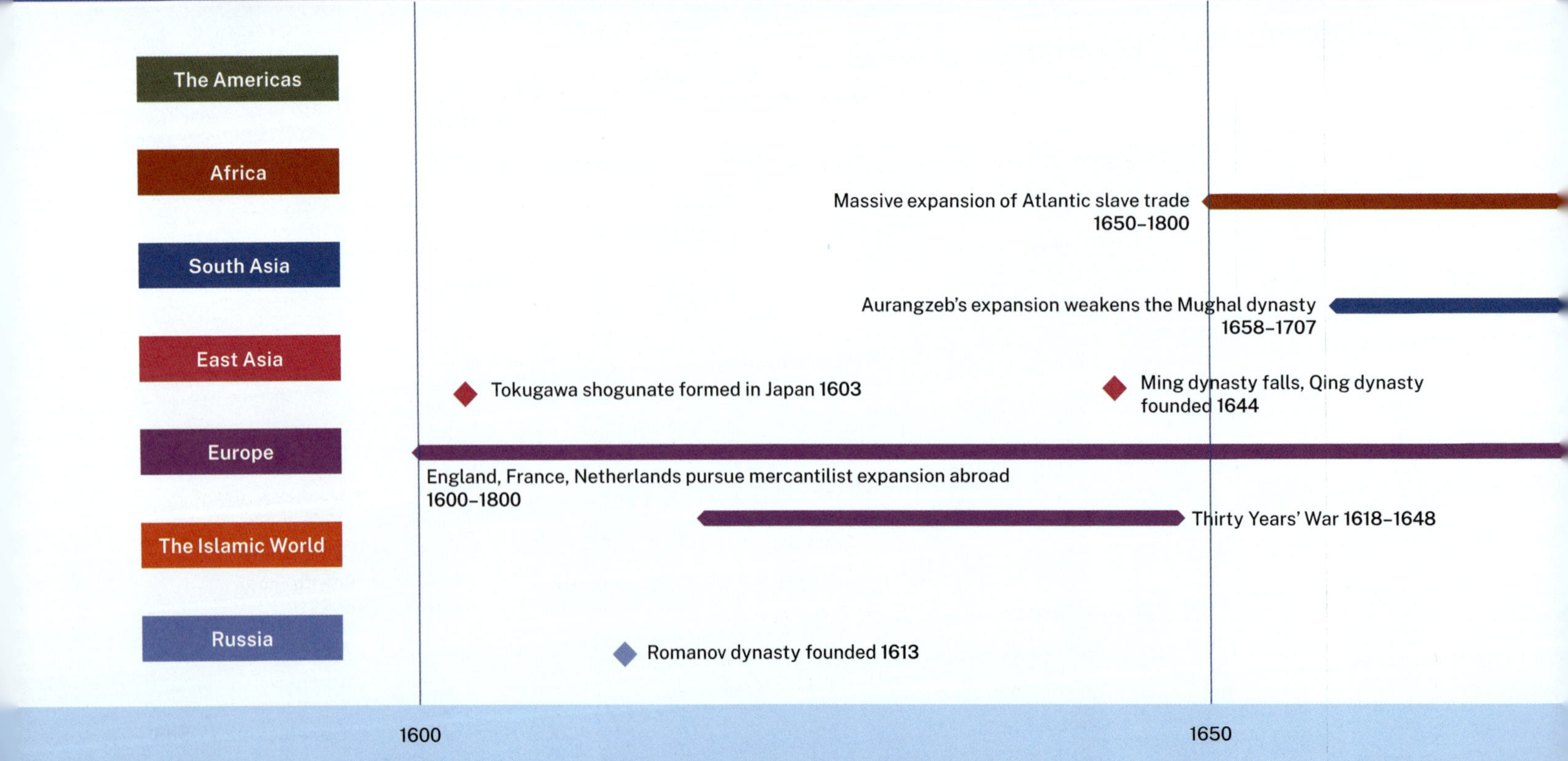

KEY TERMS

absolute monarchy p. 580
Canton system p. 568
chartered companies p. 545
enclosure p. 580
Little Ice Age p. 545
Mamluks p. 563
Manchus p. 564
mercantilism p. 545
Muscovy p. 576
Qing dynasty p. 566
Seven Years' War p. 582
Thirty Years' War p. 578
Tokugawa shogunate p. 572

THINKING ABOUT GLOBAL CONNECTIONS

Thinking about Exchange Networks and World Trade How did silver, and then sugar, transform world trade? What political and cultural forces benefited from the development of long-distance trading networks? Which groups suffered and how? Contrast the effects of long-distance trade in major world regions.

Thinking about Changing Power Relationships and World Trade The seventeenth and eighteenth centuries witnessed the rise of new powers in England, Japan, and Russia, as well as regional powers on the west coast of Africa. Several established empires continued to expand but confronted powerful new challenges to their authority. How did leaders of the Ottoman, Mughal, and Qing Empires respond to challenges to their authority? What major challenges did they face? How would you characterize the new powers that emerged around the world in this period?

Thinking about the Impact of World Trade on Gender Relations The Atlantic slave trade wreaked havoc on sex ratios both in Africa and in the slavery-ridden societies of the New World because most enslaved Africans taken across the ocean were men. How did this affect social life on New World plantations? What strategies did African communities utilize to mitigate the loss of so many men? Elsewhere around the world, increased trade challenged established social hierarchies. How did ruling elites mobilize gender to reinforce their authority?

Go to INQUIZITIVE to see what you've learned—and learn what you've missed—with personalized feedback along the way.

- Sugar complex emerges in the Caribbean region seventeenth century
- British defeat French forces in North America during the Seven Years' War 1756–1763
- French and Dutch merchants establish fur trade in North America seventeenth century
- Asante state founded 1701
- British assume control of French interests in South Asia during Seven Years' War 1756–1763
- Seven Years' War 1756–1763
- Safavid dynasty collapses 1722
- Köprülü reforms stabilize Ottoman Empire mid-seventeenth century
- Russia expands into Siberia seventeenth century
- Peter the Great reigns 1682–1725

1700 | 1750

Global Themes and Sources

Comparing Perceptions on Slavery in the Atlantic World

The documents gathered here present different aspects of slavery in the Atlantic world. For enslaved Africans, the Atlantic system was an abomination. For enslavers, merchants, and political leaders—in Africa and Europe—the slave trade was a business. Each document highlights a different aspect and presents a different perspective on Atlantic slavery.

In the first document, Olaudah Equiano describes the horrifying conditions captives endured on the African coast as they awaited the arrival of slaving ships from the point of view of a captive. In the second, Richard Ligon explains the absence of revolts by enslaved people from the planters' perspective, while in the third, the Baron de Wimpffen, a Swiss aristocrat and explorer, describes the centrality of race, as opposed to family lineage or nobility, in the colonial society of Saint-Domingue. The final three documents show data from the 1835 household census for Santiago do Iguape, Bahia, a parish in the heart of a sugar plantation region in Brazil. Created by Portuguese colonial authorities for their own purposes, the census records provide basic demographic statistics about the region's population, over half of which was enslaved.

Collectively, these documents raise comparative questions: How did different people and groups view the same institution, slavery? How did they perceive one another? How did they distinguish people like themselves from others? The statistical information, in particular, makes it possible to see how the composition of plantation society changed—to identify cause and effect—in a sugar-producing region.

ANALYZING SLAVERY IN THE ATLANTIC WORLD

- Compare the way each written source divides people into racial groups. How do the sources mark the boundaries between communities? What criteria do they use?
- Contrast de Wimpffen's account of Saint-Domingue with Ligon's history of Barbados. What are their biggest fears?
- Does the evidence from the graphs support or undermine the claims of the written sources?

PRIMARY SOURCE 13.1

The Interesting Narrative of the Life of Olaudah Equiano (1789), Olaudah Equiano

Taught to read and write by his masters, Olaudah Equiano (c. 1745–1797) published *The Interesting Narrative of the Life of Olaudah Equiano, or Gustavus Vassa, the African* (1789) after purchasing his freedom in 1766. Known as Gustavus Vassa during his lifetime, he was active in the British abolitionist movement.

- Explain the significance of nation (or community) in this document.
- What part of his captivity most troubled Equiano, and how did he cope?
- Equiano describes the punishment meted out to Whites. Explain why. How do those passages shape the meaning of the document as a whole?

The first object which saluted my eyes when I arrived on the coast, was the sea, and a slave ship, which was then riding at anchor, and waiting for its cargo. These filled me with astonishment, which was soon converted into terror, when I was carried on board. I was immediately handled, and tossed up to see if I were sound, by some of the crew; and I was now persuaded that I had gotten into a world of bad spirits, and that they were going to kill me. Their complexions, too, differing so much from ours, their long hair, and the language they spoke (which was very different from any I had ever heard), united to confirm me in this belief. Indeed, such were the horrors of my views and fears at the moment, that, if ten thousand worlds had been my own, I would have freely parted with them all to have exchanged my condition with that of the meanest slave in my own country. When I looked round the ship too, and saw a large furnace of copper boiling, and a multitude of black people of every description chained together, every one of their countenances expressing dejection and sorrow, I no longer doubted of my fate; and, quite overpowered with horror and anguish, I fell motionless on the deck and fainted. When I recovered a little, I found some black people about me, who I believed were some of those who had brought me on board, and had been receiving their pay; they talked to me in order to cheer me, but all in vain. . . .

I now saw myself deprived of all chance of returning to my native country, or even the least glimpse of hope of gaining the shore, which I now considered as friendly; and I even wished for my former slavery in preference to my present situation, which was filled with horrors of every kind, still heightened by my ignorance of what I was to undergo. I was not long suffered to indulge my grief; I was soon put down under the decks, and there I received such a salutation in my nostrils as I had never experienced in my life; so that, with the loathsomeness of the stench, and crying together, I became so sick and low that I was not able to eat, nor I had the least desire to taste anything. . . .

In a little time after, amongst the poor chained men, I found some of my own nation, which in a small degree gave ease to my mind. I inquired of these what was to be done with us? They gave me to understand, we were to be carried to these white people's country to work for them. I then was a little revived, and thought, if it were no worse than working, my situation was not so desperate; but still I feared I should be put to death, the white people looked and acted, as I thought, in so savage a manner; for I had never seen among any people such instances of brutal cruelty; and this not only shown towards us blacks, but also to some of the whites themselves. One white man in particular I saw, when we were permitted to be on deck, flogged so unmercifully with a large rope near the foremast, that he died in consequence of it; and they tossed him over the side as they would have done a brute. This made me fear these people the more; and I expected nothing less than to be treated in the same manner. . . .

At last, when the ship we were in, had got in all her cargo, they made ready with many fearful noises, and we were all put under deck, so that we could not see how they managed the vessel. But this disappointment was the least of my sorrow. The stench of the hold while we were on the coast was so intolerably loathsome, that it was dangerous to remain there for any time, and some of us had been permitted to stay on the deck for the fresh air; but now that the whole ship's cargo were confined together, it became absolutely pestilential. The closeness of the place, and the heat of the climate, added to the number in the ship, which was so crowded that each had scarcely room to turn himself, almost suffocated us. This produced copious perspirations, so that the air soon became unfit for respiration, from a variety of loathsome smells, and brought on a sickness among the slaves, of which many died. . . . The shrieks of the women, and the groans of the dying, rendered the whole a scene of horror almost inconceivable. Happily perhaps, for myself, I was soon reduced so low here that it was thought necessary to keep me almost always on deck; and from my extreme youth I was not put in fetters. In this situation I expected every hour to share the fate of my companions, some of whom were almost daily brought upon deck at the point of death, which I began to hope would soon put an end to my miseries.

Source: Olaudah Equiano, *The Interesting Narrative of the Life of Olaudah Equiano, or Gustavus Vassa, the African, Written by Himself* (New York: Norton, 2001), pp. 38–41.

PRIMARY SOURCE 13.2

A True and Exact History of the Island of Barbadoes (1673), Richard Ligon

Richard Ligon (c. 1585–1662) lost most of his fortune in the English Civil War (1642–1651). He bought half a sugar plantation on the English island of Barbados to recover from his losses and rebuild his fortune.

- How does Ligon distinguish enslavers from the enslaved?
- How does Ligon explain the absence of revolts?
- Analyze the role of religion in this document.

It has been accounted a strange thing that the Negroes, being more than double the numbers of the Christians that are there, and they accounted a bloody people where they think they have power or advantages; and the more bloody by how much they are more fearful than others: that these should not commit some horrid massacre upon the Christians, thereby to enfranchise [empower] themselves and become Masters of the Island. But there are three reasons that take away this wonder; the one is, They are not suffered [allowed] to touch or handle any weapons: The other, That they are held in such awe and slavery as they are fearful to appear in any daring act; and seeing the mustering of our men and hearing their Gun-shot (that which nothing is more terrible to them), their spirits are subjugated to so low a condition as they dare not look up to any bold attempt. Besides these, there is a third reason, which stops all designs [plans] of that kind, and that is, They are fetch'd from several parts of Africa, who speak several languages, and by that means one of them understands not another: For, some of them are fetch'd from Guinny and Binny, some from Cutchew, some from Angola, and some from the River of Gambia. And in some of these places where petty Kingdoms are, they sell their Subjects and such as they take in Battle, whom they make slaves; and some mean men sell their Servants, their Children, and sometimes their Wives; and think all good traffic [acceptable trade] for such commodities as our Merchants send them. When they are brought to us, the Planters buy them out of the Ship where they find them stark naked and therefore cannot be deceived in any outward infirmity. They choose them as they do Horses in a Market; the strongest, youthfulest, and most beautiful, yield the greatest prices. Thirty pound sterling is a price for the best man Negro; and twenty five, twenty six, or twenty seven pound for a Woman; the Children are at easier rates. . . .

When any of them die, they dig a grave, and at evening they bury him, clapping and wringing their hands and making a doleful sound with their voices. They are a people of a timorous and fearful disposition, and consequently bloody when they find advantages [opportunities]. If any of them commit a fault, give him present [immediate] punishment, but do not threaten him; for if you do, it is an even lay, he will go and hang himself to avoid the punishment. What their other opinions are in matter of Religion, I know not; but certainly they are not altogether of the sect of the Sadduces [Hebrew sect (second century BCE–first century CE) that rejected belief in the resurrection of the soul]: For, they believe a Resurrection and that they shall go into their own Country again and have their youth renewed. And lodging this opinion in their hearts, they make it an ordinary practice, upon any great fright or threatening of their Master, to hang themselves. But Colonel Walrond, having lost three or four of his best Negroes this way, and in a very little time, caused one of their heads to be cut off and set upon a pole a dozen foot high; and having done that, caused all his Negroes to come forth and march round about this head and bid them look on it, whether this were not the head of such an one that hang'd himself. Which they acknowledging, he then told them, That they were in a main error in thinking they went into their own Countries after they were dead; for, this man's head was here, as they all were witnesses of; and how was it possible the body could go without a head. Being convinc'd by this sad yet lively spectacle, they changed their opinions; and after that, no more hanged themselves.

Source: Richard Ligon, *A True and Exact History of the Island of Barbadoes* (London: Peter Parker, 1673), excerpts available online at http://nationalhumanitiescenter.org/pds/amerbegin/power/text8/LigonBarbadosSlavery.pdf.

PRIMARY SOURCE 13.3

A Voyage to Saint Domingue (1797), Alexandre-Stanislas, Baron de Wimpffen

Alexandre-Stanislas, Baron de Wimpffen, served as a captain under the French general Count Rochambeau in 1781–1782 and was an aristocratic military figure and explorer. He served in the West Indies and resigned in 1788.

- Analyze the significance of "intimacy" in this document.
- What does de Wimpffen mean by the "compulsatory precautions arising from the prejudice of colour"?
- Explain the relationship between "whites from Europe" and "white Creoles."

Although the distance between the slave and the free man is immense, yet, to avoid subdivisions, and minute distinctions, I have adopted the division of color, as the most simple. For I must further observe to you, that the male and female negroes, as well as the male and female mulattos, in spite of the acquisition of liberty, remain in a state of abjectness, which not only disqualifies them from any public employ, but forbids them to contract with the whites a sufficient degree of intimacy, I will not say to sleep with them, but even to eat. If I visit a rich mulatto, he will call me Sir, and not master, like the rest. I call him friend, dear friend, &c. he will ask me to dinner; but if he be correct, he will not presume to sit at table with me.

Such, Sir, is the total division. Each of the three classes has besides its shades—such as those which, in despite of complexion, separate the governor from the other whites, the mulatto from the free negro, &c. &c.

The compulsatory precautions arising from the prejudice of colour, have procured for the inhabitants two advantages, which in some degree compensate for the ridiculousness of it. They render the government more circumspect in its arbitrary proceedings; and they imprint on the colonists a character of haughty independence, from which despotic administrators have more than once experienced a resistance so inflexible, that the court has been finally obliged to recall a governor, whom the habit of playing the nabob [a European who returned from India, having made a fortune] in the East, has daily tempted to transgress the bounds of his authority.

The natural consequence of the order of things which prevails here, is, that all those titles of honour which are elsewhere the *pabula* [source] of emulation, of rivalry and of discord; which inspire so much pride, and create so many claims in some; so much ambition and envy in others; shrink to nothing, and entirely disappear before the sole title of WHITE. It is by your skin, however branded it may be, and not by your parchment [titles of nobility], however worm-eaten, that your pretensions to gentility are assessed. Thus you see that vanity, which on your side of the water torments and turns herself a thousand ways, to impose on the public, and usurp the tribute of respect which it accords to the claims of birth, would here lose both her time and her labor.

Each of the different classes of the inhabitants of St. Domingo has, as you will readily imagine, a turn of thinking, a style of living, more or less approximate or distinct; which, after all, has little resemblance to what you will find elsewhere; because the climate, the regimen, the manners, the wants, the occupations, the degree of reciprocal dependency, establish here connections of the slightest nature; very different from those which, with you, Sir, bind together the members of the same society. . . .

The first thing that strikes every traveller who arrives here with the faculty of observation, is, that in spite of the conformity of origin, colour and interests, the whites from Europe, and the white Creoles, form two classes, which, by their reciprocal pretentions, are so widely foundered, that necessity alone can bring them together. The former, with more breeding, more politeness, and more knowledge of the world, affect over the latter a superiority which is far from contributing to unite them. Yet, if the Creoles were a little more cautious than they are at present in their too early connections with women; if they cultivated with more care their extraordinary propensities to excel in all bodily exercises; if they seconded by a better method of education the natural facility of their genius; I am persuaded, that not having to struggle against the influence of the climate under which they were born, nor against the habitudes of a kind of life, differing essentially from that to which a European is obliged to submit himself on his arrival here, I am persuaded, I say, that all the advantages would be on their side. Nothing is wanting to the Creole, but a sufficient degree of good sense, to enable him to use, without abusing, the faculties with which nature has endued [*sic*] him.

Source: Francis Alexander Stanislaus, Baron de Wimpffen, *A Voyage to Saint Domingue, in the Years 1788, 1789, and 1790*, translated by J. Wright (London: T. Cadell, Junior, and W. Davies, 1797), pp. 62–65.

PRIMARY SOURCE 13.4

Population Statistics of the Bahia Sugar Plantations, Brazil (1835)

These documents show data from the 1835 household census for Santiago do Iguape, Bahia, a parish in the heart of a sugar plantation region in Brazil. They provide basic demographic statistics about the region's population, over half of which was enslaved. Created by colonial authorities for their own purposes, the census records make it possible to reconstruct the experience of people who left no written records themselves.

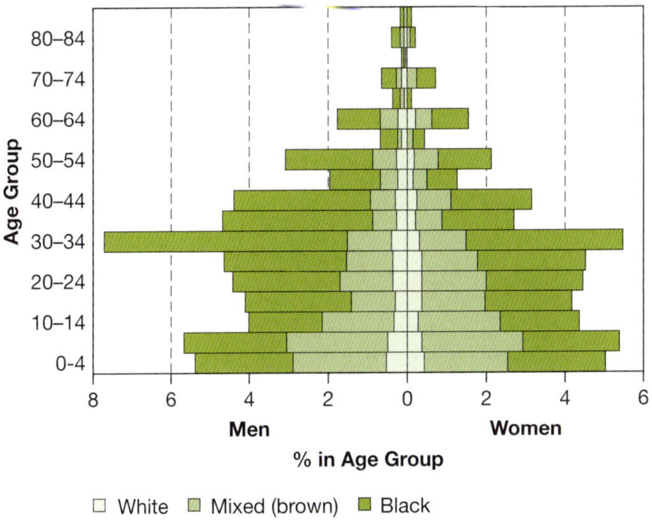

Population by Racial Classification in 1835, Santiago do Iguape

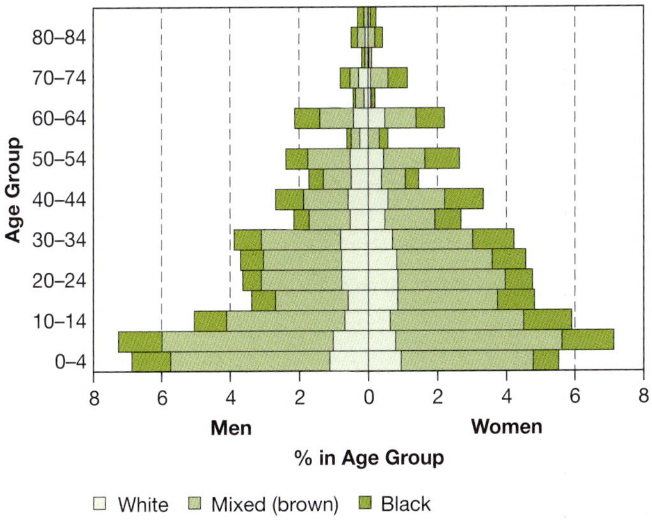

Free and Freed Population by Racial Classification in 1835, Santiago do Iguape

Population pyramids are graphs that present a population's composition by age and sex, and, here, by racial classification as well. A pyramid equally divided between men and women with a wide base represents an expanding population with a large proportion of children and young adults. Iguape's free and freed populations follow this pattern, but the enslaved population does not.

Compare the data for each racial group in the first graph, and consider why the Brazilian state organized its records according to racial categories. How do you think the demands of sugar production shaped the racial categories Brazilian officials used to sort the local population?

Considering the second two graphs, on the free and enslaved populations, how was plantation society changing? Which groups managed to achieve a level of stability, and which did not?

Describe the challenges slaves would have faced in establishing families on the sugar plantations of Santiago do Iguape, and contrast their experience with the experiences of freed people of different racial classifications.

Source: Katherine Holt, "Population by Racial Classification, Santiago do Iguape 1835," "Free and Freed Population by Racial Classification, Iguape 1835," and "Enslaved Population by Place of Birth, Santiago do Iguape, 1835," The Bahian History Project: The 1835 Santiago do Iguape Household Census Database, http://www.mappingbahia.org/project/.

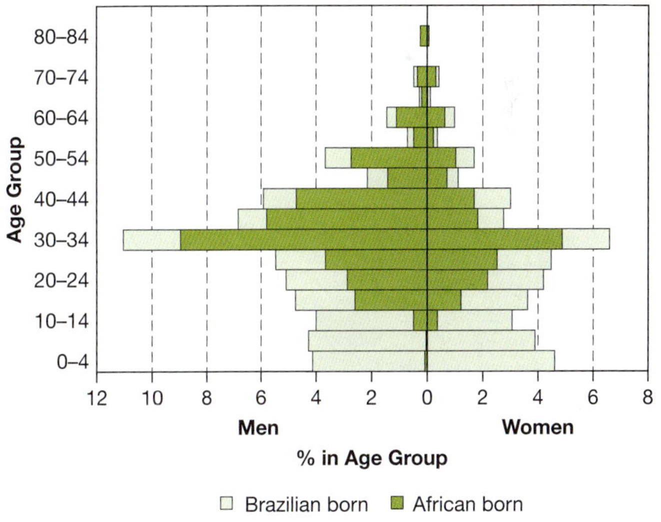

Enslaved Population by Place of Birth in 1835, Santiago do Iguape

Interpreting Visual Evidence

A World of Goods

As overseas trade generated new wealth, elites displayed this wealth in diverse ways. Some used new wealth to buy expensive local materials, while others displayed their power by incorporating foreign materials into local designs. Near commercial centers, opportunities for consumption and display of new goods also drew ordinary people into market activities. Ranging from the purely ornamental to the modest and practical, material objects reflected the identities of the people who bought and displayed them, as well as the identities of the producers who made them. They reinforced and sometimes altered status hierarchies as people's appreciation of these material objects, their beauty, and the skill that went into their production shaped the status of both consumers and producers.

The first object, *Oba with Sacrificial Animals from the Ezomo's Altar of the Hand* (eighteenth–nineteenth century), is made of brass, which signified the elite status of the royal patron—more modest men would have requested terra-cotta or wood. In the kingdom of Benin, altars like this celebrated exceptional individuals. In addition to the materials chosen, the artist used costume and scale to show the status of the figures depicted. The king, Ehenua, dressed in full military regalia, appears in the center of a group of smaller soldiers, aids, and priests. Two rows of musketeers above the frieze include Portuguese soldiers, showing the support Europeans provided Benin's leaders. The second object is a porcelain bowl produced in China for the British market, with a painting of a cricket match by the English painter Francis

Oba with Sacrificial Animals from the Ezomo's Altar of the Hand.

Chinese porcelain bowl, with painting by Francis Hayman.

Hayman (1708–1776). The third object, a Chinese lacquer tray from the Qing dynasty, likely crafted for the internal Chinese market, portrays a pastoral scene. The final object, a British-manufactured teapot, was made for middle-class consumers who could not afford imported porcelain from China. This example, with a handle, was intended to match European decorative style; the factory left off the handle for "Oriental" designs.

QUESTIONS FOR ANALYSIS

1. Describe how these objects were used. What functions did they serve?
2. Analyze the relationship between display and function in these objects. What impression do you think these objects made on people who saw them?
3. Explain the significance of these works for the people who produced them. What roles do you think artistry, craft skill, and financial gain played for the artists and artisans who produced them?
4. How did the conditions in which these objects were produced relate to the identities consumers sought to project? Consider also the relationship between the production of commodities—such as the tea and sugar associated with the final object—and consumer identity.

Tray (lacquer and mother of pearl), Chinese School, Qing dynasty.

British-manufactured teapot.

Before You Read This Chapter

GLOBAL STORYLINES

The Creation of Global Cultures

- Growing global commerce enriches rulers and merchants, who express their power through patronage for the arts.
- Distinctive cultures flourish in the major regions of the world, blending new influences with local traditions to varying degrees.
- While the Islamic and Asian worlds confidently retain their own belief systems, the Americas and Oceania increasingly face European cultural pressures.

CHAPTER OUTLINE

14

Cultures of Splendor and Power

1500–1780

FOCUS QUESTIONS

- What were the connections between cultural exchanges and the creation of a global market?
- In what ways did each culture in this period reflect the ideas of the state in which it was produced? How were the various cultures alike and different?
- What were the different responses to foreign cultures across Afro-Eurasia in the period 1500–1780? How were they similar and different?
- How did hybrid cultures emerge in the Americas, and what was the connection between these cultures and Enlightenment ideology?

In 1664, a sixteen-year-old girl from New Spain asked her parents for permission to attend the university in the capital. Although she had mastered Greek logic, taught Latin, and become a proficient mathematician, she had two strikes against her: she was a woman, and her thinking ran against the grain of the Catholic Church. So keen was she to pursue her studies that she proposed to disguise herself as a man. But her parents denied her requests, and instead of attending university she entered a convent in Mexico City. She spent the rest of her life cloistered. Fortunately, the convent turned out to be a sanctuary for her. There she studied science and mathematics and composed remarkable poetry. Sor (Sister) Juana Inés de la Cruz was the bard of a new world where people mixed in faraway places, where new wealth created new customs, and where new ideas began to take hold. One of her poems, "You Men," begins: "Silly, you men—so very adept/at wrongly faulting womankind, not seeing you're alone to blame/for faults you plant in woman's mind." Her poetry illustrates how new discoveries and new knowledge challenged old ways. But her life story also reflects the fierce resistance to new ways. Sor Juana's poetry enraged church authorities, who forced her to recant her words and who burned her books. Only the intervention of the viceroy's wife prevented officials from torching the nun's complete works before she died of plague in 1695.

Sor Juana's story attests to the progress of and resistance to new ideas—ideas that flourished as commerce and imperial consolidation fostered new knowledge and foreign borrowing. Creating new ideas and cultural practices often involved adapting from local or Indigenous peoples—usually without giving them credit. The result was a complex intermingling of worlds. Global commerce created riches that supported the arts, architecture, and scientific ventures. And yet, experimentation with new ways caused discomfort among defenders of the old order and provoked backlashes against innovation. At the same time, the mixing and combining of cultures made it harder and harder to separate "original" or "indigenous" ways of life from imported or borrowed ways.

Sor Juana Inés de la Cruz. In this portrait by Miguel Cabrera, Sor (Sister) Juana Inés de la Cruz (1651–1695) sits surrounded by scholarly artifacts, like her books, and symbols of piety. Sor Juana's writings exemplify how people around the world experimented with new cultural styles, often fusing disparate cultures. Frustrated by her exclusion from men's cultural circles, she also wrote in a personal, confessional style.

This chapter explores how global commerce enriched and reshaped cultures in the centuries after the Americas ceased to be worlds apart from Afro-Eurasia. Profiting from trade in New World commodities, many rulers and merchants displayed their power by commissioning fabulous works of art and majestic palaces and sprawling plazas. These cultural splendors were meant to impress. They also demonstrated the growing connections between distant societies, reflecting how exotic, borrowed influences could blend with domestic traditions. Book production and consumption soared, with some publications finding their way around the world. Indeed, information from distant parts became valuable; books were the medium to buy and sell it. The circulation of books and ideas, alongside the movement of peoples and commodities, intensified cultural exchanges and led to experiments in religious tolerance. As a result, people became more aware of diversity as the world's parts were laced together.

For some, this was a threat. All over the world, many people doubled down on their traditions. For others, it was an opportunity for adventure, discovery—and exploitation. So with splendor and power came a mixture of innovation and resistance. It was in Europe, however, that new knowledge gave rise to efforts to organize and systematize the world into categories—and into Europeans' ideas of hierarchy and superiority.

Trade and Culture

For many groups, the period's global cultural flourishing owed much to burgeoning world trade, which allowed some rulers to consolidate wealth, administration, and military power. These rulers were eager to patronize the arts as a way to legitimize their power and exhibit their cultural sophistication. In Europe, monarchs known as enlightened absolutists restricted the clergy and nobility and hired loyal bureaucrats who championed the knowledge of the new age. British monarchs, though not absolutists (because they shared power with Parliament), followed suit. Mughal emperors, Safavid shahs, and Ottoman sultans glorified their regimes by bringing artists and artisans from all over the world to give an Islamic flavor to their major cities and buildings. Rulers in China and Japan also looked to artists to extol their achievements. And in Africa, the wealth garnered from enslavement and the slave trade underwrote cultural productions of extraordinary merit.

Of course, some rulers and polities were more eager for change than others. Moreover, certain societies—in the Americas and the South Pacific, for example—found that contact, conquest, and commerce encroached on the autonomy of indigenous cultures. Although Europeans and native peoples exchanged ideas and practices, these transfers were unbalanced. Both Native Americans and Africans, for example, adapted to European missionizing by creating mixed forms of religious worship—but only because they were under pressure to do so. Europeans borrowed much from Native Americans and enslaved Africans but did not share sovereignty or wealth in return.

Despite the unifying aspects of world trade, each society retained core uniqueness. Ruling classes disseminated values based on cherished classical texts and long-established moral and religious principles. They used space in new ways to establish and project their power. (See Current Trends in World History: The Political Uses of Space.) They mapped geographies and wrote histories according to their traditional visions of the universe. Even as global trade drew their attention outward, societies celebrated their achievements in politics, economics, and culture with pride in their own heritages.

In 1500, the world's most dynamic cultures were in Asia, in areas profiting from the Indian Ocean and China Sea trades. It was in China and the Islamic world that the spice and luxury trades first flourished; here, too, rulers had successfully established political stability and centralized control of taxation, law making, and military force. This often involved recruiting people from diverse backgrounds and promoting secular (nonreligious) education. In the Ottoman, Ming, and Mughal Empires, for example, while older ways did not die out, both trade and empire building contributed to the spread of knowledge about distant people and foreign cultures.

Culture in the Islamic World

For centuries, Muslim elites had generously funded cultural development and mobilized ideas from a pre-Islamic past to create narratives of authenticity. As the Ottoman, Safavid, and Mughal Empires gained greater expanses of territory in the sixteenth and seventeenth centuries, they acquired new resources to fund more such pursuits. They also positioned themselves as rival heirs to an Islamic tradition as they bumped up against each other. Rulers supported new schools and building projects, and the elite produced books, artworks, and luxury goods. Cultural life reflected the politics of empire building, as emperors and elites sought greater prestige by patronizing intellectuals and artists.

Forged under different empires, Islamic cultural and intellectual life now reflected three distinct worlds. In place of an earlier Islamic cosmopolitanism, unique cultural patterns prevailed within each empire. Although the Ottomans, the Safavids, and the Mughals shared a common faith, each developed a relatively autonomous form of Muslim culture.

The Ottoman Cultural Synthesis

By the sixteenth century, the Ottoman Empire was enjoying a remarkably rich culture that blended ethnic, religious, and linguistic elements whose diversity exceeded those of previous Islamic empires. The Ottomans' cultural synthesis accommodated both **Sufis** (Islamic mystics who stressed contemplation and ecstasy through poetry, music, and dance) and ultraorthodox ***ulama*** (Islamic jurists who stressed tradition and religious law). It also balanced the interests of military men and administrators with those of clerics. Finally, it allowed autonomy to the minority faiths of Christianity and Judaism.

LAW AND OTTOMAN CULTURAL UNITY The Ottoman world achieved cultural unity, above all, by an outstanding intellectual achievement—its system of administrative law. As the empire absorbed diverse cultures and territories, the sultans realized that the *sharia* (Islamic holy law) would not suffice because it was silent on many secular matters. Moreover, the Ottoman state needed comprehensive laws to bridge differences among the many social and legal systems under its rule. Mehmed II, conqueror of Constantinople,

Islamic Scientists. This fifteenth-century Persian miniature shows Islamic scholars working with sophisticated navigational and astronomical instruments and reflects the importance that the educated classes in the Islamic world attached to observing and recording the regularities in the natural world. Indeed, many of Europe's advances in sailing drew on knowledge from the Muslim world.

Current Trends in World History

The Political Uses of Space

The use of space for political purposes is a theme we can trace across world history. In the early modern period, many kings and emperors opted to build grand palaces to create lavish power centers, from which they could project their influence over their kingdoms; petitioners and potential rivals would have to come to *them* to ask for favors or to complete their business. Monarchs sculpted these environments, creating a series of spaces, each of them open to a smaller and smaller number of the king's favorites. Both palaces and their surrounding grounds were ornate and splendid, were expensive to construct, and involved the best craftsmen and artists available, which often meant borrowing ideas and designs from neighboring cultures. Palace complexes of this type, built in Beijing, in Istanbul, in Isfahan, and just outside Paris, used space to project the rulers' power and to show who was boss.

The **Forbidden City of Beijing** was the earliest of these impressive sites of royal power (see illustration in Chapter 11, p. 479). Its construction took about four years—from 1416 to 1420—although the actual name "Forbidden City" did not appear until 1576. The entrance of the city was straddled by the Meridian Gate, the tallest structure of the entire complex, which towered over all other buildings at more than 115 feet above the ground. It was from this lofty position that the emperor extended his gaze toward his empire, as he oversaw various court ceremonies, including the important annual proclamation of the calendar that governed the entire country's agricultural and ritual activities. Foreign emissaries received by the court were also often allowed to use one of the passageways through the gate, where they were expected to be duly awed. As for the officials' daily audience with the emperor, they had to line up outside the Meridian Gate around 3 A.M. before proceeding to the Hall of Supreme Harmony. It was typical of the entire construction project that this impressive hall with vermilion walls and golden tiles was built at considerable cost. For the columns of the hall, fragrant hardwood had to be found in the tiger-ridden forests of the remote southwest, while the mountain forests of the south and southwest were searched for other timbers that eventually made their way to the capital through the Grand Canal.

The **Topkapi Palace** in Istanbul, capital of the Ottoman Empire, began to take shape in 1458 under Mehmed II and underwent steady expansion over the years (see photo in Chapter 11, p. 464). Topkapi projected royal authority in much the same way as the Forbidden City emphasized Chinese emperors' power: governing officials worked enclosed within massive walls, and monarchs rarely went outside their inner domain.

More than two centuries later, in the 1670s and 1680s, the French monarch Louis XIV built the **Palace of Versailles** on the site of a royal hunting lodge 11 miles from Paris, the French capital (see illustration in Chapter 13, p. 581). This enormously costly complex was built to house Louis's leading clergymen and nobles, who were obliged to visit at least twice a year. Louis hoped that by taking wealthy and powerful men and women away from their local power bases, and by diverting them with entertainments, he could keep them from plotting new forms of religious schism or challenging his right to rule. Going to Versailles also allowed him to escape the pressures and demands of the population of Paris. Many European monarchs—including Russia's Peter the Great—would build palace complexes modeled on Versailles.

If in China, the Ottoman Empire, and France, emperors built what were essentially private spaces in which to conduct and dominate state business, Shah Abbas (r. 1587–1629) of the Safavid Empire chose to create a great new public space instead. In the early seventeenth century, Shah Abbas oversaw the construction of the **great plaza at Isfahan**, a structure that reflected his desire to bring trade, government, and religion together under the authority of the supreme political leader. An enormous public mosque, the Shah

began the reform. By recruiting young boys, rather than noblemen, for training as bureaucrats or military men and making them accountable directly to the sultan, he fashioned a professional bureaucracy with unswerving loyalty to the ruler. Mehmed's successor, Suleiman the Magnificent and the Lawgiver, continued this work by compiling a comprehensive legal code. The code addressed subjects' rights and duties, proper clothing, and how Muslims were to relate to non-Muslims.

RELIGION AND EDUCATION A sophisticated educational system was crucial for the empire's religious and intellectual integration and for its cultural achievements. Here, too, the Ottomans tolerated difference. They encouraged three educational systems that produced three streams of talent—civil and military bureaucrats, *ulama*, and Sufi masters. The administrative elite attended hierarchically organized schools that culminated in the palace schools at Topkapi (see Chapter 11). In the religious sphere, an equally elaborate

Abbas Mosque, dominated one end of the plaza, which measured 1,667 feet by 517 feet. At the other end were trading stalls and markets. Along one side sat government offices; the other side offered the exquisite Mosque of Shaykh Lutfollah. While other rulers of this era devoted their wealth to creating rich private spaces, Shah Abbas used the vast plaza to open his city to all comers, keeping only the Mosque of Shaykh Lutfollah for his personal use.

The royal use of space says a great deal about how monarchs in this era wished to be seen and remembered and about how they wanted to rule. While some wanted to retreat from the rest of society, Shah Abbas wanted to create an open space for trade and the exchange of ideas. World history is full of palaces and plazas (the Piazza San Marco in Venice might be compared to the royal plaza at Isfahan); we can still visit and admire them. But when we do, we should also remember that space, and the architecture that either opens up to the public or sets aside privileged spaces, has always had political as well as cultural functions.

Isfahan. On the great plaza at Isfahan, markets and government offices operated in close proximity to the public Shah Abbas Mosque, shown here, and the shah's private mosque. This structure represented Shah Abbas's desire to unite control of trade, government, and religion under one leader.

QUESTIONS FOR ANALYSIS

- Choose one of the places discussed in this feature. Explain how the architectural layout shaped the political power exercised by that space.
- Contrast private spaces, like the palace at Versailles, with public spaces, like the great plaza at Isfahan. What political goals could be accomplished by each?

EXPLORE FURTHER

Babaie, Sussan, *Isfahan and Its Palaces: Statecraft, Shi'ism and the Architecture of Conviviality in Early Modern Iran* (2008).

Necipoğlu, Gülru, *Architecture, Ceremonial, and Power: The Topkapi Palace in the Fifteenth and Sixteenth Centuries* (1991).

system took students from elementary schools (emphasizing reading, writing, and numbers) on to higher schools, or *madrasas* (emphasizing law, religious sciences, the Quran, and the regular sciences). These graduates became *ulama* who served as judges, experts in religious law, or teachers. Another set of schools, *tekkes*, taught the devotional strategies and religious knowledge for students to enter Sufi orders.

Each set of schools created lasting linkages between the ruling elite and the orthodox religious elite. The *tekkes*, especially, helped integrate Muslim peoples living under Ottoman rule. The value that the Ottomans placed on education was evident in the saying that "an hour of learning is worth more than a year of prayer"—and in the advances that those schooled in Ottoman institutions made in astronomy, physics, history, geography, and politics.

NEW IDEAS AND THE ARTS If education fused state and religious authority, the Ottomans merged inherited traditions

Mehmed II. In 1480, the Venetian painter Gentile Bellini sat down to paint a portrait of the sultan Mehmed II. Bellini was on a diplomatic mission to Constantinople. The sultan admired Bellini, so when the peace treaty between the two powers was signed, he requested Bellini's skills as a portraitist. The colors, fabrics, and floral ornaments speak to the Ottoman influences, while the use of the arch and the parapet create a sense of distance between the subject and viewer, which was typical of Italian painting styles at the time. The lower left is inscribed "Victor Orbis," or "Conqueror of the World."

with new elements in art as well. For example, portraiture became popular after the Italian painter Gentile Bellini visited Istanbul. Astonished by the splendor and captivated by the colors and mixtures of the Ottoman court, Bellini composed a portrait of Mehmed II. While borrowing local styles, Bellini also left behind Italian influences in Istanbul.

In other areas, the Ottomans elaborated their own styles. Consider the magnificent architectural monuments of the sixteenth through eighteenth centuries, including mosques, gardens, tombs, forts, and palaces: these show scant western influence. Nor were the Ottomans interested in western literature or music. They generally believed that God had given the Islamic world a monopoly on truth and enlightenment and that their military successes proved his favor.

The elites' capacity to celebrate their well-being and prosperity spread to the broader public during the so-called Tulip Period during the first half of the eighteenth century. The elite had long admired the tulip's bold colors and graceful blooms, and for centuries the flower served as the sultans' symbol. In fact, both Mehmed the Conqueror and Suleiman the Magnificent grew tulips in the most prestigious courtyards at Topkapi Palace in Istanbul; the palace's walls were covered by glazed tiles with blossoming bulbs. And many Ottoman warriors heading into battle wore undergarments embroidered with tulips to ensure victory. By the early eighteenth century, tulip designs appeared on tiles, fabrics, and public buildings, and authorities sponsored elaborate tulip festivals.

Fascination with the tulip represented a widespread delight in worldly things. Commoners, too, now celebrated life's pleasures—in coffeehouses and taverns. Indeed, Ottoman demand for luxury goods (such as lemons, soap, pepper, metal tools, coffee, and wine) grew so extensive that a well-traveled diplomat looked askance at the supposed wealth of Europe. He wrote, "In most of the provinces [of Europe], poverty is widespread, as a punishment for being infidels. Anyone who travels in these areas must confess that goodness and abundance are reserved for the Ottoman realms" (Mazower, p. 116). Thus, despite challenges from western Europe and foreboding that their best days were behind them, the Ottomans took some foreign elements into their culture while preserving inherited ways.

Safavid Culture, Shiite State

The Safavid Empire in Persia (modern-day Iran) was not as long-lived as the Ottoman and Mughal Empires. Founded in 1501, it lasted until 1722, with fleeting revivals afterwards. Sandwiched between these two powerhouses, it was also the poorest of the three. Indeed, there was a significant brain drain of writers and artists from Persia, who left especially to join the Mughal court. However, the Safavid rulers did give Shiism a home base, a location for displaying Shiite culture. While adapting pre-Islamic Persianate traditions, Safavid rulers also claimed to be the true heirs to the Prophet's teachings and entangled neighboring Islamic empires in chronic feuds. The brilliant culture that emerged during the Safavid period provided a unique blend of Shiism and Persia's distinctive historical identity. The greatest of all Iranian epics, known as *Shah Namah* (*The Book of Kings*), had been written centuries earlier (see Chapter 10). Perhaps among the finest illuminated manuscripts in human history, it had involved the labor of dozens of artists, scribes, and pigment and paper makers. The work was now revived and celebrated as a great national epic. Ismail I (r. 1501–1524) used it to eulogize Persian patriotism (and to celebrate royal authority). Lavish illustrations of battles and trysts, hunting scenes and courtly romance, recovered the epic of pre-Islamic legends

The Ottomans and the Tulip. The sultan's affection for tulips was part of a wider spirit of reform, high consumption, and elite sociability during what is known as the Tulip Period. The walls of Topkapi Palace were lavishly covered with glazed floral tiles. No flower was more prominent than the tulip, brought by the Ottomans from their homeland in central Asia. Unlike modern tulips, these blossoms were prized for their long, dagger-shaped petals and their graceful bows, like those of believers bending their heads before God. The stunning blue in this tile comes from lapis lazuli, crushed from gemstones from Persia. Europeans fell in love with these flowers, imported them into their gardens, and turned them into the subject of speculative frenzies.

to represent the Safavid ruler, Shah Tahmasp (1514–1576), Ismail's son, as its heroic heir. *The Book of Kings* was also a landmark assertion of the revival of Persian language, pushing back against the spread of Arabic in the region.

THE SHIITE EMPHASIS The Safavids faced a critical dilemma when they seized power. They owed their rise to the support of Turkish-speaking tribesmen who followed a populist form of Islam. But to hold on to power, the Safavid shahs needed to cultivate powerful and conservative elements of Iranian society: Persian-speaking landowners and orthodox *ulama*. Thus, they turned away from the more popular Turkish-speaking Islamic brotherhoods with their mystical and Sufi qualities and instead built a mixed political and religious system that extolled a Shiite vision of law and society and drew on older Persian imperial traditions. Even after the Safavids lost power, Shiism remained the fundamental religion of the Iranian people. As Shiism consolidated, however, artists and writers of other Muslim faiths, particularly Sunnis, trickled out, especially to the Mughal court, where they were welcomed to a more diverse setting.

The most effective architect of a cultural life based on Shiite religious principles and Persian royal absolutism was Shah Abbas I (r. 1587–1629). The location that he chose to display the wealth and royal power of his state, its Persian and Shiite heritages, and its artistic sensibility was the new capital city of Isfahan. For this purpose, the shah hired skilled artists and architects to design a city that would dwarf even Delhi and Istanbul, the other showplaces of the Islamic world. The architectural goal was to create an earthly representation of heavenly paradise.

The Book of Kings. The sixteenth-century edition of *The Book of Kings* was the peak expression of reaching into the past to revive an epic for a new Persian identity. Lavish illustrations of battles and trysts, hunting scenes and courtly romance, recovered the epic of pre-Islamic legends to represent the Safavid ruler, Shah Tahmasp (1514–1576), Ismail's son, as its heroic heir. In this image, King Gayumars, the first Persian king, floats above his courtiers and gazes down at them and his garden like a benevolent ruler.

Ottoman Court Women. This eighteenth-century watercolor found in Topkapi Palace, in Istanbul, shows how court women, summoned to provide entertainment, played various musical instruments.

ARCHITECTURE AND THE ARTS The Safavid shahs were unique in seeking to project both absolute authority and accessibility. For example, their dwellings were unlike those of other Afro-Eurasian rulers—such as Topkapi Palace, in Istanbul; the Citadel, in Cairo; and the Red Forts of the Mughals. Those enclosed and fortified buildings enhanced rulers' power by concealing them from their subjects. In contrast, the buildings of Isfahan were open to the outside, demonstrating the Safavid rulers' desire to connect with their people.

Safavid architecture found its highest expression in the capital, Isfahan. Isfahan's centerpiece was the great plaza next to the royal palace and the royal mosque at the capital's heart. The plaza, surrounded by elaborate public and religious buildings, measured nearly 100,000 square yards, only slightly smaller than Tiananmen Square, in Beijing, and seven times bigger than the plaza of San Marco, in Venice. A suitably impressed seventeenth-century English visitor noted that the plaza was 1,000 paces from north to south and 200 from east to west—far larger than the largest urban squares in London and Paris. He added that it "is without doubt as spacious, as pleasant, and aromatic a market as any in the universe."

Other aspects of intellectual life also reflected the elites' aspirations, wealth, and commitment to Shiite principles. Safavid artists perfected the illustrated book, the outstanding example being *The Book of Kings*, mentioned earlier. Weavers produced highly ornate and beautiful silks and carpets for trade throughout the world, and artisans painted tiles in vibrant colors and created mosaics that adorned mosques and other buildings. Moreover, the Safavids developed an elaborate calligraphy that was the envy of artists throughout the Islamic world. All of these works celebrated Shiite visions of the sacred while reinforcing the authority and prestige of the empire's ruling elite.

Power and Culture under the Mughals

Like the Safavids and the Ottomans, the Mughals fostered a lavish high culture, supported primarily by taxes on agriculture but reliant on silver for its currency and, at its high point, open to global trade. But there was one crucial difference: they ruled over a large non-Muslim population. As a result, Mughal rulers created an inclusive culture. So highly did it value art and learning that it welcomed non-Muslims into its circle. Thus, while Islamic traditions dominated the empire's political and judicial systems, Hindus shared with Muslims the flourishing of learning, music, painting, and architecture. In this arena, aesthetic refinement and philosophical sophistication could bridge religious differences.

RELIGION Mughal rulers were flexible toward their realm's diverse peoples, especially in spiritual affairs. Though its primary commitment to Islam stood firm, the imperial court also patronized other beliefs, displaying a tolerance that earned it widespread legitimacy. The contrast with Europe, where religious differences drove deep fractures within and between states, was stark.

The promise of an open Islamic high culture found its greatest fulfillment under the emperor Akbar (r. 1556–1605). This skillful military leader was also a popular ruler who allowed common people as well as nobles from all ethnic groups to converse with him at court. Unlike European monarchs, who tried to enforce religious uniformity, Akbar studied comparative religion and hosted regular debates among Hindu, Muslim, Jain, Parsi, and Christian theologians. His quest for universal truths outside the strict *sharia* led him to develop a religion of his own. Ultimately, he introduced at his court a

Akbar Leading Religious Discussion. This painting depicts Akbar's many different types of advisers, books, and elaborate accounts, fit for a powerful empire. In the image, you can see a Jesuit priest in discussion with Islamic authorities over whether the Bible or the Quran is the true word of God.

Shah Jahan. In this 1629 painting, Emperor Shah Jahan is perched on the globe below angels bearing the insignia of sovereignty, as if the Mughal emperor mediated between the terrestrial and the divine with supreme authority and legitimacy. Shah Jahan took the Mughal Empire to its height, and he imagined his court—and himself—at the center of the world order.

"Divine Faith" (Dīn-i Ilāhī) that was a mix of Quranic, Hindu, Catholic, and other influences; it emphasized piety, prudence, gentleness, liberality, and a yearning for God.

A liberal religious attitude was not limited to Akbar's reign but remained an important feature of Mughal rule. Sufism was the most important expression of this attitude. Dara Shikoh, Emperor Shah Jahan's eldest son, for example, was an accomplished scholar of Sufism. He translated Sanskrit texts into Persian, including the Hindu text Upanishads, which, in turn, was translated into French and circulated in Europe. Dara Shikoh declared there was no fundamental difference between Islam and Hinduism. His open religious attitude drew the ire of the orthodox *ulama*, who pressed for the supremacy of Islamic law and upheld religious purity.

The debate between conservative and liberal attitudes carried over to Hinduism. Orthodox writers reiterated Brahman privileges and opposed the entry of women and Shudras (members of the lower caste) into the spiritual sphere. But saints of the *bhakti* (devotional) sects offered a different vision. This movement, which had led to the establishment of Sikhism (see Chapter 11), swept through northern India between the fifteenth and seventeenth centuries. Devotion to the playful cowherd Krishna, rather than rituals officiated by Brahmans, gained popularity as the path to salvation. One famous *bhakti* saint was Mirabai (1498–1547), a woman who was compelled to marry a warrior's son but preferred the company of Krishna's devotees. She composed many poems mocking marriage and asceticism. If Mirabai challenged the prohibition of women in the spiritual sphere, another *bhakti* saint, Tukaram (1608–1649), asserted the fundamental equality of human beings and challenged caste inequality. Yet another saint, Eknath (1533–1599), wrote poems that poked fun at both orthodox Hindus and Muslims and argued that true devotees of God were without caste or creed.

While Persian and Sanskrit functioned as languages of the court and the elite, the *bhakti* movement addressed the common folk in regional languages. This promoted the development of Marathi, Hindi, Bengali, and other regional vernaculars. It also produced a lively engagement between Sufism and Hindu devotionalism—so much so that scholars cannot determine which tradition is the source of which particular poem. While *bhakti* poetry narrated Krishna's story as a Sufi romance, some Sufi poetry began by invoking Allah before turning to Hindu imagery and themes. Sufism spread in popular culture with poetry and songs addressing daily life, not just an esoteric union with God. Among these were songs for women, including one for those engaged in grinding food grains or spinning thread. These songs nurtured religious devotion and amplified the role of women in popular Islam. Women regularly visited Sufi shrines and prayed for divine intervention in their daily lives.

Religious life under the Mughals at both elite and popular levels presents a rich and diverse picture of dialogue and interaction between different religions, which is at odds with the principle of Hindu-Muslim cultural separatism that some religious nationalists hold to today.

Emperor Jahangir Embracing Shah Abbas. Around 1618, Abu al-Hasan painted this image of the Mughal emperor Jahangir embracing his cousin and rival, Shah Abbas of Iran. Jahangir is represented as the dominant relative, towering over his meek cousin; the Mughal stands on top of a lion, Shah Abbas on a lamb. In fact, the relatives were constantly at war over control of Afghanistan. The painting is a good example of the hybrid styles of the Mughal court. It features cherubs holding a halo and layered images to create a sense of perspective—elements Mughal artists adopted from the European Renaissance. The purpose, however, is clear: here was a ruler prevailing over the world.

ARCHITECTURE AND THE ARTS In architecture, too, the Mughals produced masterpieces that blended styles. This was already evident as builders combined Persian, Indian, and Ottoman elements in tombs and mosques under Akbar's predecessors. His third son was Shah Jahangir (1569–1627), known as the "King of the World." Born of a Hindu mother, Jahangir kept up the mixed style and made it a tradition. While the court welcomed travelers, artists, and scholars from around the world, Jahangir patronized artists who blended Persian, Hindu, and other styles.

Jahangir's fifth son, Shah Jahan, took the mixed style to new heights. In 1630, he ordered the building in Agra of a magnificent white marble tomb for his beloved wife, Mumtaz Mahal. Like many other women in the Mughal court, she had been an important political counselor. Designed by an Indian architect of Persian origin, this structure, the **Taj Mahal**, took twenty years and 20,000 workers to build. The 42-acre complex included a main gateway, a garden, minarets, and a mosque. The translucent marble mausoleum lay squarely in the middle of the structure, enclosed by four identical façades and crowned by a majestic central dome rising to 240 feet. The stone inlays of different types and hues, organized in geometric and floral patterns and featuring Quranic verses inscribed in Arabic calligraphy, gave the surface an appearance of delicacy and lightness. Blending Persian and Islamic design with Indian materials and motifs, this poetry in stone represents the most splendid example of Mughal high culture and the combining of cultural traditions. The Taj Mahal gave a sense of refined grandeur to this empire's power and splendor. (See again Current Trends in World History: The Political Uses of Space.)

FOREIGN INFLUENCES VERSUS ISLAMIC CULTURE Under later emperors, Mughal culture slowly dimmed—though visitors continued to be awestruck. François Bernier, a seventeenth-century French traveler, admired the broad philosophical interests of Danishmand Khan, whom the emperor Aurangzeb had appointed as governor of Delhi.

The Taj Mahal. A symbol of Mughal splendor, the Taj Mahal was a mausoleum that was built of white marble. Often described as poetry in stone, it was constructed under Shah Jahan as an homage to his deceased wife, Mumtaz Mahal (*right*).

According to Bernier, Khan avidly read the works of the French philosophers Gassendi and Descartes and studied Sanskrit treatises to understand different philosophical traditions. But Aurangzeb, a pious Muslim, favored Islamic arts and sciences. He dismissed many of the court's painters and musicians and in 1669 ordered that all recently built non-Islamic places of worship be torn down. In his court, intellectuals debated whether metaphysics, astronomy, medicine, mathematics, and ethics were of use in the practice of Islam. Women, at least at court, apparently were allowed to pursue the arts, for two of Aurangzeb's daughters were accomplished poets.

Well into the eighteenth century, the Mughal nobility exuded confidence and lived in unrivaled luxury. The presence of foreign scholars and artists enhanced the courtly culture, and the elite eagerly consumed exotic goods from China and Europe. Foreign trade also brought in more silver, advancing the money economy and supporting the nobles' sumptuous lifestyles. In addition, the Mughals assimilated European military technology: they hired Europeans as gunners and military engineers in their armies, employed them to forge guns, and bought guns and cannons from them. However, Mughal appreciation for other European knowledge and technology was limited. Thus, when a representative of the English East India Company presented an edition of Mercator's *Maps of the World* to the emperor Jahangir in 1617, the emperor returned it with the remark that no one could read or understand it. Others were more curious. Jahangir's successor, Shah Jahan, seized upon Europeans' introduction of terrestrial globes. He treated them as new ornaments that allowed him to imagine himself at the center of—if not the commander of—a wider world. Courtly portraits feature the emperor posed as a kind of world king or world conqueror, holding the orb in his magnanimous hands like a delicate object that he, and only he, could grasp.

The Islamic world drew on intellectual currents that spanned the Eurasian–North African landmass, for its centers were in Istanbul, Cairo, Isfahan, and Delhi. From Islam's founding, Muslims had looked to earlier traditions as well as India and China, not to Europe, for inspiration. By the eighteenth century, the increasing wealth and power of Christian kingdoms enriched by New World colonies made those cultures more imposing. Yet even as Muslims brought a few new European elements into their cultural mix, most still regarded Europeans as rude barbarians. Bellini, the Venetian painter in Istanbul, was more an exception than a rule. More impressive in the eyes of elites in Persia, India, and the Ottoman Empire were the cultural splendors to be found to the east.

Culture and Politics in East Asia

Like the Ottomans, Safavids, and Mughals, the Chinese did not need to prove the richness of their scholarly and artistic traditions. China had long been a renowned center of learning, with its emperors and elites supporting artists, poets, musicians, scientists, and teachers. But in late Ming and early Qing China, cultural flourishing owed more to a booming internal market, as the growing population and extensive commercial networks propelled the circulation of ideas as well as goods. As a result, China's cultural sphere expanded and diversified well before similar changes occurred elsewhere.

In Japan, too, prosperity promoted cultural dynamism. Because of Japan's giant neighbor across the sea, the Japanese people had always been aware of outside influences. Like the Chinese government, the Tokugawa shogunate tried to promote Confucian notions of a social hierarchy organized on the basis of social position, age, gender, and kin. It also tried to shield the country from egalitarian ideas that would threaten the strict social hierarchy. But the forces that undermined government control of knowledge in China proved even stronger in Japan. Here, a decentralized political system enabled different cultural influences to spread, including European ideas and practices. By the eighteenth century, in struggling to define its own identity through these contending currents, the cultural scene in Japan was more lively, open, and varied than its counterpart in China.

Chinese Civil Service Exam. This is the remains of a Chinese Examination Hall in Canton (Guangzhou). For centuries, Chinese dynasts built an elaborate professional ruling class. To join this class, applicants had to pass a grueling standardized test, which lasted three days and two nights. Those who passed joined the prestigious bureaucratic machine.

China: The Challenge of Expansion and Diversity

In China, the circulation of books spread ideas among the literate, and religious rituals instilled cultural values among the broader population. Advances in cartography reflected the distinctive worldview of Chinese elites.

PUBLISHING AND THE TRANSMISSION OF IDEAS Broader circulation of ideas had more to do with the decentralization of book production than with technological innovations. After all, woodblock and movable type printing had been present in China for centuries. Initially, the state had spurred book production by printing Confucian texts, but before long, the economy's increasing commercialization weakened government controls over what got printed. Even as officials clamped down on unorthodox texts, there was no centralized system of censorship, and unauthorized opinions circulated freely.

By the late Ming era, a burgeoning publishing sector catered to the diverse social, cultural, and religious needs of educated elites and urban populations. European visitors admired the vast collections of printed materials housed in Chinese libraries, describing them as "magnificently built" and "finely adorn'd." In fact, the late Ming was an age of collections of other sorts as well. Members of the increasingly affluent elite acquired objects for display (such as paintings, ceramics, and calligraphy) as a sign of their status and refinement. Consumers could build collections by purchasing from multiple sources—from roadside peddlers to monks to gentlemen dealers—because books and other luxury goods were now more affordable. Increasingly, publishers offered a mix of wares: guidebooks for patrons of the arts, travelers, or merchants; handbooks for performing rituals, choosing dates for ceremonies, or writing proper letters; almanacs and encyclopedias; morality books; and medical manuals.

Especially popular were study aids for the civil service examination, including models for the required, highly structured eight-part essay. In 1595, Beijing reeled with scandal over news that the second-place graduate had reproduced verbatim several model essays published by commercial printers. Just over twenty years later, the top graduate plagiarized a winning essay submitted years earlier. Ironically, then, the increased circulation of knowledge led critics to bemoan a decline in real learning. Instead of mastering the classics, they charged, examination candidates were simply memorizing the work of others.

Examination hopefuls were not the only beneficiaries of the book trade, for elite women also joined China's literary culture, penetrating the formerly male-only domain as readers, writers, and editors. Anthologies of women's poetry were especially popular, not only in the market, but also, when issued in limited circulation, as a way to celebrate the refinement of the writer's family. Men of letters soon recognized the market potential of women's writings. Some also saw women's less regularized style (usually acquired through family channels rather than state-sponsored schools) as a means to challenge

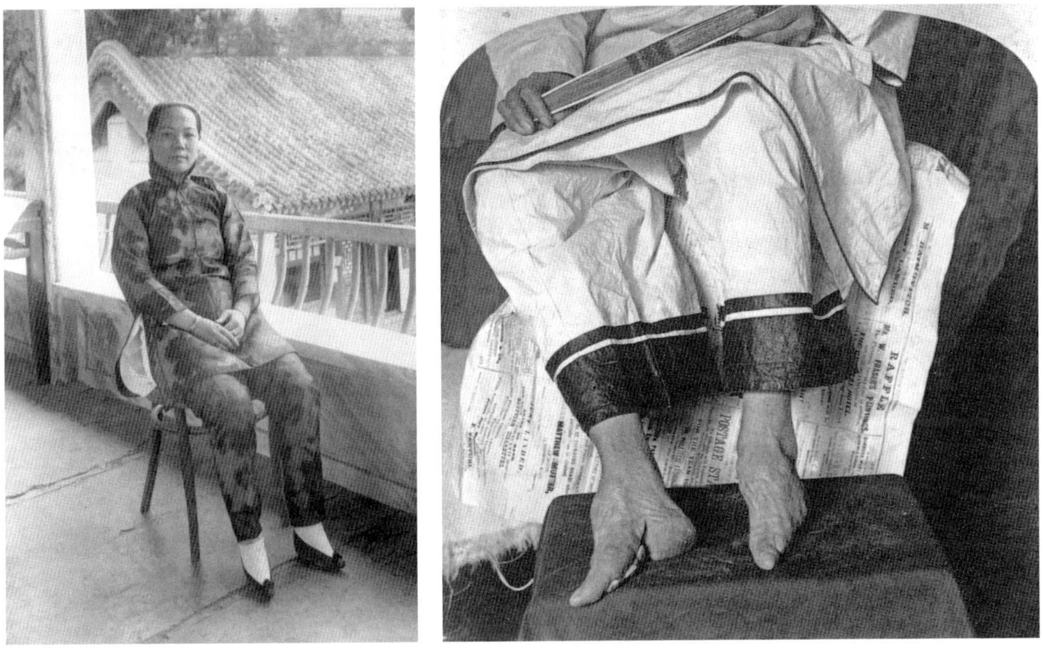

Footbinding. Two images of bound feet: (*left*) as an emblem of feminine respectability when wrapped and concealed, as on this well-to-do Chinese woman; (*right*) as an object of curiosity and condemnation when exposed for the world to see.

stifling stylistic conformity. A few women even served as publishers themselves.

Although elite women enjoyed success in the world of culture, the period brought increasing restrictions on their lives. Remarriage of widows and premarital sex might have met with disapproval in earlier times, but now they were utterly unthinkable for women from "good" families. Ironically, the thriving publishing sector indirectly promoted the stricter morality by printing plays and novels that echoed the government's conservative attitudes. Meanwhile, footbinding (which elite women first adopted around the late Tang-Song period) spread among common people, as small, delicate feet came to signify femininity and respectability.

POPULAR CULTURE AND RELIGION Important as the book trade was, it had only an indirect impact on most men and women in late Ming China. Those who could not read well or at all absorbed cultural values through oral communication, ritual performance, and daily practices. The Ming government tried to control these channels, too. It appointed village elders as guardians of local society and instituted "village compacts" to ensure shared responsibility for proper conduct and observation of the laws.

Still, the everyday life of rural and small-town dwellers went on outside these official networks. Apart from toiling in the field, villagers participated in various religious and cultural practices, such as honoring local guardian spirits, patronizing Buddhist and Daoist temples, or watching performances by touring theater groups. Furthermore, villagers often took group pilgrimages to religious sites and attended markets in nearby towns offering restaurants, brothels, and other types of entertainment. At the marketplaces the visitors gathered news and gossip or listened to itinerant storytellers and traveling monks; such open-ended cultural activities gave audiences opportunities to reinterpret official norms to serve their own purposes and to contest the government's rules. For example, commoners could take officially approved morality tales celebrating impartial officials and use them to challenge the real-life behavior of government bureaucrats.

Popular religions that mingled various traditions also reflected late Ming cultural flourishing. Here, at the grassroots level, there was little distinction among Buddhist, Daoist, and local cults. After all, the Chinese believed in cosmic unity, and although they venerated spiritual forces, they did not consider any of them to be a Supreme Being who favored one sect over another. They believed it was the emperor, rather than any religious group, who held the mandate of heaven; the enforcement of orthodox values was more a matter of political than of religious control. Unless sects posed an obvious threat, the emperor had no reason to regulate their spiritual practices. This situation promoted religious tolerance and avoided the sectarian warfare that plagued post-Reformation Europe.

TECHNOLOGY AND CARTOGRAPHY Belief in cosmic unity did not prevent the Chinese from devising technologies to master nature's operations in this world. For example, the magnetic compass, gunpowder, and the printing press were all Chinese inventions. Moreover, Chinese technicians had mastered iron casting and produced mechanical clocks centuries before Europeans did. Chinese astronomers also compiled accurate records of eclipses, comets, novae, and meteors. In part, the emperor's needs drove his interest in astronomy and calendrical science. After all, it was his job as the Son of Heaven, and thus mediator between heaven and earth, to determine the best dates for planting, holding festivities, scheduling mourning periods, and convening judicial court sessions. The Chinese believed that the empire's stability depended on correct calculation of these dates.

In the realm of cartography, the Chinese demonstrated most clearly their understanding of the world. Their maps encompassed elements of history, literature, and art—not just technical detail. It was not that "scientific" techniques were lacking; a map made as early as 1136 reveals that Chinese cartographers could readily draw to scale. Yet, because Chinese elites valued written text over visual and other forms of representation, the main goal of mapping was not geometric and mathematical precision. Reflecting the elites' worldview, most maps placed the realm of the Chinese emperor, as the ruler of "All under Heaven," at the center, surrounded by foreign countries; China's physical scale and distances to other lands were distorted. Still, some of the maps covered a vast expanse: one included an area stretching from Japan to the Atlantic, encompassing Europe and Africa.

CHINESE VIEWS OF EUROPEANS Before the nineteenth century, the Chinese had incomplete knowledge about foreign lands despite a long history of contact. The empire saw itself as superior to all others (a common feature of many cultures). A Ming geographical publication portrayed the Portuguese as men who are "seven feet tall, have eyes like a cat, a mouth like an oriole, an ash-white face, thick and curly beards like black gauze, and almost red hair" (quoted in Dikötter, p. 14). Qing authors in the eighteenth century confused France with the Portugal known during Ming times, and they characterized England and Sweden as dependencies of Holland. During this period of cultural flourishing, in short, most Chinese did not feel compelled to revise their view of the world.

Artist and Geisha at Tea. The erotic, luxuriant atmosphere of Japan's urban pleasure quarters was captured in a new art form, the *ukiyo-e*, or "pictures from a floating world." In this image set in Tokyo's celebrated Yoshiwara district, several geisha flutter about a male artist.

Cultural Identity and Tokugawa Japan

The culture that developed in Japan in this period drew on local traditions and, increasingly, foreign influences from China and Europe. Chinese cultural influence had long crossed the Sea of Japan, but under the Tokugawa shogunate there was also interest in European culture. This interest grew with the presence of the Dutch. There was also some contact with Russians. At the same time, the study of Japanese traditions and culture surged. Thus, Tokugawa Japan engaged in a three-cornered conversation that included time-honored Chinese ways (transmitted via Korea), European teachings, and distinctly Japanese traditions.

NATIVE ARTS AND POPULAR CULTURE Until the sixteenth and seventeenth centuries, the main patrons of Japanese culture were the imperial court in Kyoto, the hereditary shogunate, religious institutions, and a small upper class. These groups developed an elite culture of theater and stylized painting. Samurai (former warriors turned bureaucrats) and daimyos (regional lords) favored a masked theater, called Noh, and an elegant ritual for making tea and engaging in contemplation. In their gardens, the lords built teahouses with stages for Noh drama. These gave rise to hereditary schools of actors, tea masters, and flower arrangers. The elites also hired commoner-painters to decorate tea utensils and other fine articles and to paint the brilliant interiors and standing screens in grand stone castles. Some upper-class men created their own paintings, which conveyed philosophical thoughts. Calligraphy was proof of refinement.

Alongside the elite culture arose a rougher urban one. Here, artisans and merchants could purchase, for example, works of fiction and colorful prints (often risqué) made from carved woodblocks and could enjoy the company of female entertainers known as geisha who were skilled (*gei*) in playing

Kabuki Theater. Kabuki originated among dance troupes in the environs of temples and shrines in Kyoto in the late sixteenth and early seventeenth centuries. As kabuki spread to the urban centers of Japan, the theater designs enabled the actors to enter and exit from many directions and to step out into the audience, lending the skillful, raucous shows great intimacy.

the three-stringed instrument (*shamisen*), storytelling, and performing; some were also prostitutes. Kabuki—a type of theater that combined song, dance, and skillful staging to dramatize conflicts between duty and passion—became wildly popular. This art form featured dazzling acting, brilliant makeup, and sumptuous costumes.

Much popular entertainment chronicled the world of the common people rather than politics or high society. The urbanites' pleasure-oriented culture was known as "the floating world" (*ukiyo*), and the woodblock prints depicting it were called *ukiyo-e* (*e* meaning "picture"). Here, the social order was temporarily turned upside down. Those usually considered inferior—actors, musicians, courtesans, and others seen as possessing low morals—became idols. Even some upper-class samurai partook of this "lower" culture. But to enter the pleasure quarters, they had to leave behind their swords, a mark of rank.

Literacy in Japan now surged, especially among men. The most popular novels sold 10,000 to 12,000 copies. In the late eighteenth century, Edo had some sixty booksellers and hundreds of book lenders. In fact, the presence of so many lenders allowed books to spread to a wider public that previously could not afford to buy them. By the late eighteenth century, as more books circulated and some of them criticized the government, officials tried to censor certain publications. The government's response testified to the uncommon power wielded by people of modest means and the relative significance of popular culture in Japan.

RELIGION AND CHINESE INFLUENCE In the realm of higher culture, China loomed large in the Tokugawa world. But rather than mimic China, Japanese scholars adapted imported styles. Sometimes, they borrowed. They wrote imperial histories of Japan in the Chinese style; Chinese law codes and other books attracted a significant readership. Some Japanese traveled south to Nagasaki to meet Zen Buddhist masters and Chinese residents there. A few Chinese monks won permission to found monasteries outside Nagasaki and to give lectures and construct temples in Kyoto and Edo.

Sometimes, they drew a line against the imported cultures. Although Buddhist temples grew in number, they did not displace the native Japanese practice of venerating ancestors and worshipping gods in nature. Later called Shintō ("the way of the gods"), this practice boasted a network of shrines throughout the country. Shintō developed from time-honored beliefs in spirits, or *kami*, who were associated with places (mountains, rivers, waterfalls, rocks, the moon) and activities (harvest, fertility). Seeking healing or other assistance, adherents appealed to these spirits in nature and daily life through incantations and offerings. Some women under Shintō served as *mikos*, a kind of shaman with special divinatory powers. Reacting to the influence of Chinese Buddhism and desiring to honor their own country's greatness, some thinkers promoted intellectual traditions from Japan's past. These efforts stressed "native learning," Japanese texts, and Japanese uniqueness. In so doing, scholars formalized a Japanese religious and cultural tradition and denounced Confucianism and Buddhism as foreign contaminants.

Sometimes, scholars merged and mixed. Shintō rituals competed with a powerful strain of neo-Confucianism that issued moral and behavioral guidelines. For example, in 1762, *Greater Learning for Females* appeared—an influential text that made Confucian teachings understandable for nonscholars. In particular, it outlined social roles that stressed hierarchy based on age and gender as a way to ensure order. At the same time, merit became important in determining one's place in the social hierarchy. Doing the right thing (propriety) and being virtuous were key.

By the early eighteenth century, neo-Confucian teachings of filial piety and loyalty to superiors had become the official state creed. This philosophy legitimated the social hierarchy and the absolutism of political authorities, but it also instructed the shogun and the upper class to provide "benevolent administration" for the people's benefit. That meant taking into account petitioners' complaints and requests, whether for improved irrigation and roads or for punishment of unfair officials. Thus Japanese culture shaped state structure—and vice versa.

EUROPEAN INFLUENCES Chinese thought was not the only outside influence to compete with revived native learning. By the late seventeenth century, Japan was also tapping other sources of knowledge. By 1670, a guild of Japanese interpreters in Nagasaki who could speak and read Dutch accompanied Dutch merchants on trips to Edo. As European knowledge spread to high circles in Edo, in 1720 the shogunate lifted its ban on foreign books. Thereafter, European ideas, called "Dutch learning," circulated more openly. Scientific, geographical, and medical texts appeared in Japanese translations and in some cases displaced Chinese texts. A Japanese-Dutch dictionary appeared in 1745, and the first official school of Dutch learning followed. Students of Dutch or European teachings remained a limited segment of Japanese society, but the demand for translations intensified.

Japan's internal debates about what to borrow from the Europeans and the Chinese illustrate the changes that the world had undergone in recent centuries. A few hundred years earlier, products and ideas generally did not travel beyond coastal regions and had only a limited effect (especially inland) on local cultural practices. By the eighteenth century, though, expanded networks of exchange and new prosperity made the integration of foreign ideas feasible and, sometimes, desirable. The Japanese did not consider the embracing of outside influences as a mark of inferiority or subordination, particularly when they could put those influences to good use. This was not the case for the great Asian land-based empires, which were eager lenders but hesitant borrowers.

African Cultural Flourishing

The wealth that spurred artistic achievement and displays of power in the three major Islamic states and China and Japan also swept across African states. What is notable about this era in African history is the contrast between the cultural flourishing and the spread of captive labor. This was no coincidence: the expanding slave trade enriched African elites, who sold their captives to European enslavers and used their wealth to fund cultural activities and invigorate centuries-old artisanal and artistic traditions. As in the Islamic world and East Asia, African artisans maintained local forms of cultural production, such as wood carving, weaving, and metalworking.

Kente Cloth. Kente cloth originated among the Asante people and spread to other parts of West Africa. Threads of silk and cotton were interwoven to produce patterns with dazzling colors and geometric shapes. The colors represented different meanings important to the Asante peoples. Gray stood for healing and gold for royalty. Red was said to engender spiritual moods.

Cultural traditions in Africa varied from kingdom to kingdom, but there were patterns among them. For example, all West African elites encouraged craftsmen to produce carvings, statues, masks, and other objects that glorified the rulers' power and achievements. (Royal patrons in Europe, Asia, and the Islamic world did the same with architecture and painting.) There was also a widespread belief that rulers and their families had the gods' blessing, much as was the case in Ottoman, Safavid, Mughal, Chinese, and Japanese societies at this time. But African arts and crafts not only celebrated royal power; they also captured the energy of a universe that people believed was filled with spiritual beings. Starting in the sixteenth century and continuing through the eighteenth century when the slave trade reached its peak, African rulers had even more reason—and means—to support cultural pursuits. After all, as destructive as the slave trade was for African peoples, it made the slave-trading states wealthy and powerful.

The Asante, Oyo, and Benin Cultural Traditions

The kingdom of Asante led the way in cultural attainments, and the Oyo Empire and Benin also promoted rich artistic traditions. The Asante kingdom's access to gold and the revenues that it derived from selling captives undergirded its prosperity, making it the richest state in West Africa—perhaps even in the whole of sub-Saharan Africa. So deeply imbued with a desire to achieve economic success were the citizens of Asante that they accorded the highest respect to entrepreneurs who made money and surrounded themselves with retainers and enslaved men and women. The adages of the age were inevitably about becoming rich: "Money is king," "Nothing is as important as money." People who had wealth displayed it ostentatiously, wearing special garments signaling that they were persons of wealth and power. Those who could command the services of at least 1,000 subjects were entitled to wear a special cloth and to have a horsetail switch borne in front of them.

Artisans celebrated these traditions through the crafting of magnificent seats or stools coated with gold as symbols of authority; the most ornate were reserved for the head of the Asante federation, the Asantehene, who ruled this far-flung empire from the capital city of Kumasi. By the eighteenth century, these monarchs ventured out from the secluded royal palace only on ceremonial and feast days, when they wore sumptuous silk garments featuring many dazzling colors and geometric patterns in interwoven strips. Known as Kente cloth, this fabric was worn at first only by rulers, but later on wealthy individuals were permitted to garb themselves with it. Kings also had the golden elephant tail carried in front of them, a symbol of the greatest wealth. Held aloft on these celebratory occasions were maces, spears, staffs, and other symbols of power fashioned from the kingdom's abundant gold supplies. These reminded the common people of the Asantehene's connection to the gods.

Ife Bronze. An Ife bronze from the Yoruba peoples of present-day Nigeria. This magnificent work, one of a collection of fifteen pieces, was crafted sometime between the eleventh and fifteenth centuries and discovered by an American researcher in 1939.

Brass Oba Head. The brass head of an Oba, or king, of Benin. The kingdom's brass and bronze work was among the finest in all of Africa.

Equally resplendent were rulers of the Oyo Empire and Benin, located in the territory that now constitutes Nigeria. Elegant, refined metalwork in the form of West African bronzes reflects these rulers' awesome power and their peoples' highest esteem. The bronze heads of Ife, capital city of the Yoruba Oyo Empire, are among the world's most sophisticated artworks. According to one commentator, "Little that Italy or Greece or Egypt ever produced could be finer, and the appeal of their beauty is immediate and universal" (Tignor, p. 428). Artisans fashioned the best known of these works in the thirteenth century (before the slave trade era), but the tradition continued and became more elaborate in the seventeenth and eighteenth centuries.

Bronzes from Benin, too, displayed exquisite craftsmanship. Although historical records have portrayed Benin as one of Africa's most brutal slave-trading regimes, it also produced art of the highest order. Whether Benin's reputation for brutality was deserved or simply part of Europeans' later desire to label African rulers as "savage" in order to justify their conquest of the landmass, it cannot detract from the splendor of its artisans' creations.

Wealth acquired from the slave trade fostered cultural flourishing in Africa, notably though not exclusively in West Africa. Here, as in the Islamic world and East Asia, artisans and craftspersons drew on their own traditions. But the African artistic tradition, unlike Islamic and East Asian traditions, was little influenced by other cultures, even at a time when Africa was being drawn into global networks of exchange and political domination.

The Enlightenment in Europe

Europe also entered a phase of cultural flourishing and advanced learning in the seventeenth and eighteenth centuries. As in other world regions, intensifying commercial exchange and the consolidation of dynasties after a period of upheaval powered the burgeoning of arts and science. Europe's empires were drawing in commodities and observations from all corners of the planet, adding to the pool of

Botanical Engraving from *Metamorphosis Insectorum Surinamensium*. This painting by Maria Sibylla Merian, done while she was in Suriname, is typical of her commitment to a living portrait of natural life. Here, a ripe fruit opens to attract butterflies of the forest—possibly a trick she learned from local Indigenous people. It was not the fruit, however, that interested her, but the metamorphosis from a caterpillar munching its way across a branch to a butterfly in search of nectar.

learning that set the stage for Europe's scientific revolution. While it used to be described as Europe's creation, the change relied on global encounters, discoveries, and importation of knowledge from elsewhere.

Observations from around the world stoked a hunger for uncovering new information and borrowing knowledge from others. Consider the example of botany and **bioprospecting**, the taking of botanical information from one place and using it in another—and thereby adding value to it. Merchants from China, India, and the Arabian Peninsula had been transporting plants and minerals, like opium, pepper, and frankincense, as they traveled in caravans and ships to distant lands around the Indian Ocean and South China Sea. The rise of European overseas expansion turned the spice trade into traffic in plant information. A diverse array of people became part of this enterprise. European naturalists and explorers acquired knowledge of plants from local herbalists and apothecaries who studied them for their healing powers. They then returned to Europe to publish their findings. This gave botany added commercial value. One example was the Dutch explorer Georg Everhard Rumphius (1627–1702). He studied the natural world of the Indonesian archipelago while an employee of the Dutch East India Company (VOC) and compiled a magnificent catalogue about local plants, which started as a study of a tree resin that worked miracles for skin ailments. It would have been impossible without the aid of local herbalists and botanists like Patti Cuhu, whom Rumphius described as "a man experienced in the knowledge of plants . . . who has helped me a great deal in this work" or Iman Reti, a "Moorish priest from Buro" whom Rumphius called "my Master." Their assistance allowed the self-styled Dutch scientist to catalogue over 1,300 plants with valuable medicinal uses.

There were also European women naturalists who drew upon local sources of knowledge for global circulation. The talented German female artist-naturalist Maria Sibylla Merian traveled to Dutch Suriname to paint and draw flora, insects, and birds of the tropics based (unlike like some of her male peers) on direct observation. In 1699, she set sail with her daughter to study and catalogue rare insects and foliage. Though she came to decry the enslavement of Africans and Indigenous people, she relied upon captive labor for her work. Merian quickly learned that they knew much more about nature than the Dutch settlers did, and she turned to them to gather rare specimens, especially of fruit, caterpillars, and butterflies from the forests along the Suriname River. Their samples became her artistic subjects, though she never gave her workers credit for their role in the making of global science.

If the pool of knowledge was global, why did Europe seize greater advantage compared to China, India, and the Muslim world, where scientific work had been well in advance of Europe before the sixteenth century? Between 800 and 1450 CE, the multinational, multiethnic, and multireligious Muslim world possessed the most important centers for this study. Throughout Islam, the mathematical sciences of arithmetic, geometry, and trigonometry flourished and broke open fields of astronomy, astrology, geography, cartography, and optics. The Islamic world also excelled in medicine and philosophy, and much of Greek, Indian, and pre-Islamic Persian science had been made available to scholars in the Islamic world through translations from Pahlavi, Sanskrit, Greek, and Syriac. The breakthroughs in astronomy were extraordinary. Working independently in Damascus, Ibn al-Shatir produced non-Ptolemaic models of the planets that were similar to those put forward later by Copernicus. The Maragha Observatory (1259 and later) in Persia produced the first non-Ptolemaic planetary models; Nasir al-Din al-Tusi (1201–1271), a Persian astronomer and mathematician who was the director of the Maragha Observatory, created a diagram of the movements of the planets, written in Arabic, that some historians claim must have been seen by Copernicus and influenced his thinking of the universe.

New knowledge and new science, however, disturbed incumbent authorities. In the Islamic world, novelty provoked a reaction. The *ulama* responded to threats to their authority in conservative, even fundamentalist, ways, reiterating the importance of religious studies, which included studies of the Quran, the sayings of the Prophet (*hadith*), the *sharia*

Colbert Presents French Scientists to Louis XIV. In founding the Académie des Sciences in 1666, King Louis XIV hoped to show his support for the new science and win scientists' endorsement for his still rather fragile regime. Here his chief minister (and the inventor of mercantile policies), Jean-Baptiste Colbert, presents the scholars to the king. The central presence of maps and globes in the image tells us how much exploration of the world and conquest of colonies were part of this collaborative endeavor.

Matteo Ricci Adapts to Chinese Culture. This image depicts Jesuit father Matteo Ricci with one of his most high-profile converts to Christianity, the scholar and official Xu Guangqi. Behind them stands a painting of the Madonna and baby Jesus with a text in literary Chinese, demonstrating Ricci's commitment to adapting Christianity and European culture to the text-oriented Chinese cultural world.

(religious law), theology, poetry, and the Arabic language. They questioned the value of the foreign sciences and the study of the natural world. Occasional scholars were able to challenge the *ulama's* monopoly on learning and to look outward for inspiration, but such efforts relied on weak and scarce reformist patrons.

Take the example of Ibrahim Muteferrika, a Hungarian convert to Islam, who set up a printing press in Istanbul in 1729. Under the patronage of a reformist grand vizier, Muteferrika published works on science, geography, and history that drew on western findings. Encouraged by his success, Turkish intellectuals translated and published some of Europe's most influential scientific works. When Muteferrika's patron was killed, however, the *ulama* reasserted their control over education and publications and closed off this promising avenue of contact with western learning.

What of China? The English philosopher Francis Bacon credited the Chinese with three of the most influential inventions in the world at that time, namely the magnetic compass, gunpowder, and printing. In contrast to European scientists concerned with novel theoretical breakthroughs, Chinese scientists were bent on narrow, practical, applications and not foundational discovery. For instance, practitioners in the Middle Kingdom were less inclined than their European counterparts to mathematize the study of the natural world. Nor did they fully understand the use of the experimental method.

So, what was distinctive about Europe if knowledge was circulating globally? Europe had its fair share of conservative forces that regarded new science and arts as threats to their authority. The difference was institutional and political. First, feuds between middle-sized, aggressive, and quarreling states meant that competitors seized the opportunity to use knowledge to elbow aside their adversaries. Accordingly, kings and their courts patronized science. Second, European rulers welcomed artists and scientists who were fleeing persecution elsewhere, to get an edge on the competition. Even the persecutors eventually learned that driving out scientists and artists resulted in a loss of talent. Third, Europe had internal diffusion mechanisms for practical and theoretical discoveries. Printing presses and the circulation of scientists allowed European competitors to share the pool of breakthroughs. By contrast, commercial printing in Asia had a smaller reach. These institutional constraints in Asia allowed Europeans to leapfrog ahead, paradoxically by making use of the science and knowledge that originated abroad.

Europeans were more open to borrowing—or taking—from others because their rulers and magnates began to appreciate the value of new knowledge. By the late seventeenth century, getting an edge in the knowledge business could give rivals a strategic edge. By founding the Royal Society in 1662, for example, Charles II hoped to show not only that the crown backed scientific progress but also that England's great minds backed the crown against critics and rivals. Similar reasoning lay behind Louis XIV's founding of the French Académie des Sciences. The result was an escalation of the drive to learn.

We can see the tilt in the knowledge balance in Europe's favor by comparing how Europeans learned from China and how the Chinese learned from Europeans. Starting in the late sixteenth century, Jesuit missionaries found Chinese literati and officials extraordinarily receptive to European breakthroughs in mathematics and astronomy. Here, it seemed, was a fruitful bridge between Europe's new science and China's ruling elite. The first two Jesuit missionaries to reach China, Michele Ruggiere (1543–1607) and Matteo Ricci (1552–1610), arrived in 1582 and 1583, respectively. As was the case with many Jesuits at this time, both were brilliantly educated not just in religious and theological matters but also in Europe's evolving new science. Ricci was a unique polyglot and polymath. Not only did he master Mandarin Chinese early on in his stay in China, but he also brought with him a knowledge of mathematics, learned at the Roman College under one of the best mathematicians of his time, Christoph Clavius. With a Chinese official, Xu Guangqi (1562–1633), he translated Euclid's *Elements* into Chinese in 1607. Ricci established a mission in Nanjing in 1595 and was the first European to enter the Forbidden City of Beijing in 1601 at the invitation of the emperor.

Although the Catholic Church had banned the works of Copernicus and Galileo, both Ruggiere and Ricci were "closet Copernicans" and believed that presenting Europe's scientific achievements to the ruling classes at the emperor's court would win them favor and facilitate conversions of many Chinese to Christianity. At the time of their arrival, China was in the midst of debates over its solar calendar, which now was out of sync with the seasons and causing difficulties coordinating ceremonial rites and rituals. Thus, Chinese officials were eager to employ Jesuit knowledge of mathematics and astronomy—based on Copernicus and Galileo's heliocentrism—to assist them in bringing ceremonial dates and political and economic activities into a better relationship with the seasons. For their part, the Jesuits participated in Confucian ceremonies, hoping to win favor with the emperor and arguing that the rites were compatible with Catholicism. But to the Jesuits' great disappointment, the Chinese did not accept their religious and theological tenets, and the men made only a very small number of converts. When Pope Clement XI issued a papal bull condemning the missionaries' participation in the rites, the project of cultural exchange broke down. Offended, the Kangxi emperor, who had once been sympathetic to the missionaries, banned Christian missionaries from practicing in China. His successor went further, ordering the closing of all churches and the expulsion of the Jesuits from China. Thus, starting in the mid-eighteenth century, the European window on China and the Chinese window on Europe were closed. China turned away from European contact, most notably Europe's new science that had once intrigued the Chinese ruling classes.

Once Europeans seized their advantage and found ways to commercialize new knowledge, they reversed the knowledge gap that once separated Asian scientists from Europeans. But the more they learned in their interactions with others, and the more they succeeded in secularizing and spreading their ideas at home, the more European intellectuals became convinced not only that their culture was superior—after all, such ethnocentricity was hardly rare—but that they had discovered a set of universal laws that applied to everyone, everywhere around the globe.

The New Science

A "new science" took root in Europe, a search for stable, testable, and objective knowledge, especially in physics and astronomy. From its findings and inspiration a wider movement, the **Enlightenment**, was born. Often defined purely in intellectual terms as the spread of faith in reason and in universal rights and laws, the Enlightenment also encompassed broader developments, such as the expansion of literacy, the

Galileo. Worried that the new science would undermine the Christian faith, the Catholic Church put Italian scientist Galileo on trial in 1633 for espousing heretical beliefs and condemned him to house arrest until his death in 1642.

spread of critical thinking, the improvement of agricultural productivity, and the decline of religious persecution. As literate, middle- and upper-class men and women gained confidence in their ability to reason for themselves, to understand the world without calling on traditional authorities, and to publicly criticize what they found distasteful or wrong, they embraced an increasingly "enlightened" age.

The search for new, testable knowledge began centuries before the Enlightenment in the efforts of Nicolaus Copernicus (1473–1543) and Galileo Galilei (1564–1642) to understand the behavior of the heavens. These men were both astronomers and mathematicians. Making their own mathematical calculations and observations of the stars and planets, these scholars came to conclusions that contradicted age-old assumptions. By no means was trusting one's own work rather than the accepted authorities easy or without risk: when Galileo confirmed Copernicus's claims that the earth revolved around the sun, he was put on trial for heresy.

In the seventeenth century, a small but influential group of scholars committed themselves, similarly, to experimentation, calculation, and observation. They adopted a method for "scientific" inquiry laid out by the philosopher Sir Francis Bacon (1561–1626), who claimed that real science entailed the formulation of hypotheses that could be tested in carefully controlled experiments. Bacon believed that traditional authorities could never be trusted; only by conducting experiments could humans begin to comprehend the workings of nature. Bacon was chiefly wary of classical and medieval authorities, but his principle also applied to traditional knowledge that European scientists were encountering in the rest of the world. Confident of their calculations performed according to the new **scientific method**, scientists like Isaac Newton (1642–1727) defined what they believed were universal laws that applied to all matter and motion; they criticized older conceptions of nature (from Aristotelian ideas to folkloric and foreign ones) as absurd and obsolete. Thus, in his *Principia Mathematica*, Newton set forth the laws of motion—including the famous law of gravitation, which simultaneously explained falling bodies on earth and planetary motion.

The new science became useful science. The new math could be used for ballistics, and the new astronomy for building better clocks and navigational devices, such as the chronometer. More technical sophistication necessitated, in turn, the establishment of military schools, which increasingly stressed engineering methods, made advances in surveying and mapping, and introduced a culture of meritocracy into the previously noble-dominated armies. In rural areas, landowners began to read books about crop rotation and formed societies to discuss the latest methods of animal breeding. In Italy, numerous female natural philosophers emerged, and the genre of scientific literature for "ladies" took hold. By about 1750, even artisans and journalists were applying Newtonian

Chronometer. John Harrison (1693–1776) was an English carpenter and self-taught clockmaker at a moment in history when time was increasingly becoming money. He discovered a means to determine longitude accurately, which greatly facilitated long-distance travel. His clocks were so accurate that they kept time to within a second per month. His portable clocks, like this one, kept time to within three seconds a day. Keeping portable but accurate time and being able to measure longitudes at sea were game-changing for navigation and accurate mapping. This was just one of many devices behind the measurement revolution.

mechanics to their practical problems and inventions. A consensus emerged among proponents of the new science that useful knowledge came from collecting data and organizing them into universally valid systems, rather than from studying revered classical texts.

By the eighteenth century, the spread of the new science, together with expanding commerce and the relaxation, in some places, of censorship, began to give reform-minded Europeans hope that they were living in a *siècle des lumières*, or "century of light." In many places, this was still more hope than reality, as literacy was far from universal, peasants still suffered under arbitrary systems of taxation, and judicial regimes remained harsh. But many thinkers could now hope that Thomas Hobbes's pessimism, formed in the midst of the Little Ice Age and the terrors of the seventeenth century (see Chapter 13), had been wrong and that human societies, along with the sciences, could be improved. That hope launched the movement we now call the Enlightenment.

The Enlightenment Thinkers

Enlightenment thinkers, called **philosophes** in France, built on the achievements of the new science, insisting that scientific reasoning could and should be used to understand human societies as well as the natural world. Thinkers such as the English scientist and political writer John Locke (1632–1704), the French writers Voltaire (1694–1778) and Denis Diderot (1713–1784), and the Scottish political economist Adam Smith (1723–1790) believed in the power of human reason to criticize and improve existing institutions and practices. They claimed that oppressive governments, religious superstition, and irrational social inequalities were not ills people simply had to accept. Human beings could use their reason, Locke believed, to combat the human-made evils of intolerance and superstition. Similarly, Voltaire criticized the torture of criminals, Diderot denounced the despotic tendencies of the French kings Louis XIV and Louis XV, and Smith exposed the inefficiencies of mercantilism (see Chapter 13). Very few of these writers were political radicals or atheists (people who do not believe in any god), but their belief that Europe and the world could be improved by the universal application of law and reason appealed to reformers.

The Enlightenment touched all of Europe, but to varying extents. In the Netherlands, France, and Britain, where population density and urbanization were greatest, enlightened learning spread widely; in Spain, Poland, and Russia, enlightened circles were small and barely influenced the general population. Enlightened thought flourished in commercial centers such as Amsterdam and Edinburgh and in colonial ports such as Philadelphia and Boston. As education and literacy levels rose in these cities, book sales and newspaper circulation surged. Religious literature and Bibles were still the best-sellers, but the widening market increasingly put scientific treatises, scandalous novels, and even pornography into readers' hands.

POPULAR CULTURE The expanding reading public grew increasingly omnivorous and increasingly difficult to police. In England, the Netherlands, and Switzerland, authorities essentially gave up censoring, and radical books and pamphlets printed there were smuggled into other markets, where they found readers of many sorts. Some of the most popular works were not from high intellectuals but from more sensationalist essayists. Pamphlets charging widespread corruption, fraudulent stock speculation, and insider trading circulated widely. Sex, too, sold well. Works like *Venus in the Cloister or the Nun in a Nightgown* racked up as many sales as the now-classic works of the Enlightenment. Bawdy and irreligious, these vulgar best-sellers exploited consumer demand—but they also seized the opportunity to mock authority figures, such as nuns and priests. Some even dared to go after the royal family, portraying Marie Antoinette as having sex with her court confessor. In these cases, pornography—some of it even philosophical—spilled into the literary marketplace for political satire. Such works displayed the seamier side of the Enlightenment, but they also revealed a willingness (on the part of high and low intellectuals alike) to challenge established beliefs and institutions and to undermine royal and clerical authority.

New readerships generated new cultural institutions and practices. In Britain and Germany, book clubs and coffeehouses sprang up to cater to sober men of business and learning; here, aristocrats and well-to-do commoners could read news sheets or discuss stock prices, political affairs, and technological novelties. Similar noncourtly socializing occurred in Parisian salons, where aristocratic women presided. Speaking their minds more openly in these private settings than at court or at public assemblies, women here freely exchanged ideas with men. The number of female readers and writers soared, and the relatively new genre of the novel, as well as specialized women's journals, appealed especially to them.

Salon of Madame Geoffrin. Much of the important work—and wit—of the Enlightenment was the product of private gatherings known as salons. Often hosted, like the one depicted here, by aristocratic women, these salons also welcomed down-at-the-heels writers and artists, offering everyone, at least in theory, the opportunity to discuss the sciences, the arts, politics, and the idiocies of their fellow humans on an equal basis.

SEEKING UNIVERSAL LAWS Inspired by the new science, many thinkers sought to discover the "laws" of human behavior, an endeavor linked with criticism of existing governments. Explaining the laws of economic relations was chiefly the work of Adam Smith, whose book *The Wealth of Nations* probed the possibility of some universal economic laws. It became one of the most influential and long-lived of enlightened works. Smith claimed that releasing constraints on market exchanges allowed the individual's "trucking and bartering" nature to express itself fully. In Smith's view, the "invisible hand" of the market, rather than government regulations, would lead to prosperity and social peace because it allowed people to align their self-interests with their moral sensibilities. By pursuing personal gain, he felt, people could trade with each other and allow each other's talents to flourish. Less "civilized" (as he put it) nations could escape the trap of poverty by unfettering individuals. Many of Smith's subsequent readers treated his market-friendly prescriptions as a universal model for modernization. It is important to note, however, that Adam Smith never ceased to see humans as both moral and material agents.

The French *Encyclopédie* was perhaps the Enlightenment's most characteristic attempt to encompass universal knowledge. Edited by the brilliant and irreverent writer Denis Diderot, it ultimately comprised twenty-eight volumes containing essays by more than 130 intellectuals. It was extremely popular among the elite despite its political, religious, and intellectual radicalism. Its purpose was "to collect all the knowledge scattered over the face of the earth" and to make it useful to men and women in the present and future. The *Encyclopédie* offered a wealth of information about all manner of things, including descriptions and illustrations showing how to make pins and bind books and the latest advances in painting. One of its authors also detailed the horrors of the slave trade. "Slavery," he noted, "is a negotiation that violates all religion, moral, natural law, and human rights"—even if it yields riches for the enslavers. Although it covered all parts of the world, the project generally treated the non-European world as historically important and interesting, but also as unmodern and in need of an Enlightenment only known to Europeans. Diderot reserved for himself the space to write the entry on Africa. Though he never visited the continent, he was fascinated and urged further scientific exploration in order to create an encompassing view of all of humanity. (See Analyzing Global Developments: How Can We Measure the Impact of an Idea?)

Consequences of the Enlightenment

The Enlightenment—or, more properly, Enlightenments, as there was much variation across Europe—was a movement with numerous ambivalent consequences, both for religious

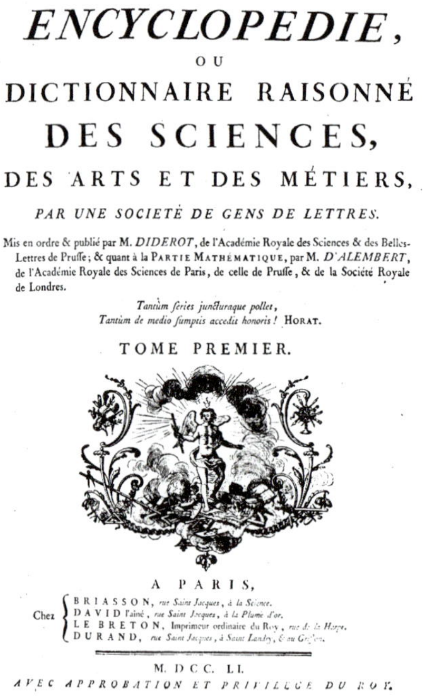

ENCYCLOPEDIE,

OU

DICTIONNAIRE RAISONNÉ

DES SCIENCES,

DES ARTS ET DES MÉTIERS,

PAR UNE SOCIETÉ DE GENS DE LETTRES.

Mis en ordre & publié par M. *DIDEROT*, de l'Académie Royale des Sciences & des Belles-Lettres de Pruſſe; & quant à la PARTIE MATHÉMATIQUE, par M. *D'ALEMBERT*, de l'Académie Royale des Sciences de Paris, de celle de Pruſſe, & de la Société Royale de Londres.

Tantùm ſeries juncturaque pollet,
Tantùm de medio ſumptis accedit honoris! HORAT.

TOME PREMIER.

A PARIS,

Chez BRIASSON, *rue Saint Jacques, à la Science.*
DAVID l'aîné, *rue Saint Jacques, à la Plume d'or.*
LE BRETON, Imprimeur ordinaire du Roy, *rue de la Harpe.*
DURAND, *rue Saint Jacques, à Saint Landry, & au Griffon.*

M. DCC. LI.

AVEC APPROBATION ET PRIVILEGE DU ROY.

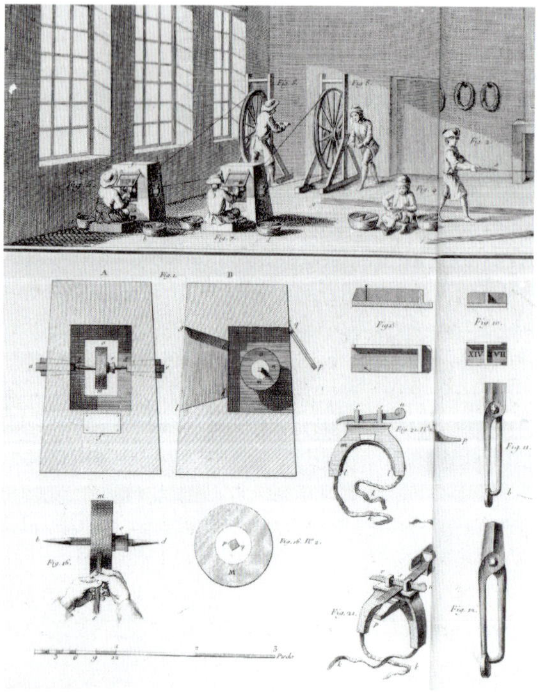

The *Encyclopédie*. Originally published in 1751, the *Encyclopédie* was the most comprehensive work of learning of the French Enlightenment. *Top:* The title page features an image of light and reason being dispersed throughout the land. The title itself identifies the work as a dictionary, based on reason, that deals not just with the sciences but also with the arts and occupations. It identifies two of the leading men of letters (*gens de lettres*), Denis Diderot and Jean le Rond d'Alembert, as the primary authors of the work. Contributors to the *Encyclopédie* included craftsmen as well as intellectuals. *Bottom:* The detailed illustrations of a pin factory and the processes and machinery employed in pin making are from a plate in the fourth volume of the *Encyclopédie* and demonstrate its emphasis on practical information.

Analyzing Global Developments

How Can We Measure the Impact of an Idea?

The single most important work of the European Enlightenment, Denis Diderot's *Encyclopédie* set out to provide an objective compendium of all human knowledge. Yet this work was very French: of its more than 130 authors, only sixteen were foreign, and, of those sixteen, seven came from the French-speaking city of Geneva, just across the border. All of them were men. Within France, the authors came primarily from the north, especially from Paris. Noble and clerical authors weighed more heavily on the list of authors than did people with such backgrounds in society at large (this had to do with literacy rates, which were much higher among the elite); most of Diderot's authors came from the Third Estate (see Chapter 15). None of those bourgeois authors had much to do with capitalism, nor did the aristocratic authors have much to do with feudalism. There were large contingents of doctors, lawyers, government officials, and skilled artisans.

We know very little about the production and diffusion of the first edition of the *Encyclopédie*, produced from 1751 to 1772 under Diderot's direction. The first four editions, in fact, were expensive luxury items, relatively unimportant in terms of diffusion. The *Encyclopédie* that circulated in prerevolutionary Europe came from cut-rate smaller-format editions published between 1777 and 1782, when the final, revised version, the *Encyclopédie méthodique*, began to appear. For these later editions, thorough records have survived, raising far-reaching questions about how ideas circulated and where during the Enlightenment, at least within Europe. (We know very little about the circulation of the *Encyclopédie* beyond Europe.) Where did the writers come from, where did their ideas go, and how, if at all, did their origins influence the content and ultimate significance of their project? We include a table of key words and their classification in thematic categories from the original edition, to give a sense of its contents and priorities.

Source: Robert Darnton, *The Business of Enlightenment: A Publishing History of the* Encyclopédie, *1775–1800* (1979).

Terms	Number of Appearances	Principal Categories
Commerce	5,713	Commerce, geography
Science	2,095	[Multiple categories]
Christ	1,821	Theology, holy scripture
Africa	1,772	Geography, history, natural history, botany
Slavery	238	Natural law, ethics, religion, ancient history
African slavery (*La traite des nègres*)	15	Commerce
Negro	536	Natural history, commerce
Saint-Domingue	96	Geography, botany
China	957	Agriculture, chemistry, history, natural history, geography, metaphysics, tapestry
Turk or Turkey	701	Geography, history
Muhammad	356	Theology, history, philosophy

QUESTIONS FOR ANALYSIS

- What does the diffusion of the *Encyclopédie* within France and across Europe tell us about its influence? How should we evaluate the influence of a book? Do you think the *Encyclopédie*'s local origins compromised its universal ambitions?
- What does the number of appearances of various terms tell us about the topics that Diderot and his contributors were most focused on?
- How do you think the social origins of the contributors shaped the kinds of topics covered by the *Encyclopédie*?

and political institutions and for Europe's relationship with the rest of the world.

RELIGION AND THE ENLIGHTENMENT Although few Enlightenment thinkers were atheists, most criticized what they perceived to be the irrational rituals, superstitions, persecutions, and expenditures defended by clergy. They insisted that the use of reason, rather than force or rote repetition of formulas, was the best way to create a community of believers and morally good people. Their critiques of church authorities and practices were highly controversial. Some governments bowed to clerical pressure and censored the most radical books or exiled writers, but many absolutist monarchs saw an advantage in reducing the church's power and introducing at least some measure of tolerance of religious minorities into their realms.

Tolerance did not mean full civil rights—for Catholics in England, for example, or for Jews anywhere in Europe. Tolerance simply meant a loosening of religious uniformity, and the population as a whole often resented even this. Few

Europeans entirely lost their faith as a result of the spread of enlightened ideas and critiques. The Enlightenment succeeded in spreading the suspicion of religious authorities and the distaste for religious persecution. It was instrumental in laying the foundation for revolutionaries' attacks on the church and for the evolution of secular states and societies in Europe in the nineteenth century.

The application of enlightened ideas to non-European religions had ambivalent effects. On the one hand, enlightened thinkers sought information about other religions and wrote books discussing similarities between Christian and non-Christian practices and beliefs. On the other hand, their imposition of enlightened categories and principles often resulted in severe misunderstandings, as differences were increasingly explained as others' "backward" refusal to evolve along European lines. For example, authors of the *Encyclopédie* portrayed Islam with the same ill will that they applied to other organized religions, condemning Muhammad as an imposter and the Quran as a book stuffed with barbaric and ignorant ideas that contradicted the laws of physics. The application of these enlightened tests to non-European religions often substituted new prejudices against "backward" religions and cultures for old prejudices against non-Christians destined for hell.

THE ENLIGHTENMENT AND POLITICS Absolutist governments did not entirely reject enlightened ideas, which included ideas that were in most cases reformist or critical of religious authorities rather than directly political. Rulers recognized the virtues of some universality (like an applicable system of taxation) and precision (as in a well-drilled army). Also, social mobility allowed more skilled bureaucrats to rise through the ranks, while commerce provided the state with new riches. The idea of collecting knowledge, too, appealed to states that wanted to exert greater control over their subjects and to extend their reach overseas. Consider Louis XIV, who was persuaded to establish a census (though he never carried it out) so that he could "know with certitude in what consists his grandeur, his wealth, and his strength." Many enlightened princes supported innovations in the arts and agriculture or sent scientific missions out to explore the world and plant their flags. Like the philosophes, they were convinced that the improvement of trade, agriculture, and national productivity was the right way forward, even though some were also beholden to the older values of the nobility and clergy. Merit and religious tolerance could also be useful in attempts to make states more profitable and armies more efficient. In this way, cultural efflorescence and secular state building in Europe went hand in hand.

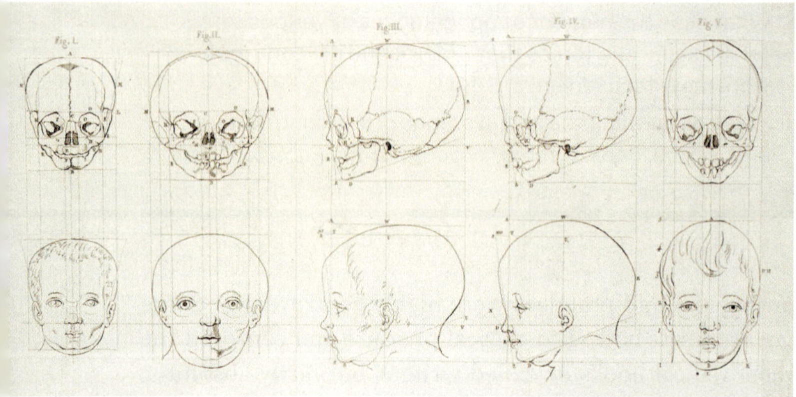

Racial "Classification." The Dutch anatomist Petrus Camper (1722–1789) advocated a theory of facial angles to create new, scientifically classified ranks of species and humans. In this drawing, Camper sought to illustrate the differences and commonalities among primates, including humans, and to devise a stratified classification system. In his system, some humans resembled apes more than other humans.

But ideas are powerful things and could not be contained within elite circles or prevented from becoming increasingly radical. If many philosophes were themselves uncomfortable with offering liberty and equality (not to mention sovereignty) to *all* people, this was doubly true of their rulers. The Enlightenment in itself was revolutionary only in thought: but thought, too, can be powerful. In the later eighteenth century, new readerships and institutions enabled the extensive spread of concepts such as freedom of conscience, religious tolerance, and equality before the law, even to women, lower-class men, and enslaved peoples whom European elites felt might not deserve it. This was perhaps the Enlightenment's most important, if unintended, legacy.

THE ENLIGHTENMENT AND THE ORIGINS OF RACIAL THOUGHT A darker side of the Enlightenment is evident in the ways in which the new science's insistence on classification and universal natural laws led to a transformation in the idea of "race." Previously, the word *race* referred to a swift current in a stream or a test of speed or a lineage (mainly that of a royal or noble family). By the late seventeenth century, a few writers were expanding the definition to designate a European ethnic lineage, identifying, for example, the indomitable spirit and freedom-loving ethos of the Anglo-Saxon race. In developing a universal knowledge, the Enlightenment created a comprehensive map of the world's advanced and "barbaric" peoples, stratifying them according to Europeans' values and definitions—with lasting effects on racial thinking.

The Frenchman François Bernier, who had traveled in Asia, may have been the first European to attempt to classify the world's peoples. He used a variety of criteria, including those that were to become standard from the late eighteenth century down to the present, such as skin color, facial features, and hair texture. Bernier published this work in his

Linnaeus's Eurocentric Classification System. The frontispiece of one of Linnaeus's books depicts Europe as a botanical monarch receiving floral tributes from the world's regions. Darker-skinned Native American and Asian women bear their offerings to the white-skinned, crowned, allegorical European queen in the center. She alone holds the keys to scientific truth.

New Division of the Earth by the Different Groups or Races Who Inhabit It (1684). Later, the Swedish naturalist Carolus Linnaeus (1707–1778); the French scholar Georges-Louis Leclerc, the comte de Buffon (1707–1788); and the German anatomist Johann Friedrich Blumenbach (1752–1840) also used racial principles to classify humankind.

Enlightened Europeans were not the first to remark on other peoples' distinctive physical features and to see themselves as superior. Chinese elites also professed racialized hierarchies. They glorified their own "white" complexions as compared to the dark skin of the peasants, the "black" skin of the wavy-haired "devils" of Southeast Asia, and the "ash-white" pallor of the Europeans. Native Americans commented critically on the hairiness and odor of European invaders. What the Enlightenment added was the drive to classify all of humankind and impose a universal hierarchy—one that put White Europeans on top.

Although Bernier may have begun the process, Linnaeus decisively pushed forward the project of creating a racial classification of humankind. His *Systema Naturae* (1735) sought to classify all the world's plants and animals by giving each a binomial, or two-word, name. His project would have been inconceivable without expeditions and collections of naturalists and an explosion of information from around the world. By championing a visual way of knowing—relying upon observation, drawing, and representations of nature—Linnaeus created a catalogue that began the process of standardizing scientific knowledge on a global scale. With knowledge *from* the world, Linnaeus produced a representation *of* the world and stratified the continents into subspecies: *Homo europaeus*, *Homo americanus*, *Homo afer*, and *Homo asiaticus*. He added a fifth category, *Homo monstrosus*, for "wild" men and "monstrous" types. Linnaeus's classifications were based on a combination of physical characteristics that included skin color and social qualities. He characterized Europeans as light skinned and governed by laws; Asians as "sooty" and governed by opinion; Indigenous American peoples as copper skinned and governed by custom; and Africans (whom he consigned to the lowest rung of the human ladder) as ruled by personal whim. The Linnaean vision culminated with Europe at the center—or top—of a world system.

It is one of the paradoxes of the Enlightenment that a movement that generated a quest for universal knowledge and spread the idea of human liberty far and wide also introduced a new form of what would be considered "scientific" racism—one marked, too, by European biases.

Creating Hybrid Cultures in the Americas

In the Americas, mingling between European colonizers and Native peoples (as well as enslaved Africans) produced hybrid cultures. But the cultural mixing grew increasingly unbalanced as Europeans imposed authority over more of the Americas. For Native Americans, the pressure to adapt their cultures to those of the colonists began from the start. Over time, Indigenous people faced mounting pressure as Europeans insisted that their conquests were not simply military endeavors but also spiritual errands. In addition to guns and germs, all of Europe's colonizers brought Bibles, prayer books, and crucifixes with the intent of Christianizing and "civilizing" Indigenous and African populations in the Americas. Yet missionary efforts produced uneven and often unpredictable outcomes. Even as Indigenous Americans and enslaved Africans adopted Christian beliefs and practices, they often retained older religious practices too.

European colonists likewise borrowed from the peoples they subjugated and enslaved. This was especially true in the sixteenth and seventeenth centuries, when the colonists' survival in the New World often depended on adapting. Before long, however, many American settlements had become stable and prosperous, and colonists preferred not to admit their past dependence on others. New hierarchies emerged, and elites in Latin America and North America increasingly followed the tastes and fashions of European aristocrats. Yet, even as they imitated Old World ways, these colonials forged identities that separated them from Europe.

Spiritual Encounters

Settlers in the New World had the military and economic power to impose their culture—especially their religion—on some Indigenous peoples. While the Jesuits had little impact in China, Christian missionaries in the Americas had armies and officials to back up their insistence that Native Americans and enslaved Africans abandon their own deities and spirits for Christ. Nonetheless, their attempts to force conversions were rarely a complete success, and some European settlers became interested in Native American culture.

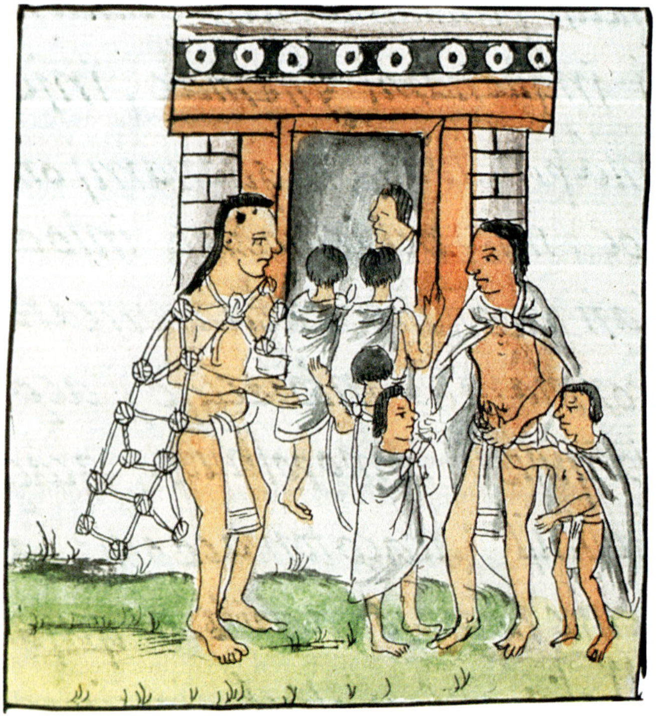

Native Americans Becoming Christians. This image is from a colonial chronicle illustrated and narrated by Indigenous scribes who had converted to Christianity. The picture of Native Americans before the conquest entering a house of prayer is intended to represent the Indigenous peoples as proto-Christians.

FORCING CONVERSIONS European missionaries, especially Catholics, used numerous techniques to bring Indigenous peoples within the Christian fold. Smashing idols, razing temples, and whipping backsliders all belonged to the missionaries' arsenal. Catholic orders (principally Dominicans, Jesuits, and Franciscans) also learned what they could about Indigenous people's beliefs and rituals—and then exploited that knowledge to convert people to Christianity. For example, many missionaries demonized local gods, subverted Indigenous spiritual leaders, and transformed Indigenous iconography into Christian symbols. But at the same time, the missionaries preserved much linguistic and ethnographic information about Indigenous communities. In sixteenth-century Mexico, the Dominican friar Bernardino de Sahagún compiled an immense ethnography of Mexican ways and beliefs. In seventeenth-century Canada, French Jesuits prepared dictionaries and grammars of the Iroquoian and Algonquian languages and translated Christian hymns into Indigenous tongues.

Neither gentle persuasion nor violent coercion produced the results that missionaries desired. When conversions did occur, the resulting Christian practices were usually hybrid forms in which Indigenous deities and rituals merged with Christian ones. Among Andean mountain people, for example, priestesses of local cults took the Christian name Maria to mask their secret worship of traditional deities. In other cases, Indigenous communities turned their backs on Christianity and accused missionaries of bringing disease and death. Those who did convert often believed that Christian spiritual power supplemented, rather than supplanted, their own religions.

MIXING CULTURES More distressing to missionaries than the blending of beliefs or outright defiance were the Indigenous peoples' successes in converting captured colonists, whom they often adopted (particularly women and children) as a way to replace lost kin. It deeply troubled the missionaries that many captured colonists accepted their adoptions and refused to return to colonial society when given the chance. Moreover, some other Europeans voluntarily chose to live in Indigenous communities. Comparing the records of cultural conversion, one eighteenth-century colonist suggested that "thousands of Europeans are Indians," yet "we have no examples of even one of those Aborigines having from choice become European" (Crevecouer, p. 306). In fact, this is untrue. With time, many Indigenous people did take on European ways, combining imported fashion with local clothing; some entered nunneries, colleges, or universities and became intellectuals. In this mixed cultural world, those familiar with both Indigenous and European ways became the intermediaries for cultural exchanges, diplomatic arrangements, and trade.

Europeans also attempted to Christianize enslaved peoples from Africa, though many enslavers doubted the wisdom of converting persons they regarded as mere property. Sent forth with the pope's blessing, Catholic priests targeted enslaved populations in the American colonies of Portugal, Spain, and France. Applying many of the same techniques that missionaries used with Indigenous "heathens," these priests produced similarly mixed results. Often converts blended Islamic or traditional African religions with Catholicism. Converted African people wove remembered practices and beliefs from their homeland into their American Christianity, transforming both along the way. In northeastern Brazil, for example, enslaved peoples combined the Yoruba faiths of their ancestors with Catholic beliefs, and they frequently attributed powers of African deities to Christian saints. Sometimes Christian and African faiths were practiced side by side. In Saint-Domingue, enslaved and free Black people practiced *vodun* ("spirit" in the Dahomey tongue); in Cuba, they practiced *santería* ("cult of saints" in Spanish), a faith of similar origins.

Just as enslavers feared, Christianity—especially in its hybrid forms—could inspire resistance, even revolt, among enslaved people. Indeed, a major freedom-seeking resistance leader in mid-eighteenth-century Suriname was a Christian. Those held in bondage in the English colonies drew inspiration from Christian hymns that promised deliverance, and they embraced as their own the Old Testament story of Moses leading the Israelites out of Egypt. By the late eighteenth century, freed men and women like the Methodist Olaudah Equiano (see Chapter 13) were asserting that slavery was unjust and incompatible with Christian brotherhood.

INTERMARRIAGE AND CULTURAL MIXING Beyond the attractions of Indigenous cultures, Europeans mixed with Indigenous peoples because there were many more men than women among the colonists. Almost all the early European traders, missionaries, and settlers were men. The British North American settlements saw more women arrive relatively early on, and as a result, English settlers were the least inclined to forge voluntary liaisons with Native peoples. And in some parts of the Andes and in Central America, where European settlement was scarcer, natives and newcomers mingled less. But in many parts of New France, New Spain, and Brazil, for instance, mixing was a norm. In response to the scarcity of women and to facilitate the spread of newcomers' culture, the Portuguese crown authorized intermarriage between Portuguese men and local women. These relations often amounted to little more than rape, but longer-lasting relationships developed in places where Indigenous peoples kept their independence—as among French fur traders and Indigenous women in Canada, the Great Lakes region, and the Mississippi Valley. Whether by coercion or consent, sexual relations between European men and Indigenous women resulted in offspring of mixed ancestry. In fact, the Mestizos of Spanish colonies and the *Métis* of French outposts soon outnumbered settlers of wholly European descent.

The increasing numbers of enslaved Africans in the Americas further complicated the mix of New World cultures.

Racial Mixing. *Left:* This *casta* painting shows racial mixing in colonial Mexico—the father is a Spaniard, the mother Native American, and the child Mestizo. (Like the word *caste*, *casta* refers to a group within a social hierarchy, in this case defined by race and racial mixing.) The image indicates that Indigenous people who married Whites achieved elevated status. *Right:* Here, too, we see a racially mixed family. The father is a Spaniard, the mother is African, and the child is what was then called "Mulatto" (a term for a person of mixed White and Black ancestry that is considered offensive today). Observe, however, the less aristocratic and markedly less peaceful portrayal of this family.

Unlike marriages between fur traders and Native women, in which the women held considerable power because of their connections to Indigenous trading partners, sexual intercourse between European men and enslaved African women was almost always forced. Children born from such unions swelled the ranks of mixed-ancestry people in the colonial population. Again, however, unlike the offspring of European fur traders and Indigenous women, who generally found an equal place in their mothers' communities or gained power as intermediaries between their parents' cultures, the children of African women and European men generally became the enslaved property of their fathers.

Forming American Identities

Colonization of the Americas brought Europeans, Africans, and Indigenous people into sustained contact, though the nature of the colonies and the character of the contact varied considerably. Where their dominance was strongest, European colonists imposed their ways on subjugated populations and imported what they took to be the chief attributes of the countries and cultures they had left behind. Yet Europeans were not immune to cultural influences from the groups they dispossessed and enslaved, and over time the colonists developed distinctive "American" identities. The cultures and identities of Indigenous people and enslaved Africans also underwent significant transformations, though often what Europeans imposed was only partially adopted.

CREOLE IDENTITIES In Spanish America, ethnic and cultural mixing produced a powerful new class, the **Creoles**—persons of European descent born in the Americas. Increasing numbers of Creoles were the offspring of mixed-race unions. In their newfound world classifications, Europeans looked down their noses at these racialized Creoles as less "white." In turn, Creoles increasingly resented the control that **Peninsulares**—men and women born in Spain or Portugal but living in the Americas—had over colonial society. Creoles especially chafed under the Peninsulares' exclusive privileges, like those that forbade Creoles from trading with other colonial ports. Also, they disliked the fact that royal ministers gave most official posts to Peninsulares.

"Americans" created their own schools of high art, often adapting Indigenous styles and motifs to European repertoires.

In many cities of the Spanish and Portuguese Empires, reading clubs and salons hosted energetic discussions of fresh Enlightenment ideas and contributed to the growing Creole identity. In one university in Peru, Catholic scholars taught their students that Spanish labor drafts and taxes on Andean natives not only violated divine justice but also offended the natural rights of free men. The Spanish crown, recognizing

Noble Indian Man of Quito. One Ecuadorean artist from the Quito School, Vicente Albán, painted six canvases illustrating the importance of native figures, fruit, and fauna as representatives of New World fecundity. He also portrayed the ways in which Andean peoples were mixing and matching styles, as in his painting *Noble Indian Man of Quito* from 1783. He was committed to showing the wealth and fertility of the Americas, especially its fine textiles and sumptuous fruits.

the role of printing presses in spreading troublesome ideas, strictly controlled the number and location of printers in the colonies. In Brazil, royal authorities banned them altogether. Nonetheless, books, pamphlets, and simple gossip allowed new notions of history and politics to circulate among literate Creoles.

The global Enlightenment also inspired a quest for modern science as a basis for Creole reform. The Spanish government sent Royal Botanical Expeditions composed of scientists and artists to Chile and Peru (1777–1788), New Granada (1783–1816), and New Spain (1787–1803). These campaigns collected and classified an astonishing array of flora; they also produced beautifully illustrated publications that launched an American style of natural painting, notable for documenting the richness of tropical habitats, and several new and marketable commodities that would change the shape of colonization forever.

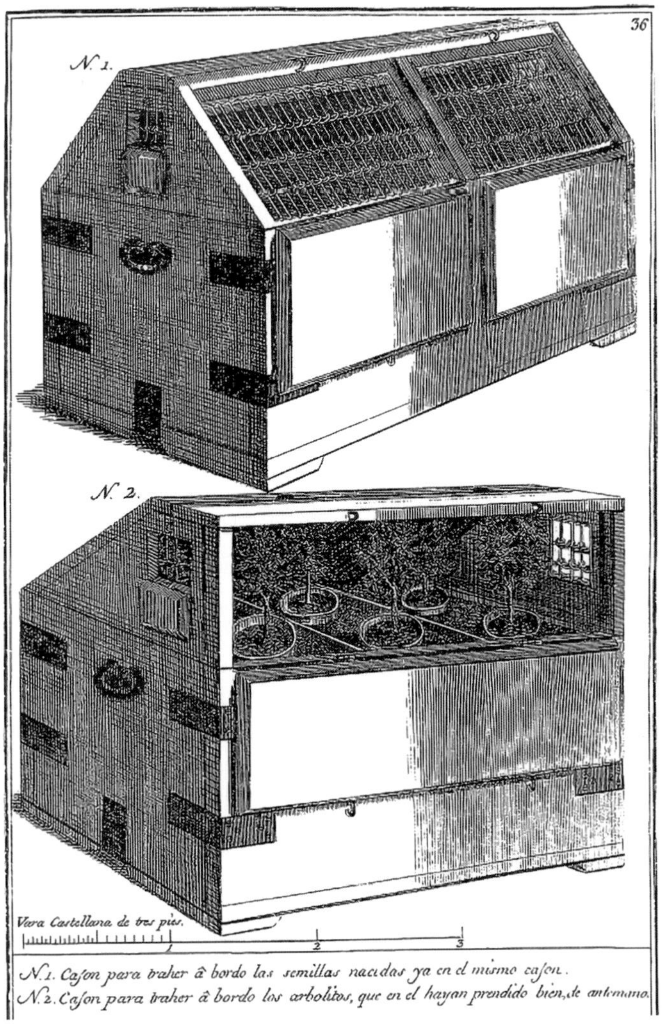

The Cinchona Plant. The Creole New Granada botanical expedition generated thousands of scientific illustrations of previously unknown tropical plants. One of the enlightened leaders of this expedition, José Celestino Mutis, recommended the intensive cultivation of the cinchona plant, whose bark could be used to make the most effective antimalarial medicine of the day, quinine. This image is of maritime crates used to transport live plants and saplings from the tropics to botanical gardens or from experimental stations in Spain to the colonies.

Perhaps the most significant of these commodities was the one popularized by José Celestino Mutis, a Spanish-born physician who had moved to New Granada as a young man. Mutis was fascinated by the medicinal properties of New World plants, and he oversaw the making of no less than 6,500 botanical illustrations from New Granada alone. He was especially interested in the cinchona plant, whose bark had been used by Indigenous people and Jesuit missionaries for centuries to cure malaria. Mutis recognized that cinchona, or quinine, if scientifically cultivated, could be the commodity that allowed more Europeans to settle in the tropics. Committed both to the Enlightenment and to Spanish mercantilism, Mutis believed—rightly, it turned out—that his scientific efforts would improve the health of all of humanity *and* yield riches for Spanish colonies.

The botanical conquest of the New World added to the global warehouse of what Europeans and Creoles knew about natural diversity. It also emboldened scientific and entrepreneurial activity in the tropics and gave Spanish American Creoles a sense that they, too, were part of the "century of light" and on the side of reform and improvement.

ANGLICIZATION In one important sense, wealthy colonists in British America were similar to the Creole elites in Iberian America: they, too, copied European ways. For example, they constructed "big houses" (in Virginia) modeled on the country estates of English gentlemen, imported opulent furnishings and fashions from the finest British stores, and exercised more control over colonial assemblies. Imitating the English also involved tightening patriarchal authority. In seventeenth-century Virginia, men had vastly outnumbered women, which gave women some power (widows, in particular, gained greater control over property and more choices when they remarried). During the eighteenth century, however, sex ratios became more equal, and women's property rights diminished as English customs took precedence. Overall, patriarchal authority was evident in family portraits, where husband-patriarchs sat or stood in front of their wives and children.

Intellectually, too, British Americans were linked to Europe. Importing enormous numbers of books and journals, these Americans played a significant role in the Enlightenment as producers and consumers of political pamphlets, scientific treatises, and social critiques. Indeed, drawing on the words of numerous Enlightenment thinkers, American intellectuals created the most famous of enlightened documents: the Declaration of Independence. It announced that all men were endowed with equal rights and were created to pursue worldly happiness. In this way, Anglicized Americans, like the Creole elites of Latin America, showed themselves to be products of both European and New World encounters.

The Influence of European Culture in Oceania

In the South Pacific, another kind of Anglicization was under way, one similarly shaped by imperialism and enlightened science. Here, even more than in Latin America, enlightened science, embodied in the voyages of Captain James Cook, had ecologically as well as culturally transformative consequences, creating replications of Europe in far distant parts of the world. The focus here is on Australia, but one could also analyze the English colonial territories of New Zealand or Canada in the same terms. Here the wiping out of local peoples and the resettlement by White Europeans—albeit many of them outcasts—created the basis for a variation on colonization marked by a greater degree of cultural transfer.

Until Europeans colonized it in the late eighteenth century, Australia was, like the Americas before Columbus, truly a world apart. Separated by water and sheer distance from other regions, Australia featured harsh natural conditions and a sparse population. At the time of the European colonization, the island was home to around 300,000 people, mostly hunters and gatherers. While Pacific seafarers may have ventured into the area in the past, there is little evidence that either Chinese or Muslim merchants had ever strayed that far south. Spices had drawn the Portuguese and Dutch into the South Pacific (see Chapter 13), and the Spanish, despite considerable resistance, had conquered Guam and the Mariana Islands by 1700. Both the Portuguese and the Dutch had seen the northern and western coasts of Australia, but they had found only sand, flies, and Aboriginals. Only after the scientific voyages of Captain James Cook (1728–1779) to the region in 1768–1779 did Europeans see Australia's more hospitable eastern coast and develop serious interest in colonization. Now the intrusion into **Oceania** (Australia, New Zealand, and the islands of the southwestern Pacific) presented Europeans with a previously unknown region that could serve as a laboratory for studying other peoples and geographical settings. (See Map 14.1.)

James Cook was a veteran sailor, a practitioner of the new science, and, as it turned out, an imperial transformer of worlds. Known to the Royal Society for his excellent maps and his successful attempts to combat scurvy, Cook was the ideal captain to guide the first of what would be three scholarly voyages to observe the movement of the planet Venus from the Southern Hemisphere. Besides Cook, the Royal Society sent along on this 1768 trip one of its members who

The Voyages of Captain James Cook. *Left:* During his celebrated voyages to the South Pacific, Cook kept meticulous maps and diaries. Although he had little formal education, he became one of the great exemplars of enlightened learning through experience and experiment. *Right:* Kangaroos were unknown in the western world until Cook and his colleagues encountered (and ate) them on their first visit to Australia. This engraving of the animal (which, unlike most animals, plants, and geographical features, actually kept the name the Aboriginals had given it) from Cook's 1773 travelogue, *A Voyage Round the World in the Years 1768–1771*, lovingly depicts the kangaroo's environs and even emotions.

The Global View

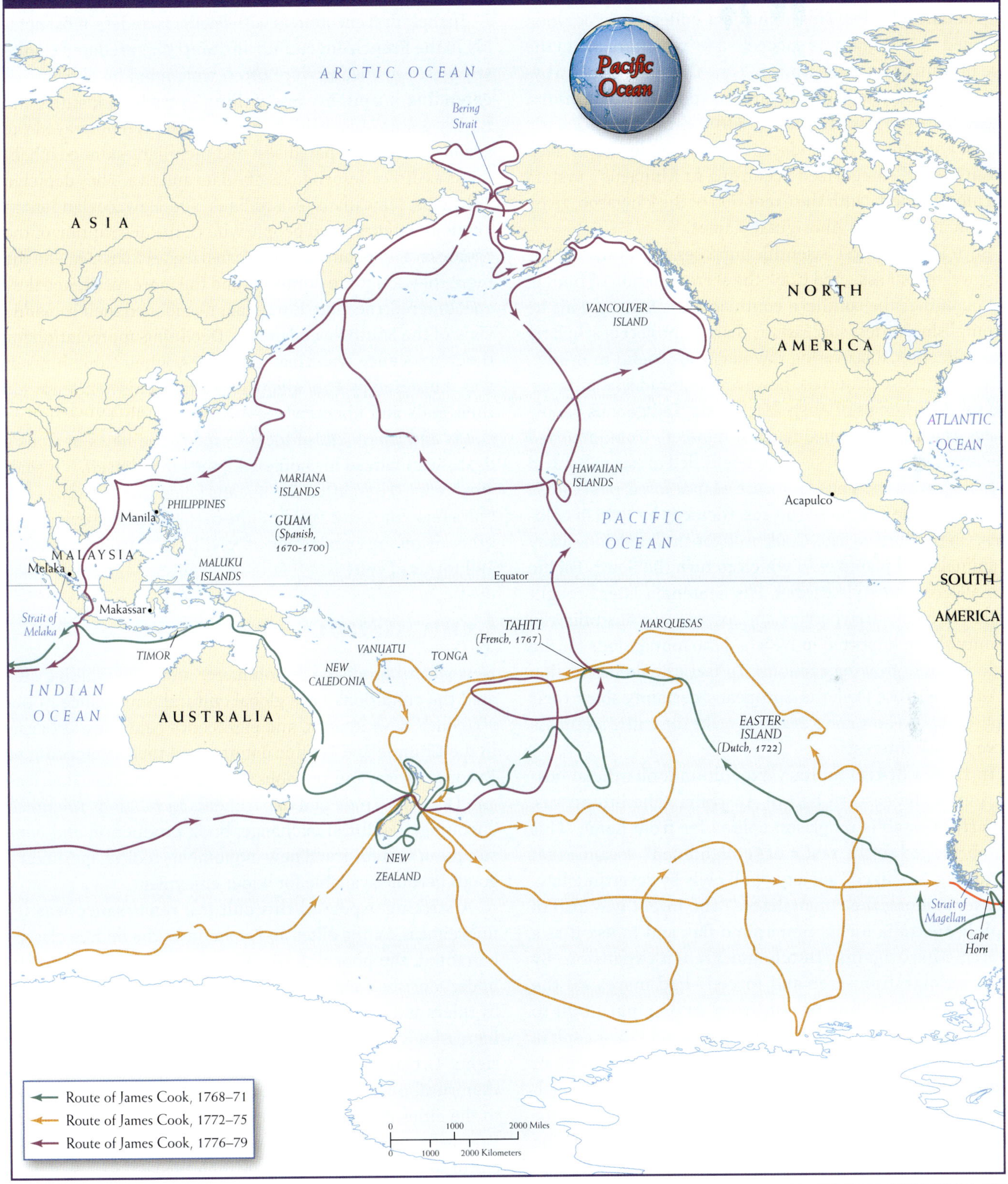

MAP 14.1 | Cook's Global Voyages

Captain Cook's voyages throughout the Pacific Ocean symbolized a new era in European exploration of other societies.

- Where did Cook explore, and what peoples did he encounter?
- Contrast the routes Cook selected for his three voyages. How do they differ? What does that tell us about his project?
- According to your reading, how did Cook's endeavors symbolize "scientific" imperialism?

was a botanist; a doctor and student of Carolus Linnaeus; and numerous artists and other scientists. The crew also carried sophisticated instruments and had instructions to keep detailed diaries. This grand data-collecting expedition returned in 1771 and was succeeded by two more. As in the case of Mutis's investigations in New Granada, Cook's voyages generated a flood of scholarly and popular publications. These featured approximately 3,000 drawings of Pacific plants, animals, birds, landscapes, and peoples never seen in Europe, all categorized according to Linnaeus's system and most of them, with the exception of the kangaroo, given English, rather than Aboriginal, names.

Beyond the voyages' scientific purposes, however, the British government assigned Cook the secret mission of finding and claiming "the southern continent" for Britain. This he accomplished no less successfully than the project of scholarly data collection, discovering raw materials useful to Britain. Extracting those materials, however, required a labor force, and the Aboriginals of Australia, like the Indigenous people of the Americas, perished in great numbers from imported diseases. Those who survived generally fled to escape control by British masters. Thus, to secure a labor force, plans arose for grand-scale conquest and resettlement by British colonists. On his third voyage, Cook brought an astonishing array of animals and plants with which to turn the South Pacific into a European-style garden. His lieutenant later brought apples, quinces, strawberries, and rosemary to Australia; the seventy sheep imported in 1788 laid the foundations for the region's wool-growing economy. In fact, the domestication of Australia arose from the Europeans' certainty about their superior know-how and a desire to make the entire landmass serve British interests.

In 1788, a British military expedition took official possession of the eastern half of Australia. The intent was, in part, to establish a prison colony far from home. This plan belonged to the realm of "enlightened" dreams: that of ridding "civilized" society of all evils by resettling lawbreakers among the "uncivilized." The intent was also to exploit Australia for its timber and flax and to use it as a strategic base against Dutch and French expansion. By 1860, immigration—free and forced—had increased the Anglo-Australian population from an original 1,000 to about 1.2 million. Importing their customs and their capital, British settlers turned Australia into a frontier version of home, just as they had done in British America. Yet such large-scale immigration had disastrous consequences for the surviving Aboriginals. Like the Native Americans, the original inhabitants of Australia were decimated by disease and increasingly forced westward by European settlement, with European ideas and institutions simply replacing local ones. Thus was Oceania, even more than Latin America and far more than the major land empires of Afro-Eurasia, made over in Europe's image.

In their first encounters with Pacific Islanders, most notably in the French encounters in Tahiti that predated Cook's voyages, Europeans were often welcomed by aboriginals extending hospitality and willing to trade foodstuffs and luxury goods. Accordingly, Europeans often portrayed the islands as "tropical paradises" and their light-skinned inhabitants as direct descendants of Adam and Eve. They depicted Tahitians, Hawaiians, Australians, and New Zealanders as virtuous, uncorrupted people who fit the description of the "noble savage" popularized by Jean-Jacques Rousseau. But the more they sought to dominate and the more resistance they encountered, the more Europeans abandoned their romantic view of the South Sea Islanders. Declining appreciation for their innocence was clear after 1779, when Cook himself was murdered by Hawaiians resentful of his contempt for their gods and his crew's less-than-friendly extraction of goods and treatment of local women. The news of Cook's death scandalized his homeland; the king himself, it is said, shed tears. Thereafter, Europeans began to emphasize the "savagery" of South Pacific cultures and insisted ever more urgently on the exportation of "civilized" European culture and forms of rule.

Conclusion

New wealth produced by commerce and state building created the conditions for a global cultural renaissance in the sixteenth, seventeenth, and eighteenth centuries. It began in the Chinese and Islamic empires and then stretched into Europe, Africa, and previous worlds apart in the Americas and Oceania. Trade and experiments in religious tolerance encouraged cultural exchange; book production and consumption soared; grand new monuments took shape; luxury goods became available for wider enjoyment.

A striking aspect of this cultural renaissance was its unevenness. While elites and sometimes the middle classes benefited, the poor did not. They remained illiterate and undernourished and were often subjected to brutal treatment by rulers and landowners. Elite women in Europe and China increasingly joined literate society, but they gained no new rights. Urban areas also profited more from the new wealth than rural ones did, so people seeking refinement flocked to the cities. Some former cultural centers, like the Italian Peninsula, lost their luster as new, more commercially and culturally dynamic centers took their place.

Among states, too, cultural inequalities were glaring. Although the Islamic and Chinese worlds confidently retained their own systems of knowing, believing, and representing, the Americas and Oceania increasingly faced European cultural pressures. Here, while hybrid practices became widespread by the late eighteenth century, European beliefs and habits predominated as the standards for judging degrees of "civilization." African cultures largely escaped this influence, though their homelands felt the impact of European expansionism through the slave trade.

From a commercial standpoint, the world was more integrated than ever before. It was also becoming more stratified into categories and classifications by Europeans. In so doing, Europeans made this hierarchy seem more scientific, more natural. The Chinese still believed in the superiority of their traditional knowledge and customs. Muslim rulers, confident of Islam's primacy, allowed others to form subordinate cultural communities within their realm and adopted European ideas only when doing so served their own imperial purposes. Above all, it was Europeans who constructed knowledge that they believed was universal and objective, and that positioned themselves atop the hierarchy they envisioned. This view would prove consequential, as well as controversial, in the centuries to come.

After You Read This Chapter

TRACING THE GLOBAL STORYLINES

FOCUS ON: The Creation of Global Cultures

The Islamic World

- The Ottomans' unique cultural synthesis accommodates not only mystical Sufis and ultraorthodox *ulama* but also military men, administrators, and clerics.
- The Safavid state proclaims the triumph of Shiism and Persian influences in the sumptuous new capital, Isfahan.
- Mughal courtly culture values art and learning and, at its high point, welcomes non-Muslim contributions.

East Asia

- China's cultural flourishing, coming from within, is evident in the broad circulation of traditional ideas, publishing, and mapmaking.
- Japan's imperial court at Kyoto develops an elite culture of theater, stylized painting, tea ceremonies, and flower arranging.

Europe

- Cultural flourishing known as the Enlightenment yields a faith in reason and a belief in humans' ability to fathom the laws of nature and human behavior.
- European thinkers articulate a belief in unending human progress.
- Europeans expand into Australia and the South Pacific.

Africa

- Slave-trading states such as Asante, Oyo, and Benin celebrate royal power and wealth through art.

The Americas

- Even as Euro-Americans participate in the Enlightenment, their culture reflects Native American and African influences.

CHRONOLOGY

The Islamic World

- Shah Abbas I builds Isfahan 1598–1629
- Taj Mahal built in Mughal dynasty 1630–1650

Africa

- Oyo and Asante kingdoms produce vibrant artistic works 1600s

Europe

East Asia

- Growing circulation of books and ideas in China 1600s
- Study aids for the civil service examination are especially popular 1600s
- Anthologies of women's poetry circulate widely 1600s
- "Floating worlds" appear in Japanese cities 1600s

The Americas

- Hybrid cultures appear 1600s

1500 | 1550 | 1600 | 1650

KEY TERMS

bioprospecting p. 610
Creoles p. 622
Enlightenment p. 613
Forbidden City of Beijing p. 596
great plaza at Isfahan p. 596
Oceania p. 624
Palace of Versailles p. 596
Peninsulares p. 622
philosophes p. 614
scientific method p. 614
Sufis p. 595
Taj Mahal p. 602
Topkapi Palace p. 596
ulama p. 595

THINKING ABOUT GLOBAL CONNECTIONS

Thinking about Exchange Networks and Cultural Change How did increased exchanges of goods and ideas change established traditions? What institutions and ideas proved most hospitable to foreign influence, even in established cultures, and why? Which fields proved more resistant to outside ideas? Why were some regions more receptive to foreign influences than others were? Consider religion, natural science, and art.

Thinking about Changing Power Relationships and Cultural Change How did established cultures respond to the inclusion of the Americas in an increasingly integrated world? Which cultures flourished, and why? What relationship(s) can you see between new wealth and cultural change?

Thinking about Environmental Impacts and Cultural Change The isolation of the Americas and Oceania paved the way for ecological catastrophe when Europeans arrived. How, in turn, did ecological catastrophes leave Indigenous cultures vulnerable? Consider the nature of religious change in the Americas and the Afro-Eurasian core regions and population movements in Australia.

Go to INQUIZITIVE to see what you've learned—and learn what you've missed—with personalized feedback along the way.

Tulip Period in Ottoman Empire
1720s

Isaac Newton publishes *Principia Mathematica*
1687

Enlightenment philosophy spreads among educated elites
1700s

Carolus Linnaeus publishes *Systema Naturae*
1735

Voyages of Captain Cook
1768–1779

Adam Smith publishes *The Wealth of Nations*
1776

Enlightenment philosophy spreads among colonial elites
eighteenth century

1700 | 1750 | 1800

Global Themes and Sources

Comparing Changes to Global Commerce and Society

Commerce spread around the globe as never before in the centuries after 1500. Although business practices differed in different settings, the same questions confronted merchants, men of letters, and political leaders everywhere trade flourished: Was trade natural—consistent with the right order of things—or unnatural? Did it bring out the best or worst in people? Did the arrival of new wealth and goods support or undermine established cultures and social elites?

Commerce was a central issue in the European Enlightenment; the first three documents all present trade as central to modern European culture. The fourth, by a Japanese merchant named Shimai Soshitsu, instructed future generations on how to keep business interests from compromising their values. The final selection, drawn from edicts issued by the Chinese Qianlong Emperor, shows both fear about the dangers business interests posed and a recognition that they were too important to abolish altogether.

To make sense of these documents, you will need to think comparatively and evaluate how a range of authors responded to the same set of issues. Given the centrality of commerce, they offer the opportunity to think about cause and effect. What change or changes can you identify?

ANALYZING CHANGES TO GLOBAL COMMERCE AND SOCIETIES

- Place the following documents on a continuum from those that support commerce to those that reject it.
- Analyze the relationship between commerce and the social order in each document. Does the document present commerce as upholding the social order or as subverting it?
- Analyze the tension between progress and backwardness in each source, from the author's point of view.

PRIMARY SOURCE 14.1

"Doux Commerce" (1748), Charles de Secondat, Baron de Montesquieu

Charles de Secondat, Baron de Montesquieu (1689–1755), was a magistrate in the *parlement* (law court) of Bordeaux and a man of letters, one of the most influential figures in the French Enlightenment. The French term *doux commerce* refers to the gentle, taming, civilizing force of commerce.

- Explain the relationship between commerce and "barbarous behavior."
- Which values does trade promote, in Montesquieu's view, and which does it stifle?
- Identify the central assumption at work in this text. What does Montesquieu take for granted, and what does he defend with argument?

Commerce is a cure for the most destructive prejudices; for it is almost a general rule, that wherever we find agreeable manners, there commerce flourishes; and that wherever there is commerce, there we meet with agreeable manners.

Let us not be astonished, then, if our manners are now less savage than formerly. Commerce has everywhere diffused a knowledge of the manners of all nations: these are compared one with another, and from this comparison arise the greatest advantages.

Commercial laws, it may be said, improve manners for the same reason that they destroy them. They corrupt the purest morals. This was the subject of Plato's complaints; and we every day see that they polish and refine the most barbarous.

Peace is the natural effect of trade. Two nations who traffic with each other become reciprocally dependent; for if one has an interest in buying, the other has an interest in selling; and thus their union is founded on their mutual necessities.

But if the spirit of commerce unites nations, it does not in the same manner unite individuals. We see that in countries [Holland] where the people move only by the spirit of commerce, they make a traffic of all the humane, all the moral virtues; the most trifling things, those which humanity would demand, are there done, or there given, only for money.

The spirit of trade produces in the mind of a man a certain sense of exact justice, opposite, on the one hand, to robbery, and on the other to those moral virtues which forbid our always adhering rigidly to the rules of private interest, and suffer us to neglect this for the advantage of others.

The total privation of trade, on the contrary, produces robbery, which Aristotle ranks in the number of means of acquiring; yet it is not at all inconsistent with certain moral virtues.

Hospitality, for instance, is most rare in trading countries, while it is found in the most admirable perfection among nations of vagabonds.

Source: Charles de Secondat, Baron de Montesquieu, *The Spirit of the Laws* (Cambridge, England: Cambridge University Press, 1989), pp. 338–39.

PRIMARY SOURCE 14.2

"The Propensity to Truck, Barter, and Exchange" (1776), Adam Smith

Adam Smith (1723–1790) was a Scottish moral philosopher and leading figure of the Scottish Enlightenment whose 1776 book, *The Wealth of Nations*, was a pioneering work of political economy.

- According to Smith, where does the division of labor come from?
- What challenges stand in the way of economic growth, in Smith's view?
- What do you think Smith would say about economic inequality?

The division of labour, from which so many advantages are derived, is not originally the effect of any human wisdom, which foresees and intends that general opulence to which it gives occasion. It is the necessary, though very slow and gradual consequence of a certain propensity in human nature which has in view no such extensive utility; the propensity to truck, barter, and exchange one thing for another.

Whether this propensity be one of those original principles in human nature of which no further account can be given; or whether, as seems more probable, it be the necessary consequence of the faculties of reason and speech, it belongs not to our present subject to inquire. It is common to all men, and to be found in no other race of animals, which seem to know neither this nor any other species of contracts. Two greyhounds, in running down the same hare, have sometimes the appearance of acting in some sort of concert. Each turns her [the hare being hunted] towards his companion, or endeavours to intercept her when his companion turns her towards himself. This, however, is not the effect of any contract, but of the accidental concurrence of their passions in the same object at that particular time.

***

As it is by treaty, by barter, and by purchase that we obtain from one another the greater part of those mutual good offices which we stand in need of, so it is this same trucking disposition which originally gives occasion to the division of labour. In a tribe of hunters or shepherds a particular person makes bows and arrows, for example, with more readiness and dexterity than any other. He frequently exchanges them for cattle or for venison with his companions; and he finds at last that he can in this manner get more cattle and venison than if he himself went to the field to catch them. From a regard to his own interest, therefore, the making of bows and arrows grows to be his chief business, and he becomes a sort of armourer. Another excels in making the frames and covers of their little huts or movable houses. He is accustomed to be of use in this way to his neighbours, who reward him in the same manner with cattle and with venison, till at last he finds it his interest to dedicate himself entirely to this employment, and to become a sort of house-carpenter. In the same manner a third becomes a smith or a brazier, a fourth a tanner or dresser of hides or skins, the principal part of the clothing of savages. And thus the certainty of being able to exchange all that surplus part of the produce of his own labour, which is over and above his own consumption, for such parts of the produce of other men's labour as he may have occasion for, encourages every man to apply himself to a particular occupation, and to cultivate and bring to perfection whatever talent or genius he may possess for that particular species of business.

The difference of natural talents in different men is, in reality, much less than we are aware of; and the very different genius which appears to distinguish men of different professions, when grown up to maturity, is not upon many occasions so much the cause as the effect of the division of labour. The difference between the most dissimilar characters, between a philosopher and a common street porter, for example, seems to arise not so much from nature as from habit, custom, and education. When they came into the world, and for the first six or eight years of their existence, they were, perhaps, very much alike, and neither their parents nor playfellows could perceive any remarkable difference. About that age, or soon after, they come to be employed in very different occupations. The difference of talents comes then to be taken notice of, and widens by degrees, till at last the vanity of the philosopher is willing to acknowledge scarce any resemblance. But without the disposition to truck, barter, and exchange, every man must have procured to himself every necessary and conveniency of life which he wanted. All must have had the same duties to perform, and the same work to do, and there could have been no such difference of employment as could alone give occasion to any great difference of talents.

As it is this disposition which forms that difference of talents, so remarkable among men of different professions, so it is this same disposition which renders that difference useful. Many tribes of animals acknowledged to be all of the same species derive from nature a much more remarkable distinction of genius, than what, antecedent to custom and education, appears to take place among men. By nature a philosopher is not in genius and disposition half so different from a street porter, as a mastiff is from a greyhound, or a greyhound from a spaniel, or this last from a shepherd's dog. Those different tribes of animals, however, though all of the same species, are of scarce any use to one another. The strength of the mastiff is not, in the least, supported either by the swiftness of the greyhound, or by the sagacity of the spaniel, or by the docility of the shepherd's dog. The effects of those different geniuses and talents, for want of the power or disposition to barter and exchange, cannot be brought into a common stock, and do not in the least contribute to the better accommodation and conveniency of the species. Each animal is still obliged to support and defend itself, separately and independently, and derives no sort of advantage from that variety of talents with which nature has distinguished its fellows. Among men, on the contrary, the most dissimilar geniuses are of use to one another; the different produces of their respective talents, by the general disposition to truck, barter, and exchange, being brought, as it were, into a common stock, where every man may purchase whatever part of the produce of other men's talents he has occasion for.

Source: Adam Smith, *An Inquiry into the Nature and Causes of the Wealth of Nations* (London: Methuen, 1904), pp. 15, 17–18.

PRIMARY SOURCE 14.3

On Inequality (1755), Jean-Jacques Rousseau

Jean-Jacques Rousseau (1712–1778) was a political philosopher from Geneva with deep connections to the Enlightenment in France and across Europe. In the nineteenth century, his work particularly influenced Karl Marx and Sigmund Freud, among many others.

- Analyze the role of private property in this text.
- What role does competition play? Does Rousseau see competition as essential for innovation or as a problem?
- What does Rousseau mean when he says, "To be and to appear became two entirely different things"?

The first man who, having enclosed a piece of ground, thought to say *this is mine*, and found people sufficiently simple to believe him, was the true founder of civil society. How many crimes, wars, murders, how many miseries and horrors Mankind would have been spared by him who, pulling up the stakes or filling in the ditch, had cried out to his kind: Beware of listening to this impostor; You are lost if you forget that the fruits are everyone's and the Earth no one's: But in all likelihood things had by then reached a point where they could not continue as they were; for this idea of property, depending as it does on many prior ideas which could only arise successively, did not take shape all at once in man's mind: Much progress had to have been made, industry and enlightenment acquired, transmitted, and increased from one age to the next, before this last stage of the state of Nature was reached. Let us therefore take up the thread earlier, and try to fit this slow succession of events and of knowledge together from a single point of view, and in their most natural order.

***

Things having reached this point, it is easy to imagine the rest. I shall not pause to describe the successive invention of the other arts, the progress of languages, the testing and exercise of talents, the inequalities of fortune, the abuse of Wealth, nor all the details that attend them and which everyone can easily add. I shall limit myself to a brief glance at Mankind placed in this new order of things.

Here, then are all our faculties developed, memory and imagination brought into play, amour propre interested, reason become active, and the mind almost at the limit of the perfection of which it is capable. Here are all natural qualities set in action, every man's rank and fate set, not only as to the amount of their goods and the power to help or to hurt, but also as to mind, beauty, strength or skill, as to merit or talents, and, since these are the only qualities that could attract consideration, one soon had to have or to affect them; for one's own advantage one had to seem other than one in fact was. To be and to appear became two entirely different things, and from this distinction arose ostentatious display, deceitful cunning, and all the vices that follow in their wake. Looked at in another way, man, who had previously been free and independent, is now so to speak subjugated by a multitude of new needs to the whole of Nature, and especially to those of his kind, whose slave he in a sense becomes even by becoming their master; rich, he needs their services; poor, he needs their help, and moderate means do not enable him to do without them. He must therefore constantly try to interest them in his fate and to make them really or apparently find their own profit in working for his: which makes him knavish and artful with some, imperious and harsh with the rest, and places him under the necessity of deceiving all those he needs if he cannot get them to fear him and does not find it in his interest to make himself useful to them. Finally, consuming ambition, the ardent desire to raise one's relative fortune less out of genuine need than in order to place oneself above others, instills in all men a black inclination to harm one another, a secret jealousy that is all the more dangerous as it often assumes the mask of benevolence in order to strike its blow in greater safety: in a word, competition and rivalry on the one hand, conflict of interests on the other, and always the hidden desire to profit at another's expense; all these evils are the first effect of property, and the inseparable train of nascent inequality.

Before its representative signs were invented, wealth could scarcely consist in anything but land and livestock, the only real goods that men can possess. Now, once inheritances had increased in number and size to the point where they covered all the land and all adjoined one another, men could no longer aggrandize themselves except at one another's expense, and the supernumeraries whom weakness or indolence had kept from acquiring an inheritance of their own, grown poor without having lost anything because they alone had not changed while everything was changing around them, were obliged to receive or to seize their subsistence from the hands of the rich; and from this began to arise, according to the different characters of the poor and the rich, domination and servitude, or violence and plunder. The rich, for their part, had scarcely become acquainted with the pleasure of dominating than they disdained all other pleasures, and using their old Slaves to subject new ones, they thought only of subjugating and enslaving their neighbors; like those ravenous wolves which once they have tasted human flesh, scorn all other food, and from then on want to devour only men.

Source: Jean-Jacques Rousseau, Second Discourse, Part 2, in *Rousseau's Political Writings: Discourse on Inequality, Discourse on Political Economy, on Social Contract* (New York: Norton, 1988), pp. 34, 42–43.

PRIMARY SOURCE 14.4

Merchant Codes in Tokugawa Japan (1610)

Shimai Soshitsu (1539–1615) was a sake merchant in Hakata, Japan. In his testament, Shimai sets out a list of instructions, echoing military codes, to help subsequent generations remain virtuous while pursuing commerce.

- Identify the values expressed in this document.
- Analyze the merchant's relationship to money. What purpose do profits serve?
- Does commerce threaten the social order or support it, in Shimai's view?

1. Live an honest and sincere life. Respect your parents, your brothers, and your relatives, and try to live harmoniously with them all. Honor and treat with respect everyone you meet, even those you see only occasionally. Never behave discourteously or selfishly. Never lie. In fact, never say anything that even resembles a lie, even something you heard from someone else.

2. Although those who are elderly may reasonably pray about the life to come, you should ignore all such issues until you are fifty. You may follow only the Pure Land or Zen Buddhist faiths, and you must have absolutely nothing to do with the Christian religion. . . . Such a faith is an intolerable obstacle to anyone devoted to his house. Not one person in ten understands the things of this life or of the next. Birds and beasts worry only about what is immediately before them, and humans are no different. In this life they first should make certain that they do not sully their reputations. If even Buddha himself is said to have known nothing of the world to come, how can any ordinary mortal know such things? Until you reach fifty, therefore, do not worry about the future life. . . .

3. Dice, backgammon, and all other forms of gambling are strictly forbidden in this life. Even *go*, chess, the martial arts, the nō chants, and the nō dances are forbidden for people under forty. . . .

4. Until you are forty, avoid every luxury, and never act or think like one above your station in life. In matters of business and moneymaking, however, work harder than anyone else. . . . Always behave as one whose station in life is half that of yours. Although some people may suggest that you [should] be more visible and assertive, ignore all such advice and maintain a low profile. Until you turn fifty, be temperate in all things, and avoid all ostentation and finery, anything, in fact, that might call attention to yourself. Do not cultivate expensive tastes, for you should ignore such things as the tea ceremony, swords, daggers, and fine clothes. . . . Do not build a new house unless you are over fifty. Those who are that old may build what they like and can afford. Yet most people are poor by the time they die, for fewer than one in ten or twenty who build a fortune by their own talent carry it to their graves, and those who inherit their wealth are even more likely to lose it and die impoverished. Remember this.

5. Until you are forty, do not invite out others or let others invite you out. Once or twice a year you may invite out your parents, brothers, or relatives, or go out at their invitation, but—do not forget—even this you may do only occasionally. . . .

***

8. Never wander outside the shop or visit places where you have no business being. . . . Since you will generally be in the house, you yourself should tend the morning and evening cooking fires and handle the firewood and embers. You should pick up all trash inside and behind the house, chop up the pieces of rope and short bits of trash to use in plaster, and use the long pieces to make rope. Collect and clean pieces of wood and bamboo longer than five *bu* and use them as firewood. Save all paper scraps, even pieces only three or five *bu* long, to use in making fresh paper. Do as I have done, and waste absolutely nothing.

9. When you need something, go and buy it yourself, regardless of whether it is firewood, two or three *bu* of small fish or sardines, other purchases from the seaside or the town, or even timber. Bargain for the items and pay as little as you can. . . .

10. In general, use few servants, especially few female ones. . . .

11. Keep a steady supply of coarse *miso* on hand for your servants, and when you make the *miso* soup in the mornings and evenings, carefully filter the *miso*. You should add to the residue salt and cucumbers, eggplants, gourd melons, and onions, and serve this as a side dish to the servants. You can give them the stalks as well, and when rice is expensive, you may feed them some sort of hodgepodge. But if you do give your servants such a dish, you and your wife should eat it as well. Even if you intend to eat rice, first sip at least a bit of the hodgepodge, for your servants will resent it if you do not. . . .

***

13. Those with even a small fortune must remember that their duty in life is to devote themselves to their house and its business. They must not become careless, for if they buy what they want, do as they please, and, in general, live sumptuously, they will soon spend that fortune. . . . Although a samurai can draw on the produce of his tenured lands to earn his livelihood, a merchant must rely on the profit from his business, for without that profit, the money in his bags would soon disappear. No matter how much profit he makes and packs into his bags, however, if he continually wastes that money, he may as well pack it into bags full of holes. Remember this.

14. Rise early in the morning, and go to bed as soon as the sun sets, for you will waste oil if you burn lamps during evenings when you have nothing important to do. . . .

***

17. Live in harmony with your wife, for the two of you must work together diligently. Both of you should live modestly and carefully and consider always the good of the house and its business. A contentious, unhappy marriage destroys a house, for it distracts the husband and wife from their work. . . .

These seventeen articles were written not for Sōshitsu's sake but for yours. They are his testament, and you should follow them closely. They should be as important to you as the Great Constitution of Prince Shōtoku. Read them every day, or even twice a day, and be careful to forget nothing. Write a vow on the back of a votive tablet promising never to violate any of the articles and put it in my coffin when I die.

Source: Wm. Theodore de Bary, Carol Gluck, and Arthur E. Tiedemann (eds.), *Sources of Japanese Tradition*, vol. 2, *1600 to 2000*, 2nd ed. (New York: Columbia University Press, 2001), pp. 268–71.

PRIMARY SOURCE 14.5

An Edict on Trade (1793), the Qianlong Emperor

The Qianlong Emperor (1711–1799) was the sixth emperor of the Manchu-led Qing dynasty in China. In the late eighteenth century, the English East India Company sought to expand its trade with China. Here the Chinese government seeks to regulate the activity of English merchants.

- What was the Qianlong Emperor trying to accomplish?
- How does the Qianlong Emperor justify trading with foreign powers?
- From the emperor's point of view, what effect does trade have on the social order?

You, O King, live beyond the confines of many seas, nevertheless, impelled by your humble desire to partake of the benefits of our civilization, you have dispatched a mission respectfully bearing your memorial. Your Envoy has crossed the seas and paid his respects at my Court on the anniversary of my birthday. To show your devotion, you have also sent offerings of your country's produce.

***

As to your entreaty to send one of your nationals to be accredited to my Celestial Court and to be in control of your country's trade with China, this request is contrary to all usage of my dynasty and cannot possibly be entertained.

***

You, O King from far, have yearned after the blessings of our civilization, and in your eagerness to come into touch with our converting influence have sent an Embassy across the sea bearing a memorial. I have already taken note of your respectful spirit of submission, have treated your mission with extreme favour and loaded it with gifts, besides issuing a mandate to you, O King, and honouring you with the bestowal of valuable presents. Thus has my indulgence been manifested.

. . . Hitherto, all European nations, including your own country's barbarian merchants, have carried on their trade with Our Celestial Empire at Canton. Such has been the procedure for many years, although Our Celestial Empire possesses all things in prolific abundance and lacks no product within its borders. There was therefore no need to import the manufactures of outside barbarians in exchange for our own produce. But as the tea, silk, and porcelain which the Celestial Empire produces are absolute necessities to European nations and to yourselves, we have permitted, as a signal mark of favour, that foreign hongs [trading firms licensed by the Chinese government] should be established at Canton, so that your wants might be supplied and your country thus participate in our beneficence. But your Ambassador has now put forward new requests which completely fail to recognize the Throne's principle to "treat strangers from afar with indulgence," and to exercise a pacifying control over barbarian tribes, the world over. . . .

Your Ambassador requests facilities for ships of your nation to call at Ningpo, Chusan, Tientsin and other places for purposes of trade. Until now trade with European nations has always been conducted at Macao, where the foreign hongs are established to store and sell foreign merchandise. Your nation has obediently complied with this regulation for years past without raising any objection. In none of the other ports named have hongs been established, so that even if your vessels were to proceed thither, they would have no means of disposing of their cargoes. Furthermore, no interpreters are available, so you would have no means of explaining your wants, and nothing but general inconvenience would result. For the future, as in the past, I decree that your request is refused and that the trade shall be limited to Macao.

Source: Gentzler J. Mason, *Changing China: Readings in the History of China from the Opium War to the Present* (New York: Praeger, 1977), pp. 23–28.

Interpreting Visual Evidence

Envisioning the World

Although maps give the impression of objectivity and geographic precision, the arrangement of names and locations, as well as the areas placed at the center and the margins, reveal the mapmakers' views of the world. In most cultures, official maps located their own major administrative and religious sites at the center of the universe and reflected local elites' ideas about how the world was organized.

There were, however, important differences. For example, Chinese maps, like the first two below, typically devoted more attention to textual explanations with moral and political messages than to locating places accurately. The Codex Xolotl presents a cartographic history, showing mountains and waterways and using hieroglyphic place-names for sites in the Valley of Mexico, marking historic conquests of an Aztec group, the Acolhuas of Texoco.

The Iranian map presents an unabashedly Islamic vision, with a grid that measures the distances from any location in the Islamic world to Mecca. The map of al-Idrisi, also from the Islamic world, shows the world as consisting of only three landmasses: Africa, Asia, and Europe.

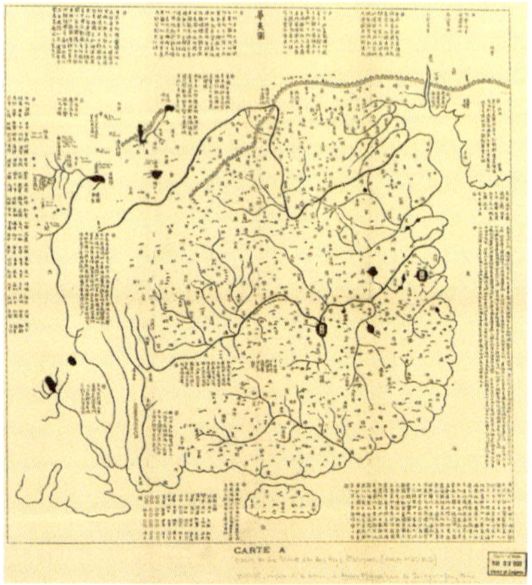

The *Huayi tu* map, 1136.

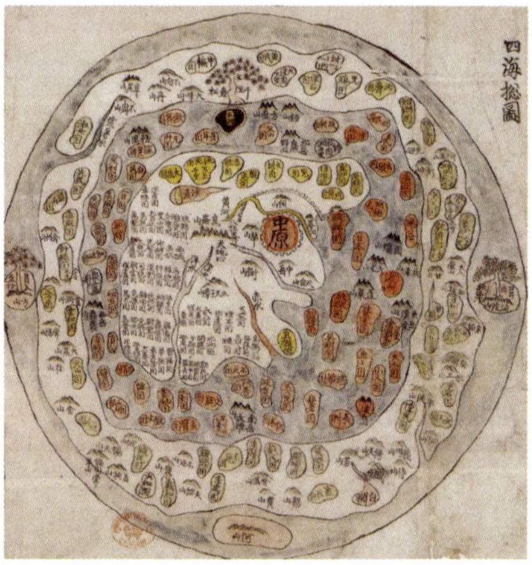

Chinese wheel map, 1760s.

Codex Xolotl, early sixteenth century.

Iranian map, seventeenth century.

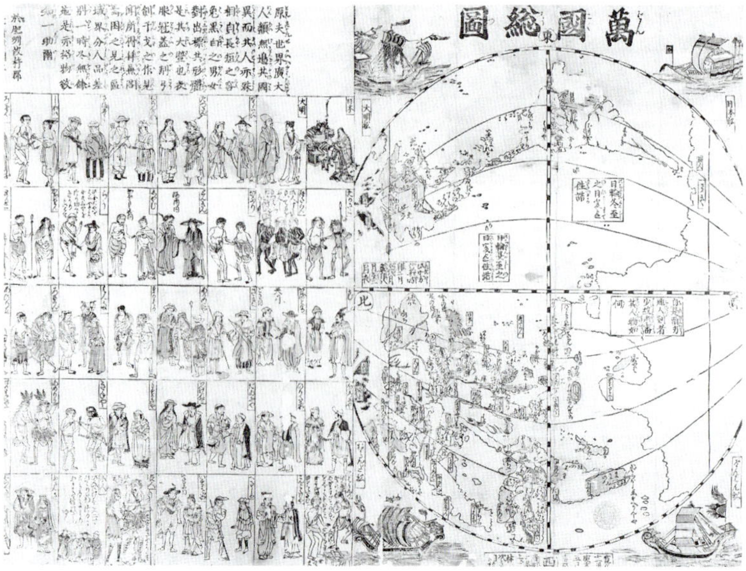

Japanese map of the world, 1761.

The Japanese map shows Dutch influence, with much information about distant lands both in the map and in the two-person images to the left. Finally, the European maps (the Waldseemüller map and the Mercator projection) appear objective at first glance, but they, too, group the rest of the world around their own territory, which they distort to make appear disproportionately large.

QUESTIONS FOR ANALYSIS

1. Describe the organizing principles, and therefore priorities, of each map.
2. Compare the maps. How are they different from one another?
3. Evaluate the relative awareness each map shows of distant cultures and territories.

Al-Idrisi map, twelfth century.

Waldseemüller map, 1507.

Mercator projection, 1569.

Before You Read This Chapter

GLOBAL STORYLINES

The Global Impact of the Atlantic and Industrial Revolutions

- A new era based on radically new ideas of freedom and the nation-state emerges in the Atlantic world.
- Enslaved and Indigenous peoples seize ideas of freedom for their own.
- The beginnings of a global consumer culture and the industrial revolution transform communities and the global economy.
- The worldwide balance of power shifts decisively toward northwestern Europe.

CHAPTER OUTLINE

15

Reordering the World

1750–1850

FOCUS QUESTIONS

- What were the new ideas of freedom, and how did they differ from earlier understandings of this term?
- How did political and economic developments in the Atlantic world compare with those in regions elsewhere?
- What key developments constituted the industrial revolution? How did these changes alter the societies that began to industrialize during this time?
- What were the patterns of global trade and economic growth, and how did they relate to political changes?
- What were the similarities and differences between groups of people who held power in each region? What changes occurred in these societies?

In 1798, the French commander Napoleon Bonaparte invaded Egypt. At the time, Europeans regarded this territory as the cradle of a once-great culture, a land bridge to the Red Sea and trade with Asia, and an outpost of the Ottoman Empire. Occupying the country would allow Napoleon to introduce some of the principles of the French Revolution and to seize control of trade routes to Asia. Napoleon also hoped that by defeating the Ottomans, who ruled over Egypt, he would augment his and France's historic greatness.

Although Napoleon's adventure would backfire, it challenged Ottoman rule and threatened the balance of power in Europe. Similar challenges were being felt worldwide. Indeed, the effect of Napoleon's actions in Africa, the Americas, and Europe, combined with ideas of revolution, laid the foundations for a new era—one based on a radically new understanding of freedom as the absence of constraint, the opposition of privileges handed down by a lord or master.

New ideas of freedom rang out from many points and reverberated around the world. They destroyed the American colonial domains of Spain, Portugal, Britain, and France; brought new nations to the stage; challenged established elites everywhere; and gave voice to the most downtrodden and excluded. The impulse for change was a belief that governments should enact laws that apply to all people, though in practice there were exceptions (women, enslaved people of all genders, and colonial subjects). Free speech, free markets, and governments freely elected by freeborn men, it was thought, would benefit everyone. The advent of new freedoms spurred a debate and conflict over who would get these freedoms. The idea of freedom also challenged systems like mercantilist control and chattel slavery that held empires together. In Europe and the Americas, though not elsewhere, the era also witnessed the emergence of the nation-state. This new form of political organization derived legitimacy from its inhabitants, often referred to as citizens, who, in theory if not always in practice, shared a common culture, language, and ethnicity.

If struggles for freedom leveled societies in some parts of the world, they yielded new forms of hierarchy. Arguments about rights to trade or hold property set the stage for depriving people of freedom. They also led inexorably to changes in the worldwide balance of power. Even as western Europeans lost their American colonies, they gained economic and military strength that further challenged Asian and African governments. In China, the ruling Manchus faced European pressure to permit expanded trade. In Egypt and the Ottoman Empire, reform-minded leaders tried to modernize. When the rise of Egypt threatened Europe's strategic interests in the eastern Mediterranean, the European states intervened to rein in that country's ambitions.

Underlying many of these political and social upheavals were major changes in the world economy. Countries began to produce goods less for their own population and more for people living in other places around the globe. This specialization for export markets further integrated the world. But results were paradoxical. While the world became more integrated and economic growth took off, social disparities grew wider—both within and across countries. What is called "the industrial revolution" set in motion great divides between Europe and North America and the rest of the world and even within industrializing societies.

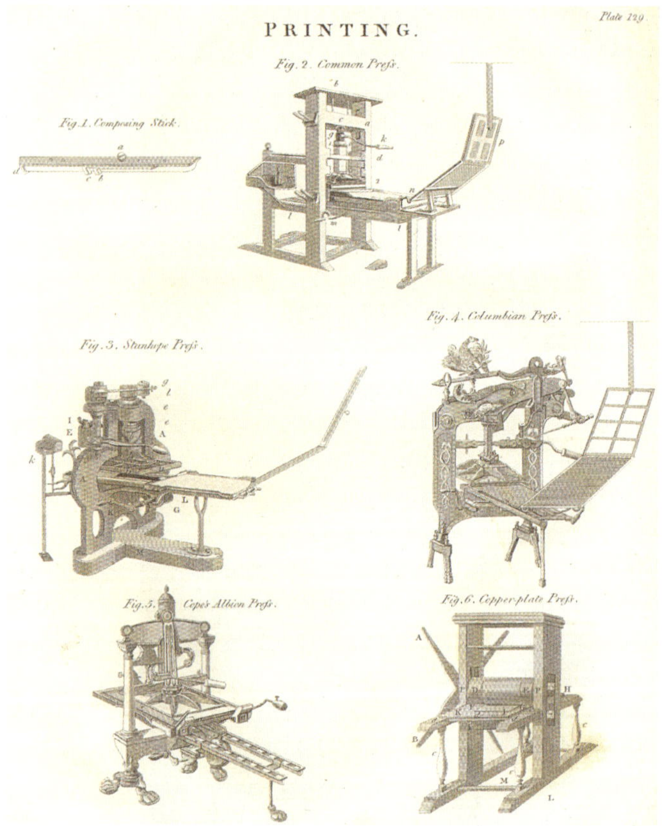

The Printing Press. The printing press underwent important transformations after 1750. This illustration shows how the original wood presses gave way to iron presses, which were more durable, printed larger sheets, and could hold movable type more easily. Eventually, cylinders could roll long sheets through the presses for a continuous flow. Hand stamping and rolling eventually ceded to steam-driven machinery.

Revolutionary Transformations and New Languages of Freedom

In the eighteenth century, the circulation of goods, people, and ideas created pressure for reform around the Atlantic world. As economies expanded, many people in Europe and the Americas felt that the restrictive mercantilist system prevented them from sharing in the new wealth and power. Similarly, an increasingly literate public called for their states to adopt just practices, including the abolition of torture and the accountability of rulers. Although elites resisted the demands for more freedom to trade and more influence in government, power holders could not stamp out these demands before they became—in several places—full-scale revolutions.

Reformers wanted to expand the franchise, to enable property holders to vote. Claims of **popular sovereignty**, the idea that political power depends on "the people," became rooted in the idea of the nation: people who share a common language, common culture, and common history. This, in turn, gave rise to the nation-state as a form of political organization. Over the course of the nineteenth century, political movements began to emphasize nationalism, the idea that peoples with a common identity should have states of their own, and democracy, the idea that the people, the *demos*, should choose their own representatives and be governed by them (see Chapter 16). In this chapter, we concentrate on the first expressions of this new thinking in four empires—British, French, Spanish, and Portuguese—where new ideas of freedom broke old loyalties.

This chapter also concentrates on far-reaching economic developments that came in tandem with revolutionary political change. Economic reformers argued that unregulated economies would produce faster economic growth. Going well beyond the work of Adam Smith, they called for **free trade** (or **laissez-faire**), unencumbered by tariffs, quotas, and fees; free markets, which would be unregulated; and free labor, which meant using paid labor rather than enslaved labor. They insisted that these economic freedoms would yield more just and more efficient societies, ultimately benefiting everyone, everywhere in the world.

Ideas and practices spread on the backs of a transformation in communications after 1750. First, changes in the media disseminated new ideas about political and economic freedom. The idea of a "people" could be shared only if there were shared stories and information. Second, faster, cheaper, and easier access to valuable information helped mobilize resources and intensify pressures to open markets around the world. As a result, newspapers, news agencies, and global reporting helped promote national identities within societies while also creating more interlinked and interdependent markets across societies.

There was a quiet revolution in how information was organized and exchanged, how it became a commodity like cotton or coal was. First, technologies changed. Iron frames replaced wood hand printing presses, then cylinders allowed continuous sheets to be printed, while steam could power bigger cylinders. Second, the circulation of information became a more complex business and eventually involved sprawling multinational news agencies with agents operating around the world. Printers became bigger businesses with elaborate divisions of labor. The most prized jobs, like typesetting, went to men. Women, too, performed printing jobs, but they were assigned the hardest ones. They worked as sheet feeders, which was not just backbreaking and mind-numbing, but also risky: a tired or distracted woman could lose a hand or fingers as the presses clamped down. Eventually, as cylinders and steam replaced flatbed stamp presses, those dangerous jobs got replaced. The creation of guilds and unions of more skilled workers ultimately drove women from the industry.

Ultimately, the cost of printing declined sharply, making newspapers, magazines, pamphlets, and broadsheets more accessible. These would become the mechanisms for spreading seditious ideas, which often spurred authorities to clamp down on their sales, frequently with mixed results. Booklets like *Common Sense* (1776) by the rebel Thomas Paine or *What Is the Third Estate?* (1789) by Abbé Sieyès explained in common language what was at stake and why common people deserved more rights than the powerful gave them. As the Spanish Empire went into convulsions along with the French and British Empires, the printing press became a weapon of war there, too. When the Venezuelan patriot Francisco de Miranda set out to liberate the colony from Spanish rule in 1804, he brought with him a printing press, which the colony did not yet have, to spread his revolutionary message.

Print technology also fostered new practices of mutual recognition to legitimize and legalize new freedoms. When Eastern and Western Cherokee gathered in the mid-1820s to discuss their own statehood, they printed hundreds of copies of their new 1827 constitution to be disseminated far and wide.

Atlantic Telegraph Cable. This painting depicts the laying of the first Atlantic telegraph cable in 1857, off the coast of Ireland. Once inventors figured out how to protect underwater cables, there was a scramble to tether the continents together after the 1851 connection from England to France. Within a few years, companies were dreaming bigger. They were also able to use other new technologies, like the steam-powered vessel especially designed to lay cable that is shown here. The breakthroughs were also labor-intensive, as this image also illustrates.

"We, the people of the Cherokee Nation," it proclaimed for all, "in National Convention assembled, in order to establish justice, insure tranquility, promote the common welfare, and secure to ourselves and our posterity the blessings of freedom . . . do ordain and establish this Constitution for the government of the Cherokee Nation." This was a declaration of independence, one that summoned the world, using print technology, to recognize indigenous sovereignty.

Many women also seized the opportunities afforded by cheap printing to claim their rights. The idea of giving them the vote might have been unthinkable, but it was hard to deny them a voice. One of the most prominent was Mary Wollstonecraft, whose *Vindication of the Rights of Woman* (1792) echoed men's demands for rights but criticized revolutionary men for their convenient hypocrisy—for claiming that women were unequal while denying them educational opportunities to be equal. It was published on both sides of the Atlantic and immediately translated into French. (See Global Themes and Sources: Primary Source 15.1.)

There was also an explosion of global news that enabled events in one part of the world to reach others more easily and more cheaply. Since long-distance transportation was still costly and relied on sailing vessels, traders tended to focus on the most valuable kinds of information: commercial and financial. In the 1820s, the news from London could still take two to three months to reach Buenos Aires or Cape Town, and over four months to reach India and then New South Wales. But the demand for commodities and markets made information ever more valuable. The maritime journal *Lloyd's List* went from publishing twice a week to six days a week in 1837, and new economic newspapers and magazines began to flourish, stoking demand for relevant news. Soon, the British Admiralty took over the running of ocean mail packet boats and made them more efficient. Then American packet boats muscled into the Royal Mail business, cutting round trips between New York and Liverpool to five weeks. When innovators figured out how to transmit messages by cable, the cost of information plunged. Long-distance and underwater cables expanded the reach and velocity of information gathering. New coatings made of colonial Malaysian latex and Bengali hemp allowed cables to be laid under water. A cable linking Dover to Calais was laid in 1851; after that, lines stretched all over the planet to link commercial and political entrepôts. The number of days it took to dispatch news from London went from one month to two days for New York, from 145 days to 3 days for Bombay, and from 97 days to 3 days for Buenos Aires.

The Boston Massacre. Paul Revere's idealized view of the Boston Massacre of March 5, 1770. In the years after the Seven Years' War, Bostonians grew increasingly disenchanted with British efforts to enforce imperial regulations. When British troops fired on and killed several members of an angry mob in what came to be called the "Boston Massacre," the resulting frenzy stirred revolutionary sentiments among the populace.

Political Reorderings

Empires became more connected with each other through the cross-border flow of commodities and information. But the expansion of world markets also led to a scramble to control these markets. Global rivalries between empires plunged them all into a crisis, and escalating mercantilist wars mired them deeper and deeper into debt. Debt meant more borrowing and thus inflation, and more taxes and thus resistance. Consequently, a global arms race ignited basic questions about the legitimacy of governments and the rights of people to defend themselves from what they saw as predatory policies. Late in the eighteenth century, revolutionary ideas spread across the Atlantic world. Fueled by social discontent, new ideas of freedom and reason appealed to revolutionaries who wanted to topple old elites. (See Map 15.1.) As more newspapers, pamphlets, and books circulated in European countries and American colonies, readers began to discuss their societies' problems and to believe they had the right to participate in governance.

The slogans of independence, freedom, liberty, and equality seemed to promise an end to oppression, hardship, and inequities. In the North American colonies and in France, revolutions ultimately brought down monarchies and blossomed in republics. The examples of the United States and France soon encouraged others in the Caribbean and Central and South America to reject the rule of monarchs. In all of these revolutionary environments, new institutions—such as written constitutions and permanent parliaments—claimed to represent the people.

The North American War of Independence, 1776–1783

The American Revolution ended British rule in parts of North America, with the major exception being Canada, where Britain continued to claim most of the northern half of the continent. It was the first in a series of revolutions to shake the Atlantic world, inspired by new ideas of freedom.

By the mid-eighteenth century, Britain's colonies in North America swelled with people and prosperity. Bustling port cities like Charleston, Philadelphia, New York, and Boston saw inflows of enslaved Africans, migrant Europeans, and manufactured goods, while agricultural staples flowed out. A "genteel" class of merchants and landowning planters dominated colonial affairs.

But with settlers arriving from Europe and enslaved peoples from Africa, land was a constant source of dispute. Large landowners struggled with yeomen (independent farmers). Sons and daughters of farmers, often unable to inherit or acquire land near their parents, moved westward, where they came into conflict with Indigenous peoples. To defend their lands, many Indigenous peoples allied with Britain's rival, France. After losing the Seven Years' War (see Chapter 13), however, France ceded its Canadian colony to Britain to secure the return of its much more lucrative Caribbean colonies, especially Saint-Domingue. This forced many Indigenous people to turn to Britain for help fending off land-hungry colonists. British officials did make some concessions to Indigenous interests, but they did not have the troops or financial strength to protect them. In many cases, Indigenous peoples tried to steer clear of the conflict, for fear of reprisals. Among the Cherokee and Iroquois, for instance, a deep split emerged on whether to remain loyal to the crown or support the rebels. Across the settlement fringe, the revolutionary war was often a violent struggle between irregular militias and Indigenous peoples defending their own sovereignty and villages, which only emboldened disgruntled settlers to complain that London neglected their interests.

ASSERTING INDEPENDENCE FROM BRITAIN Even as tensions simmered and sometimes boiled over into bloodshed on the western frontier of British North America, the situation of the British in North America still looked very strong in the mid-1760s. Political revolution seemed unimaginable. And yet, a decade later, that is what occurred.

The spark came not from the contested peripheries but from the core in London. The government of King George III insisted that colonists help pay for Britain's war with France and for the benefits of being subjects of the British Empire. It seemed only reasonable to King George and his ministers, faced with staggering war debts, that colonists contribute to the crown that protected them. Accordingly, the king's officials imposed taxes on a variety of commodities and tried to end the lucrative smuggling by which colonists had been evading the restrictions that mercantilism was supposed to impose on colonial trade. To the king's surprise and dismay, colonists objected to the new measures and protested having to pay taxes when they lacked political representation in the British Parliament.

In 1775, resistance in the form of petitions and boycotts turned into open warfare between a colonial militia and British troops in Massachusetts. Once blood was spilled, more radical voices came to the fore. Previously, leaders of the resistance to taxation without representation had claimed to revere the British Empire while fearing its corruptions. Now calls for severing the ties to Britain became more prominent. Thomas Paine, a recent immigrant from England, captured the new mood in a pamphlet he published in 1776, arguing that it was "common sense" for people to govern themselves. Later that year, the Continental Congress (in which representatives from thirteen colonies gathered) adapted part of Payne's popular pamphlet for the Declaration of Independence.

With the Declaration of Independence, the rebels announced their right to rid themselves of the English king and rule at home. The rebels immediately produced an internal rift. Many settlers remained loyal to the crown and were forced to flee to the Caribbean, or to Nova Scotia or regions north of the Great Lakes, the later provinces of Canada. But many could not escape. Many enslaved and formerly enslaved people also declared their loyalty to the king. Some British commanders wanted to arm them to subdue the rebels, especially in the plantation belts of Georgia and the Carolinas. This led to horrific violence against any Black soldier caught in a British uniform and to atrocities against free and enslaved populations of color even suspected of collusion with the enemy.

The internal fighting over loyalty to the cause posed a basic question: Who would rule at home, and how? Lofty rhetoric did not explain how these colonists (now calling themselves Americans) should organize a nonmonarchical government—or how thirteen weakly connected colonies (now calling themselves states) might survive in a world of monarchies. Nonetheless, the colonies soon became embroiled in a revolution that would turn the world upside down.

During their War of Independence, Americans designed new political arrangements. First, individual states elected delegates to state constitutional conventions, where they drafted written constitutions to govern the workings of their states. Second, by eliminating royal authority, the state constitutions gave extensive powers to legislative bodies, whose members "the people" would elect. But who constituted the people? That is, who had voting rights? Not women, whether enslaved or free. Not enslaved men. Not Indigenous peoples. Not even adult White men who owned no property.

The Global View

MAP 15.1 | Revolutions and Empires in the Atlantic World, 1776–1829

Influenced by Enlightenment thinkers and the French Revolution, colonies gained independence from European powers (and in the case of Greece, from the Ottoman Empire) in the late eighteenth and early nineteenth centuries.

- Which European powers granted independence to their colonial possessions in the Americas during this period?
- What were the first two colonial territories to become independent in the Americas?
- Based on the chronology presented in this map and on your reading, consider the relative importance of European influence and local developments in the Americas in accounting for the timing of independence in different countries. Why, in particular, did colonies in Spanish and Portuguese America obtain political independence decades after the United States won its independence?

Abigail Adams. Abigail Adams was the wife of John Adams, a leader in the movement for American independence and later the second president of the United States. Abigail's letters to her husband testified to the ways in which revolutionary enthusiasm for liberty and equality began to reach into women's minds. In the spring of 1776, Abigail wrote to implore that the men in the Continental Congress "remember the ladies, and be more generous and favorable to them than your ancestors. . . . If particular care and attention is not paid to the Ladies we are determined to foment a Rebellion, and will not hold ourselves bound by any Laws in which we have no voice, or Representation."

Despite the limited extent of voting rights, the notion that all men are created equal overturned former social hierarchies. Thus, common men no longer automatically deferred to gentlemen of higher rank. Many women claimed that their contributions to the revolution's cause (by managing farms and shops in their husbands' absence) earned them greater equality in marriage, including property rights. In letters to her husband, John Adams, who was a representative in the Continental Congress and a champion of American independence, Abigail Adams stopped referring to the family farm as "yours" and instead called it "ours." Most revolutionary of all, many enslaved people sided against the revolution, for it was the British who offered them freedom—most directly in exchange for military service. Backed by France and Spain, the Continental Army under the command of General George Washington finally broke the British back. With the Treaty of Paris (1783), the United States gained its independence.

BUILDING A REPUBLICAN GOVERNMENT Political change of this magnitude unleashed revolutionary social claims against elites. Elites struggled to contain them.

Amid the political revolution against monarchy, the prospect of a social revolution of the enslaved, women, and artisans generated a reaction against what American elites called the "excesses of democracy." Their fears increased after farmers in Massachusetts, led by Daniel Shays, interrupted court proceedings in which the state tried to foreclose on their properties for nonpayment of taxes. The farmers who joined in Shays's Rebellion in 1786 also denounced illegitimate taxation—this time, by their state's government. Acting in the interests of the fledgling government, Massachusetts militiamen defeated the rebel army. But to save the young nation from falling into "anarchy," propertied men convened the Constitutional Convention in Philadelphia a year later.

This gathering aimed to forge a document that would create a more powerful national government and a more unified nation. After fierce debate, the convention drafted a charter for a republican government in which power would rest with representatives of the people—not a king. It was controversial at home. Critics, known as Anti-Federalists, feared the growth of a potentially tyrannical national government and insisted on including a Bill of Rights to protect individual liberties from abusive government intrusions. Ultimately, the Constitution won ratification, and it was soon amended by the Bill of Rights.

This settlement did not put an end to arguments about the scope and power of the national government. One question that deeply troubled the new nation involved slavery: Could a country that declared all men to be equal tolerate a substantial enslaved population? Southern enslavers, for whom slavery was an economic mainstay, answered that question unequivocally, and individuals who would have preferred a different policy had to give way. In an uneasy truce, political leaders agreed not to let the debate over whether to abolish slavery escalate into a cause for disunion. As the frontier pushed westward, however, the question of which new states would or would not allow slavery sparked debates yet again. Initially, the existence of ample land postponed a confrontation. In 1800, Thomas Jefferson's election as the third president of the United States marked the triumph of a model of sending pioneers out to new lands in order to reduce conflict on old lands. In the same year, however, an enslaved Virginian named Gabriel Prosser raised an army of fellow freedom fighters to seize the state capital at Richmond and won support from White artisans and laborers for a more inclusive republic. But his dream of an egalitarian revolution fell victim to White terror and Black betrayal: twenty-seven

The "Tennis Court Oath." Locked out of the chambers of the Estates-General, the deputies of the Third Estate reconvened at a nearby indoor tennis court in June 1789; there they swore an oath not to disband until the king recognized the sovereignty of a national assembly.

resisters, including Prosser, went to the gallows. With them, for the moment, died the dream of a multiracial republic in which all men were truly created equal.

In a larger Atlantic world context, the American Revolution ushered in a new age based on ideas of freedom while at the same time sharpening the line that separated those with freedom and citizenship from those who enjoyed neither. As more and more colonies broke free from Europe, no longer could racial exclusion be blamed on greedy empires or distant monarchs. Instead, the new states relied on home-grown restrictions—and often suppressed freedom struggles at home.

The French Revolution, 1789–1799

Just as global war indebted the British Empire and forced it to hike taxes, the French Empire also shouldered crushing debts. But in France, it was the taxes imposed at home, not in the colonies, that ignited a wave of revolt. Partly inspired by reports from the American Revolution, French men and women soon began to call for liberty, too, and the result profoundly shook Europe's dynasties and social hierarchies. Its impact, though, reached well beyond Europe: the French Revolution, even more than the American, inspired rebels and terrified rulers around the globe. Eventually, the upheaval in France spread to the colonies—and set off the first successful revolution of the enslaved.

ORIGINS AND OUTBREAK For decades, enlightened thinkers had attacked France's old regime—the court, the aristocracy, and the church—at the risk of imprisonment or exile. But by the mid-eighteenth century, discontent had spread beyond the educated few. In the countryside, peasants grumbled about having to pay taxes and tithes to the church, whereas nobles and clergy paid almost no taxes. A combination of these pressures, as well as a fiscal crisis, unleashed the French Revolution of 1789.

The French king himself opened the door to revolution. Eager to weaken his rival, England, Louis XVI spent huge sums in support of the American rebels—and thereby overloaded the state's debt. To raise sufficient funds, he was forced to convene the Estates-General, a medieval advisory body that had not met since 1614. His subjects rejoiced. The delegates of the clergy (the First Estate) and the aristocracy (the Second Estate) hoped to restore some of the privileges they had lost to the absolutist state. The delegates representing everyone else (the Third Estate), in contrast, believed that the time had come for taxation to be shared equally.

Afraid the king would crush the reform movement, delegates of the Third Estate declared themselves to be the "National Assembly," the body that should determine France's future. On July 14, 1789, a hungry and angry Parisian crowd took to the streets, looting bakeries and attacking the headquarters of the tax collectors. They stormed a medieval armory—the Bastille—that not only was an infamous prison for political prisoners but also held a large store of gunpowder. The crowd murdered the commanding officer, then cut off his head and paraded it through the streets of Paris. On this day (Bastille Day), the king made the fateful decision not to call out the army, and the capital city belonged to the crowd. As news spread to the countryside, so did the agitation. Barely three weeks later, the French National Assembly abolished the feudal privileges of the nobility and the clergy. In the Declaration of the Rights of Man and of the Citizen, the assembly

Women March on Versailles. On October 5, 1789, a group of market women, many of them fishwives (traditionally regarded as leaders of the poor), marched on the Paris city hall to demand bread. Quickly, their numbers grew, and they redirected their march to Versailles, some 12 miles away and the symbol of the entire political order. In response to the women, the king finally appeared on the balcony and agreed to sign the revolutionary decree and return with the women to Paris.

echoed the Americans' Declaration of Independence, but in more universal language.

REVOLUTIONARY CHANGES AND CONFLICTS As in the United States, political change posed basic questions about who was a member of the nation. The French Declaration guaranteed all citizens of the French nation a new kind of liberty, defined not as a special privilege given by the king but as a freedom from constraint, including religious constraints. But who got to be a citizen?

Inspired by revolutionary rhetoric, some women argued that the new principles of citizenship should include women's rights as well. In 1791, a group of women demanded the right to bear arms to defend the revolution, but they stopped short of claiming equal rights for both sexes. In their view, women would become citizens by being good revolutionary wives and mothers, not because of any natural rights. In the same year, Olympe de Gouges composed the Declaration of the Rights of Woman and the Female Citizen, proposing rights to divorce, hold property in marriage, be educated, and have public careers. The all-male assembly countered: a "fraternity" of free *men* composed the nation. But it was a sign that revolutionary ranks were splintering, as men and women argued over the revolution's proper goals. Soon a new National Convention was elected by universal manhood suffrage, meaning that all adult males could vote—the first such election in Europe.

The radicals believed that to sweep away traditional forms of inequality and oppression, they would need to destroy the old regime's entire system of thinking and ways of speaking. So they changed street names to honor revolutionary heroes, destroyed monuments to the royal family, adopted a new flag, and insisted that everyone be addressed as "citizen." They were so exhilarated by the new world they were creating that they created a new calendar: the new ten months were given the names of natural phenomena.

As the revolution gained momentum, deep divisions emerged. In 1790, all clergy had to take an oath of loyalty to the new state. The French next declared war against Austria, and then Prussia, Britain, and Russia. Soon they had foreign armies on their soil and a civil war to contend with, when outraged peasants and dwellers in major provincial cities rose up against the revolutionary government and its wartime demands. Louis XVI was accused of conspiracy and lost his head to the guillotine in January 1793.

THE TERROR One resolution to discord was the formation of a modern dictatorship, authoritarian rule in the name of the "people." After the king's execution, radicals known as Jacobins, who wanted to extend the revolution beyond France's borders, instituted the first national draft to form, by 1794, the world's largest modern army of 800,000 soldiers. Led by the lawyer Maximilien Robespierre, the Jacobins also launched the Reign of Terror to purge the nation of its internal enemies. Jacobin leaders oversaw the execution of as many as 40,000 of these so-called enemies of the people.

By mid-1794, enthusiasm for Robespierre's measures had lost popular support, and Robespierre himself went to the guillotine on 9 Thermidor (July 28, 1794). His execution marked the end of the Terror. Several years later, following more political turmoil, a coup d'état brought to power a thirty-year-old general from the recently annexed Mediterranean island of Corsica.

The general, **Napoleon Bonaparte** (1769–1821), put security and order ahead of social reform. True, his regime retained many of the revolutionary changes, especially those associated with more efficient state government; but retreating from the Jacobins' anti-Catholicism, he allowed religion to be freely

Battle of the Pyramids. The French army invaded Egypt with grand ambitions and high hopes. Napoleon brought a large cadre of scholars along with his 36,000-man army, intending to win Egyptians to the cause of the French Revolution and to establish a French imperial presence on the banks of the Nile. This idealized portrait of the famous Battle of the Pyramids, fought on July 21, 1798, shows Napoleon and his forces crushing the Mamluk military forces.

practiced again in France. He turned away from republican principles and also rolled back the revolution's democratic push. Napoleon first was a member of a three-man consulate; then he became first consul; finally, he proclaimed himself emperor. Most important, he created a civil legal code—the Napoleonic Code—that applied throughout all of France (and the French colonies, including the Louisiana Territory). By designing a law code applicable to the nation as a whole, Napoleon created a model that would be widely imitated by emerging nation-states in Europe and the Americas in the century to come.

The Napoleonic Era, 1799–1815

Determined to extend the reach of French influence, Napoleon had his armies trumpet the principles of liberty, equality, and fraternity wherever they went. Many local populations embraced the French, regarding them as liberators. Inspired by his leadership, many non-Frenchmen, including many Poles, volunteered to fight in the army. Napoleon was not surprised to face resistance from aristocrats commanding foreign armies, but he so strongly believed that he was the great liberator that he was shocked when ordinary people rebelled against the French, as was the case in Egypt. After Napoleon defeated Mamluk troops there in 1798, the Egyptian population made it crystal clear that he was unwelcome.

In Portugal, Spain, and Russia, French troops also faced fierce popular resistance. Portuguese and Spanish soldiers and peasants formed bands of resisters called guerrillas, and British troops joined them to fight the French in the Peninsular War (1808–1813). In Germany and Italy, as local inhabitants grew tired of hearing that the French occupiers' ways were superior, many looked to their past for inspiration to oppose the French. Now they discovered something they had barely recognized before: *national* traditions and borders.

In Europe, Napoleon extended his empire from the Iberian Peninsula to the Austrian and Prussian borders. (See Map 15.2.) In 1812, he invaded Russia and marched his now-multinational army all the way to Moscow. His forces, however, were overstretched, undersupplied, and outmaneuvered by wily Russian troops. Soon, the French were forced to retreat through battle-scarred territory, suffering grievously from Russian harassment and the harsh winter. As Napoleon fled westward, all the major European powers united against him and decimated what was left of his army. Forced to capitulate in 1814, Napoleon was sent into exile, but he managed to escape soon after to lead his troops one last time. At the Battle of Waterloo in Belgium in 1815, armies from Prussia, Austria, Russia, and Britain crushed his troops as they made their last stand.

In 1815, delegates from the victorious states met at the Congress of Vienna. They agreed to respect one another's borders and to cooperate in preventing future revolutions and war. They restored thrones to monarchs deposed by the French under Napoleon, and they returned France itself to the care of a new Bourbon king.

The impact of the French Revolution and Napoleon's conquests, however, was far-reaching. The stage was now

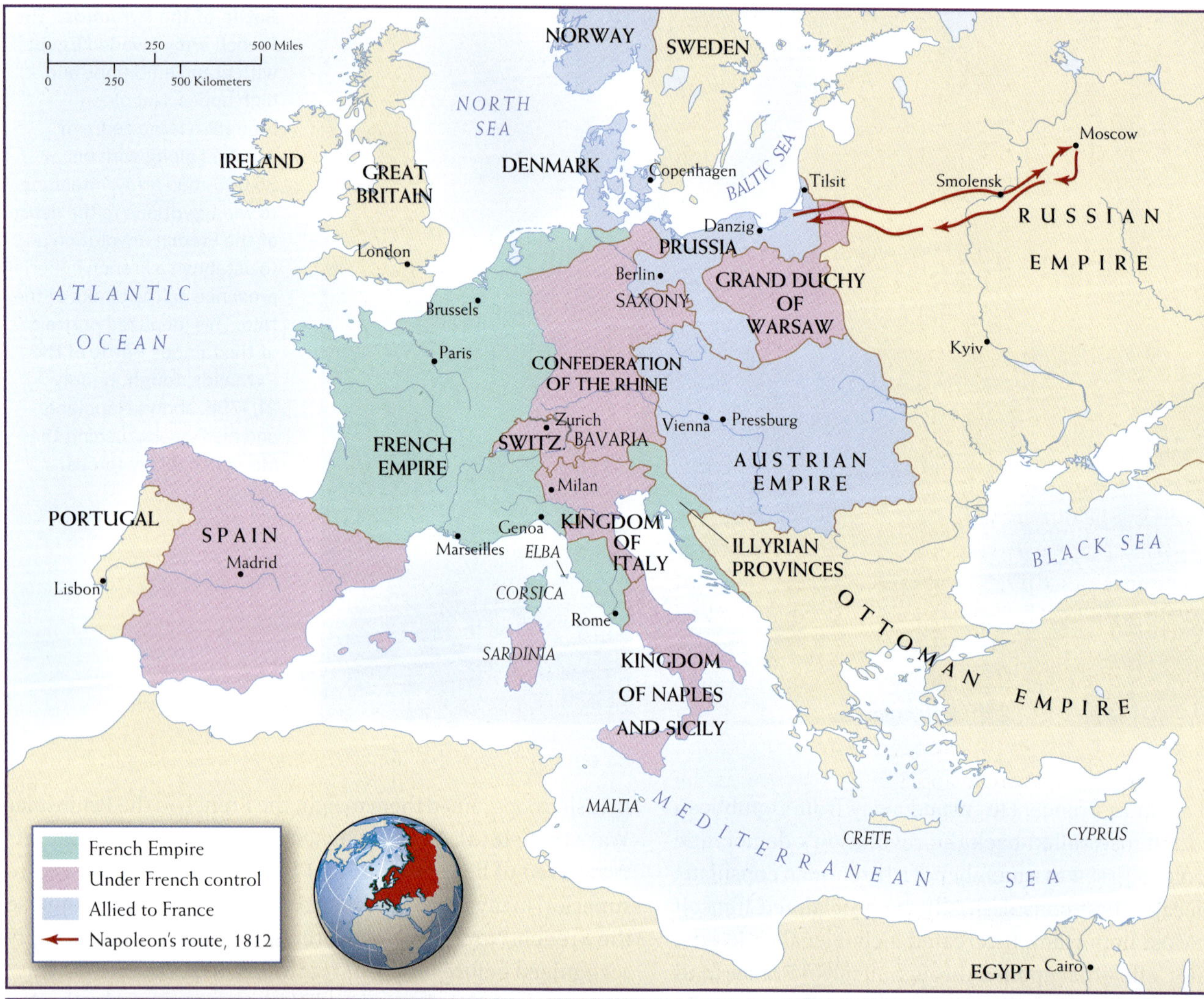

MAP 15.2 | Napoleon's Empire, 1812

Early in the first decade of the nineteenth century, Napoleon controlled almost all of Europe.

- What major states were under French control? What countries were allied with France?
- Compare this map with the European part of Map 15.1, and explain how Napoleon redrew the map of Europe. What major country was not under French control?
- According to your reading, how was Napoleon able to control and build alliances with so many states and kingdoms?

set for a century-long struggle between those who wanted to restore monarchies and hierarchies as they existed before the French Revolution and those who wanted to guarantee a more liberal order based on individual rights, limited government, and free trade.

Revolution in Saint-Domingue (Haiti)

The thirteen colonies in North America were not the only ones to secede from European masters. France also saw colonies break away in this age of new freedoms. This was the case in Saint-Domingue, presently Haiti. As in parts of British North America, the enslaved called for freedom, but unlike in British North America, they were able to mobilize into mass armies. In this Caribbean colony, freedom meant not just liberation from Europe but also emancipation from White planters. Saint-Domingue thus added a second, global dimension to the nineteenth-century struggle over freedom. Enslaved rebels dramatically posed an important question: How universal and equal were these new rights?

The French Revolution sent shock waves through this highly prized French colony. At the time, the island's enslaved Black population numbered 500,000, compared with 40,000 White French settlers and about 30,000 free "people of color" (individuals of mixed Black and White ancestry as well as freed Black people). Almost two-thirds of the enslaved were relatively recent arrivals from Africa, with fresh memories of freedom, and, for many of them, military experience. They had been brought to the colony to toil on its renowned sugar plantations, which were exceptional in their brutality. The enslaved population was an angry majority without local ties, producing wealth for rich absentee landlords of a different race.

The enslaved seized French revolutionary slogans and made them their own. Liberty, equality, and fraternity meant freedom from enslavers. But the real revolutionary energy came from the determination to defend local religious beliefs, especially the mixture of Catholic and African rituals, called *vodou*, against the anti-religious decrees from France. As civil war erupted, the enslaved seized the opportunity to take up arms against their oppressors. A massive slave revolt started in the plantation belt of the northern plains in August 1791. Panicked plantation owners called on French armies to restore order. Insurgents invaded plantations and set entire cities and hillsides ablaze. The first enslaved generals allied with France's rival, Spain, which controlled the other half of Hispaniola. Those generals promised freedom to their followers but not general emancipation. That possibility emerged later, as the war that revolutionary France waged against its European neighbors spread to the Caribbean. The British, French, and Spanish, as well as the generals of color in Saint-Domingue, promised freedom to enslaved soldiers who joined them. Even after the French revolutionary assembly, the National Convention, abolished slavery in 1793, prominent enslaved generals, like Toussaint L'Ouverture, hesitated to break their alliance with Spain, unconvinced that the new French republic would survive. Toussaint rallied to France in 1794.

Revolution in Saint-Domingue. In 1791, enslaved Black freedom fighters and free people of color rose up against White planters. This engraving was based on a German report on the uprising and depicts White enslavers' fears of rebellion as much as the actual events themselves.

Once liberated, the formerly enslaved slowly took control of the island. Planters, abandoned by the commissioners and hounded by their freed captives, fled. Insurgents began to create home-rule institutions of their own while remaining loyal to France. But their struggles were not over. Toussaint himself imposed strict labor discipline on plantations to salvage local finances, and formerly enslaved people still had to fight off British and Spanish forces. Then, after Napoleon took power in France, bringing with him a strong commitment to order and France's imperial ambitions, they had to slay their own emperor's armies. He sent a massive army to reimpose control and roll back emancipation. Thus began the most cruel and violent phase of the revolution. Again, rebel armies burned cities and farms. Yellow fever ravaged French troops. Their commanders resorted to White terror. Toussaint L'Ouverture, formerly enslaved, became the leader of the revolution—fighting not just for the abolition of slavery but for freedom from France until he was tricked by false promises of peace and was captured along with a hundred of his supporters. "You have cut down . . . only the trunk of the tree of liberty," he warned his captors. "It will spring up again from the roots, for they are numerous and they are deep." L'Ouverture died in a French prison of malnutrition and pneumonia. In 1804, General Jean-Jacques Dessalines declared the island, newly named Haiti, independent. (See Current Trends in World History: Two Case Studies in Political Change and Environmental Degradation.)

The specter of a free country ruled by formerly enslaved peoples sent shudders across the Atlantic world. What if the revolt went viral? All around the Caribbean, news of conspiracies circulated. In Florida, freedom seekers allied with the Seminole Tribes to drive European settlers into the sea. The Haitian government contributed money and some troops to insurrectionists in South America. Charleston, South Carolina, went into a panic in 1793 when enslaved Dominicans were freed. As far away as Albany, New York, authorities executed enslaved people charged with arson, fearing they were emulating the burning tactics of Saint-Domingue insurgents. Jamaican rulers went on high alert. A version of martial law was declared in Venezuela. Thomas Jefferson, author of the Declaration of Independence and the U.S. president at the time, also enslaved numerous people, and he refused to recognize Haiti. Like other American enslavers, he worried that the example of a successful uprising might inspire similar revolts in the United States and elsewhere in the Americas.

Current Trends in World History

Two Case Studies in Political Change and Environmental Degradation

Overthrowing slavery and colonial domination did not necessarily halt environmental degradation. In fact, in two important New World countries, the new nations of Haiti and Brazil, the transition to independence aggravated environmental problems created by former colonial regimes.

Two hundred and fifty years ago, Haiti, which was under French colonial rule at that time and known as Saint-Domingue, was the richest colony in the Americas, perhaps even the richest colony in the world, accounting for two-thirds of France's worldwide investment. Saint-Domingue's extraordinary wealth came from large, White-owned sugar plantations that used a massive and highly coerced enslaved population. Their lives were short and brutal, lasting on average only fifteen years; hence the wealthy planter class had to replenish their labor supplies from Africa at frequent intervals.

White planters on the island were eager to amass quick fortunes so that they could sell out and return to France. Vastly outnumbered by enslaved Africans at a time when abolitionist sentiments were gaining ground in Europe and even circulating among the enslaved in the Americas, the planters' families knew that their prosperity was unlikely to last. They gave little thought to sustainable growth and were not troubled that they were destroying their environment.

The planters greeted the onset of the French Revolution in 1789 with enthusiasm. They saw an opportunity to assert their independence from France, to engage in wider trading contacts with North America and the rest of the world, and thus to become even richer. They ignored the possibility that the ideals of the French Revolution—especially its slogan of liberty, equality, and fraternity—could inspire the island's free and enslaved Black people. Indeed, no sooner had the White planters thrown in their lot with the Third Estate in France than a rebellion broke out in Saint-Domingue. From its beginnings in 1791, it led, after great loss of life to enslaved Africans and French soldiers, to the proclamation of an independent state in Haiti in 1804, ruled by African Americans. Haiti became the Americas' second independent republican government. Although the revolt brought political independence to Haiti's Black population, it only intensified the land's environmental deterioration. Not only did sugarcane fields become scorched battlefields, but the newly freed rushed to stake out independent plots on the old plantations and in wooded areas. In both places, the new peasant class energetically cleared the land. The small country became even more deforested, and intensive cultivation increased erosion and soil depletion. Haiti fell into a more vicious cycle of environmental degradation and poverty.

The second case study of political change leading to the destruction of the environment comes from the independent Brazilian state, where the ruling elite, having achieved autonomy from Portugal, expanded the agrarian frontier. Landowners oversaw the clearing of ancient hardwood forests so that enslaved workers and free squatters could plant coffee trees. The clearing process had begun with sugarcane in the coastal regions, but it accelerated with coffee plantings in the hilly regions of São Paulo.

In fact, coffee was a worse threat to Brazil's forests than any other invader in the previous 300 years. Coffee trees thrive on soils that are neither soggy nor overly dry. Therefore, planters razed the forest, which contained a balanced variety of trees and undergrowth, and Brazil's once-fertile soil suffered rapid depletion by a single-crop industry. Whereas the forests had once been the home for more diverse plants and a high indigenous population, Indigenous peoples had fled or been taken captive and—within

The revolution in Saint-Domingue therefore tilted the scales of campaigns for liberty far beyond the island. Fear of the contagion of revolt forced some governments to rethink the commitment to slavery altogether. The British government curtailed the expansion of plantation agriculture in Trinidad. One by one, European and American governments began to question the wisdom of importing more enslaved Africans lest they lose control of their colonies. It was not just exalted ideals of liberty that fueled the abolitionist movement, but also the fear of what would happen if the enslaved rose up violently to claim rights afforded to their fellow human beings.

Revolutions in Spanish and Portuguese America

Revolutionary enthusiasm also spread through Spanish and Portuguese America. The Spanish and Portuguese empires were not immune from the heavy burdens of war and the hunger for revenues that put pressure on local populations. But unlike the colonists' war of independence that produced the United States, political upheaval in the rest of the Americas mobilized people of color and turned political revolts into a social revolution. (See Map 15.3.)

Enslaved People Cutting Cane. Sugar was the preeminent agricultural export from the New World for centuries. Owners of sugarcane plantations relied almost exclusively on enslaved Africans to produce the sweetener. Labor in the fields was especially harsh, as they worked in the blistering sun from dawn until dusk.

Toussaint L'Ouverture. In the 1790s, Toussaint L'Ouverture led his fellows in the French colony of Saint-Domingue in the world's largest and most successful insurrection of the enslaved. Toussaint embraced the principles of the French Revolution and demanded that universal rights be applied to people of African descent.

one generation—the clear-cutting led to monocrop economies. This drained the soils of nutrients and led to extensive erosion. Deteriorating land drove planters farther into the frontier to destroy even more forests and plant more coffee groves. The environmental impact was monumental: between 1788 and 1888, when slavery was abolished, Brazil produced about 10 million tons of coffee and lost 300 million tons of ancient forest biomass (the accumulated biological material from living organisms).

QUESTIONS FOR ANALYSIS

- Who intensified the deforestation and degradation in each case, and why did they do it?
- Why do you think deforestation increased in intensity after Haitians and Brazilians gained their autonomy/independence?

EXPLORE FURTHER

Diamond, Jared, and James A. Robinson (eds.), *Natural Experiments of History* (2010).

Geggus, David (ed.), *The Impact of the Haitian Revolution in the Atlantic World* (2001).

In part, rebellion was homespun. Before the French Revolution, Indigenous Andean peoples rebelled against Spanish colonial authority. From the 1740s, there had been periodic tax revolts and bread riots. The seething finally exploded in a spectacular uprising in the 1780s. Quechua-speaking peoples around the ancient Inca capital of Cuzco rose up, demanding freedom from forced labor and compulsory consumption of Spanish wares. Led by a local Quechua chief (kuraka) who called himself Túpac Amaru II, claiming to be the heir to the last Inca rebel of the sixteenth century, an Andean army took control over the region. A force of 40,000 to 60,000 Indigenous soldiers besieged Cuzco and nearly vanquished the Spanish armies. Túpac Amaru aimed to restore a version of Inca rule—though without declaring full independence from Spain. It took Spanish forces many years to take back control and eliminate the insurgents. When they finally captured Túpac Amaru, they forced him to watch as executioners tore out the tongues of his wife and son for having spoken out against Spanish rulers. They hung his son and beat his wife to death. Then, the executioners ordered that the rebel leader's limbs be tied to horses and ripped from his body. Túpac Amaru's head was placed on a spike at the entrance to Cuzco. Spanish authorities were determined to terrorize any future dissenters.

MAP 15.3 | Latin American Nation Building

Creating strong, unified nation-states proved difficult in Latin America. The map shows where boundaries were drawn in Mexico, the United Provinces of Central America, and the Republic of Colombia. In each case, the governments' territorial and nation-building ambitions failed to some degree.

- During what period did a majority of the colonies in Latin America gain independence?
- Which European countries lost the most in Latin America during this period?
- Why did all these colonies gain their independence during this time?

After this uprising, Iberian American elites who feared their Indigenous or enslaved majorities renewed their loyalty to the Spanish or Portuguese crown. They hesitated to imitate the independence-seeking Anglo-American colonists, lest they unleash a social revolution. Ultimately, however, the French Revolution and Napoleonic wars shattered the ties between Spain and Portugal and their American colonies.

BRAZIL AND CONSTITUTIONAL MONARCHY Brazil was a prized Portuguese colony whose path to independence saw little political turmoil and no social revolution. In 1807, French troops stormed Lisbon, the capital of Portugal, but not before the royals and their associates fled to Rio de Janeiro, then the capital of Brazil. There they made reforms in administration, agriculture, and manufacturing, and they established schools, hospitals, and a library. In fact, the royals' migration prevented the need for colonial claims for autonomy, because with their presence Brazil was now the center of the Portuguese Empire. Furthermore, the royal family willingly shared power with the local planter aristocracy, so the economy prospered and slavery expanded.

In 1821, the exiled Portuguese king returned to Lisbon, instructing his son Pedro to preserve the family lineage in Rio de Janeiro. Soon, however, Brazilian elites rejected Portugal altogether. Fearing that colonists might topple the dynasty in Rio de Janeiro and spark regional disputes, Pedro declared Brazil an independent empire in 1822. Shortly thereafter, he established a constitutional monarchy, which would last until the late nineteenth century. By the 1840s, Brazil had achieved a political stability unmatched in the Americas. Its socially controlled transition from colony to nation was unique in Latin America.

MEXICO'S INDEPENDENCE When Napoleon occupied Spain, he sparked a crisis in the Spanish Empire, spurring independence movements throughout the colonies. Because the ruling Spanish Bourbons fell captive to Napoleon in

Latin American Revolutionaries. Left: At the center of this Juan O'Gorman mural is the Mexican priest and revolutionary Miguel Hidalgo y Costilla, who led—as O'Gorman portrays—a multiclass and multiethnic movement. Right: Simón Bolívar fought Spanish armies from Venezuela to Bolivia, securing the independence of five countries with the greater goal of transforming the former colonies into modern republics. Among his favorite models were George Washington and Napoleon Bonaparte, whose iconic portrait by Jacques-Louis David inspired this painting of Bolívar.

1807, colonial elites in Buenos Aires (Argentina), Caracas (Venezuela), and Mexico City (Mexico) enjoyed self-rule without an emperor. Once the Bourbons returned to power in 1814 after Napoleon was crushed, **Creoles** (Spaniards born in the Americas) resented Spain's reinstatement of Peninsulares (colonial officials born in Spain). Creoles wanted to free themselves of these officials.

From 1810 to 1813, two rural priests in Mexico, Father Miguel Hidalgo y Costilla and Father José María Morelos, galvanized an insurrection of peasants, Indigenous peoples, and artisans. They sought an end to abuses by the elite, denounced bad government, and called for redistribution of wealth, return of land to the Indigenous peoples, and respect for the Virgin of Guadalupe (who later became Mexico's patron saint). The rebellion nearly choked off Mexico City, the colony's capital, which horrified Peninsulares and Creoles alike and led them to support royal armies that eventually crushed the uprising.

Despite the military victory, Spain's hold on its colony weakened. Like the Creoles of South America, the Creoles of Mexico identified themselves more as Mexicans and less as Spanish Americans. So when the Spanish king appeared unable to govern effectively abroad and even within Spain, the colonists considered home rule. Anarchy seemed to spread through Spain in 1820, and Mexican generals (with support of the Creoles) proclaimed Mexican independence in 1821. Unlike in Brazil, Mexican secession did not lead to stability.

OTHER SOUTH AMERICAN REVOLUTIONS The loosening of Spain's grip on its colonies was more prolonged and militarized than Britain's separation from its American colonies. Venezuela's Simón Bolívar (1783–1830), the son of a merchant-planter family who was educated on Enlightenment texts, dreamed of a land governed by reason. He revered Napoleonic France as a model state built on military heroism and constitutional proclamations. So did the Argentine leader, General José de San Martín (1778–1850). Men like Bolívar, San Martín, and their many generals waged extended wars of independence against Spanish armies and their allies between 1810 and 1824. In some areas, like present-day Uruguay and Venezuela, the wars left entire provinces depopulated.

What started in South America as a political revolt against Spanish colonial authority escalated into a social struggle among the enslaved Indigenous peoples, Mestizos, and Whites. The militarized populace threatened the planters and merchants; rural folk battled against aristocratic Creoles; Indigenous Andean peoples fled the mines and occupied great estates. Provinces fought their neighbors. Popular armies, having defeated Spanish forces by the 1820s, fought civil wars over the new postcolonial order.

New states and collective identities of nationhood now emerged. However, a narrow elite led these political communities, and their guiding principles were contradictory. Simón Bolívar, for instance, urged his followers to become "American," to overcome their local identities. He wanted

Chasing Enslaver Dhows. Transformed from a major proponent of the Atlantic slave trade to its chief opponent, the British used their naval forces to suppress European and African slave traders who attempted to subvert the injunction against slave trading. Here a British vessel chases an East African dhow trying to run enslaved people from the island of Zanzibar.

the liberated countries to form a Latin American confederation, urging Peru and Bolivia to join Venezuela, Ecuador, and Colombia in the "Gran Colombia." But local identities prevailed, giving way to unstable national republics. To mobilize troops, Bolívar promised freedom to enslaved people for joining the cause. This helped build popular patriotic armies, but it also further splintered elites. It was hard to generate symbols of unity when the revolutions contained so much civil strife. Both Bolívar and San Martín died feeling that they had failed. The real heirs to independence were local military chieftains, who often forged alliances with landowners, which perpetuated the power of property-owning patriarchs. In the face of so much uncertainty, for many, the prior obligation was to family and kin rather than state and public interests. Though many women yearned for more room to become educated and to choose their spouses, political instability tended to favor traditional private norms. Thus, the legacy of the Spanish American revolutions was contradictory. All the mainland colonies broke free of Spain, but social hierarchies persisted.

Change and Trade in Africa

Africa also was swept up in revolutionary tides, as increased domestic and world trade—including the selling of enslaved Africans—shifted the terms of state building across the continent. The main catalyst for Africa's political shake-up was the rapid growth and then the demise of the Atlantic slave trade. Here, in contrast to the Americas and Europe and even much of the rest of the world, ideals like liberty, equality, fraternity, and the pursuit of happiness had decidedly contrary effects. The abolition of the slave trade, which European reformers believed would lead to economic prosperity based on "legitimate trade," had the perverse effect of intensifying domestic slavery. As Africa became an exporter of raw materials rather than human beings, the hard work done on African farms and plantations—producing palm, palm kernels, peanuts, and gum for export—was done by the enslaved.

Abolition of the Slave Trade

Even as it enriched and empowered some Africans and many Europeans, the slave trade became a subject of fierce debate in the late eighteenth century. Some European and American revolutionaries argued that enslaved labor was inherently less productive than free wage labor and ought to be abolished. At the same time, another group favoring abolition of the slave trade insisted that traffic in humans was immoral. In London abolitionists created committees, often led by Quakers, to lobby Parliament for an end to the slave trade. Quakers in Philadelphia did likewise. Pamphlets, reports, and personal narratives denounced the traffic in people. (See Global Themes and Sources: Primary Source 15.4.)

In response to abolitionist efforts, North Atlantic powers moved to prohibit the slave trade. Denmark acted first in 1803, Great Britain followed in 1807, and the United States joined the campaign in 1808. Over time, the British persuaded the French and other European governments to do likewise. To enforce the ban, Britain posted a naval squadron off the coast of West Africa to prevent any slave trade above the equator and finally compelled Brazil and Cuba, the last countries to allow slavery after the end of the American Civil War, to end imports of humans. After 1850, Atlantic slave shipping dropped sharply.

But up until the 1860s, even though the British had outlawed the slave trade and the Americans had agreed to cease importing humans, enslavers continued to buy and ship captives, often illegally. British squadrons that stopped these smugglers took the freed captives to the British base at Sierra Leone and resettled them there. Liberia, too, became a territory for freed captives and for formerly enslaved people returning from the Americas.

New Trade with Africa

Even as the Atlantic slave trade died down, Europeans promoted commerce with Africa. Now they wanted Africans to export raw materials and to purchase European manufactures. What Europeans liked to call "legitimate" trade aimed to raise the Africans' standard of living by substituting trade in produce for trade in humans. West Africans responded by exporting palm kernels and peanuts. The real bonanza was in vegetable oils to lubricate machinery and make candles and in palm oil to produce soap. Africa's palm and peanut plantations were less devastating to the environment than their predecessors in the West Indies had been. There, planters had felled forests to establish sugar estates (see Chapter 12). In West Africa, where palm products became crucial exports, the palm tree had always grown wild. Although intensive cultivation caused some deforestation, the results were not as extreme as in the Caribbean. Regardless of the environmental impact, European merchants argued that by becoming vibrant export societies, Africans would earn the wealth to profitably import European wares.

SUCCESS IN THE AGE OF LEGITIMATE COMMERCE Emerging in the age of legitimate commerce, the new trade gave rise to a generation of successful West African merchants. There were many rags-to-riches stories, like that of King Jaja of Opobo (1821–1891). Kidnapped and sold into slavery as a youngster, he started out paddling canoes carrying palm oil to coastal ports. Ultimately becoming the head of a coastal canoe house, he founded the port of Opobo as a merchant-prince and chief and could summon a flotilla of war canoes on command. A freed Yoruba man, William Lewis, made his way back to Africa and settled in Sierra Leone in 1828. Starting with a few utensils and a small plot of land, he became a successful merchant and sent his son Samuel to England for his education. Samuel eventually became an important political leader in Sierra Leone.

EFFECTS IN AFRICA Just as the slave trade shaped African political communities, its demise brought sharp adjustments. For some, it was a welcome end to the constant drainage of people. For others, it was a disaster because it cut off income necessary to buy European arms and luxury goods. Many West African regimes, like the Yoruba kingdom, collapsed once chieftains could no longer use the slave trade to finance their retinues and armies.

The rise of free labor in the Atlantic world and the dwindling foreign slave trade had an unanticipated effect in Africa. It strengthened slavery there. In some areas, by the mid-nineteenth century, the enslaved accounted for more than half the population. No longer did they serve in domestic employment; instead, they toiled on palm oil plantations or, in East Africa, on clove plantations. They also served in the military forces, bore palm oil and ivory to markets as porters, or paddled cargo-carrying canoes along rivers leading to the coast. In 1850, northern Nigeria's ruling class enslaved more people than independent Brazil and almost as many as the United States. No longer the world's supplier, Africa itself had become the world's largest enslaving region.

Economic Reorderings

Behind the political and social upheavals, profound changes were occurring in the world economy. Until the middle of the eighteenth century, global trade touched only the edges of societies, most of which produced for their own subsistence. At that time, surpluses were confined to specialty goods such as porcelains and silks. They entered trade arteries but did not change the cultures that produced them. By the middle of the nineteenth century, however, global trade began to boom. Basic staples, food, fibers, and fuel became more and more important in the basket of world trade, while precious commodities and metals declined as a share of overall trade. What started with sugar, tea, and coffee spread to other basics like clothing, wheat, and meat. Likewise, what started as elite consumption percolated down to become mass consumption. This shift evinced a dramatic change in the global division of labor, with entire societies gearing more and more of their economic activity to the production of long-distance goods.

Regional and Global Origins of Industrialization

Many factors contributed to this reorganization of world trade: state policies changed, elites promoted free trade in parts of Europe and Latin America, and new technologies like steam allowed commerce to reach deeper inland and slashed the cost of transportation and information. In addition, financiers pooled their money via government bonds and private shares to invest in commercial infrastructure, such as the telegraph. But one of the most important forces in this new trading system was the industrial revolution, which slashed the prices of manufactured goods and required new staple inputs, many of which had to be imported.

One effect of this global reordering was to open a gap between the haves and the have-nots across countries. Societies that industrialized tended to see their incomes grow, sometimes substantially. Even industrialized societies with scarce resources, like land, boomed—though the identity of the landowners would determine how equally the returns were distributed. In contrast, societies that remained basically agrarian with higher population densities (and labor abundance rather than land abundance) tended to fall behind. The new international division of labor produced wealth and inequality at the same time. Global reintegration and a commercial bonanza created a new global economic divide.

MERGING SPHERES OF TRADE Access to new and cheaper commodities yielded a consumer revolution and reconfigured Europe's place in the world. The lure to consume products that had once been available as luxuries only to the wealthy classes fueled regional and global trade. More food, including new food items, and better clothes, made of cotton instead of heavy, scratchy wool, trickled down the social ladder. By the eighteenth century, other staples joined the long-distance trading business. Tea, for instance, became a beverage of world trade. Its leaves came from China, the sugar to cut its bitterness from the Caribbean, and the ceramics from which to drink a proper cup from the English Midlands.

Shopping became a verb. It denoted going out with a specific purpose: to buy. The act of shopping itself became a status symbol for people who had climbed out of the working classes; by shopping, they demonstrated that they had time for public leisure and the means to spend money on luxuries. In addition, shops increasingly marketed products not only to men but also to women and girls of the new leisured classes, who created a customer base for another new sector: fashion.

Paying attention to one's looks was no longer just for aristocrats but now also for the new rich (and even the professional middling sectors), and was for men and women alike. Men gave up long coats and knee breeches, suiting themselves with trousers and waistcoats. In women's fashion, meanwhile, it became increasingly in vogue to reveal the actual curvature of the body, freeing it from layers upon layers of heavy fabric and the steel hoops that were needed to keep the mountain of garb up. Practicality became popular, as did hygiene: people wanted to wear clothes that were lighter and more easily washed. Not to mention underwear, knitted from that liberating fiber: cotton.

By 1850, there was a booming advertising business, which in turn fueled the expansion of the press. The press, for its part, drew more and more revenue not from the sales of papers and magazines but from ads, many pitched at women. As a result, the consumer and communications revolutions became mutually reinforcing.

The Rise of Fashion. Fashion became a business just as business became a fashion. The rise of new commercial and industrial classes living in cities created a market for high-end clothing made of new fabrics, especially cotton. These were assimilated into the taste for older fabrics like silk and—as the top hat of this model German gentleman around 1800 indicates—beaver pelts. This image provides a fine display of how new urban fashion appealed to women and men alike.

This consumer revolution was not just about Europeans importing from the rest of the world. The rest of the world also imported goods from Europe. Alcohol was a major export to Indigenous peoples in North America as payment for furs and to African slave traders in return for captives. Another European export was guns. The city of Birmingham became the world firearms capital, based on gradual technological adaptations that were typical of the hardware trades (as we will see, software trades, like textiles, were a different story). By tinkering with high-precision tools and machines—for example, by boring metal, refining files, and becoming more adept at ironwork to weld barrels (without an accurate barrel, muskets and later rifles were useless)—the general machine tool industry created the right conditions for other production breakthroughs. But despite these developments, the boom in gunmaking would have been impossible without global trade. Why? The never-ending appetite for weapons to duel with world rivals made empires into military-industrial complexes. In this way, European imperial wars globalized an arms race.

Empires were also export systems selling large-scale munitions on a global scale. On the North American frontier, the bow and arrow had long been eclipsed by muskets, though Indigenous peoples still ambushed European and American soldiers with the silent accuracy of an arrow while the invaders fumbled around with their flintlocks. Birmingham gunsmiths made fortunes by supplying muskets, pistols, locks, and ordnance to the East India Company, which equipped armies of sepoys (Indian soldiers serving in the company ranks) with small arms and sold stockpiles to Indian allies (called nabobs) in the struggle to subdue Bengal after driving out the French in 1757 (the Battle of Plassey). One Scottish businessman, Lawrence Dundas, made so much money supplying British troops during the Seven Years' War that people called him "the Nabob of the North." Gunmakers also turned to the African market. By 1800, 150,000 to 200,000 guns were shipped to Africa per year.

Britain's edge in the arms race was a critical factor in boosting its global ascent in the nineteenth century. Once the Napoleonic wars ended in 1815 and gunmakers faced the prospect of a sharp contraction in demand for their commodities, they pressured the government to promote military exports to clients in warring Latin America, the Middle East, and the expanding frontiers in the United States. Competition among gunmakers produced a scramble to lower production costs and prices to gun consumers by using interchangeable parts, which put small firearms into the hands of consumers worldwide.

The combination of war-making capacities and a consumer revolution transformed the world division of labor. The expansion of European exports and imports boosted European standards of living; spurred institutions and industries connected to global trade, such as shipping and shipbuilding; and fueled financial institutions, such as insurance companies, stock exchanges, and banks. These latter institutions were to serve the Europeans, especially the British, well during the industrial revolution. They became the instruments to channel more and more money into manufacturing enterprises.

But the rise of European manufactured exports led to the world's first deindustrialization, in Asia. Access to cheap primary inputs (raw materials), pools of capital, and support from the state and war making gave Europeans an edge over native industries in India and China. European—and especially British—producers began to undercut Indians in their home market for exquisite artisanal textiles. In China, cheaper delftware from the Netherlands and stoneware from England cut deeply into the market for Chinese porcelain.

The state played an important role in nurturing European industries. States began to see the benefits of a strong merchant and manufacturing class: not only did manufacturing increase the wealth of nations, as Adam Smith had argued, but it created pools of money that the state could borrow in times of need. States also enacted new laws to defend the rights of private property owners and inventors, so they could reap rewards from patents and be encouraged to innovate further. If the state encouraged the making of money, it also agreed to protect those who loaned money. Capitalists could rely on the government to force debtors to honor their obligations, thus protecting lenders from risk. These measures formed a pact between merchants and the state that would make some parts of Europe and some colonies of Europe distinctive.

Nowhere was this new alliance clearer than in England. Critical for the takeoff of the English cotton manufacturing industry were tariffs against Indian textile imports. Here, the pressure came from the woolen and linen industries, which wanted to shut out their Indian competitors. The chief beneficiaries, however, would be cotton entrepreneurs. In 1701, the English Parliament passed a law against the importation of dyed or printed calicoes coming from China, India, and Persia. The state followed this act of Parliament by passing a law that fined anyone wearing printed or dyed calicoes, though Indian muslins were exempted.

SOCIAL AND POLITICAL CONSEQUENCES OF GLOBAL TRADE The expansion of global trade had important social and political consequences. Global trading now trickled its way down from elites to ordinary folk, especially in western Europe. Even ordinary people could purchase imported goods with their earnings. Thus, the poor began to enjoy—some would say became addicted to—coffee, tea, and sugar and eventually even felt the need to use soap. European artisans and farmers purchased tools, furnishings, and home decorations. Colonial laborers also used their meager earnings to buy imported cotton cloth made in Europe from the raw cotton they themselves had picked several seasons earlier.

As new goods flowed from ever more distant corners of the globe, immense fortunes grew. To support their enterprise, traders needed new services, in insurance, bookkeeping, and the recording of legal documents. Trade helped nurture the emergence of new classes of professionals—accountants and lawyers. The new cities of the commercial revolution, hubs like Bristol, Bombay, and Buenos Aires, provided the homes and flourishing neighborhoods for a class of men and women known as the **bourgeoisie**: urban businessmen, financiers, and other property owners without aristocratic origins.

As Europe moved to the center of this new global economic order, one class in particular moved to the top of the social ladder: the trader-financiers. Like the merchandiser, the financier did not have to emerge from the high and mighty of Eurasia's dynasties. Consider Mayer Amschel Rothschild (1744–1812): born the son of a money changer in the Jewish ghetto of Frankfurt, Rothschild progressed from coin dealing to money changing, then from trading textiles to lending funds to kings and governments. By the time of his death, he owned the world's biggest banking operation and his five sons were running powerful branches in London, Paris, Vienna, Naples, and Frankfurt.

By extending credit, families like the Rothschilds also enabled traders to ship goods across long distances without having to worry about immediate payment. All these financial changes implied world integration through the flow of goods as well as the flow of money. In the 1820s, sizable funds amassed in London flowed to Egypt, Mexico, and New York to support trade, public investment, and, of course, speculation.

The Industrial Revolution and the British Surge

Trade and finance repositioned western Europe's relationship with the rest of the world. So did the emergence of manufacturing—a big leap took place in the output of cheap industrial commodities. The heart of this process was a gradual accumulation and diffusion of technical knowledge. Lots of little inventions, their applications, and their diffusion across the Atlantic world gradually built up a stock of technical knowledge and practice. Historians have traditionally called these changes the **industrial revolution**, a term first used by the British economic historian Arnold Toynbee in the late nineteenth century. Although the term suggests radical and rapid economic change, the reality was much more gradual and less dramatic than originally believed. Yet the term still has great validity, for the major economic changes that occurred in Britain, northwestern Europe, and North America catapulted these countries ahead of the rest of the world in industrial and agricultural output and standard of living.

MANUFACTURING AND THE COTTON TEXTILE INDUSTRY Nowhere was this industrial revolution more evident than in Britain. Britain had a few natural advantages, like large supplies of coal (for cheap carbon-based energy) and iron (for cheap and durable metal). Emboldened by a war-making empire, it also had a political and social environment that allowed merchants and industrialists to invest heavily while also expanding their internal and international markets. But the cost of labor in Britain was relatively high. For the British to outsell competitors in India and China, they would have to replace expensive workers with cheap energy and sufficient capital to purchase labor-saving machines.

In addition to its coal and iron reserves, by the eighteenth century Britain could boast an abundance of inventors and entrepreneurs. Few were university educated or conversant in the ideas of the Enlightenment, though some were. What was key to their success was their experimental and observational practices. As scientific methods became more popular, new technologies became more fashionable. Intrepid young artisans, who were literate and numerate enough to lead the way, invented laborsaving devices like steam engines and mechanical spinners, crucial inventions for the cotton textile industry.

The first problem tackled by these artisanal innovators was that of how to pump water out of coal mining shafts. Using steam to make smooth rotary power, they created a cheaper and more efficient energy source than a horse or river could provide. Once rotary power was connected to spinning and weaving devices, the capacity to produce low-cost, high-volume cloth took off. Steam allowed factories to locate farther away from earlier energy sources and in swelling cities, where these units of production could grow in scale without driving up production costs. What followed was a cascade of smaller, but

A Cotton Textile Mill in the 1830s. The region of Lancashire became one of the major industrial hubs for textile production in the world. By the 1830s, mills had made the shift from artisanal work to highly mechanical mass production. Among the great breakthroughs was the discovery that cloth could be printed with designs, such as paisley or calico (as in this image), and marketed to middle-class consumers.

important, innovations. In this fashion, mechanical production eclipsed the manual production that was the basis of textile production in the rest of the world.

A good example of how the alliance of the inventor with the investor furthered the industrial revolution was the advent of the steam engine. Such engines burned coal to boil water; the resulting steam drove mechanized devices. While several tinkerers worked on the device, the most famous was James Watt (1736–1819) of Scotland, who managed to separate steam condensers from piston cylinders. This enabled pistons to stay hot and run constantly. Watt joined forces with the industrialist Matthew Boulton, who marketed the steam engine and set up a laboratory where Watt could refine his device. The steam engine catalyzed a revolution in transportation. Steam-powered engines also improved sugar refining, pottery making, and other industrial processes, generating more products at lower cost than when workers had made them by hand.

In a dramatic way, cotton became Britain's dominant industry in the nineteenth century. Even in the middle of the eighteenth century, India's cotton textile industry had dwarfed Britain's. Factories in Bengal produced 85 million pounds of yarn per year compared with 3 million in England. At the time, cotton production was entirely a hand industry, but a series of macro inventions—James Hargreaves's spinning jenny, Richard Arkwright's water frame, and Samuel Crompton's combination of the jenny and the water frame into the "mule"—enabled the British to produce yarns that rivaled India's in durability, quality, and beauty. The difference? The British product was much cheaper because it relied on fewer workers. In contrast to India, where one person, usually a woman, produced yarn on a handheld spinning wheel, in England and Scotland one person could operate a jenny, a water frame, and finally a mule and produce seventy times what a single hand-operated wheel could yield. Crompton's spectacular mule worked in pairs overseen by a single minder with the help of two boys to roll out fabric in large quantities. The largest carried up to 1,320 spindles and was as long as 150 feet. These macro inventions became the tools of the first industrial factories.

By the 1830s, Britain's dominance of world markets was unrivaled. In this decade, British cotton textile mills employed 425,000 workers and accounted for 16 percent of jobs in British manufacturing. To sustain the output of fabric, Britain's boom required imported raw cotton from Brazil, Egypt, India, and the United States. Most raw cotton for British factories had come from colonial India until 1793, when the American inventor Eli Whitney (1765–1825) patented a "cotton gin" that separated cotton seeds from fiber. After that, cotton farming spread so quickly in the southern United States that by the 1850s it was producing more than 80 percent of the world's cotton supply. In turn, every enslaved Black person in the Americas and many Indians in British India were wearing cheap, British-produced cotton shirts. In less than a century, India had gone from exporting fine textiles to Britain to exporting raw cotton, while imports of British cloth drove thousands of Bengali artisan weavers out of business. The Indian economy suffered doubly because even its cotton producers had to compete against new suppliers. Thus did the industrial revolution transform the balance of world economic power.

A NEW ECONOMIC ORDER What, in sum, was the industrial revolution? First, it should be clear that it did not always mean the creation of large-scale factories. In fact, the large factory was rare in manufacturing. Moreover, the largest production units at the time were sugar plantations of the Americas. Small-scale production remained the norm, mass production the exception. Gunmakers in Birmingham and Harpers Ferry, Virginia, and the pioneering ballistic manufacturer Honoré Blanc in France, whose interchangeable and uniform parts used in artillery dazzled buyers around the world, shipped their weapons from small plants. The silks of Lyon, cutlery of Solingen, calicoes of Alsace, and cottons of Pawtucket, Rhode Island, were all products of small firms in heavily industrialized belts.

The industrial revolution combined three decisive forces: the application of energy sources like coal that allowed production in more efficient locations, the use of machinery to augment the productivity of specialized labor, and the deployment of interchangeable parts that made machinery more effective and cheaper to use. Knowledge and science could be harnessed to the pooling of investments to launch manufacturers into a new age, an age capable of seizing the opportunity afforded by wars and empires to create demand for new products and new markets—and to crush rivals in old Asian markets.

One of the great mysteries of the industrial revolution was why China, the home of inventors of astronomical water clocks and gunpowder, did not become an epicenter of industrial production. There are three reasons. First, China did not foster experimental science and engineering of the kind that allowed Watt to stumble onto the possibility of steam or Hargreaves, Arkwright, and Crompton to invent machines to produce yarn. Chinese authorities discouraged the partnership of inventors and investors. Experimentation, testing, and the links between thinkers and investors were a distinctly Atlantic phenomenon. The Qing, like the Mughal and Ottoman dynasties, swept great minds into their bureaucracies and reinforced the old agrarian system based on peasant exploitation and tribute. Second, unlike the Europeans, Chinese rulers saw little need to engage in overseas expansion or establish trading outposts in faraway lands in search of riches. The agrarian dynasties of China and India neither showered favors on local merchants nor effectively shut out interlopers. This made them vulnerable to cheap manufactured imports from European traders backed by governments that extolled the virtues of free trade. Third, China did not have ready access to cheap sources of fuel. China's coal deposits lay in the northwest, but merchants and trading hubs were in the southeast. Cheap carbon gave European and North American manufacturers a comparative advantage. And once ahead of the industrial game, these manufacturers could drive their Asian competitors out of business.

The effects of European and North American industrialization were profound. Historically, Europe had a trade imbalance with partners to the east—it imported large quantities of furs from Russia and spices and silks from Asia. It made up for this with silver from the Americas. But the new economic order meant that by the nineteenth century western Europe had not only manufactures like textiles to export to the world but also capital. One of Europe's biggest debtors was none other than the sultan of the Ottoman Empire, whose tax system could not keep up with the daunting expenditures necessary to keep the realm together. More and more, Asian, African, and American governments found themselves borrowing from Europe's financiers just as their people were buying industrial products from Europe and selling their primary products to European consumers and producers.

Working and Living

The industrial revolution brought more demanding work routines—not only in the manufacturing economies of western Europe and North America but also on the farms and plantations of Asia and Africa. Although the European side of the story is better known, cultivators throughout the rest of the world toiled harder and for longer hours.

URBAN LIFE AND WORK ROUTINES Increasingly, Europe's workers made their living in cities. London, Europe's largest city in 1700, saw its population nearly double over the next century to almost 1 million. By the 1820s, population growth was even greater in the industrial hubs of Leeds, Glasgow, Birmingham, Liverpool, and Manchester. (See Map 15.4 and Analyzing Global Developments: Town and Countryside, Core and Periphery, in the Nineteenth Century.) By contrast, in the Low Countries (Belgium and the Netherlands) and France, where small-scale, rural-based manufacturing flourished, the shift to cities was less extreme.

For most urban dwellers, cities were not healthy places. Water that powered the mills, along with chemicals used in dyeing, went directly back into waterways that provided drinking water. Overcrowded tenements shared just a few outhouses. Most European cities as late as 1850 had no running water, no garbage pickup, and no underground sewer system. The result was widespread disease. (In fact, no European city at this time had as clean a water supply as the largest towns of the ancient Roman Empire once had.)

Often families were forced to send women and children outside the home to work. Their wages, usually less than half those paid to adult male workers, helped families survive but exposed these workers, too, to the dangers and hardships of working in factories or mines. Most worked shifts of 12 or more hours at a time, making it impossible for children to obtain the kind of education that might have made escape from the working class possible. Orphans and inhabitants of workhouses—places where debtors, drunks, or those accused of immoral behavior were sent—were treated essentially as enslaved labor.

Changes in work affected the understanding of time. Most farmers' workloads had followed seasonal rhythms, but after 1800 industrial settings imposed a rigid concept of work discipline and time. To keep the machinery operating, factory and mill owners installed huge clocks and used bells or horns to signify the workday's beginning and end. Employers also measured output per hour and compared workers' performance. Josiah Wedgwood, a maker of teacups and other porcelain, installed a Boulton & Watt steam engine in his manufacturing plant and made his workers use it efficiently. He rang a bell at 5:45 in the morning so employees could start work as day broke. At 8:30 the bell rang for breakfast, at 9:00 to call them back, and at 12:00 for a half-hour lunch; it last tolled when darkness put an end to the workday. Sometimes, though, factory clocks were turned back in the morning and forward at night, falsely extending the exhausted laborers' workday.

Despite higher production, industrialization imposed numbing work routines and paltry wages. Worse, however, was having no work at all. As families abandoned their farmland and depended on wages, being idle meant having no income. Periodic downturns in the economy put wage workers at risk, and many responded by organizing protests. In 1834, the British Parliament centralized the administration of all poor relief and deprived able-bodied workers of any relief unless they joined a workhouse, where working conditions resembled those of a prison.

SOCIAL PROTEST AND EMIGRATION While entrepreneurs accumulated private wealth, the effects of the industrial revolution on working-class families raised widespread concern. In the 1810s in England, groups of jobless craftsmen, called Luddites, smashed the machines that had left them unemployed. In 1849, the English novelist Charlotte Brontë published a novel, *Shirley*, depicting the misfortunes caused by the power loom. Charles Dickens described a mythic Coketown to evoke pity for the working class in his 1854 classic *Hard Times*. Both Elizabeth Gaskell, in England, and Émile Zola, in France, described the hardships of women whose malnourished children were pressed into the workforce too early. Gaskell and Zola also highlighted the hunger, loneliness, and illness that prostitutes and widows endured. These

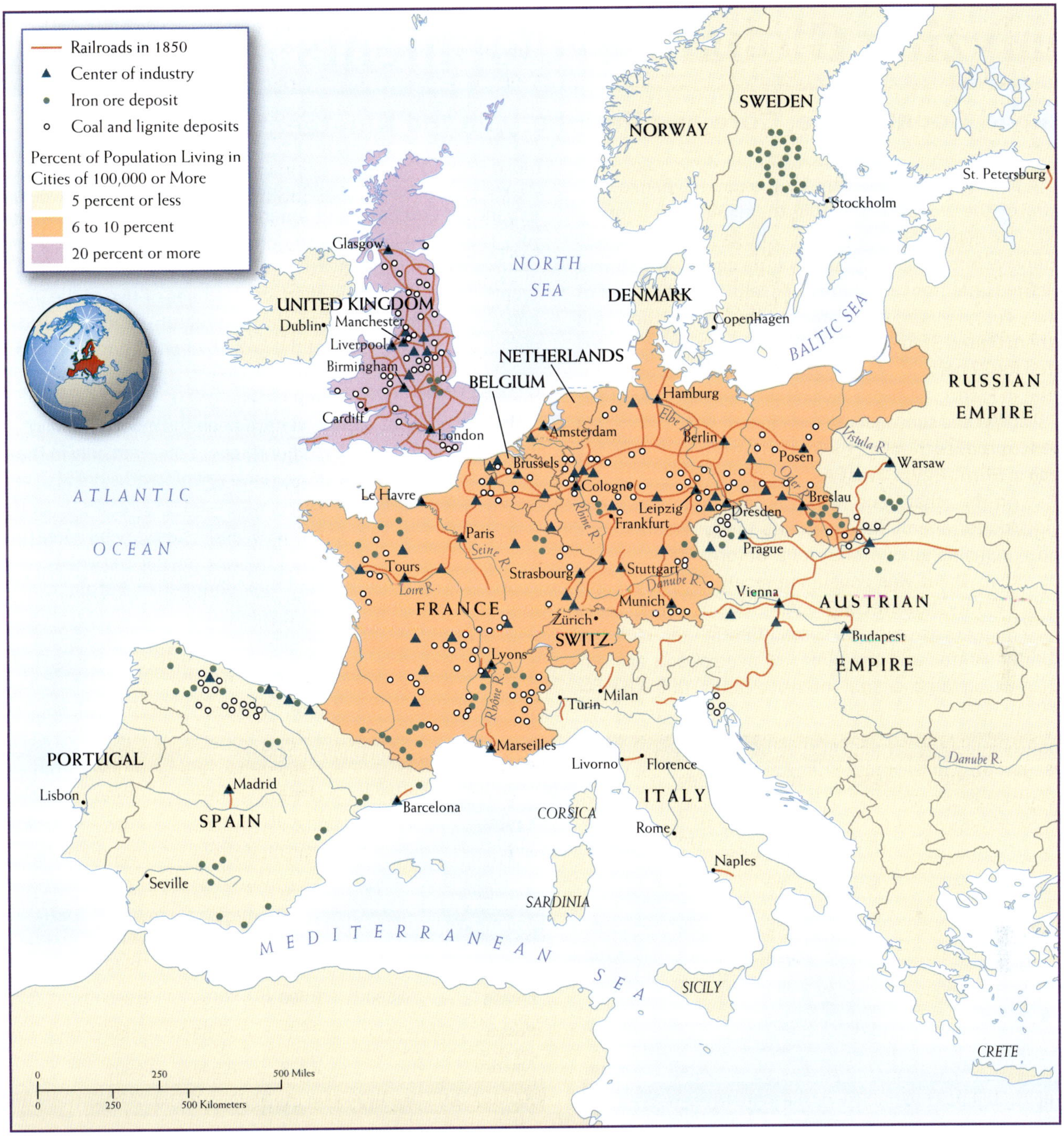

MAP 15.4 | Industrial Europe around 1850

By 1850, much of western Europe was industrial and urban, with major cities linked to one another through a network of railroads.

- According to this map, what natural resources contributed to the growth of the industrial revolution? What effects did it have on urban population densities?
- Compare the courses of major rivers with those of the railways.
- Why did the United Kingdom have such a large concentration of cities with more than 100,000 inhabitants? How was the United Kingdom able to support such large population centers?

Analyzing Global Developments

Town and Countryside, Core and Periphery, in the Nineteenth Century

The textile industry was by far the most dynamic sector of the world economy in the nineteenth century. It was dependent on cotton, whose production was labor-intensive but required relatively little capital investment and benefited little from economies of scale. In the first half of the century, cotton was primarily produced by enslaved people in the southern United States. By the late 1850s, the United States accounted for 77 percent of the cotton consumed in Britain, for 90 percent in France, and for about 92 percent in Russia. After the U.S. Civil War and subsequent emancipations, sharecroppers continued to produce the crop, though cotton production began to flourish in Brazil, Egypt, West Africa, and India.

Wheat, on the other hand, was the basic staple of European and Mediterranean diets well into the nineteenth century, and it remains vitally important. Before the advent of railroads, most wheat was consumed locally. In the second half of the century, however, vast quantities of wheat came onto world markets as railroads spread through the Midwest of the United States and the plains of central and eastern Europe. Grown on large, capital-intensive farms, that wheat—as well as rye, corn, millet, and other grains—fed radically expanding European and American industrial cities and factory towns, linking them to rich agricultural hinterlands and contributing unwittingly to the economic volatility of the nineteenth century. Here we chart the fortunes of two of the most important commodities of the nineteenth-century world—cotton and wheat—against the growth of cities and railroads.

QUESTIONS FOR ANALYSIS

- Which countries appear to have been the most dynamic? Pay attention to relative change over time—not only in the biggest cities and most extensive rail networks but also in those growing the fastest.
- How did the growth of railroads and cities vary by country? What does this tell us about the relationship between economic core regions and their peripheries and about patterns of inequality more generally?
- How did the extension of railroads, along with the economic integration they fostered, influence patterns of inequality worldwide?

Population of Major Cities (in thousands)

	1800	1830	1850	1880	1900
Alexandria	15		60	231	320
Delhi		150	152	173	209
Rio de Janeiro	43	125	166	360	523
London	1,117		2,685	4,770	6,586
Paris	576		1,053	2,269	2,714
Moscow	250		365	748	989
New York City	60	161	340	847	1,478
Tokyo	457			824	1,819

Population Estimates (in thousands)

	1800	1825	1850	1875	1900
Egypt	3,854	4,541	4,752	6,961	10,186
India	255,000	257,000	285,000	306,000	
Brazil			7,678	9,930	17,438
England	8,893	12,000	17,928	22,712	32,528
France	27,349	30,462	35,783	36,906	38,451
Russia	35,500	52,300	68,500	90,200	132,900
America	5,297	11,252	23,261	45,073	76,094
Japan	25,622	26,602	27,201	25,037	44,359

Output of Cotton (in thousand metric tons)

	1800	1825	1850	1875	1900
Egypt				132	293
India			12	533	536
America	17	121	484	1,050	2,120

Wheat Production (in thousand metric tons)

	1825	1850	1875	1900
France	4,580	6,600	7,550	8,860
Russia			53	136
America		2,722	8,546	16,302

Length of Open Railway Lines (in kilometers)

	1825	1850	1875	1900
Egypt		1,184	1,410	2,237
India		32	10,527	39,834
Brazil		14	1,801	15,316
England	43	9,797	23,365	30,079
France	17	2,915	19,351	38,109
Russia	27	501	19,029	53,234
America	37	14,518	119,246	311,160
Japan		29	62	6,300

Source: S. Beckert, "Emancipation and Empire: Reconstructing the Worldwide Web of Cotton Production in the Age of the American Civil War," *The American Historical Review* 109, no. 5 (December 2004): 1405–38; B. R. Mitchell, *International Historical Statistics: Africa, Asia, and Oceania, 1750–2005, International Historical Statistics: The Americas, 1750–2005, and International Historical Statistics: Europe, 1750–2005* (London: Palgrave Macmillan, 2007).

A Model Textile Mill. Distressed by the terrible working conditions of nineteenth-century textile mills, Welsh industrialist and reformer Robert Owen sought to create humane factories. From maintaining the orderliness of the factory floor to posting work rules on the walls, Owen's reforms saw significant improvements in the health and morale of his workers. Nonetheless, he would continue to employ children in his factories, like most of his contemporaries.

social advocates sought protective legislation for workers, including curbing child labor, limiting the workday, and, in some countries, legalizing prostitution for the sake of monitoring the prostitutes' health.

Some people, however, could not wait for legislative reform. Thus, the period saw unprecedented emigration, as unemployed workers or peasants abandoned their homes to seek their fortunes in America, Canada, and Australia. During the Irish Potato Famine of 1845–1849, at least 1 million Irish citizens left their country (and a further million or so died) when fungi attacked their subsistence crop. Desperate to escape starvation, they booked cheap passage to North America on ships so notorious for disease and malnutrition that they earned the name "coffin ships." Those who did survive faced discrimination in their new land, for many Americans feared that the immigrants would drive down wages or create social unrest.

The industrial revolution produced wealth on an unprecedented scale, but that wealth was unevenly distributed. Inequalities existed both within societies and between them. Free trade had at first led to the creation of small firms, but over time some productive workshops expanded into massive, dynamic, creative, and unstable industrial corporations.

Persistence and Change in Afro-Eurasia

As western Europe pulled ahead of the rest of the world economically and technologically, it became a threat to the remaining Afro-Eurasian empires. Western European merchants and industrialists, joined by American ones after the middle of the nineteenth century, sought closer economic and (in some cases) political ties once they commanded an advantage. They did so in the name of gaining "free" access to Asian markets and products, putting regional competitors in a tough spot. Some Afro-Asian elites wanted technologies and goods, but without strings attached. Others just resisted the whole package. Russian and Ottoman rulers responded by modernizing their military organizations and hoped to achieve similar economic strides while distancing themselves from the democratic principles of the French Revolution. The Chinese Empire remained outside the orbit of European power until the first Opium War of the early 1840s forced the Chinese to acknowledge their military weaknesses. Thus, changes in the Atlantic world unleashed new pressures around the globe, though with varying degrees of intensity.

Revamping the Russian Monarchy

Russian rulers responded to the emergent new western European commercial and industrial powerhouses by strengthening their traditional authority through modest reforms and the suppression of domestic opposition. Tsar Alexander I (r. 1801–1825) was fortunate that Napoleon committed several blunders and lost his formidable army in the Russian snows. Yet the French Revolution and its massive, patriotic armies struck at the heart of Russian political institutions, which rested upon a huge peasant population laboring as serfs. The tsars could no longer easily justify their absolutism by claiming that enlightened despotism was the most advanced form of government, since a new model, rooted in popular sovereignty and the concept of the nation, had arisen.

Decembrists in St. Petersburg. Russians energetically participated in the coalition that defeated Napoleon, but the ideas of the French Revolution greatly appealed to the educated upper classes, including aristocrats of the officer corps. In December 1825, at the death of Tsar Alexander I, some regimental officers staged an uprising of about 3,000 men, demanding a constitution and the end of serfdom. But Nicholas I, the new tsar, called in loyal troops and brutally dispersed the "Decembrists," executing or exiling their leaders.

In December 1825, when Alexander died unexpectedly and childless, there was a question over succession. Some of the Russian officers launched a patriotic revolt, hoping to convince Alexander's brother Constantine to take the throne, and guarantee a constitution, in place of a more conservative brother, Nicholas. The Decembrists, as the proponents of Constantine were called, came primarily from elite families and were familiar with western European life and institutions. A few Decembrists wanted to establish a constitutional monarchy to replace Russia's despotism; others favored a tsar-less republic and the abolition of serfdom. But the officers' conspiracy failed to win over conservative landowners and bureaucrats, who believed in the tsar's divine right to rule and did not want to see serfdom abolished. As Constantine, too, supported Nicholas's claim to power, Nicholas (r. 1825–1855) became tsar and brutally suppressed the insurrectionists.

Russia's rulers and upper classes had always both feared and been inspired by western examples. They continued to borrow western technology and modes of administration but held at bay western ideas and practices of liberty through censorship and the promotion of a distinctly Russian identity. In trying to maintain absolutist rule, Nicholas and his successors portrayed the monarch's family as the ideal historical embodiment of the nation with direct ties to the people. Nicholas himself prevented rebellion by expanding the secret police, enforcing censorship, conducting impressive military exercises, and maintaining serfdom. And in the 1830s, he introduced a conservative ideology that stressed religious faith, hierarchy, and obedience. Although in 1861 a new tsar, Alexander II, would finally abolish serfdom, throughout the nineteenth century Russia remained the most conservative of the great powers.

Reforming Egypt and the Ottoman Empire

Unlike Russia, where Napoleon's army had reached Moscow, the Ottoman capital in Istanbul never faced a threat from French troops. Still, Napoleon's invasion of Egypt shook the Ottoman Empire. Even before this trauma, imperial authorities faced the challenge posed by increased trade with Europe and the greater presence of European merchants and missionaries. In addition, many non-Muslim religious communities in the sultan's empire wanted the European powers to advance their interests. In the wake of Napoleon, who had promised to remake Egyptian society, reformist energies swept from Egypt to the center of the Ottoman domain. (See Global Themes and Sources: Primary Source 15.2.)

REFORMS IN EGYPT In Egypt, far-reaching changes came with **Muhammad Ali**, a skillful, modernizing ruler. After the French withdrawal in 1801, Muhammad Ali (r. 1805–1848) won a chaotic struggle for supreme power in Egypt and aligned himself with influential Egyptian families. Yet he looked to revolutionary France for a model of modern state building. As with Napoleon (and Simón Bolívar in Latin America), the key to his hold on power was the army. With the help of French advisers, the modernized Egyptian army became the most powerful fighting force in the Middle East.

Muhammad Ali also reformed education and agriculture. He established a school of engineering and opened the first modern medical school in Cairo under the supervision of a French military doctor. And his efforts in the countryside made Egypt one of the world's leading cotton exporters. A summer crop, cotton required steady watering when the Nile's irrigation waters were in short supply. So Muhammad Ali's public works department, advised by European

Muhammad Ali. The Middle Eastern ruler who most successfully assimilated the educational, technological, and economic advances of nineteenth-century Europe was Muhammad Ali, ruler of Egypt from 1805 until 1848.

engineers, deepened the irrigation canals and constructed a series of dams across the Nile. These efforts transformed Egypt, making it the most powerful state in the eastern Mediterranean and alarming the Ottoman state and the great powers in Europe.

Muhammad Ali's modernizing reforms, however, disrupted the habits of the peasantry. After all, incorporation into the industrial world economy involved harder work (as English wage workers had discovered), often with little additional pay. Because irrigation improvements permitted year-round cultivation, Egyptian peasants now had to plant and harvest three crops instead of one or two. Moreover, the state controlled the prices of cultivated products, so peasants saw little profit from their extra efforts. Young men also faced conscription into the state's enlarged army, while whole families had to toil, unpaid, on public works projects. In addition, a state-sponsored program of industrialization aimed to put Egypt on a par with Europe: before long, textile and munitions factories employed 200,000 workers. But Egypt had few skilled laborers or cheap sources of energy, so by the time of Muhammad Ali's death in 1849, few of the factories survived.

External forces also limited Muhammad Ali's ambitious plans. At first, his new army enjoyed spectacular success. But Muhammad Ali overplayed his hand when he sent forces into Syria in the 1830s and later when he threatened Anatolia, the heart of the Ottoman state. Fearing that an Egyptian ruler might attempt to overthrow the Ottoman sultan and threaten the balance of power in the eastern Mediterranean region, the European powers compelled Egypt to withdraw from Anatolia and reduce its army.

OTTOMAN REFORMS Under political and economic pressures like those facing Muhammad Ali in Egypt, Ottoman rulers also made reforms. Indeed, military defeats and humiliating treaties with Europe were painful reminders of the sultans' vulnerability. In 1805, Sultan Selim III tried to create a new infantry, trained by western European officers. But before he could bring this force up to fighting strength, the janissaries stormed the palace, killed its new officers, and deposed Selim in 1807. Over the next few decades, janissary military men and clerical scholars (*ulama*) cobbled together an alliance that continuously thwarted reformers.

Why did reform falter in the Ottoman state before it could be implemented? After all, in France and Spain the old regimes were also inefficient and burdened with debts and military losses. The French required a ferocious revolution to overturn the old order and to remove its supporters. But reform was possible only if the forces of restraint—especially old regime militaries—were weak or dismantled, as in France, where young officers like Napoleon Bonaparte emerged and reformers were strong and courageous. In the Ottoman Empire, the janissary class had grown powerful, providing the main resistance to change. Ottoman authority depended on clerical support, and the Muslim clergy also resisted change. Blocked at the top, Ottoman rulers were hesitant to appeal for popular support. Such an appeal, in the new age of popular sovereignty and national feeling, would be dangerous for an unelected dynast in a multiethnic and multireligious realm.

Mahmud II (r. 1808–1839), who acknowledged Europe's rising power, broke the political deadlock. He shrewdly manipulated his conservative opponents. Convincing some clerics that the janissaries neglected traditions of discipline and piety and promising that a new corps would pray fervently, the sultan won the *ulama*'s support and in 1826 established a European-style army corps. When the janissaries plotted their inevitable mutiny, Mahmud rallied clerics, students, and subjects. The schemers retreated to their barracks, only to be shelled by the sultan's artillery and then destroyed in flames. Thousands of other janissaries were rounded up and executed.

Like Muhammad Ali in Egypt, Mahmud brought in European officers to advise his forces. Here, too, military reform spilled

Indian Resistance to Company Rule. Tipu Sultan, the Mysore ruler, put up a determined resistance against the British. This painting by Robert Home shows Charles Cornwallis, the East India Company's governor, receiving Tipu's two sons as hostages after defeating him in the 1792 war. The boys remained in British custody for two years. Tipu returned to fighting the British and was killed in the war of 1799.

over into nonmilitary areas. The Ottoman modernizers created a medical college and then a school of military sciences. To understand Europe better and to create a first-rate diplomatic corps, the Ottomans schooled their officials in European languages and had European classics translated into Turkish. As Mahmud's successors extended reforms into civilian life, this era—known as the Tanzimat, or reorganization period (1826–1839)—saw legislation that guaranteed equality for all Ottoman subjects, regardless of religion.

The reforms, however, stopped well short of revolutionary change. For one thing, reform relied too much on the personal whim of rulers. Also, the bureaucratic and religious infrastructure remained committed to old ways. Moreover, any effort to reform the rural sector met resistance by the landed interests. Finally, the merchant classes profited from business with a debt-ridden sultan. By preventing the empire's fiscal collapse through financial support to the state, bankers lessened the pressure for reform and removed the spark that had fired the revolutions in Europe. Together, these factors impeded reform in the Ottoman Empire.

Colonial Reordering in India

Europe's most important colonial possession in Asia between 1750 and 1850 was British India. Unlike in North America, the changes that the British imposed in Asia did not lead to political independence. Instead, India was increasingly dominated by the **East India Company**, which the crown had chartered in 1600. The company's control over India's imports and exports in the eighteenth and nineteenth centuries, however, contradicted Britain's claims about its allegiance to a world economic system based on "free trade."

THE EAST INDIA COMPANY'S MONOPOLY Initially, the British, through the East India Company, tried to control India's commerce by establishing trading posts along the coast without taking complete political control. After conquering the state of Bengal in 1757, the company began to fill its coffers and its officials began to amass personal fortunes. Even the British governor of Bengal pocketed a portion of the tax revenues. Such unbridled abuse of power caused the Bengal army, along with forces of the Mughal emperor and of the ruler of Awadh, to revolt. Although the rebels were unsuccessful, British officials left the emperor and most provincial leaders in place—as nominal rulers. Nonetheless, the British secured the right for the East India Company to collect tax revenues in Bengal, Bihar, and Orissa and to trade free of duties throughout Mughal territory. In return, the Mughal emperor would receive a hefty annual pension. The company went on to annex other territories, bringing much of South Asia under its rule by the early nineteenth century. (See Map 15.5.)

To rule with minimal interference, however, required knowing the conquered society. This led to Orientalist

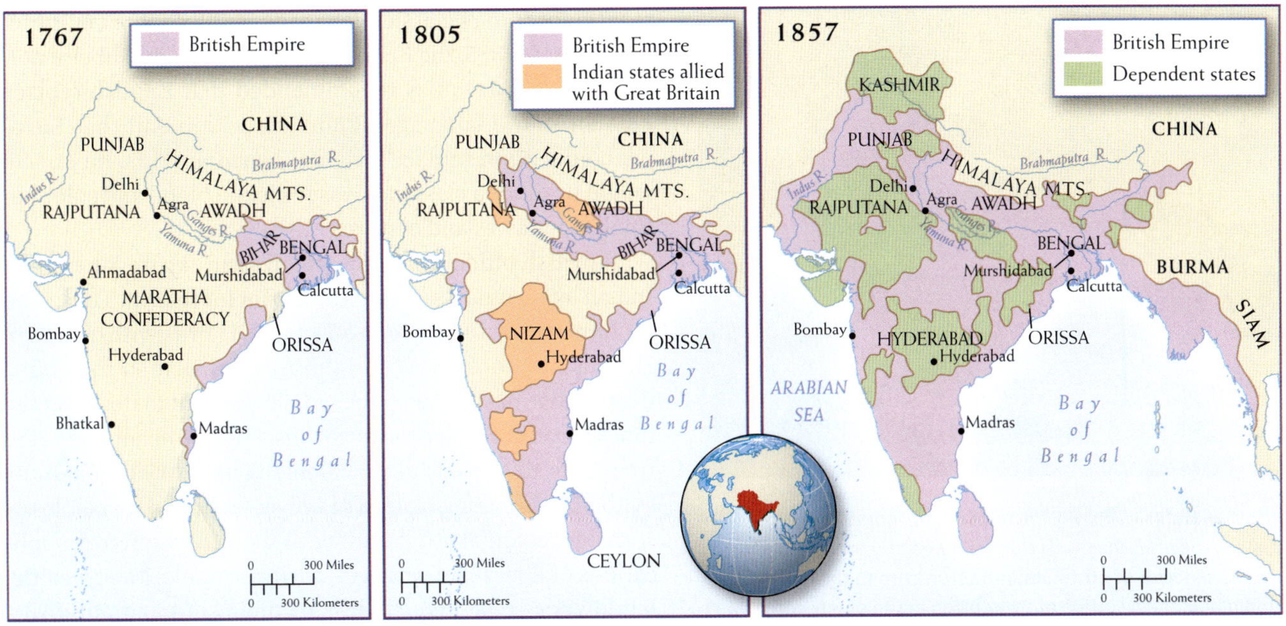

MAP 15.5 | The British in India, 1767–1857

Starting from locations in eastern and northeastern India, the British East India Company extended its authority over much of South Asia prior to the outbreak of the Indian Rebellion of 1857.

- What type of locations did the British first acquire in India?
- According to your reading, how did the British East India Company expand into the interior of India and administer these possessions?
- Why did the company choose a strategy of direct rule over some areas and indirect rule over other areas in India?

scholarship: British scholar-officials wrote the first modern histories of South Asia, translated Sanskrit and Persian texts, identified philosophical writings, and compiled Hindu and Muslim law books. Through their efforts, the company state presented itself as a force for revitalizing authentic Hinduism and recovering India's literary and cultural treasures. Although the Orientalist scholars admired Sanskrit language and literature, they still supported English colonial rule and did not necessarily agree with local beliefs.

EFFECTS IN INDIA Maintaining a sizable military and civilian bureaucracy also required taxation. Indeed, taxes on land were the East India Company's largest source of revenue. From 1793 onward, land policies required large and small landowners alike to pay taxes to the company. As a result, large estate owners gained more power and joined with the company in determining who could own property. Whenever smaller proprietors defaulted on their taxes, the company put their properties up for auction, with the firm's own employees and large estate owners often obtaining title.

Company rule and booming trade altered India's urban geography as well. By the early nineteenth century, colonial cities like Calcutta, Madras, and Bombay were the new centers at the expense of older Mughal cities like Agra, Delhi, Murshidabad, and Hyderabad. As the colonial cities attracted British merchants and Indian clerks, artisans, and laborers, their populations surged. Calcutta's reached 350,000 in 1820; Bombay's jumped to 200,000 by 1825. In these cities, Europeans lived close to the company's fort and trading stations, while migrants from the countryside clustered in crowded quarters called "black towns."

Back in Britain, the debts of rural Indians and the conditions of black towns generated little concern. Instead, calls for reform focused on the East India Company's monopoly: its sole access to Indian wealth and its protection of company shareholders and investors. In 1813, the British Parliament, responding to merchants' and traders' demands to participate in the Indian economy, abolished the company's monopoly over trade with India.

India now became an importer of British textiles and an exporter of raw cotton—a reversal of its traditional pattern of trade. In the past, India had been an important textile manufacturer, exporting fine cotton goods throughout the Indian Ocean and to Europe. But its elites could not resist

Packing Cotton Bales. This 1864 engraving of the packing of cotton bales registers the shift in cotton trade between India and Britain; from being an exporter of cotton manufactures up to the eighteenth century, India became a source of raw cotton in the nineteenth century.

the appeal of cheap British textiles. As a result, India's own industrialization stalled. In addition, the import of British manufactures caused unfavorable trade balances that changed India from a net importer of gold and silver to an exporter of these precious metals.

PROMOTING CULTURAL CHANGE Led by evangelical Christians and liberal reformers, the British did more than alter the Indian economy; they also advocated far-reaching changes in Indian culture so that its people would value British goods and culture. In 1817, James Mill, a philosopher and an employee of the East India Company, condemned what he saw as backward social practices and cultural traditions. He and his son, John Stuart Mill, argued that only dictatorial rule could bring good government and economic progress to India, whose people they considered unfit for self-rule or liberalism. Now the mood swung away from the Orientalists' respect for India's classical languages, philosophies, cultures, and texts. In 1835, the British poet, historian, and liberal politician Lord Macaulay recommended that English replace Persian as the language of administration and that European education replace Oriental learning. This, he hoped, would produce a class that was Indian in blood and color but English in tastes and culture.

If British officials saw liberalism as an excuse for empire, Indian intellectuals saw in it a blueprint for reform. Thus, Ram Mohun Roy, an Indian reformer, locked horns with orthodox Hindus and took the lead in urging the British to abolish the practice of *sati,* by which women burned to death on the funeral pyres of their dead husbands. Roy also championed the free press, unsuccessfully challenging its restriction in India by the British as a violation of universal liberal principles.

A new colonial order built with such contradictory applications of liberalism was necessarily unstable. Most wealthy landowners resented the loss of their land and authority. Peasants, thrown to the mercy of the market, moneylenders, and landlords, were in turmoil. Dispossessed artisans stirred up towns and cities. And merchants and industrialists chafed under the British-dominated economy. Even though India was part of a more interconnected world and thereby supported Europe's industrialization, it was doing so as a colony. As freedom expanded in Europe, exploitation expanded in India.

Persistence of the Qing Empire

The Qing dynasty, which had taken power in 1644, was still enjoying prosperity and territorial expansion as the nineteenth century dawned. Its court elites accepted the dynasty's authority in spite of the fact that the Manchus were not Han Chinese but came originally from Manchuria. In this regard, Chinese upper classes were unlike most of the delegates called to the Estates-General in France in 1789, who seethed with resentment against the monarchy and the aristocracy.

Calcutta. Designated the capital of British India in 1772, Calcutta became vital to the British East India Company's activities as a main exporter of goods such as cotton and opium. The wealthy British merchants and Anglo-Indians that Calcutta attracted utterly transformed its landscape, as shown in this 1910 photograph of the Great Eastern Hotel, which was commonly hailed the "Jewel of the East." This street scene of wide paved roads, carriages, and Victorian architecture would be difficult to distinguish from one of turn-of-the-century London, were it not for the Indian figures in traditional dress.

Rice Cultivation. From hand-sowing seedlings to harvesting the grains in leech-infested waters, the process of rice cultivation was so labor-intensive that multigenerational households cropped up throughout imperial China to yield the necessary workforce.

EXPANDING BOUNDARIES The Qing had a talent for extending the empire's boundaries and settling frontier lands. Before 1750, they conquered Taiwan (the stronghold of remaining Ming forces), pushed westward into central Asia, and annexed Tibet. Qing troops then eliminated the threat of the powerful Junghars in western Mongolia and halted Russian efforts to take southern Siberia in the 1750s. To secure these territorial gains, the Qing encouraged settlement of frontier lands like Xinjiang. New crops from the Americas aided this process—especially corn and sweet potatoes, which grow well in less fertile soils.

Like their European counterparts, Chinese peasants were on the move. But migration occurred in Qing China for different reasons. The state-sponsored westward movement into Xinjiang, for example, aimed to secure a recently pacified frontier region through military colonization, after which civilians would follow. So peasants received promises of land, tools, seed, and the loan of silver and a horse—all with the dual objectives of producing enough food to supply the troops and relieve pressure on the poor and arid northwestern part of the country. These efforts brought so much land under cultivation by 1840 that the region's ecological and social landscape completely changed.

Other migrants were on the move by their own initiative. The ever-growing competition for land drove them even into areas where the Qing regime had tried to restrict migration (because of excessive administrative costs), such as Manchuria and Taiwan. As the migrants introduced their own agricultural techniques, they reshaped the environment through land reclamation and irrigation projects and sparked large population increases.

PROBLEMS OF THE EMPIRE Despite their success in expanding the empire, the Qing faced nagging problems. As a ruling minority, they took a conservative approach to innovation. And only late in the eighteenth century did they deal with rapid population growth. On the one hand, the tripling of China's population since 1300 demonstrated the realm's prosperity; on the other, a population of over 300 million severely strained resources—especially soil for growing crops and wood for fuel.

In spite of the difficulties that beset the Qing, European rulers and upper classes remained eager consumers of Chinese silks, teas, carved jade, tableware, jewelry, paper for covering walls, and ceramics. The Chinese, for their part, had little demand for most European manufactures. Trade with the Europeans continued, however, even though Emperor Qianlong famously wrote in 1793, in response to a request for more trade by Britain's king, "As your ambassador can see for himself, we possess all things and have no use for your country's manufactures."

By the mid-nineteenth century, technological advances, such as steam-powered naval ships, had strengthened European powers, and the Qing could no longer dismiss their increasing demands. The first clear evidence of an altered balance of power was a British-Chinese war over a narcotic. Indeed, the **Opium Wars** exposed China's vulnerability in a new era of European ascendancy.

THE OPIUM WARS AND THE "OPENING" OF CHINA Europeans had been selling staples and intoxicants in China for a long time. For example, tobacco, a New World crop, had become widely popular in China by the seventeenth century. Initially, few people would have predicted that tobacco smoking would lead to the widespread use of opium. Previously opium was mainly eaten as a medicine or an aphrodisiac. It was only on the island of Java in the seventeenth century that opium was mixed with tobacco and smoked; from there Dutch merchants carried it to Taiwan off the eastern coast of China and to China itself. Before long, people in Southeast Asia, Taiwan, and China were smoking crude opium mixed with tobacco. By the late eighteenth century, opium smokers with their long-stemmed pipes were conspicuous, though habitual users were largely confined to the upper wealthy classes in China because of its high prices.

Although the Qing banned opium imports in 1729, the Chinese continued to smoke the drug and import it illegally. The ban was utterly unenforced, for no one was prosecuted for opium offenses within the Qing Empire from 1729 until the first decade of the nineteenth century. Sensing its economic potential, the East India Company created an opium monopoly in India in 1773, using the state of Bengal for the cultivation of poppies, from which opium was made. Because the Chinese showed little taste for British goods, the British had been financing their tea imports with exports of silver to China. But by the late eighteenth century, the company's tea purchases had become too large to finance with silver. Fortunately for the company, the Chinese were eager for Indian cotton and opium, and then mostly just opium. By the 1830s, opium had become one of the most lucrative commodities in world trade.

As Bengal produced more and more opium, the price came down and the number of Chinese smokers increased. The result was a devastating balance of trade deficit for the Chinese. By 1823, opium surpassed cotton as China's largest import, and eight years later, in 1830–31, the opium trade had a staggering value of more than £13 million. In a reversal from earlier trends, silver began to flow out of instead of into China. Once silver shortages occurred, the peasants' tax burden grew heavier because they had to pay in silver (see Chapter 13). Consequently, long-simmering unrest in the countryside gained momentum. At the Qing court, some officials wanted to legalize the opium trade so as to eliminate corruption and boost revenues. (After all, as long as opium was an illegal substance, the government could not tax its traffic.) Others wanted stiffer prohibitions. In 1838, suppression won out. The emperor sent a special commissioner to Canton, the main center of the trade, to eradicate the influx of opium. But the governor-general of Hunan and Hubei Provinces in central China, Lin Zexu, a zealot of the suppression policy, went further than the emperor ever intended. Instead of seizing opium supplies in the hands of Chinese merchants as the emperor expected, Lin went to Canton itself, ordered all the Chinese servants out of the opium factory buildings, and shut off food supplies to the 350 British, American, Dutch, and Parsi merchants now trapped inside the merchant's factories. The detentions of the traders, with their immense stocks of opium, valued at $10 million, lasted six weeks and convinced the British foreign secretary, Lord Palmerston, to take military action.

Though determined, the Chinese were overwhelmed by Britain's modern military technology. After a British fleet—including four steam-powered battleships—entered Chinese waters in June 1840, the warships bombarded coastal regions near Canton and sailed upriver for a short way. (See Map 15.6.) On land, Qing soldiers, some armed with imported matchlocks, fared badly against the modern artillery of British troops, many of whom were Indians supplied with percussion cap rifles. Along the Yangzi River, outgunned Qing forces fought fiercely, but they were no match for British gunpowder. Many of the Qing soldiers killed their own wives and children before committing suicide.

Opium. *Left:* A common sight in late Qing China was establishments catering specifically to opium smoking. Taken from a volume condemning the practice, this picture shows opium smokers idling their day away. *Right:* Having established a monopoly in the 1770s over opium cultivation in India, the British greatly expanded their manufacture and export of opium to China to balance their rapidly growing import of Chinese tea and silk. This picture from the 1880s shows an opium warehouse in India where the commodity was stored before being transported to China.

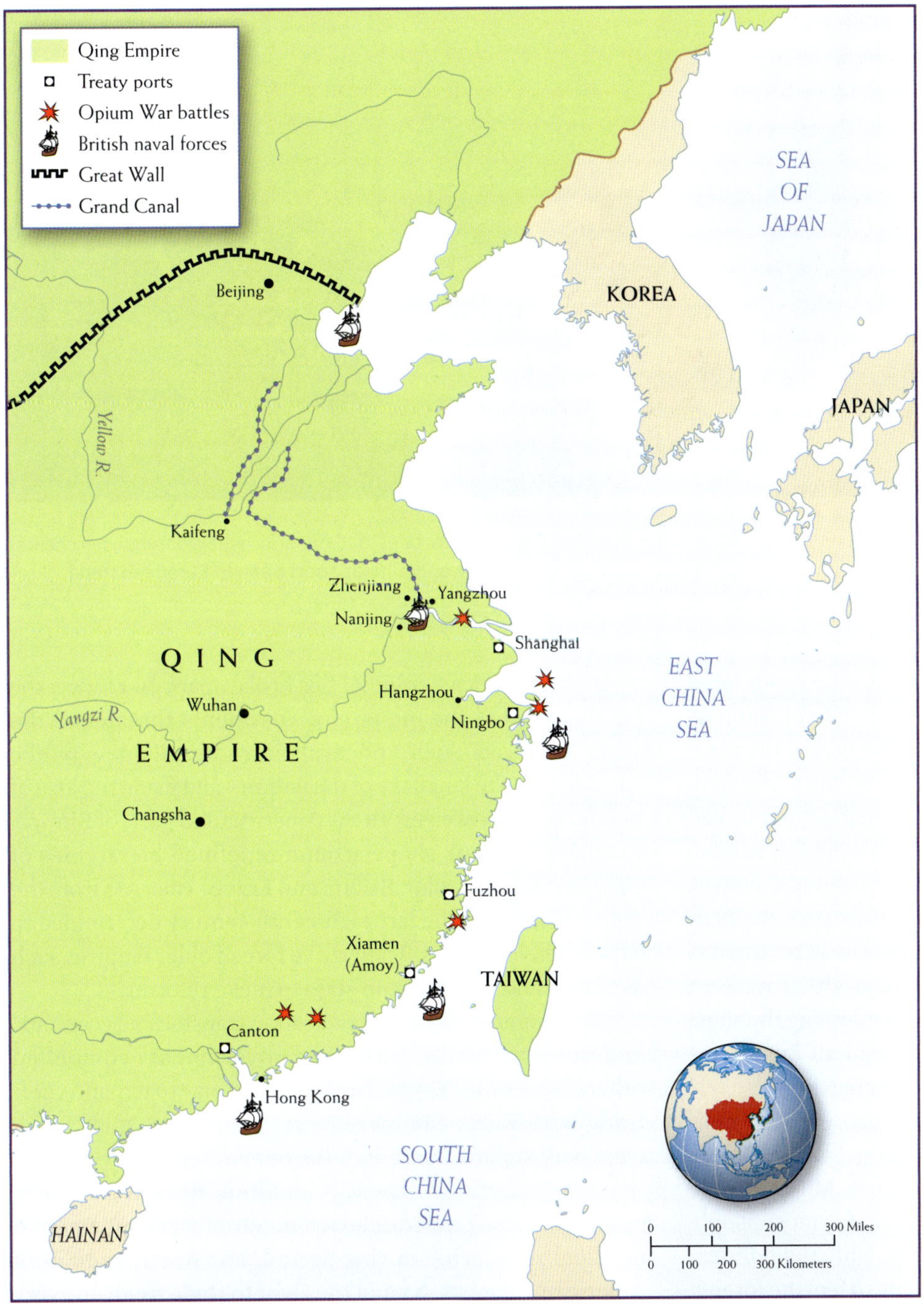

MAP 15.6 | The Qing Empire and the Opium Wars

The Opium Wars demonstrated the superiority of British military technology. Their victory granted the British control of Hong Kong and established a series of treaty ports, which gave Europeans access to Chinese trade and were subject to the laws of designated European countries.

- How many treaty ports were there after the Opium Wars? What was their significance?
- How were the treaty ports distributed along China's coastline?
- According to the text, how did the Opium Wars change relations between China and the western powers?

The British decision to go to war in defense of the opium trade was not universally popular. The traders at Canton demanded it, but the British Parliament was deeply divided. Free traders embraced the Canton merchants' argument that they had no influence on Chinese laws, tastes, and customs and bore no responsibility "for the dark side of China's foreign trade." Yet the opponents of this position were as strong and determined in Parliament as those who favored military intervention. Religious groups, temperance societies, and others, including the *Times* (London), opposed the war and favored ending the opium trade. Parliament carried the motion to go to war by a narrow vote of 271 to 262.

The Opium Wars signified a turning point in Europe's relations with China and China's attitude to the west. The European view of China had been ambivalent at the beginning of the nineteenth century. Some thinkers, like Voltaire, admired the Chinese, but a more negative view of China, stressing its despotism and cultural stagnation, also had its advocates. The British military defeat of the Chinese state and the further opening of China to western influences heightened this negative view of Chinese culture. In a similar vein, Chinese people saw the Opium Wars increase the taxation burdens on the peasantry exponentially, leading to a series of rebellions in the second half of the nineteenth century. (One of these, the Taiping Rebellion, is discussed in Chapter 16.) The Opium Wars also became a festering wound in China's sense of its importance and its superiority over outsiders. It continued to fester in Chinese consciousness, inspiring anti-European nationalism and fear and hatred of the west.

Trade in Canton. In this painting, we can see the hongs, the buildings that made up the factories, or establishments, where foreign merchants conducted their business in Canton. From the mid-eighteenth century to 1842, Canton was the only Chinese port open to European trade.

FORCING MORE TRADE The Qing ruling elite capitulated to European pressure, and with the 1842 Treaty of Nanjing, the British acquired the island of Hong Kong and the right to trade in five treaty ports. They also forced the Chinese to repay their costs for the war. Subsequent treaties guaranteed that the British and other foreign nationals would be tried in their own courts for crimes, rather than in Chinese courts, and would be exempt from Chinese law. Moreover, the British insisted that any privileges granted through treaties with other parties would also apply to them. Other western nations followed the British example in demanding the same right, and the arrangement thus guaranteed all Europeans and North Americans a privileged position in China.

Still, China did not become a formal colony. To the contrary, in the mid-nineteenth century, Europeans and North Americans were trading only on its outskirts. Most Chinese did not encounter the Europeans. Daily life for most people went on as it had before the Opium Wars. Only the political leaders and urban dwellers were beginning to feel the foreign presence and wondering what steps China might take to acquire European technologies, goods, and learning.

Conclusion

During the period 1750–1850, changes in politics, commerce, industry, and technology reverberated throughout the Atlantic world and, to varying degrees, elsewhere around the globe. By 1850, the world was more integrated economically, with Europe increasingly at the center.

In the Americas, colonial ties broke apart. In France, the people toppled the monarchy. Dissidents threatened the same in Russia. Such upheavals introduced a new public vocabulary—the language of the nation—and made the idea of revolution empowering. In the Americas and parts of Europe, nation-states took shape around redefined hierarchies of class, gender, and color. Britain and France emerged from the political crises of the late eighteenth century determined to expand their borders. Their drive forced older empires such as Russia and the Ottoman state to make reforms.

As commerce and industrialization transformed economic and political power, European governments compelled others (including Egypt, India, and China) to expand their trade with European merchants. Ultimately, such countries had to participate in a European-centered economy as exporters of raw materials and importers of European manufactures. Trade underlay much of the fundamental political reordering of this period. For North and South American colonists, having the right to trade freely in every market of the world intensified their demands for political freedom. The British fought a war with the Chinese to keep their ports open to all trade goods, including opium. European statesmen joined together to stymie Muhammad Ali's conquest of the Ottoman Empire in part because of their desire to keep eastern Mediterranean markets available to their merchants.

By the 1850s, many of the world's peoples became more industrious, producing less for themselves and more for distant markets. Through changes in manufacturing, some areas of the world also made more goods than ever before. With its emphasis on free trade, Europe began to force open new markets—even to the point of colonizing them. Gold and silver now flowed out of China and India to pay for European-dominated products like opium and textiles.

However, global reordering did not mean that Europe's rulers had uncontested control over other people or that the institutions and cultures of Asia and Africa ceased to be dynamic. Some countries became dependent on Europe commercially; others became colonies. China escaped colonial rule but was forced into unfavorable trade relations with the Europeans. Across the world, as the next chapter will illustrate, the rise of European power intensified pressure on Indigenous people as part of a global land grab—and inspired a global tide of resistance among workers, peasants, and Indigenous peoples in pursuit of alternative world orderings. In sum, dramatic changes combined to unsettle systems of rulership and to alter the economic and military balance between western Europe and the rest of the world.

After You Read This Chapter

TRACING THE GLOBAL STORYLINES

FOCUS ON: The Global Impact of the Atlantic and Industrial Revolutions

The Atlantic World

- North American colonists revolt against British rule and establish a nonmonarchical, republican form of government.
- In the wake of the American Revolution, the French citizenry proclaims a new era of liberty, equality, and fraternity and executes opponents of the revolution, notably the king and queen of France.
- Napoleon's French Empire extends many principles of the French Revolution throughout Europe.
- Enslaved and Indigenous peoples adapt revolutionary ideas for their own claims to freedom.
- In the midst of the French Revolution, enslaved Haitians throw off French rule, abolish slavery, and create an independent state.
- Napoleon's invasion of Iberia frees Portuguese and Spanish America from colonial rule.
- The British lead a successful campaign to abolish the Atlantic slave trade and promote new sources of trade with Africa.
- An industrial revolution spreads outward from Britain to a few other parts of the Atlantic world.
- The Russian monarchy strengthens its power through modest reforms and suppression of rebellion.

Africa, India, and Asia

- In Egypt, a military leader, Muhammad Ali, modernizes the country and threatens the political integrity of the Ottoman Empire.
- The British East India Company increasingly dominates the Indian subcontinent.
- The Qing Empire persists despite major European encroachments on its sovereignty.

CHRONOLOGY

The Americas: The American Revolution 1776–1783

Europe: James Watt invents the steam engine 1769

Africa

Ottoman Empire

South Asia

East Asia

1700

1750

KEY TERMS

Muhammad Ali p. 666
Napoleon Bonaparte p. 648
bourgeoisie p. 659
Creole p. 655
East India Company p. 668
free trade (laissez-faire) p. 641
industrial revolution p. 660
Opium Wars p. 671
popular sovereignty p. 640

THINKING ABOUT GLOBAL CONNECTIONS

Thinking about Exchange Networks and Sociopolitical Change How did established dynasties respond to pressures created by increased exchanges of goods, ideas, and peoples? To what degree did established elites respond by forging a partnership with "the people"? Who defined "the people," and on what terms?

Thinking about Changing Power Relationships and Sociopolitical Change What new kinds of political organizations emerged in this period? Where did new political systems take root, and where did established elites resist most successfully? In what ways did enslaved and Indigenous peoples adapt revolutionary ideas for their own claims to freedom?

Thinking about Environmental Impacts and Sociopolitical Change Although new technologies only gradually transformed agriculture—by far the most common economic activity in the world—the spread of more intensive cultivation demanded considerable capital investment. How did the relationship between town and countryside change as a result? How did living conditions change in cities as their populations swelled?

Go to INQUIZITIVE to see what you've learned—and learn what you've missed—with personalized feedback along the way.

The Haitian Revolution 1791–1804
Revolutions in Spanish America 1810–1824
The French Revolution 1789–1799
The Napoleonic Era 1799–1815
Abolition and decline of Atlantic slave trade 1803–1867
Muhammad Ali reigns in Egypt 1805–1848
Tanzimat reforms in Ottoman Empire 1826–1839
British East India Company rules India 1757–1858
Qing territorial expansion eighteenth century
First Opium War 1839–1842
Second Opium War 1856–1860

1800 | 1850 | 1900

Global Themes and Sources

Revolution for Whom?

Although Enlightenment *philosophes* argued that the laws of reason applied to everyone and the American Declaration of Independence declared that all men are created equal, their ideas immediately provoked a wide range of opposition during the political reordering of the Age of Revolution. In Europe and the United States, women and the enslaved protested their exclusion, while elite men in territories occupied by western colonizers pointed to the hypocrisy of the occupiers' egalitarian rhetoric. In different ways, they all probed the central, often hidden, assumptions of European elites about hierarchy and difference.

Two of the documents were written in wealthy corners of western Europe and the United States; one was written in Egypt, then occupied by the French army; and one was written in newly independent Haiti, recently liberated from French control. One of the texts was written by a woman; the remaining three were written by men. All four were written by elites upset at their exclusion. Collectively, they highlight tensions and divisions within Europe as well as between Europeans and others. Making sense of them requires grappling with the degree to which people around the world accepted or rejected the basic premises of Enlightenment thinkers.

The sources invite you to think comparatively about the various ways that men and women viewed the same parts of the Enlightenment tradition. They also challenge you to think about whether critiques written outside Europe were similar to those from within, and which ideas resonated most deeply and why.

ANALYZING COMPARATIVE VIEWPOINTS ON REVOLUTIONS

Analyze the role of Enlightenment ideas. Do these documents challenge those ideas or seek to apply them more fully? Do they reject the Enlightenment tradition or contend that its values have not been fully realized? Which document is the most critical? Which is the least critical?

Compare the documents written in Europe and the United States to those written in Egypt and Haiti.

Evaluate the degree to which these documents make universal arguments and the degree to which their claims are rooted in local traditions, communities, and beliefs.

PRIMARY SOURCE 15.1

On the Rights of Women (1792), Mary Wollstonecraft

One of the founding figures of modern feminism, Mary Wollstonecraft was born in London in 1759. Her *Vindication of the Rights of Woman* (1792), written in the midst of the French Revolution, took aim at notions of women as helpless, emotional adornments, dependent by their nature on men.

Identify the limits Wollstonecraft places on women's participation in politics. What role does reason play in setting those limits?

Explain what Wollstonecraft means by *virtue*.

Explain the comparison Wollstonecraft draws between male superiority and the divine right of kings.

Surely there can be but one rule of right, if morality has an eternal foundation, and whoever sacrifices virtue, strictly so called, to present convenience, or whose duty it is to act in such a manner, lives only for the passing day, and cannot be an accountable creature.

The poet then should have dropped his sneer when he says,

If weak women go astray,
The stars are more in fault than they.

For that they are bound by the adamantine chain of destiny is most certain, if it be proved that they are never to exercise their own reason, never to be independent, never to rise above opinion, or to feel the dignity of a rational will that only bows to God, and often forgets that the universe contains any being but itself and the model of perfection to which its ardent gaze is turned, to adore attributes that, softened into virtues, may be imitated in kind, though the degree overwhelms the enraptured mind.

If, I say, for I would not impress by declamation when Reason offers her sober light, if they be really capable of acting like rational creatures, let them not be treated like slaves; or, like the brutes who are dependent on the reason of man, when they associate with him; but cultivate their minds, give them the salutary, sublime curb of principle, and let them attain conscious dignity by feeling themselves only dependent on God. Teach them, in common with man, to submit to necessity, instead of giving, to render them more pleasing, a sex to morals.

Further, should experience prove that they cannot attain the same degree of strength of mind, perseverance, and fortitude, let their virtues be the same in kind, though they may vainly struggle for the same degree; and the superiority of man will be equally clear, if not clearer; and truth, as it is a simple principle, which admits of no modification, would be common to both. Nay, the order of society as it is at present regulated, would not be inverted, for woman would then only have the rank that reason assigned her, and arts could not be practiced to bring the balance even, much less to turn it.

These may be termed Utopian dreams. Thanks to that Being who impressed them on my soul, and gave me sufficient strength of mind to dare to exert my own reason, till, becoming dependent only on him for the support of my virtue, I view, with indignation, the mistaken notions that enslave my sex.

I love man as my fellow; but his sceptre, real or usurped, extends not to me, unless the reason of an individual demands my homage; and even then the submission is to reason, and not to man. In fact, the conduct of an accountable being must be regulated by the operations of its own reason; or on what foundation rests the throne of God?

It appears to me necessary to dwell on these obvious truths, because females have been insulated, as it were; and while they have been stripped of the virtues that should clothe humanity, they have been decked with artificial graces that enable them to exercise a short-lived tyranny. Love, in their bosoms, taking the place of every nobler passion, their sole ambition is to be fair, to raise emotion instead of inspiring respect; and this ignoble desire, like the servility in absolute monarchies, destroys all strength of character. Liberty is the mother of virtue, and if women be, by their very constitution, slaves, and not allowed to breathe the sharp invigorating air of freedom, they must ever languish like exotics, and be reckoned beautiful flaws in nature. Let it also be remembered, that they are the only flaw.

As to the argument respecting the subjection in which the sex has ever been held, it retorts on man. The many have always been enthralled by the few; and monsters, who scarcely have shown any discernment of human excellence, have tyrannized over thousands of their fellow-creatures. Why have men of superior endowments submitted to such degradation? For, is it not universally acknowledged that kings, viewed collectively, have ever been inferior, in abilities and virtue, to the same number of men taken from the common mass of mankind—yet have they not, and are they not still treated with a degree of reverence that is an insult to reason? China is not the only country where a living man has been made a God. *Men* have submitted to superior strength to enjoy with impunity the pleasure of the moment; *women* have only done the same, and therefore till it is proved that the courtier, who servilely resigns the birthright of a man, is not a moral agent, it cannot be demonstrated that woman is essentially inferior to man because she has always been subjugated.

Brutal force has hitherto governed the world, and that the science of politics is in its infancy, is evident from philosophers scrupling to give the knowledge most useful to man that determinate distinction.

I shall not pursue this argument any further than to establish an obvious inference, that as sound politics diffuse liberty, mankind, including woman, will become more wise and virtuous.

Source: Mary Wollstonecraft, *A Vindication of the Rights of Woman*, A Norton Critical Edition, edited by Deidre Shauna Lynch (New York: Norton, 2009), pp. 39–41.

PRIMARY SOURCE 15.2

An Egyptian Reaction to French Occupation (1798), Abd al-Rahman al-Jabarti

In 1798, revolutionary France authorized a military campaign in "the Orient," present-day Syria and Egypt, to protect French trade interests and disrupt British access to India. Napoleon Bonaparte sought to win support for the French invasion by presenting himself as a liberator and invoking the ideals of the French Revolution. Here the Cairo scholar Abd al-Rahman al-Jabarti responds.

Describe the significance of equality in this document.

Identify the criteria al-Jabarti uses to criticize Napoleon and the French.

Analyze the role of religion in this document.

On Monday news arrived that the French had reached Damanhur and Rosetta [in the Nile Delta]. . . . They printed a large proclamation in Arabic, calling on the people to obey them. . . . In this proclamation were inducements, warnings, all manner of wiliness and stipulations. Some copies were sent from the provinces to Cairo and its text is:

In the name of God, the Merciful, the Compassionate. There is no god but God. He has no son nor has He an associate in His Dominion.

On behalf of the French Republic which is based upon the foundation of liberty and equality, General Bonaparte, Commander-in-Chief of the French armies makes known to all the Egyptian people that for a long time the Sanjaqs [its Mamluk rulers] who lorded it over Egypt have treated the French community basely and contemptuously and have persecuted its merchants with all manner of extortion and violence. Therefore the hour of punishment has now come.

Unfortunately, this group of Mamluks . . . have acted corruptly for ages in the fairest land that is to be found upon the face of the globe. However, the Lord of the Universe, the Almighty, has decreed the end of their power.

O ye Egyptians . . . I have not come to you except for the purpose of restoring your rights from the hands of the oppressors and that I more than the Mamluks serve God. . . .

And tell them also that all people are equal in the eyes of God and the only circumstances which distinguish one from the other are reason, virtue, and knowledge. . . . Formerly, in the lands of Egypt there were great cities, and wide canals and extensive commerce and nothing ruined all this but the avarice and the tyranny of the Mamluks.

[Al-Jabarti then challenged the arguments in the French proclamation and portrayed the French as godless invaders, inspired by false ideals.]

Here is an explanation of the incoherent words and vulgar constructions which he put into this miserable letter.

His statement "In the name of God, the Merciful, the Compassionate. There is no god but God. He has no son, nor has He an associate in His Dominion." In mentioning these three sentences there is an indication that the French agree with the three religions [Islam, Judaism, and Christianity], but at the same time they do not agree with them, nor with any religion. They are consistent with the Muslims in stating the formula "In the name of God," in denying that He has a son or an associate. They disagree with the Muslims in not mentioning the two Articles of Faith, in rejecting the mission of Muhammad, and the legal words and deeds, which are necessarily recognized by religion. They agree with the Christians in most of their words and deeds, but disagree with them by not mentioning the Trinity, and denying the mission and furthermore in rejecting their beliefs, killing the priests, and destroying the churches. Then, their statement "On behalf of the French Republic, etc.," that is, this proclamation is sent from their Republic, that means their body politic, because they have no chief or sultan with whom they all agree, like others, whose function is to speak on their behalf. For when they rebelled against their sultan six years ago and killed him, the people agreed unanimously that there was not to be a single ruler but that their state, territories, laws, and administration of their affairs, should be in the hands of the intelligent and wise men among them. They appointed persons chosen by them and made them heads of the army, and below them generals and commanders of thousands, two hundreds, and tens, administrators and advisers, on condition that they were all to be equal and none superior to any other in view of the equality of creation and nature. They made this the foundation and basis of their system. This is the meaning of their statement "based upon the foundation of liberty and equality." Their term "liberty" means that they are not slaves like the Mamluks; "equality" has the aforesaid meaning. Their officials are distinguished by the cleanliness of their garments. They wear emblems on their uniforms and upon their heads. . . .

They follow this rule: great and small, high and low, male and female are all equal. Sometimes they break this rule according to their whims and inclinations or reasoning. Their women do not veil themselves and have no modesty. . . . Whenever a Frenchman has to perform an act of nature he does so where he happens to be, even in full view of people, and he goes away as he is, without washing his private parts after defecation. . . .

His saying "[all people] are equal in the eyes of God" the Almighty is a lie and stupidity. How can this be when God has made some superior to others as is testified by the dwellers in the Heavens and on Earth? . . .

So those people are opposed to both Christians and Muslims, and do not hold fast to any religion. You see that they are materialists, who deny all God's attributes. . . . May God hurry misfortune and punishment upon them, may He strike their tongues with dumbness, may He scatter their hosts, and disperse them.

Source: Abd al-Rahman al-Jabarti, *Al-Jabarti's Chronicle of the First Seven Months of the French Occupation of Egypt*, translated by Shmuel Moreh (Leiden: E. J. Brill, 1975), pp. 39–40, 42–43, 46–47.

PRIMARY SOURCE 15.3

The Haitian Declaration of Independence (1804)

Drafted by Jean-Jacques Dessalines, a formerly enslaved politician who went on to become the first ruler of an independent Haiti, the Haitian Declaration of Independence was issued on January 1, 1804, in the port city of Gonaïves. The Declaration marked the end of the thirteen-year-long Haitian Revolution—the only successful revolution of the enslaved in history—and established Haiti's independence from France. Haiti was the first independent nation of Latin America and only the second in the Americas, after the United States.

Identify the terms the Declaration uses to describe the French.

How does the Declaration distinguish Haitians from the French? Do you think race is a factor?

How does the Declaration explain Haiti's (temporary) defeat by the French army?

Citizens:

It is not enough to have expelled the barbarians who have bloodied our land for two centuries; it is not enough to have restrained those ever-evolving factions that one after another mocked the specter of liberty that France dangled before you. We must, with one last act of national authority, forever assure the empire of liberty in the country of our birth; we must take any hope of re-enslaving us away from the inhuman government that for so long kept us in the most humiliating torpor. In the end we must live independent or die.

Independence or death . . . let these sacred words unite us and be the signal of battle and of our reunion.

Citizens, my countrymen, on this solemn day I have brought together those courageous soldiers who, as liberty lay dying, spilled their blood to save it; these generals who have guided your efforts against tyranny have not yet done enough for your happiness; the French name still haunts our land.

Everything revives the memories of the cruelties of this barbarous people: our laws, our habits, our towns, everything still carries the stamp of the French. Indeed! There are still French in our island, and you believe yourself free and independent of that Republic, which, it is true, has fought all the nations, but which has never defeated those who wanted to be free.

What! Victims of our [own] credulity and indulgence for 14 years; defeated not by French armies, but by the pathetic eloquence of their agents' proclamations; when will we tire of breathing the air that they breathe? What do we have in common with this nation of executioners? The difference between its cruelty and our patient moderation, its color and ours, the great seas that separate us, our avenging climate, all tell us plainly that they are not our brothers, that they never will be, and that if they find refuge among us, they will plot again to trouble and divide us.

Native citizens, men, women, girls, and children, let your gaze extend on all parts of this island: look there for your spouses, your husbands, your brothers, your sisters. Indeed! Look there for your children, your suckling infants, what have they become? . . . I shudder to say it . . . the prey of these vultures.

Instead of these dear victims, your alarmed gaze will see only their assassins, these tigers still dripping with their blood, whose terrible presence indicts your lack of feeling and your guilty slowness in avenging them. What are you waiting for before appeasing their spirits? Remember that you had wanted your remains to rest next to those of your fathers, after you defeated tyranny; will you descend into their tombs without having avenged them? No! Their bones would reject yours.

And you, precious men, intrepid generals, who, without concern for your own pain, have revived liberty by shedding all your blood, know that you have done nothing if you do not give the nations a terrible, but just example of the vengeance that must be wrought by a people proud to have recovered its liberty and jealous to maintain it, let us frighten all those who would dare try to take it from us again; let us begin with the French. Let them tremble when they approach our coast, if not from the memory of those cruelties they perpetrated here, then from the terrible resolution that we will have made to put to death anyone born French whose profane foot soils the land of liberty.

We have dared to be free, let us be thus by ourselves and for ourselves. Let us imitate the grown child: his own weight breaks the boundary that has become an obstacle to him. What people fought for us? What people wanted to gather the fruits of our labor? And what dishonorable absurdity to conquer in order to be enslaved. Enslaved? . . . Let us leave this description for the French; they have conquered but are no longer free.

Let us walk down another path; let us imitate those people who, extending their concern into the future, and dreading to leave an example of cowardice for posterity, preferred to be exterminated rather than lose their place as one of the world's free peoples.

Let us ensure, however, that a missionary spirit does not destroy our work; let us allow our neighbors to breathe in peace; may they live quietly under the laws that they have made for themselves, and let us not, as revolutionary firebrands, declare ourselves the lawgivers of the Caribbean, nor let our glory consist in troubling the peace of the neighboring islands. Unlike that which we inhabit, theirs has not been drenched in the innocent blood of its inhabitants; they have no vengeance to claim from the authority that protects them.

Fortunate to have never known the ideals that have destroyed us, they can only have good wishes for our prosperity.

Peace to our neighbors; but let this be our cry: "Anathema to the French name! Eternal hatred of France!"

Natives of Haiti! My happy fate was to be one day the sentinel who would watch over the idol to which you sacrifice; I have watched, sometimes fighting alone, and if I have been so fortunate as to return to your hands the sacred trust you confided to me, know that it is now your task to preserve it. In fighting for your liberty, I was working for my own happiness. Before consolidating it with laws that will guarantee your free individuality, your leaders, who I have assembled here, and I, owe you the final proof of our devotion. . . .

Swear, finally, to pursue forever the traitors and enemies of your independence.

Source: Laurent Dubois and John D. Garrigus, *Slave Revolution in the Caribbean, 1789–1804: A Brief History with Documents* (Boston: Bedford/St. Martins, 2006), pp. 188–91.

PRIMARY SOURCE 15.4

"What to the Slave Is the Fourth of July?" (1852), Frederick Douglass

Frederick Douglass spent the first twenty years of his life enslaved, before becoming a leading abolitionist. In this public lecture, delivered on July 5, 1852, to the Ladies' Anti-Slavery Society in Rochester, New York, Douglass contrasts the freedoms and natural rights championed in the Declaration of Independence and celebrated on the Fourth of July with the substantial lack of freedom endured by enslaved African Americans.

- Analyze Douglass's use of the term *citizens*. What is the significance of citizenship?
- Analyze the role of patriotism in this document. Is this a patriotic speech?
- Explain the significance of capital punishment in this document.

Fellow-Citizens—pardon me, and allow me to ask, why am I called upon to speak here today? What have I, or those I represent, to do with your national independence? Are the great principles of political freedom and of natural justice, embodied in that Declaration of Independence, extended to us? and am I, therefore, called upon to bring our humble offering to the national altar, and to confess the benefits, and express devout gratitude for the blessings, resulting from your independence to us? . . .

But, such is not the state of the case. I say it with a sad sense of the disparity between us. I am not included within the pale of this glorious anniversary! Your high independence only reveals the immeasurable distance between us. The blessings in which you this day rejoice, are not enjoyed in common. The rich inheritance of justice, liberty, prosperity, and independence, bequeathed by your fathers, is shared by you, not by me. The sunlight that brought life and healing to you, has brought stripes and death to me. This Fourth of July is *yours*, not *mine*. *You* may rejoice, *I* must mourn. To drag a man in fetters into the grand illuminated temple of liberty, and call upon him to join you in joyous anthems, were inhuman mockery and sacrilegious irony. Do you mean, citizens, to mock me, by asking me to speak today? If so, there is a parallel to your conduct. And let me warn you that it is dangerous to copy the example of a nation whose crimes, lowering up to heaven, were thrown down by the breath of the Almighty, burying that nation in irrecoverable ruin! I can to-day take up the plaintive lament of a peeled and woe-smitten people! . . .

Fellow-citizens; above your national, tumultuous joy, I hear the mournful wail of millions! whose chains, heavy and grievous yesterday, are, to-day, rendered more intolerable by the jubilee shouts that reach them. If I do forget, if I do not faithfully remember those bleeding children of sorrow this day, "may my right hand forget her cunning, and may my tongue cleave to the roof of my mouth!" To forget them, to pass lightly over their wrongs, and to chime in with the popular theme, would be treason most scandalous and shocking, and would make me a reproach before God and the world. My subject, then fellow-citizens, is AMERICAN SLAVERY. I shall see, this day, and its popular characteristics, from the slave's point of view. Standing, there, identified with the American bondman, making his wrongs mine, I do not hesitate to declare, with all my soul, that the character and conduct of this nation never looked blacker to me than on this 4th of July! Whether we turn to the declarations of the past, or to the professions of the present, the conduct of the nation seems equally hideous and revolting. America is false to the past, false to the present, and solemnly binds herself to be false to the future. Standing with God and the crushed and bleeding slave on this occasion, I will, in the name of humanity which is outraged, in the name of liberty which is fettered, in the name of the constitution and the Bible, which are disregarded and trampled upon, dare to call in question and to denounce, with all the emphasis I can command, everything that serves to perpetuate slavery—the great sin and shame of America! "I will not equivocate; I will not excuse"; I will use the severest language I can command; and yet not one word shall escape me that any man, whose judgment is not blinded by prejudice, or who is not at heart a slaveholder [enslaver], shall not confess to be right and just. . . .

Must I undertake to prove that the slave is a man? That point is conceded already. Nobody doubts it. The slaveholders themselves acknowledge it in the enactment of laws for their government. They acknowledge it when they punish disobedience on the part of the slave. There are seventy-two crimes in the state of Virginia, which, if committed by a black man (no matter how ignorant he be) subject him to the punishment of death; while only two of these same crimes will subject a white man to the like punishment. What is this but the acknowledgment that the slave is a moral, intellectual, and responsible being. The manhood of the slave is conceded. It is admitted in the fact that southern statute books are covered with enactments forbidding, under severe fines and penalties, the teaching of the slave to read or write. When you can point to any such laws, in reference to the beasts of the field, then I may consent to argue the manhood of the slave. When the dogs in your streets, when the fowls of the air, when the cattle on your hills, when the fish of the sea, and the reptiles that crawl, shall be unable to distinguish the slave from a brute, then will I argue with you that the slave is a man!

Source: Frederick Douglass, *Narrative of the Life of Frederick Douglass, an American Slave, Written by Himself*, A Norton Critical Edition, edited by William L. Andrews and William S. McFeely (New York: Norton, 1997), pp. 123–25.

Interpreting Visual Evidence

Framing the Subject

Important currents of Enlightenment thought (which fed into classical liberalism in the nineteenth century—see Chapter 16) stressed the autonomy of the individual. All men were thought to be created equal, endowed with reason and the ability to master nature and the world around them. European liberals celebrated individual initiative, self-control, and material success through hard work as signs of virtue. They also drew from the Enlightenment a faith that the natural world follows observable laws. This faith gave rise, as we have seen, to advances in the natural sciences and then the social sciences. In the arts, that faith corresponded to a renewed interest in representing the external world in precise, objective terms, called realism. Painters sought to capture and reflect an independent, external, stable reality—this in a period before photography. It was a confident but also a self-centered view of the world.

Here we consider efforts to represent the individual in portraiture. Jean-Auguste-Dominique Ingres painted the French newspaper baron and businessman Louis-François Bertin, in a portrait from 1832. Bertin's *Journal des Débats* served as the recognized organ of the opposition to the Bourbon Restoration in early nineteenth-century France and helped put the constitutional July Monarchy in power. The painter Édouard Manet described Bertin as "the Buddha of the self-satisfied, well-to-do, triumphant bourgeoisie." Unlike Ingres, who painted a real historical figure, Jean-Léon Gérôme, in *Bashi-Bazouk* (1868–69), painted a model dressed in garments made of textiles he had acquired on a trip to the Near East, to represent the unpaid, irregular mercenary soldiers who lived from plunder and fought in Ottoman armies. Gérôme conceived and executed this painting of an Ottoman soldier in a European studio. In the *Portrait of an Indian*, French artist Anne-Louis Girodet-Trioson painted a man in Ottoman clothing. Finally, the *Portrait of the Imperial Bodyguard Zhanyinbao* was probably sketched by a (European) Jesuit artist in the Chinese court and then transferred to a silk scroll by a Chinese master.

Ingres, Louis-François Bertin.

Gérôme, Bashi-Bazouk.

QUESTIONS FOR ANALYSIS

1. Create a psychological profile for each portrait. What clues does the artist give you about the men, their values, and their standing in the world?
2. What is the effect of the sparse backgrounds and the intricate detail in the foregrounds? What do you think the artists left out of these portraits that might influence your profiles?
3. Do the painters create coherent images of their subjects? What contradictions can you see—for example, between violent aggression and delicate refinement, or between order and disorder—with respect to discipline and control?
4. Compare the two "Orientalist" paintings—the *Portrait of an Indian* and *Bashi-Bazouk*—with the other two. What does Orientalist mean in this context? How, in particular, do they differ from the *Portrait of the Imperial Bodyguard Zhanyinbao*?

Girodet-Trioson, *Portrait of an Indian.*

Portrait of the Imperial Bodyguard Zhanyinbao.

Before You Read This Chapter

GLOBAL STORYLINES

Global Challenges to Western Expansion

- Protest movements challenge the nineteenth-century order based on industrial capitalism, the nation-state, and colonization.
- Led by prophets, political radicals, and common people, the movements arise among marginal groups and regions and express visions of an ideal, utopian future.
- The movements differ markedly, depending on the local circumstances of the global forces of change.
- Although most movements are defeated, they give voice to the views of peasants and workers and have a lasting effect on the policies of ruling elites.

CHAPTER OUTLINE

16

Alternative Visions of the Nineteenth Century

FOCUS QUESTIONS

- What alternative visions challenged the ideals of industrial capitalism, colonialism, and nation-states in this period?
- How similar were the utopian goals, immediate outcomes, and long-term influence of rebel movements around the world? How did they differ?
- How did an urge for social justice animate the alternative visions?
- What role did religion play in these alternative social visions?

For centuries, the Chinese state had been marching westward while Russian influence spread eastward to converge on the borderlands of Central Asia. To many of the nomads caught in between, their territories, flocks, and commercial ways came under threat. So did their religion: many were Muslims. In 1862, the Hui (Muslim) peoples across three large Chinese provinces (Shaanxi, Gansu, and Ningxia) rose up against the Qing state. Mullahs ordered followers to hoard as many bamboo poles as possible to equip the impromptu rebels with spears and declared a Holy War. The Hui revolt led to a massive wave of violence, with Hui killing Han Chinese and Han militias lashing back. In all, Northwest China lost a population of some 21 million people due to massacres, famine, and epidemics during the 1862–1877 revolt. Known as the Hui Revolt or the Minorities War, it has been overshadowed by the rebellions in the heartland of China and the Opium Wars against western intruders. The Hui Revolt was notable not just for the ethnic cleansing, but as a sign that the Hui, like many people around the world, resisted being integrated into expanding states and empires;

Hui Revolt. Pictured are pro-Qing dynasty forces with their guns and artillery preparing for battle against Hui rebels (not pictured). The Hui rebels, in comparison, were nomadic peoples defending their Muslim faith and way of life, armed with homemade bamboo spears, who lived in Northwest China during the Hui Revolt (1862–1877).

they wanted to preserve their local and community ways, their systems of common property, their freedom to roam, and their autonomous religions. It took Qing armies years to subdue the rebels, and their campaign ended with the execution of the rebel leaders, the mass castration of their sons, and the female relatives sent as enslaved people for the conquering officers. Survivors fled inwards, many into the fringes of the Russian empire. Neighboring Turkic, Mongol, and neighboring states and khanates, like Kashgaria, seized the opportunity to turn the Chinese frontier into an ongoing chronic problem. Chinese rulers would thereafter reserve special anxiety about religious and ethnic minorities in the territorial fringes of their empire.

The struggles in the outer provinces of China echoed the many prophetic crusades that challenged an emerging nineteenth-century order of laissez-faire capitalism, the nation-state organization, new technologies, and industrial organizations, which combined now aspired to provide the dominant answers to age-old questions of who should govern and what beliefs should prevail. But these answers did not stamp out other views. A diverse assortment of political radicals, charismatic prophets, peasant rebels, and anticolonial insurgents put forward-striking counterproposals to those that capitalists, colonial modernizers, and nation-state builders had developed. The people making these counterproposals were motivated by the impending loss of their existing worlds and were energized by visions of an ideal, utopian future.

This chapter attends to the voices and visions of those who opposed a nineteenth-century world in which capitalism, colonialism, and nation-states held sway. It puts the spotlight on challengers who shared a dislike of global capitalism and European (and North American) colonialism. Beyond that similarity, they differed in significant ways, for the alternatives they proposed reflected the local circumstances in which each of them developed. Although many of the leaders and movements they inspired suffered devastating defeats, like the Hui of northwestern China, the dreams that aroused their fervor did not always die with them. Some of these alternative visions of the nineteenth century endured to propel the great transformations of the twentieth.

Reactions to Social and Political Change

The transformations of the late eighteenth and early nineteenth centuries had upset polities and economies around the globe. In Europe, the tide of political and economic revolutions either swept aside or severely battered the old order. In North America, the newly independent United States began an expansion westward. Territorial growth led to the dispossession of hundreds of Indigenous tribes and the acquisition of nearly half of Mexico by conquest. In Latin America, fledgling nation-states that now replaced the Spanish Empire struggled to control their subject populations. And in Asia and Africa, rulers and common people alike confronted the growing might of western military and industrial power. At stake were issues of how to define and rule territories and what social and cultural visions they would embody. (See Map. 16.1.)

The alternatives to the dominant trends varied considerably. Some rebels and dissidents called for the revitalization of traditional religions, and many reworked religious ideas in order to frame solutions to current social or political problems. Others wanted to strengthen village and communal bonds; still others imagined a society where there was no private property and where people shared goods equally. The actions of these dissenters depended on their local traditions and the degree of contact they had with the effects of industrial capitalism, European colonialism, and centralizing nation-states.

This era of rapid social change, when differing visions of power and justice vied with one another, offers unique opportunities to hear the voices of the lower orders—peasants, workers, women, religious minorities—whose perspectives the elites often ignored or suppressed and whose traditional historiography has been overlooked. While there are few written records that capture the views of the illiterate and the marginalized, we do have traditions of folklore, dreams, rumors, and prophecies. Handed down orally from generation to generation, these resources illuminate the visions of common folk.

The alternative visions that challenged the dominance of colonialism, capitalism, and nation-states differed markedly. In Europe and the Americas, the heartlands of industrial capitalism and the nation-state, radical thinkers dreamed of far-reaching changes. They sought nothing less than an end to private property and a socialist alternative to capitalism. In Africa, the Middle East, and China, regions not yet colonized by Europeans, dynamic religious prophets and charismatic military leaders emerged. Here, men (and sometimes women) revitalized traditional ways, rejuvenated destabilized communities, and reorganized societies in hopes of preventing the spread of unwelcome foreign ideas and institutions. Finally, in South Asia and the Americas, where indigenous groups had come under the domination of Europeans and peoples of European descent, rebellions targeted the authority of the state. Just as Wovoka inspired a revolt against the U.S. government, the Mayas similarly fought to defend their cultural and political autonomy against the power of the Mexican state. So, too, did Indian peasants and old elites join forces in a fierce revolt against their colonial masters in British India.

Prophecy and Revitalization in the Islamic World and Africa

By the end of the eighteenth century, the Islamic world and non-Islamic Africa had reached a crossroads. The Ottomans, Safavids, and Mughals had extended Muslim trading zones, facilitated cross-cultural communication, and promoted common knowledge over vast territories—but now their era of flowering had ended, and political and military declines had begun. Although much of this territory had not been colonized and was only partially involved with European-dominated trading networks, a sense of alarm intensified as Christian Europe's power spread. (See Current Trends in World History: Islam: An Enduring Alternative in Algeria.) In Egypt and the Ottoman Empire, leaders responded by attempting to modernize their states along European lines (see Chapter 15). Farther away from the main trade routes and political centers, however, this sense of alarm also bred religious revitalization movements that sought to recapture the glories of past traditions. Led by prophets who feared that Islam was in trouble, these movements spoke the language of revival and restoration as they sought to establish new, religiously based governments across lands in which Muslims ruled and Islamic law prevailed.

Prophecy also exerted a strong influence in non-Islamic Africa, where long-distance trade and population growth were upending the social order. Just as Muslim clerics and political leaders sought solutions to unsettling changes by rereading Islamic classics, African communities looked to charismatic leaders who drew strength from their peoples' spiritual and magical traditions. Often uniting disparate groups behind their dynamic visions, prophetic leaders and other "big men" gained power because they were able to resolve local crises—mostly caused by drought, a shortage of arable land, or some other issue related to the harsh environment.

Islamic Revitalization

Movements to revitalize Islam took place on the peripheries—in areas that seemed immune from the potentially threatening repercussions of the world economy. Here, religious leaders rejected westernizing influences they felt were encroaching on their authority and way of life. (See Map 16.2.) Instead, revitalization movements looked back to Islamic traditions and modeled their revolts on the life of Muhammad. But even as they looked to the past, they attempted to establish something new: full-scale theocracies. These reformers conceived of the state as the primary instrument of God's will and as the vehicle for purifying Islamic culture.

WAHHABISM One of the most powerful reformist movements arose on the Arabian Peninsula, the birthplace of the Muslim faith. In the Najd region, an area surrounded by mountains and deserts, a religious cleric named Muhammad Ibn Abd al-Wahhab (1703–1792) galvanized the population by attacking what he regarded as lax religious practices. His message found a ready response among local inhabitants who felt threatened by the new commercial activities and fresh intellectual currents swirling around them. Abd al-Wahhab demanded a return to the pure Islam of Muhammad and the early caliphs.

Although Najd was far removed from the currents of the expanding world economy, Abd al-Wahhab himself was not. Having been educated in Iraq, Iran, and the Hijaz (a region on the western end of modern Saudi Arabia, on the Red Sea), he was aware of the dramatic changes taking place around the world and feared that Islam was losing its vitality. No area seemed to have fallen into a more degraded and powerless state than its very birthplace, the Hijaz. Here, he railed against the polytheistic beliefs that had taken hold of the people, complaining that in defiance of Muhammad's tenets men and women were worshipping trees, stones, and tombs and making sacrifices to false images. Abd al-Wahhab's movement stressed the absolute oneness of Allah (hence his followers were called *Muwahhidin*, or Unitarians) and the need for Muslims to go back to what he considered the fundamental beliefs that had prevailed at the beginnings of Islam. He also severely criticized Sufi sects for extolling the lives of saints over the worship of God.

The Global View

MAP 16.1 | Global Challenges to Western Expansion in the Nineteenth Century

During the nineteenth century, a series of rebellions and revitalization movements took place worldwide pushing back against the early waves of western global capitalism.

- According to this map, how many different regions of the world did the nineteenth century rebellions and revitalization movements occur?
- Based on the geographic locations of the rebellions and movements in each area of the world, did they occur in more central or peripheral areas?
- According to the reading, what did these rebellions and movements all share in common?

Current Trends in World History

Islam: An Enduring Alternative in Algeria

Many of the alternative movements featured in this chapter derived their impetus from deeply held religious beliefs. Religion played a role in the Indian mutiny and in the visions that spurred the Taiping rebels. In Muslim locations far from the main currents of western influence, like the Arabian Peninsula and northern Nigeria, religious beliefs generated revivalist movements. But elsewhere they became a political force, and one that developed a palpably anti-European nature as well as the power to endure long beyond the victory of European invaders. World historians like to study political and social movements because they bring into relief the relationship between the colonizer and the colonized and, in the case of these alternative movements, the relationship between peoples living on the peripheries of empires and those living in the center who are part of the ruling elite, including indigenous elites.

This was the case in particular along the old Ottoman periphery, one of the major targets for European colonization. Strikingly, in the first decades of the nineteenth century, in the Ottomans' Balkan domains of Serbia and Greece, Christianity had linked together opponents against the empire. In the decades to follow, as Ottoman power receded, it left behind it Islamic groups who also used religion as the glue that bound together otherwise diverse peoples. The following example highlights the importance of Islam in galvanizing resistance to French imperialism in Algeria. But there are also other examples: in the 1840s and 1850s in the Caucasus Mountains, another Ottoman periphery, Islam linked together Chechen and other groups in opposition to Russian colonization; and in the early twentieth century, Libyans attempted to oppose Italian colonization by rallying behind the green flag of the Prophet. Unquestionably, the more Europeans sought to dominate lands inhabited by Muslims, the more they called forth in reaction Islamic alternatives and a politicized form of Islamic resistance.

In 1830, through a series of mishaps and miscalculations, the French found themselves in possession of the Regency of Algiers, a territory of 60,000 square miles where previously 10,000 Ottoman Turks had ruled over 3 million Arab and Berber tribesmen. The French invasion had been an ill-considered adventure, designed to divert attention from the fact that the backward-looking French king, Charles X, had lost his legitimacy at home. In 1830, Charles was toppled by the so-called July Revolution, but his successor, King Louis Philippe (r. 1830–1848), decided to pursue France's adventure abroad. This was a risky and ultimately costly plan, however, as the French controlled only a few coastal enclaves and the capital city of Algiers; in 1831, the European civilian population was a mere 3,228. Moreover, although the French had driven out the Turks, they had emboldened Arab tribes in the western part of the land to found their own independent state.

In seeking a leader to unite them, the Arab tribes turned to Abd al-Qadir (1808–1883), a charismatic and domineering personality even though only twenty-five years of age. His father, head of the most important Sufi brotherhood in Algeria, had groomed his son to be a leader and had taught him to despise the Ottoman overlords. Abd al-Qadir and his followers had already committed themselves to overthrowing the Ottomans, but once the French arrived, they were even more determined to rid their area of invaders they regarded as infidels who were intent on seizing their lands and imposing their way of life on them. In organizing resistance to the French, Abd al-Qadir relied on his reputation as a holy man and a scholar, rather than as merely the head

As **Wahhabism** swept across the Arabian Peninsula, the movement threatened the Ottomans' hold on the region. Wahhabism gained a powerful political ally in the Najdian House of Saud, a leading family whose followers, inspired by the Wahhabis' religious zeal, undertook a militant religious campaign. They sacked the Shiite shrines of Karbala in southern Iraq, and in 1803 they overran the holy cities of Mecca and Medina, damaging the tombs of the saints. Their assault on the Shiite sites reflected their commitment to Sunni Islam, while their destruction of the tombs of Sufi saints was an attack on the Sufi-inspired popular culture. It also stemmed from a belief that monuments to individuals whose beliefs were distant from the mainstream beliefs of Islam desecrated Islam's two holiest cities. Frightened by the Wahhabi challenge, the Ottoman sultan persuaded the provincial ruler of Egypt to send troops to the Arabian Peninsula to suppress the movement. The Egyptians defeated the Saudis in 1818, but Wahhabism and the House of Saud continued to represent a pure Islamic faith that attracted clerics and common folk throughout the Muslim world.

USMAN DAN FODIO AND THE FULANI In West Africa, Muslim revolts erupted from Senegal to Nigeria in the early nineteenth century, responding in part to increased trade with the outside world and the circulation of religious ideas from across the Sahara Desert. In this region, the Fulani of one of the tribes. In preparation for battle, he called on his soldiers to follow him in a holy war (jihad) against Christian invaders, promising those who joined him in battle that "anyone of you who dies, will die a martyr; those of you who survive will gain glory and live happily." Tribes that might not have fought together did so because they were united by their loyalty to a religious as well as a political leader. Abd al-Qadir succeeded in part because he was a forceful personality, but in part because he stood for Islam, which the native Algerians shared, whatever their kinship ties or loyalties to local leaders.

For fifteen years, Abd al-Qadir's forces held out, surrendering only to a massive French force of 108,000 men in 1847. Although often defeated in pitched battles, Abd al-Qadir used his superior knowledge of the terrain and his ability to wait in ambush for French columns to frustrate the French. The French government was finally compelled to send its most accomplished military man, Marshal Thomas-Robert Bugeaud, and to provide him with one-third of its entire military force to finish the job of "pacifying" Algeria.

The French conquest of Algeria marks one of the bloodiest episodes in the history of those two lands. No fewer than 300,000 Algerians perished during these years. Although the French portrayed Abd al-Qadir as a Muslim fanatic, determined to take his people back to a dark age, their message fell on deaf ears. The Algerians extolled him for resisting the French and later made him an iconic figure of the nationalist movement. One of the first acts carried out by the independent Algerian government in 1962 was to tear down the statue of Marshal Bugeaud and to replace it with one of Abd al-Qadir. The religiously motivated resistance leader had prevailed over the secular political conquerors after all.

Abd al-Qadir in Exile, Damascus, Syria (1862). Having surrendered to a massive French army in December 1847, Abd al-Qadir was imprisoned in France. After the Revolution of 1848, the new French president, Louis-Napoleon Bonaparte (Napoleon's nephew) released Abd al-Qadir and gave him a government pension in return for the latter's promise not to disturb Algeria.

QUESTIONS FOR ANALYSIS

- What impact did Algeria's geographic location have on its role in these revolutionary events?
- How did native Algerians view their former Ottoman rulers compared to French Europeans? What was their ultimate goal?

EXPLORE FURTHER

Brower, Benjamin Claude, *A Desert Named Peace: The Violence of France's Empire in the Algerian Sahara, 1844–1902* (2009).

Clancy-Smith, Julia, *Rebel and Saint: Muslim Notables, Populist Protest, Colonial Encounter (Algeria and Tunisia, 1800–1904)* (1994).

Danziger, Raphael, *Abd al-Qadir: Resistance to the French and Internal Consolidation* (1977).

people were decisive in religious uprisings that sought, like the Wahhabi movement, to re-create a supposedly purer Islamic past. The majority were cattle keepers, practicing a pastoral and nomadic way of life. But some were sedentary, living in settled communities, and people in this group converted to Islam, read the Islamic classics, and communicated with holy men of North Africa, Egypt, and the Arabian Peninsula. They concluded that West African peoples were violating Islamic beliefs and engaging in irreligious practices.

West Africa went through its own revolutions while the industrial revolution and the American and French Revolutions unfolded. But West Africa's upheavals were, to a great extent, reactions to European interventions in West Africa because of the slave trade. The earliest of these West African Muslim reform movements emerged in the 1690s, and such movements steadily occurred throughout the eighteenth century and into the early nineteenth century. The primary agents were the Fulani clerics, who felt their religious beliefs threatened as the European slave trade became more prominent in the interior of West Africa, reaching into the Sahel by the late eighteenth century. What troubled Fulani clerics was not the institution of slavery, which Fulani states practiced themselves, but rather the practice of capturing free-born Muslims and selling them to European enslavers, a violation of Islamic norms. Fulani Muslims believed that the Islam being practiced by the ruling and ruled classes was contrary to the Muslim principles espoused in the days of Muhammad. Although Muslim rulers called themselves emirs and sultans, their critics believed that they were not faithful practitioners of Islam; hence jihads, or holy wars, could be waged against them.

By the end of the eighteenth century, jihads had swept from the Senegal Valley, through the savannah and the Sahel, and up to what is present-day Nigeria. What was by far the most powerful of these jihadist movements flourished in modern-day northern Nigeria. Its leader was a Fulani Muslim cleric, **Usman dan Fodio** (1754–1817), who ultimately created a vast Islamic empire. Dan Fodio's movement had all the trappings of the Islamic revolts of this period. It sought inspiration in the life of Muhammad and demanded a return to early Islamic practices. It attacked false belief and heathenism and urged followers to wage holy war against nonbelievers. Usman dan Fodio's adversaries were the old Hausa rulers (leaders of city-states that had emerged between 1000 and 1200), who, in dan Fodio's view, were not sufficiently faithful to Islamic beliefs and practices. The trigger for proclaiming jihad against Hausa rulers was not the animist religious practices of the Hausa peoples but the capture of Muslim clerics, who were held not for ransom but for sale to Yoruba traders and entry into the Atlantic slave trade. Defying Hausa authorities, dan Fodio withdrew from his original habitation in Konni and established a new community of believers at Gudu, citing the ancient precedent of Muhammad's withdrawal from Mecca to establish a community of true believers at Medina (see Chapter 9). The practice of withdrawal, called *hijra* in Muhammad's time, was yet another of the Prophet's inspirations that religious reformers now invoked.

Dan Fodio was a member of the Qadiriyya, one of many Sufi brotherhoods that had helped spread Islam into West Africa. Sufism, the mystical and popular form of Islam, sought an emotional connection with God through a strict regimen of prayers, fasting, and religious exercises to obtain mystical states. Like Wovoka and Sitting Bull in North America, dan Fodio had visions that led him to challenge the West African ruling classes. In one vision, the founder of the Qadiriyya order instructed him to unsheathe the sword of truth against the enemies of Islam.

Dan Fodio blamed local leaders for what he saw as their failure to respect Islamic law. He won the support of devout Muslims in the area, who agreed that the people were not properly practicing Islam. He also gained the backing of his Fulani tribes and many of the Hausa peasantry, who had suffered under the rule of the Hausa landlord class. The revolt, initiated in 1804, resulted in the overthrow of the Hausa rulers and the creation of a confederation of Islamic emirates, almost all of which were in the hands of the Fulani allies of dan Fodio.

Fulani women of northern Nigeria made critical contributions to the success of the religious revolt. Although dan Fodio and other male leaders of the purification movement expected women to obey the *sharia* (Islamic law), being modest in their dress and their association with men outside the family, they also expected women to support the community's military and religious endeavors. In this effort, they cited women's important role in the first days of Islam. The best known of the Muslim women leaders was Nana Asma'u (1793–1864), daughter of dan Fodio. Fulani women of the upper ranks acquired an Islamic education, and Asma'u was as astute a reader of Islamic texts as any of the learned men in her society. Like other Muslim Fulani devotees, she accompanied the warriors on their campaigns, encamped with them, prepared food for them, bound up their wounds, and provided daily encouragement. According to many accounts, Asma'u inspired the warriors at their most crucial battle, hurling a burning spear into the midst of the enemy army. Her poem "Song of the Circular Journey" celebrates the triumphs of military forces that trekked thousands of miles to bring a reformed Islam to the area. (For another poem by Asma'u, see Global Themes and Sources: Primary Source 16.2.)

Usman dan Fodio considered himself a cleric first and a political and military man second. Although his political leadership was decisive in the revolt's success, thereafter he retired to a life of scholarship and writing. He delegated the political and administrative functions of the new empire to his brother and his son. An enduring decentralized state structure, which became known as the Sokoto caliphate in 1809, developed into a stable empire that helped spread Islam through the region. A century later, the faith of a small minority of people living in northern Nigeria had become the religion of the vast majority.

Charismatic Military Men in Non-Islamic Africa

Non-Islamic Africa saw revolts, new states, and prophetic movements arise from the same combination of factors that influenced the rest of the world—particularly long-distance trade and population increase. Local communities here also looked to religious traditions and, as was so often the case in African history, expected charismatic clan leaders, known as "big men," to provide political leadership.

In southern Africa, early in the nineteenth century, a group of political revolts reordered the political map. Collectively known as the ***Mfecane*** ("the crushing" in Zulu) **movement**, its epicenter was a large tract of land east of the Drakensberg Mountains, an area where growing populations and land resources existed in a precarious balance. (See again Map 16.2.) Compounding this pressure, trade with the Portuguese in Mozambique and with other Europeans at Delagoa Bay and the arrival of British colonists contesting both the earlier Dutch settlers and indigenous African communities disrupted the traditional social order. This set the stage for a political crisis for the northern Nguni (Bantu-speaking) peoples.

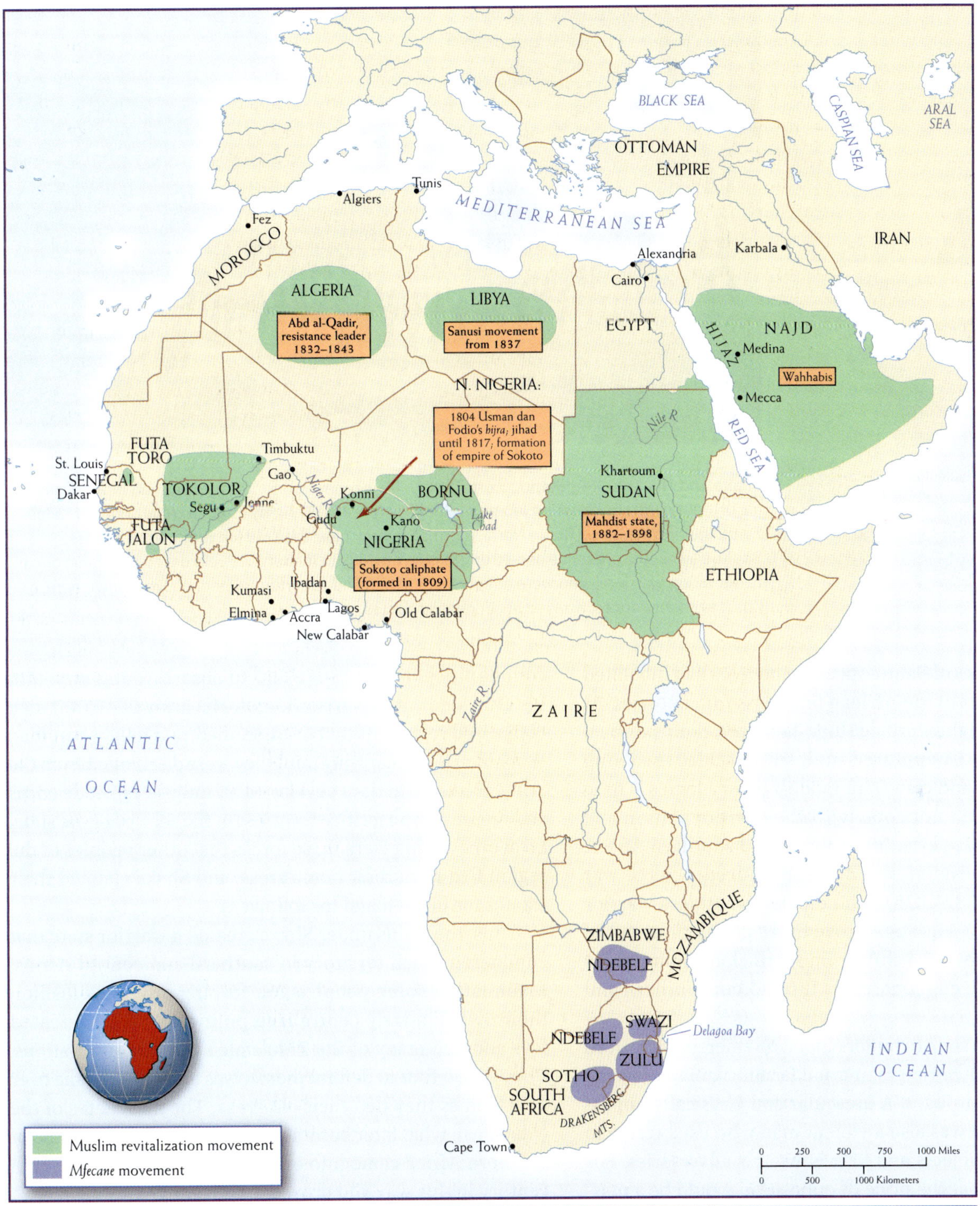

MAP 16.2 | Muslim Revitalization Movements in the Middle East and Africa and the *Mfecane* Movement in Southern Africa

During the nineteenth century, a series of Muslim revitalization movements took place throughout the Middle East and North Africa.

- According to this map, in how many different areas did the revitalization movements occur?
- Based on their geographic location within their larger regions, did these movements occur in central or peripheral areas?
- According to your reading, were any of the same factors that led to Islamic revitalization involved in the *Mfecane* developments in southern Africa?

Shaka and His Zulu Regiments. *Left*: Though he is renowned for his reforms and infamous for his brutality, the only existing image of Shaka is this engraving by English trader Henry Francis Fynn, the first White settler in Natal, a British colony near the Zulu kingdom. Nonetheless, Shaka's awesome presence and strength is as obvious to modern viewers as it would have been to his young warriors, who were deeply loyal to him and superbly trained. *Above*: Shown here, a Zulu regiment dances, arrayed in concentric circles.

Many branches of Bantu-speaking peoples had inhabited the southern part of the African landmass for centuries. At the end of the eighteenth century, however, their political organizations still operated on a small scale, revolving around families and clans and modest chieftaincies. These tiny polities could not cope with the overpopulation and competition for land that now dominated southern Africa. A branch of the Nguni, the Zulus, produced a fierce war leader, Shaka (1787–1828), who created a ruthless warrior state (1818–1828). His state drove other populations out of the region and forced a shift from small clan communities to large, centralized monarchies throughout southern and central Africa.

Shaka was the son of a minor chief who emerged victorious in the struggle for cattle-grazing and farming lands that arose during a severe drought. A muscular and physically imposing figure, Shaka was also a violent man who used terror to intimidate his subjects and to overawe his adversaries. His enemies knew that the price of opposition would be a massacre, even of women and children. Nor was he much kinder to his own people. Following the death of his beloved mother, for example, Shaka executed those who were not properly contrite and did not weep profusely. Reportedly, it took 7,000 lives to assuage his grief.

Shaka built a new state around his own military and organizational skills and the fear that his personal ferocity produced. He drilled his men relentlessly in the use of short stabbing spears and in discipline under pressure. Like the Mongols, he had a remarkable ability to incorporate defeated communities into the state and to absorb young men into his ultra-dedicated warrior forces. His army of 40,000 men comprised regiments that lived, studied, and fought together. Forbidden from marrying until they were discharged from the army, Shaka's warriors developed an intense esprit de corps and regarded no sacrifice too great in the service of the state. So overpowering were these forces that other peoples of the region fled from their home areas, and Shaka claimed their estates for himself and his followers.

Thus, the Zulus under Shaka created a warrior state that conquered much territory in southern and central Africa, assimilating some peoples and forcing others to fashion their own similarly centralized polities. Shaka's defeated foes adopted many of the Zulu state's military innovations. They did so first to defend themselves and then to take over new land as they fled their old areas. The new states of the Ndebele in what later became Zimbabwe and of the Sotho of southern Africa came into existence in the mid-nineteenth century in this way and proved long-lasting.

In turning southern Africa from a region of smaller polities into an area with larger and more powerful ones, Shaka seemed very much a man of the modern, nineteenth-century world. Yet he was, in his own unique way, a familiar kind of African leader, for he shared a charismatic and prophetic style with others who emerged during periods of acute social change. He was, in this sense, one of many big men to seek dominance. His new state built an enduring Zulu community and established its traditions against encroachments by outside European forces.

Prophecy and Rebellion in China

In the mid-nineteenth century, China witnessed an explosive popular rebellion that incorporated Christian beliefs into its long tradition of peasant revolts. Even before 1842, European opium traders had conducted a brisk trade with the Chinese through Canton, the only port open to western commerce. After the Opium Wars, however, westerners forced Qing rulers to open up a number of other ports to trade. To be sure, the dynasty retained authority over almost the whole realm, and western influence remained confined to a small minority of merchants and missionaries. Nevertheless, foreign gunboats and extraterritorial rights reminded the Chinese of the looming power of the west.

As in the Islamic world and other parts of sub-Saharan Africa, population increases in China from 250 million in 1644 to around 450 million by the 1850s—were putting considerable pressure on land and other resources. Moreover, the rising consumption of opium, grown in India and brought to China by English traders, was producing further social instability and financial crisis. As banditry and rebellions spread, the Qing dynasts turned to the gentry to maintain order in the countryside. But as the gentry raised its militia to suppress these troublemakers, it whittled away at the authority of the Qing Manchu rulers.

Searching for an alternative present and future, beginning in 1850 hundreds of thousands of disillusioned peasants joined what became known as the Taiping Rebellion. It put Qing China in a state of civil war for over a decade, costing some 20 to 30 million lives. If one regards the Taiping uprising as a civil war rather than a rebellion, as many scholars now do, it was probably the most lethal civil war of all time, the death toll being thirty times that of the American civil war (Platt, *Autumn*, p. xxiii). The uprising drew on China's long history of peasant revolts. Traditionally, these rebellions ignited within popular religious sects whose visions were egalitarian or **millenarian** (convinced of the imminent coming of a just and ideal society). Moreover, in contrast to orthodox institutions, here women played important roles. Inspired by Daoists, who revered a past golden age before the world was corrupted by human conventions, or by Buddhist sources, these sects threatened the established order. In times of political breakdown, millenarian sects could transform local revolts into large-scale rebellions. Yet the Christian influence on the Taipings and the fact that the uprising was eventually defeated with the help of the British were testaments to the new global context. Qing China and the United States were the two largest international markets for the British. With the U.S. market lost to its civil war, the British felt compelled to intervene in China to protect its interests.

The Dream of Hong Xiuquan

The story of the rebellion begins with a complex dream that inspired its founding prophet, Hong Xiuquan (1814–1864). A native of Guangdong Province in the southernmost part of the country (see Map 16.3), Hong first encountered Christian missionaries in the 1830s. He was then trying, unsuccessfully, to pass the civil service examination, which would have won him entry into the elite and a potential career in the Qing bureaucracy. Disappointed by his poor showing, Hong began to have visions, including a dream in 1837 that led him to form the Society of God Worshippers and the Taiping Heavenly Kingdom.

In this dream, a ceremonial retinue of heavenly guards escorted Hong to heaven. The group included a cock-like figure that he later identified as Leigong, the Duke of Thunder, a familiar figure in Chinese mythology. When Hong reached heaven, his belly was slit open and his internal organs were

The Port of Canton. Before the Opium Wars, Canton (now Guangzhou) was the only Chinese port open to western traders. This image depicts the "factories" or trading stations operated by a number of different countries, including Denmark, Great Britain, Sweden, the United States, and the Netherlands.

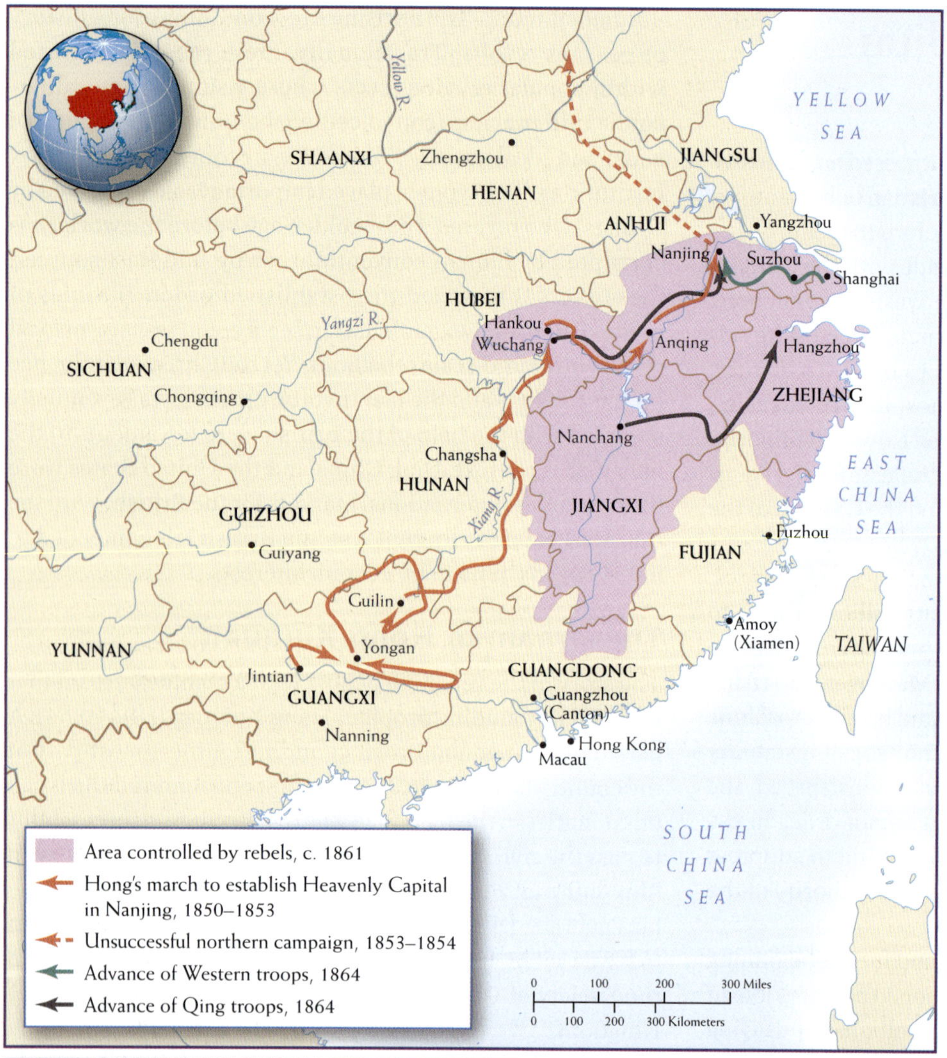

MAP 16.3 | The Taiping Rebellion in China, 1850–1864

The Taiping Rebellion started in the southwestern part of the country. The rebels, however, went on to control much of the lower Yangzi region and part of the coastal area.

- What cities did the rebels' march start and end in?
- Why do you think the Taiping rebels were so successful in southern China and not in northern regions?
- How did western powers react to the Taiping Rebellion? Would they have been as concerned if the rebellion took place farther to the north or west?

replaced with new ones. As the operation for his renewal was completed, heavenly texts were unrolled for him to read. The "Heavenly Mother" then met and thoroughly cleansed him. She addressed him as "Son" before bringing him in front of the "Old Father." Although not part of the heavenly bureaucracy, Confucius and women generals from the Song dynasty were also present. Upon meeting Hong, the "Old Father" complained that human beings had been led astray by demons, as demonstrated by the vanity of their shaven heads (a practice the Manchu Qing regime imposed), their consumption of opium, and other forms of debauchery. The "Old Father" even denounced Confucius, who, after being flogged and begging for mercy before Hong's heavenly "Elder Brother," was allowed to stay in heaven but forbidden to teach again. Still, the world was not yet free of demons. So the "Old Father" instructed Hong to leave his heavenly family behind and return to earth to rescue human beings from demons.

How much of this account has been embellished with hindsight scholars will probably never know. What we do know is that Hong, after failing the civil service exam for the third time, suffered a strange "illness" in which he had visions of combating demons. He also began proclaiming himself the Heavenly King. Relatives and neighbors thought he might have gone mad, but Hong gradually returned to his normal state. In 1843, after failing the exam for the fourth time, Hong immersed himself in a Christian tract titled *Good Words for Exhorting the Age*. Reportedly, reading this tract enabled Hong to realize the full significance of his earlier dream. All the pieces suddenly fell into place. The "Old Father," he concluded, was the Lord Ye-huo-hua (a Chinese rendering of "Jehovah"), the creator of heaven and earth. Accordingly, the cleansing ritual foretold Hong's baptism. The "Elder Brother" was Jesus the Savior, the son of God. He, Hong Xiuquan, was the younger brother of Jesus—God's other son. Just as God had previously sent Jesus to save mankind, Hong thought that God was now sending *him* to rid the world of evil. What was once a dream was now a prophetic vision.

The Rebellion

Unlike earlier sectarian leaders whose plots for rebellion were secret before exploding onto the public arena, Hong chose a more audacious path. Once convinced of his vision, he began to preach his doctrines openly, baptizing converts and destroying Confucian idols and ancestral shrines. Such assaults on the establishment testified to his conviction that he was carrying out God's will. Hong's message of revitalization of a troubled land and restoration of the "Heavenly Kingdom," imagined as a just and egalitarian order, appealed to the subordinate classes caught in the flux of social change. Drawing on a largely rural social base and asserting allegiance to Christianity, the **Taiping** ("Great Peace") **Rebellion** of 1850–1864 claimed to herald a new era of economic and social justice.

Many early followers came from the margins of local society—those whose anger at social and economic dislocations caused by the Opium Wars was directed not at the Europeans but at the Qing government. The Taipings identified the ruling Manchus as the "demons" and as the chief obstacle to realizing God's kingdom on earth. Taiping policies were strict: they prohibited the consumption of alcohol, the smoking of opium, or any indulgence in sensual pleasure. Men and women were segregated for administrative and residential purposes. At the same time, in a drastic departure from dynastic practice, women joined the army in segregated units. These female military units mostly comprised Hakka women. The Hakka are an ethnic subgroup (to which Hong Xiuquan, the founder of the Taipings, belonged) within the Han with a distinct identity. An important part of their culture was that Hakka women did not bind their feet.

There were further challenges to established social and cultural norms. For example, women could serve in the Taiping bureaucracy. Also, examinations now focused on a translated version of the Bible and assorted religious and literary compositions by Hong. Finally, all land was to be divided among the families according to family size, with men and women receiving equal shares. Once each family met its own needs for sustenance, the communities would share the remaining surplus. These were all radical departures from Chinese traditions. But the Taiping opposition to the Manchus did not involve the formation of a modern nation-state. The rebellion remained caught between the modern and the traditional.

By 1850, Hong's movement had amassed a following of over 20,000, giving Qing rulers cause for concern. When they sent troops to arrest Hong and other rebel leaders, Taiping forces repelled them and then took their turmoil beyond the southwestern part of the country. In 1851, Hong declared himself Heavenly King of the "Taiping Heavenly Kingdom" (or "Heavenly Kingdom of Great Peace"). By 1853, the rebels had captured major cities. Upon capturing Nanjing, the Taipings cleansed the city of "demons" by systematically killing all the Manchus they could find—men, women, and children. Then they established their own "heavenly" capital in the city.

Although many missionaries considered the Taiping leader, Hong Xiuquan, to be mad, they and many other European hands in China had a better opinion of his cousin Hong Rengan, who was the second-in-command of the Taiping movement, held the Taiping title of Shield King, and was in charge of the civil service in Nanking, the Taiping capital. They believed Hong Rengan would bring about the westernization and Christianization of China and fully open it to European influences. Hong Rengan had a strikingly different background from Hong Xiuquan. He had spent his early years in Hong Kong, absorbing the teachings of Protestant missionaries. Furthermore, he articulated his vision for China's modernization in a document titled "A New Work for the Aid of Government," expressing his belief that China was no longer the center of the universe and that the British now held that place. He also wrote of his desire for the Chinese to stop calling outsiders

Taiping Rebellion. The tens of thousands who had joined the "Heavenly King" became such a formidable force that they swiftly conquered and settled in many of the cities they encountered. Depicted in this mid-nineteenth-century painting are imperial Chinese troops driving the Taiping rebels from their stronghold in Tientsin.

"barbarians," believing that China could and must benefit from the achievements of the west. Although he regarded the British as the most powerful, he regarded the Americans as "the most righteous and wealthy country of all." The British government's initial neutrality to the Taipings, as well as many missionaries' attraction to the Taiping Rebellion, was owed to the pro-western and pro-Christian perspectives of Hong Rengan.

In the end, the rebellion collapsed. Several factors contributed to the fall of the Heavenly Kingdom: struggles within the leadership, excessively rigid codes of conduct, and the rallying of Manchu and Han elites around the embattled dynasty. Disturbed by the Taipings' repudiation of Confucianism and wanting to protect their property, landowning gentry led militias against the Taipings. Moreover, western governments also eventually opposed the rebellion, claiming that its doctrines represented a perversion of Christianity. Thus did army units led by foreign officers take part in suppressing the rebellion. Hong Xiuquan himself perished as his heavenly capital fell in 1864. With the Qing victory imminent, few of the perhaps 100,000 rebels in Nanjing surrendered. Their slaughter prepared the stage for a determined attempt by imperial bureaucrats and elite intellectuals to rejuvenate the Qing state. Although the Taipings' millenarian vision vanished, the desire to reconstitute Chinese society and government did not. The rebellion, in that sense, continued to inspire reformers as well as future peasant uprisings.

Like their counterparts in the Islamic world and Africa, the Taiping rebels promised to restore lost harmony. Despite all their differences in cultural and historical background, what Muhammad Ibn Abd al-Wahhab, Usman dan Fodio, Shaka, and Hong Xiuquan had in common was the perception that the present world was unjust. Thus, they sought to reorganize their communities—an endeavor that involved confronting established authorities. In this regard, the language of revitalization used by prophets in Islamic areas and China was crucial, for it provided an alternative vocabulary of political and spiritual legitimacy. Although in non-Islamic Africa the impulse was not religious revitalization, it still was an appeal to tradition—to communal solidarity and to the familiar role of "big men" in stateless societies. By mobilizing masses eager to return to an imagined golden age, these prophets and charismatic leaders gave voice to those dispossessed by global change, while producing new, alternative ways of organizing society and politics.

Congress of Vienna. At the Congress of Vienna in 1815, the Austrian prime minister Clemens von Metternich took the lead in drafting a peace settlement that would balance power among the states of Europe.

Socialists and Radicals in Europe

Europe and North America were the core areas of capitalist activity, nation-state building, and colonialism. But there, too, the main currents of thought and activity faced challenges. Prophets of all stripes—political, social, cultural, and religious—voiced antiestablishment values and dreamed of alternative arrangements. Radicals, liberals, utopian socialists, nationalists, abolitionists, and religious mavericks made plans for better worlds to come. They did so in the face of a new era dominated by conservative monarchies. This conservatism was pervasive in central Europe, where reestablished kings and aristocrats revived most of their former power and privileges. (See Map 16.4.) Restoration of the old regimes had occurred at the Congress of Vienna in 1815, at the end of the French Revolution and Napoleon's conquests (see Chapter 15). However, opposition to this arrangement was widespread, and radical voices confidently predicted the coming of a new day.

Restoration and Resistance

The social and political ferment of the efforts to restore the old order, known as the Restoration period (1815–1848), owed a great deal to the ambiguous legacies of the French Revolution and the Napoleonic wars. Kings had been toppled and replaced by republics and then by Napoleon and his relatives; these breaks in traditional forms of rule meant that Restoration-era states had political options to choose from. Most returned to monarchy, leaving many of their citizens deeply dissatisfied and eager for reform of some kind. **Radicalism**—the conviction that real change was only possible by going to the root (in Latin, *radix*) of the problem—spread. There were several key groups of radicals in this period, including surviving Jacobins (see Chapter 15), who were convinced that the revolution had not gone far enough and were devoted to restoring republican governments, even if violent action had to be taken. Other radicals had

MAP 16.4 | Civil Unrest and Revolutions in Europe, 1819–1848

Civil unrest and revolutions swept Europe after the Congress of Vienna established a peace settlement at the end of the French Revolution and Napoleon's conquests. Conservative governments had to fight off liberal rebellions and demands for change.

- How many sites of revolutionary activity can you locate on this map?
- What parts of Europe appear to have been politically stable, and what parts rebellious? Based on your reading and the map, can you explain the stability of some parts of Europe and the instability of others?

become champions of nationalism in places where empires or princely city-states still dominated, such as the Metternich German Confederation and Italy. Yet another group of radicals looked farther back in time for inspiration, to sixteenth- and seventeenth-century religious radicals such as English Puritans and German Anabaptists, who had wanted to sweep away sinful communities and remake society from the ground up. Dubbed "utopian socialists," this group combined older religious fundamentalism with an attack on the evils of the new industrialism; they hoped that by peacefully consenting to a reorganization of the workplace and the home, all of humankind could enjoy happiness on the earth.

The radicals, however, were by no means the only Europeans dissatisfied with the Restoration and eager to revive earlier ideas and models to effect change. The moderate reformers known as liberals sought not to completely overthrow or overhaul Restoration regimes but rather to work within them to establish a greater measure of liberty and equality. Liberals wanted their states to carry through the legal and political reforms envisioned in 1789—but not to attempt economic leveling in the manner of the radical Jacobins. Liberals were eager to curb the states' restrictions on trade, destroy the church's stranglehold on education, and give more people the right to vote—all the while preserving the free market, the Christian churches, and the rule of law. Proponents of **liberalism** insisted on equality under the law and on the individual's right to think, speak, act, and vote as he or she pleased, so long as no harm came to people or property. Liberals feared that powerful states would become corrupt or tyrannical and held that the proper role of government was to foster civil liberties and promote legal equality. Many of them also became proponents of nationalism as opposed to the reinstated privileges of the monarchies.

Self-conscious "reactionaries" also emerged at this time. Their crusade was not just to restore privileges to kings and nobles but also to reverse the religious and democratizing concessions that sovereigns had made during the revolutionary and Napoleonic periods. In Russia, for example, the Slavophiles touted what they regarded as "native" traditions and institutions over the excessively "westernizing" reforms introduced by Peter the Great and continued by his self-styled "enlightened despot" successors. Many Slavophiles were ardent monarchists. Their desire for a strong yet "traditional" Russia brought them into conflict with the conservative but modernizing tsarist state.

In sum, the reactionaries wanted a return to the traditionally ordered societies that existed prior to the French Revolution; the liberals wanted reforms that would limit the power of government and the church and promote the rights of individuals and free trade. For the most part, the reactionaries got their way in eastern, central, and southern Europe; but in Britain, France, and the Low Countries, liberals had greater sway. However, neither group dominated fully, and the rivalry between these two groups continued to define the political landscape until at least the 1840s.

Radical Visions

What did it really mean to be a "radical" in the Restoration era? *Radicals* were men and women who favored the total reconfiguration of the old regime's state system: going to the root of the problem and continuing the revolution, not reversing it or stopping reform. In general, radicals shared a bitter hatred for the status quo and an insistence on popular sovereignty, but beyond this consensus there was much dissension in their ranks. If some radicals demanded the equalization or abolition of private property, others (like Serbian, Greek, Polish, and Italian nationalists) were primarily interested in throwing off the oppressive overlordship of the Ottoman, Russian, and Austrian Empires and creating their own nation-states. It was the radicals' threat of a return to revolution that ultimately reconciled both liberals and reactionaries to preserving the status quo.

NATIONALISTS In the period before 1848, nationalism was a cause dear to liberals and radicals and threatened the conservative balance of power introduced into Europe at the Congress of Vienna in 1815. The age of revolutions had spread the idea of popular sovereignty (see Global Themes and Sources in Chapter 15), but the question remained: Who exactly were "the people"? For radicals who longed for liberation from the multiethnic empires, "the people" encompassed all those who shared a common language and what was thought to be a common history, and each "people" deserved its own state.

Each fledgling nationalist movement—whether Polish, Czech, Greek, Italian, or German—had different contours, but they all drew backers from the liberal aristocracy and the well-educated and commercially active middle classes. University students were especially active in these movements. Most nationalist movements were at first weak and easily crushed, such as attempted Polish uprisings inside tsarist Russia in 1830–1831 and 1863–1864. Unable to win political power, the movements' leaders instead pursued educational and cultural programs to arouse and unite their nation for eventual statehood. The Greeks did manage to wrest independence from the Ottoman Turks—but only because the European powers intervened to help a cause that did not threaten to take territory away from any European state.

Other nationalist movements were suppressed or at least slowed down with little bloodshed. In places such as the German principalities, the Italian states, and the Hungarian parts of the Habsburg Empire, secret societies of young men—students and intellectuals—gathered to plan bright republican futures. Regrettably for these patriots, however, organizations like Young Italy, founded in 1832 to promote national unification and renewal, had little popular or foreign support. Censorship and a few strategic executions suppressed them. Yet many of these movements would ultimately succeed in the century's second half, when conservatives and liberals alike in western Europe employed nationalist fervor to advance their own great power ambitions. However, in central Europe, nationalism pitted many claimants for the same territories against one another, like the Czechs, Serbs, Slovaks, Poles, and Ruthenians (Ukrainians). They did not understand why they could not have a nation-state, too.

SOCIALISTS AND COMMUNISTS Much more threatening to the ruling elite were the radicals who believed that the French Revolution had not gone far enough. They longed for a grander revolution that would sweep away the Restoration's political *and* economic order. Early socialists and communists (the terms were more or less interchangeable at the time) insisted that political reforms offered no effective answer to the more pressing "social question": What was to be done about the inequalities that industrial capitalism was introducing? The socialists worried in particular about two things. One was the growing gap between impoverished workers and newly wealthy employers. The other concern was that the division of labor—that is, the dividing up and simplifying of tasks so that each worker performs most efficiently—might make people into soulless, brainless machines. The socialists believed that the whole free market economy, not just the state, had to be transformed to save the human race from self-destruction. Liberty and equality, they insisted, could not be separated; aristocratic privilege along with capitalism belonged on history's ash heap.

No more than a handful of radical prophets hatched revolutionary plans in the years after 1815, but ordinary workers, artisans, domestic servants, and women employed in textile manufacturing joined them in staging strikes, riots, peasant uprisings, and protest meetings. A few socialists and feminists, such as the English thinker John Stuart Mill and his wife, Harriet Taylor Mill, campaigned for social and political equality of the sexes. In Britain in 1819, Manchester workers at St. Peter's Field demonstrated peacefully for increased representation in Parliament, but panicking guardsmen fired on the crowd, leaving 11 dead and 460 injured in an incident later dubbed the Peterloo Massacre. In 1839 and 1842, nearly half the adult population of Britain signed the People's Charter, which called for universal suffrage for all adult males, the secret ballot, equal electoral districts, and annual parliamentary elections. Like most such endeavors, this mass movement, known as Chartism, ended in defeat. Parliament rejected the charter in 1839, 1842, and 1848.

FOURIER AND UTOPIAN SOCIALISM Despite their many defeats, the radicals kept trying. Some sense of this age of revolutionary aspirations reveals itself in one European visionary who had big grievances and even bigger plans: Charles Fourier (1772–1837). Fourier's **utopian socialism** was perhaps the most visionary and influential of all Restoration-era alternative movements. He introduced planning, whereas the revolutionaries invoked violence, and he generally rejected the equalizing of conditions, fearing the suppression of diversity. Still, he and like-minded socialists dreamed of transforming states, workplaces, and human relations in a much more thorough way than their religious or political predecessors had done.

Fired by the egalitarian hopes and the cataclysmic failings of the French Revolution, Fourier believed himself to be the scientific prophet of the new world to come. He was a highly imaginative, self-taught man who earned his keep in the cloth trade, an occupation that gave him an intense hatred for merchants and intermediaries. Convinced that the division of labor and repressive moral conventions were destroying humankind's natural talents and passions, Fourier concluded that a revolution grander than that of 1789 was needed. But this utopian transformation of economic, social, and political conditions, he thought, could occur through organization, not through bloodshed. Indeed, by 1808, Fourier believed that the thoroughly corrupt world was on the brink of giving way to a new and harmonious age, of which he was the oracle.

First formulated in 1808, his "system" envisioned the reorganization of human communities into what he called phalanxes. In these harmonious collectives of 1,500 to 1,600 people and 810 personality types, diversity would be preserved but efficiency maintained; best of all, work would become enjoyable. All members of the phalanx, rich and poor, would work, though not necessarily at the same tasks. All would work in short spurts of no more than 2 hours, so as to make labor more interesting and sleep, idleness, and overindulgence less attractive. A typical rich man's day would begin at 3:30 A.M. for eating breakfast, reviewing the previous day, and participating in an industrial parade. At 5:30 he would hunt; at 7:00 he would turn to fishing. At 8:00 he would have lunch

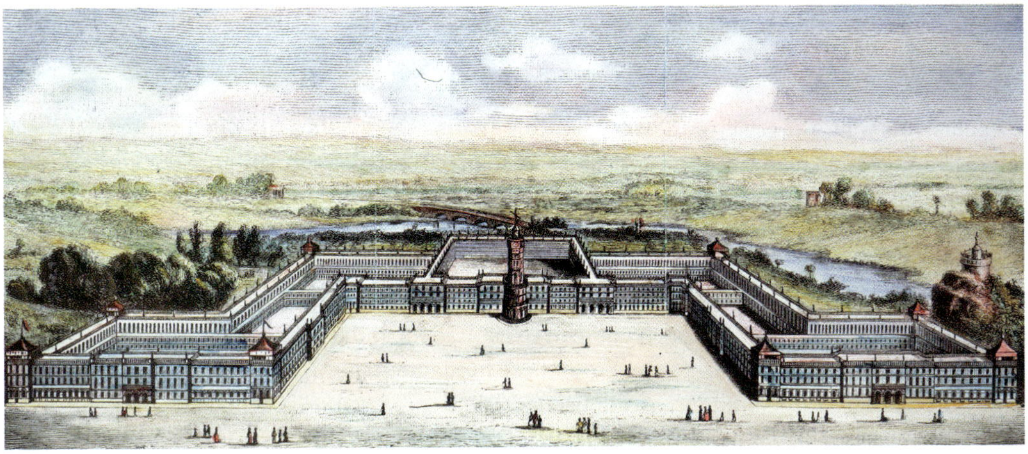

The Phalanx. The phalanx, as one of Fourier's German followers envisioned it. In this rendering, the idealized home for the residents of the cooperative social system is represented as a building architecturally similar to the home of the French kings, the Louvre.

and read the newspapers (though what news there might be in this world is hard to fathom). At 9:00 he would meet with horticulturists, and at 10:00 he would go to Mass. At 10:30 he would meet with a pheasant breeder; later he would tend exotic plants, herd sheep, and attend a concert. Each man would cultivate what he wanted to eat and learn about what he wanted to know. As for unpleasant tasks, they would become less so because they would now occur in more comfortable settings, such as warmed barns and spotless factories. Truly undesirable jobs, like sweeping out stables or cleaning latrines, would fall to young adolescents, who, Fourier argued, actually liked mucking about in filth.

Fourier's phalanx by no means constituted an Eden in which humankind lived without knowing what it was like to sweat; rather, it was a workers' paradise in which comforts and rewards made working enjoyable. However, this system of production and distribution would run without merchants. Fourier intentionally excluded intermediaries like himself from his plan for paradise. He believed that they corrupted civilization and introduced unnaturalness into the division of labor.

Fourier's writings gained popularity in the 1830s, appealing to radicals who supported a variety of causes. In France, women were particularly active in spreading his ideas. Longing for social and moral reforms that would address problems such as prostitution, poverty, illegitimacy, and the exploitation of workers (including women and children), some women saw in Fourierism a higher form of Christian communalism. By reshaping the phalanx to accommodate monogamous families and Christian values, women helped make his work more respectable to middle-class readers. In Russia, Fourier's works fired the imaginations of the young writer Fyodor Dostoyevsky. He and fourteen others in the radical circle to which he belonged were sentenced to death for their views (though their executions were called off at the last minute). In 1835–1836, both the young Italian nationalist Giuseppe Mazzini and the Spanish republican Joaquín Abreu published important articles on Fourier's thought. The German thinker Karl Marx (1818–1883) read Fourier with great care, and there are many remnants of utopian thought in his work. In *The German Ideology,* Marx describes life in an ideal communist society; in a postrevolutionary world, he predicts that "nobody has one exclusive sphere of activity but each can become accomplished in any branch he wishes, society regulates the general production and thus makes it possible for me to do one thing today and another tomorrow, to hunt in the morning, fish in the afternoon, rear cattle in the evening, [and] criticize after dinner."

MARXISM Karl Marx fell in love with philosophy at university, but in the Restoration era his socially radical and atheistic views prevented him from getting a job. To support

Karl Marx. The author (with Friedrich Engels) of *The Communist Manifesto,* Karl Marx argued that the exploitation of wage laborers would trigger a proletarian revolution and would lead to socialism supplanting capitalism.

his family, he took up a career in journalism in the Rhineland region, where he was exposed both to radical French ideas and to the plight of peasants being pushed off common land. Writing about legislative debates over property rights and taxation in Europe and America, he was forced to deal with economics. His understanding of *capitalism*, a term he was instrumental in popularizing, deepened through his collaboration with Friedrich Engels (1820–1895). Engels was a German-born radical who, after observing conditions in the factories owned by his wealthy father in Manchester, England, published a stinging indictment of industrial wage labor titled *The Condition of the Working Class in England* (1843).

Together, Marx and Engels developed what they called "scientific socialism," which they contrasted with the "utopian socialism" of others like Fourier. Scientific socialism was rooted, they argued, in a materialist theory of history: what mattered in history was the production of material goods and the ways in which society was organized into classes of producers and exploiters. History, they claimed, consisted of successive forms of exploitative production and rebellions against them. Capitalist exploitation of the wage worker was only the latest, and worst, version of class conflict, Marx and Engels contended. In industrialized societies, capitalists owned the means of production (the factories and machinery) and exploited the wage workers. Marx and Engels were confident that the clashes between industrial wage workers—or **proletarians**—and capitalists would end in a colossal transformation of human society and would usher in a new world of true liberty, equality, and fraternity. These beliefs constituted the fundamentals of **Marxism**. For Marx and Engels, history inevitably moved through stages: from feudalism to capitalism and then to communism.

From these fundamentals, Marx and Engels issued a comprehensive critique of post-1815 Europe. They identified a whole class of the exploited—the working class. They believed that more and more people would fall into this class as industrialization proceeded and that the masses would not share in the rising prosperity that capitalists monopolized. Marx and Engels predicted that there would be overproduction and underconsumption, which would lead to lower profits for capitalists and, consequently, lower wages or unemployment for workers—which would ultimately spark a proletarian revolution. This revolution would result in a "dictatorship of the proletariat" and the end of private property. With the destruction of capitalism, the men claimed, exploitation would cease and the state would wither away.

After a decade of hardship across Europe known as the hungry forties, in 1848 a series of revolutions shook the Restoration regimes. These were not proletarian revolutions. Modern industry had not developed beyond a few key locations, mostly in northern and western Europe. Instead, the revolutions were cross-class affairs made up of an uneasy coalition of liberal doctors, lawyers, students, urban artisans, wage workers, and social outcasts. As a group, they shared little more than a frustration with the old elites and a desire for an independent nation. But in 1848, that was enough to create a wave of uprisings in France, Austria, Russia, Italy, Hungary, and the German states. After hearing that revolution had broken out in France, Marx and Engels published *The Communist Manifesto,* calling on the workers of all nations to unite in overthrowing capitalism. (See Global Themes and Sources: Primary Source 16.5.) But the men were sorely disappointed (not to mention exiled) by the reactionary crackdowns that followed the 1848 revolutions.

After 1850, Marx and Engels took up permanent residence in England, where they tried to organize an international workers' movement. In the doldrums of the midcentury, they turned to science, but they never abandoned the dream of total social reconfiguration. Nor would their many admirers and heirs. The failure of the 1848 revolutions did not doom prophecy itself or diminish commitment to alternative social landscapes.

Insurgencies Against Colonizing and Centralizing States

Outside Europe, for Indigenous peoples in the Americas and for Britain's colonial subjects in India, the greatest threat to traditional worlds was the colonizing process itself, not industrial capitalism and centralizing states. While European radicals looked back to revolutionary legacies in imagining a transformed society, Indigenous insurgents in the Americas and rebels in British India drew on their traditional cultural and political resources to imagine local alternatives to foreign impositions. Like the peoples of China, Africa, and the Middle East, Indigenous groups in the Americas and India met the period's challenges with prophecy, charismatic leadership, and rebellion. Everywhere the insurgents spoke in languages of the past, but the new worlds they envisioned bore unmistakable marks of the present as well.

Indigenous Prophets in North America

Like other Indigenous peoples threatened by imperial expansion, the Indigenous peoples of North America dreamed of a world in which intrusive colonizers disappeared. Taking such dreams as prophecies, many Indigenous peoples in 1805 in the Ohio Valley flocked to hear the revelations of a Shawnee prophet named Tenskwatawa. Facing a dark present and a darker future, they enthusiastically embraced Tenskwatawa's visions, which (like that of the Paiute prophet Wovoka nearly a century later) foretold how invaders would vanish if Indigenous people returned to their customary ways and traditional rites.

EARLY CALLS FOR RESISTANCE AND A RETURN TO TRADITION Tenskwatawa's visions—and the anticolonial uprising they inspired—drew on a long tradition of visionary leaders. From the first encounters with Europeans, Indigenous seers had periodically encouraged their peoples to purge their worlds of colonial influences and to revitalize their own traditions. Often these prophets had aroused their followers not only to engage in cleansing ceremonies but also to cooperate in violent anticolonial uprisings. In 1608, for example, the Spanish government decided to turn New Mexico into a royal province. Spanish expansion was dramatic and by 1630, there were fifty Catholic churches and monasteries in New Mexico, as well as some 3,000 Spaniards. Roman Catholic missionaries claimed that 86,000 Pueblos had embraced Christianity by the end of the seventeenth century. Resentment among the Indigenous peoples increased as the Spanish invaded their lands and stripped them of their ancestral ways of life. The resentment finally boiled over in 1680, when previously divided Pueblo villagers in New Mexico united behind the prophet Popé to chase Spanish missionaries, soldiers, and settlers out of that colony. After their victory, Popé's followers destroyed all things European: they torched wheat fields and fruit orchards, slaughtered livestock, and ransacked Catholic churches. Hundreds of Spanish settlers and more than twenty priests were reportedly killed while 2,400 survivors were forced to flee. For a dozen years, the Indigenous peoples of New Mexico reclaimed control over their lands, but eventual divisions within their ranks ultimately allowed for Spanish reconquest in 1692.

Seventy years later and half a landmass away, the charismatic oratory of the Delaware shaman Neolin encouraged Indigenous peoples of the Ohio Valley and Great Lakes to take up arms against the British, leading to the capture of several British military posts. Although the British put down the uprising, imperial officials learned a lesson from the conflict: they assumed a less arrogant posture toward Ohio Valley and Great Lakes Indigenous peoples, and to preserve peace, they forbade colonists from trespassing on lands west of the Appalachian Mountains. The British, however, were incapable of restraining the flow of settlers across the mountains, and the problem became much worse for the Indigenous peoples once the American Revolution ended. With the Ohio Valley transferred to the new United States, American settlers crossed the Appalachians and flooded into Kentucky and Tennessee.

Despite the settlers' considerable migration, much of the territory between the Appalachian Mountains and the Mississippi River, which Americans referred to as the "western country," remained the country of Indigenous peoples. North and south of Kentucky and Tennessee, Indigenous warriors more than held their own against American forces. As in previous anticolonial campaigns, the visions of various prophets bolstered the confidence and unity of Indigenous warriors, who twice joined together to rout invading American armies. But their confederation failed in a third encounter, in 1794, and their leaders had to surrender lands in what is now the state of Ohio to the United States. (See Map 16.5.)

TENSKWATAWA: THE SHAWNEE PROPHET The Shawnees, who lost most of their holdings, were among the most bitter—and bitterly divided—of Indigenous peoples living

MAP 16.5 | Indigenous Peoples' Revolts in the United States and Mexico

The new world order of expanding nation-states and industrial markets strongly affected Indigenous peoples in North America.

- According to this map, where did the fiercest resistance to centralizing states and global market pressures occur?
- What regions of the United States were Indigenous peoples forced to leave?
- According to your reading, to what extent, if any, did the Indigenous peoples' alternative visions create or preserve an alternative to the new emerging order?

Visions of Indigenous Unification. *Left*: A portrait of Tenskwatawa, the "Shawnee Prophet," whose visions stirred thousands of Indigenous peoples in the Ohio Valley and Great Lakes to renounce dependence on colonial imports and resist the expansion of the United States. *Right*: A portrait of his brother, Tecumseh, who succeeded in building a significant pan-Indigenous confederation, although it unraveled following his death at the Battle of the Thames in 1813.

in the Ohio Valley. Some Shawnee leaders concluded that their people's survival now required that they cooperate with American officials and Christian missionaries. This strategy, they realized, entailed wrenching changes in Shawnee culture. European reformers, after all, insisted that Indigenous men give up hunting and take up farming, an occupation that the Shawnees and their neighbors had always considered "women's work." Moreover, the Shawnees were pushed to abandon communal traditions in favor of private property rights. Of course, missionaries prodded Indigenous people to quit their "heathen" beliefs and practices and become faithful, "civilized" Christians. For many Shawnees, these demands went too far; worse, they promised no immediate relief from the dispossession and impoverishment that now marked Indigenous daily lives. Young men, especially, grew angry and frustrated.

Among the demoralized Shawnees was **Tenskwatawa** (1775–1836), whose story of overcoming personal failures through religious visions and embracing a strict moral code has uncanny parallels with that of Hong Xiuquan, the Taiping leader. In his first thirty years, Tenskwatawa could claim few accomplishments. He had failed as a hunter and as a medicine man, had blinded himself in one eye, and had earned a reputation as an obnoxious braggart. All this changed in the spring of 1805, however, after he fell into a trance and experienced a vision, which he vividly recounted to one and all. In this dream, Tenskwatawa encountered a heaven where the virtuous enjoyed the traditional Shawnee way of life and a hell where evildoers suffered punishments. Additional revelations followed, and Tenskwatawa soon stitched these together into a new social gospel that urged disciples to abstain from alcohol and return to traditional customs.

Like other prophets, Tenskwatawa exhorted Indigenous peoples to reduce their dependence on European trade goods and to sever their connections to Christian missionaries, even as his own vision of heaven and hell, like Wovoka's and Hong Xiuquan's, borrowed from the messages of those missionaries. Thus, he urged his audiences to replace imported cloth and metal tools with animal skins and implements fashioned from wood, stone, and bone. Livestock, too, was to be banished, as Indigenous men again gathered meat by hunting wild animals with bows and arrows, instead of guns and powder. If Indigenous people obeyed these dictates, Tenskwatawa promised, the deer, which "were half a tree's length under the ground," would come back in abundant numbers to the earth's surface. Likewise, he claimed, Indigenous people killed in conflict with colonial intruders would be resurrected, while evil Americans would depart from the country west of the Appalachians. (See Global Themes and Sources: Primary Source 16.1.)

Like the Qing who encountered Hong's visions, American officials initially dismissed Tenskwatawa as deluded but harmless; their concerns grew, however, as the Shawnee Prophet gathered more followers. These converts came not only from among the Shawnees but also from Delaware, Ottawa, Wyandot, Kickapoo, and Seneca villages. The spread of Tenskwatawa's message raised anew the specter of a pan-Indigenous confederacy. Hoping to undermine the Shawnee Prophet's claims to supernatural power, territorial governor William Henry Harrison challenged Tenskwatawa to make the sun stand still. But Tenskwatawa one-upped Harrison. Having learned of an impending eclipse from White astronomers, Tenskwatawa assembled his followers on June 16, 1806. Right on schedule, and as if on command, the sky darkened. Claiming credit for the eclipse, Tenskwatawa

Indigenous Peoples' Removals after 1815. After the failure of efforts to forge solidarity among Indigenous peoples in the United States, the American government forced many of them to relocate west of the Mississippi. Often these measures were extremely violent, as in the case of the removal of the Cherokee Nation from its southern lands to present-day Oklahoma, an event so traumatic for the Cherokee as to be known afterwards as "The Trail of Tears."

saw his standing soar, as did the ranks of his disciples. Now aware of the growing threat, American officials tried to bribe Tenskwatawa, hoping that cash payments might dim his vision and quiet his voice. Failing that, they wondered if one of the prophet's Indigenous adversaries might be encouraged to assassinate him.

In fact, Tenskwatawa had made plenty of enemies among his fellow Indigenous peoples. His visions, after all, consigned drinkers to hell (where they would be forced to swallow molten metal) and singled out those who cooperated with colonial authorities for punishment in this world and the next. Indeed, Tenskwatawa condemned as witches those Indigenous people who rejected his preaching in favor of the teachings of Christian missionaries and American authorities. (To be sure, Tenskwatawa's damnation of Christianized Indigenous people was somewhat paradoxical, for missionary doctrines obviously influenced his vision of a burning hell for sinners and his crusade against alcohol.)

TECUMSEH AND THE WISH FOR INDIGENOUS PEOPLES' UNITY Although Tenskwatawa's accusations alienated some Indigenous people, his prophecies gave heart to many more. This was particularly the case once his brother, Tecumseh (1768–1813), helped circulate the message of an Indigenous renaissance among Indigenous villages from the Great Lakes to the Gulf Coast. On his journeys after 1805, Tecumseh did more than spread his brother's visions; he also wed them to the idea of a renewed and enlarged Indigenous confederation. Moving around the Great Lakes and traveling across the southern half of the western country, Tecumseh preached the need for Indigenous unity. He repeatedly urged Indigenous people to resist any American attempts to get them to sell more land. In response, thousands of followers renounced their ties to colonial ways and prepared to combat the expansion of the United States.

By 1810, Tecumseh had emerged, at least in the eyes of American officials, as even more dangerous than his brother. Impressed by Tecumseh's charismatic organizational talents, William Harrison warned that this new "Indian menace" was forming "an Empire that would rival in glory" that of the Aztecs and the Incas. In 1811, while Tecumseh was traveling among southern tribes, Harrison had his troops attack Tenskwatawa's village, Prophet's Town, on the Tippecanoe River in what is now the state of Indiana. The resulting battle was evenly fought, but the Indigenous warriors eventually gave ground, and American forces burned Prophet's Town. That defeat discredited Tenskwatawa, who had promised his followers protection from destruction at American hands. Spurned by his former disciples, including his brother, Tenskwatawa fled to Canada.

Tecumseh soldiered on. Although he mistrusted the British, he recognized that only a British victory over the Americans in the War of 1812 could check further American expansion. So he aligned himself with the British. Commissioned as a brigadier general in the British army, Tecumseh recruited many Indigenous warriors to the British cause, though his real aim remained the building of a pan-Indigenous union. But in 1813, with the war's outcome in doubt and the pan-Indigenous confederacy still fragile, Tecumseh perished at the Battle of the Thames, north of Lake Erie.

INDIGENOUS PEOPLES' REMOVALS The discrediting of Tenskwatawa and the death of Tecumseh damaged the cause of Indigenous unity; then British betrayal dealt it a fatal blow. Following the war's end in 1814, the British withdrew their support and left the Indigenous Peoples south of the Great Lakes to fend for themselves against land-hungry American settlers and the armies of the United States. By 1815, American citizens outnumbered Indigenous peoples in the western country by a seven-to-one margin, and this gap dramatically widened in the next few years. Recognizing the hopelessness of military resistance, Indigenous peoples south of the Great Lakes resigned themselves to relocation. During the 1820s, most of the peoples north of the Ohio River were removed to lands west of the Mississippi River. During the 1830s, the southern tribes were cleared out, completing what amounted to an ethnic cleansing of Indigenous peoples from the region between the Appalachians and the Mississippi.

In the midst of these final removals, Tenskwatawa died, though his dream of an alternative to American expansion had faded for his people years earlier. Through the rest of the nineteenth century, however, other Indigenous prophets emerged, and their visions continued to inspire followers with the hope of an alternative to life under the colonial rule of the United States. In the restored world imagined by Indigenous seers, Indigenous peoples maintained control of their homelands, retained traditional gender roles and identities in which men could hunt abundant game, and sustained communal customs at odds with the acquisitive individualism that American reformers, styling themselves "Friends of the Indian," had sought to impose on defeated Indigenous peoples.

The Caste War of Yucatán

As in North America, the creation of expansionist nation-states in Latin America sparked widespread revolts by Indigenous peoples. The difference was that after the secession from Spain and Portugal, Latin America went through decades of political instability. Across the region, rural people seized the opportunity to resist encroachers. The Maya revolt in Yucatán was the most protracted. It started in 1847, and its flames were doused only with the full occupation of Yucatán by Mexican national troops in 1901.

EARLY MAYA AUTONOMY The strength and endurance of the Maya revolt stemmed in large measure from the unusual features of the Spanish conquest in southern Mesoamerica. Because this area was not a repository of precious metals or fertile lands, Spain and its rivals focused their efforts elsewhere—on central and northern Mexico and the Caribbean islands. Cultivation and commerce were much less disruptive to Indigenous lives in Yucatán than elsewhere in the New World.

After Mexico gained independence, it plunged into a series of civil wars, which culminated in the loss of its northern provinces, first Texas and then, in the wake of a disastrous war with the United States, almost half of the rest of its territory from California to New Mexico. For Mayas, this was largely a relief; they could survive without much intrusion from the federal government and its troops. Their villages still constituted the chief political domain, ruled by elders; breaking away from Spain meant that old colonial institutions, notably the Catholic Church, weakened, while new republican ideas could be adapted to village self-government. Ownership of land remained collective, the property of families and not individuals. Even food retained its communal and spiritual significance. Corn, a mere staple to White consumers, continued to enjoy sacred status in Maya culture.

GROWING PRESSURES Mexican independence did not, however, mean blessed autonomy for distant provinces. First, regional elites—mainly White, but often with the support of Mestizo populations—bickered for supremacy so long as the central authority of Mexico City remained weak. Weaponry flowed freely through the peninsula, and some rivals even appealed for Maya support. Second, regional and international trade spurred the spread of sugar estates and commercial farming, which threatened traditional corn cultivation. Over the decades, plantations slowly encroached on Maya properties. Planters used several devices to lure independent Mayas to work, especially in the harvest. The most important device, debt peonage, involved giving small cash advances to Indigenous families, which obligated fathers and sons to work for meager wages to pay off the debts. Back in the village, it fell to women and daughters to till the land and defend collective property. The real threat came from tax collectors. Mexico's costly wars, culminating in a showdown with the United States in 1846, drove tax collectors and army recruiters into villages in search of revenues and soldiers. There they confronted subsistence farmers, many of them women, struggling to hang on.

This was the pressure cooker when General Zachary Taylor invaded Mexico and American warships blockaded Mexican ports. Suddenly, all the internal tensions in Yucatán blew open. Rival political elites took up arms and appealed to the peasantry for support. Peasants, in turn, mobilized into militia, starting as foot soldiers of urban clans—but soon became independent rebel fighting forces that took half a century to subdue. The rebels were primarily free Mayas who had not yet been absorbed into the sugar economy. They wanted to dismantle old definitions of Indigenous peoples as a caste—a status that deprived the Indigenous people of rights to defend their sovereignty on equal legal footing with Whites and that also subjected the Indigenous people to special taxes. Thus, local Maya leaders, like Jacinto Pat and Cecilio Chi, upheld a

Caste War of Yucatán. The conflict in the Yucatán Peninsula came to be called the "Caste War" and came to symbolize Indigenous resistance in Mexico. For twentieth-century muralists like Fernando Castro Pacheco, it became the subject for a public memorial for Indigenous resistance against Mexican elites. This mural, like so many of its kind in Mexico, hangs in the government palace in Mérida, the capital city of the region that was nearly overrun by Maya insurgents in the late 1840s. Note the use of peasant tools, like the machete, as weapons; the muscular posing, angry faces, and fiery coloration of the insurgents; and the huddling, naked, innocents behind the protective arm of the rebel.

republican model of formal equality of all political subjects and devotion to a spiritual order that did not distinguish between Christians and non-Christians. "If the Indians revolt," one Maya rebel explained, "it is because the Whites gave them reason; because the Whites say they do not believe in Jesus Christ, because they have burned the cornfield."

THE "CASTE WAR" Horrified, the local White elites reacted to the uprising with vicious repression and dubbed the ensuing conflict a caste war. In their view, the bloody conflict, which became known as the **Caste War of Yucatán**, was a struggle between forward-looking liberals and backward-looking Indigenous peoples. This narrative helped frighten Whites into a common cause. The irony is that the classification of Mayas as a "caste" was the effect, not the cause, of the war—and the narrative helped justify the repression that ensued.

At first, Whites and Mestizos were no match for the determined peasants, whose forces seized town after town, demolishing as they did so the whipping posts where Indigenous people had endured public humiliation and punishment. By 1848, Indigenous armies controlled three-quarters of the peninsula and were poised to take Yucatán's largest city, Mérida. In a panic, embattled Whites appealed for U.S. and British help, offering the peninsula for foreign annexation in return for military rescue from the Mayas.

In the end, luck helped save Yucatán's Whites. The Maya farmers, who had taken up arms to defend their world, returned to their farms when planting season came, declaring that "the time has come for us to make our planting, for if we do not we shall have no Grace of God to fill the bellies of our children." Like many ordinary people, the farmers were unaware of international changes that had an impact on their situation. In 1848, the Mexican-American War ended with Washington paying the Mexican government $15 million for giving up its northern provinces. The Mexican government plowed the money into a force of 17,000 soldiers to wage a scorched-earth campaign to drive back the depleted Maya forces.

What ensued was a protracted counterinsurgency. Mexican armies set Indigenous villages ablaze. Between 30 and 40 percent of the Maya population perished in the war and its repressive aftermath. The White governor even sold captured Indigenous people into slavery to Cuban sugar planters. Indeed, the White narrative of the caste nature of the war eventually became a self-fulfilling prophecy.

RECLAIMING A MAYA IDENTITY Many poor people tried to keep their heads down and avoid the carnage. But the violence swept up even bystanders. In doing so, it kindled a new kind of Maya identity, one that reflected the Mayas' exclusion from the Mexican republic.

Warfare prompted a spiritual transformation that reinforced the value of a purely Maya identity to counter the Mexican invaders' efforts to create a strong, centralized state. Thus, a struggle that began with demands for legal equality and relative cultural autonomy became a crusade for spiritual salvation and the complete cultural separation of the Maya people. A particularly influential group under José María Barrera retreated to a hamlet called Chan Santa Cruz. There, at the site where he found a cross shape carved into a mahogany tree, Barrera had a vision of a divine encounter. Thereafter, a swath of Yucatán villages refashioned themselves as moral communities orbiting around Chan Santa Cruz. Leaders created a polity, with soldiers, priests, and tax collectors pledging loyalty to the Speaking Cross. As with the followers of Hong Xiuquan in China's Taiping Rebellion, Indigenous rebels forged an alternative religion: it blended Christian rituals, faiths, and icons with Maya legends and beliefs. At the center was a stone temple, Balam Na ("House of God"), 100 feet long and 60 feet wide. Through pious pilgrimages to Balam Na and the secular justice of Indigenous judges, many Mayas soon governed their autonomous domain in Yucatán, almost completely cut off from the rest of Mexico.

Among the fugitives were women. The old Catholic Church had confined them to duties as tenders of altars and as protectors of private domesticity—making women the instruments of piety and subordination. Disenchantment with colonial spiritual authority presented opportunities for women to press for access to schools as a condition to fulfill sacred duties, new and old. One woman teacher in the town of Dzemul, Josefa Ortega, argued that educating "the fairer sex" was key to preserving "civil order."

This alternative to Latin American state formation, however, faced formidable hurdles. For example, disease ravaged the people of the Speaking Cross. Once counting 40,000 inhabitants, the villages dwindled to 10,000 by 1900. Also, a new crop, henequen (also known as sisal), used to bind bales for North American farms and to stuff the seats of automobiles, began to spread across Yucatán. The peninsula that had once supported mixed agrarian societies now became a desiccated region producing a single crop, driving the people to seek refuge farther into the interior. As profits from henequen production rose, White landowners began turning Yucatán into a giant plantation.

Finally, the Mexican oligarchy, having resolved its internal disputes, threw its weight behind the strong-arm ruler General Porfirio Díaz (r. 1876–1911). The general sent one of his veteran commanders, Ignacio Bravo, to do what no other Mexican could accomplish: defeat Chan Santa Cruz and drive Mayas into the henequen cash economy. When General Bravo finally entered the town, he found the once-imposing temple Balam Na covered in vegetation. Nature was reclaiming the territories of the Speaking Cross. Hunger and arms finally drove the Mayas to work on White Mexican plantations; the alternative vision was vanquished.

The Rebellion of 1857 in India

Like the Indigenous peoples of the Americas, the peoples of nineteenth-century India had a long history of opposition to colonial domination. Armed revolts had occurred since the onset of rule by the British East India Company (see Chapter 15). Nonetheless, the uprising of 1857 was unprecedented in its scale, and it posed a greater threat than had any previous rebellion. (See Analyzing Global Developments: Alternative Movements in Asia and Africa.) Though led primarily by the old nobility and petty landlords, it was a popular uprising with strong support from the lower orders of Indian society. The rebels appealed to bonds of local and communal solidarity, invoked religious sentiments, and reimagined traditional hierarchies in egalitarian terms. They did this to pose alternatives to British rule and the deepening involvement of India in a network of capitalist relationships. Karl Marx, with his hope for revolution dashed in Europe, cast his eyes on the revolt in British India, eagerly following the events and commenting on them in daily columns for the *New-York Daily Tribune*.

INDIA UNDER COMPANY RULE When the revolt broke out in 1857, the East India Company's rule in India was a century old. During that time, the company had become an increasingly autocratic power whose reach encompassed the whole region. Mughal rule still existed in name, but the emperor lived in Delhi, all but forgotten and without any effective power. For a while, the existence of several princely states with which the British had entered into alliances prevented the British from exercising complete control over all of India. These princely domains enjoyed a measure of fiscal and judicial authority within the British Empire. They also contained landed aristocrats who held the right to shares in the produce and maintained their own militias.

Believing that the princely powers and landed aristocracies were outdated, the company instituted far-reaching changes in administration in the 1830s and 1840s. The Charter Act of 1833 ended almost all of the East India Company's trading activities. It gave absolute power to the governor-general of India, enabling him to make laws that all the courts had to administer. In addition, it required the East India Company to recruit its officials by merit on the basis of competitive exams. In short, the Charter Act made clear that the East India Company was no longer a commercial enterprise but a governing body. The government dispatched the noted Whig historian and political figure Thomas Macaulay to India. During his three-year stint in the country he was expected "to legislate for a conquered race, to whom the blessings of our constitution cannot as yet be extended. Macaulay produced a comprehensive code of laws that bore no relationship to traditional Indian laws or any legislation that the company had introduced.

These changes infuriated local peoples and laid the foundations for one of the world's most violent and concerted movements of protest against colonial authority. Lord Dalhousie, upon his appointment as governor-general in 1848, immediately began annexing what had been independent princely domains

Analyzing Global Developments

Alternative Movements in Asia and Africa

During the nineteenth century, five uprisings of global significance occurred in Africa and Asia. Two of these were carried out on a massive scale (the Taiping Rebellion and India's Great Rebellion); the other three involved much smaller numbers. The two large-scale uprisings did not last as long as the three movements in sub-Saharan Africa and the Arabian Peninsula and were put down with great loss of life. In contrast, the political and cultural successes of the Wahhabi Revolt in the Arabian Peninsula, Shaka's Zulu state in southern Africa, and the Fulani Revolt in northern Nigeria can be seen clearly even to this day.

QUESTIONS FOR ANALYSIS

- Why were Europeans involved in suppressing the larger-scale uprisings in China and India but not the smaller-scale ones in Africa and the Arabian Peninsula?
- Although all five movements suffered stinging military defeats (the Fulani at the hands of the British in 1900, the Zulu state at the hands of the British in 1878, the Wahhabis at the hands of Egyptian troops at the beginning of the nineteenth century, the Taiping rebels at the hands of the Qing rulers, and the Indian rebels at the hands of British soldiers), were their long-term consequences markedly different?
- What holds these diverse movements together and allows us to represent them as alternatives to the main developments underway in western Europe and North America, the regions that had become dynamic centers of historical change?

Movement/Leader	Short-Term Consequences	Long-Term Consequences
Smaller-Scale Uprisings		
Fulani Revolt, Northern Nigeria (1804–1817)	• Created largest state in sub-Saharan Africa • Occupied two-thirds of present-day Nigeria	• Gained independence in 1960 • Fulani elite families who worked with British now rule over present-day Nigeria
Usman dan Fodio (1754–1817)	• British conquered it in early twentieth century	
Shaka's Zulu state	• Created an army of 40,000 warriors	• British conquered Zulu state in 1878
Shaka (1787–1828)	• Created Zulu state covering 11,500 square miles in southern Africa	• Zulus maintained their identity through apartheid • Population of 11 million today
Wahhabi Revolt, Arabian Peninsula (1744–1818)	• Ruled over much of the Arabian Peninsula	• Created the House of Saud, which rules over Saudi Arabia today
Muhammad Ibn Abd al-Wahhab (1703–1792)	• Defeated by Egyptian army in 1812	• Retains commitment to Wahhab principles today
Larger-Scale Uprisings		
Taiping Rebellion (1850–1864)	• Accrued half a million members	• Rebellion caused 20 million deaths by 1853
Hong Xiuquan (1814–1864)	• Leader Hong and rebels ruled over central and southern China from Nanjing for eleven years	• Nearly toppled Qing dynasty; Mao Zedong viewed it as precursor to peasant-led communist movement; now viewed as threat to social order due to large-scale violence
Indian Rebellion (1857–1858)	• Indian sepoys of East India Company started revolt	• British crown ended company rule after brutally suppressing rebellion
Geographical leaders, no monolithic figure	• Sepoys pledged support to Mughal emperor; revolt included sepoys, peasants, small landholders, and religious leaders across northern India	• Laid the foundation for later Indian populist and nationalist resistance

Sources: William Dalrymple, *The Last Mughal: The Fall of a Dynasty: Delhi, 1857* (2007); Carolyn Hamilton (ed.), *The Mfecane Aftermath: Reconstructive Debates in Southern African History* (1995); Mervyn Hiskett, *The Sword of Truth: The Life and Times of the Shehu Usman dan Fodio* (1994); Jonathan Spence, *God's Chinese Son: The Taiping Heavenly Kingdom of Hong Xiuquan* (1996).

MAP 16.6 | Indian Rebellion of 1857

The Indian Rebellion of 1857 broke out first among the Indian soldiers of the British army. Other groups soon joined the struggle.

- According to this map, how many centers of rebellion were located in British territory and how many in dependent states?
- Why do you think the rebellion occurred in the interior of the subcontinent rather than along the coasts?
- In what way was the East India Company's expansion into formerly autonomous areas during the first half of the nineteenth century a factor in the rebellion?

and stripping native aristocrats of their privileges. Swallowing one princely state after another, the British removed their former allies. The government also decided to collect taxes directly from peasants, displacing the landed nobles as intermediaries. In disarming the landed nobility, the British threw the retainers and militia of the notables into unemployment, and by demanding high taxes from peasants, the British forced them to rely on moneylenders, who could take ownership of land when peasant proprietors failed to pay. Meanwhile, the company transferred judicial authority to an administration that was insulated from the Indian social hierarchy.

The most prized object for annexation was the kingdom of Awadh in northern India. (See Map 16.6.) Founded in 1722 by an Iranian adventurer, it was one of the first successor states to have gained a measure of independence from the Mughal ruler in Delhi. With access to the fertile resources of the Ganges plain, its opulent court in Lucknow was one place where Mughal splendor still survived. In 1765, the company imposed a treaty on Awadh under which the ruler paid an annual tribute for British troops stationed in his territory to "protect" his kingdom from internal and external enemies. The British constantly ratcheted up their demands for tribute and abused their position to monopolize the lucrative trade in cotton, indigo, textiles, and other commodities. But the more successful they were in exploiting Awadh, the more they longed to annex it completely. Thus, Dalhousie declared in 1851 that Awadh was "a cherry which will drop into our mouths some day."

TREATY VIOLATIONS AND ANNEXATION In 1856, citing misgovernment and deterioration in law and order, the East India Company violated its treaty obligations and sent its troops to Lucknow to take control of the province. Nawab Wajid Ali Shah, the poet-king of Awadh, whom the British saw as effete and debauched, refused to sign the treaty of abdication. Instead, he came dressed in his mourning robes to meet with the British official charged to take over the province. After pleading unsuccessfully for his legal rights under the treaty, he handed over his turban to the official and then left for Calcutta to argue his case before Dalhousie. There was widespread distress at the treatment he received. Dirges were recited, and religious men rushed to Lucknow to denounce the annexation.

In fact, the annexation of princely domains and the abolition of feudal privileges formed part of the developing practices of European imperialism. To the policy of annexation, Dalhousie added an ambitious program of building railroads, telegraph lines, and a postal network to unify the disjointed territory into a single "network of iron sinew" under British control. Dalhousie saw these infrastructures as key to developing India into a productive colony—a supplier of raw materials for British industry and a market for its manufactures.

A year after Dalhousie's departure in 1856, India went up in flames. The spark that ignited the simmering discontent into a furious rebellion—the Rebellion of 1857 (Great Rebellion)—was the "greased cartridge" controversy. At the end of 1856, the British army, which consisted of hundreds of thousands of Hindu and Muslim recruits (sepoys) commanded by British officers, introduced the new Enfield rifle to replace the old-style musket. To load the rifle, soldiers had to bite the cartridge open. Although manufacturing instructions stated that linseed oil and beeswax be used to grease the cartridge, a rumor circulated that cow and pig fat had been used. But biting into cartridges greased with animal fat meant violating the Hindu and Muslim sepoys' religious traditions. The sepoys became convinced that there was a plot afoot to defile them and to compel their conversion to Christianity. So a wave of rebellion spread among the 270,000 Indian soldiers, who greatly outnumbered the 40,000 British soldiers employed to rule over 200 million Indians.

REBELLION BREAKS OUT The mutiny broke out on May 10, 1857, at the military barracks in Meerut. The previous day, the Indian soldiers had witnessed eighty-five of their comrades being manacled and shackled in irons and marched off to the prison for refusing to load their rifles. The next day, all three regiments at Meerut mutinied, killed their British officers, and marched 30 miles south to Delhi, where their comrades in regiments there welcomed them joyfully. Together, they "restored" the aging Bahadur Shah as the Mughal emperor, which lent legitimacy to the uprising. The Mughal capital quickly swarmed with rebel soldiers and religious leaders who gathered there from near and distant territories.

The revolt turned from a limited military mutiny into a widespread civil rebellion that involved peasants, artisans, day laborers, and religious leaders. While the insurgents did not eliminate the power of the East India Company, which managed to retain the loyalty of princes and landed aristocrats in some places, they did throw the company into a crisis.

Rebellion of 1857. Russian painter Vasili Vereshchagin depicts the cruel and unusual method in which British officers executed the Indian rebels—by strapping them to the mouths of cannons. The inhumanity of this practice was not soon forgotten by Europeans; this particular reproduction of the painting comes from "Raubstaat England" ("Robber State England"), an anti-British pamphlet published by the Nazis during World War II.

The Indian Sepoys. Pictured here are Indian soldiers, or sepoys, who were armed, drilled, and commanded by British officers. The sepoys were drawn from indigenous groups that the British considered "martial races." This photograph shows the Sikhs, designated as one such "race."

The Rani of Jhansi. The Rani of Jhansi, who was deposed by the British, rose up during the revolt of 1857. In subsequent nationalist iconography, as this twentieth-century watercolor illustrates, she is remembered as a heroic rebel, all the more so because of her gender.

Before long, the mutineers in Delhi issued a proclamation declaring that because the British were determined to destroy the religion of both Hindus and Muslims, it was the duty of the wealthy and the privileged to support the rebellion. (See Global Themes and Sources: Primary Source 16.3.) To promote Hindu-Muslim unity, rebel leaders asked Muslims to refrain from killing cows in deference to Hindu sentiments.

Triumphant in Delhi, the rebellion spread to other parts of India. In Awadh, proclamations in Hindi, Urdu, and Persian called on Hindus and Muslims to revolt. Troops at the garrison in Lucknow, Awadh's capital, did just that. Seizing control of the town, the rebels urged all classes to unite in expelling the British and succeeded in compelling the colonial forces to retreat.

Although the dispossessed aristocracy and petty landholders led the rebellion, leaders also appeared from the lower classes. Bakht Khan, who had been a junior noncommissioned officer in the British army, became commander in chief of the rebel forces in Delhi, replacing one of the Mughal emperor's sons. And Devi Singh, a wealthy peasant, set himself up as a peasant king. Dressed in yellow, the insignia of Hindu royalty, he constituted a government of his own, modeling it on the British administration. While his imitation of company rule showed his respect for the British bureaucracy, he defied British authority by leading an armed peasantry against the hated local moneylenders.

The call to popular forces also marked the rebel career of Maulavi Ahmadullah Shah, a Muslim theologian. He stood at the head of the rebel forces in Lucknow, leading an army composed primarily of ordinary soldiers and people from the lower orders. Claiming to be an "Incarnation of the Deity" and thus inspired by divine will, he emerged as a prophetic leader of the common people. He voiced his undying hatred of the British in religious terms, calling on Hindus and Muslims to destroy British rule and warning his followers against betrayal by landed authorities.

PARTICIPATION BY THE PEASANTRY The presence of popular leadership points to the important role of the lower classes as historical actors. Although feudal chieftains often brought them into the rebellion, the peasantry made it their own. The organizing principle of their uprising was the common experience of oppression. Thus, they destroyed anything that represented the authority of the company: prisons, factories, police posts, railway stations, European bungalows, and law courts. Equally significant, the peasantry attacked local moneylenders and power holders who had purchased land at government auctions and were seen as benefiting from company rule.

Vigorous and militant as the popular rebellion was, it was limited in its territorial and ideological horizons. To begin with, the uprisings were local in scale and vision. Peasant rebels attacked the closest seats of administration and sought to settle scores with their most immediate and visible oppressors. They generally did not carry their action beyond the village or collection of villages. Their loyalties remained intensely local, based on village attachments and religious, caste, and clan ties. Nor did popular militants seek to undo traditional hierarchies of caste and religion.

THE BRITISH RESPONSE Convinced that the rebellion was the result of plotting by a few troublemakers, the British reacted with a brutal, vengeful counterinsurgent campaign. Villages were torched, and rebels were tied to cannons and blown to bits to teach Indians a lesson in power. Delhi fell in

September 1857, Lucknow in March 1858. The British exiled the unfortunate Mughal emperor to Burma, where he died, and murdered his sons. Most of the other rebel leaders were either killed in battle or captured and executed. When, at the same time, the British also moved to annex the state of Jhansi in northern India, its female leader, Lakshmi Bai, mounted a counterattack. After a two-week siege, Jhansi fell to the British; Lakshmi Bai escaped on horseback, only to die in the fighting for control of a nearby fortress. Her intelligence, bravery, and youth (she was twenty-eight) made her the subject of many popular Indian ballads in the decades to follow.

By July 1858, the vicious campaign to restore British control had achieved its goal. Yet, in August, the British Parliament abolished company rule and the company itself and transferred responsibility for the governing of India to the crown. In November, Queen Victoria issued a proclamation guaranteeing religious toleration, promising improvements, and allowing Indians to serve in the government. She promised to honor the treaties and agreements with princes and chiefs and to refrain from interfering in religious matters. The insurgents had risen up not as a nation but as a multitude of communities acting independently, and their determination to find a new order shocked the British and threw them into a panic. Having crushed the uprising, the British resumed the work of transforming India into a modern colonial state and economy. But the desire for radical alternatives and traditions of popular insurgency, though vanquished, did not vanish.

The rebellion was the result of a last-ditch effort by the East India Company to hold on to power in the face of swelling discontent in India and grumbling in the British Parliament. In reality, the company was unsure of its ability to bring westernization and modernity to India. Its insecure hold on power caused it to become increasingly authoritarian, which transformed discontent into an insurgency. This was why the violence was most acute in northern India, where the opposition to company rule ran deep, where the company had only recently imposed itself, and where it wielded only limited military capacity. It was there that the rebels posed the greatest threat to British rule and thus had to be quashed mercilessly.

Secundra Bagh Palace Courtyard. The Sepoy Rebellion's aftermath was captured by Italian photographer Felice Beato, who covered conflicts across Asia and is regarded as the first global wartime photographer. Beato arrived in Lucknow in 1858 to record the wreckage after most of the fighting in the Rebellion was squashed. In this photo, he relied on local witnesses to move bones and skulls around in the foreground to dramatize the violence.

Conclusion

The nineteenth century was a time of turmoil and transformation. While powerful forces reconfigured the world as a place for capitalism, colonialism, and nation-states, so, too, did prophets, charismatic leaders, radicals, peasant rebels, and anticolonial insurgents arise to offer alternatives. Reflecting local circumstances and traditions, the struggles of these men and women for a different future opened up spaces for the ideas and activities of subordinate classes.

Conventional historical accounts either neglect these struggles or fail to view them as a whole. These individuals were not just romantic, last-ditch resisters, as some scholars have argued. Even after defeat, their messages remained alive within their communities. Nor were their actions isolated and atypical events, for when viewed on a global scale, they bring to light a world that looks very different from the one that became dominant. To see the Wahhabi movement in the Arabian Peninsula together with the Shawnee Prophet in North America, the utopians and radicals in Europe with the peasant insurgents in British India, and the Taiping rebels with the Mayas in Yucatán is to glimpse a world of marginalized regions and groups. It was a world that more powerful groups endeavored to suppress but could not erase.

In this world, prophets and rebel leaders usually cultivated power and prestige locally; the emergence of an alternative polity in one region did not impinge on communities and political organizations in others. As much as these individuals had in common, they envisioned widely different kinds of futures. Even Marx, who called the workers of the world to unite, was acutely aware that the call for a proletarian revolution applied only to the industrialized countries of Europe. Other dissenters had even more localized horizons. A world fashioned by movements for alternatives meant a world with multiple centers and different historical paths.

What gave force to a different mapping of the world was the fact that common people were at the center of these alternative visions, and their voices, however muted, gained a place on the historical stage. The quest for social justice in various forms defined efforts to reconstitute alternative worlds. In Islamic regions, the egalitarianism practiced by revitalization movements was evident in their mobilization of all Muslims, not just the elites. Likewise, charismatic military leaders in Africa, for all their use of raw power, used the framework of community to build new polities. The Taiping Rebellion distinguished itself by seeking to establish an equal society of men and women in service of the Heavenly Kingdom. Operating under very different conditions, the European radicals imagined a society free from aristocratic privileges and bourgeois property. Anticolonial rebels and insurgents depended on local solidarities and proposed alternative moral communities. In so doing, these movements compelled ruling elites to adjust the way they governed. The next chapter explores this challenge.

After You Read This Chapter

TRACING THE GLOBAL STORYLINES

FOCUS ON: Global Changes to Western Expansion

Europe

- European socialists and radicals envision a world free of exploitation and inequalities, while nationalists work to create new independent nation-states.

The Americas

- Indigenous prophets in the United States imagine a world restored to its customary ways and traditional rites.
- Mayas in Yucatán defy the central Mexican government in a rebellion known as the Caste War.

The Islamic World and Africa

- Revivalist movements in the Arabian Peninsula and West Africa demand a return to traditional Islam.
- A charismatic warrior, Shaka, creates a powerful state in southern Africa.

Semicolonial China

- An inspired prophetic figure, Hong Xiuquan, leads the Taiping Rebellion against the Qing dynasty and European encroachment on China.

Colonial India

- Indian troops mutiny against the British and attempt to restore Mughal rule.

CHRONOLOGY

The Islamic World and Africa

- Fulani Revolt in West Africa 1804–1817
- Wahhabis wage militant religious campaign in Arabian Peninsula 1813–1815
- Shaka creates Zulu state in southern Africa 1818–1828

China

- Taiping Rebellion 1850–1864

Europe

- Free markets spread 1830s
- Fourier's utopian socialism gains popularity 1830s
- Revolutions across Europe; Marx and Engels publish *The Communist Manifesto* 1848

The Americas

- Tecumseh's rebellion in North America 1810–1813

India

- Indian Rebellion 1857–1858

1800

1850

KEY TERMS

Caste War of Yucatán p. 710

Usman dan Fodio p. 694

liberalism p. 702

Marxism p. 704

***Mfecane* movement** p. 694

millenarian p. 697

proletarians p. 704

Radicalism p. 700

Taiping Rebellion p. 699

Tenskwatawa p. 707

utopian socialism p. 703

Wahhabism p. 692

THINKING ABOUT GLOBAL CONNECTIONS

Thinking about Exchange Networks and Alternative Visions How did people around the world respond to the major changes of the French, American, and industrial revolutions? What difference did proximity to the European and American "core" make?

Thinking about Changing Power Relationships and Alternative Visions What kind of challenges did the new order provoke? What kinds of traditions did those challenges draw on, and what kind of success did they have?

Thinking about Gender and Alternative Visions Describe the role women played in millenarian protest movements during the nineteenth century, and explain the significance of gender to those movements.

Go to INQUIZITIVE to see what you've learned—and learn what you've missed—with personalized feedback along the way.

Caste War in Yucatán, Mexico
1847–1901

Ghost Dance movement in North America
1889–1890

1900

1950

Global Themes and Sources

Comparing Alternatives to Nineteenth-Century Capitalism

While European capitalism and colonialism drove transformative changes in the nineteenth century, protest movements around the world envisioned a future based on other values. These selections provide radically different visions for the future—different from European capitalism and colonialism, and different from one another.

Tenskwatawa, Nana Asma'u, and Bahadur Shah all sought to revive local traditions, reject outside influences, and return to what they viewed as a pure, authentic past that had existed before market forces and new ideas began to unsettle the social order. The Taiping leaders, inspired by a millenarian Christianity, challenged central values of conventional Chinese society; they confronted the central role of the family and ancestral worship and urged their followers to see themselves as belonging to a single family. *The Communist Manifesto* sought nothing less than the complete transformation of society everywhere, starting from the industrial heartland of Europe and taking advantage of the technical advances of the machine age to satisfy everyone's basic needs and put an end to class conflict.

These sources highlight the causes behind the development of these alternative visions and provide an opportunity for comparison. It is particularly important to note the impact that market forces and new ideas of citizenship and equality had on these protests. Some of the protesters came in close contact with market forces and new ideas of citizenship and equality, while others flourished beyond their immediate influence. Consider how each society or group responded, and how it was shaped by the ideas and forces that emerged from the North Atlantic core in the period from 1750 to 1850. Finally, consider what common elements all of these documents share and where they part company.

ANALYZING ALTERNATIVES TO NINETEENTH-CENTURY CAPITALISM

- Analyze the influence of market forces and new ideas of equality in each document.
- Analyze the role of religion—whether explicit or implicit—in each document. Pay special attention to ideas of virtue, sin, and redemption.
- The creators of these sources all opposed capitalism and colonialism, but they reacted differently to what they viewed as outside influences. Place the authors of these sources on a continuum in terms of their rejection of those influences and their efforts to recapture an unsullied past.

PRIMARY SOURCE 16.1

Visions of the Great Good Spirit (1810), Tenskwatawa

In the first decade of the nineteenth century, the Shawnee leader Tenskwatawa recalled an earlier, happier time for the Indigenous peoples of the Great Lakes and Ohio Valley—it was a time before the coming of the Europeans. In this speech, Tenskwatawa recounts how contact with the "white men's goods" contaminated and corrupted the Indigenous peoples. He urges them to reject the ways of White Americans and return to the pure ways of a precolonial past.

- Identify the commodities and habits that led to the decline of Indigenous peoples in the United States.
- What rules did "Our Creator" give Tenskwatawa to help him make his people what they were before?
- Compare Tenskwatawa's view of commodities and exchange to the view expressed in *The Communist Manifesto.*

I died and went to the World Above, and saw it.

The punishments I saw terrify you! But listen, those punishments will be upon you unless you follow me through the door that I am opening for you!

Our Creator put us on this wide, rich land, and told us we were free to go where the game was, where the soil was good for planting. That was our state of true happiness. We did not have to beg for anything. Our Creator had taught us how to find and make everything we needed, from trees and plants and animals and stone. We lived in bark, and we wore only the skins of animals.

Thus were we created. Thus we lived for a long time, proud and happy. We had never eaten pig meat, nor tasted the poison called whiskey, nor worn wool from sheep, nor struck fire or dug earth with steel, nor cooked in iron, nor hunted and fought with loud guns, nor ever had diseases which soured our blood or rotted our organs. We were pure, so we were strong and happy.

For many years we traded furs to the English or the French, for wool blankets and guns and iron things, for steel awls and needles and axes, for mirrors, for pretty things made of beads and silver. And for liquor. This was foolish, but we did not know it. We shut our ears to the Great Good Spirit. We did not want to hear that we were being foolish.

But now those things of the white men have corrupted us, and made us weak and needful. Our men forgot how to hunt without noisy guns. Our women don't want to make fire without steel, or cook without iron, or sew without metal awls and needles, or fish without steel hooks. Some look in those mirrors all the time, and no longer teach their daughters to make leather or render bear oil. We learned to need the white men's goods, and so now a People who never had to beg for anything must beg for everything!

Some of our women married white men, and made half-breeds. Many of us now crave liquor. He whose filthy name I will not speak, he who was I before, was one of the worst of those drunkards. There are drunkards in almost every family. You know how bad this is.

And so you see what has happened to us. We were fools to take all these things that weakened us. We did not need them then, but we believe we need them now. We turned our backs on the old ways. Instead of thanking the Great Spirit for all we used to have, we turned to the white man and asked them for more. So now we depend upon the very people who destroy us! This is our weakness! Our corruption! Our Creator scolded me, "If you had lived the way I taught you, the white men could never have got you under their foot!"

And that is why Our Creator purified me and sent me down to you full of the shining power, to make you what you were before!

No red man must ever drink liquor, or he will go and have the hot lead poured in his mouth!

No red man shall take more than one wife in the future. No red man shall run after women. If he is single, let him take a wife, and lie only with her.

Any red woman who is living with a white man must return to her people, and must leave her children with the husband, so that all nations will be pure in their blood.

Now hear what I was told about dealing with white men! These things we must do, to cleanse ourselves of their corruption!

Do not eat any food that is raised or cooked by a white person. It is not good for us. Eat not their bread made of wheat, for Our Creator gave us corn for our bread. Eat not the meat of their filthy swine, nor of their chicken fowls, nor the beef of their cattle, which are tame and thus have no spirit in them. Their foods will seem to fill your empty belly, but this deceives you for food without spirit does not nourish you.

There are two kinds of white men. There are the Americans, and there are the others. You may give your hand in friendship to the French, or the Spaniards, or the British. But the Americans are not like those. The Americans come from the slime of the sea, with mud and weeds in their claws, and they are a kind of crayfish serpent whose claws grab in our earth and take it from us. . . .

Remember it is the wish of the Great Good Spirit that we have no more commerce with white men!

We may keep our guns, and if we need to defend ourselves against American white men, the guns will kill them because they are a white man's weapon. But arrows will kill American intruders, too! You must go to the grandfathers and have them teach you to make good bows and shape arrowheads, and you must recover the old hunting skills. . . .

We will no longer do the frolic dances that excite lust. The Great Good Spirit will teach me the old dances we did before the corruption, and from these dances we will receive strength and happiness!

Source: Elizabeth Cobbs Hoffman, Edward J. Blum, and Jon Gjerde (eds.), *Major Problems in American History*, vol. 1, *To 1877*, 3rd ed. (Boston: Wadsworth Cengage Learning, 2012), pp. 207–9.

PRIMARY SOURCE 16.2

A Female Muslim Voice in Africa (1838–1839), Nana Asma'u

The Islamic scholar, writer, and poet Nana Asma'u was the daughter of Usman dan Fodio, the leader of the Fulani Revolt in northern Nigeria at the turn of the nineteenth century. She was also deeply attached to her brother, Muhammad Bello, who succeeded their father as head of the Sokoto caliphate. Nana Asma'u composed this poem in praise of her brother, underlining his commitment to an Islamic way of life.

- Identify the values that the poet celebrates. What does she praise?
- What threats to the community does the poem identify? What is their nature, and where do they come from? Do they come from the outside world or the community's inner failings, or from some combination of these?
- What role does gender play in the poem? Why does Nana Asma'u write about her brother?

I give thanks to the King of Heaven, the One God. I invoke blessings on the Prophet and set down my poem.

The Lord made Heaven and earth and created all things, sent prophets to enlighten mankind.

Believe in them for your own sake, learn from them and be saved, believe in and act upon their sayings.

I invoke blessings on the Prophet who brought the Book, the Qur'an: he brought the *hadith* to complete the enlightenment.

Muslim scholars have explained knowledge and used it, following in the footsteps of the Prophet.

It is my intention to set down Bello's characteristics and explain his ways.

For I wish to assuage my loneliness, requite my love, find peace of mind through my religion.

These are his characteristics: he was learned in all branches of knowledge and feared God in public and in private.

He obeyed religious injunctions and distanced himself from forbidden things: this is what is known about him.

He concentrated on understanding what is right to know about the Oneness of God.

He preached to people and instructed them about God: he caused them to long for Paradise.

He set an example in his focus on eternal values: he strove to end oppression and sin.

He upheld the *shari'a,* honored it, implemented it aright, that was his way, everyone knows.

And he made his views known to those who visited him: he said to them "Follow the *shari'a,* which is sacred."

He eschewed worldly things and discriminated against anything of ill repute; he was modest and a repository of useful knowledge.

He was exceedingly level-headed and generous, he enjoyed periods of quietude: but was energetic when he put his hand to things.

He was thoughtful, calm, a confident statesman, and quick-witted.

He honored people's status: he could sort out difficulties and advise those who sought his help.

He had nothing to do with worldly concerns, but tried to restore to a healthy state things which he could. These were his characteristics.

He never broke promises, but faithfully kept them: he sought out righteous things. Ask and you will hear.

He divorced himself entirely from bribery and was totally scrupulous: He flung back at the givers money offered for titles.

One day Garange [chief of Mafora] sent him a splendid gift, but Bello told the messenger Zitaro to take it back.

He said to the envoy who had brought the bribe, "Have nothing to do with forbidden things."

And furthermore he said, "Tell him that the gift was sent for unlawful purposes; it is wrong to respond to evil intent."

He was able to expedite matters: he facilitated learning, commerce, and defense, and encouraged everything good.

He propagated good relationships between different tribes and between kinsmen. He afforded protection; everyone knows this.

When strangers came he met them, and taught about religious matters, explaining things: he tried to enlighten them.

He lived in a state of preparedness, he had his affairs in order and had an excellent intelligence service.

He had nothing to do with double agents and said it was better to ignore them, for they pervert Islamic principles.

He was a very pleasant companion to friends and acquaintances: he was intelligent, with a lively mind.

He fulfilled promises and took care of affairs, but he did not act hastily.

He shouldered responsibilities and patiently endured adversities.

He was watchful and capable of restoring to good order matters which had gone wrong.

He was resourceful and could undo mischief, no matter how serious, because he was a man of ideas.

He was gracious to important people and was hospitable to all visitors, including non-Muslims.

He drew good people close to him and distanced himself from people of ill repute.

Those are his characteristics. I have recounted a few examples that are sufficient to provide a model for emulation and benefit.

May God forgive him and have mercy on him: May we be united with him in Paradise, the place we aspire to.

For the sake of the Prophet, the Compassionate, who was sent with mercy to mankind.

May God pour blessings on the Prophet and his kinsmen and all other followers.

May God accept this poem. I have concluded it in the year 1254 ah [after *hijra,* the Muslim dating system].

Source: "Gikku Bello," in *One Woman's Jihad: Nana Asma'u, Scholar and Scribe,* by Beverly B. Mack and Jean Boyd (Bloomington: Indiana University Press, 2000), pp. 97–99.

PRIMARY SOURCE 16.3

The Azamgarh Proclamation (1857), Bahadur Shah

The Indian leaders of the Rebellion of 1857 issued numerous proclamations. The Azamgarh Proclamation, excerpted below, is one of many. The emperor, Bahadur Shah, issued it in August 1857 on behalf of the mutineers who had seized the garrison town of Azamgarh. It attacks the British for subverting Indian traditions and calls on the rebellion's followers to restore the precolonial order.

Identify the rebels' main grievances against the English.

Analyze the role of religion in the rebellion.

Explain the significance of commerce and property for the rebels.

25th. August, 1857.

It is well known to all, that in this age the people of Hindoostan, both Hindoos and Mohammedans, are being ruined under the tyranny and oppression of the infidel and treacherous English. It is therefore the bounden duty of all the wealthy people of India, especially of those who have any sort of connection with any of the Mohammedan royal families, and are considered the pastors and masters of their people, to stake their lives and property for the well being of the public. With the view of effecting this general good, several princes belonging to the royal family of Delhi, have dispersed themselves in the different parts of India, Iran, Turan, and Afghanistan, and have been long since taking measures to compass their favourite end; and it is to accomplish this charitable object that one of the aforesaid princes has, at the head of an army of Afghanistan, &c., made his appearance in India; and I, who am the grandson of Abul Muzuffer Serajuddin Bahadur Shah Ghazee, King of India, having in the course of circuit come here to extirpate the infidels residing in the eastern part of the country, and to liberate and protect the poor helpless people now groaning under their iron rule, have, by the aid of the *Majahdeens* [religious warriors], erected the standard of Mohammed, and persuaded the orthodox Hindoos who had been subject to my ancestors, and have been and are still accessories in the destruction of the English, to raise the standard of Mahavir.

Several of the Hindoo and Mussalman chiefs, who have long since quitted their homes for the preservation of their religion, and have been trying their best to root out the English in India, have presented themselves to me, and taken part in the reigning Indian crusade, and it is more than probable that I shall very shortly receive succours from the West. Therefore, for the information of the public, the present *Ishtahar*, consisting of several sections, is put in circulation, and it is the imperative duty of all to take it into their careful consideration, and abide by it. Parties anxious to participate in the common cause, but having no means to provide for themselves, shall receive their daily subsistence from me; and be it known to all, that the ancient works, both of the Hindoos and the Mohammedans, the writings of the miracle-workers, and the calculations of the astrologers, pundits, and rammals, all agree in asserting that the English will no longer have any footing in India or elsewhere. Therefore it is incumbent on all to give up the hope of the continuation of the British sway, side with me, and deserve the consideration of the Badshahi, or imperial Government, by their individual exertion in promoting the common good, and thus attain their respective ends; otherwise if this golden opportunity slips away, they will have to repent of their folly, as it is very aptly said by a poet in two fine couplets, the drift whereof is "Never let a favourable opportunity slip, for in the field of opportunity you are to meet with the ball of fortune; but if you do not avail yourself of the opportunity that offers itself, you will have to bite your finger through grief."

No person, at the misrepresentation of the well-wishers of the British Government, ought to conclude from the present slight inconveniences usually attendant on revolutions, that similar inconveniences and troubles should continue when the Badshahi Government is established on a firm basis; and parties badly dealt with by any sepoy or plunderer, should come up and represent their grievances to me, and receive redress at my hands; and for whatever property they may lose in the reigning disorder, they will be recompensed from the public treasury when the Badshahi Government is well fixed. . . .

Section II—Regarding Merchants. It is plain that the infidel and treacherous British Government have monopolized the trade of all the fine and valuable merchandise, such as indigo, cloth, and other articles of shipping, leaving only the trade of trifles to the people, and even in this they are not without their share of the profits, which they secure by means of customs and stamp fees, &c. in money suits, so that the people have merely a trade in name. Besides this, the profits of the traders are taxed, with postages, tolls, and subscriptions for schools, &c. Notwithstanding all these concessions, the merchants are liable to imprisonment and disgrace at the instance or complaint of a worthless man. When the Badshahi Government is established, all these aforesaid fraudulent practices shall be dispensed with, and the trade of every article, without exception, both by land and water, shall be open to the native merchants of India, who will have the benefit of the Government steam-vessels and steam-carriages for the conveyance of their merchandise gratis; and merchants having no capital of their own shall be assisted from the public treasury. It is therefore the duty of every merchant to take part in the war, and aid the Badshahi Government with his men and money, either secretly or openly, as may be consistent with his position or interest, and forswear his allegiance to the British Government.

Section III—Regarding Public Servants. It is not a secret thing, that under the British Government, natives employed in the civil and military services, have little respect, low pay, and no manner of influence; and all the posts of dignity and emolument in both the departments, are exclusively bestowed on Englishmen for natives in the military service, after having devoted the greater part of their lives, attain to the post of soobadar (the very height of their hopes) with a salary of 60r. or 70r. per mensem; and those in the civil service obtain the post of Sudder Ala, with a salary of 500 r. a month, but no influence, jagheer, or present. . . .

Therefore, all the natives in the British service ought to be alive to their religion and interest, and, abjuring their loyalty to the English, side with the Badshahi Government, and obtain salaries of 200 or 300 rupees per month for the present, and be entitled to high posts in future. If they, for any reason, cannot at present declare openly against the English, they can heartily wish ill to their cause, and remain passive spectators of passing events, without taking any active share therein. But at the same time they should indirectly assist the

Badshahi Government, and try their best to drive the English out of the country. . . .

Section IV—Regarding Artisans. It is evident that the Europeans, by the introduction of English articles into India, have thrown the weavers, the cotton dressers, the carpenters, the blacksmiths, and the shoemakers, &c., out of employ, and have engrossed their occupations, so that every description of native artisan has been reduced to beggary. But under the Badshahi Government the native artisans will exclusively be employed in the services of the kings, the rajahs, and the rich; and this will no doubt ensure their prosperity. Therefore these artisans ought to renounce the English services, and assist the *Majahdeens*, engaged in the war, and thus be entitled both to secular and eternal happiness.

Section V—Regarding Pundits, Fakirs and other learned persons. The pundits and fakirs being the guardians of the Hindoo and Mohammedan religions respectively, and the Europeans being the enemies of both the religions, and as at present a war is raging against the English on account of religion, the pundits and fakirs are bound to present themselves to me, and take their share in the holy war. . . .

Lastly, be it known to all, that whoever, out of the above named classes, shall after the circulation of this Ishtahar, still cling to the British Government, all his estates shall be confiscated, and his property plundered, and he himself, with his whole family, shall be imprisoned, and ultimately put to death.

Source: Ainslie T. Embree (ed.), *1857 in India: Mutiny or War of Independence?* (Boston: D. C. Heath, 1963), pp. 1–3.

PRIMARY SOURCE 16.4

The Principles of the Heavenly Nature (1854), Taiping Heavenly Kingdom

In this excerpt from 1854, written after the Taipings had established a capital in Nanjing and after initial victories had given way to a decline in morale and cohesion, the Taiping leaders envision a radically new community based on the values of a messianic Christianity.

- Explain the significance of the family. Why do the authors speak of their members as brothers and sisters?
- What do the authors mean by "degeneration"? What "degenerated" and why?
- Analyze the relationship between external challenges and internal weakness in this text.

We marquises and chancellors hold that our brothers and sisters have been blessed by the Heavenly Father and the Heavenly Elder Brother, who saved the ensnared and drowning and awakened the deluded; they have cast off worldly sentiments and now follow the true Way. They cross mountains and wade rivers, not even ten thousand *li* being too far for them to come, to uphold together the true Sovereign. Armed and bearing shield and spear, they carry righteous banners that rise colorfully. Husband and wife, men and women, express common indignation and lead the advance. It can be said that they are determined to uphold Heaven and to requite the nation with loyalty.

In the ten thousand nations of the world everyone is given life, nourished, protected, and blessed by the Heavenly Father, the Supreme Ruler and Lord God-on-High. Thus the Heavenly Father, the Supreme Ruler and Lord God-on-High, is the universal father of man in all the ten thousand nations of the world. There is no man who should not be grateful, there is no man who should not reverently worship Him. . . .

However, worldly customs daily degenerated. There were even those who likened themselves to rulers, and, being deluded in heart and nature, arrogant yet at fault, and falsely self-exalted, forbade the prime minister and those below to sacrifice to Heaven. Then [these men] competed in establishing false gods and worshiping them, thus opening up the ways of the devilish demons. The people of the world all followed in like fashion, and this became firmly fixed in their minds. Thereupon, after a considerable time, they did not know their own errors. Hence the Heavenly Father, the Lord God, in view of mortal man's serious crime of disobedience, at his first anger, sent down forty days and forty nights of heavy rain, the vast waters spreading in all directions and drowning mortal man. Only Noah and his family had unceasingly worshiped the Heavenly Father, the Supreme Ruler and Lord God-on-High; therefore, relying on the Heavenly grace, they were fortunate and they alone were preserved. In this, the first instance of the Heavenly Father's great anger, was the great proof of his great powers displayed.

After the Flood, the devilish king of Egypt, whose ambition was mediocrity and who was possessed by the demons, envied the Israelites in their worship of God and bitterly persecuted them. Therefore, the Heavenly Father in his great anger led the Israelites out of Egypt. In this, the second instance of the Heavenly Father's great anger, was the great proof of his great powers displayed.

However, the rulers and people of that time still had not completely forgotten the Heavenly grace. But since the emergence of Daoism in the [Chinese] Qin [dynasty] and the welcoming of Buddhism in the Han [dynasty], the delusion of man by the demons has day by day increased, and all men have forgotten the grace and virtue of the Heavenly Father. . . . The Heavenly Father once again became greatly angered; yet if he were to annihilate them completely, he could not bear it in his heart; if he were to tolerate them, it would not be consonant with righteousness. At that time, the elder son of the Heavenly Father, the Heavenly Elder Brother Jesus, shouldered the great burden and willingly offered to sacrifice his life to redeem the sins of the men of the world. . . .

Let us ask your elder and younger brothers: formerly the people sacrificed only to the demons; they worshiped the demons and appealed to the demons only because they desired the demons to protect them. Yet how could they think that the demons could really protect them? . . . To worship them is of no avail. However, the men of the world sank even deeper, not knowing how to awaken themselves. Therefore, the Heavenly Father again became angry.

In the *dingyou* year [1837], our Heavenly Father displayed the heavenly grace and dispatched angels to summon the Heavenly King up to Heaven. There He clearly pointed out the demons' perversities and their deluding of the world. He also invested the Heavenly King with a seal and a sword; He ordered the Savior, the Heavenly Elder Brother, Jesus, to take command of the Heavenly soldiers and Heavenly generals and to aid the Heavenly King, and to attack and conquer from Heaven earthward, layer by layer, the innumerable demons. After their victory they returned to Heaven and the Heavenly Father, greatly pleased, sent the Heavenly King down upon the earth to become the true Taiping Sovereign of the ten thousand nations of the world and to save the people of the world. He also bade him not to be fearful and to effect these matters courageously, for whenever difficulties appeared, the Heavenly Father would assume direction and the Heavenly Elder Brother would shoulder the burden.

***

We brothers and sisters, enjoying today the greatest mercy of our Heavenly Father, have become as one family and are able to enjoy true blessings; each of us must always be thankful. Speaking in terms of our ordinary human feelings, it is true that each has his own parents and there must be a distinction in family names; it is also true that as each has his own household, there must be a distinction between this boundary and that boundary. Yet we must know that the ten thousand names derive from the one name, and the one name from one ancestor. Thus our origins are not different. Since our Heavenly Father gave us birth and nourishment, we are of one form though of separate bodies, and we breathe the same air though in different places. This is why we say, "All are brothers within the four seas." Now, basking in the profound mercy of Heaven, we are of one family. . . .

We brothers, our minds having been awakened by our Heavenly Father, joined the camp in the earlier days to support our Sovereign, many bringing parents, wives, uncles, brothers, and whole families. It is a matter of course that we should attend to our parents and look after our wives and children, but when one first creates a new rule, the state must come first and the family last, public interests first and private interests last. Moreover, as it is advisable to avoid suspicion [of improper conduct] between the inner [female] and the outer [male] and to distinguish between male and female, so men must have male quarters and women must have female quarters; only thus can we be dignified and avoid confusion. There must be no common mixing of the male and female groups, which would cause debauchery and violation of Heaven's commandments. Although to pay respects to parents and to visit wives and children occasionally are in keeping with human nature and not prohibited, yet it is only proper to converse before the door, stand a few steps apart and speak in a loud voice; one must not enter the sisters' camp or permit the mixing of men and women. Only thus, by complying with rules and commands, can we become sons and daughters of Heaven.

At the present time, the remaining demons have not yet been completely exterminated and the time for the reunion of families has not yet arrived. We younger brothers and sisters must be firm and patient to the end, and with united strength and a single heart we must uphold God's principles and wipe out the demons immediately. With peace and unity achieved, then our Heavenly Father, displaying his mercy, will reward us according to our merits. Wealth, nobility, and renown will then enable us brothers to celebrate the reunion of our families and enjoy the harmonious relations of husband and wife. Oh, how wonderful that will be! The task of a thousand times ten thousand years also lies in this; the happiness and emoluments of a thousand times ten thousand years also lie in this; we certainly must not abandon it in one day.

Source: Wm. Theodore de Bary and Richard Lufrano (eds.), *Sources of Chinese Tradition*, vol. 2, *From 1600 through the Twentieth Century*, 2nd ed. (New York: Columbia University Press, 2000), pp. 226–30.

PRIMARY SOURCE 16.5

Bourgeoisie and Proletariat (1848), Karl Marx and Friedrich Engels

At the behest of an international revolutionary organization, the Communist League, in 1847 Karl Marx and Friedrich Engels set out to draft a confession of faith. While Engels's initial draft was set in the form of a catechism, the final document, rewritten by Marx, took the following, combative, critical form. Published in January 1848, just before revolution in Paris set off rebellion across Europe, *The Communist Manifesto* foretold the inevitable overthrow of bourgeois-dominated capitalism by the working classes.

- According to Marx and Engels, how does class conflict change over time? Pay special attention to the range of groups opposed to one another.
- Define the term ***bourgeois***. How are the bourgeoisie different from all the prior dominant classes in history?

This document was initially conceived as a declaration of faith. What role, if any, does religion play in this final version?

A spectre is haunting Europe—the spectre of communism. . . .

The history of all hitherto existing society is the history of class struggles.

Freeman and slave, patrician and plebeian, lord and serf, guild-master and journeyman, in a word, oppressor and oppressed, stood in constant opposition to one another, carried on an uninterrupted, now hidden, now open fight, a fight that each time ended, either in a revolutionary reconstitution of society at large, or in the common ruin of the contending classes.

In the earlier epochs of history, we find almost everywhere a complicated arrangement of society into various orders, a manifold gradation of social rank. In ancient Rome we have patricians, knights, plebeians, slaves; in the Middle Ages, feudal lords, vassals, guild-masters, journeymen, apprentices, serfs; in almost all of these classes, again, subordinate gradations.

The modern bourgeois society that has sprouted from the ruins of feudal society has not done away with class antagonisms. It has but established new classes, new conditions of oppression, new forms of struggle in place of the old ones.

Our epoch, the epoch of the bourgeoisie, possesses, however, this distinct feature: it has simplified class antagonisms. Society as a whole is more and more splitting up into two great hostile camps, into two great classes directly facing each other—Bourgeoisie and Proletariat.

From the serfs of the Middle Ages sprang the chartered burghers of the earliest towns. From these burgesses the first elements of the bourgeoisie were developed. . . .

The bourgeoisie, wherever it has got the upper hand, has put an end to all feudal, patriarchal, idyllic relations. It has pitilessly torn asunder the motley feudal ties that bound man to his "natural superiors," and has left remaining no other nexus between man and man than naked self-interest, than callous "cash payment.". . .

We see then: the means of production and of exchange, on whose foundation the bourgeoisie built itself up, were generated in feudal society. At a certain stage in the development of these means of production and of exchange, the conditions under which feudal society produced and exchanged, the feudal organisation of agriculture and manufacturing industry, in one word, the feudal relations of property became no longer compatible with the already developed productive forces; they became so many fetters. They had to be burst asunder; they were burst asunder. . . .

It is enough to mention the commercial crises that by their periodical return put the existence of the entire bourgeois society on its trial, each time more threateningly. In these crises, a great part not only of the existing products, but also of the previously created productive forces, are periodically destroyed. In these crises, there breaks out an epidemic that, in all earlier epochs, would have seemed an absurdity—the epidemic of over-production. . . .

Because there is too much civilisation, too much means of subsistence, too much industry, too much commerce. The productive forces at the disposal of society no longer tend to further the development of the conditions of bourgeois property; on the contrary, they have become too powerful for these conditions, by which they are fettered, and so soon as they overcome these fetters, they bring disorder into the whole of bourgeois society, endanger the existence of bourgeois property. The conditions of bourgeois society are too narrow to comprise the wealth created by them. . . .

The weapons with which the bourgeoisie felled feudalism to the ground are now turned against the bourgeoisie itself.

But not only has the bourgeoisie forged the weapons that bring death to itself; it has also called into existence the men who are to wield those weapons—the modern working class—the proletarians. . . .

Owing to the extensive use of machinery, and to the division of labour, the work of the proletarians has lost all individual character, and, consequently, all charm for the workman. He becomes an appendage of the machine, and it is only the most simple, most monotonous, and most easily acquired knack, that is required of him. Hence, the cost of production of a workman is restricted, almost entirely, to the means of subsistence that he requires for maintenance, and for the propagation of his race. But the price of a commodity, and therefore also of labour, is equal to its cost of production. . . .

Modern Industry has converted the little workshop of the patriarchal master into the great factory of the industrial capitalist. Masses of labourers, crowded into the factory, are organised like soldiers. As privates of the industrial army they are placed under the command of a perfect hierarchy of officers and sergeants. Not only are they slaves of the bourgeois class, and of the bourgeois State; they are daily and hourly enslaved by the machine, by the overlooker, and, above all, by the individual bourgeois manufacturer himself. The more openly this despotism proclaims gain to be its end and aim, the more petty, the more hateful and the more embittering it is. . . .

But with the development of industry, the proletariat not only increases in number; it becomes concentrated in greater masses, its strength grows, and it feels that strength more. The various interests and conditions of life within the ranks of the proletariat are more and more equalised, in proportion as machinery obliterates all distinctions of labour, and nearly everywhere reduces wages to the same low level. The growing competition among the bourgeois, and the resulting commercial crises, make the wages of the workers ever more fluctuating. The increasing improvement of machinery, ever more rapidly developing, makes their livelihood more and more precarious; the collisions between individual workmen and individual bourgeois take more and more the character of collisions between two classes. Thereupon, the workers begin to form combinations (Trades' Unions) against the bourgeois; they club together in order to keep up the rate of wages; they found permanent associations in order to make provision beforehand for these occasional revolts. Here and there, the contest breaks out into riots.

Now and then the workers are victorious, but only for a time. The real fruit of their battles lies, not in the immediate result, but in the ever expanding union of the workers. This union is helped on by the improved means of communication that are created by modern industry, and that place the workers of different localities in contact with one another. It was just this contact that was needed to centralise the numerous local struggles, all of the same character, into one national struggle between classes. But every class struggle is a political struggle. And that union, to attain which the burghers of the Middle Ages, with their miserable highways, required centuries, the modern proletarian, thanks to railways, achieve in a few years. . . .

Of all the classes that stand face to face with the bourgeoisie today, the proletariat alone is a really revolutionary class. The other classes decay and finally disappear in the face of Modern Industry; the proletariat is its special and essential product. . . .

The advance of industry, whose involuntary promoter is the bourgeoisie, replaces the isolation of the labourers, due to competition, by the revolutionary combination, due to association. The development of Modern Industry, therefore, cuts from under its feet the very foundation on which the bourgeoisie produces and appropriates products. What the bourgeoisie therefore produces, above all, are its own grave-diggers. Its fall and the victory of the proletariat are equally inevitable.

Source: *The Marx-Engels Reader*, edited by Robert C. Tucker (New York: Norton, 1972), pp. 335–45.

Interpreting Visual Evidence

The Gender of Nations

Nations are abstractions. They have no material form. The scholar Benedict Anderson famously referred to them as "imagined communities," groups of people who have never met, who may not even speak the same language or worship the same god(s), and yet who come to think of themselves as sharing something profound in common, such as being American, or Egyptian, or Chinese. In order to create this sort of community, nationalists have had to represent their nations visually, often in human form and more often as women than as men. For every John Bull (England) or Uncle Sam (the United States), there were several Mariannes (France) or Ranis of Jhansi (India). Especially in areas where few people could read, images and iconography played a vital role in spreading the idea of nationalism to the masses.

The attributes of the chosen figures provide insight into different nationalist movements. The figures' ties to real or invented historical traditions often reflect how these movements defined themselves in opposition to established authorities. In the first image, *Liberty Leading the People* (1830), the French Romantic painter Eugène Delacroix represents a barefoot, bare-chested woman, Marianne, leading a cross-class group of rebels against King Charles X. She wears a Phrygian bonnet, an image of freedom borrowed from antiquity, which had become popular during the Revolution of 1789–1799. In the 1890s, an Egyptian Jew named Ya'qub Sanu'a published a nationalist journal in Paris called *Abu Naddara*, which helped introduce Egypt to cartoons. In one issue he presents a veiled Egypt, with France and Russia by her side, confronting Great Britain. A similar use of allegory is at work in the Brazilian artist Manuel Lopes Rodrigues's painting of a woman. But the allusions are mixed. The woman wears the Phrygian bonnet and thus establishes her connection to French principles and the ancient world. She also wields a sword of justice. Unlike Marianne, the Brazilian heroine is in command, looking confidently but calmly into the future. Finally, the Rani of Jhansi was the queen of the Maratha-ruled state of Jhansi

Delacroix, *Liberty Leading the People.*

Sanu'a, cartoon in *Abu Naddara.*

in the north-central part of India and a leading figure in the Rebellion of 1857. She later became a nationalist icon, as the twentieth-century watercolor here illustrates, and a symbol of heroic resistance against the British.

QUESTIONS FOR ANALYSIS

1. Why do you think nationalists in all of these countries, unlike those in Great Britain and the United States, used female symbols for the nation? What kind of established political authority did they challenge, and how did that challenge differ from the British and American cases?
2. Why do you think Rodrigues, like other artists around the world, borrowed French imagery so explicitly? What does that tell us about Brazilian politics, the challenges the Brazilian people faced, and their reservoirs of strength?
3. Why do you think Sanu'a, a cosmopolitan liberal who had criticized the subordination of women, presented Egypt as a fully covered, veiled woman? To whom do you think he was appealing?
4. To what extent does the image of the Rani of Jhansi look backward and invoke history, at least implicitly? To what extent does it look forward and make claims about the nature of contemporary India?

Rodrigues, *Efígie da República.*

The Rani of Jhansi.

Before You Read This Chapter

GLOBAL STORYLINES

How Nation-States Became Global Empires

- Nation-state building and imperialism change the map of the world.
- Industrialization, science, and technology enable states in North America and western Europe—and, to a lesser extent, Japan—to overpower other regions politically, militarily, and economically.
- European, American, and Japanese imperialists encounter significant opposition in Africa and Asia.

CHAPTER OUTLINE

17

Nations and Empires

1850–1914

FOCUS QUESTIONS

- Which institutions enabled elites in western Europe, the Americas, and Japan to consolidate nation-states, and to what degree did they succeed during this period?
- How did industrialization, science, and technology affect the expansion of powerful states into the rest of the world?
- In what ways were the reactions to imperialism in Asia and Africa alike, and in what ways were the reactions different? How effective were these responses?
- To what extent did colonies contribute to the wealth and political strength of the nation-states that controlled them?

In 1895, the Cuban patriot José Martí launched a rebellion against the last Spanish holdings in the Americas. The anti-Spanish struggle continued until 1898, when Spain withdrew from Cuba and Puerto Rico. Martí hoped to bring freedom to a new Cuban nation and equality to all Cubans. But even as he helped secure freedom from the declining Spanish Empire, he could not prevent Cuba's military occupation and political domination by the world's newest imperial power, the United States.

Martí's hopes and frustrations found parallels around the world. After 1850, the building of nation-states and the expansion of their empires changed the map of the world, exhilarating some peoples and frustrating others. It was a worldwide phenomenon, spanning Japan's northern islands, the indigenous Lakota empire in the heart of North America, and dreams of Arab unity across the Middle East. But the communities that benefited most were Europeans and peoples of European descent. During these decades, the nation-states of Europe, now locked in intense political and economic rivalry, projected their power across the entire world. Much of the rivalry among European states intensified through disruptions in the European balance of power, caused by the unification of two new states (Italy and Germany). Across the Atlantic, the United States forsook its anticolonial origins and annexed overseas possessions and in so doing ran into rivals in the south, north, and west, each with their own visions.

Imperial expansion did not go unchallenged. It encountered fierce resistance from communities that did not want to be part of someone else's empire. In Asia, Africa, and across the Americas, resisters struggled to repel their invaders, often demanding the right to govern themselves.

The second half of the nineteenth century witnessed the simultaneous—and entwined—advance of nationalism and imperialism. These decades also saw the further expansion of the industrial revolution, and with it the economic and social resources to power expansion and integration of market and political forces. Taken together, the era's developments allowed western Europe and the United States to attain greater primacy in world affairs. But tensions inside these nations and their empires, as well as within other states, made the new world order anything but stable.

Consolidating Nations and Constructing Empires

During the second half of the nineteenth century, the idea of building nation-states engulfed the globe. In the previous century, a series of wars, ending with the Napoleonic wars, had made Europeans increasingly conscious of political and cultural borders and of the power of new bureaucracies. Enlightenment thinkers had emphasized the importance of nations, defined as peoples who share a common past, territory, culture, and tradition. To many people it seemed natural that once absolutist rulers had fallen, the state should draw its power and legitimacy from those who lived within its borders and that the body of institutions governing each territory should be uniquely concerned with promoting the welfare of that particular people. While this was a cultural project, new technologies played a vital role in augmenting states' powers to make nations, especially in communications, with the arrival of the telegraphic cable and cheaper printing presses; and transportation, with the advent of steamships, screw propellers, and railways. These breakthroughs collapsed distances, accelerated mobilities, and permitted new states and their leaders to integrate their peoples and expand their frontiers.

Building Nationalism

Nations did not usually well up from people's longings for liberty and togetherness. More often than not, ruling elites created nations. They did so by compelling diverse groups of people and regions to accept a unified network of laws, a central administration, time zones, national markets and currencies, and a single regional dialect as the "national" language. To overcome strong regional identities, state administrators broadened public education in the national language and imposed universal military service to build a national army. These efforts nurtured the notion of a one-to-one correspondence between a "people" and a nation-state, and they radiated the values and institutions of dominant elites outward to regions throughout each nation-state and beyond their national borders.

The world's major nation-states of the late nineteenth century were not all alike, however. They took many forms. Some had been in existence for years, such as Japan, England, France, Spain, and Portugal; here, citizens embraced their national identities. Some were colonial breakaways, like the United States, Brazil, Haiti, and much of Spanish America; here, multi-racial societies had to create unity out of their diversity. Some nation-states, such as Germany and Italy, were entirely new, forged through strategic military conquests. Elsewhere, plans for nation-states in central Europe, the Balkans, Poland, and Ukraine were chiefly the inventions of local elites; their plans displeased Russian, Austrian, and Ottoman monarchs and were of little interest to the multilingual, multiethnic peasantry in these areas. In many parts of the world, intellectuals were the primary agents agitating for new nation-states, often urging new states to break away from existing empires. That secessionist impulse posed a particularly thorny challenge to the rulers of multinational empires like Russia and Austria.

Expanding the Empires

In countries that became nation-states, the processes of nation building and the acquisition of new territories, often called **imperialism**, went hand in hand. Their rulers measured national strength not only by their people's unity and the possession of the most modern means of production, but also by the conquest of new territories. Thus, Germany, France, the United States, Russia, and Japan rivaled Britain by expanding and modernizing their industries and seizing nearby or far-off territories. By the century's end, gaining new territory had become so important that these states scrambled to colonize peoples from Africa to the Amazon, from California to Korea. (See Map 17.1.)

Never before had there been such a rapid reshuffling of peoples and resources. As transportation costs declined, workers left their homelands in search of better opportunities. Japanese moved to Brazil, Indians to South Africa and the Caribbean, Chinese to California, and Italians to New York and Buenos Aires. At the same time, American capitalists invested outside the United States, and British investors financed the construction of railroads in China and India. Raw materials from Africa and Southeast Asia flowed to the manufacturing nations of Europe and the Americas.

Imperial rule facilitated a widespread movement of labor, capital, commodities, and information. As scholars studied previously unknown tribes and races, new schools taught colonized peoples the languages, religions, scientific practices, and cultural traditions of their colonizers. Publications and products from the "mother country" circulated widely among indigenous elites. Yet empire builders did not extend to the people of color who inhabited their colonies the same rights that they gave to inhabitants of their own nations; here, nation and empire were incompatible—and a divide opened across the world between peoples who belonged to nations and began to enjoy rights as citizens and those who lived in colonial or semi-colonial societies with few or no rights. Not only were colonial subjects largely prohibited from participating in their own governments, but they were, with few exceptions, also not considered members of the nation at all. As a result, imperialism produced diametrically opposed reactions: exultation among the colonizers and bitterness among the colonized.

Expansion and Nation Building in the Americas

Once freed from European control, the elites of the Americas used new techniques, from schools to censuses, and technologies, especially in commercial printing, to create political communities of their own. By the 1850s, they shared a desire both to create widespread loyalty to their political institutions and to expand territorial domains. This required refining the tools of government to include national laws and court systems, standardized money, and national political parties. It also meant finding ways to settle hinterlands that previously belonged to indigenous populations. Having once been European colonies, New World territories became vibrant nation-states based on growing prosperity and industrialization.

Although nation-states took shape throughout the world, the Americas saw the most complete assimilation of new possessions. Instead of treating outlying areas as colonial outposts, American nation-state builders turned them into new provinces. With the help of rifles, railroads, schools, and land surveys, frontiers became staging areas for the expanding populations of North and South American societies. For indigenous peoples, however, such national expansion meant the loss of traditional lands on a vast scale and many lost lives. In some cases, it also meant creating empires of their own.

Not all national consolidations in the Americas were the same. The United States, Canada, and Brazil, for example, experienced different processes of nation building, territorial expansion, and economic development. Each one incorporated frontier regions into national polities and economies, although they used different techniques for subjugating indigenous peoples and administering their new holdings.

The United States

Military might, fortuitous diplomacy, and the power of numbers enabled the United States to claim territory that spanned the North American continent. (See Map 17.2.) At its independence, the new nation had been a barely united confederation of states. Indigenous resistance and Spanish and British rivalry hemmed in the "Americans" (as Americans of European descent came to call themselves). At the same time, the disunited states threatened to fracture into northern and southern polities, for questions of states' rights and slavery versus free labor intruded into national politics. Yet, rallying to the rhetoric of **Manifest Destiny**, a term first coined in 1845 for the idea that it was God's will for the United States to "overspread" North America, Americans pushed their territorial claims and boundaries westward. They acquired territories via purchase agreements and treaties with France, Spain, and Britain and via warfare and treaties with diverse Indigenous Native American nations and Mexico. (See Global Themes and Sources: Primary Source 17.1.)

"Acquiring" territories is a nice way to put what was, to Indigenous peoples, a land grab. For many, it meant expulsion and removal to make way for Euro-American settlers. By the late 1840s, some 100,000 Indigenous Americans out of more than 300,000 living west of the Mississippi River were forced to live in "Indian Territory"—which would in turn later be raided by subsequent waves of settlement. For some Indigenous peoples, the pressure spurred the creation of empires of their own. The Lakota people, for instance, created a vast, powerful alliance in the west. Responding to the call of Ptesánwin, White Buffalo Calf Woman, a supernatural being who guided them to bison herds and spiritual fulfilment, Lakota leaders established a heartland beyond the Missouri River. With Cheyennes, Arapahos, Kiowas, Shoshones, and many others, they too expanded their reach, bought weapons, sold hides, and kept settlers at bay. Farther south, Comanches did the same. They became an equestrian superpower, and became active trading partners with nearby settlers, like Iowa farmers who were desperate to survive. Mobile, powerful, and wealthy, these inland empires used the same technologies of conquest as non-Indigenous Americans—guns, money, and treaties—to create a sense of united peoplehood. It also set the stage for a lasting clash in the heartlands of North America, which would affect the makings of the Mexican, American, and Canadian nations.

The Global View

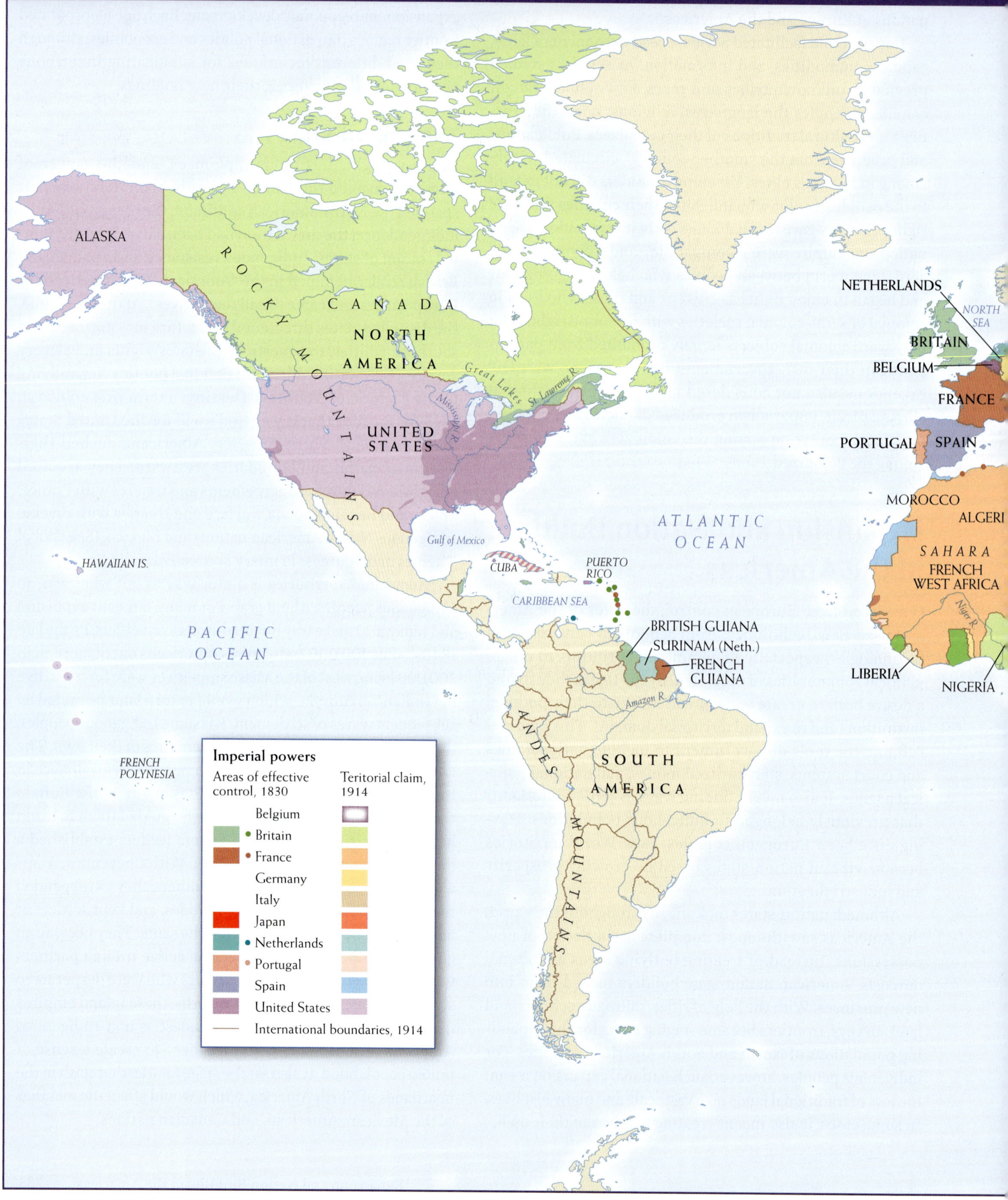

MAP 17.1 | From Nation-States to Global Empires, 1830–1914

Across the nineteenth century into the early twentieth century, countries worldwide first turned into nation-states and then transformed themselves into global empires through colonization.

- According to the map legend, which westernized countries were the most heavily involved in colonizing other peoples around the world?
- According to the map, which regions of the world were most impacted by nineteenth-century imperialism?
- According to the reading, what did these colonizing efforts share in common? What were the different models of colonialism?

MAP 17.2 | U.S. and Canadian Westward Expansion, 1803–1912

Americans and Canadians expanded westward in the second half of the nineteenth century, aided greatly by railways.

- How do you account for the differences between the transcontinental railroads in the United States and Canada?
- When did Canada and the United States complete their respective territorial expansions? Why were these expansions not continuous, moving from east to west?

African American Gains and Losses. *Above*: In the immediate aftermath of the American Civil War, "Radical Republicans" asserted political control by passing laws and constitutional amendments ending slavery, guaranteeing equal rights, and enfranchising freedmen. One result was the election of African Americans to the U.S. Congress. During the 1870s, however, White leaders retreated from the commitment to Black rights, allowing ex-Confederates to reassert control over Southern politics. *Right*: The Ku Klux Klan terrorized African Americans in the post–Civil War South. Klan violence reversed many of the legal and political gains made by freedpeople and helped restore planters to power in the South.

As part of the territories taken from Mexico after the Mexican-American War (1846–1848), the United States gained California, where the discovery of gold brought migration on an unprecedented scale. As news of the find spread, hopeful prospectors raced to stake their claims. In the next few years, over 100,000 Americans took to the overland trails and to the seas in quest of California's riches.

The California gold rush, however, was not only a great American migration; it also inspired tens of thousands of individuals from Latin America, Australia, Asia, and Europe to pour into California. What had just a few years earlier been a sparsely populated corner of northwestern Mexico was transformed almost overnight into the most cosmopolitan place on earth. In the 1850s, California was truly where worlds came together.

CIVIL WAR AND STATES' RIGHTS Ironically, California and the territories that the United States took from Mexico also spurred the coming apart of the American nation. The deeply divisive issue was whether these lands would be open to slavery or restricted to free labor. Following the 1860 election of Abraham Lincoln, who pledged to halt the expansion of slavery, the United States divided between North and South and plunged into a gruesome Civil War (1861–1865).

The bloody conflict led to the abolition of slavery, and the struggle to extend voting and citizenship rights to freedpeople qualified the Civil War as a second American Revolution. It gave the nation a new generation of heroes and martyrs, such as the assassinated president, Abraham Lincoln. Lincoln promised a new model of freedom for a nation reborn out of bloodshed. Its cornerstone would be the incorporation of freedpeople as citizens of the United States. Alas, the experiments in biracial democracy during the Reconstruction period (1867–1877) were short-lived. In the decades after the Civil War, counterrevolutionary pressure led to the denial of voting rights to African Americans and the restoration of (White) planter rule in the Southern states. This pressure was spearheaded by the terrorism of the Ku Klux Klan, a group of former Confederates that sought to undermine African Americans' legal and political gains and to restore White planters to power in the South.

Nonetheless, the war brought enduring changes across the United States. The defeat of the South established the preeminence of the national government. After the Civil War, Americans learned to speak of their nation in the singular ("the United States is" in contrast to "the United States are"). With an invigorated nationalism came an enlarged national government.

ECONOMIC AND INDUSTRIAL DEVELOPMENT Even more dizzying were social and economic changes. Within ten years of the war's end, the industrial output of the United States had climbed by 75 percent. Symbolizing this growth was the expansion of railroad lines. In 1865, the United States boasted 35,000 miles of track. By 1900, nearly 200,000 miles of track connected the Atlantic to the Pacific and crisscrossed the American territory in between. Increasingly, steam-powered machines replaced human muscle as the engine of production, bringing dramatic improvements in output. Before the Civil War, it took 61 hours of labor to produce an acre of wheat; by 1900, new machinery cut the time to a little over 3 hours. Mechanization boosted production on farms and in factories, and rapid railroad transportation permitted the shipment of more goods at lower prices across greater distances. Americans made such impressive industrial gains that the United States soon joined Britain and Germany atop the list of economic giants.

A potent instrument of capital accumulation appeared at this time—the **limited-liability joint-stock company**. Firms such as Standard Oil and U.S. Steel mobilized capital from shareholders, who left the running of these enterprises to paid managers. Intermediaries, like J. Pierpont Morgan, the New York financial giant who became the world's wealthiest man, loaned money and brokered big deals on the New York Stock Exchange. So great were the fortunes amassed by leading financiers and industrialists that by 1890 the richest 1 percent of Americans owned nearly 90 percent of the nation's wealth.

As mechanized production churned out ever more goods, farms and factories produced more than Americans needed or could afford to purchase. In the 1890s, overproduction plunged the American economy into a harsh depression. Millions of urban workers lost their jobs; others suffered sharp cuts in wages. Soon, radical labor leaders called for the dismantling of the industrial capitalist state and strikes proliferated. In the countryside, declining prices and excessive railroad freight charges pushed countless farmers toward bankruptcy.

Meanwhile, Americans were continuing their migrations west. Joined by throngs of immigrants from Europe, they were attracted by homestead acts promising nearly free acreage to settlers and by the railroad's real estate promoters. (Railroad corporations had been given enormous land grants as a subsidy for building transcontinental lines.) The migrations sparked another round of wars with Indigenous peoples, some of them genocidal.

INDIGENOUS RELATIONS IN THE AMERICAN WEST In the mid-nineteenth century, Indigenous peoples living in the Great Plains had signed many treaties with the U.S. government in which tribal boundaries were agreed to and which provided for safe passage of settlers through their tribal lands. As the waves of settlers continued to increase and the treaty provisions were repeatedly violated, a series of "Indian Wars" broke out in the 1860s and 1870s after the Sand Creek Massacre. During the late 1860s, after the initial wave of wars, the U.S. government once again forced the Indigenous peoples to leave their legally recognized ancestral hunting lands and move to remote federal reservations where they were to learn how to farm and be out of the way of settlers. Peace was fleeting after the repeated incursions of gold prospectors into Indigenous lands resulted in the Great Sioux War of 1876. After fifteen months of intense and deadly

Oklahoma Land Rush. This photograph captures the rush of homesteaders to claim lands on the "Cherokee Strip" on September 16, 1893. The opening of land that had previously been restricted to Indigenous peoples set off several similar rushes in the Oklahoma Territory.

battles, Indigenous peoples returned to the federal reservations, where many died from disease and starvation.

By the late nineteenth century, territorial expansion in the United States confined almost all Indigenous peoples to reservations. The buffalo that once supported many tribes disappeared: White settlers built towns, farms, and railroads through the buffalo's natural habitat, and Indigenous peoples overhunted the shrinking herds. Across the American West, many Indigenous people fell into despair. One was a Paiute Indian named Wovoka. But in 1889, he had a vision of a much brighter future. In his dream, the "Supreme Being" told Wovoka that if Indigenous people lived harmoniously, shunned White ways (especially alcohol), and performed the cleansing **Ghost Dance**, then the buffalo would return and they, including the dead, would be reborn to live in eternal happiness.

As word spread of Wovoka's vision, Indigenous people from hundreds of miles around made pilgrimages to the lodge of this new prophet. Many proclaimed him the "Indians' messiah" or the "Red Man's Christ," an impression fostered by scars on his hands. Especially among the Shoshone, Arapaho, Cheyenne, and Sioux peoples of the northern Plains, Wovoka's message inspired new hope. Soon increasing numbers joined in the ritual Ghost Dance, hoping it would restore the good life that English colonialism in the Americas had extinguished. Among the hopefuls was Sitting Bull, a revered Sioux chief who was himself famous for his visions. Yet, less than two years after Wovoka's vision, Sitting Bull died at the hands of police forces on a Sioux reservation. A few days later, on December 29, 1890, the U.S. Seventh Cavalry Regiment massacred Sioux Ghost Dancers at a South Dakota creek called Wounded Knee. It was a dark moment and time for sure for Indigenous peoples in the United States, but it would not be their end, either.

By now the United States had become a major world power. It boasted an economy that despite its troubles in the 1890s had expanded rapidly over the last decades of the nineteenth century. It also was a more integrated nation after the Civil War, with an amended constitution that claimed to uphold the equality of all members of the American nation. But there was no agreement on what that equality should involve or how the country would adjust to a new century in which the nation's "destiny" had already been fulfilled.

Canada

Canadians also built a new nation, enjoyed economic success, and followed an expansionist course. Like the United States, Canada had access to a vast frontier prairie for growing agricultural exports. And as in the United States, these lands became the homes and farms of more European immigrants. However, whereas the United States had waged a war to gain independence, Canada's separation from Britain was peaceful. From the 1830s to the 1860s, Britain gradually passed authority to the colony, leaving Canadians to grapple with the task of creating a shared national community while moving into territories where Native peoples had created their own homelands.

BUILDING A NATION Sharp internal divisions made that task especially difficult. For one thing, there was a well-established French population. It had remained after the British took control of France's northernmost North American colony in 1763. Wanting to keep their villages, their culture, their religion, and their language intact, these French Canadians did not feel integrated into the emerging Canadian national community. Nor were they eager to join the English-speaking population in settling new areas, lest such migration dilute their French Canadian presence.

The English speakers were equally unenthusiastic about creating an independent nation. Fear of being absorbed into the American republic reinforced these Canadians' loyalty to the British crown and made them content with colonial status. Indeed, when Canada finally gained its independence in 1867, it was by an Act of Parliament in London and not by revolution.

TERRITORIAL EXPANSION Lacking cultural and linguistic unity, not to mention an imperial overlord, Canadians used territorial expansion to build an integrated state. But their process differed from that of their neighbor to the south. In response to the U.S. purchase of Alaska from Russia and the movement of settlers onto the American plains, Canadian leaders realized that they had to incorporate their own western territories, lest these, too, fall into American hands. Pioneers seemed unwilling to venture to these prairies—it was far, it was cold, and the growing season was cruelly short. So the state lured emigrant farmers from Europe and the United States with subsidized railway rates and the promise of fortunes to be made. It also offered attractive terms to railway companies to connect agrarian hinterlands with Montreal and Toronto (see again Map 17.2) and *not* with commercial cities in the United States.

The Canadian state also faced friction with Indigenous peoples. Frontier warfare threatened to drive away investors and settlers, who could always find property south of the border instead. To prevent the kind of bloodletting that characterized the United States' westward expansion, the Canadian government signed treaties with Indigenous peoples to ensure strict separation between these communities and newcomers. It also created a special police force, the Royal Canadian Mounted Police, to patrol the territories.

Canadian expansion was hardly bloodless, however. Many Indigenous and mixed-blood peoples (*Métis*) resented the treaties. Moreover, the Canadian government was often less than honest in its dealings. As in the United States, the Canadian government sought either to push them into out-of-the-way

Abolition in Brazil. The abolition of slavery in Brazil was by far the most popular act of the country's monarchy, though it immediately alienated the planter class and led to the bloodless downfall of the royal family. *Left*: A large crowd is gathered before the Imperial Palace in Rio de Janeiro to applaud Princess Isabel in particular. Observe the number of umbrellas used to protect against the sun. *Right*: Although the abolition of slavery had widespread support, it was immediately turned into a political symbol. In *Libertação dos Escravos* (1889), the painter Pedro di Figueredo Americo idealizes the act as a republican gesture of salvation for pleading freedom seekers who are surrounded by ennobled Whites (represented as women) who shower their praise on the royal liberator. Note how the artist relegates the monarch to the background, in contrast to the immense support she receives in the photo. Note also the racial stratification suggested by the depiction of enlightened Whites and prostrate, bawling, Blacks. Such racist imagery makes for a sharp contrast with the uniform, unified scene in the black-and-white photograph.

territories or turn Indigenous peoples into farmers and then incorporate them into Canadian society. As in the United States, heartland peoples created their own nations and empires to resist the intruders.

One difference between Canada and the United States, however, was the role of the government. The need to accommodate resident French speakers, prevent American intrusion north of the border, and the relative scarcity of land-hungry settlers willing to endure shorter growing seasons and harsher conditions in Canada, meant that state authorities had greater autonomy to bargain with and recognize the rights of Indigenous peoples. They acquired powers to intervene, regulate, and mediate social conflict and relations. In 1870, for instance, to create a new province of Manitoba, the national government gave the Red River Métis 1.4 million prized acres to ease tensions—though in practice, the lands got sold off and led to ongoing court battles over Aboriginal title, which recently ended with Supreme Court rulings holding the federal government responsible for failing to honor its deal. But even though the state was relatively strong, the sense of a national identity was comparatively weak. Expansionism helped Canada remain an autonomous state, but it did not solve the question of what it meant to belong to a Canadian nation.

Latin America

Latin American elites also engaged in nation-state building and expanded their territorial borders. But unlike the situation in the United States and Canada, expansion did not create homesteader frontiers that could help expand democracy and forge national identities. Instead, civil conflict fractured certain countries in the region and rural elites hung on to their private properties and political privileges (see Chapters 15 and 16).

Far more than in North America, the richest lands in Latin America went not to small farmers but to large estate holders producing exports such as sugar, coffee, or beef. The result: while Latin America shared in the world's frontier expansion and general economic growth, elites hoarded opportunities at the expense of the poor, the Indigenous people, and people of color.

CONSOLIDATION VERSUS FRAGMENTATION Indigenous peoples and peasant uprisings were a major worry in new Latin American republics. Fearing insurrections, elites devised governing systems that protected private property and investments while limiting the political rights of the poor and the propertyless. Likewise, the specter of revolts by enslaved resisters, driven home not just by earlier, brutal events in Haiti (see Chapter 15) but also by daily rumors of rebellions, kept elites in a state of alarm. One Argentine writer, Domingo Faustino Sarmiento, echoed the concern about giving too much power to the masses, and he described the challenge of nation-state building in Latin America as a struggle between elitist "civilization" and popular "barbarism." Creating strong nations, it seemed to many Latin American elites, required excluding large groups of people from power.

BRAZIL: AN "EXCLUSIVE" NATION-STATE Brazil illustrates the process by which Latin American rulers built nation-states that excluded much of the population from both the "nation" and the "state." Through the nineteenth century, rulers in Rio de Janeiro defused political conflict by allowing planters to retain the reins of power. Moreover, although the Brazilian government officially abolished the slave trade in 1830, it allowed illegal imports of enslaved human beings to continue for another two decades (until, in 1851, British pressure compelled Brazil to enforce the ban).

The end of the slave trade, coupled with freedom seekers' resistance, began to choke the planters' system by driving up the price of the enslaved within the region. Sensing that the system of forced labor was unraveling, enslaved people began to flee the sugar and coffee plantations, and army personnel refused to hunt them down. In the 1880s, even while laws still upheld enslaved labor, country roads in the state of São Paulo were filled with freedom seekers looking for relatives or access to land. Finally, in 1888, the Brazilian emperor abolished slavery.

Thereafter, as in the United States, Brazilian elites followed two strategies in creating a new labor force for their estates. They retained some formerly enslaved men and women as gang-workers or sharecroppers, and they also imported new workers—especially from Italy, Spain, and Portugal. These laborers often came as seasonal migrant workers or indentured tenant farmers. Indeed, European and even Japanese migration to Brazil helped planters preserve their holdings in the post-slavery era. In all, 2 million Europeans and some 70,000 Japanese moved to Brazil.

The Brazilian state was exclusive by design. The constitution of 1891 established a federal system and proclaimed Brazil a republic, but its electoral rules barred all women and the vast majority of men from voting. After all, with the abolition of slavery, the sudden enfranchisement of millions of freedmen would have threatened to flood the electoral lists with propertyless, potentially uncontrollable voters. As in the United States, politicians responded by slapping severe restrictions on suffrage and by rigging rules to reduce political competition. However, given the greater share of the Black population in Brazil, restrictions there excluded a larger share of the potential electorate than in the United States.

BRAZIL: EXPANSION AND ECONOMIC DEVELOPMENT Like Canada and the United States, the Brazilian state extended its reach to distant areas and incorporated them as provinces. The largest land grab occurred in the Amazon River basin, the world's largest drainage watershed and tropical forest. It had built up over millennia around the meandering tributaries that convey runoffs from the eastern slopes of the Andes all the way to the Atlantic Ocean. It was a massive yet delicate habitat of balanced biomass suspended by towering trees with a canopy of leaves and vines that kept the basin ecologically diverse. Here, the Brazilian state gave giant concessions to local capitalists to extract rubber latex. When combined with sulfur, rubber was a key raw material for tire manufacturing in European and North American bicycle and automobile industries.

Opera House in Manaus. The turn-of-the-century rubber boom brought immense wealth to the Amazon jungle. As in many boom-and-bust cycles in Latin America, the proceeds flowed to a small elite and diminished when the rubber supply outstripped the demand. But the wealth produced was sufficient to prompt the local elite to build temples of modernity in the midst of the jungle. Pictured here is the Opera House in the rubber capital of Manaus. Like other works built by Latin American elites of the period, this one emulated the original in Paris.

As Brazil became the world's exclusive exporter of rubber, its planters, merchants, and workers prospered. Rich merchants became lenders and financiers, not only to workers but also to landowners themselves. The mercantile elites of Manaus, the capital of the Amazon region, designed and decorated their city to reflect their new fortune. Although the streets were still paved with mud, the town's elites built a replica of the Paris Opera House, and Manaus became a regular stopover for European opera singers on the circuit between Buenos Aires and New York. Rubber workers also benefited from the boom. Men migrated from farms and villages around the Amazon and from the impoverished northeast. Many moved into and mingled with local populations, like the Amahuaca, who hunted, fished, and sold survival goods to the rubber

Rubber Plantation Workers. *Left*: A worker harvests latex, a milky fluid that is secreted from a rubber tree via taps in its trunk. *Right*: The worker must work quickly to collect and process it into dry rubber before it coagulates.

tappers. As in North America, when the pressure on them mounted, the Amahuaca were fully prepared to lash back and make frontier life miserable for the newcomers. What was distinctive about rubber is that it was not the land but the native trees that were prized; so instead of pushing people off the land and selling it to settlers, most rubber empresarios wanted to draft them to tap the latex. Mostly either Indigenous peoples or mixed-blood people, they saved meager sums to take home to their kin. Meanwhile, women and girls took care of subsistence plots or worked as domestics. In this fashion, the benefits of the commodity boom in the Amazon trickled down to the poor. In practice, though, Indigenous peoples and the poor newcomers were not so much dispossessed of land as much as they were exploited as workers.

The Brazilian rubber boom soon went bust. One problem was the ecosystem: such a diversified biomass could not tolerate a regimented form of production that emphasized the cultivation of rubber trees at the expense of other vegetation and made the forest vulnerable to nonhuman predators. Leaf blight and ferocious ants destroyed all experiments at creating more sustainable rubber plantations. Moreover, it was expensive to haul the rubber latex out of the jungle all the way to the coast along the slow-moving Amazon River. Another problem was that Brazilian rubber faced severe competition after a British scientist smuggled rubber plant seeds out of Brazil in 1876. Following years of experimentation, British patrons transplanted a blight-resistant hybrid to the British colony of Ceylon (present-day Sri Lanka). As competition led to increased supplies and reduced prices, Brazilian producers went bankrupt. Merchants called in their loans, landowners forfeited their titles, and rubber workers returned to their subsistence economies. Tropical vines crept over the Manaus Opera House, and it gradually fell into disrepair.

Throughout the Americas, nineteenth-century elites adapted older models of politics while attempting to satisfy popular demands for inclusion. Although the ideal was to construct nation-states that could reconcile differences among their citizens and pave the way for economic prosperity, in fact political autonomy did not bring prosperity, or even the right to vote, to all. As each nation-state expanded its territorial boundaries, many new inhabitants were left out of the political realm.

Consolidation of Nation-States in Europe

In Europe, no "frontier" existed into which new nations could expand. Instead, nation-states took shape out of older monarchies and empires, and their borders were determined by diplomats or by battles between rival claimants. In the wake of the French Revolution, the idea caught on that "the people" should form the basis for the nation and that nations should be culturally homogeneous—but no one could agree on who "the people" should be. Yet, over the course of the nineteenth century, as literacy, the cities, industrial production, and the number and prosperity of property owners expanded, ruling elites had no choice but to share power with a wider group of citizens. These citizens, in turn, increasingly defined themselves as, say, Frenchmen or Germans, rather than as residents of Marseilles or subjects of the king of Bavaria.

Defining "the Nation"

For a very long time, in most places, "the nation" was understood to comprise kings, clergymen, nobles—and occasionally rich merchants or lawyers—and no one else. Although some peoples, such as the English and the Spanish, were already self-conscious about their unique histories, only in the late eighteenth century did elites start to put the crucial building blocks of European nationalism in place.

Technologies played a vital role in nation building. During the nineteenth century, a huge expansion of literacy and the periodical press made it possible for people all across Europe to read books and newspapers in their own languages. At the same time, the emerging industrial economy made merchants anxious to standardize laws, taxation policies, and weights and measures. States invested huge sums in building roads and then railroads, linking provincial towns with bigger cities and laying the foundations for a closer political integration.

But who were the people, and what constituted a viable nation-state? Few of Enlightenment pamphlets clarified exactly who the communities were that belonged to a specific territory and shared cultural or religious traditions. For some people, the nation was a collection of all those who spoke one language; for others, it was all those who lived under a certain prince or who shared a religious heritage. This was a particularly acute problem in multiethnic central and southeastern Europe, where many people were multilingual, rich and poor alike. But some who shared the same language objected to being lumped into one nation-state. The Irish, for example, spoke English but were predominately Catholics and wanted to be free from Anglican rule.

The Europe-wide revolutions of 1848 (see Chapter 16) sought to put "the people" in power; in many cases, too, rebels sought to create unified nation-states, each of which would serve one particular cultural and linguistic group. (Examples include the Czechs and Italians, both of whom wanted states independent from the Habsburg Empire.) But the revolutions ran into difficulties defining who "the people" were and how to fashion new nations out of Europe's multiethnic empires. Deep divisions opened among ethnic groups and between middle-class liberals and radicals, some of whom wanted to share out the nation's wealth. Monarchs took advantage of the chaos and restored their regimes. The troubling questions continued to agitate Europe for many years to come.

Unification in Germany and Italy

Two of Europe's fledgling nation-states came into being when the dynastic states of Prussia and Piedmont-Sardinia swallowed their smaller, linguistically related neighbors, creating the German and Italian nation-states. (See Map 17.3.) In both regions, conservative prime ministers—Count Otto von Bismarck of Prussia and Count Camillo di Cavour of Piedmont—exploited radical, and especially liberal, nationalist sentiment to rearrange the map of Europe.

BUILDING UNIFIED STATES The unification of Germany and Italy posed all the familiar problems of who the people were and who should be included in the new nation-states. To begin with, German speakers were spread all across central and eastern Europe; after 1815, many, but not all, resided in the Austrian-dominated German Confederation. They continued to live, as they had for centuries, in largely autonomous states of diverse size, wealth, and religious and ethnic makeup. Similarly, Italians had lived separately in city-states and small kingdoms on the Italian Peninsula and spoke a range of dialects. The historical experiences and economic developments had made Bavarian Germans (Catholic) quite different from Prussian Germans (Protestant); likewise, the Milanese (who lived in a wealthy urban industrial center) shared little with the typical Sardinian peasant. But liberal nationalists had made the case that their high culture—especially their musical and theatrical traditions—overrode all these differences, and emotional appeals by poets, composers, and orators convinced many people that this was indeed the case.

Ultimately, Bismarck and Cavour merged nationalist rhetoric with clever diplomacy to forge united German and Italian nations. But both had to go to war to accomplish their aims. In a famous address in 1862, Bismarck bellowed: "Not through speeches and majority decisions are the great questions of the day decided—that was the great mistake of 1848 and 1849—but through blood and iron." True to his word, Bismarck unified the northern German states under the Prussian crown by means of war: with Denmark in 1864, Austria in 1866, and France (over the western provinces of Alsace and Lorraine) in 1870–1871. Italy also was united under the banner of Piedmont-Sardinia through a series of small conflicts, many of them engineered to prevent the establishment of more radical republics.

INTERNAL CONFLICTS These "unified" states were favorable to some liberal principles, but rejected democracy. The new Italy was a constitutional monarchy, not a republic; less than 5 percent of the 25 million people could vote. The new German Empire (the Reich) did have an assembly elected by all adult males (the Reichstag), but it was ruled by aristocrats and bureaucrats under a monarch. In fact, Bismarck continued to dominate Prussian politics for twenty-eight years, until fired in 1890 by Kaiser Wilhelm II.

The new states, especially the Germans, enjoyed brisk economic growth, which simply highlighted the fact that they remained internally fragmented. In Italy, Piedmontese liberals in the north hoped that centralized rule would transform southern Italy into a prosperous, commercial, and industrial region like their own. The south was agricultural, isolated from modernizing impulses, and little attracted to northern customs. The north, industrialized and more fully developed

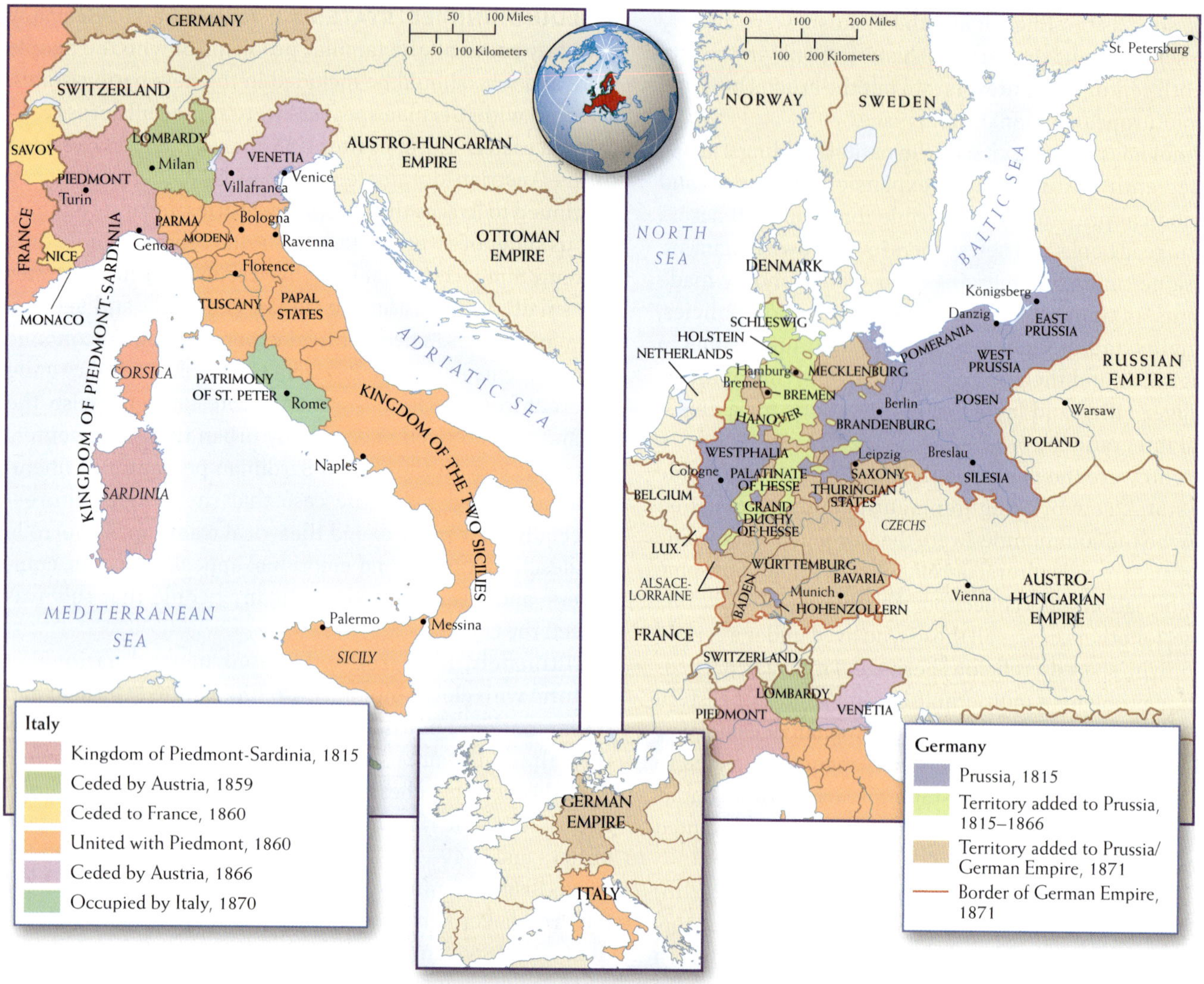

MAP 17.3 | Italian Unification and German Unification, 1815–1871

Italian unification and German unification altered the political map of Europe.

- What were the names of the two original states that grew to become Italy and Germany?
- Who were the big losers in these territorial transfers?
- According to your reading, what problems did the new Italian and German states face in creating strong national communities?

economically, had important commercial links with Switzerland and France. In Germany, many non-Germans—Poles in Silesia, French in Alsace and Lorraine, Danes in the provinces of Schleswig-Holstein—became "national minorities" whose rights remained in question. In the 1870s, Bismarck branded both Catholics and socialists as traitors to the new state; both retaliated by forming powerful political movements. By the 1890s, both Italy and Germany were seething with internal feuds, which turned nationalism into a more belligerent, expansionist, and ultimately destabilizing force.

Nation Building and Ethnic Conflict in the Austro-Hungarian Empire

Bismarck's wars of unification came at the expense of Habsburg supremacy in central Europe and of French territory and influence in the west. Following Germany's swift victory over the Austrian army in 1866, the Hungarian nobles who controlled the eastern Habsburg Empire forced the weakened dynasts to grant them home rule within a larger empire. But this move did not solve Austria-Hungary's nationality problems. On the contrary: Czechs, Poles, and other Slavs now began to clamor for their own autonomous national homelands. The problems were only exacerbated after Austria-Hungary occupied the territory of Bosnia-Herzegovina in 1878 (annexed in 1908), a formerly Ottoman region where the Austrians now ruled over hundreds and thousands of discontented Serbs, Croatians, and Bosnian Muslims.

Domestic Discontents in France and Britain

Nation builders also faced detractors in Britain and France. For the French, dealing with military defeat at the hands of the Germans was the primary national concern in the decades leading up to World War I. For the British, issues of Irish separatism, the rise of the working class, and feminists' demands troubled the political arena.

DESTABILIZATION IN FRANCE Bismarck launched the Franco-Prussian War of 1870–1871 to complete the unification of Germany. The sound drubbing that the French troops received and the capture of Napoleon III early in the conflict embarrassed French patriots. Even more catastrophic was the German siege of Paris, which lasted for more than three months. Having escaped the city by balloon so as to continue the war, the provisional government left Paris without leadership and without food. Parisians resorted to eating all sorts of things, including two zoo elephants. When, in early 1871, the government signed a humiliating peace treaty, furious Parisians vented their rage and established a socialist commune proclaiming the city a utopia for workers. The leftist commune lasted until the provisional national government's predominantly peasant army stormed Paris a few months later. At least 25,000 Parisians died in the bloody mop-up that followed. A "Third Republic" took the place of Napoleon III's empire. Its conservative leaders were wary of the socialists and workers.

Nationalist elites were also bent on revenge for their humiliation in 1871. The years to follow would bring three unsettling developments: first, increasingly sharp conflict between classes over the shape of the republic; second, rising anti-German resentment; and third, French nationalists turned their resentment and search for redemption onto colonial subjects, who now experienced more virulent forms of racism masquerading as a French civilizing mission.

IRISH NATIONALISM IN GREAT BRITAIN The kingdom of England—which was composed of England, clearly the dominant state, and Wales—became the kingdom of Great Britain when it united with Scotland in 1707 and Ireland in 1801. Although the English had long thought of themselves as a nation, the idea that all Britons belonged in the same state was much more problematic. Great Britain was home to people whose historical experiences, religious backgrounds, and economic opportunities were very different. In the nineteenth century, British leaders wrestled in particular with lower-class agitation and demands for independence from Irish nationalists. Beginning in 1832, Britain responded to class conflict by extending political rights to most men but not women, then finally established universal suffrage for adult males after World War I. In 1918, roughly one-quarter

The Irish Potato Famine. Many families in Ireland were left desperate and starving in the aftermath of the potato crop failure and were forced to find sustenance wherever they could. In this engraving from the late nineteenth century, a group of people by the coast collect limpets and seaweed to eat.

of British women gained the right to vote, and the rest did so a decade later.

Yet Ireland remained England's Achilles' heel. Although in 1836 Irish Catholics finally became equal to Protestants before the law, the two communities' political and economic conditions remained very uneven. English and Irish Protestants owned the vast majority of the land and attempted to squeeze Irish smallholders to give up their plots. Over the course of the early nineteenth century, more and more Irish peasants had planted energy-rich and easy-to-cultivate potatoes on their remaining rocky and sandy land. A relatively healthy diet of potatoes and milk had fueled population growth and put more pressure on the land. When a continent-wide potato blight ravaged the island's crops in 1845, this monoculture turned into a recipe for widespread famine. Although the blight continued to decimate harvests for the next four years, the English stuck to their laissez-faire principles and were slow to send grain to relieve Irish suffering, resulting in the death of as many as a million and the emigration of about the same number. Many of these Irish emigrants made their way to England, seeking either passage to North and South America or work in the English mill towns. Like their Scottish brethren, they did not assimilate easily and often got the lowliest jobs. All of this, on top of 300 years of repressive English domination, spawned a mass movement for Irish home rule that continued into the twentieth century.

Born in opposition to the old monarchical regimes, European nationalism by the end of the nineteenth century had become a means used by liberal and conservative leaders alike to unite "the people" behind them. But this did not mean that everyone had equal access to power. Women, the poor, and minority ethnic and religious groups, in particular, did not have a just share. Moreover, by 1900, European nationalisms and bitterness, sowed by the wars of unification, were producing deeper enmities between states and within multinational empires. Nationalism had transformed the map of old European dynasties and given more people a voice in political decision-making and a share in the cultural life than ever before. But it had made Europe a more volatile place.

Eiffel Tower. This 1890 photograph of an illuminated Eiffel Tower encapsulates the fact and spirit of early twentieth-century technological innovation, from the architectural breakthrough of the tower itself to the harnessing of electricity to truly render Paris its nickname—the City of Light.

Industry, Science, and Technology

A powerful combination of industry, science, and technology created the conditions for nationalist conceptions of "the people" to spread. These forces also reordered the relationships between different parts of the world and made them more interdependent. One critical factor was that after 1850, western Europe and North America experienced a new phase of industrial development—essentially a second industrial revolution. Japan, too, joined the ranks of industrializing nations as its state-led program of industrial development started to pay dividends. These changes transformed the global economy and intensified rivalries among industrial societies. For example, Britain now had to contend with competition from the United States, Germany, and Japan.

New Materials, Technologies, and Business Practices

New materials and new technologies were vital in late nineteenth-century economic development. The period witnessed major technological changes with the arrival of new organic sources of power (oil) and new ways to get old organic sources (like coal) to processing plants. These changes freed manufacturers from having to locate their plants close to their fuel sources. Not only did the most important source of energy—electricity—permit factories

Railroad Workers. The construction of railroad lines across the United States was dangerous work, much of it done by immigrant laborers, including large numbers of Chinese, such as those in this photograph taken in 1886.

to arise in areas with plenty of skilled workers, but it also slashed production costs. **Steel**, which was more malleable and stronger than iron, became essential for industries like shipbuilding and railways. The world output of steel shot up from half a million tons in 1870 to 28 million tons in 1900. The miracle of steel was celebrated through the construction of the Eiffel Tower in Paris (completed in 1889), an aggressively modern monument that loomed over the picturesque cityscape and was double the height of any other building in the world at the time. Steel was part of a bundle of innovations that included chemicals, oil, pharmaceuticals, and mass transportation vehicles like trolleys, buses, taxis, and trains. Scientific research, too, boosted industrial development. German companies led the way in creating laboratories where university-trained chemists and physicists conducted research to serve industrial production. The United States likewise wedded scientific research with capitalist enterprise: universities and corporate laboratories produced swelling ranks of engineers and scientists, as well as patents.

The breakthroughs of the second industrial revolution ushered in new business practices, especially mass production and the giant integrated firm. No longer would modest investments suffice, as they had in Britain a century earlier. Now large banks were the major providers of funds. In Europe, limited-liability joint-stock companies were as wildly successful in raising capital on stock markets as they were in the United States. Companies like Standard Oil, U.S. Steel, and Siemens mobilized capital from a large number of investors, the shareholders. The scale of these firms was awesome. U.S. Steel alone produced over half the world's steel ingots, castings, rails, and heavy structural shapes—and nearly half of all its steel plates and sheets, which were vital in the construction of buildings, railroads, ships, and the like.

Integration of the World Economy

Not only did industrial change concentrate power in North Atlantic societies, but it also reinforced their power on the world economic stage and created a more integrated world economy. Of course, Europe and the United States increased their exports of new products; but at the same time, they grew

Suez Canal. The Suez Canal opened to world shipping in 1869 and reduced the time it took to sail between Europe and Asian ports. Although the French and the Egyptians supplied most of the money and the construction plans and Egyptians were the main workforce, British shipping dominated canal traffic from the outset.

eager to control the importation of tropical commodities such as cocoa and coffee. While the North Atlantic societies were still largely self-sufficient in coal, iron, cotton, wool, and wheat (the major commodities of the first industrial revolution), the second industrial revolution bred a need for rubber, copper, oil, and bauxite (an ore used to make aluminum), which were not available domestically. Equally important, large pools of money became available for investing overseas. London may have lost its industrial leadership, but it retained dominance over the world's financial operations. By 1913, the British had the huge sum of £4 billion invested overseas—funds that generated an annual income of £200 million, or one-tenth of Britain's national income.

MOVEMENTS OF LABOR AND TECHNOLOGY Because the more integrated world economy needed workers for fields, factories, and mines, vast movements of the laboring population took place. Indians moved thousands of miles to work on sugar plantations in the Caribbean, Mauritius, and Fiji; to labor in South American mines; and to build railroads in East Africa. Chinese workers constructed railroads in the western United States and toiled on sugar plantations in Cuba. The Irish, Poles, Jews, Italians, and Greeks flocked to North America to fill its burgeoning factories. Italians also moved to Argentina to harvest wheat and corn.

New technologies of warfare, transportation, and communication eased global economic integration—and strengthened European domination. With steam-powered gunboats and breech-loading rifles, Europeans opened new territories for trade and conquest. At home and in their colonial possessions, imperial powers constructed networks of railroads that carried people and goods from hinterlands to the coasts. From there, steamships bore them across the seas. Completion of the Suez Canal in 1869 shortened ship voyages between Europe and Asia and lowered the costs of interregional trade. Information moved even faster than cargoes, thanks to the laying of telegraph cables under the oceans, supplemented by overland telegraph lines.

CHARLES DARWIN AND NATURAL SELECTION Although machines were the most visible evidence that humans could master the universe, perhaps the most momentous shift in the conception of nature derived from the travels of one British scientist: **Charles Darwin** (1809–1882). Longing to see exotic fauna, he signed on for a four-year voyage in 1831 on a surveying vessel bound for Latin America and the South Seas. As the ship's naturalist, Darwin collected large quantities of specimens and recorded observations daily. After returning to England, he became convinced that the species of organic life had evolved under the uniform pressure of natural laws, not by means of a special, one-time creation as described in the Bible.

Darwin's theory, articulated in his *On the Origin of Species* (1859), laid out the principles of **natural selection**. Inevitably, he claimed, populations grow faster than the food supply; this condition creates a "struggle for existence" among species. In later work he showed how the passing on of individual traits is also determined by what he called sexual selection—according to which the "best" mates are chosen for their strength, beauty,

Charles Darwin. Engraving of Darwin testing the speed of a tortoise in the Galápagos Islands. It was during his visit to these islands that Darwin developed many of the ideas that he would put forth in his 1859 *On the Origin of Species.*

or talents. The outcome: the "fittest" survive to reproduce, while the less adaptable do not. The "economy of nature" is, Darwin confessed, a painful reality: people would rather behold "nature's face bright with gladness" than recognize that some animals must be others' prey and that shortages are, ultimately, part of nature's "miraculous efficiency." Although Darwin's book dealt exclusively with nonhuman animals (and mostly with birds), his readers immediately wondered what his theory implied for humans.

A passionate debate began among scientists and laypeople, clerics and anthropologists. Some read Darwin's doctrine of the "survival of the fittest" to mean that it was natural for the strong nations to dominate the weak or justifiable to allow disabled persons to die—something Darwin explicitly refuted. In later work, however, Darwin's own ideas about evolution began to echo some public views about racial superiority and hierarchies. As more groups (mis)interpreted Darwin's theory to suit their own objectives, a set of beliefs known as social Darwinism legitimated the suffering of the underclasses in industrial society: it was unnatural, social Darwinists claimed, to tamper with natural selection. In subsequent years, Europeans would repeatedly suggest that they had evolved more than Africans and Asians. Extending Darwinian ideas far beyond the scientist's intent, some Europeans came to believe that nature itself gave them the right to rule others.

Imperialism and Resistance

Increasing rivalries among nations and social tensions within them produced an expansionist wave late in the nineteenth century. Although Africa became the primary focus of interest, a frenzy of territorial conquest overtook Asia as well. The period witnessed the French occupation of Vietnam, Cambodia, and Laos and the British expansion in Malaya (present-day Malaysia). In China's territories, competition by foreign powers to establish spheres of influence heated up in the 1890s. And in India, imperial ambitions provoked the British to conquer Burma (present-day Myanmar). Moreover, Britain and Russia competed for preeminence from their respective outposts in Afghanistan and central Asia. In the Americas, expansion usually involved the incorporation of new territories as provinces, making them integral parts of the nation.

In Asia and Africa, however, European imperialism turned far-flung territories into colonial possessions. Here, inhabitants were usually designated as subjects of the empire without the rights and privileges of citizens. Britain's imperial regime in India provided lessons to a generation of European colonial officials in Africa and other parts of Asia. Yet, even as Europe's colonial administrators looked to earlier imperial practices in India and the Caribbean for use in Africa, they also regarded Africans as less economically and culturally developed than Asian communities. Hence, they believed that Africans would require an extended period of colonial tutelage.

The exponents of European and North American colonization argued that colonial rule produced benefits for both the colonial peoples and the colonizers. They insisted that there was a moral justification for material pursuits. Economically, colonies would be drawn into and profit from an emerging world economy. They would export primary products in high

Sinews of the Raj. The British allowed several native princes to remain in power as long as they accepted imperial paramountcy. This photograph shows a roadbuilding project in one such princely state. Officials of the Muslim princely ruler and British advisers supervise the workers.

Railways in India. Following the uprising of 1857, after which India became a kingdom of the British Empire and was no longer a concession of the East India Company, the British built an extensive system of railroads to develop India as a profitable colony and to maintain military security. Railways and telegraphs, which connected the interior of the country to the cities and ports of the coast, were more instrumental than anything else in integrating the colony—and eventually the nation. This engraving shows the East India Railway around 1863. The train and the telegraph post overshadow the lush vegetation in the background and cheering Indians watch in idealized marvel.

demand in the industrialized parts of the global economy—like cocoa, diamonds, gold, and copper from Africa; rubber from the Dutch East Indies and Brazil; sugar from the Caribbean; cotton from India and Egypt; and beginning mainly after World War I, oil from the Middle East to fuel industrial economies. In return, colonial peoples would import finished manufactured goods—clothing made from their raw cotton; processed foods made from coffee, cocoa, and sugar; railway engines; and oceangoing vessels. Were the benefits truly evenly distributed, as some imperialist proponents claimed? The consensus is no. While countries that produced tropical commodities experienced rapid growth, the rewards were unevenly spread. Profits flowed mainly to European-run export-import firms, large global banks, wealthy industrialists, and elites tied to their businesses in tropical societies.

Not surprisingly, colonized peoples resisted the imposition of economic systems that favored colonial extractors. There were myriad ways to taking back some control, like seeking freedom from plantation life, stealing cash crops to sell in local markets, and disobeying orders. Sometimes, the colonized defied authorities and organized collectively to strike, occupy estates, and eventually to join mass organizations to demand national self-determination. In many parts of colonial Asia, early forms of resistance, usually put down with savage reprisals, were followed by organized political protest and the formation of nationalist political parties. The African continent, the last to be colonized, at first went through an early phase of armed resistance to colonial rule, which was bloodily repressed. After World War I, colonial critics followed in the footsteps of the Asian anticolonial nationalists. They, too, created anticolonial, mainly nonviolent, political organizations, seeking at first the redress of colonial grievances, such as lost lands. Many of these nations would have to wait until the post–World War II period to achieve full independence. For the most part, however, most resistance defended household and village autonomy and dispossession through local and everyday forms of resistance. Mass nationalist mobilizing had to wait until the turn of the twentieth century or later.

India and the Imperial Model

Having suppressed the Indian Rebellion of 1857 (see Chapter 16), authorities revamped the colonial administration and created what many British colonial officials regarded as a model system of imperial rule. Indians were not to be appeased—and certainly not to be brought into British public life. But they did have to be governed, and the economy had to be revived. So, after replacing East India Company rule by crown government in 1858, the British set out to make India into a more secure and productive colony. This period of British sovereignty was known as the **Raj** ("rule").

The most urgent tasks facing the British in India were those of modernizing its transportation and communication systems and transforming the country into an integrated colonial state. These changes had begun under the governor-general of the East India Company, Lord Dalhousie, who oversaw the development of India's modern infrastructure. When he left office in 1856, he boasted that he had harnessed India to the "great engines of social improvement—I mean Railways, uniform Postage, and the Electric Telegraph." A year later, northern India exploded in the 1857 rebellion. But the rebellion also demonstrated the military value of railroads and telegraphs, for these modern systems were useful tools for

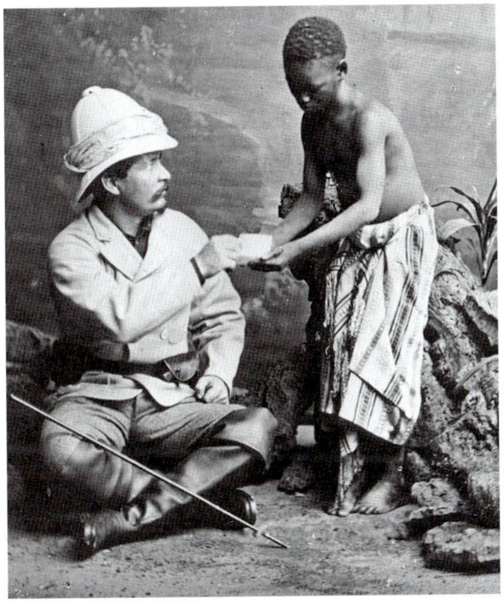

Europeans in Africa. *Left*: Henry Morton Stanley was one of the most famous of the nineteenth-century explorers in Africa. He first made his reputation when he located the British missionary-explorer David Livingstone, feared dead, in the interior of Africa, uttering the famous words, "Dr. Livingstone, I presume." Stanley worked on behalf of King Leopold, establishing the Belgian king's claims to territories in the Congo and often using superior weaponry to cow African opponents. *Right*: The ardent British imperialist Cecil Rhodes endeavored to bring as much of Africa as he could under British colonial rule. He had an ambition to create a swath of British-controlled territory that would stretch from the Cape in South Africa to Cairo in Egypt, as this cartoon shows.

rushing British troops to severely affected regions. After the British suppressed the revolt, they took up the construction of public works with renewed vigor. Railways were a key element in this project, attracting approximately £150 million of British capital. (Though it came from British investors, Indian taxpayers paid off the debt through their taxes.) The first railway line opened in 1853, and by 1910 India had 30,627 miles of track in operation—the fourth largest railway system in the world.

Construction of other public works followed. Engineers built dams across rivers to tame their force and to irrigate lands; workers installed a grid of telegraph lines that opened communication between distant parts of the region. These public works served imperial and economic purposes: India was to become a consumer of British manufactures and a supplier of primary staples such as cotton, tea, wheat, vegetable oil, seeds, and jute (used for making rope or burlap sacking). The control of India's massive rivers allowed farmers to cultivate the rich floodplains, transforming them into lucrative cotton-producing provinces. On the hillsides of the island of Ceylon and the northeastern plains of India, the British established vast plantations to grow tea—which was then marketed in England as a healthier alternative to Chinese green tea. India also became an important consumer of British manufactures, especially textiles, in an ironic turnaround to its centuries-old tradition of exporting its own cotton and silk textiles.

The reform efforts of the Raj made India into a unified territory and enabled its inhabitants to regard themselves as "Indians." These were the first steps to becoming a "nation" like Italy and the United States, but there were profound differences. Above all, as colonial subjects, Indigenous peoples did not have basic civic and human rights. Other European powers, in parallel with the British example, tried to modernize and integrate their colonies economically without welcoming colonial peoples into the life of the nation.

Dutch Colonial Rule in Indonesia

Decades before the British government took control of India away from the East India Company, Holland had terminated the rule of the Dutch East India Company over Indonesia. Beginning in the 1830s, the Dutch government took administrative responsibility over Indonesian affairs. Holland's new colonial officials envisioned a more regulated colonial economy than that of their British counterparts in India. For example, they ordered Indonesian villagers to allocate one-third of their land for cultivating coffee beans, an important export. In return, the colonial government paid a set price (well below world market prices) and placed a ceiling on rents owed to landowners.

These policies had dreadful local consequences. For example, increased production of the export crops of coffee beans, sugar, and tobacco meant reduced food production for the local population. By the 1840s and 1850s, famine spread across Java; over 300,000 Indonesians perished from starvation. Surviving villagers voiced growing discontent, prompting harsh crackdowns by colonial forces. Back in Holland, the embarrassing spectacle of colonial oppression prompted calls for reform. Thus, in the 1860s the Dutch government introduced what it called an ethical policy for governing Asian colonies: it reduced governmental exploitation and encouraged Dutch settlement of the islands and more private enterprise. For Indonesians, however, the replacement of government agents with private merchants made little difference. In some areas, islanders put up fierce resistance. On the sprawling island of Sumatra, for instance, armed villagers fought off Dutch invaders. After decades of warfare, Sumatra was finally subdued in 1904. The shipping of Indonesian staples continued to enrich the Dutch.

Colonizing Africa

No region felt the impact of European colonialism more powerfully than Africa. In 1880, the only two large European colonial possessions in Africa were French Algeria and two British-ruled South African territories, the Cape Colony and Natal. But within a mere thirty years, seven European states had carved almost all of Africa into colonial possessions. (See Map 17.4.)

PARTITIONING THE AFRICAN LANDMASS A major moment in initiating the European scramble for African colonies occurred in 1882 when the British invaded and occupied Egypt. This action provoked the French, who had regarded Egypt as their special sphere of influence ever since Napoleon's 1798 invasion. Indeed, Britain's move not only intensified the two powers' rivalry to seize additional territories in Africa but also alarmed the other European states, fearful that they might be left behind. As these powers joined the scramble, Portugal called for an international conference to discuss claims to Africa. Meeting in Berlin between 1884 and 1885, delegates from Germany, Portugal, Britain, France, Belgium, Spain, Italy, the United States, and the Ottoman Empire agreed to carve up Africa and to recognize the acquisitions of any European power that had achieved occupation on the ground. Colonizers rushed to plant their flags as widely as possible, lest they be outmaneuvered by their rivals.

The consequences for Africa were devastating. Nearly 70 percent of the newly drawn borders failed to correspond to older demarcations of ethnicity, language, culture, and commerce—for Europeans knew little of the landmass beyond its coast and rivers. They based their new colonial boundaries on European trading centers rather than on the location of African population groups. In West Africa, for example, the Yoruba were split between the French in Dahomey and the British in southwestern Nigeria, and a segment of the very large and dynamic Mandara peoples came under British-ruled Nigeria, with another Mandara group being administered by the Germans in Cameroon. (See again Map 17.4.) In fact, Nigeria became an administrative nightmare, as the British attempted to integrate the politically centralized Muslim populations of the north with the city-state Yoruba dwellers and small tribes of the Ibos of the south.

Several motives led the European powers into their frenzied partition of Africa. Although European businesses were primarily interested in Egypt and South Africa, where their investments were lucrative, small-scale traders and investors harbored fantasies of great treasures locked in the vast uncharted interior. Politicians, publicists, and the reading public also took an interest. The writings of explorers like David Livingstone (1813–1873), a Scottish doctor and missionary, and Henry Morton Stanley (1841–1904), an adventurer in the pay of the *New York Herald*, excited readers with accounts of Africa as a continent of unlimited economic potential.

Battle of Adwa. Portrait of King Menelik, who defeated the Italian forces at the Battle of Adwa in 1896, thus saving his country from European colonization.

The most determined of the African empire builders was Leopold II (r. 1865–1909), king of the Belgians. (See Current Trends in World History: Africa's Newest Hunters and Gatherers: Greed, Environmental Degradation, and Resistance.) But in southern Africa, Cecil Rhodes (1853–1902), the British champion of imperialism, brought the Rhodesias, Nyasaland, Bechuanaland, the Transvaal, and the Orange Free State into the British Empire as part of a design to have British territories stretching all the way from the Cape of Good Hope, in South Africa, to Cairo, in Egypt.

Other Europeans saw Africa as a grand opportunity for converting souls to Christianity. In fact, Europe's civilizing mission was an important motive in the scramble for African territory. In Uganda, northern Nigeria, and central Africa, missionaries went ahead of European armies, begging the European statesmen to follow their lead.

AFRICAN RESISTANCE Contrary to European assumptions, Africans did not welcome European "civilization." Resistance, however, was largely futile. Africans faced two unappealing options: they could capitulate to the Europeans and negotiate to limit the loss of their autonomy, or they could fight to preserve their sovereignty. Only a few chose

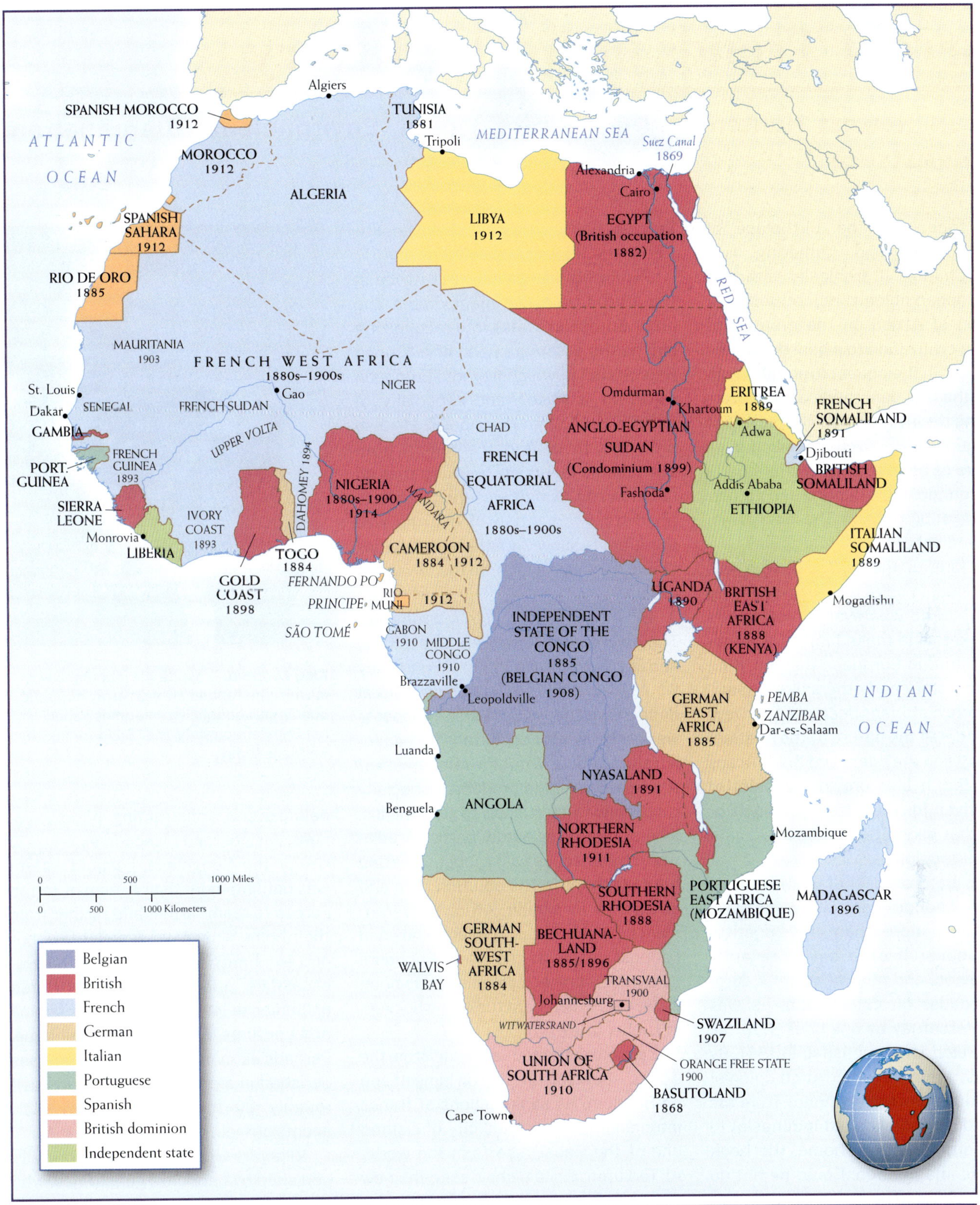

MAP 17.4 | Partition of Africa, 1880–1914

The partition of Africa took place between the early 1880s and the outbreak of World War I.

- Which two European powers gained the most territory in Africa?
- Which two African states managed to remain independent? What kind of economic and political gain did European powers realize through the colonization of Africa? Did any of the European states realize their ambitions in Africa?

Current Trends in World History

Africa's Newest Hunters and Gatherers: Greed, Environmental Degradation, and Resistance

Africa was the birthplace of hunting and gathering (see Chapter 1). Ironically, although the European colonizers justified their partition of Africa on the grounds of bringing civilization to a benighted people, in fact, in their quest to enrich themselves, the first generation of colonizers exploited the most available resources of the continent, enslaved and killed huge numbers of people, and returned parts of the continent to a hunting and gathering mode of production. The most driven and greediest of these figures was Leopold II, king of the Belgians, who was determined, in spite of sweet-sounding rhetoric, to do whatever it took to line his pockets and make himself a formidable figure in European politics. King Leopold's story and others like it fascinate world historians because it conveys in stark detail the nature of the relationship between the rulers and the Africans they ruled. It also provides a point of comparison for the different models of ruling that each European power instituted in its colonies.

Even before ascending the throne in 1865, Leopold cast about for ways to become more than the constitutional monarch of a small, recently established, and neutral state. A voracious reader on colonialism, he was struck forcefully by one book: *How the Dutch Ruled Java*, published in 1861. By demonstrating how the Dutch colonial state had expropriated money from the East Indies (today called Indonesia) to spend on projects at home, the book fired his imagination. Could he not do the same? Could he not stake out a colony, take money from it to swell his own exchequer, and use some of it on public works at home—to beautify the cities of Belgium the way Paris had been beautified in the 1850s and 1860s?

Fixing his gaze on central Africa in the 1880s, Leopold manipulated the other European states into recognizing him as the sovereign head of a "Congo Free State," in which he led a European effort to "civilize" (and especially to exploit) the Congo River basin. He also promised to defend the region from any Islamic incursion, warning that an uncolonized Congo was vulnerable to Jihadists. A condition of his rule was therefore to allow Christian missionaries to add their moral labor to the "civilizing mission."

But how to make these lands pay off? They were almost entirely unexplored and unsurveyed, and though in time they would yield some of the richest mineral deposits in the world, these prospects were unknown to Leopold and his administrators at first. What the rain forests of Africa had was wild products, especially rubber and ivory. But how to get Africans, who at that point hardly participated in world trade, to tap wild rubber vines and hunt elephants? The solution here and elsewhere in similar African environments was to recruit soldiers (known in Leopold's state as the Force Publique) who would compel local villagers to bring in baskets of elephant tusks and buckets of rubber latex.

Leopold extracted vast sums from the Congo, spending lavishly on himself and on Belgium. He sank millions of francs into making the seaside city of Ostend one of the finest resorts in the world. At Tervuren, while a choir sang the new Congo anthem, Leopold laid the foundation stone of a world college for overseas colonial administration. In Brussels he spent over $5 million renovating royal palaces and constructing parks, avenues, casinos, and racecourses.

King Leopold. Despite the inhumane way in which he funded his vast array of public buildings, Leopold is sometimes called, not unaffectionately, the "Builder King" by Belgians today.

For the Congolese, Leopold's state was nothing more than a reign of terror. Forced to roam farther and farther from their home villages in search of rubber and elephants to keep pace with ever-escalating quotas, villagers suffered an immense loss of life through famine and conflicts with the Force Publique. Perhaps as many as 10 million Africans perished in a population that had been roughly 20 million before Leopold's agents arrived.

Villagers who resisted were brutally punished by Leopold's gendarmes, who routinely chopped the hands off those who protested. A man called Nsala brought the remains of his daughter to a Christian mission station as evidence

Exploitation of the Congo. Leopold II, king of the Belgians, gained wealth from a brutal exploitation of the Congo—wealth that he garnered from the killing of elephants for their ivory tusks and that he used to enhance his own personal riches and to beautify Belgian cities.

Nsala from the town of Walla. This photo of Nsala from the town of Walla was taken by Alice Seeley Harris and set off a humanitarian crusade to put an end to atrocities in Congo.

of the atrocities. Alice Seeley Harris, one of the missionaries used her camera—a new device for the time—and took Nsala and his daughter's photo and sent the negative back to Britain; the image stoked humanitarian outrage. As villagers began to testify to journalists and investigators, Belgian rulers were finally forced to strip their emperor of his moral and material claims. In 1908, a year before his death, Leopold was compelled, against his wishes, to turn the administration of the Congo over to the Belgian parliament.

QUESTIONS FOR ANALYSIS

- Why was King Leopold such an important figure in the European partition of Africa?
- While the Congo story is one of the most brutal stories of colonial exploitation and environmental degradation, which other episodes in world history does it remind you of and why?

EXPLORE FURTHER

Harms, Robert, *Land of Tears: The Exploration and Exploitation of Equatorial Africa* (2019).

Hochschild, Adam, *King Leopold's Ghost* (1998).

the course of moderation. Lat Dior, a Muslim warlord in Senegal, refused to let the French build a railway through his kingdom. "As long as I live, be well assured," he wrote the French commandant, "I shall oppose with all my might the construction of this railway. I will always answer no, no, and I will never make you any other reply. Even were I to go to rest, my horse, *Malay*, would give you the same answer." Conflict was inevitable, and Lat Dior lost his life in a battle with the French in 1886.

Only Menelik II of Ethiopia repulsed the Europeans, for he knew how to play rivals off one another. By doing so, he procured weapons from the French, British, Russians, and Italians. He also had a united, loyal, and well-equipped army. In 1896, his troops routed Italian forces at the Battle of Adwa, after which Adwa became a celebrated moment in African history. Its memory inspired many of Africa's later nationalist leaders.

Most resisters were ignorant of the disparity in military technology between Africans and Europeans—especially the killing power of European breech-loading weapons and the Maxim machine gun. In addition, the European armies had better tactics and a more sustained appetite for battle. Africa's armies fought during the nonagricultural season, engaging in open battles so as to achieve quick and decisive results and then returning to their farms. Such military traditions were effective in fighting neighbors, but not well-equipped invaders.

Some African forces did adapt their military techniques to the European challenge. For example, Samori Touré (1830–1900) proved a stubborn foe for the French, employing guerrilla warfare and avoiding full-scale battles in the savanna lands of West Africa. From 1882 until 1898, Touré eluded the French. Dividing his 35,000-man army, Touré had one contingent take over territories not yet conquered by the French and there reestablish a fully autonomous domain. A smaller contingent conducted a scorched-earth campaign in the regions from which it was retreating, leaving the French with parched and wasted new possessions. But these tactics only delayed the inevitable. The French finally defeated and captured Touré and sent him into exile in Gabon, where he died in 1900.

COLONIAL ADMINISTRATIONS IN AFRICA Once the euphoria of partition and conquest had worn off, power fell to "men on the spot"—military adventurers, settlers, and entrepreneurs whose main goal was to get rich quick. As these individuals established near-fiefdoms in some areas, Africans (like Native Americans on the other side of the Atlantic) found themselves confined to territories where they could barely provide for themselves. To uphold such an invasive system at minimal expense, Europeans created permanent standing armies by equipping their African supporters, whom they either bribed or compelled to join their side. Such armies bullied local communities into doing the colonial authorities' bidding.

Eventually, these rough-and-ready systems led to violent revolts from aggrieved Africans, and in their aftermath the colonial rulers had to create more efficient administrations dedicated to providing health care and education for the colonized. As in India, colonial powers in Africa laid the foundations for future nation-state organizations. Once information trickling out of Africa revealed that the imperial governments were not realizing their goal of bringing "civilization" to the "uncivilized," each European power implemented a new form of colonial rule, stripping the strongman conquerors of their

Tuareg Resistance. Tuareg warriors put up stiff resistance against European intruders. The Tuareg people ran the caravan routes across the Sahara from North to West Africa and became powerful and wealthy thanks to expanding trade. Since they were also nomadic, they had large herds of camels, which they deployed in battle with peerless skill. Trade also gave them access to weapons and they played European rivals against one another. The Sahara, therefore, was a perennial source of resistance to colonization. This image depicts Tuareg warriors wiping out a French patrol in the early twentieth century at a time when publics in Europe were starting to question the legitimacy of empire.

absolute powers, monitoring them more closely, and assuming greater responsibility for the conquered peoples.

However much the colonial systems of the European states differed, all had three similar goals. First, the colony was to pay for its own administration. Second, administrators on the spot had to preserve the peace; nothing brought swifter criticism from the mother country than a colonial rebellion. Third, colonial rule was to attract other European groups, such as missionaries, settlers, and merchants. Missionaries came to convert "heathens" to Christianity, convinced that they were battling with Islam for the soul of the continent. Settlers went only to those parts of Africa that had climatic conditions similar to those in Europe. They poured into Algeria and South Africa but only trickled into Kenya, Southern Rhodesia, Angola, and Mozambique, attracted by advertising at home that stressed comfortable living conditions and promised that these areas would someday become White man's territories. Moreover, colonial governments' promises to construct railroads, roads, and deep-water facilities persuaded European merchants and investors to take out bigger commercial stakes in Africa.

Europeans brought their extreme racial attitudes toward peoples of color into Africa. They discovered similar views toward Whiteness and Blackness within African societies and were quick to take advantage of this overlap. In West Africa, the British, French, and Germans lacked a large administrative staff and were wholly dependent on noncommissioned African soldiers and police forces to maintain their authority. They quickly gravitated to those ethnic groups who regarded themselves as superior, at least those willing to make themselves available as collaborators with their conquerors. The Tuareg peoples, the Arabs, or Fulani, and the notables among the Songhai peoples looked down on others, many of whom were their vassals or were actually enslaved to them. They used the Arabic words for the colors White (*bidan*) and Black (*sudan*) as markers of their superiority and the inferiority of others. In particular, the Tuareg and Fulani ruling elites accepted European rule in hopes that the colonial period would be a short one, from which they would emerge with powers intact. In response, the Europeans delegated much local authority to these former rulers.

Colonial rulers found precolonial West African societies profoundly divided between nomad and sedentary, enslaver and enslaved, and Black and White. To a considerable extent, notions of race, while not being inalterably associated with skin color, stemmed from the impact of Muslim and Arab thought throughout West Africa. Illustrative of Arab/Muslim writings on sub-Saharan Africans was the work of the geographer al-Masudi (896–956), who claimed that "merriment dominates the black man because of his defective brain, whence all the weakness of his intelligence" (quoted in Hall, p. 45). Even the famed and otherwise tolerant historian Ibn Khaldun scorned sub-Saharan Africans, mainly because of their torrid climate, which he claimed held them back, though he also affirmed that "adherence to Islam redeemed all other differences."

Eventually, stabilized colonies began to deliver on their economic promise. Whereas early imperialism in Africa had relied on the export of ivory and wild rubber, after these resources became depleted, the colonies pursued other exports. From the rain forests came cocoa, coffee, palm oil, and palm kernels.

Diamond Mine. The discovery of diamonds and gold in South Africa in the late nineteenth century led to the investment of large amounts of overseas capital, the mobilization of severely exploited African mine workers, and the Boer War of 1899–1902, which resulted in the incorporation of the Afrikaner states (created by Boer settlers) of the Transvaal and the Orange Free State into the Union of South Africa.

Analyzing Global Developments

Imperialism and the African Trade Revolution

The colonial period initiated a trade revolution in Africa, which, as we have seen, had been a supplier of human labor to the Americas from the fifteenth century until the middle of the nineteenth century (see Chapter 13). Even as the Europeans endeavored to eradicate the African institution of slavery and slave trading within the continent, they also promoted the reintegration of African economies into the world economy through the export of important, often new cash crops like cocoa from West Africa and significant minerals like gold and diamonds from South Africa and the import of European manufactures. To this end, the colonial powers financed railways and deepened harbors. Already by the outbreak of World War I, West Africa had become the leading exporter of cocoa, South Africa the leading exporter of diamonds and gold, and Egypt, along with the United States, the leading exporter of high-quality cotton.

QUESTIONS FOR ANALYSIS

- Is there a correlation between the increase in the number of railroads built and the amount of natural resources taken out of Africa? If so, how can you tell?
- During what period were the largest increases in the construction of the railroads and the largest exportation of cocoa and gold?
- Do you think the general trend toward increasing production continued well into the twentieth century, or do you think this was the high point? Explain your answer.

Length of Railway Line Opened (in kilometers)

Year	Africa
1880	4,579
1885	6,813
1890	9,202
1895	11,962
1900	16,319
1905	25,574
1910	37,768
1915	47,624

Cocoa Exports from the Gold Coast and Nigeria (in tons)

Year	Gold Coast	Nigeria
1900	536	202
1905	5,090	470
1910	22,600	2,932
1915	77,300	9,105
1920	125,000	17,155

Union of South Africa Gold (in ounces)

Year	Total Output	Estimated % of World Output
1897	2,744	24%
1907	6,451	32.4%
1913	8,799	39.3%
1916	9,297	42.3%
1921	8,129	50.9%

Sources: B. R. Mitchell, *International Historical Statistics: Africa, Asia, and Oceania, 1750–2005* (2007); Polly Hill, *The Gold Coast Cocoa Farmer: A Preliminary Survey* (1965); Sara Berry, *Cocoa, Custom and Socio-Economic Change in Western Nigeria* (1975); S. Herbert Frankel, *Capital Investment in Africa: Its Course and Effects* (1938).

From the highlands of East Africa came tea, coffee, sisal (used in cord and twine), and pyrethrum (a flower used to make insecticide). Another important commodity was long-staple, high-quality cotton, grown in Egypt and the Anglo-Egyptian Sudan. Indeed, tropical commodities from all across Africa (as from India and Latin America) flowed to industrializing societies. (See Analyzing Global Developments: Imperialism and the African Trade Revolution.)

The boom in late nineteenth-century colonial trade had far-reaching effects. It facilitated western corporations' land acquisitions in the global and colonized south, much of it in colonial Africa. It also made it possible for the industrialized nations of western Europe and North America to gain access to valuable resources beyond their borders. The results were stunning. Textile factories in Europe and North America benefited hugely from the expansion of cotton cultivation. For example, between 1800 and 1914 world production of cotton rose by a factor of twenty-five; by the end of the century cotton cultivation covered an area the size of the United Kingdom. Moreover, 1.5 percent of the world's population was involved in growing and shipping the crop and turning it into textiles. In addition, the export of the many products from colonized areas that took place on a vast scale disrupted traditional family life.

The best example of the disruption of African family life comes from South Africa, where the discovery of diamonds and gold in the late nineteenth century not only created unheard-of fortunes for ardent imperialists like Cecil Rhodes but also threatened family life and traditional agriculture all over the region. The mining of both metals required an immense number of laborers, many of whom were recruited forcibly. By the turn of the century, the gold mines of Witwatersrand in South Africa required a workforce of 100,000, drawing miners from as far away as Mozambique, the Rhodesias, and Nyasaland as well as South Africa itself. Because work belowground was hazardous and health services were inadequate, workers often tried to flee. But armed guards and barbed wire fences kept them in the mines. While European-run companies made huge profits, the absence of adult African males meant that the task of maintaining small, mainly subsistence farms fell to those who remained behind—older men and women, wives of mine workers, and children.

To observers, the European empires in Africa seemed solid and durable, but in fact, European colonial rule there was fragile. For all of British Africa, the only all-British force was 5,000 men garrisoned in Egypt. Elsewhere, European officers depended on African military and police forces. And prior to 1914, the number of British administrative officers available for the whole of northern Nigeria was less than 500. These were hardly strong foundations for statehood. It would not take much to destabilize the European order in Africa.

Uncle Sam Leading Cuba. In the years before the Spanish-American War, cartoonists who wished to see the United States intervene on behalf of Cuba in the islanders' struggle for independence from Spain typically depicted Cuba as a White woman in distress. By contrast, in this and other cartoons following the Spanish-American War, Cubans were drawn as Black and usually as infants or boys unable to care for themselves and in need of the benevolent paternal rule of the United States.

The American Empire

The United States, like Europe, plunged into the mania of stretching nation-building into imperial expansion. Echoing the rhetoric of Manifest Destiny from the 1840s, the expansionists of the 1890s claimed that Americans still had a divine mission to spread their superior civilization and their Christian faith around the globe. However, America's new imperialists followed the European model of colonialism from Asia and Africa: colonies were to provide harbors for American vessels, supply raw materials to American industries, and purchase the surplus production of American farms and factories. These new territorial acquisitions were not intended for American settlement or statehood. Nor were their inhabitants to become American citizens, for foreigners of color were considered unfit for incorporation into the American nation.

The pressure to expand came to a head in the late 1890s, when the United States declared war on Spain and invaded the Philippines, Puerto Rico, and Cuba. From 1895, Cuban patriots had been slowly pushing back Spanish troops and occupying sugar plantations—some of which belonged to American planters. Fearing social revolution off the shores of Florida, the American expansionists presented themselves as the saviors of Spanish colonials yearning for freedom, while at the same time safeguarding property for foreign interests during the Spanish-American War (1898). After defeating Spanish regulars in Cuba, American forces began disarming Cuban rebels and returning lands to their owners.

Although the Americans claimed that they were intervening to promote freedom in Spain's colonies, they quickly forgot their promises. The United States annexed Puerto Rico after minimal protest, but Cubans and Filipinos resisted becoming colonial subjects. Bitterness ran particularly high among Filipinos, to whom American leaders had promised independence if they joined in the war against Spain. Betrayed, Filipino rebels launched a war for independence in the name of a Filipino nation. In two years of fighting, over 5,000 Americans and perhaps 200,000 Filipinos perished. The outcome: the Philippines became a colony of the United States.

Colonies in the Philippines and Cuba laid the foundations for a revised model of U.S. expansionism. The earlier pattern had been to turn Native American lands into privately owned farmsteads and to extend the Atlantic market across the continent. But in this new era, there was no intention of making new possessions part of the nation. Instead, the United States repeatedly sent troops to many Caribbean and Central American countries to keep them in line with business interests. The Americans preferred to turn these regimes into dependent client states, rather than making them part of the United States itself (as with Alaska and Hawaii) or converting them into formal colonies (as the Europeans had done in Africa and Asia). The entire world was an object for the powerful states to shape to their needs.

Imperialism and Culture

Europeans and Americans set out to bring "civilization" to the peoples of their colonies. At least since the Crusades, Europeans had regularly written and thought about other peoples. These images and ideas had grown more numerous and varied as commerce and colonialism in Asia and the Atlantic world increased; they served various purposes, including informing, entertaining, and flattering Europeans as well as criticizing their culture. As Europeans began to exert more control over various parts of the world, they found it easier to muscle into distant cultures and to carry away treasures. As Europeans and Americans grew more and more confident in their achievements, they became convinced that their arts and sciences were superior—and curiosity often turned to disdain. In time, Europeans presumed that the only

The Civilizing Mission. This advertisement for Pears soap shamelessly tapped into the idea of Europeans bringing civilization to the people of their colonies. It said that use of Pears soap would teach the virtues of cleanliness to the "natives" and implied that it would even lighten their skin.

The Women of Algiers in Their Apartment. An oil painting by Eugène Delacroix (1798–1863) of Algerian women being attended by a Black servant. European painters in the nineteenth century often used images of women to portray Arab Muslim society.

true modern civilization was their own; other peoples might have reigned over great empires in antiquity but had since fallen into decadence and decline. In literature and painting, for example, a new genre known as Orientalism portrayed nonwestern peoples as exotic, sensuous, and economically backward. Rather than depicting Egyptian dock workers or middle-class Algerian women, these paintings featured snake charmers and inhabitants of the harem, thereby suggesting that the whole region was inhabited by people of these types, in contrast to a uniformly progressive Europe, inhabited by industrial workers and men of science.

Europeans also employed scientific reasons to explain hierarchies of world civilizations and especially races. Darwin himself wavered on the nature of race. Sometimes he argued that all humans as God's creatures—had the same abilities to evolve. He was an avowed opponent of slavery. But he also believed in a hierarchical order. Sometimes he ratified a view of "lower" and "higher" races, the former stuck in the past and the latter anointed by God or by nature itself to define and dictate civilization's future. "Social Darwinists" took these ideas to extremes. Europeans' relationship to others might now be one of condescending sympathy or of ruthless exploitation, but the bottom line was that it was up to White Europeans and Americans to create modern culture; darker people, the cultural Darwinians argued, were not nearly as fully "evolved" as the Europeans and could not hope to catch up (or to offer a viable alternative model for poetry or painting, for example). At best, they could be taught European languages, sciences, and religions and perhaps be made to evolve more quickly. It is telling that French colonial subjects who did well at French schools were known as *evolués*, "the evolved ones."

CELEBRATING IMPERIALISM Especially in middle- and upper-class circles, Europeans celebrated their imperial triumphs. After the invention of photographic film and the Eastman Kodak camera in 1888, imperial images surfaced in popular forms such as postcards and advertisements. Imperial themes also decorated packaging materials; tins of coffee, tea, tobacco, and chocolates featured pictures highlighting the commodities' colonial origins. Cigarettes often had names like "Admiral," "Royal Navy," "Fighter," and "Grand Fleet." Some of this served as propaganda, produced by investors in imperial commodities or by colonial pressure groups.

Propaganda promoted imperialism abroad but also inspired changes at home. For example, champions of empire argued that if the British population did not grow fast enough to fill the world's sparsely settled regions, then the population of other nations would. Population was power, and the number of healthy children provided an accurate measure of global influence. "Empire cannot be built on rickety and flat-chested citizens," warned a British member of Parliament in 1905. In addition, writers for young audiences often invoked colonial settings and themes. Whereas girls' literature stressed domestic service, child-rearing, and nurturing, boys' readings depicted exotic locales, devious Orientals, savage Africans, and daring colonial exploits.

Imperialists did not simply create a world in their image. Many back home were indifferent to far-away adventures and were even skeptical about their governments doing the bidding for big trading interests. Many grew increasingly restless at the news of atrocities. They may not have believed in world equality; but the news and pictures of their soldiers committing horrible acts upon innocent people was a violation of the principles of civilization their rulers claimed to be exporting. After a group of US Marines were photographed slaughtering Filipino families, many Americans denounced US imperialism. Notable figures like the African-American sociologist W.E.B DuBois and the writer Mark Twain denounced the US government for hypocrisy. Some missionaries began to identify with the colonized and became fierce anti-imperialists, or at least called for humanitarian reform.

Pressures of Expansion in Japan, Russia, and China

The challenge of integrating political communities and extending territorial borders was a problem not just for western Europe and the United States. Indeed, in some areas of the world, western European and North American sprawl was a response to non-western expansion, especially coming from Russia and Japan. Empires were on the march all over the place. And some older empires, like the Ottoman and Qing China got increasingly squeezed.

Japan's Transformation and Expansion

Starting in the 1860s, Japanese rulers tried to recast their country less as an old dynasty and more like a modern nation-state. Since the early seventeenth century, the Tokugawa shogunate had kept outsiders within strict limits and thwarted internal unrest. But after an American naval officer, Commodore Matthew Perry, entered Edo Bay in 1853 with a fleet of steam-powered ships, other Americans, Russians, Dutch, and British followed in his wake. These outsiders forced the Tokugawa rulers to sign humiliating treaties that opened Japanese ports, slapped limits on Japanese tariffs, and exempted foreigners from Japanese laws. Younger Japanese, especially among the military (samurai) elites, felt that Japan should respond by adapting, not rejecting, western practices.

In 1868, a group of reformers toppled the Tokugawa shogunate and promised to return Japan to its mythic greatness by creating a modern empire with a proper emperor, as in Britain, Russia, and France. Emperor Mutsuhito—the Meiji ("Enlightened Rule") Emperor—became the symbol of a new Japan. He ruled over a professionalized military that sidelined the old samurai class while the aristocratic daimyos gave way to a parliament. Even women emerged from private seclusion; the empress led the way by donning western outfits, Victorian-style shoes, and elaborate hats in public. Schools for women like the "Tokyo Women's School," popped up around the country. Furthermore, the cult of "a good wife and a wise mother" authorized women to take a more important role in promoting national welfare.

Mutsuhito's reign (1868–1912) was called the **Meiji Restoration**. By founding schools, initiating a propaganda campaign, and revamping the army to create a single "national" fighting force, the Meiji government promoted a political community that stressed linguistic and ethnic homogeneity as well as superiority compared with others. In this way, the Meiji leaders overcame age-old regional divisions, subdued local political authorities, and mobilized the country to face rivals for Pacific supremacy.

ECONOMIC DEVELOPMENT One of the Meiji period's remarkable achievements was the nation's economic transformation. After 1871, when the government banned the feudal system and allowed peasants to become small landowners, farmers improved their agrarian techniques and saw their standard of living rise. The energetic new government unified the currency around the yen, created a postal system, introduced tax reforms, laid telegraph lines, formed compulsory foreign trade associations, launched campaigns to promote exports and personal savings, established an advanced civil service system, began to build railroads, and hired thousands of foreign consultants. In 1889, the Meiji government introduced a constitution (based largely on the German model). The following year, 450,000 people—about 1 percent of the population—elected Japan's first parliament, the Imperial Diet.

As the government sold valuable enterprises to the people it knew best, it created private economic dynasties. The new large companies (such as Sumitomo, Yasuda, Mitsubishi, and Mitsui) were family organizations. Fathers, sons, cousins, and uncles ran different parts of large integrated corporations—some in charge of banks, some running the trade wing, some overseeing factories. Women played a crucial role, not just as custodians of the home but also as cultivators of important family alliances, especially among potential marriage partners. In contrast to American limited-liability firms, which issued shares on stock markets to anonymous buyers, Japan's version of large-scale managerial capitalism was a personal affair.

CONFLICT WITH NEIGHBORS As in many other emerging nation-states, expansion was a tempting prospect. It offered the promise of more markets for selling goods and obtaining staples, and it was a way to burnish the image of national superiority and greatness. Japanese ventures abroad were initially spectacularly successful. The Meiji moved first to take

Perry Arrives in Japan. A Japanese woodblock print portraying the uninvited arrival in Edo (Tokyo) Bay on August 7, 1853, of a tall American ship, which was commanded by Matthew Perry. This arrival marked the end of Japan's ability to fully control the terms of its interactions with foreigners.

The Imperial Diet. Japan's rush to modernize and nation build during the Meiji Restoration also led its new leaders to borrow and adapt models and mores from Europeans. This included the idea of a parliament or house of commons, called the Imperial Diet. Observe how the Japanese parliamentarians in this image dress in English suits and black leather lace-up shoes and sprout English-style moustaches and the occasional beard. Even the backbenchers can be seen to cheer (or holler) in the back, as was customary for English lawmakers. And yet the scene is undoubtedly Japanese. The colors and fabrics are Japanese, as are the teapots on the speaker's desk.

over the kingdom of the Ryūkyūs, southwest of Japan. (See Map 17.5.) A small show of force, only 160 Japanese soldiers, was enough to establish the new Okinawa Prefecture there in 1879. The Japanese regarded the people of the Ryūkyūs as an ethnic minority and refused to incorporate them into the nation-state on equal terms. In contrast with the British in India or the Americans in Puerto Rico, the Japanese conquerors refused to train an Indigenous Ryūkyūan governing class. Meiji intellectuals insisted that the "backward" Okinawans were unfit for local self-rule and representation.

Even while incorporating surrounding territories into the state, the Japanese also engaged in imperial expansion. In 1876, the Japanese fixed upon Korea, which put their plans on a collision course with China's sphere of influence. In a formal treaty, the Japanese recognized Korea as an independent state, opened Korea to trade, and won extraterritorial rights. As a result, the Chinese worried that soon the Japanese would try to take over Korea. These fears were well founded: Japanese designs on Korea eventually sparked the Sino-Japanese War of 1894–1895, in which the upstart Japan delivered a humiliating defeat to the Chinese military.

The Sino-Japanese War accelerated Japan's rapid transformation to a nation-state and a colonial power with no peer in Asia. Having lost the war, China ceded the province of Taiwan to the Japanese. Japan also annexed Korea in 1910 and converted Taiwan and Korea into the twin jewels of its young empire. Like the British in India, the Japanese regarded their colonial subjects as racially inferior and unworthy of the privileges of citizenship. And like other imperial powers, the Japanese expected their possessions to serve the metropolitan center. Densely populated and short of land, Japan wanted these colonies to become granaries, sending rice to the mother country. Moreover, the Meiji regime exploited Taiwanese sugar exports to relieve a Japanese economy heavily dependent on imports. Meanwhile, other Pacific powers, like Great Britain and especially the United States, eyed Japanese grandeur with increasing alarm. Especially in the United States, military strategists began to call for heavy naval investment to preempt Tokyo's influence over the Pacific. The decision to go to war against Spain was in part taken to thwart Japanese influence over the Philippines.

Russian Transformation and Expansion

Russian expansion was motivated by both a civilizing mission and a need to defend against other countries expanding along its immense border. Facing an emerging Germany, a British presence in the Middle East and Persia, a consolidating China, and an ascendant Japan, Russia knew it would have to

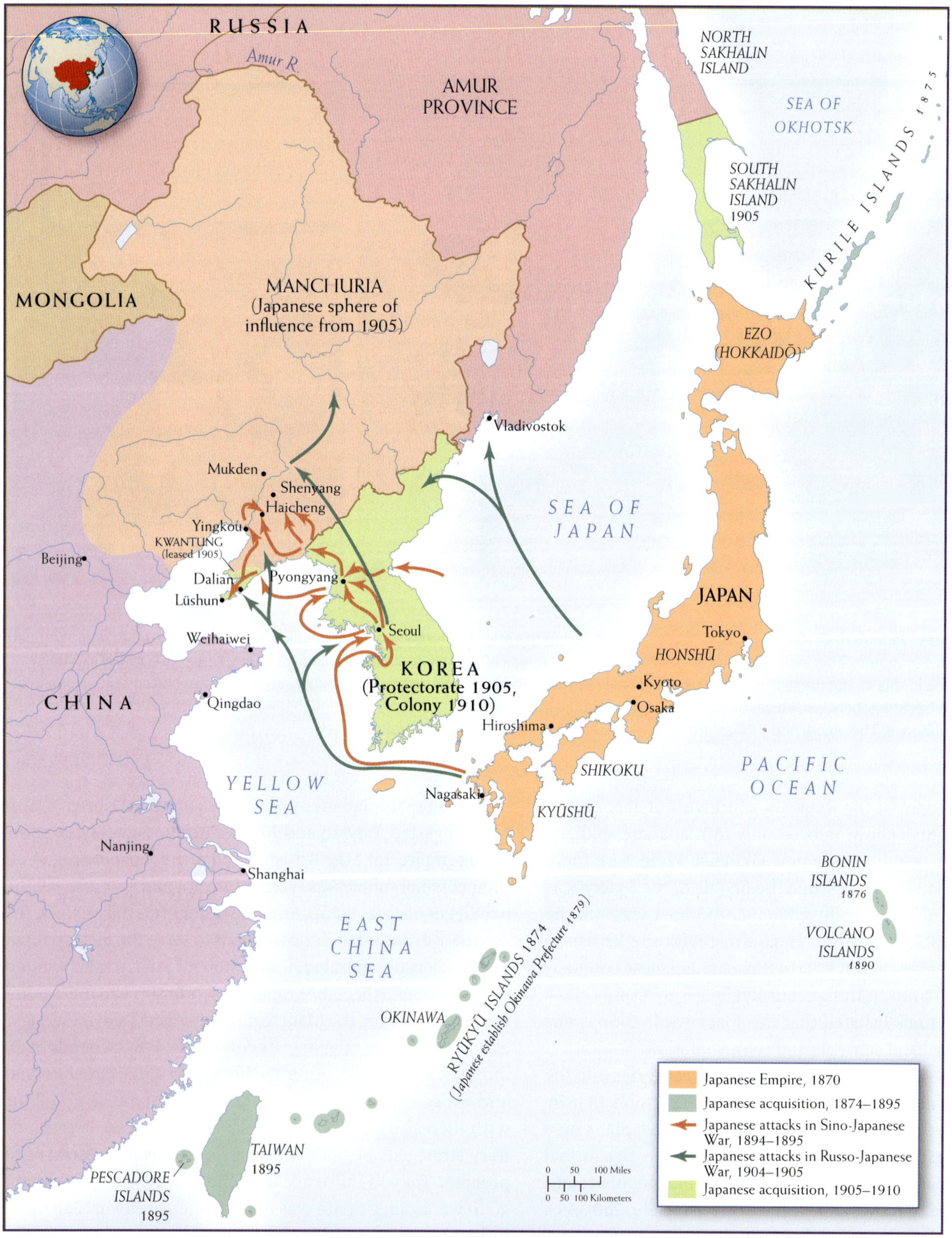

MAP 17.5 | Japanese Expansion, 1870–1910

Under the Meiji Restoration, the Japanese state built a strong national identity and competed with foreign powers for imperial advantage in East Asia.

- According to the map, what were the first areas that the Japanese Empire acquired as it started to expand?
- What two empires' spheres of influence were affected by Japan's aggressive attempts at expansion?
- According to your reading, what were the new Japanese state's objectives? How were they similar to or different from those of expansionist European states in the same period?

Economic Transformation of Japan. During the Meiji period, the government transformed the economy by building railroads, laying telegraph lines, founding a postal system, and encouraging the formation of giant firms known as zaibatsu, which were family organizations consisting of factories, import-export businesses, and banks. Here we see a raw-silk-reeling factory that was run by one of the zaibatsu.

enlarge its already large territorial domain. So it established a number of expansionist fronts simultaneously: southwest to the Black Sea, south into the Caucasus and Turkestan, and east into Manchuria. (See Map 17.6.) Success depended on annexing territories and establishing protectorates over vulnerable conquered peoples.

Looking west and south, Russia invaded the Ottoman territories of Moldavia (present-day Moldova) and Walachia (present-day Romania) in 1853. The invasion provoked opposition from Britain and France, which joined with the Ottomans to defeat Russia in the Crimean War (1853–1856). By exposing Russia's lack of modern weapons and its problems in supplying troops without a railway system, the defeat spurred a course of aggressive modernization and expansion.

MODERNIZATION AND INTERNAL REFORM In the 1860s, Tsar Alexander II launched a wave of "Great Reforms" to make Russia more modern and to preserve its status as a great power. Autocratic rule continued, but officials reintegrated the society. In 1861, for example, a decree emancipated peasants from serfdom. Other changes included a sharp reduction in the duration of military service, a program of education for the conscripts, and the beginnings of a mass school system to teach children reading, writing, and Russian culture. Starting in the 1890s, as railroads and factories expanded, so did the steel, coal, and petroleum industries. But while the reforms strengthened the state, they did not enhance the lives of common people. Workers in Russia were brutally exploited, even by the standards of the industrial revolution. Also, large landowners had kept most of the empire's fertile land, and the peasants had to pay substantial redemption fees for the poorer-quality plots they received.

The reforms revealed a fundamental problem: the rulers were eager to reform society, but not the basis of government (autocracy). This caused liberals, conservatives, and malcontents alike to question the state-led modernizing mission. Before long, in the press, courtrooms, and streets, men and women denounced the regime. Revolutionaries engaged in terror and assassination. In 1881, a terrorist bomb blew the tsar to pieces. In the 1890s, following another famine, the radical doctrines of Marxism (see Chapter 16) gained popularity in Russia. Even aristocratic intellectuals, such as the author of *War and Peace*, Count Leo Tolstoy, lamented their despotic government.

TERRITORIAL EXPANSION Yet the critics of internal reform did not hold back the Russian expansionists, who believed they had to take over certain lands to keep them out of rivals' hands. So they conquered the highland people of the Caucasus Mountains to prevent Ottomans and Persians from encroaching on Russia's southern flank. And they battled the British over areas between Turkestan and British India, such as Persia (Iran) and Afghanistan. Although some Russians

MAP 17.6 | Russian Expansion, 1801–1914

The Russian state continued to expand in the nineteenth century.

- According to this map, what lands did Russia acquire during the period 1796–1855? What lands did it acquire next?
- Compare this map of Russian expansion with Map 13.7. How did the direction of Russia's expansion change in the nineteenth century?
- Which states did the expanding Russian Empire more resemble in this era, western European states (such as Great Britain) or American states (such as the United States)?

emigrated to these lands, they never became a majority there. The new provinces were multiethnic, multireligious communities that were only partially integrated into the Russian nation.

Perhaps the most impressive Russian expansion occurred in East Asia, where the underpopulated Amur River basin boasted rich lands, mineral deposits, and access to the Pacific Ocean. The Chinese also wanted to colonize this area, which lay just north of Manchuria. After twenty years of struggle, Russia claimed the land north and south of the Amur River and in 1860 founded Vladivostok, a port on the Pacific Ocean whose name signified "Rule the East." Deciding to focus on these areas in Asia, the Russian government sold its one territory in North America (Alaska) to the United States. Then, to link the capital (Moscow) and the western part of the country to its East Asian spoils, the government began construction of the Trans-Siberian Railroad. When it was completed in 1904, the new railroad bridged the east and the west. Russia then began to eye the Korean Peninsula, on which Japan, too, had set its sights.

GOVERNING A DIVERSE NATION Russia was a huge empire whose rulers were only partially effective at integrating its diverse regions into a political community. In 1897, during the first complete population census, ethnographers struggled over what to call all the empire's peoples: nations or tribes. In the end, authorities chose the term *nationalities*, recognizing 104 of them, speaking 146 languages and dialects.

The Trans-Siberian Railroad. Russia's decision to build a railway across Siberia to the Pacific Ocean derived from a desire to expand the empire's power in East Asia and to forestall British advances in Asia. The colossal undertaking, which claimed the lives of thousands of workers, reached completion just as Russia clashed militarily with Japan. The new railroad ferried Russian troops over long distances to battles, such as the one at Mukden, in Manchuria, which was then the largest land battle in the history of warfare.

Ethnic Russians accounted for slightly more than half of the population.

Counting and categorizing peoples formed part of the state's attempts to figure out how to govern this diverse realm. As the United States did, Russia made conquered regions into full parts of the empire. But unlike the United States, Russia was suspicious of decentralized federalism, fearing it would lead groups to demand secession. Moreover, the tsars were terrified by the idea of popular sovereignty. Preferring the tried-and-true method of centralized autocracy, they divided most of the empire into governorships ruled by appointed civilian or military governors who were supposed to function like local tsars or autocrats.

Unlike the United States, which displaced or slaughtered Indigenous populations during its expansion across an entire continent, Russia tolerated and taxed the new peoples. In this daunting task, the state's approach ranged from outright repression (of Poles and Jews) to favoritism (toward Baltic Germans and Finns), although the beneficiaries of favoritism often later lost favor if they became too strong. Further, unlike the United States, which managed to pacify borders with its weaker neighbors, Russia faced the constant suspicions of Persians and Ottomans and the menace of British troops in Afghanistan. And in East Asia, a clash with expansionist Japan loomed on the horizon.

China under Pressure

While the Russians and Japanese scrambled to copy European models of industrialism and imperialism, the Qing were slower to mobilize against threats from the west. Even as the European powers were dividing up China into spheres of influence, Qing officials were much more worried about internal revolts and threats from their northern borders. Into the 1850s and 1860s, many Qing officials still regarded the increasing European incursions and demands as a lesser danger by comparison.

ADOPTING WESTERN LEARNING AND SKILLS A growing number of Chinese officials, however, recognized the superior armaments and technology of rival powers and were deeply troubled by the threat posed by European military might. Starting in the 1860s, reformist bureaucrats sought to adopt elements of western learning and technological skills—but with the intention of keeping the core Chinese culture intact.

This so-called **Self-Strengthening movement** included a variety of new ventures: arsenals, shipyards, coal mines, a steamship company to contest the foreign domination of coastal shipping, and schools for learning foreign ways and languages. Most interesting was the dispatch abroad of about 120 schoolboys under the charge of Yung Wing. The first Chinese graduate of an American college (Yale University, 1854), Yung believed that western education would greatly benefit Chinese students, so he took his charges to Connecticut in the 1870s to attend school and live with American families. Conservatives at the Qing court were soon dismayed by reports of the students' interest in Christianity and aptitude for baseball. In 1881, after the U.S. government refused to admit the boys into military academies, the court summoned the students home.

Yung Wing's abortive educational mission was not the only setback for the Self-Strengthening movement, for skepticism about western technology was rife among conservative officials. Some insisted that the introduction of machinery would lead to unemployment; others worried that railways would facilitate western military maneuvers and lead to an invasion; still others complained that the crisscrossing tracks disturbed the harmony between humans and nature. The first short railway track ever laid in China was torn up in 1877 shortly after being built, and the country had only 288 kilometers of track prior to 1895.

Although they did not acknowledge the railroad's usefulness, the Chinese did adopt other new technologies to access a wider range of information. For example, by the early 1890s there were about a dozen Chinese-language newspapers (as distinct from the foreign-language press) published in major cities, with the largest ones having a circulation of 10,000 to 15,000. To avoid government intervention, these papers sidestepped political controversy; instead, they featured commercial news and literary contributions. In 1882, the newspaper *Shenbao* made use of a new telegraph line to publish dispatches within China.

INTERNAL REFORM EFFORTS China's defeat by Japan in the Sino-Japanese War (1894–1895), sparked by quarrels over Korea, prompted the first serious attempt at reform by the Qing. Known as the Hundred Days' Reform, the episode lasted only from June to September 1898. The force behind it was a thirty-seven-year-old scholar named Kang Youwei and his twenty-two-year-old student Liang Qichao. Citing rulers such as Peter the Great of Russia and Emperor Meiji of Japan as their inspiration, the reformers urged Chinese leaders to develop a railway network, a state banking system, a modern postal service, and institutions to foster the development of agriculture, industry, and commerce.

The reformers' opportunity to accelerate change came in the summer of 1898 when the twenty-seven-year-old Guangxu emperor decided to implement many of their ideas, including changes in the venerable civil service examination system. But the effort was short-lived, for conservative officials rallied behind Guangxu's aunt, the Empress Dowager Cixi, who emerged from retirement to overturn the reforms. The young emperor was put under house arrest. Kang and Liang fled for their lives and went into exile. It would take still more military defeats to finally jolt the Qing court into action, but by then it was too late to save the regime.

The reforms of the Self-Strengthening movement were ineffectual, too modest, and poorly implemented. Very few Chinese acquired new skills. Despite talk of modernizing, the civil service examination remained based on Confucian classics and still opened the only doors to government service. Governing elites were not yet ready to reinvent the principles of their political community, and they adhered instead to the traditional dynastic structure.

By the late nineteenth century, the success of the Qing regime in expanding its territories a century earlier seemed like a distant memory, as various powers repeatedly forced it to make economic and territorial concessions. Unlike Japan or Russia, however, the Qing government resisted any comprehensive social reforms (until after the turn of the twentieth century), and its policies left the country vulnerable to both external aggression and internal instability.

Conclusion

Between 1850 and 1914, empire and imperialism carried European, American, and, to a lesser extent, Japanese power and culture throughout the world. In terms of the size of populations that the peoples of European descent ruled, this era was the high point of European and Euro-American predominance. Although most of the world's people lived either in landed empires or under the authority of colonial rulers, the dominant political institution of Europeans, Euro-Americans, and the Japanese was the nation-state. This powerful political organization owed its full emergence in the nineteenth century to the inspiration of European and American reformers seeking a new political framework that expressed popular sentiments alongside the economic, cultural, and political interests of the ruling classes.

Although the ideal of "a people" united by territory, history, and culture grew increasingly popular worldwide, it was not easy to make it a reality. Official histories, national heroes, novels, poetry, and music helped, but central to the process of nation formation were the actions of bureaucrats. Asserting sovereignty over what it claimed as national territory, the state "nationalized" diverse populations by creating a unified system of law, education, military service, and government.

Colonization beyond borders was another part of nation building in many societies. In these efforts, territorial conquests took place under the banner of nationalist endeavors. In Europe, the Americas, Japan, and to some extent Russia, the intertwined processes of nation building and territorial expansion were most effective. The Amazon River basin, Okinawa, and especially the North American West became important provinces of integrated nation-states, populated with settlers who produced for national and international markets.

However, the integrating impulses of emerging nations did not wipe out local differences, mute class antagonisms, or eliminate gender inequalities. Even as Europeans and Americans came to see themselves as chosen—by God or by natural selection—to rule the rest, they suffered deep divisions. Not everyone identified with the nation-state or the empire or agreed on what it meant to belong or to conquer. But by the century's end, racist advocates and colonial lobbyists seem to have convinced many that their interests and destinies were bound up with their nations' unity, prosperity, and global clout.

Ironically, imperial expansion, based on the might of nation-states, had an unintended consequence, for self-determination could also apply to racial or ethnic minorities at home and in the colonies. Armed with the rhetoric of progress and uplift, colonial authorities tried to subjugate distant people, but colonial subjects themselves often asserted the language of "nation" and accused imperial overlords of betraying their own lofty principles. As the twentieth century opened, Filipino and Cuban rebels used Thomas Jefferson's Declaration of Independence to oppose American invaders, Koreans defined themselves as a nation crushed under Japanese heels, and Indian nationalists made colonial governors feel shame for violating English standards of "fair play."

After You Read This Chapter

TRACING THE GLOBAL STORYLINES

FOCUS ON: How Nation-States Became Global Empires

The Americas and Europe: Consolidating Nations

- Residents of the United States claim territory across the North American continent after fighting a bloody civil war to preserve the union and abolish slavery, creating conflict with Indigenous peoples.
- Canadians also build a new nation and expand across the continent, creating conflict with Indigenous peoples.
- Brazilians create a prosperous nation-state that excludes much of the population from the privileges of belonging to the "nation" and the "state."
- The dynastic states of Prussia and Piedmont-Sardinia create German and Italian nation-states at the expense of France and the Austrian Empire.

Industry, Science, and Technology on a Global Scale

- Continued industrialization transforms the global economy.
- New technologies of warfare, transportation, and communication lead to greater global economic integration.
- Charles Darwin's *On the Origin of Species* overturns previous conceptions of nature, arguing that present-day life-forms evolved from simpler ones over long periods.

Empires

- After suppressing the Indian Rebellion of 1857, the British reorganize their rule in India, providing a model for other imperial powers.
- European powers partition the entire African continent (except for Ethiopia and Liberia) despite intense African resistance.
- Americans win the Spanish-American War, annex Puerto Rico, and establish colonial rule over the Philippines.
- The expansionist aims of Japan, Russia, and China lead to clashes over possessions in East Asia, with Russia gaining much territory and Japan defeating the Chinese.
- Colonial rule spurs nationalist sentiments among the colonized.

CHRONOLOGY

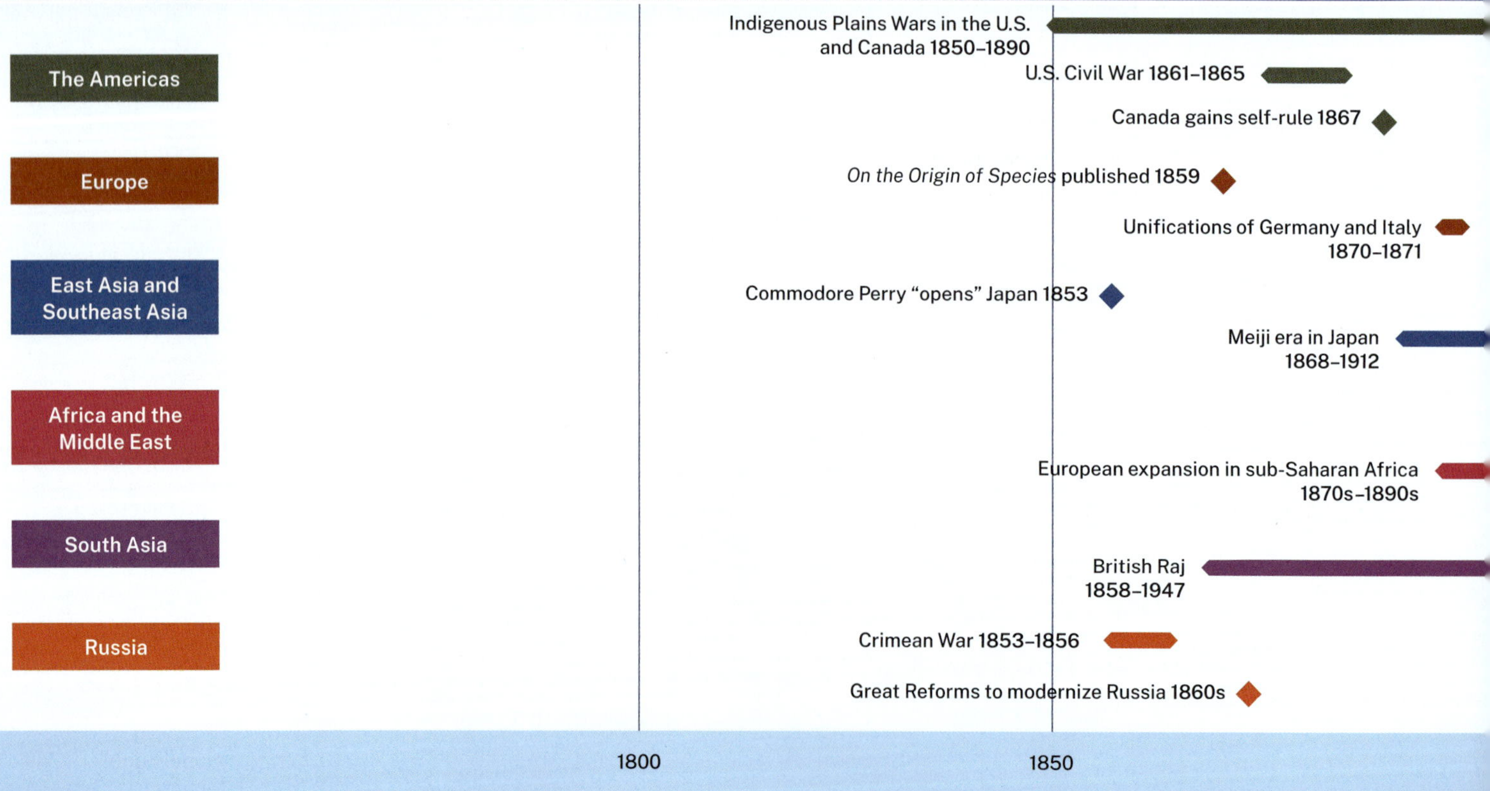

KEY TERMS

Charles Darwin p. 748
imperialism p. 732
limited-liability joint-stock company p. 738
Ghost Dance p. 739
Manifest Destiny p. 733
Meiji Restoration p. 762
natural selection p. 748
Raj p. 750
Self-Strengthening movement p. 768
steel p. 747

THINKING ABOUT GLOBAL CONNECTIONS

Thinking about Worlds Together, Worlds Apart and Nations & Empires Compare the eighteenth-century empires of Spain, Portugal, and Britain with the new empires arising in Africa at the end of the nineteenth century. What were the sources of their wealth and power? How and to what degree were colonial territories and economies integrated with their imperialist states?

Thinking about Changing Power Relationships and Nations & Empires How did the growth of western influence and Japanese power lay the basis for opposition movements in Africa and Asia? How did people respond to imperialism? Where was resistance most effective?

Thinking about Environmental Impacts and Nations & Empires Describe the second industrial revolution and explain how it differed from the first industrial revolution. Pay special attention to the new technologies used in the late nineteenth century, especially the sources of power and new materials that were used.

Go to INQUIZITIVE to see what you've learned—and learn what you've missed—with personalized feedback along the way.

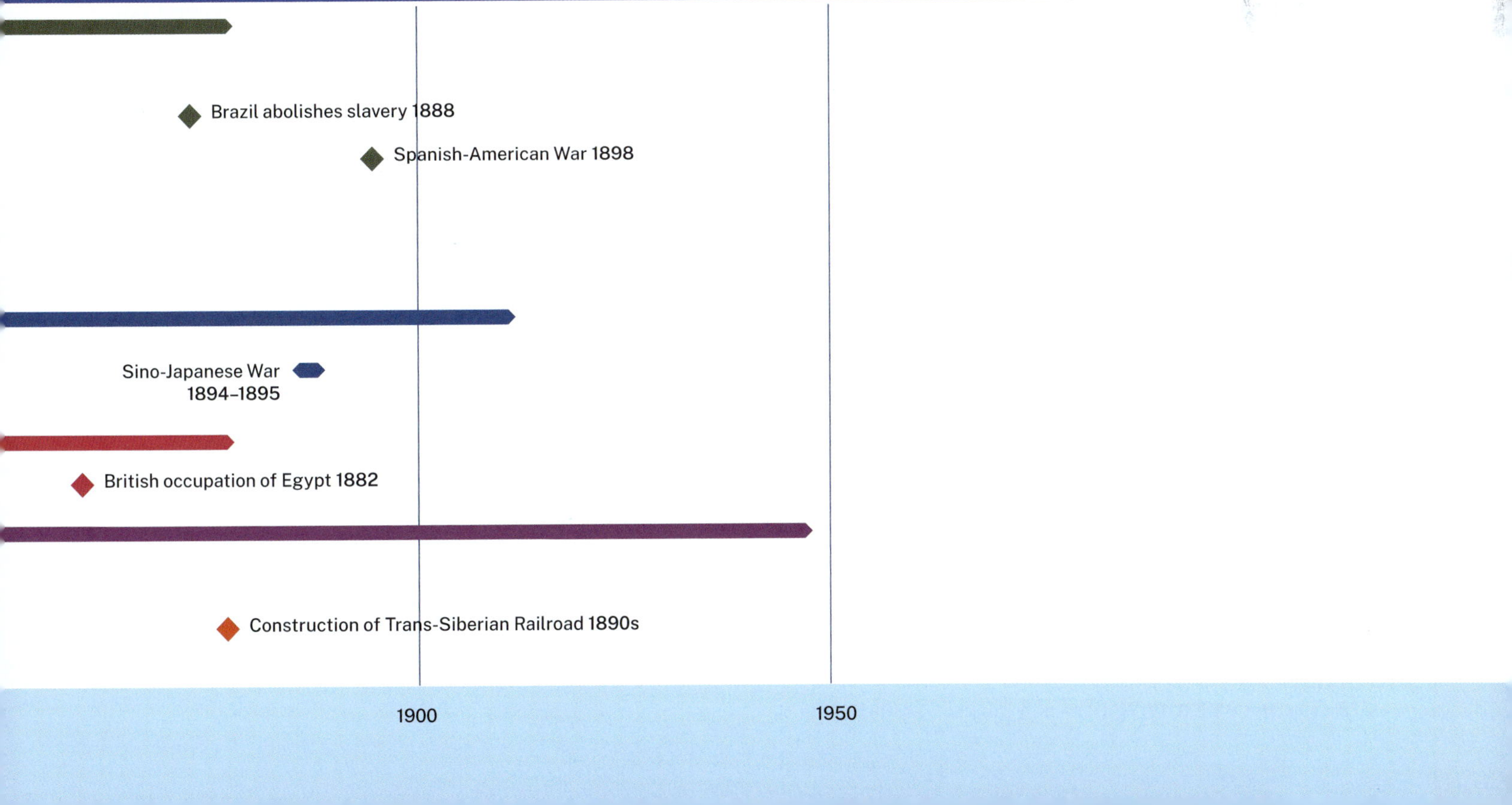

Global Themes and Sources

Contextualizing the Scramble for Empire

In the second half of the nineteenth century, a handful of nation-states, most but not all of them in Europe, renewed their competition for colonial territory. Class conflict at home and resistance to their efforts abroad bred a new, conflictual vision that stressed competition and struggle in nature as well as human affairs. Doubts arose about the progressive nature of the changes ushered in by the era of the French and industrial revolutions, in particular the idea that granting more people the vote and spreading free markets would lead to peace and prosperity for everyone. Colonizers increasingly believed that they must control ever-greater expanses of territory or risk defeat by rival powers.

The documents presented here show imperialist powers' efforts to explain their actions, to defend their right to rule others, and to mark boundaries of inclusion and exclusion. The sources start in the Americas, where John L. O'Sullivan asserts divine support for "Anglo-Saxon" expansion westwards. Next, Count Shigenobu Okuma celebrates Japanese dynamism over the course of the prior generation. Then, in Russia, writing in the context of the empire's expansion eastward, Prince Esper Ukhtomskii considers his country's role as a colonial power in Asia by comparing the Romanov regime to its rivals. In the final document, the General Act of the Conference of Berlin concerning the Congo, the great powers of Europe set ground rules for their competition for territory in Africa.

All written at roughly the same time, these documents demand attention to historical context. Each, in different ways, asserts its country's right to dominate others. Pay special attention to the justifications each mobilizes and the authors' efforts to distinguish colonizer from colonized, those with the right to rule from everyone else.

ANALYZING THE CONTEXT OF THE SCRAMBLE FOR EMPIRE

- How do the authors justify their country's right to rule others? What kind of reasons do they present (ethnic, moral, technological)?
- Compare the efforts to divide insiders from outsiders in these documents.
- Evaluate the balance between confidence and insecurity in each source.

PRIMARY SOURCE 17.1

"Manifest Destiny" (1845), John L. O'Sullivan

John L. O'Sullivan (1813–1895) was an American newspaper columnist and editor who urged the annexation of Texas to the United States in this 1845 article. He justified it on the basis of what he called "manifest destiny."

- Why does O'Sullivan dismiss slavery as a cause for U.S. expansion?
- Explain the relationship between the United States and Mexico in this document.
- What role does technology play in O'Sullivan's justification for U.S. expansion?

No—Mr. Clay was right when he declared that Annexation was a question with which slavery had nothing to do. The country which was the subject of Annexation in this case, from its geographical position and relations, happens to be—or rather the portion of it now actually settled, happens to be—a slave country. But a similar process might have taken place in proximity to a different section of our Union; and indeed there is a great deal of Annexation yet to take place, within the life of the present generation, along the whole line of our northern border. Texas has been absorbed into the Union in the inevitable fulfilment of the general law which is rolling our population westward; the connexion of which with that ratio of growth in population which is destined within a hundred years to swell our numbers to the enormous population of *two hundred and fifty millions* (if not more), is too evident to leave us in doubt of the manifest design of Providence in regard to the occupation of this continent. It was disintegrated from Mexico in the natural course of events, by a process perfectly legitimate on its own part, blameless on ours; and in which all the censures due to wrong, perfidy and folly, rest on Mexico alone. And possessed as it was by a population which was in truth but a colonial detachment from our own, and which was still bound by myriad ties of the very heart-strings to its old relations, domestic and political, their incorporation into the Union was not only inevitable, but the most natural, right and proper thing in the world—and it is only astonishing that there should be any among ourselves to say it nay. . . .

California will, probably, next fall away from the loose adhesion which, in such a country as Mexico, holds a remote province in a slight equivocal kind of dependence on the metropolis. Imbecile and distracted, Mexico never can exert any real governmental authority over such a country. The impotence of the one and the distance of the other, must make the relation one of virtual independence; unless, by stunting the province of all natural growth, and forbidding that immigration which can alone develop[e] its capabilities and fulfil the purposes of its creation, tyranny may retain a military dominion which is no government in the legitimate sense of the term. In the case of California this is now impossible. The Anglo-Saxon foot is already on its borders. Already the advance guard of the irresistible army of Anglo-Saxon emigration has begun to pour down upon it, armed with the plough and the rifle, and marking its trail with schools and colleges, courts and representative halls, mills and meeting-houses. A population will soon be in actual occupation of California, over which it will be idle for Mexico to dream of dominion. They will necessarily become independent. All this without agency of our government, without responsibility of our people—in the natural flow of events, the spontaneous working of principles, and the adaptation of the tendencies and wants of the human race to the elemental circumstances in the midst of which they find themselves placed. And they will have a right to independence—to self-government—to the possession of the homes conquered from the wilderness by their own labors and dangers, sufferings and sacrifices—a better and a truer right than the artificial title of sovereignty in Mexico a thousand miles distant, inheriting from Spain a title good only against those who have none better. Their right to independence will be the natural right of self-government belonging to any community strong enough to maintain it—distinct in position, origin and character, and free from any mutual obligations of membership of a common political body, binding it to others by the duty of loyalty and compact of public faith. This will be their title to independence; and by this title, there can be no doubt that the population now fast streaming down upon California will both assert and maintain that independence.

Whether they will then attach themselves to our Union or not, is not to be predicted with any certainty. Unless the projected rail-road across the continent to the Pacific be carried into effect, perhaps they may not; though even in that case, the day is not distant when the Empires of the Atlantic and Pacific would again flow together into one, as soon as their inland border should approach each other. But that great work, colossal as appears the plan on its first suggestion, cannot remain long unbuilt. Its necessity for this very purpose of binding and holding together in its iron clasp our fast settling Pacific region with that of the Mississippi valley—the natural facility of the route—the ease with which any amount of labor for the construction can be drawn in from the overcrowded populations of Europe, to be paid in the lands made valuable by the progress of the work itself—and its immense utility to the commerce of the world with the whole eastern coast of Asia, alone almost sufficient for the support of such a road—these considerations give assurance that the day cannot be distant which shall witness the conveyance of the representatives from Oregon and California to Washington within less time than a few years ago was devoted to a similar journey by those from Ohio; while the magnetic telegraph will enable the editors of the "San Francisco Union," the "Astoria Evening Post," or the "Nootka Morning News" to set up in type the first half of the President's Inaugural, before the echoes of the latter half shall have died away beneath the lofty porch of the Capitol, as spoken from his lips.

Away, then, with all idle French talk of *balances of power* on the American Continent. There is no growth in Spanish America! Whatever progress of population there may be in the British Canadas, is only for their own early severance of their present colonial relation to the little island three thousand miles across the Atlantic; soon to be followed by Annexation, and destined to swell the still accumulating momentum of our progress. And whosoever may hold the balance, though they should cast into the opposite scale all the bayonets and cannon, not only of France and England, but of Europe entire, how would it kick the beam against the simple solid weight of the two hundred and fifty, or three hundred millions—and American millions—destined to gather beneath the flutter of the stripes and stars, in the fast hastening year of the Lord 1945!

Source: John L. O'Sullivan, "Manifest Destiny," in *The American West: A Source Book*, edited by Clark C. Spence (New York: Crowell, 1966), pp. 108–11.

PRIMARY SOURCE 17.2

Fifty Years of New Japan (1909), Count Shigenobu Okuma

Count Shigenobu Okuma (1838–1922) held high-ranking positions in the Meiji government and served as prime minister of Japan during World War I (1914–1916). The founder of Waseda University, he was an early advocate of western science and culture in Japan. In this document, he celebrates Japan's ability to draw on foreign influences.

- Identify the sources of Japan's strength, according to Okuma.
- Compare the justification for expansion in this document to the justifications in the documents by O'Sullivan and Ukhtomskii.
- Evaluate the balance in this document between internal sources of Japanese strength and borrowed foreign influences.

By comparing the Japan of fifty years ago with the Japan of today, it will be seen that she has gained considerably in the extent of her territory, as well as in her population, which now numbers nearly fifty million. Her government has become constitutional not only in name, but in fact, and her national education has attained to a high degree of excellence. In commerce and industry, the emblems of peace, she has also made rapid strides, until her import and export trades together amounted in 1907 to the enormous sum of 926,000,000 yen. Her general progress, during the short space of half a century, has been so sudden and swift that it presents a rare spectacle in the history of the world. This leap forward is the result of the stimulus which the country received on coming into contact with the civilization of Europe and America, and may well, in its broad sense, be regarded as a boon conferred by foreign intercourse. Foreign intercourse it was that animated the national consciousness of our people, who under the feudal system lived localized and disunited, and foreign intercourse it is that has enabled Japan to stand up as a world power. We possess today a powerful army and navy, but it was after Western models that we laid their foundations by establishing a system of conscription in pursuance of the principle "all our sons are soldiers," by promoting military education, and by encouraging the manufacture of arms and the art of shipbuilding. We have reorganized the systems of central and local administration, and effected reforms in the educational system of the empire. All this is nothing but the result of adopting the superior features of Western institutions. That Japan has been enabled to do so is a boon conferred on her by foreign intercourse, and it may be said that the nation has succeeded in this grand metamorphosis through the promptings and the influence of foreign civilization. For twenty centuries the nation has drunk freely of the civilizations of Korea, China, and India, being always open to the different influences impressed on her in succession. Yet we remain politically unaltered under one Imperial House and sovereign, that has descended in an unbroken line for a length of time absolutely unexampled in the world. We have welcomed Occidental civilization while preserving their old Oriental civilization. They have attached great importance to Bushido, and at the same time held in the highest respect the spirit of charity and humanity. They have ever made a point of choosing the middle course in everything, and have aimed at being always well-balanced. We are conservative simultaneously with being progressive; we are aristocratic and at the same time democratic; we are individualistic while also being socialistic. In these respects we may be said to somewhat resemble the Anglo-Saxon race.

Source: Count Shigenobu Okuma, *Fifty Years of New Japan* (*Kaikoku Gojunen Shi*), 2nd ed., edited by Marcus B. Huish, vol. 2 (London: Smith, Elder, 1910), pp. 554–55, 571–72.

PRIMARY SOURCE 17.3

Russia's Imperial Destiny (1896), Prince Esper Ukhtomskii

Prince Esper Ukhtomskii (1861–1921), a poet, publisher, and ardent advocate of eastern expansion, was a close confidant of Tsar Nicholas II of Russia. He accompanied Nicholas on an Asian tour in 1890–1891, before the latter assumed the throne. Nicholas approved each chapter of Ukhtomskii's three-volume account of the journey before publication, which was part of his preparation to assume the throne.

- How does Ukhtomskii justify Russian influence in Asia?
- What role does technology play in Russian expansion, according to Ukhtomskii?
- Which rival powers does Ukhtomskii discuss? What role do those rivalries play in Russian expansion?

Our stay at Saigon, the base of French operations in the advance against important borderlands of China, will in its turn be marked by enthusiasm in the greeting of a friendly nation. For us Russians, who scarcely ever visit the distant lands of Asia to study the powers and the means of European colonists, a visit to the central point of the "Indo-Chinese" empire governed from Paris, will be doubly instructive, doubly useful after seeing the British domains and patriarchally protected Java. This will be the more appropriate in that every figure, every vivid detail, every living fact, must and will lead us to reflect, in what a marked degree we Russians, as regards our prestige in Asia, voluntarily resign to every comer from Europe our historical part and our inherited mission as leaders of the East.

In such an abnormal state of affairs all the gain, as regards material prosperity, falls to the share of the representatives of Western principles—representatives foreign in spirit, and in reality hateful to those peoples of an ancient type on whom they have forced themselves by means of their cannon. Burmah, Cambodia, and Annam are no more; Siam is on the eve of dangerous external catastrophes; Japan is on the threshold of terrible internal dissensions; China alone, standing guard over its own, and unconsciously over Russian, interests, holds its ground with the wisdom of the serpent, gathers its forces against the foe from beyond the seas, and anxiously glances towards the silent North, where is situated the only State from which the Celestial Empire, educated in autocratic principles, can expect moral support, disinterested assistance, and a practical alliance based on community of interests.

This northern land of mist, forest, and ice, the extreme east of Siberia, opened up by Khabaroff, and other bold pioneers like him, the land re-united to Russia by the genius of Mooravioff-Amoorsky—is still a realm of primitive quiet, of deepest stillness and stagnation. It is only with the end of the century, with the opening up of new ways of communication with our eastern coast, that a new era with all its unforeseen consequences may begin. Meanwhile the land bears the stamp of something unformed and sad, like the life of its original settlers. All the more attention and unprejudiced judgment, then, is required of any one who would draw a parallel between the lands of the Pacific south now opening out before us, with the emerald island of Java, the inexhaustible natural riches of the Indo-Chinese soil, the self-confident vitality of the Celestial Empire, and the marshes and retired nooks, the boundless desert borders, of the country whose mission, in spite of all this, is to be a source of light for the neighbouring expanse, with its countless population.

The tiny kingdom of Holland holds sway in Asia over more than thirty million human beings (and that, too, at the equator, in an earthly paradise), while in the third part of the same continent the most important Power in it cannot reckon up one-half the number.

European colonisers, though not without envy and enmity, have shared among them the best coast-districts of these lands. Towns of such universal commercial importance as Hong-Kong and Singapore are the most eloquent witnesses to the indefatigable enterprise of Europeans amidst the prevailing Asiatic torpor. But while drawing the juices out of this gigantic continent, and, wherever possible, holding hundreds of millions in a state of economic slavery, do the pioneers of civilisation hope for final success? Holding on to the brink and ledges of a precipice, are they not in a state of constant alarm, lest the stones should give way and hurl them into the abyss? When the whole East awakes, as it will sooner or later: when it realises its mighty power and determines to speak its mind, then threats, violence, and superficial victories will not remedy the internal discord. This is why it is Russia's part to grow in power unobserved amidst the wastes and deserts of the North in expectation of the conflict between two worlds, in which the decision will depend on neither of them.

The idea of invading a complex foreign life, of using Asia as a tool for the advancement of the selfish interests of modern, so-called civilised, mankind, was repugnant to us. For more than two hundred years we have remained at home; for our natural union with Turkestan and the region of the Amur cannot be regarded as political annexations. We have remained at home with our traditional carelessness and indolence, while the Pacific has become the arena of Western European advance against a native world with an ancient political constitution and an undoubted civilisation of its own.

The results are patent. The strangers have dethroned and oppressed the East. Coming here to live and make money, they do not find a home. (But any Asiatic borderland soon becomes a home for a Russian.) The natives are not brothers in humanity to them; for them the land is one of voluntary exile, and the people are considered as miserable and inferior beings. The latter gradually realise the meaning of these outrageous views, and repay their "masters" with intense hatred. But where and how are they to find protection and a bulwark against the foreign foe?

But the mythologising spirit is still alive amongst them. The more actively Europe presses on Asia, the brighter becomes the name of the White Tsar in popular report and tradition.

***

From that remote period when our great golden-domed Moscow, which but a little earlier was no more than a small town in an insignificant subordinate principality, received the blessing of the saints and was irradiated by the creative glow of the autocratic idea, the East, advancing on us with fire and sword, has masterfully drawn toward it the eyes of the Russians: has wakened in them sleeping powers and heroic daring: and now calls them onward to deeds of glory, to advancement beyond the bounds of a dull reality, to a bright, glorious, and ineffable future! There neither is nor ever has been a nation whose past is so closely bound up with its future, as may be seen in the growth of the Russian Empire. The man of the West (the German, the Frenchman, the Englishman, the Italian) must cross the seas to find relief from the pressure which overwhelms him at home. Far from his native land, he must build his temporal prosperity on a foundation of sand, and the more firmly he takes root there under conditions of the most favourable nature, the more evident does it become that his old home, and he the voluntary exile, belong to two perfectly alien worlds. Beyond the seas, away from the life of his native land, he may gain money and position, but cannot (except artificially and but for a short time) retain completely untouched the spirit of his people, their ideals and traditions.

Source: Prince E. Ukhtomskii, *Travels in the East of Nicholas II Emperor of Russia, When Cesarewitch, 1890–1891*, vol. 2 (London: Archibald Constable and Company, 1890), pp. 142–43, 444–46.

PRIMARY SOURCE 17.4

General Act of the Conference of Berlin concerning the Congo (1885)

The Berlin Conference of 1884–1885 (also known as the Congo Conference) regulated European trade and colonization in sub-Saharan Africa in the late nineteenth century. The following selection is an excerpt from the General Act of the Conference.

The document opens by expressing a desire for mutual understanding and a desire for economic growth. What challenges to progress and economic prosperity does the document suggest?

Identify the priorities expressed in this document.

What limits, if any, does this document impose on the colonizers?

In the name of Almighty God:

. . . Wishing to regulate in a spirit of good mutual understanding the conditions most favorable to the development of commerce and of civilization in certain regions of Africa, and to assure to all peoples the advantages of free navigation upon the two principal African rivers which empty into the Atlantic ocean; desirous on the other hand to prevent misunderstandings and contentions to which the taking of new possessions on the coast of Africa may in the future give rise, and at the same time preoccupied with the means of increasing the moral and material well being of the indigenous populations, have resolved, upon the invitation which has been addressed to them by the Imperial Government of Germany in accord with the Government of the French Republic, to assemble for this object a Conference at Berlin. . . .

Chapter I.

Declaration relative to the liberty of commerce in the basin of the Congo, its embouchures and neighboring country, and dispositions connected therewith.

Article 1.

The commerce of all nations shall enjoy complete liberty. . . .

Article 2.

All flags, without distinction of nationality, shall have free access to all the littoral of the territories above enumerated, to the rivers which there empty into the sea, to all the waters of the Congo and its affluents including the lakes, to all the ports situated upon the borders of these waters, as well as to all the canals which may in the future be excavated with the object of connecting together the water courses or lakes comprised in the whole extent of the territories described in Article 1. They may undertake every kind of transport and exercise the coastwise navigation by sea and river as also small boat transportation upon the same footing as the allegiants.

Article 3.

Merchandise of every origin imported into these territories, under whatever flag it may be, by route of sea or river or land, shall have to discharge no other taxes than those which may be collected as an equitable compensation for expenses useful to commerce and which, under this head, must be equally borne by the allegiants and by strangers of every nationality.

All differential treatment is prohibited in respect to ships as well as merchandise.

Article 4.

Merchandise imported into these territories shall remain free from entrance and transit dues.

The Powers reserve to themselves to decide, at the end of a period of twenty years, whether freedom of entry shall or shall not be maintained.

Article 5.

Every Power which exercises or shall exercise rights of sovereignty in the territories under consideration shall not concede there either monopoly or privilege of any kind in commercial matters.

Strangers shall enjoy there without distinction, for the protection of their persons and their goods, the acquisition and transmission of their movable and immovable property and for the exercise of the professions, the same treatment and the same rights as the allegiants.

Article 6.

Depositions relative to the protection of the natives, of missionaries and of travelers, and also to religious liberty.

All Powers exercising rights of sovereignty or an influence in the Said territories engage themselves to watch over the conservation of the indigenous populations and the amelioration of their moral and material conditions of existence and to strive for the suppression of slavery and especially of the negro slave trade; they shall protect and favor without distinction of nationality or of worship, all the institutions and enterprises religious, scientific or charitable, created and organized for these objects or tending to instruct the natives and to make them understand and appreciate the advantages of civilization.

The christian missionaries, the savants, the explorers, their escorts, properties and collections shall be equally the object of special protection.

Liberty of conscience and religious toleration are expressly guaranteed to the natives as well as to allegiants and to strangers.

The free and public exercise of all forms of worship, the right to erect religious edifices and to organize missions belonging to all forms of worship shall not be subjected to any restriction or hindrance.

***

Chapter II.

Declaration concerning the slave trade.

Article 9.

Conformably to the principles of the law of nations, as they are recognized by the signatory Powers, the slave trade being interdicted, and as the operations which, by land or sea, furnish slaves to the trade ought to be equally considered as interdicted, the Powers who exercise or shall exercise rights of sovereignty or an influence in the territories forming the conventional basin of the Congo declare that these territories shall not serve either for a market or way of transit for the trade in slaves of any race whatever. Each of these Powers engages itself to employ all the means in its power to put an end to this commerce and to punish those who are occupied in it.

Chapter III.

Declaration relative to the neutrality of the territories comprised in the conventional basin of the Congo.

Article 10.

In order to give a new guarantee of security to commerce and to industry and to favor, by the maintenance of peace, the development of civilization in the countries mentioned in Article 1 and placed under the regime of commercial liberty, the high signatory parties of the present Act and those who shall subsequently adhere to it engage themselves to respect the neutrality of the territories or parts of territories depending on said countries, including therein the territorial waters, so long as the Powers who exercise or shall exercise rights of sovereignty or protectorate over these territories, making use of the option to proclaim themselves neutrals, shall fulfill the duties which belong to neutrality.

***

Article 17.

There is instituted an International Commission charged to assure the execution of the dispositions of the present navigation Act.

The signatory Powers of this Act, as well as those who shall adhere to it hereafter, can, at all times, have themselves represented in the said Commission, each by one delegate. No delegate can dispose of more than one vote even in the case where he may represent several governments.

***

Article 19.

. . . In case of an abuse of power or of an injustice on the part of an agent or employé of the International Commission, the individual who shall regard himself as injured in his person or in his rights may address himself to the consular agent of his nation. The latter shall examine the complaint; if he finds it prima facie reasonable, he shall have the right to present it to the Commission. Upon his initiative, the Commission represented by at least three of its members, shall join itself to him to make an investigation touching the conduct of its agent or employé. If the consular agent considers the decision of the Commission as giving rise to objections of right, he shall make a report of it to his government which may have recourse to the Powers represented in the Commission and invite them to come to agreement upon the instructions to be given to the Commission.

***

Chapter VI.

Declaration relative to the conditions essential to be fulfilled in order that new occupations upon the coasts of the African continent may be considered as effective.

Article 34.

The Power which henceforth shall take possession of a territory upon the coast of the African continent situated outside of its present possessions, or which, not having had such possessions hitherto, shall come to acquire them, and likewise, the Power which shall assume a protectorate there, shall accompany the respective act with a notification addressed to the other signatory Powers of the present Act, in order to put them in a condition to make available, if there be occasion for it, their reclamations.

Source: "The Treaty of Berlin," *American Journal of International Law* 3, no. 1, supplement: Official Documents (January 1909): 7–24.

Interpreting Visual Evidence

Occidentalism: Representing Western Influence

Ever since the publication of Edward Said's landmark work *Orientalism* (1978), scholars have carefully examined European and American efforts to represent nonwestern peoples in disciplines ranging from art, languages, and literature to law, biology, and philosophy. The field of postcolonial studies that emerged in Said's wake has emphasized the degree to which western descriptions of "Orientals" were really efforts to describe themselves—as the rational, disciplined opposite of the supposedly sensual Orient—and to affirm their own values. More recently, scholarly attention has turned to different peoples' efforts to make sense of European and American influences on their societies—representations that we might call "Occidentalism" (the "Occident" meaning the west).

Here we consider a range of visual materials that both reflected and shaped ordinary people's views of western influence. These depictions circulated widely; notice the combination of text and images, for those who could not read. While Japan was not colonized, the Meiji Restoration relied heavily on European models for its constitution and economic plans. In the first image, *Bake-Bake Gakkō* (School of Demons) from the series *Kyosai Rakuga* (1874), Kawanabe Kyosai satirizes the European-inspired Japanese school reforms of the Meiji Restoration. The second image, *The Beating of the (Foreign) Devils and the Burning of the (Christian) Books* (c. 1890), shows Chinese Boxer rebels attacking foreign influence. In the final image, the Mexican caricaturist José

Kawanabe Kyosai's *Bake-Bake Gakkō*, number 3 of the *Kyosai Rakuga* series (Kawanabe Kyosai Memorial Museum).

The Beating of the (Foreign) Devils and the Burning of the (Christian) Books.

Guadalupe Posada mocks American influence in *The American Mosquito* (1910–1913). Whether the mosquitoes in question represent American tourists, the Americans brought in by Mexico's President Díaz to manage railroads and mines, or the American dollar remains unclear.

EL MOSQUITO AMERICANO

El Mosquito Americano
Ahora acaba de llegar;
Dicen se vino á pasear
A este suelo mexicano.

Dizque el domingo embarcó
Allá en Laredo de Texas,
Y que al Saltillo llegó
Picándoles las orejas,
En la Estación á unas viejas
Que bien las hizo marchar,
Hasta las hizo sudar
Este animal inhumano;
Luego empiezan á gritar:
El Mosquito americano.

A Guanajuato marchó,
Esto es cosa de reir;
Él al centro no llegó,
Pero si estuvo en Marfil.
Ya no podrán sufrir
Tan malcriado y altanero,
Pues le picó en el trasero
A un militar veterano.
Porque es mucho, muy grosero
El Mosquito americano.

Tomó el rumbo de Irapuato
Y por Pénjamo pasó;
De allí luego regresó
Por el pueblo de Uriangato,
La hacienda de Villachato
La dejó muy derrotada;
Toda la gente asustada
La encontró el vale Mariano,
Nana Emeteria gritaba:
El Mosquito americano.

Por la puerta de San Juan
Piedra Gorda y la Sandía,
Una viejecita decía:
¡Jesús, qué fiero animal!
Dígame usted Don Pascual
¿No le ha llegado el Mosquito?
Dicen que es muy chiquitite,
Y también muy inhumano;
¿Qué dice tata Pachito
El Mosquito americano?

The American Mosquito.

QUESTIONS FOR ANALYSIS

1. Compare the representation of foreign influence in all three works. Are those influences purely oppressive? Do any local actors appear to find outside influence appealing? What is the greater threat, according to these images, internal weakness or a coercive foreign intervention?
2. Analyze the relationship between local traditions and progress in each work. Do the images present a vision of progress? From the perspective of the artists, what is the relationship, if any, between foreign influence and progress?
3. Do the artists present a homegrown vision of progress, or is progress something that comes from abroad? Is it possible, from the artists' points of view, to be Japanese, Chinese, or Mexican and modern at the same time?
4. What messages do these works convey about their own societies? Do the artists present their own people as powerless victims, as vulnerable and divided, as caught between their own autocratic rulers and outside invaders, or perhaps as unified and defiant?

Before You Read This Chapter

GLOBAL STORYLINES

The Global Impact of Modernity

- Numerous factors lead to global instability: vast population movements, worldwide financial crises, class conflict, the rise of women's consciousness, and hatred of colonial domination.
- Class conflict, economic instability, and great power rivalry within Europe combine with growing protest from overseas to undermine Europe's dominant position in world affairs.
- New forms of scientific thinking and artistic expression, known as cultural modernism, challenge the dominant western view of progress and open Europe and North America to the cultural achievements of nonwestern societies.

CHAPTER OUTLINE

FOCUS QUESTIONS

- What was the connection between migration and the development of nationalism in this period?
- How did China's responses to imperialism compare with those in Africa?
- What political, economic, and social crises swept through the world in this period? What impact did they have on different regions of the world?
- How did new cultural forms at the turn of the century reflect challenges to the world order as it then existed?
- In what ways did race, nation, and religion unify populations but also make societies more difficult to govern and economies more difficult to manage?

18

An Unsettled World

1890–1914

In 1905, a young African man, Kinjikitile Ngwale, began to move among various ethnic groups in German East Africa, spreading a message of opposition to German colonial authorities. In the tradition of visionary prophets (see Chapter 16), Kinjikitile claimed that by anointing his followers with blessed water (*maji* in Swahili), he could protect them from European bullets and drive the Germans from East Africa. Kinjikitile's reputation spread rapidly, drawing followers from across 100,000 square miles of territory. Although German officials soon executed Kinjikitile, they could not prevent a broad uprising, called the Maji Maji Revolt. The Germans brutally suppressed the revolt, killing between 200,000 and 300,000 Africans.

The Maji Maji Revolt and its aftermath revealed the intensity of resistance to the world of nations and their empires. In Europe and North America, critics who felt deprived of the full benefits of industrializing nation-states—especially women, workers, and frustrated nationalists—demanded far-reaching reforms. In Asia, Africa, and Latin America, anticolonial critics and exploited classes protested European domination. Ironically, at the very moment when peoples of European descent seemed to have established preeminence in international affairs, they, too, began to feel that they had lost control over a world changing at an alarming rate. While continuing to trumpet the wonders of European civilization to the colonized abroad, Europeans at home began the search for new forms of social organization and cultural expression suitable to a deeply unsettled age.

This chapter tackles the anxieties and insecurities that unsettled the world around the turn of the twentieth century. It ties them in particular to three key factors: (1) the uprooting of millions of people from countryside to city and from one continent to another; (2) discontent with the poverty that many suffered even as economic production leaped upward; and (3) resentment of and resistance to European domination. Around the globe, this tumult caused a questioning of old ideas that led to a flowering of new thinking and fresh artistic expression under the label of "modernism." Championed by some and despised by others, modernism *meant* to be unsettling—to represent the world in shocking new ways—and thus tells us a great deal about the conflicts and crises that defined this era.

Progress, Upheaval, and Movement

The period from 1890 to 1914 brought unprecedented prosperity and anxiety, integration and resistance. Rapid economic progress brought challenges to the established order and the people in power. In Europe, the United States, and Latin America, radicals and middle-class reformers agitated for political and social change. In areas colonized by European countries and the United States, resentment focused on either colonial rulers or Indigenous elites. Even in nations such as China, which had not been formally colonized but which faced repeated intrusions, popular discontent targeted domination by Europeans. In China, Mexico, and Russia, angry peasants and workers allied with frustrated reformers to topple autocratic regimes.

In the late nineteenth century, a larger concentration of capital made possible more intensive forms of agriculture and more mechanized forms of manufacturing, fueling economic growth. But advanced capitalism also spurred inequalities within industrial countries and, especially, between the world's industrial and nonindustrial regions. It also brought unwelcome changes in how and where people worked and lived. Rural folk flocked into the cities, hoping to escape the poverty that encumbered most people in the countryside. In the cities, even though public building projects produced sewer systems, museums, parks, and libraries, the poor had little access to them. Anxieties intensified when economic downturns left thousands out of work. This led, in some cases, to organized opposition to authoritarian regimes or to the free market system.

With so much upheaval in the air, a new generation of young artists, writers, and scientists broke with older conventions and sought new ways of seeing and describing the world. Many of these innovators were energized by the idea of moving beyond traditional forms of art, literature, music, and science. At the same time, this generation's exuberance provoked reactions by those who were not ready to give up their cultural traditions and institutions.

Peoples in Motion

If the world was being *unsettled* by political, economic, and cultural changes, it was also being *resettled* by mass emigration. (See Map 18.1.) A "Caucasian tsunami," in the memorable words of historian Alfred Crosby, resulted in emigration of an unprecedented number of Europeans to North America, Australia, Argentina, Africa, and Cuba. This "tsunami" began after the Napoleonic wars and gathered momentum in the 1840s, when the Irish fled their starving communities to seek better lives in places like Ontario (Canada), New York (United States), and Patagonia (Argentina); the Irish exodus and the end of the slave trade meant that, for the first time, European migration eclipsed that of African captives. The United States was the favored destination, with European migrants exceeding by sixfold the number of Europeans who migrated to Argentina (the second-place receiving country) between 1871 and 1920. The high point occurred between 1901 and 1910, when over 6 million Europeans entered the United States. This was nothing less than a demographic revolution. For receiving countries, it was also a way to "whiten" the local population, especially in the Americas, where there were large populations descended from enslaved or Indigenous populations.

EMIGRATION, IMMIGRATION, INTERNAL MIGRATION Europeans were not the only peoples on the move. Between the 1840s and the 1940s, 29 million South Asians migrated into the Malay Peninsula and Burma (British colonies), the Dutch Indies (Indonesia), East Africa, and the Caribbean. Most were recruited to labor on plantations, railways, and mines in British-controlled territories. Merchants followed laborers, making the South Asian migrant populations more diverse. Meanwhile, the Chinese, too, emigrated in significant numbers. Between 1845 and 1900, forces such as population pressure, a shortage of cultivable land, and social turmoil drove 800,000 Chinese to seek new homes in North and South America, New Zealand, Hawaii, and the West Indies. Close to four times as many settled in Southeast Asia.

At the same time, industrial changes caused millions to migrate *within* their own countries or to neighboring ones, seeking employment in the burgeoning cities or other opportunities in frontier regions. In North America, hundreds of thousands headed west, while millions relocated from the countryside to the cities. In Asia, about 10 million Russians went east to Siberia and central Asia, and 2 million Koreans moved northwest to Manchuria. In Africa, small numbers of South Africans moved north into Northern and Southern Rhodesia in search of arable land and precious metals. Across the world, gold rushes, silver rushes, copper rushes, and a diamond rush took people across landmasses and across oceans. Mostly men, these emigrants were hell-bent on profit and were often willing to destroy the land in order to extract precious commodities as quickly as possible.

People traveled with varying credentials and goals. Some went as colonial officials or soldiers, some as missionaries or big-game hunters—most of these folks did not plan to stay. Merchants and traders were more likely to settle in for the long term. Several million East Asians (mostly Chinese) scattered all over Asia, East and South Africa, North America, the Pacific Coast of South America, and the Caribbean, replacing men and women who were formerly enslaved on plantations, or doing construction. Japanese laborers migrated to Peru to mine guano for fertilizer and to Hawaii to harvest sugar.

Migrants took big risks. Travel was often hazardous, and leaving behind native cultures and kin groups was painful. Many experienced conflicts with resident populations, as did Chinese migrants who ventured into Taiwan and other frontier regions. In the cities, tensions mounted as migrant workers faced low wages, poor working and living conditions, and barriers to higher-paying positions. In China, women without male relatives to protect them sometimes suffered abuse or exploitation. And yet, the economic rewards were substantial enough that the risks of sending the men abroad seemed worth taking.

Until 1914, governments imposed almost no controls on immigration or emigration. In China, the Qing government tried to restrict emigration into the Manchus' northeastern homelands, but it failed. Eager to add both laborers and consumers to its expanding territory, the United States allowed entry to anyone who was not a prostitute, a convict, or a "lunatic," but in 1882 racist reactions spurred legislation that barred entry to almost all Chinese. Travel within Europe required no passports or work permits; foreign-born criminals were subject to deportation, but that was the extent of immigration policy. (See Analyzing Global Developments: Migration and the Origin of Border Control Policies.)

URBAN LIFE AND CHANGING IDENTITIES Cities boomed, with both positive and negative repercussions. The population of Buenos Aires climbed from 180,000 in 1869 to 1.58 million in 1914, and London's passed 6.5 million. Local governments undertook massive rebuilding and beautification projects,

Urban Transportation. *Left*: Streetcars in Tokyo, Japan's capital, are watched over by sword-bearing patrolmen in 1905, during the Russo-Japanese War. The first electric streetcar began running in Japan in 1895. Note the elevated electricity lines, which date to the 1880s. *Right*: Heavy traffic in London, in about 1910, points to an urban population on the move. Note the many kinds of transportation—motor buses as well as horse-drawn wagons; the railings in the foreground mark the entrance to the underground, or subway.

The Global View

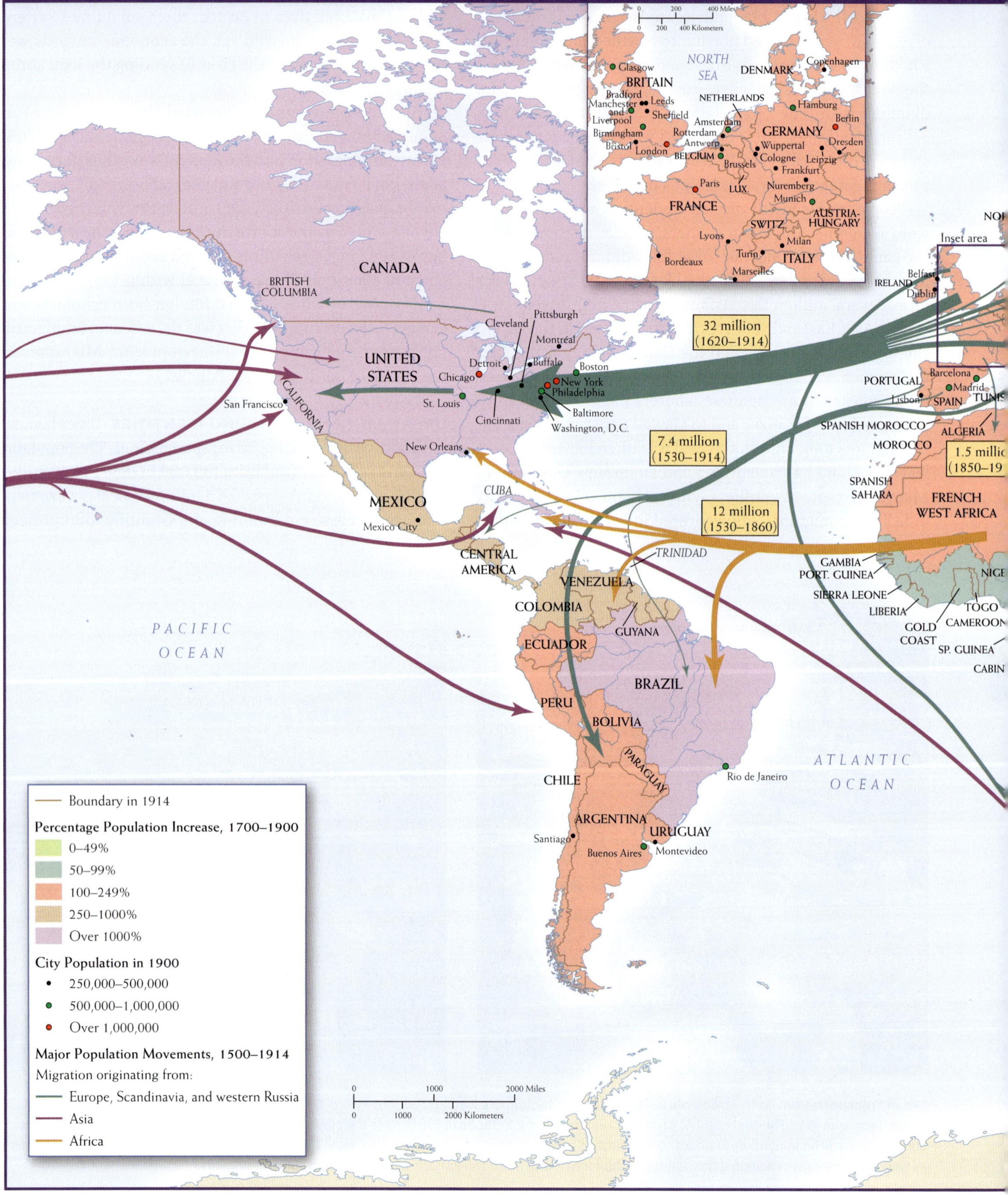

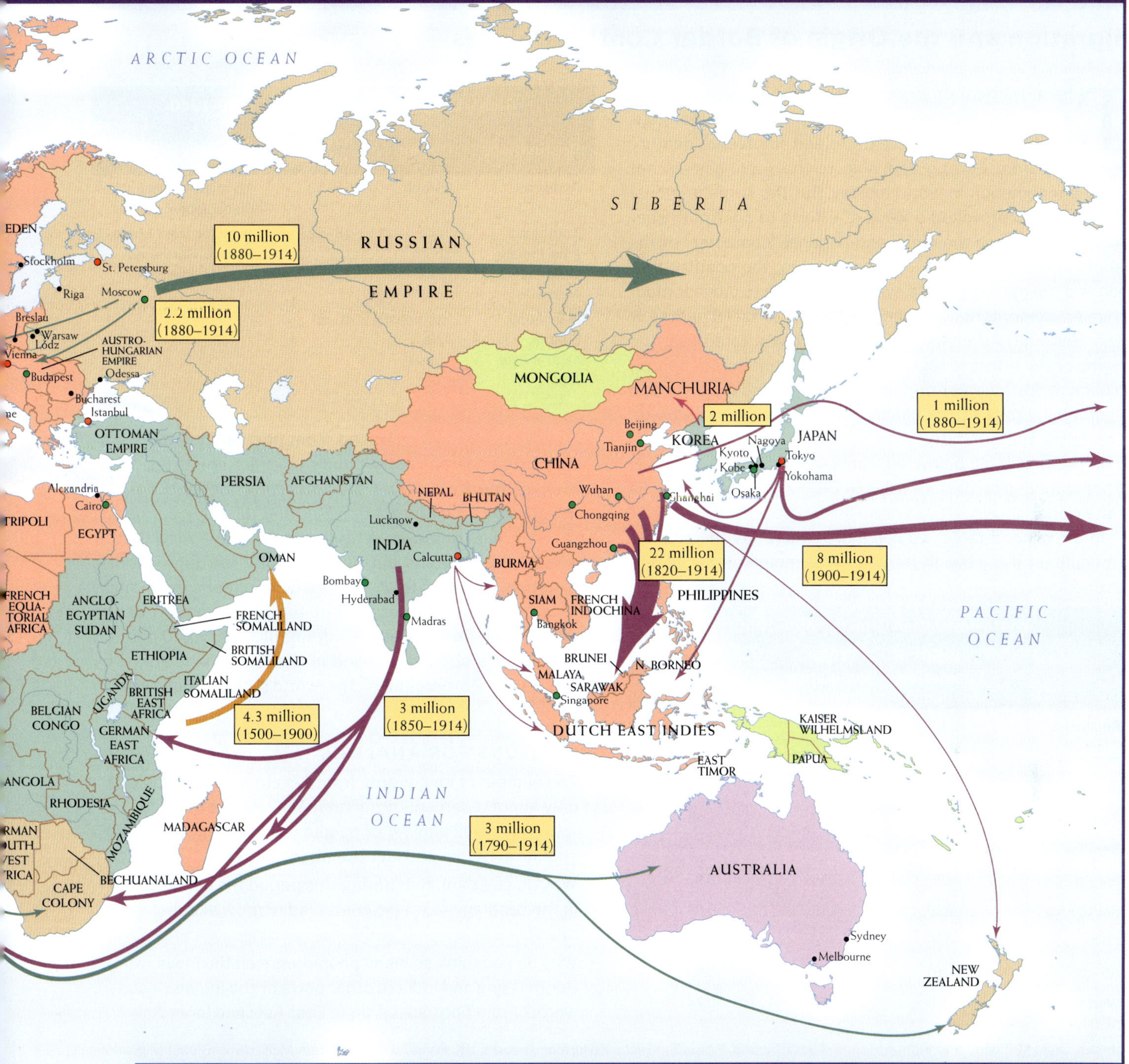

MAP 18.1 | Nineteenth-Century Migration

The nineteenth century witnessed a demographic revolution in terms of migration, urbanization patterns, and population growth. The world's population also rose from roughly 625 million in 1700 to 1.65 billion in 1900 (a two-and-a-half-fold increase).

- To what areas did most of the migrants from Europe go? What about the migrants from China, India, and Africa?
- What four areas saw the greatest population increase by 1900?
- How were migration flows and urbanization connected? What factors most accounted for these global population changes? Was internal growth more important than external migration in the case of the world's population growth? In what countries was population growth most affected by external or internal migration?

Analyzing Global Developments

Migration and the Origin of Border Control Policies

The movement of large numbers of people within and across regions—namely, the spread of the Mongols, the Atlantic world slave trade, and nineteenth-century migrations from Europe and Asia to the Americas—is not a new phenomenon in world history. But the surge in global migration also provoked a wave of efforts to control it, specifically to manage the racial and national "character" of the people within borders. The United States, the country that received the most migrants, was also the one to pioneer modern migration practices, especially the use of racial quotas or bans. Historian Adam McKeown has demonstrated that the origins of the effort to regulate and document border control go back to late nineteenth-century America and the efforts to substantially restrict the number of Asian immigrants trying to enter the United States.

In the first table below, we see a comparison of the rates of population growth from 1850 to 1950 in the major regions of the world.

In the second table, we see more concretely the number of people on the move in terms of their points of origin and destinations.

World Population Growth, 1850–1950

	1850 Population (millions)	1950 Population (millions)	Average Annual Growth (%)
Receiving			
Americas	59	325	1.72
North Asia	22	104	1.57
Southeast Asia	42	177	1.45
Sending			
Europe	265	515	0.67
South Asia	230	445	0.66
China	420	520	0.21
Africa	81	205	0.93
World	1,200	2,500	0.74

Global Long-Distance Migration, 1840–1940

Destinations	Origins	Migrants (millions)	Auxiliary Origins
Americas	Europe	55–58	2.5 million from India, China, Japan, Africa
Southeast Asia, Indian Ocean Rim, Australasia	India, South China	48–52	5 million from Africa, Europe, Northeast Asia, Middle East
Manchuria, Siberia, central Asia, Japan	Northeast Asia, Russia	46–51	

These data were compiled from port and customs statistics at significant entry points to major countries. What we see in the data is that the "receiving" nations' populations grew by a factor of 4.0–5.5 during this 100-year period and that their overall growth was more than twice that of the "sending" regions during this time. Not only was the population growth rate of the receiving nations much more dramatic during this period, but the redistribution of the world's population was equally dramatic. In 1850, 10 percent of the world's population lived in the "receiving" areas; by 1950, nearly 25 percent of the world's population lived in those areas.

QUESTIONS FOR ANALYSIS

- The number of immigrants from Asia to the Americas was only about 3 percent of the total. Why do you think such a relatively small number of people would cause a dramatic change in border and identification control?
- Why do you think that during this period the populations in the sending areas also continued to grow at substantial rates?
- Why do you think so many people were on the move from South China and India to other parts of the Indian Ocean world? From northeast Asia to East Asia and Inner Asia?

Sources: Colin McEvedy and Richard Jones, *Atlas of World Population History* (Harmondsworth, UK: Penguin, 1978); Adam McKeown, "Global Migration, 1846–1940," *Journal of World History* 15 (2004): 155–89; Adam M. McKeown, *Melancholy Order: Asian Migration and the Globalization of Borders* (New York: Columbia University Press, 2008).

but severe housing shortages remained. This was the era in which city planning came into its own—to widen and regularize thoroughfares for train and streetcar traffic and to make crowded city life attractive to new inhabitants. City governments in Paris, New York, Cairo, Buenos Aires, and Brussels spent lavishly on opera houses, libraries, sewers, and parks, hoping to ward off disease and crime and to impress others with their modernity.

Rebuilding medieval cities meant opening them up—to traffic, to consumption, to public enlightenment, to light and

Coney Island in 1905. As societies grew richer and more consumer oriented, cities cleared space for promenades, parks, and beaches for leisure time. Coney Island in New York became a model for local escapes from the work week and the bustle of the metropolis. Sites like this were designed to be spectacular and to provide images for even distant consumers to gawk at. Visiting Coney Island meant leaving with memorabilia to show off—like the postcard pictured here.

air—but it also meant reorganizing them along class lines. In Vienna, for example, a wide, circular boulevard, the *Ringstrasse,* replaced medieval walls. It showcased a grand imperial theater, a neo-Renaissance opera house, and a neoclassical parliament. In Paris, fashionable new apartment houses and cafés edged out strategic but dilapidated workers' hovels; wide, well-lit avenues replaced narrow, dark streets. The small, narrow streets of Tokyo, which had 2 million inhabitants by 1905, escaped such engineering, but the city also acquired a new national museum in a city park.

Tokyo, like so many other booming cities, had also made cities safe for the new leisured classes to enjoy their wealth through recreation. For instance, in Europe, parks and broad sidewalks, like the famous Champs-Élysées in Paris, were made to stroll in, to see and to be seen. Women, no longer cooped up in the domestic sphere, donned the latest furs and dresses; men were no less fashion conscious. Cities pushed their smelly and pestilent ports to the outskirts. Shores were ideal, in good weather, for public bathing. In Buenos Aires, for instance, it was no longer shameful to show some flesh on municipal beaches. Despite the influence of the Catholic Church, migrants from Italy, Spain, and Russia, as well as Indigenous-born Argentine women, congregated and pushed fashion trends to the edge with ever more revealing bathing suits. The same happened on New York's Coney Island beaches.

In theory the new public institutions were accessible to all, but in practice they mostly benefited the elite, and in many cases poorer people were forced to leave their downtown dwellings and take up residence in shabby suburbs. For these urbanites, life continued to revolve around long hours at work, and they continued to inhabit overcrowded and unsanitary living conditions and to die from diseases such as cholera and tuberculosis.

Even the poorest, however, felt that the metropolis offered opportunities unavailable in small towns or in the countryside; here one could at least *hope* to change one's lot in life. For western women, in particular, the cities offered new possibilities. Some of those who had worked as domestic servants, textile workers, or agricultural laborers now took positions as shop girls, secretaries, or—thanks to educational opportunities—teachers; a very few became doctors, although their practices were largely limited to treating other women. Increasing female literacy and the falling price of books and magazines gave western women access to new models of acceptable behavior. In cities it became respectable, even fashionable, for women to be seen on the boulevards. The availability in some places of ready-made clothes and packaged goods changed the way wealthier women shopped and cooked. Yet, for most women, leisure time, professional work, and luxury consumption remained dreams rather than realities.

Increased population density made possible more collective action—and collective amusement—but did not necessarily lead to greater social harmony. The turn of the century was marked by the construction of new parks, soccer and baseball stadia, theaters, and pubs, but also by an increasing number of conflicts between workers and business owners or police. Social clubs, political organizations, and charitable associations met more and more frequently—but often battled with one another for members or influence. As cities grew, they often developed ethnically homogeneous neighborhoods—"Little Italies" or "Chinatowns" in the United States, Basque *barrios* in Buenos Aires, and Jewish or Irish neighborhoods in England—where inhabitants kept to themselves and were sometimes feared and hated by their neighbors. Seeking to unify nations internally, many writers, artists, and political leaders created mythic histories that aimed to give diverse groups a common story of nationhood. Such inventions were crucial in nation building, but they also fueled conflict among nations that in 1914 erupted in the Great War, an event that would generate another huge wave of emigration and urban expansion—and hostility to "foreigners."

Discontent with Imperialism

In the decades before the Great War, opposition to European domination in Asia and Africa gathered strength. During the nineteenth century, as Europeans touted imperialism as a "civilizing mission," local prophets voiced alternative visions contesting European supremacy (see Chapter 16). While imperialists consolidated their hold, suppression of unrest in the colonies required ever more force and bloodshed. As the cycle of resistance and repression escalated, many Europeans back home questioned the harsh means of controlling their colonies. By 1914, these questions were intensifying as colonial subjects across Asia and Africa challenged imperial domination. In China, too, where Europeans were scrambling for trading opportunities without actually establishing formal colonial power, local populations resisted foreign influences.

Unrest in Africa

Africa witnessed many anticolonial uprisings in the first decades of colonial rule. (See Map 18.2.) Violent conflicts embroiled not only the Belgians and the Germans, who ruled autocratically, but also the British, who placed traditional African rulers as mediators in a system called "indirect rule." These uprisings made Europeans uneasy: Why were Africans resisting regimes that had huge advantages in firepower and claimed to bring the bounty of their "civilizing mission"? Some Europeans concluded that Africans were too stubborn or unsophisticated to appreciate Europe's generosity. Others, shocked by the spectacle of colonial cruelty, called for reform. A few radicals even demanded an end to imperialism. Colonial uprisings shook the confidence of imperialists.

In African, organized armies and villagers rose up to challenge the European conquest. Everywhere, Europeans responded with savage repression bordering on ethnic cleansing. And yet, Africans did not back down against forced labor, increased taxes, and appropriated land.

THE ANGLO-BOER WAR The continent's most devastating anticolonial uprising occurred in South Africa. This unique struggle pitted two White communities against each other: the British in the Cape Colony and Natal against the Afrikaners, descendants of original Dutch settlers who lived in the Transvaal and the Orange Free State. (See Map 18.2 inset.) Although two White regimes were the main adversaries, the Anglo-Boer War (1899–1902) involved the area's 4 million Black inhabitants as fully as its 1 million Whites.

The war's origins lay in the discovery of gold in the Transvaal in the mid-1880s. As the area rapidly became Africa's richest state, the prospect that Afrikaner republics might become the powerhouse in southern Africa was more than British imperialists could accept. They also fretted over rumors of German influence on Afrikaners.

Fighting a relentless guerrilla campaign, Afrikaners waged a war that would last three years and cost Britain 20,000 soldiers and £200 million. Britain's difficulties containing the Afrikaner insurgency led commanders to devise a strategy that cut insurgents off from the local civilian population. Barbed wire had been invented in Texas to manage herds of

The Anglo-Boer War. The British sent a large contingent of troops to South Africa to deal with the resistance of the two Boer republics—the Orange Free State and the Transvaal. The loss of life and the cruelties inflicted on soldiers and civilians alike during the war, which lasted from 1899 to 1902, did much to undermine the British people's views of their imperial mission. The Transvaal and the Orange Free State fought valiantly to keep from becoming part of the British Empire. In the end, they lost.

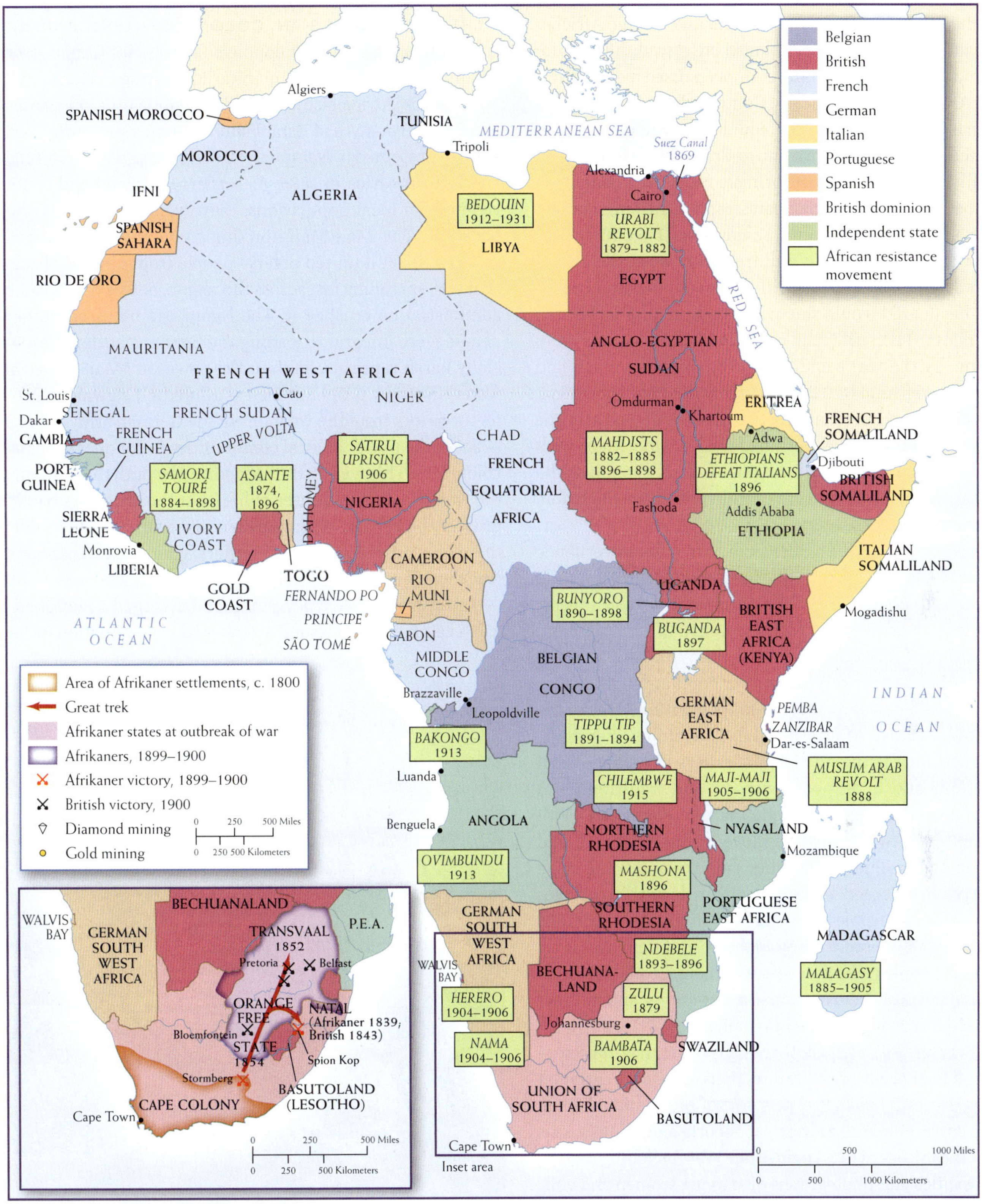

MAP 18.2 | Uprisings and Wars in Africa

The European partition and conquest of Africa were violent affairs.

- How many separate African resistance movements can you count on this map?
- Where was resistance the most prolonged?
- According to your reading, why were Ethiopians (see Chapter 17), who sustained their autonomy, able to do what other African opponents of European armies were not?

cattle; the Portuguese used it to contain and subdue Africans in Mozambique in 1895, the Spanish borrowed the idea for Cuba, and the British, watching their peers, used it extensively against Afrikaners and Africans. Commanders also borrowed a Spanish innovation from the counterinsurgency in Cuba: the concentration camp. Meant to drain all civilians', and especially women's, support for male rebels, concentration camps became humanitarian catastrophes. At one moment in the war, giant prison camps penned over 155,000 people, many of them women and children. Nor were the camps restricted to Afrikaners. The British also rounded up Africans whom they feared would side with the "anticolonial" Dutch descendants. The suffering and loss in these camps were appalling; by the war's end, 28,000 Afrikaner women and children, as well as 14,000 Black Africans, had perished there. On one thing the Boers and British agreed: do not arm the African population! They both had fresh memories of wars against the Zulu and other local populations, though as the war dragged on, Africans were recruited for transportation, or as scouts and messengers.

This war exemplified a new form of frontier governance and a new legal use of words like indigenous or tribal. While populations crossed borders in ever larger numbers, governments also systematized forms of racial segregation, containment, and isolation of those they did not want. While this war was ostensibly between two White settler populations, the more devastating effect was on indigenous populations. One of the architects of Native Affairs of Natal, Theophilus Shepstone, had argued for relying on "tribal" leaders to manage local populations and to respect "customs and traditions"—in order to keep them local, hemmed in, and contained. With the disputes between settlers more or less resolved, and borrowing techniques from other empires and frontiers, a global system emerged of "indigenous" rule within reserves or territories ostensibly to preserve customs and traditions within them while controlling mobility and denying rights for "tribal" peoples who moved out of them. From Argentina to Afghanistan, a system of camps, reservations, and indirect rule by chiefs or elders came into being.

The war also signaled another change, one that ran sometimes in diametrically opposite directions to the concentration of state powers. Thanks to a new sort of international actor, the war correspondent, newspaper reports and photographs brought the misery of the **Anglo-Boer War**, including reports of its atrocities and photographs of starving women and children, back to Europe. The horrors of the war traumatized the British, who were used to regarding themselves as Europe's most enlightened and efficient colonial rulers. They were scandalized, too, by how long it had taken for the "empire on which the sun never sets" to subdue such a ragtag opponent; but they did, eventually, win the war, bringing the Transvaal and the Orange Free State—with their vast gold reserves—into their empire.

OTHER STRUGGLES IN COLONIZED AFRICA If the Anglo-Boer War and Leopold's abuses in Congo (see Chapter 17) sparked humanitarian outrage, Germany's atrocities in Africa also whipped up public opinion against empire. Germany had established colonies in South West Africa (present-day Namibia), Cameroon, and Togo in 1884 and in East Africa in 1885. As settlers took land and water rights from local populations, they eventually provoked a backlash. The Maji Maji uprising (1905–07) was not well organized. Yet it united diverse people from different backgrounds, spreading fast across the region, before the German administration crushed it. The Ngoni, Matumbi, and other people were integral to leading the fight and suffered especially harsh reprisals. Faith in the power of "Maji" (special water) given by prophets such as Kinjikiteli Ngwale to protect warriors from the weapons of the German army led to a belief in the power of local communities to conquer German colonizers. This was further supported by faith that not only the "maji ya uzima" (water of life), but the ancestors would protect the rebels. With gods and ancestors on their side, the rebels proved a threat to settlers, who panicked about a "race war."

In return, the German commander waged a scorched-earth campaign and issued a genocidal extermination order

Extermination of the Herero. The Germans carried out a campaign of near-extermination against the Herero population in German South West Africa in 1904–1906. Nearly 90 percent of the Herero were killed. In this 1906 photograph, a German soldier stands guard over Herero women and children in a prison camp.

Maji-Maji Warriors. This image shows a group of Maji-Maji warriors in traditional dress, armed with spears, bows and arrows, knobkieries, and leather shields.

against the local population. They also unleashed a war of gunpowder against the spirits and spears, especially using the Maxim gun (the world's first recoil-operated fully automatic heavy machine gun) against guerrillas. Portraying Africans as either accepting subjects or childlike primitives, Europeans redoubled their efforts to impose colonial order. The problem, in their view, was not that empire building destroyed local ways of life, but that they had not yet succeeded in imposing civilization on a stubbornly "backward" world. And yet, the news and photos of atrocities was unsettling at home and provoked reform, the creation of the Colonial Department in 1907, and a shift to administrative rather than militaristic government by the Germans.

The Boxer Uprising in China

At the turn of the century, forces from within and without also unsettled China. Although not formally under colonial rule, but divided into spheres of influence, the Chinese, like the Africans, deeply resented European and Japanese intrusions. As the population swelled to over half a billion and outstripped the country's resources, problems of landlessness, poverty, and peasant discontent (constants in China's modern history) led many to mourn the decay of political authority. In response, in 1898 the Qing emperor tried to modernize industry, agriculture, commerce, education, and the military. But opponents blocked the emperor's designs. Before long, conservatives within the palace placed the emperor under house arrest. In his place, the Empress Dowager Cixi seized control on behalf of those who resisted change and opening.

EXTERNAL FACTORS The breakdown of dynastic authority originated largely with foreign pressure. For one thing, China's defeat in the Sino-Japanese War of 1894–1895 (see Chapter 17) was deeply humiliating. Although Japan, which acquired Taiwan as its first major colony, was the immediate beneficiary of the war, Britain, France, Germany, and Russia quickly scrambled for additional concessions from China. They demanded that the Qing government grant them specific areas within China as their respective "spheres of influence." (See Map 18.3.) The United States also pushed the Qing to accept western norms of political and economic exchange. The Americans, however, were in favor of an "open-door" policy that would keep access available to all traders, while supporting missionary efforts to spread Christianity.

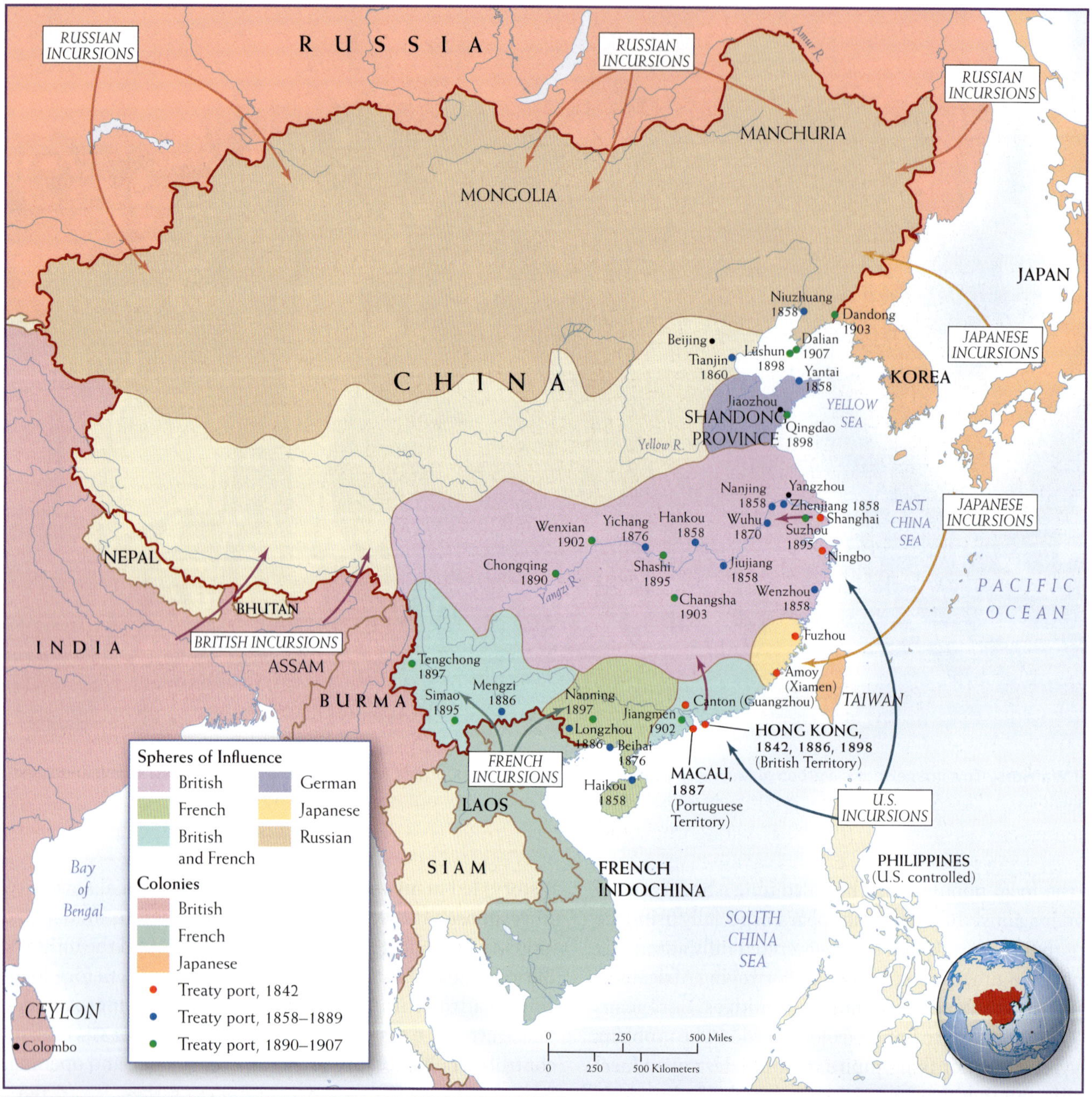

MAP 18.3 | Foreign Spheres of Influence in China, 1842–1907

While technically independent, the Qing dynasty could not prevent foreign penetration and domination of its economy during the nineteenth century.

- Which five powers established spheres of influence in China?
- At what time was the greatest number of treaty ports established?
- According to your reading, what did the foreign powers hope to achieve within their spheres of influence? What kinds of local opposition did the foreign influence inspire?

The most explosive reaction to these pressures, the **Boxer Uprising**, started within the peasantry. Like colonized peoples in Africa, the Boxers violently resisted European meddling in their communities. And as in the Taiping Rebellion decades earlier (see Chapter 16), the story of the Boxers was tied to missionary activities. Whereas in earlier centuries Jesuit missionaries had sought to convert the court and the elites, by the mid-nineteenth century the missionary goal was to convert commoners. After the Taiping Rebellion, Christian missionaries had streamed into China, impatient to make new

Cixi's Allies. The Empress Dowager Cixi emerged as the most powerful figure in the Qing court in the last decades of the dynasty, from the 1860s until her death in 1908. Highly able, she approved many of the early reforms of the Self-Strengthening movement, but her commitment to the preservation of the Manchu Qing dynasty made her suspicious of more fundamental and wide-ranging changes. Here she is shown surrounded by court eunuchs; Cixi relied upon them, especially as her relationships with orthodox officials were often ambivalent.

converts in the hinterlands and confident of their governments' backing. With the Qing dynasty in a weakened state, Christian missionaries became more aggressive.

An incident in 1897, in which Chinese residents killed two German missionaries in the northern province of Shandong, brought tensions to a boil. In retribution, the German government demanded the right to construct three cathedrals, to remove hostile local officials, and to seize the northeastern port of Jiaozhou. As tensions mounted, martial arts groups in the region began to attack the missionaries and converts, calling for an end to the Christians' privileges. In early 1899, several of these groups united under the name Boxers United in Righteousness and adopted the slogan "Support the Qing, destroy the foreign." Like the African followers of Kinjikitile, the Boxers believed that divine protection made them immune to all earthly weapons. As one fighter noted, "We requested the gods to attach themselves to our bodies. When they had done so, we became Spirit Boxers, after which we were invulnerable to swords and spears, our courage was enhanced, and in fighting we were unafraid to die and dared to charge straight ahead."

INTERNAL FACTORS The Boxer movement flourished especially where natural disasters and harsh economic conditions increased hardships. Shandong Province had suffered floods throughout much of the decade, followed by prolonged drought in the winter of 1898. Idle, restless, and often hungry, many peasants, boatmen, and peddlers turned to the Boxers for support. They also liked the Boxers' message that the gods were angry over the foreign presence in general and Christian activities in particular.

As these activists, many of them young men, swelled the Boxers' ranks, women also found a place in the movement. The so-called Red Lanterns were mostly teenage girls and unmarried women who announced their loyalty by wearing red garments. Although the Red Lanterns were segregated from the male Boxers—they worshipped at their own altars and practiced martial arts at separate boxing grounds—they were important to the movement in counteracting the influence of Christian women. Indeed, one of the Boxers' greatest fears was that cunning Christian women would use their guile to weaken the Boxers' spirits. The rebels believed that their invulnerability came from spirit possession and that the inherent polluting power of women threatened their "magic." However, they claimed that the "purity" of the Red Lanterns could counter this threat. The Red Lanterns were supposedly capable of incredible feats: they could walk on water or fly through the air. Belief in their magical powers provided critical assistance for the uprising.

As the movement gained momentum, the Qing vacillated between viewing the Boxers as a threat to order and embracing them as a force to check foreign intrusion. Early in 1900, Qing troops clashed with the Boxers in an escalating cycle of violence. By spring, however, the Qing could no longer control the tens of thousands of Boxers roaming the vicinities of Beijing and Tianjin. Embracing the Boxers' cause, the empress dowager declared war against the foreign powers in June 1900.

Acting without any discernible plan or leadership, the Boxers went after Christian and foreign symbols and persons. They harassed and sometimes killed Chinese Christians in parts of northern China, destroyed railroad tracks and telegraph lines, and attacked owners of foreign objects such as lamps and clocks. In Beijing, the Boxers besieged foreign embassy compounds, where diplomats and their families cowered in fear.

FOREIGN INVOLVEMENT AND AFTERMATH In August 1900, a foreign army of 20,000 troops crushed the Boxers. About half came from Japan; the rest came primarily from Russia, Britain, Germany, France, and the United States. Thereafter, the victors forced the Chinese to sign the punitive Boxer Protocol. Among other punishments, it required the regime to pay an exorbitant compensation in gold (about twice the empire's annual income) for damages to foreign life and property. The protocol also authorized western powers to station troops in Beijing. The effect: a crippling blow to the dynasty's standing.

Even in defeat, the Boxers' anti-western uprising showed how much had changed in China since the Taiping Rebellion. Although the Boxers were primarily peasants, even they had felt the unsettledness generated by European inroads into China. Indeed, the Europeans' commercial and spiritual reach, once confined to elites and port cities, had extended across much of China. Whereas the Taiping Rebellion had mobilized millions against the Qing, the Boxers remained loyal to the dynasty and focused their wrath on foreigners and Chinese Christians. The Boxer Uprising was, in many ways, like the Maji Maji Revolt in East Africa. Both were widespread protests against increased western influence. But whereas African protesters wanted to restore their precolonial societies, the Boxers sought to banish from their land all symbols and elements of a western way of life that angered their gods and ruined their world.

The Boxer Uprising in China. The Boxer Uprising was eventually suppressed by a foreign army made up of Japanese, European, and American troops that arrived in Beijing in August 1900. The picture here shows fighting between the foreign troops and the combined forces of Qing soldiers and the Boxers. After a period of vacillation, the Qing court, against the advice of some of its officials, finally threw its support behind the quixotic struggle of the Boxers against the foreign presence, laying the ground for the military intervention of the imperialist powers.

Worldwide Insecurities

Protests against European intrusion in Africa and China were distant movements that most Europeans could disregard. There were dissenters like the African American intellectual W. E. B. Du Bois, who denounced the violence in China while meeting at the first Pan-African Conference in 1900; the English economist John A. Hobson, who decried the war in South Africa; and the American novelist Mark Twain, who accused President Theodore Roosevelt of hypocrisy in the bloody occupation war in the Philippines. But for the most part, news of distant wars reinforced public belief in the supposed inferiority of other cultures. For example, when news of butchery in the suppression of the Maji Maji reached the British media, it was instantly trumpeted as a sign of German savagery; for their part, Germans gloated in the same way over news of South African concentration camps. At the same time, however, conflicts closer to home tore at European and North American confidence. These included rivalries among western powers, the booms and busts of expanding industrial economies, new types of class conflict, challenges about the proper roles of women, and problems of uncontrolled urbanization. (See again Map 18.1.)

Imperial Rivalries at Home

The rise of a European-centered world deepened rivalries within Europe and promoted instability there. Numerous factors fostered conflict, including France's smoldering resentment at its defeat in the Franco-Prussian War (see Chapter 17), but tension increased as the European states competed for raw materials and colonial footholds. Even as these powers built up their supply of weapons, as well as ships and railroads to transport troops, not everyone supported the buildup. Many Europeans, for example, disapproved of spending on massive steam-powered warships. Others warned that the arms race would end in a devastating war.

The formation of new empires destabilized the heart of Europe. The unifications of Germany and Italy at the expense of France and the Austrian Empire had smashed the old balance of power in Europe. Then, new alliances after 1890 compounded the tensions. German–French hostility persisted; German–Russian friendship crumbled. This left

Germany surrounded by foes: Britain and France to the west, Russia to the east. Meanwhile, ethnic nationalism fractured the multinational Ottoman and Habsburg Empires as Arabs, Turks, Czechs, and southern Slavs challenged their old masters. The Balkans in particular became a hotbed. Roiled by internal conflicts, the two venerable empires created power vacuums in central and southeastern Europe. Sensing conflict on the horizon, Britain, Germany, France, and Russia entered into a massive arms race.

FINANCIAL, INDUSTRIAL, AND TECHNOLOGICAL INSECURITIES Economic leaps helped make powers "great," but they could also unsettle societies. Indeed, pride about wealth and growth coincided with laments about changes in national and international economies. To begin with, Americans and Europeans recognized that the small-scale, laissez-faire capitalism championed by Adam Smith (see Chapter 14) was giving way to an economic order dominated by huge, heavily capitalized firms. Gone, it seemed, was Smith's vision of many small producers in vigorous competition with one another, all benefiting from efficient—but not exploitative—divisions of labor.

Instead of progressing smoothly, the economy of the west in the nineteenth century bounced between booms and busts: long-term business cycles of rapid growth followed by stagnation. Late in the century, the pace of economic change accelerated. Large-scale steel production, railroad building, and textile manufacturing expanded at breakneck speed, while waves of bank closures, bankruptcies, and agricultural crises ruined many small property owners, including farmers. By the century's end, a few large firms, such as John D. Rockefeller's Standard Oil and the large banking institutions, dominated in France, Britain, Germany, and the United States. The same was true in Japan, where *zaibatsu*—large companies with banking subsidiaries for finance and industrial wings dominating different sectors of the market—like Sumitomo, Mitsui, and Mitsubishi were the engine of Japan's extraordinary economic growth.

GLOBAL FINANCIAL AND INDUSTRIAL INTEGRATION These were years of heady international financial integration. More and more countries joined the world system of borrowing and lending; more and more countries were linked financially because their national currencies were all backed by gold. At the hub of this world system were the banks of London, which since the Napoleonic wars had been a major source of capital for international borrowers.

The rise of giant banks and huge industrial corporations caused alarm, for it seemed to signal an end to free markets and competitive capitalism. In the United States, an entire generation of journalists cut their teeth exposing the skullduggery (shady dealings) of financial and industrial giants. Ida Tarbell grew up in company towns in Pennsylvania and watched as bigger oil firms drove out little ones until they fell under one mantle: the Standard Oil Company of John D. Rockefeller. As one of the investigative "muckraker" journalists, Tarbell published a celebrated book about Standard Oil in 1904, a work that heavily influenced the drafting of new regulatory policies. In Europe, too, critics lamented a similar trend in which lack of competition created greater disparities of wealth between the owners of firms and the workforce.

Rather than longing for the return of truly free markets, many critics sought reforms that would protect people from economic instability. To cope with an unruly market, farmers created cooperatives. For their part, big industrialists fashioned monopolies, or cartels, in the name of improving efficiency, correcting failures in the market, and heightening profits. At the same time, government officials and academic specialists worried that modern economies were inherently unstable, prone to overproduce, and vulnerable to bankruptcy and crisis. The solution, many economists thought, was for the state to manage the national economies.

FINANCIAL CRISES Banking especially seemed in need of closer government supervision. Many industrial societies already had central banks (banks that issued national currencies, fixed underlying interest rates, and in general

Ida Tarbell. Ida Minerva Tarbell (1857–1944) grew up near oilfields in Pennsylvania, where her father was an oilman. Her family was rocked by the boom and bust of American finance when their savings were wiped out in the Panic of 1857, only to recover with the oil boom in 1859. Tarbell attended college and began her career as a teacher, eventually becoming an intrepid investigative reporter. She parlayed her research into the abuses of oil magnates into a series of articles in *McClure's* magazine, exposing the ruthless practices of Standard Oil. Such "muckraking" became a new model for investigative journalism directed against the high and the mighty.

controlled monetary policy), and London's Bank of England had long since overseen local and international money markets. But public institutions did not yet have the resources to protect all investments during times of economic crisis. Between 1890 and 1893, fully 550 American banks collapsed, and only the intervention of J. P. Morgan prevented the depletion of the nation's gold reserves. In 1907, a more serious crisis threatened, caused by a panic on Wall Street that led to a run on the banks. Once again, it fell to J. P. Morgan to rescue the American dollar from financial panic. Morgan himself lost $21 million and emerged from the bank panic convinced that some sort of public oversight was needed. In 1913, the U.S. Congress ratified the Federal Reserve Act, creating boards to monitor the supply and demand of the nation's money.

The crisis of 1907 showed how national financial matters could quickly become international affairs. The sell-off of the shares of banks and trusts in the United States also led American investors to withdraw their funds from other countries that relied on American capital. As a result, Canada, for instance, suffered a bank crisis of its own. Countries like Egypt and Mexico, far apart geographically yet linked through international capital, also suffered either withdrawal of investors' funds or a suspension of new investments and a string of bankruptcies. Although the head of Mexico's government, General Porfirio Díaz, tried to regain investors' confidence and their funds, Mexico fell into a severe recession as U.S. capital dried up. In turn, Mexicans lost faith in their own economic—and political—system. Unemployed and suffering new hardships, many Mexicans flocked to Díaz's political opponents, who eventually raised the flag of rebellion in 1910. A year later, the entire regime collapsed in revolution (discussed later in this chapter).

INDUSTRIALIZATION AND THE MODERN ECONOMY

Just as financial circuits linked nations as never before, so did industrialization. Backed by big banks, industrialists could afford to extend their enterprises physically and geographically, so heavy industries now came to new places. In Russia, for example, industrial activity quickened. With loans from European (especially French, Belgian, and British) investors, Russia built railways, telegraph lines, and factories and developed coal, iron, steel, and petroleum industries. By 1900, Russia was producing half of the world's oil and a considerable amount of steel. Yet industrial development remained uneven: southern Europe and the American South continued to lag behind northern regions. The gap was even more pronounced in colonial territories, which contained few industrial enterprises aside from railroad building and mining.

Labor Disputes. The late nineteenth century witnessed a surge in industrial strife, worker strikes, and violent suppression of labor movements. *Left*: One of the deadliest confrontations in the United States occurred in May 1892, when a strike against the Carnegie Steel Company escalated into a gunfight, which left ten dead and many more wounded. Here, a group of striking workers keeps watch over the steel mill in Homestead, Pennsylvania. *Right*: Striking dock workers rally in London's Trafalgar Square in 1911. By this time, residents of European cities were used to seeing crowds of protesters pressing for improved working conditions or political reform.

By 1914, the factory and the railroad had become global symbols of the modern economy—and of its positive and negative effects. Everywhere, the coming of the railroad to one's town or village was a big event: for some, it represented an exhilarating leap into the modern world; for others, a terrifying abandonment of the past. Ocean liners, automobiles, and airplanes, likewise, could be both dazzling and disorienting.

For ordinary people, the new economy brought benefits and drawbacks. Factories produced cheaper goods, but they belched clouds of black smoke. Railways offered faster transport, but they ruined small towns unlucky enough to be left off the branch line. Machines (when operating properly) were more efficient than human and animal labor, but workers who used them felt reduced to machines themselves. Indeed, the American Frederick Winslow Taylor proposed a system of "scientific management" to make human bodies perform more like machines, maximizing the efficiency of workers' movements. But workers did not want to be managed or to cede control of the pace of production to employers. "Taylorization" was the source of great resistance and strike waves. For strikers, as for conservatives, progress had taken an unsettling turn.

The "Woman Question"

Complicating the struggle over social inequalities was the increasingly urgent issue of how women fit into the world's rapidly changing economies and societies. Male advocates of empire, interestingly, had drawn attention early on to the hardships suffered by women in Asia and Africa; imposing reforms here was one way that imperial architects felt they could justify colonial regimes. At the same time, in the west, female advocates were demanding that women be given more rights as citizens, and more radical voices called for fundamental changes to the family and the larger society. Like the labor and socialist movements, feminists also formed cross-border alliances and, thanks to the media, followed each other's news. When the English suffragette Emily Davison dashed into the lanes at the aristocratic Epsom Derby horserace and got trampled to death by the king's horse, the news made headlines around the world. The clamor for women's rights was a truly global one. Komako Kimura, trained in Japanese dance and theater and raised to be a "proper wife," was also an avid reader of western literature and developed a reputation as a rebel for her daring performances. She soon became one of Japan's early suffragettes and cofounded the True New Woman's Association and labored to send her magazine to Europe and North America. She finally traveled to the United States in 1917 to study how American activists had succeeded in winning the vote there. She was among the celebrities who marched through New York that October demanding women's emancipation worldwide.

Komako Kimura. Komako Kimura (1887–1980) was a pioneering Japanese feminist. She traveled widely and drew inspiration from suffragist movements in Europe and North America to campaign in Japan. But she also became a global celebrity, making the case for women's suffrage in an international crusade. Conscious that mass politics was becoming a media phenomenon, she used her training in dance and theater to cultivate her public persona. She also got in trouble. The Japanese government censored her magazine, *The True Woman*, for advocating women's right to choose their husbands and practice birth control. In this photo, she poses during a massive suffragist march in New York in October 1917.

In fact, few of the world's polities made significant progress in giving women opportunities or compensation equivalent to their male counterparts in this era. The most that could be said was that more people were now aware that the question of how society treated 50 percent of the population was a question worth asking.

Radical women met stiff repression wherever they challenged the established order. In 1903, China's Qiu Jin (1875–1907) left her husband and headed to Japan to study. There she befriended other radicals and made a name for herself by dressing in men's clothing, carrying a sword, and trying her hand at bomb making. Returning to China in 1906, she founded the *Chinese Women's Journal* (*Zhongguo nübao*) and wrote articles urging women to fight for their rights and to leave home if necessary. Qing authorities executed Qiu Jin after she participated in a failed attempt to topple the dynasty.

WOMEN'S STATUS IN THE COLONIES In the colonial world, the woman question was a contentious issue—but it was mainly argued among men. European authorities liked to boast that colonial rule improved women's status. Citing examples of traditional societies' subordination of women, they criticized as barbaric the veiling of women in Islamic societies, the binding of women's feet in China, widow burning (*sati*) in India, and female genital mutilation in Africa. Europeans believed that prohibiting such acts was a justification for colonial intervention.

And yet, for women in Africa, the Middle East, and India, colonialism added to their burdens. As male workers headed into the export economy, formerly shared agricultural work fell exclusively on women's shoulders. In Africa, for example, the opening of vast gold and diamond mines drew thousands of men away to work in the mines, leaving women to fend for themselves. Similarly, the rise of European-owned agricultural estates in Kenya and Southern Rhodesia depleted surrounding villages of male family members, who went to work on the estates. In these circumstances, women kept the local, food-producing economy afloat.

Nor did colonial "civilizing" rhetoric improve women's political or cultural circumstances. In fact, European missionaries preached a message of domesticity to Asian and African families, emphasizing that a woman's place was in the home raising children and that women's education should be different from men's. Thus, males overwhelmingly dominated the new schools that Europeans built. Moreover, customary law in colonial Africa, as interpreted by chiefs who collaborated with colonial officials, favored men. As a result, African women often lost landholding and other rights that they had enjoyed before the Europeans' arrival.

WOMEN'S ISSUES IN THE WEST In western countries, for most of the nineteenth century, a belief in "separate spheres" had supposedly confined women to domestic matters, while leaving men in charge of public life and economic undertakings. (In practice, only women from middle- and upper-class families avoided working outside the home for wages.) Men did not mind having women work for their charities or churches or educate their daughters at home. But most men as well as most women continued to think that higher education and public activism were not suitable for "ladies"—and that, if possible, these "ladies" should not have to labor outside the home or acquire a profession. Urbanization and advancing capitalism did begin to change this picture, especially in western Europe and America. Some women who craved new opportunities increasingly found work as teachers, secretaries, typists, department store clerks, social workers, and telephone operators. These jobs offered greater economic and social independence, at least for a few. But women in eastern and southern Europe and in Latin America were largely left out of these developments and remained subordinate members of their communities.

Advances toward political equality for women came even more slowly. By midcentury, several women's suffrage movements had appeared, but these campaigns bore little immediate fruit. In 1868, women received the right to vote in local elections in Britain. Within a few years, Finland, Sweden, and some American states allowed single, property-owning women the right to cast ballots—again, only in local elections. Women obtained the right to vote in national elections in New Zealand in 1893, in Australia in 1902, in Finland in 1906, and in Norway in 1913. Despite these modest gains, male alarmists portrayed women's suffrage and women's rights as the beginning of civilization's end.

Quietly, and without conferring with one another, many women began to take charge of their lives in another way, and that was to assert control over reproduction. Although in numerous countries the use of contraceptive devices was illegal, women still found ways to limit the number of children they bore. The French birthrate fell so precipitously in the second half of the nineteenth century that commentators began to worry about France's "degeneration." Declining birthrates, along with improved medicine, also meant that fewer women died in childbirth and more would see their children reach adulthood. Even in the first years of the twentieth century, these demographic changes, together with urbanization, resulted in much greater changes in women's lives than did political movements.

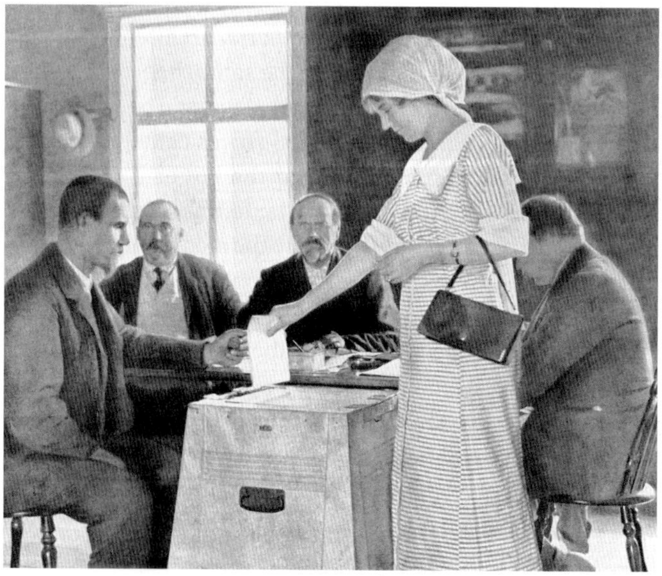

Women's Suffrage in Finland. The British and then the French introduced the concept of citizenship with universal rhetoric, but in practice the category of citizen was generally restricted to property-holding males. Finland granted its women the right to vote in 1906, earlier than most countries. In this photograph, a Finnish woman casts her ballot in the election of 1906.

Social Conflict in a New Key

Capitalism's volatility shook confidence in free market economies and sharpened conflicts between classes; the tone of political debates was transformed as new, more strident voices called for radical change. Although living conditions for European and North American workers improved over time, widening inequalities in income and the slow pace of reform led to frustration. Most workers remained committed to peaceful agitation, but some radicals turned to violence. Often, especially in eastern Europe and Russia, the closed character of political systems fueled frustration—and radicalism. This was also the case in Latin America, where even the middle classes were largely shut out of politics until new parties offered fresh opportunities for political expression. In Argentina, for example, urban workers found outlets for protest within movements known as **syndicalism** (the organization of workplace associations that included unskilled laborers), socialism, and **anarchism** (the belief that society should be a free association of members, not subject to government, laws, or police).

STRIKES AND REVOLTS In the Americas and in Europe, radicals adopted numerous tactics for asserting the interests of the working class. In Europe, the franchise was gradually expanded in hopes that the lower classes would prefer voting to revolution—and indeed, most of the new political parties that catered to workers had no desire to overthrow the state. But conservatives feared them anyway, especially as they gained electoral clout. The Labour Party, founded in Britain in 1900, quickly boasted a large share of the vote. By 1912, the German Social Democratic Party was the largest party in the Reichstag. But it was not the legally sanctioned parties that sparked violent street protests and strikes. A whole array of syndicalists, anarchists, radical royalists, and revolutionary socialists sprang up in this period, making work stoppages everyday affairs.

Although the United States did not have similarly radical factions or successful labor parties, American workers were also organizing. The labor movement's power burst forth dramatically in 1894 when the American Railway Union launched a strike that spread across the nation. Spawned by wage cuts and firings following an economic downturn, the Pullman Strike (directed against the maker of railway sleeping cars, George Pullman) involved approximately 3 million workers. The strike's conclusion, however, revealed the enduring power of the status quo. After hiring replacement workers to break the strike, Pullman requested federal troops to protect his operation. When the troops arrived, infuriated strikers reacted with violence—which led to a further crackdown by the government against the union. After its leaders were jailed, the strike collapsed. Although strikes and protests in the United States often failed to achieve their immediate goals, they worried those in power and ultimately led to important changes.

The Mexican Revolution. *Left*: By 1915, Mexican peasants, workers, and farmers had destroyed much of the old elitist system. This was the first popular, peasant revolution of the twentieth century. Among the most famous leaders were Pancho Villa and Emiliano Zapata. They are pictured here in the presidential office in the capital. Villa took the president's chair jokingly. Zapata, carrying the broad hat typical of his people, refused to wear military gear and glowered at the camera suspiciously. *Right*: By the 1920s, Mexican artists and writers were putting recent events into images and words. Pictured here is a detail from a mural by Diego Rivera. Notice the nationalist interpretation: Porfirio Díaz's troops defend foreign oil companies and White aristocrats against middle-class and peasant (and darker-skinned) reformers who call for a "social revolution." Observe also the absence of women in this epic mural.

REVOLUTION IN MEXICO Perhaps the most successful revolution of the prewar era occurred in Mexico. A peasant uprising, it thoroughly transformed the country. Fueled by the unequal distribution of land and by disgruntled workers, the **Mexican Revolution** erupted in 1910 when political elites split over the succession of General Porfirio Díaz after decades of his strong-arm rule. Dissidents balked when Díaz refused to step down, and peasants and workers rallied to the call to arms.

What destroyed the Díaz regime and its powerful army was the swelling flood of peasants, farmers, cattlemen, and rural workers who were desperate for a change in the social order. From the north (led by the charismatic Pancho Villa) to the south (under the legendary Emiliano Zapata), rural folk helped topple the Díaz regime. In the name of providing land for farmers and ending oligarchic rule, peasant armies defeated Díaz's troops and then proceeded to destroy many large estates. The fighting lasted for ten brutal years, during which almost 10 percent of the country's population perished.

Thereafter, political leaders had to accept popular demands for democracy, respect for the sovereignty of peasant communities, and land reform. As a result, the Constitution of 1917 incorporated widespread reform, and by 1920 an emerging generation of politicians recognized the power of a militarized peasantry and initiated deep-seated changes in Mexico's social structure. These leaders also realized that their new regime had to appeal ideologically to common folk. Revolutionaries gave trade unions sweeping rights to organize, paving the way for nationalizing the country's mines and oil industries. But perhaps the radicals' most lasting legacy was the creation of rural communes for Mexico's peasantry. These communal village holdings, called *ejidos*, sought to revive a precolonial way of life. The revolution thus spawned a set of new national myths, based on the heroism of rural peoples, Mexican nationalism, and a celebration of the Aztec past.

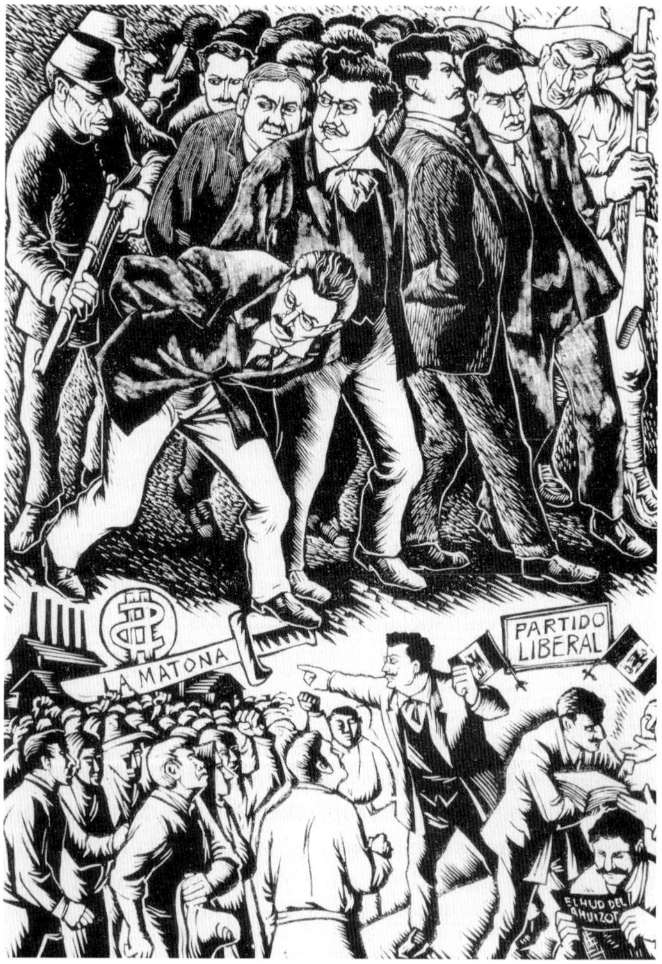

Díaz and the Liberal Party. In this 1910 print, the Mexican satirist José Guadalupe Posada portrays the leaders of the popular Liberal Party as being literally under the feet of the elitist followers of General Porfirio Díaz.

PRESERVING ESTABLISHED ORDERS Although the Mexican Revolution succeeded in toppling the old elite, elsewhere in Latin America the ruling establishment remained united against assaults from below. Already in 1897, the Brazilian army had mercilessly suppressed a peasant movement in the northeastern part of the country. Moreover, in Cuba, the Spanish and then the American armies crushed tenant farmers' efforts to reclaim land from sugar estates. In Guatemala, Indigenous Maya lost land to coffee barons.

Much the same occurred in Europe and the United States, where the preservation of established orders did not rest on repression alone. Here, too, elites grudgingly agreed to gradual change. Indeed, by the end of the nineteenth century, left-wing agitators, muckraking reporters, and middle-class reformers began to win meaningful social improvements. Unable to suppress the socialist movement, Otto von Bismarck, the German chancellor, defused the appeal of socialism by enacting social welfare measures in 1883–1884 (as did France in 1904 and England in 1906). He enacted legislation insuring workers against illness, accidents, and old age, and establishing maximum working hours. In the United States, it took lurid journalistic accounts of unsanitary practices in Chicago slaughterhouses, a series of bank failures (discussed earlier), and anxieties about the ill effects of the "**closing of the frontier**" in the American West to spur the federal government into action. In 1906, President Theodore Roosevelt signed the Federal Meat Inspection Act, which provided for government supervision of meatpacking operations. In other cases (banking, steel production, railroads), the federal government's enhanced supervisory authority served corporate interests as well.

These consumer and family protection measures reflected a broader reform movement, one dedicated to creating a more efficient society and correcting the undesirable consequences of urbanization and industrialization. At local and state levels, **progressive reformers** attacked corrupt city governments that had allegedly fallen into the hands of immigrant-dominated "political machines." The progressives also attacked other vices, such as gambling, drinking, and prostitution—all associated with industrialized, urban settings. The creation of city parks preoccupied urban planners, who hoped parks' green spaces would serve as the city's "lungs" and offer healthier forms of entertainment than houses of prostitution, gambling dens, and bars. From Scandinavia to California, the proponents of old-age pensions and public ownership of utilities put pressure on lawmakers. Thousands of associations took shape against capitalism's excesses, and they occasionally succeeded in changing state policies.

The period leading up to World War I was one of rapid social changes and of new social conflicts. Women and workers pressed for new rights, strikes disrupted industrial output, and revolutions broke out in Mexico and Russia. As financial crises reverberated across the globe, European elites were forced to make reforms, though they tended to be limited, especially in the colonial world.

Pablo Picasso. The Franco-Spanish artist Pablo Picasso was one of the first to incorporate "primitive" artistic forms into his work, as displayed in his breakthrough canvas *Les Demoiselles d'Avignon* (*The Courtesans of Avignon*; 1907), which was inspired by the artist's study of African sculpture and masks.

Cultural Modernism

As revolutionaries and reformers wrestled with increasing social and economic tensions, the intellectuals, artists, and scientists began to recognize that a new cultural world, along with a new century, was dawning. What we call **modernism**—the sense of having broken with tradition—came to prominence in many fields, from physics to architecture, from painting to the social sciences. The experimental thinking of this era was shaped by turn-of-the-century anxieties and opportunities; its leaders sought not to please the public or make slight changes to older scientific theories but to question all the old rules and test the limits of the arts and sciences. Often older Enlightenment ideals of rationality and clarity were challenged in favor of the exploration of more primitive and darker sources of meaning and inspiration; in the sciences, probabilities replaced certainties.

Emblematic of the new ideas was the work of Pablo Picasso (1881–1973), a Spanish painter who spent much of his life in Paris: inspired by African masks in Paris's Ethnographic Museum, Picasso broke with the Renaissance style of representation in producing *Les Demoiselles d'Avignon* (1907). Shocking in its form, this painting also depicted a series of nude prostitutes, who confront the viewer and seem to say, "Go ahead and look at me and here see what really lies beneath your civilized exterior." No wonder modernism remained, throughout its existence, controversial: it meant to break the rules and sometimes to terrorize the rule makers.

Modernist movements were notably international. Egyptian social scientists read the works of European thinkers, while French and German painters flocked to museums to inspect artifacts from Africa and Oceania. The Mexican writer and, later, minister of education José Vasconcelos became an avid reader of the Indian intellectual Swami Vivekananda, popularizer of yoga and champion of Hinduism as one of the world's great religions. His spiritual nationalism helped shape Vasconcelos's and other Latin Americans' anticolonial reforms. Thanks to the efforts of the publisher Eugen Diederichs, Germans at the turn of the century could read translations of modernist works originally written in Swedish, English, Russian, and Chinese. As travel times decreased, students, scholars, artists, social reformers, and writers crossed oceans and inspired one another with new ideas.

Popular Culture Comes of Age

From the late eighteenth to the late nineteenth century, production and consumption of the arts, books, music, and sports changed dramatically. The change derived mainly

Impressionism. Emerging in Paris in the last third of the nineteenth century, Impressionism was an artistic movement that was radical in its day. Impressionists stressed the changing qualities of light, the passage of time, and movement as they sought to capture perceptions of a modern world in rapid flux, as seen here in Claude Monet's *The Gare Saint-Lazare* (*left*) and Camille Pissarro's *Sunset over the Boieldieu Bridge at Rouen* (*right*).

from new urban settings, technological innovations, and increased leisure time. As education (especially in America and Europe) became nearly universal, there were many more readers and museumgoers. At the same time, cultural works now found their way down to nonelite members of society. Middle-class art lovers who could not afford original paintings eagerly purchased lithographs and mass-produced engravings; millions who could not attend operas and formal dress balls attended dance halls and vaudeville shows (entertainment by singers, dancers, and comedians). People flocked to hear lectures given by travelers, often accompanied by slide shows. For the first time, sports attracted mass followings. Soccer in Europe, baseball in the United States, and cricket in India had wildly devoted middle- and working-class fans. Thus did a truly **popular culture** emerge, delivering affordable and accessible forms of art and entertainment to the masses.

By the century's close, the press constituted a major form of popular entertainment and information. This was partly because publishers were offering different wares to different classes of readers and partly because many more people could read, especially in Europe and the Americas. The "yellow press" was full of stories of murder and sensationalism that appealed to the urban masses. By now, the English *Daily Mail* and the French *Petit Parisien* boasted circulations of over 1 million. In the United States, urban dwellers, many of whom were immigrants, avidly read newspapers—some in English, others in their native languages. Here, too, banner headlines, sensational stories, and simple language drew in readers with little education or poor English skills. Books, too, proliferated and fell in price; penny novels about cowboys, murder, and romance became the rage.

By now the kind of culture one consumed had become a reflection of one's real (or desired) status in society, a central part of one's identity. For many Latin American workers, for example, reading one's own newspaper or comic strip was part of the business of being a worker. Argentina's socialist newspaper, *La Vanguardia*, was one of Buenos Aires's most prominent periodicals, read and debated at work and in the cafés of working-class neighborhoods. Anyone seen reading the bourgeois paper, *La Prensa*, faced heckling and ridicule by proletarian peers.

As the community of cultural consumers broadened and as ideas from across the globe flooded in, writers, artists, and scholars struggled to adapt. Their attempts to confront the brave new world in the making resulted in the remarkable innovations that characterize modernism—the breaking with tradition.

Modernism in European Culture

In intellectual and artistic terms, Europe at the turn of the twentieth century experienced perhaps its richest age since the Renaissance. Artists' work reflected their ambivalence about the modern, as represented by the railroad, the big city, and the factory. While the artists and writers of the mid-nineteenth century had largely celebrated progress, the painters and novelists of the century's end took a darker view. They turned away from enlightened clarity and descriptive prose, searching for more instinctual truths. Now the primitive came to symbolize both Europe's lost innocence and the forces that reason could not control,

Paul Gauguin's *Where Do We Come From? What Are We? Where Are We Going?* In this large-scale painting, Gauguin used Tahitian rather than European biblical figures to pose some of humanity's deepest questions about the meaning of life, the relationship between humans and gods, and our destinies after death.

such as sexual drives, religious fervor, or brute strength. The painter who led the way in incorporating these themes into modern art was Paul Gauguin (1848–1903), who left Europe for Tahiti in 1891 and there found new forms of contentment and new ways of representing the world that he believed were less artificial than those practiced in Europe. In paintings such as *Where Do We Come From? What Are We? Where Are We Going?* (1897), Gauguin posed humankind's great questions and intimated that the Polynesians—despite European contempt for their religious rituals and lack of "progress"—might have more answers than did his "civilized" compatriots back home.

However, the arts alone did not undermine older views of the world. Even science, in which the Enlightenment had placed so much faith, worked a disenchanting magic on the midcentury bourgeois worldview. After the century's turn, pioneering physicists and mathematicians like Albert Einstein took apart the Enlightenment's conviction that humans could achieve full knowledge of, and control over, nature. In his later work, Einstein drew on the previously ridiculed work of the Indian physicist Satyendra Nath Bose (1894–1974), who understood light to be a gas composed of particles. These particles were too tiny to be distinguished by any microscope, but their existence could be hypothesized through the application of statistics. The work of Einstein, Bose, and other scholars of their generation laid the foundations for today's quantum physics. In this modernist form of science, probabilities took the place of certainties.

In philosophy and the social sciences, some European modernists began to question rationality itself. From the time of the Enlightenment, Europeans had prided themselves on their "reason." To be rational was to be civilized and to master irrational urges; respectable middle-class nineteenth-century men were thought to embody these virtues. But in the late nineteenth century, faith in rationality began to falter. Perhaps reason was *not* humankind's highest attainment, said some; perhaps reason was too hard for mortal beings to sustain, said others. Friedrich Nietzsche (1844–1900) claimed that conventional European attempts to assert The Truth—including science and Judeo-Christian moral codes—were nothing more than life-destroying quests for power; individuals would do better to dispense with the old forms and invent new forms of truth to live by. In 1895, the French social psychologist Gustave Le Bon (1841–1931) wrote a treatise in which he equated the unconscious volatility of crowds (including crowds of striking workers) with the irrationality of women and "primitives." Le Bon's work became wildly popular, appealing to Benito Mussolini in Italy and Vladimir Lenin in Russia and inspiring the work of Sigmund Freud (1856–1939) on "the collective unconscious." By this time, Freud had already begun to excavate layers of the human subconscious, where irrational desires and fears lay buried. For Freud, human nature was not as simple as it had seemed to Enlightenment thinkers. Instead, he asserted, humans were driven by sexual longings and childhood traumas, some revealed only as neuroses, in dreams, or during extensive psychoanalysis.

Neither Nietzsche nor Freud was well loved among liberal elites. But in the new century, Nietzsche would become the prophet for many antiliberal, antirational causes, from nudism to Nazism, and Freud's dark vision would become central to the twentieth century's understanding of the self.

Sigmund Freud, at Work in His Study in Vienna. Freud surrounded himself not only with books but also with Egyptian figurines and African masks, expressions of universal artistic prowess—and irrational psychological drives.

Cultural Modernism in China

What it meant to be modern sparked debate beyond western Europe. Europeans provided one set of answers; thinkers elsewhere offered quite different answers. Chinese artists and scientists at the turn of the century selectively engaged western ideas and transformed them. Indeed, some scholars have described the late Qing period as a time of competing cultural modernities, in contrast to the post-Qing era, which pursued a single, western-oriented modernity. These forms of modernity involved critical reflection on Chinese traditions and mixed reactions to western culture.

As in the west, Chinese writers now had a wider readership. By the later nineteenth century, more than 170 presses in China were serving a potential readership of 2 to 4 million, concentrated mostly in the urban areas. These cities were more economically and culturally vibrant than the hinterlands. Not only was there an expanding body of readers, but newly rich beneficiaries of the treaty-port economy now patronized the arts.

Painters from the Lower Yangzi region congregated in Shanghai. Collectively known as the **Shanghai School**, these classically trained painters appropriated western technical novelties into their artistic practice. Consider the self-portrait of the artist Ren Xiong (1820–1857): bareheaded and legs apart, he stands upright and stares straight at the viewer. Ren Xiong's work reflected the influence of photography, a new visual medium. Similarly, experimental writers drew on

Ren Xiong, *Self-Portrait*. This famous self-portrait of Ren Xiong was most likely produced in the 1850s. Ren Xiong was probably familiar with the new practice of portrait photography in the treaty ports. Although his self-portrait reproduced some old conventions of Chinese scholarly art, such as the unity of the visual image with a lengthy self-composed inscription, it is also clear that through its rather unconventional pose and image, it reflects the trend of cultural modernism in China during this period.

modern science, sometimes to explore the question of China's future relations with the west. The novel *New Era* (1908) by Bigehuan Zhuren, for example, put its opening scenes in the year 1999, by which time, as the story envisioned, China would be a supreme world power and a constitutional monarchy. Depicting China at war with western powers, *New Era* celebrated military strength but also introduced inventions such as electricity-repellent clothing and bulletproof satin. More visionary still was *The Stone of Goddess Nüwa* (1905), whose male author, Haitian Duxiaozi, imagined a technologically advanced feminist utopia. Its female residents studied subjects ranging from the arts to physics, drove electric cars, and ate purified liquid food extracts. Their mission was to save China by eliminating corrupt male officials. Such works, combining the fanciful with the critical, offered a new and provocative vision of China.

Yet the integration of western modes of knowledge into Chinese culture was an intellectual challenge. Did being modern mean giving up China's scholarly traditions and values? Many Chinese scholars, for example, recognized and promoted the usefulness of western science and technology, although most of them considered these a way to acquire national wealth and power rather than a way to understand the world. Indeed, many of the elite in this period still insisted that Chinese learning remain the principal source of all knowledge. What kind of balance should exist between western thought and Chinese learning, or even whether the ancient classics should keep their fundamental role, was an issue that would haunt generations to come. In this respect, the Chinese dilemma reflected a worldwide challenge to accepting the impulses of modernism.

Modernism arose at a time when intellectuals began to question the values that had sustained Europe and North America throughout most of the nineteenth century. It reflected discontent with industrialization, income inequality, and colonial repression. Even though modernism had its origins and most profound impact in Europe, in many ways, especially in art, it drew upon nonwestern traditions and spread its influence throughout Asia and Africa among the educated classes.

Rethinking Race and Reimagining Nations

Ironically, at this time of huge population transfers and shared technological modernization, individuals and nations became passionate defenders of the idea that identities were deeply rooted and unchangeable and were based on physical as well as cultural characteristics. Although physical characteristics had always played *some* role in identifying persons, by the late nineteenth century the Linnaean classifications (see Chapter 14) had become the means for ranking the worth of whole nations and for defining who could belong to the nation and enjoy its rights and privileges.

By the century's close, racial roots had become a crucial part of national identity. This was the era of ethnographic museums, folkloric collectors, national essence movements, eugenics, and racial genealogies. People wanted to know who they (and their neighbors) were—especially in terms of *biological* ancestry. Now the idea of inheritance took on new weight, in both cultural and biological forms. Doctors, officials, and novelists described the genetic inheritance of mental illness, alcoholism, criminality, and same-sex attraction; nationalists spoke of the uniqueness of the Slavic soul, the German mind, and the Hispanic race. They spoke of Hindu spirituality and of Islamic principles as if there were no variations or conflicts within these categories. The preoccupation with race reflected a worldwide longing for fixed roots in an age that seemed to be burning all its bridges to the past.

Nationalist and racial ideas were different in different parts of the world, and they produced a variety of nationalist or sometimes panethnic movements. In Europe and America, debates about race and national purity reflected several concerns: fear of losing individuality in a technological world, rising tensions among states, and fear of being overrun by Brown, Black, and East Asian peoples beyond the borders of "civilization." By contrast, in India these ideas were part of the anticolonial debate. This was also the case in China, Latin America, and the Islamic world, where discussions of identity went hand in hand with opposition to western domination and corrupt indigenous elites.

Racial nationalisms were not necessarily to the taste of political leaders. Panethnic movements such as pan-Germanism, for example, looked beyond the nation-state, envisioning a Germanic community whose formation would require the breakup of the Habsburg Empire and economic ruin in multiethnic cities such as Vienna and Prague. Pan-Islamic movements, too, threatened to cause havoc in the Ottoman and British Empires. Behind these movements was the notion that political communities should be built on racial purity or unsullied indigenous traditions, but it was unclear *which* traditions could actually claim any sort of purity. Racial language might unify some communities—such as White Americans—but it also threatened the existence of the multiethnic empires and flourishing metropolises.

Nation and Race in North America and Europe

In Europe and the United States, the changing mood was striking. Americans and Europeans greeted the end of the century with a combination of chest-beating pride and shoulder-slumping pessimism, and this mood influenced attitudes about national identity, race, and religion. In the

Current Trends in World History

Adapting to the Environment: Russian Peasants Take on the Steppe

The Eurasian steppe extends for some 5,000 miles north of the Caucasus Mountains, from northern China and Mongolia to Hungary, and below the forest belt of the original Muscovy. When historians mention these grasslands at all, it is generally to treat them as a military highway for armies of nomads that formed their own short-lived empires and harassed others. In this telling, when steppe warriors stood in the way of imperial Russian state expansion, they were wiped out or bribed to enter into bargains with the state. In the case of the powerful freebooters of the Don River basin, known as Cossacks, the Russian Empire offered grants of land and respect for Cossack self-government in exchange for the Cossacks' help in defending the empire's southern frontier. But there is another, lesser known environmental history of the steppe—one that tells of wheat fields and locusts, of snowstorms and boundless skies, and of the ways in which peasant migrants from northern, watered forests learned to adapt their farming methods to the land.

Russians first became aware of the environmental peculiarities of this region soon after Catherine the Great annexed a large swath of the southern steppe, dubbing it "New Russia." The tsarina had hoped to use this rich earth to feed Russians living on poorer northern lands. But already by the late eighteenth century, it was clear that increased farming was not yielding great increases in food production. Why not? Catherine sent officials to investigate, and at first they blamed the land, pointing to natural vegetation, recurring droughts, and other special qualities of the steppe environment. Over time, however, they realized that the problem lay in the farmers' practices, not in the land itself. The peasants were practicing farming as they had up north, grateful for the land but ignorant of it. Gradually, painfully, peasants as well as officials learned that because the steppe was different—hot and dry—it required different methods. The old implements did not work either: a new type of plow was needed to break the heavier-rooted plant life, especially steppe fescue (feather grass).

A breakthrough occurred when a Mennonite farmer observed topsoil blowing off his field. He planted a line of trees to break the wind and, in winter, to help retain snow for moisture. Similarly, an agronomist noticed that ravines near the river were widening and advised peasants to leave a band of steppe grasses in place as they plowed, since the grasses would help hold down the soil. At first, many peasants resisted sowing less of the land. Eventually, however, they discovered that the advice enabled them to increase crop production because of reduced erosion. In other words, environmental awareness spread—and made a difference.

The geologist Vasily Dokuchaev (1846–1903) turned the environmental awareness of the settlers and peasants into the first form of soil science. Dokuchaev's breakthrough idea was this: the problem with steppe farming was not the steppe but the farmer. He made extensive studies across Russian regions, developed a theory of soil formation in relation to climate and human usage, and created the first soil classification system. He recommended

early 1890s, for example, Americans flocked to extravagant commemorations of the 400th anniversary of Christopher Columbus's discovery. The largest was the Columbian Exposition in Chicago. Such events displayed the most modern machinery and celebrated the nation's marvelous destiny. Yet, at the same time, Americans—like many Europeans—feared for their future, viewing the 1890s not only as the last decade of the nineteenth century but more broadly as the end of an era.

RESTRICTING IMMIGRATION For many White Americans, concerns about the end of an era triggered cultural alarms and political reforms. In his 1893 essay "The Significance of the Frontier in American History," which became one of the most enduring and influential interpretations of the American past, the historian Frederick Jackson Turner called attention to the U.S. Census Bureau's 1890 announcement that the "American frontier" had "closed." According to Turner, that closing threatened the future access to new lands (new to him, though not to those lands' Indigenous populations) that had long shaped the individualistic nature of the American people and the democratic character of their political institutions.

Such fears fueled the rise of nativist political movements that sought to curb immigration into the United States, which often involved discriminations based on race, ethnicity, or religion. Animosity toward Chinese workers was particularly fervent in the American West and led to the 1882 Exclusion Act, which prohibited almost all immigration from China. After the Spanish-American War brought the United States new colonies in the Pacific and the Caribbean, darker peoples from the Philippines, Puerto Rico, and Cuba became a

***Harvest in the Ukraine* (1880)** This 1880 painting by Vladimir Orlovsky shows Ukrainian peasants bringing in the rich harvest of the steppe.

crop rotations, longer fallow periods, and lighter plowing (to preserve topsoil). He wanted peasants to become stewards, not just exploiters, of the land.

By the latter part of the nineteenth century, agriculture in the steppe had taken off. Cossacks, too, had become successful farmers. New Russia, which was also called Ukraine, became a breadbasket (which it still is to a large extent). Imperial Russia became the world's leading agricultural exporter, feeding both Germany and Britain in the run-up to World War I.

Russia's environment was transformed. And yet, the agriculture of the steppe was not what we would call "sustainable." The minimal woods in the area were depleted (peasants continued to act as if they still lived in northern forests with endless supplies of timber), and the black-earth topsoil was significantly diminished. Later, this would spur the introduction of chemical fertilizers—which would increase crop yields but once again change the steppe ecosystem, adding pollutants to rivers. Like human history, the natural history of the steppe never stands still.

QUESTIONS FOR ANALYSIS

- How did the steppe lands' usefulness to the Russian Empire change during the period described?
- How did peasants, officials, and scientists learn to think differently about steppe lands?

EXPLORE FURTHER

Moon, David, *The Plough That Broke the Steppes: Agriculture and Environment on Russia's Grasslands, 1700–1914* (2013).

focus for those who feared the loss of "White America." Even more threatening at the turn of the century because they numbered in the millions were "swarthy" immigrants from southern and eastern Europe. To many White Americans of northwestern European heritage, these newcomers from the other end of Europe were barely more "White" than immigrants from Asia and Latin America. Reducing the flow from southern and eastern Europe, if not halting it entirely, galvanized anti-immigration movements in the first decades of the twentieth century (and culminated in the passage of severe restrictions during the 1920s).

FACING NEW SOCIAL ISSUES Like Americans, Europeans also expressed concerns about trends at home. For example, intellectuals suggested that mechanization deprived men of their vitality. Darwinist theory provoked new anxieties about **degeneration**, the fear that inherited diseases and racial mixing were causing "civilized" people to become soft, weak, and sickly. Sexual relations between European colonizers and indigenous women—and their mixed offspring—had almost always been a part of European expansionism, but as racial identities hardened, many saw racial mixing as harmful to the supposedly "superior" White races and to the moral fiber of the whole nation. Talk of virility arose, partly provoked by doctors' and scientists' involvement in treating social problems. Before long, English and American schoolboys were encouraged to play sports, to avoid becoming too weak to defend the nation. In addition, medical attention focused on homosexuality, regarding it as a disease and a threat to Anglo-Saxon civilization. In France, the falling birthrate seemed to signal a period of decadence characterized by weak, sickly men and irrational women.

Some people tied degeneration to debates about whether Jews—defined by religious practice or, increasingly, by ethnicity—could be fully assimilated into European society. Even though Jews had gained rights as citizens in most European nations by the late nineteenth century, powerful prejudices persisted. In the 1880s and 1890s, violent pogroms, often involving police complicity, targeted the large Jewish populations in the Russian Empire's western territories and pushed the persecuted farther westward. These emigrants' presence, in turn, stirred up fear and resentment, especially in Austria, Germany, and France. Reactionaries began to talk about the "pollution" of the European races by mixing with Semites and to circulate rumors about Jewish bankers' conspiratorial powers. Perhaps because nothing else seemed stable and enduring, wealthy White male Europeans (like their American counterparts) promoted programs of racial purity to shore up the civilizations they saw coming apart at the seams.

PROTECTING THE ENVIRONMENT In addition to immigration restriction, the dawning recognition about limitations on new lands and other vital natural resources prompted a rethinking of attitudes and policies about the environment on both sides of the North Atlantic. In the United States, the near extinction of the buffalo by hunters, the dramatic reduction of timber stands by logging companies, the rapid depletion of grasslands from overgrazing, and the pressing need to find water to sustain agriculture on the often-parched lands of the American West attested to the passing of the frontier. When Theodore Roosevelt became president of the United States in 1901, he translated concerns about protecting natural resources into government policy. The market, insisted Roosevelt and like-minded conservationists, could not be trusted to sustain natural resources. Instead, federal action and regulation were necessary. This led in 1902 to the passage of the National Reclamation Act, which provided funding for large-scale dams and irrigation projects. Three years later, the Roosevelt administration orchestrated the establishment of the National Forest Service to manage the development of millions of acres of permanent public lands.

Similar worries and remedies were at work in Europe. In France, nostalgia about vanishing pastoral landscapes and anxieties about widespread deforestation provoked efforts to restore at least portions of the countryside. As in the United States, conservation efforts were spearheaded not by rural inhabitants but by urban bourgeoisie, with newly protected landscapes often becoming tourist destinations for city dwellers. In Russia, however, it was peasant farmers and local officials, seeking to make the steppe lands more productive, who laid the foundation for a new kind of soil science. (See Current Trends in World History: Adapting to the Environment: Russian Peasants Take on the Steppe.)

Brazilian Modernization. These photographs convey two aspects of Brazilians' drive to civilize. To the left is an image of the military leader Cândido Mariano da Silva Rondon, himself of mixed-blood descent, who was raised as an orphan in military schools—which were important institutions for racial blending and modernization. He made a career surveying the Amazon for telegraph lines and became a great defender of Indigenous peoples. Here he is in 1910, posing as the civilizer-protector and receiving gifts from Indigenous people in the Guaporé River valley near the Bolivian border. Contrast this scene of peaceful uplift with the image at right, of Café do Rio, one of the elite hot spots in the capital of Rio de Janeiro in 1912. Cafés were the symbol of Europeanization, fostering the spread of new customs of gentlemanly socializing among writers, politicians, and military leaders. The fashion of the day was to wear Panama hats, to sport bicolored shoes, and to drink local spirits. Note the absence of women. And there appears to be only one Afro-Brazilian customer (seated, with hat on, at the central table). For all its modernizing rhetoric, this elite culture was still highly exclusive.

Race-Mixing and the Problem of Nationhood in Latin America

In Latin America, debates about identity chiefly addressed ethnic intermixing and the legacy of a system of government that, unlike much of the North Atlantic world, excluded rather than included the populace. After all, social hierarchies reaching back to the sixteenth century ranked White Iberians (Whites born in Spain and Portugal) at the top, Creole elites in the middle, and Indigenous and African populations at the bottom. Thus, the higher on the social ladder, the more likely the people were to be White.

CONTESTED MIXTURES It is important to note that "mixing" did not lead to a shared heritage. Nor did it necessarily lead to homogeneity. In fact, the "racial" order did not stick, since some Iberians occupied the lower ranks, while a few people of color did manage to ascend the social ladder. Moreover, starting in the 1880s, the racial hierarchy saw further disruption by the deluge of poor European immigrants; they were flooding into prospering Latin American countrysides or into booming cities like Buenos Aires in Argentina and São Paulo in Brazil. Latin American societies, then, did not easily become homogeneous "nations." Indeed, many Latin American observers wondered whether national identities could survive these transformations at all.

In an age of acute nationalism, the mixed racial composition of Latin Americans generated special anxieties. In the 1870s in Mexico, it was common to view Indigenous peoples as obstacles to change. One demographer, Antonio García Cubas, considered Indigenous people "decadent and degenerate." According to him, their presence deprived the republic of the right kind of citizens. In Cuba and Brazil, observers made the same claims about Black people. According to many modernizers, Latin America's own people were holding it back. The solution, argued some writers, was to attract White immigrants and to establish educational programs that would "uplift" Indigenous, Blacks, and people of mixed descent. Thus, many intellectuals joined the crusade to modernize and westernize their populations. In the effort to "whiten" their republics, many Latin American governments made especially strong pitches for northern European migrants, despite the mounting evidence that they often made inferior farmers and did not work well with others. So, even by 1900, some of the shine of "pure" White races was rubbing off, not least because European migrants did not live up to the propagandists' expectations.

Diego Rivera's *History of Mexico*. This is one of the most famous works of Mexican art, a portrait of the history of Mexico by the radical nationalist painter Diego Rivera. In this chapter and in Chapter 12, we have shown details from this mural. In stepping back to view the whole work, which is in the National Palace in Mexico City, we can see how Rivera envisioned the history of his people generally. Completed in 1935, this work seeks to show a people fighting constantly against outside aggressors; it winds like a grand epic from their glorious preconquest days (lower center) to the conquest, the colonial exploitation, the revolution for independence, nineteenth-century invasions from France and the United States, and the popular 1910 Mexican Revolution. It culminates in an image of Karl Marx, framed by a "scientific sun" (not shown here)—pointing to a future of progress and prosperity for all, as if restoring a modern Tenochtitlán of the Aztecs. This work captured many Mexicans' efforts to return to the Indigenous roots of the nation and to fuse them with modern scientific ideas.

PROMOTING NATIONHOOD BY CELEBRATING THE PAST For their part, Latin American leaders began to exalt bygone glories as a way to promote national identity and foster unity. Inventing successful myths could make a government seem more legitimate—as the heir to a rightful struggle of the past. Thus, in Mexico, General Díaz took the bell that Father Hidalgo had tolled on September 16, 1810, to mark the beginning of the war against Spain (see Chapter 15) and placed it in the National Palace in Mexico City. In the month of that centennial in 1910, grand processions wound through the capital. Many of the parades celebrated Aztec grandeur, thereby creating a mythic arc from the greatness of the Aztec past to the triumphal story of Mexican independence—and to the benevolence and progress of the Díaz regime. As the government glorified the Aztecs with pageants, statues, and pavilions, however, it continued to ignore modern Aztec descendants, who lived in squalor.

Some thinkers now began to celebrate ancient heritages as a basis for modern national identities. For example, in Mexico and eventually in the Andes, the pre-Spanish past became a crucial foundation stone of the nation-state. The young Mexican writer José Vasconcelos (1882–1959) grew disenchanted with the brutal rule of Díaz and his westernizing ambitions. Nonetheless, he endorsed Díaz's celebration of the Indigenous past, for he believed that Mexicans were capable of a superior form of civilization. He insisted that if they had fewer material concerns, their combined Aztec and Spanish Catholic origins could create a spiritual realm of even higher achievement. In Vasconcelos's view, Mexico's greatness flowed not in spite of, but because of, its mixed nature.

Sun Yat-sen and the Making of a Chinese Nation

Just as Latin Americans celebrated an authentic past, Chinese writers emphasized the power and depth of Chinese culture—in contrast to the Qing Empire's failing political and social strength. Here, writers used race to emphasize the superiority of the Han Chinese. Here, too, the pace of change generated a desire to trace one's roots back to secure foundations. Moreover, traditions were reinvented in the hope of saving a "Chinese culture" threatened by modernity.

In China, as elsewhere, scholars and political mobilizers took up the challenge of redefining identities. By the century's end, prominent members of both groups had abandoned their commitment to preserving the old order but were not ready to fully adopt western practices. Their attempts at combining traditions and values from home and abroad gave rise to the modern Chinese intelligentsia and modern Chinese nationalism.

PROMOTING HAN NATIONALISM Symbolizing the challenge of nation building were the endeavors of **Sun Yat-sen** (1866–1925), who was part of an emerging generation of critics of the old regime. Like his European counterparts, Sun dreamed of a political community reshaped along national lines. Born into a modest rural household in southern China, he studied medicine in the British colony of Hong Kong and then turned to politics during the Sino-Japanese War. When the Qing government rejected his offer of service to the Chinese cause, he became convinced that China's rulers were out of touch with the times. Subsequently, he established an organization based in Hawaii to advocate the Qing downfall and the cause of republicanism. The cornerstone of his message was Chinese nationalism—specifically, Han (the majority of the population) nationalism.

Sun blasted the feeble rule by the non-Han "outsiders," the Manchus, and trumpeted a sovereign political community of "true" Chinese. No ruler, he argued, could enjoy legitimacy without the nation's consent. He envisioned a new China free of Manchu rule, building a democratic form of government and an economic system based on equalized land rights. In this fashion, Sun claimed, China would join the world of nation-states and have the power to defend its borders.

Sun's nationalism did not catch on immediately in China itself, partly because the Qing regime persecuted all dissenters. His ideas fared better among the hundreds of thousands of Chinese who had emigrated in the second half of the nineteenth century. Often facing discrimination in their adopted homelands, these overseas communities applauded Sun's racial nationalism and democratic ideas. In addition, Chinese students studying abroad found inspiration in his message.

REPLACING THE QING AND RECONSTITUTING A NATION Sun's nationalist and republican call resonated more powerfully as the Qing Empire grew weaker early in the twentieth century. Military defeat at the hands of neighboring Japan and the fiasco of the Boxer Uprising further shook the dynasty. Realizing that reforms were necessary, the Manchu court began overhauling the administrative system and the military after the turn of the century. Yet these changes came too late. The old elites grumbled, and the new class of urban merchants, entrepreneurs, and professionals (who often benefited from business with westerners) regarded the government as outmoded. Moreover, peasants and laborers resented the high cost of the reforms, which seemed to help only the rulers.

A mutiny, sparked in part by the government's nationalization of railroads and its low compensation to native Chinese investors, broke out in the city of Wuchang in central China in 1911. It signaled the start of what became known as the 1911 Revolution as unrest spread to other parts of the country, and Sun Yat-sen hurried home from traveling in the United States. Few people rallied to the emperor's cause, and the

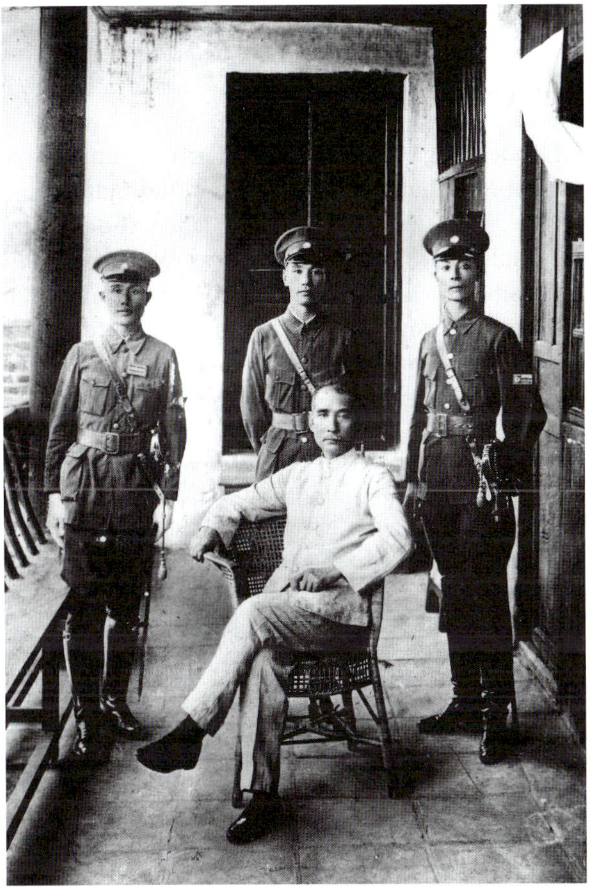

Sun Yat-sen. These two images of Sun Yat-sen (1866–1925), the man generally known as the "father of the Chinese nation," capture the evolution of China's cultural identity during this period. *Left*: In early 1912, Sun and the officials of the new republic, all of them civilians, in public in full western-style jackets and ties. *Right*: Sun is pictured here shortly before his death, surrounded by generals. Chiang Kai-shek (1887–1975), standing behind him, had just been appointed commandant of the Whampoa Military Academy. By the time this photo was taken, China was sliding into civil war, and Sun was relying increasingly on the army. He feared that sovereignty could be assured only through a strong military.

Qing dynasty collapsed—bringing an abrupt end to a dynastic tradition of more than 2,000 years.

China would soon be reconstituted, and Sun's ideas, especially those regarding race, would play a central role. The original flag of the republic, for example, consisted of five colors representing the citizenry's major racial groups: red for the Han, yellow for the Manchus, blue for the Mongols, white for the Tibetans, and black for the Muslims. But Sun had reservations about this multiracial flag, believing there should be only one Chinese race. The existence of different groups in China, he argued, was the result of incomplete assimilation—a problem that the modern nation now had to confront.

Nationalism and Invented Traditions in India

British imperial rule persisted in India, but the turn of the century saw cracks in its stranglehold. Four strands had woven the territory together: the consolidation of colonial administration, the establishment of railways and telegraphs, the growth of western education and ideas, and the development of colonial capitalism. Now it was possible to speak of India as a single unit. And it was also possible for anticolonial thinkers to imagine seizing and ruling India by themselves. Thus, a new form of resistance emerged, different from peasant rebellions of the past. Now, dissenters talked of Indians as "a people" who had both a national past and national traditions.

A MODERNIZING ELITE Leaders of the nationalist opposition were western-educated intellectuals from colonial cities and towns. Although a tiny minority of the Indian population, they gained influence through their access to the official world and their familiarity with European knowledge and history. This elite group used their knowledge to develop modern cultural forms. For example, they turned colloquial languages (such as Hindi, Urdu, Bengali, Tamil, and Malayalam) into standardized, literary forms for writing novels and dramas. Now the publication of journals, magazines, newspapers, pamphlets, novels, and dramas surged, facilitating communication throughout British India.

Along with print culture came a growing public sphere where intellectuals debated social and political matters. By 1885, voluntary associations in big cities had united to establish a political party, the **Indian National Congress**. Lawyers, prominent merchants, and local notables dominated its early leadership. The congress demanded greater representation of Indians in administrative and legislative bodies, criticized the government's economic policies, and encouraged India's industrialization.

Underlying this political nationalism, embodied by the Indian National Congress, was cultural nationalism. The nationalists claimed that Indians might not be a single race but were at least a unified people because of their unique culture and common colonial history. Indeed, nationalism in India (unlike in Europe) developed with an acute awareness of Indians as colonial subjects. The critical question was, Could India be a modern nation *and* hold on to its Indian identity?

BUILDING A MODERN IDENTITY ON REWRITTEN TRADITIONS The recovery of traditions became a way to establish a modern Indian identity without acknowledging the recent subjugation by British colonizers. So Indian intellectuals (like those in Latin America) turned to the past and rewrote the histories of ancient empires and kingdoms. In this way, Indian intellectuals promoted the idea of the nation-state even though the region had no integrated, national history prior to colonization.

To portray Indians as a people with a unifying religious creed, intellectuals reconfigured Hinduism so that it resembled western religion. This was no easy task, for traditional Hinduism did not have a supreme textual authority, a monotheistic God, an organized church, or an established creed. Nonetheless, nationalist Hindu intellectuals combined various philosophical texts, cultural beliefs, social practices, and Hindu traditions into a mix that they labeled the authentic Hindu religion. Other Indian revivalists, too, explored the roots of a national culture. Some researched ancient Indian contributions to astronomy, mathematics, algebra, chemistry, and medicine and called for a national science. In the fine arts, intellectuals constructed an imaginary line of continuity to the glorious past to promote a specifically Indian art and aesthetics (sense of beauty).

While fashioning hybrid forms, revivalists also narrowed the definition of Indian traditions. As Hindu intellectuals looked back, they identified Hindu traditions and the pre-Islamic past as the only sources of India's culture. Other contributors to the region's mosaic past were forgotten; the Muslim past, in particular, had no prominent role. However, the Muslims and other religious, ethnic, and linguistic groups also attempted to mobilize their communities for modern, secular purposes. The Indian National Muslim League, for example, which formed in 1906, advanced the *political* interests of Muslims, not the Islamic religion.

HINDU REVIVALISM Hindu revivalism became a powerful political force in the late nineteenth century, when the nationalist challenge to the colonial regime took a militant turn. New leaders rejected constitutionalism and called for militant agitation. The British decision to partition Bengal in 1905 into two provinces—one predominantly Muslim, the other Hindu—drew militants into the streets to urge the boycott of British goods. Rabindranath Tagore, a famous Bengali poet and future Nobel laureate, composed stirring nationalist poetry. Activists formed voluntary organizations, called Swadeshi ("one's own country") Samitis ("societies"), that championed indigenous enterprises for manufacturing soap, cloth, medicine, iron, and paper, as well as schools for imparting nationalist education. Although few of these ventures succeeded, they asserted Indians' autonomy as a people. But the movement's Hindu revivalist flavor alienated the Muslims. Even Tagore, who had served as the poet laureate of the Swadeshi movement, was so troubled by its divisiveness that he went on to pen a novel, *Home and the World* (1916), that lamented the narrow-mindedness of nationalism.

Meanwhile, the Swadeshi movement swept aside the moderate leadership of the Indian National Congress and installed a radical leadership that broadened the nationalist

Modern Indian Art. Painter Raja Ravi Varma's 1889 portrait of Maharani Chimnabai incorporates elements typical to western art while retaining the palette, the patterns, and the focus on prominent individuals that reach back to India's glorious past.

Rabindranath Tagore. The Bengali writer, philosopher, and teacher Rabindranath Tagore became the poet laureate of the Swadeshi movement in Bengal in 1903–1908. The first Asian Nobel laureate, he became disenchanted with nationalism, viewing it as narrow and not universalistic. The photo shows Tagore reading to a group of his students in 1929.

agitation. Although the people did not topple the colonial regime, Indian mass mobilization was enough to alarm the British rulers, who turned to force to keep the colony intact. When the movement slipped into a campaign of terrorism in 1908, the government responded by imprisoning militant leaders. However, the colonial administrators annulled their partition of Bengal in 1911.

Late nineteenth-century Indian nationalism posed a kind of challenge to the British that was different from that of the suppressed 1857 rebellion. Back then, insurgents had wanted to preserve local identities against the encroaching modern state and colonial economy. Now, in contrast, nationalist leaders imagined a modern national community. Invoking religious and ethnic symbols, they formed modern political associations to operate in a national public arena. Unlike the insurgents of 1857, they did not seek a radical alternative to the colonial order; instead, they fought for the political rights of Indians as a national community. In these new nationalists, British rulers discovered an enemy not so different from themselves.

The Pan Movements

India and China were not the only places where activists dreamed of founding new states. Across the globe, groups had begun to imagine new communities based on ethnicity or, in some cases, religion. **Pan movements** (from the Greek *pan*, "all") sought to link people across state boundaries. The grand aspiration of all these movements—which included pan-Asianism, pan-Islamism, pan-Africanism, pan-Slavism, pan-Turkism, pan-Arabism, pan-Germanism, and Zionism—was the rearrangement of borders to unite dispersed communities. But such remappings posed a threat to rulers of the Russian, Austrian, and Ottoman Empires, as well as to overseers of the British and the French colonial empires.

PAN-ISLAMISM Within the Muslim world, intellectuals and political leaders begged their coreligionists to put aside sectarian and political differences so that they could unite under the banner of Islam in opposition to European incursions. The leading spokesman for pan-Islamism was the well-traveled Jamal al-Din al-Afghani (1838–1897). Born in Iran and given a Shiite upbringing, he nonetheless called on Muslims worldwide to overcome their Sunni and Shiite

Sultan Abdul Hamid II Agrees to a Constitution. In 1876, the new Ottoman sultan, Abdul Hamid II, agreed to reign as a constitutional monarch. Thanks in part to a war with Russia, which commenced the next year, and in part to the sultan's own dictatorial instincts, within two years' time the Ottoman Empire had reverted to absolute monarchy, and the sultan had begun to promote himself as a Muslim leader.

differences so that they could work together against the west. During a sojourn in Egypt, he joined with a young Egyptian reformer, Muhammad Abduh (1849–1905), to inspire an Islamic protest against Europe. Later, Afghani and Abduh (then living in Paris) published a pan-Islamic newspaper. Afghani subsequently made his way to Istanbul, where he supported the pan-Islamic ambitions of Sultan Abdul Hamid II, who promoted the defense of Islam as a way to thwart European schemes to divide up the Ottoman Empire.

The pan-Islamic appeal only added to Muslims' confusion as they confronted the west. Indeed, Arab Muslims living as Ottoman subjects had many calls on their loyalties. Should they support the Ottoman Empire to resist European encroachments? Or should they embrace the Islamism of Afghani? Most decided to work within the fledgling nation-states of the Islamic world, looking to a Syrian or Lebanese identity as the way to deal with the west and gain autonomy. But Afghani and his disciples had struck a chord in Muslim culture, and their Islamic message has long retained a powerful appeal.

PAN-GERMANISM AND PAN-SLAVISM Pan-Germanism found followers across central Europe, where it often competed with a pan-Slavic movement that sought to unite all Slavs against their Austrian, German, and Ottoman overlords. This area had traditionally been ruled by German-speaking elites, who owned the land farmed by Poles, Czechs, Russians, and other Slavs. German elites began to feel increasingly uneasy as Slavic nationalisms (spurred by the midcentury revivals of traditional Czech, Polish, Serbian, and Ukrainian languages and cultures) became more popular. Even more threatening was the fact that the Slavic populations were growing faster than the German. As pogroms in the Russian Empire's borderlands in the 1880s, as well as economic opportunities, drove crowds of eastern European Jews westward, German resentment toward these newcomers also increased.

What made pan-Germanism a movement, however, was the intervention of a former liberal, Georg von Schönerer (1842–1921). In 1882, Schönerer, outraged by the Habsburg Empire's failure to favor Germans, founded the League of German Nationalists. It brought together students, artisans, teachers, and small businessmen in the interest of uniting German Austrians with the Germans in Bismarck's Empire. Schönerer detested the Jews, defining them by their "racial characteristics" rather than by their religious practices. After his election to the Austrian upper house, he attempted to pass anti-Jewish legislation modeled on the American Chinese Exclusion Act of 1882.

The rhetoric of pan-Germanism motivated central Europeans to think of themselves as members of a German *race*, their identities determined by blood rather than defined by state boundaries. This, too, was the lesson of pan-Slavism. Both movements led fanatics to take actions that were dangerous to existing states. The organization of networks of radical southern Slavs, for example, unsettled Serbia and Herzegovina (annexed by the Austrians in 1908). Indeed, it was a Serbian proponent of plans to carve an independent Slav state out of Austrian territory in the Balkans who assassinated the heir to the Habsburg throne in June 1914. By August, the whole of Europe had descended into mass warfare, bringing much of the rest of the world directly or indirectly into the conflict as well. Eventually, the Great War would fulfill the pan-Slav, pan-German, and anti-Ottoman Muslim nationalist longing to tear down the Ottoman and Habsburg Empires.

Intellectuals articulated the pan movements, and aspiring political leaders and secret societies took up their ideologies, leaving Europe and much of Asia at the end of the nineteenth century boiling with ideas on how to create new political communities that could go beyond the nations and transcend the borders of the states.

Conclusion

Ever since the Enlightenment, Europeans had put their faith in "progress." Through the nineteenth century, educated elites took pride in their booming industries, bustling cities, and burgeoning colonial empires. Yet by the century's end, urbanization and industrialization seemed more disrupting than uplifting, more disorienting than reassuring. Moreover, colonized people's resistance to the "civilizing mission" fueled doubts about the course of progress.

Especially unsettling to the ruling elite was the realization that "the people" not only were against them but also were developing ways to unseat them. In colonial settings, nationalists learned how to mobilize large populations. In Europe, socialist and right-wing leaders challenged liberal political power. By contrast, old elites, whose politics relied on closed-door negotiations between "rational" gentlemen, were unprepared to deal with modern ideas and identities.

Nor were the elites able to control the scope of change, for the expansion of empires had drawn ever more people into an unbalanced global economy. Everywhere, disparities in wealth appeared—especially in Africa, Asia, and Latin America. Moreover, the size and power of industrial operations threatened small firms and made individuals seem insignificant. Even some cities seemed too big and too dangerous. All these social and economic challenges stretched the capacities of gentlemanly politics.

Yet anxieties stimulated creative energy and experimental thinking that found expression in a movement that became known as modernism. Western artists borrowed nonwestern images and vocabularies; noneastern intellectuals looked to the west for inspiration, even as they formulated anti-western ideas. The upheavals of modern experience propelled scholars to study the past and to fabricate utopian visions of the future.

Revivals and dislocations, as well as cultural and political movements, influenced the reformulating of identities. However, this was an incomplete process. For even as these changes unsettled the European-centered world, they intensified rivalries among Europe's powers themselves. Thus, this order was unstable at its center—Europe itself. And in the massive conflict that destroyed this era's faith in progress, Europe would ravage itself. The Great War would yield an age of even more rapid change—and even more violent consequences.

After You Read This Chapter

TRACING THE GLOBAL STORYLINES

FOCUS ON: The Global Impact of Modernity

Global Trends

- Mass migrations and unprecedented urban expansion challenge national identities.

Africa and China: Anticolonialism

- The Anglo-Boer War and violent uprisings against colonial rule in Africa call Europe's imperializing mission into question.
- The Chinese rebel against European encroachments in the Boxer Uprising.

Europe and North America: Mounting Tensions

- Intense political rivalries, financial insecurities and crises, rapid industrialization, feminism, and class conflict roil Europe and spread to the rest of the world.

Mexico: Resentment toward Elites

- The most widespread revolution from below takes place in Mexico.

Cultural Modernism

- Increased earning power gives workers in wealthy nations the leisure to enjoy music, vaudeville shows, sports, and other forms of popular culture and to read mass circulation newspapers.
- Elite culture explores new forms in painting, architecture, music, literature, and science in order to break with the past and differentiate itself more dramatically from popular culture.
- New ideas of race emerge, as does a renewed emphasis on the nation-state and nationalism.

CHRONOLOGY

Africa

The Americas

Jim Crow laws in the United States 1890s

Europe

South Asia

Indian National Congress founded 1885

East Asia

1870

1880

1890

KEY TERMS

anarchism p. 799
Anglo-Boer War p. 790
Boxer Uprising p. 792
closing of the frontier p. 800
degeneration p. 807
Indian National Congress p. 811
Mexican Revolution p. 800
modernism p. 801
pan movements p. 813
popular culture p. 802
progressive reformers p. 801
Shanghai School p. 804
Sun Yat-sen p. 810
syndicalism p. 799

THINKING ABOUT GLOBAL CONNECTIONS

Thinking about Crossing Borders and an Unsettled World How did mobility of different kinds unsettle established certainties in this period? Think in particular of the massive flight of farmers toward cities and the erosion of traditional social hierarchies; the prevalence of steamships and rail travel, which made long-distance journeys easier than ever before; and the emergence of the telephone and telegraph, which revolutionized communications.

Thinking about Changing Power Relationships and an Unsettled World To what extent were challenges to western influence internal to the western tradition—the product of growing doubts and contradictions within the Enlightenment project—articulated by Europeans like Nietzsche and Freud? To what degree were they external to that tradition—a reaction against the massive concentration of wealth and power centered in the west and the values that supported western dominance?

Thinking about Women and Gender in an Unsettled World To what degree did the economic and technological breakthroughs of the nineteenth century improve women's lives? To what extent were women able to make claims on governments in different parts of the world? How did ordinary women take control of their bodies and their lives, and how did feminists challenge patriarchal cultures?

Go to INQUIZITIVE to see what you've learned—and learn what you've missed—with personalized feedback along the way.

Anglo-Boer War 1899–1902
Herero Revolt 1904–1906
Maji Maji Revolt 1905–1907
Labor unrest 1880s–1910s
Progressive reforms in the United States 1900–1920
Mexican Revolution 1910–1920
Social welfare laws enacted in many states 1880s–1910
Labor unrest 1880s–1910s
Picasso unveils *Les Demoiselles d'Avignon* 1907
Boxer Uprising 1899–1900
Chinese Republican Revolution 1911

1900 | 1910 | 1920

Global Themes and Sources

Global Feminisms

The word *feminist* first entered common usage in French in the 1890s; shortly thereafter, it appeared in English and then in a wide array of languages. Demands for women's rights, however, emerged long before that, as we have seen, and they did so around the world.

Here we present a range of women's voices on women's rights. From the middle of the nineteenth century to the early twentieth, all four women spoke up on behalf of women and basic justice. All invoked religion in their writings. But they made their cases in very different ways: they differed in particular in their appreciation (or rejection) of women's difference from men and, in varying degrees, in their views of work, education, and the importance of motherhood. Sojourner Truth (c. 1797–1883) became known as a powerful abolitionist orator and preacher after her emancipation. Though unable to read or write, she left an indelible mark with her speeches. In the speech reprinted here, delivered at a women's rights convention in Akron, Ohio, in 1851, she rebukes the antifeminist statements of White male ministers. The next three documents were written by privileged women. Argentine writer María Eugenia Echenique centers her argument on equality of opportunity in an article published in a feminist journal. In a public speech Qiu Jin urges Chinese women to take their destiny into their own hands and encourages those who marry to be full partners with their husbands, while Bahithat al-Badiya concentrates in her lecture on equality in the workplace for Egyptian women.

Compare these documents. Pay attention to the different ways in which they all challenge women's exclusion.

ANALYZING GLOBAL FEMINISMS COMPARATIVELY

- Explain what women's rights means to these authors. What supports rights, in their view, and what stands in the way of rights? Do the authors agree or disagree with one another?
- What social classes did these women represent? Explain the significance of class in each document.
- Compare the opinions of marriage and motherhood expressed in these documents.
- Compare the distinctions the texts draw between the private and public life.

PRIMARY SOURCE 18.1

"Ain't I a Woman?" (1851), Sojourner Truth

Born into slavery in New York State, Sojourner Truth gained her freedom in 1827 and became well known as an abolitionist speaker and advocate of women's rights. This document is an extemporaneous speech to a women's convention in Akron, Ohio, in 1851, as remembered later by Frances D. Gage.

- Why did the other women at the meeting ask Gage not to allow Sojourner Truth to speak? What were they afraid of?
- What does Truth mean when she says, "Ain't I a woman?"
- What role does religion play in this document?

Reminiscences by Frances D. Gage. Sojourner Truth.

The leaders of the movement trembled on seeing a tall, gaunt black woman in a gray dress and white turban, surmounted with an uncouth sun-bonnet, march deliberately into the church, walk with the air of a queen up the aisle, and take her seat upon the pulpit steps. A buzz of disapprobation was heard all over the house, and there fell on the listening ear, "An abolition affair!" "Woman's rights and niggers!" "I told you so!" "Go it, darkey!"

I chanced on that occasion to wear my first laurels in public life as president of the meeting. At my request order was restored, and the business of the Convention went on. Morning, afternoon, and evening exercises came and went. Through all these sessions old Sojourner, quiet and reticent as the "Lybian Statue," sat crouched against the wall on the corner of the pulpit stairs, her sun-bonnet shading her eyes, her elbows on her knees, her chin resting upon her broad, hard palms. At intermission she was busy selling the "Life of Sojourner Truth," a narrative of her own strange and adventurous life. Again and again, timorous and trembling ones came to me and said, with earnestness, "Don't let her speak, Mrs. Gage, it will ruin us. Every newspaper in the land will have our cause mixed up with abolition and niggers, and we shall be utterly denounced." My only answer was, "We shall see when the time comes."

The second day the work waxed warm. Methodist, Baptist, Episcopal, Presbyterian, and Universalist ministers came in to hear and discuss the resolutions presented. One claimed superior rights and privileges for man, on the ground of "superior intellect"; another, because of the "manhood of Christ; if God had desired the equality of woman, He would have given some token of His will through the birth, life, and death of the Saviour." Another gave us a theological view of the "sin of our first mother."

There were very few women in those days who dared to "speak in meeting"; and the august teachers of the people were seemingly getting the better of us, while the boys in the galleries, and the sneerers among the pews, were hugely enjoying the discomfiture, as they supposed, of the "strong-minded." Some of the tender-skinned friends were on the point of losing dignity, and the atmosphere betokened a storm. When, slowly from her seat in the corner rose Sojourner Truth, who, till now, had scarcely lifted her head. "Don't let her speak!" gasped half a dozen in my ear. She moved slowly and solemnly to the front, laid her old bonnet at her feet, and turned her great speaking eyes to me. There was a hissing sound of disapprobation above and below. I rose and announced, "Sojourner Truth," and begged the audience to keep silence for a few moments.

The tumult subsided at once, and every eye was fixed on this almost Amazon form, which stood nearly six feet high, head erect, and eyes piercing the upper air like one in a dream. At her first word there was a profound hush. She spoke in deep tones, which, though not loud, reached every ear in the house, and away through the throng at the doors and windows.

"Wall, chilern, whar dar is so much racket dar must be somethin' out o' kilter. I tink dat 'twixt de niggers of de Souf and de womin at de Norf, all talkin' 'bout rights, de white men will be in a fix pretty soon. But what's all dis here talkin' 'bout?

"Dat man ober dar say dat womin needs to be helped into carriages, and lifted ober ditches, and to hab de best place everywhar. Nobody eber helps me into carriages, or ober mud-puddles, or gibs me any best place!" And raising herself to her full height, and her voice to a pitch like rolling thunder, she asked, "And a'n't I a woman? Look at me! Look at my arm! (and she bared her right arm to the shoulder, showing her tremendous muscular power). I have ploughed, and planted, and gathered into barns, and no man could head me! And a'n't I a woman? I could work as much and eat as much as a man—when I could get it—and bear de lash as well! And a'n't I a woman? I have borne thirteen chilern, and seen 'em mos' all sold off to slavery, and when I cried out with my mother's grief, none but Jesus heard me! And a'n't I a woman?

"Den dey talks 'bout dis ting in de head; what dis dey call it?" ("Intellect," whispered some one near.) "Dat's it, honey. What's dat got to do wid womin's rights or nigger's rights? If my cup won't hold but a pint, and yourn holds a quart, wouldn't ye be mean not to let me have my little half-measure full?" And she pointed her significant finger, and sent a keen glance at the minister who had made the argument. The cheering was long and loud.

"Den dat little man in black dar, he say women can't have as much rights as men, 'cause Christ wan't a woman! Whar did your Christ come from?" Rolling thunder couldn't have stilled that crowd, as did those deep, wonderful tones, as she stood there with outstretched arms and eyes of fire. Raising her voice still louder, she repeated, "Whar did your Christ come from? From God and a woman! Man had nothin' to do wid Him." Oh, what a rebuke that was to that little man.

Turning again to another objector, she took up the defense of Mother Eve. I can not follow her through it all. It was pointed, and witty, and solemn; eliciting at almost every sentence deafening applause; and she ended by asserting: "If de fust woman God ever made was strong enough to turn de world upside down all alone, dese women togedder (and she glanced her eye over the platform) ought to be able to turn it back, and get it right side up again! And now dey is asking to do it, de men better let 'em." Long-continued cheering greeted this. "'Bleeged to ye for hearin' on me, and now ole Sojourner han't got nothin' more to say."

Amid roars of applause, she returned to her corner, leaving more than one of us with streaming eyes, and hearts beating with gratitude. She had taken us up in her strong arms and carried us safely over the slough of difficulty turning the whole tide in our favor. I have never in my life seen anything like the magical influence that subdued the mobbish spirit of the day, and turned the sneers and jeers of an excited crowd into notes of respect and admiration. Hundreds rushed up to shake hands with her, and congratulate the glorious old mother, and bid her God-speed on her mission of "testifyin' agin concerning the wickedness of this 'ere people."

Source: Sojourner Truth, "Ain't I a Woman?" in *History of Woman Suffrage*, vol. 1, 2nd ed., edited by Elizabeth Cady Stanton, Susan B. Anthony, and Matilda Joslyn Gage (Rochester, NY: Charles Mann, 1889), 115–17.

PRIMARY SOURCE 18.2

"The Emancipation of Women" (1876), María Eugenia Echenique

In Argentina, the young writer María Eugenia Echenique (1851–1878) advocated scientific education for women. She presented her views in a leading women's newspaper, *La Ondina del Plata*, in July 1876, in reply to a critic who celebrated women's role as mothers who were responsible for the home and could only be corrupted by public life.

- What, according to Echenique, is the principal obstacle standing in the way of women's rights?
- What is the relationship between motherhood and women's rights?
- Explain the significance of biological difference in this document.

When emancipation was given to men, it was also given to women in recognition of the equality of rights, consistent with the principles of nature on which they are founded, that proclaim the identity of soul between men and women. Thus, Argentine women have been emancipated by law for a long time. The code of law that governs us authorizes a widow to defend her rights in court, just as an educated woman can in North America, and like her, we can manage the interests of our children, these rights being the basis for emancipation. What we lack is sufficient education and instruction to make use of them, instruction that North American women have; it is not just recently that we have proclaimed our freedom. To try to question or to oppose women's emancipation is to oppose something that is almost a fact, it is to attack our laws and destroy the Republic.

So let the debate be there, on the true point where it should be: whether or not it is proper for women to make use of those granted rights, asking as a consequence the authorization to go to the university so as to practice those rights or make them effective. And this constitutes another right and duty in woman: a duty to accept the role that our own laws bestow on her when extending the circle of her jurisdiction and which makes her responsible before the members of her family.

This, assuming that the woman is a mother. But, are all women going to marry? Are all going to be relegated to a life of inaction during their youth or while they remain single? Is it so easy for all women to look for a stranger to defend their offended dignity, their belittled honor, their stolen interests? Don't we see every day how the laws are trodden underfoot, and the victim, being a woman, is forced to bow her head because she does not know how to defend herself, exposed to lies and tricks because she does not know the way to clarify the truth?

Far from causing the breakdown of the social classes, the emancipation of women would establish morality and justice in them; men would have a brake that would halt the "imperious need" that they have made of the "lies and tricks" of litigations, and the science of jurisprudence, so sacred and magnificent in itself but degenerated today because of abuses, would return to its splendor and true objective once women take part in the forum. Generous and abnegated by nature, women would teach men humanitarian principles and would condemn the frenzy and insults that make a battlefield out of the courtroom.

"Women either resolve to drown the voice of their hearts, or they listen to that voice and renounce emancipation." If emancipation is opposed to the tender sentiments, to the voice of the heart, then men who are completely emancipated and study science are not capable of love. The beautiful and tender girl who gives her heart to a doctor or to a scientist, gives it, then, to a stony man, incapable of appreciating it or responding to her; women could not love emancipated men, because where women find love, men find it too; in both burns the same heart's flame. I have seen that those who do not practice science, who do not know their duties or the rights of women, who are ignorant, are the ones who abandon their wives, not the ones who, concentrated on their studies and duties, barely have time to give them a caress.

Men as much as women are victims of the indifference that ignorance, not science, produces. Men are more slaves of women who abuse the prestige of their weakness and become tyrants in their home, than of the schooled and scientific women who understand their duties and are capable of something. With the former the husband has to play the role of man and woman, because she ignores everything: she is not capable of consoling nor helping her husband, she is not capable of giving tenderness, because, preoccupied with herself, she becomes demanding, despotic, and vain, and she does not know how to make a happy home. For her there are no responsibilities to carry out, only whims to satisfy. This is typical, we see it happening every day.

The ignorant woman, the one who voluntarily closes her heart to the sublime principles that provoke sweet emotions in it and elevate the mind, revealing to men the deep secrets of the All-Powerful; the woman incapable of helping her husband in great enterprises for fear of losing the prestige of her weakness and ignorance; the woman who only aspires to get married and reproduce, and understands maternity as the only mission of women on earth—she can be the wife of a savage, because in him she can satisfy all her aspirations and hopes, following that law of nature that operates even on beasts and inanimate beings.

I would renounce and disown my sex if the mission of women were reduced only to procreation, yes, I would renounce it; but the mission of women in the world is much more grandiose and sublime, it is more than the beasts', it is the one of teaching humankind, and in order to teach it is necessary to know. A mother should know science in order to inspire in her children great deeds and noble sentiments, making them feel superior to the other objects in the universe, teaching them from the cradle to become familiar with great scenes of nature where they should go to look for God and love Him. And nothing more sublime and ideal than the scientific mother who, while her husband goes to cafes or to the political club to talk about state interests, she goes to spend some of the evening at the astronomical observatory, with her children by the hand to show them Jupiter, Venus, preparing in that way their tender hearts for the most legitimate and sublime aspirations that could occupy men's minds. This sacred mission in the scientific mother who understands emancipation—the fulfillment of which, far from causing the abandonment of the home, causes it to unite more closely—instead of causing displeasure to her husband, she will cause his happiness.

The abilities of men are not so miserable that the carrying out of one responsibility would make it impossible to carry out others. There is enough time and competence for cooking and mending, and a great soul such as that of women, equal to that of their mates, born to embrace all the beauty that exists in Creation of divine origin and end, should not be wasted all on seeing if the plates are clean and rocking the cradle.

Source: María Eugenia Echenique, "The Emancipation of Women," translated by Francisco Manzo Robledo, in *Reading about the World*, vol. 2, edited by Paul Brians et al. (Boston: Harcourt Brace College Publishing, 1999).

PRIMARY SOURCE 18.3

Injustices to Chinese Women (early twentieth century), Qiu Jin

Qiu Jin (1875–1907) was a Chinese revolutionary, feminist, and writer. She left her two children and an abusive marriage behind in 1903 to travel to Japan, where she wore men's clothing and learned to make bombs. She joined a range of overseas Chinese groups that strove to overthrow the Qing Empire and was later executed for her role in an abortive nationalist uprising. In the public address reprinted here, Qiu speaks out against arranged marriages and urges women to take charge of their own future.

- According to Qiu Jin, what is the principal obstacle standing in the way of women's rights?
- On what basis does Qiu criticize arranged marriages?
- What significance, if any, does motherhood have in this document? Does Qiu demand women's rights as mothers and educators of children or on some other basis?

An Address to Two Hundred Million Fellow Countrywomen

Alas! The greatest injustice in this world must be the injustice suffered by our female population of two hundred million. If a girl is lucky enough to have a good father, then her childhood is at least tolerable. But if by chance her father is an ill-tempered and unreasonable man, he may curse her birth: "What rotten luck: another useless thing." Some men go as far as killing baby girls while most hold the opinion that "girls are eventually someone else's property" and treat them with coldness and disdain. In a few years, without thinking about whether it is right or wrong, he forcibly binds his daughter's soft, white feet with white cloth so that even in her sleep she cannot find comfort and relief until the flesh becomes rotten and the bones broken. What is all this misery for? Is it just so that on the girl's wedding day friends and neighbors will compliment him, saying, "Your daughter's feet are really small"? Is that what the pain is for?

But that is not the worst of it. When the time for marriage comes, a girl's future life is placed in the hands of a couple of shameless matchmakers and a family seeking rich and powerful in-laws. A match can be made without anyone ever inquiring whether the prospective bridegroom is honest, kind, or educated. On the day of the marriage the girl is forced into a red and green bridal sedan chair, and all this time she is not allowed to breathe one word about her future. After her marriage, if the man doesn't do her any harm, she is told that she should thank Heaven for her good fortune. But if the man is bad or if he ill-treats her, she is told that her marriage is retribution for some sin committed in her previous existence. If she complains at all or tries to reason with her husband, he may get angry and beat her. When other people find out they will criticize, saying, "That woman is bad; she doesn't know how to behave like a wife." What can she do? When a man dies, his wife must mourn him for three years and never remarry. But if the woman dies, her husband only needs to tie his queue with a blue thread. Some men consider this to be ugly and don't even do it. In some cases, three days after his wife's death, a man will go out for some "entertainment." Sometimes, before seven weeks have passed, a new bride has already arrived at the door. When Heaven created people it never intended such injustice because if the world is without women, how can men be born? Why is there no justice for women? We constantly hear men say, "The human mind is just and we must treat people with fairness and equality." Then why do they greet women like black slaves from Africa? How did inequality and injustice reach this state?

Dear sisters, you must know that you'll get nothing if you rely upon others. You must go out and get things for yourselves. In ancient times when decadent scholars came out with such nonsense as "men are exalted, women are lowly," "a virtuous woman is one without talent," and "the husband guides the wife," ambitious and spirited women should have organized and opposed them. When the second Chen ruler popularized footbinding, women should have challenged him if they had any sense of humiliation at all. . . . Men feared that if women were educated they would become superior to men, so they did not allow us to be educated. Couldn't the women have challenged the men and refused to submit? It seems clear now that it was we women who abandoned our responsibilities to ourselves and felt content to let men do everything for us. As long as we could live in comfort and leisure, we let men make all the decisions for us. When men said we were useless, we became useless; when they said we were incapable, we stopped questioning them even when our entire female sex had reached slave status. At the same time we were insecure in our good fortune and our physical comfort, so we did everything to please men. When we heard that men like small feet, we immediately bound them just to please them, just to keep our free meal tickets. As for their forbidding us to read and write, well, that was only too good to be true. We readily agreed. Think about it, sisters, can anyone enjoy such comfort and leisure without forfeiting dearly for it? It was only natural that men, with their knowledge, wisdom, and hard work, received the right to freedom while we became their slaves. And as slaves, how can we escape repression? Whom can we blame but ourselves since we have brought this on ourselves? I feel very sad talking about this, yet I feel that there is no need for me to elaborate since all of us are in the same situation.

I hope that we all shall put aside the past and work hard for the future. Let us all put aside our former selves and be resurrected as complete human beings. Those of you who are old, do not call yourselves old and useless. If your husbands want to open schools, don't stop them; if your good sons want to study abroad, don't hold them back. Those among us who are middle-aged, don't hold back your husbands lest they lose their ambition and spirit and fail in their work. After your sons are born, send them to schools. You must do the same for your daughters and, whatever you do, don't bind their feet. As for you young girls among us, go to school if you can. If not, read and study at home. Those of you who are rich, persuade your husbands to open schools, build factories, and contribute to charitable organizations. Those of you who are poor, work hard and help your husbands. Don't be lazy, don't eat idle rice. These are what I hope for you. You must know that when a country is near destruction, women cannot rely on the men anymore because they aren't even able to protect themselves. If we don't take heart now and shape up, it will be too late when China is destroyed.

Sisters, we must follow through on these ideas!

Source: Qiu Jin, "An Address to Two Hundred Million Fellow Countrywomen," in *Chinese Civilization: A Sourcebook*, 2nd ed., edited by Patricia Buckley Ebrey (New York: Free Press, 1993), pp. 342–44.

PRIMARY SOURCE 18.4

Industrialization and Women's Freedom in Egypt (1909), Bahithat al-Badiya

Malak Hifni Nasif (1886–1918) was born into a literary, middle-class Cairo family that encouraged her education. She was a member of the first graduating class of the Girls' Section of the 'Abbas Primary School in 1901 and continued her schooling in the Saniyyah Teacher Training College but had to quit when she married. She moved to the desert and began writing under the pseudonym Bahithat al-Badiya ("Seeker in the Desert").

How does the author's social background shape her views?

Analyze the relationship between public and private in this text. What is the author's view of the idea of separate spheres for men and women?

Explain al-Badiya's support for the veil.

A Lecture in the Club of the Umma Party

Ladies, I greet you as a sister who feels what you feel, suffers what you suffer and rejoices in what you rejoice. . . .

Our meeting today is not simply for getting acquainted or for displaying our finery but it is a serious meeting. I wish to seek agreement on an approach we can take and to examine our shortcomings in order to correct them. . . . At the moment there is a semi-feud between us and men because of the low level of agreement between us. Men blame the discord on our poor upbringing and haphazard education while we claim it is due to men's arrogance and pride. This mutual blame which has deepened the antagonism between the sexes is something to be regretted and feared. God did not create man and woman to hate each other but to love each other and to live together so the world would be populated. If men live alone in one part of the world and women are isolated in another both will vanish in time.

Men say when we become educated we shall push them out of work and abandon the role for which God has created us. But, isn't it rather men who have pushed women out of work? Before, women used to spin and to weave cloth for clothes for themselves and their children, but men invented machines for spinning and weaving and put women out of work. In the past, women sewed clothes for themselves and their households but men invented the sewing machine. The iron for these machines is mined by men and the machines themselves are made by men. Then men took up the profession of tailoring and began to make clothes for our men and children. Before women winnowed the wheat and ground flour on grinding stones for the bread they used to make with their own hands, sifting flour and kneading dough. Then men established bakeries employing men. They gave us rest but at the same time pushed us out of work. . . .

I do not mean to denigrate these useful inventions which do a lot of our work. Nor do I mean to imply that they do not satisfy our needs. But, I simply wanted to show that men are the ones who started to push us out of work and that if we were to edge them out today we would only be doing what they have already done to us.

The question of monopolising the workplace comes down to individual freedom. One man wishes to become a doctor, another a merchant. Is it right to tell a doctor he must quit his profession and become a merchant or vice versa? No. Each has the freedom to do as he wishes. . . .

Specialised work for each sex is a matter of convention. It is not mandatory. We women are now unable to do hard work because we have not been accustomed to it. . . .

Nothing irritates me more than when men claim they do not wish us to work because they wish to spare us the burden. We do not want condescension, we want respect. They should replace the first with the second. . . .

Men criticise the way we dress in the street. They have a point because we have exceeded the bounds of custom and propriety. We claim we are veiling but we are neither properly covered nor unveiled. I do not advocate a return to the veils of our grandmothers because it can rightly be called being buried alive, not *hijab*, correct covering. The woman used to spend her whole life within the walls of her house not going out into the street except when she was carried to her grave. I do not, on the other hand, advocate unveiling, like Europeans, and mixing with men, because they are harmful to us. . . .

If we had been raised from childhood to go unveiled and if our men were ready for it I would approve of unveiling for those who want it. But the nation is not ready for it now. . . .

Veiling should not prevent us from breathing fresh air or going out to buy what we need if no one can buy it for us. It must not prevent us from gaining an education nor cause our health to deteriorate. When we have finished our work and feel restless and if our house does not have a spacious garden why shouldn't we go to the outskirts of the city and take the fresh air that God has created for everyone and not just put in boxes exclusively for men. But, we should be prudent and not take promenades alone and we should avoid gossip. We should not saunter moving our heads right and left. . . .

The imprisonment in the home of the Egyptian woman of the past is detrimental while the current freedom of the Europeans is excessive. I cannot find a better model of today's Turkish woman. She falls between the two extremes and does not violate what Islam prescribes. She is a good example of decorum and modesty. . . .

If we pursue everything western we shall destroy our own civilisation and a nation that has lost its civilisation grows weak and vanishes.

Source: Bahithat al-Badiya, "A Public Lecture for Women Only in the Club of the Umma Party," from "Industrialization and Women's Freedom in Egypt," in *Opening the Gates: A Century of Arab Feminist Writing*, edited by Margot Badran and Miriam Cooke (Bloomington: Indiana University Press, 1990), pp. 228–34, 236.

Interpreting Visual Evidence

Global Modernism

Modernism was an international cultural movement that reacted against established traditions and sought to mark a break between the old and the new. In Europe, the movement's center, modernists challenged the Enlightenment belief in stable, universal truth. They criticized realism—the attempt to reproduce the natural world and human interactions faithfully, like a photograph—as naïve and superficial; they believed realists compressed a three-dimensional reality into two and left out the passions and often-irrational urges that motivate human behavior.

When the Franco-Spanish artist Pablo Picasso first showed his painting *Les Demoiselles d'Avignon* (*The Courtesans of Avignon*; 1907), his friends accused him of wasting his talents, and outraged critics likened the canvas to a broken pane of glass. Picasso broke all the rules of the art academies. He abandoned perspective and proportion, distorted shapes, and borrowed from what at the time were considered primitive cultures in order to criticize the hypocrisies of bourgeois European culture. Rather than idealizing the human form of nymphs or classical goddesses, Picasso rendered it in jagged, jarring terms, presenting five common prostitutes in a brothel.

Influenced by Europe, modernists elsewhere challenged a different set of established traditions, but they too set out to redefine what it meant to be modern. For them, the problem was how to be Bengali, Chinese, or Egyptian, for example, and modern at the same time. In *Playing the Flute* (painted

Picasso, *Les Demoiselles d'Avignon*.

Ren Bonian, *Playing the Flute*.

between 1860 and 1880), the Shanghai School artist Ren Bonian relied on old conventions in Chinese art like the use of text and folk elements (the solitary, meditative figure). But he also drew inspiration from international currents in the use of colors and naturalist imagery. Note, for instance, the gnarled roots. Like many European Romantics, Ren Bonian offers a pastoral scene, a retreat from the noisy urban world alluded to by the wall or tall fence. This fades into a plain white background, as if to clear room for imported western motifs among the established traditions of Chinese art.

The Indian artist Abanindranath Tagore painted a number of works that drew inspiration from Mughal art. His best-known work, *Bharat Mata* (Mother India; 1905), presents a young woman with four arms, in the manner of Hindu gods, holding symbols of India's national aspirations—a book, sheaves of rice, Hindu prayer beads, and a white cloth—in an effort to create nationalist feeling in Indians across the subcontinent.

Tagore, *Bharat Mata*.

QUESTIONS FOR ANALYSIS

1. Identify similarities in these works. Do you see connections in terms of the use of color or other artistic techniques? What characteristics, if any, do they share?
2. Who do you think made up the audiences for these works? With whom were the artists trying to communicate? To whom were they responding? How broad do you think they imagined their public was, compared to the audiences for the images reproduced in the Interpreting Visual Evidence section of Chapter 17?
3. What do you think each artist understood by the term *modern*, and how is this reflected in his work?

Before You Read This Chapter

GLOBAL STORYLINES

World War I and the Growth of Mass Societies

- The Great War (World War I) engulfs the globe, exhausts Europe, and promotes production and consumption on a mass scale.
- The victors' peace imposed on Germany produces resentment and economic instability, while Woodrow Wilson's League of Nations struggles to keep the peace.
- European countries' efforts to rebuild their economies after the Great War by cutting expenses and returning to the gold standard cause the Great Depression, whose severe repercussions reverberate globally.
- Three strikingly different visions for building a better world compete: liberal democracy, authoritarianism, and anticolonialism.

CHAPTER OUTLINE

19

Global Crisis

1910–1939

FOCUS QUESTIONS

- What were the causes of World War I, and how did the war disrupt societies around the world?
- In what ways did the development of modern, mass societies cause the stock market crash of 1929 and the Great Depression? How were they affected by it?
- What were the ideologies of liberal democracy, authoritarianism, and anticolonialism? How were they alike, and how were they different? How successful was each during this period?
- In what ways did access to consumer goods and other aspects of mass society influence political conflict in Asia, Africa, and Latin America?

When the Ottoman Empire entered the First World War on October 29, 1914, nearly three months after the major European powers had taken up arms, a European conflict went global. Although there were minor skirmishes in East Asia and East Africa, the Ottoman decision spread the conflict across the Middle East—and militarized the struggle for control of a vital resource that would determine the course of the war: oil. Control over the seas, land, and air depended on battleships, submarines, tanks, and airplanes. They all needed petroleum.

This was the first major industrial-age war. It relied on control over not only global resources but also industrial-scale armies, navies, and supply lines. To raise so many troops meant that empires had to mobilize their entire imperial domains. As a result, the soldiers and civilians involved in these clashes were the most international of the war. Every ethnicity and religion of South Asia joined with the British forces who fought alongside Canadians, Australians, and New Zealanders, while the French deployed

North African, Senegalese, and Sudanese soldiers. These Triple Entente armies slammed up against Turkish, Arab, Kurdish, Caucasian and (early on) some Armenian soldiers in the Ottoman army alongside their German and Austrian comrades who composed the Central Powers. The Ottoman front pitched global, multilingual, and multicolored armies at each other for control of land passages and sea-lanes that connected east and west—and also, crucially, for access to precious oil reserves that would help determine the outcome of the world's first industrial war.

In this fashion, the first industrial war became an imperial war—and thus a world war. Empires aligned with each other into a gruesome, drawn-out struggle for survival. The Ottomans threw in their lot with the Central Powers to maintain their empire and to reclaim lost territories. The British, French, and Russians sought nothing less than the demolition of the Ottoman Empire. The British and French became even more determined to achieve this goal when Russia dropped out of the war in 1917. Russia wanted access to the Mediterranean through the Dardanelles. The British had their eyes on Palestine and Iraq, leaving Syria to the French. The Germans, hemmed in on the west and east, yearned to extend their sphere of influence across the Middle East. In the end, the stress on these empires led to revolutionary breakdowns, most dramatically in Russia, which flipped from being a near-absolutist regime to a communist one before the war's end.

This fight to the death over the fate of empires and the future of the Middle East also revealed a new face of war. It would not just be a contest between armies. A struggle over survival wrapped civilians into the carnage. Indeed, civilians and their lands became the prime targets. Hitherto, wars over social survival had largely been confined to colonial and frontier conflicts—like the dispossession of native people and the famous concentration camps in Cuba, South Africa, and Namibia (see Chapter 18). But 1914 not only yielded the first global war but also made extermination of entire peoples a new, permanent practice of war. This practice hit minorities especially hard. The most notorious example involved the treatment of ethnic Armenians (who were Christians) in the Middle East. In a frenzy of paranoia about enemies within their empire, Ottoman authorities systematically expelled and exterminated up to 1.5 million Armenian civilians. Starvation camps, death marches, and mass executions became part of the conduct of war at the dawn of the twentieth century.

Raging from August 1914 to November 1918, World War I shook the moral and material foundations of the European-centered world. It sowed disillusionment at home and with European rule in far-flung colonies. It kindled dreams of freedom and self-determination worldwide and posed challenges for elites grappling with competing visions for building a dynamic, modern society amid ongoing international rivalries. In the end, it set the stage for the implosion of the European world order built up over the course of the nineteenth century. The 1930s was first of all defined by an economic calamity. The British economist John Maynard Keynes called this calamity a "Great Slump" in 1930, and it subsequently became known as the Great Depression. It also ushered in political and social crises that fanned the embers of ethnic hatreds and imperial rivalries of the First World War.

Armenian Genocide. Armenian civilians being escorted by Ottoman troops to a mass prison in Mezireh in April 1915. As the war ground to a stalemate, Talaat Pasha, the minister of the navy, became the dictator of Syria and suspected Christians of colluding with Ottoman enemies. He became known as "the Blood Shedder" for his cruelty to unarmed civilians.

This chapter deals with that war and its global impact. First, because the war was fought among European powers with sprawling empires, it prompted production and consumption on a mass scale. Wartime leaders also used new media such as radio and film to promote national loyalties and to discredit enemies—and thereby helped spread mass culture. Wartime practices of mobilization offered a new political model as well. Second, the terms of the peace settlement and the absence of international leadership unbalanced the global economy and laid the groundwork for the Great Depression. Third, political turmoil surrounding the war inflamed disputes over how to manage new mass societies and build a better world. To this end, three strikingly different visions arose: liberal democracy, authoritarianism, and anticolonialism. These ideologies competed for preeminence in the decades leading up to World War II as powerful countries pressed their preferred visions on other societies.

The Great War

Few events were more decisive in drawing men and women worldwide into national and international politics than the **Great War**, as it was known before 1939. For over four years, millions of soldiers from Europe, its dominions, and its colonies killed and mutilated one another. Such carnage damaged European claims to civilized superiority and encouraged colonial subjects to break from imperial masters. Among Europeans, too, the war's effects shook the hierarchies of prewar society. Above all, the war made clear how much the power of the state now depended on the support of the people.

The war's causes were complex. Underlying European tensions were great-power rivalries, which pitted a rising Germany and a conflict-ridden Austria-Hungary against Britain, France, and Russia. Through most of the nineteenth century, Britain had been the preeminent power. By century's end, however, Germany's industrial output had surpassed Britain's, and Germany had begun building a navy. For the British, who controlled the world's seas, the German navy was an affront; for the French, still seething from their defeat in the Franco-Prussian War of 1870–1871 (see Chapter 17), German military buildup seemed a mortal threat; for the Germans, it was a logical step in their expanding ambitions. British hawks, wielding their might in the international financial system, wanted to destroy German power. German hawks felt surrounded—by the French to the west, the Russians to the east—and argued for launching war before Russia grew too strong militarily. Germany joined Austria-Hungary to form the **Central Powers** (later adding the Ottoman Empire), and Britain affiliated itself with France and Russia in the Triple Entente (called the **Allied Powers** later, after Italy joined).

Well armed and secretly pledged to defend their partners, the rivals were provided with a spark in June 1914, when the heir to the Habsburg throne was assassinated in Sarajevo, the capital of Austrian-annexed Bosnia. The assassin, a teenage Bosnian Serb named Gavrilo Princip, hoped to trigger an independence movement that would unite South Slav territories in the Austro-Hungarian Empire (see Chapter 18) with independent Serbia. The Austro-Hungarian emperor decided to take a firm stand, and the German kaiser backed him; the Russians declared support for the Serbs in an effort to uphold state prestige and stifle domestic political opposition. The British and French were determined to prevent Germany and Austria from taking advantage of a possible Ottoman collapse and were keen to realize their own ambitions at German expense in the colonial world. Unable to diffuse mounting tensions diplomatically, contestants braced for war.

Battle Fronts, Stalemate, and Carnage

At the outset, the belligerents expected the war to end quickly. But it soon became infamous for its duration and horrors. As casualties mounted, the war became more intractable, each side determined to slug it out for a final victory that never came. It began on July 29 with a massive Austrian bombardment of Serbian Belgrade, followed by the invasion of Austro-Hungarian troops who committed atrocities against civilians. The German offensive, a thrust through neutral Belgium into France, ran into French and Belgian resistance. German troops came close to Paris at the First Battle of the Marne in September 1914. (See Map 19.1.) A stalemate ensued. Instead of a quick war, vast land armies dug trenches along the Western Front—from the English Channel through Belgium and France to the Alps—installing barbed wire and setting up machine-gun posts.

The Germans had a scheme to tip the scales. It meant sabotaging rival empires by stirring up their colonies and destabilizing borderlands; if they could inflame resistance, it might bring London, Paris, and Moscow to kneel. Berlin pressured the Ottomans to join—and urged the sultan to proclaim a jihad against the British, French, and Russians so the Muslim world inside those empires would rise up. The worldwide Muslim population at the time totaled 240 million, of whom 100 million lived under British colonial rule. Another 20 million resided in the French empire, and an additional 20 million lived under the Russian tsar's rule. In the end, the scheme did not work. But it helped spread the European conflict globally and turned the Middle East into a cauldron of war for the rest of the century.

It would be hard to exaggerate the terror and futility. Lord Kitchener—who had conquered Sudan in part by unleashing

MAP 19.1 | World War I: The European and Middle Eastern Theaters

Most of the fighting in World War I occurred in Europe, and most of it was concentrated across a few agonizingly static fronts. Millions of soldiers perished over relatively thin belts of land, which became pulverized lunar landscapes.

- Which countries had to fight a two-front war?
- Did the armies of the Central Powers or the Allies gain the most territory during the war?
- According to your reading, how did those territorial gains affect the war's outcome?

Trenches in World War I. The anticipated war of mobility turned out to be an illusion; instead, armies dug trenches and filled them with foot soldiers and machine guns. To advance entailed walking into a hail of machine-gun fire. Life in the trenches meant cold, dampness, rats, disease, and boredom.

the machine gun on Sudanese warriors—had predicted to the British cabinet that the war in Europe "will not end until we have plumbed our manpower to the last military man." The fear of having to "go over the top" and into the withering fire and gas of "no man's land" to attack the enemy's entrenched position drove large numbers of soldiers insane. Between panic attacks and bombardment, soldierly life in the trenches combined boredom, dampness, vermin, and disease.

The war quickly ground to a gruesome standstill. Although neither the Allies nor the Central Powers could substantially advance, they refused to negotiate peace. At Ypres in 1915, the Germans tried to break the stalemate by introducing poison gas, but a countermove of equipping soldiers with gas masks nullified that advantage. In July 1916, the British launched an offensive along the Somme River in northeastern France. By November, when the futile attack halted, approximately 600,000 British and French and 500,000 Germans had perished. When the smoke lifted, the battle lines had hardly budged.

On the other side of Europe, Russian troops advanced into German East Prussia and Austria-Hungary along the Eastern Front. Although they defeated Austro-Hungarian troops in Galicia (between present-day Poland and Ukraine) and scored initial victories in eastern Germany, they suffered devastating reversals once the Germans threw in well-trained divisions that were better armed and better provisioned than the Russian troops.

Attempts to win by opening other fronts—in Turkey, the Middle East, and Africa—only added to the carnage. The sprawling Ottoman Empire battled British- and Russian-led forces in Egypt, Iraq, Anatolia, and the Caucasus. In 1915–1916, Ottoman forces massacred or deported 1.5 million Armenians, accused of collaborating with the Russians. Some analysts regard these attacks as the world's first genocide, the intentional elimination of a whole people.

If the Ottomans saw butchery as a last-ditch effort to save the empire, it also lured their enemies into dreams of taking over the region and securing access to the oil fields of the Persian Gulf. Russia craved control of the Turkish Straits, which would provide its grain-exporting ships with unfettered access to the Mediterranean, as well as control of the borderlands of Armenia and Crimea. Germany also had designs on the Straits and Ottoman-controlled Arab lands. All sides appealed to nationalism in what was once a multicultural and multireligious empire. No one foresaw the consequences of the hastily drawn-up postwar borders and the drive to "unmix" the pluralistic communities of the region. (See Map 19.2.)

Legacies of Mobilization

A war of this scale, toll, and duration forced governments to call up more men than ever before. More than 70 million men worldwide fought in the war, including almost all of Europe's young adult males. From 1914 to 1918, 13 million served in the German army; in Russia, some 15 million served. The British Empire mobilized nearly 9 million soldiers. In France, around 8 million served, nearly 80 percent of the fifteen to forty-nine age-group.

The Global View

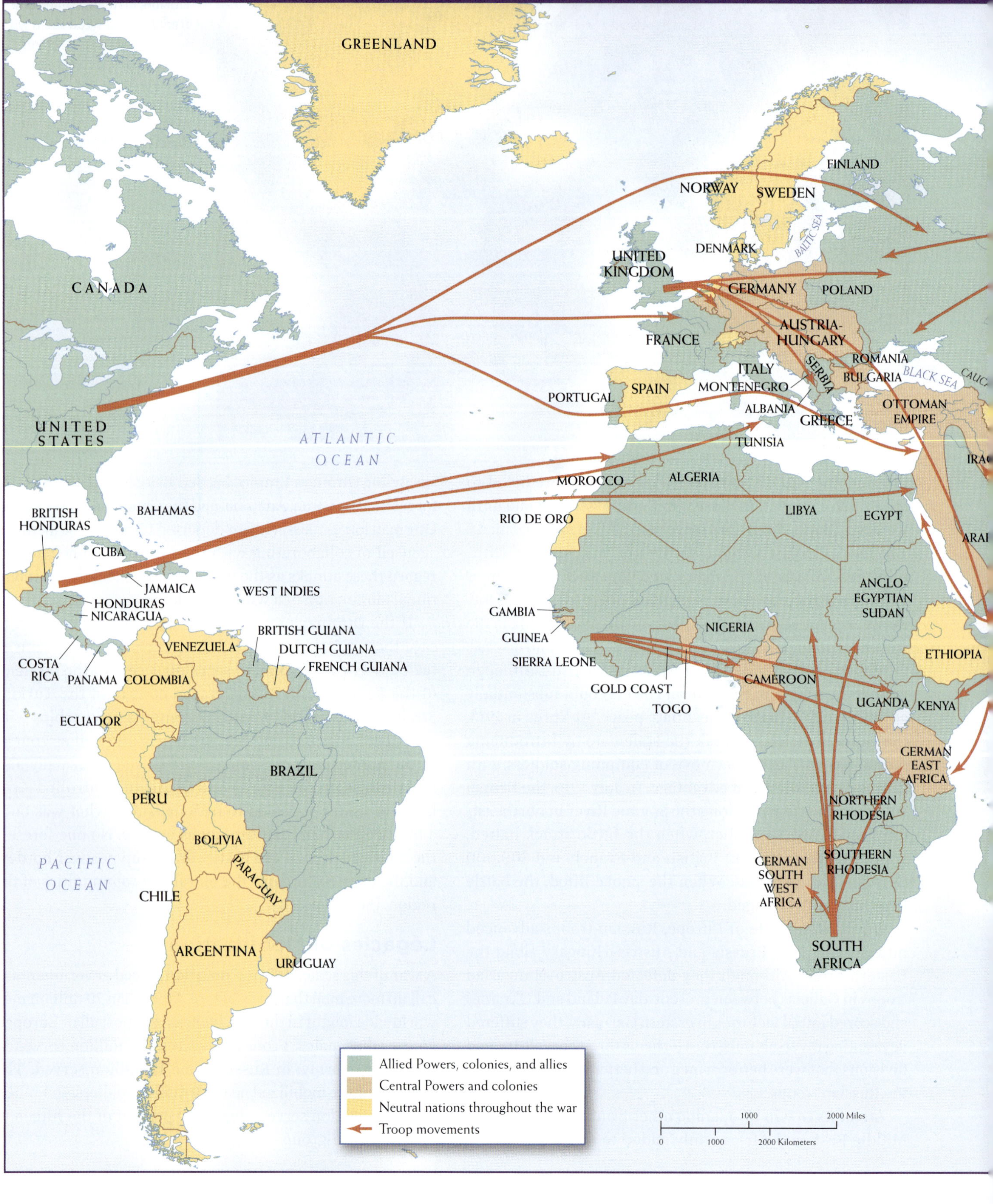

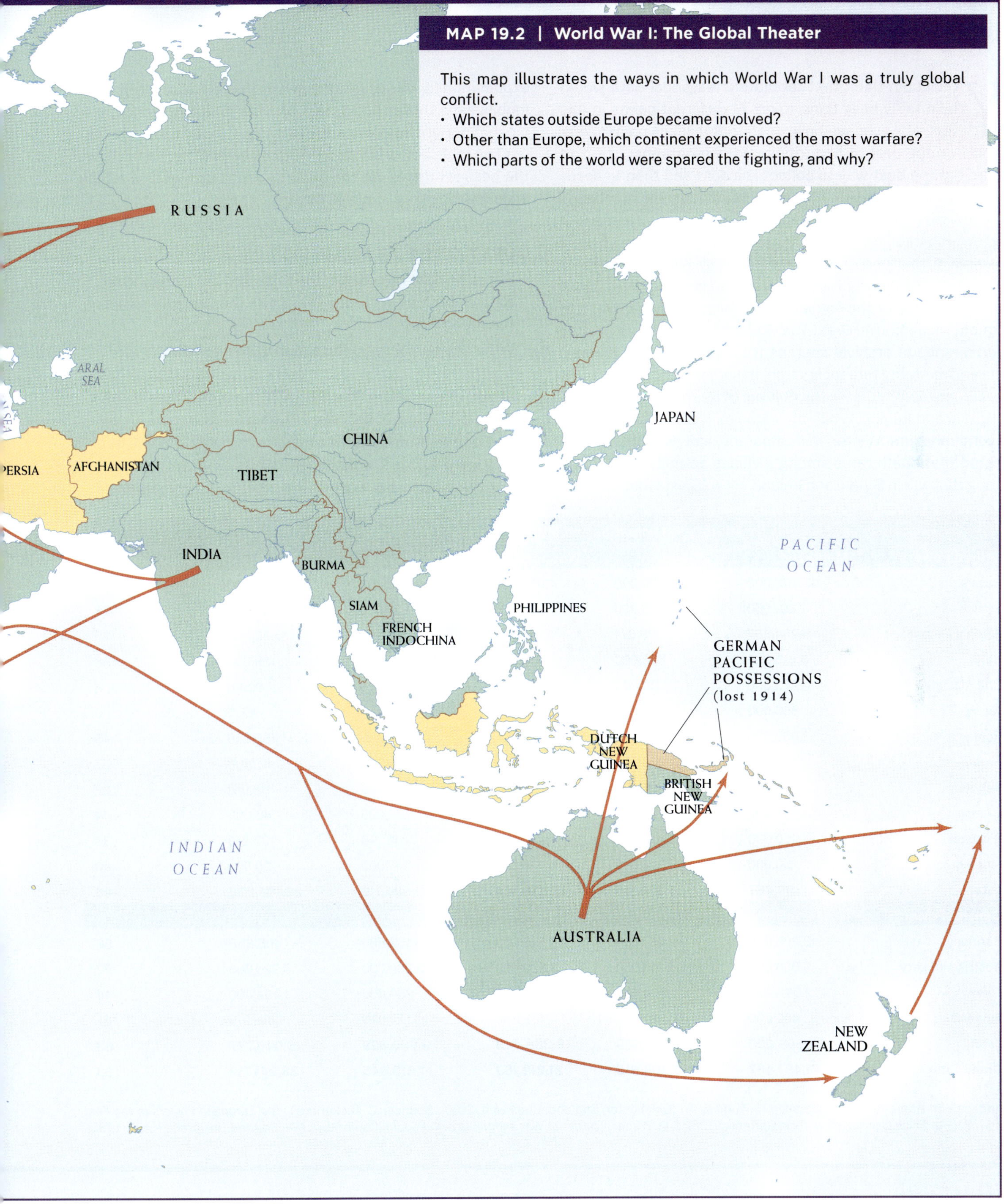

MAP 19.2 | World War I: The Global Theater

This map illustrates the ways in which World War I was a truly global conflict.

- Which states outside Europe became involved?
- Other than Europe, which continent experienced the most warfare?
- Which parts of the world were spared the fighting, and why?

Analyzing Global Developments

Measuring Casualties in World War I

You would think that tabulating historical data would be a fairly easy thing to do. At different points in this text, however, we have seen that it takes painstaking efforts on the part of historians and demographers first to figure out the best way to collect the data and then to accurately categorize and count them. Figuring out the number of Africans that left on enslaver ships and where they embarked and disembarked during the Atlantic slave trade is an obvious example of this kind of work. Historian Jay Winter and others have worked tirelessly for thirty years to come up with accurate death tolls for the soldiers and civilians in World War I. In a landmark book, *The Great War and the British People,* Winter used a range of archival sources from government agencies' data and mortality rate tables from major insurance companies to estimate and calculate the number of deaths among people in Britain and Ireland. While the carnage in World War I seems beyond measure, Winter, in one paradoxical finding, demonstrated that death rates among civilians actually went down during that war in Britain and Ireland. He suggests that the best explanation for this development was the efforts of the state to mobilize the civilian population, provide health insurance, and, most important, improve nutrition.

The table below builds on Winter's early efforts and shows the best estimates for the military death tolls across all the major participants in World War I.

QUESTIONS FOR ANALYSIS

- Based on data provided in the table, did the mobilization for the war have a greater impact on the Central Powers or the Allied Powers? Justify your answer.
- While the number of people mobilized was a factor of 1.5 greater for the Central Powers, why do you think their dead, wounded, and missing/POW rates were nearly twice as high as those of the Allied Powers?
- The United States played a major role in World War I, but why were its dead, wounded, and missing/POW rates so low compared with those of the other major combatants?

Military Participation and Military Losses in World War I

Allied Powers	Mobilized	Dead	Wounded	POW/Missing	Total	% Casualties
Russia	15,798,000	1,800,000	4,950,000	2,500,000	9,250,000	59
France	7,891,000	1,375,800	4,266,000	537,000	6,178,800	78
GB, incl. empire	8,904,467	908,371	2,090,212	191,652	3,190,235	36
Italy	5,615,000	578,000	947,000	600,000	2,125,000	38
United States	4,273,000	114,000	234,000	4,526	352,526	8
Japan	800,000	300	907	3	1,210	0
Romania	1,000,000	250,706	120,000	80,000	450,706	45
Serbia	750,000	278,000	133,148	15,958	427,106	57
Belgium	365,000	38,716	44,686	34,659	118,061	32
Greece	353,000	26,000	21,000	1,000	48,000	14
Portugal	100,000	7,222	13,751	12,318	33,291	33
Montenegro	50,000	3,000	10,000	7,000	20,000	40
Total	**45,899,467**	**5,380,115**	**12,830,704**	**3,984,116**	**22,194,935**	**48**
Central Powers						
Germany	13,200,000	2,037,000	4,216,058	1,152,800	7,405,858	56
Austria-Hungary	9,000,000	1,100,000	3,620,000	2,200,000	6,920,000	77
Turkey	2,998,000	804,000	400,000	250,000	1,454,000	48
Bulgaria	400,000	87,500	152,390	27,029	266,919	67
Total	**25,598,000**	**4,028,500**	**8,388,448**	**3,629,829**	**16,046,777**	**63**
Grand Total	**71,497,467**	**9,408,615**	**21,219,152**	**7,613,945**	**38,241,712**	**53**

Sources: John Horne (ed.), *A Companion to World War I* (Chichester, England: Blackwell, 2010); Spencer C. Tucker (ed.), *The European Powers in the First World War: An Encyclopedia* (New York: Garland, 1996); J. M. Winter, *The Great War and the British People* (Cambridge, MA: Harvard University Press, 1985).

More than half of the mobilized men died, were wounded or taken prisoner, or were reported missing in action. (See Analyzing Global Developments: Measuring Casualties in World War I.) Over four years, military deaths exceeded 9 million. Another 21 million soldiers were wounded. Vast numbers of survivors bore artificial limbs, had trouble breathing, or walked the streets with disfigured faces. Naval blockades and aerial bombardments had aggravated food shortages and left people susceptible to epidemics, like influenza. As demobilizing soldiers spread disease into their communities, influenza claimed perhaps 50 million people worldwide.

Mass mobilization changed expectations about the state. Civilian pressure forced many states to make promises they would have to fulfill after the war, such as welfare provisions, expanded suffrage, and pensions for widows and the wounded. Mass mobilization also undermined traditional gender boundaries. Tens of thousands of women served at or near the front as doctors, nurses, and technicians. Even more women mobilized on the "home front," taking on previously male occupations—especially in munitions plants. But women could also turn against the state. Particularly in central Europe and Russia, the war's demands for soldiers and supplies left farms untended and caused food shortages. Bread riots and peaceful protests by women trying to feed their children put states on notice that their citizens expected compensation for their sacrifices.

Military demobilization, meanwhile, hit societies hard, especially working women; when soldiers hobbled home, women faced layoffs from their wartime jobs. Still, their wartime roles helped women win the vote in Denmark (1915), the former Russian Empire (1917), Britain (1918), Germany (1918), and the United States (1920). (France held out until 1944.) Young, unmarried women went out in public unescorted, dressed as they saw fit, and maintained their own apartments, to the shock of cultural conservatives.

Because this was a war between empires, it became a global war. To increase their forces, the British and the French conscripted colonial subjects: India provided 1 million soldiers; more than 1 million Africans fought in Africa and Europe for their colonial masters, and another 3 million transported war supplies. Even the sparsely populated British dominions of Australia, New Zealand, and Canada dispatched over 1 million young men to fight for the empire. Colonial recruits were also put to work in factories. In France, the international labor force numbered over 250,000, including workers from China, Vietnam, Egypt, India, the West Indies, and South Africa. The fighting in Africa would pit German colonial armies against neighboring Allied colonial armies, with the heaviest fighting in Central and East Africa. The results were twofold: over 100,000 African soldiers died in the fighting, and over 300,000 civilians died from war-related famine and disease.

Women's War Effort. With armies conscripting almost all able-bodied men, women filled their places in factories, especially in those that manufactured war materials, such as the French plant pictured here in 1916.

Despair and disillusionment at the prolonged, bloody war turned into revolt and revolution. In British-ruled Nyasaland, a mission-educated African, John Chilembwe, directed his compatriots to refuse British military demands and to stand up for "Africa for the Africans." Although the British suppressed the insurrection and executed the rebel leader, Chilembwe's death did not stop the growing desire to undo bonds to the imperial power.

The Russian Revolution

The war ravaged all empires; some it destroyed. The first to go was Romanov Russia. In February 1917, with its capital in revolt, Tsar Nicholas II stepped down under pressure from his generals. They wanted to quash the mass unrest in St. Petersburg, which, they believed, threatened the war effort along the Eastern Front. Some members of the suspended Russian parliament formed a "provisional" government; at the same time, grassroots councils (soviets) sprang up in factories and urban garrisons. With the tsar removed, millions of peasants seized land, soldiers and sailors abandoned the front, and borderland non-Russian groups split from the crumbling empire.

Russia became free in a chaotic way. The unelected Provisional Government had no local organs of rule, while the grassroots soviets had no levers of national power. As the despised tsarist police fell apart, so did public order. The tsar's downfall incited widespread hopes that the hated war would now end, but the Provisional Government would not abandon its allies Britain and France by signing a separate peace with Germany and Austria-Hungary. That was a fatal decision. Waves of infuriated rank-and-file soldiers, sailors, and workers deserted their posts.

Chaos led to decomposition and civil war. In October, left-wing socialists calling themselves **Bolsheviks**, who validated the peasants' land seizure and promised to end the war, seized power. Led by Vladimir Lenin and Leon Trotsky, the Bolsheviks drew support among the radicalized members of the soviets. Arresting Provisional Government members, they claimed power in the name of the soviets. In December, Soviet Russia held the then-largest free election in world history; nearly 40 million men and women elected delegates to a constitutional convention, or constituent assembly. But the Bolsheviks disbanded the body after one day. In March 1918, as the Russian army further disintegrated, Soviet Russia at Lenin's insistence signed the Treaty of Brest-Litovsk, acknowledging German victory on the Eastern Front and sacrificing vast territories to safeguard the socialist revolution. For additional protection, the Bolshevik leadership relocated the capital from St. Petersburg to Moscow, where they set about building a revolutionary dictatorship to combat tsarist defenders known as "White Russians."

The Fall of the Central Powers

On April 2, 1917, the United States declared war on Germany. This occurred after German submarines sank several American merchant ships and after a secret telegram came to light in which German officials sought Mexican support by promising to help Mexico regain territories it had lost to the United States in 1848.

The entry of U.S. troops tilted the balance of military power in Europe. The Allies turned the tide at the Second Battle of the Marne in July 1918 and pushed German soldiers back into Belgium. Starving and sick German troops then began to surrender en masse. Before long, Germany tottered on the edge of civil war as the Allied blockade caused starvation in the cities. Finally, German generals agreed to an armistice in November 1918. After Kaiser Wilhelm II fled into exile, the German Empire became a republic. The last Habsburg emperor also abdicated, and Austria-Hungary dissolved into several new states. With the collapse of the Ottoman Empire, the war claimed a fourth dynasty among its casualties.

The Peace Settlement and the Impact of the War

Once the Axis alliance collapsed, the question became not how to end an endless war but how to create a durable peace. To decide the future of the modern world, the victors convened five peace conferences, one for each of the Central Powers. Most important was the conference to negotiate peace with Germany, held in Versailles, France, in January 1919. Delegates drew many of their ideas from American president Woodrow Wilson's "Fourteen Points," a blueprint he had issued in 1918 to counter Germany's occupation of eastern Europe. Wilson insisted that postwar borders be redrawn by following the principle of "self-determination of nations" and that an international **League of Nations** be established to negotiate future quarrels. Though the League earned a toothless reputation, it was nonetheless a milestone in the creation of an idea of global cooperation.

The Russian Revolution. *Right:* The July 1917 demonstrations in Petrograd were among the largest in the Russian Empire during that turbulent year of war and revolution. In this photo, marchers carry banners reading "Down with the Ministers-Capitalists" and "All Power to the Soviets of Worker, Soldier, and Peasant Deputies." *Left:* Vladimir Lenin died just six years and three months after the October 1917 revolution, but he lived on in his writings and in images, such as this painting by Pavel Kuznetsov. Artists and propagandists helped make Lenin a ubiquitous icon of the new Soviet order.

In practice, bitterness overwhelmed high-minded ideas. The French and Belgians, on whose territories so much of the devastation had occurred, wanted recompense and revenge. The Versailles treaty held the Germans solely responsible for the war, demanded that Germany pay reparations for the damages it had inflicted, and compelled the Germans to return Alsace and Lorraine, taken by Germany after the Franco-Prussian War of 1870–1871 (see Chapter 17), to France. There was a frenzy over parts of the German Empire. The treaty redistributed German colonies in Africa among the British, French, Belgians, and South Africans. Nor was Germany the only target: Greek nationalists wanted to gouge Turkish lands. A hobbled Woodrow Wilson was dismayed. Then Americans rounded on him at home. When a League of Nations was established in 1920, the United States refused to join.

Broken Promises and Political Turmoil

A major challenge for world peace was how to reckon with seething resentments and nationalism. Home fronts suffered grim impoverishment as states failed the challenges of a total war their rulers had launched. Left-wing elements grew stronger even as they divided between moderate socialists and communists; the right underwent a radical and dangerous mutation toward fascism; and the center tried to accommodate itself to mass democracy. The polarization also unfolded on racial lines. Anti-Semitism spread everywhere. African American soldiers who returned from service in Europe walked into a storm of racial hatred and lynching. Violence became an enduring part of politics.

Part of the problem lay in the very foundation of a peace premised on free, self-determining, and democratic nations. President Wilson had intended his ideology, especially his Fourteen Points, to apply principally to the ethnic minorities within the Russian and Austro-Hungarian Empires and to European peoples still under Ottoman rule. Self-determination was for European provinces of old dynastic empires, not necessarily for colonies overseas (or for many racial minorities at home). When Japan and others lobbied at the peace talks for an equality clause for all peoples, they were struck down. Moreover, applying the principle of self-determination was exceedingly difficult in practice. Suddenly, 60 million people in central and eastern Europe emerged as inhabitants of new nation-states. (See Map 19.3.) Many were unhappy, as perhaps 25 million now lived in states where they were ethnic minorities and thus vulnerable to persecution in the tumultuous years after the armistice. Much of the ethnic conflict that had simmered beneath the surface of the old empires now broke into the open.

Beyond Europe, colonial peoples also seized upon the rhetoric of self-determination. But France's and Britain's imperial ambitions dashed these sentiments. After a long-drawn-out military campaign in 1919, the British suppressed a rebellion in Egypt, albeit only after promising Egyptian nationalists a limited form of autonomy. The Syrians, too, did not understand why they were less deserving of self-rule than the Czechoslovaks or Yugoslavs, but the French put down a Syrian nationalist revolt. In India, similarly inspired by Wilsonian ideals, peaceful protesters gathered in a garden in the city of Amritsar in the Punjab. The British army mowed down 370 men and women and wounded 2,000 (although Indian eyewitnesses claimed that the dead totaled more than 1,000). The brutality emboldened Indian critics—and shocked sensibilities back home. In China, students offended by the minor status accorded to their country at Versailles launched a widespread protest in the name of Wilsonianism that solidified nationalist sentiment for this generation of students and later ones.

The bloodiest of all conflicts occurred in Iraq, where nearly 600,000 people—more than 20 percent of the population—rose up against British military efforts to force them into a colonial state. The rebellion's first stages were so successful that the Iraqis established an independent state in the Middle Euphrates region, one that brought together Sunni and Shiite leaders and Arab officers and soldiers who had formerly served with the Ottoman army but desired an independent Iraqi state. Ultimately, British forces totaling 73,000, of whom 63,000 were Indian soldiers, were needed to crush the rebellion.

A final set of broken promises triggered an Arab nationalist movement led by the emir of Mecca, Sharif Husayn. Believing that he had British military and political support to create an independent Arab state in Syria, parts of Palestine, Jordan, and Iraq, Sharif Husayn led a general Arab rebellion against the Ottoman Turks. He was taken aback when the Bolsheviks published secret peace agreements that had been negotiated between the British and the French during the war. One of these was the Sykes-Picot Agreement (signed by Mark Sykes on behalf of the British and François Georges-Picot for the French), which divided the Arab east between Britain and France. (See Map 19.4.) A second promise, for a homeland for the Jews in Palestine, also angered Arab nationalists: the Balfour Declaration of November 2, 1917, took the form of a letter sent by the British foreign secretary, Arthur James Balfour, to Baron Rothschild, leader of the British Jewish community, and fulfilled a Zionist aspiration for a national homeland for the Jewish people in Palestine. The declaration did acknowledge the rights of the local residents, stating that it was "clearly understood that nothing shall be done which may prejudice the civil and religious rights of existing non-Jewish communities in Palestine, or the rights and political status enjoyed by Jews in any other country." Nonetheless, the declaration failed to reconcile competing claims, and it ultimately led, along with subsequent events, to the creation of the state of Israel and numerous Arab-Israeli wars.

MAP 19.3 | Outcomes of World War I in Europe, North Africa, and Some of the Middle East

The political map of Europe and the Middle East changed greatly after the peace treaty of 1919.

- Comparing this map with Map 19.1, which shows the European and Middle Eastern theaters of war, identify the European countries that came into existence after the war.
- What happened to the Ottoman Empire, and what powers gained control over many territories of the Ottoman state?
- What states emerged from the Austro-Hungarian Empire?

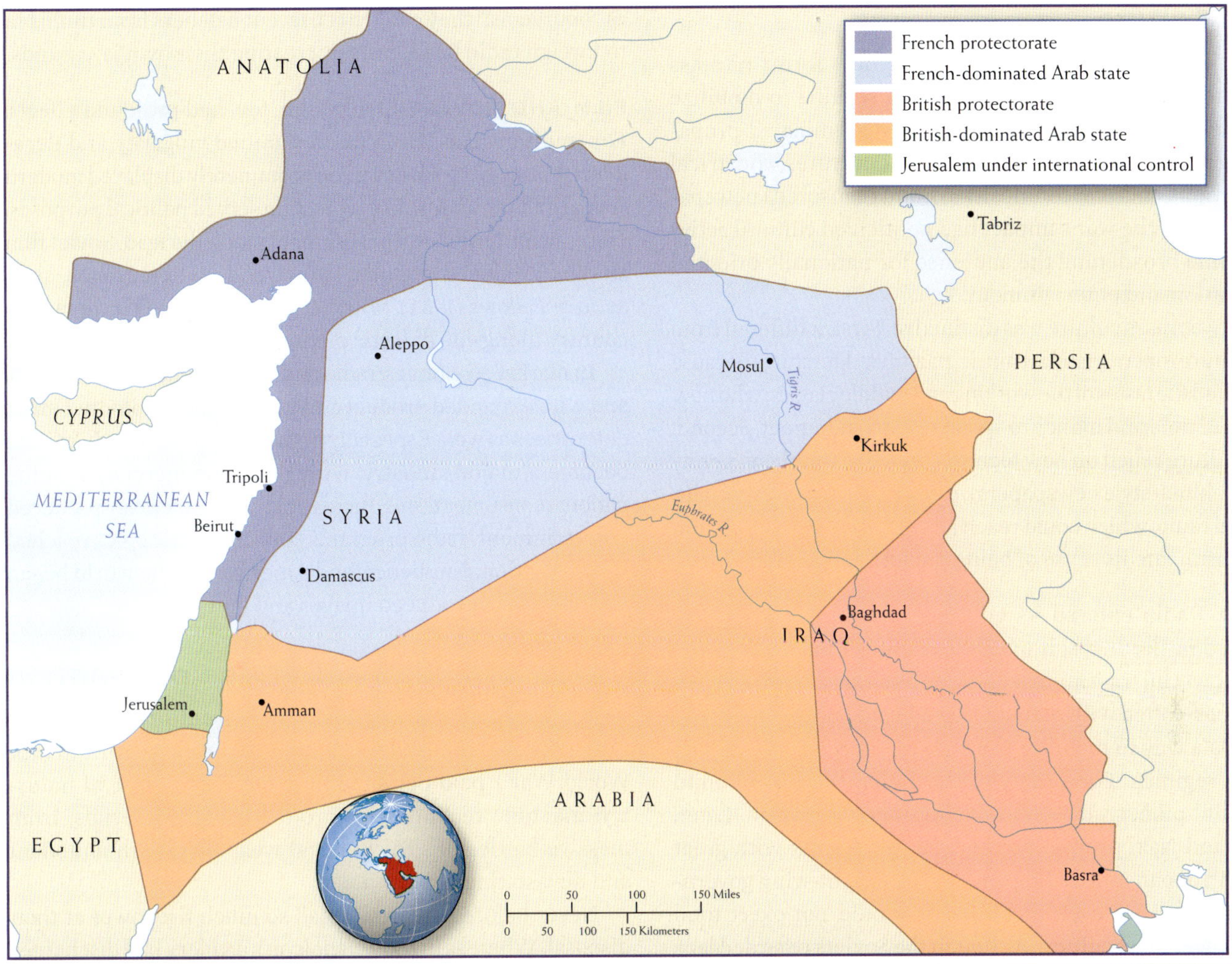

MAP 19.4 | The Sykes-Picot Agreement

The Sykes-Picot Agreement was a secret pact negotiated between British diplomat Mark Sykes and French diplomat François Georges-Picot in 1916. While the agreement reserved protectorates for the French in Syria and the British in Iraq, it also supported the creation of a politically independent Arab state or confederation of Arab states under an Arab chief.

- Why did the British and French governments want to divide up the Arab provinces of the Ottoman Empire?
- Compare the areas that were to be the Arab confederation, though dominated by the French and the British, with the map of ISIS (the Islamic State) that appears in Chapter 22 (Map 22.3). How similar are the territories in both maps?
- Why do you think that Arabs in particular and Muslims in general believed that this agreement was antithetical to their wishes and was an inadequate recompense for their contributions to the war effort? Why do you think that it continues to this day to fuel powerful grievances against the west?

Mass Society: Culture, Production, and Consumption

The war also contributed to another modern phenomenon: mass societies. Even before World War I mobilized entire societies to produce shells, uniforms, and rations, democratic regimes had begun to extend the right to vote, in many cases making non–property holders and women eligible to cast ballots. Authoritarian regimes, meanwhile, had begun to mobilize the people via rallies and mass organizations. And new technologies, such as radio, were helping to create mass cultures that spanned geographical and class divides. The radio, coupled with mass-circulation tabloids featuring vivid snapshot photography, created the means to turn wider circles of listeners and readers into integrated communities—like nations. Mass consumer culture only compounded the challenge of a peace that needed nations to cooperate rather than compete with one another. Ultimately, world peace collapsed under the weight of mass-culture-induced national rivalries.

Mass Culture

Indicative of the modern world were new forms of mass communication and entertainment. In seeking to mobilize populations for total war, leaders had disseminated propaganda as never before—through public lectures, theatrical productions, musical compositions, and (censored) newspapers. Indeed, the war's impact had politicized cultural activities while broadening the audience for nationally oriented information and entertainment.

Postwar mass culture was distinctive. First, it differed from elite culture (opera, classical music, paintings, literature) because it reflected the tastes of the working and middle classes, who now had more time and money to spend on entertainment. Second, mass culture relied on new technologies, like the cheap penny press (tabloid-style newspapers), photography, and, especially, film and radio, which could reach an entire nation's population and consolidate its sense of being a single nation-state.

RADIO Radio entered its golden age after World War I. Invented in the 1890s, it made little impact until the 1920s, when powerful transmitters permitted stations to reach larger audiences—often with nationally syndicated programs. Radio also was a way to mobilize the masses, especially in authoritarian regimes. For example, the Italian dictator Benito Mussolini pioneered the radio address to the nation. Later, Soviet and Nazi propagandists used this format with great effect. In Japan, too, radio promoted the right-wing government's goals. But even dictatorships could not exert total control over mass culture. Although the Soviets regarded jazz as "bourgeois," they could not prevent listeners from tuning in to foreign radio broadcasts or creating their own jazz bands.

FILM AND ADVERTISING Film, too, had profound effects. For traditionalists, Hollywood signified vulgarity and decadence because the silver screen prominently displayed modern sexual habits. But just like radio, film served political purposes. Here, again, antiliberal governments took the lead. Soviet film studios produced popular Hollywood-style musicals, such as *Jolly Fellows* (1934), with catchy songs sung by the whole country, alongside didactic pictures about socialist triumphs.

In market economies, radio and film became big businesses, and with expanded product advertising, they promoted other enterprises as well. Especially in the United States, advertising became a major industry, with radio commercials shaping national consumer tastes. Increasingly, too, American-produced entertainment, radio programs, and cinematic epics reached an international audience, and America and the world began to share mass-produced images and fantasies.

Mass Production and Mass Consumption

The technologies that boosted mass culture also transformed production and consumption on a mass scale. In fact, World War I paid perverse tribute to the power of industry: machine technologies produced war materials, from massive battleships to chemical weaponry, with abundant and devastating effect.

Never before had armies had so much firepower at their disposal. Whereas in 1809 Napoleon's artillery had discharged

Mass Cultural Propaganda. *Left:* The movie poster for the Soviet propaganda film *Jolly Fellows* by Grigori Aleksandrov. *Right:* The shooting of *Triumph of the Will*, directed by Leni Riefenstahl, who made a series of films for the annual Nazi Party rallies in Nuremberg. This one, perhaps the greatest propaganda film ever, won gold medals in Venice in 1935 and at the World's Fair in 1937.

90,000 shells over two days during the largest battle waged in Europe to that point, by 1916 German guns were firing 100,000 rounds of shells per hour over the course of 12 hours in the Battle of Verdun. To sustain military production, millions of men and women worked in factories at home and in the colonies. Producing huge quantities of identical guns, gas masks, bandage rolls, and boots, these factories reflected the modern world's demands for greater volume, faster speed, reduced cost, and standardized output—key characteristics of mass production.

The war reshuffled the world's economic balance of power. It left belligerents with huge debts—all but the United States, which emerged not only unscathed but an industrial powerhouse. As its share of world industrial production climbed above one-third in 1929 (roughly equal to that of Britain, Germany, and Russia combined), people around the globe regarded the United States as a "working vision of modernity" in which not only production but also consumption boomed. But as the United States was emerging as the world's powerhouse and creditor, the world was also becoming dependent on America's volatile financial sector.

THE AUTOMOBILE ASSEMBLY LINE The most outstanding example of the relationship between mass production and consumption was the motor car, which symbolized American ingenuity. Before World War I, the automobile had been a rich man's toy made by skilled tradesmen. Then came Henry Ford, who founded the Ford Motor Company in 1903. Five years later, he began production of the Model T, a car that at $850 was within the reach of middle-class consumers. Soon popular demand outstripped supply. Seeking to make more cars faster and cheaper, Ford used mechanized conveyors to send the auto frame along a track, or assembly line, where each worker performed one simplified, repetitious task. By standardizing the manufacturing process, subdividing work, and substituting machinery for manual labor, Ford's assembly line vastly expanded output while lowering costs.

By the 1920s, a finished car rolled off Ford's assembly line every 10 seconds. Although workers complained about becoming "cogs" in a depersonalized labor process, Ford's factory near Detroit employed 68,000 workers—making it the largest factory in the world. In addition, millions of cars required millions of tons of steel alloys, as well as vast amounts of glass, rubber, textiles, and petroleum. Cars also needed roads and service stations. Altogether, nearly 4 million jobs related directly or indirectly to the automobile—an impressive total in a labor force of 45 million workers.

After World War I, automobile ownership became more common among Americans. By the 1920s, assembly-line production had dropped the Model T's price to $290. Ford further expanded the market for cars by paying his own workers $5 per day—approximately twice the nation's average manufacturing wage. He understood that without mass consumption, increased middle-class purchasing power, and the public's appetite for goods, there could be no mass production. Whereas in 1920 Americans owned 8 million motor cars, a decade later they owned 23 million. The automobile's rapid spread seemed to demonstrate that mass production worked. From Germany, the Soviet Union, and Brazil, industrialists traveled to the massive River Rouge automobile plant in Michigan to admire the feat of economic engineering.

Car Assembly Line. Mass production was made possible by the invention of the electric motor in the 1880s, and it involved three principles: the standardization of core aspects of products, the subdivision of work on assembly lines, and the replacement of manual labor by machinery as well as by reorganizing flow among shops. The greatest successes occurred in the auto plants of Henry Ford. With each worker along the line assigned a single task, millions of automobiles rolled off Ford assembly lines like the one shown in this 1930 photograph, and millions of Americans became owners of automobiles.

THE GREAT DEPRESSION The advent of mass societies and mass markets heightened the sense of instability. Societies were more dependent than ever, but economic relations were underregulated and subject to rigid principles, like the gold standard. Many worried that democracies were vulnerable to the whims of public opinion. Furthermore, economists worried about underlying market problems. Just as the peace treaties did not put an end to war, they could not wind the economic clock back to the prewar global prosperity. Instead, the world economy went through seismic ups and downs—and finally crashed dramatically in 1929, bringing a decade of misery, political polarization, and eventually nationalist-fueled war.

World War I had several lingering effects on the world economy. Primary producers of foodstuffs and fibers struggled to adjust to the new industrial age. In frontier areas like the North American West or in colonial plantation regions of West Africa, farmers began to overproduce their wheat and palm oil, driving down their prices by the late 1920s. These edges of the world market turned into weak links.

The war also led to runaway inflation. Conservative governments, desperate to restore stability, turned to austerity measures to place their countries back on a creaky gold standard. Some societies never fully recovered from the economic trauma of the first wave of mass unemployment caused by government policy.

Finally, the war left all belligerents burdened with massive public debts. France and Britain, once big lenders, became net borrowers; they owed creditors a whopping $8.5 billion in 1918. Germany, the crippled powerhouse at the center of Europe's economy, was stuck not only with its war debts but with the burden of indemnities. The Treaty of Versailles imposed reparations on Germany that totaled $33 billion, of which it ultimately paid $21 billion. The whole financial system became dependent on loans from the United States. Through the 1920s, American lenders recycled old loans while European debtors struggled to pay them off. This meant that if there was ever a crisis in the nerve center of New York, it would send riptides around the world.

The world market was interdependent. But it had no coordinating authorities to deal with a crisis. This made it fragile. Sure enough, when American authorities who worried about overheated markets at home raised the cost of money, the real debtors were pushed into insolvency. Western farmers could not pay the banks, the banks started to go belly up, and New York financiers started to call in their loans abroad.

This set off a spiral into the **Great Depression**. Bankers panicked, stock prices plunged, debtors walked away from their loans, banks failed, and as big lending from New York slammed shut, countries went off the gold standard one by one, letting their currencies fall.

Financial turmoil undermined world trade. As governments abandoned the gold standard and devalued their currencies, their exports suddenly became cheaper and this set off a scramble for markets. Striving to protect workers and investors from the influx of cheap foreign goods, governments raised tariff barriers against imports in tit-for-tat protectionism. Although Woodrow Wilson had dreamed of an American-led world order, the retreat of the United States from open markets caused worldwide damage. In the summer of 1930,

German Reparations. The Versailles peace treaty imposed heavy burdens on the German people. Stripped of colonial possessions, coal from the Saar region, and industries in other provinces, Germany still shouldered heavy "reparations" payments. When Germany fell into arrears, Belgian and French forces began to invade industrial pockets. This 1923 photo captures French troops moving into the manufacturing heartland of the Ruhr. In response, German coal and rail workers refused to work. The country plunged off a hyperinflationary cliff, stabilizing only after French withdrawal and a financial bailout. The economic cost and the memory of hurt pride led to lasting German grievances.

Congress approved a major hike in import duties, named the Smoot-Hawley Tariff Act after its sponsors, Senator Reed Smoot and Representative Willis C. Hawley. Country after country followed suit. Where possible, empires tried to create their own protectionist zones. The British Empire, once the bastion of free trade liberalism, retreated into a shell during a landmark summit in Ottawa at which it declared preferences for its own imperial products. Led by the world powers that had once buoyed international markets, nations and empires took shelter behind borders. World trade collapsed. Manufacturers cut back production, laid off millions of workers, and often went out of business. World prices for Argentine beef, Chilean nitrates, and Indonesian sugar all dropped sharply. Shrinking markets and drastic shortages of credit forced industries and farms worldwide into bankruptcy.

The Great Depression forced economists to rethink the core of laissez-faire liberalism (see Chapter 15), the idea that free markets regulate themselves and free trade leads to economic progress. By the late 1930s, the exuberant embrace of private mass production had ceded to a new conviction: state intervention to regulate the economy was critical to prevent disaster. In 1936, the British economist John Maynard Keynes published a landmark treatise, *The General Theory of Employment, Interest, and Money*. He argued that the market could not always adjust to its own failures and that sometimes the state had to stimulate it by increasing the money supply and creating jobs. Although the "Keynesian Revolution" took years to transform economic orthodoxy and to produce state policies designed to enhance citizens' lives, otherwise known as the welfare state, many governments had doubts about whether capitalism could be saved. The Great Depression did more than any other event to challenge the belief that liberal democracy and capitalism were the best way to achieve political stability and economic progress.

Mass Politics: Competing Visions for Building Modern States

The turmoil of war and its aftermath upset class, gender, and colonial relations. On battlefronts and home fronts, workers, peasants, women, and colonial subjects had sacrificed and now expected to share in the fruits of peace as full-fledged citizens. Even in victorious nations, many lost confidence in traditional authorities who had caused the human wastage. Then came the Depression, which did nothing to embolden the reputation of old elites.

No longer contained in genteel chambers, politics shifted to the street. Variants of socialism gained throngs of new adherents even to some extent in the individualism-obsessed United States, where many thought socialism would never take root. In the Soviet Union, Bolsheviks began to construct a society whose rules defied capitalist principles. Elsewhere, mass movements of paramilitaries sought to replace imperiled liberal democratic states, first in Italy, then in Germany and Spain. Liberal democratic empires, such as Britain and France, also faced challenges to square their rule over colonial subjects with their rhetoric of freedom. And a hybrid political order, mixing democratic and authoritarian institutions, emerged in Latin America. (See Current Trends in World History: Population Movements: Filling Up the Empty Spaces and Spreading Capitalism.)

Stock Traders after the Crash. On October 29, 1929, "Black Thursday," the American stock market crashed. Here traders are pictured congregating in the financial district of New York City. As stock values plummeted, panic gripped Wall Street and soon spread across the nation. The market crash was followed by even more devastating bank runs as the Great Depression overtook the world.

Current Trends in World History

Population Movements: Filling Up the Empty Spaces and Spreading Capitalism

As we have seen in Chapters 12 and 13, the European discovery of the Americas resulted in a vast movement of peoples across the Atlantic Ocean from Europe and Africa into the Western Hemisphere. These population movements, among the largest in world history up to that point, pale when measured against the long-distance migrations that occurred in the hundred years between 1840 and 1940. During these years, 150 million individuals of European and Asian descent filled up the less populated parts of the world, moving from Europe, South Asia, and China into the Americas, Southeast Asia, and northern Asia in unprecedented numbers and spreading a capitalist mode of production wherever they moved. A great many of the migrants went as laborers in the factories and on the plains of the Americas and on the rubber, sugar, tea, and coffee plantations springing up in the Dutch East Indies and East and southern Africa. They were as essential to the expansion of the capitalist system in these regions as the 12 million African captives transported to the Americas during the Atlantic slave trade were for the economic expansion of the Americas. Although the new watchword in economic relations was free labor, not all of the men and women who moved were in fact free workers. Indentured servitude—that is, agreeing to work for a certain number of years, usually between three and seven, in return for transportation to the region, food, housing, and clothing—was widely used with Chinese and Indian workers.

A good example of the movement and use of semi-coerced or indentured workers in less developed regions comes from East Africa. There, the British and Germans were engaged in a furious political rivalry to extend their control over territories, and British officials believed that constructing a railway from the coast of East Africa at the port of Mombasa to Kisumu at Lake Victoria would enhance their territorial ambitions in East Africa. They also concluded that they would be unable to recruit a sufficient supply of African workers to accomplish the task. Not surprisingly, they looked to the government of India to assist them in providing the necessary workforce.

The British government of India did more than help them. In all, it made available nearly 35,000 indentured South Asian workers on three-year contracts for the construction of what was known as the Uganda Railway, whose track, covering a distance of 582 miles, was completed in a mere five years, from 1896 to 1901. The work was arduous and the living conditions in the work camps were horrific, yet the British official overseeing the construction concluded that had it not been for this workforce, the project probably could not have been completed in less than twenty years. The building of the Uganda Railway is one of many examples in which we see significant numbers of people moving to new places and regions, sometimes by their own choosing and sometimes not, to play an important role in the expansion of the capitalist system and the rivalries between colonial powers.

The Uganda Railway. Indian workers cut rock for the Uganda Railway, built in 1896 to 1901, during the European scramble to colonize Africa.

QUESTIONS FOR ANALYSIS

- Why do you think that in some cases, like the building of the Uganda Railway, governments had to be involved in forcibly moving workers to where they were needed rather than letting market forces draw the workers to where work was available?
- What do you see as some of the similarities and differences between the treatment of enslaved Africans and the treatment of the forced or indentured servants during this period?

EXPLORE FURTHER

McKeown, Adam, *Melancholy Order: Asian Migration and the Globalization of Border* (2008).

In the search for solutions to mass unemployment and alternatives to mass uncertainty, authoritarian models grew increasingly popular, especially as the communist Soviet Union, fascist Italy, Nazi Germany, dictatorial Portugal and Spain, and militaristic Japan projected images of national strength and pride. Outside Europe, liberal models could not cope with the scale and diversity of the new politics. By the late 1930s, the few remaining democracies appeared weak. Dictators seemed to be riding the wave of the future while colonies sought to go their own separate ways.

Liberal Democracy under Pressure

Fighting a total war had offered European states the opportunity to experiment with illiberal policies. Indeed, the war brought both the suspension of parliamentary rule and democratic rights and an effort by governments to manage industry and distribution of goods and wealth. States on both sides of the conflict jailed many individuals who opposed the war. Governments regulated both production and, through rationing, consumption. Above all, the war revolutionized the size and scope of the state.

BRITISH AND FRENCH RESPONSES TO ECONOMIC CRISES Britain and France retained their parliamentary systems, but even here, old-fashioned liberal democracy was on the run. Strife rippled across the British Empire, and in the home isles Britain gave independence to what became the Republic of Ireland in 1922. Britain's working-class Labour Party came to power twice between 1923 and 1931, but either alone or in coalition with Liberals and Conservatives, Labour could not lift the country out of its economic crisis.

Disorder was even more pronounced in France, which had lost 10 percent of its young men and had seen destruction in vast territory. In 1932–1933, six government coalitions came and went over just nineteen months. Against the threat of a rightist coup, a coalition of the moderate and radical left, including the French Communist Party, formed the Popular Front government (1936–1939). It introduced the right of collective bargaining, a 40-hour workweek, two-week paid vacations, and a minimum wage.

THE AMERICAN NEW DEAL In the United States, too, markets and liberalism faced questions. When the Great Depression shattered the nation's fortunes, pressure intensified to create a more secure political and economic system.

In contrast to postwar Europe, where labor parties and socialist movements surged, the 1920s saw a conservative tide engulf American politics in response to wartime government activism. The Republican Warren Harding won the presidency in 1920 with a resounding 60 percent of the popular vote. Four years later, Calvin Coolidge scored an even greater landslide, remarking that the "business of America is business" (and not government interference in free enterprise). Herbert Hoover's election in 1928 continued Republicans' presidential triumphs. During these years of conservative ascendance, the United States restricted mass immigration and approved a constitutional amendment to prohibit "the manufacture, sale, or transportation of intoxicating liquors." Prohibition, as the ban on alcohol came to be called, was a signature of the moral reaction against the uncertainties of modern life. The proponents of Prohibition, mostly native-born Protestants living in rural America, looked upon alcohol

"Jim Crow." "Jim Crow" laws mandated the segregation of races in the American South, with African Americans forced to use separate, and usually unequal, facilities, including schools, hotels, and theaters, such as this one in Mississippi.

Josephine Baker. The African American entertainer Josephine Baker, unable to perform in America because of her race, was a sensation on the stage in Paris after World War I. Many of her shows exoticized or even caricatured her African descent.

consumption as an urban vice associated with immigrants in the cities.

In addition to targeting immigrants, nativists targeted African Americans in the South. "Jim Crow" laws enforced social segregation, economic inequality, and political disenfranchisement. Millions of Black women and men quit the countryside and moved to northern cities such as New York and Chicago, seeking relief from the legal barriers to their opportunities and rights, but discrimination up north restricted their residences to urban ghettos. Still, within Black neighborhoods, most famously New York City's Harlem, the New Negro movement, or Harlem Renaissance, showcased Black novelists, poets, painters, and musicians, many of whom used their art to protest racial subordination.

The Great Depression took its toll on free market liberalism. By the end of 1930, more than 4 million American workers had lost their jobs. As President Hoover insisted that citizens' thrift and self-reliance, not government handouts, would restore prosperity, the economic situation worsened. By 1933, industrial production had dropped by a staggering 50 percent since 1929 as unemployment reached 25 percent. Hard times were even worse in the countryside, where farm income plummeted by two-thirds between 1929 and 1932.

In the 1932 presidential election, a Democrat, Franklin Delano Roosevelt, won by a landslide. He promptly launched what came to be called the **New Deal**, a set of programs and regulations that dramatically expanded the scope of the American national government and its role in the nation's economic life. In his first 100 days in office, Roosevelt obtained legislation to provide relief for the jobless and to rebuild the shattered economy. Among his administration's experiments were the Federal Deposit Insurance Corporation to guarantee bank deposits up to $5,000, the Securities and Exchange Commission to monitor the stock market, and the Federal Emergency Relief Administration to help states and local governments assist the needy. Subsequently, the Works Progress Administration put nearly 3 million people to work building roads, bridges, airports, and post offices. In addition, the Social Security Act inaugurated old-age pensions supported by the federal government. Never before had the U.S. federal government expended so much on social welfare programs or intervened so directly in the national economy. Nonetheless, Roosevelt refrained from substantially redistributing national income. Likewise, although his administration established public agencies to build dams and oversee the irrigation of arid lands and the electrification of rural districts, these were exceptions. Privately owned enterprises continued to dominate American society. Roosevelt's aim was not to destroy but to save capitalism. In this regard the New Deal succeeded, for it staved off authoritarian solutions to modern problems.

During the 1920s and 1930s, liberal democratic regimes respected elections and defended private property against challenges from labor movements and socialist critics. But they intervened in markets and regulated people's lives in ways that prewar governments would never have contemplated.

Authoritarianism and Mass Mobilization

Like the liberal systems they challenged, authoritarian regimes came in various stripes. Italy, Germany, and Japan saw the triumph of right-wing dictatorships. Although differing in important respects, all disliked the left-wing dictatorship of the Soviet Union. And the Soviets had no liking for the fascists. Yet all the postwar dictatorships shared a visceral dislike of liberal democracy as weak and corrupt, unsuited to muscular nations. These regimes touted their success in mobilizing the masses to create dynamic yet orderly societies. They also had charismatic leaders who personified the power and unity of the societies over which they ruled.

Although rejecting liberal democracy, post–World War I dictators insisted that they had their people's support. True, they treated their people as a mass conscript army that needed firm leadership to build new societies and guarantee well-being. But their demands, the leaders maintained, would yield robust economies, restore order, and renew pride. In addition, dictators gained support by embracing public welfare programs. They also vowed to deliver prosperity, national pride, and technology without having to endure the class divisions, unemployment, urban-industrial squalor, or moral decay of liberal societies. For a time, many believed them.

THE SOVIET UNION AND SOCIALISM The most dramatic blow to liberal capitalism occurred in Russia, where the radical Bolshevik Party established a socialist regime. Fearing the spread of revolution, Britain, France, Japan, and the United States sent armies to Russia to contain Bolshevism. But after executing Tsar Nicholas II and his family, the Bolsheviks rallied support by defending the homeland against its invaders. They also mobilized people to fight and win a horrific civil war (1918–1921). The conflict pitted an array of tsarists, social democrats, and independent peasant armies against the Bolshevik dictatorship and its supporters (including many soldiers, sailors, workers, and state functionaries).

In the all-out mobilization against those whom they labeled the Whites, or counterrevolutionaries, the Bolsheviks, calling themselves the Reds, began to rebuild state institutions. Their forced requisitions of grain from the peasantry caused a severe famine between 1921 and 1923 in which some 7 to 10 million people died from hunger and disease.

To revive a ravaged economy, the Bolsheviks grudgingly legalized private trade in the countryside while retaining state control over most industries. In 1924, with the country still recovering from civil war, the leader of the revolution, Lenin, died. No one had done more to shape the institutions of the revolutionary regime, including creating expectations for a single ruler. After eliminating his rivals, **Joseph Stalin** (1878–1953) emerged as the new leader of the Communist Party and the country, which had become the Union of Soviet Socialist Republics (USSR), or Soviet Union.

Since socialism as a fully developed social and political order had never existed, no one was sure in the 1920s how the USSR would actually be built and work. Stalin resolved this dilemma by defining Soviet or revolutionary socialism in opposition to capitalism. Since many capitalist states had "bourgeois" parliaments, said to serve the interests of the rich, socialism would have soviets (councils) of worker and peasant deputies. Since capitalism had unregulated and unruly markets, socialism would have economic planning and full employment. And since capitalism relied on the "exploitation" of private ownership, socialism would outlaw private trade and private property. In short, socialism would eradicate capitalism and then invent socialist forms in housing, culture, values, dress, and even modes of reasoning.

War brought down the Romanov regime; why not use war to build a socialist one? Stalin launched class war, beginning in the heavily populated countryside. Rich peasants, derided as *kulaks*, were to be deported to remote areas. Villages had to fill quotas for deportation; often those selected were people who had slept with someone's wife rather than those who owned the most cows. Personal animosities, greed, and ambition spurred this class war. The remaining peasants were forced to combine their farms into larger units worked collectively and run by regime loyalists. Tens of thousands of urban activists seeking to build a new world led the forced drive to establish collective farms and to sell their grain and livestock at state-run collection points at depressed state prices. In protest, hundreds of thousands of peasants burned their crops, slaughtered their livestock, and destroyed their farm implements. The government responded by deporting protesters to remote areas. In the chaos of 1931–1933, a second famine claimed between 5 and 7 million lives.

When it came to industry, the regime rolled out Five-Year Plans to "catch and overtake" the leading capitalist countries. Millions of enthusiasts (as well as deported peasants) set about building a socialist urban utopia founded on advanced

Stalin. Joseph Stalin posing at the Allies' "Big Three" conference in Yalta, on Soviet soil, in February 1945. Much had changed since Stalin became leader of the Communist Party of the Soviet Union in 1922.

technology, most of it purchased from Depression-mired capitalist countries. Tens of millions of people built thousands of factories, hospitals, and schools. Huge hydroelectric dams, automobile and tractor factories, and heavy-machine-building plants symbolized the promise of Soviet-style modernity. Many of these entailed colossal waste, but they wiped out unemployment. While the capitalist world remained mired in the Depression, Soviet socialism and its promises gained adherents around the world.

Soviet authorities also promoted socialism in the borderlands. In 1922, the USSR joined the independent states of Ukraine, Belorussia (Belarus), and the Transcaucasian Federation with Soviet Russia to form a single federal state. The USSR also soon acquired several new republics, some from central Asia; eventually there were fifteen (see Map 19.5), all of which secured their own state institutions—but under centralized rule from Moscow. In the 1930s, collectivization and mass arrests devastated the peasants and nomads as well as the officials of the republics, but industrialization and urbanization gave opportunities to new people and empowered new indigenous elites.

Collectivized Agriculture. Soviet plans for the socialist village envisioned the formation of large collectives supplied with advanced machinery, thereby transforming peasant labor into an industrial process. The realities behind the images of smiling farmers—such as in this poster, exhorting "Give first priority to gathering the Soviet harvest!"—were low productivity, enormous waste, and often broken-down machinery.

MASS TERROR AND STALIN'S DICTATORSHIP The Soviet political system became more despotic as the state expanded. Police power grew the most, partly from forcing peasants into collectives and organizing mass deportations. As the Communist Party's ranks swelled, ongoing loyalty verifications also led to the removal of party members, even when they professed absolute loyalty. From 1936 to 1938, more than 2 million supposedly treasonous "enemies of the people" were arrested, and more than 750,000 were executed; others faced long sentences in forced labor camps, collectively known as the Gulag. Such purges decimated the loyal Soviet elite—party officials, state officials, intelligentsia, army officers, and even members of the police who had enforced the terror. In the end, the terror manifested highly petty motives as well as a desire to participate in the violent crusade of building socialism in a hostile world, full of internal and external enemies. (See Global Themes and Sources: Primary Source 19.2.)

ITALIAN FASCISM The liberal model also faced a challenge from the right. Italy had been on the winning side of the Great War, but the outcome hardly seemed like a victory. Mass strikes, occupations of factories, and peasant land seizures swept the country in 1919 and 1920. Amid this disorder, rightists rose up in response. Their leader was **Benito Mussolini** (1883–1945), a former socialist journalist who in 1919 organized disaffected veterans and adventurers into a mass political movement called **fascism**.

Mussolini mixed aggressive nationalism with social radicalism to sweep away all the institutions discredited by the war. Fascist supporters demanded the annexation of "Italian" lands in the Alps (Austria) and on the Dalmatian coast (Yugoslavia) and called for female suffrage, an 8-hour workday, a share of factory control for workers, a tax on capital, and land redistribution.

Fascists attracted numerous followers. Their violence-prone shock troops wore black shirts and baggy trousers tucked into high black leather boots and saluted with a dagger thrust into the air. In 1920, the squads received money from landowners and industrial magnates to beat up socialist leaders, after which Italian fascism became fully identified with the right. Still, the fascists saw themselves as champions of the little guy, of peasants and (nonsocialist) workers, as well as of war veterans, students, and white-collar types—they considered themselves an all-class movement.

MAP 19.5 | The Soviet Union

The Union of Soviet Socialist Republics (USSR) came into being after World War I.

- How did its boundaries compare with those of the older Russian Empire, as shown in Map 17.5?
- Identify the Soviet republics other than Russia.
- What does the large number of Soviet republics suggest about the ethnic diversity within the Soviet Union?

Mussolini. Benito Mussolini, known as Il Duce, liked to puff out his chest, particularly when appearing in public. He pioneered radio addresses to the people and encouraged fascist versions of the mass spectacles that also became common in Soviet Russia.

In 1922, Mussolini announced a march on Rome. The march was a bluff, yet it intimidated the king, who disliked fascist ruffians but feared bloodshed more. So he withheld use of the army against the lightly armed marchers. When the Italian government resigned in protest, the monarch invited Mussolini to become prime minister, even though fascists had won only a small minority of seats in the 1921 elections. By 1924, taking advantage of disarray in the parliament, Mussolini began to outlaw other parties and force through a dictatorship.

Mussolini's dictatorship cut deals with big business and the church, thus falling short of a total social revolution. Nonetheless, it skillfully used parades, films, radio, and visions of recapturing Roman imperial grandeur to boost support during the troubled times of the Depression. The cult of the leader, Il Duce, also provided cohesion. As the first antiliberal, antisocialist alternative, the early phase of Italian fascism served as a model for other countries.

GERMAN NAZISM In Germany, too, fear of Bolshevism and anger over the war propelled the right to power. After a small workers' movement dedicated to winning workers over from socialism took shape in Munich, the army high command ordered a young demobilized corporal to infiltrate the group. That corporal, **Adolf Hitler** (1889–1945), soon dominated the nationalist workers' movement, whose name he changed to the National Socialist German Workers' Party (*National-Sozialistische Arbeits-Partei,* or **Nazis**).

Unlike Mussolini, the young Hitler was never a socialist. The first Nazi Party platform, set forth in 1920, combined nationalism with a heavy dose of anticapitalism. It also called for the renunciation of the Treaty of Versailles and for discrimination against Jews. It was an assertion of Germany's grievances against the world and of the small man's grievances against those whom the Nazis perceived as the rich. At first, Hitler and the Nazis were unsuccessful, and Hitler himself was arrested. Although sentenced to five years in prison for treason, he served less than a year. While in prison he wrote an autobiographical and fanatically anti-Semitic treatise called *Mein Kampf* (*My Struggle*, 1925), which was an initial flop but incorporated many of the ideas he would apply later as dictator.

What catapulted Hitler and the radical right to power was a combination of the Great Depression and the actions of traditional conservatives. Fearing popular support for the Communist and Socialist Parties and convinced that he could control Hitler, Germany's president appointed Hitler chancellor (prime minister) in January 1933, even though the Nazis had never won a majority of the vote and their share was declining. Traditional conservatives believed they could control Hitler while benefiting from his mass political base. Thus, like Mussolini, Hitler came to power peacefully and legally.

Hitler used fears of a communist conspiracy, crystallized by a mysterious fire at the German Reichstag, to repress the leftist parties and the free press, robbing opponents of the ability to criticize the regime publicly. Hitler then proposed legislation that would enable him to promulgate laws on his authority as chancellor without the parliament's approval. By July 1933, the Nazis were the only legal party and Hitler was dictator of Germany. The first concentration camps (initially to house political prisoners) filled up. Like Mussolini, Hitler

Hitler. Adolf Hitler and his advisers mastered the staging of mass rallies. These rallies and marches projected an image of dynamism and collective will, which Hitler claimed to embody.

relied on choreographed mass rallies, new media like film and radio, and his personal charisma to mobilize a mass following.

Hitler also unleashed a campaign of persecution against Jews, believing that assimilated Jews controlled the banks and that eastern Jewish emigrants carried disease. Like many other right-wing Germans, Hitler also believed that a Jewish-socialist conspiracy had stabbed the German army in the back, causing its surrender in World War I, and that intermarriage with Jews was destroying the supposed purity of the Aryan race (which included northern, White Europeans). Hitler and the Nazis did not believe that religious practice defined Jewishness; instead, they held, it was transmitted biologically from parents to children. In 1935, Hitler instituted legal measures, known as the Nuremberg Laws, that excluded Jews from the civil service and the professions, forced them to sell their property, deprived them of citizenship, and forbade them to marry or have sex with Aryans. Hitler also encouraged the use of terror against Jews, destroying their businesses, homes, and marriages with non-Jews and frightening them into leaving Germany, with the ultimate aim of eliminating all traces of Jewish life and culture in Nazi-dominated central Europe.

Although some Germans opposed Hitler's illiberal activism, the Nazis won popular support by reviving the economy and restoring national pride. In 1935, defying the Treaty of Versailles, Hitler announced a vigorous rearmament program. The state also financed public works, including reforestation, swamp drainage projects, and highway building, that absorbed the unemployed; organized leisure, entertainment, travel, and vacations; and built public housing. Nazism mixed anti-Semitism with full employment and social welfare programs that privileged racially approved groups. (See Global Themes and Sources: Primary Source 19.3.)

Seeing how liberal regimes retreated to their imperial blocs, Hitler nursed expansionist aspirations. Initially, Hitler called his state the Third Reich (the first being the Holy Roman Empire, or Reich, and the second the Reich created by Bismarck in 1871). He claimed that like the Holy Roman Empire, his empire would last 1,000 years. Hitler also harbored grand aspirations to impose racial purity and German power in Europe and perhaps beyond.

DICTATORSHIPS IN SPAIN AND PORTUGAL As authoritarian regimes spread across Europe, the military instituted dictatorships in Spain and Portugal. Their effort to seize power in Spain provoked a brutal civil war from 1936 to 1939, which left 250,000 dead.

The Spanish civil war was, from the start, an international war. When the Spanish republican government introduced reforms to break the hold of the church and landlords on the state, the military launched a coup and received weapons, advisers, and other backing from fascist Italy and Nazi Germany. The Soviet Union supported the republic with weapons and advisers, and many volunteers fought in international brigades. Britain and France dithered, leading Stalin and many others to conclude that the democratic powers would not stand up to fascism. The leader of the military coup, Generalissimo Francisco Franco (who had risen to prominence as an army officer in the campaign to establish a Spanish protectorate over what became Spanish Morocco), gained the upper hand in the civil war thanks to foreign support, his brutal tactics, and his forging of a broad political coalition of the traditional and radical right.

MILITARIST JAPAN Unlike authoritarian regimes in Europe, Japan's emerging right-wing movement did not suffer wounded power and pride during World War I. In fact, because wartime disruptions reduced European and American competition, Japan expanded production, exporting munitions, textiles, and consumer goods to Asian and western markets. During the war, the Japanese gross national product (GNP) grew 40 percent, and the country built the world's third-largest navy. After a devastating earthquake and fire in 1923, Tokyo was rebuilt with steel and reinforced concrete, symbolizing the new, modern Japan.

Initially, post–World War I Japan seemed headed down the liberal democratic road. Mass political parties and expanded suffrage in 1925 increased the electorate roughly fourfold. But along with democratization came repressive measures. Although the Meiji Constitution remained in effect, a new Peace Preservation Law specified up to ten years' hard labor for any member of an organization advocating change in the political system or abolition of private property. The law served as a club against the mass leftist parties.

Japan veered from the liberal democratic road after Emperor Hirohito came to power in 1926. Here, as in Germany, the Great Depression spurred the eventual shift to dictatorship. Japan's trade with the outside world had more than tripled between 1913 and 1929, but after 1929 China and the United States imposed barriers on Japanese exports in preference for domestic products. These measures contributed to a 50 percent decline in Japanese exports, and unemployment surged. Such turmoil invited calls for stronger leadership, which military commanders were eager to provide. As in Germany and Italy, Japanese rulers dreamed of empire to defend the homeland against rivals.

It was in the Japanese Empire that militarism and expansionism received a boost. In 1931, a group of army officers arranged an explosion on the Japanese-owned South Manchurian Railroad as a pretext for taking over Manchuria. In 1932, Japan added Manchuria to its Korean and Taiwanese colonies, proclaiming the puppet state of Manchukuo. (See Map 19.6.) In response, the League of Nations imposed sanctions on Japanese aggression—which led the Japanese to withdraw from the League and contribute

Hirohito. A portrait of Crown Prince Hirohito of Japan in 1925, the year before he ascended the Japanese throne. Hirohito presided over Japan's war in Asia, beginning with the 1931 seizure of Manchuria and culminating in the 1945 surrender, but he remained emperor for another four decades. When he died in 1989, his wartime responsibility was still a difficult subject for many.

to the crumbling of the feeble postwar order. (See Global Themes and Sources: Primary Source 19.4.) Meanwhile, at home, "patriotic societies" waged a campaign of terror against uncooperative businessmen and critics of the military. By 1940, Hirohito and his closest advisers had merged all political parties into the Imperial Rule Association, ending even the semblance of democracy, and they advocated a form of racial purity. The Imperial Army divided Asian peoples into "master races," "friendly races," and "guest races," reserving a dominant position for the Japanese "Yamato Race."

COMMON FEATURES OF AUTHORITARIAN REGIMES

Despite important differences, the major authoritarian regimes—the communist Soviet Union, fascist Italy, Nazi Germany, and militarist Japan—shared many traits. All rejected parliamentary rule and sought to revive their country's power through authoritarianism, violence, and a cult of the leader. (See Global Themes and Sources: Primary Source 19.1.)

All claimed that modern economies required state direction. Japan's government fostered huge business conglomerates; Italy's encouraged big business to form cartels. The German state also regarded the private sector as the vehicle of economic growth, but it expected entrepreneurs to support the Nazis' racial, antidemocratic, and expansionist aims. The most thorough economic coordination occurred in the Soviet Union, which adopted American-style mass production while eliminating private enterprise. Instead, the Soviet state owned and managed all the country's industry.

Another common feature involved using mass organizations for state purposes. The Soviet Union, Italy, and Germany had single mass parties; Japan had various rightist groups until the 1940 merger. All promoted dynamic youth movements, such as the Hitler Youth and the Union of German Girls, the Soviet Communist Youth League, and the Italian squads marching to the anthem "Giovinezza" (Youth). State-organized labor forces replaced independent labor unions.

All these regimes, except the Soviet Union, were ambivalent about women in public roles. Even the Soviets, who claimed to support gender equality, eventually restricted abortion and

Manchurian Incident. Taken from among the throng of Japanese troops, this September 1931 photograph documents the Japanese invasion of Manchuria after the bombing of the South Manchurian Railroad, later known as the Manchurian Incident.

MAP 19.6 | The Japanese Empire in Asia, 1933

Hoping to become a great imperial power like the European states, Japan established numerous colonies and spheres of influence early in the twentieth century.

- What were the main territorial components of the Japanese Empire?
- How far did the Japanese succeed in extending their political influence throughout East Asia?
- According to your reading, what problems did the desire to extend Japanese influence in China present to Japanese leaders?

rewarded mothers who had many children. Officials sought to honor new mothers as a way to repair the loss of so many young men during the Great War. Yet many more women were also entering professional careers, and some were becoming their family's primary wage earners. In Italy, fascist authorities had to accept *la maschetta*—the new woman, or flapper, who wore short skirts, bobbed her hair, smoked cigarettes, and engaged in freer sex. In Japan, the *mogā* or *modangāru* ("modern girl") phenomenon provoked considerable negative comment, but authorities could not suppress it.

Finally, all the dictatorships used violence and terror as tools for remaking the sociopolitical order. The Italians and the Japanese openly arrested political opponents, particularly in their colonies. However, it was the Nazis and the Soviets who filled concentration and labor camps with alleged enemies of the state, whether Jews or supposed counterrevolutionaries.

Still, brutal as these regimes were, their successes in mastering the masses drew envious glances even from those following the liberal democratic road. They also attracted imitators. British and French fascists and communists, though never coming to power, formed national parties and proclaimed support for foreign models. Certain politicians, intellectuals, and labor organizers in South and North America admired Hitler, Lenin, and Stalin. Many hoped to use the methods of mass mobilization and mass violence for their own ends.

The Hybrid Regimes in Latin America

Latin American nations felt the same pressures that produced liberal democratic and authoritarian responses in Europe, the Soviet Union, and Japan. However, Latin American leaders devised solutions that combined democratic and authoritarian elements. What they shared with European and Asian counterparts was the need to cope with the developing effects of the Depression and the breakdown of world trade and finance by shoring up domestic mass consumption and protecting native industries. As elsewhere, governments in Latin America turned inward. But they also aimed to integrate previously excluded and marginal peoples to bring legitimacy to the new order. So, with spreading mass consumption, new Latin American rulers expanded mass politics and fomented nationalism—which took democratic and autocratic forms. One such instance is called corporatism.

ECONOMIC TURMOIL Latin American countries had abstained from fighting in World War I, but their export economies had suffered. As trade plummeted, popular confidence in traditional oligarchic regimes fell, and radical agitation surged. During the war years, trade unionists in Buenos Aires took control of the city's docks, and the women of São Paulo's needle trades inspired Brazil's first general strike. Bolivian tin miners, inspired by events in Russia, proclaimed a full-blown socialist revolution.

As in Europe, Latin American governments stepped in to manage volcanic economic markets. More than in any other region, the Depression battered Latin America's trading and financial systems because they were most dependent on the exports of basic staples, from sugar to wheat, and faced stiff protection or evaporating demand for their commodities. The region, in fact, suffered a double whammy because it had borrowed so much money to invest in infrastructure and expansion. When the world's major banks failed, creditors called in

Hitler Youth. Like the communists in the Soviet Union, the Nazis organized and indoctrinated boys and girls in the hopes of making them strong supporters of the regime. Pictured here are members of the Hitler Youth, about 1939.

their loans from Latin America. This move drove borrowers to default. In response, Latin American governments—with backing from the middle classes, nationalist intellectuals, and urban workers—turned to their domestic rather than foreign markets as the main engine of growth. Here, too, the state took on a more interventionist role in market activity than it was expected to do under the model of classical liberalism.

After the war, Latin American elites confronted the age of mass politics by establishing mass parties and encouraging interest groups to associate with them. Collective bodies such as chambers of commerce, trade unions, peasant associations, and organizations for minorities like Blacks and Indigenous people all operated with state sponsorship. This form of modern politics, often labeled corporatist, used social groups to bridge the gap between ruling elites and the general population.

CORPORATIST POLITICS IN BRAZIL Corporatist politics took hold especially in Brazil, where the Old Republic collapsed in 1930. In its place, a coalition led by the skilled politician Getúlio Vargas (1883–1954) cultivated a strong following by enacting socially popular reforms.

Dubbing himself the "father of the poor," Vargas encouraged workers to organize, erected monuments to national heroes, and supported the building of schools and the paving of roads. Striving to appeal to Black Brazilians, who had been excluded from public life since the abolition of slavery, he legalized many previously forbidden Afro-Brazilian practices, such as the ritual *candomblé* dance, whose African and martial overtones seemed threatening to White elites. Vargas also supported samba schools, organizations that not only taught popular dances but also raised funds for public works. Moreover, Vargas addressed maternity and housing policies and enfranchised women (although they had to be able to read, as did male voters). Although he condemned the old elites for betraying the country to serve the interests of foreign consumers and investors, he arranged foreign funding and developed plans with foreign technical advisers to build steel mills and factories. However, he promoted domestic industry so that Brazil would not be so dependent on imports.

Ruling as a patriarch enabled Vargas to squelch dissent and build new lines of loyalty. When he revamped the constitution in 1937, he banned competitive political parties and created forms of national representation along corporatist lines. Each social sector, or class, would be represented by its function in society (for example, as workers, industrialists, or educators), and each would pledge allegiance to the all-powerful state. Although his opponents complained about losing democratic rights, Vargas also created rights for previously excluded groups like trade unions, which now could use their corporatist representatives to press for demands. One demand was to secure rights to basic economic needs, like food and shelter. To bolster the system, he employed a small army of modern propagandists who used billboards, loudspeakers, and radio to broadcast the benevolence of "Father" Vargas. Among this campaign's objectives was the persecution of "speculators" and "oligarchs" who were believed to deprive Brazilian workers of their basic social rights. The "father of the poor" in turn protected national industries that produced manufactured goods for popular consumption. In this way, Vargas's corporatist aims created a new alliance of consuming commoners and new industrialists to eclipse the old rural order.

Getúlio Vargas. This cartoon of Vargas, governor of the southern state of Rio Grande do Sul, portrays him as a country bumpkin even as he leads the way in overthrowing Brazil's Old Republic.

Samba Dancers. The dance started in the shanty towns of Rio de Janeiro and eventually became popular throughout the world, thanks to films, photographs, and long-playing records that featured samba music.

The Vargas appeal had echoes around a world struggling with economic depression and scarcity. Fueled by nationalism, policies protected domestic markets and tried to secure impoverished workers. The same kinds of claims were voiced in the colonial worlds of Africa and Asia. But here the fact that colonial peoples had no access to the instruments of a national government meant that their welfare demands went unanswered and heightened anticolonialism.

Anticolonial Visions of Modern Life

The changes in the world economy highlighted colonial inequalities. Lack of access to consumer goods and other aspects of mass society turned the spotlight on local disparities and fueled nationalist protest movements. Mostly, the leading parties represented the aspirations of the educated and well-off, seeking a way of life like that of developed societies. But individuals like Gandhi and anticolonial socialists and communists championed the interests of the poor and spurned the desires of the middle classes. Increasingly, anticolonial movements assumed the forms of mass politics seen worldwide, with political parties, trade unions, street protest, and consumer boycotts spreading.

The Great War cast a massive pall over Europe's civilizing mission. The war, the recovery, and the subsequent Depression forced empires to double down on their colonies to extract wealth at the very same time that colonial subjects were embracing mass politics. The result was the beginning of a global uprising against Europe's empires and the ripening of anticolonial alternative visions.

Debates over liberal democratic versus authoritarian models engaged the world's colonial and semicolonial regions. But in Asia and Africa there was a larger concern: what to do about colonial authority. Throughout Asia, most educated people wanted to roll back the European and American imperial presence. Some Asians even accepted Japanese imperialism as an antidote, under the slogan "Asia for the Asians." In Africa, intellectuals questioned whether the British and the French were sincerely committed to African improvement or were instead obstacles to African peoples' well-being. (See again Current Trends in World History: Population Movements: Filling Up the Empty Spaces and Spreading Capitalism.)

In Africa as well as Asia, anticolonialism was the preeminent vision. To overcome the contradictions of European democratic liberalism, educated Asians and Africans proposed various forms of nationalism.

Behind the Asian and African nationalist movements were profound disagreements about how best to govern nations once they gained independence and how to define citizenship. For many intellectuals, the imperial powers' democratic ethos was appealing. Others liked the radical authoritarianism of fascism and communism, with their promises of a rapid leap to modernity. Whatever their political preferences, most literate colonials also regarded their own religious and cultural traditions as sources for political mobilization. Thus, Muslim, Hindu, Chinese, and African values were part of nationalist campaigns as leaders appealed for support from the rank and file. The colonial figures involved in political and intellectual movements insisted that the societies they sought to establish were going to be modern *and* at the same time retain their indigenous characteristics.

SUB-SAHARAN AFRICAN STIRRINGS Africa contained the most recent territories to come under the Europeans' control, so anticolonial nationalist movements there were quite young. After 1918, African peoples probed more deeply for the meaning of Europe's imperial presence.

In some regions, environmental degradation contributed to the resentment. In the peanut belt of Senegal, for example, African cultivators pushed into more arid regions, cutting down trees and eventually exhausting the soil. In Kenya, where African peoples were confined to specific locations to make land available to European settlers, Africans began to overgraze and overcultivate their lands. A severe problem occurred among the Kamba people living near Nairobi. Their herds had become so large that the government attempted to implement a forcible campaign of culling. Refusing to cooperate, the Kamba joined the chorus of African protesters against British authority.

There was some room (but not much) for voicing African interests under colonialism. The French had long sought to assimilate their colonial peoples into French culture. In France's primary West African colony, Senegal, four coastal cities had traditionally elected one delegate (of mixed African and European ancestry) to the French National Assembly. This practice lasted until 1914, when Blaise Diagne (1872–1934), an African candidate, ran for election to the Assembly and won, invoking his African origins and garnering the African vote. While the British allowed Africans to elect delegates to municipal bodies, they refused to permit colonial representatives to sit in Parliament. Committed to democracy at home, the European powers remained steadfastly against it in their colonies.

Excluded from representative bodies, Africans experimented with various forms of protest, but such opposition ran up against not only colonial administrators but also western-educated African elites. Yet even this privileged group began reconsidering its relationship to colonial authorities. In Kenya, immediately after World War I, a contingent of mission-educated Africans called on the British to provide more and better schools and to return lands they claimed European settlers had stolen. The young nationalists drew important lessons from their confrontation with the authorities. Their new spokesperson, Jomo Kenyatta (1898–1978), invoked their precolonial Kikuyu traditions as a basis for resisting colonialism. These early anticolonial movements laid

Blaise Diagne. Diagne was the first African elected to the French National Assembly. He won the election to the French parliament in 1914, beating White and mixed-race candidates by appealing to the majority-Black African population that lived in the four communes of Senegal.

the foundations for more widespread resistance to colonial rule after World War II.

IMAGINING AN INDIAN NATION As Africans explored the use of modern politics against Europeans, in India opposition took a different form. World War I and its aftermath brought full-blown challenges to British rule. Indeed, the Indian nationalist challenge provided inspiration for other anticolonial movements.

For over a century, Indians had heard British authorities extol the virtues of parliamentary government, yet they were excluded from participation. In 1919, the British slightly enlarged the franchise in India and allowed more local self-government, but these moves did not satisfy Indians' nationalist longings. During the 1920s and 1930s, the nationalists, led by **Mohandas Karamchand (Mahatma) Gandhi** (1869–1948), laid the foundations for an alternative, anticolonial movement.

GANDHI AND NONVIOLENT RESISTANCE Gandhi had studied law in England and had worked in South Africa on behalf of Indian immigrants before returning to India in 1915. Thereafter, he assumed leadership in local struggles and became the focus of the Indian nationalist movement. He also spelled out the moral and political philosophy of *satyagraha,* or **nonviolent resistance**, which he had developed while in South Africa. His message to Indians was simple: develop your own resources and inner strength and control the instincts and activities that encourage participation in colonial economy and government, and you shall achieve *swaraj* ("self-rule"). Faced with Indian self-reliance and self-control pursued nonviolently, Gandhi claimed, the British eventually would have to leave.

The Amritsar massacre (discussed earlier in this chapter) and other conflicts spurred the nationalists to oppose cooperation with government officials, to boycott goods made in Britain, to refuse to send their children to British schools, and to withhold taxes. Gandhi added his voice, calling for an all-India *satyagraha*. He also formed an alliance with Muslim leaders and began turning the Indian National Congress from an elite organization of lawyers and merchants into a mass organization open to anyone who paid modest dues, including the illiterate and the poor.

When the Depression struck India in 1930, Gandhi singled out salt as a testing ground for his ideas on civil disobedience. Every Indian used salt, whose production was a heavily taxed government monopoly. Thus, salt symbolized the Indians' subjugation to a colonial government. To break that monopoly, Gandhi began a 240-mile march from western India to the coast to gather sea salt for free. Accompanying him were seventy-one followers representing different regions and religions of India. News wire services and mass-circulation newspapers worldwide reported on the drama of the sixty-one-year-old Gandhi, wooden staff in hand, dressed in coarse homespun garments, leading the march. Thousands of people gathering en route were moved by the sight of the frail apostle of nonviolence encouraging them to seek independence from colonial rule. The air thickened with tension as observers speculated on the British reaction to Gandhi's arrival at the sea. After nearly three weeks of walking, Gandhi waded into the surf, picked up a lump of natural salt, held it high, confessed that he had broken the salt law, and invited every Indian to do the same.

Inspired by Gandhi's example, millions of Indians joined strikes, boycotted foreign goods, and substituted indigenous hand-woven cloth for imported textiles. Many Indian officials in the colonial administration resigned in solidarity. The colonizers were taken aback by the mass mobilization. Yet British denunciations of Gandhi only added to his personal aura and to the anticolonial crusade. By insisting that Indians follow their conscience (always through nonviolent protest), by exciting the masses through his defiance of colonial power, and by using symbols like homespun cloth to counter foreign, machine-spun textiles, Gandhi instilled in the people a sense of pride, resourcefulness, and Indian national awareness.

A DIVIDED ANTICOLONIAL MOVEMENT Unlike the charismatic authoritarians who dominated Italy, Germany, and Russia, Gandhi did not aspire to dictatorial power. Moreover, his program met opposition from within, for not everyone shared his vision of a unified national community as the source of public life. As elsewhere, the winds of modern social change were blowing in new ideologies and aspirations. Cambridge-educated Jawaharlal Nehru (1889–1964), for example, believed that only by embracing science and technology could India develop as a modern nation. And radical activists wanted revolution, not peaceful protest. These activists organized rural peasants and the growing industrial proletariat in the cities to overthrow colonial domination.

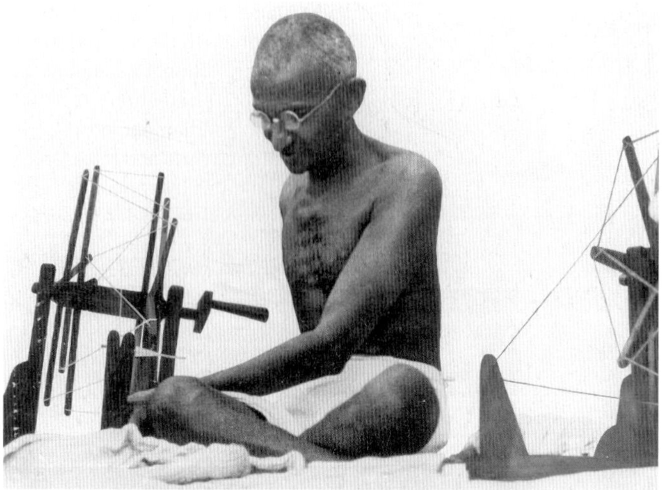

Gandhi and the Road to Independence. *Left:* Gandhi launched a civil disobedience movement in 1930 by defying the British government's tax on salt. Calling it "the most inhuman poll tax the ingenuity of man can devise," Gandhi, accompanied by his followers, set out on a monthlong march on foot covering 240 miles to Dandi, on the Gujarat coast. The picture shows Gandhi arriving at the sea, where he and his followers broke the law by scooping up handfuls of salt. *Right:* Gandhi believed that India had been colonized by becoming enslaved to modern industrial civilization. Indians would achieve independence, he argued, when they became self-reliant. Thus, he made the spinning wheel a symbol of *swaraj* and handspun cloth the virtual uniform of the nation.

Their stress on class conflict ran against Gandhi's ideals of national unity.

The era of mass politics brought lower castes and Dalits ("untouchables") onto the public stage, where they demanded an end to caste discrimination. This demand was articulated most powerfully by the brilliant Dalit leader B. R. Ambedkar. Born in 1891 to a poor family of the "untouchable" caste, Ambedkar graduated from Bombay University in 1912 and earned doctorates from Columbia University and the London School of Economics in the 1920s. On his return to India, he emerged as the most important Dalit leader and engaged Gandhi in a fierce debate over the relationship between caste and the nation. Gandhi argued that the unity of Hindu society, which included the Dalits, formed the bedrock of national unity. Ambedkar responded that the achievement of national unity demanded a rejection of Hinduism, which divided the society into castes and perpetuated social discrimination. Only social equality and democracy, not a caste-ridden Hindu society, could build nationhood, he claimed. The removal of Dalits' civil disabilities, such as untouchability and prohibition from entry into temples, that Gandhi proposed was not the answer. What was required, Ambedkar insisted, was the wholesale destruction of the caste system.

Religion, too, threatened to fracture Gandhi's hope for anticolonial unity. The Hindu-Muslim alliance crafted by nationalists in the early 1920s splintered over who represented them and how to ensure their political rights. The Muslim community found a leader in Muhammad Ali Jinnah, who set about making the Muslim League the sole representative organization of the Muslim community. In 1940, the Muslim League passed a resolution demanding independent Muslim states in provinces where Muslims constituted a majority, on the grounds that they were not a religious minority of the Indian nation, but a nation themselves.

Hindus also sought a political role on the basis of religious identity. Leaders committed to revitalizing Hinduism began organizing Hindus as a religious nation. Hindu symbols and a Hindu ethos colored the fabric of Indian nationalism woven by Gandhi and the Indian National Congress Party.

A further challenge came from women. Long-standing efforts to "uplift" women now escalated into a demand for women's rights, including suffrage. Following the formation of the All India Women's Conference in 1927, activists addressed issues relating to women's work, health, employment, education, and literacy and demanded legislative seats for women. The Indian National Congress Party, however, elevated its nationalist agenda above women's demands, just as it had done in dealing with the lower castes and the relations between Hindus and Muslims.

In 1937, the British belatedly granted India provincial assemblies, a bicameral (two-chamber) national legislature, and a self-governing executive. By then, however, India's people were deeply politicized. The Indian Congress Party, which inspired the masses to overthrow British rule, struggled to incorporate divergent ideologies and new political institutions, such as labor unions, peasant associations, religious parties, and communal organizations. Seeking a path to economic modernization, Gandhi, on one side, envisioned independent India as an updated collection of village republics organized around the benevolent authority of male-dominated households.

Gandhi and Nehru Sharing a Light Moment. Despite their divergent views on modernity, Gandhi was personally close to Nehru, who was his chosen political heir.

Nehru, on another side, hoped for a socioeconomic transformation powered by science and state-sponsored planning. Both believed that India's traditions of collective welfare and humane religious and philosophical practices set it apart from the modern west. By the outbreak of World War II, India was well on its way toward political independence, but British policies and India's divisions foretold a violent end to imperial rule (see Chapter 20).

CHINESE NATIONALISM Unlike India and Africa, China was never formally colonized. But foreign powers' "concession areas" on Chinese soil compromised its sovereignty. Indeed, foreign nationals living in China enjoyed many privileges, including immunity from Chinese law. Furthermore, unequal treaties imposed on the Qing government had robbed China of its customs and tariff autonomy. Thus, Chinese nationalists' vision of a modern alternative echoed that of Indian nationalists: ridding the nation of foreign domination was the initial condition of national fulfillment. For many, the 1911 Revolution (as the fall of the Qing dynasty came to be known; see Chapter 18) symbolized the first step toward transforming a crumbling agrarian empire into a modern nation.

Despite high hopes, the new republic could not establish legitimacy. For one thing, factional and regional conflicts made the government little more than a loose alliance of gentry, merchants, and military leaders. Its intellectual inspiration came from the ideas of the nationalist leader Sun Yat-sen. In 1912, after the Qing emperor stepped down, a military strongman, Yuan Shikai, forced Sun Yat-sen to concede the presidency to him. Although Sun had organized his followers into a political party, the Guomindang, Yuan dismissed all efforts to further democracy and dissolved the parliament. Only Yuan's death in 1916 ended his attempt to establish a new personal dynasty.

The republic endured another blow when the Treaty of Versailles awarded Germany's old concession rights in the Shandong Peninsula to Japan. On May 4, 1919, thousands of Chinese students demonstrated in Beijing. As the protests spread to other cities, students appealed to workers and merchants to join their ranks. In what became known as the May Fourth movement, workers went on strike and merchants closed shops. Across the country, the Chinese boycotted Japanese goods.

As the Guomindang, still led by Sun Yat-sen, tried to rejuvenate itself, it looked to students and workers as well as the Russian Revolution for inspiration. Under the banner of anti-imperialism, the reorganized party sponsored mass organizations of workers' unions, peasant leagues, and women's associations.

In 1926, amid a renewed tide of antiforeign agitation, **Chiang Kai-shek** (1887–1975) seized control of the party following Sun's death. Chiang launched a partially successful military campaign to reunify the country and established a new national government in 1928 with its capital in Nanjing.

Chiang, like his Chinese communist rivals, believed that the Chinese masses had to be mobilized in order for China to succeed as a modern nation and escape colonial rule. The New Life movement, launched with a torchlight parade in 1934 in Nanchang, exemplified his aspiration for a new Chinese national consciousness. Drawing on diverse ideas (from Confucian precepts to social Darwinism) and fascist practices such as the militarization of everyday life in the name of sacrificing for the nation, the movement aimed to instill discipline and moral purpose into a unified citizenry. It promoted dress codes for women, condemned casual sexual liaisons, and campaigned against spitting, urinating, and smoking in public.

PEASANT POPULISM IN CHINA: WHITE WOLF For many Guomindang leaders, the peasant population represented a backward class. Thus, the leadership failed to tap into the revolutionary potential of the countryside, which was alive with grassroots movements such as that of White Wolf.

Chiang Kai-shek. Riding the current of anti-imperialism, Chiang Kai-shek, shown here in 1924 in military dress, led the Guomindang on a military campaign in 1926–1928 and seized power, establishing a new national government based in Nanjing.

From late 1913 to 1914, Chinese newspapers circulated reports about a roving band of armed men led by a mysterious figure known as White Wolf said to have almost magical power. It is unlikely that the band, rumored to have close to a million followers, had more than 20,000 members at its height. But the White Wolf movement's impact reverberated well beyond its physical presence.

Popular myth depicted White Wolf's mission to rid the country of injustice. The band was known to raid major trade routes and market towns. It was said that once the band captured a town, "cash and notes were flung out to the poor." Such stories won the White Wolf army many followers in rural China. Although the army lacked the power to restore order to the countryside, its presence reflected the changing market forces that had come to China. For example, in the northwestern province of Shaanxi (Shensi), where the band held its most famous march, markets that formerly flourished with trade in Chinese cotton now awaited cotton bales shipped from Fall River, Massachusetts.

A POSTIMPERIAL TURKISH NATION Of all the postwar anticolonial movements, none was more successful or more committed to European models than that of **Mustafa Kemal Ataturk** (1881–1938), who helped forge the modern Turkish nation-state. Until 1914, the Ottoman Empire was a colonial power in its own right. But having fought on the losing German side, it saw its realm shrink to a part of Anatolia under the Treaty of Sèvres, which ended the war between the Allies and the Ottoman Empire.

Some of its former territories, such as those in southern Europe, became independent states; others, such as those in the Middle East, came under British and French administration as mandates of the League of Nations. Fearing that the rest of the empire would be colonized, Ottoman military leaders, many of whom had resisted Turkish nationalism, now embraced the cause. What made modern Turkish nationalism so successful was its ability to convert the mainstay of the old regime, the army, to the goal of creating a Turkish nation-state. These men, in turn, mobilized the masses and launched a state-led drive for modernity.

In 1920, an Ottoman army officer and military hero named Mustafa Kemal harnessed this groundswell of Turkish nationalism into opposition to Greek troops who had been sent to enforce the peace treaty. Rallying his own troops to defend the fledgling Turkish nation, Kemal reconquered most of Anatolia and the area around Istanbul and secured international recognition for the new state in 1923 in the Treaty of Lausanne. Thereafter, a forcible exchange of populations occurred. Approximately 1.2 million Greek Christians left Turkey to settle in Greece, and 400,000 Muslims relocated from Greece to Turkey.

With the Ottoman Empire gone, Kemal and his followers moved to build a state based on Turkish national consciousness. First they deposed the sultan. Then they abolished the Ottoman caliphate and proclaimed Turkey a republic, whose supreme authority would be an elected House of Assembly. Later, after Kemal insisted that the people adopt European-style surnames, the assembly conferred on Kemal the mythic name Ataturk, "father of the Turks."

In forging a Turkish nation, Kemal looked to construct a European-style secular state and to eliminate Islam's hold over civil and political affairs. The Turkish elite replaced Muslim religious law with the Swiss civil code, instituted the western (Christian) calendar, and abolished the once-powerful dervish religious orders. They also suppressed Arabic and Persian words from Turkish, substituted Roman script for Arabic letters, forbade polygamy, made wearing the fez (a brimless cap) a crime, and instructed Turks to wear European-style hats. The veil, though not outlawed, was denounced as a relic. In 1934, the government enfranchised Turkish women, granted them property rights in marriage and inheritance, and allowed them to enter the professions. Schools, too, were placed under state control and, along with military service, became the chief instrument for making the masses conscious of belonging to a Turkish nation. Yet many villagers did not accept Ataturk's non-Islamic nationalism, remaining devoted to Islam and resentful of the prohibitions against dervish dancing.

Ataturk. In the 1920s, Mustafa Kemal, known as Ataturk, introduced the Latin alphabet for the Turkish language as part of his campaign to modernize and secularize Turkey. He underscored his commitment to change by having a photographer record his demonstration of the new alphabet.

In imitating Europe, Kemal borrowed many of its antidemocratic models. Inspired by the Soviets, he inaugurated a five-year plan for the economy emphasizing centralized coordination. Turkish nationalists also drew on Nazi examples by advocating racial theories that posited central Asian Turks as the founders of all civilizations. In another authoritarian move, Kemal occasionally rigged parliamentary elections, while using the police and judiciary to silence his critics. The Kemalist revolution in Turkey was the most far-reaching and enduring transformation that had occurred outside Europe and the Americas up to that point. It offered an important model for the founding of secular, authoritarian states in the Islamic world.

NATIONALISM AND THE RISE OF THE MUSLIM BROTHERHOOD IN EGYPT Elsewhere in the Middle East, where France and Britain had expanded their holdings at the Ottomans' expense, anticolonial movements borrowed from European models while putting their own stamp on nation-making and modernization campaigns. In Egypt, British occupation predated the fall of the Ottoman Empire, but here, too, World War I energized the forces of anticolonial nationalism.

When the war ended, Sa'd Zaghlul (1857–1927), an educated Egyptian patriot, pressed for an Egyptian delegation to attend the peace conference at Versailles. He hoped to present Egypt's case for national independence. Instead, British officials arrested and exiled him and his most vocal supporters. When news of this action came out, the country burst into revolt. Rural rebels broke away from the central government, proclaiming local republics. Villagers tore up railway lines and telegraph wires, the symbols of British authority.

After defusing the conflict, British authorities tried to mollify Egyptian sensibilities. In 1922, Britain proclaimed Egypt independent, though it retained the right to station British troops on Egyptian soil. Ostensibly, this provision would protect traffic through the Suez Canal and foreign populations residing in Egypt, but it also enabled the British to continue influencing Egyptian politics. Two years later, elections placed Zaghlul's nationalist party, the Wafd, in office. But the British prevented the Wafd from exercising real power.

This subversion of independence and democracy provided an opening for antiliberal variants of anticolonialism. During the Depression years, a fascist group, Young Egypt, garnered wide appeal. Much more influential and destined to have an enduring influence throughout the Arab world was an Islamic group founded in 1928, the Muslim Brotherhood, which attacked liberal democracy as a façade for middle-class, business, and landowning interests. The Muslim Brotherhood was anticolonial and anti-British, but its members considered mere political independence insufficient. Egyptians, they argued, must also renounce the lure of the west (whether liberal capitalism or "godless" communism) and return to a purified form of Islam. For the Muslim Brotherhood, Islam offered a complete way of life. A "return to Islam" through the nation-state created yet another model of modernity for colonial and semicolonial peoples.

Conclusion

The Great War and its aftermath accelerated both the trend toward mass society in a broad range of activities and the debate over how to define progress and organize the people. Because mass society meant production and consumption on a staggering scale, satisfying the populace became a pressing concern for rulers worldwide. Competing programs vied for ascendancy in the new, broader, public domain.

Most programs fell into one of three categories: liberal democratic, authoritarian, or anticolonial. Liberal democracy defined the political and economic systems in most of western Europe and the Americas in the decade following World War I. Resting on faith in free enterprise and representative democracy (with a restricted franchise), liberal regimes had already been unsettled before the Great War. Turn-of-the-century reforms broadened electorates and brought government oversight and regulation into private economic activity. But during the Great Depression, dissatisfaction again deepened. Only far-reaching reforms, introducing greater regulation and more aggressive government intervention to provide for the citizenry's welfare, saved capitalist economies and democratic political systems in Britain, France, and North America from collapse.

Through the 1930s, liberal democracy was in retreat. Authoritarianism seemed better positioned to satisfy the masses while representing the dynamism of modernity. While authoritarians differed about the faults of capitalism, they joined in the condemnation of electoral democracy. Authoritarians mobilized the masses to put the interests of the nation above the individual. That mobilization often involved brutal repression, yet it seemed also to restore pride and purpose to ordinary people.

Meanwhile, the colonial and semicolonial world searched for ways to escape European domination. In Asia and Africa, anticolonial leaders sought to eliminate foreign rule while turning colonies into nations and subjects into citizens. Some looked to the liberal democratic west for models of nation building, but others rejected liberalism because it was associated with colonial rule. Instead, socialism, fascism, and a return to religious traditions offered more promising paths.

The two decades after the end of World War I brought great political upheavals and deep economic dislocations. At times, powerful states stood behind the competition between liberal democracy, authoritarianism (both right and left), and anticolonial nationalism. Yet the traumas were tame compared with what followed with the outbreak in 1939 of World War II.

After You Read This Chapter

TRACING THE GLOBAL STORYLINES

FOCUS ON: World War I and the Growth of Mass Societies

The Great War

- The war destroys empires, starting with the Bolshevik Revolution against the tsarist regime in Russia, followed by the defeat and dissolution of the German, Austro-Hungarian, and Ottoman Empires.
- Mass mobilization sees almost 70 million men join the fighting, undermines traditional gender boundaries, and forces states to recognize their peoples' demands for compensation afterward.
- Mass culture spreads as leaders use the new media of radio and film to promote national loyalties and discredit enemies.
- Liberal democracies in France, Britain, and the United States survive the Great Depression by enacting far-reaching changes in their political systems and free market economies.
- Authoritarian (communist and fascist) dictatorships with many political similarities emerge in the Soviet Union, Italy, Germany, Spain, and Portugal.
- Latin American leaders devise hybrid solutions that combine democratic and authoritarian elements.
- Peoples living under colonial rule in Asia and Africa mobilize traditional values to oppose imperial rulers.
- Key individuals emerge in the struggle to define newly independent nations: Kenyatta, Gandhi, Chiang Kai-shek, and Ataturk.

CHRONOLOGY

The Americas
- United States enters World War I 1917

Europe
- World War I 1914–1918
- Mussolini takes over Italy 1922

Soviet Union
- Bolshevik Revolution 1917
- Russian civil war 1918–1921

East Asia

South Asia

Middle East
- Sykes-Picot Agreement 1916
- Balfour Declaration 1917
- Mustafa Kemal creates modern Turkish nation-state 1

1900 | 1910 | 1920

KEY TERMS

Allied Powers p. 829
Mustafa Kemal Ataturk p. 860
Bolsheviks p. 835
Central Powers p. 829
Chiang Kai-shek p. 859
fascism p. 848
Mohandas Karamchand (Mahatma) Gandhi p. 857
Great Depression p. 842
Great War (World War I) p. 829
Adolf Hitler p. 850
League of Nations p. 836
Benito Mussolini p. 848
Nazis p. 850
New Deal p. 846
nonviolent resistance p. 857
Joseph Stalin p. 847

THINKING ABOUT GLOBAL CONNECTIONS

Thinking about Transformation and Conflict and Visions of the Modern What was the relationship between war and progress in the early twentieth century? What new political, social, and cultural movements grew out of the Great War? Think in particular of the role of former soldiers in politics; the adaptation in peacetime of production practices developed for the war effort; and governments' willingness and ability to regulate the economy and people's everyday lives.

Thinking about Changing Power Relationships and Visions of the Modern What, if anything, was left in this period of the tradition of classical liberalism, which trusted markets to regulate themselves and believed progress would result when individuals pursued their own self-interest? What role did government intervention—in the economy and society—play for the three major traditions discussed in this chapter: liberal democratic, authoritarian, and anticolonial? How central was state intervention to their respective views of progress and modernity?

Thinking about Gender and Visions of the Modern What role did women play in the social transformations of the early twentieth century, both as participants and as symbols? Pay special attention to the role of women workers in war production and, increasingly, in professional careers thereafter; to women consumers in an era of mass production; and to governments' commitment to the ideal of gender equality and their (faltering) willingness to abide by that ideal.

Go to INQUIZITIVE to see what you've learned—and learn what you've missed—with personalized feedback along the way.

- Great Depression begins 1929
- Vargas becomes leader of Brazil 1930
- New Deal reforms (United States) 1933–1941
- Hitler takes over Germany 1933
- Popular Front rules France 1936–1939
- Collectivization and Five-Year Plans instituted 1928–1935
- Political purges 1936–1938
- Chiang Kai-shek becomes leader of China 1928
- Japan annexes Manchuria 1932
- Gandhi's Salt March 1930
- Muslim Brotherhood founded in Egypt 1928

1930 | 1940 | 1950

Global Themes and Sources

Comparing and Contextualizing Totalitarianism

The term *totalitarianism* emerged in the early twentieth century to refer to regimes that aspired to intervene more directly into people's everyday lives than previous dictatorships had done. While some writers gave the term a positive meaning, most used it critically, to condemn the erosion of basic freedoms. During the Cold War, anticommunist intellectuals in Europe and the United States linked Nazi Germany and the Soviet Union, and sometimes imperial Japan, and contrasted them with the "free world" of liberal democracies. Since the end of the Cold War, historians have largely abandoned the term, calling attention to the notable differences between Nazi Germany and the Soviet Union and to the role of ordinary people in policing one another in all the interwar dictatorships.

Hannah Arendt gave classic expression to the term *totalitarianism* in her 1951 *Origins of Totalitarianism*. The next two sources provide a more ambivalent view of state power: the letter to Marfa Gudzia shows one woman shaming another in Soviet Magnitogorsk for her husband's supposed failure as a worker and a man, while Victor Klemperer's diary shows ordinary Germans uninterested in Nazi propaganda. The final document demonstrates the Japanese militarist state's open aggression to pursue their own interests knowing the declining League of Nations would not be able to stop them.

These sources invite you to compare and contextualize. Each provides a different window into the workings of power in authoritarian dictatorships. To what degree did the governments impose their will on their people? What space, if any, for resistance, was left?

ANALYZING THE CONTEXT OF TOTALITARIANISM

How does Arendt's view of totalitarianism apply to the three subsequent documents?

What role do ordinary people play in supporting or resisting the regime in the second and third documents?

Identify the nature and limits of state power in the final three documents.

PRIMARY SOURCE 19.1

The Origins of Totalitarianism (1951), Hannah Arendt

One of the most influential political philosophers of the twentieth century, Hannah Arendt (1906–1975), a Jew, fled Nazi Germany in 1933 and ultimately settled in the United States, where she received American citizenship in 1950. Her first major book, *The Origins of Totalitarianism*, linked Nazi Germany and the Soviet Union.

Arendt claims that totalitarianism marks a fundamentally new form of politics. On what grounds does she make this claim?

Explain the significance of the private sphere—"the whole sphere of private life"—in this passage.

What is the relationship between ruler and ruled in this excerpt?

The question we raised at the start of these considerations and to which we now return is what kind of basic experience in the living-together of men permeates a form of government whose essence is terror and whose principle of action is the logicality of ideological thinking. That such a combination was never used before in the varied forms of political domination is obvious. Still, the basic experience on which it rests must be human and known to men, insofar as even this most "original" of all political bodies has been devised by, and is somehow answering the needs of, men.

It has frequently been observed that terror can rule absolutely only over men who are isolated against each other and that, therefore, one of the primary concerns of all tyrannical government is to bring this isolation about. Isolation may be the beginning of terror; it certainly is its most fertile ground; it always is its result. This isolation is, as it were, pretotalitarian; its hallmark is impotence insofar as power always comes from men acting together, "acting in concert" ([Edmund] Burke); isolated men are powerless by definition.

Isolation and impotence, that is the fundamental inability to act at all, have always been characteristic of tyrannies. Political contacts between men are severed in tyrannical government and the human capacities for action and power are frustrated. But not all contacts between men are broken and not all human capacities destroyed. The whole sphere of private life with the capacities for experience, fabrication and thought are left intact. We know that the iron band of total terror leaves no space for such private life and that the self-coercion of totalitarian logic destroys man's capacity for experience and thought just as certainly as his capacity for action.

Source: Hannah Arendt, *The Origins of Totalitarianism* (1951; repr., San Diego: Harcourt Brace, 1973), p. 474.

PRIMARY SOURCE 19.2

Letter to Marfa Gudzia (1930s)

In this letter, a woman named Anna Kovaleva, wife of the best locomotive driver in the Soviet factory town of Magnitogorsk, writes to Marfa Gudzia, the wife of the worst, to criticize her for her husband's many shortcomings.

Analyze the role of gender in this document. What is the source of Kovaleva's pride? How does she contribute to society?

How does state power operate in this document?

How did Kovaleva and her husband get their apartment?

Dear Marfa!

We are both wives of locomotive drivers of the rail transport of Magnitka. You probably know that the rail transport workers of the MMK [Magnitogorsk Metallurgical Complex] are not fulfilling the plan, that they are disrupting the supply of the blast furnaces, open hearths, and rolling shops. . . . All the workers of Magnitka accuse our husbands, saying that the rail workers hinder the fulfillment of the [overall] industrial plan. It is offensive, painful, and annoying to hear this. And moreover, it is doubly painful, because all of it is the plain truth. Every day there were stoppages and breakdowns in rail transport. Yet our internal factory transport has everything it needs in order to fulfill the plan. For that, it is necessary to work like the best workers of our country work. Among such shock workers is my husband, Aleksandr Panteleevich Kovalev. He always works like a shock worker, exceeding his norms, while economizing on fuel and lubricating oil. His engine is on profit and loss accounting. . . . My husband trains locomotive drivers' helpers out of unskilled laborers. He takes other locomotive drivers under his wing. . . . My husband receives prizes virtually every month. . . . And I too have won awards. . . .

My husband's locomotive is always clean and well taken care of. You, Marfa, are always complaining that it is difficult for your family to live. And why is that so? Because your husband, Iakov Stepanovich, does not fulfill the plan. He has frequent breakdowns on his locomotive, his locomotive is dirty, and he always overconsumes fuel. Indeed, all the locomotive drivers laugh at him. All the rail workers of Magnitka know him—for the wrong reasons, as the worst driver. By contrast, my husband is known as a shock worker. He is written up and praised in the newspapers. . . . He and I are honored everywhere as shock workers. At the store we get everything without having to wait in queues. We moved to the building for shock workers [*dom udarnika*]. We will get an apartment with rugs, a gramophone, a radio, and other comforts. Now we are being assigned to a new store for shock workers and will receive double rations. . . . Soon the Seventeenth Party Congress of our Bolshevik Party will take place. All rail workers are obliged to work so that Magnitka greets the Congress of Victors at full production capacity.

Therefore, I ask you, Marfa, to talk to your husband heart to heart, read him my letter. You, Marfa, explain to Iakov Stepanovich that he just can't go on working the way he has. Persuade him that he must work honorably, conscientiously, like a shock worker. Teach him to understand the words of comrade Stalin, that work is a matter of honor, glory, valor, and heroism.

You tell him that if he does not correct himself and continues to work poorly, he will be fired and lose his supplies. I will ask my Aleksandr Panteleevich to take your husband in tow, help him improve himself and become a shock worker, earn more. I want you, Marfa, and Iakov Stepanovich to be honored and respected, so that you live as well as we do.

I know that many women, yourself included, will say: "What business is it of a wife to interfere in her husband's work. You live well, so hold your tongue." But it is not like that. . . . We all must help our husbands to fight for the uninterrupted work of transport in the winter. OK enough. You catch my drift. This letter is already long. In conclusion, I'd like to say one thing. It's pretty good to be a wife of a shock worker. It's within our power. Let's get down to the task, amicably. I wait your answer.

Anna Kovaleva

Source: Stephen Kotkin, *Magnetic Mountain: Stalinism as a Civilization* (Berkeley: University of California Press, 1995), pp. 218–19.

PRIMARY SOURCE 19.3

Victor Klemperer's Diary (1938)

Victor Klemperer (1881–1960) was a scholar of the French Enlightenment whose diaries, published in Germany in 1995, shed light on everyday life in Nazi Germany.

According to Klemperer, how did the public respond to Goering's speech?

Based on Klemperer's account, how would you characterize the relationship between rulers and ruled, between the Nazi state and ordinary Germans?

Evaluate the influence of Nazi ideology in this document.

September 11, Sunday

For the third time Georg has remitted 500M to me from the blocked account "of the deceased Frau Maria Kl." My joy is already no longer as great as the first two times. Because this time I was almost counting on the sum. Also it is only a very partial help; also I feel more humiliated than before, since he has not written me a single line since October and replied neither to my letter of condolence nor to my birthday greetings. Nevertheless the sum (which by the way I do not yet have in my hands, and no one knows what is going to happen tomorrow, everything is uncertain and every hour may bring new coercive measures and war), so nevertheless the money is a great relief to me at the moment. Eva was always preaching: Let the Öhlmanns come here during their holiday, then we can go for a trip with Grete. I had vacillated, the Öhlmanns' holiday came to an end, and Grete took the train to Kudowa. In view of the 500M we announced our visit to the Öhlmanns and drove to Leipzig yesterday. Luck with the weather and a very successful drive via Niederwartha, Meissen [. . .]. New rest house in Lonnewitz. Village just before Oschatz, "Long Distance Lorry Drivers' Restaurant." The huge vehicles outside, the huge portions inside. The Party Rally was coming over the loudspeaker. Announcement, the arrival of Field Marshal Goering. Introductory march, roars of triumph, then Goering's speech, about the tremendous rise, affluence, peace and workers' good fortune in Germany, about the absurd lies and hopes of its enemies, constantly interrupted by well-drilled roars of applause. But the most interesting thing about it all was the behavior of the customers, who all came and went, greeting and taking their leave with "Heil Hitler." But no one was listening. I could barely understand the broadcast because a couple of people were playing cards, striking the table with loud thumps, talking very loudly. It was quieter at other tables. One man was writing a postcard, one was writing in his order book, one was reading the newspaper. And landlady and waitress were talking to each other or to the cardplayers. Truly: Not one of a dozen people paid attention to the radio for even a single second, it could just as well have been transmitting silence or a foxtrot from Leipzig.

At the Öhlmanns' by two and then like the last time in early spring coffee and conversation in her little room until six. According to Trude Öhlmann's stories from the Deutsche Bücherei, where they get a great deal of official information, war is virtually certain. The air-raid precautions (we too have just had several practices, blackout, sirens), the preparations for mobilization all point to it. Mood of the public, of the workers in particular, is bad. If I talk to the butcher or the butter man here in Dresden, then there will certainly be peace, but if (as the day before yesterday) I listen to Wolf, the car man, then so many of his mates have been fetched straight from work to the army again: "Things are coming to a head now!" If I read the newspaper, see and hear the film reports, then we're doing soooo well, we love the Führer soo much and sooo unanimously—what is real, what is happening? That's how one experiences history. We know even less about today than about yesterday and no more than about tomorrow.

Source: Victor Klemperer, *I Will Bear Witness: The Diaries of Victor Klemperer*, translated by Martin Chalmers (London: Weidenfeld & Nicolson, 1998) pp. 267–68.

PRIMARY SOURCE 19.4

Japanese Foreign Minister's Speech on Manchuria at League of Nations (1932)

In September 1931, Japanese forces invaded the Chinese territory of Manchuria and created a puppet state. In so doing, they violated a principle of the postwar order, which called for the League of Nations to impose sanctions on countries for their acts of aggression against other countries. When European states sided with Chinese appeals over the annexation of Manchuria at the League of Nations, the Japanese delegation stormed out. In one of his last speeches in Geneva, the Japanese foreign minister, Yosuke Matsuoka, laid out his reasons for Japan's policies.

- How did Japanese rulers view neighboring China?
- How did Matsuoka justify Japan's intervention?
- What were Matsuoka's views of the purpose of the League of Nations?

December 8, 1941

Today, Japan is confronted with grave dangers. Conditions in China are worse than ever, despite the assurance of our Chinese Colleague to the contrary. In a word, Japan is today faced with an appalling situation throughout Eastern Asia, and is fighting single-handed to save the Far East—not to start war in the Far East; far from it. And we are confronting that situation with Soviet Russia still outside the League of Nations.

One speaker referred to nationalism and internationalism. He spoke as though some peoples in Europe were on a higher plane, while the Japanese were on a lower plane. I cannot quite see my way to agree to such a representation of Japan and other Powers. We Japanese, I think, can state, without fear of contradiction, that Japan has in the past contributed to internationalism, if not throughout the world, at least in the Far East, and has contributed to world peace in an indirect way, if not in a direct way. We believe that a real internationalism can only be achieved through a healthy nationalism. We believe it, and if that speaker meant to criticize Japan for holding such belief, I accept the criticism.

Again, several speakers have stated that the League is the lifeline of their existence. This statement is, as I understand it, primarily made for the promotion of the self-interest of each individual Member. In Japan, we entertain a similar notion when we refer to Manchuria. That idea we base first on self-interest, and secondly on that great policy of Japan to which I have had occasion to refer—the maintenance of peace and order in Eastern Asia. Nevertheless, primarily we refer to Manchuria as our lifeline from the standpoint of our own self-interest. I do not claim to know exactly the intentions of these speakers in referring to the "lifeline," but I do say that these gentlemen, when they speak of the League of Nations as their own lifeline, admit that they are speaking primarily from self-interest, and I submit that it is only fair to allow us Japanese to present our case and make contentions based on the self-interests of Japan.

I will say a few words about Manchukuo. As I have already had occasion to point out, the conditions in Manchukuo are improving and the situation compares favorably with that of China proper today. Its administration is working in a better way; its finances are assured; the most difficult question of currency offers no reason for anxiety. Our idea is that the healthy development of Manchukuo will eventually contribute to the attainment of the high object for which the League stands.

Source: Full text of "Japan's case in the Sino-Japanese dispute as presented before the Special session of the Assembly of the League of Nations," https://archive.org/stream/japanscaseinsino00leag/japanscaseinsino00leag_djvu.txt.

Interpreting Visual Evidence

Men, Machines, and Mass Production

Mass production of consumer goods reshaped economies and societies in the early twentieth century. Powered by coal and later electricity, the modern factory transformed work, first in Europe, the United States, and Japan and then, especially from 1950 onwards, around the world. The images gathered here provide several perspectives on mass production and its cult of efficiency—its efforts to streamline, to standardize productive activity, to maximize output and minimize cost—and its consequences for workers.

Large-scale manufacturing on assembly lines demands coordinated action. Engineers like Frederick Winslow Taylor (see Chapter 18) developed the field of "scientific management," the forerunner of ergonomics, to streamline the production process. Rather than shaping production to the needs and desires of skilled workers, Taylor tried to adapt machines and human bodies to one another. He and his followers broke down complex tasks into standardized, repeatable actions and then timed workers, imposing a predictable uniformity and minimizing accidents and error. Gone were the days when farmers organized their days by the light of the sun.

The French inventor-scientist Étienne-Jules Marey (1830–1904) set the stage for the scientific study of labor. He developed stop-action photography in 1882, with a photographic "gun" that took twelve frames per second, which helped pave the way for modern cinema. Here we look at a series of studies of human movement that would influence Taylor and facilitate the study of labor practices around the world.

Inspired by Pablo Picasso and Karl Marx, among others, the Mexican muralist Diego Rivera (1886–1957) was fascinated by labor. His Detroit mural (1923) of the Ford Motor Company depicted workers on an assembly line, celebrating the physical force of cosmopolitan groups of industrial workers. The final two images include a photograph of a Ford assembly line in Detroit and one from a Mitsubishi electric plant in Japan in the 1930s, representing iconic examples of modern factories, with standardized, streamlined production processes powered by electricity and massive machines.

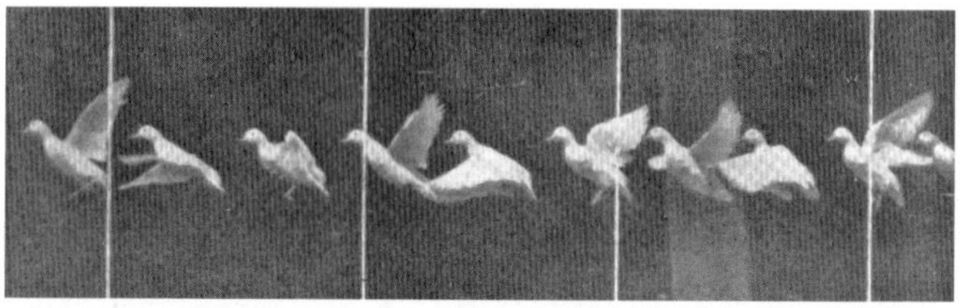

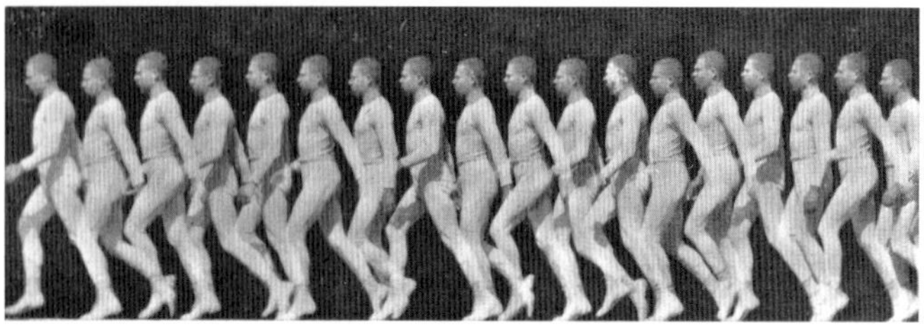

Photographs by Étienne-Jules Marey.

Mural in Detroit by Diego Rivera.

Car assembly line at Ford plant.

Mitsubishi Electric Factory.

QUESTIONS FOR ANALYSIS

1. Describe the relationship between workers and machines in these images, from the point of view of the workers.
2. Explain how engineers like Taylor, who were interested in maximizing production, could also use Marey's images to improve working conditions.
3. Explain the relationship between factory production and factory workers, as depicted in these images, and mass consumption and consumers, as presented in this chapter.
4. On balance, do the images of the human body and industrial work presented here promise alienation or liberation for workers?

Before You Read This Chapter

GLOBAL STORYLINES

World War II and the Emergence of the First, Second, and Third Worlds during the Cold War

- World War II shatters the European-centered global order, weakening Europe and Japan and unsettling empires.
- The United States and its liberal democratic allies (the First World) engage in a cold war with the Soviet Union and its communist allies (the Second World).
- Decolonized states in Asia, Africa, and Latin America (the Third World) struggle to find a "third way" but find themselves caught between rival superpowers.

CHAPTER OUTLINE

20

The Three-World Order

1940–1975

FOCUS QUESTIONS

- How did World War II contribute to the creation of the three-world order after 1945?
- To what extent was World War II a global war?
- What roles did the United States and the Soviet Union play in the Cold War?
- What were the goals of Third World countries during this period, and to what degree were these goals achieved?
- How similar and different were civil rights issues in the First, Second, and Third Worlds? In what ways did each "world" address these and other rights?

In February 1945, the three leaders of the World War II Allies—President Franklin Delano Roosevelt of the United States, Prime Minister Winston Churchill of Great Britain, and Premier Joseph Stalin of the Soviet Union—met to prepare for the postwar world. By then, Germany, Italy, and Japan were losing the war. Reordering would prove deeply contentious, for the three leaders had profoundly different visions. Roosevelt, who envisioned independent nation-states kept at peace by an international body, had no interest in restoring the old European empires. Churchill, however, resisted liquidation of the British Empire. Stalin left no doubt that he intended to secure influence in eastern Europe and Asia and to weaken Germany so that it could never again menace the Soviet Union.

The war had complex and often contradictory effects. All belligerents saw their state powers bolstered to wage a long total war. At the same time, as old empires groaned under the weight of war requirements, demands for freedom spread across Asia and Africa; colonial peoples wanted states of their own. When the fighting finally stopped, it was clear that the European-centered order, shocked by World War I, had been shattered by World War II. But it was not just the European-centered order that was on the ropes; after centuries of carving the world into hierarchies, the very concept of empire had lost its legitimacy. Nation-states filled the void. Moreover, the state's reach had expanded to make war; when the war was over, these capacities were repurposed for postwar reconstruction.

But this new world of nation-states did not mean that all states were alike. Rulers organized into three rough alignments of nation-states, each with ideological underpinnings, which struggled for supremacy in the postwar order. In this chapter, we will use the terms *First World, Second World,* and *Third World* for these groupings; those were the terms used at the time to describe a global geography in which a liberal capitalist ("First") world was opposed both by a communist ("Second") world and a ("Third") world made up largely of postcolonial nations that wanted to assert their right to stand apart from both of the Cold War's major geopolitical blocs.

The war also kindled efforts to make a lasting peace; the treaties that ended the First World War gave rise to the first international peacemaking devices. Despite their differences, the victors of 1945 agreed to give internationalism a new life with new organizations. Institutions, like the United Nations, aimed to restrain new and old nations from wielding their powers for excessively competitive purposes, lest they spin into the ruinous spiral of rivalry of the 1930s.

The result was a delicate balance of rising nationalism and internationalism that framed the contest over a three-world order after 1945. Heading the "First World" was the United States, which with its allies championed capitalism and democracy as the best way to bring unprecedented prosperity in the decades after 1945. Leading the "Second World" was the Soviet Union, the crucial ally of the United States during World War II, which became its chief adversary in the protracted Cold War that followed. As leader of the communist bloc, the Soviet Union contested capitalist societies' claims and trumpeted socialism's accomplishments. Caught in between (and sometimes literally caught in the crossfire when the Cold War turned hot) were formerly colonized and semicolonized people. Lumped together as the "Third World" by western intellectuals and by Asian and African leaders who embraced the idea of an alternative to the dominant blocs, these nations emerged from the war eager to mold the world order to their ideas of freedom.

Competing Blocs

The roots of the world's division into three blocs lay in the breakup of Europe's and Japan's empires and the demise of European world leadership. The destruction of Europe and the defeat of Japan left a power vacuum, which the United States and the Soviet Union rushed to fill. Both believed that their respective systems—capitalism and communism—had universal application. They were now superpowers because of the size of their economies and arsenals, the transcontinental reach of their political influence, and the fact that each embodied a model of civilization applicable to the whole world. As their spheres of influence expanded, they engaged in a bitter ideological rivalry known as the Cold War because no direct military conflict occurred between the superpowers, both of which after 1949 possessed the atomic bomb.

While the capitalist and communist blocs embarked on a cold war, conflicts in the Third World got very hot. In Asia and Africa, anticolonial leaders launched campaigns for independence. Winning popular support by mobilizing deep-seated desires for justice and freedom, they asserted their claims for national independence. Latin American countries, too, sought progress and nationhood. But newfound political freedom did not easily translate into economic development or social equity. Moreover, as the two superpowers looked for allies and client states, they militarized rival states and factions within the Third World.

Each superpower also faced internal problems. Even as the United States maintained that its booming industrial economy, abundant consumer goods, liberal democracy, and vibrant popular culture were proof of capitalism's superiority, the nation also wrestled with racism and became involved in unpopular wars to stop the spread of communism—most notably in Vietnam. The Soviet Union celebrated its own economic prowess and social welfare policies, but it continued to imprison and persecute reformers and dissenters and to operate a command economy, oriented to heavy industrial products and armaments. By the 1960s, the USSR's use of military force to crush socialist reform efforts within the Soviet bloc was undermining communism's allure.

By the 1960s and the early 1970s, tensions were simmering in the three-world order. The United States and the Soviet Union faced discontent within their societies and opposition within their respective blocs. At the same time, the rising economic might of Japan and the other Pacific economies, the emerging clout of oil-rich states, and the specter of radical revolution in Africa, Asia, and Latin America suggested a shift in the balance of wealth and power away from the First and Second Worlds.

World War II and Its Aftermath

World War II grew out of the bitter experiences of both World War I and the failures of the peace. It also resulted from the aggressive ambitions and racial theories of Germany and Japan. Both states sought to impose racial hierarchies through conquest and coerced labor. By the late 1930s, German and Japanese ambitions to become imperial powers brought these conservative dictatorships (which along with Italy constituted the **Axis Powers**) into conflict with France, Britain, the Soviet Union, and eventually the United States (the **Allied Powers**).

Compared to the First World War, the Second World War was more global, stretching across Europe, Africa, and Asia; the Atlantic and the Pacific Oceans; and the Northern and Southern Hemispheres. Belligerents mobilized entire societies, including the colonized, into armed forces and placed enormous demands on civilians. Civilians in places such as India and Greece, Yugoslavia and Korea, Poland and the Philippines suffered terrible hardships, including famines, reprisal killings, and deportations in the course of this war without mercy. Moreover, as aerial bombardment of cities caused colossal civilian casualties, the total war erased the old distinction between soldiers and civilians. Women—as victims and as collaborators, as volunteers and as forced laborers, as workers behind the scenes and as witnesses to the conflict—were involved as never before. They, together with children, the infirm, and the elderly, also swelled the enormous population of refugees seeking safety in the midst of worldwide chaos.

World War II also completed the decline of European world dominance that World War I had set in motion. The unspeakable acts of barbarism perpetrated during the Second World War, including the Nazi genocides directed against Jews and others, robbed Europe of its lingering claims of superiority. In the war's wake, anticolonial movements demanded national self-determination from battered and morally bankrupted European powers.

Kent, 1940. During the Battle of Britain in 1940, English civilians often had to take cover from Nazi bombers at a moment's notice. In this image, originally published in *Life* magazine, the children of hops farmers in the southwestern English county of Kent anxiously watch the skies from a hastily dug air-raid trench.

The War in Europe

World War II began in September 1939 with Germany's invasion of Poland and the British and French decision to oppose it. Before it was all over in 1945, much of Europe, including Germany, had been leveled.

BLITZKRIEG AND TOTAL WAR Germany's early success was staggering. After Germany signed a nonaggression pact with the Soviet Union in August 1939, Nazi troops overran western Poland; the Soviets then invaded from the east and occupied Poland's eastern half. Nazis and Soviet invaders murdered or deported thousands of Poles. Hitler then attacked to the west, sweeping across France, Norway, Denmark, Luxembourg, Belgium, and Holland. Within less than two years, the Germans controlled virtually all of Europe from the English Channel to the Soviet border. (See Map 20.1.) Only Britain escaped Axis control, although Nazi bombers pulverized British cities. Hitler waited to strike to

Leningrad, Winter 1941–1942. Surrounded by German forces for more than 900 days, the city of Leningrad experienced terrible hunger and cold. Here two women brave the bitter cold to collect the remains of a horse that has died in the street—probably from exhaustion and hunger.

MAP 20.1 | World War II: The European Theater

The Axis armies enjoyed great success during the early stages of World War II.

- Which parts of the European theater did the Allies control? The Axis? Which countries were neutral in 1941?
- Where did the major Allied and Axis campaigns take place?
- What was Germany's greatest geographic obstacle during World War II?

the east until June 1941, when Germany broke its pact and invaded the Soviet Union with 170 divisions, 3,000 tanks, and 3.2 million men—an invasion force of a size unmatched before or since. Here, as elsewhere, the Germans fought a *blitzkrieg* ("lightning war") of tank-led assaults followed by motorized infantrymen and then foot soldiers.

The Soviet response was a massive counteroffensive. Stalin threw everything he had into the war. It took a full two years of industrial mobilization and terrible bloodletting before the Soviets could start to push Hitler's army slowly westward. At the Battle of Stalingrad, the German army and its allies suffered 1.5 million men killed, wounded, or captured while 75,000 Soviet troops suffered the same fate. Six months later, the two industrial powerhouses slammed into each other at the Battle of Kursk. The largest tank battle in history, Kursk saw German armored divisions of 2,000 tanks fall to a Soviet tank force twice its size. Before 1944, the Soviets bore the brunt of the European fighting but in turn caused more than 85 percent of all German casualties. The British attacked the Nazis in the air and on the sea and, along with American troops, stopped a German advance across North Africa into Egypt. With Canadians, they launched an offensive from North Africa to drive Axis forces from Italy. The spectacular D-Day landing of western Allied forces in Normandy on June 6, 1944 (when the Germans had a mere 15 divisions in France, compared to more than 300 divisions on the Eastern Front), brought the Germans face to face with American, Canadian, and British troops. On April 30, 1945, as Soviet and Anglo-American forces converged on Berlin, Hitler committed suicide. Days later, Germany surrendered unconditionally. At last, the devastating war in Europe—more "total" than any before—was over.

RACIAL WAR AND THE HOLOCAUST The Nazi war was not just a grab for land and raw materials; it was also a crusade for a new order based on race. Hitler considered Slavic peoples to be subhuman and was prepared to kill or starve them to make room for German Aryans. But his most powerful racial hatred was directed at Europe's Jewish population. Hitler had long talked of "freeing" Europe of all Jews. At the war's outset, the Nazis herded Jews into ghettos and labor camps and seized their property. As the German army moved eastward, more and more Jews came under the Nazis' control. At first the Nazi bureaucrats contemplated deportation, but they then ruled out transporting "subhumans" as too costly and settled for starving them and crowding them together in unsanitary ghettos. By the summer of 1941 special troops operating behind the army on the Eastern Front had begun mass shootings of communists and Jewish civilians, and by fall 1941 Hitler and the SS (the *Schutzstaffel*, or special security forces) were building a series of killing centers. When the German invasion of Russia stalled in the winter of 1941, the German leaders abandoned their plans to ship Jews to locations beyond the Ural Mountains. At a conference in Wannsee, just outside Berlin, in late January 1942, German decision makers finalized plans to kill all the Jews of Europe. This murderous departure from the work camps and ghettos meant a systematic eradication of Jews to clear the way for Nazi settlement in the east and racial purification across Europe. Accordingly, cattle cars shipped Jews from all over Europe to extermination sites in the east where Nazis used the latest technology, including the cyanide-based poison gas Zyklon B, to kill men, women, and children. The largest facility, Auschwitz, combined an extermination center and work camp in a single complex.

The deliberate racial extermination of the Jews, known as the **Holocaust**, claimed around 6 million European Jews. About half of this number died in the gas chambers of concentration camps; the others perished in face-to-face executions or from starvation, disease, or exhaustion. The Nazis also turned their mass killing apparatus against Sinta and Roma people, gay people, communists, and Slavs, with deportations to the death camps continuing to the very end of the war. Nazi genocides stood as a powerful challenge to European claims that science, technology, and an efficient bureaucracy would make life better for everyone. Lamenting connections between European culture and the Holocaust, the German philosopher Theodor Adorno wrote in 1949, "To write poetry after Auschwitz is barbaric."

COLLABORATION AND RESISTANCE Nazi occupation created massive social, economic, and political upheavals throughout Europe. Hitler established puppet governments that complied with deportation orders against Jews and dissidents. In occupied territories, most people simply struggled to survive and to take care of their families as best they could. A large number of collaborators, however, worked with the Germans, spurred by a mixture of ideology, opportunism, and fear. Hitler's giant police state also spawned resistance fighters, who opposed German occupiers for varying reasons. Among the resistance movements were both nationalists (who opposed German domination) and communists (who wanted to defeat both fascism and capitalism), who would fight among themselves even after the war was won.

The Ovens at Auschwitz (Reconstruction). One of the most horrifying aspects of Nazi behavior during World War II was the attempt to make mass killing efficient, scientific, and hygienic. At Auschwitz, the deadliest of the extermination camps, more than 1 million Jews and other racial and political "enemies" of the regime were murdered according to carefully designed plans. Many of the bodies were then burned in specially built ovens like these so the Nazis could avoid digging potentially unhygienic mass graves and could hide the evidence that genocide was being committed. Still, prisoners and guards at the camp reported enduring the terrible smell of burning flesh and the falling of ash containing fragments of human bones.

Analyzing Global Developments

World War II Casualties

World War II was the most destructive armed conflict in recorded history. This chart lists the number mobilized, military deaths, and estimated total deaths during World War II for some of the countries and colonial regions where the loss of life was greatest. In many cases, civilian casualties are difficult to estimate because of the chaos that reigned both during and after the war. The war mobilized more than 120 million military personnel; more than 20 million died. The death toll of civilian populations was substantially greater. Civilian deaths directly caused by the war, including genocide, bombing, starvation, and disease, are now estimated to range from 30 million to 55 million, or slightly more than 60 percent of total losses; figures vary widely because of the difficulty of arriving at accurate numbers in places where loss of life was extremely high and chaos continued after the war, such as China, the USSR, and India. Historians now put the total human losses at roughly 60 million dead, including the 6 million Jews killed in the Holocaust, more than double the number killed in World War I.

QUESTIONS FOR ANALYSIS

- Which countries endured the greatest loss of life in World War II, and why?
- Contrast civilian and military casualties in World War II, and explain why civilian casualty rates were so much higher than military losses. (To arrive at civilian casualty figures, subtract the military death toll from the estimated total death figures.) Why was this particularly the case in colonial territories such as India, the Dutch East Indies, and French Indochina?
- Compare and contrast the casualties for World Wars I and II. (See the Analyzing Global Developments feature in Chapter 19.)
- Many historians regard World War I as a greater turning point in European and western history than World War II, despite the latter war's extraordinarily high loss of life. Why do you think historians would hold to this view? What is your view of the relative global importance of the two wars?

World War II Casualties

Nation	Population in 1939	Max. No. Mobilized	Military Deaths	Estimated Total Deaths
USSR	108,377,000	12,500,000	8,800,000–10,700,000	27,000,000+
China	517,568,000	5,000,000	2,220,000	14,000,000–20,000,000
Germany	69,622,500	9,200,000	5,553,000	6,600,000–8,600,000
Poland	34,775,700	1,000,000	240,000	5,800,000

THE BITTER COSTS OF WAR The war in Europe had devastating human and material costs. This was particularly the case in eastern Europe, where German forces leveled more than 70,000 Soviet villages, obliterated one-third of the Soviet Union's wealth, and inflicted 7 million Soviet military deaths (by contrast, the Germans lost 3.5 million soldiers) and at least 20 million civilian deaths. German bombing of British cities, such as London, inflicted a heavy toll on civilians and buildings, as did Allied bombing of war plants and Axis cities like Dresden and Tokyo. Urban casualties were perhaps greatest in Leningrad, a city that was surrounded and besieged for 900 days; 900,000 people lost their lives during this struggle. By the war's end, Poland had lost 6 million people and Great Britain had lost 400,000. (See Analyzing Global Developments: World War II Casualties.) "What is Europe now?" mused British prime minister Winston Churchill. "A rubble heap, a charnel house, a breeding ground of pestilence and hate."

The War in the Pacific

Like the war in Europe, the conflict in the Pacific transformed the military and political landscape. (See Map 20.2.) The war broke out when Japan's ambitions to dominate Asia targeted American interests and might.

World War II Casualties

Nation	Population in 1939	Max. No. Mobilized	Military Deaths	Estimated Total Deaths
Dutch East Indies	69,435,000	N/A	N/A	3,500,000
Japan	71,380,000	6,095,000	2,120,000	2,600,000–3,100,000
India	311,820,000	2,150,000	87,000	1,500,000–2,500,000
Yugoslavia	5,510,100	500,000	305,000	1,505,000
French Indochina	24,568,000	N/A	N/A	1,000,000–1,500,000
Hungary	9,129,000	350,000	300,000	580,000
France	40,000,000	5,000,000	217,600	567,000
Greece	7,221,900	414,000	20–35,000	300,000–800,000
Italy	44,394,000	4,000,000	301,400	457,000
United Kingdom	47,760,000	4,683,000	383,400	450,700
United States	131,028,000	16,353,659	407,000	419,400
Philippines	16,000,300	105,000	N/A	118,000

Total World War II Deaths: 60 million (including 6 million Jews)

Sources: Data compiled from: Alan Axelrod (ed.), *Encyclopedia of World War II*, vol. 1 (New York: Facts on File, 2007); Rana Mitter, *Forgotten Ally: China's World War II, 1937–1945* (Boston: Houghton Mifflin Harcourt, 2013); I. C. B. Dear (ed.), *The Oxford Companion to World War II* (Oxford: Oxford University Press, 1995); The National WWII Museum, New Orleans. Note: Casualty figures vary for most of these countries, in some cases widely. These are at best estimates.

JAPAN'S EFFORTS TO EXPAND Japan's efforts to expand in Asia were already underway in the 1930s, but the outbreak of war in Europe opened opportunities for further expansion. Japan's military invaded and occupied Manchuria in 1931 and then launched an offensive against the rest of China in 1937. What ensued for the next eight years was a brutal struggle for control over China. It exacted a terrible toll on the population. Most infamous was the ravaging of Nanjing, in which Japanese aggressors slaughtered at least 100,000 civilians and raped thousands of women in the Chinese city between December 1937 and February 1938.

After concluding a pact with Germany in 1940, the Japanese seized French Indochina in 1941 and squeezed the Dutch East Indies for oil and rubber. Now the chief obstacle to further expansion in the Pacific was the United States, which already had imperial interests in places like China and the Philippines as well as other Pacific islands. Hoping to strike the United States before it was prepared for war, the Japanese launched a surprise air attack on the American naval base at Pearl Harbor, in Hawaii, on December 7, 1941.

Now Japan's expansion shifted into high gear. With French Indochina already under their control, the Japanese turned against the American colony of the Philippines and

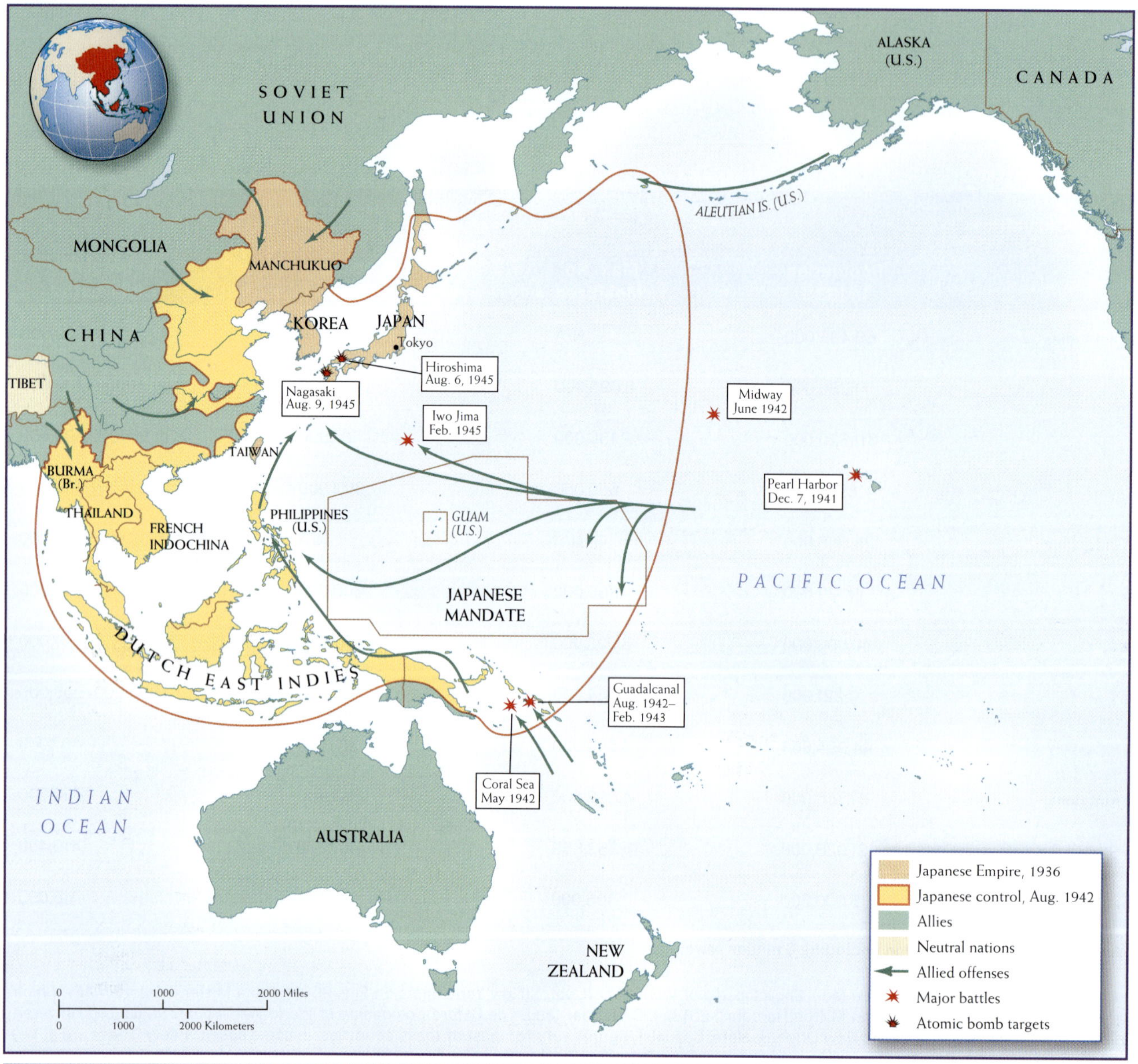

MAP 20.2 | World War II: The Pacific Theater

Like Germany and Italy, Japan experienced stunning military successes in the war's early years.

- In August 1942, which areas in the Pacific theater were under the control of the Japanese, and which were under Allied control?
- What does tracing the routes of the Allied offense tell you about the Allies' main strategy?
- What geographic factors influenced the American decision to drop atomic bombs on Hiroshima and Nagasaki to end the war, instead of invading Japan?

against the Dutch East Indies, both of which fell in 1942. By coordinating their army, naval, and air force units and using tactical surprise, the Japanese seized a huge swath of territory that included British-ruled Hong Kong, Singapore, Malaya, and Burma, while threatening the British Empire's hold on India as well.

Japan justified its aggression on the grounds that it was anticolonial and pan-Asian; Japan promised to drive out the European imperialists and to build a new order reflecting "Asia for Asians." In practice, however, the Japanese made terrible demands on fellow Asians for resources, developed myths of Japanese racial purity and supremacy, and treated

Chinese and Koreans with brutality. During the war, Japan put up to 4 million Koreans to work for its empire, forcibly imported another 700,000 Korean men as laborers, and pressed up to 200,000 young women into service as prostitutes for Japanese soldiers. (In a similar move, the Nazi war effort in Europe involved forcing 12 million foreign laborers—including 2 million prisoners of war—to settle and work in Germany.)

ALLIED ADVANCES AND THE ATOMIC BOMB As the war escalated, the edge fell to the powers that could mobilize more industrial and scientific resources. Japan and Germany succeeded at the quick strike; by 1943, the tide was turning due to the Allies' ability to roll entire fleets and air divisions off their assembly lines. Like the Germans in their war against Russia, the Japanese could not sustain their military successes against the United States. By mid-1943, U.S. forces had put the Japanese on the defensive. Fighting from island to island, American troops recaptured the Philippines, and a combined force of British, American, and Chinese troops returned Burma to Britain. The Allies then moved toward the Japanese mainland. By summer 1945, American bombers had all but devastated the major cities of Japan. Yet Japan did not surrender.

Anticipating that an invasion of Japan would cost hundreds of thousands of American lives, U.S. president Harry Truman unleashed the Americans' secret weapon. It was the work of a team of scientists who were predominantly European refugees. On August 6, 1945, an American plane dropped an atomic bomb on the city of Hiroshima, killing or maiming over 100,000 people and poisoning the air, soil, and groundwater for decades to come. Three days later, the Americans dropped a second atomic bomb on Nagasaki, and on Japan's western flank the Russians prepared to invade. Within days, Emperor Hirohito announced Japan's surrender, bringing the war to an end. Japan's dreams of East Asian supremacy had been defeated, at the cost of millions displaced, wounded, widowed, and orphaned. Asians, like Europeans, were relieved that six years of globalized horror had finally ended, but neither could guess what transformations the postwar world would bring.

Japanese Aggression. The brutal Battle of Shanghai (August–November 1937) marked the beginning of what turned out to be World War II in Asia. Claiming to be "protecting" China from European imperialists and expecting a relatively easy victory, the Japanese instead met with stiff resistance from the Chinese troops under Chiang Kai-shek. Here we see Japanese marines parading through the streets of the city after they finally broke through Chinese defenses. About a quarter of a million Chinese soldiers, close to 60 percent of Chiang's best troops, were killed or wounded in the campaign, a blow from which Chiang's regime never recovered. The Japanese sustained more than 40,000 casualties.

Internationalism and the Cold War

The destruction of Europe and the defeat of Japan left a power vacuum, which the United States and the Soviet Union rushed to fill. Avoiding direct warfare, the Americans and Soviets vied for influence in postwar Europe and around the globe. The ruin of war, and especially the toll it took on innocent civilians, motivated a surge in international efforts to curb rivalry and competition.

Even in the darkest moment of the war in 1941, U.S. president Franklin Delano Roosevelt and British prime minister Winston Churchill staked out a vision for a postwar world. Called the Atlantic Charter, it identified basic pillars for peace resting on a notion of rights. Ever since, world affairs have been dominated by notions of rights, and not just balance of powers. The first was the right for all people to belong to a political community in which they were free from fear or want. The second was the right of all nations to be free from outside interference, which included imperial meddling or bullying neighbors. It was a visionary document and laid out many of the principles that have informed global governance since 1945. But there was also a tension between its precepts. How could states be compelled to recognize individuals' rights without conforming to external rules and norms that might intrude on their rights to be sovereign?

To resolve this challenge, as armies and navies enclosed on Germany and Japan, political leaders planned the creation of new international organizations. The best known was the United Nations, formed in 1945 in San Francisco even as warships and bombers were pushing Japan to the brink. Its principal mandate was to promote world peace through mutual understanding and recognition of shared rules, like laws banning wars of aggression. One of the signature achievements came in 1948 with the adoption of the Universal Declaration of Human Rights, which underscored that all humans were entitled to be free from political and religious persecution.

Applied inconsistently, the Declaration nonetheless aspired to give new moral ballast to a war-torn world.

The growth of international institutions extended to the management of the world economy. In 1944, delegates from Asia, Latin America, Europe, and North America gathered in a hotel in Bretton Woods, New Hampshire, to outline a governance structure for the world economy. Determined to prevent the competitive protectionism and foreign exchange rate instability that had sent governments spiraling into the Great Depression, they laid the groundwork for the **International Monetary Fund (IMF)** (which gave countries relief from short-term payment difficulties) and the International Bank for Reconstruction and Development (which became better known as the **World Bank** and earmarked loans to recover and invest in needed infrastructure). The idea was to make good on the Atlantic Charter's call to replace international competition with cooperation.

In practice, these institutions functioned better at stabilizing international relations than equalizing them. Indeed, many critics, especially from the emerging Third World, would come to resent their elitism. Often, they accused the IMF and the U.N. of behaving in ways that harkened back to the meddling of old empires. And since so many of these new global institutions relied on the backing of the United States, they became tangled up with rising anti-Americanism in the 1960s and 1970s.

Postwar Planning at Yalta. The "Big Three" allies confer about the end of the war at the Black Sea resort of Yalta in February 1945. On the left is British prime minister Winston Churchill, at the center is American president Franklin Roosevelt, and on the right is Soviet premier Joseph Stalin.

Rebuilding Europe

For the time being, the new international institutions of 1945 focused on rebuilding war-torn Europe. As much as possible, this meant keeping Europe from sliding into the orbit of the Soviet Union. In Europe, communism and liberal democracy offered competing approaches to rebuilding states and societies after World War II. Many of the interwar democracies had been corrupt or ineffectual. By contrast, communism gained new appeal because its credo promised a clean slate. Many eastern Europeans, reacting to the horrors of fascism and not knowing the extent of Stalin's crimes, looked to the Soviets for answers.

Europe's leftward tilt alarmed U.S. policymakers. As President Truman began advocating a policy of containment to prevent the further advance of communism, an American journalist popularized the term **Cold War** in 1946 to describe a new form of struggle in which both sides endeavored to avoid direct warfare.

Truman's containment policy was tested when the Soviets attempted to seize control of Berlin. Like the rest of Germany, Berlin had been partitioned into British, French, American, and Soviet zones of occupation, but the city was an island within the Soviet zone. In 1948, the Soviets attempted to cut the city off from western access by blocking western routes to the capital. The United States and its western allies responded with the Berlin Airlift, which involved transporting supplies in planes to western Berlin to keep the population from capitulating to the Soviets. This crisis lasted for almost a year, until Stalin relented in May 1949 and trucks once again rolled through the eastern zone.

In that same year, occupied Germany was split into two hostile states: the democratic Federal Republic of Germany (West Germany) in the west and the communist German Democratic Republic (East Germany) in the east. In 1961, leaders in the German Democratic Republic built a wall around West Berlin to insulate the east from capitalist propaganda and to halt a flood of émigrés fleeing communism. The Berlin Wall became the great symbol of a divided Europe and of the Cold War.

U.S. policymakers wanted to shore up democratic governments in Europe, so Truman promised American military and economic aid. Containing the spread of communism meant securing a capitalist future for western Europe, a job that fell to Truman's secretary of state, General George C. Marshall. He launched the Marshall Plan, an ambitious program that provided over $13 billion in grants and credits to reconstruct Europe and facilitate an economic revival. U.S. policymakers hoped the aid would dim communism's appeal by fostering economic prosperity, muting class tensions, and integrating western European nations into an alliance of capitalist democracies.

Soviet troops had occupied eastern European nations at the war's end, and both communist and leftist members of other parties formed Soviet-backed coalition governments there. By tricking their moderate leftist allies and repressing their critics and opponents, the communists established dictatorships in Bulgaria, Romania, Hungary, and Czechoslovakia in 1948.

The Berlin Airlift. In summer 1948, a new currency was issued for the united occupation zones of West Germany. It began to circulate in Berlin at more favorable exchange rates than the eastern zone's currency, and Berlin seemed poised to become an outpost of the west inside the Soviet occupation zone. The Soviets responded by blocking western traffic into Berlin; the west countered with an airlift, forcing the Soviets to back down in May 1949 but hastening the division of Germany into two countries.

The Americans offered Marshall Plan aid to eastern Europe, too, which Stalin saw as a threat to Soviet security. He felt the same about the formation in 1949 of the **North Atlantic Treaty Organization (NATO)**, a military alliance between countries in western Europe and North America. He believed that the Soviet Union, having sacrificed millions of people in the war against fascism, deserved to be dominant in eastern Europe. In 1955, the Soviets formally allied themselves with Europe's communist nations in the **Warsaw Pact**, a military alliance of their own. (See Map 20.3.) Each alliance concentrated military forces (and later atomic weapons) directly at each other. The tense confrontations between NATO nations and Warsaw Pact nations in Europe and other parts of the world in the 1950s and 1960s brought the world to the brink of an atomic World War III.

War in the Nuclear Age: The Korean War

The dropping of the atomic bombs on Japan in 1945 changed military strategies and international relations forever. Spurred by the onset of the Cold War, the Soviets worked hard to catch up to the Americans and in 1949 tested their first nuclear bomb. Thereafter, each side rushed to stockpile nuclear weapons and update its military technologies. By 1960, the explosive power of these weapons had increased so greatly that nuclear war had the potential to destroy the world without a single soldier firing a shot. This sobering realization changed the rules of the game. Each side now possessed the power to inflict total destruction on the other, a circumstance that inhibited direct confrontations but sparked smaller conflicts in parts of Asia where the postwar settlement was murky.

In 1950, North Korean troops backed by the Soviet Union invaded U.S.-backed South Korea, setting off the Korean

Atom Bomb Anxiety. Schoolchildren taking shelter under their desks during an A-bomb drill in Brooklyn, New York, in 1951. The Soviets had exploded their first test bomb in 1949. Underground bomb shelters were built in many American urban areas as places in which to survive a doomsday attack.

MAP 20.3 | NATO and Warsaw Pact Countries

The Cold War divided Europe into two competing blocs: those allied with the United States in the North Atlantic Treaty Organization (NATO) and those linked to the Soviet Union under the Warsaw Pact.

- Which nations had borders with nations belonging to the opposite bloc?
- Comparing this map with Map 20.1, explain how combat patterns in World War II shaped the dividing line between the two blocs.
- According to the map, where would you expect Cold War tensions to be the most intense?

MAP 20.4 | The Korean War

The Korean War was an early confrontation between the capitalist and communist blocs during the Cold War era.

- What were the dates of each side's farthest advance into the other side's territory?
- Why was the Korean Peninsula strategically important?
- According to your reading, how did the outcome of the war shape political affairs in East Asia for the next several decades?

War. (See Map 20.4.) Claiming this violated the Charter of the United Nations, which had been established in 1945 to safeguard world peace and protect human rights, President Truman ordered American troops to drive back the North Koreans. The U.N. Security Council, thanks to a Soviet boycott, also sent troops from fifteen nations to restore peace. Within a year, the invaders had been routed and were near collapse. When U.N. troops advanced to the Chinese border, however, Stalin maneuvered his communist Chinese allies into rescuing the communist regime in North Korea and driving the South Korean and U.N. forces back to the old boundary in the middle of the Korean Peninsula. Across the Korean isthmus, communist and American-led U.N. troops waged a seesaw war. The fighting continued until 1953, when an armistice divided the country at roughly the same spot as at the start of the war. Nothing had been gained. Losses, however, included 33,000 Americans, at least 250,000 Chinese, and up to 3 million Koreans.

The Korean War energized America's anticommunist commitments and spurred a rapid increase in NATO forces. The United States now saw Japan as a bulwark against communism and resolved to rebuild Japanese economic power. Like West Germany, Japan went from being the enemy in World War II to being a valued U.S. ally as the Cold War rivalry between the United States and the Soviet Union propelled both sides to shore up alliances around the globe.

The Long March. In China, the Long March of 1934–1935 has been commemorated by the ruling communists as one of the most heroic episodes in the party's history. This photo shows communist partisans crossing the snow-covered mountains in the western province of Sichuan in 1935. Despite their efforts, the ranks of the party were decimated by the end of the 6,000-mile journey from the southeastern to the northwestern part of the country; fewer than one in eight reached their destination.

Decolonization

The disastrous effects of World War II on all empires, including Japan's prewar and wartime empire and the longer-standing colonies belonging to the European powers, inspired colonial peoples to reconsider their political future. The process of **decolonization** and nation building, creating national identities to replace previous colonial and precolonial loyalties, followed four patterns: civil war; wars of independence; negotiated independence; and incomplete decolonization. All of them yielded new nations to join international organizations stressed by Cold War rivalries.

The Chinese Revolution

In China, the ousting of Japanese occupiers intensified a civil war that brought the communists to power. The communist movement in China had its origins in the struggle since the early twentieth century to free the country from western domination. Founded in 1921, the Communist Party sought power but was outgunned by Chiang Kai-shek's Nationalist regime and driven from China's cities; its members retreated into the interior, where they founded base camps. In 1934, under attack by Chiang's forces, the communists, led by **Mao Zedong** (1893–1976), abandoned their largest base and undertook an arduous 6,000-mile journey through the rugged terrain of northwestern China. (See Map 20.5.) In the course of this great escape, glorified in communist lore as the Long March, fewer than 10,000 of the approximately 80,000 people who started the journey reached their destination. Fortunately for the communists, the Japanese invasion in 1937 diverted Nationalist troops and offered Mao and the survivors a chance to regroup.

The Japanese forces not only inflicted irreparable damage on the Nationalist military but also further debilitated the capacity of Chiang's regime to govern areas that had not fallen to the invaders. Nationalist soldiers and citizens alike were often left to fend for themselves and became increasingly demoralized and disaffected. When the Japanese invaders seized China's major cities but were unable to control the countryside, the communists expanded their support among the vast peasantry.

Mao's followers cultivated popular support by advocating the lowering of taxes, cooperative farming, and policies aimed at women, such as the outlawing of arranged marriages and

MAP 20.5 | The Long March, 1934–1935

During the Long March, which took place during the struggle for power between the Nationalist Guomindang and the communists within China, communist forces traveled over 6,000 miles to save their lives and their movement.

- What route did the communist forces take?
- Why did the communists take this particular route?
- How did this movement affect the outcome of this internal struggle in the long run?

The Founding of the People's Republic of China. Mao Zedong speaks at a national flag-raising ceremony at Shanghai, celebrating the founding of the People's Republic of China on October 1, 1949. Although most Chinese knew little about the Communist Party, many had high hopes for a new, independent, and liberated China.

the legalization of divorce. Like many anticolonial reformers, Mao regarded women's emancipation as a key component in building a new nation, since he considered their oppression to be both unjust and an obstacle to progress.

Communist expansion in the rural areas during World War II swelled the membership of the Communist Party from 40,000 in 1937 to over a million in 1945. After Japan's surrender, China's civil war between Nationalists and communists resumed. But communist forces now had the numbers, the guns (supplied by the Soviet Union and captured from the Nationalists), and the popular support to assault Nationalist strongholds and seize power. By contrast, although the Nationalist government had weapons and financing from the United States, as well as control of the cities, it had not recovered from its defeat at the hands of the Japanese. No match for the invigorated communists, the Nationalists fled to the island of Taiwan, where they established a rival Chinese state.

In 1949, Mao proclaimed that China had "stood up" to the world and had experienced a "great people's revolution." Subsequently, many of his ventures proved disastrous failures (see later in this chapter), but China's model of an ongoing people's revolution provided much hope in the Third World. (See Global Themes and Sources: Primary Source 20.1.)

Negotiated Independence in India and Africa

In India and most of colonial Africa, gaining independence involved little bloodshed, although the aftermaths were often extremely violent. The British, realizing that they could no longer rule India without coercion, bowed to the inevitable and withdrew. Much the same happened in Africa, where nationalists also succeeded in negotiating independence from European empires, although, as we shall see, there were notable exceptions.

INDIA Unlike China, India achieved political independence without an insurrection. But it did veer dangerously close to civil war. As anticolonial elites in the Indian National Congress Party negotiated a peaceful transfer of power from British rule, they disagreed about what kind of state an independent India should have. Should it, as Gandhi wished, be a nonmodern utopia of self-governing village communities, or should it emulate western and Soviet models with the goal of establishing a modern nation-state? Even more pressing was the question of relations between the Hindu majority and the Muslim minority.

For the most part, the congress leadership retained tight control over the mass movement that it had mobilized in the 1920s and 1930s. Even Gandhi hesitated to leave the initiative to the common people, believing that they had not yet assimilated the doctrine of nonviolence. Accordingly, Gandhi and the leadership worked hard to convince the British that they, the middle-class leaders, spoke for the nation. At the same time, the threat of a mass peasant uprising with radical aims (as was occurring in China) encouraged the British to transfer power quickly.

As negotiations moved forward, Hindu-Muslim relations deteriorated. Whose culture would define the new nation?

Jawaharlal Nehru. Nehru, the leader of independent India, sought to create a "mixed economy" of private and public sectors with democracy to chart an independent path for India. This photo shows him speaking at the opening ceremonies for the Bhakra Dam in 1963.

The Indian nationalism that had existed in the late nineteenth century reflected the culture of the Hindu majority. Yet this movement masked the multiplicity of regional, linguistic, caste, and class differences *within* the Hindu community, just as Muslim movements that arose in reaction to Hindu-dominated Indian nationalism overlooked divisions within their own ranks. Now the prospect of defining "India" created a grand contest between newly self-conscious communities. Riots broke out between Hindus and Muslims in 1946, which increased the mutual distrust between congress and Muslim League leaders. The leader of the Muslim League demanded that British India be partitioned into separate Hindu and Muslim states if there were no constitutional guarantees for Muslims. The specter of civil war haunted the proceedings, as outgoing colonial rulers decided to divide the subcontinent into two states: India and Pakistan.

On August 14, 1947, Pakistan gained independence from Britain; a day later, India did the same. The euphoria of decolonization, however, drowned in a frenzy of brutality. Shortly after independence, up to 1 million Hindus and Muslims killed one another. Fearing further violence, 12 million Hindus and Muslims left their homes to relocate in the new countries where they would be in the majority. Distraught by the rampage, Gandhi fasted, refusing sustenance until the killings stopped. The violence abated. This was perhaps Gandhi's finest hour. But animosity and fanaticism remained. Less than six months later, a Hindu zealot shot Gandhi dead as he walked to a prayer meeting.

Had Gandhi lived, he would not have approved of the direction independent India took. He had already voiced disapproval of industrialization and of equipping the Indian state with an army and police forces. But Jawaharlal Nehru, India's first prime minister, and other leaders of the Indian National Congress Party were committed to building a strong state capable of modernizing India. Accordingly, they backed the Dalit leader B. R. Ambedkar, who drafted a constitution for a parliamentary democracy that guaranteed basic individual freedoms while equipping the state with substantial powers to foster social equality. Inspired by Soviet-style planned development but also committed to democracy, the new state under Nehru sought, as he put it, to build a "socialistic pattern of society" based on a mixed economy of public and private sectors. Declaring that he wanted to give India the "garb of modernity," Nehru asked Indians to consider hydroelectric dams and steel plants the temples of modern India. He made his watchwords "education" and "economic development," believing that these would loosen the hold of religion on Muslims and encourage them to join the national mainstream. He also hoped that the diminished role of religious traditions would improve the condition of women. Such a vision allowed Nehru, until his death in 1964, to guide Indian modernization along a third path. (See Global Themes and Sources: Primary Source 20.2.)

AFRICA FOR AFRICANS Shortly after Indian independence, most African states also gained their national sovereignty. Except for southern Africa, where minority White rule persisted, the old colonial states ceded to indigenous rulers. One reason for this rapid decolonization was that nationalist movements had made gains during the interwar period. These years had taught a generation of nationalists to seek wider support for their political parties. World War II, then, swelled the ranks of anticolonial political parties, as many African soldiers expected tangible rewards for serving in imperial armies.

The postwar years also saw throngs of Africans flock to the cities in search of a better life. As expanding educational systems produced a wave of primary and secondary school graduates, these educated young people and other new urban dwellers became disgruntled when attractive employment opportunities were not forthcoming. The three groups—former servicemen, the urban unemployed or underemployed, and the educated—led the nationalist agitation that began in the late 1940s and early 1950s. (See Map 20.6.)

Faced with rising nationalist demands, and too much in debt themselves to invest more in pacifying the discontented, European powers agreed to decolonize. The new world powers, the Soviet Union and the United States, also favored decolonization. Thus, decolonization in most of Africa was a rapid and relatively sedate affair. In 1957, the Gold Coast (renamed Ghana), under Prime Minister Kwame Nkrumah, became tropical Africa's first independent state. Other British colonial territories followed in rapid succession, so that by 1963 all of British-ruled Africa except for Southern Rhodesia was independent. In these former colonial possessions,

Kwame Nkrumah. West Africa's leading nationalist, Kwame Nkrumah, mobilized the peoples of the Gold Coast and, through electoral successes, convinced the British to confer independence on the Gold Coast, which was renamed Ghana in 1957.

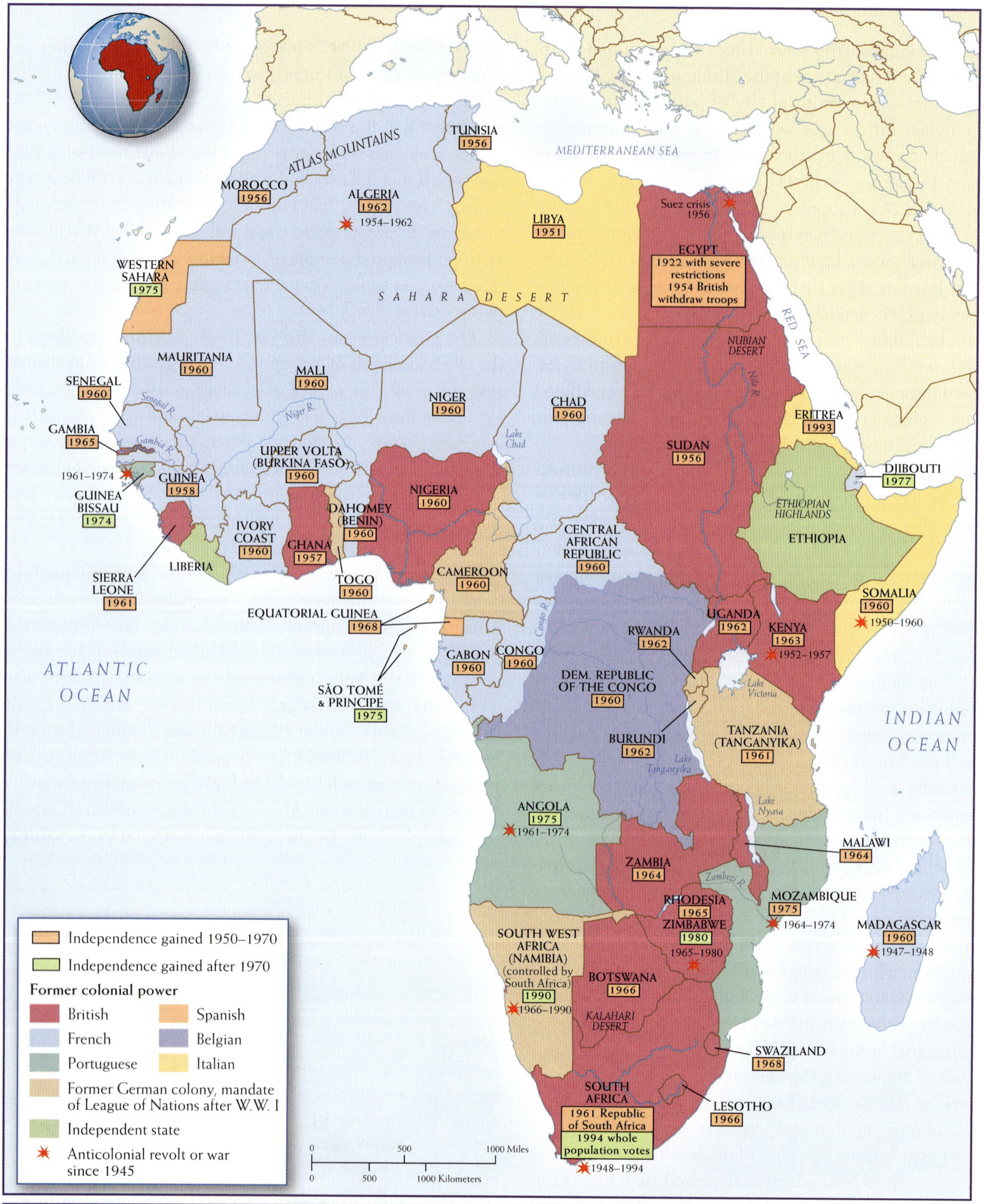

MAP 20.6 | Decolonization in Africa

African decolonization occurred after World War II, largely in the 1950s, 1960s, and 1970s.

- Find at least four areas that won independence in the 1950s, and identify which former colonial power had ruled each area.
- What areas took longer to gain independence?
- According to your reading, what problems and tensions contributed to this uneven process across Africa?

charismatic nationalist leaders became the authorities to whom the British ceded power. Many of the new rulers had obtained a western education but were committed to returning Africa to the Africans.

Decolonization in much of French-ruled Africa followed a similarly smooth path, although the French were initially resistant. Believing their own culture to be unrivaled, the French treated decolonization as assimilation: instead of negotiating independence, they tried first to accord fuller voting rights to their colonial subjects, even allowing Africans and Asians to send delegates to the French National Assembly. In the end, however, the French electorate had no desire to share the privileges of French citizenship with overseas populations. Nor did African leaders wish to submerge their identities in a Greater France. Thus, France dissolved its political ties with French West Africa and French Equatorial Africa in 1960, having given protectorates in Morocco and Tunisia their independence in 1956. Algeria, always considered an integral part of France overseas, was a different matter. Its independence did not come quickly or easily (as we will discuss shortly).

Léopold Sédar Senghor. Senghor combined sharp intellect with political savvy. An accomplished poet and essayist and one of the founders of the Negritude movement among Francophone intellectuals, he became Senegal's first president when the country gained full independence in 1960.

Patrice Lumumba. Lumumba championed the freedom of the Congo from Belgian rule and became the country's first prime minister in 1960. His call for liberation across Africa frightened White settlers in Rhodesia and South Africa, who schemed with European and American covert operators to sew unrest in the fledgling Republic of Congo. When he turned to the Soviet Union for help, he was toppled in a coup d'état, arrested, and executed on January 17, 1961.

The most chaotic and ill-prepared African decolonization unfolded in the Belgian Congo. It would end in a monumental human tragedy: the killing and dismemberment of the only democratically elected prime minister of the Congo, Patrice Lumumba. While Britain and France contemplated giving their African colonies independence, the Belgians doubled down on their paternalistic form of colonialism, hoping it would enable them to remain in control. But the Belgians' stubborn refusal to leave turned a local political vacuum into a violent struggle for power. One last indignity remained for the independent Congo to endure. In January 1961, American covert operators plotted against the Congo's firebrand leader, Patrice Lumumba. With U.S. covert support, the Congolese army seized him. Then, Lumumba's captors shot him, burned his body with acid, and buried him in an unmarked grave. In an effort to deprive his followers of a gathering place and a symbol of a better future, Lumumba's enemies disinterred him, dismembered him, and reburied him along the border with Southern Rhodesia.

Promoting Africa for Africans gave way to a mood of despair. The leaders of African independence believed that Africa's precolonial traditions would enable the region to move from colonialism right into a special African form of socialism, escaping the ravages of capitalism. Without rejecting western culture completely, they extolled the so-called African personality, exemplified by the idea of "Negritude" developed by Senegal's first president, Léopold Sédar Senghor. (See Global Themes and Sources: Primary Source 20.3.) Negritude, they claimed, was steeped in communal solidarities and able to embrace social justice and equality, while rejecting the naked individualism that Africans felt lay at the core of European culture. Unfortunately, this creed of unity could not make up for deep-seated divides within fledgling nation-states.

Violent and Incomplete Decolonizations

Although transfers of power in most of Africa and Asia ultimately occurred peacefully, there were notable exceptions. In Palestine, Algeria, and southern Africa, the presence of European immigrant groups created violent conflicts that aborted any peaceful transfer of power—or left the process incomplete. In Vietnam, the process was also violent and delayed, partly because of France's desire to reimpose colonial control and partly from the power politics of Cold War competition.

PALESTINE, ISRAEL, AND EGYPT In Palestine, Arabs and Jews had been on a collision course since the end of World War I. Before that war, a group of European Jews, known as Zionists, had argued that only an exodus from existing states to their place of origin in Palestine could lead to Jewish self-determination. **Zionism** combined a yearning to realize the ancient biblical injunction to return to the holy lands with a fear of anti-Semitism and anguish over increasing Jewish assimilation. Zionists wanted to create a Jewish state, and they won a crucial victory during World War I when the British government, under the Balfour Declaration, promised a homeland for the Jews in Palestine. But when the British awarded themselves Palestine as a mandate after 1918, they also guaranteed the rights of Palestinian Arabs and sought to mediate between an increasing number of Zionist settlers and their Arab and Christian neighbors.

As more Jews settled in Palestine, buying up land and seeking to increase their political influence, tensions rose between Zionists and Palestinian Arabs. Meanwhile, both groups grew dissatisfied with British rule. Arabs resented the presence of Jews, who displaced farmers who had lived on the land for generations, and openly sought their own independent state. The Zionists became especially enraged when British authorities wavered in supporting their demands for greater immigration. After World War II, the pressure for Jewish immigration increased as hundreds of thousands of concentration camp survivors clamored for entry into Palestine, and Zionist militants began using force to attempt to gain control of the state.

In late 1947, the British could no longer control the festering region and announced that they would leave negotiations over the area's fate to the United Nations; in May 1948, the British turned their old League of Nations mandate in Palestine over to the U.N. That body then voted to partition Palestine into Arab and Jewish territories. The Arab states rejected the partition, and the Jewish Agency, a nongovernmental agency that supported the immigration of Jews to Israel, only reluctantly accepted it. When the British withdrew their troops in 1948, a Jewish provisional government proclaimed the establishment of the state of Israel. Although the Jews were delighted to have an independent state, they were unhappy about its small size, its indefensible borders, and the fact that it did not include all the lands that had belonged to ancient Israel. For their part, the Palestinians were shocked at the partition, and they looked to their better-armed Arab neighbors to regain the territories set aside for the new state of Israel.

The ensuing Arab-Israeli War of 1948–1949 shattered the legitimacy of Arab ruling elites. Arab states entered the war poorly prepared to take on the well-run and enthusiastically supported Israeli Defense Force. By the time the United Nations finally negotiated a truce, Israel had extended its boundaries

The Creation of the State of Israel. Standing beneath a portrait of Theodor Herzl, the founder of the Zionist movement, David Ben-Gurion, the first Israeli prime minister, proclaimed independence for the state of Israel in May 1948.

and more than 1 million Palestinians had become refugees in surrounding Arab countries.

Embittered by this defeat, a group of young army officers in Egypt plotted to overthrow the Egyptian regime, which they felt was corrupt and still under British influence. One of the officers, Gamal Abdel Nasser, became the head of a secret organization of junior military officers—the Free Officers Movement. These men had ties with communists and other dissident groups, including the Muslim Brotherhood, which favored a return to Islamic rule. They launched a successful coup in 1952, forcing the king to abdicate and leave the country. Then they enacted a land reform scheme that deprived large estate owners of lands in excess of 200 acres and redistributed these lands to the landless and smallholders, who instantly became ardent supporters of the new regime. The new regime also dissolved the parliament, banned political parties (including the communists and the Muslim Brotherhood), and stripped the old elite of its wealth.

In 1956, Nasser moved to nationalize the Suez Canal Company (an Egyptian company, mainly run by French businessmen and experts), inciting the Israelis, the British, and the French to invade Egypt and seize territory along the Suez Canal. Opposition by the United States and the Soviet Union forced them to withdraw, providing Nasser with a spectacular diplomatic triumph. As Egyptian forces reclaimed the canal, Nasser's reputation as leader of the Arab world soared. He became the chief symbol of a pan-Arab nationalism that swept across the Middle East and North Africa and especially through the camps of Palestinian refugees.

The Anglo-Egyptian Treaty. This photo shows Egyptian president Nasser signing the Anglo-Egyptian Treaty with the British minister of state in 1954. The agreement ended the stationing of British troops on Egyptian soil and called for the withdrawal of British troops stationed at the Suez Canal military base. But shortly after the last British soldiers left Egypt in early 1956, Britain invaded the country in a vain effort to block Nasser's nationalization of the Suez Canal Company and to remove the Egyptian leader from power.

THE ALGERIAN WAR OF INDEPENDENCE The appeal of Arab nationalism was particularly strong in Algeria, where a sizable French settler population (the Colons) of 1 million stood in the way of a complete and peaceful decolonization. Indeed, French leaders claimed that Algeria was an integral part of France, an overseas department that was legally no different from Brittany or Normandy. Although the Colons were a minority, they held the best land and lived in wealthy residential quarters in the major cities. And although all residents of Algeria were supposedly entitled to the same rights as the French citizenry, in fact the Colons, mainly living in the country's coastal cities, controlled Algeria's finances and all its public institutions.

As elsewhere, anticolonial nationalism in Algeria gathered force after World War II. The Front de Libération Nationale (FLN), the leading nationalist party, used violence to provoke its opponents and to make the local population choose between supporting the nationalist cause or the Colons. The full-fledged revolt that erupted in 1954 pitted FLN troops and guerrillas against thousands of French troops. Atrocities and terrorist acts occurred on both sides.

The war dragged on for eight years, at a cost of perhaps 300,000 lives. On the French mainland, the war came as a terrible shock. Many French citizens had accepted the idea that Algeria was not a colonial territory but part of France itself. The Colons insisted that they had emigrated to Algeria in response to their government's promises and that yielding power to the nationalists would be a betrayal. After an insurrection led by Colons and army officers brought down the French government in 1958, the new French president, Charles de Gaulle, negotiated a peace accord.

The peace, however, led to an exodus. After handing over power to FLN leaders, more than 800,000 Colons left Algeria. By late 1962, over 90 percent of the European population had departed. Their catchphrase was "the suitcase or the coffin." At independence, then, Algeria had a population mix no different from that of the other North African countries.

While struggling for independence, the FLN and its Armée de Libération Nationale (ALN) became a symbol for decolonizing movements worldwide. Frantz Fanon, who served as a physician and psychiatrist in Algeria and supported the FLN, believed that Algeria pointed the way for countries emerging from colonialism. Yasser Arafat, the champion of Palestinian rights, claimed that the FLN was "the window through which we appear to the West." (For more on the Third World movement, see below.)

EASTERN AND SOUTHERN AFRICA The bloody conflict in Algeria highlights a harsh reality of African decolonization: the presence of European settlers prevented the smooth transfer of power. Even in British-ruled Kenya, where the European settler population had never been large, a violent

Mau Mau Rebellion. A large segment of the Kikuyu population rose up against the British colonial occupation of Kenya. This revolt, which began in 1952, was finally suppressed by British arms and Kikuyu "loyalists." Nonetheless, the Mau Mau Uprising led to Kenya's independence from British rule.

war of independence broke out between European settlers and African nationalists. Employing secrecy and intimidation, the Kikuyu peoples, Kenya's largest ethnic group, organized a revolt. This uprising, which began in 1952, forced the British to fly in troops to suppress it, but ultimately the British government conceded independence to Kenya in 1963. Decolonization proved even more difficult in the southern third of the continent, where Portuguese Angola, Portuguese Mozambique, and British Southern Rhodesia (present-day Zimbabwe) did not gain independence until 1980.

Women played vital roles in these decolonization struggles. In Egypt, for example, the leading nationalists were all men, but they gained crucial support from educated and modernizing women, many of whom organized impressive demonstrations on their behalf. The wife of Sa'd Zaghlul, Egypt's most dynamic nationalist figure after World War I, gained a large following and a reputation as mother of the nation. Moreover, during Kenya's battle against British colonial rule, women supplied the fighters with food, medical resources, and information about the British. Those who were caught ended up in concentration camps and suffered brutal treatment from their prison guards. Yet, once independence was achieved, most women reverted to their traditional subordinate status.

South Africa, which held the continent's largest and wealthiest settler population (a mixture of Afrikaans- and English-speaking peoples of European descent), defied Black majority rule longer than other African states. After winning the elections of 1948, the White Afrikaner-dominated National Party enacted an extreme form of racial segregation known as **apartheid**. Under apartheid, laws stripped Africans, Indians, and colored persons (those of mixed descent) of their few political rights. Racial mixing of any kind was forbidden, and schools were strictly segregated. The Group Areas Act, passed in 1950, divided the country into separate racial and tribal areas and required Africans to live in their own racial areas, called homelands. Pass laws prohibited Africans from traveling outside their homelands without special work or travel passes.

The ruling party tolerated no protest. Nelson Mandela, one of the leaders of the African National Congress (ANC) who campaigned for an end to discriminatory legislation, was repeatedly harassed, detained, and tried by the government, even though he urged peaceful resistance. After the Sharpeville massacre in 1960, in which police killed demonstrators who were peacefully protesting the pass laws, Mandela and the ANC decided to oppose the apartheid regime with

Apartheid Protest. In Johannesburg, South Africans march in the street to protest the new restrictions on African citizens, soon to be known worldwide as apartheid, implemented by the White minority government of Daniel Malan. During the Malan administration (1948–1954), informal discrimination was systematically made law, and all electoral, housing, civil, and employment rights of African citizens were dismantled.

violence. Subsequently, the government announced a state of emergency, banned the ANC, and arrested those of its leaders who had not fled the country or gone underground. A South African court sentenced Mandela to life imprisonment. Other Black leaders were tortured or beaten to death. Here, too, women kept resistance flames burning. The most dynamic of these individuals was Winnie Mandela, wife of the imprisoned Nelson Mandela. Unlike many of the ANC leaders, who opposed the regime from exile, she remained behind and openly and courageously spoke out against the apartheid government. Despite such human rights violations, the Whites retained external support. Through the 1950s and 1960s, western powers (especially the United States) saw South Africa as a bulwark against the spread of communism in Africa.

Ho Chi Minh. Ho Chi Minh's formation of the League for the Independence of Vietnam, or Viet Minh, in 1941 set the stage for his rise at the end of World War II. Here he attends a youth rally in October 1955, just over a year after the victory of his forces at Dien Bien Phu, which resulted in the ousting of the French from Vietnam.

VIETNAM The same desire to contain communism also drew the United States into support for a conservative and pro-western regime in Vietnam. Vietnam had come under French rule in the 1880s, and by the 1920s approximately 40,000 Europeans were living among and ruling over roughly 19 million Vietnamese. To promote an export economy of rice, mining, and rubber, the colonial rulers granted vast land concessions to French companies and local collaborators, while leaving large numbers of peasants landless.

The colonial system also generated a new intelligentsia. Primarily schooled in French and Franco-Vietnamese schools, educated Vietnamese worked as clerks, shopkeepers, teachers, and petty officials. Yet they had few opportunities for advancement in the French-dominated colonial system. Discontented, they thus turned from the traditional ideology of Confucianism to modern nationalism. Vietnamese intellectuals overseas, notably Ho Chi Minh, took the lead in imagining a new Vietnamese nation-state.

Ho had left Vietnam at an early age and found his way to London and Paris. During the interwar period he read the writings of Marx, Engels, and Lenin, and he discovered not only an ideology for opposing French exploitation but also a vision for transforming the common people into a political force. He was a founding member of the French Communist Party and subsequently founded the Indochinese Communist Party. After the Japanese occupied Indochina, he traveled to China, embraced the idea of an agrarian revolution, and established the Viet Minh, a liberation force, in 1941. Back in Vietnam, the communist-led Viet Minh became a powerful nationalist organization as it mobilized the peasantry.

When the French tried to restore their rule in Vietnam after Japan's defeat in 1945, Ho led the resistance. War with France followed (1946–1954), featuring guerrilla tactics to undermine French positions. The Viet Minh was most successful in the north, but even in the south its campaign bled the French. Finally, in 1954, the anticolonial forces won a decisive military victory. At the Geneva Peace Conference, Vietnam (like Korea) was divided into two zones. Ho controlled the north, while a government with French and American support took charge in the south.

Although the French departed, decolonization in Vietnam was incomplete. North Vietnam supported the Viet Cong—communist guerrillas—who combined anti-imperialist nationalism with a land reform program that appealed greatly to the peasants. Determined to contain the spread of communism in Southeast Asia, the United States began smuggling arms to the regime in the south. During the early 1960s, U.S. involvement escalated. In 1965, large numbers of American troops entered the country to fight on behalf of South Vietnam, while communist North Vietnam turned to the Soviet Union for supplies. Over the next several years, the United States sent some 500,000 soldiers to fight the Vietnam War, but peasant support enabled the Viet Cong to continue fierce guerrilla fighting. Even the bombing of villages and the deployment of counterinsurgency forces failed to prevent the spread of communism in Southeast Asia. In 1975, just two years after the final withdrawal of American troops, the South Vietnamese government collapsed.

Thus, the process of decolonization varied across regions. Although most of the lands in Asia and Africa had gained independence by the mid-1960s, there were significant exceptions in Africa (South Africa, Southern Rhodesia, and the Portuguese colonies) and in Asia (notably, Vietnam). Although the British and French realized that they no longer had the resources to stem the nationalist tide spreading through the Third World, they tried to use military might to regain control

Agriculture and Decolonization. Women pose with their farming implements before hoeing a field of maize in South Africa around 1923. Since men were often recruited for seasonal and mining work away from the village, women took charge of farms. When White settlers encroached on villages for their land, they often pushed women off their plots. Over the years, dispossessed women joined the vanguard of opposition to White and European rule.

in areas with large European settlements, such as Kenya and Algeria. Here, too, however, local nationalists or communists eventually would seize control, ending direct imperial rule—but not western or Soviet attempts to interfere in the affairs of other states.

WOMEN, NATIONALISM, AND DECOLONIZATION Decolonization mobilized women in struggles all over the world. Some of the most dramatic examples of their participation come from colonial Africa. In Kenya immediately after World War I, Kikuyu women assembled outside the prison where the colonial authorities were holding Harry Thuku, the leader of the first African political party in Kenya. The women indeed had much to protest. The British had expropriated substantial amounts of land for distribution to European settlers—land that the Kikuyu believed belonged to them. Land dispossession affected all segments of Kikuyu society, none more profoundly than women, who bore major responsibilities for feeding and looking after their families. Confined to reserves that they considered inadequate for feeding and supporting their families, particularly when the colonial authorities forcibly recruited many young adult males to work on settler estates, the women rallied to support Thuku and denounced colonial authorities for allowing their lands to be seized for settlers.

Much the same happened in 1929 in southeastern Nigeria, where Ibo women and women from other ethnic communities, believing that the colonial authorities planned to tax them as well as men, similarly feared that they would be unable to look after their families. Here, they turned against the British-appointed African warrant chiefs, who served as native-born officers of the empire. Surrounding the homes of these chiefs, the women insulted them and demeaned their manhood. This form of protest, called "sitting on a man," had traditionally been employed against men who had illegitimately wielded their powers over women, and was revived under British rule. The uprising was perhaps the biggest women's protest movement in colonial history at the time, covering an area of 6,000 square miles with an estimated population of 2 million. Fifty-five women lost their lives, and the British colonial administration, so deeply troubled by the women's uprising, abolished the system of warrant chiefs. They even appointed women to serve on African courts.

Three Worlds

World War II and postwar decolonization created a three-world order in which the liberal democratic and capitalist First World and the communist Second World competed for global influence, notably among the newly decolonized Third World states. Possessing nuclear weapons, superior armies, and industrial might, the Soviet Union and the United States had emerged from the war as the world's only superpowers. As decolonization spread, these Cold War belligerents offered new leaders their models for modernization. On one side, the United States, together with its western European allies and Japan, had developed democratic forms of governance and a dynamic capitalist economy that produced immense quantities of affordable consumer goods. The Soviet Union, on the other side, trumpeted the Communist Party's egalitarian ideology and its rapid transition from "backward" to highly industrialized. Both the First World and the Second World expected the decolonized Third World to adopt their models.

The decolonized, however, had their own ideas about how to modernize. Under Mao's leadership, China established full autonomy from the Cold War superpowers and implemented its own very radical form of modernization. Other postcolonial leaders, such as Nehru in India, developed unique mixtures of democracy and state planning. But in many decolonized nations in Asia and Africa, economies that had been exploited or left underdeveloped by colonial powers could not leap into industrial development, and they remained economically or politically dependent on western or Soviet states.

The First World

As the Cold War spread in the early 1950s, western Europe and North America became known as the First World, or "the free world." Later on, Japan joined this group. Following the principles of liberal modernism, First World states sought to organize the world on the basis of capitalism and democracy. Yet, in struggling against communism, the free world sometimes aligned with Third World dictators, thereby sacrificing its commitment to freedom and democracy for the sake of propping up pro-western regimes.

WESTERN EUROPE The reconstruction of western Europe after World War II was a spectacular success. By the late 1950s, most nations' economies there were thriving, thanks in part to massive American economic assistance. Improvements in agriculture were particularly impressive. With increased mechanization and the use of pesticides, fewer farmers were feeding more people. In 1950, for example, each French farmer had produced enough food for seven people; by 1962, one farmer could feed forty. And as industrial production boomed and wages rose, goods that had been luxuries before the war—refrigerators, telephones, automobiles, indoor plumbing—became commonplace. Prosperity and the dismantling of national military establishments allowed governments to expand social welfare systems, such that by the late 1950s education and health care were within the reach of virtually all citizens. The success of reconstruction blunted the appeal of the communist camp.

THE UNITED STATES While Europe lay in ruins, the United States boomed. The majority of Americans could afford more consumer goods than ever before—almost always U.S. manufactures. Home ownership became more common, especially in the burgeoning suburbs. Stimulating suburban development was a baby boom that reversed more than a century of declining birth rates.

Yet anxieties about the future of the First World abounded. Following the Soviet Union's explosion of an atomic bomb, the communist revolution in China, and the outbreak of the Korean War, fear of the communist threat prompted increasingly harsh rhetoric. In fact, anticommunist hysteria led the Republican senator from Wisconsin, Joseph McCarthy, to initiate a campaign to uncover closet communists in the State Department and in Hollywood. Televised congressional hearings broadcast his views to the entire nation, compelling elected officials to support a strong anticommunist foreign policy and a large military budget.

Levittown. In the decades after World War II, the American population shifted from the cities to the suburbs. To satisfy the demand for single-family homes, private developers, assisted by government policies, built thousands of new communities on the outskirts of urban centers. Places like Long Island's Levittown (pictured here), made affordable by the use of standard designs and construction, enabled many middle-class Americans to own their own home.

Anticommunism. As the Cold War heated up, anticommunist fervor swept the United States. Leading the charge against the "communist conspiracy" was Wisconsin senator Joseph McCarthy, pictured here with his aide, the attorney Roy Cohn.

Civil Rights Movement. *Left:* The 1955 arrest of Rosa Parks for refusing to relinquish her seat on a bus in Montgomery, Alabama, led to a boycott that brought Martin Luther King Jr. to prominence and galvanized the challenge to legal racial segregation in the American South. *Right:* Borrowing from Gandhi's tactics of nonviolent civil disobedience, protesters staged "sit-ins" across the southern United States in the 1950s and early 1960s, as in this photograph of Black and White students seated together at a segregated lunch counter in Jackson, Mississippi.

Postwar American prosperity did not benefit all citizens equally. During the 1950s, nearly a quarter of the American population lived in poverty. But many African Americans, a group disproportionately trapped below the poverty line, participated in a powerful movement for equal rights and the end of racial segregation. The National Association for the Advancement of Colored People (NAACP) won court victories that mandated the desegregation of schools. Boycotts, too, became a weapon of the growing **civil rights movement**, with Martin Luther King Jr. (1929–1968) leading a successful strike against injustices in the bus system of Montgomery, Alabama. Here and in subsequent campaigns against White supremacy, King borrowed his most effective weapon—the commitment to nonviolent protest and the appeal to conscience—from Gandhi. As the civil rights movement spread, the federal government gradually supported programs for racial equality.

THE JAPANESE "MIRACLE" Japan reemerged as an economic powerhouse in this period. The war had ended with Japan's unconditional surrender in 1945, its dreams of dominating East Asia dashed, and its homeland devastated. But after 1945, in an attempt to incorporate Japan into the First World, the United States provided military protection, investment, and transfers of technology to help rebuild Japanese society. The Japanese government guided this economic development through directed investment, partnerships with private firms, and protectionist policies. By the mid-1970s, Japan, formerly a dictatorship, was a politically stable civilian regime with a thriving economy, enjoying considerable American guidance and the replacement of the emperor's power with a parliamentary system.

The Second World

The Soviet Union and eastern European satellites, together with Mongolia and North Korea, constituted the communist Second World. The scourge of World War II and the shadow

Soviet Model. The rapid infrastructural development under Stalin was certainly a great feat, though it came at the cost of a great loss of human life. Displayed in this East German poster is a map of new canals constructed in this period as part of Stalin's Five-Year Plan.

of the Cold War fell heavily on the Soviets. Having lost 70,000 towns and villages, 32,000 factories, 82,000 schools, one-third of its gross domestic product (GDP), and 27 million people, the Soviet Union was determined to insulate itself from future aggression from the west. That meant turning eastern Europe, as well as parts of northeastern Asia, into a bloc of communist buffer states.

THE APPEAL OF THE SOVIET MODEL The Soviet model's egalitarian ideology and success with rapid industrialization made it seem a viable alternative to capitalism. Here there was no private property and thus, in Marxist terms, no exploitation. The Soviet state promised full employment and immunity from capitalism's upturns and downturns. The model also promised rapid development—which would make it appealing for ambitious Third World leaders. It forced agrarian collectivization and rapid introduction of heavy industry. This spelled doom for independent producers. In the Arctic region, for instance, Indigenous peoples like the Chukchi who lived off whaling and hunting reindeer were forced into collectives and required to fill production quotas, while their children received Russian educations and were taught how to speak Russian. Across the tundra, Soviet engineers and geologists moved in to make the landscape more productive through the extraction of natural resources for the nation. Along with them came the Gulag camps filled with political prisoners and criminals who provided forced labor to extract natural resources. Eventually, these labor camps would turn into major industrial sites and cities that drove Soviet growth. But they also further impinged on the lives of the Indigenous Arctic peoples. Many Chukchi complained. "I am the master of myself," protested one man who refused to give up his reindeer. "Under the reign of the Chukchi life is better."

Indigenous Arctic Peoples. Indigenous peoples like the Chukchi, who lived off whaling and hunting reindeer in the Soviet Siberian tundra, wanted to continue their traditional ways of life but were forced into collectives and required to fill production quotas as part of the Soviet Union's effort to modernize the country.

Soviet propaganda touted protections for workers, inexpensive mass transit, paid maternity leave, free health care, and universally available education. By the 1950s, the literacy rate soared above 80 percent. True, Soviet policies did not provide material abundance of the sort that First World nations were enjoying. But if consumer goods were often scarce, in state stores they were cheap. Likewise, while it sometimes took ten years or more to obtain a small apartment through waiting lists at work, when one's turn finally came the apartment carried low annual rent and could be passed on to one's children.

Because of censorship, few inhabitants of the Soviet zone knew how people lived in the First World, so it was easy to believe in the advantages of the Soviet system. Yet, even when people learned about the prosperity of western Europe and the United States (usually from intercepting forbidden western TV and radio programs), many still contended that the Soviet Union was the more just society. Theirs, they believed, was a land with no racial or class divisions, no drive for foreign colonies, no imperialist wars over markets. If members of the Soviet elite lived in privileged circumstances, their luxurious lifestyles were often well concealed. Indeed, many of socialism's internal critics did not typically seek to overthrow the system and restore capitalism. Rather, they demanded that the Soviet regime introduce reforms that would create "socialism with a human face."

REPRESSION OF DISSENT Few outside the Soviet sphere knew just how inhuman Soviet communism was, and few within knew the extent of the brutality. Under Stalin, anyone suspected of opposing the regime risked imprisonment, forced labor, and often torture or execution. After the war, Stalin and the leadership tightened their grip. Surviving soldiers who had been prisoners of war in Germany and civilians who had survived enslaved labor at the hands of the Germans—and had therefore seen the better living conditions of the west—were sent to special screening camps. Many disappeared. By the time of Stalin's death in 1953, the vast gulag (labor camp complex) confined several million people, who dug for gold and uranium and survived on hunks of bread and gruel.

Stalin's successors had to face hard questions, including what to do with so many prisoners, many of whom were incarcerated for fabricated political crimes. This problem became acute when mass strikes rocked the camps in 1953 and 1954, forcing the regime's hand. In 1956, the new party leader, Nikita Khrushchev, delivered a speech at a closed session of the Communist Party Congress in which he attempted to

The Gulag. The Soviet labor camp system was an integral part of the Soviet economy. At any given time, around 3 million prisoners labored in camps, like this one in Perm, Siberia, felling timber, building railroads, or digging for gold. Several million more were forced into exile in isolated locales. During World War II, the gulag population fell drastically, as inmates were sent to certain death at the front or perished from starvation. Between the war's end and Khrushchev's rise to power (following Stalin's death) in the 1950s, the gulag system reached its peak, with the imprisonment of German and Japanese POWs, the deportation of entire nations, and the internment of Soviet returnees from German camps.

separate Stalin's crimes from true communism. The speech was never published in the Soviet Union, but party members discussed it widely and it was leaked abroad. The extent of the arrests and executions under Stalin that Khrushchev revealed came as a terrible shock.

Repercussions were far-reaching. Eastern European leaders interpreted Khrushchev's speech as an endorsement for political liberation and economic experimentation. Right away, Polish intellectuals began a drive to break free from the communist ideological straitjacket. Soon Polish workers organized a general strike in Poznań—first over bread and wages, then against Soviet occupation. Emboldened by these events, Hungarian intellectuals and students held demonstrations demanding an uncensored press, free elections with genuine alternative parties, and the withdrawal of Soviet troops. The Hungarian Party leader, Imre Nagy, endorsed the campaign for reform and threatened to withdraw from the Warsaw Pact.

But the seeming liberalization promised by Khrushchev's speech proved short-lived. Rather than let eastern Europeans stray, the Soviet leadership crushed dissent. In Poland, the security police massacred strikers. In Hungary, tanks from the Soviet Union and other Warsaw Pact members invaded, and the Soviet Union installed a new government that aimed to smash all "counterrevolutionary" activities; Nagy was kidnapped, then murdered. After the revolts, Hungary and Poland did win some economic and cultural autonomy, but unquestionably, the Second World remained very much the dominion of the Soviet Union.

Despite the self-inflicted stains from its crackdowns and arrests of nonconformists, the Soviet Union was undeniably a superpower. In fact, its status surged after the launching of Sputnik, the first satellite, into space in 1957. Students from Third World countries flocked to the Soviets' excellent education system for training as engineers, scientists, army commanders, and revolutionaries. The updated 1961 Communist Party program predicted euphorically that within twenty years the Soviet Union would surpass the United States and eclipse the First World, but the overwhelming emphasis on heavy industry left terrible scars both on the population and on the landscape. (See Current Trends in World History: Soviet Ecocide.)

The Third World

In the 1950s, French intellectuals coined the term **Third World** (*tiers monde*) to describe countries that, like the "Third Estate" in the 1789 French Revolution, represented the majority of the world's population but were oppressed. The term became a slogan of resistance and a declaration of autonomy from the other two blocs, the capitalist west and the communist east. The Third World's defenders believed capitalist countries were too materialistic and were ruled by oligarchic corporations, while they thought communist countries were soulless, godless, and tended toward dictatorship. Third Worlders aimed to defeat imperialism, which they regarded as a sinister force. They also challenged global inequality. By the early 1960s, most of the countries in Asia, Africa, and Latin America, having emerged from colonial domination, aimed to create more just societies than those of the First and Second Worlds. Their leaders believed that they could even build democratic societies and promote rapid economic development through economic planning.

The early 1960s were years of heady optimism in the Third World. Ghanaian prime minister Kwame Nkrumah trumpeted pan-Africanism as a way to increase the power of African nations in global politics. Egyptian president Gamal Abdel Nasser boasted that his democratic socialism was neither western nor Soviet and that Egypt would remain neutral in the Cold War struggle. Indian prime minister Jawaharlal Nehru blended democratic politics and vigorous state planning to promote India's quest for political independence and economic autonomy. Around Latin America, governments aggressively promoted industrialization and agrarian reform to break their dependence on exports and to break the grip of old elites.

LIMITS TO AUTONOMY Charting a third way proved difficult. Both the Soviets and the Americans saw the Third World as "underdeveloped" and as a place where they could showcase their competing virtues. Moscow championed central planning solutions, while Washington, D.C., sought to ensure that market structures and private property underlay modernization. American-led institutions, like the World Bank and the International Monetary Fund, functioned to make the Third World more friendly to capitalism.

Another force that threatened Third World economic autonomy was the multinational corporation. In the rush to acquire advanced technology, Africans, Asians, and Latin Americans struck deals with multinationals to import their know-how. Owned primarily by American, European, and Japanese entrepreneurs, firms such as United Fruit, Firestone, and Volkswagen expanded cash cropping and plantation activities and established manufacturing branches worldwide. But such corporations impeded the growth of indigenous firms. Although the world's nations were more economically interdependent, the west still made the decisions—and reaped most of the profits.

Whether dealing with the west or the Soviet Union, Third World leaders had limited options because they faced pressure to choose one side or the other in the Cold War. To create more subservient client states, the Soviet Union backed communist insurgencies around the globe, while the United States supported almost all leaders who declared their anti-communism. Indeed, to contain communist expansion, the United States formed a number of military alliances. Following the 1949 creation of NATO, similar regional arrangements took shape in Southeast Asia (SEATO) and in the Middle East (the Baghdad Pact). These organizations brought many Third World nations into American-led alliances and allowed the United States to establish military bases in foreign territories. The Soviet Union countered by positioning its own forces in other Third World countries.

Nowhere was the militarization of Third World countries more threatening to economic development than in Africa. Whereas in the colonial era African states had spent little on military forces, this trend ended abruptly once the states became independent and were drawn into the Cold War. Civil wars, like the one that splintered Nigeria between 1967 and 1970, were opportunities for the great powers to wield influence. When the west refused to sell weapons to the Nigerian government so it could suppress the breakaway eastern province of Biafra, the Soviets supplied MIG aircraft and other vital weapons. A similar situation occurred in Egypt, a strategic region to both superpowers. After the founding of Israel, Egypt's new military rulers insisted that their country never again be caught militarily unprepared. Aware of the west's support for Israel, the Egyptians turned to the Soviet bloc. The resulting arms race between Egypt and Israel left the region bristling with modern weaponry.

Thus, Third World nations now confronted a situation that has been called **neocolonialism**. How were they to apply liberal or socialist models to their own situations? How were they to deal with economic structures and institutions that seemed to reduce their autonomy and limit their development? And how might they escape being puppets of the west or the Soviet Union? No wonder Third World nations grew frustrated about prospects for an alternative way to modernity.

By the late 1960s, as the euphoria of decolonization evaporated and new states became mired in debt and dependency, many Third World nations fell into dictatorship and authoritarian rule. Although some dictators still spoke about forging a third way, they did so mainly to justify their own corrupt regimes. They had forgotten the democratic commitments that were made at independence. Most also had been drawn into the Cold War, the better to extract arms and assistance from one of the superpowers.

The Global View

MAP 20.7 | The Emergence of the First, Second, and Third Worlds during the Cold War, 1945–1991

In the post–World War II era, a three-world order emerged in the backdrop of an ideological Cold War that pitted liberal democracies against communist states.

- According to the map, what two countries played the largest role in the Cold War?
- According to the map, how geographically widespread was the Cold War? How do you know?
- According to the reading, what was the role of the colonized worlds in the Cold War?

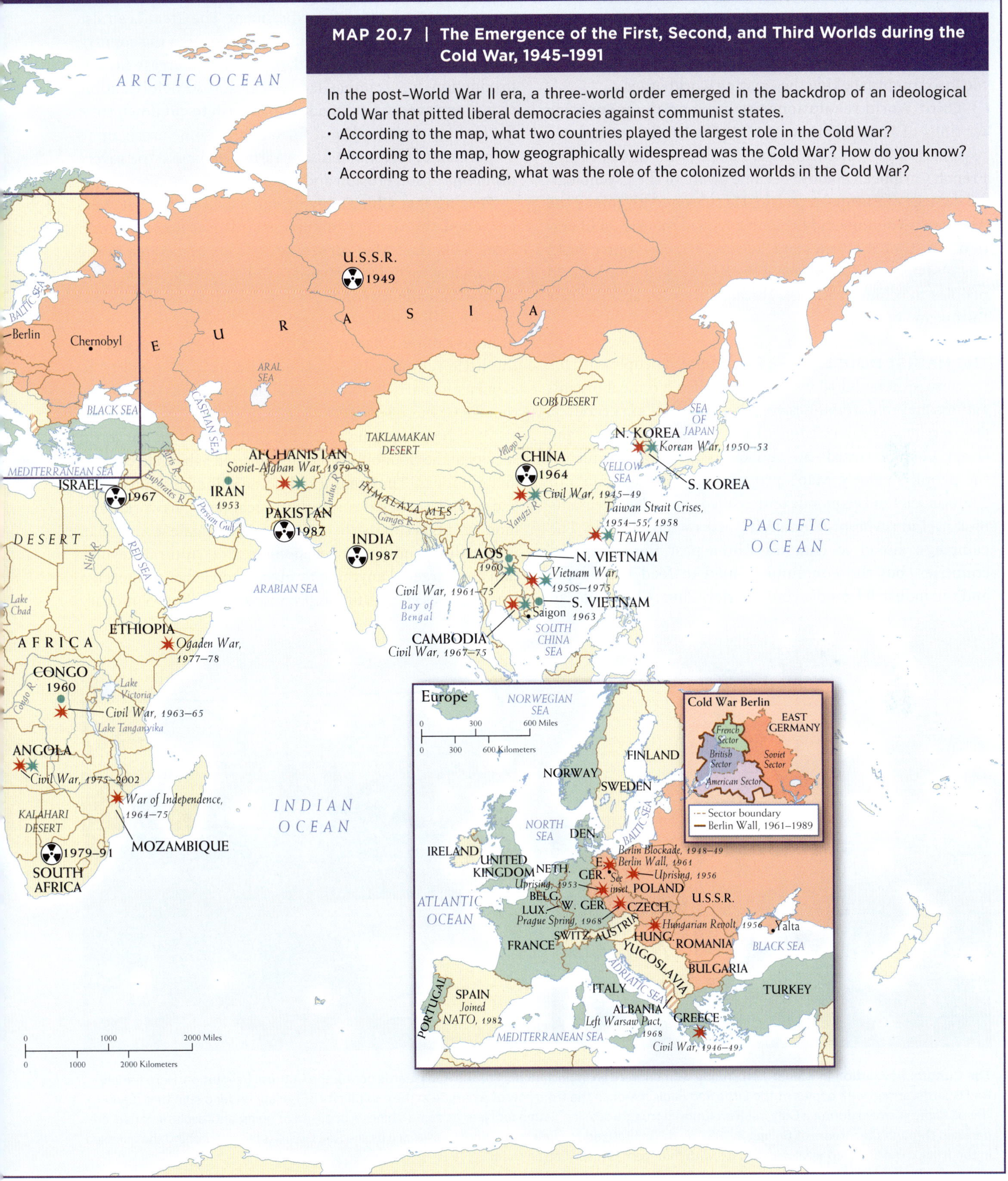

REVOLUTIONARIES AND RADICALS Against the background of bitterly disappointed expectations, Third World radicalism emerged as a powerful force. Revolutionary movements in the late 1950s and the 1960s sought to transform their societies. But while some radicals seized power, they, too, had trouble shaking the existing world order.

Third World revolutionaries drew on the pioneering writings of Frantz Fanon (1925–1961). While serving as a psychiatrist in French Algeria, Fanon (who was born in a French Caribbean colony) became aware of the psychological damage of European racism. He subsequently joined the Algerian revolution and became a radical theorist of liberation. (See Global Themes and Sources: Primary Source 20.4.) His 1961 book *The Wretched of the Earth* urged Third World peoples to achieve catharsis through violence against their European oppressors.

THE MAOIST MODEL While Fanon moved people with his writings, others did so by building radical political organizations and undertaking revolutionary social experiments. One model was Mao Zedong. In 1958, Mao introduced the Great Leap Forward—an audacious attempt to unleash the people's energy. Mao's program organized China into 24,000 social and economic units, called communes. Peasants took up industrial production in their own backyards. The campaign aimed to catapult China past the developed countries, but the communes failed to feed the people and the industrial goods were inferior. Thus, China took an economic leap backward. By 1961, as many as 45 million people had perished from famine and malnutrition, forcing the government to abandon the experiment. The Great Leap also exacted a devastating environmental cost from the country. The drive for a dramatic—and unrealistic—increase in steel production, for example, led to widespread deforestation, as farmers everywhere made a mad dash to cut down trees for fuel for their backyard furnaces. In some areas, up to 80 percent of forestland disappeared, leading to the severe problems of soil erosion and water loss.

Fearing that China's revolution was losing spirit, Mao launched the Great Proletarian Cultural Revolution in 1966. This time Mao turned against his associates in the Communist Party and appealed to China's young people. They enthusiastically responded. Organized into "Red Guards," over 10 million of them journeyed to Beijing to participate in huge rallies. Chanting, crying, screaming, and waving the little red book of Mao's quotations, they pledged to cleanse the party of its corrupt elements and to thoroughly remake Chinese society.

With help from the army, the Red Guards set out to rid society of the "four olds"—old customs, old habits, old culture, and old ideas. They ransacked homes, libraries, museums, and temples. They destroyed classical texts, artworks, and monuments. With its rhetoric of struggle against American imperialism and Soviet revisionism, the Cultural Revolution also targeted anything foreign. Knowledge of a foreign language was enough to compromise a person's revolutionary

The Cultural Revolution in China. *Left:* Young women were an important part of the Red Guards during the Cultural Revolution. Here female Red Guards, armed with copies of the *Little Red Book*, march in the front row of a parade in the capital city of Beijing under a sign that reads "Rise." *Right:* A crowd during a Cultural Revolution "struggle session" laugh and jeer as some Chinese, accused of being antirevolutionaries, are paraded through the streets of Beijing in 1967 by the militarized student revolutionaries known as the Red Guard (standing behind the accused in the truck). The accused wear dunce caps with their names inscribed on them.

credentials. The Red Guards attacked government officials, party cadres, or just plain strangers in an escalating cycle of violence. Even family members and friends were pressured to denounce one another; all had to prove themselves faithful followers of Chairman Mao. As chaos mounted, in late 1967 the army moved in to quell the disorder and reestablish control. To forestall further disruption, the government created an entire "lost generation" when, between 1967 and 1976, it deprived some 17 million Red Guards and students of their formal education and relocated them to the countryside "to learn from the peasants."

Given the costs of the Great Leap Forward and the Cultural Revolution, many of Mao's revolutionary policies were hard to admire. But in spite of the upheaval inside China, the Maoist model had great appeal outside China for people seeking radical alternatives to the three-world order. For example, a young philosopher from Ayacucho in Peru, Abimael Guzmán, traveled to Beijing in 1965 to learn about the miracles of Maoism and to meet the legendary chairman. Like thousands of other activists, he came away dazed. "It was one of the most transcendental and unforgettable experiences of my life," he reported. When Guzmán returned to Peru, he vowed to lead a peasant revolution in the Andes; disseminated translations of Mao's *Little Red Book*; converted teachers, especially women; and organized guerrilla militias. Peruvians woke up to graffiti all over prominent walls announcing, "Viva Beijing!" Guzmán renamed himself "Chairman Gonzalo" in honor of Chairman Mao and formed an insurgency movement that plunged Peru into a spiral of violence in the 1980s that left tens of thousands dead.

LATIN AMERICAN REVOLUTION Most Third World radicals did not go as far as Mao, but they still dreamed of overturning the social order. In Latin America, such dreams excited those who wished to throw off the influence of U.S.-owned multinational corporations and local elites.

Reform programs in Latin America addressed numerous concerns. Economic nationalists urged greater protection for domestic industries and sought to curb the multinationals. Liberal reformers wanted to democratize political systems and redistribute land, lest discontent erupt into full-blown revolutions like China's. But when liberals and nationalists joined forces, as in Guatemala in the 1950s, their reforms met resistance from local conservatives and from the United States. In Guatemala, the banana-producing American multinational United Fruit Company (which was the largest landowner and controlled the country's railroads and its major port) opposed land reform. Still, the progressive and nationalist regime of Jacobo Arbenz persevered with plans for agrarian reform and proposed taking over uncultivated land owned by United Fruit. Despite Arbenz's intention of compensating the company for its land, the U.S. Central Intelligence Agency (CIA) plotted with sectors of the Guatemalan army to put an end to reform, culminating in a coup d'état. Through moves such as this, the United States warned other governments that Washington would not tolerate assaults on its national interests in what it deemed its backyard.

In Cuba, the failure to address political, social, and economic concerns spurred a revolution. Since the Spanish-American War of 1898, Cuba had been ruled by governments better known for their compliance with U.S. interests than with popular sentiment. In 1933, during the crisis resulting from the Great Depression, Sergeant Fulgencio Batista emerged as a strongman, and in 1952 he led a military coup that deposed a corrupt civilian government and made him dictator. Under the Batista dictatorship, sugar planters, casino operators, and North American investors prospered, but middle- and working-class Cubans did not. The latter demanded a voice in politics and a new moral bond between the people and their government. In 1953, a group composed heavily of university students launched a botched assault on a military garrison. One of the leaders, a law student named **Fidel Castro** (1926–2016), gave a stirring speech at the rebels' trial, which made him a national hero. After his release from prison in 1955, he fled to Mexico. Several years later, he returned and started organizing guerrilla raids from mountain jungles. In early 1959, his band of bearded rebels swept into the capital, Havana.

Castro then set about consolidating power, elbowing aside rivals and wresting control of the economy from the wealthy elite, who fled into exile. As his policies grew increasingly radical, American leaders began to plot his demise. When

Fidel Castro and Cuba's National Liberation. The Cuban Revolution of 1958–1959 was a powerful model for many national liberation movements elsewhere in the world. No sooner did Cuban rebels force a break with the United States in 1959 than they discovered that they needed outside support to survive. The Soviet Union, eager to place a toehold for communism close to the United States, began to provide economic and military subsidies to its Caribbean ally. Here Castro grasps the hand of Nikita Khrushchev atop the Lenin Mausoleum during Moscow's May Day parade in 1963.

Castro announced a massive redistribution of land and the nationalization of foreign oil refineries, the United States ended all aid and sealed off the American market to Cuban sugar. Then, in 1961, the CIA mounted an invasion by Cuban exiles, landing at the Bay of Pigs. The invasion not only failed to overthrow Castro but further radicalized his ambitions for Cuba. He now declared himself a socialist and aligned himself with the Soviet Union. It was over Cuba and its radicalizing revolution that the world came closest to nuclear Armageddon in the Cuban Missile Crisis of 1962. To deter further U.S. attacks, Castro appealed to the Soviet Union to install nuclear weapons in Cuba—a mere 90 miles off the coast of Florida. When U.S. intelligence detected the weapons, President John F. Kennedy ordered a blockade of Cuba just as weapons-bearing Soviet ships were heading toward Havana. For several weeks, the world was paralyzed with anxiety as Kennedy, Khrushchev, and Castro matched threats. In the end, Kennedy succeeded in getting the Soviets to withdraw their nuclear missiles from Cuba.

The Cuban Revolution was a turning point in the making of the Third World. By rejecting the power of capitalist industrial societies, Castro and his followers promoted revolution, not reform, as a way to achieve Third World liberation. The symbol of this new spirit was Castro's closest lieutenant, Ernesto "Che" Guevara (1928–1967). "El Che" grew up in Argentina and traveled widely around Latin America as a student. Shortly after receiving his medical degree in 1953, he arrived in Guatemala in time to witness the CIA-backed overthrow of the progressive Arbenz government. Thereafter, Guevara became increasingly bitter about American influences in Latin America. He joined Castro's forces and helped topple the pro-American regime of Fulgencio Batista in Cuba in 1958. After 1959, he held several posts in the Cuban government but grew restive for more action. Latin America, he felt, should challenge the world power of the United States. Soon his casual military uniform, his patchy beard, his cigar, and his moral energy became legendary symbols of revolt.

The idea of revolution as a way to overcome underdevelopment and to free Third World societies spread beyond Latin America. Che became Castro's envoy to world meetings and summits of Third World state leaders, where he celebrated the Cuban road to freedom. Returning to Latin America, Che set up his center of operations in highland Bolivia in 1966, among South America's most downtrodden Indigenous people. "We have to create another Vietnam in the Americas with its center in Bolivia," he proclaimed. Guevara did not, however, know the local Indigenous language, and he had little logistical support. He and his two dozen fighters launched their regionwide war in absolute isolation. Thus, it took little time for the Bolivian army and CIA operators to capture the rebels. After a brief interrogation, Bolivian officers ordered that the guerrilla commander be killed on the spot.

To combat the germ of revolution, the Kennedy administration sent American advisers throughout Latin America to dole out aid, explain how to reform local land systems, and demonstrate the benefits of liberal capitalism. Working with American advisers, Latin American militaries were trained to root out radicalism. They learned that gaining the support of indigent civilians was the key to defeating the guerrillas. Even Salvador Allende's democratically elected socialist government in Chile was not spared; the CIA and

Che Guevara. Ernesto "Che" Guevara, shown here addressing a conference in Uruguay in 1961 at which he denounced U.S. interventions in Latin America, was a chief lieutenant to Cuba's Fidel Castro and a fierce champion of Third World radicalism.

Latin American Human Rights. By the early 1980s, human rights movements were gaining strength all over Latin America, even in Chile under the repressive General Pinochet. Here, a crowd of 400,000 demonstrates against his rule in November 1983.

U.S. policymakers aided General Augusto Pinochet's military coup against the regime in 1973 and looked the other way while political opponents were butchered. By 1975, rebel forces had been liquidated in Argentina, Uruguay, Brazil, Mexico, Bolivia, and Venezuela.

Tensions within the Three Worlds

Third World radicalism did not alter the balance of global wealth and power, but it exposed vulnerabilities in the three-world order. So did the continuation of the Vietnam War, which opened fissures within the First World. As antiwar and civil rights movements mushroomed, the United States experienced social unrest on a scale not seen since the Great Depression. In the Second World, too, dissent challenged the Soviet Union's hold on world communism. Satellite states in eastern Europe sought more flexible orbits, while Mao's China charted a course at odds with Soviet designs. Finally, in the 1970s, the rising fortunes of oil-producing nations and of Japan introduced new problems within and between worlds.

Tensions within the First World

Although the First World enjoyed great prosperity in the decades after World War II, a variety of issues created friction within these societies and between allies.

WOMEN'S ISSUES AND CIVIL RIGHTS In the First World, groups that believed they had been left behind in the surge of economic growth expressed deep unhappiness. One such group was women, whose economic and political opportunities remained severely restricted. In Italy, France, and Belgium, women did not obtain the right to vote until the end of World War II, and everywhere governance and high-paying jobs remained almost entirely in the hands of men. Although women made gains in employment outside the home, they still awaited a decrease in domestic responsibilities.

Another group, European students, expressed concerns about the deployment of nuclear weapons and about exclusive and unresponsive educational institutions that preserved the power and high culture of the elite few. Protests reached their peak in Paris in 1968 when workers joined with students in a general strike and clashed violently with police.

In the United States, a crescendo of protests against racial discrimination propelled the U.S. government to enact civil rights legislation and to promote programs designed to end poverty. The Civil Rights Act of 1964 banned segregation in public facilities and outlawed racial discrimination in employment, and the Voting Rights Act of 1965 gave millions of previously disenfranchised African Americans an opportunity to exercise equal political rights. The Lyndon Baines Johnson administration also supported programs bolstering social security, health, education, and assistance to the poor. Aided by impressive economic growth, the War on Poverty nearly halved the U.S. poverty rate.

Urban Riots. Racial tensions boiled over in a number of American cities during the 1960s. This photograph of a man being taken into custody was snapped on July 23, 1967, the first day of what turned out to be five days of rioting in Detroit. The unrest left 43 people dead, 467 injured, and more than 2,000 buildings burned down.

But legacies of racism and inequality were not easy to overcome. In spite of Supreme Court decisions, most schools remained racially homogeneous not only in the South but across the United States, as "White flight" to the suburbs left inner-city neighborhoods and schools to minorities. Especially in Atlanta, Philadelphia, Detroit, Miami, and St. Louis, African Americans' frustration over discrimination and lack of jobs led to violence. Militant voices, like those of Malcolm X and the Black Panthers, became prominent. Instead of integration, these radicals advocated Black separatism; instead of Americanism, they espoused pan-Africanism.

African American struggles inspired Native Americans, Mexican Americans, homosexuals, and women to initiate their own campaigns for equality and empowerment. Women now questioned a life built around taking care of home and family. In fact, the introduction of the birth control pill in 1960 and the publication of Betty Friedan's *The Feminine Mystique* in 1963 stand as watershed moments in American women's history. Because oral contraception allowed women to limit childbearing and to have sex with less fear of pregnancy, the resulting freedom helped unleash a sexual revolution. Moreover, Friedan blasted the myth of middle-class domestic contentment, describing the idealized 1950s suburban home as a "comfortable concentration camp" from which women must escape. Despite rising numbers of married women and college-educated women in the workforce, their compensation and opportunity for advancement lagged far behind those of men.

ENVIRONMENTAL CONCERNS AND THE VIETNAM WAR A year before Friedan authored her challenge to the subordination of women, Rachel Carson published *Silent*

Women Protest Sexism. Insisting that "the private is public," many women in the 1960s and 1970s argued that the problem of sexism went beyond equal rights and income equality: women's oppression began in the home, where they were treated merely as homemakers or as sex objects. At this 1971 rally in London, protesters suggested that women were being "crucified" by their association with these everyday objects: an apron, a net shopping bag, silk stockings, and an item of washing.

Spring, a book that was equally revolutionary in its attack against long-held practices. In particular, Carson's book took on the use of synthetic pesticides such as dichlorodiphenyltrichloroethane (DDT), which she said caused cancer, devastated wildlife, and destroyed natural ecosystems. Although chemical manufacturers responded that pesticides had vastly multiplied agricultural yields, *Silent Spring* stirred opposition that ultimately led to the banning of DDT in the United States in 1972. More broadly, Carson's book spurred the development of an environmental movement that questioned many of the ideas about economic progress and material prosperity upon which the "American Dream" had rested.

The escalation of the war in Vietnam prompted many American college students to question the ideals of American society. As the United States increased troop levels there in the 1960s, it conscripted more men. Tens of thousands of young Americans fled the country to escape the draft. Upward of 250,000 simply did not register; another 100,000 burned their draft cards. After President Richard Nixon sent American troops into Cambodia in 1970 to root out North Vietnamese soldiers, students at over 500 campuses occupied buildings and closed down universities. At Kent State University in Ohio, National Guardsmen attempting to stop the protests killed four students.

One of the tactics used by the U.S. military was the spraying of the herbicide known as Agent Orange, which was used to destroy North Vietnamese crops and jungle hideouts. This chemical, which got its name from the orange barrels in which it was transported, gained notoriety as veterans and Vietnamese civilians claimed that this weaponized herbicide—more powerful than DDT—had caused severe damage to their health. The spectacle of destruction, mounting body bags filled with American soldiers, and news of atrocities committed by American troops drained the war of support at home. The United States withdrew from Vietnam in 1973, but not before the divisions created by the war had strained the country almost to the breaking point.

Tensions within the Second World

The unity of the communist world also came under increasing pressure. As early as 1948, Yugoslavia had broken free of the Soviet yoke and embarked on its own road to building socialism. Other satellites within the Soviet bloc had more trouble freeing themselves. In 1956, Poland and Hungary had been forced back in line. Twelve years later, Czechoslovakia experienced the Prague Spring, in which communist authorities experimented with creating a democratic and pluralist socialist world. Workers and students rallied behind the reformist government of Alexander Dubček, calling for more freedom of expression, more autonomy for workers and consumers, and more debate within the ruling monopoly party. Once again, Soviet tanks crushed what the Soviets branded a "counterrevolutionary" movement. As the tanks rolled into Prague, the Czech capital, one desperate student doused himself with gasoline and lit a match—his public suicide a gesture of defiance against communist rule.

Thereafter, the Prague Spring served as a symbol for dissenters, who were divided between those who still wanted to reform socialism and those who wanted to overturn it. Underground reading groups proliferated throughout eastern Europe, and some Russians renewed their faith in Orthodox Christianity, their prerevolutionary religion. Many dissidents were exiled from the Soviet Union. Most famous by the early 1970s was the Russian novelist Aleksandr Solzhenitsyn. His masterwork, *The Gulag Archipelago*, repudiated the notion

Prague Spring. In the spring of 1968, a movement demanding economic self-determination and freedom of speech took hold in Czechoslovakia, especially among students in its capital city, Prague. The Soviets allowed the movement to unfold for several months, but in late August they organized an invasion with troops and tanks from the USSR and several other Warsaw Pact countries. Although Czech students rallied to oppose the invaders—shouting "Ivan, go home!"—the Soviets suppressed the movement, afterward purging intellectuals from all leadership positions.

that socialism could be reformed by a turn away from Stalin's policies. Yet almost no one in the Soviet Union could obtain copies of Solzhenitsyn's exposé, which had been published abroad and was a best-seller in the west. In 1974, the author himself was expelled from the USSR and took up residence in Vermont.

Still, there were important changes within the Second World. During the 1950s and 1960s, "national communism" became the rule throughout eastern Europe, even in countries that experienced Soviet invasions. National variations also arose within the Soviet Union, where Moscow conceded some autonomy to the Communist Party machines of its fifteen republics—in exchange for fundamental loyalty. Dissidents were still persecuted, but by the 1970s many fewer were executed or even arrested outright, and the population of the gulags declined.

Shared antipathy for the United States had created a Sino-Soviet alliance in the years just after the Chinese Revolution of 1949. By the late 1950s, the Soviet Union had contributed massive military and economic aid to China. But the Chinese increasingly sought to define their own brand of Marxism and criticized Khrushchev's efforts to distance himself from Stalin and reduce tensions with the United States and the west. Preferring to accentuate confrontation, the Chinese acquired their own nuclear weapons and began to tout themselves as a peasant-socialist alternative to the Soviet model of development, especially for Third World countries. The fissure raised China's profile throughout Asia and even in eastern Europe. Indeed, Romania achieved a measure of autonomy in foreign policy by playing off China and the Soviet Union. Albania declared its allegiance to China. African nations, interested in Soviet aid, increased their demands with subtle hints that they might consider deepening ties with China instead. In the 1970s, U.S. president Richard Nixon seized the opportunity offered by the Sino-Soviet split to woo Mao's China at Soviet expense.

Tensions within the Third World

In contrast to the First and Second Worlds, the Third World was never unified by economic, military, or political alliances. Despite a common history of domination and the shared search for a "third way," the Cold War polarized Third World nations. It pushed them to choose between alignment with the First World or the Second. Nonetheless, radicalism nourished new hopes for unifying and empowering the Third World.

One effort at collaboration was the formation in 1960 of a cartel of oil exporters. The Organization of the Petroleum Exporting Countries (OPEC)—which included Algeria, Ecuador, Gabon, Indonesia, Iran, Iraq, Kuwait, Libya, Nigeria, Qatar, Saudi Arabia, the United Arab Emirates, and Venezuela—had little impact in raising oil revenues through the 1960s, even though several members nationalized their oil fields. But after the fourth major Arab-Israeli war broke out in 1973, OPEC's Arab members decided to pressure Israel's First World allies by halting oil exports to them. Overnight, the embargo raised oil prices more than threefold, a bonanza that enriched all oil producers and led to an oil crisis in the west. To many, the bulging treasuries of OPEC nations seemed like the Third World's revenge. Here were Saudi Arabian princes, Venezuelan magnates, and Indonesian ministers dictating world prices to industrial consumers.

But the realignment was incomplete. Third World producers of raw materials such as coffee and rubber tried unsuccessfully to duplicate OPEC's model, and OPEC itself had trouble controlling the world's oil market. During the 1970s, discoveries in the North Sea, Mexico, and Canada reduced pressures on the large oil-consuming states to be more fuel efficient. With supply up, prices fell. To compensate for lost revenue, various OPEC states raised their own production, putting further downward pressure on prices.

Nor did oil revenues help overcome poverty and dependency in the Third World as a whole. To the contrary, most revenue surpluses from OPEC simply flowed back to First World banks or boosted real-estate holdings in Europe and the United States. Some of the money was in turn reloaned to the world's poorest countries in Africa, Asia, and Latin America, at high

Current Trends in World History

Soviet Ecocide

Before the twentieth century, the spread of peasant agriculture, as well as settlement in the steppe and forest zones and the hunting of fur-bearing forest animals, brought profound changes to the Russian environment, including soil degradation, deforestation, and depopulation of species. But the environmental impact of Soviet-era industrialization was staggering. No other industrial civilization poisoned its land, air, water, and people so systematically and over so long a time. Scholars have deemed the Soviet environmental catastrophe an "ecocide."

Soviet economic planners and propagandists celebrated the plumes of purple and orange smoke in their skies as evidence of the country's huge industrial production. Pollution control devices remained unheard of well after their 1950s introduction in Europe and the United States; even when installed in Soviet factories, they were rarely turned on so as not to depress output. Sulfur dioxide, hydrogen sulfide, and solid phenols in the water, the food supply, and the air caused epidemic levels of respiratory and intestinal ailments, blood diseases, and birth defects. The giant steel plant at Magnitogorsk, once the pride of Stalin's industrial leap, became a zone of atmospheric and soil devastation 120 miles long and 40 miles wide; inside it, chronic bronchitis, asthma, and cancers attacked the population. In agriculture, the Soviet Union continued to use the insecticide DDT long after its 1972 banning in the United States.

In the 1970s, despite the socialist country's overall development, Soviet life expectancy began to decline and infant mortality to rise. By 1989, Soviet men lived an average of 63.9 years from birth, down from 66.1 in 1965. By the late 1980s, infant mortality rose to 25.4 per 1,000, roughly the same as in Malaysia, a developing country, and Harlem. Alcoholism also contributed mightily to adverse health trends.

The April 1986 Chernobyl nuclear disaster exposed 20 million people in Ukraine and Belarus to excess radiation. Although there was no bomb concussion, the accident spewed more radioactive material into the atmosphere than had been released by the atomic bombs over Hiroshima and Nagasaki. The Chernobyl cleanup claimed around 7,000 lives.

Few symbols of Soviet ecocide surpass the Aral Sea—once a huge saline lake at the border between Kazakhstan and Uzbekistan. Because inflow into the lake was blocked by dams built for wasteful power plants and excess irrigation for cotton production, the lake shrank by two-thirds, giving way to huge white, lifeless salt flats. Soviet cosmonauts, looking down from space in 1975, were astonished to see immense storms of dust and salt over central Asia. Toxic salt rain wreaked enormous damage on human and animal lungs. Yet, despite the human toll, Soviet Uzbekistan, with twice the population of Soviet Belarus, was served by only one-third the hospitals.

Beginning in the 1950s, Lake Baikal, the world's largest body of fresh water, and once among the cleanest, suffered from the construction of factories on its perimeter, especially a cellulose cord plant (for tires on Soviet bombers) and pulp plant (for paper). The threat to Baikal, as well as the Aral Sea catastrophe,

interest rates, to pay for more expensive imports—including oil! The biggest bonanza went to multinational petroleum firms whose control over production, refining, and distribution yielded enormous profits.

For all the talk in the mid-1970s of changing the balance of international economic relations between the world's rich and poor countries, fundamental inequalities persisted. Those few Third World nations that appeared to break out of the cycle of poverty, like South Korea and Taiwan, did not achieve success through international markets. Rather, these states regulated markets, nurtured new industries, educated the populace, and required multinationals to work collaboratively with local firms. These were exceptions that proved the general rule: the international economy reinforced existing structures.

Conclusion

The three-world order arose on the ruins of European empires and their Japanese counterpart. World War II affirmed the nation-state rather than the empire as the primary form for organizing communities. In spite of the rhetoric of individualism and the free market, the war and postwar reconstruction also enhanced the reach and functions of the modern state. In the Third World, too, leaders of new nations saw the state as the primary instrument for promoting economic development.

Aral Sea Catastrophe. What was once one of the largest lakes in the world shrank to less than 10 percent of its original size due to the aggressive Soviet construction of irrigation canals in the 1960s to bolster cotton production. Here, a shipping vessel is moored on the bed of the former Aral Sea, in present-day Kazakhstan.

sparked grassroots environmental activism in an otherwise tightly controlled Soviet society. Scientists led the way in breaking censorship taboos, and people from all walks of life turned up at unsanctioned meetings and signed their names to petitions to stop the damage and protect the environment.

QUESTIONS FOR ANALYSIS

- Why do you think environmental degradation was so much more severe in the Soviet Union than in western countries?
- Why do you think environmental awareness developed much sooner in the United States than in the Soviet Union?

EXPLORE FURTHER

Feshbach, Murray, and Alfred Friendly Jr., *Ecocide in the USSR: Health and Nation under Siege* (1992).

Micklin, Philip, N.V. Aladin, and Igor Plotnikov (eds.), *The Aral Sea: The Devastation and Partial Rehabilitation of a Great Lake* (2014).

Weiner, Douglas R., *A Little Corner of Freedom: Russian Nature Protection from Stalin to Gorbachev* (1999).

The organization of the world into three blocs lasted into the mid-1970s. This arrangement fostered the economic recovery of western Europe and Japan from the wounds inflicted by war. These nations' recovery grew out of a Cold War alliance with the United States, where anticommunist hysteria accompanied an economic boom. The Cold War also cast a shadow over the citizens of the Soviet Union and eastern Europe. Gulags and political surveillance became widespread, while the Soviets and their satellite regimes mobilized resources for military purposes. The Third World, squeezed by its inability to reduce poverty, on the one hand, and by superpower rivalry, on the other, struggled to pursue a "third way." While some states maintained democratic institutions and promoted economic development, many tumbled into dictatorships and authoritarian regimes and often suffered irreparable environmental damage.

In this context, Third World revolutionaries sought radical social and political transformation, seeking paths different from both western capitalism and Soviet communism. Though not successful, they energized considerable tensions in the three-world order. These tensions intensified in the late 1960s and early 1970s as Vietnamese communists defeated the United States, an oil crisis struck the west, and protests escalated in the First and Second Worlds. Thirty years after the war's end, the world order forged after 1945 was beginning to give way.

After You Read This Chapter

TRACING THE GLOBAL STORYLINES

FOCUS ON: World War II and the Emergence of the First, Second, and Third Worlds during the Cold War

World War II

- World War II grows out of unresolved problems connected to World War I, especially the aggressive plans of Germany and Japan to expand their political and economic influence.
- The war brings huge human and material costs and ushers in an age of nuclear weapons.
- At the war's end, the United States, fearing the spread of communism and Soviet influence, rebuilds war-torn Europe and Japan and creates military and political alliances to contain Soviet expansionist ambitions.

A New Global Order

- The Soviet Union and the United States become superpowers.
- Japan emerges as an economic powerhouse and a U.S. ally.
- A weakened Europe cannot resist demands for independence from Asian and African nationalists.
- Chinese communists engineer a revolution, while Indian nationalists and many African leaders achieve independence through negotiations.
- Elsewhere, especially in territories with large settler populations, decolonization is violent (Palestine, Israel, Egypt, Algeria, and Kenya) or incomplete (southern Africa).
- Actions by Latin American reformers and revolutionary insurgents spark counterinsurgency efforts by the United States and its regional allies.
- An insecure three-world order emerges after most Asian and African states achieve independence.

CHRONOLOGY

The Americas
- United States emerges as a global superpower 1945
- U.S. civil rights movement 1950s–1960s

Europe
- World War II 1939–1945
- NATO formed 1949

Soviet Union
- Soviet Union emerges as a global superpower, creates client states in eastern Europe 1945
- Stalin dies 1953

Africa
- Decolonization 1950s–1970s

Middle East
- Decolonization 1940s–1950s
- The United Nations partitions Palestine 1948

South Asia
- British Raj ends, India and Pakistan declare independence 1947

East Asia
- World War II 1937–1945
- Vietnamese fight for independence, first from France and then from the United States 1946–1975
- Communist victory in Chinese civil war 1949
- Korean War 1950–1953
- Japanese economic "miracle" 1950s–1970s

1930 | 1940 | 1950

KEY TERMS

Allied Powers p. 873
apartheid p. 892
Axis Powers p. 873
Fidel Castro p. 903
civil rights movement p. 896
Cold War p. 880
decolonization p. 884
Holocaust p. 875
International Monetary Fund (IMF) p. 880
Mao Zedong p. 884
neocolonialism p. 899
North Atlantic Treaty Organization (NATO) p. 881
Third World p. 899
Warsaw Pact p. 881
World Bank p. 880
Zionism p. 890

THINKING ABOUT GLOBAL CONNECTIONS

Thinking about Worlds Together, Worlds Apart and the Three-World Order Explain how the collapse of a Europe-centered world changed how states interacted with one another. In what ways did the division of the globe into three rival worlds differ from the dominance of the European "great powers" that preceded it? Which world order do you think was more stable, the Europe-centered world or the three-world order that followed it? Do you think one system was more equitable than the other?

Thinking about Changing Power Relationships and the Three-World Order Analyze Third World revolutionaries' ability to alter the dynamic of the Cold War. Where do you think power was located in this period? To what degree did Washington and Moscow determine the course of world affairs, and to what degree were politicians in places like Cuba, Vietnam, and Algeria able to play the superpowers off against each other? How and to what degree were revolutionaries able to make claims on the First and Second Worlds for economic, political, or military assistance?

Thinking about Environmental Impacts and the Three-World Order In this period, for the first time, organized groups set out to defend the environment. What sparked their protests? Where were those organizations most fully developed? Where was ecological devastation most extreme? What force or forces opposed environmentalists?

Go to INQUIZITIVE to see what you've learned—and learn what you've missed—with personalized feedback along the way.

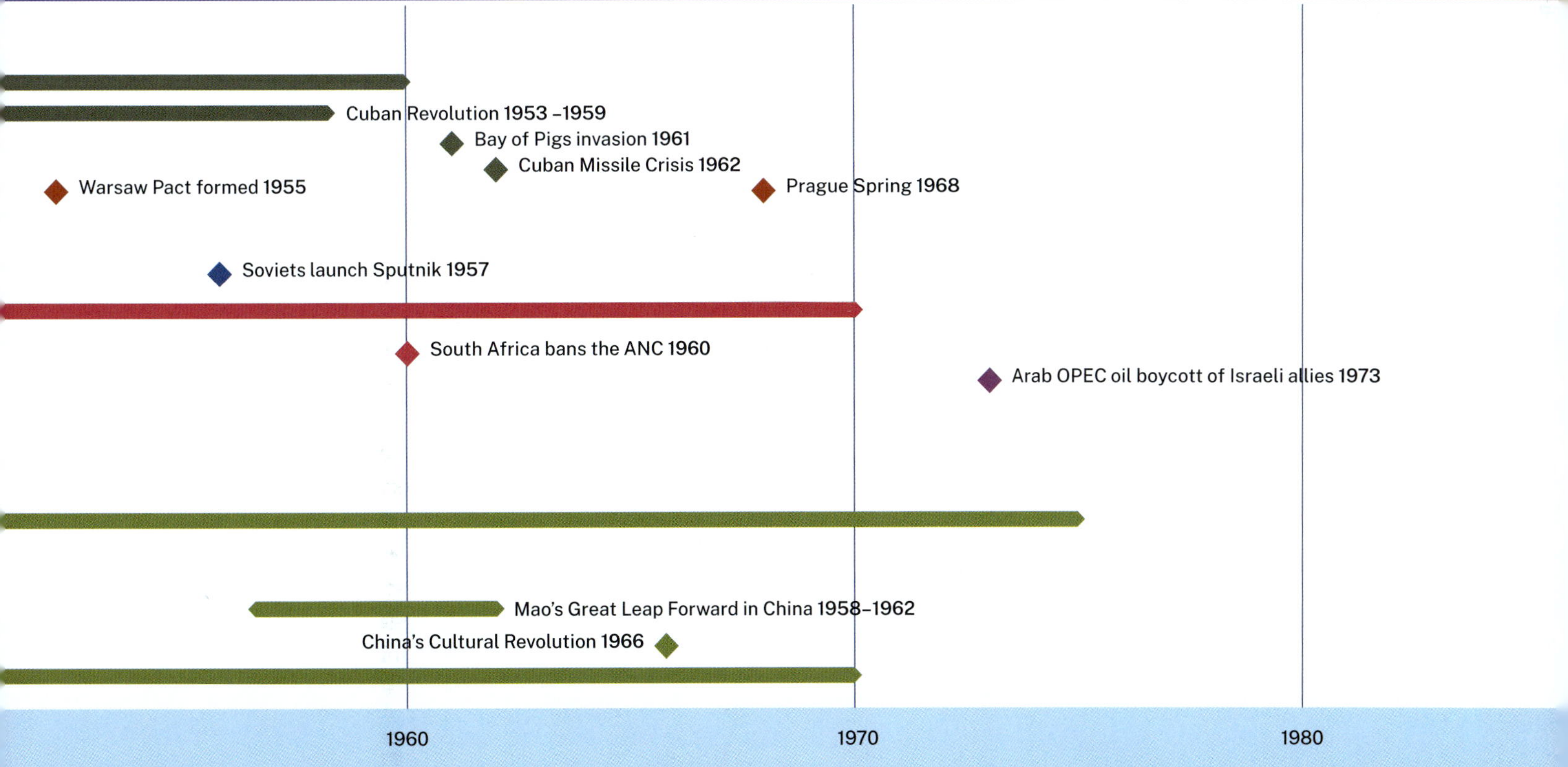

Global Themes and Sources

Comparing Independence and Nation Building

Intellectuals and political activists in the Third World sought to expel foreign colonizers and build new societies. As their nations struck out on their own, the overwhelming majority of these thinkers and leaders wanted to borrow at least some elements from their own established traditions, on the one hand, and from foreign influences, on the other.

In his "New Democracy" (1940), Mao Zedong set forth a new democratic culture—nationalistic, scientific, and mass based—that he regarded as a transitional stage to the communist utopia of the future. Jawaharlal Nehru also celebrated science and technology in his "Note to the Members of the National Planning Committee" (1940), which sought a "third way" between capitalism and communism. In his speech on Negritude, Léopold Sédar Senghor presented a Black culture different from, but not inferior to, European cultural forms. Frantz Fanon, inspired by Mao as well as Marx and Lenin, celebrated the power of violence to restore the self-respect of the colonized; only through violence and a rejection of all that the colonizers stood for, he thought, could the colonized ever truly free themselves.

These selections invite comparison. From a wide range of backgrounds, the authors represented here all drew inspiration in varying degrees from Marx and Lenin in their efforts to emancipate their countries and build new futures for their people. But for all that each of these authors sought to blend foreign influences with homegrown traditions, the balances they proposed and the pace and nature of the changes they sought differed markedly.

ANALYZING INDEPENDENCE AND NATION BUILDING COMPARATIVELY

All of these authors came from overwhelmingly rural societies. Explain why they drew on the ideas of Karl Marx, who famously likened peasants to a "sack of potatoes" and thought modern industry essential to end oppression of all kinds.

Identify the balance between indigenous tradition and foreign influence in each selection. Which text draws most heavily on foreign sources, and which rejects outside influences most completely?

Analyze the relationship between the individual and the community described in each of these readings.

Which of the readings do you consider most revolutionary, and why? Do you think the idea of revolution was important to the authors?

PRIMARY SOURCE 20.1

"New Democracy" (1940), Mao Zedong

As chairman of China's Communist Party, Mao Zedong (1893–1976) ruled the People's Republic of China from its founding in 1949 until his death. This document was written as Mao sought to adapt communism to Chinese traditions and distance himself from Soviet influence.

Explain what Mao means by "democracy of the Chinese type."

What, if any, foreign influence can you see in this text?

What elements, if any, of the Chinese past does Mao want to preserve?

The Chinese Revolution Is Part of the World Revolution

The historical feature of the Chinese revolution consists in the two steps to be taken, democracy and socialism, and the first step is now no longer democracy in a general sense, but democracy of the Chinese type, a new and special type—New Democracy. How, then, is this historical feature formed? Has it been in existence for the past hundred years, or is it only of recent birth?

If we make only a brief study of the historical development of China and of the world, we shall understand that this historical feature did not emerge as a consequence of the Opium War but began to take shape only after the first imperialist world war and the Russian October Revolution.

After these events, the Chinese bourgeois-democratic revolution changes its character and belongs to the category of the new bourgeois-democratic revolution and, so far as the revolutionary front is concerned, forms part of the proletarian-socialist world revolution.

This "world revolution" refers no longer to the old world revolution—for the old bourgeois world revolution has long become a thing of the past—but to a new world revolution, the socialist world revolution. Similarly, to form "part" of the world revolution means to form no longer a part of the old bourgeois revolution but of the new socialist revolution. This is an exceedingly great change unparalleled in the history of China and of the world.

This correct thesis propounded by the Chinese Communists is based on Stalin's theory.

As early as 1918, Stalin wrote in an article commemorating the first anniversary of the October Revolution:

> The great worldwide significance of the October Revolution chiefly consists in the fact that:
>
> 1. It has widened the scope of the national question and converted it from the particular question of combating national oppression in Europe into the general question of emancipating the oppressed peoples, colonies, and semi-colonies from imperialism.
>
> 2. It has opened up wide possibilities for their emancipation and the right path toward it, has thereby greatly facilitated the cause of the emancipation of the oppressed peoples of the West and the East, and has drawn them into the common current of the victorious struggle against imperialism.
>
> 3. It has thereby erected a bridge between the socialist West and the enslaved East, having created a new front of revolutions against world imperialism, extending from the proletarians of the West, through the Russian revolution to the oppressed peoples of the East.

Since writing this article, Stalin has again and again expounded the theoretical proposition that revolutions in colonies and semi-colonies have already departed from the old category and become part of the proletarian-socialist revolution.

The first step in, or the stage of, this revolution is certainly not, and cannot be, the establishment of a capitalist society under the dictatorship of the Chinese bourgeoisie; on the contrary, the first stage is to end with the establishment of a new-democratic society under the joint dictatorship of all Chinese revolutionary classes headed by the Chinese proletariat. Then the revolution will develop into the second stage so that a socialist society can be established in China.

New-Democratic Politics

As to the question of "political structure" [in the New Democracy], it is the question of the form of structure of political power, the form adopted by certain social classes in establishing their organs of political power to oppose their enemy and protect themselves. Without an adequate form of political power there would be nothing to represent the state. . . . But a system of really universal and equal suffrage, irrespective of sex, creed, property, or education, must be put into practice so that the organs of government elected can properly represent each revolutionary class according to its status in the state, express the people's will and direct revolutionary struggles, and embody the spirit of New Democracy. Such a system is democratic centralism. Only a government of democratic centralism can fully express the will of all the revolutionary people and most powerfully fight the enemies of the revolution.

The state system—joint dictatorship of all revolutionary classes. The political structure—democratic centralism. This is new-democratic government; this is a republic of New Democracy, the republic of the anti-Japanese united front, the republic of the new Three People's Principles with the three cardinal policies, and the Republic of China true to its name.

New-Democratic Economy

We must establish in China a republic that is politically new-democratic as well as economically new-democratic.

Big banks and big industrial and commercial enterprises shall be owned by this republic.

Enterprises, whether Chinese-owned or foreign-owned, that are monopolistic in character or that are on too large a scale for private management, such as banks, railways, and airlines, shall be operated by the state so that private capital cannot dominate the livelihood of the people. This is the main principle of the control of capital.

This was also a solemn statement contained in the Manifesto of the First National Congress of the Nationalists during the period of the Nationalist-Communist cooperation; this is the correct objective for the economic structure of the new-democratic republic under the leadership of the proletariat. The state-operated industries are socialist in character and constitute the leading force in the national economy as a whole; but this republic does not take over other forms of capitalist private property or forbid the development of capitalist production that "cannot dominate the livelihood of the people," for China's economy is still very backward.

This republic will adopt certain necessary measures to confiscate the land of landlords and distribute it to those peasants having no land or only a little land, carry out Dr. Sun Yat-sen's slogan of "land to the tillers," abolish the feudal relations in the rural areas, and turn the land into the private property of the peasants. In the rural areas, rich peasant economic activities will be tolerated. This is the line of "equalization of land ownership." The correct slogan for this line is "land to the tillers." In this stage, socialist agriculture is in general not yet to be established, though the various types of cooperative enterprises developed on the basis of "land to the tillers" will contain elements of socialism.

New-Democratic Culture

A given culture is the ideological reflection of the politics and economy of a given society. There is in China an imperialist culture, which is a reflection of the control of imperialism over China politically and economically. This part of culture is advocated not only by the cultural organizations run directly by the imperialists in China but also by a number of shameless Chinese. All culture that contains a slave ideology belongs to this category. There is also in China a semi-feudal culture, which is a reflection of semi-feudal politics and economy and has as its representatives all those who, while opposing the new culture and new ideologies, advocate the worship of Confucius, the study of the Confucian canon, the old ethical code, and the old ideologies. Imperialist culture and semi-feudal culture are affectionate brothers, who have formed a reactionary cultural alliance to oppose China's new culture. This reactionary culture serves the imperialists and the feudal class and must be swept away.

Some Errors on the Question of the Nature of Culture

So far as national culture is concerned, the guiding role is fulfilled by Communist ideology, and efforts should be made to disseminate socialism and communism among the working class and to educate, properly and methodically, the peasantry and other sections of the masses in socialism.

A National, Scientific, and Mass Culture

New-democratic culture is national. It opposes imperialist oppression and upholds the dignity and independence of the Chinese nation. . . . China should absorb on a large scale the progressive cultures of foreign countries as an ingredient for her own culture; in the past we did not do enough work of this kind. We must absorb whatever we today find useful, not only from the present socialist or new-democratic cultures of other nations, but also from the older cultures of foreign countries, such as those of the various capitalist countries in the age of enlightenment. However, we must treat these foreign materials as we do our food, which should be chewed in the mouth, submitted to the working of the stomach and intestines, mixed with saliva, gastric juice, and intestinal secretions, and then separated into essence to be absorbed and waste matter to be discarded—only thus can food benefit our body; we should never swallow anything raw or absorb it uncritically. So-called wholesale Westernization is a mistaken viewpoint. China has suffered a great deal in the past from the formalist absorption of foreign things. Likewise, in applying Marxism to China, Chinese Communists must fully and properly unite the universal truth of Marxism with the specific practice of the Chinese revolution; that is to say, the truth of Marxism must be integrated with the characteristics of the nation and given a definite national form before it can be useful; it must not be applied subjectively as a mere formula. . . .

Communists may form an anti-imperialist and anti-feudal united front for political action with certain idealists and even with religious followers, but we can never approve of their idealism or religious doctrines. A splendid ancient culture was created during the long period of China's feudal society. To clarify the process of development of this ancient culture, to throw away its feudal dross, and to absorb its democratic essence is a necessary condition for the development of our new national culture and for the increase of our national self-confidence; but we should never absorb anything and everything uncritically.

The Twofold Task of the Chinese Revolution and the Chinese Communist Party

To complete China's bourgeois-democratic revolution (the new-democratic revolution) and to prepare to transform it into a socialist revolution when all the necessary conditions are present—that is the sum total of the great and glorious revolutionary task of the Communist Party of China. All members of the party should strive for its accomplishment and should never give up halfway. Some immature Communists think that we have only the task of the democratic revolution at the present stage but not that of the socialist revolution at the future stage; or that the present revolution or the agrarian revolution is in fact the socialist revolution. It must be emphatically pointed out that both views are erroneous. Every Communist must know that the whole Chinese revolutionary movement led by the Chinese Communist Party is a complete revolutionary movement embracing the two revolutionary stages, democratic and socialist, which are two revolutionary processes differing in character, and that the socialist stage can be reached only after the democratic stage is completed. The democratic revolution is the necessary preparation for the socialist revolution, and the socialist revolution is the inevitable trend of the democratic revolution. And the ultimate aim of all Communists is to strive for the final building of socialist society and communist society.

Source: Mao Zedong, *Selected Works*, in *Sources of Chinese Tradition*, 2nd ed., vol. 2, edited by Wm. Theodore de Bary and Richard Lufrano (New York: Columbia University Press, 2000), pp. 418–23.

PRIMARY SOURCE 20.2

"A Note to the Members of the National Planning Committee" (1940), Jawaharlal Nehru

Jawaharlal Nehru (1889–1964) was the first prime minister of India and a leading figure in Indian politics before and after independence. Here he combines a universalist, technocratic faith in planning with local traditions.

- Evaluate the balance of foreign influence and Indian tradition in this document.
- What does Nehru think planning can achieve? What risks does he want to avoid?
- What is Nehru's view of entrepreneurship and free markets?

Planning for the Future

To some it may appear that this is a most unsuitable time for planning, which is essentially a labour of peaceful co-operation. It may be argued that we should wait for better times and more stable conditions, for who knows what the outcome of the present conflict will be? On what foundation shall we build, when no man can foretell what that foundation will be? And yet though we are so uncertain of the future, this we know well that the future will be very different from the past or even from this changing present. Already we see vast political and economic changes taking shape in the womb of the future. Can we plan in India with all this doubt and uncertainty?

These considerations fill our minds, as they should, and we must give careful thought to them. And yet these very considerations lead us to a contrary conclusion. For it is this very time of change and uncertainty that demands mental activity and a vision of the future that we desire. If we are mere onlookers now, and passive and helpless agents of circumstances or the will of others, we barter away our claim to that future. Instead of preparing for it, we hand the reins to others. Every conflict ends sometime or other, every war is followed by a peace, temporary or more enduring, every work of destruction has to be followed by construction. That construction will be chaotic and wasteful unless previous thought has been given to it. A period of war and dynamic change therefore demands, even more than the static times of peace, the planned activity of the mind, so that, when time and opportunity come, this may be translated with all speed into the planned activity of the nation.

For, thinking and planning for the future is essential if that future is not to end in misdirected energy and chaos. It is foolish to imagine that when the present crisis at long last ends, a new or better arrangement of world affairs or our national affairs will automatically emerge out of it. It is equally unwise to allow matters to drift, protesting occasionally perhaps, but otherwise looking on helplessly, for fear that what we may do might involve a risk or be taken unfair advantage of by our opponents. The world is full of risks and dangers today. We cannot escape them. The greatest risk and danger is to drift and not give thought and energy to finding a way out. It is manifest that the old order has had its day and is dissolving, whether we like this or not. It has led to wars and upheavals and continuing conflicts which involve not only passion and hatred and an enormous waste of energy and resources, but also prevent us from achieving what is otherwise easily attainable. We have to understand the conflicts of forces that dominate the world today and seek to resolve these conflicts. It is certainly a possibility that the world may inevitably be led to social dissolution. We have to avoid that, if we can, but we cannot do so by shutting our eyes to the fact that the existing order is incapable of preventing this catastrophe. Something else, more in keeping with modern conditions, has to be evolved. Politics, in our country as elsewhere, dominates the scene and occupies men's minds. But the real changes that are shaping the world are deeper than politics. If we plan, we must consider them and have clear minds about them.

We shall thus have to consider, at this stage or later, the basic and fundamental policies that must govern our planning. Without a definite and clear-cut objective in view, and an understanding of the path we must pursue, we shall plan ineffectively or perhaps even in vain.

Already the NPC has given some thought to this matter and we have come to some general but fundamental decisions. It is well to recapitulate some of them. We are aiming at a free and democratic state, which has full political and economic freedom. In this state the fundamental rights of the individual and the group—political, economic, social and cultural—will be guaranteed, and the corresponding duties and obligations laid down. The state will be progressive and will utilize all scientific and other knowledge for the advancement of the people as a whole, and for the promotion of their happiness and material as well as cultural and spiritual well-being. The state will not permit the exploitation of the community by individuals or groups to the disadvantage of the former and to the injury of the nation as a whole. To realize the social objectives, the state has to plan through its representatives for the nation (whenever possible, in co-operation with other nations) and to co-ordinate the various activities of the nation so as to avoid waste and conflict and attain the maximum results. This planning will deal with production, distribution, consumption, investment, trade, income, social services, and the many other forms of national activity which act and react on each other. Briefly put, planning aims at the raising of the material and cultural standard of living of the people as a whole. In India our standards are so terribly low and poverty is so appalling that this question of raising standards is of the most vital importance. The NPC has suggested that national wealth should be increased between two and three times within the next ten years, and this should be so planned as to raise the general standard at least in a like measure.

Source: Jawaharlal Nehru, "A Note to the Members of the National Planning Committee," May 1, 1940, *Report: National Planning Committee* (Bombay: Vora & Co. Publishers, 1949), pp. 114–25.

PRIMARY SOURCE 20.3

On Negritude (1959), Léopold Sédar Senghor

Léopold Sédar Senghor (1906–2001) was a Senegalese poet and politician. A leading figure in the Negritude movement,

Senghor served as the first president of Senegal (1960–1980). This selection, drawn from a lecture at Oxford University and reprinted many times, provides a concise overview of the movement; Senghor initially expressed these ideas in poetry.

Define Negritude.

Explain the relationship between reason and emotion in this text.

What does Senghor mean when he says that Negritude does not oppose European values but complements them?

Paradoxically it was the French who first forced us to seek its essence, and who then showed us where it lay . . . when they enforced their policy of assimilation *and thus deepened our despair. . . . Early on, we had become aware within ourselves that assimilation was a failure; we could assimilate mathematics or the French language, but we could never strip off our black skins nor root out our black souls. And so we set out on a fervent quest for the Holy Grail: our Collective Soul. And we came upon it.*

It was not revealed to us by the "official France" of the politicians who, out of self interest and political conviction defended the policy of assimilation. Its whereabouts was pointed out to us by that handful of freelance thinkers—writers, artists, ethnologists, and prehistorians—who bring about cultural revolutions in France. It was, to be quite precise, our teachers of Ethnology who introduced us to the considerable body of work already achieved in the understanding of Africa, by the University of Oxford.

What did we learn from all those writers, artists and teachers? That the early years of colonisation and especially, even before colonisation, the *slave trade* had ravaged black Africa like a bush fire, wiping out images and values in one vast carnage. That Negroid civilisation had flourished in the Upper Paleolithic Age, and that the Neolithic Revolution could not be explained without them. That their roots retained their vigour, and would one day produce new grass and green branches. . . .

Negritude is *the whole complex of civilised values—cultural, economic, social and political—which characterise the black peoples,* or, more precisely, the Negro-African world.

All these values are essentially informed by intuitive reason. Because this sentient reason, the reason which comes to grips, expresses itself emotionally, through that self-surrender, that coalescence of subject and object; through myths, by which I mean the archetypal images of the collective Soul, above all through primordial rhythms, synchronised with those of the Cosmos.

In other words, the sense of communion, the gift of myth-making, the gift of rhythm, such are the essential elements of Negritude, which you will find indelibly stamped on all the works and activities of the black man. . . .

In opposition to European racialism, of which the Nazis were the symbol, we set up an "anti-racial racialism." The very excesses of Naziism, and the catastrophes it engendered, were soon to bring us to our senses. Such hatred, such violence, above all, such weeping and such shedding of blood produced a feeling of revulsion—it was so foreign to our continent's genius: our *need to love.*

And then the anthropologists taught us that there is no such thing as a pure race: scientifically speaking, races do not exist. They went one better and forecast that, with a mere two hundred million people, we would in the end disappear as a "black race," through miscegenation.

At the same time they did offer us some consolation. "The focal points of human development," wrote Teilhard de Chardin, in 1939, "always seem to coincide with the points of contact and anastomosis of several nerve paths," that is, in the ordinary man's language, of several races.

If then we were justified in fostering the values of Negritude, and arousing the energy slumbering within us, it must be in order to pour them into the mainstream of cultural miscegenation (the biological process taking place spontaneously). They must flow towards the meeting point of all Humanity; they must be our contribution to the Civilisation of the Universal.

Biological miscegenation, then, takes place spontaneously, provoked by the very laws which govern Life, and in the face of all policies of Apartheid. It is a different matter in the realm of culture. Here, we remain wholly free to cooperate or not, to provoke or prevent the synthesis of cultures. This is an important point. For, as certain biologists point out, the psychological mutations brought about by education are incorporated in our genes, and are then transmitted by heredity. Hence the major role played by *Culture.*

Seen within this prospect of the Civilisation of the Universal, the colonial policies of Great Britain and France have proved successful complements to each other, and black Africa has benefited.

The policies of the former tended to reinforce the traditional native civilisation. As for France's policy, although we have often reviled it in the past, it too ended with a credit balance, through forcing us actively to assimilate European civilisation. This fertilised our sense of Negritude.

Today, our Negritude no longer expresses itself as opposition to European values, but as a *complement* to them. Henceforth, its militants will be concerned, as I have often said, *not to be assimilated, but to assimilate.* They will use European values to arouse the slumbering values of Negritude, which they will bring as their contribution to the Civilisation of the Universal.

Nevertheless, we still disagree with Europe: not with its values any longer (with the exception of Capitalism) but with its theory of the Civilisation of the Universal. . . .

In the eyes of the Europeans, the "exotic civilisations" are static in character, being content to live by means of archetypal images, which they repeat indefinitely. The most serious criticism is that they have no idea of the *pre-eminent dignity of the human person.*

My reply is this. Just as much as black Africa, taking this as an example, Europe and its North American offspring live by means of archetypal images. For what are Free Enterprise, Democracy, Communism, but *myths*, around which hundreds of millions of men and women organise their lives?

Negritude itself is a myth (I am not using the word in any pejorative sense), but a living, dynamic one, which evolves with its circumstances into a form of humanism.

Actually, our criticism of the [European] thesis is that it is monstrously anti-humanist. For if European civilisation were to be imposed, unmodified, on all Peoples and Continents, it could only be by force. That is its first disadvantage. A more serious one is that it would not be *humanistic*, for it would cut itself off from the complementary values of the greater part of humanity. As I have said elsewhere, it would be a universal civilisation; it would not be the Civilisation of the Universal.

Whereas our revised Negritude is humanistic. I repeat, it welcomes the complementary values of Europe and the white man, and indeed, of all other races and continents.

But it welcomes them in order to fertilise and re-invigorate its own values, which it then offers for the construction of a civilisation which shall embrace all Mankind.

The *Neo-Humanism* of the twentieth century stands at the point where the paths of all Nations, Races and Continents cross, where the Four Winds of the Spirit blow.

Source: Léopold Sédar Senghor, "What Is Negritude?" *Negro Digest*, April 1962, pp. 3–6.

PRIMARY SOURCE 20.4

On Decolonization (1961), Frantz Fanon

Frantz Fanon (1925–1961) was a psychiatrist and writer from the Caribbean island of Martinique. Fanon joined the Algerian Front de Libération Nationale and treated torture victims during the Algerian War of Independence (1954–1962). This selection, written at the very end of his life, drew on his wartime experience.

- Analyze the role of religion in this passage.
- Is this text Eurocentric?
- What role do traditional Muslim religious leaders ("the caids and the customary chiefs") play in this text?

In decolonization, there is therefore the need of a complete calling in question of the colonial situation. If we wish to describe it precisely, we might find it in the well-known words: "The last shall be first and the first last." Decolonization is the putting into practice of this sentence. That is why, if we try to describe it, all decolonization is successful.

The naked truth of decolonization evokes for us the searing bullets and bloodstained knives which emanate from it. For if the last shall be first, this will only come to pass after a murderous and decisive struggle between the two protagonists. That affirmed intention to place the last at the head of things, and to make them climb at a pace (too quickly, some say) the well-known steps which characterize an organized society, can only triumph if we use all means to turn the scale, including, of course, that of violence.

You do not turn any society, however primitive it may be, upside down with such a program if you have not decided from the very beginning, that is to say from the actual formulation of that program, to overcome all the obstacles that you will come across in so doing. The native who decides to put the program into practice, and to become its moving force, is ready for violence at all times. From birth it is clear to him that this narrow world, strewn with prohibitions, can only be called in question by absolute violence.

***

As soon as the native begins to pull on his moorings, and to cause anxiety to the settler, he is handed over to well-meaning souls who in cultural congresses point out to him the specificity and wealth of Western values. But every time Western values are mentioned they produce in the native a sort of stiffening or muscular lockjaw. During the period of decolonization, the native's reason is appealed to. He is offered definite values, he is told frequently that decolonization need not mean regression, and that he must put his trust in qualities which are well-tried, solid, and highly esteemed. But it so happens that when the native hears a speech about Western culture he pulls out his knife—or at least he makes sure it is within reach. The violence with which the supremacy of white values is affirmed and the aggressiveness which has permeated the victory of these values over the ways of life and of thought of the native mean that, in revenge, the native laughs in mockery when Western values are mentioned in front of him. In the colonial context the settler only ends his work of breaking in the native when the latter admits loudly and intelligibly the supremacy of the white man's values. In the period of decolonization, the colonized masses mock at these very values, insult them, and vomit them up.

***

But it so happens that for the colonized people this violence, because it constitutes their only work, invests their characters with positive and creative qualities. The practice of violence binds them together as a whole, since each individual forms a violent link in the great chain, a part of the great organism of violence which has surged upward in reaction to the settler's violence in the beginning. The groups recognize each other and the future nation is already indivisible. The armed struggle mobilizes the people; that is to say, it throws them in one way and in one direction.

The mobilization of the masses, when it arises out of the war of liberation, introduces into each man's consciousness the ideas of a common cause, of a national destiny, and of a collective history. In the same way the second phase, that of the building-up of the nation, is helped on by the existence of this cement which has been mixed with blood and anger. Thus we come to a fuller appreciation of the originality of the words used in these underdeveloped countries. During the colonial period the people are called upon to fight against oppression; after national liberation, they are called upon to fight against poverty, illiteracy, and underdevelopment. The struggle, they say, goes on. The people realize that life is an unending contest.

We have said that the native's violence unifies the people. By its very structure, colonialism is separatist and regionalist. Colonialism does not simply state the existence of tribes; it also reinforces it and separates them. The colonial system encourages chieftaincies and keeps alive the old Marabout confraternities. Violence is in action all-inclusive and national. It follows that it is closely involved in the liquidation of regionalism and of tribalism. Thus the national parties show no pity at all toward the caids and the customary chiefs. Their destruction is the preliminary to the unification of the people.

At the level of individuals, violence is a cleansing force. It frees the native from his inferiority complex and from his despair and inaction; it makes him fearless and restores his self-respect. Even if the armed struggle has been symbolic and the nation is demobilized through a rapid movement of decolonization, the people have the time to see that the liberation has been the business of each and all and that the leader has no special merit. From thence comes that type of aggressive reticence with regard to the machinery of protocol which young governments quickly show. When the people have taken violent part in the national liberation they will allow no one to set themselves up as "liberators." They show themselves to be jealous of the results of their action and take good care not to place their future, their destiny, or the fate of their country in the hands of a living god. Yesterday they were completely irresponsible; today they mean to understand everything and make all decisions. Illuminated by violence, the consciousness of the people rebels against any pacification. From now on the demagogues, the opportunists, and the magicians have a difficult task. The action which has thrown them into a hand-to-hand struggle confers upon the masses a voracious taste for the concrete. The attempt at mystification becomes, in the long run, practically impossible.

Source: Frantz Fanon, *The Wretched of the Earth*, trans. Constance Farrington (New York: Grove Press, 1963), pp. 37, 43, 93–95.

Interpreting Visual Evidence

War and Propaganda

Both the Allies and the Axis Powers made major efforts to mobilize consent and win support, not only among soldiers but on the home front as well. Governments used propaganda—information and ideas that are spread in order to promote a certain political point of view—to shape public opinion during World War II. While Joseph Goebbels and the Nazi Ministry for Public Enlightenment and Propaganda were the most famous for their efforts to demonize the enemy and foster a sense of solidarity at home and among Germany's allies, they had analogs in Washington, London, Moscow, and Tokyo. Propaganda offices around the world enlisted journalists, cartoonists, and other visual artists, as well as radio and film, to spread their messages.

The first image, "Victory or Bolshevism," a poster by Hans Schweitzer, known as Mjölnir (the name of the Norse god Thor's hammer), contrasts a wholesome German community with the bleak prospect of a Soviet occupation after the German defeat at Stalingrad (1942–1943). The next two images show European propaganda that celebrates the loyalty of colonial subjects in their empires' war efforts. A recruitment poster for the British army shows seven uniformed soldiers from across the empire, prepared to fight

German poster, "Victory or Bolshevism."

British poster, "Together."

Free French troops train in Bouar.

for a common future. The photograph shows Free French troops—Resistance fighters who supported the Allies and opposed collaborationist Vichy France—marching in Bouar, in French Equatorial Africa (today the Central African Republic). The final image shows a Japanese representation of the United States. It depicts a demonic Franklin Delano Roosevelt with grasping hands and an evil smile.

Japanese poster portraying a villainous President Roosevelt.

QUESTIONS FOR ANALYSIS

1. Contrast the stereotypes presented to celebrate cooperation with those presented to demonize enemies. Do they differ in any meaningful ways?
2. How does the medium—poster, caricature, or photograph—shape the message these images convey? How is the photograph similar to or different from the posters and caricature? Do photos appeal to audiences in the same way?
3. Analyze the role of gender in these images. How do the artists use masculine and feminine imagery, and to what effect?

Before You Read This Chapter

GLOBAL STORYLINES

The Emergence of Modern Globalization

- Following the collapse of the three-world order, new global markets and communications networks integrate the world but also create deep inequalities.
- New technologies and vast population movements make global culture more homogeneous.
- Globalization, supranational organizations (like the World Bank, the European Union, and the United Nations), and religious fundamentalism erode the power of the nation-state.

CHAPTER OUTLINE

FOCUS QUESTIONS

- What transnational forces eroded the power of the nation-state in the last third of the twentieth century, and how did they do so?
- What was the relationship between global migration, new technologies, and the spread of cultural influences during and after the Cold War?
- How did globalization and population changes affect the environment, and vice versa?
- To what degree did globalization change societies? How similar and different was globalization after the Cold War as compared with earlier forms of globalization?

21

Globalization

1970–2000

Consider the following comparison. In the thirteenth century, few people could imagine moving beyond their local region. Venetian explorer Marco Polo, who voyaged through China, and Arab scholar Ibn Battuta, who traversed the Islamic world, were rare exceptions. In contrast, by the late twentieth century, people crossed in a matter of hours the distances that it took Marco Polo and Ibn Battuta years to cover. By the end of the twentieth century, many slept while flying at 30,000 feet over what Marco Polo took months to cover on a horse. And many others stayed at home while "traveling" the world via the Internet, Instagram, books, newspapers, and streaming shows on Netflix from South Korea to Israel.

But not all travelers moved about so comfortably. Many migrants—desperate to escape political chaos, religious persecution, climate calamities, or poverty—slipped across borders in the dark of night, traveled as human cargo inside containers, or used their own feet or boarded rickety boats to flee their homelands. Billions of others still had no access to the global age's technological wonders and economic opportunities. Thus, while **globalization** (the development of integrated worldwide cultural and economic structures) created possibilities for some, it also caused deeper disparities.

Globalization also mixed up the world, creating more diversity in some places and uniformity in other places. Again, consider two different settings: a fishing village in the Amazon River basin and cosmopolitan Los Angeles. Picture an elderly Amazonian fisherman trying to teach his children their parents' tongue, Cocama-Cocamilla, but to no avail. All his children speak Spanish instead. "I tried to teach them," the old man laments. "It's like paddling against the current." Seven centuries ago, over 500 languages rang throughout the Amazon River basin. As of the year 2000, only 57 languages survived there.

Evidently, one effect of globalization is to reduce diversity. But it can also increase local diversity. For example, Los Angeles, once the emblem of White, suburban America, became a cacophonous city with over 100 languages spoken in its public schools—and Los Angeles paled beside other cities. Fully 58 percent of Miami's population was foreign-born in 2023; in Toronto, Canada that number was 49 percent, and in Sydney, Australia 45 percent.

This chapter observes the impact of globalization in several ways: (1) the movement of families and groups, as well as goods and ideas, across boundaries that once divided religious, ethnic, and national communities; (2) the role of international financial organizations in addressing world financial issues; (3) the power of multinational corporations in transforming local markets into international ones; and (4) unexpected effects, such as galvanizing discontent, sparking a revival of traditional religions (to counter secular and materialist influences), and driving deeper divisions among and within the world's regions—even while bringing them closer together.

Global Integration

The full impact of globalization, a process that began in the 1970s, is still unfolding. Lately, much of it is negative; since 2009, there has been a backlash almost everywhere. But there is no denying the historic shift. By the late twentieth century, the forces driving global integration—and inequality—were no longer the empires of old. For centuries, these empires had been the engines of convergence and conflict. By the mid-twentieth century, however, they were in retreat. The Cold War and decolonization movements produced the three-world order. But within three decades, the three-world order was also in retreat. Power structures in the First World, under such stress in the 1970s, did not crack. But those in the Second World did. The Cold War ended with the implosion of the Soviet bloc. The Third World also splintered, with some areas becoming highly advanced and others falling into deep poverty; the term **developing world** obscured these differences. Now a new architecture of power organized the world into a unified marketplace with unhindered flows of capital, commerce, culture, and labor. By 2000, most societies had endorsed electoral systems and adopted some form of market economy.

Because the United States promoted these changes, globalization has looked to some like Americanization. The United States unquestionably stood as the world's most influential society, with its music, food, principles of representative government, and free markets spreading worldwide. Yet the process did not run one way. The world also came to America and shaped its society: people living in the United States—along with their inventions, sports stars, and musical inspirations—increasingly came from somewhere else.

Nor was the United States immune from transnational forces challenging the power of the nation-state itself. In the United States, as elsewhere, globalization functioned through networks of investment, trade, and migration that operated relatively independently of nation-states. In the process, globalization shook entrenched forms of political and social identification, including religious and military authority. Members of societies now often identified more with local, subnational, or international movements or cultures rather than with nation-states. To be sure, nation-states remained essential for establishing democratic institutions and protecting human rights, but supranational institutions like the European Union and the International Monetary Fund (see later discussion) often impinged on their autonomy. As borders became more open, money, goods, and people flowed back and forth, further undermining the autonomy of nation-states.

Removing Obstacles to Globalization

In the mid-1970s, political practices and institutions associated with the three-world order started to deteriorate. By the late 1980s, the communist Second World was disintegrating. The collapse of the Soviet Union brought the Cold War to an end. At the same time, the capitalist First World gave up its last colonial possessions, and the remnants of White settler supremacy disintegrated. But as this occurred, the formerly colonized Third World's dream of a "third way" also vanished. As empires withdrew, they revealed a world integrated by markets for capital, labor, culture, and technology rather than by forced loyalties to imperial masters or other foreign powers.

Ending the Cold War

A world split between hostile factions limited the prospects for a global exchange of peoples, ideas, and resources. There was widespread exchange within the rival blocs—that is, among socialist countries and among capitalist countries—but for other countries the pressure from the Soviet Union and the United States to align with a superpower constrained their choices. Any perceived threat of deviating from the alignment could bring on cruel intervention, as in Nicaragua or Poland.

Some larger countries could find some autonomy. Egypt had enough clout to leave the Soviet orbit in the 1970s and changed the political geography of the Arab world. At the same time, the rivalry between blocs posed rising tolls. The cost was highest in contested hot spots of the Third World, but even the superpowers paid a price. Eventually, economic pressures, technological changes, and political crumbling brought down the walls that defined the three-world order and widened the scope for an explosion of trade, migration, and cultural exchange across borders.

MOUNTING COSTS The many regional conflicts of the Cold War era (Vietnam, Afghanistan, Nicaragua) were deadly for countries caught in the ideological crossfire. Vietnam became a battleground for Russian, Chinese, and American ambitions. This war spilled over into Laos and Cambodia, dragging them to ruin along with Vietnam. China attracted several client states in the competition for influence in the Third World and within the communist bloc. In Afghanistan, Moscow propped up a puppet regime, only to fall into a bloody war against Islamic and tribal guerrillas financed and armed by the United States, Saudi Arabia, and Pakistan. In Central America, U.S. president Ronald Reagan and his advisers opposed the victory of the left-leaning Nicaraguan Sandinista coalition in 1979. During the 1980s the U.S. government pumped millions of dollars to the Contras (right-wing opponents of the left-wing Sandinistas) and lent military and monetary assistance to other Central American anticommunist forces. Thus, for much of the world, the Cold War was a real confrontation with tremendously high costs for local powers.

Rivalry was costly to the superpowers, too: the 1970s and 1980s saw the largest peacetime accumulation of arms in history. Despite myriad treaties and summits, the United States and the Soviet Union stockpiled nuclear and conventional weaponry. Furthermore, in 1983 Reagan unveiled the Strategic Defense Initiative ("Star Wars"), a plan to use satellites and space missiles to insulate the United States from incoming nuclear bombs. For both sides, military spending sprees brought economic troubles. The U.S. national debt increased; Soviet life expectancy began to decline and infant mortality began to rise.

Cracks on either side of the conflict appeared in the 1970s. The intelligence organizations of both the Soviet Union and the United States produced secret memos questioning whether the Soviet bloc could sustain its global position. As stalemate in Afghanistan undermined the image of the mighty Soviet armed forces, mothers of Soviet soldiers protested the regime's refusal to acknowledge the very fact of the war in which their sons were fighting and in some cases dying. The eastern European satellites became dependent on western European loans and consumer goods. At the same time, the western alliance itself faced internal tensions. In Europe and North America, the antinuclear movement rallied millions to the streets. Western industrialists worried about competition from Japan, which had been pouring money into rapid industrialization rather than arms. Political leaders also grappled with distressingly high unemployment rates. Thus, both sides shared a common crisis: fatigue from the Cold War and an economic challenge from East Asia.

THE SOVIET BLOC COLLAPSES In the end, the Soviet bloc collapsed. (See Map 21.1.) Even though planned economies employed the entire Soviet population, they failed to fill stores with sufficient consumer goods. Socialist health care and benefits lagged behind those of the capitalist welfare states. Authoritarian political structures relied on deception and coercion rather than elections and civic activism. (See Global Themes and Sources: Primary Source 21.1.) Although the Communist Party had promised to beat capitalism by building socialism on the way to achieving full communism, the latter paradise was nowhere on the horizon. The gap between socialism and capitalism turned into a chasm.

Lech Wałęsa. A Polish electrician from the Lenin Shipyard in the Baltic port city of Gdańsk, Wałęsa spearheaded the formation of Solidarity, a mass independent trade union of workers who battled the communist regime that ruled in their name. He later was elected president of post-communist Poland.

MAP 21.1 | Collapse of the Communist Bloc in Europe

The Soviet Union's domination of eastern Europe ended precipitously in 1989. The political map of eastern and central Europe took on a different shape under European integration.

- What significant event in many communist countries signaled the collapse of communism?
- In what part of eastern and central Europe did the most political instability and conflict occur?
- According to your reading, why did the end of communist rule cause the reshuffling of political boundaries in the region?

One catalyst in socialism's undoing was Poland. A critical event was the naming of a Polish archbishop as pope in 1978. The first non-Italian pope in 455 years, John Paul opposed the Soviet form of socialism. In 1979, he made a pilgrimage to his native Poland, holding enormous outdoor masses; in 1980, he supported mass strikes at the Gdańsk shipyard, which led to the formation of the Soviet bloc's first independent trade union, Solidarity, led by a Polish nationalist and critic of Soviet control, Lech Wałęsa. As Communist Party members in Poland defected to its side, the union became a society-wide movement; it aimed not to reform socialism (as in Czechoslovakia in 1968; see discussion of the Prague Spring in Chapter 20) but to overcome it. A crackdown by the Polish military and police put most of Solidarity's leadership in prison and drove the movement underground, but Soviet intelligence officials secretly worried that Solidarity could not be easily eradicated.

The most consequential factor in the collapse of the Soviet superpower was Mikhail Gorbachev, who became general secretary of the Soviet Communist Party in 1985 and launched an effort to reform the Soviet system. He focused on political changes first. Under this effort (*perestroika*, "reconstruction"), Gorbachev permitted contested elections for a new Congress of Peoples' Deputies, relaxed censorship, sanctioned civic associations, legalized small nonstate businesses, granted autonomy to state firms, and encouraged the republics to be responsible for their own affairs within the Soviet Union. His foreign policy also upended decades of Soviet central control. He sought arms control to lessen the burdens on the Soviet Union. He pulled troops from Afghanistan and informed eastern European leaders that they could not count on Moscow's armed intervention to prop up their regimes.

Gorbachev wanted to rescue socialism; instead, he destabilized it. His political changes allowed civic groups to call not for the system's reform but for its liquidation. Eastern Europe bolted from the Soviet orbit, and some of the union republics began to push for independence. In response, disgruntled factions within the KGB (the main security agency of the Soviet Union from 1954 to 1991) and the Soviet military tried to hang on by staging a coup in 1991. It was a botch job. The former Communist Party boss of Moscow, Boris Yeltsin, rallied the opposition, faced down the hardliners, and was elected president of the Russian republic in the Soviet Union's first democratic election in 1991. Beleaguered Soviet elites saw an opportunity. They abandoned the socialist cause and divided up state property among themselves—and became the so-called oligarchs of the post-Soviet order.

When communist regimes collapsed, the European and Asian political maps changed dramatically. Old states died; new ones sprouted. In Asia, the division between North and South Korea lived on. But in Vietnam and China, Communist Parties embraced western capitalism. In Europe, East Germany dissolved; West Germany absorbed its remnants after the Berlin Wall came down in 1989. Soon after, Yeltsin and the leaders of Ukraine and Belarus formally dissolved the old USSR into independent states. (See Map 21.2.)

But the end of Soviet-style socialism was not entirely peaceful. The worst carnage occurred in the former Yugoslavia, where political quarrels between regions, neighbors, and ethnic groups decomposed into a horrific civil war in Europe. Serbs and Croats, in particular, engaged in savage struggles over territories in the Balkans.

The fall of the Berlin Wall and the collapse of the Soviet Union allowed eastern European states to resume their cultural, political, and economic ties with western Europe and the United States, ties previously severed by the 1945 partition of Europe. No sooner had the Berlin Wall come down than new countries lined up to join the European Union. With the Cold War over, traditionally neutral countries

The Berlin Wall. The breaching of the Berlin Wall in November 1989 spelled the end of the Soviet bloc. Decades of debate over whether communism could be reformed turned out to be moot. In the face of competition from the richer, consumer-oriented west, communism collapsed.

MAP 21.2 | The Breakup of the Soviet Union

The Soviet Union broke apart in 1991. Compare this map with Map 17.6, which illustrates Russian expansion in the nineteenth century.

- Which parts of the old Russian Empire remained under Russian rule, and which of its territories established their own states?
- In what areas did large migrations accompany the breakup, and for what reasons?
- According to your reading, how did the breakup of the Soviet Union change Russia's status in Europe and Asia?

like Austria and Sweden applied for admission. Then came a flood of eastern European, Balkan, and Baltic applicants. By 2004, the European Union had grown from 322 million people to 495 million. European integration and the turn west went beyond economic matters. Many of the countries that joined the European Union also entered the **North Atlantic Treaty Organization (NATO)** alliance, much to the distaste of Russia.

By historical standards the Cold War had been relatively brief, spanning four decades. But communism had played a major role in the military conflicts and the headlong modernization of Russia and China, and it exercised important influence on India and elsewhere in the Third World, where proxy wars were devastating. Communism, however, faced a trilemma: it could not keep up the Cold War *and* deliver the good life to its adherents *and* survive in a more competitive world economy. Ultimately, it was the inability to keep up with the consumption and technology race more than the inability to keep up with the arms race that doomed the USSR and unleashed in the early 1990s economic and cultural energies that would buoy global integration.

Africa and the End of White Rule

Although the aftermath of World War II saw the dismantling of most of Europe's empires, remnants of colonial rule remained in southern Africa. (See Chapter 20, Map 20.6.) Here, Whites clung to centuries-old notions of their racial superiority over non-Europeans. Final decolonization meant that self-rule would return to all of Africa. The end of colonialism also set the stage for former colonies to find new trading and investment partners and to become more integrated with the wider world.

THE LAST HOLDOUTS The last fortresses under direct European control were the Portuguese colonies of southern and western Africa. However, by the mid-1970s, efforts to suppress African nationalist movements had exhausted Portugal's resources. As African nationalist demands led to a hurried Portuguese withdrawal from Guinea-Bissau, Angola, and Mozambique, formal European colonialism in Africa came to an end.

But White rule still prevailed elsewhere in Africa. In Rhodesia, a White minority resisted all international pressure to allow Black rule. In the end, independent African neighbors helped support a liberation guerrilla movement under Robert Mugabe. Surrounded, Rhodesian Whites finally capitulated. Mugabe swept to power with massive electoral support in 1979. The new constitutional government renamed the country Zimbabwe, erasing from Africa's map the name of the long-deceased British expansionist Cecil Rhodes (see Chapter 17). At first, President Mugabe worked well with the agriculturally and financially powerful former White ruling elite, but over time, under pressure from elements in his own party, he promoted land redistribution and turned against the White elite in ways that led to a steep economic decline and massive inflation.

SOUTH AFRICA AND NELSON MANDELA The final outpost of White rule was South Africa, where a European minority was larger, richer, and more entrenched than elsewhere in the region—and highly invulnerable to outside pressures. Although powerful international firms operated there, they were reluctant to risk their investments by boycotting the racist regime. In addition, the U.S. government regarded South Africa's large army as a useful tool to fight Soviet allies elsewhere in southern Africa. In any case, the ruling

The End of Apartheid. Nelson Mandela, running for president in 1994 as the candidate of the African National Congress, here casts a ballot in the first all-races election in South Africa. This election ended apartheid and saw the African National Congress take control of the Republic of South Africa.

Afrikaner-led National Party used ruthless tactics against internal critics. Yet, in the countryside and cities, defiance of White rule was growing. Africans lobbed rocks and crude bombs (Molotov cocktails) at tanks and organized mass strikes in the multinational-owned mines.

The spectacle of violence in western media coincided with a rising human rights movement, which triggered mounting pressures from abroad to end the racist apartheid system. The International Olympic Committee banned South African athletes starting in 1970. American students insisted that their universities divest themselves of companies with investments in South Africa. As international pressures grew, foreign governments—even that of the United States, once South Africa's staunchest ally—applied economic sanctions against South Africa. A swelling worldwide chorus demanded that **Nelson Mandela** (1918–2013), the imprisoned leader of the African National Congress (ANC), be freed. The White political elite eventually realized that it was better to negotiate new arrangements than to endure international condemnation and years of internal warfare against a majority population. In 1990, President F. W. de Klerk (of the National Party) released Mandela from prison and legalized the ANC and the Communist Party of South Africa. Ensuing negotiations produced South Africa's first free, mass elections in 1994. These brought an overwhelming victory to the ANC, with Nelson Mandela elected as president. Majority rule had finally come to South Africa, and for the first time in centuries, Africans ruled over all of Africa. The triumph over White rule also became a global emblem for the effectiveness of international human rights campaigning and solidarity.

In Nelson Mandela, South Africa's White rulers found a man of exceptional integrity and political savvy. He had spent more than two decades in prison, much of it at hard labor. But he looked beyond past injustices to ease the transition to full democracy. Besides, he was aware that with the country veering toward civil war, only a negotiated change would preserve South Africa's industries, wealth, and educational system.

The leaders of independent Africa faced immense problems in building stable political communities. Although they set out to destroy the vestiges of colonial political structures and to erect African-based public institutions, local contests for political power impeded this process. Ethnic and religious rivalries, held in check during the colonial period, now blazed forth. Civil wars erupted in many countries (most violently in Nigeria, Sudan, and Zaire), and military leaders were drawn into politics. Coups d'état were common. Nigeria, for instance, had six military coups between 1966 and 1999. By the 1990s, the continent was aflame with civil strife; armed conflicts that started with the Cold War endured well after it ended, even though White rule had finally come to an end throughout the entire continent.

Unleashing Globalization

As obstacles to international integration began to dissolve, capital, commodities, people, and culture crossed borders with ever-greater freedom. Even though trade, foreign investment, migration, and cultural borrowing had long been hallmarks of modern history, the global age changed their scale. At the same time, never had there been such unequal access to the fruits of globalization. Several factors contributed to increasing integration and to new power arrangements: international banking, expanded international trade, population migrations, and technical breakthroughs in communications that facilitated the worldwide spread of cultural influences.

Finance and Trade

The increased international flow of goods and capital was well underway in the 1970s, but the end of the Cold War removed many impediments to globalization. During the 1990s, even the strongest nation-states felt the effects of economic globalization.

GLOBAL FINANCE AND DEREGULATED MARKETS Major transformations occurred in the world's financial system in the 1970s. America's budget and trade deficits prompted President Richard Nixon to take the dollar off the gold standard, an action that enabled the yen, the lira, the pound, the franc, and other national currencies to cut their ties to the American dollar. Now international financiers enjoyed greater freedom from national regulators and found fresh business opportunities.

The primary agents of the heightened global financial activity were banks. Based mainly in London, New York, and Tokyo, big banks attracted large amounts of capital for lucrative ventures around the world. Revenues from oil producers provided a large infusion of cash into the global economy in the 1970s. At the same time, banks joined forces to issue mammoth loans to developing nations.

No international financial organization was more influential than the International Monetary Fund (IMF), which came into existence after World War II with a view to raising capital from all the participating states so as to be able to lend funds to states coping with balance-of-payments shortages. During the 1980s, it emerged as a central player, especially in response to a global debt crisis. This would be the first in a series of worldwide financial shocks that summoned new global actors above and beyond nation-states. Throughout the 1970s, European, Japanese, and North American banks had loaned money on very easy terms to cash-strapped developing countries and eastern-bloc borrowers. But what was once good business soon turned sour. In 1982, a wave of defaults threatened to overrun Latin America in particular. After Mexico threatened to default, South Korea, Egypt, and the Philippines also got hit. Throughout the 1980s, international banks and the IMF kept heavily indebted customers solvent. The IMF offered short-term loans to governments on strict conditions: balance budgets; compel civilian populations to give up subsidies on essential products, especially food products; slash imports; and boost exports. Latin Americans led the way in deregulating markets, privatizing state assets, reorganizing their finances, and promoting a return to a growth model based on exports and foreign markets. All across the world, tariffs and other barriers to foreign trade crumbled, state enterprises became private firms, and foreign banks and multinational companies took a greater interest in investing in these newly reformed economies. It was in developing countries, however, that the shift to globalism was most dramatic—and most destabilizing.

EFFECTS OF INTEGRATED NETWORKS New technologies and institutions enabled many more financial investors and traders to participate in the integrated networks of world finance. The Internet and online trading accelerated the mobility—and volatility—of capital across borders. Volatility soon created problems, however. In the 1990s, currency devaluations in Mexico, in Russia, and across East Asia shocked financiers. When the Mexican economy became paralyzed in 1994, the crisis was so extreme that not even the IMF could bail it out; the U.S. Treasury had to issue the largest international loan in history to pull Mexico out of its economic tailspin. Despite its role as the lender in that instance, the United States emerged in the new financial order as the world's largest borrower, because it imported far more than it exported. Early in the new millennium, its net foreign debt soared past $2 trillion—a 700-percent increase since the early 1990s. Much of this debt was owed to China, which racked up huge trade surpluses with the United States.

Globalization deepened commercial, as well as financial, interdependence. The total value of world trade increased nearly tenfold between 1973 and 1998, and trade in Asia grew even faster. In 1960, trade accounted for 24 percent of the global gross domestic product (GDP; the total value of all goods and services produced in a country in a single year). By 1995, that share had almost doubled. Where an American would once have worn American-made clothes (Levi's), driven an American car (a Ford), and watched an American television (Zenith), such was rarely the case by century's end. Increasingly, consumers bought foreign goods and services and manufacturers sold a greater share of their own output abroad. This pattern had always been true of smaller regions like Central America and southern Africa. But in the 1980s, it intensified as countries with cheap and skilled labor, like China, India, and Brazil, could set up their own manufacturing capacity and outbid their competitors, who then entered a long cycle of what is called deindustrialization. It was in this fashion that globalization led to the worldwide spread of manufacturing.

International trade also shifted the international division of labor. After World War II, Europeans and North Americans dominated manufacturing, while developing countries supplied raw materials. But by the 1990s, this was no longer the case. Brazil became a major airplane maker, South Korea

Globalization. In the 1970s, East Asian countries, starting with Japan and South Korea, and China in the 1990s, became major exporters of manufactured goods while North America and Europe began their long deindustrialization. Shipping containers (like those pictured here) were crucial to this new global division of labor. Invented to haul expensive military hardware for the U.S. war in Vietnam, they proved instrumental in lowering shipping costs. They allowed ever-more-fragile goods, like electronics, to be transported safely and did away with labor-intensive systems of loading and unloading massive transport vessels. The results were massive layoffs from manufacturing and transportation jobs in some parts of the world and rapid industrialization in emerging economies.

exported millions of automobiles, and China emerged as the world's largest source of textiles, footwear, and electronics.

The most remarkable global shift involved East Asian industry and commerce. Manufactured goods, including high-technology products, now issued from the eastern fringe of Afro-Eurasia as often as from its western fringe. Japan blazed the Asian trail: between 1965 and 1990, its share of world trade doubled to almost 10 percent. China, too, flexed its economic muscle, especially after Deng Xiaoping took power in 1978. (See Analyzing Global Developments: Deng Xiaoping and China's So-Called Economic Miracle.) It's hard to imagine now, but at the time China was very poor. Even as late as 1990, China's per capita income was 30 percent lower than that of the countries of sub-Saharan Africa. Moreover, China barely registered on the global economic scale, commanding a mere 1.6 percent of global GDP. To improve China's economy, Deng threw open the country's doors to foreign trade and investment. In addition, study missions abroad brought back ideas and encouragement. By globalizing China, Deng turned it into an economic powerhouse. By 2010, China had become the world's second-largest economy, producing 8.6 percent of global GDP. It muscled past Germany, the United States, and Japan to become the largest exporter of goods in the world. China's per capita income was now three times that of sub-Saharan Africa. For the three decades from 1990 to 2019, China chalked up astounding 10 percent annual growth rates, even maintaining 6 percent GDP growth during the global recession of 2008 to 2010 (see Chapter 22).

For East Asia as a whole, the share of world exports doubled in the same period, with smaller countries like Singapore, Taiwan, South Korea, and Hong Kong becoming mini-powerhouses. By the early 1990s, these countries and Japan were major investors abroad. As East Asia's share of world production quickly increased, the U.S. and European shares decreased.

REGIONAL TRADE BLOCS AND GROWING DISPARITIES

Industrialization of previously less developed countries, combined with lower trade barriers, increased the pressures of world competition on national economies. Some areas responded by establishing regional trade blocs in an effort to create larger markets for themselves and stay competitive in an even more integrated world economy.

Meanwhile, the most complete regional integration occurred in Europe. Indeed, Europeans slashed trade barriers and harmonized their commercial policies toward the rest of the world. In 1993, the Maastricht Treaty established the **European Union (EU),** and what had been conceived as a trading and financial bloc began to evolve into a political union as well. In hopes of establishing permanent peace and prosperity, European states agreed to give up aspects of their sovereignty and allow European-wide legislative and judicial bodies (the European Parliament and the Court of Justice of the European Union) to make binding political and legal decisions. In 1990, EU members agreed to eliminate border controls and visas and created a vast open migrant zone across

"Great. You move to Mexico, and we all end up working at McDonald's."

Trade Blocs and Outsourcing. The creation of regional trade agreements led to more trade and migration within blocs, such as between Europe and North America. But as manufacturers sought out new locations for their factories to take advantage of cheaper labor elsewhere, they generated backlash from workers. Many had to seek out new jobs in the service sectors as assembly lines closed. This cartoon captures the resentments directed against business elites.

the old Cold War divide. The result was a migration from the east to the west. A generation later, there would be a wave from the Middle East and Africa.

The core of the European Union, however, remained a common economy. In 2002, a number of the European Union states deepened their economic interdependence by adopting a single currency, the euro. A few nations—most notably the United Kingdom—did not want to give up control of their own currency. By 2020, the European Union had twenty-seven members, with nineteen members using the euro.

European countries may have gone the farthest in dismantling national borders and sovereignties. But they were not alone. The Unites States, Mexico, and Canada agreed in 1994 to create a common trade bloc. In South America, Brazil and Argentina formed the backbone of a regional fusion. And Asian countries formed what is often called a "noodle bowl" of trade agreements to create regional partnerships and multilateral agreements to liberalize trade among countries of the Asian Pacific.

Although international trade thus increased, it also became increasingly unequal. High-technology and high-value goods now occupied an ever-greater share of the manufacturing and exports of the world's richest countries. For "rich" countries as a whole, about half of total GDP reflected the production and distribution of such goods and services, giving those countries a competitive advantage. In general, where global incomes were lower and people were less educated, peoples' incomes lagged because they were less productive and faced a steeper climb up the social ladder. Poor nations remained, with few exceptions, locked in the production of low-tech goods and the export of raw materials. Increasingly, technology and knowledge now divided the world into affluent, technically sophisticated countries and poor, technically underdeveloped regions.

Migration

Migration, a constant feature of world history, became more pronounced in the twentieth century. (See Map 21.3.) After 1970, fewer Europeans were on the move, but many more Asians, Africans, and Latin Americans were chasing jobs in the richer countries. By 2000, there were 120 million migrants scattered across 152 countries, up from 75 million in 1965.

PATTERNS OF MIGRATION Migratory flows often followed the contours of past colonial and political ties. Where North America and Europe had had colonies or dependencies, their political withdrawal left tracks for migrants to follow. Indians and Pakistanis moved to Britain. Dominicans, Haitians, and Mexicans went to the United States. Algerians and Vietnamese moved to France. And where emerging rich societies cultivated close diplomatic ties, these relations opened migratory gates. This was true of Germany's relationship with Turkey, of Japan's with South Korea, and of Canada's with Hong Kong. In most cases, economic factors propelled migrants across national borders.

International migration was often an extension of regional and national migration from poorer, rural areas to urban centers. In Nigeria, for example, rural-urban migration intensified after 1970. In 1900, Nigeria's capital at the time, Lagos, had a population of 41,847. At the century's end, Lagos had more than 10 million people, with predictions that it would double by 2025. The key to Lagos's boom in the 1970s was the existence of large oil reserves inside the country and the high prices that oil fetched in international markets. When the Organization of the Petroleum Exporting Countries (OPEC) sent oil prices soaring, money poured into Nigeria. The government kept most of it in its largest city. That, in turn, spurred people to move to Lagos. This rural-urban migration increased Lagos's population by 14 percent per year in the 1970s and 1980s. No government—least of all a new, weakly supported one like Nigeria's—could cope with such a huge influx. Electricity supplies failed regularly. There were never enough schools, teachers, or textbooks. But the city burst with the vitality of new arrivals, prompting one immigrant to exclaim: "It's a terrible place; I want to go there!"

One of the biggest changes in world migration patterns took place in the United States. Having all but closed its coastal borders on the Pacific in the late nineteenth century and on the Atlantic in the 1920s, the United States enacted a major immigration reform in 1965 that opened its gates to the world's migrants. By 2000, 27 million immigrants lived there, accounting for almost 10 percent of the population—double the share in 1970 and approaching levels not seen since the early twentieth century. The profile of migration also changed. In 1970, there were more Canadians or Germans living in the United States than Mexicans. Over the next thirty years, the Mexican influx rose tenfold and by 2000 accounted for almost one-third of immigrants in the United States. The numbers migrating from Asia also surged, accounting for over 40 percent of all immigrants to the United States in the 1990s.

TEMPORARY MIGRANTS Some migrants moved for temporary sojourns. At least that was the original intent. In the 1950s and 1960s, southern Europeans moved northward; yet when Spain, Portugal, Greece, and Italy also became wealthy societies, not only did the exodus decline, but these countries also became magnets for Middle Eastern, North African, South Asian, and then eastern European migrants. The economic downturn in Europe in the 1970s, however, resulted in high unemployment and made integration difficult. Most migrants from Asia and Africa went initially to Europe in search of temporary jobs as guest workers. With time, they and their families who followed

Analyzing Global Developments

Deng Xiaoping and China's So-Called Economic Miracle

Deng Xiaoping (1904–1997) is the person most closely associated with China's opening to the outside world and its rapid economic growth rate, which pulled half a billion people out of poverty between 1990 and 2019. Physically he was not an imposing figure. He was a mere 5 feet tall and so deaf in one ear that he had difficulty hearing remarks made at meetings of the Politburo and other important gatherings. Often his deafness precluded his participation in discussions. Even so, his commanding personality caused all eyes to fix on him when he entered a room. His communist credentials were impeccable. As a young man, he won an opportunity to travel to France, where he hoped to study. But funds ran out, and for two and a half years he earned a living as a factory worker. Dispirited by the way the French scorned the Chinese living in France—workers as well as students and businesspeople—he joined the Chinese Community Party, founded in China in 1921, and a French branch established a year later. Eventually, he left factory work to become an apparatchik in the Chinese Community Party in France. Deng spent five years in France and another year in the Soviet Union, an experience that served him well and set him off from other communists, like Mao, who had seen little of the outside world. He then returned to China and became a military commander in the fight against the Japanese and the Guomindang (the Nationalist Party). His support of Mao Zedong was ardent; he accompanied Mao on the Long March and rose in the hierarchy of the party, which seized power in 1949.

Later, Mao and Deng had a falling out, and Deng was exiled to the countryside, or rusticated, for three and a half years (1969–1973), during China's Cultural Revolution (1966–1976). During this period, China was ruled by military men and inexperienced revolutionary zealots, who sent party officials, university professors, and students to the countryside and governed chaotically and ruthlessly. The circumstances compelled Deng to think creatively about what had gone wrong in China and produced such suffering and how best to mold China's political, cultural, and economic future. After Mao's death in 1976, Deng's star rose. He became the preeminent leader in 1978, a position that enabled him to impose his vision of a transformed China on the nation.

In power, Deng was the opposite of Mao. He recognized that although Mao had used his personality cult to unify a diverse country and champion a virtuous communist ideology, he had created a number of catastrophic programs, notably the Great Leap Forward (1958–1962)—a plan designed to turn China from an agrarian society to an industrial economy that had left 30 million dead in its wake—and the Cultural Revolution. Spurning the cult of personality, Deng had no statues made of himself and he did not insist that government offices and other venues display his photo, as Mao had required. In fact, he did not even occupy the top positions in the Communist Party (the secretary-general) or the government (premier), confining himself to the positions of the vice-chairman of the party and the vice-premier. The only top position that he held was chairman of the Central Military Commission. Nonetheless, his preeminence was recognized in China itself and abroad; he made a number of visits to the United States, Britain, and other countries, where he was always fêted as China's ruler.

By 1978, Deng was seventy-four years old and was convinced that China had to open itself to the outside world. This process became easier when U.S. president Richard Nixon and his secretary of state, Henry Kissinger, created a liaison office between China and the United States (1973–1978), which ultimately resulted in the United States' recognition of the People's Republic of China in 1979. Deng and many Chinese officials, even those who had not traveled extensively outside the country, were aware of the astonishing economic progress of the Asian Tigers, notably Japan, Hong Kong, Taiwan, South Korea, and Singapore. Deng put the matter well when he declared, "Recently, our comrades had a look abroad. The more we see the more we realize how backward we are" (Vogel, p. 218). Trade and study missions were sent to Hong Kong, Japan, and eastern and western Europe. With the assistance of the British high commissioner of Hong Kong, a special free trade zone, known as the Shenzhen Economic Zone, was established between Hong Kong and the part of mainland China in proximity to Hong Kong. Its existence enabled Chinese businesspeople to meet and discuss financial issues with their Hong Kong counterparts and to manufacture goods with cheap Chinese labor for export abroad.

The most influential of these missions was the one sent to western Europe, led by Gu Wu. It visited France, Switzerland, Germany, Denmark, and Belgium between May 2, 1978, and June 6, 1978. The members chosen for this and other missions were expected to head ministries and sectors of the economy for which they gathered data during these overseas missions. In western Europe, mission members expected to find an impoverished workforce and business and government officials who were hostile and secretive to the Chinese delegation, as Chinese government officials were to both foreigners and Chinese non-employees who visited Chinese factories. Instead, the members of the mission were stunned by the generosity and warmth of the European hosts, their seeming eagerness to provide capital and technological support to China, and the high living standards enjoyed by Europe's working classes.

After the four missions returned, Li Xiannian, whom Deng had put in charge of economic issues, prepared a report, *Principles to Guide Four Modernizations*, which was intended to show how China could take advantage of the new opportunities for borrowing technology and capital from the developed economies of the world. On September 7, 1978, Li Xiannian announced that a new age had arrived, adding that

China could no longer remain closed to the outside world, but must import foreign technologies, equipment, capital, and management skills. He predicted, in a wildly optimistic spirit, that China would import $18 billion worth of goods and equipment between 1978 and 1985.

Although Deng Xiaoping stepped down in 1992 and died in 1997, just as rapid economic progress was occurring, he made sure that the Chinese ruling class chose as successors individuals who were committed to his program of economic growth and Communist Party control. Moreover, as a dedicated communist, he affirmed his belief that it was only the Chinese Communist Party that had the right financial and economic skills and the right governing capabilities to lead China's opening to the outside world in a way that would ensure both economic growth and political stability.

The following tables show overall economic growth rates in Britain during the industrial revolution (1750s–1870), the United States from 1850 to 1989, and China from 1961 to 2018. They demonstrate just how colossal the economic growth rate in China was, compared with the rates in these two other fast-growing countries. Deng believed that China could industrialize and grow rapidly economically without responding to citizens' demands for political participation and the end of communist control over the political and economic system. Whether this belief will continue to hold true remains to be seen.

China's Overall GDP Annual Growth Rates	
1961–69	3.37%
1970–79	7.14%
1980–89	9.74%
1990–99	10.00%
2000–09	11.29%
2010–18	7.79%

China's GDP per Capita Annual Growth Rates	
1961–69	1.20%
1970–79	5.27%
1980–89	8.09%
1990–99	8.76%
2000–09	8.74%
2010–18	7.25%

Britain's Overall GDP Annual Growth Rates	
1760s–1780s	0.83%
1780s–1801/10	1.62%
1801/10–1830s	1.85%
1830s–1861/70	2.34%

Britain's GDP per Capita Annual Growth Rates	
1760s–1780s	0.10%
1780s–1800s	0.53%
1800s–1830s	0.41%
1830s–1860s	1.16%

United States' Overall GDP Annual Growth Rates	
1800–55	3.99%
1855–90	4.0%
1890–1927	3.50%
1929–66	3.18%
1966–89	2.69%

United States' GDP per Capita Annual Growth Rates	
1800–55	0.93%
1855–90	1.55%
1890–1927	1.86%
1929–66	1.73%
1966–89	1.67%

QUESTIONS FOR ANALYSIS

- How do China's GDP overall growth rates and per capita growth rates compare with those of Britain during the industrial revolution and the United States from 1850 to 1989? How do you account for any extreme differences?
- Why have Deng Xiaoping and his successors been able to resist demands for democracy and maintain the dominant political position of the Chinese Communist Party?
- Based on your reading, compare Gorbachev's *perestroika* reform movement with Deng's vision for economic and political reform in China.
- Do you think the Chinese are likely to maintain high growth rates over the long run, given the experience of Britain and the United States? Explain your answer.

Sources: Justin Yifu Lin, "China and the Global Economy," *China Economic Journal* 4, no. 1 (2011): 1–14; Ezra F. Vogel, *Deng Xiaoping and the Transformation of China* (Cambridge, MA: Belknap Press, 2011). The figures for Britain during the industrial revolution are from Stephen Broadberry et al., *British Economic Growth, 1270–1870* (Cambridge, England: Cambridge University Press, 2015); and Nicholas Crafts and Terence Mills, "Six Centuries of British Economic Growth: A Time Series Perspective," *European Review of Economic History* 21, no. 2 (May 2017): 141–58. Those for the United States are from Stanley L. Engerman and Robert E. Gallman, *The Cambridge Economic History of the United States*, vol. 3 (Cambridge, England: Cambridge University Press, 2000), p. 8. The Chinese GDP data are derived from the World Bank reports, *World Development Indicators*, for the years involved.

The Global View

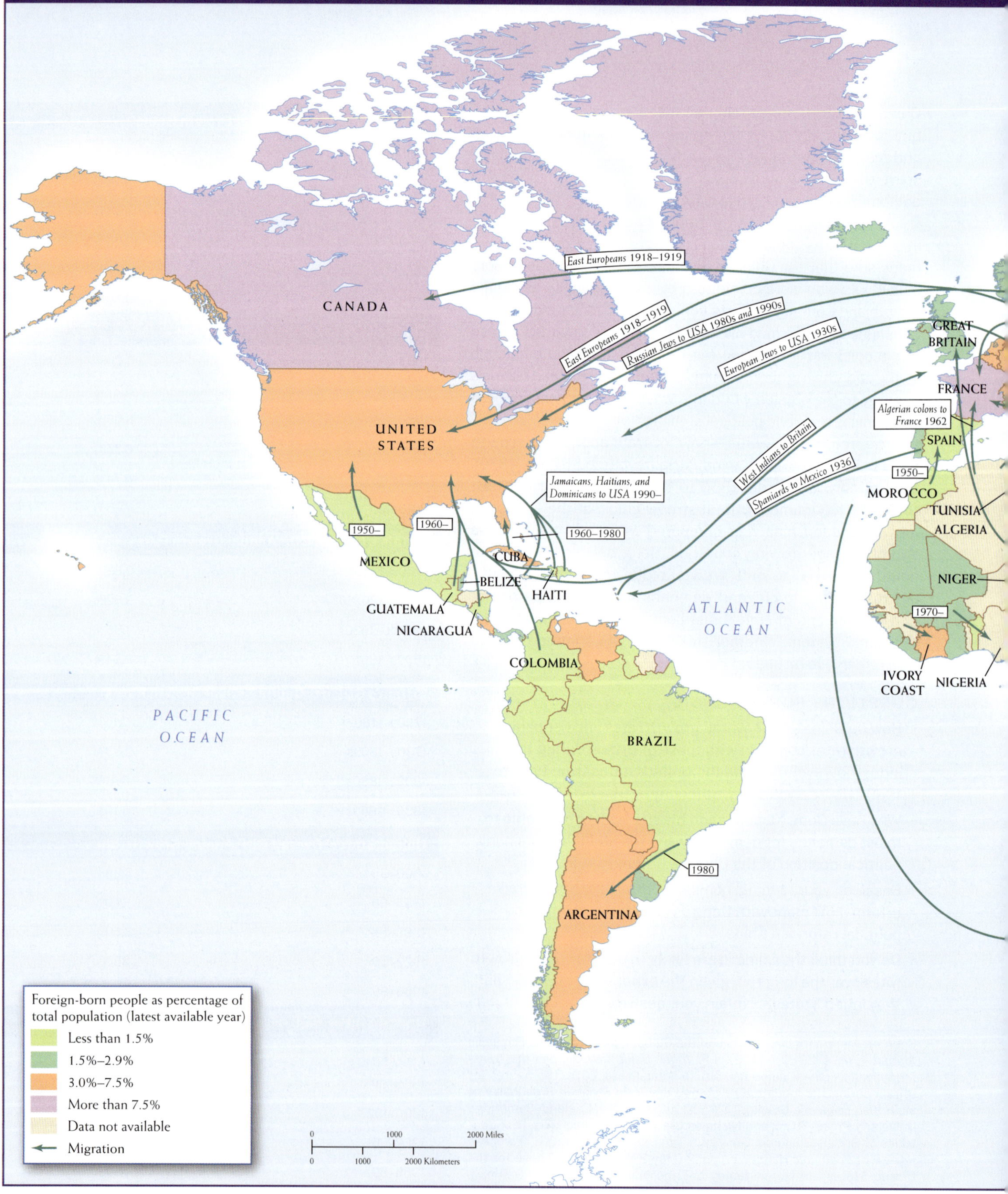

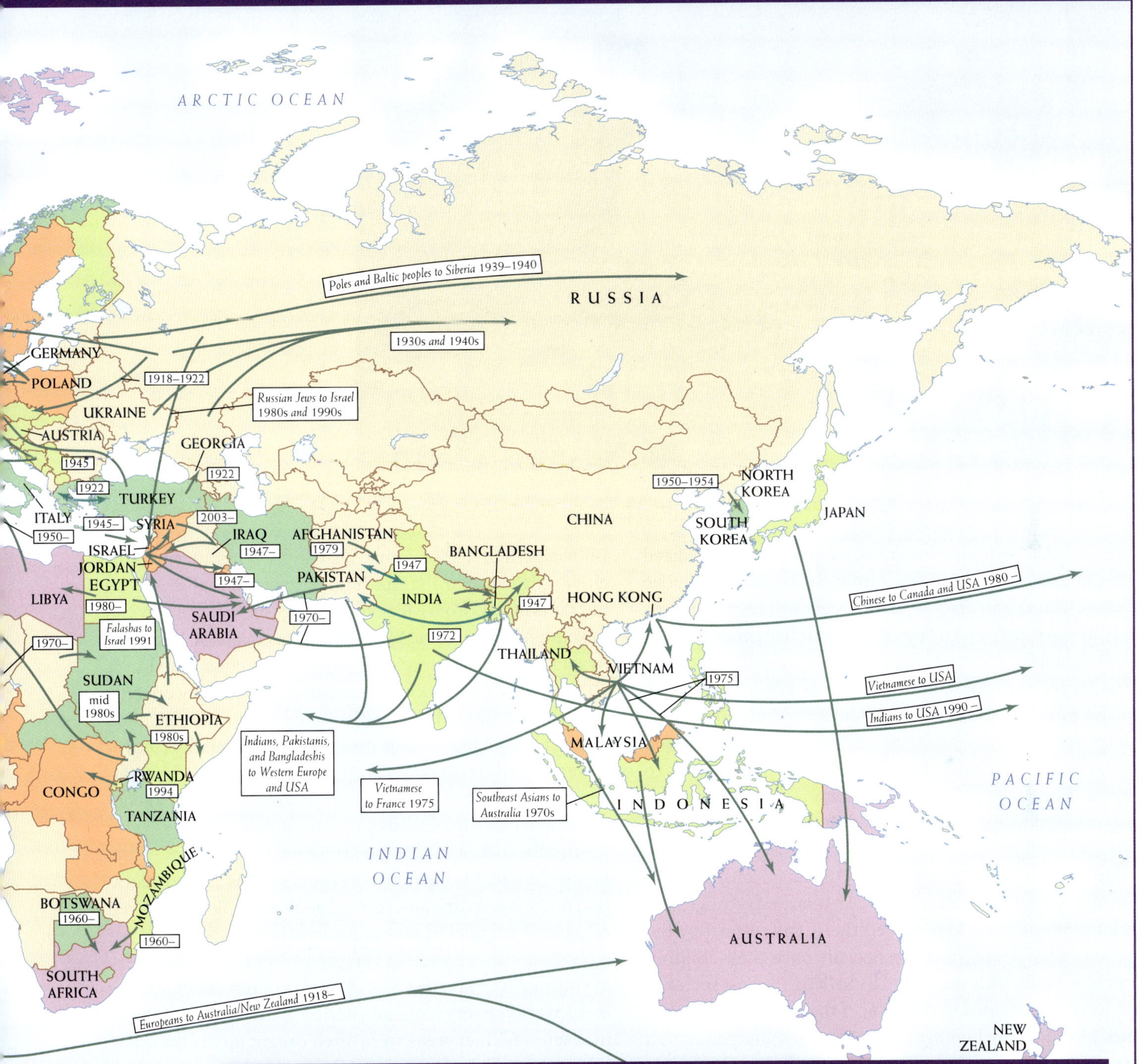

MAP 21.3 | World Migration, 1918–1998

The world's population continued to grow and move around in the twentieth century.

- Looking at this map, identify the countries that had the greatest increase in foreign-born people as a percentage of total population.
- Compare the areas of most rapid population growth during the nineteenth century with the parts of the world that, according to this map, had the highest percentage of foreign-born people in the twentieth century. What are the similarities and differences?
- During the twentieth century, which parts of the world were the sending areas, and which were the receiving territories? See also Map 18.1.

Lagos, Nigeria. During the twentieth century, Lagos was one of the fastest-growing and most crowded cities in Africa.

them settled in their host countries, often living in dilapidated public housing projects, isolated from city centers and public services. The existence of welfare programs made them less likely to leave and return "home" than earlier generations of labor migrants.

In Japan, too, immigrants were not easily incorporated. Tokyo's policy in the 1970s resembled the European guest worker program. Discouraging permanent settlement and immigration, Japan encouraged mainly itinerant workers to move to the country, and yet its economy required increasing numbers of these sojourners. Indeed, Japan's deep reluctance to integrate migrants led to dire labor shortages.

After Japan, the economic tigers of Hong Kong, Taiwan, and Malaysia all became hosts for temporary migrants. Millions of guest workers moved there, and ultimately the migrants sank deeper roots, especially once their children entered schools. This presented a challenge to host societies that were accustomed to thinking of their national communities as ethnically homogeneous. At times, discrimination led to violent conflicts between recent immigrants, long-time residents, and the state's security forces. Governments also grappled with the challenge of extending citizenship rights to and culturally assimilating newcomers who wanted to dress according to religious custom, as in the case of Muslims in France (10 percent of that country's population).

RESIDENT NONCITIZENS AND REFUGEES In the United States, arguments in Los Angeles over schools and health care for resident noncitizens became part of a global debate. In Argentina, up to 500,000 undocumented Peruvians, Bolivians, and Paraguayans also lived without rights as citizens. Even more staggering, between 3 and 8 million migrants moved from Mozambique, Zimbabwe, and Lesotho to South Africa. In some Middle Eastern countries, like Saudi Arabia and Kuwait, foreign-born workers constituted over 70 percent of the workforce. In general, migrants were only partially accommodated, while many were fully excluded from host societies. Thus, even though population movements flowed across political, kinship, and market networks, demographic reshuffling heightened national concerns about the ethnic makeup of political communities.

Finally, forced migrations remained a hallmark of the modern world. In contrast to earlier centuries' forced migration of enslaved Africans, recent involuntary flows involved refugees fleeing civil war and torture. Many suffered for weeks, months, or years in refugee camps on the periphery of violence. The greatest concentration of refugees occurred in the world's poorest region—Africa. Those Africans unable to reach wealthier areas were often caught up in ethnic and religious conflicts that generated vast refugee camps, where survival depended on the generosity of host governments and international contributions.

Global Culture

Migrations and new technologies helped create a more global entertainment culture. In this domain, globalization was often equated with Americanization. Yet American entertainments themselves reflected artistic practices from across the globe as one mass culture met another. On a global scale,

African Refugees. During the late twentieth century, Africa became a continent of displaced persons and refugee camps. Pictured here is a camp in Chad for Sudanese driven out of the Darfur region by government-sponsored raids.

there was less diversity in 2000 than in 1300, but in terms of individuals' everyday experience, the potential for experiencing cultural diversity (if one could afford the technology to do so) increased.

NEW MEDIA Technology was key in spreading entertainment. In the 1970s, for example, cassette tapes became the dominant medium for popular music, sidelining the long-playing record and the short-lived eight-track tape. Bootleggers illegally mass-reproduced cassette tapes and sold them cheaply to young consumers. Television was another globalizing force, as American producers bundled old dramas and situation comedies to stations worldwide. Brazilian soap operas began to penetrate Spanish-language American TV markets in the 1980s, often inducing Mexican viewers to rush home from work to catch the latest episode. Latin American television shows and music were distributed in the United States in areas with large Spanish-speaking populations. Bombay also produced its fair share of programs for viewers of British television and today produces roughly twice as many films per year as Hollywood. (See Current Trends in World History: Urbanization as a Global Phenomenon: Transforming Bombay to Mumbai.) In terms of box-office revenues, Hollywood remains the world's leading producer of films, helped in no small measure by its ability to export movies across borders and turn actors from around the world into global celebrities.

Television's globalizing effects were especially evident in sports. Soccer (known as football outside the United States) became an international passion, with devoted national followings for national teams. Indeed, by the 1980s, soccer was *the* world sport, with television ratings increasingly determining its schedule. Organizers of the 1986 World Cup in Mexico insisted that big soccer matches take place at midday so that games could be televised live at prime time in Europe, despite teams' having to play under the scorching sun. In many parts of the globe, major American sports made particularly deep inroads as more foreigners participated in them and as television broadcast American games in other countries. The National Basketball Association (and the athletic footwear firm Nike) was particularly successful in international marketing; in the process, it made Michael Jordan the world's best-known athlete in the late twentieth century.

CULTURAL EXCHANGES Technology was not the only driving force of world cultures, for migration and exchange were also important. For example, as people moved around, they brought their own musical tastes and borrowed others. Reggae, born in the 1960s among Jamaica's Rastafarians, became a hit sensation in London and Toronto, where large West Indian communities had migrated. Reggae lyrics and realist imagery invoked a Black countercultural sensibility and a redemptive call for a return to African roots. Soon, Bob Marley and the Wailers, reggae's flagship band, played to audiences worldwide. In northeastern Brazil, where African culture emerged from decades of disdain, Bob Marley became a folk hero. In Soweto, South Africa, populated by Black workers, he was a symbol of resistance.

Reggae propelled a shift in Black American music. In broadcasting reggae, disc jockeys merged sounds and chanted lyrics over a beat, a "talkover" form that soon characterized

Current Trends in World History

Urbanization as a Global Phenomenon: Transforming Bombay into Mumbai

The city has played a pivotal role in world history since it first emerged thousands of years ago along the Tigris and Euphrates Rivers in Mesopotamia (modern-day Iraq). People have flocked to cities ever since for the social and economic advantages that these locations offer. By the end of the twentieth century, the proportion of people living in cities—usually defined as places having populations over 5,000 or 10,000—exceeded 50 percent in the wealthiest countries and was approaching that proportion in the less developed countries.

Of the burgeoning cities in the developing world, one of the most dynamic is Mumbai, in the state of Maharashtra, India. Acquired in the sixteenth century by the Portuguese, who then transferred its control to the English East India Company, Bombay (as it was named at the time) developed as a port city for colonial commerce. It profited from the cotton trade, developed a vibrant textile industry, attracted migrants from the countryside, and acquired a cosmopolitan image. India gained its independence from Britain in 1947, and in 1996 Bombay was renamed "Mumbai." It still epitomizes the modern face of the nation, and its increasingly heterogeneous population reflects the larger Indian melting pot.

Beginning in the 1980s, however, the nature of the city's relationship with the world economy started to change. The cotton textile industry, Bombay's economic backbone, went into a decline. Industrial employment fell sharply. The share of informal household enterprises, small shops, petty subcontractors, and casual labor rose, along with employment in banking and insurance. Economic liberalization removed hurdles for foreign businesses and brought the city directly into the global economy.

Today Mumbai occupies a strategic place in transnational geography. This is evident in the increasing presence of financial institutions, trading organizations, insurance companies, telecommunications corporations, and information technology enterprises with worldwide operations. Even the city's vibrant film industry addresses a global, not just a national, audience. Rather appropriately, Bombay cinema has been nicknamed "Bollywood." The city, however, still attracts a large number of poor migrants who live in slums or call the pavements their home. The gap between Mumbai's rich and poor has grown alarmingly. The millions who eke out a miserable living stand in stark contrast to a tiny elite enriched by the global economy.

Globalization has also affected Mumbai residents' identity. In the 1990s, the political party then in power in Maharashtra was the Shiv Sena, a nativist regional party named after a seventeenth-century Maratha chieftain who opposed the Mughal Empire. As the industrial economy and trade unions gave way to the service sector and unorganized labor, the Shiv Sena utilized the social and political fluidity produced by globalization to win support for its nativist ideology. Mumbai's cosmopolitan image went up in smoke in 1992–1993, when the Shiv Sena led pogroms against the city's Muslim residents. In response, a Muslim underworld don, according to police investigations, engineered a series of bomb blasts in March 1993. Since then, the city has experienced episodes of violence, none more gruesome than the terrorist attacks on two luxury hotels, a crowded railway station, and a Jewish center in November 2006. Ironically, the terrorists chose to attack Mumbai because of its economic importance and reputation as a cosmopolitan city.

Mumbai today illustrates the uneven effects of globalization. The society is sharply divided, economic disparities are great, and the city's politics is a cauldron of conflicting identities. These are the local forms in which this vast and influential city experiences globalization.

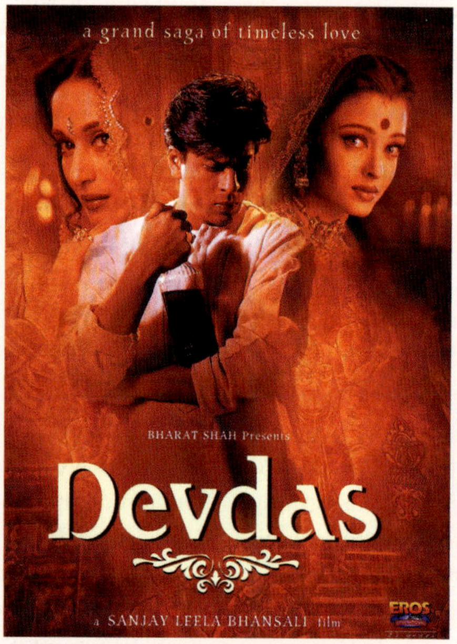

Bollywood. Bombay cinema, or Bollywood, has an increasing global presence. This poster advertises *Devdas*, a three-hour romance that won awards in India and around the world.

QUESTIONS FOR ANALYSIS

- Contrast migration to Mumbai, as described here, with that to other parts of the world, notably western Europe and Japan, as described in the body of the chapter.
- How does Mumbai fit into the larger theme of "Worlds Together, Worlds Apart"?

EXPLORE FURTHER

Anand, Nikhil, *Hydraulic City: Water and the Infrastructures of Citizenship in Mumbai* (2017).

Mehta, Suketu, *Maximum City: Bombay Lost and Found* (2005).

Prakash, Gyan, *Mumbai Fables* (2010).

Bob Marley. In the 1970s, young Europeans and North Americans began to listen to music from the developing countries. Among the most popular was Jamaican-based reggae, and its most renowned artist was Bob Marley. Marley's music combined rock and roll with African rhythms and lyrics about freedom and redemption for the downtrodden of the world.

rap music as well. This was a disruptive concept in the late 1970s, but within ten years rap had become mainstream. Rap lyrics emulated reggae realism by focusing on Black problems, but they also opened a new domain of controversies involving gang worldviews. On the world stage, Latino rappers stressed multicultural themes, often in "Spanglish." Asian rap stressed the genre as a vehicle for cross-cultural sharing.

The effects of migration on global music were also evident in Latin American transformations of North American genres. Latin music came into its own thanks to Latin American migrants to the United States. In New York and New Jersey, Puerto Ricans and Dominicans popularized boogaloo, salsa, and merengue. In Los Angeles, Mexican *corridos* (ballads) became pop hits.

Baseball Goes International. The 1980s and 1990s saw an influx of ballplayers from Latin America and quite a few from Asia as well. *Left:* Boston Red Sox slugger David Ortiz hails from the Dominican Republic. *Right:* New York Yankees superstar Ichiro Suzuki is from Japan.

What reinforced cross-cultural borrowing was not just the medium of production and distribution of entertainment across borders, but also the message. Increasingly, world popular culture was youth culture—especially its message of generational opposition. Consider Egypt's popular TV serial *The School of Troublemakers*, which carried a resolutely antiestablishment message: it showed schoolboys challenging their teachers' authority and then reveling in the chaos that resulted. In Argentina, rock and roll was crucial to the counterculture during the military dictatorship of the 1970s and 1980s. Charlie García urged Buenos Aires audiences to defy authorities by daring to dream of a different order. Indeed, in countries where repressive regimes quashed public cultures, pop culture was usually counterculture.

The same globalizing effects influenced sports. Consider the staple of American identity, baseball, whose major league teams took on a more global cast. Beginning in the 1960s, the number of Latin Americans playing in North American professional leagues grew steadily. Notable in the 1980s was the Mexican pitcher Fernando Valenzuela, whose exploits as a member of the Los Angeles Dodgers made him a hero to that city's Mexican population and in his native land as well. The Dodgers also took the lead in reaching for Asian talent. In the 1990s, as Los Angeles experienced a growing Asian immigrant population, the Dodgers signed the Japanese pitcher Hideo Nomo. Meanwhile, in the Dominican Republic, baseball fans were riveted by their favorite players in the big leagues: slugger Sammy Sosa and ace pitcher Pedro Martínez. The emergence of so many Latin American and Asian baseball players epitomized the ability of what were once purely American cultural forms to spread their influences and to bring peoples all over the world together.

LOCAL CULTURE World cultures may have become more integrated and homogeneous, but they did not completely replace national and local cultures. Indeed, technology and migration often reinforced the appeal of "national" cultural icons as national celebrities gained popularity among immigrant groups abroad. Inexpensive new technology introduced these stars to more and more people. In Egypt, the most popular singer of the Nasser years was Umm Kulthum, who became the favorite of the middle classes via radio. In 1975, she was given a state funeral, the likes of which had rarely been seen.

As the market for world cultures grew increasingly competitive and integrated, performers borrowed from one another and employed a wider variety of styles, with some becoming commercial sensations. The result was often a challenge to convention. Consider the Indian movie industry, which has become one of the world's behemoth entertainers. When Bombay's Hindi cinema was cut off from the world, it never developed new themes and forms. But now it did. In place of

Fairuz. Street art depicting the singer Fairuz. Born in Lebanon in 1934, Fairuz is an icon in the Arab world. Her record sales top 150 million worldwide. Although she was raised in a conservative Christian household, her voice and lyrics crossed religious and sectarian divides. Even through the horrors of the Lebanese civil wars of the 1970s and 1980s, she appealed to all sides and refused to abandon her country. Occasionally, however, her crossovers upset her fans. For instance, in 2008, when Syrian dictator Bashar al-Assad's troops occupied part of Lebanon, Fairuz performed in Syria, claiming that culture should not be politicized. Some accused her of turning a blind eye.

the timeworn east versus west theme, it confidently embraced the global space with glamorous romance, breakout dancing, and chart-topping music. The local Hindi film became a global Indian phenomenon, at home in London, Sydney, and New York, and portrayed a global lifestyle. Bombay cinema also acquired a new brand, Bollywood, which came to increasingly depend on revenues from the United States, Europe, and the Middle East, where South Asian migrants flocked to see the latest blockbusters.

Among the breakthroughs that have occurred since the 1970s was the triumph of Black performers (Bob Marley, Whitney Houston, Michael Jackson), Black athletes (Pelé, Michael Jordan, Carl Lewis), and Black writers (Toni Morrison, Chinua Achebe). Competition also shattered some biases of gender and sexuality. Female performers like Madonna became popular icons. So did gay performers, starting with the Village People, whose campy multicultural anthem "YMCA" created a place for a new generation of gay or bisexual artists. In American television, the comedian and talk show host Ellen DeGeneres broke barriers as a popular lesbian performer who could elicit peals of laughter from gay and straight audiences alike. Of course, beyond Europe and North America, flirting with sexual conventions had its limits. In the Middle East, female video artists wore headscarves—but they still swung their hips. What were once relatively homogeneous national cultures, often dominated by men representing the ethnic majority, gave way to a wide variety of entertainers and artists who broke loose of confining local cultures.

Communications

Computer technology revolutionized global communications. In the late 1980s, while working in Switzerland, the British physicist Tim Berners-Lee devised a means to pool data stored on various computers. Whereas previous electronic links had existed only between major universities and research stations, Berners-Lee made data more accessible by creating the World Wide Web. With each use and each connection, and as people entered more data, however, the Web grew unmanageably crowded and difficult to navigate. The early 1990s saw the first commercial browsers used in navigating the so-called Internet. Suddenly people were communicating across global networks more easily than with neighbors and more inexpensively than with local phone calls.

The change created a new generation of wealth. CEOs of top companies like General Motors, Royal Dutch Shell, and Merck had less net worth than Michael Dell (hardware maker), Bill Gates (software maker), and Jeff Bezos (creator of Amazon). Shares of Internet firms, known as dot-coms, swept the world's stock markets. Money from these companies flowed globally as they established offices worldwide. Software and Internet technologies developed enormous economies of scale and thus became prone to monopolization as they took over small companies.

Hardware, software, and the Internet were not purely American innovations. Within a few years of their invention, personal computers were being made in Mexico and computer chips were being mass-produced in Taiwan. The brains behind the Internet were likely to be students from Indian institutes of technology. Originally engineering schools, these institutes trained a whole generation of pioneering computing engineers, many of whom resettled in California's Silicon Valley. By 1996, Indians held half of the 55,000 temporary work visas issued by the U.S. government for high-tech employees. Roughly half of Silicon Valley start-up companies in the late 1990s were the brainchildren of Indian entrepreneurs. Google, the biggest of them all, was founded by a couple of graduate students

Family Planning in China. To control China's burgeoning population, the government enacted the one-child policy in 1979, which restricted each household to one child. While the policy was generally effective, numerous cases of forced abortions by zealous party officials and overwhelming numbers of female orphans revealed the need for a less stringent approach to population control. This 1996 propaganda billboard in Wuhan reads: "Family planning is the need of mankind." It is no accident that the single child in the ideal family illustrated beneath the slogan is a girl.

at Stanford. One of them, Sergey Brin, was a Jewish Russian fugitive. The current CEO of the giant firm is Sundar Pichai, who grew up in Chennai, India, before moving to the United States for graduate studies.

While the Internet revolution provided new means to share and sell information, it also reinforced hierarchies between haves and have-nots. Great swaths of the world's population living outside big cities had no access to the Internet. According to World Bank calculations, in the late 1990s countries with low-income economies had, on average, 26 phone lines per 1,000 people; countries with high-income economies had 550 lines per 1,000 people. The biggest losers were the billions living in rural areas or towns neglected by state and private communications providers. The have-nots were poor not just from lack of capital but from lack of access to knowledge and new media.

Characteristics of the New Global Order

While providing access to an unimaginable array of goods and services, globalization also deepened world inequalities. Families changed, and life spans increased. Education and good health determined one's status in society as never before. Populations expanded dramatically, requiring greater industrial and agricultural output from all parts of the world. While many regions consumed more than ever before, others struggled with famine. And as tropical rain forests were destroyed and the burning of fossil fuels increased, **global climate change** threatened the world's population.

The Demography of Globalization

It took 160 years (1800–1960) for the world's population to increase from 1 billion to 3 billion; over the next 40 years (1960–2000), it jumped from 3 billion to over 6 billion. Behind this steepening curve were two important developments: a decline in mortality, especially among children, and a rise in life expectancy.

Population growth was hardly equal worldwide. (See Map 21.4.) In Europe, population growth peaked around 1900, and it moved upward only gradually from 400 million to 730 million during the twentieth century, with little growth after the 1970s. North America's population quadrupled over the same period, mainly because of immigration. The population booms in the twentieth century occurred in Asia (400 percent), Africa (550 percent), and Latin America (700 percent). China and India each passed the billion-person mark. Increases were greatest in the cities. By the 1980s, the world's largest cities were Asian, African, and Latin American. Greater Tokyo-Yokohama had 30 million inhabitants; Mexico City, 20 million; São Paulo, 17 million; Cairo, 16 million; Calcutta, 15 million; and Jakarta, 12 million.

Population growth slowed most dramatically in richer societies. For some, like Italy, the growth rate declined to zero. More recently enriched societies like Korea, Taiwan, and Hong Kong also had fewer births. Societies that did not see their birthrates decline by the same rate (much of Africa, southern Asia, and impoverished parts of Latin America) had difficulty raising income levels. But even among poor nations, birthrates declined after the 1970s.

The most remarkable turnaround occurred in China, where the government instituted a "one-child family" policy

MAP 21.4 | World Population Increases, 1950–1997

The world's population more than doubled between 1950 and 1997, rising from approximately 2.5 billion to nearly 6 billion.

- Which countries had the largest population increases over these five decades? Why do you suppose these countries experienced such high population increases?
- According to your reading, why did western Europe and Russia have the lowest population increases?

with rewards for compliance and penalties for transgression. Inducements included cash subsidies, preferential access to nurseries and kindergartens, priority in medical care, and the promise of favored treatment in housing, education, and employment. The policy also prompted an imbalance in sex ratio at birth. The bias in favor of sons (long a feature of China's patrilineal system, which emphasized descent through the male line), together with the availability of ultrasound scanners, promoted the widespread—albeit illegal—practice of prenatal sex selection.

In general, however, declining family size resulted from choice. In rich countries, more women deferred having children as education, career prospects, and birth control devices provided incentives and methods to postpone starting a family. In addition, love became a precondition to marriage and family formation in societies that had traditionally emphasized arranged marriages.

FAMILIES In many countries, the legal definition of families became more fluid in this period. Here again, the change reflected women's choices and the relationship between love and marriage. First, couples chose to end their marriages at unprecedented rates. In the United States, for example, the divorce rate doubled between 1970 and 1998; by the century's end, one in two marriages ended in divorce. In Belgium and Britain late in the twentieth century, fewer than half of all marriages survived. China's divorce rate soared, too. In Beijing, by century's end it approached 25 percent—double the 1990 rate. As of 2000, women initiated more than 70 percent of divorces.

As marriages became shorter-lived, new forms of childrearing proliferated. Europeans, including the supposedly more traditional Italians and Greeks, abandoned nuclear family conventions. In those European countries where divorce remained difficult, more couples lived together without getting married. In the United States, out-of-wedlock childbirths constituted one-third of all births in the late 1990s, with only about half of American children living in households with both parents (compared with nearly three-quarters of children in the early 1970s).

AGING Longer life spans also affected family fortunes, as more infants survived childhood and lived to be old. The population of industrial nations "grayed" considerably as the

Wedding Ceremonies. *Left:* A bride bends down to allow the groom to tie the mangalsutra, or sacred necklace, around her neck, symbolizing their union in this Hindu wedding ceremony in India. *Right:* South Korean martial artist Kim Jong-bok holds his bride, actress Song Hee-jung, during their 2005 wedding ceremony, held on the Tokdo islets off the Korean Peninsula to protest Japan's claim of the territory.

median age increased and the percentage over age sixty-five grew. In western Europe and Japan, graying rates were even more marked. Japan's birthrate plummeted, and the citizenry aged at such a rate that the country began to depopulate. From a population of 127 million in 2000, estimates forecast a decline to 105 million by 2050.

The aging population presented new challenges for families. For centuries, being a parent meant providing for children until they could be self-sufficient. Old age, the years of relatively unproductive labor, was brief. Communities and households absorbed the cost of caring for the elderly. Household savings became family bequests to future, not older, generations. But as populations aged, retirees needed society's savings to survive. So public and private pension funds swelled to accumulate future pools of money for the retired. In Germany, over 30 percent of the government's social policy spending went into the state pension fund. Chinese demographers warned that the one-child policy might create an unbalanced population structure. In a society in which the family still largely provided the safety net, many people worried about having to support two parents and four grandparents.

In Africa, where publicly supported pension funds were rare, the aged faced bleaker futures. Whereas in earlier times the elderly were respected founts of wisdom, colonial rule and the postcolonial world elevated the young—especially those with western educations and lifestyles. Then, in the 1970s, as birthrates soared, the demand on family resources to care for infants and children rose at the very moment when society's resource base began to shrink. The elderly could no longer work, but neither could they rely on the household's support.

HEALTH The distribution of contagious diseases also reflected inequities in the globalized world. Although microbes have no respect for borders, the effects of public health regulations, antibiotics, and vaccination campaigns reduced the spread of contagions. By the late twentieth century, not only did nutrition and healthy habits count (as they always had), but access to medicines did, too.

What used to be universal afflictions in previous centuries (such as the Black Death) now just affected certain peoples. Water treatment and proper sewerage, for example, had banished cholera from most urban centers by the mid-twentieth century. More recently, however, its deadly grip again reached across Asia and into the eastern Mediterranean, parts of Latin America, and much of sub-Saharan Africa. From the 1970s, Africa suffered frequent outbreaks. The crucial cause of the respread of cholera was urban developers' failure to keep sanitation systems growing apace with the demand for water. Thus, diseases proliferated where urban squalor was most acute—in cities with the greatest post-1970s population growth.

In the 1970s, entirely new diseases began to devastate the world's population. Consider **HIV/AIDS**, an epidemic that, in its first two decades, killed 12 million people. Acquired immunodeficiency syndrome (AIDS) is caused by the human immunodeficiency virus (HIV), which spreads through blood and other body fluids. The virus may remain dormant in the bodies of infected people for some time, but eventually attacks the immune system, leaving victims unable to fight off even the most common microbes. First detected in 1981, HIV/AIDS was initially stigmatized as a "gay cancer" (as it then appeared primarily in gay men) and received little attention. Gay activists in San Francisco, New York, Toronto, and Rio de Janeiro mobilized and pressured public authorities to be more responsive; at first, they were greeted with derision. But as the disease spread to heterosexuals and public awareness about it increased, a new campaign urged the practice of safe sex, control of blood supplies, and restrictions on sharing hypodermic needles. In Europe and North America, where

HIV/AIDS Treatment and Education. *Left:* At the Thirteenth International AIDS Conference in Durban, South Africa, in July 2000, AIDS activists express their displeasure at the high prices and unavailability of lifesaving drugs for most of those in the developing countries who are affected by AIDS. *Right:* African governments did not tackle the problem of HIV/AIDS in their severely affected continent with the energy warranted. Pictured here, however, a doctor seeks to impress on the youth of a local community how they should conduct their social and sexual lives in light of the AIDS crisis.

the campaigns intensified and new drugs kept the virus under control, HIV/AIDS rates stabilized. Unfortunately, the affliction went global.

New treatments were very expensive, however, leaving the poor and disadvantaged still vulnerable to infection. By 2000, 33 million people had AIDS (the vast majority in poor countries) and even more were infected with HIV. (See Map 21.5.) At least two-thirds of those with AIDS lived in sub-Saharan Africa. In India, 7 million carried HIV; in China, the figure topped 1 million. At present, the most afflicted country is South Africa, with almost 8 million people living with HIV.

Other factors behind the geographical and demographic prevalence of HIV/AIDS were schooling and literacy. Better education led to safer sexual practices. Worldwide, more educated men and women showed higher use of condoms.

EDUCATION Access to decent education increasingly separated the haves from the have-nots. Moreover, because educational opportunities usually favored men, schooling shaped differences between the lives of men and women. In sub-Saharan Africa and in India, for example, literacy rates were, respectively, 63 and 64 percent for men and only 39 and 40 percent for women as of 2000. In the Arab world, the gap between men and women decreased somewhat by the end of the twentieth century. Yet low levels of literacy overall and the depressed levels for women continued to impede each region's efforts to combat poverty. (See Global Themes and Sources: Primary Source 21.3.)

Gender bias also remained in rich societies. For decades, however, women and girls pressed for equal access, with some astounding results. In the United States, by the late 1980s, more than half of all college degrees went to women (up from 38 percent in 1960). Chinese women made even greater strides, although roadblocks persisted. Ironically, with China's recent market reforms, women's access to basic education regressed, as families, particularly in rural areas, reverted to spending their limited resources on educating

African Women and Education. Though women's education lagged behind that of men in Africa, a number of women, like Stella Kenyi, pictured here (*left*), graduated from African high schools and attended universities at home or abroad. Kenyi taught business skills to men and women in Sudan after completing an undergraduate degree at Davidson College in North Carolina.

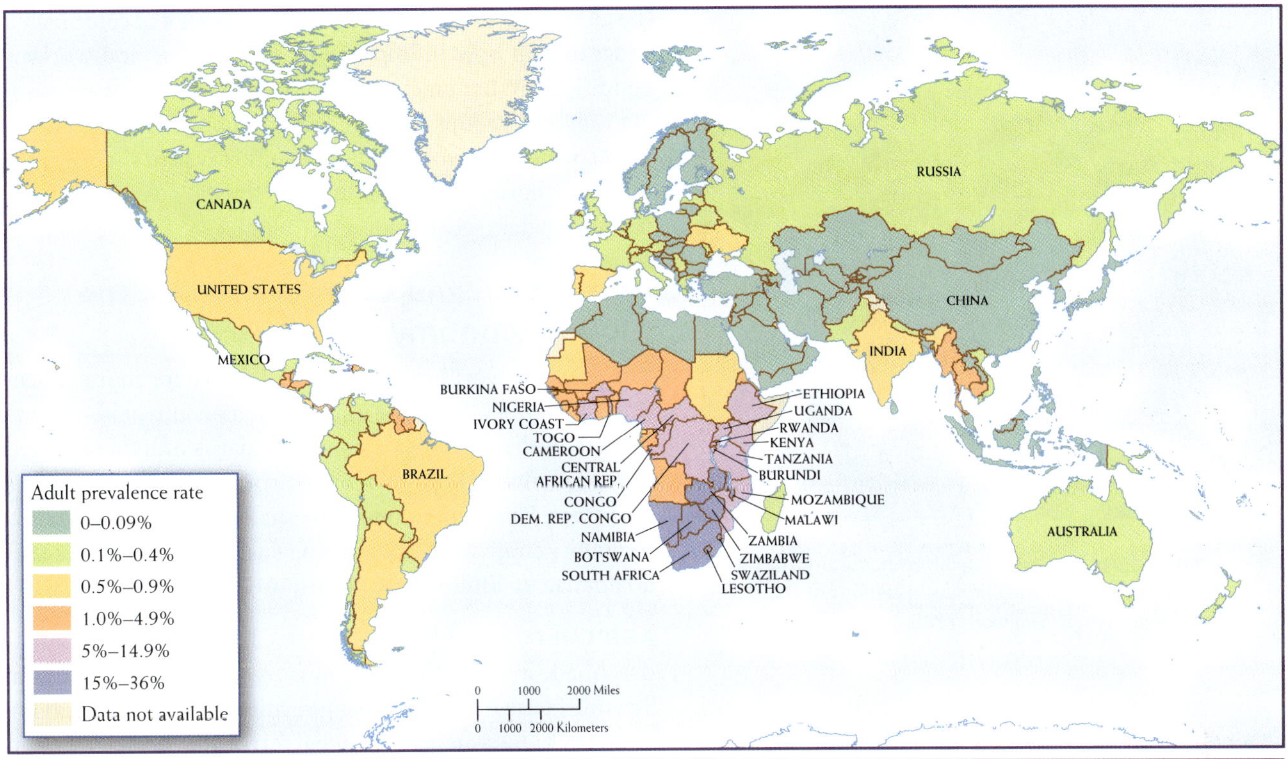

MAP 21.5 | HIV Infection across the World, 1999

HIV, which leads to AIDS, spread across the whole world within two decades, providing further evidence of global interconnectedness. The outbreak began in Africa.

- Where in Africa have the highest rates of HIV infection occurred?
- Which countries *outside* the African continent have had the highest rates of infection, and why is this so?
- Which countries have the lowest rates of HIV infection, and why is this so?

sons. Thus, in 2000, up to 70 percent of China's 140 million illiterates were women.

WORK Although more women held jobs outside the home, they lacked full equity at work. Limited by job discrimination and burdens of child-rearing, women's participation in the workforce reached a fairly stable level by the 1980s. The percentage of women at the top of the corporate pyramid was considerably smaller than their proportion in the labor force or their college graduation rates. In 1995, the Chinese government claimed that Chinese women had made better advances than their U.S. counterparts: there were more Chinese women (10 percent) than American women (3 percent) in senior managerial posts. Still, Chinese women graduates complained of discrimination in the job market. In 2000, some 60 percent of China's unemployed were women, and the number was growing. Women worldwide had difficulties breaking through the "glass ceiling"—a seemingly invisible barrier to women's advancement. Consequently, while income disparities between men and women narrowed, a significant gap persisted.

Working outside the home led to problems inside the home. Who would take care of the children? Changing gender norms in rich countries sparked major migration streams. Jamaican and Filipino women migrated by the thousands in the 1970s and 1980s to Canada and Australia to work as nannies to raise money to send back home, where they had often left their own children. In South Africa and Brazil, local women served as domestic servants and nannies. They were doing the jobs that once belonged to middle- and upper-class homemakers, women who now wanted the same rights as men: to parent *and* to work.

FEMINISM The deeply ingrained inequality between men and women prompted calls for change. Feminist movements arose mainly in Europe and North America in the 1960s and then became global in the 1970s. In 1975, the first truly international women's forum took place in Mexico City. But becoming global did not necessarily imply overturning local customs. What feminists called for was not the abolition of gender differences but equal treatment—equal pay and equal opportunities for obtaining jobs and advancement. In

Forum on Women. Women representing different cultures of the world hold out a "peace torch" at the opening ceremony of the U.N. World Conference on Women in Beijing in 1995.

general, then, in spite of rapid population growth, women's inequities between and within societies remained prominent in this period. The most glaring were between the rich and poor countries, although well-to-do classes of women emerged everywhere and tended to congregate in big cities.

Women took increasingly active stances against discrimination in government and in the workplace. Indeed, as economic integration intensified with regional trade pacts (usually negotiated by men in the interest of male-owned and male-run firms), women struggled to ensure that globalization did not cut them out of new opportunities. For instance, after Argentina, Uruguay, Paraguay, and Brazil negotiated the Mercosur free trade pact, traffic across South American borders soared. But as trade grew, so did government efforts to monitor illegal commerce and foster approved trade along new highways and bridges. Women were responsible for one kind of illicit commerce, because for generations they had transported goods across the river separating Argentina and Paraguay. When customs officers tried to stop this practice in the mid-1990s, Argentine and Paraguayan women locked arms to occupy the new bridge that male truckers used to ship Mercosur products, protesting the restrictions on their age-old enterprise.

The rising tide of global feminism culminated in a U.N. conference on women in Beijing in 1995. Government delegates from more than 180 countries attended the Fourth World Conference on Women to produce "a platform for action" regarding women's rights in politics, business, education, and health. Alongside the official conference was a parallel conference for nearly 30,000 representatives at the NGO Forum for Women. These grassroots activists represented 2,000 nongovernmental organizations from every corner of the globe. Representatives planned strategies and coordinated programs on how to improve women's living and working conditions. What emerged from the conference were associations and groups that pledged to lobby for the rights of women and girls worldwide. One effect was to spotlight the ongoing shortage of opportunities for the advancement of women leaders worldwide.

Production and Consumption in the Global Economy

The growing world population, the desire for more education and better health, the entry of women into paid employment, and the promise of rising standards of living spurred unprecedented production and consumption of the world's resources. The most immediate challenge was how to feed so many people while developing sustainable practices that do not use up limited natural resources.

AGRICULTURAL PRODUCTION Changing agrarian practices made a huge difference in increasing food production. Starting in the 1950s, the "green revolution," largely involving nonfarm inputs such as chemical fertilizers, herbicides, and pesticides, produced dramatically larger harvests. Then, in the 1970s, biologists began offering genetically engineered crops that multiplied yields at an even faster rate.

But these breakthroughs were not evenly distributed. American farmers, the biggest innovators, were the greatest beneficiaries. For example, by century's end they produced approximately one-ninth of the world's wheat and two-fifths of its corn. From this output, American exports accounted for about one-third of the world's international wheat trade and four-fifths of all corn exports. At the heart of the innovation was political power, for farmers had the clout to force officials to maintain roads, subsidize credit and prices, and mop up surplus supply. But Asian rice farmers made impressive innovations, too. In Taiwan and Korea, chemical and biological breakthroughs allowed rice yields to jump by 53 and 132 percent, respectively, between 1965 and 1985. And as Indian wheat farmers deployed chemical fertilizers, new seed varieties, and irrigation systems to double their output, the Ganges River basin supported an ever-larger urban population. The most miraculous transformation occurred in China. Beginning in the late 1970s, the Chinese government broke up some of the old collective farms and restored the individual household as the basic economic unit in rural areas. Thereafter, agricultural output surged by roughly 9 percent per year between 1978 and 1986.

Other agricultural producers also replied to world demand, but sometimes their added production was disruptive. While biology and chemistry allowed some farmers to get more out of their land, others simply opened up new lands to cultivation. Lacking access to credit, seed, and good land, small farmers had to go where land was cheap. In Java, farmers cleared sloping woodland to make way for coffee plantings. In southern Colombia, peasants moved into semitropical woodlands to cultivate coca bushes (the source of cocaine) at profits that other cultivators could never realize.

The most notorious frontier expansion occurred in the Amazon River basin. Populations flocked to the Amazon frontier, largely from impoverished areas in northeastern Brazil. They cleared (by fire) cheap land, staked their claims, and, like nineteenth-century American homesteaders, tried to climb the social ladder by cultivating crops and raising livestock. But the promise of bounty failed: the soils were poor and easily eroded, and land titles provided little security, especially once large speculators moved into the area. So the dwellers on the frontier moved farther inland to repeat the cycle. By the 1980s, migrants to the Amazon River basin had burned away much of the jungle, contaminated the biosphere (the environment in which life exists), reduced the stock of diverse plant and animal life, and fostered social conflict in the Brazilian hinterland.

Nor were "breadbasket areas" always able to feed exploding populations. This was especially true in Africa from the 1970s onward, when domestic food production could not keep pace with population growth. (See Map 21.6.) Food shortages thereafter increased in frequency and duration, wiping out large numbers of sub-Saharan peoples. The protruding ribs on African children became a typical image of the region.

What explained Africa's famines? As the Indian Nobel Prize–winning economist Amartya Sen observed, famines—and their increasing frequency—are not natural disasters; they are human-made. (See Global Themes and Sources: Primary Source 21.4.) Food shortages in Africa stemmed largely from governments that ignored the rural sector and its politically unorganized farmers. Unable to persuade their governments to raise prices for their crops, the farmers lacked incentives to expand production. Food shortages were also by-products of global inequities. African countries, earmarking hefty chunks of their economies to agrarian exports to repay debts incurred in the 1970s, could not produce enough foodstuffs domestically and thus became food importers.

NATURAL RESOURCES AND THE ENVIRONMENT While American farmers now produced a large share of the world's food, Americans also consumed a high proportion of its

Saving the Amazon. The rise of an international environmental movement in the 1970s led to alliances with local Indigenous and environmental leaders, especially in the Amazon. *Top:* Farmers and ranchers cut and burned the Amazon at a ferocious rate in pursuit of frontier lands. In these remote regions, it was hard for local authorities to enforce conservation laws. *Bottom:* One of the most prominent advocates of the rights of Indigenous people and the need to protect imperiled jungles was the British musician Sting. Here he is pictured alongside one of the Amazon's foremost Indigenous leaders, Bep Koroti Paiakan.

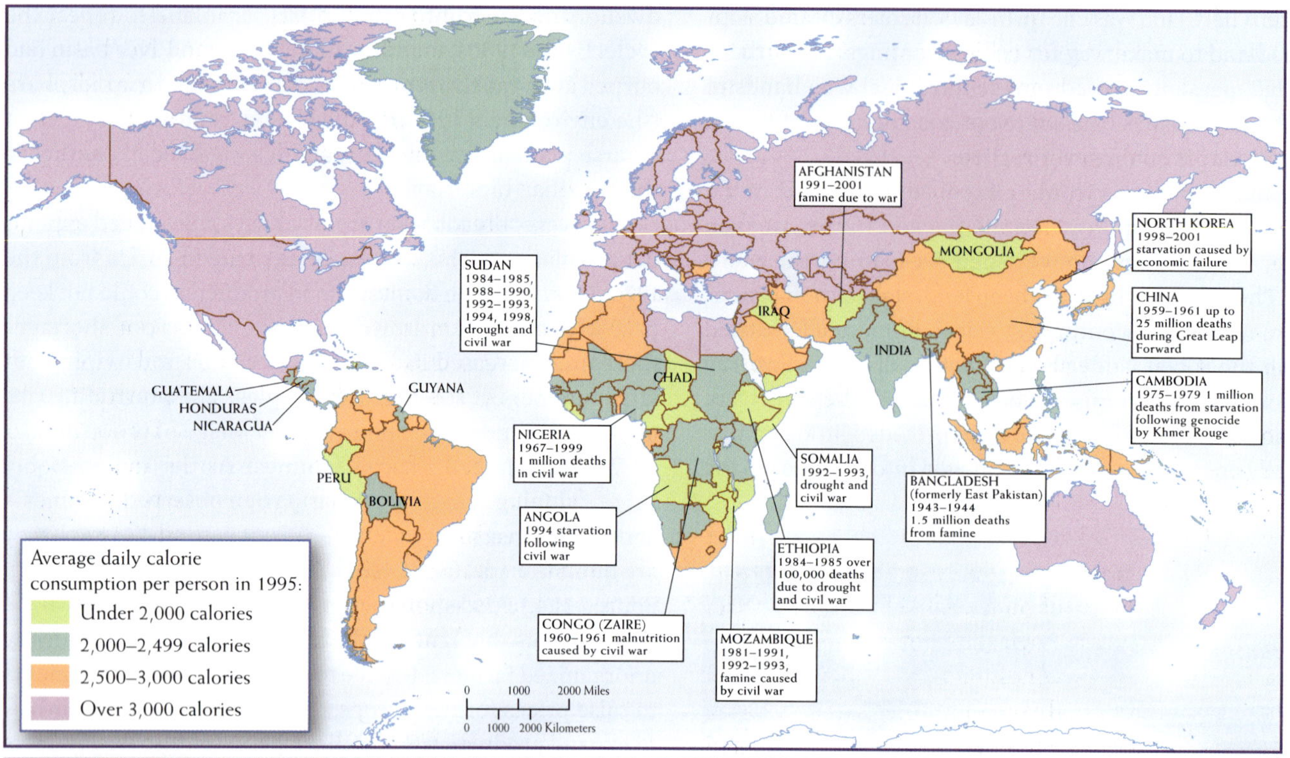

MAP 21.6 | Food Consumption and Famine since the 1940s

There is perhaps no better indicator of the division of the world into rich and poor, haves and have-nots, than average food consumption and famine.

- Which parts of the world have had the most difficulty in feeding their populations?
- What have been some of the causes of famine and malnourishment in these regions?
- How much have famine and malnourishment been due to human actions, and how much to climate and other matters over which human beings have little control?

natural resources. Energy consumption presented a similar story, although America's enormous appetite for fossil fuels generated a domestic debate about reliance on foreign sources and pollution of the environment. In the 1970s, OPEC raised the price of crude oil (see Chapter 20). The cartel weakened in the 1980s, partly because new oil fields opened elsewhere in the world and partly because internal struggles divided the exporters.

The harshest conflict over oil occurred in the mid-1980s between Iran and Iraq, followed by the 1990 Iraqi invasion of Kuwait. Iraq was poised to become dominant in the area and thus to control oil policies. The conquest of Kuwait would have given Iraq control over about 7 percent of the world's oil supplies and nearly 20 percent of the world's known reserves. Only Iraq's neighbors, Saudi Arabia and Iran, would have been larger oil exporters, and Iraq would have been in a position to menace both. As the situation threatened to unsettle the regional balance of power, the U.S. government moved to restore it. Rallying a coalition of other nations, the Americans and their allies turned to the United Nations to gain approval for a military invasion called Operation Desert Storm. The ensuing Gulf War, which ended with Iraq's expulsion from Kuwait, restored an order in which the global distribution of power favored oil consumers over producers and preserved a regional balance of power.

The consumption of water, oil, and other natural resources became matters of international concern late in the twentieth century. So did pollution control and the disposal of waste products. Part of this internationalization reflected the recognition that individual nations could not solve environmental issues on their own. Air and water, after all, do not stop flowing at political boundaries.

Americans consumed a disproportionate share of the world's natural resources. By 2000, they were using water at a per capita rate of three times the world's average. Indeed, extensive irrigation was crucial to California's agricultural sector, the most productive and profitable in the world. Gathering more water also allowed a desert metropolis like Los Angeles to grow.

In the United States and Canada, attempts to curb energy consumption saw little success, and the United States grew more dependent on oil imports. In the late 1990s, North American demand for fuel-guzzling sport utility vehicles intensified oil imports. Dependence on foreign sources locked oil importers into recurring clashes with oil exporters.

As Canadians saw their northern lakes fill up with acid rain (precipitation laced with sulfur, mainly from coal-fired plants), they urged their southern neighbor to curb emissions. Thus, reciprocal agreements between Canada and the United States took shape in the 1980s. Europeans, also beset by acidification, likewise negotiated regional environmental treaties. But some polluters simply moved overseas to poorer and less powerful nations. As the west cleaned up its environment, the rest of the world paid the price.

Other problems crossed human-made borders as well, especially the growing problem of climate change. The world was now confronted with the greenhouse effect and **global warming** (worldwide rising temperatures caused in large part by the release into the air of human-made carbons), ocean pollution, and declining biological diversity. An increase in vehicles, factories, and air-conditioned homes—the general betterment of middle-class living—meant more combustion of coal, gas, and oil. Moreover, liberalizing world trade and industrializing Asia released 4 billion metric tons of carbon into the atmosphere in 1970; the figure by 2009 was 10 billion. Fully half of the fossil fuel–induced carbon dioxide emissions worldwide since 1750 took place after 1985.

People around the planet were emitting more carbon and at the same time were increasingly aware of the catastrophic risks. On June 26, 1974, *Time* magazine announced provocatively to the world that our "prolonged streak of exceptionally good climate has probably come to an end." But it took years to turn words and science into action plans. In 1992, Rio de Janeiro hosted a massive Earth Summit of state and NGO leaders, as well as scientists from around the world, that spotlighted the global threat of climate change. The follow-up in Kyoto, Japan, did lead to a major treaty that pledged countries to curb carbon emissions. But when President George W. Bush entered the White House in early 2001, he scrapped the Kyoto Protocol—to the dismay of many scientists, activists, and partner governments.

The response to environmental crises has been uneven at best. Where environmentalists acquired political power, they forced regulators to curb carbon emissions, a problem that grew with the rise of automobile traffic in cities like Tokyo, Mexico City, and Los Angeles. But control of fossil fuels depended on power and wealth, for it was hard to impose restrictions in societies where high energy use seemed a necessity of economic life. Even the Japanese, pioneers of clean fuel as early as the 1960s, were polluters in other spheres long thereafter. With increasing controls at home, Japanese industrialists went

Kyoto Protocol. That America would no longer participate in the Kyoto Protocol was especially infuriating to the global audience, as America is the largest emitter of carbon dioxide and other major greenhouse gases. Here, Greenpeace environmental activists look on as one of their cohorts, dressed as Bush, brandishes a flaming globe in a dramatic protest outside the U.S. embassy in Mexico City.

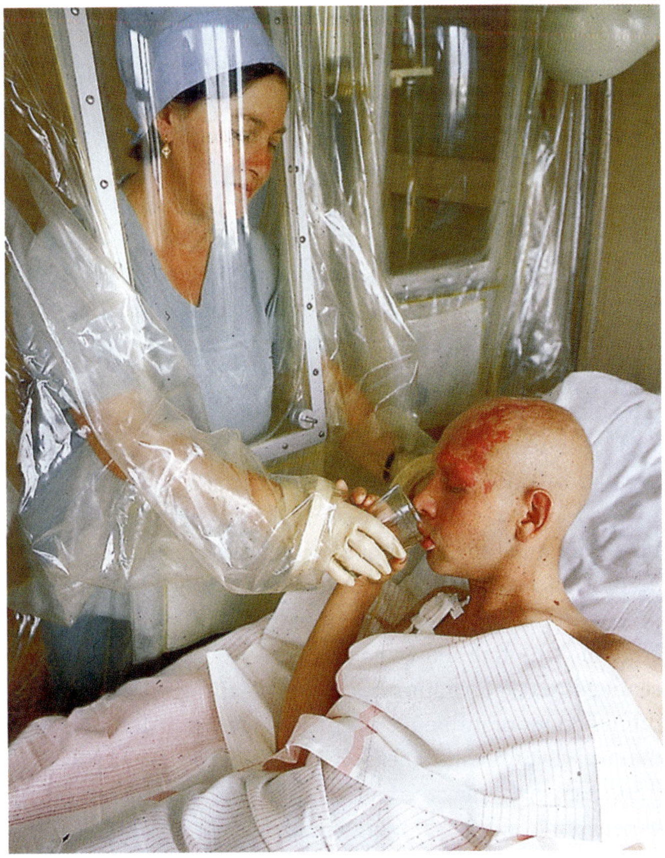

Chernobyl and Protest. Among the victims of the 1986 explosion at the Chernobyl power plant, history's worst nuclear meltdown, were firefighters, such as the man pictured here, sent in to put out the blaze. Chernobyl turned Mikhail Gorbachev's *glasnost*, or openness, into more than a slogan, and it became a rallying cry for the populace, which hoped for political change and improvements in daily life.

abroad to unload hazardous wastes. U.S. industrialists did the same, sending hazardous wastes to Mexico. Argentina and Canada sent their nuclear waste not abroad but to poor provinces desperate for jobs.

Environmental problems gained new urgency after the meltdown of a Soviet nuclear reactor in Chernobyl in 1986. Initially, communist authorities tried to cover up the disaster; but when the fallout reached Sweden, they had to accept responsibility. The delayed response was disastrous for Ukraine and Belorussia (present-day Belarus). Being relatively powerless under a centralized authoritarian regime, they had no political voice to cry out for help in addressing the contamination. As Chernobyl and global warming demonstrated, environmental concerns do not observe boundary lines. Yet at the end of the twentieth century, global guidelines for regulating the impact of human activities on the environment had eluded the world's leaders.

Citizenship in the Global World

Globalization distributed its benefits unequally. In general, people with access to better education and more opportunities profited from the border-crossing freedoms that the new order permitted. For most of the world's population, however, the new power structure was not so kind. Finding little opportunity in the globalized world, disadvantaged groups often invoked older religious and nationalist ideals. As globalization fostered human rights, environmental and labor standards, and women's rights worldwide, critics claimed that the language of international rights and standards was promoting neocolonial power in the form of a new "civilizing mission."

In particular, globalization posed massive problems for the nation-state. Since the nineteenth century, nation-states were supposed to be key in defining the rights of citizens. But now the rapid movement of ideas, goods, capital, and people across national boundaries undercut the authority of even the most powerful nations. Accordingly, other political spheres emerged to define and defend citizens. After the 1970s, people realized that international and supranational organizations often had more influence over their lives than did their own national governments. These organizations became increasingly important in shaping the meaning of citizenship. This was true especially in the developing countries, where nation-states struggled hardest to accommodate globalization.

Fourth World Struggles

Across the world, new ideas emerged from the disenchantments with older national ideas of belonging and citizenship. The idea of human rights, the proposition that nations should be held accountable by other nations for how they treated their own citizens, grew. It was not enough to leave the fate of humans to sovereign states. International solidarity movements like Amnesty International and Human Rights Watch grew. The environmental movement expanded. There were calls for the creation of a whole new world economic order, as Latin American, African, and Asian leaders called for an end to the Bretton Woods system and the creation of a more equitable order, one governed by new, more inclusive, institutions.

George Manuel. A pioneering leader in the modern-day global Indigenous movement, George Manuel was the first elected national chief of the National Indian Brotherhood in Canada (1970–1976). The organization would later change its name to the Assembly of First Nations in 1982 after undergoing a major change, with chiefs of the First Nations serving as representatives to create a more direct relationship with the Nations. After publication of *The Fourth World: An Indian Reality*, Manuel then founded and served as the first president of the World Council of Indigenous Peoples (1975–1981).

Nowhere was the drive to rethink global citizenship more profound than in the way global Indigenous movements expanded and linked from the 1970s to become influential forces today. After many centuries of colonialism and national expansion at the expense of Indigenous peoples, their leaders employed the language of rights to challenge Eurocentric conceptions of states and sovereignty and to demand their own systems of representation. In southern Chile, Mapuche leaders challenged dictators and democrats alike to acknowledge centuries of violence and exclusion. In Bolivia, Indigenous farmers and miners demanded that native languages like Aymara be recognized as an official tongue. Australian and New Zealand aborigines demanded both recognition and autonomy from White, Euro-descendant rule. In the early 1970s, Julius Kambarage Nyerere, the Tanzanian activist met with the Canadian Indigenous-rights champion George Manuel, chief of the National Indian Brotherhood. After meeting with Nyerere and other anticolonial activists around the world, Manuel went on to publish *The Fourth World: An Indian Reality* in 1974, which denounced the colonialisms of the First,

Second, and Third World nationalist projects. It was a sensation, as Métis, Dene, and First Nations across Canada mobilized at a time in which the country was embarking on deep constitutional changes. The combination of the earlier conversations with Nyerere and other anticolonnial leaders around the world and the success of the essay inspired Manuel to form the World Council of Indigenous Peoples in 1975. In 1977 at the Second General Assembly of the World Council of Indigenous Peoples in Sweden, Manuel proposed drafting an international declaration to uphold and protect the rights of Indigenous peoples worldwide. This declaration would substantially inform the United Nations Declaration on the Rights of Indigenous Peoples, which would be adopted in 2007. (See Chapter 22 for further discussion.) Manuel would go on to participate in the Canadian constitutional talks in 1980–81. Ultimately, when it appeared that First Nation Indigenous rights would not receive serious attention in the updated constitution, Manuel led the Constitution Express, a group made up hundreds of Indigenous activists who succeeded in getting new language incorporated into the updated Canadian constitution that recognized the ancestral and treaty rights of Indigenous Peoples in Canada, particularly concerning land claims. The Canadian experience echoed around the world and set off efforts to create global Indigenous alliances focused on hot spots like the Amazon, the upper woodlands of Burma, and Australia—areas where the growing claims for Indigenous rights clashed with global extractive frontiers for minerals, timber, and seafood. The concept of Fourth Worldism soon became synonymous with struggles of the colonized, excluded, and displaced who refused to identify with the dominant nation-building ideas of the others' worlds.

By the 1980s, globalization, new rights for the excluded, and fourth-world movements were leading to a full-scale push for reckoning with the past through truth commissions, as well as the organization of states that made them less centralized and nationalized, in order to be more accountable. One example of this was the surge of activism in southern Mexico in the early 1990s. Under the umbrella of a new "Zapatista" movement, which harkened back to the peasant and indigenist traditions of the Mexican Revolution, Mayan-descended farmers challenged Mexican centralism and nationalism while also lashing out against the exclusivism of the new world economic order. (See Primary Source 21.2.)

In the United States, Indigenous peoples grew steadily more frustrated after the social programs of the 1960s failed to alleviate their deeply impoverished economic conditions. The American Indian Movement (AIM) was formed in 1968 to promote "Red Power," which led to the famous occupations of Alcatraz Island in California and Wounded Knee in South Dakota by Indigenous activists. The result of these "sit-in" protests were renewed discussions about Indigenous Americans' grievances with the U.S. government. Ultimately, Indigenous peoples would move to a more successful strategy—taking individual states and the U.S. government to court using existing treaties upon which they could base their claims for the re-establishment of tribal lands, financial restitution, and stronger sovereignty (self-rule).

Supranational Organizations

If nation-states started to devolve more authority to autonomous local groupings, globalization also propelled more cross-border activism and organization. New organizations with international responsibilities took shape after World War II for the purpose of facilitating global activities. These **supranational organizations** (organizations that transcend national boundaries) often successfully managed crisis situations, but they also impinged on the autonomy of all but the most powerful states.

Among the most prominent supranational organizations were the World Bank and the International Monetary Fund, which provided vital economic assistance to poorer nations. The World Bank, originally named the International Bank for Reconstruction and Development, was designed primarily to provide vital economic assistance for big development projects. In contrast, the International Monetary Fund provided funds and technical assistance to countries whose economies were in trouble. A good example of the World Bank's agenda was the financial support that it gave to the government of Ghana for the Volta River Project, which was intended to create an electrical grid for that country. Indeed, these international organizations financed and offered technical information for some of the largest development programs in the developing countries. The World Bank also made available funds for a system of national parks in the Philippines to help indigenous people manage rain forests, coral reefs, and other threatened ecological zones. Nonetheless, the World Bank and the IMF required that recipient governments implement far-reaching economic reforms, such as devaluation of the currency and the privatization of public-sector companies. Many of these policies were deeply unpopular, leading to riots and charges that these international groups were agents of a new kind of imperialism.

Another set of supranational bodies, international nongovernmental organizations (NGOs), also stepped forward late in the twentieth century. Many championed human rights or highlighted environmental problems. Others, like the International Committee of the Red Cross, once dedicated to war relief, became more active in peacetime, sheltering the homeless or providing food for famine victims. What united NGOs was not so much their goals but the way they pursued them: autonomously from state power. NGOs created a layer of international forces that rivaled the political power of nation-states.

International NGOs reached a new level of influence in the 1970s because most nation-states at that time were still

Bosnia in the Midst of War. Despite extensive destruction and perpetual sniper fire, the multiethnic population of Sarajevo refused to abandon their city. With the help of U.N. soldiers and aid workers, they kept alive the hope for the peaceful coexistence of Muslims, Serbs, and Croats in Bosnia.

not democracies. Of the 121 countries in 1980, only 37 were democracies, accounting for only 35 percent of the world population. People found it difficult to rely on authoritarians to uphold their rights as citizens. Indeed, despite adopting a Universal Declaration of Human Rights in 1948, the United Nations (another international organization created after World War II and intended to provide a forum for settling international disputes) itself was a latecomer to enforcing human rights provisions, largely because many of its own members were the self-same authoritarians.

NGOs, then, took the lead in trying to make the language of human rights stick. The brutality of military regimes in Latin America inspired the emerging network of international human rights organizations to take action. After the overthrow of Chile's Salvador Allende in 1973, solidarity groups proliferated to protest the military junta's harsh repression. When the Argentine military began killing tens of thousands of innocent civilians in 1976 and news of their torture techniques leaked out, human rights movements again took action. Prominent among them was Amnesty International. Formed in 1961 to defend prisoners of conscience (detained for their beliefs, color, sex, ethnic origin, language, or religion), Amnesty International catalogued human rights violations worldwide. By 2000, an extensive network of associations was informing the public, lobbying governments, and pressuring U.N. member nations to live up to commitments to respect the rights of citizens.

Violence

International organizations and NGOs could play only a limited role in preserving peace and strengthening human rights. The end of the Cold War left entire regions in such turmoil that even the most effective humanitarian agencies could not prevent mass killings.

Consider the Balkans in the 1990s. In the territorial remains of Yugoslavia, groups of Serbs, Croats, Bosnians, ethnic Albanians, and others fought for control. Former neighbors, fueled by opportunistic leaders' rhetoric, no longer saw themselves as citizens of pluralistic political communities. Instead, demagogues trumpeted the superiority of ethnic Serbs. When international agencies moved in to try to bolster public authority, they failed as Yugoslavia's ethnic mosaic imploded into civil war and ethnic cleansing. The Dayton Accords of 1995 ended the bloodshed by partitioning Bosnia and assigning several international organizations to maintain peace. But in 1999, Serbian president Slobodan Milošević sent troops to suppress unrest in the province of Kosovo; only NATO air strikes on Serbia's capital, Belgrade, convinced Milošević to back down. Subsequently, Milošević was indicted by the International Criminal Tribunal on sixty-six counts of war crimes and crimes against humanity, but he died of a heart attack before he could be found guilty.

Some of the most gruesome scenes of political violence occurred in Africa, where nation-states struggled to uphold the rule of law for all citizens. Here, tension often erupted in conflict between ethnic groups. The failure of African agriculture to sustain growing populations, as well as unequal access to resources like education, made ethnic rivalries worse. Droughts, famine, and corruption ignited the rivalries into riots and killings—even into bitter civil war and the breakdown of centralized authority.

Events in Rwanda reflected Africa's horrifying experience with political violence. Friction grew between the majority Hutus (agrarian people, who were often very poor) and the minority Tutsis (herders, who were better educated, were wealthier, and had been chosen by the Belgians during the colonial period to rule over the Hutus) after the two peoples had intermarried and lived side by side for many generations. Some resentful Hutus blamed the Tutsis for all their woes. As tensions mounted, the United Nations dispatched peacekeeping

Rwandan Refugees. Perhaps as many as 800,000 Tutsis and moderate Hutus were killed in 1994 as the Hutus turned against the local Tutsi population while Rwanda was being invaded by a Tutsi-led army from Uganda. Not surprisingly, the massacre led to an enormous refugee crisis.

troops. Moderate Hutus urged peaceful coexistence, only to be shouted down by government forces in command of radio stations and a mass propaganda machine. Although alerted to the impending problem, U.N. forces, fearing a clash and uncertain of their mandate, failed to prevent the violence.

The failure on the part of the international community, including the United States, which did not have troops on the ground and which had no clear policy toward Rwanda, gave the Hutu government an implicit green light to wipe out opponents. In 100 days of carnage in 1994, Hutu militias massacred 800,000 Tutsis and moderate Hutus. This was not, as many proclaimed, the militarization of ancient ethnic rivalries, for many Hutus were butchered as they tried to defend Tutsi friends, relatives, and neighbors. Meanwhile, the ensuing refugee crisis destabilized neighboring countries. The civil war in Rwanda sent riptides across eastern and central Africa, creating a whole new generation of conflicts.

Some societies, however, tried to put political violence behind them. In Argentina, El Salvador, Guatemala, and South Africa, the transition to democracy compelled elected rulers to establish inquiries into past rulers' human rights abuses. These **truth commissions** were vital for creating a new aura of legitimacy for democracies and for promising to uphold the rights of individuals. In South Africa, many Black constituents backed the new president, Nelson Mandela, but also demanded a reckoning with the punitive experience of the apartheid past. To avoid a backlash against the former White rulers, the South African leadership opted to record the past events rather than avenge them. Truth, the new leaders argued, would be powerful enough to heal old wounds. The Truth and Reconciliation Commission, chaired by Nobel Peace Prize winner and longtime opponent of apartheid Bishop Desmond Tutu, called on all who had been involved in political crimes, Whites as well as Blacks, to come before its tribunal and speak the truth. Although the truth alone did not fully settle old scores, a more open discussion of basic liberties fostered new bonds between public authorities and citizens.

The genocide in Rwanda represented the most egregious failure of the international community to deal with a severe humanitarian crisis. To some extent, the failure to respond was the result of the rapidity and ferocity with which the enmity toward the Tutsis exploded, catching off guard countries with the resources to deal with this level of violence. In other less politically charged crises, like famines, especially in Africa, international organizations like the Red Cross and Catholic Charities mobilized support and provided much relief.

Religious Foundations of Politics

Secular concerns for human rights and international peace were not the only foundations for politics after the Cold War. In many regions, people wanted religion to define the moral fabric of political communities. Very often, religion provided a way to reimagine the nation-state just as globalization was undermining national autonomy.

HINDU NATIONALISM In India, Hindu nationalism offered a communal identity for a country being rapidly transformed by globalization. In the 1980s, India freed market forces, privatized state firms, and withdrew from its role as welfare provider. Economic reforms under the ruling Congress Party sparked economic growth, thereby creating Asia's largest, best-educated, and most affluent middle class. But because these changes also widened the gap between rich and poor, lower classes and castes formed political parties to challenge the traditional elites. With established hierarchies and loyalties eroding, Hindu nationalists argued that religion could now fill the role once occupied by a secular state. Claiming that the ideology of Hindutva ("Hinduness") would bring the help that secular nationalism had failed to provide, Hindu militants trumpeted the idea of India as a nation of Hindus (the majority), with minorities relegated to a lesser status.

The chief beneficiary of the politics established by economic liberalization was a Hindu nationalist party, the Bhartiya Janata Party (BJP), or Indian People's Party. It was the political arm of an alliance of Hindu organizations devoted to establishing India as a Hindu state. By the late 1980s, the BJP and other like-minded parties were advancing an anti-minority (chiefly anti-Muslim) ideology. Claiming that the state had systematically appeased the minorities and trampled on the rights of the majority, they urged Hindus to overthrow "pseudo-secularism." This communal ideology was a winning formula, and in 1998 a BJP coalition came to power. Hindu nationalists sought to transform the secular nation-state into a moral community, but without challenging the economic forces of globalization.

Ayatollah Khomeini. After fifteen years of exile in France due to his outspoken opposition to the shah, Ayatollah Ruhollah Khomeini returned to Tehran in 1979 to the ardent welcome of his supporters.

ISLAMIC CONSERVATISM In some cases, religion provided a way to resist seemingly American-dominated globalization. One of the most spirited challenges arose in the Islamic Middle East. Here, many people believed that modernizing and westernizing programs were leading their societies toward rampant materialism and unchecked individualism. Critics included traditional clerics and young western-educated elites whose job prospects seemed bleak and who felt that the promise of modernization had failed. Having criticized modernizing processes since the nineteenth century, Islamic conservatives flourished once more in the 1970s, as global markets and social dislocations undermined the moral foundations of secular leadership.

The most revolutionary Islamic movement arose in Iran, where clerics forced the shah from power in 1979. The revolt pitted a cadre of religious officials possessing only pamphlets, tracts, and tapes against the military arsenal and the vast intelligence apparatus of the Iranian state. Shah Mohammad Reza Pahlavi had enjoyed U.S. technical and military support since the Americans had helped place him on the throne in 1953. His bloated army and police force, as well as his brutally effective intelligence service, had crushed all challenges to his authority. The shah had also benefited from oil revenues, which soared after 1973. Yet the uneven distribution of income, the oppressive police state, and the royal family's ostentatious lifestyle fueled widespread discontent. As discontent rose, so did repression. And as repression intensified, so did the feeling that the government had abandoned the people.

The most vociferous critique came from the mullahs (Muslim scholars or religious teachers), who found in the Ayatollah Ruhollah Khomeini a courageous leader. Khomeini used his traditional Islamic education and his training in Muslim ethics to accuse the shah's government of gross violations of Islamic norms. He also identified the shah's ally, America, as the great Satan. With opposition mounting, the shah fled the country in 1979. In his wake, Khomeini established a theocratic state ruled by a council of Islamic clerics. Although some Iranians grumbled about aspects of this return to Islam (women's reduced status, leaders' arbitrariness, ruptured relations with the west, and the failure to institute democratic procedures), they prided themselves on having inspired a revolution based on principles other than those drawn from the west.

RELIGIOUS CONSERVATISM IN THE UNITED STATES The search for moral foundations of politics in the global age reached beyond nonwestern societies. Indeed, in the United States, religion became a potent force after the 1970s as the membership and activism of conservative, fundamentalist Protestant churches eclipsed those of mainline

American Hostage Crisis in Iran. The United States was stunned in 1979 by Iran's Islamic Revolution, which overthrew the shah and brought the exiled cleric Ayatollah Khomeini to power. After radical students captured the U.S. embassy, as well as fifty-three hostages, an American rescue raid failed, leading to celebration by Iranians, as shown here.

denominations. Insisting on literal interpretation of the Bible, Protestant fundamentalists railed against secularizing trends in American society. This traditionalist crusade took up a broad range of cultural and political issues. Religious conservatives (predominantly evangelical Protestants, but including some Catholics and Orthodox Jews) attacked many of the social changes that had emerged from liberation movements of the 1960s. Shifting sexual and familial relations were sore points, but the religious conservatives especially targeted public leaders who, they felt, had abandoned the moral purpose of authority by legalizing abortion and supporting secular values.

Acceptance of and Resistance to Democracy

New sources of power and new social movements drastically changed politics in the global age. Increasingly, international organizations were decisive in defining the conditions of democratic citizenship. Perhaps most remarkable was how much democracy spread toward the end of the twentieth century. In South Africa, Russia, and Guatemala, elections now decided politicians' fate. In this sense, the world's societies embraced the idea that people have a right to choose their own representatives. Nevertheless, democracy did not triumph everywhere.

An important holdout was China. Mao Zedong died in 1976, and within a few years his successor, Deng Xiaoping, opened the nation's economy to market forces. But Deng and other Chinese Communist Party leaders resisted multiparty competition. Instead of capitalism and western-style democracy, they maintained that China should follow its own path to modernity. By the late 1980s, economic reforms had produced spectacular increases in production and rising standards of living for most of China's people. But the widening gap between rich and poor, together with increasing public awareness of corruption within the party and the government, triggered popular discontent. Worker strikes and slowdowns, peasant unrest, and student activism spread. On April 22, 1989, some 100,000 people gathered in **Tiananmen Square** at the heart of Beijing in silent defiance of a government ban on assembling. The following month brought a greater show of defiance when television cameras and world journalists converged on China to cover the historic visit of Soviet leader Mikhail Gorbachev. Several hundred students, flanked by thousands of supporters, began a hunger strike at the square to demand democratic reform. Tiananmen Square was now their stage and the world their audience. Within days, the strike spread to other cities. In Beijing, where well over a million people filled the city center, a carnivalesque atmosphere prevailed as the students sang and danced to rock songs and folk ballads.

The regime responded by declaring martial law. Two huge protest demonstrations followed, and residents erected barricades to defend the city against government troops. As the protest's momentum waned, a 28-foot icon, partly inspired by the Statue of Liberty, was unveiled at the square, capturing the imagination of the crowd and the attention of the cameras. But by then the government had assembled troops to crush the

Tiananmen Square. This white plaster and Styrofoam statue, inspired in part by the Statue of Liberty and dubbed the Goddess of Democracy, was created by students in Beijing in the spring of 1989. It was brought to Tiananmen Square and unveiled at the end of May in an attempt to reinvigorate the democracy movement and the spirits of the protesters. For five days it captured worldwide attention, until it was toppled by a tank on June 4 and crushed as the Chinese People's Liberation Army cleared the square of its democracy advocates.

movement. In a night of terror that began at dusk on June 3, the People's Liberation Army turned their guns against the people. Most students in the square negotiated a safe passage; those who lost their lives—estimates vary from 2,000 to 7,000—were the nameless people who wielded Molotov cocktails, sticks, or bricks in a futile attempt to repel the troops.

The Chinese government weathered the storm. It continued to suppress unofficial social organizations; to control access to information, including that obtained over the Internet; and to crack down on dissidents. But it could not completely control the forces of globalization. Some organizations, like the quasi-religious group Falun Gong, eluded authorities and even used the Internet to enlist international support. At the dawn of the twenty-first century, signs of change were apparent. A visible urban entrepreneurial class had emerged, whose top echelon conducted its global businesses over nearly ubiquitous cellular phones. Rural dwellers paid what little they had to be smuggled abroad, at great risk and often with lethal consequences, so that they could make a better living in America or Europe. Within China, tens of millions of people lived a transient existence, with tens of thousands daily leaving the countryside for the cities. There they often suffered economic and social exploitation, as well as abuse from police and other government officials. Existing at the margins of the new prosperity, they, too, served as reminders of the uneven effects of globalization.

In Mexico, democracy finally triumphed as the single party that had dominated the country for seventy-one years fell after the election of Vicente Fox in 2000. Until that time, Mexican rulers had combined patronage and rigged elections to stay in office. By the 1980s, corruption and abuse permeated the system. The abuse of democratic rights fell hardest on poor communities, especially those with large numbers of indigenous people.

Consider the state of Chiapas. An impoverished area with many Maya descendants, Chiapas had trouble coping with social and economic change in the 1980s. The president stripped Indigenous peoples of their right to communal land and let the ruling party run Chiapas like a fiefdom. By the early 1990s, the province was demanding material betterment, cultural recognition of Indigenous rights, and local democracy. When one group of rebels, the Zapatistas, rose up in Mexico City against the government in 1994, the government prepared to crush the insurgents. (See Global Themes and Sources: Primary Source 21.2.) But no one anticipated how supranational forces would play a role in helping local democracy: Cable News Network (CNN) broadcast the clash worldwide, and the rebel leader created a website that drew thousands of hits. Thereafter, international news media flooded Chiapas, filming Indigenous people waving flags and pronouncing victory. Leaders in Mexico City, deeply embarrassed, asked local church authorities to negotiate peace and spearhead a commission to hear the villagers' concerns. In 2000, national elections toppled the ruling party (including its representatives in Chiapas), and Mexico dismantled its one-party ruling system.

Mexico, South Africa, and China were powerful examples of how men and women in every corner of the earth yearned to choose their own leaders. In 1994, millions of previously disenfranchised South Africans lined up for hours to cast a vote for their new Black African president, Nelson Mandela. In 2000, the Mexican electorate turned out the ruling party, while in China the ruling Communist Party had to call in the army to prevent regime change and democratic reforms.

With the fall of the Soviet Union, new social grievances fueled new political actors, leading to a global wave of demands on governments for freedom, for human and democratic rights, and for welfare support to shelter the have-nots from the very forces unleashed by economic globalization. There

Protests in Mexico. *Top:* Among the great Mexican muralists of the twentieth century, David Alfaro Siqueiros was the strongest advocate for class struggle. In this 1957 mural image, *The People in Arms,* Siqueiros portrays Mexican peasants as they pick up arms in 1910 to fight for a new order. Paintings such as these provided inspiration for movements such as the Zapatista rebellion, depicted below. *Bottom:* After generations of oppression and exclusion, the peasants of Chiapas, in southern Mexico, called for democracy and respect for their right to land. When Mexican authorities refused to bend, peasants took up arms. While they knew that they posed no military threat to the Mexican army, the Zapatista rebels used the world media and international organizations to embarrass the national political establishment into allowing reforms.

were significant breakthroughs—in South Africa and a number of other African states, in many Latin American societies, and in eastern Europe, which was released from the pall of the east-west divide. Even so, dictatorial regimes like those in China, parts of Africa, and parts of the Middle East held out against protest movements and maintained their autocracies.

Conclusion

In the thirteenth century (as long before), a few travelers like Ibn Battuta and Marco Polo ventured over long distances to trade, to explore, and to convert souls; yet communications technology was rudimentary, making long-distance mobility and exchange expensive, rare, and perilous. The world was more a series of communities set apart than a world bound together by culture, capital, and communications networks.

By the late twentieth century, that balance had changed. Food, entertainment, clothing, and even family life were becoming more similar worldwide. To be sure, some local differences remained. In 2000, local cultures lived on and in some cases were revived through challenges to the authority of nation-states. No longer did the nation-state or any single level of community life define collective identities. At the same time, worldwide purveyors of cultural and commercial resources offered local communities the same kinds of products, from aspirin to Nike shoes. Exchanges across local and national boundaries became easier. For the first time, many of the world's peoples felt they belonged to a global culture.

New technologies, new methods of production and investment, and the greater importance of personal health and education for human betterment created new possibilities—and greater inequalities. Indeed, the disparities between haves and have-nots in 2000 were astonishing. For as humanity harnessed new technologies to accelerate exchanges across and within cultures, an ever-larger gulf separated those who participated in global networks from those who languished on the margins. This inequality produced a range of divergent political and cultural forms after the collapse of the three-world order. Thus, as the world became more integrated, it also grew apart along ever-deeper lines.

After You Read This Chapter

TRACING THE GLOBAL STORYLINES

FOCUS ON: The Emergence of Modern Globalization

Removing Obstacles to Globalization

- Communism's fall and the end of the Cold War improve prospects for global exchange of peoples, ideas, and resources.
- Final decolonization in Angola, Mozambique, and Guinea-Bissau and the end of apartheid in South Africa return self-rule throughout Africa.

Unleashing Globalization

- Financial deregulation and the end of gold and silver standards allow money to move freely across borders but lead to a Third World debt crisis.
- Widespread migrations occur as people in Africa, Asia, and Latin America move to Europe and America, following the tracks of their former colonizers.
- Revolutions in culture and communications make cultural diversity more possible for those who can afford it.

The New Global Order

- Globalization leads to dramatic population expansion, requiring greater agricultural and industrial output.
- Family structure changes, life spans increase, and more goods are available, yet inequalities deepen as education and good health determine social status as never before.
- As globalization erodes the power of the nation-state, greater violence occurs between and within states. Nongovernmental organizations (NGOs) and religion become resources for dealing with violence and inequality and for reimagining the nation-state.

CHRONOLOGY

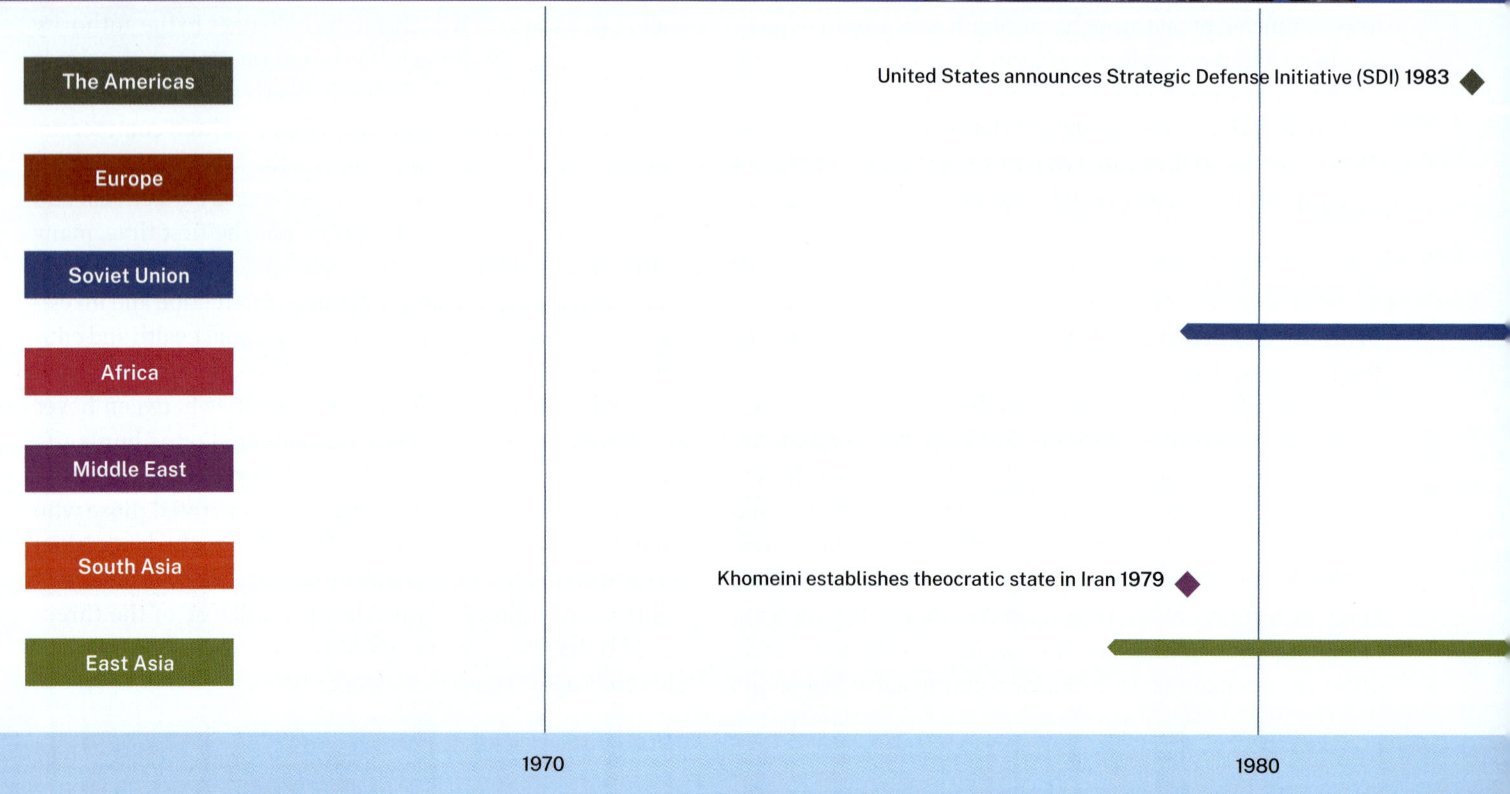

KEY TERMS

developing world p. 924
European Union (EU) p. 932
global climate change p. 943
globalization p. 924
global warming p. 951
HIV/AIDS p. 945
Nelson Mandela p. 930
North Atlantic Treaty Organization (NATO) p. 928
supranational organizations p. 953
Tiananmen Square p. 957
truth commissions p. 955

THINKING ABOUT GLOBAL CONNECTIONS

Thinking about Worlds Together, Worlds Apart and Globalization How did globalization shape patterns of inequality? After the Cold War, trade, migration, and communications reshaped the terms on which peoples interacted with one another around the world. Industry, agriculture, culture, and the arts all linked peoples and regions together in different ways. Consider differences in all these domains. What kinds of inequalities were most significant?

Thinking about Changing Power Relationships and Globalization What kind of resistance movements did globalization generate, both within the world's wealthiest societies and elsewhere? How did the feminist, labor, and environmental reform movements resemble and differ from their predecessors? How did Hindu nationalism and religious conservatism differ from each other and from earlier nationalist and religious or pan movements?

Thinking about Environmental Impacts and Globalization Explain the relationship between globalization, climate change, and the environment. The consumption of water, oil, and other natural resources became major national and international issues in this period. How did the organization of agricultural and industrial production change, and what influence did those changes have on global warming, acid rain, and pollution? Identify efforts to limit damage to the environment and evaluate their success.

Go to INQUIZITIVE to see what you've learned—and learn what you've missed—with personalized feedback along the way.

- North American Free Trade Agreement approved 1992
- Zapatista rebellion in Mexico 1994
- Eastern European communist regimes collapse 1989
- Yugoslavia dissolves, ethnic cleansing ensues 1989–1995
- European Union formed 1993
- Soviet-Afghan War 1979–1989
- Gorbachev assumes power 1985
- Chernobyl nuclear accident 1986
- Dissolution of the Soviet Union 1991
- Mandela released from prison 1990
- Free elections in South Africa 1994
- Genocide in Rwanda 1994
- BJP heads up government in India 1998
- Deng Xiaoping reforms China 1978–1992
- Chinese state cracks down on Tiananmen Square protests 1989

1990 2000

Global Themes and Sources

Comparing the Power of Grassroots Democracies

Despite the enormous economic and technological advances of the past 200 years, famine and dire poverty remain problems in many places. These problems have been particularly severe where unrepresentative, authoritarian leaders prevent foreign aid from reaching the needy and ordinary people from achieving self-sufficiency. Self-sufficiency has been further undermined by pervasive discrimination against women, which has limited their access to education and has therefore compromised economic growth for everyone, men and women alike.

Written by a dissident dramatist (and future politician) in 1978, the first document, excerpted from a long essay in political philosophy, explores the possibility for individuals to maintain their independence and dignity, and ultimately to undermine the communist dictatorships of eastern Europe. In the second document, from the General Council of the Zapatista Army of National Liberation (EZLN), a group of mostly Indigenous peoples living in a jungle region in Chiapas, Mexico, seeks international support for its conflict with Mexican authorities. In the third, researchers for the World Bank report that better education, and especially better education for girls, improves economic development among the poor. The final selection, from economist and Nobel laureate Amartya Sen (1933–), argues that no major famine has occurred in a democratic country with a free press.

The selections presented here all call attention to the importance of grassroots democracy and equality in responding to political, economic, and ecological disasters and achieving at least a measure of autonomy. They raise big questions about the nature and location of power and the possibility of change. While there is an important comparative dimension to these selections—each understands the promise of grassroots democracy differently—they are all the product of a common context, a common reaction against monolithic, authoritarian forms of rule. Collectively, they call for both comparison and contextualization.

ANALYZING THE POWER OF GRASSROOTS DEMOCRACIES COMPARATIVELY AND CONTEXTUALLY

On what basis do the authors of these documents claim authority? In whose name do they speak? What goals do they seek to attain?

What does justice mean from the perspectives of these four documents? Do the authors agree or disagree on what is just?

What is the relationship between individual and collective rights in these documents? To what degree does each text consider individual liberties essential or harmful to the common good? Pay special attention to differences between the first document and the next three.

PRIMARY SOURCE 21.1

"The Power of the Powerless" (1978), Václav Havel

Václav Havel (1936–2011) was a Czech dramatist; a founder of Charter 77, a civic initiative under communism (1976–1982) that defended human rights; and the president of Czechoslovakia (1989–1992) and then the Czech Republic (1993–2003). His essay *The Power of the Powerless*, originally written in 1978, provided a model of what he called "living within the truth," a form of resistance against communism.

What does Havel mean by "living within the truth"?

Explain the significance of law in this document.

Compare this selection with the excerpt from Karl Marx and Friedrich Engels's *Communist Manifesto* in Primary Source 16.5. Is Havel's view of politics compatible with the manifesto?

A spectre is haunting eastern Europe: the spectre of what in the West is called "dissent." This spectre has not appeared out of thin air. It is a natural and inevitable consequence of the present historical phase of the system it is haunting. It was born at a time when this system, for a thousand reasons, can no longer base itself on the unadulterated, brutal, and arbitrary application of power, eliminating all expressions of nonconformity. What is more, the system has become so ossified politically that there is practically no way for such nonconformity to be implemented within its official structures.

***

And so the post-totalitarian system behaved in a characteristic way: it defended the integrity of the world of appearances in order to defend itself. For the crust presented by the life of lies is made of strange stuff. As long as it seals off hermetically the entire society, it appears to be made of stone. But the moment someone breaks through in one place, when one person cries out, "The emperor is naked!"—when a single person breaks the rules of the game, thus exposing it as a game—everything suddenly appears in another light and the whole crust seems then to be made of a tissue on the point of tearing and disintegrating uncontrollably.

When I speak of living within the truth, I naturally do not have in mind only products of conceptual thought, such as a protest or a letter written by a group of intellectuals. It can be any means by which a person or a group revolts against manipulation: anything from a letter by intellectuals to a workers' strike, from a rock concert to a student demonstration, from refusing to vote in the farcical elections, to making an open speech at some official congress, or even a hunger strike, for instance. If the suppression of the aims of life is a complex process, and if it is based on the multifaceted manipulation of all expressions of life, then, by the same token, every free expression of life indirectly threatens the post-totalitarian system politically, including forms of expression to which, in other social systems, no one would attribute any potential political significance, not to mention explosive power.

***

Like ideology, the legal code is an essential instrument of ritual communication outside the power structure. It is the legal code that gives the exercise of power a form, a framework, a set of rules. It is the legal code that enables all components of the system to communicate, to put themselves in a good light, to establish their own legitimacy. It provides their whole game with its "rules" and engineers with their technology. Can the exercise of post-totalitarian power be imagined at all without this universal ritual making it all possible, serving as a common language to bind the relevant sectors of the power structure together? The more important the position occupied by the repressive apparatus in the power structure, the more important that it functions according to some kind of formal code. . . .

If the exercise of power circulates through the whole power structure as blood flows through veins, then the legal code can be understood as something that reinforces the walls of those veins. Without it, the blood of power could not circulate in an organized way and the body of society would haemorrhage at random. Order would collapse.

A persistent and never-ending appeal to the laws—not just to the laws concerning human rights, but to all laws—does not mean at all that those who do so have succumbed to the illusion that in our system the law is anything other than what it is. They are well aware of the role it plays. But precisely because they know how desperately the system depends on it—on the "noble" version of the law, that is—they also know how enormously significant such appeals are. Because the system cannot do without the law, because it is hopelessly tied down by the necessity of pretending the laws are observed, it is compelled to react in some way to such appeals. Demanding that the laws be upheld is thus an act of living within the truth that threatens the whole mendacious structure at its point of maximum mendacity.

Over and over again, such appeals make the purely ritualistic nature of the law clear to society and to those who inhabit its power structures. They draw attention to its real material substance and thus, indirectly, compel all those who take refuge behind the law to affirm and make credible this agency of excuses, this means of communication, this reinforcement of the social arteries outside of which their will could not be made to circulate through society. They are compelled to do so for the sake of their own consciences, for the impression they make on outsiders, to maintain themselves in power (as part of the system's own mechanism of self-preservation and its principles of cohesion), or simply out of fear that they will be reproached for being "clumsy" in handling the ritual. They have no other choice: because they cannot discard the rules of their own game, they can only attend more carefully to those rules.

***

Hope for those who would liberate themselves, therefore, lies in a symbiosis of the moral and the social, of humanity and democracy, in the realization of a social order in which the formalized and functionalized structure of society will be regulated and controlled by this "newly discovered" spontaneous civic activity, which will be a permanent and essential source of social self-awareness, while the bureaucracies ruling society shrink to assume merely compliant executive roles.

Source: Václav Havel, "The Power of the Powerless," in *The Power of the Powerless: Citizens against the State in Central-Eastern Europe*, ed. John Keane (Armonk, NY: M. E. Sharpe, 1985), pp. 23, 42–43, 74–77, 108–9.

PRIMARY SOURCE 21.2

Declaration of War against the Mexican Government (1993), EZLN

The Zapatista Army of National Liberation (EZLN) is a revolutionary political organization based in Chiapas, the southernmost state in Mexico. On January 1, 1994, it took up arms against the government, calling for a restoration of the principles of the Mexican Revolution and protesting the confiscation of poor people's land rights. This document, released in 1993, issues a call to arms.

The document opens, "We are a product of 500 years of struggle." Who is "we"? Who does the document include as insiders, and whom—whether individuals or broad social forces—does it exclude?

On what basis do the authors speak for the nation?

What is the relationship between this declaration and the rule of law? Do the authors claim to uphold the law, or do they reject it and seek to overthrow it?

To the People of Mexico: Mexican Brothers and Sisters:

We are a product of 500 years of struggle: first against slavery, then during the War of Independence against Spain led by insurgents, then to avoid being absorbed by North American imperialism, then to promulgate our constitution and expel the French empire from our soil, and later the dictatorship of Porfirio Diaz denied us the just application of the Reform laws and the people rebelled and leaders like Villa and Zapata emerged, poor men just like us. We have been denied the most elemental preparation so they can use us as cannon fodder and pillage the wealth of our country. They don't care that we have nothing, absolutely nothing, not even a roof over our heads, no land, no work, no health care, no food nor education. Nor are we able to freely and democratically elect our political representatives, nor is there independence from foreigners, nor is there peace nor justice for ourselves and our children.

But today, we say ENOUGH IS ENOUGH.

We are the inheritors of the true builders of our nation. The dispossessed, we are millions and we thereby call upon our brothers and sisters to join this struggle as the only path, so that we will not die of hunger due to the insatiable ambition of a 70 year dictatorship led by a clique of traitors that represent the most conservative and sell-out groups. They are the same ones that opposed Hidalgo and Morelos, the same ones that betrayed Vicente Guerrero, the same ones that sold half our country to the foreign invader, the same ones that imported a European prince to rule our country, the same ones that formed the "scientific" Porfirista dictatorship, the same ones that opposed the Petroleum Expropriation, the same ones that massacred the railroad workers in 1958 and the students in 1968, the same ones [that] today take everything from us, absolutely everything.

To prevent the continuation of the above and as our last hope, after having tried to utilize all legal means based on our Constitution, we go to our Constitution, to apply Article 39 which says:

> "National Sovereignty essentially and originally resides in the people. All political power emanates from the people and its purpose is to help the people. The people have, at all times, the inalienable right to alter or modify their form of government."

Therefore, according to our constitution, we declare the following to the Mexican federal army, the pillar of the Mexican dictatorship that we suffer from, monopolized by a one-party system and led by Carlos Salinas de Gortari, the maximum and illegitimate federal executive that today holds power.

According to this Declaration of War, we ask that other powers of the nation advocate to restore the legitimacy and the stability of the nation by overthrowing the dictator.

We also ask that international organizations and the International Red Cross watch over and regulate our battles, so that our efforts are carried out while still protecting our civilian population. We declare now and always that we are subject to the Geneva Accord, forming the EZLN as our fighting arm of our liberation struggle. We have the Mexican people on our side, we have the beloved tri-colored flag highly respected by our insurgent fighters. We use black and red in our uniform as our symbol of our working people on strike. Our flag carries the following letters, "EZLN," Zapatista National Liberation Army, and we always carry our flag into combat.

Beforehand, we refuse any effort to disgrace our just cause by accusing us of being drug traffickers, drug guerrillas, thieves, or other names that might be used by our enemies. Our struggle follows the constitution which is held high by its call for justice and equality.

Therefore, according to this declaration of war, we give our military forces, the EZLN, the following orders:

First: Advance to the capital of the country, overcoming the Mexican federal army, protecting in our advance the civilian population and permitting the people in the liberated area the right to freely and democratically elect their own administrative authorities.

Second: Respect the lives of our prisoners and turn over all wounded to the International Red Cross.

Third: Initiate summary judgments against all soldiers of the Mexican federal army and the political police that have received training or have been paid by foreigners, accused of being traitors to our country, and against all those that have repressed and treated badly the civil population and robbed or stolen from or attempted crimes against the good of the people.

Fourth: Form new troops with all those Mexicans that show their interest in joining our struggle, including those that, being enemy soldiers, turn themselves in without having fought against us, and promise to take orders from the General Command of the Zapatista National Liberation Army.

Fifth: We ask for the unconditional surrender of the enemy's headquarters before we begin any combat to avoid any loss of lives.

Sixth: Suspend the robbery of our natural resources in the areas controlled by the EZLN.

To the People of Mexico: We, the men and women, full and free, are conscious that the war that we have declared is our last resort, but also a just one. The dictators are applying an undeclared genocidal war against our people for many years. Therefore we ask for your participation, your decision to support this plan that struggles for work, land, housing, food, health care, education, independence, freedom, democracy, justice and peace. We declare that we will not stop fighting until the basic demands of our people have been met by forming a government of our country that is free and democratic.

Join the Insurgent Forces of the Zapatista National Liberation Army.

General Command of the EZLN 1993

Source: "First Declaration from the Lacandon Jungle," http://struggle.ws/mexico/ezln/ezlnwa.html (http://struggle.ws/mexico.html).

PRIMARY SOURCE 21.3

Why Gender Matters (2000), World Bank

The *World Development Report* is an annual report published since 1978 by the International Bank for Reconstruction and Development. The report for 2000–2001, which included this selection, was devoted to the topic "Attacking Poverty."

Describe the effect of tuition on girls' school attendance.

Evaluate the relative importance of barriers to girls' education posed by culture on the one hand and poverty on the other.

What effect does expanding educational opportunity for girls have on boys?

Using Subsidies to Close Gender Gaps in Education

Evaluations of recent initiatives that subsidize the costs of schooling indicate that demand-side interventions can increase girls' enrollments and close gender gaps in education. A school stipend program established in Bangladesh in 1982 subsidizes various school expenses for girls who enroll in secondary school. In the first program evaluation girls' enrollment rate in the pilot areas rose from 27 percent, similar to the national average, to 44 percent over five years, more than twice the national average. After girls' tuition was eliminated nationwide in 1992 and the stipend program was expanded to all rural areas, girls' enrollment rate climbed to 48 percent at the national level. There have also been gains in the number of girls appearing for exams and in women's enrollments at intermediate colleges. While boys' enrollment rates also rose during this period, they did not rise as quickly as girls'.

Two recent programs in Balochistan, Pakistan, illustrate the potential benefits of reducing costs and improving physical access. Before the projects there were questions about whether girls' low enrollments were due to cultural barriers that cause parents to hold their daughters out of school or to inadequate supply of appropriate schools. Program evaluations suggest that improved physical access, subsidized costs, and culturally appropriate design can sharply increase girls' enrollments.

The first program, in Quetta, the capital of Balochistan, uses a subsidy tied to girls' enrollment to support the creation of schools in poor urban neighborhoods by local NGOs. The schools admit boys as long as they make up less than half of total enrollments. In rural Balochistan the second program has been expanding the supply of local, single-sex primary schools for girls by encouraging parental involvement in establishing the schools and by subsidizing the recruitment of female teachers from the local community. The results: girls' enrollments rose 33 percent in Quetta and 22 percent in rural areas. Interestingly, both programs appear to have also expanded boys' enrollments, suggesting that increasing girls' educational opportunities may have spillover benefits for boys.

Source: The World Bank, from "Using Subsidies to Close Gender Gaps in Education," World Bank. 2001. *World Development Report 2000–2001: Attacking Poverty*, p. 122, Box 7.2. © World Bank. http://openknowledge.worldbank.org/handle/10986/11856 License: Creative Commons Attribution license (CC BY 3.0).

PRIMARY SOURCE 21.4

"Democracy as a Universal Value" (1999), Amartya Sen

This selection is drawn from Amartya Sen's work on the economics and politics of famines as well as political philosophy. In many famines, Sen has shown, food supplies remained adequate, while unemployment, rising prices, and unresponsive governments led to catastrophe. The current selection comes from a keynote address delivered in New Delhi, titled "Building a Worldwide Movement for Democracy."

What does Sen mean by democracy?

What, according to Sen, is the relationship between democracy and economic dynamism?

Explain the significance of famines to Sen's argument.

In the summer of 1997, I was asked by a leading Japanese newspaper what I thought was the most important thing that had happened in the twentieth century. . . .

I did not, ultimately, have any difficulty in choosing one as the preeminent development of the period: the rise of democracy.

***

It is often claimed that nondemocratic systems are better at bringing about economic development. This belief sometimes goes by the name of "the Lee hypothesis," due to its advocacy by Lee Kuan Yew, the leader and former president of Singapore. He is certainly right that some disciplinarian states (such as South Korea, his own Singapore, and postreform China) have had faster rates of economic growth than many less authoritarian ones (including India, Jamaica, and

Costa Rica). The "Lee hypothesis," however, is based on sporadic empiricism, drawing on very selective and limited information, rather than on any general statistical testing over the wide-ranging data that are available. A general relation of this kind cannot be established on the basis of very selective evidence. For example, we cannot really take the high economic growth of Singapore or China as "definitive proof" that authoritarianism does better in promoting economic growth, any more than we can draw the opposite conclusion from the fact that Botswana, the country with the best record of economic growth in Africa, indeed with one of the finest records of economic growth in the whole world, has been an oasis of democracy on that continent over the decades. We need more systematic empirical studies to sort out the claims and counterclaims.

There is, in fact, no convincing general evidence that authoritarian governance and the suppression of political and civil rights are really beneficial to economic development. Indeed, the general statistical picture does not permit any such induction. . . . The directional linkage seems to depend on many other circumstances, and while some statistical investigations note a weakly negative relation, others find a strongly positive one. If all the comparative studies are viewed together, the hypothesis that there is no clear relation between economic growth and democracy in *either* direction remains extremely plausible. Since democracy and political liberty have importance in themselves, the case for them therefore remains untarnished. . . .

We must go beyond the narrow confines of economic growth and scrutinize the broader demands of economic development, including the need for economic and social security. In that context, we have to look at the connection between political and civil rights, on the one hand, and the prevention of major economic disasters, on the other. Political and civil rights give people the opportunity to draw attention forcefully to general needs and to demand appropriate public action. The response of a government to the acute suffering of its people often depends on the pressure that is put on it. The exercise of political rights (such as voting, criticizing, protesting, and the like) can make a real difference to the political incentives that operate on a government.

I have discussed elsewhere the remarkable fact that, in the terrible history of famines in the world, no substantial famine has ever occurred in any independent and democratic country with a relatively free press. We cannot find exceptions to this rule, no matter where we look: the recent famines of Ethiopia, Somalia, or other dictatorial regimes; famines in the Soviet Union in the 1930s; China's 1958–61 famine with the failure of the Great Leap Forward; or earlier still, the famines in Ireland or India under alien rule. China, although it was in many ways doing much better economically than India, still managed (unlike India) to have a famine, indeed the largest recorded famine in world history: Nearly 30 million people died in the famine of 1958–61, while faulty governmental policies remained uncorrected for three full years. The policies went uncriticized because there were no opposition parties in parliament, no free press, and no multiparty elections. Indeed, it is precisely this lack of challenge that allowed the deeply defective policies to continue even though they were killing millions each year. The same can be said about the world's two contemporary famines, occurring right now in North Korea and Sudan.

Famines are often associated with what look like natural disasters, and commentators often settle for the simplicity of explaining famines by pointing to these events: the floods in China during the failed Great Leap Forward, the droughts in Ethiopia, or crop failures in North Korea. Nevertheless, many countries with similar natural problems, or even worse ones, manage perfectly well, because a responsive government intervenes to help alleviate hunger. Since the primary victims of a famine are the indigent, deaths can be prevented by recreating incomes (for example, through employment programs), which makes food accessible to potential famine victims. Even the poorest democratic countries that have faced terrible droughts or floods or other natural disasters (such as India in 1973, or Zimbabwe and Botswana in the early 1980s) have been able to feed their people without experiencing a famine.

Famines are easy to prevent if there is a serious effort to do so, and a democratic government, facing elections and criticisms from opposition parties and independent newspapers, cannot help but make such an effort. Not surprisingly, while India continued to have famines under British rule right up to independence (the last famine, which I witnessed as a child, was in 1943, four years before independence), they disappeared suddenly with the establishment of a multiparty democracy and a free press. . . .

The issue of famine is only one example of the reach of democracy, though it is, in many ways, the easiest case to analyze. The positive role of political and civil rights applies to the prevention of economic and social disasters in general. When things go fine and everything is routinely good, this instrumental role of democracy may not be particularly missed. It is when things get fouled up, for one reason or another, that the political incentives provided by democratic governance acquire great practical value.

Source: Amartya Sen, "Democracy as a Universal Value," *Journal of Democracy* 10, no. 3 (1999): 3, 6–9.

Interpreting Visual Evidence

Chimerica

The term "Chimerica" refers to the idea that the People's Republic of China and the United States of America make up a single, dominant economic entity. It was coined by the historian Niall Ferguson and the economist Moritz Schularick to describe the interdependent relationship that began in the last two decades of the twentieth century and has extended into the first decades of the twenty-first century. China began to open its economy in the early 1980s, and its exports of manufactured goods, especially to the United States—which rose from $51.5 billion in 1996 to $102 billion in 2001—eventually fueled the world economy. Combined, the two countries make up roughly 13 percent of the world's land surface, a quarter of its population, more than a third of its economic production, and, by some estimates, nearly half of all economic growth in the first decade of the new millennium. Chimerica is also a play on the word *chimera*: a fire-breathing female monster in Greek mythology, or an unrealizable dream, an illusion.

Like Japan and Germany after World War II, China in this period concentrated on export-led industrial growth. But unlike those countries, China refused to let workers' wages rise as the economy grew, and its leaders refused to apply international standards to workplace safety, intellectual property, or environmental protections. In developed

Modern Beijing.

Foxconn factory with suicide nets.

Retirement community near Phoenix, Arizona.

Walmart Supercenter.

Unofficial Apple store in Tehran.

economies, where those protections applied and wages were higher, production costs were higher. As a result, competition from China cost millions of jobs in developed countries, including 2.9 million jobs in the United States alone from 2001 to 2012. Chinese leaders instead invested the surplus revenues abroad, mostly in the United States, where the influx of Chinese investment kept interest rates low. U.S. consumers used the resulting easy credit to purchase homes, cars, and goods like tablets and mobile phones, many of them manufactured in China.

The images presented here portray different aspects of what Ferguson and Schularick call Chimerica. The first shows modern Beijing, with massive new buildings, roadways, and smog; it shows both the robust growth of the Chinese economy—notice how new the buildings are—and its environmental costs. The second photograph shows protective nets around a factory run by Foxconn, one of Apple's leading suppliers in China, after a series of suicides in 2010 drew world attention to the company's labor practices. This image reflects some of the dire costs of producing consumer goods at low prices. The third image shows a massive retirement community near Phoenix, Arizona, filled with homes purchased at low interest rates, thanks to Chinese investment. The fourth image shows a Walmart Supercenter in Albany, New York, filled with inexpensive goods, many of them produced in China. Such "big-box" retail stores provide many jobs, but at much lower wages than the industrial jobs that have disappeared. The final image shows an unofficial Apple store in Tehran, Iran; it illustrates the dominance of global brands for Chinese-made consumer items.

QUESTIONS FOR ANALYSIS

1. Explain the relationship between China and the United States presented by these images. How has each country benefited from this relationship, and what sacrifices has each made?
2. Looking at the first two images, identify the sacrifices ordinary Chinese people have made as a result of the policies that enabled their country to invest in the United States. What group or groups in China do you think benefited from these policies, and how?
3. With the second, third, and fourth images in mind, analyze the trade-offs for ordinary Americans that have resulted from Chinese investment in the United States.
4. Examine the final image and consider the likely consequences of the growth of Chimerica for ordinary consumers and workers around the world.

Before You Read This Chapter

GLOBAL STORYLINES

The Impact of Modern Globalization Today

- The global "war on terror" achieves successes and failures in its fight against fundamentalist terrorists.
- The benefits of a globally integrated economy are unequally distributed, creating substantial tensions within and across societies.
- Mounting geopolitical and economic uncertainties lead to a rise in populist politics and economic nationalism, polarizing many countries politically. Heightened political polarization helped bring expanding state violence, racial justice demonstrations, and LGBTQ rights into focus.
- Twenty-first-century globalization contributes to an increasing incidence and prevalence of pandemics.
- Economic development and human consumption cause climate change, with substantial negative effects on biodiversity, water quality, and food production.

CHAPTER OUTLINE

22

Twenty-First-Century Global Challenges

2001–the Present

FOCUS QUESTIONS

- What is modern globalization? How is it different from earlier forms of global integration?
- What are some of the global challenges we face in the twenty-first century?
- In what ways has climate change affected the world, and what can be done to lessen or reverse the impact of climate change?
- Who are the beneficiaries of modern globalization? Who has not benefited? Why is this?
- How has globalization contributed to a resurgence in political populism and economic nationalism?

The new millennium closed the chapter on the bloody wars and ideological rivalries of the twentieth century. Although the Cold War was over and global integration seemed greater than ever before in human history, the new millennium brought explosive hostilities and fresh economic tensions over the makeup of the world order. Extreme **globalization** brought contradictory effects. It made societies more interdependent. Societies benefited from the work and ideas of others. But interdependence brought anxiety and risks—from climate change to the policies and competitive urges of others.

The year 2001 exposed this tension between opportunity and hazard. That year, communist China joined the World Trade Organization and folded into the world market, putting an apparent end to centuries of east-west commercial divides. That same year, on September 11, 2001, nineteen hijackers commandeered four commercial airplanes—one of the hallmarks of globalization in the jet age and mass travel. The hijackers slammed two of the planes into the World Trade Center in New York City and a third into the Pentagon, home of the U.S. Department of Defense, in Washington, D.C. The fourth plane was deterred from its intended target by the courageous actions of its passengers and crashed in a field in Pennsylvania. Television sets around the world projected horrifying images of the Trade Center's twin towers engulfed in flames, then crumbling in a heap of ash and twisted metal, in real time. A little-known Muslim militant organization, al-Qaeda, headed by an equally obscure Saudi, Osama bin Laden, claimed responsibility for the attacks that took the lives of more than 3,000 Americans. What followed was a predictable and determined American military response—the invasions of Iraq, incorrectly blamed for engineering the attacks, and Afghanistan, where a fundamentalist Islamic government provided a haven for bin Laden and his al-Qaeda affiliates.

Economic turmoil added to the turbulence of terrorism and wars. The global economy and technologies had brought the world together as never before, but the benefits of integration were unequally distributed. Consequently, when an economic crisis broke out, as it did in 2008, its effects were felt globally but experienced unequally, causing despair and discontent. As people across the world came to grips with the shadow of mounting geopolitical and economic uncertainties, a populist politics of "us versus them" swept many parts of the world. The wake of the economic meltdown of 2008 also saw the rise of right-wing populist politicians, led by Donald J. Trump, elected as president of the United States in 2016. In the United States, Brazil, India, Turkey, Britain, and parts of eastern Europe, ethnic and religious nationalists emerged, claiming to represent the "real" and virtuous people in a face-off against out-of-touch liberal elites. Many were lashing out against the "globalists"—a term used to decry the champions of international cooperation—for betraying their nations economically and admitting too many foreigners.

Interdependence also facilitated pandemics. Along with ideas, goods, and people, viruses and fungi also crossed borders. The outbreaks of SARS and Ebola foreshadowed the COVID-19 outbreak of 2020, which brought the world to a halt. An outbreak of this scale had not been seen since the Spanish flu pandemic of 1918, a century previously, which had killed millions worldwide.

Even as the world became more fractured and nations grew further apart, a global awareness of our common challenges intensified. Populists were gaining the upper hand in many countries, but many citizens worried about the future of the planet as climate change, looming economic and military tensions, and pandemics seemed to promise ever more hazards that required global cooperation.

Global Challenges

War on Terror

The 9/11 terrorist attack created revulsion across the world. Anger focused on Osama bin Laden and al-Qaeda, the loosely organized militant networks of Islamist groups that

9/11. *Left*: With the North Tower already aflame, this photograph captures a second hijacked jet an instant before it crashed into the South Tower of New York's World Trade Center on September 11, 2001. *Right*: A firefighter calls for ten more rescue workers to help search for survivors in the smoldering ruins.

had organized the attack. The militants claimed that it was a response to America's imperialist policies in the Middle East and retribution for American troops' presence in Saudi Arabia (during the first Iraq War). In the months and years that followed, countries grappled with a "war on terror," conflicts with militant Islamic groups, and a global economic crisis. George W. Bush, who had become president after a close and disputed election the year before, gained broad public support for his tough talk about bringing terrorists to justice. Domestically, Bush pushed for security measures to curb future terrorist violence, protect freedom, and secure the American homeland. His nation-first reaction anticipated a wider turn toward aggressive and ultra-competitive responses to international threats.

Internationally, President Bush declared a "**global war on terror**." With the backing of the majority of the American people, as well as strong support from many nations, Bush sent American forces to Afghanistan in October 2001 to hunt down bin Laden, destroy al-Qaeda training camps, and topple the Taliban government that had provided a haven for the terrorists. Expanding the battlefront of the war on terror, the Bush administration ordered an invasion of Iraq in 2003, falsely charging its brutal dictator, Saddam Hussein, with abetting the terrorist assault of 9/11 and wielding weapons of mass destruction. As in Afghanistan, the initial offensive went well, but defeating the Iraqi army and finding Hussein proved easier than restoring order to the country, improving living standards, and persuading the population to rally around the American vision of a democratic polity.

Moreover, the failure to find weapons of mass destruction or to uncover indisputable links between Saddam Hussein and al-Qaeda, together with mounting American losses from an

Iraqi Elections. Iraqis voted on December 15, 2005, while the country was under American and allied military occupation. Voters' fingers were stained after voting so that they could not vote twice; many walked away from the polling booth showing their stained finger with pride.

ongoing insurgency, left many U.S. citizens questioning the wisdom of this war.

In Afghanistan, the situation deteriorated. U.S.-led coalition forces found themselves in a quagmire like the one that the Soviets had fallen into two decades earlier (see Chapter 21). Coalition forces had some early success in maintaining stability. But they were more successful at toppling the old regime than building a new one. Their task became more difficult when local warlords, using personal power to achieve their own goals, challenged the corrupt and inept government in Kabul—the warlords then filled the political vacuum. Matters worsened when the Taliban regrouped in neighboring Pakistan. Kabul became an island in a sea of discord.

While the campaigns in Iraq and Afghanistan faltered, the United States accelerated its campaign to hunt down terrorist leaders, and on May 2, 2011, under President Barack

Withdrawal from Kabul. As the United States officially withdrew from Afghanistan, hundreds of Afghans swarmed and climbed aboard the landing gears of a U.S. Air Force aircraft taxiing for take off to ferry international diplomats to safety on a runway at Kabul's Hamid Karzai International Airport in Afghanistan on Monday, August 16, 2021, in a desperate effort to leave Kabul.

Obama, a daring operation in Pakistan ended with the death of Osama bin Laden. Even so, the American image suffered internationally due to exposés of programs of extensive surveillance (including that of U.S. citizens), the use of coercive interrogation techniques, "rendition" of suspected militants to sites where they could be tortured to extract information, the inhumane treatment of Iraqi prisoners at the Abu Ghraib prison, and the harsh and indefinite detention of suspected terrorists at Guantánamo. The domestic support for the Bush administration also eroded.

Helped by a growing chorus of disapproval of the Iraq War, Barack Obama secured the American presidency in 2008. Following his campaign promise, President Obama announced plans to end the Iraq War and refocus attention on Afghanistan. The Iraq occupation ended in 2011. Obama then began reducing troop deployments in Afghanistan. Finally, under the presidency of Joe Biden, the last American and allied troops withdrew from what had become America's longest war. Unfortunately, twenty years of conflict had created an Afghan state utterly reliant on western aid. Beyond the capital of Kabul, the new regime enjoyed little influence. Immediately upon the heels of the troop withdrawal, the ousted Taliban toppled the shaky government and claimed power—and just as immediately began to roll back liberties, taking special aim at the rights of women to education, work, and public expression. The fall of Kabul revealed another feature of the new era of contested globalization and the retreat of (often wobbly) liberal democracy: a surge in the exodus of Afghans to places like Kyrgyzstan, Rwanda, and Britain, where they joined the millions of other displaced people seeking shelter and asylum from hostile or neglectful regimes.

Crisis and Inequality in the Global Economy

Beginning in 2007, the world economy entered its worst crisis since the 1930s. The problem began in the financial sector, the most globally interlinked of all. Seeking new sources of profits, investors from around the world poured their money into an ever-expanding housing market, employing riskier and riskier investments—many of which were so complex that not even the regulators in charge of monitoring the financial sector could understand them.

The signals of an approaching financial disaster were apparent to many, but were ignored in part because Alan Greenspan, the guru of monetary policy at the Federal Reserve, America's central bank, was an ardent economic libertarian and free marketer. He believed that the marketplace would bring about necessary corrections. In reality, risk and indebtedness were at record levels. Commercial and investment banks and insurance companies had tripled their indebtedness over the three decades leading up to 2008. Even when the Hongkong and Shanghai Banking Corporation (HSBC), based in London since 1991 and the seventh-largest bank in the world in terms of assets, reported massive losses in its subprime housing loans and Countrywide Financial Corporation filed for bankruptcy, President George W. Bush and Congress did not react. Only when a leading financial investment firm, Bear Stearns, collapsed in March 2008 because of its heavy exposure to subprime mortgage loans did the Treasury Department intervene, providing a loan of nearly $30 billion to JPMorgan Chase to buy out Bear Stearns. But no support was forthcoming on September 18, 2008, when Lehman Brothers, a firm that had been in existence since 1850 and had survived the Civil War, World Wars I and II, and the Great Depression, filed for bankruptcy. Had the Treasury provided anywhere from $12 billion to $60 billion, the roiling financial crisis might have been averted. But it did not, and what had already been a dramatic economic and financial meltdown in the United States spread quickly to the United Kingdom, Ireland, Spain, and Iceland. As the shockwaves reverberated throughout Europe, Asia, Latin America, and parts of Africa, millions lost their livelihoods and houses, corporations failed, and trillions of dollars in financial wealth vaporized. In the words of one close observer, "The once mighty U.S. economy [was brought] to its knees, [leaving] all levels of government gasping for tax revenue."

The **Great Recession** of 2008, as it soon came to be called, did not last as long as the Great Depression of 1929. The unemployment rate in the United States cratered at 10 percent, not 25 percent, and hundreds of banks, not thousands, failed. The fact that the financial downturn of 2008 was not as sharp or persistent as the 1929 depression was largely due to the innovative policies championed by Ben Bernanke at the Federal Reserve and officials at the U.S. Treasury. It was perhaps fortuitous that Bernanke was at the Fed and Christina Romer was a high-ranking economic adviser in the Obama administration. Both had studied the Great Depression during their academic careers and were committed to monetary and fiscal policies that they believed would have pulled the United States out of the 1929 depression. Specifically, they thought it essential to shore up the U.S. financial system because it integrated so much of the world economy. This meant protecting the big banks, stimulating the economy with easy credit to keep consumers buying commodities, resisting protectionism, and promoting international cooperation. In keeping with these policies, the Treasury bailed out fourteen financial firms, including such heavy hitters as Goldman Sachs, Morgan Stanley, Merrill Lynch, Bank of America, Citigroup, and JPMorgan Chase, as well as two automobile manufacturers, General Motors and Chrysler. Big companies pressured a bewildered Congress into setting aside the stupendous sum of $700 billion in a program labeled TARP (Troubled Asset Relief Program). Although the majority of Americans thought the program was wrongheaded,

Occupy Wall Street. Inspired by other stirrings around the world, this largely national movement was fueled by methods as novel as social media and as traditional as a sit-in. Here, an Occupy Wall Street rally joins a labor union demonstration outside the New York County Courthouse in 2011.

rewarding banks that had brought on the financial disaster, TARP was, according to one top adviser, "among the most successful—but least understood—economic policy innovations in our nation's history" (Blinder, p. 178). In fact, the Treasury disbursed only $430 billion of the allocated $700 billion and eventually turned a profit of $25 billion when the businesses repaid their debts. Still, the bailout of Wall Street while Main Street suffered was a lasting source of grievance and contributed to the sense that political brokers were in the pockets of the rich—who would soon be called "the 1 percent."

While the crisis started in the United States, it whiplashed the world economy. American authorities had less success getting European authorities to follow suit. Monetary authorities there were leery about bailing out troubled countries and were determined to keep the euro currency stable. But this meant that the European economy entered a prolonged slump and recovered very slowly. Among the debtor countries in southern Europe, like Greece and Italy, and eastern Europe, notably Ukraine and Hungary, there was no help. Grievances soon piled up amid rising unemployment, especially for young people. Meanwhile, the Chinese government gave the green light to state firms to continue spending, and these firms embarked on a borrowing spree that was more monumental and more lasting than the American corporate bailouts. Together, U.S. and Chinese spending and lending were enough to keep the financial crash of 2008 from turning into a full-blown economic depression.

While a depression was averted, the crisis revealed underlying tensions and produced new scars. The risks of interdependence brought attention to the winners and losers from globalization. Developing countries like China and India saw a rising middle class, but this was not the case in the United States, where the middle class shrank and a small number of individuals held the lion's share of the wealth. This situation was due in large part to the exportation of American manufacturing jobs to cheaper locations around the world and the decline in the power of labor unions, which had been critical in dramatically expanding the middle class in America after World War II.

The crisis also exposed how globalization had concentrated wealth in the hands of a few in the United States and other industrialized economies and the enormous power that big corporations exercised over the political system. Vital to the political power of corporate America were a number of crucial Supreme Court decisions, the most important of which was the 2010 *Citizens United* ruling. In a 5–4 vote, the court ruled that in campaign financing the free speech of the First Amendment of the Constitution prohibited restricting the financial contributions of businesses as well as nonprofit corporations, trade unions, and other associations.

Even as economies emerged from the Great Recession, **economic inequality** among individuals and between regions led to new challenges. This sparked protests, none more powerful and dramatic than those conducted by Occupy Wall Street (OWS), a movement that started in September 2011 in New York and was organized by a Canadian environmental activist group called Adbusters. A charismatic Canadian writer, Naomi Klein, also emerged as a prominent voice in denouncing the model of globalization dominated by corporate interests. Her voice, among others, and the movement

Hurricane Katrina. As the hurricane dissipated in the tail end of August 2005, the U.S. Coast Guard surveyed the affected areas by aircraft and conducted damage assessment of what would be the costliest natural disaster in American history. This Coast Guard photograph captures New Orleans immediately after the passing of Katrina.

Social Media and the Right to Privacy Controversy. Robert Weissman, president of Public Citizen, speaks during a protest against Facebook policies, including the social media giant's political stances, data security lapses, politicalization, privacy violations, and misinformation outside their offices in Washington, D.C., May 25, 2021.

known as "Occupy" were themselves global. These activists drew inspiration from the upheavals and demonstrations in the Middle East, notably the Iranian Green Movement and the Spanish Indignados. Occupations spread to Madrid and Buenos Aires, Beirut and Istanbul, highlighting growing social and economic inequality and challenging the power of banks and corporations.

OWS was one among a wide range of emergent political upheavals around the world. Each one had a character specific to the region. Yet together they represented a new phenomenon. Almost all of them took shape outside conventional politics and ideological agendas. Expressing antiestablishment ideals and using social media to mobilize, the young took the lead in these new popular upsurges and became a permanent fixture on the political landscape worldwide. But instead of rallying to traditional parties, they preferred to take their activism to the streets and public squares.

Social Media

Globalization from 1992 coincided with the emergence of revolutionary media of the digital age. Indeed, it is hard to disentangle economic integration from the hyper-acceleration of information flows. The Internet, the rise of social media platforms like Facebook, founded in 2004, and Twitter, founded in 2006, were the source of initial euphoria about a borderless, free-flowing world. Going online affected not just how people communicated, but what they learned and watched. Online education firms like Coursera and edX exploded onto the scene in 2012; universities and colleges invested in their distance teaching capabilities. When the global COVID-19 pandemic hit in early 2020, the world's higher education system flipped to Zoom. Many of you reading this book now will do so in its electronic version. The same effect swept global entertainment. Instead of watching television, people turned on their computers to watch YouTube videos. Streaming services like Netflix not only eclipsed traditional networks like NBC in the United States, Britain's BBC, and Canada's CBC; they brought hit series like the South Korean *Squid Game* and the Spanish *Money Heist* to far-away viewers.

But as a handful of giant firms consolidated their grip over media, many began to worry about excessive concentration of power. Google, Facebook, and others used their platforms to sell the attention of their "users" to advertisers, effectively commercializing private data, often without the consent or even awareness of people who turned on their laptops or opened apps on their smartphones to convey to marketers their location, viewing habits, and personal preferences. States got into the act, too. New media became means for governments to watch their citizens' behavior. Using facial recognition and means to analyze massive amounts of data, even democratic states encroached on personal liberties. In the hands of autocratic regimes like China, new media became means to exercise explicit social control and repression of minorities like Muslim Uighurs.

If the new millennium saw excitement about new forms of connectivity and "social" media, by 2023, a worldwide chorus of concern about social control and exploitation of private data fueled efforts to roll back the hegemony of technology firms. European regulators paved the way in 2023 by suing giants like Google for exploiting their dominance in advertising to undermine competitors. That year, they did the same to Meta (formerly Facebook) for violating privacy rules. Even Washington rumbled with rumors that legislators were going to crack down. What fueled the regulators was the general social anxiety about the use of new media. More evidence was pouring out that algorithms were designed to produce online addictions; young women suffered from growing anxiety, especially for their self-esteem as digital platforms celebrated distorted images of women; teen depression was soaring—and was highly correlated with social media consumption. Most of all, social media was turning the Internet into a cauldron of unreliable information, conspiracy theories, and autocratic control. New terms, like "surveillance capitalism" edged aside the more benign language of social media.

Destruction by Hurricane Sandy on Ortley Beach, New Jersey. Hurricane Sandy, moving ashore in New Jersey on October 29, 2012, was the second-costliest hurricane in U.S. history. Its high winds struck twenty-four states, including the entire eastern seaboard from Florida to Maine.

Climate Change

Climate change has emerged as one of the most pressing issues for the new millennium. Scientists and activists had been ringing the alarm bells about rising atmospheric temperatures since the 1980s. By 2019, the evidence of systemic changes to the biosphere was undeniable. The Intergovernmental Science-Policy Platform on Biodiversity and Ecosystem Services (IPBES) published a definitive report in May 2019, concluding that climate change was responsible for significant and irreversible reductions in global biodiversity. A few months later, in August, the United Nations reported that **global climate change** was responsible for vast reductions in water supplies, especially in the tropics, and threatened food supplies, especially for large, precarious population belts. The threat of climate change mobilized global cooperation. The IPBES report, compiled by 145 environmental experts from 50 countries with inputs from another 310 contributors, and based on a review of 15,000 scientific and governmental sources, warned that 1 million of the 8 million plant and animal species in existence today would become extinct within the next two decades if the present trends in climate warming continue. This would be a rate of extinction hundreds of times higher than the averages of the last 10 million years. Moreover, innumerable climate reports made clear that humans were utterly responsible for an impending disaster that threatens all regions of the world. More than a third of the world's land surface is now devoted to crop or livestock production. Tropical rain forests, essential for planetary control of global warming, have decreased by 50 percent since 1950 to make way for agriculture and livestock grazing. The oceans and rivers have been overfished. Since 1980 greenhouse gas emissions have doubled, raising global temperatures by at least 0.7°C. The reports called for transformative change in humanity's approach to the earth, stating that the various plans thus far accepted by the world's countries were inadequate. Much more needed to be done, and much more quickly, to make the planet carbon free and to reverse the decline of forests, the deterioration of the oceans and rivers, and the steady increase of lands devoted to agriculture and livestock.

Climate change demands shared solutions by the world's national governments. Yet there is no international agency with teeth to enforce a global accord. The result has been a series of often frustrating global summits, usually ending with countries deeply divided over solutions. With few exceptions, however, no country denies the causes: the reliance on fossil fuels for energy sources. But China objected that it would have to curb fossil fuel dependence when it has a much lower per capita income than, for instance, Germany. And the United States balked at the idea that it had to finance "poor countries'" adjustment to carbon reduction on the grounds that some of them, like China, were direct economic competitors. A major breakthrough occurred in Paris in 2015 when, under the sponsorship of the United Nations Framework Convention on Climate Change, most of the nations of the world gathered to hammer out an agreement that would limit the emission of greenhouse gases and hold the increase in global temperature to less than 2°C. (See Global Themes and Sources: Primary Source 22.1.) The accord, scheduled to go into effect in 2020, set a higher standard, aiming to achieve a less than 1.5°C increase in global temperature. No fewer than 194 countries signed the accord on December 12, 2015, and by the end of that year 132 countries had ratified the agreement. The two heaviest polluters, China and the United States, are crucial signatories. Yet the implementation of the agreement is reserved to the nations, each of which has to file reports with the United Nations.

The new American president, Donald Trump, decided to withdraw the United States from the Paris Agreement, claiming that climate change was a hoax, invented by the Chinese to slow down American economic growth. (See Global Themes and Sources: Primary Source 22.2.) In reality, America was part of a wave of defections and noncompliance, though few nations had the temerity to leave the pact formally. (The Biden administration had America rejoin the agreement in 2021.) Most, like Australia, Japan, and Canada, just ignored its provisions. Some, like Russia, Turkey, and Iran, never signed it. The new Brazilian president, Jair Bolsonaro, approved loggers' demands to clear the Amazon forest, the world's biggest carbon sink (a large and dense concentration of flora capable of transforming carbon dioxide into oxygen). But China and India, two countries that rely heavily on coal, have made strides in meeting their carbon reduction targets. Tiny emitters, like Morocco and Gambia, have been standout examples in switching to renewable energy sources. (See Global Themes and Sources: Primary Sources 22.3 and 22.4.)

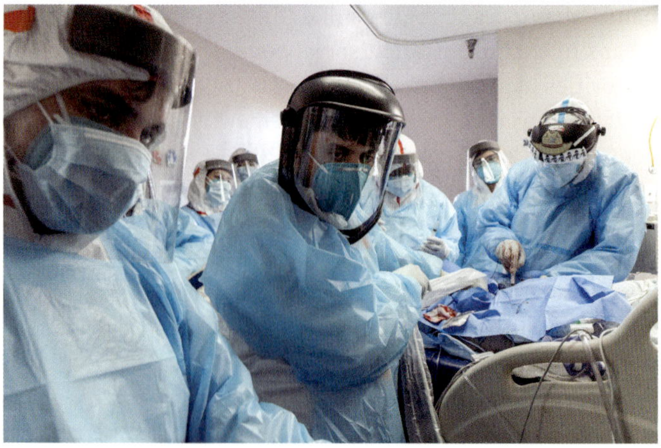

COVID-19 Pandemic. A medical staff member operates an ultrasonography machine while other medical staff members perform a procedure for hypothermia treatment on a patient in the COVID-19 intensive care unit (ICU) on Christmas Eve at the United Memorial Medical Center in Houston, Texas.

Pandemics

In late 2019, news started to leak out of the province of Hubei, China, of a new virus. As it ripped through the capital of Wuhan, Chinese authorities struggled to make sense of the threat—and to control the public relations fallout. At first, it looked like other deadly viruses before it. But it soon became clear that this virus possessed a cunning ability to spread undetected. Southern China was especially vulnerable to the transmission of viruses from other species. The numerous wet markets, where live animals were sold in unsanitary conditions, were one source. More dangerous were the massive chicken and pork farms in Hubei Province. As China lifted itself out of poverty and its cities boomed, these farms expanded—and they soon became disease incubators. Crowded, in close proximity to dense cities, and neglected by inspectors, the meat production industry in China created the conditions for a perfect epidemic storm.

On December 31, 2019, China officially informed the World Health Organization (WHO) of the "unknown disease," and on January 9, 2020, Chinese researchers released the map of the virus's genetic makeup. When the first case appeared in Bangkok a few days later, the viral implications were clear. By then, reporters from around the world were swarming into Wuhan as the virus was flowing out. Faced with mounting evidence, the WHO announced on March 10 that this mysterious disease was now a pandemic, which meant that it no longer had one point of origin—it was thoroughly global.

This was not the first **pandemic** in history. But its global shock was unprecedented. While the Black Death of the 1340s ravaged an interconnected world in the fourteenth century, eruptive fevers devastated the Indigenous populations of the Americas after 1492, and the influenza of 1918–1919 killed millions of war-fatigued people, none of these slammed the brakes so violently on an interdependent world as did COVID-19. Country after country went into lockdown. Those that dithered after the first infections, like Italy, Great Britain, the United States, and Brazil, paid a heavy human toll. Those that acted quickly and deployed testing systems, like South Korea and Taiwan, were less scathed. One source of their relative success was that they had learned from earlier pandemics and were more prepared. Societies with weak health care systems saw hospitals overwhelmed.

What started as a public health crisis exploded into an economic and social calamity. Airports worldwide emptied out. Borders between trading nations were sealed. As interdependent economies seized up, the ranks of unemployed soared—within weeks the U.S. jobless rate hit 15 percent. Middle-class people lined up at food banks. In the first two months of France's lockdown, its economy shrank by 20 percent. The most hard-hit economies were those most dependent on foreign trade. Oil exporters reeled as prices plunged; on April 20, 2020, the U.S. benchmark for crude oil dropped as low as *minus* $40 a barrel. Oil producers were paying people to buy their fuel. Across the board, global trade dropped in just a few weeks by more than it had dropped in the three years after the stock market crash of 1929. The World Trade Organization predicted that

Lockdown in India. The worldwide spread of COVID-19 forced countries to lock down their economies. In India, this meant clearing the streets of vendors and paralyzing an important part of the national economy, the informal sector. This photo of the city of Kolkata in March 2020 shows a practically deserted streetscape, with empty stalls lining the sidewalks.

global trade would shrink by one-third by the end of 2020. The collapse in world trade in turn crippled heavily indebted countries in the Global South. Argentina defaulted on a major interest payment to lenders and threatened to set off a cascade of defaults across Latin America and Africa.

The economic crisis sparked a social one. Despite the rhetoric about how viruses do not respect status or citizenship, this was a disease that afflicted the have-nots especially hard. No social group was more punished than migrants and the households that depended on them. For millions of poor migrant workers, their remittances to families back home dried up. And as cities and countries went into lockdowns, many migrant workers faced an agonizing predicament: How could they get home if the transportation systems were paralyzed? Kenyan workers were forced to leave the Gulf States and returned empty-handed to a draconian curfew. In India, when Prime Minister Narendra Modi closed the economy down overnight, millions of migrant workers began to walk home, often hundreds of miles, with no wages for their families. Salvadoran migrants to the United States also stopped sending money home, thereby choking a fifth of El Salvador's GDP. Sub-Saharan Africa is full of millions of Somali migrant workers, and this diaspora normally sends modest sums back to poverty-stricken Somalia every day, accounting for almost one-third of the country's GDP. But when COVID-19 struck, these workers were unable to send remittances back to their families. Furthermore, women's savings clubs (known as *hagbad* in Somali), which are vital to family survival, had to close down for lack of funds.

Such peacetime suffering had few modern parallels. But it also spawned remarkable displays of solidarity. In northern Italy, people went out on their balconies in the evenings as hospital workers changed shifts to applaud their selflessness. China dispatched personal protective equipment to Europe and Africa. In Berlin, when Muslims entered their fasting month of Ramadan, one pastor, Monika Matthias, invited Muslims to hold their Friday prayers in her church—provided they observe social distancing norms. She said, "During prayer, I could only say yes, yes, yes, because we have the same concerns and we want to learn from you. And it is beautiful to feel that way about each other."

The United States, the European Union, and Japan

Although the global challenges of the twenty-first century touched virtually every corner of the world, countries and regions experienced specific local changes often related to globalizing forces.

The United States

In the United States, the Obama administration sought to cope with the economic crisis while introducing health care reform; it encountered a conservative backlash in 2009 in the shape of the Tea Party movement, which espoused the ideals of small government and market freedom and contributed to a stinging defeat of the Democrats in the 2010 congressional elections. From the opposite side of the ideological spectrum arose the aforementioned Occupy Wall Street movement in 2011. Claiming to speak on behalf of the 99 percent against the wealthy 1 percent, the Occupy activists, consisting largely of young people, railed against the banks and financial institutions that the federal government had rescued from bankruptcy by providing immense loans. Although the movement ran out of steam by the end of the year, it succeeded in inserting the growing inequality into political discussions. Partially helped by the focus on inequality brought about by the Occupy movement, Obama won reelection and his Democratic party fared better in the 2012 elections. But the political pendulum swung back toward the Republicans in the 2014 midterm elections.

The most stunning event in the second decade of the twenty-first century was the election of Donald Trump to the presidency. Above all, he repudiated globalization and championed what he called "America First" values. He also threatened the multilateral fabric of the post-1945 order. Trump, who had never held political office, appealed to voters by inveighing against "inner-city" crime, immigrants, international trade, and America's traditional allies and foreign alliances. His coalition relied on swing votes in some key upper-midwestern states as well as traditional conservatives motivated by economic and religious concerns. More modest and poor rural voters who had been left feeling hopeless also rallied to his angered rhetoric. This latter group was responding to a severe economic decline and an opioid drug crisis, which were ravaging their communities as America continued to move away from manufacturing- and natural-resource-based industries and toward a globally integrated service- and information-based economy. After four turbulent and polarizing years, Obama's former vice president, Joe Biden, unseated Trump in the 2020 elections—elections that Trump and legions of his supporters believed to be "stolen." Biden managed to champion some important environmental legislation, but he could not patch together a persistently polarized and anxious republic to move his longer-term agenda forward beyond primarily issuing executive orders. As in so many other parts of the world, earlier consensus over the post-1945 welfare model and the post-1989 globalization model had come apart.

A Changing Western Europe

The American invasion of Iraq fractured the alliance between the United States and western Europe. Far more serious divisions, however, emerged over the fate of NATO and of the coherence of the European Union, whose membership peaked at twenty-eight countries, including ten that formerly had been part of the Soviet bloc. The sprawling European Union incorporated debtor and creditor countries, low-productivity and high-productivity workers, frontline immigration societies and those that kept migrants out. After the shocks of the 2008 economic slump, the divisions came to the fore. Early warning signs included votes in France and the Netherlands rejecting the EU constitution. Then came the 2016 referendum on EU membership in Britain in which "Leave," known as Brexit, secured a majority. The Brexit vote brought down a succession of British prime ministers: David Cameron, who had called for the vote, expecting a "Remain" vote; Theresa May, whose efforts to negotiate the terms of Britain's departure from the European Union failed to win a parliamentary majority; and the legally-challenged Boris Johnson, who finally did complete the terms of Brexit with the European Union, only to be mired in scandal; followed by Liz Truss; and most recently Rishi Sunak. The revolving door of British premiers and the trauma of separation from Europe left Britain scarred, polarized, and angry. They also left Britons economically more impoverished; average incomes in 2023 were lower than they were in 2007.

The rest of Europe avoided this extreme form of nativist and anti-integration politics. But only barely. While the adoption of a single currency, the euro, by seventeen EU members had indeed facilitated commerce, it had also caused economic damage. Monetary integration, in the absence of corresponding fiscal integration, meant that countries with different economies could no longer adjust for imbalances and competitiveness by currency devaluations. Unemployment rose dramatically and remained high in Europe's southern tier, even as the northern tier did better. The calamity was most visible in Greece, where northern country debtors were protected at the expense of Greek jobs and the Greek standard of living, all in the name of preserving Greece's EU membership. The euro, which had promised prosperity, became a symbol of immiseration.

The divisions also spilled into the open over how to respond to waves of migrants from Africa and the Middle East. In the summer of 2015, columns of refugees crossed into Europe through the Balkans. Many came by boat, setting sail from

British Voters Protest the Referendum to Leave the European Union. In a hotly contested referendum in which 72 percent of registered voters cast ballots, 52 percent of the electorate chose to withdraw from the European Union.

Turkey and Libya—and their crowded, rickety dinghies and rafts were sometimes no match for the waves. Thousands died, creating a massive humanitarian outcry. By year's end, Germany admitted an astonishing 1 million refugees. Many Europeans, especially in eastern Europe and in Italy, however, were less than welcoming.

The combination of fears over unfettered immigration, crystallized by the war in Syria and the resulting flow of desperate refugees into Europe, and the elites' mismanagement of the euro and the economy created fertile ground for self-styled populist politics. The EU's signature identity, democratic institutions, experienced significant erosion, beginning in Hungary and then Poland before spreading to much of the rest of the continent. Europe's malaise put the long-term future of integration to the test.

Demographic Issues in Western Countries

Two threats to future peace and prosperity in Europe—and the United States and Japan as well—are the interlocking issues of aging and immigration. Women in the European Union would have to bear 2.1 children on average to maintain its population of 500 million, but women in the European Union now average only 1.5 offspring. Adding to the demographic and labor pressures is the aging of the European population. With the percentage of elderly Europeans rising rapidly, sustaining the present workers-to-retirees ratio and paying for the region's burgeoning number of pensioners will require the European Union to attract around 15 million immigrants annually.

That number has not been reached. European populations have been boosted by millions of immigrants, many of them Muslims, but sustainable economic growth has proven elusive. Islam has become the fastest-growing religion in Europe. In France, the Muslim population exceeds 11 percent of the total. These immigrants often live in isolated and impoverished circumstances, and in many countries their status as guest workers (see Chapter 21) denies them the full benefits of citizenship. Their presence in Europe's larger cities threatens those who still equate Europe with Christendom and challenges those who believe that European integration requires complete assimilation of all inhabitants.

Europe is not alone in confronting the problems of an aging population and the integration of immigrants. (See Analyzing Global Developments: The Sharp Decline in Global Fertility Rates: Causes and Implications.) As its baby boom generation ages, the United States faces a similar imbalance between retirees and workers that endangers its Social Security system. Likewise, the flood of immigrants, particularly from Asia and Latin America, continues to shift the nation's ethnic composition. According to the U.S. Census Bureau, in 2010 people of Latin American descent in the United States numbered nearly 48 million (about 15.5 percent of the population). The presence of so many Spanish-speaking residents appears to threaten those who think the United States should remain an English-only country, and the degree to which immigrants should be required to assimilate remains a contentious issue. More heated still are debates about illegal immigration, which Donald Trump, pledging to "build a wall" across the U.S.-Mexico border, made central to his campaign for the presidency in 2016. Once in office, his efforts to "build a wall" became so divisive that they led to the longest shutdown of the federal government in American history. For over a month in late 2018 and early 2019, lawmakers argued over how much funding the Trump administration would receive to extend the existing sections of border fencing. (For a global look at population growth and life expectancies, see Maps 22.1 and 22.2.)

In many respects, the dilemma of aging presses hardest today on Japan. Like Europeans and North Americans, the Japanese are marrying later and having fewer children. Japan's female population now averages barely 1.37 children, compared with nearly 3.7 in 1950. At the same time, Japanese life expectancy has reached eighty-five, the highest in the world, which further tilts the nation's age pyramid. In 1970, the elderly (those over age sixty-five) represented around 7 percent of the population; in 2005, they reached 20 percent and are expected to hit 40 percent by 2050. Analysts surmise that Japan's population peaked at around 128 million and might decline to perhaps 120 million by 2050, with a substantial number of those over the working age. Such a downturn bodes ill for Japan's dynamic economy, which is currently the world's third largest in terms of total GDP, China having moved into second place in 2012.

Like Europe and North America, Japan relies on immigrants to fill out its labor force. In the 1960s, the nation's booming economy experienced labor shortages, but neither the government nor major corporations chose to invite in foreign laborers. They preferred automation or recruitment of workers of Japanese descent from abroad. By the 1980s, however, deepening labor shortages and the yen's rising value led to an expanded dependence on immigrant workers. Recent estimates put the number of foreign nationals in Japan at nearly 2 million, or around 1.5 percent of the total population. Most of them hail from the Korean Peninsula, the Philippines, Indochina, Brazil, and Iran, countries with a surplus of skilled workers.

Anti-immigrant Sentiments in Western Countries

In Europe, where unemployment rates remain higher than in Japan or North America, the political reaction against immigration has been sharpest. Far-right groups have demanded that immigration be halted or "foreigners" expelled, a stance

Analyzing Global Developments

The Sharp Decline in Global Fertility Rates: Causes and Implications

Migrants from less developed—and politically challenged—societies to the developed world have occurred on a massive scale during the first two decades of the twenty-first century. The inhabitants of Honduras, Guatemala, and El Salvador, fleeing poverty and criminal gangs, have sought better lives for themselves in the United States. During his campaign for the presidency, Donald Trump said that he would build a wall along the border between Mexico and the United States in order to prevent immigrants from entering the country. In Germany, Chancellor Angela Merkel's willingness to take up to 1 million immigrants fleeing the Middle East and Africa for better lives has led to the emergence of a right-wing, neo-Nazi party, the Alternative für Deutschland Party (AfD), opposed to Merkel's immigration policies. Many states in the European Union have emulated Donald Trump's plans to erect fences and walls along their borders to keep families fleeing African and Middle Eastern violence and economic deprivation from entering their countries. Even Great Britain's exit from the European Union has been an effort to return Britain to a solidly Anglo-Saxon country. The sharp decline in global fertility rates will only intensify the problems leading to the flight of people from less developed societies to the more developed parts of the world.

Global fertility rates, calculated as the average number of children born to a cisgender woman over her reproductive lifetime, are on the decline. Although fertility rates have been decreasing worldwide, in many parts of the world—especially in highly developed countries—these declines have resulted in what demographers call *below replacement rates*. For a country to maintain its population (other than through immigration), it needs a fertility rate of 2.1; in other words, the average woman must bear 2.1 children. Thus, a country's rate is below replacement if it falls below 2.1.

In 1950, only 6 countries—the Czech Republic, Estonia, Hungary, Japan, Latvia, and Ukraine, representing only 5 percent of the world's population—had fertility rates slightly below replacement levels. The global fertility rate at that time was 4.7 children per woman. By 2010, below replacement rates had occurred in 83 countries, holding nearly half the world's population. The world rate was halved to 2.4 per woman between 1950 and 2016. By 2050, if present patterns continue, more than 130 countries, or about two-thirds of the world's population, are projected to have fertility rates below 2.1 per woman.

These facts are stunning, as are their implications. People are having fewer children, which means that as these children grow up, countries will have smaller working-age populations, who must then support an ever-increasing elderly population. The problem is most severe among the more economically developed countries, including most of Europe, the United States, South Korea, Japan, China, and Australia. It is important to note that the overall number of people living in these countries is not on a similar decline; one must also factor in declining death rates as well as immigration.

A number of causes contribute to the problem of declining fertility rates worldwide. Late marriage ages, delayed childbearing, lower marriage rates, the increasing availability of contraceptives, and women's and families' decisions to have fewer children—or no children—are all factors. So are women's empowerment, ambitions, and accomplishments in the work force, undoubtedly brought about through improvements in the global education of women and girls, and aspirations for higher standards of living. The proportion of U.S. women between the ages of 40 and 44 who chose not to have children doubled between 1976 and 2006, encompassing one-fifth of women. Such was also the case in Austria, Germany, Japan, Spain, and the United Kingdom in 2010.

Some governments presiding over populations with low fertility rates have enacted policies of selective immigration to maintain their workforces and slow the pace of population aging. Others have attempted to increase childbearing by enacting policies that make marriage (or other child-rearing arrangements) attractive. These states have paid mothers to have babies, provided maternal and paternal leaves, and encouraged flexible work schedules. Denmark, France, Sweden, and Great Britain have each committed 4 percent of their GDP to family benefits in order to address low fertility. In contrast, the United States offers only 1 percent of its GDP. So far, these policies have produced only modest results.

The problem of low fertility rates is particularly severe in China, which enacted a one-child policy in 1979, modified it in the 1980s to allow rural parents to have a second child if the first was a daughter, and finally eliminated it in 2015. By this time, China's fertility rate had fallen to 1.6. The one-child policy and a cultural preference for boy children over girl children led to a disproportionate number of male births caused by abortions and even infanticide. The problem has become so severe in China that President Xi Jinping, speaking to the nineteenth National Congress of the Communist Party, guaranteed that China's childbirth policy would henceforth be closely coordinated with effective social and economic policies.

Yet in spite of sharply declining global fertility rates, the world population continues to grow. Having topped 8 billion,

Current Fertility Statistics Throughout the World

Ten Most Populous Countries in the World and Total Fertility Rates in 2018

Country	Population (in Millions)	Total Fertility Rate
China	1,394	1.8
India	1,371	2.3
United States	328	1.8
Indonesia	265	2.4
Brazil	209	1.7
Pakistan	201	3.1
Nigeria	196	5.5
Bangladesh	166	2.1
Russia	147	1.6
Mexico	131	2.2

Ten Most Populous Countries in 2050 If Present Trends Continue

Country	Population (in Millions)
India	1,680
China	1,344
Nigeria	411
United States	390
Indonesia	320
Pakistan	307
Brazil	231
Dem. Rep. Congo	216
Bangladesh	201
Ethiopia	191

Ten Countries with the Highest Total Fertility Rates in 2018

Country	Total Fertility Rate
Niger	7.2
Chad	6.4
Dem. Rep. Congo	6.3
Somalia	6.3
Angola	6.2
Mali	6.0
Burkina Faso	5.5
Nigeria	5.5
Burundi	5.5
Gambia	5.4

Total Fertility Rates of the Ten Countries with the Largest Gross National Product (GNP) per Capita in 2018

Country	Total Fertility Rate
United States	1.8
Japan	1.4
Germany	1.6
Britain	1.8
France	1.9
China	1.8
Italy	1.3
Canada	1.5
Brazil	1.7
Spain	1.3

the global population is projected to reach 8.5 billion people in 2030, 9.7 billion in 2050, and 10.9 billion by 2100, largely because of high fertility rates in sub-Saharan Africa.

In addition to these figures, the world population is growing older. The percentage of people over 65 years of age in 1960 was 5 percent. It had grown to 9 percent by 2018, and if present trends continue, it will reach 16 percent of the world's population in 2050. By that year, those under the age of 24 will have declined from 54 percent of the world's population in 1960 to 14 percent, leaving only 49 percent of those between 25 and 64 to support those 65 and over.

QUESTIONS FOR ANALYSIS

- Why do the countries with the highest per capita GNP rates have reproduction rates of less than 2.1 children per woman? What are countries with such low fertility rates doing, if anything, to deal with their population issues? In your opinion, how should states address their low fertility rates?
- Why are the highest fertility rates all concentrated in sub-Saharan Africa?
- What accounts for the fact that the countries with low fertility rates have been the most vigorous in keeping immigrants out?

Sources: Christopher Murray et al., "Population and Fertility by Age and Sex for 195 Countries and Territories, 1950–2017: A Systemic Analysis for the Global Burden of Disease Study, 2017," *Lancet* 392, no. 10159 (November 10–16, 2018): 1995–2051; Population Reference Bureau, *2018 World Population Data Sheet,* 2018, https://www.prb.org/wp-content/uploads/2018/08/2018_WPDS.pdf, and *2019 World Population Data Sheet,* 2019, https://www.prb.org/2019-world-population-data-sheet/.

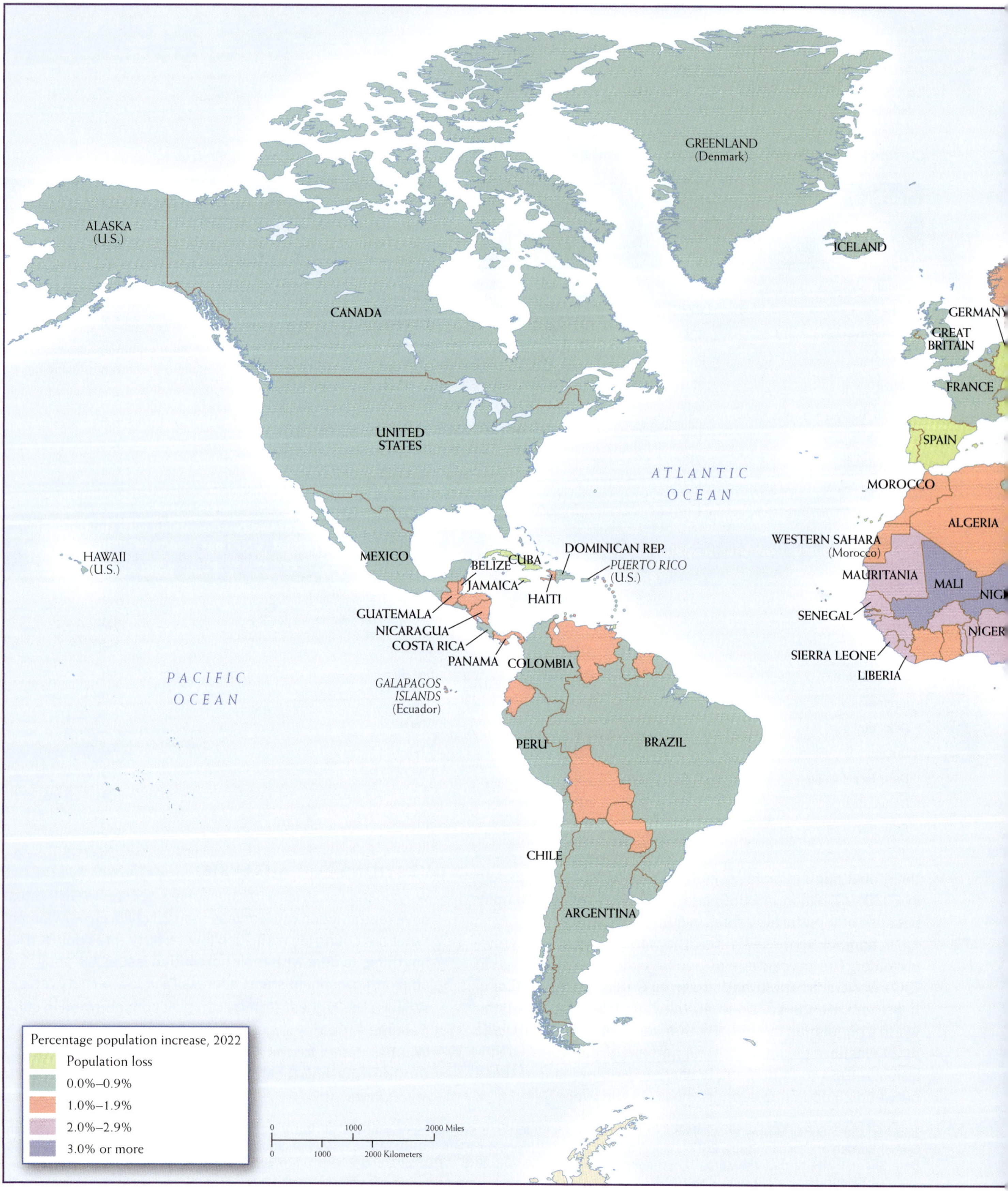
GREENLAND
(Denmark)
ICELAND
ALASKA
(U.S.)
CANADA
GERMANY
GREAT
BRITAIN
FRANCE
SPAIN
UNITED
STATES
ATLANTIC
OCEAN
MOROCCO
ALGERIA
WESTERN SAHARA
(Morocco)
MAURITANIA
MALI
HAWAII
(U.S.)
MEXICO
BELIZE
CUBA
JAMAICA
DOMINICAN REP.
PUERTO RICO
(U.S.)
HAITI
GUATEMALA
NICARAGUA
COSTA RICA
PANAMA
COLOMBIA
SENEGAL
SIERRA LEONE
LIBERIA
NIGER
PACIFIC
OCEAN
GALAPAGOS
ISLANDS
(Ecuador)
PERU
BRAZIL
CHILE
ARGENTINA
Percentage population increase, 2022
Population loss
0.0%–0.9%
1.0%–1.9%
2.0%–2.9%
3.0% or more
0
1000
2000 Miles
0
1000
2000 Kilometers

MAP 22.1 | Population Growth, 2022

The demographic patterns observed early in the twenty-first century pose major problems for the industrialized societies of western Europe, North America, and Japan. As life expectancy increases and population growth slows, these regions' economies face labor shortages that have fueled immigration.

- According to this map and Map 22.2, which regions of the world are prime candidates for sending migrants to the industrialized world?
- What cultural and political dilemmas does this phenomenon create?
- Which states within the industrialized world do you think have created the best environment for immigrant residents?

GREENLAND
(Denmark)
ICELAND
ALASKA
(U.S.)
CANADA
GERMANY
GREAT
BRITAIN
FRANCE
SPAIN
UNITED
STATES
ATLANTIC
OCEAN
MOROCCO
ALGERIA
WESTERN SAHARA
(Morocco)
MAURITANIA
MALI
HAWAII
(U.S.)
MEXICO
CUBA
DOMINICAN
REP.
PUERTO RICO
(U.S.)
BELIZE
JAMAICA
HAITI
GUATEMALA
NICARAGUA
COSTA RICA
PANAMA
COLOMBIA
SENEGAL
SIERRA LEONE
LIBERIA
NIGERIA
GALAPAGOS
ISLANDS
(Ecuador)
PACIFIC
OCEAN
PERU
BRAZIL
CHILE
ARGENTINA
Life expectancies, 2023
50–59
60–69
70–79
Over 80
No data
0
1000
2000 Miles
0
1000
2000 Kilometers

MAP 22.2 | Life Expectancies in Global Perspective, 2023

Increased attention to public health, medicine, nutrition, and education since the early nineteenth century has contributed to prolonging life expectancy around the world, as have the many scientific breakthroughs and technological advancements of the twentieth and twenty-first centuries.

- According to Map 22.1 and this map, which regions experienced population increases but low life expectancies? Population decreases and high life expectancies? Explain.
- Which countries do not match the life expectancy trends of their geographic regions? Why?
- Do you note any correlations between a region's life expectancy and its physical environment? Why or why not?

Muslim Bans. *Left:* During French president Sarkozy's state visit to India in 2010, Indian Sikh students held a demonstration in New Delhi calling for the lifting of the French ban on wearing the turban, a religious practice that dates back to the eighteenth century. *Right:* Protesters against the U.S. Supreme Court's decision to uphold President Donald Trump's ban on travel from several mostly Muslim countries expressed their indignation on June 26, 2018, in New York.

now adopted by politicians across the far-right spectrum. Support levels vary in each country, but across Europe the far right's electoral base appears to be around 15 percent; in some countries it is above 25 percent. The Freedom Party in Austria and the Northern League and National Alliance in Italy regularly place cabinet representatives in coalition governments. Ultra-right forces such as France's National Front (renamed National Rally in 2018), Denmark's People's Party, and the League of Polish Families sometimes pressure governing coalitions to slow EU integration and immigration, especially from Muslim countries. The issue of accepting Muslim refugees from war-torn Syria has galvanized supporters and opponents in the EU's most powerful country, Germany.

The issue of immigration has become intertwined with terrorism and the assimilation of Muslims in European societies. In Holland, the precipitant was the grisly murder of filmmaker Theo van Gogh by Mohammed Bouyeri in 2004. Bouyeri claimed he was fulfilling his duty as a Muslim by killing van Gogh, who had made a film about the abuse of Muslim women. Following the assassination, many in Holland questioned the nation's traditional tolerance of diversity and expressed concern that Muslims were too alien in their values to ever fit in Dutch society. Several terrorist attacks further inflamed the debate. In 2004, a series of bombings of commuter trains in Madrid killed 191 people and wounded more than 2,000; in 2005, terrorists struck London's subways, leaving 52 dead and 700 injured. In both cases, authorities pinned responsibility on al-Qaeda. But investigators also alleged that the operations were the work of Muslim residents of Spain or Britain.

France confronted a similar debate after rioting rocked a series of poor neighborhoods, notably in Paris, in 2005, protesting police brutality and the country's failure to offer equal opportunity to all. These riots caused a nativist backlash that often blamed Muslims in general for the country's problems. Nicolas Sarkozy, who was interior minister at the time, ordered the deportation of immigrants convicted of rioting, while Jean-Marie Le Pen, leader of the far-right National Front, demanded that even naturalized rioters be stripped of their citizenship. The French satirical weekly magazine *Charlie Hebdo* became the target of two terrorist attacks after publishing deliberately irreverent depictions of Muhammad. The cartoonists aggressively defended their right to lampoon any figure in the way they saw fit. The first assault, a firebombing of the offices in 2011, followed an issue equating Islam and Muhammad with oppression of women under *sharia* law; in the second assault, which occurred in 2015 after the magazine printed caricatures of the Prophet, two gunmen shouting "God is great" and the "Prophet is avenged" murdered twelve staff members, including the publisher and prominent cartoonists.

Although the Europeans stepped up their security procedures and intensified intelligence gathering, further violence occurred. On November 13, 2015, terrorists claiming allegiance to the Islamic State in Iraq and Syria (ISIS) carried out a series of coordinated attacks; while one group struck outside a Paris stadium where France was playing Germany in a football (soccer) match, others attacked restaurants and cafes. In all, 130 were killed and many more were injured. Just a few months later, a Tunisian, Anis Amri, also asserting allegiance to the Islamic State, struck in a market in Berlin, killing twelve. In the United States, meanwhile, anti-immigrant sentiments also gathered popular support, fueled by candidate, and later president, Donald Trump's nativist attacks on immigrants and restrictions on immigration from Muslim countries (the so-called Muslim ban). His administration separated children from parents who crossed the U.S.-Mexico border without documentation and sought to end the Deferred Action for Childhood Arrivals (DACA) policy of his predecessor, Barack Obama. In the

Families at the Border. In November 2016, prior to the Trump administration's escalation of family separation, U.S. Border Patrol agents stood at an open gate on the fence along the U.S.-Mexico border to allow relatives on opposite sides to hug one another during Universal Children's Day.

summer of 2020, the U.S. Supreme Court rejected the Trump administration's efforts to strip DACA students of their rights to remain and have access to education.

In just a few years, the mood of the world's most advanced industrial societies has shifted decisively. The triumphant atmosphere that ushered in the new millennium has given way to a pessimistic outlook. In the year 2000, talk of the blessings of global integration dominated the political and economic scene; now prognosticators warn about the dangers emanating from disaffected members of their societies and from radicals, especially Islamic radicals, willing and able to unleash terror anywhere in the world.

Russia, China, and India

Fueling anti-immigrant fires in Europe, Japan, and North America is the increasing number of jobs being "outsourced" to China, India, and other countries. In the past, businesses had turned to immigrants to fill low-wage positions (and to keep all wages down). But at the end of the twentieth and the beginning of the twenty-first centuries, it became more economical to relocate manufacturing to places where cheap labor was already available.

Economic Globalization and Political Effects

In the twenty-first century, business mobility is not limited to low-skilled and low-wage jobs. Technological advances—particularly in computers and communication—have enabled all sorts of enterprises to operate from almost any point on the globe. No longer do educated workers have to leave India and China for employment in Europe or North America, because it is increasingly cost-effective for corporations to shift certain operations to those countries. The playing field has been leveled in the globalized market economy, although countries with vast labor reserves such as China, India, and Russia still have a long way to go to achieve the per capita income levels enjoyed in the older capitalist societies like the United States, Europe, and Japan. Nonetheless, China, India, and Russia have had healthy economic growth in the first years of the new century. As the gap closed, China in particular has moved from being a trading partner to a trade competitor. It once sent cheap commodities to Europe and North America in return for capital goods and advanced technology; now, it is selling 5G wireless technology and cornering the market on strategic technologies like solar panels.

Russia: Economic Expansion and Aggressive Nationalism

With the price of oil regularly topping $60 per barrel and spiking at $140 per barrel in 2008, Russia enjoyed windfall energy revenues that boosted budget and trade surpluses and expanded personal incomes. Between 1999 and 2008, Russia's gross domestic product climbed at an average rate of more than 7 percent per year—an impressive achievement after the steep economic decline that followed the Soviet Union's dissolution in 1991.

Current Trends in World History

Has *Homo sapiens* Entered a New Epoch—the Anthropocene?

The earth came into being more than 4 billion years ago, and the first life-forms appeared around 2 billion years ago. From the nineteenth century onward, geologists, earth scientists, evolutionary biologists, and others have been fine-tuning a timescale of earth history, which they divide into eons, four of which have thus far existed and each of which spans hundreds and thousands of millions of years. The eons themselves are subdivided into eras, periods, epochs, and ages. Earth scientists base their geological divisions of the earth's history on the major changes that have taken place in the environment and climate of our planet and its life-forms. Using these categories, they have created a geological time scale (GTS). Today, we live in the Cenozoic Era and the Holocene Epoch. The Cenozoic Era, which began roughly 65 million years ago with the extinction of the dinosaurs, has been called the Age of Mammals because the largest land animals of the era have been mammals. The Holocene Epoch, which began about 12,000 years ago, after the last major ice age, has had a stable climate and has been increasingly dominated by *Homo sapiens*. The term *Holocene* itself, meaning whole and recent, was first proposed by the British scientist Charles Lyall in 1833 and was adopted by the International Geological Congress in 1885 as the title for our epoch.

However, two scientists, Paul J. Crutzen and Eugene F. Stoermer, believe that we have entered a new geological epoch, dominated by the impact of humankind on the earth's environment, particularly its stratosphere. They first proposed the term *Anthropocene* to represent humankind's dominance in this new epoch. Their proposal appeared in an article published in May 2000 in the newsletter of the International Geosphere-Biosphere Programme (IGBP). Although their statement was only a short one, these authors dealt with virtually all the factors that led them and their followers to assert that the environmental and geological impact of *Homo sapiens* has been so decisive that the world has indeed entered a new geological age. They stressed human population growth, the extinction of other species, the increase in atmospheric greenhouse gases, notably carbon dioxide and methane, and the destruction of rain forests. They concluded their essay by observing that "it seems to us more than appropriate to emphasize the central role of mankind in geology and ecology by proposing the term 'anthropocene' for the current geological epoch." Evidence from glacial ice cores showing a dramatic rise in greenhouse gas concentrations since the latter part of the eighteenth century caused them to argue that the Anthropocene began at the time of the industrial revolution.

Thus far, it has been mainly environmental historians who have taken up the challenge of studying the impact of humankind on the environment, though only a few have used the term *Anthropocene* proposed by Crutzen and Stoermer. They have, however, elaborated on the factors that Crutzen and Stoermer first laid out. Two environmental historians, J. R. McNeill and Peter Engelke, in their essay "Into the Anthropocene: People and Their Planet," contend that "a new history of the earth has begun, that the Holocene is over, and something new has begun: the Anthropocene." They prefer the twentieth century rather than Crutzen and Stoermer's claim for the later eighteenth century as the starting point of this epoch and conclude "that humankind emerged as the most powerful influence upon the global ecology." They cite the enormous expansion of the human population: a tenfold increase over three centuries, producing the present world population of 7.6 billion. The growth of the human population was exceedingly slow up to the beginning of the nineteenth century—only about 0.05 percent per year—but reached a full 2 percent per year in 1970. In their view, "no primate, perhaps no mammal, has ever engaged in such a frenzy of reproduction." As for the loading of the atmosphere with carbon dioxide, three-quarters of this loading took place during the most recent six and a half decades (between 1945 and 2011). The number of vehicles increased from 40 million to 800 million during the same period. Moreover, the number of residents of cities expanded from about 200 million to 3.5 billion. Until it became possible to use fossil fuels such as coal, oil, and natural gas for energy, human beings relied on their own muscles to do most work. Fossil fuels have led to rapid economic progress throughout the world, but have also created problems of smog, general pollution,

At the same time that Russia's economy was opening to the world, its political system seemed to be closing in on itself, with far-reaching economic consequences. In addressing the anarchy of the Yeltsin era (see Chapter 21), President Putin presided over a rebuilding of the central Russian state, which was widely welcomed in Russia. But the means Putin used to reassert central state power led, once again, to personal rule. The president forcibly repossessed the two principal television stations from billionaires and reassigned other valuable private properties, especially oil and gas companies, to the state, to be run by his former colleagues from the Soviet-era KGB. He also eliminated elections for regional executives and prohibited nongovernmental organizations from receiving foreign financing.

and the thinning of the ozone layer in the atmosphere that shields the earth from harmful radiation, as well as the critical problem of global warming.

Crutzen and Stoermer were optimistic in 2000 that world leaders would pay attention to the evidence, revealed by earth scientists, that human beings were upsetting the ecology and environment of the earth. Short of "an enormous volcanic eruption, an unexpected epidemic, a large scale nuclear war, an asteroid impact, a new ice age, or continued plundering of Earth's resources, [they expected] . . . mankind [to] remain a major geological force for many millennia, maybe millions of years to come." Yet, are earth scientists and well-informed political leaders and ruling elites nearly so sanguine these days?

EXPLORE FURTHER

Crutzen, Paul J., and Eugene F. Stoermer, "The 'Anthropocene,'" *IGBP Newsletter*, no. 41 (May 2000): 17–18.

McNeill, J. R., *Something New under the Sun: An Environmental History of the Twentieth Century* (2000).

McNeill, J. R., and Peter Engelke, "Into the Anthropocene: People and Their Planet," in Akira Iriye (ed.), *Global Interdependence: The World after 1945* (2014), pp. 365–533.

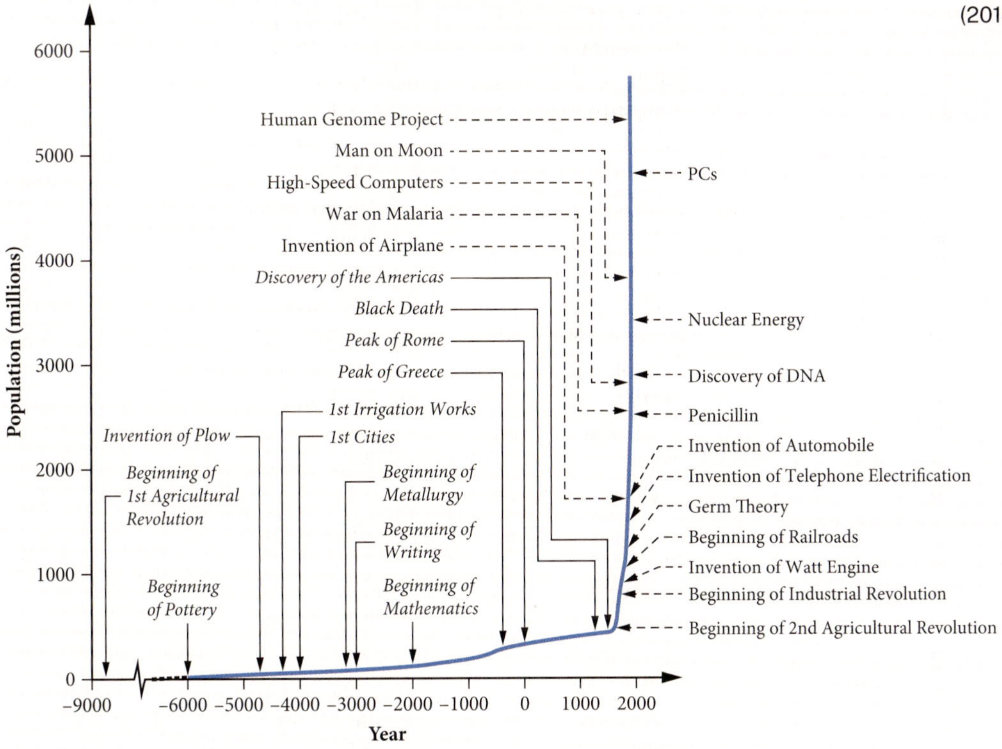

Population and Technology. This graph tracks the world's increasing population over time alongside major technological developments. Where one skyrockets, so does the other, suggesting a starting point for the Anthropocene.

Source: Figure 1 from "Catching up with the Economy," *American Economic Review* 89(1): 1–12. Copyright American Economic Association.

The result has been an authoritarian political system dominated by the executive; higher levels of corruption among runaway officials who are unchecked by the judiciary or press; economic stagnation; and a public sphere suffused with propaganda and outright lies.

The Gorbachev-Yeltsin era's promise of a real legislature, an independent judiciary, and an end to arbitrary rule gave way, in the yearning for order and stability, to aggressive nationalism and mass emigration. President Putin, after his reelection to a third (nonconsecutive) term in 2012, seized the Crimean Peninsula in a short war in 2014, much to the delight of large numbers of Russians. The annexation of Crimea came after a brief war with Georgia in 2008 that resulted in Russian recognition of two breakaway enclaves, Abkhazia and

Russian Invasion of Ukraine. A war-crimes prosecutor and a woman stand among the rubble after Russian aircraft launched thirteen missiles on the resort town of Zatoka early Tuesday, July 26, 2022, causing massive destruction.

North Ossetia, and it was followed by Russian promotion of a separatist war in the eastern Ukrainian territories bordering Russia. In addition, Russian-state-sponsored violence against Crimea's LGBTQ community was part of a wider campaign to rub out LGBTQ activism across the country. President Putin justified his actions by citing the expansion of NATO to Russia's borders and NATO's announcement that it was considering membership for Georgia and Ukraine. Russia also cited western involvement in the popular overthrow of the elected president of Ukraine, Viktor Yanukovych, who fled into exile in Russia.

Putin's aggression culminated in his full-scale invasion of Ukraine in early 2022. Bristling with resentment and claiming that Ukraine was a "made up nation" that really belonged to Russia, he sent columns of ill-prepared troops and tanks into Ukraine, bombarded cities, targeted schools, hospitals, and shopping malls to terrorize his neighbors. But the Ukrainian army fought back valiantly. With the support of NATO, and under the charismatic leadership of Volodymyr Zelenskyy, Ukrainian soldiers and citizens halted the Russian advance and began cataloguing the extent of Russian atrocities and war crimes until the two sides were bogged down in bloody see-saw battles over borderland villages. Meanwhile, both sides resorted to new means of twenty-first century wars, turning to economic sabotage, sanctions, and the use of drone warfare to send unmanned aircraft behind enemy lines. While some global leaders and more extreme conservative groups strongly committed to nationalism were supportive of Putin and the war, the general consensus in the West was that Zelenskyy's government needed and deserved aid.

China: Market Reforms and Shifting Foreign Policy

The Chinese have followed a path similar to that of the Russians, encouraging market economic reforms while quashing the possibilities for political liberalization. Their economic strategies seem to be successful. Over the last three decades, China's economy has maintained an average growth rate of over 9 percent annually, although it has shown signs of slowing down recently, with the rate dropping to under 7 percent in the years from 2015 to 2018. Some analysts have suggested that the Chinese government is reluctant to reveal the "real" rate, which might be even lower. Still, it remains true that consumer goods made in China dominate so many markets that it is virtually impossible, as several newspaper reporters have found, to supply an American family's needs on "China-free" products. Indeed, the Chinese economy has been the second largest in the world since late 2010, and some projections suggest that China might have the world's largest economy by midcentury, even though its per capita income will still lag behind that of the United States.

In many ways, China's fortunes illustrate both the promises and the pitfalls of the economic reforms undertaken by many developing countries in the era of globalization. On the one hand, despite the continued monopoly of political power by the Chinese Communist Party at home, China's entry into the World Trade Organization (WTO) in 2001 signified its full integration into the global capitalist economy. On the other hand, the reforms have caused political, social, and environmental problems that defy easy solutions. The disparity between

An Economic Boom in China. The opening of the Chinese economy in the 1980s made the country an export powerhouse. Today, computers, office machine parts, and electronics dominate China's export list. But at the outset, it was mainly textiles and low-tech assembly that powered the industrial boom. This photo was taken in 2007. Now female-dominated textile manufacturing has moved away from China to lower-wage producers, like Bangladesh.

the relatively prosperous coastal areas and the poor interior of the country—a problem that the communist government pledged to redress after it came to power in 1949—has once again become a glaring challenge.

While the Chinese government insists that the gap between the rich and the poor has been closing, albeit at a modest rate, a 2016 report from Peking University, a leading Chinese academic institution, found that 1 percent of Chinese households controlled a third of the country's assets, with the poorest 25 percent of households owning just 1 percent of the country's wealth. A 2015 survey found that there were more billionaires (in terms of U.S. dollars) in China (596) than in the United States (537). There are concerns, to be sure, both in China and worldwide, about the environmental impact of China's economic development. China's homes and factories, for instance, use 40 percent more coal than those in the United States, and Chinese city dwellers suffer from some of the world's worst smog and air quality. But as China's energy consumption and economy have soared, so has its global standing.

CHINA'S TRADE WAR WITH AMERICA The rise of China coincided with—and fueled—a disenchantment with globalization. Trade relations soon became the source of friction between partners. In the United States, traditionally the herald of multilateral free trade, the mood shifted dramatically. In his 2016 presidential campaign, Donald Trump excoriated American trade policies, claiming that they robbed Americans of jobs, created large trade deficits, and brought about large transfers of wealth to China and other countries. Upon coming to office, he immediately repudiated the Trans-Pacific Partnership (TPP) agreement, which had been signed on February 4, 2016, by countries with ports on the Pacific, though not the Chinese. During the campaign he also criticized the North American Free Trade Agreement (NAFTA), brought into effect on January 1, 1994, involving the United States, Canada, and Mexico. According to Trump, it was the worst American trade agreement ever negotiated, and he said that if he were elected president, he would either renounce it or renegotiate it. He did in fact renegotiate it in September 2018. The new treaty, known as the United States-Mexico-Canada Agreement (USMCA), provides for some improvements, like raising the percentage of automobile parts that must be made in North America and requiring that at least 40 percent of the parts in an automobile must be made by workers making at least $16 an hour (3 times the wage that current auto parts workers in Mexico make). While providing some beneficial updates to

Chinese Environmental Concerns. Despite its prosperity, Hong Kong, like other major Chinese cities, suffers from severe air pollution, which threatens its future as a hub of international commerce. This picture shows part of the city's waterfront shrouded in smog.

the now-twenty-five-year-old NAFTA treaty, these improvements did not fundamentally change the original agreement.

In reality, Trump's chief economic target was China and the massive trade imbalance with the Chinese, brought about because of the American appetite for Chinese goods and the unwillingness or inability of the Chinese to purchase American exports. The American trade deficit with China had ballooned from $10 billion dollars in 1990 to $419 billion in 2018, by which time it constituted more than half the American trade deficit of $621 billion. Trump believed that the trade deficit with China was caused by China's manipulation of its currency in order to make Chinese exports cheap. He also accused the Chinese of carrying out industrial espionage, stealing business and professional secrets.

Claiming that trade wars were easily won, Trump began his tariff war with China on March 22, 2018, by applying steep tariffs on $50 to $60 billion worth of Chinese goods. China retaliated by placing tariffs on 128 U.S. imports to China, notably aluminum, airplanes, cars, and soybeans. The tit-for-tat trade war escalated. Larry Kudlow, Trump's chief adviser, stated that tariffs on Chinese imports would have little effect on the pocketbooks of American consumers. Most economists disagreed, for that is not how tariffs usually work. Sure, the government will collect the tariff and increase its revenue, and to a very limited extent the exporters may reduce the cost of their products. But the main groups to be hurt will be American businesses and consumers, who will have to pay more for valuable Chinese imports or go without them. Independent financial surveys estimated that the new tariffs would cost American households an average of $200 a year on top of the $831 imposed by the already existing tariffs. In addition, these tariffs would affect low-income families more directly than the earlier tariffs, which were mainly imposed on industrial products. As the costs became clear, however, American negotiators began to carve out exceptions. On September 1, 2019, President Trump postponed his tariff implementation, citing pressure from business and consumer groups. He also removed a number of items from the list, notably those that consumers would likely purchase at Christmastime, such as shoes and electronic equipment. As the two trade partners squared off, the COVID-19 pandemic devastated global trade and put a hold on talks. President Biden inherited and largely continued the policy of stand-off negotiations with China, focusing not just on products but on intellectual property and technology transfers, especially the highly strategic area of chip manufactures. The two sides continued to exchange symbolic volleys and threats.

HONG KONG PROTESTS On July 1, 1997, the British ceded Hong Kong Island, Kowloon, and the New Territories to the People's Republic of China, effectively bringing an end to the British Empire. Hong Kong had been part of the British Empire for 156 years and had achieved a level of prosperity and personal freedom unknown on mainland China. The agreement between the British and Chinese governments, known as the "one country, two systems" accord, stipulated that the socialist system of the People's Republic would not be practiced in Hong Kong, where a capitalist way of life

The Umbrella Movement. Hong Kong became a hotbed of pro-democracy demonstrations in 2014 as protesters registered their anger at tightened control from Beijing. As officials toed the Chinese government line, the streets became the scenes for mass mobilization of what became called the Umbrella Movement. Umbrellas, especially yellow ones, became its symbol, as they were used to deflect the police's pepper spray and tear gas canisters.

would be maintained for fifty years. Further, the agreement stated that the chief executive of Hong Kong as well as the legislature would be selected by a committee composed of professional and business leaders until 2017, at which time both the chief executive and members of the legislature would be chosen by all of Hong Kong's citizens. Alas, the People's Republic of China has chipped away at these arrangements, and ultimately Hong Kong's chief executive, Carrie Lam, elected in 2017, brought before the Hong Kong legislature an extradition law that would allow the government of Hong Kong to extradite Hong Kong citizens for trial on the mainland. Thousands of Hong Kongers, perhaps as many as 1 million out of a total of a little more than 6 million, turned out in protest on the grounds that the law violated the spirit of the original accord. Although the chief executive has withdrawn the law from the legislature, she has not repudiated the law, leading to further protests and clashes with the police. However, as the COVID-19 pandemic spread, forcing Hong Kong dissidents off the streets, Beijing seized the opportunity to extend new national security laws to the city, curbing its autonomy and slashing its cherished civil liberties. The effect only inflamed relations. As one eighteen-year-old leader of the youth democracy movement proclaimed, "I am 100 percent Hong Kong, 0 percent China."

India: Economic Liberalization and Its Effects

India has registered impressive economic growth in the new millennium. Building on economic reforms initiated in 1991, the Indian economy became increasingly open to the global economy in the twenty-first century. Under Congress Party rule, the growth rate topped 9 percent annually between 2004 and 2009, declining to only 7 percent during the next five years when it was affected by the global economic downturn. As the state control over the economy loosened, over $20 billion in foreign investments poured in annually. The nation's information technology sector boomed, and India became a favorite destination for global corporations, attracted by its sizable English-speaking population. The state increased investments in infrastructure development, promoting public-private partnerships, to facilitate business development. Imports and exports grew, and agriculture registered an annual growth rate of over 2 percent each year. In some respects, India became a model of market-driven growth, an alternative to the state-dominated Chinese model. Its middle classes were booming and the wealthy lived more opulently than ever. But it was also unfair and fragile. When the COVID-19 pandemic hit, India's economy was sent reeling; many migrant workers and members of the middle class suddenly saw their precarious gains vanish.

India also experienced some social gains alongside economic ones. In 2005 Prince Manvendra Singh Gohil became the world's first openly gay royal, and in 2006 Nobel laureate Amartya Sen and other public figures urged the repeal of section 377 of the Indian penal code, due to its British-era provision that criminalized homosexuality. Another milestone arrived in 2008, when five Indian cities held LGBTQ pride parades for the first time. A decade later, in 2018, after many legal battles, India's Supreme Court decriminalized homosexuality in a victory for equality. Nonetheless, these gains need to be viewed side by side with rampant and violent homophobia, including numerous vigilante murders of gay, lesbian, and transgender people.

Unfortunately, the benefits of economic liberalization were experienced unequally. High inflation hit the income of the salaried class hard. The government initiated several welfare schemes of rural employment to cushion economic distress, but problems of inequality and poverty remained acute. In an effort to boost a capitalist economy, the government also declared an open season on land acquisition for real estate development, industrial parks, and mining, leading to the eviction of farmers and forest dwellers. The displaced people responded with armed insurgencies. Discontent mounted. High growth also created rising expectations and a drive for personal empowerment, and that stood at odds with the language of state patronage and welfare. Compounding the problem for the Congress government was that it became ensnared in a number of corruption scandals after 2012. A booming economy and new wealth had created opportunities for corrupt practices for which the government had failed to establish institutional controls. Riding on the widespread revulsion against corruption, the Bharatiya Janata Party (BJP), under Narendra Modi, swept the national elections and came to power in 2014, and again in 2019 with an even larger majority in parliament.

Internal Divisions, External Rivalries

Internal divisions and external rivalries have threatened to undo many benefits of economic globalization in India, China, and Russia. In India, for example, the BJP, while advocating the free market, also aggressively championed *Hindutva* ("Hinduness") as the bedrock of Indian identity. Nowhere were the effects of this twin strategy of economic liberalism and Hindu nationalism more visible than in the western state of Gujarat. Home to merchant communities for centuries, Gujarat has been in the forefront of capitalist manufactures and commerce. While aggressively participating in the global economy, the state has also been a fertile ground for Hindu nationalism.

Violence erupted in February 2002 after sixty Hindus perished in a fire that consumed a train compartment. Although

Violence and Oppression in Myanmar. Rohingya refugees shout slogans during a protest against the repatriation process at the Unchiprang refugee camp in Cox's Bazar in Bangladesh, November 15, 2018, after Bangladesh's prime minister Sheikh Hasina told a visiting U.N. official that hundreds of thousands of Rohingya refugees must go back to their ancestral home in Myanmar from crowded camps in neighboring Bangladesh.

the circumstances of the fire remain disputed, a rumor immediately spread, authenticated by the BJP government in Gujarat, then under Narendra Modi, that Muslims and a "foreign hand" were responsible. For the next few months, Hindu mobs went on a rampage, burning Muslim homes and hacking the residents to death. Newspapers reported that government leaders and the police force assisted in this carnage or looked the other way as over 2,000 Muslims lost their lives. In the provincial elections of December 2002, the BJP aggressively projected itself as a Hindu nationalist and pro-business party. This strategy paid rich dividends, and the BJP was reelected to power with a commanding majority. It repeated its impressive electoral feat once again in the 2012 elections and finally triumphed in the national elections two years later.

Hindu nationalists also took aim at Muslim-majority regions. Bolstered by his impressive win in the 2019 elections, Prime Minster Modi announced on August 8, 2019, that the part of Kashmir that was under Indian administration was being stripped of its autonomy. He claimed that his action would improve the lot of the poor and minorities and enhance the political and economic development of the region. But the action deprived 8 million Kashmiris of local self-rule, their own prime minister, and protections against non-Kashmiri Indians seeking to move to the province. Many of these limits on the authority of the Kashmiri administration had been lost over time. But making this situation formal was an affront to Muslims in India and India's Muslim neighbors. Modi's actions infuriated Pakistan and heightened tensions with Bangladesh, which was itself reeling from an influx of Muslim refugees coming from Myanmar, many of them spilling into India.

Indeed, Modi's ethno-nationalism was being echoed by neighbors like Myanmar. The democratically elected Aung San Suu Kyi turned a blind eye to ethnic cleansing in provinces like Rakhine, where Muslim populations were attacked and driven out by Buddhist nationalists. The army joined the effort until millions of Rohingya people were forced to flee to neighboring Bangladesh. Aung San Suu Kyi defended the actions—but only stoked military grievances until she herself was placed under house arrest and the generals took over, doubled down on the expulsion of minorities, and locked up domestic dissenters. The world's largest refugee camp, located in the town of Cox's Bazar in Bangladesh, became a makeshift home for nearly a million Rohingya people who were expelled from Myanmar.

The spiking tension with neighboring Pakistan was especially alarming due to the long conflictual history of the two countries. Flexing its nationalist muscle, the Indian government exploded a nuclear device in 1998. Pakistan responded by exploding its own bombs, casting an ominous shadow over the two nations' unresolved conflict over Kashmir. In that contested province, terrorist violence repeatedly disturbed the peace and brought the nuclear-armed neighbors close to a potentially devastating war. The tension between the two countries escalated in 2008 when a small band of terrorists from Pakistan carried out raids in Mumbai, slaughtering many civilians and security personnel before being subdued.

Right-Wing Hindu Nationalism. Not long after Indian independence in 1947, Hindu nationalists began to organize against the idea of a secular, multicultural state. They recruited young men and women and trained them in the arts of street and paramilitary violence. The Bharatiya Janata Party (BJP), a coalition of right-wing Hindu nationalists, has been in power since 2014. Street violence and persecution of minorities and pro-democracy activists have been on the rise ever since. *Left*: In 2002, Gujarat was consumed by sectarian riots, set off by a train fire in which sixty Hindu pilgrims died. Although an Indian government investigation concluded that the fire was accidental, the incident sparked an orgy of violence by Hindu mobs against Muslims. Shown here is an angry right-wing Hindu Party activist. *Right*: Members of the women's wing of a Hindu nationalist group perform a self-defense exercise.

Projecting recent trends into the future, many observers forecast a rearrangement of the world's economic order, with China and India especially moving to the fore during the twenty-first century. Yet China, India, and Russia, like other parts of the world, have not escaped from the past. These societies, too, struggle with widening internal divisions and potentially devastating external rivalries. (For a global look at hunger and disparities in income, see Maps 22.3 and 22.4.)

The Middle East, Africa, and Latin America

The Middle East: Radical Change or Continuity?

In the Middle East, radical changes brought about by the Arab Spring and the growth of Islamic militancy have taken place, while more than a few countries in Africa have begun to achieve economic progress and gained political stability through democratic elections.

THE ARAB SPRING The trigger for what became known as the Arab Spring occurred on December 17, 2010. A twenty-six-year-old Tunisian vegetable vendor, whose income helped support a large family, set himself on fire outside a provincial office to protest constant police harassment. This singular act aroused the entire population of Tunisia against the ruling elite. Not only had the police confiscated Mohamed Bouazizi's vegetable stand (and not for the first time), but a policewoman had slapped him in the face. In explaining his decision to take his life, his sister exclaimed, "In Sidi Bouzidi [where he resided] those with no connections and no money for bribes are humiliated and insulted and not allowed to live." As the story circulated through the country, large numbers poured out into the

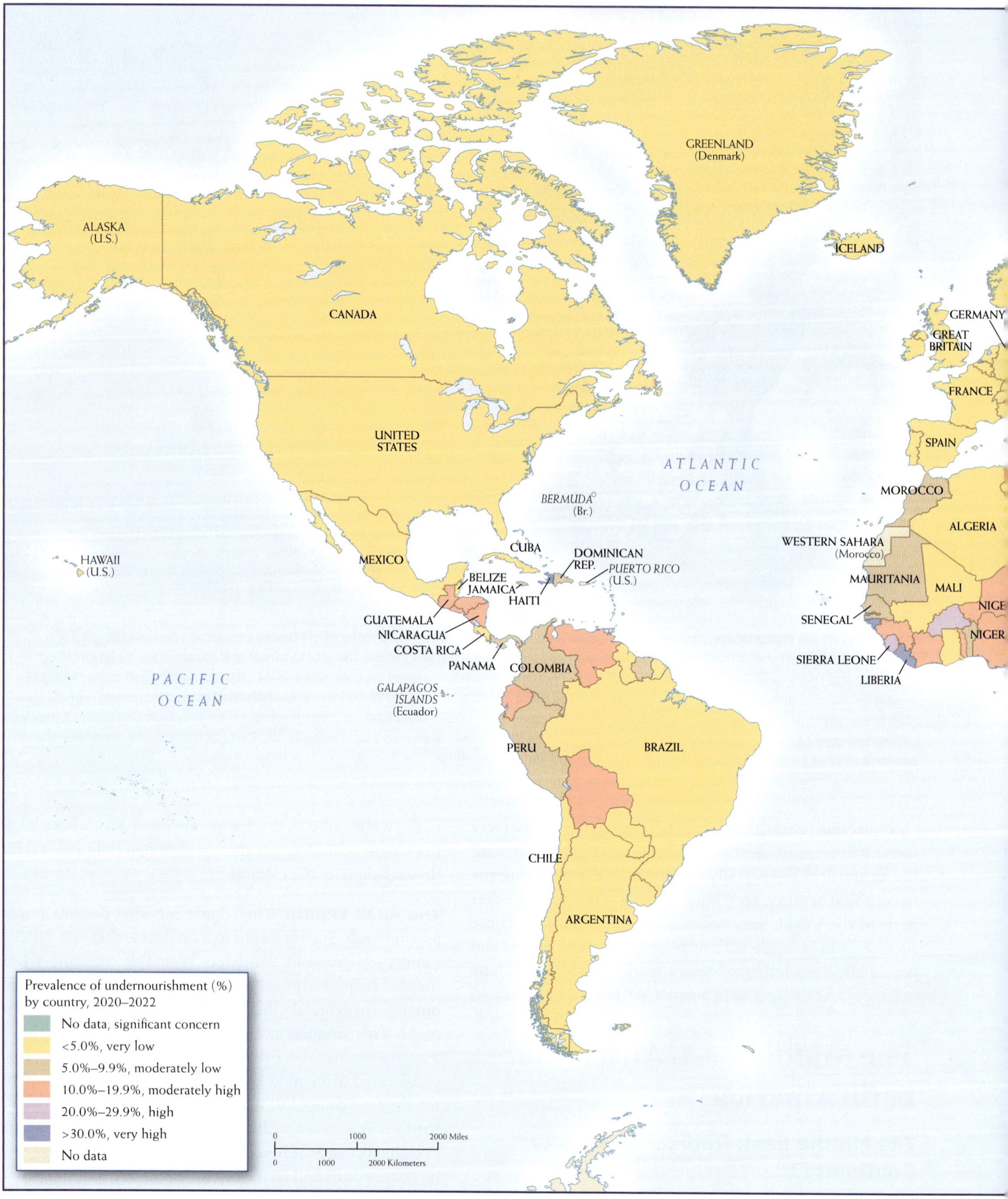
GREENLAND
(Denmark)
ICELAND
ALASKA
(U.S.)
CANADA
GERMANY
GREAT
BRITAIN
FRANCE
SPAIN
UNITED
STATES
ATLANTIC
OCEAN
MOROCCO
BERMUDA
(Br.)
ALGERIA
WESTERN SAHARA
(Morocco)
HAWAII
(U.S.)
MEXICO
CUBA
DOMINICAN
REP.
PUERTO RICO
(U.S.)
BELIZE
JAMAICA
HAITI
MAURITANIA
MALI
NIGER
NIGERIA
SENEGAL
GUATEMALA
NICARAGUA
COSTA RICA
PANAMA
COLOMBIA
SIERRA LEONE
LIBERIA
PACIFIC
OCEAN
GALAPAGOS
ISLANDS
(Ecuador)
PERU
BRAZIL
CHILE
ARGENTINA
Prevalence of undernourishment (%)
by country, 2020–2022
No data, significant concern
<5.0%, very low
5.0%–9.9%, moderately low
10.0%–19.9%, moderately high
20.0%–29.9%, high
>30.0%, very high
No data
0 1000 2000 Miles
0 1000 2000 Kilometers

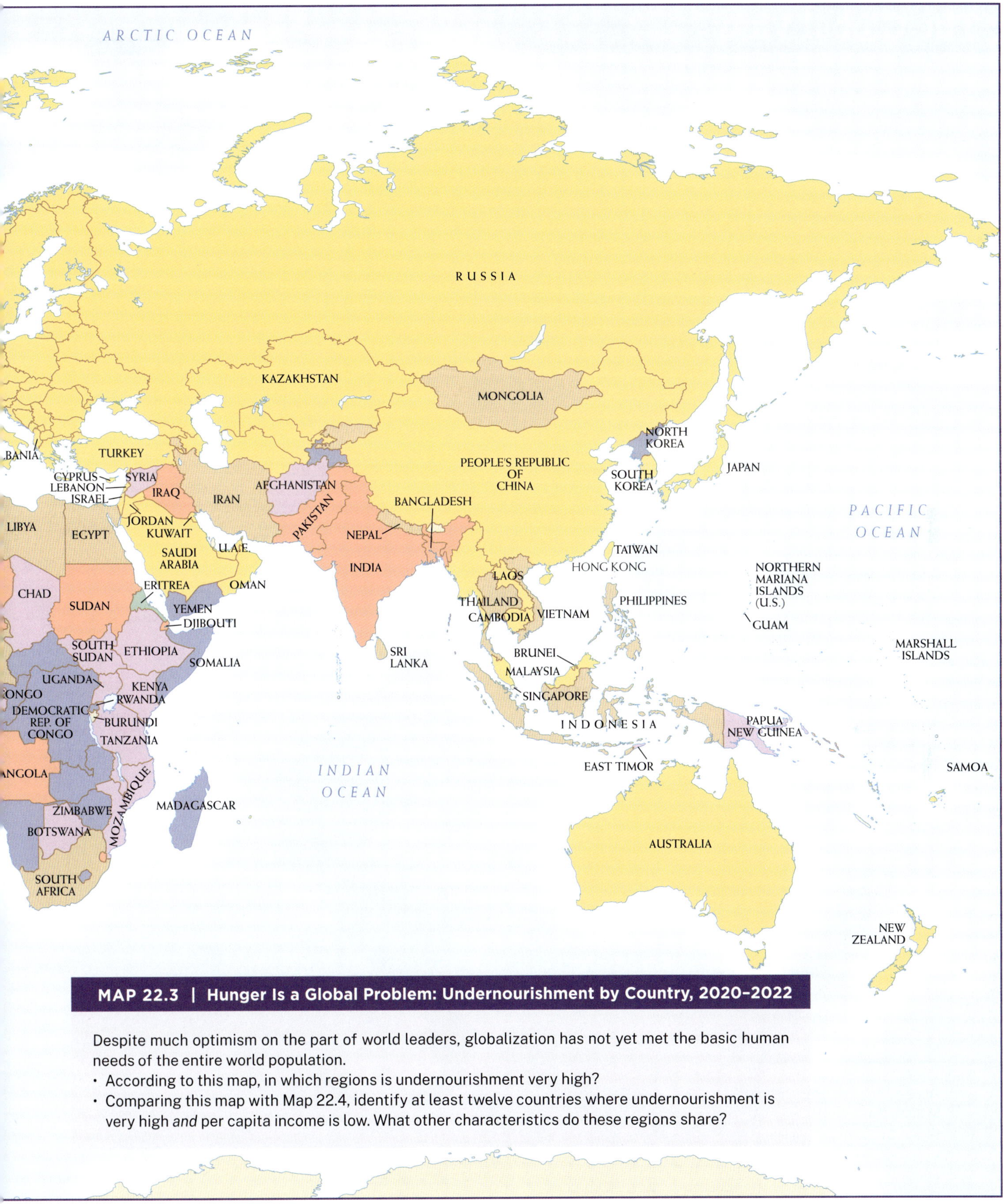

MAP 22.3 | Hunger Is a Global Problem: Undernourishment by Country, 2020–2022

Despite much optimism on the part of world leaders, globalization has not yet met the basic human needs of the entire world population.

- According to this map, in which regions is undernourishment very high?
- Comparing this map with Map 22.4, identify at least twelve countries where undernourishment is very high *and* per capita income is low. What other characteristics do these regions share?

The Global View

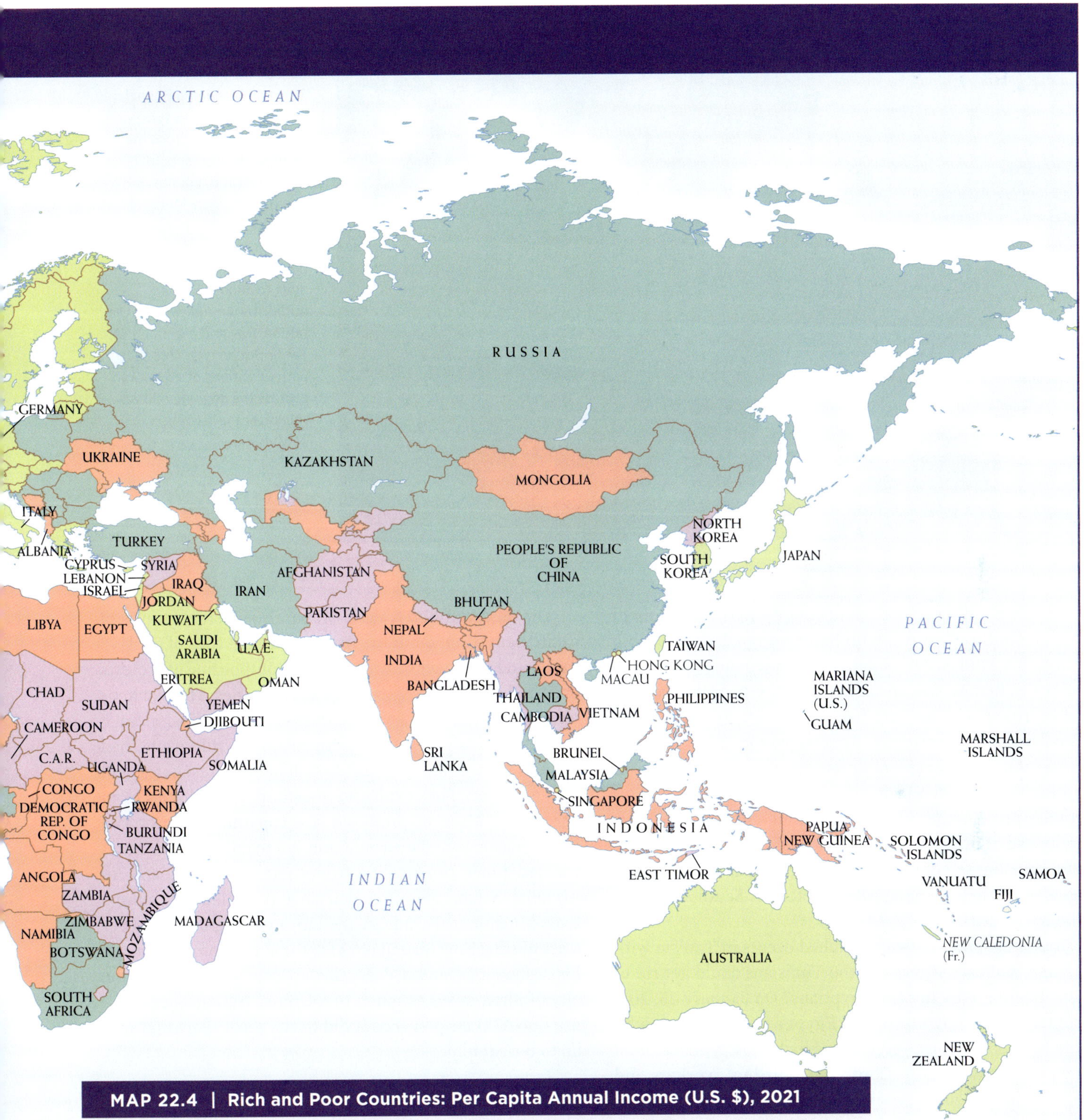

MAP 22.4 | Rich and Poor Countries: Per Capita Annual Income (U.S. $), 2021

Wealth and income derived from globalization have not been shared equally among the regions of the world, a problem which has been exacerbated by the ongoing COVID-19 pandemic since 2020.

- Using this map, identify the regions with the highest per capita income and those with the lowest. What factors do you think account for this disparity? What historical antecedents helped create this disparity?
- According to your reading, why have India and China, despite recent economic growth, failed to catch up with the United States, western European countries, and Japan in terms of per capita income?

Arab Spring. The deaths of Egyptian Khaled Said (left on the poster) and Tunisian Mohamed Bouazizi (right) provided martyrs for an upheaval across the Arab world and toppled undemocratic regimes, like that of Hosni Mubarak in Egypt in 2011. In this photograph, one demonstrator holds the martyrs' images aloft to denounce the authoritarian rule around the region. Day and night, Cairo's Tahrir Square was thronged with Egyptians of all ages to protest the ongoing military rule after the ousting of Mubarak.

streets, demanding an end to the long-term dictatorship of Zine al-Abidine Ben Ali, who had taken over from Habib Bourguiba, Tunisia's president from independence in 1956 until 1978. Ben Ali was an easy target for reproach. Not only had he ruled with an iron fist, but his second wife, Leila Trabelsi, was a notoriously corrupt person, a former hairdresser who lived in splendor and spent lavishly on herself and her prominent European and Arab guests. Ben Ali's promises to change his behavior convinced no one. The catchword of the protesters was *dégage*, "get out." With the army refusing to suppress the dissenters and the security police overwhelmed, Ben Ali departed for Saudi Arabia on January 14, 2011.

Young Egyptian radicals watched events in Tunisia with growing interest. After all, if the Tunisians could get rid of their dictator, why not the Egyptians? On January 25, 2011 (ironically a holiday to honor Egypt's police forces, who were by then an object of people's hatred), Egyptians of all backgrounds and ages—Copts and Muslims, workers and professionals, men and women—assembled in Cairo's major plaza, Midan al-Tahrir, or Liberation Square, to inform Egypt's president, Hosni Mubarak (in office since 1981), that he was no longer wanted. Their watchword, *irhal*, meaning "scram" in Arabic, expressed the protesters' utter contempt for him and his rule. On February 11, 2011, just three weeks after the first mass demonstration, Hosni Mubarak left office, turning the reins of power over to the Supreme Command of the Armed Forces, a small group of officers whom the president had chosen to lead Egypt's army.

The ouster of Ben Ali and Mubarak sent shock waves of excitement throughout the Arab world. Decades of pent-up rage could no longer be contained. An outpouring of protests occurred in all of the Arab world's major cities. The demands were consistent—the end of repression, the establishment of democratic institutions, and the ousting of rulers who had stayed in power too long and who did not represent the will of the people. The results were astonishing. Monarchs in Jordan and Morocco promised new constitutions; they said that going forward they would rule, not reign. Bahraini Shiites exacted a new constitution from their Sunni king, and Ali Abdullah Saleh, ruler of Yemen since 1978, fled the country. Even Muammar al-Qaddafi, the Libyan strongman, in power since ousting King Idris in 1969, felt the sting of protest, though his ouster and eventual execution on October 20, 2011, in the city of Sirte, owed as much to a United Nations–approved use of NATO air power as it did to the rebel army that rose up to unseat him.

CONTRIBUTING FACTORS Although much of the world had misunderstood the causes of these uprisings, they were not hard to discern after the fact. In the first place, Arab populations, 60 percent of whom were under thirty years of age and had known no other rulers, resented the fact that the wave of democratic reforms that had swept through Russia, much of eastern and central Europe, and large parts of sub-Saharan Africa had passed them by. They saw no reason why they, too, should not have leaders who represented their wishes rather than rigged elections and fraudulent referendums that supported the wishes of the ruling elites. The young came to be known as the generation in waiting—waiting for jobs that never seemed to appear; waiting to have enough money to move out of their parents' homes; and waiting to get married and start families. The fact that Hafez al-Assad of Syria had passed power to his son, Bashar al-Assad, and Hosni Mubarak of Egypt was grooming his son, Gamal, heightened the rage. Although the uprisings often took names that suggested peaceful protest—the Jasmine Revolution in Tunisia followed by the White Revolution in Egypt—in reality these outbursts reflected deep-seated and long-standing fury at rulers who were repressive, corrupt, and unresponsive to their people.

ARAB SPRING BECOMES AN ARAB WINTER The early results led euphoric protesters to believe that they could create new and more open societies. Dictators were ousted in Egypt, Tunisia, Libya, and Yemen; free elections were held; and new constitutions were promised. But the progress was hard to sustain. In Bahrain, where the king promised a more democratic constitution and appeared willing to make concessions to his Shiite subjects, violence in the capital persuaded the Saudi army to intervene and suppress the protest movement. Tunisia has accomplished more than the other states so far, owing to a strong civilian bureaucracy, high levels of education, and the strongest and most independent labor movement in the Arab world. It is, however, not out of the woods.

Egypt, too, held elections that were won by the Muslim Brotherhood party, Justice and Development, but nullified by the courts. It also elected a Muslim Brotherhood president, Mohamed Morsi. In an effort to be seen as a ruler of all the people, Morsi resigned from the Brotherhood. Yet he issued a decree granting himself powers beyond the reach of the Egyptian judiciary and failed to establish an inclusive government. He was ousted and put in prison by Egypt's military leader, General Abdel Fattah al-Sisi, who was commander in chief of the armed forces and minister of defense in the Morsi government. Once in power, Sisi dealt with the Muslim Brotherhood in a savage way, imprisoning at least 30,000, perhaps even 60,000, and massacring at least 1,000 Muslim Brotherhood protesters in Cairo on August 14, 2013. In early 2014, Sisi resigned from the military and ran for the presidency against a single opponent. While he won 96 percent of the vote, many eligible voters boycotted the election as a protest against the new government. On June 4, 2014, Sisi was sworn in as Egypt's sixth president. On April 23, 2019, he carried out a referendum that would allow him to remain as president until 2030, by which time he would be 75 years old.

By far, the most lethal outcome of the Arab Spring has occurred in Syria. Beginning on March 15, 2011, protesters demanded the ouster of President Bashar al-Assad, formed the Free Syrian Army, gained international recognition for their movement from the United States and European states, and led protests that resulted in violent confrontation with Assad's forces. Yet little has gone well for the opposition forces. Even while the Americans and many others considered Assad's days to be numbered, the Syrian president defied the protesters and western critics by gaining financial aid from Iran and crucial—indeed, regime-saving—military support from Hezbollah (a Shiite party established in Lebanon) and Russia. Assad's retaking of the rebel stronghold of Aleppo in January 2017 marked a significant military triumph for the Syrian president, driving the Free Syrian Army and its supporters into the governorates of Idlib and Hama in northwest Syria, near the border with Turkey, and calling into question whether the different groups battling the Assad regime could topple his government.

The turmoil of the Syrian civil war has produced catastrophic suffering. Eight years of war cost 500,000 lives, left over 1 million injured, displaced half the population, and reduced the economy to one-third the size it was at the outset of the conflict. In 2018, the United Nations High Commission for Refugees estimated that Syria had the largest number of the 70,800,000 worldwide refugees, returnees, internally displaced persons, and stateless persons. Indeed, more than half of the people in the refugee category came from Syria (5.5 million), Afghanistan (2.5 million), and South Sudan (2.3 million). Of the Syrian refugees, 600,000 found refuge in Germany. Assad won the war, but his country is in misery.

Nor have events gone as the protesters wanted in Yemen and in other countries like Libya. The ousting of President Ali Abdullah Saleh created a political and leadership vacuum, which a marginalized Shiite Houthi community in north Yemen attempted to fill. Houthi forces invaded the southwest and established a new government, but the Saudi regime intervened militarily against the Houthis. The civil war in that country rages on and has pushed 10 million people to the brink of famine and nearly a quarter million to catastrophic levels of food insecurity in a population of 29 million.

The Arab Spring began with such excitement and optimism, but nearly everywhere it has failed to deliver on its promises. The reasons for failure vary from country to country. In general, however, in Egypt, Syria, Saudi Arabia, and other Arab countries, like Morocco and Jordan, that retained their ruling elites, the regular militaries stayed in power and asserted their authority after the early protests. Nor did the original liberal leaders, almost all young people, create strong political parties or emerge as charismatic leaders. Sectarianism was also a factor, although it should not be overstated. In recent days, mainly young, liberal protesters in Iraq and Lebanon have demanded that the primarily Shiite government in Iraq and the multireligious elites step aside and allow less religious, more nationalist political elites to assume power.

ISIS Fighters. ISIS assembled a powerful group of soldiers, many from foreign countries (including the United States and European nations), and created a territorial state in western Syria and northern Iraq.

ISLAMIC MILITANCY As the old tyrants shook and states grew weak, one of the beneficiaries was Islamic movements. The militant movement was dominated by al-Qaeda in the 1990s, but changed significantly with the emergence of ISIS (the Islamic State in Iraq and Syria) in the early 2000s. As the Americans clipped the power of al-Qaeda, killing many of its important leaders, including Osama bin Laden, ISIS rose to take its place, becoming an even more formidable opponent of the United States and western influence in the Middle East. Islamic militancy has deep historical roots: its advocates look back with favor on early Muslim warriors who carried out their conquests inspired by the doctrine of jihad. In the twentieth century, some Muslim intellectuals urged Muslims to embrace this earlier form of jihad, promoting the use of violence to challenge the west and to create a powerful Islamic state. One of the most influential of these individuals was Sayyid Qutb, an Egyptian Muslim Brother who argued that the Quran sanctioned the use of force against corrupt and repressive Muslim rulers. In his influential book *Milestones*—written while Qutb was in prison, smuggled out, published in 1964, and circulated widely in Muslim societies—he argued that "the West has lost its vitality and Marxism has failed. At this crucial and bewildering juncture, the time of Islam and the Muslim community has arrived."

Al-Qaeda's agenda of challenging the west was based on the belief that the west, and especially the Americans, was the main force standing in the way of Islam's rise. Thus, the first order of business was to challenge American power: hence the attack on the Twin Towers and the Pentagon. The leaders of al-Qaeda (notably the Saudi Osama bin Laden and the Egyptian Ayman al-Zawahiri) came from elite families and believed that an Islamic state could emerge only after American power had been eroded. They were also extremely uncomfortable with the kinds of violence that more radical Islamists, like the founders of ISIS, urged upon their followers, such as beheadings and burning opponents of their state in prison cells. Their movement was explicitly transnational, always seeking to create branches in other Islamic countries. Nonetheless, al-Qaeda, lacking a state structure, required the protection of the Taliban in Afghanistan to form a base from which to organize its attacks on the west. Once al-Qaeda lost this protection, as it did when the Americans invaded Afghanistan in 2001, its leaders had to take refuge wherever they could. U.S. Navy SEALs killed Osama bin Laden in 2011 when he was hiding out, though really in plain sight, in Abbottabad, Pakistan. Zawahiri was killed by U.S. forces eleven years later in 2022.

Despite the apparent strength and sprawl of radical Islamic movements, it is worth noting that they have been deeply effective overall. The founder of the other major Islamic movement, ISIS, was Abu Musab al-Zarqawi, an unlikely leader. A heavy drinker, a brawler, and a high school dropout, little more than a thug, he found religion, in his case militant Islam, as his salvation and the purpose of his life. After being released from a Jordanian prison in 1992, al-Zarqawi made his way to Afghanistan to meet Osama bin Laden, whom he idolized. Although the leaders of al-Qaeda considered him too violent and hotheaded, nonetheless some high-ranking members of al-Qaeda accepted him into their ranks. The Americans chased al-Zarqawi out of Afghanistan, but eventually he made his way to Iraq, anticipating that the Americans would invade and that he could put his form of radical and militant Islam into action there.

What bolstered ISIS was the ham-fisted work of its enemy and the weakness of Middle Eastern states. The American invasion of Iraq, the failure of the Arab Spring in most Arab countries, the dismantling of the Iraqi army and civil bureaucracy, and the rise of Shiite dominance in Iraq catapulted al-Zarqawi's vision of a violent, jihadi world to prominence in Iraq. Here, his willingness to employ violence of a particularly repulsive nature earned him the nickname "the Sheikh of the Slaughterers." Although his hatred of the Americans was boundless, his rage against Iraqi Shiites was even more intense. In a country where the Sunni minority had exercised power for centuries, the dominance of Shiites in the new government of Nuri al-Maliki, a determined Shiite who refused to share power with any other group, enraged al-Zarqawi and his Sunni followers.

Al-Zarqawi's rise to prominence proved short-lived, however. American troops tracked him to a safe house just outside Baghdad and killed him on June 7, 2006. With his death, al-Qaeda in Iraq went into steep decline. The next two leaders were incompetent individuals, prompting Michael Hayden, director of the CIA, to consider al-Qaeda in Iraq to be moribund. President Obama went even further, claiming that al-Qaeda in Iraq was "amateurish" and likening it to "a junior varsity team that puts on Lakers uniforms," but adding "that doesn't make them Kobe Bryant" (Gerges, p. 2).

The American president and the director of the CIA underestimated the capabilities of al-Qaeda in Iraq to resurrect itself. Al-Qaeda had splintered into several new groups, and the most prominent was ISIS. The new leader of ISIS, Abu Bakr al-Baghdadi, was as unlikely a man to rally the organization as al-Zarqawi was to be its founder. Baghdadi had neither military nor bureaucratic experience when he assumed leadership of ISIS in May 2010. He was an Islamic scholar who had trained in some of the minor Iraqi Muslim schools and had eventually gained his doctorate by writing an exegesis of the Quran. Like so many of the members of ISIS, he had been imprisoned by the American military in Camp Bucca in Iraq, which was called "the Qaeda School" because strong anti-American and anti-Shiite discussions took place among the inmates. But he had something that the parent organization, al-Qaeda, lacked: a territorial state, based originally in northern and central Iraq, that became even more formidable following the departure of American forces from the country. Drawing on Iraqi Baathist bureaucrats dismissed by the Americans and discharged Iraqi army officers, his state surrounded itself with experienced military officers and bureaucrats. After moving into war-torn Syria and conquering Mosul in northern Iraq in 2014, ISIS also took the name the Islamic Caliphate, and Baghdadi announced to the world that he was the new Islamic State's first caliph.

TABLE 22.1 | Population of Shiite Muslims, 2009

	ESTIMATED 2009 SHIITE POPULATION	APPROXIMATE PERCENTAGE OF MUSLIM POPULATION THAT IS SHIITE
Iran	66–70 million	90–95
Iraq	19–22 million	65–70
Yemen	8–10 million	35–40
Azerbaijan	5–7 million	65–75
Syria	3–4 million	15–20
Lebanon	1–2 million	45–55
Kuwait	500,000–700,000	20–25
Bahrain	400,000–500,000	65–75
World total	154–200 million	10–13

Source: *"Mapping the Global Muslim Population," Pew Research Center, October 7, 2009.*

The conquest of Mosul meant that ISIS controlled territories in central Syria and northern Iraq were as large as those constituting the United Kingdom. It also had a population of between 6 and 9 million; an army of 30,000; a capital city, Raqqa, in Syria; and large financial resources, amassed through oil revenues, looting, and taxes. (For a look at the territory held by the Islamic State and the population of Shiite Muslims in the Middle East, see Map 22.5 and Table 22.1.) In addition, ISIS benefited from intellectuals who promoted Baghdadi's vision of a territorial state that they believed would capture the imagination of Muslims around the world. One of the most widely read individuals of this group was Abu Bakr Naji, whose manifesto, *The Management of Savagery*, appeared on the Internet in 2004. In it, Naji contended that "it is naught but violence, crudeness, terrorism, frightening others, and massacres" that will strike fear in enemies and rally supporters and near-supporters to ISIS's causes.

By 2017, ISIS was losing its strongholds in Iraq and Syria. First to fall was the city of Mosul, the biggest and largest ISIS city in its caliphate. Compelled to retreat to its Syrian capital, Raqqa, it was finally dislodged there in 2019, overrun by anti-ISIS forces led by a well-disciplined and well-armed Kurdish force. On October 26–27, 2019, Baghdadi killed himself by detonating a suicide vest as he was about to be seized by an American military unit. Nonetheless, although ISIS is no longer a state, its appeal, like that of al-Qaeda, remains potent. Not only does it have deep roots in the writings of many earlier, and now modern, Muslim theoreticians, but it continues to

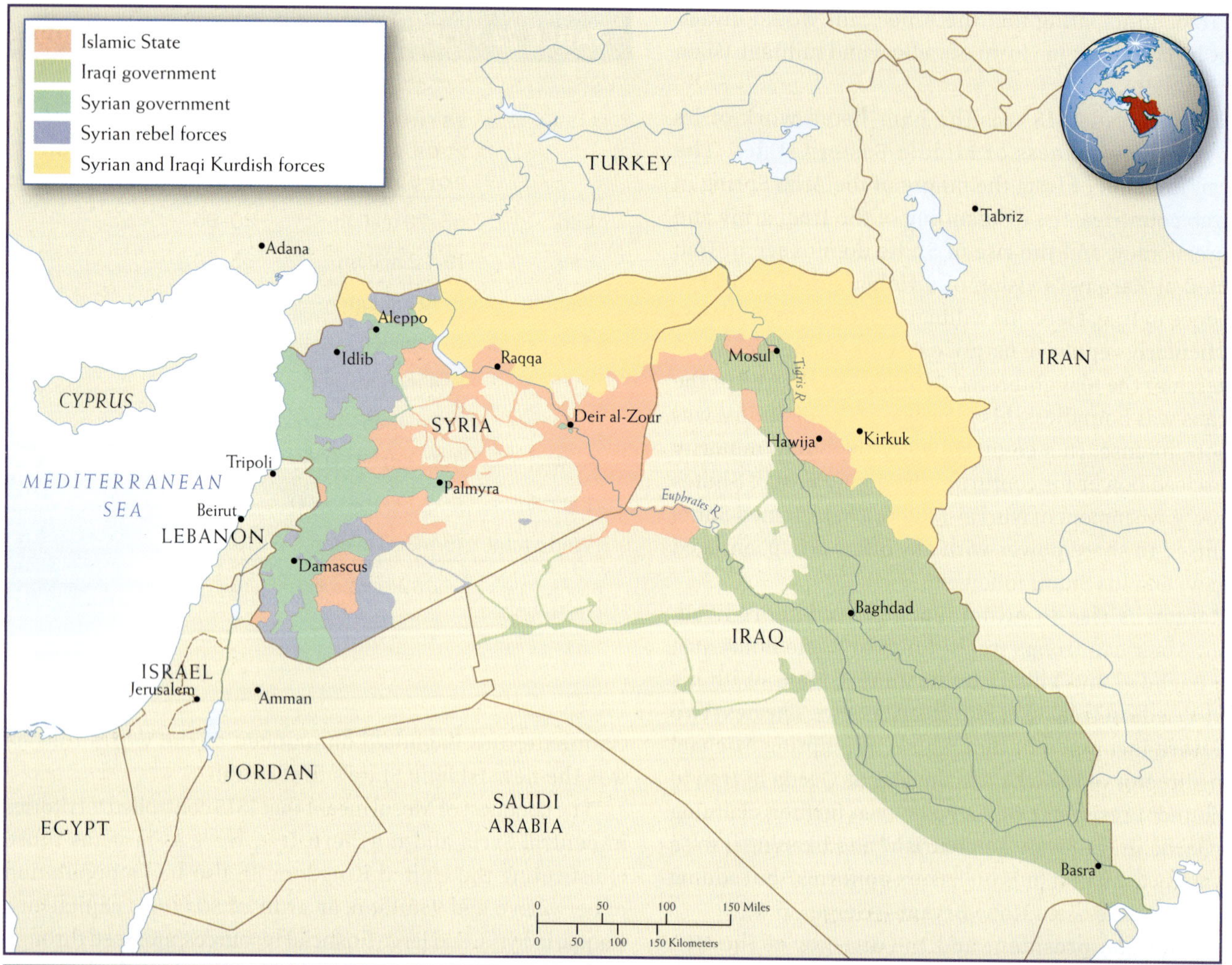

MAP 22.5 | Warring Factions in Iraq and Syria, March 27, 2017

This map shows the territories held by Kurdish fighters, ISIS, rebel Syrian fighters, and the Iraqi and Syrian governments.

- Compare the territories held by ISIS with the map of the boundaries set by the Sykes-Picot agreement (see Map 19.4). How similar are the territories that ISIS held in March 2017 to those that Sykes-Picot reserved for an Arab confederation?
- ISIS contends that the British-French agreements for the division of the Arab world after World War I need to be abolished. Why does ISIS hold these views?
- Why would the Turkish, Iraqi, and Syrian governments be dismayed that the Kurds have become the strongest militia fighting against ISIS?

appeal to marginalized Muslim groups around the world. It will be a force to be reckoned with for years.

THE IRANIAN NUCLEAR DEAL In mid-June 2015, Iran and the United States, Russia, China, Britain, France, Germany, and the European Union reached an agreement on an issue that had troubled Iran's relations with the outside world for more than a decade and that had resulted in the imposition of severe economic sanctions on Iran. The agreement dealt with Iran's nuclear program, which the Iranians claimed was entirely for civil use, but the United States and many other countries believed was to create nuclear weapon capability. The 2013 elections in Iran placed the government in the hands of moderate politicians, many of whom, like President Hassan Rouhani, believed that the sanctions placed on Iran by the west were undermining the country's standard of living and turning the state into an international pariah. The U.S. government, led by Secretary of State John Kerry, took full advantage of the situation and, along with five other states, negotiated a nuclear agreement that was to run for ten years and would allow inspections of the Iranian nuclear facilities while permitting the Iranians to enrich uranium for civil but not military uses. The negotiating foreign powers agreed to lift the financial and economic sanctions, thus permitting Iran to engage in trade with the rest of the world and to gain access to its substantial financial resources, which were tied up in western banks.

In keeping with his aversion to treaties and constraints, on May 6, 2018, President Donald Trump pulled out of the Iranian nuclear deal. While some countries in the Middle East endorsed Trump's action, including Israel, Saudi Arabia, Egypt, and the United Arab Emirates, the other signatories of the Iranian nuclear deal did not. They worried about a lethal arms race in the Persian Gulf. European governments struggled to shore up the deal, to little avail. In response, Iran breached significant parts of the agreement, exceeding a critical limit on how much fuel it could possess and enriching uranium beyond the purity it had agreed to. Iranian-American tensions reached a boiling point, coming close to outright war, in July 2019 when the Iranians shot down an American drone over the Persian Gulf. Only minutes after accepting the advice of Secretary of State Mike Pompeo and National Security Adviser John Bolton to send missiles against a series of Iranian missile sites, Trump changed his mind. Biden inherited the cauldron while trying to keep the United States out of sticky commitments. Ironically, it was the growing American-led campaign to shore up world democracies that pushed the old rivals of Iran and Saudi Arabia into the same camp; they disagreed with each other on basic matters of faith and their rival client regimes fighting across the Middle East. But they were increasingly agreeable to safeguarding their autocracies by allying against Washington.

THE FUTURE OF ISRAEL As in much of the rest of the world, where politicians favored national sovereignty over global laws and norms, a hard-line government took hold in Israel. Though it represented an unstable coalition of extremist and nationalist parties, its cunning leader and the country's longest-serving prime minister, Benjamin Netanyahu, has managed to survive and tilt the political spectrum ever further to anti-Palestinian positions. Despite corruption scandals, he has managed to win elections and cling to power—now through an unstable emergency alliance with his rivals. By 2023, however, his brand of nationalism and populism was growing increasingly autocratic. Millions of Israelis took to the streets across the spring and summer of 2023 to protest Netanyahu's plan to reduce the control of the Supreme Court over the national government.

Africa: Poverty, Disease, Genocide, and Progress

Globalization lifted many out of poverty, especially in China and elsewhere in East and Southeast Asia. But it also spread the benefits unfairly. So, while poverty decreased on the whole, inequality increased—and became more concentrated in specific regions. The result: in much of the developing world, poverty, disease, and violence persist. The new millennium did not begin auspiciously for the peoples of Africa. The region remained the poorest in the world and suffered the uncontrolled and uncontrollable spread of HIV/AIDS. Of the thirty-eight sub-Saharan African countries surveyed in the *World Bank Development Report* for 2009, all but seven were low-income countries. The poorest of the poor (Burundi, the Republic of the Congo, and Liberia) reported per capita incomes of $150 or less. Botswana, which enjoyed the second-highest per capita income level at $6,120 (behind only mineral-rich Gabon), was so devastated by HIV/AIDS that life expectancy, once the highest in Africa at close to seventy years, had tumbled to fifty-one years in 2007 and was one of the lowest in the world. (For a global look at HIV/AIDS incidence, see Map 22.6.)

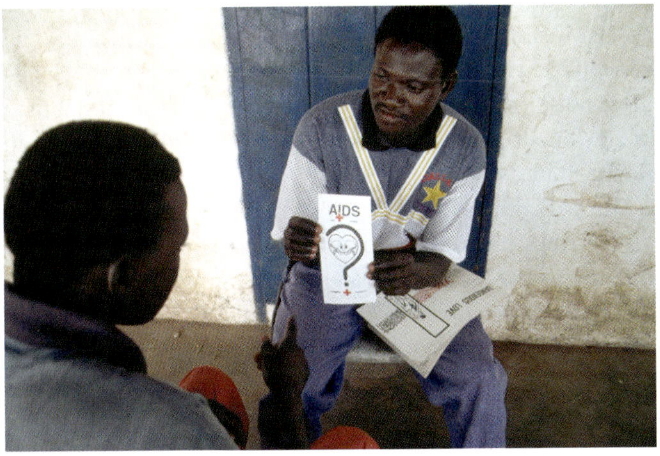

HIV/AIDS Awareness. *Left*: A Gambian health worker offers HIV/AIDS awareness literature. *Right*: Due, in part, to the high cost of medicines, HIV/AIDS has taken a deadly toll on Africans, prompting this memorial in the Netherlands on December 1 (which has been designated World AIDS Day), 2009. The crosses represented the millions of Africans unable to gain access to HIV/AIDS medications.

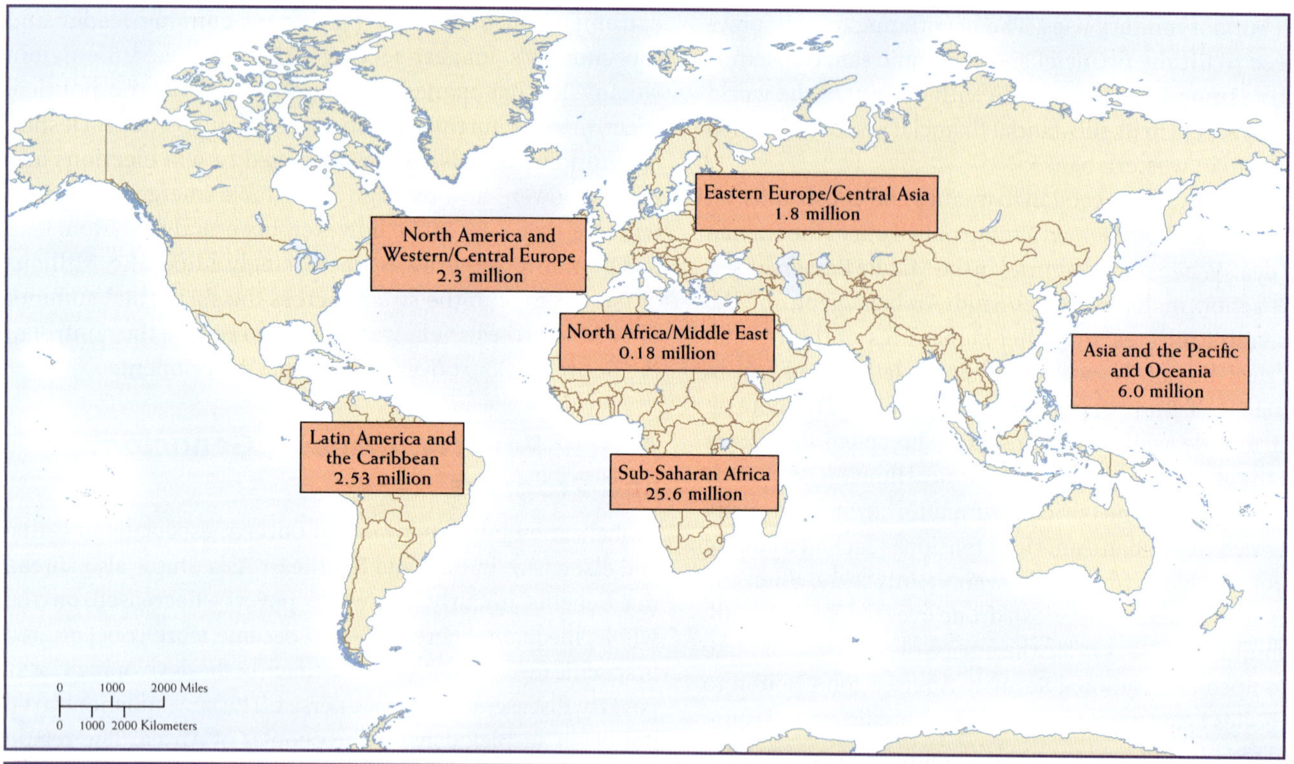

MAP 22.6 | Numbers of HIV-Positive People Worldwide, 2021

The spread of HIV/AIDS threatens the development of human capital in the twenty-first century.

- According to this map, which region has the highest rate of HIV infection?
- Using Maps 22.3 and 22.4 for reference, what connections do you see between poverty and HIV/AIDS prevalence?
- How does the spread of HIV/AIDS compromise economic development in poorer regions of the world?

There are nonetheless promising signs of political and economic progress. Ghana embraced parliamentary and presidential elections. Civil strife ended in Mozambique and Angola. South Africa convened a Truth and Reconciliation Commission to put the trauma of apartheid behind it and to stay on the course of parliamentary democracy while addressing the gross disparities of income between Whites and Blacks that were legacies of the twentieth century. Rwanda has made a spectacular comeback from the genocide of 2008 to achieve high levels of economic growth and educational achievement. In Kenya, Nigeria, South Africa, and many other African countries, in spite of glaring income inequalities, an emerging middle class has taken shape. In late 2016, Gambian voters elected a new president, sending the man who had been the country's dictator for more than two decades into exile.

Elsewhere, however, political instability wrought misery and devastation. Many of West Africa's countries (Liberia, Sierra Leone, Mali, the Ivory Coast, and the Central African Republic) were torn asunder because of ethnic and personal rivalries and required foreign intervention. Nigeria finally rid itself of unwanted military dictatorial control and moved to a civil, parliamentary system. But Nigeria's democratically elected presidents have barely been able to hold the country together. The peoples of the Niger delta in the south continue to rebel and demand a larger share of the oil wealth that is produced in their region, while in the impoverished northeast a Muslim group calling itself Boko Haram (meaning "no western learning") has carried out shocking violence. The most notorious of Boko Haram's actions was the kidnapping of 276 female students from a secondary school in Chibok in Borno State, Nigeria.

In 2011, just when Africa's longest-running civil war, pitting the animist and Christian southern Sudanese against the northern Muslim peoples, had seemingly been resolved through the creation of a new state carved out of Sudan and known as South Sudan, an ongoing dispute in western Sudan kept the Sudanese government in civil strife. In the region of Darfur, the state allowed local horse-riding, nomadic tribesmen to carry out ethnic-cleansing campaigns against settled agriculturalists. Thus, as in Rwanda in the 1990s (see Chapter 21), genocide has once more visited Africa. The conflict in Darfur has also led to one of Africa's worst cases

Secondary School Girls Kidnapped by Boko Haram. On the night of April 14, 2014, Boko Haram descended on a secondary school in northeastern Nigeria and kidnapped 276 girls, 98 of whom remain in captivity.

Liberia's President. Ellen Johnson Sirleaf after her inauguration at the Capitol Building in Monrovia on January 16, 2006. Johnson Sirleaf was Africa's first elected woman president; she enjoyed strong U.S. support and worked to fight graft and rebuild her country after years of war.

of displacement: as of 2021 over 4 million refugees had fled government terror and civil war to huddle in vast, miserable camps. But there is some reason for hope. In the West African country of Liberia, after years of pitiless civil war, the belligerents agreed to put down their guns in 2004. In 2005, remarkable elections swept Africa's first woman president, Ellen Johnson Sirleaf, into office.

Latin America: Deepening Inequalities

Globalization has contributed to economic inequality in some of the poorest parts of the world. In some cases, it worsened domestic chasms. Compared with sub-Saharan Africa, Latin America's situation is not so bleak. But within the region and countries, the divide between haves and have-nots has widened what has historically been the world's most unequal region. The very rich in Buenos Aires live like the very rich in Paris; magnates of Mexico City drive the same cars, eat the same food, read the same books, and vacation in the same spots as their social cousins from New York. They send their children to private schools in the United States and the United Kingdom to join a cosmopolitan elite. To Latin American elites, globalization has been a boon to their wealth and has facilitated integration into the international circulation of goods, ideas, and people. Many, in fact, identify less and less with a particular place in the world.

Some of the same features hold for the social bottom. Being disadvantaged and poor in southern Mexico looks a lot like being on the losing end in southern Africa: people cling to tiny parcels of land, migrate long distances for seasonal jobs, and fight against insensitive authorities for their basic needs. Globalization has offered few opportunities to make it at home. Old factories closed in Rosario, Argentina, when faced with competition from Japan; maize farmers in Mexico must contend with imports from Iowa. In many cases, thanks to globalization, the main solution to the problem has been to leave—to move to the city or across borders in search of opportunities elsewhere.

Latin Americans responded to these challenges in many ways. One sweeping trend was for voters to elect left-wing governments. In Brazil, Chile, Argentina, and Uruguay, left-wing governments offered policies to soften the blows of globalization and meet basic needs for land, schools, and decent housing. Yet, the same pressures of globalization that contributed to leftist electoral triumphs limit what these fledgling governments could do. In Venezuela, Ecuador, and Bolivia, a more nationalist and populist brand of politics has emerged, one that decried globalization altogether. The presidents of these countries promised to reverse the bad effects of globalization; they criticized imperialism and challenged American influence. Some turned more autocratic. The Nicaraguan government of Daniel Ortega, for instance, muzzled domestic dissent, gave favors to insiders, and criticized Washington. Other left-wing regimes hung on, often with calamitous results for the country. In Venezuela, a once-wealthy country that is now racked with a 44-percent unemployment rate, a "revolutionary" government has dragged the society into mass poverty and polarization. Up to 6 million people, 20 percent of the population, have

The Amazon Ablaze. Fire is a common method for clearing the Amazon forest. After Jair Bolsonaro was elected president of Brazil in 2018, loggers and land speculators began to torch thousands of acres of woodland. Satellites caught images of the alarming spread. This photo, taken in August 2019, is just one snapshot of the more than 900,000 hectares that were destroyed that year.

fled, creating a refugee crisis in neighboring Colombia and Brazil. (See Interpreting Visual Evidence: Global Inequality and the Refugee Crisis.) Others had a softer touch. The progressive president of Mexico, Andrés Manuel López Obrador (known commonly as AMLO), deftly avoided inflammatory relations with his mercurial neighbor Donald Trump while subtly undermining press and academic freedoms.

But the left-wing turn boomeranged. Parts of Latin America followed the Indian, Russian, and American tilt to nativist, right-wing politics. This was most dramatic in Brazil, where the Workers' Party lost elections in 2018, bringing the nativist firebrand Jair Bolsonaro to power on a wave of racism and sexist sloganeering. Like other populists, he stoked resentments against minorities and women and blamed outside forces for the country's woes.

Few paid a higher price than the indigenous people of the Amazon. Their forests had been under assault from ranchers and land speculators for years. Bolsonaro removed all restraints against an extractive invasion. Twenty thousand gold miners swarmed into Yanomami territory alone. In his first three years, Bolsonaro let 34,000 square kilometers burn (8.4 million acres), an area larger than Belgium. The mass destruction of their homelands invigorated Indigenous resistance and appeals for international pressures on Bolsonaro. They threw their weight behind the Workers' Party leader, known simply as Lula, and tilted a narrowly decided election against Bolsonaro in 2022. Lula, in turn, promised to reverse the deforestation. He named prominent Indigenous leaders

São Paulo, Brazil. An aerial view of one of São Paulo's biggest slums, Favela Morumbi; it borders one of the city's richest neighborhoods, which is also called Morumbi. Haves and have-nots live cheek by jowl, creating intimate frictions within cities and neighborhoods.

Anti-globalization. Anti-globalists target annual summits of the leaders of the eight most-industrialized countries. This photo shows riot police driving back protesters during the June 2007 summit in Germany. Notice the New York Yankees baseball cap on one of the protesters.

Prime Minister Modi, of India, Meeting with President Erdogan, of Turkey. President Recep Tayyip Erdogan (right), of Turkey, met with Prime Minister Shri Narendra Modi, of India, on November 16, 2015. Both men have used religion to enhance their popularity and the parties that they head, Erdogan fostering Islamism, and Modi Hinduism.

Marina Silva and Sônia Guajajara to important positions of power in Brazil; Silva became head of the Ministry of Environment and Climate Change and Guajajara was tasked to lead the Ministry for Indigenous Peoples.

A Global Trend Toward Populist Politics and Authoritarian Regimes

As globalization gave way to disenchantment, populist politics flourished in the second decade of the twenty-first century. Stoked by the financial crisis of 2008, which marginalized large segments of the world's population and heightened awareness of gross wealth inequalities and political powerlessness, populists blamed migrants, free-traders, and cosmopolitan urbanites for breaking up their nations and exposing them to the vagaries of world markets. Voters gravitated to leaders whose messages were directed to "the people" and against illegitimate "others"; elite populist politicians portrayed immigrants and ethnic and religious minorities as enemies of the people. Successful efforts to rescue the big banks and biggest investors of the global financial system, many of which had caused the crisis while ordinary people largely became its victims, led to widespread anger that was initially ignored—until political entrepreneurs perceived an opportunity.

Populism took many forms. In some countries, it was highly autocratic. In democracies like Britain, continental Europe, and the United States, it led to the rise of ethnic nationalists and the election or emergence of strong right-wing parties. In Britain, it fueled the winning vote to leave the European Union and ultimately led to the prime ministership of Boris Johnson, a hard-line Brexit advocate.

Populism pits national sentiment against internationalism in a zero-sum fashion. Populism is also often a politics less of opportunity but of resentment and grievance, division and polarization. However real the anger and the injustices, populism's ability to deliver for its angry constituents is seldom as strong as its ability to mobilize them.

A strong example of the growth of populism occurred in India, where Prime Minister Narendra Modi rose to become that nation's strongman, claiming to embody the interests of the nation. With opposition parties dispirited and weak, he skillfully used social media to portray himself as a leader working tirelessly to advance India's interests against its foreign and domestic enemies. Taking a cue from their leader's aggressive nationalism, BJP politicians and Hindu vigilante groups targeted minorities, particularly Muslims. Critics of the government's policies toward Muslims and Dalits were tarred as anti-national. In November 2016, Modi's government demonetized high-currency notes, claiming the policy to be a measure directed against unaccounted wealth, the underground economy, and counterfeit money. This move shocked the financial system and caused grave distress to the significant sector of the economy that is based on cash transactions. However, Modi successfully framed demonetization as a nationalist act; those opposed to it were labeled as anti-national and pro–"black money." Claiming to be the *chowkidar*, the watchman, for India, Modi won a stunning landslide victory for his BJP party in 2019 and gave Hindu nationalists their largest majority in modern India.

The pendulum, however, has shown signs of swinging back against the populist politicians. For example, Donald Trump's policies energized the Democratic Party, failed to benefit his nonprivileged supporters, and led to the loss of the Republican majority in the House of Representatives in the 2018 election. When he went down to defeat in 2020, he openly embraced anti-constitutional ways to cling to power, inciting a shocking riot on January 6, 2021, purportedly to prevent Biden from being sworn in. And in Turkey, Prime Minister Recep Tayyip Erdogan's chosen candidate for mayor of Istanbul suffered a crushing defeat in the June 2019 election that revealed opposition not only to Erdogan's Justice and Development Party but also to Erdogan himself. Finally, Boris Johnson, in one of his first acts as prime minister of the United Kingdom, visited Scotland, Wales, and Northern Ireland and was roundly booed. Scottish nationalists, wishing to stay in the European Union, have wondered if they should secede from the United Kingdom, and many Northern Irelanders have revived their long-standing desire to join the Republic of Ireland. Even the people of Wales, which had voted for Brexit, worried about a no-deal exit from the European Union and expressed their displeasure to Johnson.

STATE VIOLENCE AND THE STRUGGLES FOR RACIAL JUSTICE AND INDIGENOUS AND LGBTQ RIGHTS If the shocks to globalization revealed underlying injustices and the unequal effects of climate change and public health threats, the spotlight also turned to the ways in which states openly discriminated and harassed some of their own citizens, while drawing ever-harder lines in excluding noncitizens. Consider the role of police violence. In France, Britain, Turkey, and the United States—not to mention countries with even more repressive regimes like Syria and Hong Kong—policing became synonymous with a defense of privileged sectors and racial hierarchies.

One significant human rights development during this tumultuous period was the passage in 2007 of the United Nations Declaration on the Rights of Indigenous Peoples. The declaration calls for promotion and protection of Indigenous culture, Indigenous participation in all key decisions that will affect their lives, confirms Indigenous right to self-determination and recognizes subsistence rights, rights to land, territories, and resources, recognizes their right to fair redress, and outlaws discrimination against Indigenous peoples. While the declaration is non-binding, it has since been ratified by 148 countries, and sets a global standard for the treatment of Indigenous peoples that activists worldwide can draw on to promote Indigenous rights.

Violence also escalated as police and military forces were summoned to uphold what were seen—especially by racialized minorities—as environmental injustices. In the United States, the struggle over police violence and repression flared up in the wake of the Great Recession of 2008. Across the American West, Indigenous peoples intensified their political and legal mobilizations to improve their economic position (numerous sovereign peoples embraced the building of casinos on their reservations, which have generated over $22 billion in revenue since their inception in the 1980s, although only parts of the monies have been re-invested in the reservations), promote the learning of their ancestral languages, and defend their land and water rights. Their sovereignty and environmental struggles peaked in a

Indigenous Protests against the Gas Pipelines in North Dakota. Defiant Dakota Access Pipeline water protectors at the Oceti Sakowin camp on the edge of the Standing Rock Sioux Reservation faced off with various law enforcement agencies on the day the camp was slated to be raided. Many protesters and independent journalists, who were all threatened with multiple felony charges if they didn't leave, were met with militarized police on the road abutting the camp. At least six were arrested, including a journalist who reportedly had sustained a broken hip.

Black Lives Matter in 2020. On May 25, 2020, a Black civilian named George Floyd was choked to death by a White police officer in front of onlookers who pleaded to let Floyd live. Videos of the murder went viral. Across American cities and around the world, people demonstrated. Floyd, painted here in a mural in Nairobi, Kenya, became an emblem of defiance against police violence.

fight over oil and gas pipelines crossing Indigenous lands; the Standing Rock Sioux Tribe in North Dakota led mass demonstrations to block bulldozers until police and legal injunctions dispersed them. After years of dramatic standoff and litigation, the U.S. Supreme Court sided with the pipeline opponents—and ordered that the firm had to follow a legally mandated environmental review, which all but killed the project. In Canada, the landmark Truth and Reconciliation Commission of Canada (2008–15) was formed as the result of the legal settlement of court cases dealing with the abuse of Indigenous children in "Indian" Residential Schools. The final commission report in 2015 documented these abuses and others and ultimately called for 94 points of action designed to bring reconciliation between settler-Canadians and Indigenous peoples. To date, a limited number of those points have been acted on. Similar efforts to defend Indigenous land and water rights also happened in Canada against extractive developers in British Columbia, where pressures to hook up the oil and gas fields of the Canadian West to energy-hungry China with pipelines to the Pacific ran into Wet'suwet'en defenders who argued that the Canadian government was reneging on its promises at reconciliation for past abuses. The Wedzin Kwa (Morice River), their chief source of drinking water and spawning ground for salmon they live off of, was in danger of pollution. But some threats were too much for even the most resilient Indigenous communities. In the Andes, global warming quickly melted glaciers; brown mountainsides replaced a regular source of water for highland agriculture. The desiccated environments of Peru and Bolivia led Indigenous villagers to pack their few belongings and move to cities like Lima and La Paz for work.

As with Indigenous politics, there was a new turn in racial politics in the United States and elsewhere. The struggle to reform policy became a social movement under the banner of **Black Lives Matter**. In 2013, a White "neighborhood watchman" named George Zimmerman was acquitted of killing Trayvon Martin, a Black teenager who had been on the way to his father's house in Florida. A rash of news reports about brutal killings and torture hit the headlines. The deaths from excessive use of force by police of Eric Garner in New York, Michael Brown in Ferguson, Missouri, and others also prompted mass demonstrations. In 2015, twenty-eight-year-old Sandra Bland, who was arrested on a traffic stop and held for three days in a Texas jail, died in police custody. Black Lives Matter evolved quickly from a protest wave to a movement—one cofounded by three Black women, Alicia Garza, Patrisse Cullors, and Opal Tometi, two of whom identify with the LGBTQ community. They called for deep police and penal reform.

The drive to reform and restore some sense of equal citizenship gained momentum in late spring 2020 in the United States, which had emerged as the symbolic epicenter of a global movement. On May 25, a White Minneapolis police officer, Derek Chauvin, looked into cameras for 8 minutes and 47 seconds as his knee sank into the neck of a Black man named George Floyd. As onlookers called for help and warned Chauvin that George was choking, Floyd's eyes fluttered shut, he stopped breathing, and he died. The footage of the murder went viral. In the midst of a pandemic lockdown, the people of Minneapolis took to the streets to protest the long history of police abuse. Within days, small towns and cities across America became the stage for the largest single civilian

Transgender Activism. Laverne Cox, a prominent American actress and defender of the rights of LGBTQ people, became a standard-bearer for transgender activism. Here she serves as grand marshal of the New York City Pride March in 2014. Beside her is a framed picture of Islan Nettles, a young trans woman who was murdered in Harlem earlier that year, held by Nettles's mother. After the election of Donald Trump, Cox became increasingly active, working on lawsuits to defend against discrimination and appearing at rallies and demonstrations against police violence in the summer of 2020.

mobilization since the protests against the Vietnam War in the 1960s. The protest also went global as citizens of other countries turned to their own police forces and called out local injustices. Thousands of protesters took to the streets in Japan, England, Denmark, Senegal, Spain, Turkey, Canada, Portugal, South Korea, Brazil, and France. This time, calls to defund or even abolish the police joined the calls for reform and the demands to hold individual officers accountable for their use of excessive force. Social media played a vital role as viral, smartphone-shot videos of police teargassing and shooting rubber bullets at unarmed protesters and members of the press—and of protesters wearing masks to reduce the risk of spreading COVID-19—lit up the Internet.

The call for equal protection and rights for citizens also spurred mobilization for the rights of people who resist heterosexual norms and the binary gender labels of man or woman. The past decade has seen many global triumphs, as well as heightened visibility in the media and the public sphere, for **LGBTQ** people. The United Nations Human Rights Council (UNHRC) passed its first resolution affirming LGBTQ rights in 2011; actress and advocate Laverne Cox became the first transgender person on the cover of *Time* magazine in 2014; and *Moonlight* became the first LGBTQ-themed film to win the Best Picture award at the Oscars in 2017. In 2018, the Vatican used the acronym "LGBT" in an official document for the first time. In 2019, Mattel released the world's first line of gender-neutral dolls, and Pete Buttigieg became the first openly gay Democratic presidential candidate in U.S. history—to name just a few milestones. As of August 2023, thirty-four countries recognize marriage for same-sex couples. Canada became the first country outside of Europe to legally recognize same-sex marriages through the Civil Marriage Act (2005). Only a single country, Iran, is still thought to enforce the death penalty for same-sex sexual intercourse. In an ever-swinging pendulum, even as some rights are gained, others are contested or taken away; in 2020, during a pandemic, the Trump administration rescinded Obama-era health care protections for transgender people.

The events of 2019 and 2020 revealed the frustrations with both the old-style globalists and the newly minted nativists; neither side had good answers or alternatives to the worldwide impasse. Meanwhile, global challenges like climate change and pandemics continued to bear down on marginalized groups. In Africa, at the border of Zimbabwe and Zambia, the Kariba Dam—which was installed by profiteering European colonial powers and the World Bank in the 1950s over the objections of local people—is on the brink of collapse due to climate change. A tsunami will rage through southern Africa when the dam falls. In the United States, enduring and systemic social inequities mean that Black people and Indigenous people have a hospitalization rate from COVID-19 five times higher than that of (non-Hispanic) White people, and Hispanic or Latinx people are hospitalized at four times the rate of White people. Worldwide, in 2022, a total of 327 transgender and gender-diverse people were reported murdered, down just a bit from 369 in 2018; the majority of the homicides were catalogued in Brazil, and the vast majority of the victims were transgender women of color.

Conclusion: Globalization and Its Discontents

Globalization has had transforming effects, many of them decidedly good for large segments of the world's population, but some of them unsettling. Freer markets and international trade have created a global middle class, pulling nearly half a million Chinese out of poverty and equally huge proportions of the poor in India, Southeast Asia, Egypt, Nigeria, South Africa, and many other communities around the world. Members of the new international middle class communicate with one another, read the same newspapers and journals, see the same films, wear the same clothes, and eat the same foods. Nor is everything made in America, as the Nobel Prizes in Literature, the leading film actors in the world, and the major commentators on increasingly international television and radio networks demonstrate. The extremely high economic growth rates enjoyed by states once regarded as part of the developing world but now seen as economic powerhouses—countries like China, India, Brazil,

Mexico, Indonesia, South Korea, Kenya, South Africa, and Mozambique, among others—could not have been achieved without international trade networks and significant free trade agreements.

Nonetheless, the negative impacts of globalization have been much in evidence, especially since the financial crisis of 2008. While major banks and large multinational corporations were bailed out, the less well-off populace, the so-called residents of Main Street, suffered grievously. Homes were foreclosed, and workers lost good-paying jobs. In America, the hardest hit were White workers between the ages of forty-five and fifty-four who lack a high school education. Their death rates were alarmingly high, the result of suicide, drug addiction and overdosing, and alcoholism, bringing about for the first time an overall decline in the average life span of White males. The same affected industrial workers in France and Argentina. Perhaps the country that most felt the effects of precipitous deindustrialization was Russia, which went from being a powerhouse during the Cold War to highly reliant on fossil fuel extraction. No wonder Putin's supporters seethed with anxiety. Likewise, the sickness and death rates from the COVID-19 pandemic in the United States and many parts of the world fully revealed the vulnerability of poorer and more marginalized peoples.

The marginalized no longer remain silent, however. Around the world, they entered the political arena with a vengeance. But they forked. Some voted for nativist, antiglobal movements. They voted for Brexit (Britain's departure from the European Union) and contributed to the rise of Islamic militancy, Hindu nationalism, Turkey's turn toward Islamism and authoritarianism, and the increasing popularity of right-wing, ethnic nationalist parties in Europe, many of which oppose immigrant communities and balk at allowing refugees into their countries. America's marginalized segment embraced candidate Trump's 2016 campaign promises to keep Muslims out of the country and expel illegal entrants from Mexico. But they also rallied to fledgling progressive alliances and movements, from global Black Lives Matter to coalitions to stigmatize and divest from fossil fuel companies. As with the world economy, global politics became more interdependent and more fractured at the same time. In short, globalization has drawn the world more closely together, opening doors for migrants and enhancing the life prospects for many. But trade competition and new technologies have threatened groups who, through a lack in education and skills, are ill-equipped to take advantage of globalism's opportunities.

After You Read This Chapter

TRACING THE GLOBAL STORYLINES

FOCUS ON: The Impact of Modern Globalization Today

The United States, the European Union, and Japan

- The Great Recession and battles over health care, immigration, and job exportation polarize the United States politically and reveal the growing tension over inequality within the country in the forms of expanded state violence, racial justice protests, and the struggle for LGBTQ rights.
- The European Union membership begins to fracture as the Great Recession exposes major ideological fault lines over issues like immigration, domestic terrorism, and support for debtor countries.
- A severely aging and declining population in Japan creates the need for substantial immigration to fill jobs and stabilize the economy.

Russia, China, and India

- A return to an authoritarian political system in Russia and the high price of oil lead to substantial rises in personal income, state surpluses, and aggressive nationalism.
- China emerges as one of the world's largest trader and creditor nations, leading to substantial trade imbalances and frictions with countries like the United States. Chinese economic growth exacerbates internal inequalities, and political authoritarianism increases, particularly toward Hong Kong, resulting in major protests.
- India experiences high rates of economic growth driven by foreign investment in the information technology sector. High inflation rates, political corruption, internal divisions (Hindu nationalism), and external divisions (conflicts in Kashmir and Pakistan) threaten to undermine the economic gains.

The Middle East, Africa, and Latin America

- The Arab Spring generates revolutionary fever over issues like inequality in many countries (like Tunisia and Egypt) without creating lasting change, while others are torn apart by civil war (Syria) or by internal warfare with militant Islamic groups like ISIS (Iraq). Israeli and Palestinian relations are locked in a downward spiral, while American and Iranian relations worsen.
- While Africa benefits from globalization, the rewards are unevenly spread, so many countries continue to struggle with violence and unrest, HIV/AIDS, the COVID-19 pandemic, and other diseases. Ghana, South Africa, Kenya, Rwanda, and Nigeria achieve political and economic successes. West African countries suffer the most violence due to ethnic and personal rivalries.
- Globalization in Latin America deepens inequalities between haves and have-nots. Wealthy urbanites live like their counterparts in Paris, London, and New York, while factories close and farmers work small plots of land, causing many to migrate long distances for seasonal jobs or to leave their countries in search of work elsewhere.

CHRONOLOGY

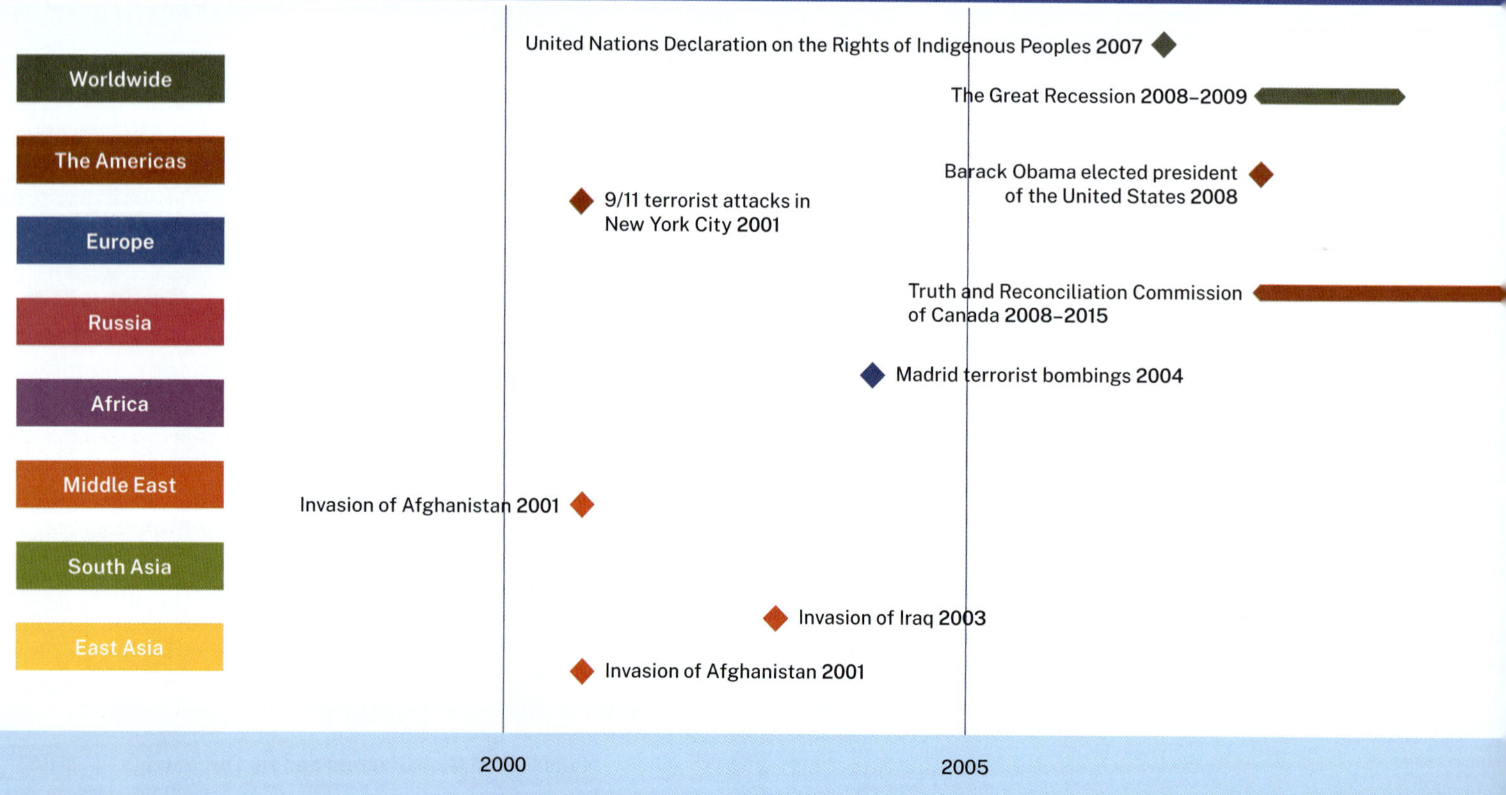

KEY TERMS

Black Lives Matter p. 1013
economic inequality p. 975
global climate change p. 977
global war on terror p. 973
globalization p. 971
Great Recession p. 974
LGBTQ p. 1014
pandemic p. 978

THINKING ABOUT GLOBAL CONNECTIONS

Thinking about Worlds Together, Worlds Apart and Twenty-First-Century Challenges. Identify the political, technological, and economic forces that brought core regions of Europe, Asia, and the Americas into ever-closer contact, coming to resemble one another as never before, and the forces that excluded developing nations, especially in Africa and Latin America, from those networks of wealth, power, and influence.

Thinking about Environmental Impacts and Twenty-First-Century Challenges. Describe the key causal factors driving global climate change and pandemic disease. To what degree are they connected and to what degree are they distinct phenomena?

Thinking about Changing Power Relationships and Cultural Change and Twenty-First-Century Challenges. How has technological change, especially the emergence of computers and the Internet, changed the transmission of culture worldwide? Where are the leading centers of the film and music industries located today?

Go to INQUIZITIVE to see what you've learned—and learn what you've missed—with personalized feedback along the way.

- Tea Party movement begins 2009
- UHNRC affirms LGBTQ rights 2011
- Occupy Wall Street movement 2011
- Black Lives Matter movement 2013
- Ethnic cleansing in Darfur 2011
- Arab Spring 2010–2011
- Syrian civil war begins 2011
- Osama bin Laden killed 2011
- Russia seizes Crimean Peninsula 2014
- Narendra Modi becomes prime minister of India 2014
- ISIS becomes Islamic Caliphate 2014–2019
- Iranian nuclear deal 2015
- Adoption of Paris Agreement on Climate Change 2015
- *Charlie Hebdo* terrorist attacks in Paris 2015
- Massive waves of migration from Middle East and Africa begin 2015
- Donald Trump elected president of the United States 2016
- 700 thousand Rohingya refugees flee Myanmar military crackdown 2017
- U.S.-China tariff war 2018–2019
- Andrés Manuel López Obrador becomes president of Mexico 2018
- Jair Bolsonaro gains power in Brazil 2018
- USMCA treaty negotiated 2018
- U.S.-China tariff war 2018–2019
- Hong Kong protests 2019
- United Nations' reports on climate change 2019
- Hong Kong protests 2019
- Racial justice protests 2020
- COVID-19 pandemic 2020–2022
- United Kingdom leaves European Union 2020
- January 6th Mob Riots at U.S. Capitol Building 2021
- U.S. withdraws from Afghanistan 2021
- World Population exceeds 8 Billion 2022
- Russian Invasion of Ukraine 2022

2010 | 2015 | 2020 | 2023

Global Themes and Sources

Analyzing the Responses to Global Climate Change

Climate change, directly caused by human activity, threatens the planet. While greenhouse gases are necessary for life on earth, the quantities, especially of carbon dioxide, produced by modern industry, deforestation, and large-scale agriculture have increased to levels that threaten irreversible harm. From droughts that ruin harvests and exacerbate conflict, to extreme weather such as deadly hurricanes, to rising sea levels that threaten catastrophic flooding, the challenges posed by climate change are both global and unprecedented.

Taking notice of these facts, world leaders met in 2015 at the United Nations Climate Change Conference in Paris to discuss how to slow the impact of global warming. The agreement was signed by 195 nations, yet some prominent world leaders continue to disregard the scientific consensus on climate change or have otherwise refused to comply with the efforts to curb carbon emissions.

The documents here reveal many responses to the Paris Agreement on Climate Change.[1] The first, produced by the nonprofit National Resources Defense Council (NRDC), summarizes the agreement, setting out the commitments of the participants—both developed and developing nations—to limit the emissions of greenhouse gases and the measures of accountability they all pledged to accept. The second is a speech by U.S. president Donald Trump, pulling the United States out of the agreement. The third is a speech by then-sixteen-year-old environmental activist Greta Thunberg, delivered at the United Nations Climate Action Summit, challenging global leaders to go beyond the targets established in Paris. The final document is the executive summary of a United Nations report on greenhouse gas emissions.

ANALYZING GLOBAL RESPONSES TO THE PARIS AGREEMENT ON CLIMATE CHANGE

Identify the core components of the Paris Agreement on Climate Change and the commitments of developed and developing nations.

Compare and contrast Trump and Thunberg's speeches. What concerns each of them about the agreement? Do the speeches share any common ground?

Evaluate the first document (the summary of the Paris Agreement) in light of the third (Thunberg's speech). What progress, if any, has been made? How should we evaluate the Paris Agreement?

[1]In these excerpts, the term $GtCO_2e$ stands for gigatons of equivalent carbon dioxide and is a simplified way to express the amount of carbon dioxide escaping into the atmosphere. UNFCCC stands for the United Nations Framework Convention on Climate Change.

PRIMARY SOURCE 22.1

NRDC Summary of the Paris Agreement on Climate Change (2015)

The U.S. nonprofit advocacy group National Resources Defense Council (NRDC) was founded in 1970 by environmentalists after a successful legal challenge to Consolidated Edison's effort to build a power plant on Storm King Mountain in New York. The nonprofit worked with the United Nations to produce a summary of the landmark international Paris Agreement on Climate Change.

Identify the nations and regions that produce the most greenhouse gases.

Contrast the targets established by the United States, China, India, and the European Union.

What kind of enforcement mechanism did the agreement create?

The Paris Agreement requires all countries—developed and developing—to make significant commitments to address climate change. Countries responsible for 97 percent of global emissions have already pledged their Nationally Determined Contributions (NDCs) for how they will address climate change. Countries will revisit their current pledges by 2020 and, ideally, strengthen their emissions reduction targets for 2030. The Paris Agreement includes a stronger transparency and accountability system for all countries—requiring reporting on greenhouse gas inventories and projections that are subject to a technical expert review and a multilateral examination. Countries will continue to provide climate finance to help the most vulnerable adapt to climate change and build low-carbon economies. While the Paris Agreement does not "solve" climate change, it allows us to start the next wave of global climate actions, creating a virtuous cycle for more aggressive action in the decades to come.

In Paris on December 12, 2015, countries adopted an international agreement to address climate change that requires deeper emissions reduction commitments from all countries—developed and developing. Countries responsible for 97 percent of global emissions submitted their climate commitments prior to the conference. These commitments will now be enshrined in the coming months once countries formally join the agreement. The agreement contains provisions to hold countries accountable to their commitments and mobilize greater investments to assist developing countries in building low-carbon, climate-resilient economies.

Encouragingly, businesses, investors, states, provinces, cities, financial institutions, and others have also pledged actions to help governments implement the agreement and even exceed their commitments.

While the Paris Agreement does not "solve" climate change, it is a critical inflection point. It brings us much closer to a safer climate trajectory and creates an ambitious path forward for decades to come. Countries have put forth an agreement that helps strengthen national action by ensuring that the current commitments are the floor—not the ceiling—of ambition. The agreement will also help spur greater action by cities, states, provinces, companies, and financial institutions. The Paris Agreement has created a virtuous cycle of increased ambition over time.

What Are the Key Elements of the Paris Agreement?

The agreement in Paris was built on the foundations of the United Nations Framework Convention on Climate Change (UNFCCC) and the Copenhagen and Cancun Agreements. This new agreement has set countries' minimum obligations, implemented mechanisms to spur additional action in developing countries, supported the most vulnerable countries in addressing climate change, and established systems to hold countries to their commitments. The Paris Agreement will be strengthened over time using its solid framework.

What New Emissions Reduction Targets Have Countries Agreed to Implement?

Countries responsible for more than 80 percent of global greenhouse gas emissions made specific commitments to reduce their emissions by 2020 as a part of the Copenhagen and Cancun agreements. The Paris agreement includes commitments that go beyond 2020, reflecting a greater level of ambition than in the previous commitments. . . . The 187 countries responsible for more than 97 percent of the world's climate pollution have announced specific reduction plans also known as Nationally Determined Contributions (NDCs). . . .

How Will the Agreement Track Country-Level Progress?

. . . Countries must report their greenhouse gas inventories and progress towards their emissions reduction targets every two years. . . .

What Are Countries' Post-2020 Climate Targets?

Prior to the Paris climate conference, countries submitted their proposed climate commitments, including specific targets for emissions reductions. So far, 187 countries—accounting for 97 percent of global greenhouse gas emissions—have submitted their climate pledges. These commitments can now be formally submitted as part of the Paris agreement.

United States: cut economy-wide emissions of greenhouse gas emissions by 26 to 28 percent below its 2005 level by 2025 and make best efforts to reduce its emissions by 28 percent.

China: peak carbon emissions no later than 2030, increase non-fossil fuels to 20 percent of the energy mix, and reduce carbon emissions per unit of gross domestic product (GDP) by 60 to 65 percent from 2005 levels by 2030.

India: reduce emissions intensity by 33 to 35 percent from 2005 levels by 2030, increase cumulative electric power installed capacity from non-fossil fuel energy resources to 40 percent by 2030, and create additional carbon sequestration of 2.5 to 3 billion tons of carbon dioxide equivalent by 2030. . . .

European Union: reduce emissions to at least 40 percent below 1990 levels by 2030 through only domestic measures.

Source: https://unfccc.int/process-and-meetings/the-paris-agreement/the-paris-agreement

PRIMARY SOURCE 22.2

Statement on the Paris Climate Accord (2017), Donald Trump

In June 2017, President Donald Trump announced that the United States would stop participating in the 2015 Paris Agreement on Climate Change. He promised to create more high-paying jobs for Americans by reducing environmental rules and regulations that he regarded as onerous for the fossil fuel industry. According to the agreement's Article 28, however, signatories cannot announce withdrawal for three years after the country's effective start date (November 2016 for the United States). The Trump administration announced plans to pull out again in 2019, with final withdrawal set for November 2020. The international community united in its criticism of the U.S. decision.

- How does President Trump justify pulling the United States out of the Paris Agreement?
- Evaluate the moral claims made in Trump's speech.
- Do you think the United States should have pulled out of the Paris Agreement? Should it have rejoined?

On these issues and so many more, we're following through on our commitments. And I don't want anything to get in our way. I am fighting every day for the great people of this country.

Therefore, in order to fulfill my solemn duty to protect America and its citizens, the United States will withdraw from the Paris Climate Accord—(applause)—thank you, thank you—but begin negotiations to reenter either the Paris Accord or a really entirely new transaction on terms that are fair to the United States, its businesses, its workers, its people, its taxpayers. So we're getting out. But we will start to negotiate, and we will see if we can make a deal that's fair. And if we can, that's great. And if we can't, that's fine. (Applause.)

As President, I can put no other consideration before the wellbeing of American citizens. The Paris Climate Accord is simply the latest example of Washington entering into an agreement that disadvantages the United States to the exclusive benefit of other countries, leaving American workers—who I love—and taxpayers to absorb the cost in terms of lost jobs, lower wages, shuttered factories, and vastly diminished economic production.

Thus, as of today, the United States will cease all implementation of the non-binding Paris Accord and the draconian financial and economic burdens the agreement imposes on our country. This includes ending the implementation of the nationally determined contribution and, very importantly, the Green Climate Fund which is costing the United States a vast fortune.

Compliance with the terms of the Paris Accord and the onerous energy restrictions it has placed on the United States could cost America as much as 2.7 million lost jobs by 2025 according to the National Economic Research Associates. This includes 440,000 fewer manufacturing jobs—not what we need—believe me, this is not what we need—including automobile jobs, and the further decimation of vital American industries on which countless communities rely. They rely for so much, and we would be giving them so little.

According to this same study, by 2040, compliance with the commitments put into place by the previous administration would cut production for the following sectors: paper down 12 percent; cement down 23 percent; iron and steel down 38 percent; coal—and I happen to love the coal miners—down 86 percent; natural gas down 31 percent. The cost to the economy at this time would be close to $3 trillion in lost GDP and 6.5 million industrial jobs, while households would have $7,000 less income and, in many cases, much worse than that.

Not only does this deal subject our citizens to harsh economic restrictions, it fails to live up to our environmental ideals. As someone who cares deeply about the environment, which I do, I cannot in good conscience support a deal that punishes the United States—which is what it does—the world's leader in environmental protection, while imposing no meaningful obligations on the world's leading polluters.

For example, under the agreement, China will be able to increase these emissions by a staggering number of years—13. They can do whatever they want for 13 years. Not us. India makes its participation contingent on receiving billions and billions and billions of dollars in foreign aid from developed countries. There are many other examples. But the bottom line is that the Paris Accord is very unfair, at the highest level, to the United States. . . .

China will be allowed to build hundreds of additional coal plants. So we can't build the plants, but they can, according to this agreement. India will be allowed to double its coal production by 2020. Think of it: India can double their coal production. We're supposed to get rid of ours. Even Europe is allowed to continue construction of coal plants.

In short, the agreement doesn't eliminate coal jobs, it just transfers those jobs out of America and the United States, and ships them to foreign countries. This agreement is less about the climate and more about other countries gaining a financial advantage over the United States. . . .

We have among the most abundant energy reserves on the planet, sufficient to lift millions of America's poorest workers out of poverty. Yet, under this agreement, we are effectively putting these reserves under lock and key, taking away the great wealth of our nation. . . .

The agreement is a massive redistribution of United States wealth to other countries. At 1 percent growth, renewable sources of energy can meet some of our domestic demand, but at 3 or 4 percent growth, which I expect, we need all forms of available American energy, or our country—(applause)—will be at grave risk of brownouts and blackouts, our businesses will come to a halt in many cases, and the American family will suffer the consequences in the form of lost jobs and a very diminished quality of life.

Even if the Paris Agreement were implemented in full, with total compliance from all nations, it is estimated it would only produce a two-tenths of one degree—think of that; this much—Celsius reduction in global temperature by the year 2100. Tiny, tiny amount. . . .

My job as President is to do everything within my power to give America a level playing field and to create the economic, regulatory and tax structures that make America the most prosperous and productive country on Earth, and with the highest standard of living and the highest standard of environmental protection. . . .

The Paris Agreement handicaps the United States economy in order to win praise from the very foreign capitals and global activists that have long sought to gain wealth at our country's expense. They don't put America first. I do, and I always will. (Applause.)

The same nations asking us to stay in the agreement are the countries that have collectively cost America trillions of dollars through tough trade practices and, in many cases, lax contributions to our critical military alliance. You see what's happening. It's pretty obvious to those that want to keep an open mind.

At what point does America get demeaned? At what point do they start laughing at us as a country? We want fair treatment for its citizens, and we want fair treatment for our taxpayers. We don't want other leaders and other countries laughing at us anymore. And they won't be. They won't be.

I was elected to represent the citizens of Pittsburgh, not Paris. (Applause.) I promised I would exit or renegotiate any deal which fails to serve America's interests. Many trade deals will soon be under renegotiation. Very rarely do we have a deal that works for this country, but they'll soon be under renegotiation. The process has begun from day one. But now we're down to business. . . .

As President, I have one obligation, and that obligation is to the American people. The Paris Accord would undermine our economy, hamstring our workers, weaken our sovereignty, impose unacceptable legal risks, and put us at a permanent disadvantage to the other countries of the world. It is time to exit the Paris Accord—(applause)—and time to pursue a new deal that protects the environment, our companies, our citizens, and our country.

It is time to put Youngstown, Ohio, Detroit, Michigan, and Pittsburgh, Pennsylvania—along with many, many other locations within our great country—before Paris, France. It is time to make America great again. (Applause.) Thank you. Thank you. Thank you very much.

Source: https://www.whitehouse.gov/briefings-statements/statement-president-trump-paris-climate-accord/

PRIMARY SOURCE 22.3

Speech to the U.N. Climate Action Summit (2019), Greta Thunberg

Greta Thunberg (b. 2003), a Swedish environmental activist and the *Time* magazine Person of the Year for 2019, was invited to address the United Nations on climate change. Her 2019 speech took world leaders to task for failing her generation.

- What is Thunberg's position on the Paris Agreement?
- Evaluate the moral claims in her speech.
- How does she see the relationship between science, the environment, and economic prosperity?

My message is that we'll be watching you.

This is all wrong. I shouldn't be up here. I should be back in school on the other side of the ocean. Yet you all come to us young people for hope. How dare you!

You have stolen my dreams and my childhood with your empty words. And yet I'm one of the lucky ones. People are suffering. People are dying. Entire ecosystems are collapsing. We are in the beginning of a mass extinction, and all you can talk about is money and fairy tales of eternal economic growth. How dare you!

For more than 30 years, the science has been crystal clear. How dare you continue to look away and come here saying that you're doing enough, when the politics and solutions needed are still nowhere in sight.

You say you hear us and that you understand the urgency. But no matter how sad and angry I am, I do not want to believe that. Because if you really understood the situation and still kept on failing to act, then you would be evil. And that I refuse to believe.

The popular idea of cutting our emissions in half in 10 years only gives us a 50 percent chance of staying below 1.5 degrees [Celsius], and the risk of setting off irreversible chain reactions beyond human control.

Fifty percent may be acceptable to you. But those numbers do not include tipping points, most feedback loops, additional warming hidden by toxic air pollution or the aspects of equity and climate justice. They also rely on my generation sucking hundreds of billions of tons of your CO_2 out of the air with technologies that barely exist.

So a 50 percent risk is simply not acceptable to us—we who have to live with the consequences.

To have a 67 percent chance of staying below a 1.5 degrees global temperature rise—the best odds given by the [Intergovernmental Panel on Climate Change]—the world had 420 gigatons of CO_2 left to emit back on Jan. 1st, 2018. Today that figure is already down to less than 350 gigatons.

How dare you pretend that this can be solved with just "business as usual" and some technical solutions? With today's emissions levels, that remaining CO_2 budget will be entirely gone within less than 8½ years.

There will not be any solutions or plans presented in line with these figures here today, because these numbers are too uncomfortable. And you are still not mature enough to tell it like it is.

You are failing us. But the young people are starting to understand your betrayal. The eyes of all future generations are upon you. And if you choose to fail us, I say: We will never forgive you.

We will not let you get away with this. Right here, right now is where we draw the line. The world is waking up. And change is coming, whether you like it or not.

Thank you.

Source: Greta Thunberg, "The World is Waking Up," from *No One Is Too Small to Make a Difference* (New York: Penguin Books, 2019), pp. 96–99.

PRIMARY SOURCE 22.4

United Nations Environment Programme—Emissions Gap Report 2019: Executive Summary

This document, produced by the United Nations, provides an assessment of current and estimated greenhouse gas emissions and compares them to a least-cost pathway to achieve the goals set out in the Paris Agreement.

Define the "emissions gap" laid out in the report.

Evaluate efforts to reduce emissions.

Identify any encouraging signs highlighted in the report.

How much will the world have to reduce greenhouse gas emissions each year by 2030 in order to limit global warming to below 2°C?

Introduction

This is the tenth edition of the United Nations Environment Programme (UNEP) Emissions Gap Report. It provides the latest assessment of scientific studies on current and estimated future greenhouse gas (GHG) emissions and compares these with the emission levels permissible for the world to progress on a least-cost pathway to achieve the goals of the Paris Agreement. This difference between "where we are likely to be and where we need to be" has become known as the "emissions gap." . . .

The summary findings are bleak. Countries collectively failed to stop the growth in global GHG emissions, meaning that deeper and faster cuts are now required. However, behind the grim headlines, a more differentiated message emerges from the ten-year summary. A number of encouraging developments have taken place and the political focus on the climate crisis is growing in several countries, with voters and protestors, particularly youth, making it clear that it is their number one issue. In addition, the technologies for rapid and cost-effective emission reductions have improved significantly. . . .

As regards the scientific perspective, the Intergovernmental Panel on Climate Change (IPCC) issued two special reports in 2019: the Climate Change and Land report on climate change, desertification, land degradation, sustainable land management, food security and greenhouse gas fluxes in terrestrial ecosystems, and the Ocean and Cryosphere in a Changing Climate report. Both reports voice strong concerns about observed and predicted changes resulting from climate change and provide an even stronger scientific foundation that supports the importance of the temperature goals of the Paris Agreement and the need to ensure emissions are on track to achieve these goals. . . .

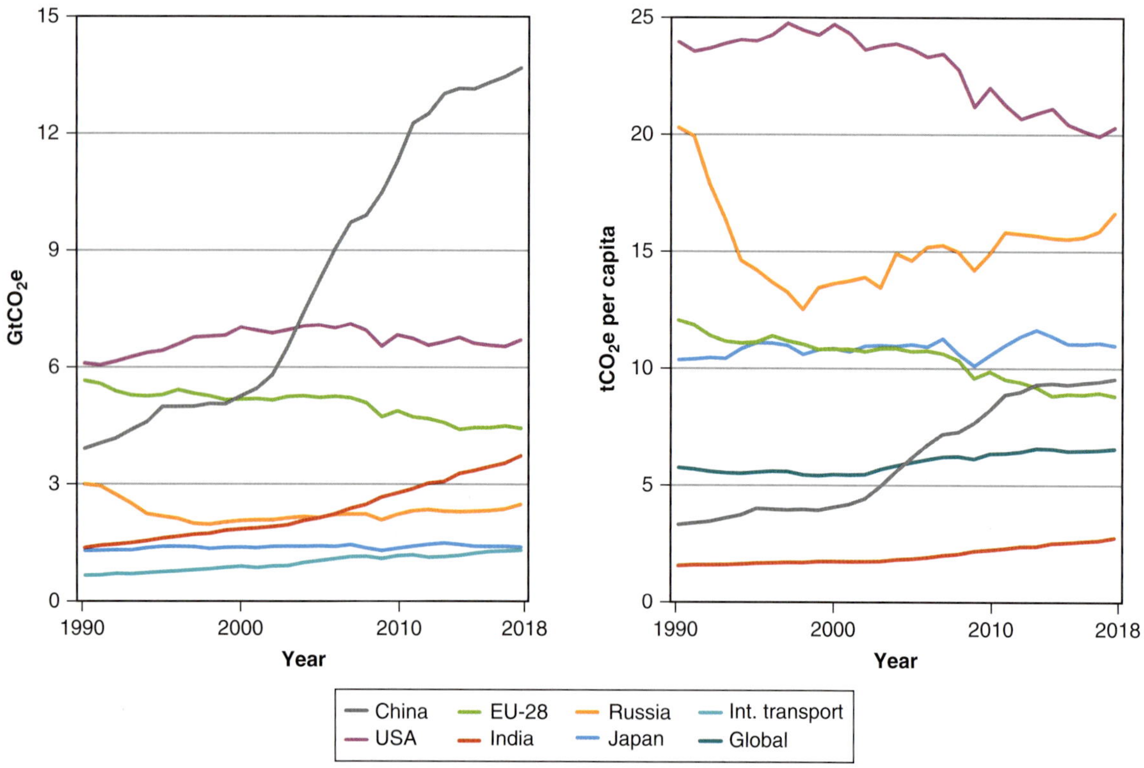

Top greenhouse gas emitters, excluding land-use change emissions due to lack of reliable country-level data, on an absolute basis (*left*) and per capita basis (*right*).

GHG emissions continue to rise, despite scientific warnings and political commitments.

- GHG emissions have risen at a rate of 1.5 per cent per year in the last decade, stabilizing only briefly between 2014 and 2016. Total GHG emissions, including from land-use change, reached a record high of 55.3 $GtCO_2e$ in 2018.
- Fossil CO_2 emissions from energy use and industry, which dominate total GHG emissions, grew 2.0 per cent in 2018, reaching a record 37.5 $GtCO_2$ per year.
- There is no sign of GHG emissions peaking in the next few years; every year of postponed peaking means that deeper and faster cuts will be required. By 2030, emissions would need to be 25 per cent and 55 per cent lower than in 2018 to put the world on the least-cost pathway to limiting global warming to below 2°C and 1.5°C respectively.

***

Although the number of countries announcing net zero GHG emission targets for 2050 is increasing, only a few countries have so far formally submitted long-term strategies to the UNFCCC.

***

Decarbonizing the global economy will require fundamental structural changes, which should be designed to bring multiple co-benefits for humanity and planetary support systems.

- . . . Climate protection and adaptation investments will become a precondition for peace and stability, and will require unprecedented efforts to transform societies, economies, infrastructures and governance institutions.

Source: United Nations Environment Programme, *Emissions Gap Report 2019: Executive Summary* (Nairobi: United Nations Environment Programme, 2019), pp. iv–vii, x.

Interpreting Visual Evidence

Global Inequality and the Refugee Crisis

By 2020, the population of forcibly displaced people topped 70 million, the highest number since World War II. Three decades from now, according to the United Nations, up to 1 billion people might be displaced due to climate change and its political fallout. As climate change grows more acute and wipes out agrarian systems and floods cities, the population of people with no states will grow—and grow. The photographs in this sequence illustrate the personal dimensions of the massive, involuntary, human uprooting of recent and coming years.

Refugees are people who are driven from their states and into other states—which is what makes forced migration a global crisis. It is also a political one. Refugees cannot turn to their own governments for support: often, they are fleeing oppressive regimes, like Syria's or Myanmar's. Sometimes, they leave obscenely negligent ones, like Venezuela's.

Because they do not have states, refugees rely on private family networks, civic and religious organizations, and systems of global protection like the United Nations High Commission for Refugees, which administers sprawling camps in Africa, the Middle East, and Asia. Some camps, like the one in Bangladesh featured in the first image, are the size of cities. But more often, refugees hide in plain sight, living and working as individuals or families in host country neighborhoods. The photo of the German chancellor visiting a school in Rostock captures her unexpected encounter with a Palestinian fourteen-year-old named Reem. Looking at the third image, you can see the way in which Venezuelan families have moved into barrios in Colombia or Ecuador and become hard to distinguish from their host country neighbors; the newcomers are notable mainly for their accents and sorrow.

In recent decades, the measure of global equality can be gauged by access to state resources and protection. In short: the poor are excluded from welfare, protection, or political rights altogether, while the wealthy can count on states to shelter their property and communities and in many places gain privileged access to political power. It is the degree of citizenship that determines the pattern of inequality within and across countries. Asylum seekers, like Reem, may grow up in host communities, but their rights to stay are precarious. Not surprisingly, those without states or living in neglectful or hostile states are often the most destitute.

The global refugee crisis also shook up politics within nation-states. The debate over whether to welcome or reject

Refugee Camp in Bangladesh. Since 2012, over a million Muslim Rohingya people have been driven from Myanmar. Almost all have fled to Bangladesh since 2017. There are two official camps. Most Rohingya have created impromptu settlements like this massive camp at Cox's Bazar, which now holds the largest concentration of refugees in the world, nearly 1 million people. On May 14, 2020, the first case of COVID-19 was detected there.

A Young Palestinian in Germany. On July 15, 2015, German chancellor Angela Merkel met with a gymnasium full of teenagers to talk about "Good Life in Germany." During the conversation, one girl named Reem explained in fluent German that she was Palestinian and that as refugees she and her family were threatened with deportation. "I have goals like anyone else. I want to study like them," Reem explained. When Merkel countered that Germany could not take more refugees and that everyone had to comply with the screening process, Reem broke down in tears in front of her friends. Merkel was shocked and in front of the cameras struggled to console the weeping girl. The image brought home to millions of Germans not just that many refugees had grown up in their country but that deportation was ripping apart friends and families. Six weeks later, Reem's family received their residency permit.

Middle-Class Refugees in Latin America. Venezuela has been collapsing for almost a decade. After Syria, it accounts for the most refugees in the world. Over 5 million have fled, mostly to neighboring countries. Many are middle-class and took airplanes and buses to find safety and jobs elsewhere. The result is shattered and scattered families. This photograph, taken in September 2018 by Dolores Ochoa, portrays a young woman who is leaving her father behind in Ecuador while she travels back home to Venezuela. Very often, the refugee crisis crosses all social classes.

The Plight of Syrian Refugees. On September 2, 2015, Turkish photojournalist Nilüfer Demir found the body of a three-year-old Syrian boy named Aylan Kurdi washed up on the beach. He had drowned. The shocked Demir started to take photos and stayed until an emergency worker arrived. Later, a Turkish court sentenced two smugglers for the death of the boy. In the meantime, this image horrified the world and shifted public opinion to recognize the plight of Syrian refugees.

refugees coincided with a revolution in communications, specifically the turn to digital circulation of information and images. Images were central in swaying public opinion. As you look at these photographs, think about how they influenced public debate, and consider that in some cases they were taken in order to affect the debate, because the scenes were so emotion laden.

Societies divided, sometimes bitterly, over whether to accept refugees. All of these images were powerful instruments for mobilizing a diverse array of emotions, from fear to sympathy, from hopelessness to guilt. The photo of the Syrian three-year-old boy, Aylan Kurdi, washed up on a Turkish beach sparked a massive debate worldwide. In Canada, there was outrage. The Canadian government had just rejected the Kurdi family's appeal for asylum, which was why Aylan's father decided to take his two young sons on an ill-fated crossing. In a national election later that autumn, voters trounced the government in Ottawa.

Elsewhere, especially in nations that neighbor refugees' home countries, there was more forbearance. In Bangladesh, swollen camps like Cox's Bazar conveyed an impression of a problem too vast for anyone to solve, which often led to resignation. Many Venezuelans were accepted in neighboring countries, with the notable exception of Brazil, whose government liked to blame outsiders for its problems.

Often, many reacted to these images with fears of an invasion of needy strangers. Though the vast majority of refugees did not reach Europe or North America, it was there that the debate was most heated, with public displays of rejection and support, as the photos of Americans and Germans wielding signs illustrate. National elections and plebiscites (direct votes of all the members of an electorate) turned on the conflict about whether to admit or deport and restrict refugees.

QUESTIONS FOR ANALYSIS

1. The debate over refugees is an intensely emotional one. What range of emotions do these images evoke in you?
2. Compare the images of host country reactions in Germany and the United States. How might historical context inform their different reactions?
3. Observe the faces of the refugees in these photos. What emotional stories do they convey? How might someone on Facebook or Instagram react to these images?

American Xenophobia. As the global migrant crisis intensified, it tilted the political balance in North America and Europe. Although most refugees stayed in the Global South and found sanctuary in neighboring countries, many Americans lashed out against the perceived threat of an invasion. The election of Donald Trump in November 2016 emboldened many to drive out refugees. Not long after his inauguration, President Trump ordered a travel ban on Muslims. His supporters, like these demonstrators outside Los Angeles International Airport, rushed to defend the ban even as the policy would go to the courts—and be struck down.

German Support for Refugees. Often, the images of the global refugee crisis emphasize the plight and exclusion of fugitives. But displacement is also about welcoming. Among affluent countries, Germany was remarkably open—and took almost 1 million refugees in one year. In this image, we see the fans of two soccer teams from Dortmund and Hanover set aside their fierce rivalry to demonstrate their support for helping refugees. The photo was taken at the onset of the wave of migrants. By the time 1 million had arrived and Germans faced the task of integrating refugees, images of welcome had started to become more scarce.

Further Readings

CHAPTER 10: BECOMING "THE WORLD," 1000–1300 CE

Allsen, Thomas, *Commodity and Exchange in the Mongol Empire: A Cultural History of Islamic Textiles* (1997). A study that uses golden brocade, the textile most treasured by Mongol rulers, as a lens through which to analyze the vast commercial networks facilitated by the Mongol conquests and control.

———, *Culture and Conquest in Mongol Eurasia* (2001). A work that emphasizes the cultural and scientific exchanges that took place across Afro-Eurasia as a result of the Mongol conquest.

Bagge, Svere, Michael Gelting, and Thomas Lundkvist (eds.), *Feudalism: New Landscapes of Debate* (2011). A collection of essays on interpretations of feudalism by experts on the topic.

Bartlett, Robert, *The Making of Europe: Conquest, Colonization and Cultural Change, 950–1350* (1993). The modes of cultural, political, and demographic expansion of feudal Europe along its frontiers, especially in eastern Europe.

Bay, Edna G., *Wives of the Leopards: Gender, Politics, and Culture in the Kingdom of Dahomey* (1998). A work that stresses the role of women in an important West African society and dips into the early history of this area.

Beach, D. N., *Shona and Zimbabwe, 900–1850: An Outline of Shona History* (1980). A good place to start for exploring the history of Great Zimbabwe.

Broadbridge, Anne F., *Women and the Making of the Mongol Empire* (2018). By examining the lives of women in Chinggis Khan's orbit, this study uncovers not only details about the lives of well-known elite Mongol women but also a larger picture of the roles of women in kinship strategies binding Mongol tribes, the economy fueling nomadic life, and the political machinations driving conquest.

Brooks, George E., *Landlords and Strangers: Ecology, Society, and Trade in Western Africa, 1000–1630* (1993). A survey assembled from primary sources of early West African history that stresses transregional connections.

Bulliet, Richard W., *Cotton, Climate, and Camels in Early Islamic Iran* (2009). An analysis of the upswing of the Iranian plateau economy after the Muslim conquest and its subsequent decline as a result of climate change.

Buzurg ibn Shahriyar of Ramhormuz, *The Book of the Wonders of India: Mainland, Sea and Islands*, ed. and trans. G. S. P. Freeman-Greenville (1981). A collection of stories told by sailors, both true and fantastic; they help us imagine the lives of sailors of the era.

Chappell, Sally A. Kitt, *Cahokia: Mirror of the Cosmos* (2002). A thorough and vivid account of the "mound people"; it explores not just what we know of Cahokia but how we know it.

Christian, David, *A Short History of Russia, Central Asia, and Mongolia*, vol. 1, *Inner Eurasia from Prehistory to the Mongol Empire* (1998). Essential reading for students interested in interconnections across the Afro-Eurasian landmass.

Curtin, Philip, *Cross-Cultural Trade in World History* (1984). A groundbreaking book on intercultural trade with a primary focus on Africa, especially the cross-Saharan trade and Swahili coastal trade.

Dawson, Christopher, *Mission to Asia* (1980). Accounts of China and the Mongol Empire brought back by Catholic missionaries and diplomats after 1240.

De Nicola, Bruno, *Women in Mongol Iran: The Khātūns, 1206–1335* (2017). Drawing on a wide range of source material, De Nicola explores the political, economic, and religious influence of women in Mongol society from the pre-imperial steppe nomadic context to the settled empire, in particular the Il-Khanate of Persia.

Di Cosmo, Nicola, Allen J. Frank, and Peter Golden (eds.), *The Cambridge History of Inner Asia: The Chinggisid Age* (2009). A definitive study of the Mongol period, written by the leading scholars of this period.

Ellenblum, Ronnie, *The Collapse of the Eastern Mediterranean: Climate Change and the Decline of the East, 950–1072* (2012). An analysis of the impact of freezing temperatures and drought on the societies of the eastern Mediterranean.

Flecker, Michael, "A 9th-Century Arab or Indian Shipwreck in Indonesian Waters," *International Journal of Nautical Archaeology* 29, no. 2 (2000): 199–217. Offers an early detailed description of the Belitung dhow's excavation, likely place of origin, construction, and cargo.

———, "A 9th-Century Arab or Indian Shipwreck in Indonesian Waters: Addendum," *International Journal of Nautical Archaeology* 37, no. 2 (2008): 384–86. An update on the origin of the Belitung dhow that, based on a comparative analysis of wood fibers, argues that the ship's timbers suggest it was built in Oman or Yemen (on the southern coast of the Arabian Peninsula), not India as was earlier considered to be a possibility.

———, "A 9th-Century Arab Shipwreck in Indonesia," in Regina Krahl et al. (eds.), *Shipwrecked: Tang Treasures and Monsoon Winds* (2010), pp. 100–119. Flecker's most recent consideration of the Belitung dhow, published in a collection of essays to accompany an exhibition focused on the important shipwreck.

Foltz, Richard C., *Religions of the Silk Road: Overland Trade and Cultural Exchange from Antiquity to the Fifteenth Century* (1999). A study of the populations and the cities of the Silk Roads as transmitters of culture across long distances.

Franklin, Simon, and Jonathan Shepherd, *The Emergence of Rus: 750–1200* (1996). The formation of medieval Russia between the Baltic and Black Seas.

Gibb, Hamilton A. R., *Saladin: Studies in Islamic History*, ed. Yusuf Ibish (1974). A sympathetic portrait of one of Islam's leading political and military figures.

Glahn, Richard von, "Re-examining the Authenticity of Song Paper Money Specimens," *Journal of Song-Yuan Studies* 36 (2006): 79–106. Provides a close examination, including descriptions, images, and translations, of many examples of paper money from the Song and Yuan dynasties. The article offers a detailed discussion (on pp. 93–94) of the flying cash example reproduced in Chapter 10.

Goitein, S. D., *Letters of Medieval Jewish Traders* (1973). The classic study of medieval Jewish trading communities based on the commercial papers deposited in the Cairo Geniza (a synagogue storeroom) during the tenth and eleventh centuries CE; it explores not only commercial activities but also the personal lives of the traders around the Indian Ocean basin.

———, *A Mediterranean Society: An Abridgment in One Volume*, rev. and ed. Jacob Lassner (1999). A portrait of the Jewish merchant community with ties across the Afro-Eurasian landmass, based largely on the documents from the Cairo Geniza (of which Goitein was the primary researcher and interpreter).

———, "New Light on the Beginnings of the Karim Merchant," *Journal of Social and Economic History of the Orient* 1 (1958). Goitein's description of Egyptian trade.

Goitein, S. D., and Mordechai A. Friedman, *India Traders of the Middle Ages: Documents from the Cairo Geniza* (2008). Collection of documents (translated into English) and authoritative essays that explore the eleventh- and twelfth-century trade conducted by several prominent Jewish families along the Mediterranean and Indian Ocean routes.

Harris, Joseph E., *The African Presence in Asia: Consequences of the East African Slave Trade* (1971). One of the few books that look broadly at the impact of Africans and African enslavement on the societies of Asia.

Hartwell, Robert, "Demographic, Political, and Social Transformations of China, 750–1550," *Harvard Journal of Asiatic Studies* 42 (1982): 365–442. A pioneering study of the demographic changes that overtook China during the Tang and Song dynasties, which are described in light of political reform movements and social changes in this crucial era.

Historical Relations across the Indian Ocean: Report and Papers of the Meeting of Experts Organized by UNESCO at Port Louis, Mauritius, from 15 to 19 July, 1974 (1980). Excellent essays on the connections of Africa with Asia across the Indian Ocean.

Hitti, Philip, *An Arab-Syrian Gentleman and Warrior in the Period of the Crusades: Memoirs of Us mah ibn-Munqidh* (1929). The Crusaders seen through Muslim eyes.

Hodgson, Natasha, *Women, Crusading, and the Holy Land in Historical Narrative* (2007). A book dealing with the Crusades and focusing on the place of women in them.

Holt, P. M., *The Age of the Crusades: The Near East from the Eleventh Century to 1517* (1984). The Crusades period as seen from the eastern Mediterranean and through the lens of a leading British scholar of the area.

Huff, Toby E., *The Rise of Early Modern Science* (2009). A bold attempt to look at the rise of scientific work in the Islamic world, premodern China, and Europe, seeking to explain why the scientific revolution occurred in Europe rather than the Islamic world or China.

Hymes, Robert, and Conrad Schirokauer (eds.), *Ordering the World: Approaches to State and Society in Sung Dynasty China* (1993). A collection of essays that traces the intellectual, social, and political movements that shaped the Song state and its elites.

Ibn Battuta, *The Travels of Ibn Battuta*, trans. H. A. R. Gibb (2002). A readable translation of the classic book, originally published in 1929.

Ibn Fadlan, Ahmad, *Ibn Fadlan's Journey to Russia: A Tenth Century Traveler from Baghdad to the Volga River*, translated with commentary by Richard Frye (2005). A coherent summary of the observations of an envoy who traveled from Baghdad to Russia.

Irwin, Robert, *The Middle East in the Middle Ages: The Early Mamluk Sultanate, 1250–1582* (1986). Egypt under Mamluk rule.

Jeppie, Shamil, and Souleymane Bachir Diagne (eds.), *The Meanings of Timbuktu* (2008). New materials on the ancient Muslim city of Timbuktu by scholars who have been preserving its manuscripts and writing about its historical importance.

Khazanov, Anatoly M., *Nomads and the Outside World*, 2nd ed., trans. Julia Crookurden, with a foreword by Ernest Gellner (1994). A classic overview of nomadism, based on years of research, covering all the nomadic communities of Afro-Eurasia.

Lambourn, Elizabeth A., *Abraham's Luggage: A Social Life of Things in the Medieval Indian Ocean World* (2018). Uses Abraham Ben Yiju's 173-item luggage list to unpack a fascinating social and economic history of a North African Jewish trader living in southern India.

Lancaster, Lewis, Kikun Suh, and Chai-shin Yu (eds.), *Buddhism in Koryo: A Royal Religion* (1996). A description of Buddhism at its height in the Koryo period, when the religion made significant contributions to the development of Korean culture.

Levtzion, Nehemia, and Randall L. Pouwels (eds.), *The History of Islam in Africa* (2000). A useful general survey of the place of Islam in African history.

Lewis, Bernard (trans.), *Islam: From the Prophet Muhammad to the Capture of Constantinople*, vol. 2, *Religion and Society* (1974). A fine collection of original sources that portray various aspects of classical Islamic society.

Lopez, Robert S., *The Commercial Revolution of the Middle Ages, 950–1350* (1976). An account focusing on the development around the Mediterranean of commercial practices such as the use of currency, accounting, and credit.

Lyons, Malcolm C., and D. E. P. Jackson, *Saladin: The Politics of the Holy War* (1984; reprint, 2001). The fundamental revisionist work on one of the more important historical figures of the time.

Maalouf, Amin, *The Crusades through Muslim Eyes*, trans. Jon Rothschild (1984). The European Crusaders as seen by the Muslim world.

Marcus, Harold G., *A History of Ethiopia* (2002). An authoritative overview of the history of this great culture.

Mass, Jeffrey, *Yoritomo and the Founding of the First Bakufu: The Origins of Dual Government in Japan* (1999). A revisionist account of how the Kamakura military leader Minamoto Yoritomo established the "dual polity" of court and warrior government in Japan.

McDermott, Joseph, *A Social History of the Chinese Book: Books and Literati Culture in Late Imperial China* (2006). The history of the book in China since the Song dynasty, with comparisons to the book's role in other civilizations, particularly the European.

McEvitt, Christopher, *The Crusaders and the Christian World of the East: Rough Tolerance* (2008). Excellent work on the relations of religious groups in the Crusader kingdoms.

McIntosh, Roderik, *The Peoples of the Middle Niger: The Island of Gold* (1988). A historical survey of an area often omitted from other textbooks.

Moore, Jerry D., *Cultural Landscapes in the Ancient Andes: Archaeologies of Place* (2005). The most recent and up-to-date analysis of findings based on recent archaeological evidence, emphasizing the importance of local cultures and diversity in the Andes.

Mote, Frederick W., *Imperial China, 900–1800* (1999). Still the best work on this period, written by an expert on the full scope of Chinese history. The chapter on the Mongols is superb.

Niane, D. T. (ed.), *Africa from the Twelfth to the Sixteenth Century*, vol. 4 of *General History of Africa* (1984). The fourth volume of UNESCO's history of Africa covers four centuries of African history. This work features the scholarship of Africans.

Oliver, Roland (ed.), *From c. 1050 to c. 1600*, vol. 3 of *The Cambridge History of Africa*, ed. J. D. Fage and Roland Oliver (1977). Another general survey of African history. This volume draws heavily on the work of British scholars.

Peters, Edward, *The First Crusade* (1971). The Crusaders as seen through their own eyes.

Petry, Carl F. (ed.), *Islamic Egypt, 640–1517*, vol. 1 of *The Cambridge History of Egypt* (1998). A solid overview of the history of Islamic Egypt up to the Ottoman conquest.

Plokhiy Serheii, (2006). *The Origins of the Slavic Nations: Premodern Identities: Russia, Ukraine, Belarus*. An excellent starting point for those looking at regional histories and identities.

Polo, Marco, *The Travels of Marco Polo*, ed. Manuel Komroff (1926). A solid translation of Marco Polo's famous account.

Popovic, Alexandre, *The Revolt of African Slaves in Iraq in the 3rd/9th Century*, trans. Leon King (1999). The account of a massive revolt against their enslavers by enslaved Africans taken to labor in Iraq's mines and fields.

Riasonovsky, Nicholas V. and Mark. D. Stteinberg, *A History of Russia*, 9th ed. (2018). A great place to begin. Chapters 1–4 of the book cover Ukraine and Russia.

Rossabi, Morris, *A History of China* (2014). Part of the Blackwell History of the World series and an excellent overview of Chinese history.

_____, *Voyager from Xanadu: Rabban Sauma and the First Journey from China to the West* (2010). Rossabi's exploration in this second/revised edition uses additional historical sources and speculation to imaginatively expand on E. A. Wallis Budge's 1920s translation of Bar Sāwmā's late thirteenth-century account of his westward travels from Mongol territories to European cities like Rome and Paris.

Scott, Robert, *Gothic Enterprise: A Guide to Understanding the Medieval Cathedral* (2003). The meaning and social function of religious building in medieval cities in northern Europe.

Shaffer, Lynda Norene, *Maritime Southeast Asia to 1500* (1996). A history of the peoples of the southeast fringe of the Eastern Hemisphere, up to the time that they became connected to the global commercial networks of the world.

Shimada, Izumi, "Evolution of Andean Diversity: Regional Formations (500 BCE–CE 600)," in Frank Salomon and Stuart Schwartz (eds.), *South America*, vol. 3 of *The Cambridge History of the Native Peoples of the Americas* (1999), pt. 1, pp. 350–517. A splendid overview that contrasts the varieties of lowland and highland cultures.

Steinberg, David Joel, et al., *In Search of Southeast Asia: A Modern History*, rev. ed. (1987). An account of the emergence of the modern Southeast Asian polities of Cambodia, Burma, Thailand, and Indonesia.

Tanner, Harold M., *China: A History* (2009). Along with Rossabi (2014), an excellent overview of the full history of China.

Tyerman, Christopher, *God's War: A New History of the Crusades* (2006). The balance of religious and nonreligious motivations in the Crusades.

Waley, Daniel, *The Italian City-Republics*, 3rd ed. (1988). The structures and culture of the new cities of medieval Italy.

Watson, Andrew, *Agricultural Innovation in the Early Islamic World: The Diffusion of Crops and Farming Techniques, 700–1100* (1983). An impressive study of the spread of new crops throughout the Muslim world.

Weatherford, Jack, *Genghis Khan and the Making of the Modern World* (2004). Going beyond the violence of conquest, this book describes and analyzes the ways in which Mongol rule brought consistency (and some would say advancement) to disparate societies that lived under Mongol control.

West, Charles, *Reframing the Feudal Revolution: Political and Social Transformation between Marne and Moselle, c. 800–c. 1100* (2013). Big change seen through an intensely studied region.

Wickham, Chris, *Sleepwalking into a New World: The Emergence of Italian City Communes in the Twelfth Century* (2015). Origins of the city democracies of medieval Italy.

CHAPTER 11: CRISES AND RECOVERY IN EURASIA, 1300–1500

Barkey, Karen, *Empire of Difference: The Ottomans in Comparative Perspective* (2008). A revisionist view of the rise and flourishing of the Ottoman Empire.

Belich, James., *The World the Plague Made: The Black Death and the Rise of Europe* (2022). A vital survey of the comparative effects of the Bubonic plague of the fourteenth century, arguing that it left Europe underpopulated and fragmented into different states.

Bois, Guy, *The Crisis of Feudalism: Economy and Society in Eastern Normandy, c. 1300–1550* (1984). A good case study of a French region that illustrates the turmoil in fourteenth-century Europe.

Brook, Timothy, *Praying for Power: Buddhism and the Formation of Gentry Society in Late Ming China* (1994). An analysis of the role of a significant religious force in the political and social developments of the Ming.

Clunas, Craig, and Jessica Harrison-Hall (eds.), *Ming: 50 Years That Changed China* (2014). Developed to accompany an exhibition at the British Museum, this catalog includes richly illustrated scholarly essays that explore clothing, jewelry, courtly objects, and commerce during the Ming dynasty.

Dardess, John, *A Ming Society: T'ai-ho County, Kiangsi, Fourteenth to Seventeenth Centuries* (1996). A work that covers the different changes and developments of a single locality in China through the centuries.

Dols, Michael Walter, *The Black Death in the Middle East* (1977). One of the few scholarly works to examine the Black Death outside Europe.

Dreyer, Edward, *Early Ming China: A Political History, 1355–1435* (1982). A useful account of the early years of the Ming dynasty.

_____, *Zheng He: China and the Oceans in the early Ming Dynasty, 1405–1433* (2005). Biography of Zheng He, which considers why Chinese and European explorations diverged.

Eisenstein, Elizabeth, *The Printing Revolution in Early Modern Europe*, 2nd ed. (2012). Makes a strong argument in favor of the printing press's significance to European history.

Faroqhi, Suraiya N., and Kate Fleet (eds.), *The Cambridge History of Turkey*, vol. 2, *The Ottoman Empire as a World Power, 1453–1603* (2013). An overview of this crucial period in Ottoman history, written by experts in the field.

Febvre, Lucien and Henri-Jean Martin, *The Coming of the Book: The Impact of Printing, 1450–1800.* An exploration of the changes wrought in Europe by the printing press. Insightful argument about the significance of printing to early modern European states.

Finkel, Caroline, *Osman's Dream: The Story of the Ottoman Empire, 1300–1923* (2005). The most authoritative overview of Ottoman history.

Finnane, Antonia, *Changing Clothes in China: Fashion, History, Nation* (2008). An exploration of changing Chinese identities from the perspective of clothing.

Green, Monica, "The Four Black Deaths," *American Historical Review* 125, no. 5 (2020): 1601–1631. An article that provocatively explores the origins and circulation of the Black Death in Central Asia and elsewhere.

Hale, John, *The Civilization of Europe in the Renaissance* (1994). A beautifully crafted account of the politics, economics, and culture of the Renaissance period in western Europe.

He, Yuming, *Home and the World: Editing the "Glorious Ming" in Woodblock-Printed Books of the Sixteenth and Seventeenth Centuries* (2013). An insightful exploration of Ming society through a close look at its vibrant print culture and market for books.

Hodgson, Marshall, *The Venture of Islam: Conscience and History in a World Civilization*, vol. 3 (1974). A good volume on the workings of the Ottoman state.

Hoffman, Philip T., *Why Did Europe Conquer the World?* (2015). Makes an interesting case for the importance of Europe's use of gunpowder technologies.

Itzkowitz, Norman, *Ottoman Empire and Islamic Tradition* (1972). Another good book on the Ottoman state.

Jackson, Peter, *The Delhi Sultanate* (1999). A meticulous, highly specialized political and military history.

Jackson, Peter, and Lawrence Lockhart (eds.), *The Cambridge History of Iran*, vol. 6 (1986). A volume that deals with the Timurid and Safavid periods in Iran.

Jones, E. L., *The European Miracle* (1981). A provocative work on the economic and social recovery from the Black Death.

Kafadar, Cemal, *Between Two Worlds: The Construction of the Ottoman State* (1995). A thorough reconsideration of the origins of one of the world's great land empires.

Karamustafa, Ahmed, *God's Unruly Friends: Dervish Groups in the Islamic Later Middle Period, 1200–1550* (1994). A book that describes the unorthodox Islamic activities that were occurring in the Islamic world prior to and alongside the establishment of the Ottoman and Safavid Empires.

Levathes, Louise, *When China Ruled the Seas: The Treasure Fleet of the Dragon Throne, 1405–33* (1994). A book that provides a lively account of the Zheng He expeditions.

Lowry, Heath W., *The Nature of the Early Ottoman State* (2003). New perspectives on the rise of the Ottomans to prominence.

McNeill, William, *Plagues and Peoples* (1976). A pathbreaking work with a highly useful chapter on the spread of the Black Death throughout the Afro-Eurasian landmass.

Morgan, David, *Medieval Persia, 1040–1797* (1988). Contains an informative discussion of the Safavid state.

Peirce, Leslie, *The Imperial Harem: Women and Sovereignty in the Ottoman Empire* (1993). A work that describes the powerful place that imperial women had in political affairs.

Pirenne, Henri, *Economic and Social History of Medieval Europe* (1937). A classic study of the economic and social recovery from the Black Death.

Reid, James J., *Tribalism and Society in Islamic Iran, 1500–1629* (1983). A useful account of how the Mongols and other nomadic steppe peoples influenced Iran in the era when the Safavids were establishing their authority.

Savory, Roger, *Iran under the Safavids* (1980). A standard and still-useful work on Safavid history.

Schäfer, Dagmar, *The Crafting of the 10,000 Things: Knowledge and Technology in Seventeenth-Century China* (2011). An innovative study of the philosophy of technology and crafts in the late Ming period with important implications for the global history of science.

Singman, Jeffrey L. (ed.), *Daily Life in Medieval Europe* (1999). An introductory description of the social and material world experienced by Europeans of different walks of life.

Tuchman, Barbara W., *A Distant Mirror: The Calamitous Fourteenth Century* (1978). A book that shows, in a vigorous way, how war, famine, and pestilence devastated Europeans in the fourteenth century.

Walton, Linda., *Middle Imperial China, 900–1350* (2023). A comprehensive study of Song China and its integration into the Mongol Empire, with important insight on Han relations with peoples beyond their borders.

Wittek, Paul, *The Rise of the Ottoman Empire* (1958). A work that contains vital insights on the emergence of the Ottoman state amid the political chaos in Anatolia.

CHAPTER 12: CONTACT, COMMERCE, AND COLONIZATION, 1450–1600

Axtell, James, *Beyond 1492: Encounters in Colonial North America* (1992). A wonderfully informed speculation about Indigenous reactions to Europeans.

Brady, Thomas A., Heiko A. Oberman, and James D. Tracy (eds.), *Handbook of European History 1400–1600: Late Middle Ages, Renaissance, and Reformation*, vol. 1, *Structures and Assertions* (1996). A good synthetic survey of recent literature and historiographical debates.

Brook, Timothy, *Vermeer's Hat: The Seventeenth Century and the Dawn of the Global World* (2008). An interesting look at the connections forged across the globe through the works of a well-known European artist.

Casale, Giancarlo, *The Ottoman Age of Exploration* (2010). The author places Ottoman exploration in a comparative context alongside European overseas expansion.

Cass, Victoria, *Dangerous Women: Warriors, Grannies, and Geishas of the Ming* (1999). An original study of Chinese female archetypes in memoirs, miscellanies, short stories, and novels.

Chaudhuri, K. N., *Trade and Civilisation in the Indian Ocean: An Economic History from the Rise of Islam to 1750* (1985). An excellent, comprehensive work that deals with the Indian Ocean economy and the appearance of European merchants there from the sixteenth century onward.

Clendinnen, Inga, *Aztecs: An Interpretation* (1991). Brilliantly reconstructs the culture of Tenochtitlán in the years before its conquest.

Crosby, Alfred W., *The Columbian Exchange: Biological and Cultural Consequences of 1492* (1972). A provocative discussion of the ecological consequences that followed the European "discovery" of the Americas.

———, *Ecological Imperialism: The Biological Expansion of Europe, 900–1900* (1986). Another important work on the ecological consequences of European expansion.

Curtin, Philip, *Cross-Cultural Trade in World History* (1984). A work stressing the role of trade and commerce in establishing cross-cultural contacts.

Faroqhi, Suraiya N. (ed.), *The Cambridge History of Turkey*, vol. 3, *The Later Ottoman Empire, 1603–1839* (2008). Definitive articles on this important period in Ottoman history.

Faroqhi, Suraiya N., and Kate Fleet (eds.), *The Cambridge History of Turkey*, vol. 2, *The Ottoman Empire as a World Power, 1453–1603* (2013). A collection of articles written by leading scholars of this crucial period in Ottoman history.

Febvre, Lucien, *The Problem of Unbelief in the Sixteenth Century: The Religion of Rabelais* (1982). A tour de force of intellectual history by the man who moved the study of the Reformation away from great men to the broader question of religious revival and mentalities.

Flynn, Dennis, and Arturo Giráldez (eds.), *Metals and Monies in an Emerging Global Economy* (1997). Contains several articles relating to silver and the Asian trade.

Frank, Andre Gunder, *ReOrient: Global Economy in the Asian Age* (1998). A reassessment of the role of Asia in the economic development of the world from around 1400 onward.

Giraldez, Arturo, *The Age of Trade: The Manila Galleons and the Dawn of the Global Economy* (2015). The best analysis of the origins and effects of the Spanish colonization of the Philippines and the making of the Pacific Ocean world.

Glahn, Richard von, *The Economic History of China: From Antiquity to the Nineteenth Century* (2016). A masterful new survey of Chinese economic history.

———, *Fountain of Fortune: Money and Monetary Policy in China, 1000–1700* (1996). Includes an excellent analysis of the history of silver in Ming China.

Greer, Allan, *Property and Dispossession: Native, Empires, and Land in Early Modern North America* (2018). A comparative account of English, French, and Spanish early settlements and the role that Indigenous peoples played in the making of empires from the Arctic to the Caribbean.

Gruzinski, Serge, *The Conquest of Mexico* (1993). An important work on the conquest of Mexico.

Habib, Irfan, *The Agrarian System of Mughal India* (1963). One of the best studies on the subject.

Hall, Richard Seymour, *Empires of the Monsoon: A History of the Indian Ocean and Its Invaders* (1996). A very engaging journalistic account with fabulous details.

Hodgson, Marshall, *The Venture of Islam*, vols. 2 and 3 (1974). A magisterial work that includes the Indian subcontinent in its careful study of the political and cultural history of the whole Islamic world.

Hulme, Peter, *Colonial Encounters: Europe and the Native Caribbean, 1492–1797* (1986). Presents an interesting interpretation of the encounters of Europeans and Native Americans.

Lach, Donald F., *Asia in the Making of Europe*, 5 books in 3 vols. (1965–). Perhaps the single most comprehensive and innovative guide to the European voyages of discovery.

Lockhart, James, and Stuart Schwartz, *Early Latin America* (1983). One of the finest studies of European expansion in the late fifteenth century.

McCann, James, *Maize and Grace: Africa's Encounter with a New World Crop, 1500–2000* (2005). A significant study of how maize, a New World crop, became Africa's most widely grown grain.

Melville, Elinor G. K., *A Plague of Sheep: Environmental Consequences of the Conquest of Mexico* (1994). A history of the transformation of a valley in Mexico from the Aztec period to the era of Spanish rule.

Mignolo, Walter D., *The Darker Side of the Renaissance: Literacy, Territoriality, and Colonization* (1995). Uses literary theory and literary images to present provocative interpretations of the encounter of Europeans and Native Americans.

Ozbaran, Salih, *Ottoman Expansion toward the Indian Ocean in the 16th Century* (2009). An important treatment of the Ottoman entry into the Indian Ocean at a time when the Portuguese were also expanding there.

Pagden, Anthony, *European Encounters with the New World* (1993). A complex look at the deep and lasting imprint of the New World on its conquerors.

Parker, Geoffrey, *The Military Revolution: Military Innovation and the Rise of the West, 1500–1800* (1996). Traces the changes in technology and tactics in the early modern period and discusses the political significance of this "revolution."

Pelikan, Jaroslav, *Reformation of Church and Dogma (1300–1700)* (1988). An important overview of major religious controversies.

Phillips, William D., and Carla Rahn Phillips, *The World of Christopher Columbus* (1992). One of the finest studies of European expansion in the late fifteenth century.

Remensnyder, Amy G., *La Conquistadora: The Virgin Mary at War and Peace in the Old and New Worlds* (2014). The author illuminates the continuities of the spiritual reconquest of Iberia and the conquest of the Americas and the symbolic importance of the Virgin as the mother of conversion in a man's world.

Roper, Lyndal, *Martin Luther: Renegade and Prophet* (2016). A magisterial biography that demonstrates the ways in which Luther was a rebel but also a man of his time.

Russell-Wood, A. J. R., *The Portuguese Empire, 1415–1808* (1992). An important survey of early Portuguese exploration.

Tutino, John, *The Mexican Heartland: How Communities Shaped Capitalism, A Nation, and World History* (2018). A view of global integration after 1492 seen from the view of central Mexico.

CHAPTER 13: WORLDS ENTANGLED, 1600–1750

Alam, Muzaffar, *The Crisis of Empire in Mughal North India* (1993). Represents the best of the new scholarly interpretations of the subject.

Bay, Edna, *Wives of the Leopard: Gender, Politics, and Culture in the Kingdom of Dahomey* (1998). A useful treatment of gender issues in Dahomey.

Blackburn, Robin, *The Making of New World Slavery: From the Baroque to the Modern, 1492–1800* (1997). A good place to begin when studying African enslavement and the Atlantic slave trade, this book compares the early expansion of the plantation systems across the Atlantic and throughout the Americas.

Blom, Philipp, *Nature's Mutiny: How the Little Ice Age of the Long Seventeenth Century Transformed the West and Shaped the Present* (2019). The author explains how climate change altered how Europeans viewed nature, risk, and science, and prepared the way for an intellectual revolution.

Bushkovitch, Paul, *Peter the Great* (2016). An updated version of a standard work, offering a concise overview of one of Russia's most celebrated and energetic rulers.

Calloway, Colin G., *One Vast Winter Count: The Native American West before Lewis and Clark* (2003). A sweeping survey of Indigenous North American histories prior to the nineteenth century.

Crossley, Pamela, *A Translucent Mirror: History and Identity in Qing Imperial Ideology* (1999). The author deals with the formation of identities such as "Manchu" and "Chinese" during the Qing period.

Dale, Stephen F., *The Muslim Empires of the Ottomans, Safavids, and Mughals* (2010). A comparative overview of Islam's three most powerful empires of the sixteenth and seventeenth centuries.

Eltis, David, and David Richardson, *Atlas of the Transatlantic Slave Trade* (2010). This work contains the most up-to-date data on the Atlantic slave trade, including the numbers transported, where the captives came from, and where they landed.

Flynn, Dennis O., and Arturo Giráldez (eds.), *Metals and Money in an Emerging World Economy* (1997). A collection of articles about the place of silver in the world economy.

Forsyth, James, *A History of the Peoples of Siberia: Russia's North Asian Colony 1581–1990* (1992). A narrative overview of a violent history reminiscent of the western expansion of the United States.

Glahn, Richard von, *Fountains of Fortune: Money and Monetary Policy in China, 1000–1700* (1996). A discussion of the place of silver in the Chinese economy.

Halperin, Charles J., *Russia and the Golden Horde: The Mongol Impact on Medieval Russian History* (1985). A book on the rise of Muscovy, forebear of the Russian Empire, from within the Mongol realm.

Hämäläinen, Pekka, *The Comanche Empire* (2008). A book that inverts the conventional history of empires in North America by arguing that the Comanches were the most successful expansionist power in the middle of the continent during the eighteenth century.

Hartley, Janet, *Siberia: A History of the People* (2014). A vivid portrait of the diverse conquerors—fur traders, Cossack adventurers, political criminals—of a region larger than almost all continents.

Hattox, Ralph S., *Coffee and Coffeehouses: The Origins of a Social Beverage in the Medieval Near East* (1985). This work shows how widespread and popular coffee consumption and coffeehouses were around the world.

Herzog, Tamar, *Frontiers of Possession: Spain and Portugal in Europe and the Americas* (2015). An exploration of how Spanish and Portuguese rulers carved up the New World, less by military action and diplomatic treaties than by quarrels over land settlement and rights to trade and travel.

Heywood, Linda M., and John K. Thornton, *Central Africans, Atlantic Creoles, and the Foundation of the Americas, 1585–1660* (2007). Examines how Africans repopulated the Americas and created hybrid cultures.

Huang, Ray, *1587, A Year of No Significance: The Ming Dynasty in Decline* (1981). An insightful analysis of the problems confronting the late Ming.

Koch, Alexander, et al., "Earth System Impacts of the European Arrival and Great Dying in the Americas after 1492," *Quarternary Science Review* 207 (March 2019): 13–39. The findings of a group of climatologists at the University of London on the impact of the morbidity of Native American populations on the climate.

Lensen, George, *The Russian Push toward Japan: Russo-Japanese Relations 1697–1875* (1959). A discussion of why and how Japan established its first border with another state and how Russia pursued its ambitions in the Pacific.

Lockhart, James, *The Nahuas after the Conquest* (1992). A landmark study of the social reorganization of Mesoamerican societies under Spanish rule.

Lovejoy, Paul, *Transformations in Slavery: A History of Slavery in Africa* (1983). An excellent discussion of African enslavement.

Mathee, Rudi, *Persia in Crisis, Safavid Decline, and the Fall of Isfahan* (2012). A study of the disintegration of the Safavid state.

Mikhail, Alan, *Nature and Empire in Ottoman Egypt: An Environmental History* (2011). An important study of the impact of the environment on Egypt in the eighteenth century.

Monahan, Erika, *The Merchants of Siberia: Trade in Early Modern Eurasia* (2016). A stirring account of entrepreneurs battling the harshest imaginable conditions to establish trading networks connecting the far-flung territories north of the ancient Silk Roads.

Moon, David, *The Plough That Broke the Steppes: Agriculture and Environment in Russia's Grasslands, 1700–1913* (2013). A bold incorporation of environmental aspects to retell the epic story of Russia's most numerous social group.

Nakane, Chie, and Shinzaburo Oishi (eds.), *Tokugawa Japan: The Social and Economic Antecedents of Modern Japan* (1990). First-rate essays on Japanese village society, urban life, literacy, and culture.

Nwokeji, G. Uko, *The Slave Trade and Culture in the Bight of Biafra: An African Society in the Atlantic World* (2010). A study of the Aro peoples of southeastern Nigeria and their use of their commercial powers to promote a vigorous trade with European enslavers on the coast.

Pamuk, Sevket, *A Monetary History of the Ottoman Empire* (2000). A discussion of the place of silver in the Ottoman Empire.

Parker, Geoffrey, *Global Crisis: War, Climate Change, and Catastrophe in the Seventeenth Century* (2013). A comprehensive and exhaustively researched study of the effects of the Little Ice Age on the governments and societies of the entire world in the seventeenth century.

——— (ed.), *The Thirty Years' War* (1997). The standard account of the conflict and its outcomes.

Pendergrast, Mark, *Uncommon Grounds: The History of Coffee and How It Transformed Our World* (2010). A narrative of coffee's history and attendant culture, from its Abyssinian origins to the present day.

Perdue, Peter C., *China Marches West: The Qing Conquest of Central Asia* (2005). This volume chronicles the expansion of the Qing Empire to its northwest, drawing comparisons to other colonial empires and their legacies.

Platonov, S. F., *Ivan the Terrible* (1986). Covers the controversies over Russia's infamous tsar.

Rawski, Evelyn, *The Last Emperors: A Social History of Qing Imperial Institutions* (1998). This volume explores the mechanisms and processes through which the Qing court negotiated its Manchu identity.

Reid, Anthony, *Charting the Shape of Early Modern Southeast Asia* (1999). A collection of articles by a leading historian of Southeast Asia.

Reséndez, Andrés, *The Other Slavery: The Uncovered Story of Indian Enslavement in America* (2016). The most comprehensive treatment of how Europeans tried to enslave Indigenous people of the Americas.

Spence, Jonathan, and John Wills (eds.), *From Ming to Ch'ing: Conquest, Region, and Continuity in Seventeenth-Century China* (1979). Covers the various aspects of a tumultuous period of dynastic transition.

Subramanyam, Sanjay, *From the Tigris to the Ganges: Explorations in Connected History* (2012). A study that demonstrates that Afro-Eurasia in the seventeenth and eighteenth centuries contained a porous network of empires, cultures, and economies.

Subramanyam, Sanjay, and Muzaffar Alam, *Indo-Persian Travels in the Age of Discoveries, 1400–1800* (2012). A lively portrait of cultural exchanges between Persia, central Asia, and India as seen in travel literature.

Taylor, Alan, *American Colonies: The Settling of North America* (2001). Brings together British, French, and Spanish colonial histories and shows how the fortunes of each were entangled with one another and with those of diverse Native American peoples.

Thornton, John K., *Africa and Africans in the Making of the Atlantic World, 1400–1800* (1998). A wonderful discussion of the large role enslaved Africans played in the formation of the Atlantic world.

———, *The Kongolese Saint Anthony: Dona Beatriz Kimpa Vita and the Antonian Movement, 1684–1706* (1998). An excellent monograph on religious movements in Kongo.

Toby, Ronald P., *State and Diplomacy in Early Modern Japan: Asia in the Development of the Tokugawa Bakufu* (1984). The author shows that the Japanese, far from being isolated from the outside world, engaged in vigorous and successful diplomacy.

Van Dusen, Nancy E., *Global Indios: The Indigenous Struggle for Justice in Sixteenth-Century Spain* (2015). A remarkable study of the ways that Spanish rulers enslaved Indigenous people in the Americas and even exported them back to Europe.

Vilar, Pierre, *A History of Gold and Money* (1991). An excellent study of the development of the early silver and gold economies.

White, Sam, *A Cold Welcome: The Little Ice Age and Europe's Encounter with North America* (2017). A discussion of the problems encountered by the first European settlers in mainland North America.

CHAPTER 14: CULTURES OF SPLENDOR AND POWER, 1500–1780

Axtell, James, *The Invasion of America: The Contest of Cultures in Colonial North America* (1985). Discusses the strategies of Christian missionaries in converting Indigenous people in North America, as well as the success of Indigenous people in converting Europeans.

Babaie, Sussan, *Isfahan and Its Palaces: Statecraft, Shi'ism and the Architecture of Conviviality in Early Modern Iran* (2008). An overview of the city of Isfahan as the capital of the Safavid state.

Barmé, Geremie R., *The Forbidden City* (2008). A concise introduction to the history of one of the most important physical emblems of Chinese imperial power.

Berlin, Ira, *Many Thousands Gone: The First Two Centuries of Slavery in North America* (1998). Surveys the development of African American culture in colonial North America.

Bleichmar, Daniela, *Visible Empire: Botanical Expeditions and Visual Culture in the Hispanic Enlightenment* (2012). A fascinating and beautifully illustrated history of Creole botanical expeditions in the eighteenth century.

———, *Visual Voyages: Images of Latin American Nature from Columbus to Darwin* (2017). The author explains how important pictures and images of nature shaped scientific pursuits.

Brook, Timothy, *The Confusions of Pleasure: Commerce and Culture in Ming China* (1999). An insightful survey of Ming society.

Canby, Sheila R., *The Shahnama of Shah Tahmasp: The Persian Book of Kings* (2014). A beautiful volume of the epic story of the founding of Persian kings to service a narrative of Safavid rulers.

Clunas, Craig, *Superfluous Things: Material Culture and Social Status in Early Modern China* (1991). A good account of the late Ming elite's growing passion for material things.

Collcutt, Martin, Marius Jansen, and Isao Kumakura, *A Cultural Atlas of Japan* (1988). A sweeping look at the many different forms of Japanese cultural expression over the centuries, including the flourishing urban culture of Edo.

Crèvecoeur, Hector St. John de, *Letters from an American Farmer*, reprinted from the original edition, with a prefatory note by W. P. Trent and an introduction by Ludwig Lewisohn (1904). Powerful and informative letters of a French settler in the Americas in the eighteenth century.

Darnton, Robert, *The Business of the Enlightenment: A Publishing History of the* Encyclopédie, *1775–1800* (1979). The classic study of Europe's first great compendium of knowledge.

Dash, Mike, *Tulipomania: The Story of the World's Most Coveted Flower and the Extraordinary Passions It Aroused* (1999). A global perspective on and lively account of the spread of the tulip around the world as a flower signifying both beauty and status.

Dikötter, Frank, *The Discourse of Race in Modern China* (1992). A good survey of Chinese discussions of race in the modern era.

Doniger, Wendy, *The Hindus: An Alternative History* (2009). A deeply scholarly yet accessibly written history of Hinduism that considers both texts and popular practices and contains a lively account of dissenting traditions.

Elman, Benjamin A., *On Their Own Terms: Science in China, 1550–1900* (2005). A study of the development of "native" Chinese science and how the process interacted with the introduction of western science to China over the course of three and a half centuries.

Eze, Emmanuel Chukwudi (ed.), *Race and the Enlightenment: A Reader* (1997). Readings examining the idea of race in the context of the Enlightenment.

Fleischer, Cornell, *Bureaucrat and Intellectual in the Ottoman Empire: The Historian Mustafa Ali (1540–1600)* (1986). Offers good insight into the world of culture and intellectual vitality in the Ottoman Empire.

Gómez, Nicolás Wey, *The Tropics of Empire: Why Columbus Sailed South to the Indies* (2008). Argues that early scientific efforts to study hotter tropical latitudes were the origins of Europe's new science.

Grafton, Anthony, April Shelford, and Nancy Siraisi, *New Worlds, Ancient Texts: The Power of Tradition and the Shock of Discovery* (1995). A concise discussion of the impact of the New World on European thought.

Gutiérrez, Ramón, *When Jesus Came, the Corn Mothers Went Away: Marriage, Sexuality, and Power in New Mexico, 1500–1846* (1991). A provocative dissection of the spiritual dimensions of European colonialism in the Americas.

Harley, J. B., and David Woodward (eds.), *The History of Cartography*, vol. 2, book 2, *Cartography in the Traditional East and Southeast Asian Societies* (1994). An authoritative treatment of the subject.

Hart, Roger, *Imagined Civilizations: China, the West, and Their First Encounter* (2013). A treatment of the Jesuit mission to China as the first contact between Chinese and European cultures.

Horton, Robin, *Patterns of Thought in Africa and the West: Essays on Magic, Religion, and Science* (1993). Reflections on African patterns of thought and attitudes toward nature, which can help us understand African American religious beliefs and resistance movements.

Huff, Toby, *Intellectual Curiosity and the Scientific Revolution: A Comparative Perspective* (2011). This book deals with Europe's scientific revolution comparatively, asking why it occurred in Europe and not in China or the Islamic world.

Kai, Ho Yi (ed.), *Science in China, 1600–1900: Essays by Benjamin Elman* (2015). Elman, an expert on Chinese science, offers his latest word on China's scientific achievements in a context of Europe's transmission of science through the Jesuit mission.

Keene, Donald, *The Japanese Discovery of Europe: Honda Toshiaki and Other Discoverers, 1720–1798* (1952). A study of the ways Japan managed to incorporate knowledge from the outside world with the development of national traditions.

Ko, Dorothy, *Teachers of the Inner Chambers: Women and Culture in Seventeenth-Century China* (1994). Explores the lives of elite women in late Ming and early Qing China.

Lewis, Bernard, *Race and Color in Islam* (1979). Examines the Islamic attitude toward race and color.

Mazower, Mark, *Salonica, City of Ghosts: Christians, Muslims and Jews, 1430–1900* (2006). An overview of one of the most important cities of the Ottoman Empire.

Mokyr, Joel, *A Culture of Growth: The Origins of the Modern Economy* (2016). Traces how the search for new knowledge yielded practical and valuable applications and set the stage for Europe's economic breakthrough.

Morgan, Philip D., *Slave Counterpoint: Black Culture in the Eighteenth-Century Chesapeake and Lowcountry* (1998). Describes the development of African American culture in colonial North America.

Munck, Thomas, *The Enlightenment: A Comparative Social History, 1721–1794* (2000). A wonderful survey, with unusual examples from the periphery, especially from Scandinavia and the Habsburg Empire.

Necipoğlu, Gülru, *Architecture, Ceremonial, and Power: The Topkapi Palace in the Fifteenth and Sixteenth Centuries* (1991). A magnificently illustrated book that shows the enormous artistic talent that the Ottoman rulers poured into their imperial structure.

Parker, Kenneth, *Early Modern Tales of the Orient: A Critical Anthology* (1999). A collection of travelers' accounts of the Near East.

"Publishing and the Print Culture in Late Imperial China," special issue, *Late Imperial China* 17, no. 1 (June 1996). Contains a collection of important articles with a foreword by the French cultural historian Roger Chartier.

Qaisar, Ahsan Jan, *The Indian Response to European Technology, AD 1498–1707* (1998). A meticulous, scholarly work on this little-studied subject.

Ramaswamy, Sumathi, "Conceit of the Globe in Mughal Visual Practice," *Comparative Studies in Society and History* 49, no. 4 (2007): 751–82. An excellent article that shows how Mughal rulers were aware of the world and adapted its discoveries to their Indo-centric visions.

Rizvi, Athar Abbas, *The Wonder That Was India*, vol. 2, *A Survey of the History and Culture of the Indian Sub-continent from the Coming of the Muslims to the British Conquest, 1200–1700* (1987). A deeply learned work in intellectual history.

Safier, Neil, *Measuring the New World: Enlightenment Science and South America* (2008). Examines the ways in which European, and especially Parisian, surveyors set about gauging the curvature of the earth, starting in Quito, Ecuador. Along the way, they learned much more about local natural history, which flowed back to Paris to inform the Enlightenment.

Smith, Bernard, *European Vision and the South Pacific* (1985). An excellent cultural history of Cook's voyages.

Smith, Richard J., *Chinese Maps: Images of "All under Heaven"* (1996). Provides a good introduction to the history of cartography in China.

Sorkin, David, *The Religious Enlightenment: Protestants, Jews, and Catholics from London to Vienna* (2008). Discusses a wide range of thinkers who were able to reconcile Enlightenment thought with religious belief.

Subrahmanyam, Sanjay, *Courtly Encounters: Translating Courtliness and Violence in Early Modern Eurasia* (2012). Explores the place of South Asia as a point of convergence for artists and scientists and the role of the Mughal court as a hub for global exchange.

Tignor, Robert L., "W. R. Bascom and the Ife Bronzes," *Africa: Journal of the International African Institute* 60, no. 3 (1990): 425–34. Explores controversies over issues of where antiquities of great artistic value like the Ife bronzes should reside.

Welch, Anthony, *Shah Abbas and the Arts of Isfahan* (1973). Describes the astonishing architectural and artistic renaissance of the city of Isfahan under the Safavid ruler Shah Abbas.

Whitfield, Peter, *The Image of the World: Twenty Centuries of World Maps* (1994). A good introduction to the history of cartography in different parts of the world.

Wilks, Ivor, *Forests of Gold: Essays on the Akan and the Kingdom of Asante* (1993). A study that focuses on the Asantes' drive for wealth.

Zilfi, Madeline C., *The Politics of Piety: The Ottoman Ulema in the Post-Classical Age (1600–1800)* (1988). Explores the cultural flourishing that took place within the Islamic world in this period.

CHAPTER 15: REORDERING THE WORLD, 1750–1850

Allen, Robert C., *The British Industrial Revolution in Global Perspective* (2009). The most recent and authoritative study of the industrial revolution in Britain and its implications around the world.

———, *Global Economic History: A Very Short Introduction* (2011). A more globally oriented overview of industrialization than Robert Allen's book on British industrialization from a comparative perspective (above).

Anderson, Fred, *Crucible of War: The Seven Years' War and the Fate of Empire in British North America, 1754–1766* (2000). The best synthesis of the "great war for empire" that set the stage for the American Revolution.

Bayly, C. A., *Indian Society and the Making of the British Empire* (1998). A useful work on the early history of the British conquest of India.

Blackburn, Robin, *The American Crucible: Slavery, Emancipation and Human Rights* (2011). This book offers a comprehensive account of the rise of abolitionism across the Atlantic empires. The author argues that enslaved people and radical thinkers formed coalitions that created the foundations of modern human rights.

———, *The Overthrow of Colonial Slavery, 1776–1848* (1988). Places the abolition of the Atlantic slave trade and colonial slavery in a large historical context.

Cassel, Par Kristoffer, *Grounds of Judgment: Extraterritoriality and Imperial Powers in Nineteenth-Century China and Japan* (2012). A study of the idea and practice of extraterritoriality within the context of the triangular relationship between China, Japan, and the west.

Chaudhuri, K. N., *The Trading World of Asia and the East India Company, 1660–1760* (1978). An authoritative economic history of the East India Company's operations.

Crafts, N. F. R., *British Economic Growth during the Industrial Revolution* (1985). A pioneering study that emphasizes a long-term, more gradual process of adaptation to new institutional and social circumstances.

Daly, M. W. (ed.), *Cambridge History of Egypt*, vol. 2, *Modern Egypt, from 1517 to the End of the Twentieth Century* (1998). Contains authoritative essays on all aspects of modern Egyptian history, including the impact of the French invasion and the rule of Muhammad Ali.

Diamond, Jared, and James A. Robinson (eds.), *Natural Experiments of History* (2010). This book consists of eight comparative studies drawn from history, archaeology, economics, economic history, geography, and political science, covering a spectrum of approaches, ranging from a nonquantitative narrative style to quantitative statistical analyses.

Eacott, Jonathan, *Selling Empire: India in the Making of Britain and America, 1600–1830* (2016). Argues that the conquest of India and the resources extracted from India were vital to attitudes toward expansion in the Americas and the financing of Britain's American empire.

Elvin, Mark, *The Retreat of the Elephants: An Environmental History of China* (2004). A study of the different ways in which China's natural environment was shaped.

Findley, Carter, *Bureaucratic Reform in the Ottoman Empire: The Sublime Porte, 1789–1922* (1980). A useful guide to Ottoman reform efforts in the nineteenth century.

Geggus, David (ed.), *The Impact of the Haitian Revolution in the Atlantic World* (2001). A lively effort to disentangle the effects of the Haitian Revolution from those of the French Revolution.

Hevia, James, *Cherishing Men from Afar: Qing Guest Ritual and the Macartney Embassy of 1793* (1995). Offers a definitive interpretation of the nature of Sino-British conflict in the Qing period.

Hobsbawm, Eric, *Nations and Nationalism since 1780* (1990). An important overview of the rise of the nation-state and nationalism around the world.

Howe, Daniel Walker, *What Hath God Wrought: The Transformation of America, 1815–1848* (2007). A Pulitzer Prize–winning interpretation of how new technologies and new ideas reshaped the economy, society, culture, and politics of the United States in the first half of the nineteenth century.

Hunt, Lynn, *Politics, Culture and Class in the French Revolution* (1984). Examines the influence of sociocultural shifts as causes and consequences of the French Revolution, emphasizing the symbols and practice of politics invented during the revolution.

Inikori, Joseph, *Africans and the Industrial Revolution in England* (2002). Demonstrates the important role that Africa and Africans played in facilitating the industrial revolution.

Isset, Christopher Mills, *State, Peasant, and Merchant in Qing Manchuria, 1644–1862* (2007). A study of the relationships between sociopolitical structures and peasant lives in a key region during the Qing.

James, C. L. R., *The Black Jacobins: Toussaint L'Ouverture and the San Domingo Revolution* (1938). This classic chronicle of the only successful revolt of the enslaved in history provides a critical portrait of its leader, Toussaint L'Ouverture.

John, Richard R., and Jonathan Silberstein-Loeb (eds.), *Making News: The Political Economy of Journalism in Britain and America from the Glorious Revolution to the Internet* (2015). An indispensable collection of essays about the transformation of communication and printing, and the rise and fall of the modern newspaper industry.

Jones, E. L., *Growth Recurring* (1988). Discusses the controversy over why the industrial revolution took place in Europe, stressing the unique ecological setting that encouraged long-term investment.

Kinsbruner, Jay, *Independence in Spanish America* (1994). A fine study of the Latin American revolutions that argues that the struggle was as much a civil war as a fight for national independence.

Landers, Jane, *Atlantic Creoles in the Age of Revolutions* (2011). A collection of fascinating and unique portraits of Atlantic world Creoles who managed to move freely and purposefully through French, Spanish, and English colonies, and through Indigenous territory, in the unstable century between 1750 and 1850.

Lieven, Dominic, *Russia against Napoleon* (2010). Explains how outnumbered Russian forces were able to defeat the massive army that Napoleon assembled for his conquest of Russia.

Mokyr, Joel, *Enlightened Economy: An Economic History of Britain, 1700–1850* (2009). Perspectives on the evolution of the British economy in the era that produced the industrial revolution.

———, *The Lever of Riches* (1990). An important study of the causes of the industrial revolution that emphasizes the role of small technological and organizational breakthroughs.

Naquin, Susan, and Evelyn Rawski, *Chinese Society in the Eighteenth Century* (1987). A survey of mid-Qing society.

Neal, Larry, *The Rise of Financial Capitalism* (1990). An important study of the making of financial markets.

Nikitenko, Aleksandr, *Up from Serfdom: My Childhood and Youth in Russia, 1804–1824* (2001). One of the very few recorded life stories of a Russian serf.

Parthasarathi, Prasannan, *Why Europe Grew Rich and Asia Did Not: Global Economic Divergence, 1600–1800* (2011). A work that places the British industrial revolution in a global context, with much emphasis on India's textile industry before it was superseded by British manufacturers.

Perdue, Peter, *China Marches West: The Qing Conquest of Central Asia* (2004). This volume shows how China continued to expand as a territorial empire until the early nineteenth century.

Walker, Charles, *The Túpac Amaru Rebellion* (2014). This is the definitive account of the largest Indigenous uprising in the Andes against Spanish authorities in the 1780s.

Platt, Stephen R., *Imperial Twilight: The Opium War and the End of China's Last Golden Age* (2018). A major work on the lead-up to and the long-term impact of the Opium Wars.

Pomeranz, Kenneth, *The Great Divergence: Europe, China, and the Making of the Modern World Economy* (2000). Offers explanations of why Europe and not some other place in the world, like parts of China or India, forged ahead economically in the nineteenth century.

Popkin, Jeremy D., *You Are All Free: The Haitian Revolution and the Abolition of Slavery* (2010). The most up-to-date survey of the events leading to the Haitian Revolution, this book calls attention to the role of local factors in the emancipation of enslaved Haitians and explores the ways in which insurgency of the enslaved transformed revolutionary politics in Europe.

Tackett, Timothy, *The Coming of the Terror in the French Revolution* (2017). An authoritative account of the most controversial phase of the French Revolution.

Taylor, Alan, *American Revolutions: A Continental History, 1750–1804* (2016). A sweeping interpretation of the founding of the United States that places the War of Independence in a North American perspective, bringing together the diverse revolutions that transformed societies and borders across the continent.

Wakeman, Frederic, Jr., "The Canton Trade and the Opium War," in John K. Fairbank (ed.), *The Cambridge History of China*, vol. 10 (1978), pp. 163–212. The standard account of the episode.

Wong, R. Bin, *China Transformed: Historical Change and the Limits of European Experience* (2000). Draws attention to the relative autonomy of merchant capitalists in relation to dynastic states in Europe as compared with China.

Wood, Gordon S., *Empire of Liberty: A History of the Early Republic, 1789–1815* (2009). An excellent synthesis of the history of the United States in the tumultuous years between the ratification of the Constitution and the War of 1812.

Wortman, Richard, *Scenarios of Power: Myth and Ceremony in Russian Monarchy*, 2 vols. (1995–2000). Examines how dynastic Russia confronted the challenges of the revolutionary epoch.

CHAPTER 16: ALTERNATIVE VISIONS OF THE NINETEENTH CENTURY

Anderson, David M., *Revealing Prophets: Prophets in Eastern African History* (1995). Good discussion of the prophets in eastern Africa.

Beecher, Jonathan, *The Utopian Vision of Charles Fourier* (1983). A fine biography of this important thinker.

Boyd, Jean, *The Caliph's Sister: Nana Asma'u, 1793–1865, Teacher, Poet, and Islamic Leader* (1988). A study of the most powerful female Muslim leader in the Fulani religious revolt.

Brower, Benjamin Claude, *A Desert Named Peace: The Violence of France's Empire in the Algerian Sahara, 1844–1902* (2009). Examines colonial violence across a few fields of research and through multiple stories to reveal some unexpected causes—for instance, France's difficult revolutionary past and its sway on the military's institutional culture.

Caplan, Karen D., *Indigenous Citizens: Local Liberalism in Early National Oaxaca and Yucatán* (2009). Shows the ways in which Indigenous people adapted liberalism for their own political imaginations and practices.

Clancy-Smith, Julia, *Rebel and Saint: Muslim Notables, Populist Protest, Colonial Encounter (Algeria and Tunisia, 1800–1904)* (1994). Examines Islamic protest movements against western encroachments in North Africa.

Clogg, Richard, *A Concise History of Greece* (1997). A good introduction to the history of Greece in its European context.

Dalrymple, William, *The Last Mughal: The Fall of a Dynasty: Delhi, 1857* (2007). A deeply researched and riveting account of Delhi during the 1857 revolt.

Danziger, Raphael, *Abd al-Qadir: Resistance to the French and Internal Consolidation* (1977). Still the indispensable work on this important Algerian Muslim leader.

Dowd, Gregory E., *A Spirited Resistance: The North American Indian Struggle for Unity, 1745–1815* (1992). Emphasizes the importance of prophets like Tenskwatawa in the building of pan-Indigenous confederations in the era between the Seven Years' War and the War of 1812.

Ellis, Elizabeth, *The Great Power of Small Nations: Indigenous Diplomacy in the Gulf South* (2023). A superb example of how Indigenous communities created alternative sovereignties in the age of national integration.

Guardino, Peter, *The Dead March: A History of the Mexican-American War* (2017). A definitive account of the war from the Mexican side of the struggle.

Guha, Ranajit, *Elementary Aspects of Peasant Insurgency in Colonial India* (1983). Not specifically on the Indian Rebellion of 1857, but includes it in its pioneering "subalternist" interpretation of South Asian history.

Hämäläinen, Pekka, *Lakota America: A New History of Indigenous Power* (2019). A study of how a river people became an empire of horse people in central North America and shaped the course of U.S. history.

———, *Indigenous Continent: The Epic Contest for North America* (2022). This book explains how the history of North America was less one of White settlement and expansion than of Indigenous adaptation, diplomacy, and successful resistance.

Hamilton, Carolyn (ed.), *The Mfecane Aftermath: Reconstructive Debates in Southern African History* (1995). Debates on Shaka's *Mfecane* movement and its impact on southern Africa.

Hiskett, Mervyn, *The Sword of Truth: The Life and Times of the Shehu Usman dan Fodio* (1994). An authoritative study of the Fulani revolt in northern Nigeria.

Johnson, Douglas H., *Nuer Prophets: A History of Prophecy from the Upper Nile in the Nineteenth and Twentieth Centuries* (1994). Deals with African prophetic and charismatic movements in eastern Africa.

Keddie, Nikki, *An Islamic Response to Imperialism: Political and Religious Writings of Sayyid Jamal ad-Din "al-Afghani" (1968)*. Definitive information on the Afghani's life and influence, coupled with a translation of one of his most important essays.

Lovejoy, Paul E., *Jihād in West Africa during the Age of Revolutions* (2016). This book should be read alongside the one by Lamin Sanneh (below), since these two scholars look at the revolutionary movements taking place in West Africa from differing perspectives. Lovejoy stresses jihads, while Sanneh emphasizes the peaceful uses of Islam.

Michael, Franz, and Chung-li Chang, *The Taiping Rebellion: History and Documents*, 3 vols. (1966–1971). The basic source for the history of the Taipings.

Mukherjee, Rudrangshu, *Awadh in Revolt, 1857–58* (1984). A careful case study of the Indian Rebellion.

Omer-Cooper, J. D., *The Zulu Aftermath: A Nineteenth-Century Revolution in Bantu Africa* (1966). A good place to start in studying Shaka's *Mfecane* movement, which greatly rearranged the political and ethnic makeup of southern Africa.

Ostler, Jeffrey, *The Plains Sioux and U.S. Colonialism from Lewis and Clark to Wounded Knee* (2004). Uses the lens of colonial theory to track relations between the Sioux and the United States, offering fresh insights about the Ghost Dance movement.

Peires, J. B. (ed.), *Before and After Shaka* (1981). Discusses elements in the debate over Shaka's *Mfecane* movement.

Pilbeam, Pamela, *French Socialists before Marx: Workers, Women and the Social Question in France* (2001). Describes the development of a variety of socialist ideas in early nineteenth-century France.

Platt, Stephen R., *Autumn in the Heavenly Kingdom: China, the West, and the Epic Story of the Taiping Civil War* (2012). A study of the Taiping Rebellion from a global perspective.

———, *Provincial Patriots: The Hunanese and Modern China* (2007). A well-argued essay on the important role that leaders born in Hunan have played in modern Chinese history. The book includes information on the role of Hunanese leaders in suppressing the Taiping uprising, and on Mao Zedong, whose home province was Hunan.

Reed, Nelson, *The Caste War of Yucatan* (1964). A classic narrative of the Caste War of Yucatán.

Restall, Matthew, *The Maya World* (1997). Describes in economic and social terms the origins of the Yucatán upheaval in southern Mexico.

Robinson, David, *Muslim Societies in African History* (2004). A valuable overview of Muslim Africa, written by an expert on African Islam.

Rugeley, Terry, *Rebellion Now and Forever: Mayans, Hispanics, and Caste War Violence in Yucatán, 1800–1880* (2009). Explains the combination of economic and cultural pressures that drove the Maya in Yucatán to revolt in the Caste War.

———, *Yucatán's Maya Peasantry and the Origins of the Caste War* (1996). This book examines the ways in which agrarian pressures, new taxes, and military recruitment put increasing strain on Maya farmers.

Sanneh, Lamin, *Beyond Jihad: The Pacifist Tradition in West African Islam* (2016). A powerful and often persuasive argument that the Muslim clerics in West Africa preferred peaceful means rather than violence to spread the tenets of Islam.

Spence, Jonathan, *God's Chinese Son: The Taiping Heavenly Kingdom of Hong Xiuquan* (1996). A fascinating portrayal of the Taiping movement through the prism of its founder.

Sperber, Jonathan, *Karl Marx: A Nineteenth-Century Life* (2013). An engaging and authoritative biography of Marx that emphasizes his role as a radical journalist.

Stedman Jones, Gareth, *Karl Marx: Greatness and Illusion* (2016). Now the authoritative biography of the founder of communism, showing Marx's own ambivalence about what he had created.

Wagner, Rudolf, *Reenacting the Heavenly Vision: The Role of Religion in the Taiping Rebellion* (1982). A brief but insightful analysis of the religious elements in the Taipings' doctrines.

Ware, Rudolph T., III, *The Walking Qur'an: Islamic Education, Embodied Knowledge, and History in West Africa* (2014). An overview of the Muslim clerics in Senegambia from the origins of Islam in the region up to the present.

White, Richard, *The Middle Ground: Indians, Empires, and Republics in the Great Lakes Region, 1650–1815* (1991). A pathbreaking exploration of intercultural relations in North America that offers a provocative interpretation of the visions of Tenskwatawa and the efforts of Tecumseh to resist the expansion of the United States.

Wilson, Jon, *The Chaos of Empire: The British Raj and the Conquest of India* (2018). This book challenges the image of an efficient British regime posed against decaying Indian kingdoms. It reveals just how brutal and improvised the conquest of India was.

CHAPTER 17: NATIONS AND EMPIRES, 1850–1914

Berry, Sara, *Cocoa, Custom and Socio-Economic Change in Western Nigeria* (1975). Innovative study based on interviews with local farmers that suggests that farmer enterprise and microeconomic theory better explain the spectacular growth in cocoa production than grand economic theory.

Cain, P. A., and A. G. Hopkins, *British Imperialism: Innovation and Expansion, 1688–1914* (1993). An excellent discussion of British imperialism, especially British expansion into Africa.

Clark, Christopher, *Iron Kingdom: The Rise and Downfall of Prussia, 1600–1947* (2009). Includes an excellent discussion of the rise of German nationalism and Prussian power.

Cooper, Frederick, *Colonialism in Question: Theory, Knowledge, History* (2005). A collection of essays by one of the leading scholars of colonial studies.

Cronon, William, *Nature's Metropolis: Chicago and the Great West* (1991). Makes connections among territorial expansion, industrialization, and urban development.

Davis, John, *Conflict and Control: Law and Order in Nineteenth-Century Italy* (1988). A superb study of the north-south and other rifts after Italian political unification.

Demuth, Bathsheba, *Floating Coast: An Environmental History of the Bering Strait* (2019). An illuminating study of how humans and other animals of the Arctic coped woith encroaching empires and extractive economies.

Forth, Aidan, *Barbed-Wire Imperialism: Britain's Empire of Camps, 1876–1903* (2017). The author shows the origins of concentration camps out of efforts to control pandemics and insurgencies.

Frankel, S. Herbert, *Capital Investment in Africa: Its Course and Effects* (1938). A careful study based on a mass of detailed figures and statistics on the general economic development of states in sub-Saharan Africa.

Friesen, Gerald, *The Canadian Prairies* (1984). The most comprehensive account of Canadian westward expansion.

Gluck, Carol, *Japan's Modern Myths: Ideology in the Late Meiji Period* (1985). A study of how states fashion useful historical traditions to consolidate and legitimize their rule.

Hall, Bruce S., *A History of Race in Muslim West Africa, 1600–1960* (2011). A study of racial consciousness in precolonial Africa and the uses made of it by the colonial conquerors of West Africa.

Harms, Robert, *Land of Tears: The Exploration and Exploitation of Equatorial Africa* (2019). A thorough and gripping account of the role scientists and surveyors played in the penetration of the interior of Africa and the pursuit of ivory and rubber.

Headrick, Daniel R., *The Tools of Empire: Technology and European Imperialism in the Nineteenth Century* (1981). A useful general study of the relationship between imperialism and technology.

Herbst, Jeffrey, *States and Power in Africa: Comparative Lessons in Authority and Control* (2000). An overview of the impact of colonial rule on contemporary African states.

Hill, Polly, *The Gold Coast Cocoa Farmer: A Preliminary Survey* (1965). A socioeconomic report detailing three issues facing the cocoa farmer: labor; indebtedness and pledging; and income and expenditure.

Hine, Robert V., and John Mack Faragher, *The American West: A New Interpretive History* (2000). Presents an excellent synthesis of the conquests by which the United States expanded from the Atlantic to the Pacific.

Hobsbawm, Eric J., *Nations and Nationalism since 1780: Programme, Myth, Reality* (1993). An insightful survey of the origins and development of nationalist thought throughout Europe.

Hochschild, Adam, *King Leopold's Ghost* (1998). A full-scale, eminently readable study of Europe's most egregiously destructive colonial regime in Africa.

Judson, Peter, *The Habsburg Empire: A New History* (2016). An innovative history of the relationship between "the people" and the state in a multiethnic empire.

Khalid, Adeeb, *Central Aisa: A New History from Imperial Conquest to the Present* (2021). This is a magnificent study of how borderlanders of inner Asia got partitioned into competing empires and forced them to become more multicultural.

Lee, Leo Ou-fan, and Andrew Nathan, "The Beginnings of Mass Culture: Journalism and Fiction in the Late Ch'ing and Beyond," in David Johnson, Andrew Nathan, and Evelyn Rawski (eds.), *Popular Culture in Late Imperial China* (1985), pp. 360–95. An important article on the emergence of a mass-media market in late nineteenth- and early twentieth-century China.

Lieven, Dominic, *Empire: The Russian Empire and Its Rivals* (2000). A comparison of the British, Ottoman, Habsburg, and Russian Empires.

Mackenzie, John M., *Propaganda and Empire* (1984). Contains a series of useful chapters showing the importance of the empire to Britain.

Mamdani, Mahmood, *Citizen and State: Contemporary Africa and the Legacy of Late Colonialism* (1996). A survey of the impact of European colonial powers on African political systems.

McClintock, Anne, *Imperial Leather: Race, Gender and Sexuality in the Colonial Contest* (1995). A study of the imperial relationship between Victorian Britain and South Africa from the point of view of cultural studies.

McNeil, William, *Europe's Steppe Frontier: 1500–1800* (1964). An excellent study of the definitive victory of Russia's agricultural empire over grazing nomads and independent frontier people.

Mitchell, B. R., *International Historical Statistics: Africa, Asia, and Oceania, 1750–2005* (2007). This comparative volume provides data from over two centuries for all principal areas of economic and social activity in both eastern and western Europe.

Montgomery, David, *The Fall of the House of Labor: The Workplace, the State, and American Labor Activism, 1865–1925* (1987). An excellent discussion of changes in work in the late nineteenth century.

Myers, Ramon, and Mark Peattie (eds.), *The Japanese Colonial Empire, 1895–1945* (1984). A collection of essays exploring different aspects of Japanese colonialism.

Needell, Jeffrey, *A Tropical Belle Epoque: Elite Culture and Society in Turn-of-the-Century Rio de Janeiro* (1987). Shows the strength of the Brazilian elites at the turn of the century.

Pan, Lynn (ed.), *The Encyclopedia of Chinese Overseas* (1999). A comprehensive coverage of the history of the Chinese diaspora.

Porter, Bernard, *The Absent-Minded Imperialists: What the British Really Thought about Empire* (2004). A careful dissection of the ways in which empire changed the British—and did not.

Prasad, Ritika, *Tracks of Change: Railways and Everyday Life in Colonial India* (2016). A detailed analysis of how railways transformed the everyday experience of Indians under colonial rule.

Rosenthal, Jean-Laurent, and R. Bin Wong, *Before and Beyond Divergence: The Politics of Economic Change in China and Europe* (2011). The authors challenge Kenneth Pomeranz's claims that China and Europe were roughly at the same level economically at the beginning of the eighteenth century and that Europe's industrial revolution, led by Great Britain, did not happen in China because of unique factors in Britain and the rest of Europe.

Ross, Corey, *Ecology and Power in the Age of Empire: Europe and the Transformation of the Tropical World* (2017). Marshals evidence that western corporations used empire to gain access to tropical raw materials, thus changing the relationship between the west and the rest of the world and altering work routines around the world.

Stengers, Jean, *Combien le Congo a-t-il coûté à la Belgique* (1957). A detailed financial accounting of how much Leopold put into the Congo and how much he took out, underscoring just how ruthlessly he exploited this possession.

Topik, Steven, *The Political Economy of the Brazilian State, 1889–1930* (1987). An excellent discussion of the Brazilian state, and especially of its elites.

Walker, Mack, *German Home Towns: Community, State, and the General State, 1648–1871* (1971; reprint, 1998). A brilliant, street-level analysis of the Holy Roman Empire (the First Reich) and the run-up to the German unification of 1871 (the Second Reich).

Wasserman, Mark, *Everyday Life and Politics in Nineteenth-Century Mexico* (2000). Wonderfully captures the way in which people coped with social and economic dislocation in late nineteenth-century Mexico.

Weeks, Theodore R., *Nation and State in Late Imperial Russia: Nationalism and Russification on the Western Frontier, 1863–1914* (1996). A good discussion of the Russian Empire's responses to the concept of the nation-state.

White, Richard, *Railroaded: The Transcontinentals and the Making of Modern America* (2011). A searing exposé of the corruptions, and a startling critique of the economic and environmental costs, associated with the expansion of railroad lines across Canada, the United States, and Mexico.

Wilson, Jon, *India Conquered: Britain's Raj and the Chaos of Empire* (2016). Stresses the violence and chaos involved in the British conquest and administration of Indian societies.

Yung, Wing, *My Life in China and America* (1909). The autobiography of the first Chinese graduate of an American university.

Zarrow, Peter, *After Empire: The Conceptual Transformation of the Chinese State, 1885–1924* (2012). A history of the changing ideas regarding the Chinese state that eventually led to the abandonment of monarchical rule by the Chinese people.

CHAPTER 18: AN UNSETTLED WORLD, 1890–1914

Aydin, Cemil, *The Idea of the Muslim World: A Global Intellectual History* (2017). Explores the creation of pan-Islamism in the nineteenth century and its complex relations with pan-Arabism, with a particular focus on the intellectual currents from Egypt to Indonesia.

Bayly, C. A., *The Birth of the Modern World, 1780–1914: Global Connections and Comparisons* (2004). A general study of the key political, economic, social, and cultural features of the modern era in world history.

Bergère, Marie-Claire, *Sun Yat-sen* (1998). Originally published in French in 1994, this is a judicious biography of the man generally known as the father of the modern Chinese nation.

Brinkley, Douglas, *Wilderness Warrior: Theodore Roosevelt and the Crusade to Save America* (2010). An important account of Roosevelt's environmental policies, based on new research.

Chatterjee, Partha, *The Nation and Its Fragments* (1993). One of the most important works on Indian nationalism by a leading scholar of "subaltern studies."

Conrad, Joseph, *Heart of Darkness* (1899). First published in a magazine in 1899, this novella contained a searing critique of King Leopold's oppressive and exploitative policies in the Congo and was part of a growing concern for the effects that European empires were having around the world, especially in Africa.

Esherick, Joseph, "How the Qing Became China," in Joseph W. Esherick, Hasan Kayali, and Eric Van Young (eds.), *Empire to Nation: Historical Perspectives on the Making of the Modern World* (2006). A study of the processes through which the Qing Empire became the nation-state of China.

——, *The Origins of the Boxer Uprising* (1987). The definitive account of the episode.

Everdell, William R., *The First Moderns: Profiles in the Origins of Twentieth-Century Thought* (1997). A rich account of the many faces of modernism, focusing particularly on science and art.

Finnane, Antonia, *Changing Clothes in China: Fashion, History, Nation* (2008). An exploration of changing Chinese identities from the perspective of clothing.

Gay, Peter, *The Cultivation of Hatred* (1994). A provocative discussion of the violent passions of the immediate pre–Great War era.

Gilmartin, Christina, et al. (eds.), *Engendering China: Women, Culture, and the State* (1994). Analyzes politics and society in modern China from the perspective of gender.

Hochschild, Adam, *King Leopold's Ghost: A Story of Greed, Terror, and Heroism in Colonial Africa* (1998). A well-written account of the violent colonial history of the Belgian Congo under King Leopold in the late nineteenth century.

Judge, Joan, *The Precious Raft of History: The Past, the West, and the Woman Question in China* (2008). An insightful exploration of the "woman question" in China at the turn of the twentieth century.

Katz, Friedrich, *The Life and Times of Pancho Villa* (1998). An exploration of the Mexican Revolution that shows how Villa's armies destroyed the forces of Díaz and his followers.

Keddie, Nikki, *An Islamic Response to Imperialism: Political and Religious Writings of Sayyid Jamal ad-Din "al-Afghani"* (1968). Definitive information on Afghani's life and influence, coupled with a translation of one of his most important essays.

Kern, Stephen, *The Culture of Time and Space 1880–1918* (1986). A useful study of the enormous changes in the experience of time and space in the age of late industrialism in Europe and America.

Kuhn, Philip, *Chinese among Others: Emigration in Modern Times* (2008). An overview of the history of Chinese migration.

McKeown, Adam, *Melancholy Order: Asian Migration and the Globalization of Borders* (2008). An examination of global migration patterns since the mid-nineteenth century and how regulations designed to restrict Asian migration to other parts of the world led to the modern regime of migration control.

Meade, Teresa, *"Civilizing" Rio: Reform and Resistance in a Brazilian City, 1889–1930* (1997). A wonderful study of cultural and class conflict in Brazil.

Mishra, Pankaj, *From the Ruins of Empire: The Intellectuals Who Remade Asia* (2012). Argues that an Asian tradition of thinking came into being in the late nineteenth century as a result of rising European empires and the emergence of Japan as an alternative model of modernization.

Moon, David, *The Plough That Broke the Steppes: Agriculture and Environment on Russia's Grasslands, 1700–1914* (2013). A pathbreaking study of Russian environmental history before the twentieth century.

Morris, Edmund, *Theodore Rex* (2002). A thorough biography of Theodore Roosevelt.

Nightingale, Carl H., *Segregation: A Global History of Divided Cities* (2012). Shows how, in the late nineteenth century, migration, investment, and booming exports coincided with increasing social partition within global cities.

Pick, Daniel, *Faces of Degeneration: A European Disorder, c. 1848–c. 1918* (1993). A study of Europe's fear of social and biological decline, particularly focusing on France and Italy.

Pretorius, Fransjohn (ed.), *Scorched Earth* (2001). A study of the Anglo-Boer War in terms of its environmental impacts.

Saler, Michael (ed.), *The Fin de Siècle World* (2014). A comprehensive anthology of essays on turn-of-the-century politics and culture across the world.

Sarkar, Sumit, *The Swadeshi Movement in Bengal* (1973). A comprehensive study of an early militant movement against British rule.

Schorske, Carl E., *Fin-de-Siècle Vienna: Politics and Culture* (1980). The classic treatment of the birth of modern ideas and political movements in turn-of-the-century Austria.

Trachtenberg, Alan, *The Incorporation of America: Culture and Society in the Gilded Age* (1982). A provocative synthesis of changes in the American economy, society, and culture in the last decades of the nineteenth century.

Wang, David Der-wei, *Fin-de-Siècle Splendor: Repressed Modernities of Late Qing Fiction, 1849–1911* (1997). A fine work that attempts to locate the "modern" within the writings of the late Qing period.

Warren, Louis, *Buffalo Bill's America: William Cody and the Wild West Show* (2005). A superb portrait of William F. Cody, the person; of Buffalo Bill, the persona Cody (and others) created; and of the popular culture his Wild West shows brought to audiences in Europe and North America.

Warwick, Peter, *Black People and the South African War, 1899–1902* (1983). An important study that reminds readers of the crucial involvement of Black South Africans in this bloody conflict.

Womack, John, Jr., *Zapata and the Mexican Revolution* (1968). A major work on the Mexican Revolution that discusses peasant struggles in the state of Morelos in great detail.

CHAPTER 19: GLOBAL CRISIS, 1910–1939

Akcam, Taner, *The Young Turks' Crime against Humanity: The Armenian Genocide and Ethnic Cleansing in the Ottoman Empire* (2012). An exhaustive examination of the factors that impelled the Turkish authorities to carry out ethnic cleansing against the Armenians during World War I.

Akin, Yiğit, *When the War Came Home: The Ottomans' Great War and the Devastation of an Empire* (2018). A social history of the reactions of Ottoman citizenry to conscription and the efforts of the state to fight a modern war with modern means.

Aksakal, Mustafa, *The Ottoman Road to War in 1914: The Ottoman Empire and the First World War* (2008). A detailed treatment of the Ottomans' decision to align with Germany rather than with Britain, France, and Russia, and to not remain neutral throughout the conflict.

Anderson, Scott, *Lawrence in Arabia: War, Deceit, Imperial Folly, and the Making of the Middle East* (2013). A new and authoritative biography of T. E. Lawrence, with significant new material on British policies in the Middle East as seen through the eyes of a strong pro-Arab figure.

Bloxham, Donald, *The Great Game of Genocide: Imperialism, Nationalism, and the Destruction of the Ottoman Armenians* (2005). The definitive work on the Armenian genocide, set in a wide historical context.

Boyce, Robert, *The Great Interwar Crisis and the Collapse of Globalization* (2009). How the collapse of the world trading system and the failure of national leaders to resolve the effects of World War I led to the Great Depression.

Brown, Judith, *Gandhi: Prisoner of Hope* (1990). A biography of Gandhi as a political activist.

Clark, Christopher, *The Sleepwalkers: How Europe Went to War in 1914* (2013). A rigorous examination of how interlaced European elites went to war with one another.

De Grazia, Victoria, and Ellen Furlough (eds.), *The Sex of Things: Gender and Consumption in Historical Perspective* (1996). Pathbreaking essays on how gender affects consumption.

Dumenil, Lynn, *The Modern Temper: America in the 1920s* (1995). A general discussion of American culture in the decade after World War I.

Eichengreen, Barry, *Gold Fetters: The Gold Standard and the Great Depression, 1919–1939* (1992). The definitive work on the Great Depression as a global crisis.

Fainsod, Merle, *Smolensk under Soviet Rule* (1989). The most accessible and sophisticated interpretation of the Stalin revolution in the village.

Friedman, Edward, *Backward toward Revolution: The Chinese Revolutionary Party* (1974). An insightful look at the failure of liberalism in early republican China through the prism of the short-lived Chinese Revolutionary Party.

Gelvin, James, *Divided Loyalties: Nationalism and Mass Politics in Syria at the Close of Empire* (1998). Offers important insights into the development of nationalism in the Arab world.

Gingeras, Ryan, *Fall of the Sultanate: The Great War and the End of the Ottoman Empire, 1908–1922* (2016). An essay on why the Ottomans entered the war and the consequences thereof.

Horne, John (ed.), *State, Society, and Mobilization during the First World War* (1997). Essays on what it took to wage total war among all the belligerents.

Johnson, G. Wesley, *The Emergence of Black Politics in Senegal* (1971). A useful examination of the stirrings of African nationalism in Senegal.

Kennedy, David M., *Freedom from Fear: The American People in Depression and War, 1929–1945* (1999). A wonderful narrative of turbulent years.

Kershaw, Ian, *Hitler*, 2 vols. (1998–2000). A masterpiece combining biography and context.

Kieser, Hans-Lukas, *Talaat Pasha: Father of Modern Turkey, Architect of Genocide* (2018). An important biography of one of the most important Ottoman statesmen, who took Turkey into the war and carried out the Armenian genocide.

Kimble, David, *A Political History of Ghana* (1963). An excellent discussion of the beginnings of African nationalism in Ghana.

Kotkin, Stephen, *Magnetic Mountain: Stalinism as a Civilization* (1995). Recaptures the atmosphere of a time when everything seemed possible, even creating a new world.

———, *Stalin*, vol. 1, *Paradoxes of Power* (2014). A sweeping history of the tsarist regime, world war, Russian Revolution, civil war, and rise of Stalin.

Lambert, Nicholas A., *Planning Armageddon: British Economic Warfare and the First World War* (2012). Mines new archives to show that the British had an aggressive plan before the war to destroy Germany financially, which the British government approved and began to enact until the United States forced it to back off.

LeMahieu, D. L., *A Culture for Democracy: Mass Communication and the Cultivated Mind in Britain between the Wars* (1988). One of the great works on mass culture.

Leonhard, Jörn, *Pandora's Box: A History of the First World War* (2018). A masterful account of how a war predicted to produce a swift victory became so unwinnable for all sides.

Lyttelton, Adrian, *The Seizure of Power: Fascism in Italy, 1919–1929* (1961). Still the classic account.

Marchand, Roland, *Advertising the American Dream: Making Way for Modernity, 1920–1945* (1985). An excellent discussion of the force of mass production and mass consumption.

Martin, Jamie, *The Meddlers: Sovereignty, Empire, and the Birth of Global Economic Governance* (2022). This book explains how many of the post-1945 institutions governing the world economy were based on experiments and ideas from the inter-war years.

Mazower, Mark, *Dark Continent: Europe's Twentieth Century* (1999). A wide-ranging overview of Europe's tempestuous twentieth century.

McGirr, Lisa, *The War on Alcohol: Prohibition and the Rise of the American State* (2016). Emphasizes the power of cultural reaction against modernity that brought about Prohibition and the irony that its enforcement helped expand the power of the modern state.

McKeown, Adam, *Melancholy Order: Asian Migration and the Globalization of Border* (2008). A major study of the vast movement of peoples around the globe between the middle of the nineteenth and the twentieth centuries.

Morrow, John H., Jr., *The Great War: An Imperial History* (2004). Places World War I in the context of European imperialism.

Musgrove, Charles D., *China's Contested Capital: Architecture, Ritual, and Response in Nanjing* (2013). An exploration of how the Chinese Nationalist capital of Nanjing served as a focal point for the making of a nation and a new form of mass politics.

Nottingham, John, and Carl Rosberg, *The Myth of "Mau Mau": Nationalism in Kenya* (1966). Dispels the myths in describing the roots of nationalism in Kenya.

Patel, Kiran Klaus, *The New Deal: A Global History* (2016). A view that places Franklin Delano Roosevelt's New Deal in a global perspective, pointing out the ways in which other powers, mainly European, responded to the Great Depression, the gold standard, and Keynesianism.

Pedersen, Susan, *The Guardians: The League of Nations and the Crisis of Empire* (2015). Skillfully reexamines the neglected effort to regulate the colonial world under a so-called mandate system.

Rogan, Eugene, *The Fall of the Ottomans: The Great War in the Middle East* (2015). Emphasizes how international the war became when the Ottomans decided to join with the Central Powers.

Rosenberg, Clifford, *Policing Paris: The Origins of Modern Immigration Control between the Wars* (2006). Explores the first systematic efforts to enforce distinctions of nationality and citizenship status in a major urban setting.

Rutledge, Ian, *Enemy on the Euphrates: The British Occupation of Iraq and the Great Arab Revolt, 1914–1921* (2014). An impassioned investigation of Britain's effort to take control of the oil-rich territory of Iraq and the determined resistance of the Iraqi peoples.

Smith, S. A., *Russia in Revolution: An Empire in Crisis, 1890–1928* (2018). A masterpiece that shows how the Russian Empire went to war, how war created a civil war, and how out of civil war revolutionaries triumphed.

Strand, David, *An Unfinished Republic: Leading by Word and Deed in Modern China* (2011). A study of how the need for popular support led to a new political culture characterized by public speaking and performance in early twentieth-century China.

Suny, Ronald Gregor, *"They Can Live in the Desert but Nowhere Else": A History of the Armenian Genocide* (2015). A careful, document-based analysis of the Armenian genocide.

Taylor, Jay, *The Generalissimo: Chiang Kai-shek and the Struggle for Modern China* (2009). The first serious biographical study of Chiang Kai-shek in English, although its reliance on Chiang's own diary as a source does raise some questions of historical interpretation.

Thorp, Rosemary (ed.), *Latin America in the 1930s* (1984). An important collection of essays on Latin America's response to the shakeup of the interwar years.

Tsin, Michael, *Nation, Governance, and Modernity in China: Canton, 1900–1927* (1999). An analysis of the vision and social dynamics behind the Guomindang-led revolution of the 1920s.

Vianna, Hermano, *The Mystery of Samba* (1999). Discusses the history of samba, emphasizing its African heritage as well as its persistent popular content.

Wakeman, Frederic, Jr., *Policing Shanghai, 1927–1937* (1995). An excellent account of Guomindang rule in China's largest city during the Nanjing decade.

Wilder, Gary, *Freedom Time: Negritude, Decolonization, and the Future of the World* (2015). Illustrates how anticolonialism grew into a global movement committed to a new idea of racial freedom and equality.

Winter, J. M., *The Experience of World War* (1988). A comprehensive presentation of the many sides of the twentieth century.

Yergin, Daniel, *The Prize: The Epic Quest for Oil, Money, and Power* (1990). An excellent global history of the petroleum industry from the 1850s through 1990.

Young, Louise, *Japan's Total Empire: Manchuria and the Culture of Wartime Imperialism* (1998). An innovative case study of Japanese imperialism and mass culture with broad implications.

CHAPTER 20: THE THREE-WORLD ORDER, 1940–1975

Aburish, Said K., *Nasser: The Last Arab* (2004). An impressive look at Egypt's most powerful political leader in the 1950s and 1960s.

Adelman, Jeremy., and Prakash, Gyan (eds.), *Inventing the Third World: In Search of Freedom for the Postwar Global South* (2022). A collection of essays about south-south solidarity and peacemaking.

Anderson, Jon Lee, *Che Guevara: A Revolutionary Life* (1997). A sweeping study of the radicalization of Latin American nationalism.

Bayly, Christopher, and Tim Harper, *Forgotten Armies: Britain's Asian Empire and the War with Japan* (2004). A brilliant social and military history of the Second World War as fought and lived in South and Southeast Asia.

Bruce-Lockhart, Katherine, "'Unsound Minds' and Broken Bodies: The Detention of 'Hardcore' Mau Mau Women at Kamiti and Gitamayu Detention Camps in Kenya, 1954–1960," *Journal of Eastern African Studies* 8, no. 4 (2014): 590–608. Examines a newly discovered British archive on the Mau Mau Uprising that reveals that the British opened a second detention camp for hardcore Mau Mau women at Gitamayu and sheds light on the treatment doled out by the British to women detained in both detention camps.

Byrne, Jeffrey James, *Mecca of Revolution: Algeria, Decolonization, and the Third World Order* (2016). Stresses the widespread influence of the Algerian revolution on other struggles for independence from imperial powers.

Chatterjee, Partha, *Nationalist Thought and the Colonial World: A Derivative Discourse* (1986). An influential interpretation of the ideological and political nature of Indian nationalism and the struggle for a postcolonial nation-state.

Cook, Alexander C. (ed.), *Mao's Little Red Book: A Global History* (2014). A look at the global impact of the Chinese Cultural Revolution through the lens of the iconic "little red book" of quotations from Mao.

Crampton, R. J., *Eastern Europe in the Twentieth Century and After*, 2nd ed. (1997). Comprehensive overview covering all Soviet-bloc countries.

Dikötter, Frank, *Mao's Great Famine: The History of China's Most Devastating Catastrophe, 1958–1962* (2010). A recent detailed account of one of the greatest man-made disasters in twentieth-century history.

Dower, John W., *Embracing Defeat: Japan in the Wake of World War II* (1999). A prize-winning study of the transformation of one of the war's vanquished.

Elkins, Caroline, *Imperial Reckoning: The Untold Story of Britain's Gulag in Kenya* (2005). Pulitzer Prize–winning study of the brutal war to suppress the nationalist uprising in Kenya in the 1950s that ultimately led to independence for that country.

———, *Legacy of Violence: A History of the British Empire* (2022). The author explains how deeply contested and violent British imperialism and the retreat of its empire was.

Evans, Martin, *Algeria: France's Undeclared War* (2011). Gives the history of the Algerian nationalist movements and provides an overview of the Algerian war for independence.

Feshbach, Murray, and Alfred Friendly, Jr., *Ecocide in the USSR: Health and Nation under Siege* (1992). A crucial study of ecological disasters in the Soviet Union.

Gerard, Emmanuel, and Bruce Kuklick, *Death in the Congo: Murdering Patrice Lumumba* (2015). The most recent study of the Congo independence movement and the execution of its major nationalist.

Getachew, Adom, *Worldmaking after Empire: The Rise and Fall of Self-Determination* (2019). An excellent study of how decolonization spread the national form of sovereignty while economic integration then weakened the idea of political self-determination.

Hargreaves, John D., *Decolonization in Africa* (1996). A good place to start when exploring the history of African decolonization.

Hasan, Mushirul (ed.), *India's Partition: Process, Strategy and Mobilization* (1993). A useful anthology of scholarly articles, short stories, and primary documents on the partition of India.

Iriye, Akira, *Power and Culture: The Japanese-American War, 1941–1945* (1981). A discussion that goes beyond the military confrontation in Asia.

Jackson, Kenneth T., *Crabgrass Frontier: The Suburbanization of the United States* (1985). An insightful and influential consideration of the movement of the American population from cities to suburbs.

Jalal, Ayesha, *The Sole Spokesman: Jinnah, the Muslim League and the Demand for Pakistan* (1985). A study of the high politics leading to the violent partition of British India.

Keep, John L. H., *Last of the Empires: A History of the Soviet Union, 1945–1991* (1995). A detailed overview of the core of the "Second World."

Lovell, Julia, *Maoism: A Global History* (2019). Traces the myth of Mao's revolution and its dissemination across the Third World as well as Europe and North America.

Mba, Nina Emma, *Nigerian Women Mobilized: Women's Political Activity in Southern Nigeria, 1900–1965* (1982). An overview of women's political protests against the British in southern Nigeria.

Micklin, Philip, N.V. Aladin, and Igor Plotnikov (eds.), *The Aral Sea: The Devastation and Partial Rehabilitation of a Great Lake* (2014). Catalogues how Soviet irrigation plans drained a giant lake and destroyed the habitat of locals who depended on it for survival.

Morris, Benny, *Righteous Victims: A History of the Zionist-Arab Conflict, 1881–1999* (2000). A book on the Arab-Israeli War of 1948.

Pantsov, Alexander V., *Mao: The Real Story*, trans. Steven I. Levine (2012). A well-researched biography of Mao Zedong.

Patterson, James T., *Grand Expectations: The United States, 1945–1974* (1996). Synthesizes the American experience in the postwar decades.

Patterson, Thomas, *Contesting Castro* (1994). The best study of the tension between the United States and Cuba. Culminating in the Cuban Revolution, it explores the deep American misunderstanding of Cuban national aspirations.

Presley, Cora Ann, *Kikuyu Women, the Mau Mau Rebellion, and Social Change in Kenya* (1992). An overview of the impact of British policies on the most colonized group of African women.

Roberts, Geoffrey, *Stalin's Wars: From World War to Cold War, 1939–1953* (2007). A reassessment of Stalin's wartime leadership that conveys the vast scale of what took place.

Saich, Tony, and Hans van de Ven (eds.), *New Perspectives on the Chinese Communist Revolution* (1995). A collection of essays reexamining different aspects of the Chinese communist movement.

Schram, Stuart, *The Thought of Mao Tse-tung* (1989). Standard work on the subject.

Tignor, Robert L., *W. Arthur Lewis and the Birth of Development Economics* (2006). An intellectual biography of the Nobel Prize–winning, West Indian–born economist, who proposed formulas to promote the economic development of less developed societies and then sought to implement them in Africa and the West Indies.

Turshen, Meredeth, "Algerian Women in the Liberation Struggle and the Civil War: From Active Participants to Passive Victims?" *Social Research: An International Quarterly* 69, no. 3 (Fall 2002): 889–911. How women participated in Algeria's war of independence from France, and the benefits this brought women afterwards.

Van Allen, Judith, "'Sitting on a Man': Colonialism and the Lost Political Institutions of Igbo Women," *Canadian Journal of African Studies* 6, no. 2 (1972): 165–81. A crucial and early article on the women's uprising against the warrant chiefs in southeastern Nigeria.

Weiner, Douglas R., *A Little Corner of Freedom: Russian Nature Protection from Stalin to Gorbachev* (1999). A groundbreaking book about Russian environmentalism.

Weiss, Herbert, "The Congo's Independence Struggle Viewed Fifty Years Later," *African Studies Review* 55, no. 1 (April 2012): 109–15. A statement by an American scholar who was in the Congo at the time of its independence.

Williams, Suan, *White Malice: The CIA and Covert Recolonization of Africa* (2021). A revealing study of how U.S. intervention in central and southern Africa turned decolonization into endemic warfare.

Zubkova, Elena, *Russia after the War: Hopes, Illusions, and Disappointments, 1945–1957* (1998). Uses formerly secret archives to catalogue the devastation and difficult reconstruction of one of the war's victors.

CHAPTER 21: GLOBALIZATION, 1970–2000

Anand, Nikhil, *Hydraulic City: Water and the Infrastructures of Citizenship in Mumbai* (2017). Illustrates how huge cities rely on basic infrastructures, like water circulation and treatment, and shows how the uneven distribution of water is a major cause of poverty and inequality. In the case of Mumbai, access to water maps onto access to power.

Collier, Paul, *The Bottom Billion: Why the Poorest Countries Fail and What Can Be Done about It* (2007). Shows that despite the world's advancing prosperity, more than a billion people have been left behind in abject poverty.

Connelly, Matthew, *Fatal Misconception: The Struggle to Control World Population* (2008). A savage attack on mainly American and United Nations population specialists, who supported China's autocratic one-child policy and other efforts to reduce fertility rates largely in Third World countries.

Davis, Deborah (ed.), *The Consumer Revolution in Urban China* (2000). A look at the different aspects of the recent, profound social transformation of urban China.

Davis, Mike, *City of Quartz: Excavating the Future in Los Angeles* (1990). Offers provocative reflections on the recent history, current condition, and possible future of Los Angeles.

Dutton, Michael, *Streetlife China* (1999). A fascinating portrayal of the survival tactics of those inhabiting the margins of society in modern China.

Eichengreen, Barry, *Globalizing Capital: A History of the International Monetary System* (1996). An insightful analysis of how international capital markets changed in the period from 1945 to 1980.

Ferguson, Niall, and Moritz Schularick, "'Chimerica' and the Global Asset Market Boom," *International Finance* 10, no. 3 (Winter 2007): 215–39. Coined the term "Chimerica" to designate a single, intertwined economic entity made up of a productive partner, China, and a consuming partner, the United States.

Gourevitch, Philip, *We Wish to Inform You That Tomorrow We Will Be Killed with Our Families: Stories from Rwanda* (1999). A volume that reveals the hatreds that culminated in the Rwanda genocide.

Guillermoprieto, Alma, *Looking for History: Dispatches from Latin America* (2001). A collection of articles by the most important journalist reporting on Latin American affairs.

Han Minzhu (ed.), *Cries for Democracy: Writings and Speeches from the 1989 Chinese Democracy Movement* (1990). A collection of documents from the events leading up to the incident in Tiananmen Square on June 4, 1989.

Herbst, Jeffrey, *States and Power in Africa: Comparative Lessons in Authority and Control* (2000). Explores the political dilemmas facing modern African polities.

Honig, Emily, and Gail Hershatter, *Personal Voices: Chinese Women in the 1980's* (1988). A record of Chinese women during a period of rapid social change.

Huang, Yasheng, *Capitalism with Chinese Characteristics: Entrepreneurship and the State* (2008). A sharp, unsentimental inside look at China's market economy and its future prospects.

Jacques, Martin, *When China Rules the World: The End of the Western World and the Birth of a New Global Order* (2009). A provocative essay on the rise of China as a world power and the overthrow of western cultural, political, and economic dominance.

Kavoori, Anandam P., and Aswin Punathambekar (eds.), *Global Bollywood* (2008). A collection of essays by leading scholars of Indian cinema on different aspects of the processes by which the Hindi film industry became Bollywood.

Kershaw, Ian, *The Global Age: Europe, 1950–2017* (2018). An overview of European developments from the end of World War II to the present.

Klitgaard, Robert, *Tropical Gangsters* (1990). On the intimate connections between corrupt native elites and international aid agencies.

Kotkin, Stephen, *Armageddon Averted: The Soviet Collapse, 1970–2000* (2001). Places the surprise fall of the Soviet Union in the context of the great shifts in the post–World War II order.

Lin, Justin Yifu, "China and the Global Economy," *China Economic Journal* 4, no. 1 (2011): 1–14. Originally presented as a luncheon address to businesspeople, this article provides useful statistics on China's economic and financial development from 1990 to 2010.

Macekura, Stephen, *Of Limits and Growth: The Rise of Global Sustainable Development in the Twentieth Century* (2016). Explores the rise of global environmental politics in the 1970s and 1980s and the debate about resources and climate change.

Maddison, Angus, *Chinese Economic Performance in the Long Run, 960–2030 AD*, 2nd ed., revised and updated (2007). Full of useful financial and economic statistics, this report is the best resource on China's economic miracle.

Mamdani, Mahmood, *When Victims Become Killers: Colonialism, Nativism, and the Genocide in Rwanda* (2001). Discusses the genocide in Rwanda in light of the legacy of colonialism.

McFarland, Victor, *Oil Powers: A History of the U.S.-Saudi Alliance* (2020). A comprehensive study of how the United States became drawn into the Middle East to manage oil dependence after 1970.

Mehta, Suketu, *Maximum City: Bombay Lost and Found* (2005). Examines one of the great, and contradictory, cities in the era of globalization.

Miller, Chris, *The Struggle to Save the Soviet Economy: Mikhail Gorbachev and the Collapse of the USSR* (2016). An insightful analysis of internal debates in Moscow over rival directions for the Soviet economy and the response to Chinese reforms after 1978.

Mottahedeh, Roy, *The Mantle of the Prophet: Religion and Politics in Iran*, 2nd ed. (2008). Perhaps the best book on the 1979 Iranian Revolution and its aftermath.

Nathan, Andrew, and Perry Link, *The Tiananmen Papers* (2002). An inside look at the divisions within the Chinese elite in connection with the 1989 crackdown.

Portes, Alejandro, and Rubén G. Rumbaut, *Immigrant America*, 2nd ed. (1996). A good comparative study of how immigration has transformed the United States.

Prakash, Gyan, *Mumbai Fables* (2010). A spirited account of the rise of India's most modern city, a center of intellectual, commercial, and political vitality.

Prunier, Gerald, *Africa's World War: Congo, the Rwandan Genocide, and the Making of a Continental Catastrophe* (2009). A chilling discussion of the spillover effects of the Rwandan genocide on central, eastern, and southern Africa.

Punathambekar, Aswin, *From Bombay to Bollywood: The Making of a Global Media Industry* (2013). A study of the transformation of the Indian film industry that globalizes its content and reach.

Rao, D. S. Prasada, and Bart van Ark, *World Economic Performance: Past, Present and Future* (2013). Essays in honor of economist Angus Maddison, including an essay by Maddison on China's long-term economic performance.

Reinhart, Carmen, and Kenneth Rogoff, *This Time Is Different: Eight Centuries of Financial Folly* (2009). Explains the latest financial crash using historical perspective.

Ruggie, John Gerard, *Just Business: Multinational Corporations and Human Rights* (2013). Shows how even big businesses became involved in human rights advocacy.

Sen, Amartya, *Poverty and Famines: An Essay on Entitlement and Deprivation* (1982). A major study that reoriented the study of famines from a narrow concentration on food supply to broader questions of ownership, exchange, and democracy.

Sikkink, Kathryn, *The Justice Cascade: How Human Rights Prosecutions Are Changing World Politics* (2011). Shows how new forms of global organizing and new social norms are changing the political rules across borders.

Stein, Judith, *Pivotal Decade: How the United States Traded Factories for Finance in the Seventies* (2010). A comprehensive study of the rise of American banking and the decline of heartland industries.

Ther, Philipp, *Europe since 1989: A History* (2016). A concise account of European integration and neoliberalism since the fall of the Berlin Wall.

Van Der Wee, Hermann, *Prosperity and Upheaval: The World Economy, 1945–1980* (1986). Describes very well the transformation and problems of the world economy, particularly from the 1960s onward.

Vogel, Ezra F., *Deng Xiaoping and the Transformation of China* (2011). The definitive biography of China's leading reformer, based on exhaustive interviews and full source material.

Westad, Odd Arne, *The Global Cold War: Third World Interventions and the Making of Our Times* (2007). A genuinely global perspective on the Cold War and its consequences.

Winn, Peter, *Americas: The Changing Face of Latin America and the Caribbean* (1992). A useful portrayal of Latin America since the 1970s.

CHAPTER 22: TWENTY-FIRST-CENTURY GLOBAL CHALLENGES, 2001–THE PRESENT

Achcar, Gilbert, *Morbid Symptoms: Relapse in the Arab Uprising* (2016). An up-to-date overview of the difficulties that the proponents of the Arab Spring encountered, with long and detailed treatments of Syria and Egypt.

Blas, Javier, and Jack Farchy, *The World for Sale: Money, Power, and the Traders Who Barter the Earth's Resources* (2021). A thorough study of the role that international commodity trading firms play in shaping the world economy.

Blinder, Alan S., *After the Music Stopped: The Financial Crisis, the Response, and the Work Ahead* (2013). A definitive and detailed treatment of the Great Recession.

Chamie, Joseph, "Replacement Fertility Declines Worldwide," YaleGlobal Online, July 12, 2018, https://archive-yaleglobal.yale.edu/content/replacement-fertility-declines-worldwide. A useful article on worldwide fertility rates.

Christensen, Thomas J., *The China Challenges: Shaping the Choices of a Rising Power* (2015). A survey of China's rise and the challenges and choices the country faces in the contemporary world.

Cleveland, William L., and Martin Bunton, *A History of the Modern Middle East*, 6th ed. (2016). The sixth edition of an important textbook that covers the whole of the Middle East from 1800 to the present.

Coates, Ta-Nehisi, *Between the World and Me* (2015). This is a beautiful memoir of growing up in Baltimore in the middle of the globalization changes and the transformation of racial politics in the United States.

Cooper, Frederick, *Africa in the World: Capitalism, Empire, Nation-State* (2014). An overview of Africa's place in global history, based on the most recent scholarship.

Crutzen, Paul J., and Eugene F. Stoermer, "The 'Anthropocene,'" *IGBP Newsletter*, no. 41 (May 2000): 17–18. The first coining of the term *Anthropocene* and the argument for a new geologic epoch.

Darwall, Rupert, *The Age of Global Warming: A History* (2013). An accessible narrative describing how scientists became increasingly aware of the threat of climate change and the multinational effort to reduce carbon emissions.

Deaton, Angus, *The Great Escape: Health, Wealth, and the Origins of Inequality* (2013). An examination of rising inequality by a Nobel Prize–winning authority who emphasizes that contemporary well-to-do individuals have largely failed to help those not so fortunate to achieve their potential.

Eichengreen, Barry J., *Hall of Mirrors: The Great Depression and the Great Recession, and the Uses—and Misuses—of History* (2015). The expert on the Great Depression now writes about the Great Recession.

Esposito, John L., Tamara Sonn, and John O. Voll, *Islam and Democracy after the Arab Spring* (2016). An analysis of the prospects of democracy in Muslim countries, with case studies of Tunisia, Egypt, and Turkey, among others.

Ferguson, James, *Give a Man a Fish: Reflections on the New Politics of Distribution* (2015). An analysis of social welfare programs in southern Africa, which involve cash payments to the poorest members of societies, and their implications for neoliberal capitalism.

Franco, Jean, *Cruel Modernity* (2013). An examination of the cultural dimensions of Latin America's experience with recent neoliberal policies and the tensions and violence of relatively stateless societies.

Gallagher, James, "Remarkable Decline in Fertility Rates," BBC News, November 9, 2018, https://www.bbc.com/news/health-46118103. Written by the health and science correspondent for BBC News, this article provides the best overview of Christopher Murray et al.'s definitive article on fertility (see below), which is packed with statistics and details.

Gerges, Fawaz A., *ISIS: A History* (2016). One of a series of books that explores the rise of ISIS and stresses the place of violence in building a new Islamic state.

Guillen, Mauro F., *The Architecture of Collapse: The Global System in the 21st Century* (2015). A work that stresses the interconnectedness and complexity of the global capitalist system and argues that global financial systems have an "intrinsic propensity to instability, disruption, and crisis."

Jaffrelot, Christophe, *Saffron Modernity in India: Narendra Modi and His Experiment with Gujarat* (2014). A political history of how Narendra Modi emerged dominant in Gujarat using anti-Muslim nationalist ideology, captured the leadership of the BJP, and built a personality cult that catapulted him to national leadership.

Judis, John, *The Populist Explosion: How the Great Recession Transformed American and European Politics* (2016). A book by a journalist and political analyst that argues that the contemporary populist upsurges on both the right and the left are responses to neoliberal globalization.

Krastev, Ivan and Stephen Holmes, *The Light That Failed: A Reckoning* (2019). The authors look at how the illiberal backlash in Russia and eastern Europe was a reaction to the global migration changes and limits of liberal promises.

Lepore, Jill, *The Whites of Their Eyes: The Tea Party's Revolution and the Battle over American History* (2011). A history of the American far right and the Tea Party and their imagination of a nostalgic American past.

Lynch, Marc, *The New Arab Wars: Uprisings and Anarchy in the Middle East* (2016). Brings the narrative of the Arab Spring and the ambitions of its diverse proponents up to the present.

McCants, William, *The ISIS Apocalypse: The History, Strategy, and Doomsday Vision of the Islamic State* (2015). An important study of ISIS based on a wide reading of its own publications.

McNeill, J. R., *Something New under the Sun: An Environmental History of the Twentieth Century* (2000). An important overview of the environmental history of the twentieth century, with considerable statistical data that underscore the impact of humans on the environment and the atmosphere.

McNeill, J. R., and Peter Engelke, "Into the Anthropocene: People and Their Planet," in Akira Iriye (ed.), *Global Interdependence: The World after 1945* (2014), pp. 365–533. Two environmental historians embrace the concept of the Anthropocene Epoch.

Milankovic, Brian, *Global Inequality: A New Approach for the Age of Globalization* (2016). Using the most up-to-date data on worldwide incomes, the author shows how the last quarter century has yielded a convergence in global income distribution across societies and the widening of a gap within societies.

Moubayed, Sami, *Under the Black Flag: At the Frontier of the New Jihad* (2015). A study of the rise of jihadism within the Arab world, with a concentration on Syria.

Muller, Jan-Werner, *What Is Populism?* (2016). The sharpest analysis yet of the nature and prospects of populism, especially its relations to political establishments, which it condemns but on which it depends.

Murray, Christopher, et al., "Population and Fertility by Age and Sex for 195 Countries and Territories, 1950–2017: A Systemic Analysis for the Global Burden of Disease Study, 2017," *Lancet* 392, no. 10159 (November 10–16, 2018): 1995–2051. The definitive article on total fertility worldwide.

Owen, Roger, *The Rise and Fall of Arab Presidents for Life, with a New Afterword* (2014). A study that examines the emergence of Arab leaders who endeavored to hold on to power for as long as they lived, with insights into the actions of those who brought many of those leaders down during the Arab Spring.

Pietz, David A., *The Yellow River: The Problem of Water in Modern China* (2015). A critical look at health and environmental issues in China today, from a historical perspective through the lens of one of its major rivers.

Population Reference Bureau, *2018 World Population Data Sheet*, 2018, https://www.prb.org/wp-content/uploads/2018/08/2018_WPDS.pdf, and *2019 World Population Data Sheet*, 2019, https://www.prb.org/2019-world-population-data-sheet/. Useful statistics on world population.

Radelet, Steven, *Emerging Africa: How Seventeen Countries Are Leading the Way* (2010). An Afro-optimist sees many African countries enjoying economic growth and political stability, proving that Africa can join much of the rest of the world in achieving economic and political progress.

———, *The Great Surge: The Ascent of the Developing World* (2015). An overview of the extraordinary progress that many of the countries in what once was called the Third World have achieved in the economic and political realms.

Reid, Michael, *Forgotten Continent: The Battle for Latin America's Soul* (2009). A journalistic account of how Latin America grappled with market openings, new democratic forces, and the search for policies to close the gap between the haves and have-nots.

Sanderson, Henry, *Volt Rush: The Winners and Losers in the Race to Go Green* (2022). An expose of the challenges of the energy transition and how it will not alter world interdependence.

Shambaugh, David, *China Goes Global: The Partial Power* (2013). An analysis of China's role in the global arena and its impact, from economics to culture.

Thompson, Helen, *Disorder: Hard Times in the 21st Century* (2022). A superb study of how global finance and energy markets changed geopolitics.

Tooze, Adam, *Crashed: How a Decade of Financial Crises Changed the World* (2018). To date, this is the authoritative account of the Great Recession of 2008, spotlighting the differences between the U.S. and European responses and some of the long-term consequences for fracturing the world.

Trenin, Dmitri, *Should We Fear Russia?* (2016). A clear-eyed view of what contemporary Russia is and is not.

Warwick, John, *Black Flags Flying: The Rise of ISIS* (2015). A detailed account of the leadership groups within ISIS and its relationship to al-Qaeda.

Weiss, Michael, and Hassan Hassan, *ISIS: Inside the Army of Terror* (2015). An account based on interviews and wide reading of western and Arab sources on the rise of ISIS.

Wright, Lawrence, *The Looming Tower: Al-Qaeda and the Road to 9/11* (2006). A Pulitzer Prize–winning study of the origins and evolution of al-Qaeda.

———, *The Terror Years: From al-Qaeda to ISIS* (2016). Primarily a study of the decline of the power of al-Qaeda, which created an opening for the more territorially based ISIS.

Glossary

Abd al-Rahman III Islamic ruler in Spain who held a countercaliphate and reigned from 912 to 961 CE.

aboriginals Original, indigenous inhabitants of a region, as opposed to invaders, colonizers, or later peoples of mixed ancestry.

absolute monarchy Form of government in which one body, usually the monarch, controls the right to tax, judge, make war, and coin money. The term *enlightened absolutist* was often used to refer to state monarchies in seventeenth- and eighteenth-century Europe.

acid rain Precipitation containing large amounts of sulfur, which comes mainly from coal-fired power plants.

adaptation Ability to alter behavior and to innovate, finding new ways of doing things.

African National Congress (ANC) Multiracial organization founded in 1912 in an effort to end racial discrimination in South Africa.

Afrikaners Descendants of the original Dutch settlers of South Africa; formerly referred to as Boers.

Agones Athletic contests in ancient Greece.

Ahmosis Egyptian ruler in the southern part of the country who ruled from 1550 to 1525 BCE; Ahmosis used Hyksos weaponry—chariots in particular—to defeat the Hyksos themselves.

Ahura Mazda Supreme God of the Persians, believed to have created the world and all that is good and to have appointed earthly kings.

AIDS *See* HIV/AIDS.

Akbarnamah Mughal intellectual Abulfazl's *Book of Akbar*, which attempted to reconcile the traditional Sufi interest in the inner life within the worldly context of a great empire.

Alaric II Visigothic king who issued a simplified code of innovative imperial law.

Alexander the Great (356–323 BCE) Leader who used novel tactics and new kinds of armed forces to conquer the Persian Empire, which extended from Egypt and the Mediterranean Sea to the interior of what is now Afghanistan and as far as the Indus River valley. Alexander's conquests broke down barriers between the Mediterranean world and Southwest Asia and transferred massive amounts of wealth and power to the Mediterranean, transforming it into a more unified world of economic and cultural exchange.

Alexandria Port city in Egypt named after Alexander the Great. Alexandria was a model city in the Hellenistic world. It was built up by a multiethnic population from around the Mediterranean world.

al-Khwarizmi Scientist and mathematician who lived from 780 to 850 CE and is known for having modified Indian digits into Arabic numerals.

Allied Powers Name given to the alliance between Britain, France, Russia, and Italy, all of which fought against Germany and Austria-Hungary (the Central Powers) in World War I. In World War II, the name was used for the alliance between Britain, France, and the United States, all of which fought against the Axis Powers (Germany, Italy, and Japan).

allomothering System in which mothers relied on other women, including their own mothers, daughters, sisters, and friends, to help in the nurturing and protecting of their children.

alluvium Area of land created by river deposits.

alphabet A mid-second-millennium BCE Phoenician system of writing based on relatively few letters (twenty-two) that combined to make sounds and words. Adaptable to many languages, the alphabet was simpler and more flexible than writing based on symbols for syllables and ideas.

American Railway Union Workers' union that initiated the Pullman strike of 1894, which led to violence and ended in the leaders' arrest.

Amnesty International Nongovernmental organization formed to defend "prisoners of conscience"—those detained for their beliefs, race, sex, ethnic origin, language, or religion.

Amorites Name, which means "westerners," used by Mesopotamian urbanites to describe the transhumant herders who began to migrate into their cities in the late third millennium BCE.

Amun Once-insignificant Egyptian god elevated to higher status by Amenemhet I (1985–1955 BCE). *Amun* means "hidden" in Ancient Egyptian; the name was meant to convey the god's omnipresence.

Analects, The Texts that included the teachings and cultural ideals of Confucius.

anarchism Belief that society should be a free association of its members, not subject to government, laws, or police.

Anatolia The area now mainly known as modern Turkey. In the sixth millennium BCE, people from Anatolia, Greece, and the Levant took to boats and populated the Aegean. Their small villages endured almost unchanged for two millennia.

Angkor Wat Magnificent temple complex that crowned the royal palace of the Khmer Empire in Angkor, adorned with statues representing the Hindu pantheon of gods.

Anglo-Boer War (1899–1902) Anticolonial struggle in South Africa between the British and the Afrikaners over the gold-rich Transvaal. In response to the Afrikaners' guerrilla tactics and in order to contain the local population, the British instituted the first concentration camps. Ultimately, Britain won the conflict but at a terrible cost.

animal domestication Gradual process that occurred simultaneously with or just before the domestication of plants, depending on the region.

annals Historical records. Notable annals are the cuneiform inscriptions that record successful Neo-Assyrian military campaigns.

Anti-Federalists Critics of the U.S. Constitution who sought to defend the people against the power of the federal government and insisted on a Bill of Rights to protect individual liberties from government intrusion.

apartheid Racial segregation policy of the Afrikaner-dominated South African government. Legislated in 1948 by the Afrikaner National Party, it had existed in South Africa for many years.

Arab-Israeli War of 1948–1949 Conflict between Israeli and Arab armies that arose in the wake of a U.N. vote to partition Palestine into Arab and Jewish territories. The war shattered the legitimacy of Arab ruling elites.

Aramaic Dialect of a Semitic language spoken in Southwest Asia; it became the lingua franca of the Persian Empire.

Aristotle (384–322 BCE) Philosopher who studied under Plato but came to different conclusions about nature and politics. Aristotle believed in collecting observations about nature and discerning patterns to ascertain how things worked.

Aryans Nomadic charioteers who spoke Indo-European languages and entered South Asia in 1500 BCE. The early Aryan settlers were herders.

Asante state State located in present-day Ghana, founded by the Asantes at the end of the seventeenth century. It grew in power in the next century because of its access to gold and its involvement in the slave trade.

ascetic One who rejects material possessions and physical pleasures.

Asiatic Society Cultural organization founded by British Orientalists who supported native culture but still believed in colonial rule.

Aśoka Emperor of the Mauryan dynasty from 268 to 231 BCE; he was a great conqueror and unifier of India. He is said to have embraced Buddhism toward the end of his life.

Assur One of two cities on the upper reaches of the Tigris River that were the heart of Assyria proper (the other was Nineveh).

Aśvaghosa First known Sanskrit writer. It is believed that he lived from 80 to 150 CE and composed a biography of the Buddha.

Ataturk, Mustafa Kemal (1881–1938) Ottoman army officer and military hero who helped forge the modern Turkish nation-state. He and his followers deposed the sultan, declared Turkey a republic, and constructed a European-like secular state, eliminating Islam's hold over civil and political affairs.

Atlantic system New system of trade and expansion that linked Europe, Africa, and the Americas. It emerged in the wake of European voyages across the Atlantic Ocean.

atma Vedic term signifying the eternal self, represented by the trinity of deities.

atman In the Upanishads, an eternal being who exists everywhere. The atman never perishes, but is reborn or transmigrates into another life.

Attila Sole ruler of all Hunnish tribes from 434 to 453 CE. Harsh and much feared, he formed the first empire to oppose Rome in northern Europe.

Augustus Latin term meaning "the Revered One"; title granted by the Senate to the Roman ruler Octavian in 27 BCE to signify his unique political position. Along with his adopted family name, *Caesar*, the military honorific *imperator*, and the senatorial term *princeps*, *Augustus* became a generic term for a leader of the Roman Empire.

australopithecines Hominin species, including *anamensis*, *afarensis* (Lucy), and *africanus*, that appeared in Africa beginning around 4 million years ago and, unlike other animals, sometimes walked on two legs. Their brain capacity was a little less than one-third of a modern human's. Although not humans, they carried the genetic and biological material out of which modern humans would later emerge.

Austro-Hungarian Empire Dual monarchy established by the Habsburg family in 1867; it collapsed at the end of World War I.

authoritarianism Centralized and dictatorial form of government, proclaimed by its adherents to be superior to parliamentary democracy and especially effective at mobilizing the masses. This idea was widely accepted in parts of the world during the 1930s.

Avesta Compilation of Zoroastrian holy works transmitted orally by priests for millennia and eventually recorded in the sixth century BCE.

Awadh Kingdom in northern India; one of the first successor states to have gained a measure of independence from the Mughal ruler in Delhi, and the most prized object for annexation by the East India Company.

Axial Age Pivotal period in the mid-first millennium BCE when radical thinkers, such as Zoroaster in Persia, Confucius and Master Lao in East Asia, Siddhartha Gautama (the Buddha) in South Asia, and Socrates in the Mediterranean, offered dramatically new ideas that challenged their times.

Axis Powers The three aggressor states in World War II: Germany, Japan, and Italy.

Aztec Empire Mesoamerican empire that originated with a league of three Mexica cities in 1430 and gradually expanded through the Central Valley of Mexico, uniting numerous small, independent states under a single monarch who ruled with the help of counselors, military leaders, and priests. By the late fifteenth century, the Aztec realm may have embraced 25 million people. In 1521, the Aztecs were defeated by the conquistador Hernán Cortés.

baby boom Post–World War II upswing in U.S. birthrates, which reversed a century of decline.

Bactria (c. 250–50 BCE) Hellenistic kingdom in Gandhara region (modern Pakistan) that became an independent state around 200 BCE, with a major city at Aï Khanoum. Its people and culture are sometimes called "Indo-Greek" because of the blending of Indian and Greek populations and ideas.

Bactrian camel Two-humped animal domesticated in central Asia around 2500 BCE. The Bactrian camel was heartier than the one-humped dromedary and became the animal of choice for the harsh and varied climates typical of Silk Road trade.

Baghdad Capital of the Islamic empire under the Abbasid dynasty, founded in 762 CE (located in modern-day Iraq). In the medieval period, it was a center of administration, scholarship, and cultural growth for what came to be known as the Golden Age of Islamic science.

Baghdad Pact (1955) Middle Eastern military alliance between countries friendly with America that were also willing to align themselves with the western countries against the Soviet Union.

Balam Na Stone temple and place of pilgrimage for the Maya people of Mexico's Yucatán Peninsula.

Balfour Declaration Letter (November 2, 1917) written by Lord Arthur J. Balfour, British foreign secretary, that promised a homeland for the Jews in Palestine.

Bamboo Annals Shang stories and foundation myths that were written on bamboo strips and later collected.

Bantu Language first spoken by people who lived in the southeastern region of modern Nigeria around 1000 CE.

Bantu migrations Waves of population movement from West Africa into eastern and southern Africa during the first millennium CE, bringing new agricultural practices to these regions and absorbing much of the hunting and gathering population.

barbarian Derogatory term used to describe pastoral nomads, painting them as enemies of civilization; the term *barbarian* used to have a more neutral meaning than it does today.

barbarian invasions Violent migration of people in the late fourth and fifth centuries CE from the frontiers of the Roman Empire into its western provinces. These migrants had long been used as non-Roman soldiers.

basilicas Early Christian churches modeled on Roman law-court buildings that could accommodate over a thousand worshippers.

Battle of Adwa (1896) Battle in which the Ethiopians defeated Italian colonial forces; it inspired many of Africa's later national leaders.

Battle of Wounded Knee (1890) Bloody massacre of Sioux Ghost Dancers by U.S. armed forces.

Bay of Pigs (1961) Unsuccessful invasion of Cuba by Cuban exiles supported by the U.S. government. The invaders intended to incite an insurrection in Cuba and overthrow the communist regime of Fidel Castro.

Bedouins Nomadic pastoralists in the deserts of Southwest Asia.

Beer Hall Putsch (1923) Nazi intrusion into a meeting of Bavarian leaders in a Munich beer hall in an attempt to force support for their cause; Adolf Hitler was imprisoned for a year after the incident.

Beghards Eccentric sixteenth-century European group whose members claimed to be in a state of grace that allowed them to do what they pleased—ranging from adultery, free love, and nudity to murder; also called Brethren of Free Speech.

bell beaker Ancient drinking vessel, an artifact from Europe, so named because its shape resembles an inverted bell.

Berenice of Egypt Egyptian queen who helped rule over the kingdom of the Nile from around 320 to 280 BCE.

Beringia Prehistoric thousand-mile-long land bridge that linked Siberia and North America (which had not been populated by hominins). About 30,000 years ago, *Homo sapiens* edged into this landmass.

Berlin Airlift (1948) Supply of vital necessities to West Berlin by air transport, primarily under U.S. auspices, initiated in response to a land and water blockade of the city instituted by the Soviet Union in the hope that the Allies would be forced to abandon West Berlin.

Berlin Wall Wall dividing the city of Berlin, built in 1961 by communist East Germany to prevent its citizens from fleeing to West Germany; torn down in 1989.

bhakti Religious practice that grew out of Hinduism and emphasizes personal devotion to gods.

big men Leaders of the extended household communities that formed village settlements in African rain forests.

big whites Literal translation of *grands blancs*; French plantation owners in Saint-Domingue (present-day Haiti) who created one of the wealthiest enslaver societies.

Bilad al-Sudan Arabic for "the land of the Blacks"; it consisted of the land lying south of the Sahara.

bilharzia Debilitating waterborne illness that was widespread in Egypt, where it infected peasants who worked in the irrigation canals.

Bill of Rights First ten amendments to the U.S. Constitution; ratified in 1791.

biomes Distinct biological systems, including humans, that have formed in response to shared physical conditions.

bioprospecting Transferring knowledge about biological, chemical, and botanical resources from one location on the planet to another with commercial aims, especially in agriculture and pharmaceuticals. Often, this involves the exploitation of indigenous forms of knowledge. In the modern age, it frequently leads to patents, which reward the owner of the patent and not necessarily the discoverer of the knowledge.

bipedalism Walking on two legs, thereby freeing hands and arms to carry objects such as weapons and tools; one of several traits that distinguished hominins.

Black Death Plague pandemic that ravaged Europe, East Asia, and North Africa in the fourteenth century, killing large numbers of people, including perhaps as much as two-thirds of the European population.

Black Jacobins Nickname for the rebels in Saint-Domingue, including Toussaint L'Ouverture, a formerly enslaved man who led the enslaved people of this French colony in the world's largest and most successful insurrection of its kind.

Black Lives Matter A decentralized and eventually global movement founded in 2013 that champions nonviolent civil disobedience in resistance to police brutality and violence against Black people.

Black Panthers Radical African American group in the 1960s and 1970s that advocated Black separatism and pan-Africanism.

black shirts Fascist troops of Mussolini's regime; these squads received money from Italian landowners to attack socialist leaders.

Black Tuesday (October 29, 1929) Historic day when the U.S. stock market crashed, plunging the United States and international trading systems into crisis and leading the world into the Great Depression.

blitzkrieg "Lightning war"; type of warfare waged by the Germans during World War II, using coordinated aerial bombing campaigns along with tanks and infantry in motorized vehicles.

bodhisattvas In Mahayana Buddhism, enlightened beings who have earned nirvana but remain in this world to help others reach it.

Bolívar, Simón (1783–1830) Venezuelan leader who urged his followers to overcome their local identities and become "American." He wanted the liberated South American countries to form a Latin American confederation, urging Peru and Bolivia to join Venezuela, Ecuador, and Colombia in the "Gran Colombia."

Bolsheviks Former members of the Russian Social Democratic Party who advocated the destruction of capitalist political and economic institutions and seized power in Russia in 1917 when the Russian Empire collapsed. In 1918, the Bolsheviks changed their name to the Russian Communist Party.

Book of the Dead Ancient Egyptian funerary text that contains drawings and paintings as well as spells describing how to prepare the jewelry and amulets that were buried with a person in preparation for the afterlife.

bourgeoisie A French term originally designating non-noble city dwellers (*Bürger* in German). They sought to be recognized not by birth or aristocratic title but by property and ability. In the nineteenth century, *bourgeois* came to refer to non-noble property owners, especially those who controlled modern industry. A bourgeois was an individual. We can refer to "bourgeois values." *Bourgeoisie* refers to the entire class, as in the French bourgeoisie as a whole.

Boxer Protocol Written agreement between the victors of the Boxer Uprising and the Qing Empire in 1901 that placed western troops in Beijing and required the regime to pay exorbitant damages for foreign life and property.

Boxer Uprising (1899–1900) Chinese peasant movement that opposed foreign influence, especially that of Christian missionaries; it was put down after the Boxers were defeated by an army composed mostly of Japanese, Russians, British, French, and Americans.

Brahma One of three major deities that form a trinity in Vedic religion. Brahma signifies birth. *See also* Vishnu *and* Shiva.

Brahmans Vedic priests who performed rituals and communicated with the gods. Brahmans provided guidance on how to live in balance with the forces of nature as represented by the various deities. Brahmanism was reborn as Hinduism sometime during the first half of the first millennium CE.

British Commonwealth of Nations Union formed in 1926 that conferred "dominion status" on Britain's White settler colonies in Canada, Australia, and New Zealand.

British East India Company *See* East India Company.

bronze Alloy of copper and tin brought into Europe from Anatolia; used to make hard-edged weapons.

brown shirts Troops of German men who advanced the Nazi cause by holding street marches, mass rallies, and confrontations and by beating Jews and anyone who opposed the Nazis.

Buddha "Enlightened One." The term was applied to Kshatriya-born Siddhartha Gautama (c. 563–483 BCE), whose ideas—about the relationship between desire and suffering and how to eliminate both through wisdom, ethical behavior, and mental discipline in order to achieve contentment (nirvana)—offered a radical challenge to Brahmanism.

Buddhism Major South Asian religion that aims to end human suffering through the renunciation of desire. Buddhists believe that removing the illusion of a separate identity would lead to a state of contentment (nirvana). These beliefs challenged the traditional Brahmanic teachings of the time and provided the peoples of South Asia with an alternative to established traditions.

bullion Uncoined gold or silver.

Byzantium Modern term for the Eastern Roman Empire (which would last until 1453), centered at its "New Rome," Constantinople, which was founded in 324 CE by Constantine on the site of the Greek city Byzantium.

Cahokia Commercial city on the Mississippi for regional and long-distance trade of commodities such as salt, shells, and skins and of manufactured goods such as pottery, textiles, and jewelry; marked by massive artificial hills, akin to earthen pyramids, used to honor spiritual forces.

calaveras Allegorical skeleton drawings by the Mexican printmaker and artist José Guadalupe Posada. The works drew on popular themes of betrayal, death, and festivity.

caliphate Islamic state, headed by a caliph—chosen either by election from the community (Sunni) or from the lineage of Muhammad (Shiite)—with political authority over the Muslim community.

Calvin, Jean (1509–1564) A French theologian during the Protestant Reformation. Calvin developed a Christianity that emphasized moral regeneration through church teachings and laid out a doctrine of predestination.

candomblé Yoruba-based religion in northern Brazil; it interwove African practices and beliefs with Christianity.

Canton system System officially established by imperial decree in 1759 that required European traders to have Chinese guild merchants act as guarantors for their good behavior and payment of fees.

caravan cities Cities (like Petra and Palmyra) that were located along land routes of the Silk Roads and served as hubs of commerce and cultural exchange between travelers and merchants participating in long-distance trade.

caravans Companies of men who transported and traded goods along overland routes in North Africa and central Asia; large caravans consisted of 600–1,000 camels and as many as 400 men.

caravanserais Inns along major trade routes that accommodated large numbers of traders, their animals, and their wares.

caravel Sailing vessel suited for nosing in and out of estuaries and navigating in waters with unpredictable currents and winds.

carrack Ship used on open bodies of water, such as the Mediterranean.

Carthage City in what is modern-day Tunisia; emblematic of the trading aspirations and activities of merchants in the Mediterranean. Pottery and other archaeological remains demonstrate that trading contacts with Carthage were as far-flung as Italy, Greece, France, Iberia, and West Africa.

cartography Mapmaking.

caste system Hierarchical system of organizing people and distributing labor.

Caste War of Yucatán (1847–1901) Conflict between Indigenous Maya and the Mexican state over Indigenous autonomy and legal equality, which resulted in the Mexican takeover of the Yucatán Peninsula.

Castro, Fidel (1926–2016) Cuban communist leader who seized power in January 1959. Castro became increasingly radical as he consolidated power, announcing a massive redistribution of land and the nationalization of foreign oil refineries; he declared himself a socialist and aligned himself with the Soviet Union in the wake of the 1961 CIA-backed Bay of Pigs invasion.

Çatal Hüyük Site in Anatolia discovered in 1958. It was a dense honeycomb of settlements filled with rooms whose walls were covered with paintings of wild bulls, hunters, and pregnant women. Çatal Hüyük symbolizes an early transition to urban dwelling and dates to the eighth millennium BCE.

cathedra Bishop's seat, or throne, in a church.

Catholic Church *See* Roman Catholicism.

Cato the Elder (234–149 BCE) Roman statesman, often seen as emblematic of the transition from a Greek to a Roman world. He wrote a manual for the new economy of plantation slavery in agriculture, invested in shipping and trading, learned Greek rhetoric, and added the genre of history to Latin literature.

caudillos South American local military chieftains.

cave drawings Images on cave walls. The subjects are most often large game, although a few are images of humans. Other elements are impressions made by hands dipped in paint and pressed on a wall as well as abstract symbols and shapes.

Celali revolts (1595–1610) Peasant and artisan uprisings against the Ottoman state.

Central Powers Alliance of Germany and Austria-Hungary in World War I.

Chan Chan City founded around 900 CE by the Moche people in what is now modern-day Peru. It became the largest city of the Chimú Empire with a core population of 30,000 inhabitants.

Chan Santa Cruz Separate Maya community formed as part of a crusade for spiritual salvation and the complete cultural separation of the Maya people; means "little holy cross."

Chandragupta Maurya (r. 321–297 BCE) Also called Chandragupta Mori (and mentioned, though not by name, in many contemporary Greek sources); founder of South Asia's first empire, as the Mauryan dynasty of India, in the power vacuum left by the withdrawal of Alexander of Macedon's Greek forces from the region.

Chandragupta I (r. c. 320–335 CE) Founder of the Gupta dynasty of India who took the title "King of Kings" and significantly expanded the territory of his empire to include all of the northern plain of India.

Chandragupta II (r. c. 380–415 CE) Grandson of Chandragupta I who further expanded Gupta territories and was a literary patron. During his reign the renowned Sanskrit author Kalidasa is thought to have flourished.

Chandravansha One of two main lineages (the lunar one) of Vedic society, each with its own creation myth, ancestors, language, and rituals. Each lineage included many clans. *See also* Suryavansha.

chapatis Flat, unleavened Indian bread.

chariot Horse-drawn vehicle with two spoked and metal-rimmed wheels. Made possible by the interaction of pastoralists and settled communities, the chariot revolutionized warfare in the second millennium BCE.

charismatic Person who uses personal strengths or virtues, often laced with a divine aura, to command followers.

Charlemagne Emperor of the west and heir to Rome from 768 to 814 CE.

chartered companies Private firms that were awarded monopoly trading rights over vast areas by European monarchs (for example, the Virginia Company and the Dutch East India Company).

Chartism (1834–1848) Mass democratic movement to pass the Peoples' Charter in Britain, granting male suffrage, secret ballot, equal electoral districts, and annual parliaments and absolving the requirement of property ownership for members of the parliament.

chattel slavery Form of slavery in which people were sold as property, the rise of which coincided with the expansion of city-states. Chattel slavery was eschewed by the Spartans, who also rejected the innovation of coin money.

Chavín Agrarian people living from 1400 to 200 BCE in complex societies in what is now Peru. They manufactured goods (ceramics, textiles, and precious metals), conducted limited long-distance trade, and shared an artistic and religious tradition, most notably at Chavín de Huántar.

Chernobyl (1986) Site in the Soviet Union (in present-day Ukraine) of the meltdown of a nuclear reactor.

Chiang Kai-shek (1887–1975) Leader of the Guomindang following Sun Yat-sen's death who mobilized the Chinese masses through the New Life movement. In 1949, he lost the Chinese Revolution to the communists and moved his regime to Taiwan.

Chimú Empire South America's first empire, centered at Chan Chan, in the Moche Valley on the Pacific coast from 1000 through 1470 CE, whose development was fueled by agriculture and commercial exchange.

chinampas Floating gardens used by Aztecs in the 1300s and 1400s to grow crops.

China's Sorrow Name for the Yellow River, which, when it changed course or flooded, could cause mass death and waves of migration.

chinoiserie Chinese silks, teas, tableware, jewelry, and paper; popular among Europeans in the seventeenth and eighteenth centuries.

Christendom Entire portion of the world in which Christianity prevailed.

Christianity New religious movement originating in the Eastern Roman Empire in the first century CE, with roots in Judaism and resonance with various Greco-Roman religious traditions. The central figure, Jesus, was tried and executed by Roman authorities, and his followers believed he rose from the dead. The tradition was spread across the Mediterranean by his followers, and Christians were initially persecuted—to varying degrees—by Roman authorities. The religion was eventually legalized in 312 CE, and by the late fourth century CE it became the official state religion of the Roman Empire.

Church of England Established form of Christianity in England dating from the sixteenth century.

city Highly populated concentration of economic, religious, and political power. The first cities appeared in river basins, which could produce a surplus of agriculture. The abundance of food freed most city inhabitants from the need to produce their own food, which allowed them to work in specialized professions.

city-state Political organization based on the authority of a single, large city that controls outlying territories.

Civil Rights Act (1964) U.S. legislation that banned racial segregation in public facilities, outlawed racial discrimination in employment, and marked an important step in correcting legal inequality.

civil rights movement Powerful movement for equal rights and the end of racial segregation in the United States that began in the 1950s with court victories against school segregation and nonviolent boycotts.

civil service examinations Set of challenging exams instituted by the Tang to help assess potential bureaucrats' literary skill and knowledge of the Confucian classics.

Civil War, American (1861–1865) Conflict between the northern and southern states of America that led to the abolition of slavery in the United States.

clan A social group comprising many households, claiming descent from a common ancestor.

clandestine presses Small printing operations that published banned texts in the early modern era, especially in Switzerland and the Netherlands.

closing of the frontier In 1893, responding to the recent U.S. Census, the historian Frederick Jackson Turner popularized the idea that the western frontier—so long crucial to the making of American identity—had closed. His announcement spurred many to worry that having lost the manliness and self-reliance nurtured by the hard life on the frontier, Americans would grow soft and weak.

Clovis people Early humans in America who used basic chipped blades and pointed spears in pursuing prey. They extended the hunting traditions they had learned in Afro-Eurasia, such as establishing campsites and moving with the herds. They were known as "Clovis people" because the type of arrowhead point that they used was first found by archaeologists at a site near Clovis, New Mexico.

Code of Manu Brahmanic code of law that took shape in the third to fifth centuries CE and expressed ideas going back to Vedic times. Framed as a conversation between Manu (the first human and an ancient lawgiver) and a group of wise men, it articulated the rules of the hierarchical *varna* system.

codex Early form of book, with separate pages bound together; it replaced the scroll as the main medium for written texts. The codex emerged around 300 CE.

cognitive skills Skills such as thought, memory, problem solving, and—ultimately—language. Hominins were able to use these skills and their hands to create new adaptations, like tools, which helped them obtain food and avoid predators.

Cohong Chinese merchant guild that traded with Europeans under the Qing dynasty.

coins Form of money that replaced goods, which previously had been bartered for services and other products. Originally used mainly to hire mercenary soldiers, coins became the commonplace method of payment linking buyers and producers throughout the Mediterranean.

Cold War (1945–1990) Ideological rivalry in which the Soviet Union and eastern Europe opposed the United States and western Europe, but no direct military conflict occurred between the two rival blocs.

colonies Regions under the political control of another country.

Colons French settlers in Algeria.

Colosseum Huge amphitheater in Rome completed by Titus and dedicated in 80 CE. Originally begun by Flavian, the structure is named after a colossal statue of Nero that formerly stood beside it.

Columbian exchange Movements between Afro-Eurasia and the Americas of previously unknown plants, animals, people, diseases, and products that followed in the wake of Columbus's voyages.

commanderies The thirty-six provinces (*jun*) into which Shi Huangdi divided territories. Each commandery had a civil governor, a military governor, and an imperial inspector.

Communist Manifesto, The Pamphlet published by Karl Marx and Friedrich Engels in 1848 at a time when political revolutions were sweeping Europe. It called on the workers of all nations to unite in overthrowing capitalism.

Compromise of 1867 Agreement between the Habsburg state and the peoples living in Hungarian parts of the empire that the state would be officially known as the Austro-Hungarian Empire.

concession areas Territories, usually ports, where Chinese emperors allowed European merchants to trade and European people to settle.

Confucian ideals The ideals of honoring tradition, emphasizing the responsibility of the emperor, and respecting the lessons of history, promoted by Confucius, which the Han dynasty made the official doctrine of the empire by 50 BCE.

Confucianism Ethics, beliefs, and practices stipulated by the Chinese philosopher Kong Qiu, or Confucius, which served as a guide for Chinese society up to modern times.

Confucius (551–479 BCE) Radical thinker whose ideas—especially about how ethical living that was centered on *ren* (benevolence), *li* (proper ritual), and *xiao* (filial piety toward ancestors living and dead) shaped the politically engaged superior gentleman—transformed society and government in East Asia.

cong tube Ritual object crafted by the Liangzhu, made of jade and used in divination practices.

Congo Free State Large colonial state in Africa created by Leopold II, king of Belgium, during the 1880s and ruled by him alone. After rumors of mass slaughter and enslavement, the Belgian parliament took possession of the colony.

Congress of Vienna (1814–1815) International conference to reorganize Europe after the downfall of Napoleon. European monarchies agreed to respect one another's borders and to cooperate in guarding against future revolutions and war.

conquistadors Spanish military leaders who led the conquest of the New World in the sixteenth century.

Constantine Roman emperor who converted to Christianity in 312 CE. In 313, he issued a proclamation that gave Christians new freedoms in the empire. He also founded Constantinople (at first called "New Rome").

Constantinople Capital city of Byzantium, which was founded as the New Rome by the emperor Constantine.

Constitutional Convention (1787) Meeting to formulate the Constitution of the United States of America.

Contra rebels Opponents of the Sandinistas in Nicaragua; they were armed and financed by the United States and other anticommunist countries (1980).

conversos Jewish and Muslim converts to Christianity in the Iberian Peninsula and the New World.

Coptic Form of Christianity practiced in Egypt. It was doctrinally different from Christianity elsewhere, and Coptic Christians had their own views of the nature of Christ.

Corn Laws Laws that imposed tariffs on grain imported to Great Britain, intended to protect British farming interests. The Corn Laws were abolished in 1846 as part of a British movement in favor of free trade.

cosmology Branch of metaphysics devoted to understanding the order of the universe.

cosmopolitans Meaning "citizens of the world," as opposed to a city-state, this term refers particularly to inhabitants of the large, multiethnic cities that were nodes of exchange in the Hellenistic world.

Council of Nicaea Church council convened in 325 CE by Constantine and presided over by him as well. At this council, a Christian creed was articulated and made into a formula that expressed the philosophical and technical elements of Christian belief.

Counter-Reformation Movement to counter the spread of the Reformation; initiated by the Catholic Church at the Council of Trent in 1545. The Catholic Church enacted reforms to attack clerical corruption and placed a greater emphasis on individual spirituality. During this time, the Jesuits were founded to help revive the Catholic Church.

coup d'état Overthrow of an established state by a group of conspirators, usually from the military.

creation narratives Narratives constructed by different cultures that draw on their belief systems and available evidence to explain the origins of the world and humanity.

creed From the Latin *credo*, meaning "I believe," an authoritative statement of belief. The Nicene Creed, formulated by Christian bishops at the Council of Nicaea in 325 CE, is an example of one such formal belief statement.

Creoles Persons of mixed European and African (or other) descent who were born in the Americas.

Crimean War (1853–1856) War waged by Russia against Great Britain and France. Spurred by Russia's encroachment on Ottoman territories, the conflict revealed Russia's military weakness when Russian forces fell to British and French troops.

crossbow Innovative weapon used at the end of China's Warring States period that allowed archers to shoot their enemies with accuracy, even from a distance.

Crusades Wave of attacks launched in the late eleventh century by western European Christians against Muslims. The First Crusade began in 1095, when Pope Urban II appealed to the warrior nobility of France to free Jerusalem from Muslim rule. Four subsequent Crusades were fought over the next two centuries.

Cuban Missile Crisis (1962) Diplomatic standoff between the United States and the Soviet Union that was provoked by the Soviet Union's attempt to base nuclear missiles in Cuba; it brought the world close to a nuclear war.

cult Religious movement, often based on the worship of a particular god or goddess.

cultigen Organism that has diverged from its ancestors through domestication or cultivation.

cuneiform Wedge-shaped form of writing. As people combined rebus symbols with other visual marks that contained meaning, they became able to record and transmit messages over long distances by using abstract symbols or signs to denote concepts; such signs later came to represent syllables, which could be joined into words. By impressing these signs into wet clay with the cut end of a reed, scribes engaged in cuneiform.

Cyrus the Great Founder of the Persian Empire. This sixth-century ruler (559–529 BCE) conquered the Medes and unified the Iranian kingdoms.

czar *See* tsar.

daimyo Ruling lord who commanded a private army in pre-Meiji Japan.

dan Fodio, Usman (1754–1817) Fulani Muslim cleric whose visions led him to challenge the Hausa ruling classes, who he believed were insufficiently faithful to Islamic beliefs and practices. His ideas gained support among those who had suffered under the Hausa landlords. In 1804, his supporters and allies overthrew the Hausa in what is today northern Nigeria.

Daoism East Asian philosophy of the Axial Age introduced by Master Lao and expanded by his student Zhuangzi. It was remarkable for its emphasis on following the *dao* (the natural way of the cosmos) and held that the best way to do that was through *wuwei* (doing nothing).

dar al-Islam Arabic for "the House of Islam"; describes a sense of common identity.

Darius I (r. 522–486 BCE) Leader who put the emerging unified Persian Empire onto solid footing after Cyrus the Great's death.

Darwin, Charles (1809–1882) British scientist who became convinced that the species of organic life had evolved under the uniform pressure of natural laws, not by means of a special, one-time creation as described in the Bible.

D-Day (June 6, 1944) Day of the Allied invasion of Normandy under General Dwight Eisenhower to liberate western Europe from German occupation.

Dear Boy Nickname of an early human skull discovered in 1931 by a team of archaeologists named the Leakeys. Other objects discovered with Dear Boy demonstrated that by his time, early humans had begun to fashion tools and to use them for butchering animals and possibly for hunting and killing smaller animals.

Decembrists Russian army officers who were influenced by events in revolutionary France and formed secret societies that espoused liberal governance. They launched a revolt that was put down by Nicholas I in December 1825.

Declaration of Independence U.S. document stating the theory of government on which America was founded.

Declaration of the Rights of Man and of the Citizen (1789) French charter of liberties formulated by the National Assembly that marked the end of dynastic and aristocratic rule. The seventeen articles later became the preamble to the new constitution, which the assembly finished in 1791.

decolonization End of empire and emergence of new independent nation-states in Asia and Africa as a result of the defeat of Japan in World War II and weakened European influence after the war.

degeneration In the later nineteenth century, many Europeans began to fear that Darwin had been wrong: urbanization, technology, racial hybridity, the emergence of the "modern" woman, and over-refinement were causing Europeans not to progress as a species but to degenerate. This fear was often combined with anxieties about colonialism, homosexuality, emigration, and/or the advancement of women.

Delhi Sultanate (1206–1526) A Turkish Muslim regime in northern India that, through its tolerance for cultural diversity, brought political integration without enforcing cultural homogeneity.

democracy The idea that people, through membership in a nation, should choose their own representatives and be governed by them.

Democritus Thinker in ancient Greece who lived from around 460 to 370 BCE; he deduced the existence of the atom and postulated that there was such a thing as an indivisible particle.
demotic writing The second of two basic forms of ancient Egyptian writing. Demotic was a cursive script written with ink on papyrus, on pottery, or on other absorbent objects. It was the most common and practical form of writing in Egypt and was used for administrative record keeping and in private or pseudo-private forms like letters and works of literature. *See also* hieroglyphs.
developing world Term applied to poor countries of the Third World and the former eastern communist bloc seeking to develop viable nation-states and prosperous economies. The term has come under sustained criticism for suggesting that there is a single path of economic growth that countries everywhere follow. It has been replaced by equally problematic terms like "advanced economy" and "emerging markets."
devshirme The Ottoman system of taking non-Muslim children in place of taxes in order to educate them in Muslim ways and prepare them for service in the sultan's bureaucracy.
dhamma Moral code espoused by Aśoka in the Kalinga edict, which was meant to apply to all—Buddhists, Brahmans, and Greeks alike.
***dhimma* system** Ottoman law that permitted followers of religions other than Islam, such as Armenian Christians, Greek Orthodox Christians, and Jews, to choose their own religious leaders and to settle internal disputes within their religious communities as long as they accepted Islam's political dominion.
dhows Ships used by Arab seafarers whose large sails were rigged to maximize the capture of wind.
Dien Bien Phu (1954) Site of a defining battle in the war between French colonialists and the Viet Minh that secured North Vietnam for Ho Chi Minh and his army and left the south to form its own government with French and American support.
Diogenes Greek philosopher who lived from around 412 to 323 BCE and who espoused a doctrine of self-sufficiency and freedom from social laws and customs. He rejected cultural norms as out of tune with nature and therefore false.
Directory Temporary military committee in France that took over affairs of the state from the radicals in 1795 and held control until the coup of Napoleon Bonaparte.
divination Rituals used to communicate with gods or royal ancestors and to foretell future events. Divination was used to legitimize royal authority and demand tribute.
Djoser Ancient Egyptian king who reigned from 2630 to 2611 BCE. He was the second king of the Third Dynasty and celebrated the Sed festival in his tomb complex at Saqqara.
domestication Bringing a wild animal or plant under human control.
Dominion in the British Commonwealth Canadian promise to keep up the country's fealty to the British crown, even after its independence in 1867. Later applied to Australia and New Zealand.
Dong Zhongshu Emperor Wu's chief minister, who advocated a more powerful view of Confucius by promoting texts that focused on Confucius as a man who possessed aspects of divinity.
double-outrigger canoes Vessels used by early Austronesians to cross the Taiwan Straits and colonize islands in the Pacific. These sturdy canoes could cover over 120 miles per day.
Duma Russian parliament.
Dutch learning Broad term for European teachings that were strictly regulated by the shoguns inside Japan.
dynastic cycle Political narrative in which influential families vied for supremacy. Upon gaining power, they legitimated their authority by claiming to be the heirs of previous grand dynasts and by preserving or revitalizing the ancestors' virtuous governing ways. This continuity conferred divine support.
dynasty Hereditary ruling family that passed control from one generation to the next.
Earth Summit (1992) Meeting in Rio de Janeiro between many of the world's governments in an effort to address international environmental problems.
East India Company (1600–1858) British charter company created to outperform Portuguese and Spanish traders in Asia; in the eighteenth century the company became, in effect, the ruler of a large part of India.
Eastern Front Battlefront between Berlin and Moscow during World War I and World War II.
economic inequality Systematically uneven distribution of both income and opportunity among different groups of people or different nations.
economic nationalism An ideology that supports state interventionism over other means of regulating a nation's market, often involving restrictions on the movement of capital, labor, and goods.
Edict of Nantes (1598) Edict issued by Henry IV to end the French Wars of Religion. The edict declared France a Catholic country but tolerated some Protestant worship.
Eiffel Tower Steel monument completed in 1889 for the Paris Exposition. It was twice the height of any other building at the time.
eight-legged essay Highly structured essay form with eight parts, required on Chinese civil service examinations.
Ekklesia Church or early gathering committed to leaders chosen by God and fellow believers.
Ekpe Powerful slave trade institution that organized the supply and purchase of enslaved people inland from the Gulf of Guinea in West Africa.
Elamites A people with their capital in the upland valley of modern Fars who became a cohesive polity that incorporated transhumant people of the Zagros Mountains. A group of Elamites who migrated south and west into Mesopotamia helped conquer the Third Dynasty of Ur in 2400 BCE.
empire Group of states or ethnic groups governed by a single sovereign power with varying degrees of centralization using a range of methods, including common language, shared religious beliefs, trade, political systems, and military might.
Enabling Act (1933) Emergency act passed by the Reichstag (German parliament) that helped transform Hitler from Germany's chancellor, or prime minister, into a dictator following the suspicious burning of the Reichstag building and a suspension of civil liberties.
enclosure A movement in which landowners took control of lands that traditionally had been common property serving local needs.

encomenderos Recipients of grants of land and special privileges from the Spanish crown. Commanders of the labor services of the colonized peoples in Spanish America.

encomiendas Grants from European Spanish governors to control the labor services of colonized peoples.

Endeavor Ship of Captain James Cook, whose celebrated voyages to the South Pacific in the late eighteenth century supplied Europe with information about the plants, birds, landscapes, and people of this uncharted territory.

Engels, Friedrich (1820–1895) German social and political philosopher who collaborated with Karl Marx on many publications, including *The Communist Manifesto*.

English Navigation Act of 1651 Act stipulating that only English ships could carry goods between the mother country and its colonies.

English Peasants' Revolt (1381) Uprising of serfs and free farm workers that began as a protest against a tax levied to raise money for a war on France. The revolt was suppressed, but led to the gradual emergence of a free peasantry as labor shortages made it impossible to keep peasants bound to the soil.

enlightened absolutists Seventeenth- and eighteenth-century monarchs who claimed to rule rationally and in the best interests of their subjects and who hired loyal bureaucrats to implement the knowledge of the new age.

Enlightenment Intellectual movement in eighteenth-century Europe, which extended the methods of the natural sciences, especially physics, to society, stressing natural laws and reason as the basis of authority.

entrepôts Multiethnic trading stations, often supported and protected by regional leaders, where traders exchanged commodities and replenished supplies in order to facilitate long-distance trade.

Epicurus Greek philosopher who espoused emphasis on the self. He lived from 341 to 279 BCE and founded a school in Athens called The Garden. He stressed the importance of sensation, teaching that pleasurable sensations were good and painful sensations bad. Members of his school sought to find peace and relaxation by avoiding unpleasantness or suffering.

Estates-General French quasi-parliamentary body called in 1789 to deal with the financial problems that afflicted France. It had not met since 1614.

Etruscans A dominant people on the Italian Peninsula until the fourth century BCE. The Etruscan states were part of the foundation of the Roman Empire.

eunuchs Surgically castrated men who rose to high levels of military, political, and personal power in several empires (for instance, the Tang and the Ming Empires in China; the Abbasid and Ottoman Empires; and the Byzantine Empire).

Eurasia The combined area of Europe and Asia.

European Union (EU) Supranational body organized in the 1950s as an attempt at reconciliation between Germany and the rest of Europe. It emerged from the European Coal and Steel Community and initially aimed to forge closer industrial cooperation. By 1993, through various treaties, many European states had relinquished important elements of their sovereignty, and the cooperation became a full-fledged union with a common parliament and a common currency. By 2020, all twenty-seven member states of the EU except Denmark had adopted, or pledged to adopt, the euro as their currency.

evolution Process by which species of plants and animals change over time, as a result of the favoring, through reproduction, of certain traits that are useful in that species' environment.

Exclusion Act of 1882 U.S. congressional act prohibiting nearly all immigration from China to the United States; fueled by animosity toward Chinese workers in the American West.

Ezo Present-day Hokkaido, Japan's fourth main island.

Farang Persian word meaning "Frank," which was used to describe Crusaders.

fascism Form of hypernationalism that emerged in Europe after the Great War (World War I), in which a charismatic leader was followed by a mass party and supported by established elites and churches and existing government institutions. Fascist movements were widespread but came to power only in Italy and Germany.

Fatehpur Sikri Mughal emperor Akbar's temporary capital near Agra.

Fatimids Shiite dynasty that ruled parts of the Islamic empire beginning in the tenth century CE. They were based in Egypt and founded the city of Cairo.

February Revolution (1917) The first of two uprisings of the Russian Revolution, which led to the end of the Romanov dynasty.

Federal Deposit Insurance Corporation (FDIC) Organization created in 1933 to guarantee all bank deposits up to $5,000 as part of the New Deal in the United States.

Federal Republic of Germany (1949–1990) Country formed from the areas of Germany occupied by the Allies after World War II. Also known as West Germany, this country experienced rapid demilitarization, democratization, and integration into the world economy.

Federal Reserve Act (1913) U.S. legislation that created a series of boards to monitor the supply and demand of the nation's money.

Federalists Supporters of the ratification of the U.S. Constitution, which was written to replace the Articles of Confederation.

feminist movements Movements that call for equal treatment for men and women—equal pay and equal opportunities for obtaining jobs and advancement. Feminism arose mainly in Europe and in North America in the 1960s and then became global in the 1970s.

Fertile Crescent An area in Southwest Asia, bounded by the Mediterranean Sea in the west and the Zagros Mountains in the east; site of the world's first agricultural revolution.

feudalism System instituted in medieval Europe after the collapse of the Carolingian Empire (814 CE) whereby each peasant was under the authority of a lord. *See also* manorialism.

fiefdoms Medieval economic and political units.

First World Term invented during the Cold War to refer to western Europe and North America (also known as the "free world" or the west); Japan later joined this group. Following the principles of liberal modernism, First World states sought to organize the world on the basis of capitalism and democracy.

five pillars of Islam Five practices that unite all Muslims: (1) proclaiming that "there is no God but God and Muhammad is His Prophet"; (2) praying five times a day; (3) fasting during the daylight hours of the holy month of Ramadan; (4) traveling on pilgrimage to Mecca; and (5) paying alms to support the poor.

Five-Year Plan Soviet effort launched under Stalin in 1928 to replace the market with a state-owned and state-managed economy in order to promote rapid economic development over a five-year period and thereby "catch and overtake" the leading capitalist countries. The First Five-Year Plan was followed by the Second Five-Year Plan (1933–1937), and so on, until the collapse of the Soviet Union in 1991.

Flagellants European social group that came into existence during the Black Death in the fourteenth century; they believed that the plague was the wrath of God.

floating population Poor migrant workers in China who supplied labor under Emperor Wu.

fluitschips Dutch shipping vessels that could carry heavy, bulky cargo with relatively small crews.

flying cash Letters of exchange—early predecessors of paper money—first developed by guilds in the northern Song province Shanxi that eclipsed coins by the thirteenth century.

fondûqs Complexes in caravan cities that included hostels, storage houses, offices, and temples; from the Arabic word for "hotel."

Forbidden City of Beijing Palace city of the Ming and Qing dynasties.

Force Publique Colonial army used to maintain order in the Belgian Congo; during the early stages of King Leopold's rule, it was responsible for bullying local communities.

Fourierism Form of utopian socialism based on the ideas of Charles Fourier (1772–1837), who envisioned communes where work was made enjoyable and systems of production and distribution were run without merchants. His ideas appealed to the middle class, especially women, as a higher form of Christian communalism.

free labor Wage-paying rather than enslaved labor.

Free Officers Movement Secret organization of Egyptian junior military officers who came to power in a coup d'état in 1952, forced King Faruq to abdicate, and consolidated their own control through dissolving the parliament, banning opposing parties, and rewriting the constitution.

free trade (laissez-faire) Domestic and international trade unencumbered by tariff barriers, quotas, and fees.

Front de Libération Nationale (FLN) Algerian anticolonial, nationalist party that waged an eight-year war against French troops, beginning in 1954, that forced nearly all of the 1 million European colonists to leave.

Fulani Muslim group in West Africa that carried out religious revolts at the end of the eighteenth and the beginning of the nineteenth centuries in an effort to return to the pure Islam of the past.

fur trade Trading of animal pelts (especially beaver skins) by Indigenous people for European goods in North America.

Gandharan style Style of artwork, especially statuary, originating in the Gandharan region of modern Pakistan, that blends Hellenistic artistic influences with Buddhist stylistic features and subjects.

Gandhi, Mohandas Karamchand (Mahatma) (1869–1948) Indian leader who led a nonviolent struggle for India's independence from Britain.

garrison towns Stations for soldiers originally established in strategic locations to protect territorial acquisitions. Eventually, they became towns. Alexander the Great's garrison towns evolved into cities that served as centers from which Hellenistic culture was spread to his easternmost territories.

garrisons Military bases inside cities; often used for political purposes, such as protecting rulers, putting down domestic revolts, or enforcing colonial rule.

gauchos Argentine, Brazilian, and Uruguayan cowboys who wanted a decentralized federation, with autonomy for their provinces and respect for their way of life.

Gdańsk shipyard Site of mass strikes in Poland that led in 1980 to the formation of the first independent trade union, Solidarity, in the Soviet bloc.

gender relations A relatively recent development that implies roles emerged only with the appearance of modern humans and perhaps Neanderthals. When humans began to think imaginatively and in complex symbolic ways and give voice to their insights, perhaps around 150,000 years ago, gender categories began to crystallize.

genealogy History of the descent of a person or family from a distant ancestor.

Geneva Peace Conference (1954) International conference to restore peace in Korea and Indochina. The chief participants were the United States, the Soviet Union, Great Britain, France, the People's Republic of China, North Korea, South Korea, Vietnam, the Viet Minh party, Laos, and Cambodia. The conference resulted in the division of North and South Vietnam.

Genoa One of two Italian cities (the other was Venice) that linked Europe, Africa, and Asia as nodes of commerce in 1300. Genoese ships linked the Mediterranean to the coast of Flanders through consistent routes along the Atlantic coasts of Spain, Portugal, and France.

German Democratic Republic (1949–1990) Country formed from the areas of Germany occupied by the Soviet Union after World War II. Also known as East Germany.

German Social Democratic Party Founded in 1875, the most powerful socialist party in Europe before 1917.

Ghana The most celebrated medieval political kingdom in West Africa.

Ghost Dance Ritual performed by Indigenous peoples in North America in the nineteenth century in the hope of restoring the world to precolonial conditions.

Gilgamesh, Epic of Heroic narrative written in the Babylonian dialect of Semitic Akkadian. This story and others like it were meant to circulate and unify the kingdom.

Girondins Liberal revolutionary group that supported the creation of a constitutional monarchy during the early stages of the French Revolution.

global climate change A wide range of phenomena caused by global warming. These changes encompass not only rising temperatures, but also changes in precipitation patterns; ice mass loss on mountain glaciers around the world; shifts in the life cycles and migration patterns of flora and fauna; extreme weather events; and sea level rise.

global war on terror Global crusade to root out anti-American, anti-western Islamist terrorist cells; launched by President George W. Bush as a response to the 9/11 attacks.

global warming Upward temperature trends worldwide due to the release of carbon into the air, mainly by the burning of fossil fuels and other human activities.

globalization Development of integrated worldwide cultural and economic structures.

globalizing empires Empires that cover immense territory; exert significant influence beyond their borders; include large, diverse populations; and work to integrate conquered peoples.

Gold Coast Name that European mariners and merchants gave to the part of West Africa from which gold was exported. This area was conquered by the British in the nineteenth century and became a British colony; upon independence, it became Ghana.

Goths One of the groups of "barbarian" migrants into Roman territory in the fourth century CE.

government schools Schools founded by the Han dynasty to provide an adequate number of officials to fill positions in the administrative bureaucracy. The Imperial University had 30,000 members by the second century BCE.

Gracchus brothers Two tribunes, the brothers Tiberius and Gaius Gracchus, who in 133 and 123–121 BCE attempted to institute land reforms that would guarantee all of Rome's poor citizens a basic amount of land that would qualify them for army service. Both men were assassinated.

Grand Canal A thousand-mile-long connector between the Yellow and Yangzi Rivers created in 486 BCE to link the north and south of China.

grand unity Guiding political idea embraced by Qin rulers and ministers with an eye toward joining the states of the Central Plains into one empire and centralizing administration.

"greased cartridge" controversy Controversy spawned by the rumor that cow and pig fat had been used to grease the shotguns of the sepoys in the British army in India. Believing that this was a British attempt to defile their religions and speed their conversion to Christianity, the sepoys mutinied against the British officers.

Great Depression Worldwide depression following the U.S. stock market crash on October 29, 1929.

great divide The division between economically developed nations and less developed nations.

Great East Asia Co-Prosperity Sphere Term used by the Japanese during the 1930s and 1940s to refer to Hong Kong, Singapore, Malaya, Burma, and other states that they seized during their attempt to dominate Asia.

Great Flood One of many traditional Mesopotamian stories that were transmitted orally from one generation to another before being recorded. The Sumerian King List refers to this crucial event in Sumerian memory and identity. The Great Flood narrative assigned responsibility for Uruk's demise to the gods.

Great Game Competition over areas such as Turkistan, Persia (present-day Iran), and Afghanistan. The British (in India) and the Russians believed that controlling these areas was crucial to preventing their enemies' expansion.

Great League of Peace and Power Iroquois alliance that united previously warring communities.

Great Leap Forward (1958–1961) Plan devised by Mao Zedong to achieve rapid agricultural and industrial growth in China. The plan, which failed miserably, may have led to the deaths of as many as 45 million people from famine and malnutrition.

great plaza at Isfahan The center of Safavid power in the seventeenth century created by Shah Abbas (r. 1587–1629) to represent the unification of trade, government, and religion under one supreme political authority.

Great Proletarian Cultural Revolution (1966–1976) Mass mobilization of urban Chinese youth inaugurated by Mao Zedong in an attempt to reinvigorate the Chinese Revolution and to prevent the development of a bureaucratized Soviet style of communism; with this movement, Mao turned against his longtime associates in the Communist Party.

Great Recession The economic downturn, with global reverberations, provoked by the financial crash of 2008.

Great Trek Afrikaner migration to the interior of Africa after the British Empire abolished slavery in 1833.

Great War (World War I) (August 1914–November 1918) A total global war involving the armies of Britain, France, and Russia (the Allies) against those of Germany, Austria-Hungary, and the Ottoman Empire (the Central Powers). Italy joined the Allies in 1915, and the United States joined them in 1917, helping tip the balance in favor of the Allies, who also drew upon the populations and material of their colonial possessions.

Greek Orthodoxy Branch of eastern Christianity, originally centered in Constantinople, that emphasizes the role of Jesus in helping humans achieve union with God.

Greek philosophers "Wisdom lovers" of the ancient Greek city-states, including Socrates, Plato, Aristotle, and others, who pondered such issues as self-knowledge, political engagement and withdrawal, and evidence-based inquiry to understand the order of the cosmos.

Greenbacks An American political party of the late nineteenth century that worked to advance the interests of farmers by promoting cheap money.

griots Counselors and other officials serving the royal family in African kingships. They were also responsible for the preservation and transmission of oral histories and repositories of knowledge.

Group Areas Act (1950) Act that divided South Africa into separate racial and tribal areas and required Africans to live in their own separate communities, including the "homelands."

guerrillas Portuguese and Spanish peasant bands who resisted the revolutionary and expansionist efforts of Napoleon; after the French word *guerre*.

guest workers Migrants seeking temporary employment abroad.

Gulag Administrative name for the vast system of forced labor camps under the Soviet regime; it originated in a small monastery near the Arctic Circle and spread throughout the Soviet Union and to other Soviet-style socialist countries. Penal labor was required of both ordinary criminals (rapists, murderers, thieves) and those accused of political crimes (counterrevolution, anti-Soviet agitation).

Gulf War (1991) Armed conflict between Iraq and a coalition of thirty-two nations, including the United States, Britain, Egypt, France, and Saudi Arabia. It was started by Iraq's invasion of Kuwait, which it had long claimed, on August 2, 1990.

gunpowder Explosive powder. By 1040, the first gunpowder recipes were being written down. Over the next 200 years, Song entrepreneurs invented several incendiary devices and techniques for controlling explosions.

gunpowder empires Muslim empires of the Ottomans, Safavids, and Mughals that used cannonry and gunpowder to advance their military causes.

Guomindang Nationalist Party of China, founded just before World War I by Sun Yat-sen and later led by Chiang Kai-shek.

Habsburg Empire Ruling house of Austria, which once ruled both Spain and central Europe but came to settle in lands along the Danube River; it played a prominent role in European affairs for many centuries. In 1867, the Habsburg Empire was reorganized into the Austro-Hungarian Empire, and in 1918 it collapsed.

hadith Sayings, attributed to the Prophet Muhammad and his early converts, used to guide the behavior of Muslim peoples.

Hagia Sophia Enormous and impressive church sponsored by Justinian and built starting in 532 CE. At the time, it was the largest church in the world.

hajj Pilgrimage to Mecca; an obligation for Muslims.

Hammurabi's Code Legal code created by Hammurabi (r. 1792–1750 BCE). The code divided society into three classes—free, dependent, and enslaved—each with distinct rights and responsibilities.

Han agrarian ideal Guiding principle for the free peasantry that made up the base of Han society. In this system, peasants were honored for their labors, while merchants were subjected to a range of controls, including regulations on luxury consumption, and were belittled for not engaging in physical labor.

Han Chinese Inhabitants of China proper who considered others to be outsiders and felt that they were the only authentic Chinese.

Han Fei Chinese state minister who lived from 280 to 233 BCE; a proponent and follower of Xunzi.

Han military Like its Roman counterpart, a ruthless military machine that expanded the Han Empire and created stable conditions that permitted the safe transit of goods by caravans. Emperor Wu heavily influenced the transformation of the military forces and reinstituted a policy that made military service compulsory.

Hangzhou City and former provincial seaport that became the political center of the Chinese people in their ongoing struggles with northern steppe nomads. It was also one of China's gateways to the rest of the world by way of the South China Sea.

Hannibal Great general from Carthage whose campaigns in the third century BCE swept from Spain toward the Italian Peninsula. He crossed the Pyrenees and the Alps with war elephants. He was unable, however, to defeat the Romans in 217 BCE.

Harappa One of the two largest of the cities that, by 2500 BCE, began to take the place of villages throughout the Indus River valley (the other was Mohenjo Daro). Each covered an area of about 250 acres and probably housed 35,000 residents.

harem Secluded women's quarters in a Muslim household.

Harlem Renaissance Cultural movement in the 1920s that was based in Harlem, a part of New York City with a large African American population. The movement gave voice to Black novelists, poets, painters, and musicians, many of whom used their art to protest racism; also referred to as the "New Negro movement."

harnesses Tools made from wood, bone, bronze, and iron for steering and controlling chariot horses. Harnesses discovered by archaeologists reveal the evolution of headgear from simple mouth bits to full bridles with headpiece, mouthpiece, and reins.

Hatshepsut Leader known as ancient Egypt's most powerful woman ruler. Hatshepsut served as regent for her young son, Thutmosis III, whose reign began in 1479 BCE. She remained co-regent until her death.

Haussmannization Redevelopment and beautification of urban centers; named after the city planner who "modernized" mid-nineteenth century Paris.

Heian period Period from 794 to 1185 CE during which the pattern of regents ruling Japan in the name of the sacred emperor began.

Hellenism Process by which the individuality of the cultures of the earlier Greek city-states gave way to a uniform culture that stressed the common identity of all who embraced Greek ways. This culture emphasized the common denominators of language, style, and politics to which anyone, anywhere in the Afro-Eurasian world, could have access.

hieroglyphs One of two basic forms of Egyptian writing that were used in conjunction throughout antiquity. Hieroglyphs are pictorial symbols; the term derives from a Greek word meaning "sacred carving." They were employed exclusively in temple, royal, and divine contexts. *See also* demotic writing.

hijra Tradition of Islam whereby one withdraws from one's community to create another, holier, one. The practice is based on the Prophet Muhammad's withdrawal from the city of Mecca to Medina in 622 CE.

Hinayana Buddhism (termed "Lesser Vehicle" Buddhism by the Mahayana/"Greater Vehicle" school; also called Theraveda Buddhism) A more traditional, conservative branch of Buddhism that accepted the divinity of the Buddha but not of bodhisattvas.

Hindu revivalism Movement to reconfigure traditional Hinduism to be less diverse and more amenable to producing a narrowed version of Indian tradition.

Hinduism Ancient Brahmanic Vedic religion that emerged as the dominant faith in India in the third century CE. It reflected rural and agrarian values and focused on the trinity of Brahma (birth), Vishnu (existence), and Shiva (destruction).

Hiroshima Japanese port devastated by an atomic bomb on August 6, 1945.

Hitler, Adolf (1889–1945) German dictator and leader of the Nazi Party who seized power in Germany after its economic collapse in the Great Depression. Hitler and his Nazi regime started World War II in Europe and systematically murdered Jews and other non-Aryan groups in the name of racial purity.

Hittites An Anatolian chariot warrior group that spread east to northern

Syria, though they eventually faced weaknesses in their own homeland. Rooted in their capital at Hattusa, they interacted with contemporary states both violently (as at the Battle of Qadesh against Egypt) and peacefully (as in the correspondence of the Amarna letters).

HIV/AIDS An epidemic of acquired immunodeficiency syndrome (AIDS) caused by the human immunodeficiency virus (HIV), which compromises the ability of the infected person's immune system to ward off other diseases. First detected in 1981, AIDS killed 12 million people in the two decades that followed.

Holocaust Deliberate racial extermination by the Nazis of Jews, along with some other groups the Nazis considered "inferior" (including Sinta and Roma [gypsies], Jehovah's Witnesses, gay people, and people with mental illness), which claimed the lives of around 6 million European Jews.

Holy Roman Empire Enormous realm that encompassed much of Europe and aspired to be the Christian successor state to the Roman Empire. In the time of the Habsburg dynasts, the empire was a loose confederation of principalities that obeyed an emperor elected by elite lower-level sovereigns. Despite its size, the empire never effectively centralized power; it was split into Austrian and Spanish factions when Charles V abdicated to his sons in 1556.

Holy Russia Name applied to Muscovy and then to the Russian Empire by Slavic Eastern Orthodox clerics who were appalled by the Muslim conquest in 1453 of Constantinople (the capital of Byzantium and of eastern Christianity) and who were hopeful that Russia would become the new protector of the faith.

home charges Fees India was forced to pay to Britain as its colonial master; these fees included interest on railroad loans, salaries to colonial officers, and the maintenance of imperial troops outside India.

hominids The family, in scientific classification, that includes gorillas, chimpanzees, and humans (that is, *Homo sapiens*, in addition to our now-extinct hominin ancestors such as the various australopithecines as well as *Homo habilis*, *Homo erectus*, and *Homo neanderthalensis*).

hominins A scientific classification for modern humans and our now-extinct ancestors, including australopithecines and others in the genus *Homo*, such as *Homo habilis* and *Homo erectus*. Researchers once used the term *hominid* to refer to *Homo sapiens* and extinct hominin species, but the meaning of *hominid* has been expanded to include great apes (humans, gorillas, chimpanzees, and orangutans).

Homo The genus, in scientific classification, that contains only "true human" species.

Homo caudatus "Tailed man," believed by some European Enlightenment thinkers to be an early human species.

Homo erectus Species that emerged about 1.8 million years ago, had a large brain, walked truly upright, migrated out of Africa, and likely mastered fire. *Homo erectus* means "standing human."

Homo habilis Species, confined to Africa, that emerged about 2.5 million years ago and whose toolmaking ability truly made it the forerunner, though a very distant one, of modern humans. *Homo habilis* means "skillful human."

Homo sapiens The first humans; emerged in Africa as early as 300,000 years ago and migrated out of Africa beginning about 180,000 years ago. They had bigger brains and greater dexterity than previous hominin species, whom they eventually eclipsed.

homogeneity Uniformity of the languages, customs, and religion of a particular people or place. It can also be demonstrated by a consistent calendar, set of laws, administrative practices, and rituals.

horses Animals used by full-scale nomadic communities to dominate the steppe lands in western Afro-Eurasia by the second millennium BCE. Horse-riding nomads moved their large herds across immense tracts of land within zones defined by rivers, mountains, and other natural geographic features. In the arid zones of central Eurasia, the nomadic economies made horses a crucial component of survival.

Huguenots French Protestants who endured severe persecution in the sixteenth and seventeenth centuries.

humanism The Renaissance aspiration to develop a greater understanding of the human experience than the Christian scriptures offered by reaching back into ancient Greek and Roman texts.

Hundred Days' Reform (1898) Abortive modernizing reform program of the Qing government of China.

hunting and gathering Lifestyle in which food is acquired through hunting animals, fishing, and foraging for wild berries, nuts, fruit, and grains, rather than planting crops, vines, or trees. As late as 1500 CE, as much as 15 percent of the world's population still lived by this method.

Hyksos Chariot-driving, axe- and composite-bow-wielding, Semitic-speaking people (their name means "rulers of foreign lands") who invaded Egypt, overthrew the Thirteenth Dynasty, set up their own rule over Egypt, and were expelled by Ahmosis to begin the period known as New Kingdom Egypt.

Ibadat Khana "House of Worship" in which the Mughal emperor Akbar engaged in religious debate with Hindu, Muslim, Jain, Parsi, and Christian theologians.

Ibn Sina Philosopher and physician who lived from 980 to 1037 CE. He was also schooled in the Quran, geometry, literature, and Indian and Euclidian mathematics.

ideology Dominant set of ideas of a widespread culture or movement.

Il Duce (leader) Name used by the fascist Italian leader Benito Mussolini.

Iliad Epic Greek poem about the Trojan War, composed several centuries after the events it describes. It was based on oral tales passed down for generations.

Il-Khanate Mongol-founded dynasty in thirteenth-century Persia.

imam Muslim religious leader and politico-religious descendant of Ali; believed by some to have a special relationship with Allah.

Imperial University Institution founded in 136 BCE by Emperor Wu (Han Wudi) not only to train future bureaucrats in the Confucian classics but also to foster scientific advances in other fields.

imperialism Acquisition of new territories by a state and the incorporation of these territories into a political system as subordinate colonies.

Imperium Latin word used to express Romans' power and command over their subjects. It is the basis of the English words *empire* and *imperialism*.

Inca Empire Empire of Quechua-speaking rulers in the Andean valley of Cuzco that encompassed a population of 4 to 6 million. The Incas lacked a clear inheritance system, causing an internal split that Pizarro's forces exploited in 1533.

Indian Institutes of Technology (IIT) Institutions originally designed as engineering schools to expand knowledge and to modernize India, which produced a generation of pioneering computer engineers, many of whom moved to the United States.

Indian National Congress Formed in 1885, a political party deeply committed to constitutional methods, industrialization, and cultural nationalism.

Indian National Muslim League Founded in 1906, an organization dedicated to advancing the political interests of Muslims in India.

Indo-European migrations The migrations, tracked linguistically and culturally, of the peoples of a distinct language group (including Sanskrit, Persian, Greek, Latin, and German) from central Eurasian steppe lands into Europe, Southwest Asia, and South Asia.

Indo-Greek Of or relating to the fusion of Indian and Greek culture in the area under the control of the Bactrians, in the northwestern region of India, around 200 BCE.

Indu Name used for what we would today call India by Xuanzang, a Chinese Buddhist pilgrim who visited the area in the 630s and 640s CE.

indulgences Church-sponsored fund-raising mechanism that gave certification that one's sins had been forgiven in return for money.

industrial revolution Gradual accumulation and diffusion of old and new technical knowledge that led to major economic changes in Britain, northwestern Europe, and North America. It resulted in large-scale industry and the harnessing of fossil fuels, which allowed economic growth to outpace the rate of population increase.

innovation Creation of new methods that allowed humans to make better adaptations to their environment, such as the making of new tools.

Inquisition General term for a tribunal of the Roman Catholic Church that enforced religious orthodoxy. Several inquisitions took place over centuries, seeking to punish heretics, witches, Jews, and those whose conversion to Christianity was called into doubt.

internal and external alchemy In Daoist ritual, use of trance and meditation or chemicals and drugs, respectively, to cause transformations in the self.

International Monetary Fund (IMF) Agency founded in 1944 to help restore financial order in Europe and the rest of the world, to revive international trade, and to offer financial support to Third World governments.

invisible hand As described in Adam Smith's *The Wealth of Nations*, the idea that the operations of a free market produce economic efficiency and economic benefits for all.

iron Malleable metal found in combined forms almost everywhere in the world; it became the most important and widely used metal in world history after the Bronze Age.

Iron Curtain Term popularized by Winston Churchill after World War II to refer to a rift that divided western Europe, under American influence, from eastern Europe, under the domination of the Soviet Union.

irrigation Technological advance whereby water delivery systems and water sluices in floodplains or river-basin areas were channeled or redirected and used to nourish soil.

Islam A religion that dates to 610 CE, when the Prophet Muhammad believed God came to him in a vision. Islam (which means submission—in this case, to the will of God) requires its followers to act righteously, to submit themselves to the one and only true God, and to care for the less fortunate. Muhammad's most insistent message was the oneness of God, a belief that has remained central to the Islamic faith ever since.

Jacobins Radical French political group that came into existence during the French Revolution; executed the French king and sought to remake French culture.

Jacquerie (1358) French peasant revolt in defiance of feudal restrictions.

jade The most important precious substance in East Asia; associated with goodness, purity, luck, and virtue. Jade was carved into such items as ceremonial knives, blade handles, religious objects, and elaborate jewelry.

Jagat Seths Enormous trading and banking empire in eastern India during the first half of the eighteenth century.

Jainism System of thought, originating in the seventh century BCE, that challenged Brahmanism. Spread by Vardhamana Mahavira, Jainism encouraged purifying the soul through self-denial and nonviolence.

Jaja (1821–1891) A merchant prince who founded the Opobo city-state, in what is known in modern times as the Rivers state of Nigeria.

janissaries Corps of infantry soldiers conscripted as children under the *devshirme* system of the Ottoman Empire and brought up with intense loyalty to the Ottoman state and its sultan. The sultan used these forces to clip local autonomy and to serve as his personal bodyguards.

jatis Social groups as defined by Hinduism's *varna* (caste) system.

Jesuits Religious order founded by Ignatius Loyola to counter the inroads of the Protestant Reformation; the Jesuits, or the Society of Jesus, were active in politics, education, and missionary work.

jihad Literally, "striving" or "struggle." This word also connotes military efforts, or "striving in the way of God." In addition, it came to mean spiritual struggles against temptation or inner demons, especially in Sufi, or mystical, usage.

Jih-pen Chinese for "Japan."

Jim Crow laws Laws that codified racial segregation and inequality in the southern part of the United States after the Civil War.

jizya Special tax that non-Muslims were forced to pay to their Islamic rulers in return for which they were given security and property and granted cultural autonomy.

jongs Large oceangoing vessels built by Southeast Asians that plied the regional trade routes from the fifteenth century to the early sixteenth century.

Judah The southern kingdom of David, which had been a Neo-Assyrian vassal until 612 BCE, when it became a vassal of Neo-Assyria's successor, Babylon, against whom the people of Judah rebelled, resulting in the destruction of Jerusalem in the sixth century BCE.

Julius Caesar Formidable Roman general who lived from 100 to 44 BCE. He was also a man of letters, a great orator, and a ruthless military man who boasted that his campaigns had led to the deaths of over a million people.

junks Large seafaring vessels used in the South China Sea after 1000 CE, which helped make shipping by sea less dangerous.

Justinian Roman or Byzantine emperor who ascended to the throne in 527 CE. In addition to his many building projects and military expeditions, he issued a new law code.

kabuki Theater performance that combined song, dance, and skillful staging to dramatize conflicts between duty and passion in Tokugawa Japan.

kamikaze Japanese for "divine winds," or typhoons; such a storm saved Japan from a Mongol attack.

kanun Highly detailed system of Ottoman administrative law that jurists developed to deal with matters not treated in the religious law of Islam.

karim Loose confederation of shippers banding together to protect convoys.

karma Literally, "fate" or "action"; in Confucian thought, a universal principle of cause and effect.

Kassites Nomads who entered Mesopotamia from the eastern Zagros Mountains and the Iranian plateau as early as 2000 BCE. They gradually integrated into Babylonian society by officiating at temples. By 1745 BCE, they had asserted order over the region, and they controlled southern Mesopotamia for the next 350 years, creating one of the territorial states.

Keynesian Revolution Post-Depression economic ideas developed by the British economist John Maynard Keynes, wherein the state took a greater role in managing the economy, stimulating it by increasing the money supply and creating jobs.

KGB Soviet political police and spy agency, formed as the Cheka not long after the Bolshevik coup in October 1917. Grew to more than 750,000 operatives with military rank by the 1980s.

khan Mongol ruler acclaimed at an assembly of elites, who was supposedly descended from Chinggis Khan on the male line; those not descended from Chinggis continually faced challenges to their legitimacy.

khanate Major political unit of the vast Mongol Empire. There were four khanates, including the Yuan Empire in China, forged by Chinggis Khan's grandson Kublai.

Kharijites Radical sect from the early days of Islam. The Kharijites seceded from the "party of Ali" (who themselves came to be known as the Shiites) because of disagreements over succession to the role of the caliph. They were known for their strict militant piety.

Khmer A people who created the most powerful empire in Southwest Asia between the tenth and thirteenth centuries in what is modern-day Cambodia.

Khomeini, Ayatollah Ruhollah (1902–1989) Iranian religious leader who used his traditional Islamic education and his training in Muslim ethics to accuse Shah Reza Pahlavi's government of gross violations of Islamic norms. He also identified the shah's ally, America, as the great Satan. The shah fled the country in 1979; in his wake, Khomeini established a theocratic state ruled by a council of Islamic clerics.

Khufu A pyramid, among those put up in the Fourth Dynasty in ancient Egypt (c. 2613–2494 BCE), which is the largest stone structure in the world. It is in an area called Giza, just outside modern-day Cairo.

Khusro I Anoshirwan Sasanian emperor who reigned from 531 to 579 CE. He was a model ruler and was seen as the personification of justice.

Kikuyu Kenya's largest ethnic group; organizers of a revolt against the British in the 1950s.

King, Martin Luther, Jr. (1929–1968) Civil rights leader who borrowed his most effective weapon—the commitment to nonviolent protest and the appeal to conscience—from Gandhi.

Kingdom of Jerusalem What Crusaders set out to liberate from Muslim rule when they launched their attacks.

Kizilbash Mystical, Turkish-speaking tribesmen who facilitated the Safavid rise to power.

Knossos Area in Crete where, during the second millennium BCE, a primary palace town existed.

***Koine* Greek** Simpler than regional versions of Greek such as Attic or Ionic, this "common Greek" dialect became an international language across the regions influenced by Hellenism and facilitated trade of goods and ideas.

Köprülü reforms Reforms named after two grand viziers who revitalized the Ottoman Empire in the seventeenth century through administrative and budget trimming as well as by rebuilding the military.

Korean War (1950–1953) Cold War conflict between Soviet-backed North Korea and U.S.- and U.N.-backed South Korea. The two sides seesawed back and forth over the same boundaries until 1953, when an armistice divided the country at roughly the same spot as at the start of the war. Casualties included 33,000 Americans, at least 250,000 Chinese, and up to 3 million Koreans.

Koryo dynasty Leading dynasty of the northern-based Koryo kingdom in Korea. It is from this dynasty that the name "Korea" derives.

Kremlin Moscow's walled city center, whose name was once synonymous with the Soviet government.

Kshatriyas Originally the warrior *varna* (caste) in Vedic society, the dominant clan members and ruling *varna* who controlled the land.

Ku Klux Klan Racist organization that first emerged in the U.S. South after the Civil War and then gained national strength as a radically traditionalist movement during the 1920s.

Kublai Khan (1215–1294) Mongol leader who seized southern China after 1260 and founded the Yuan dynasty.

kulak Originally a pejorative word used to designate better-off peasants, a term used in the late 1920s and early 1930s to refer to any peasant, rich or poor, perceived as an opponent of the Soviet regime. Russian for "fist."

Kumarajiva Renowned Buddhist scholar and missionary who lived from 344 to 413 CE. He was brought to China by Chinese regional forces from Kucha, modern-day Xinjiang.

Kushans Northern nomadic group that migrated into South Asia around 50 CE. They unified the tribes of the region and set up the Kushan Empire, which embraced a large and diverse territory and played a critical role in the formation of the Silk Roads.

Kyiv City that became one of the greatest cities of Europe after the eleventh century. It was built to be a small-scale Constantinople on the Dnieper.

Labour Party Political party founded in Britain in 1900 that represented workers and was based on socialist principles.

laissez-faire The concept that the economy works best when it is left alone—that is, when the state does not regulate or interfere with the workings of the market.

"Land under the Yoke of Ashur" Lands not in Neo-Assyria proper, but under its authority, which had to pay the Neo-Assyrian Empire exorbitant amounts of tribute.

language System of communication reflecting cognitive abilities. Natural language is generally defined as words arranged in particular sequences to convey meaning and is unique to modern humans.

language families Related tongues with a common ancestral origin; language families contain languages that diverged from one another but share grammatical features and root vocabularies. More than a hundred language families exist.

Laozi Also known as Master Lao; perhaps a contemporary of Confucius, and the person after whom Daoism is named. His thought was elaborated upon by generations of thinkers.

latifundia Broad estates that produced goods for big urban markets, including wheat, grapes, olives, cattle, and sheep.

League of Nations Organization founded after World War I to solve international disputes through arbitration; it was dissolved in 1946 and its assets were transferred to the United Nations.

Legalism Also called Statism, a system of thought about how to live an ordered life. Developed by Master Xun, or Xunzi (310–237 BCE), it is based on the principle that people, being inherently inclined toward evil, require authoritarian control to regulate their behavior.

Lenin, Vladimir (1870–1924) Leader of the Bolshevik Revolution in Russia and the first leader of the Soviet Union.

LGBTQ Acronym for people who identify as lesbian, gay, bisexual, transgender, or queer.

Liangzhu Culture spanning centuries from the fourth to the third millennium BCE that represented the last new Stone Age culture in the Yangzi River delta. One of the Ten Thousand States, it was highly stratified and is known for its jade objects.

liberalism Political and social theory that advocates representative government, free trade, and freedom of speech and religion.

limited-liability joint-stock company Company that mobilized capital from a large number of investors, called shareholders, who were not to be held personally liable for financial losses incurred by the company.

Linear A and B Two linear scripts first discovered on Crete in 1900. On the island of Crete and on the mainland areas of Greece, documents of the palace-centered societies were written on clay tablets in these two scripts. Linear A script, apparently written in Minoan, has not yet been deciphered. Linear B was first deciphered in the early 1950s.

"Little Europes" Urban landscapes between 1100 and 1200 composed of castles, churches, and towns in what are today Poland, the Czech Republic, Hungary, and the Baltic States.

Little Ice Age A period of global cooling—not a true ice age—that extended roughly from the sixteenth to the nineteenth century. The dates, especially for the start of the period, remain the subject of scientific controversy.

Liu Bang Chinese emperor from 206 to 195 BCE; after declaring himself the prince of his home area of Han, in 202 BCE, Liu declared himself the first Han emperor.

llamas Animals domesticated in the Americas that are similar in utility and function to camels in Afro-Eurasia. Llamas can carry heavy loads for long distances.

Long March (1934–1935) Trek of over 6,000 miles (or 10,000 kilometers) by Mao Zedong and his communist followers to establish a new base of operations in northwestern China.

Longshan peoples Peoples who lived in small agricultural and river-basin villages in East Asia during the third millennium BCE. They set the stage for the Shang dynasty in terms of a centralized state, urban life, and a cohesive culture.

lord Privileged landowner who exercised authority over the people who lived on his land.

lost generation The 17 million former members of the Red Guard and other Chinese youth who were denied education from the late 1960s to the mid-1970s as part of the Chinese government's attempt to prevent political disruptions.

Louisiana Purchase (1803) American purchase of French territory from Napoleon that included much of the present-day United States between the Mississippi River and the Rocky Mountains.

Lucy Relatively intact skeleton of a young adult female australopithecine unearthed in the valley of the Awash River in 1974 by an archaeological team working at a site in present-day Hadar, Ethiopia. The researchers nicknamed the skeleton Lucy. She stood just over 3 feet tall and walked upright at least some of the time. Her skull contained a brain within the ape size range, but her jaw and teeth were humanlike. Lucy's skeleton was relatively complete and at the time was the oldest hominin skeleton ever discovered.

Luftwaffe German air force.

Luther, Martin (1483–1546) A German monk and theologian who sought to reform the Catholic Church; he believed in salvation through faith alone, the importance of reading scripture, and the priesthood of all believers. His Ninety-Five Theses, which enumerated the abuses by the Catholic Church as well as his reforms, started the Protestant Reformation.

Maastricht Treaty (1993) Treaty that formed the European Union, a fully integrated trading and financial bloc with its own bureaucracy and elected representatives.

ma'at Term used in ancient Egypt to refer to stability or order, the achievement of which was the primary task of Egypt's ruling kings, the pharaohs.

Maccabees Leaders of a riot in Jerusalem in 167 BCE that was a response to a Seleucid edict outlawing the practice of Judaism.

Madhyamika (Middle Way) Buddhism Chinese branch of Mahayana Buddhism established by Kumarajiva (344–413 CE) that used irony and paradox to show that reason is limited.

madrasas Higher schools of Muslim education that taught law, the Quran, religious sciences, and the regular sciences.

magnetic needle compass A navigational instrument invented by the Chinese that helped guide sailors on the high seas after 1000 CE.

Mahayana Buddhism "Great Vehicle" Buddhism; an accessible form of

Buddhism that spread along the Silk Roads and included in its theology a divine Buddha as well as bodhisattvas.

Mahdi The "chosen one" in Islam whose appearance was believed to foretell the end of the world and the final day of reckoning for all people.

maize Grains, the crops that the settled agrarian communities across the Americas cultivated, along with legumes (beans) and tubers (potatoes).

Maji Maji Revolt (1905–1907) Swahili insurrection against German colonialists; inspired by the belief that those who were anointed with specially blessed water (*maji*) would be immune to bullets. It resulted in 200,000 to 300,000 African deaths.

Mali Empire West African empire, founded by the legendary king Sundiata in the early thirteenth century. It facilitated thriving commerce along routes linking the Atlantic Ocean, the Sahara, and beyond.

Mamluks (Arabic for "owned" or "possessed") Military men who ruled Egypt as an independent regime from 1250 until the Ottoman conquest in 1517.

Manaus Opera House Opera house built in the interior of Brazil in a lucrative rubber-growing area at the turn of the twentieth century.

Manchukuo Japanese puppet state in Manchuria in the 1930s.

Manchus Descendants of the Jurchens who helped the Ming army recapture Beijing in 1644 after its seizure by the outlaw Li Zicheng. The Manchus numbered around 1 million but controlled a domain that included perhaps 250 million people. Their rule lasted more than 250 years and became known as the Qing dynasty.

mandate of heaven Religious ideology established by Zhou leaders to communicate legitimate transfer and retention of royal power as the will of their supreme god. The mandate later became Chinese political doctrine.

Mande A people who lived in the area between the bend in the Senegal River to the west and the bend in the Niger River to the east and between the Senegal River to the north and the Bandama River to the south. Also known as the Mandinka. Their civilization emerged around 1100.

Mandela, Nelson (1918–2013) Leader of the African National Congress (ANC) who was imprisoned for more than two decades by the apartheid regime in South Africa for his political activities, until worldwide protests led to his release in 1990. In 1994, Mandela won the presidency in South Africa's first free mass elections.

Manifest Destiny Belief that it was God's will for the American people to expand their territory and political processes across the North American continent.

manorialism System in which the manor (a lord's home, its associated industry, and surrounding fields) served as the basic unit of economic power; an alternative to the concept of feudalism (the hierarchical relationships of king, lords, and peasantry) for thinking about the nature of power in western Europe from 1000 to 1300 CE.

Mao Zedong (1893–1976) Chinese communist leader who rose to power during the Long March (1934–1935). In 1949, Mao and his followers defeated the Nationalists and established a communist regime in China.

maroon community Sanctuary for formerly enslaved freedom seekers in the Americas.

Marshall Plan Economic aid package given by the United States to Europe after World War II in hopes of a rapid period of reconstruction and economic gain that would protect the countries that received the aid from a communist takeover.

martyr Literally meaning "witness," a person executed by Roman authorities for maintaining his or her Christian beliefs rather than worshipping the emperor.

Marx, Karl (1818–1883) German philosopher and economist who created Marxism and believed that a revolution of the working classes would overthrow the capitalist order and create a classless society.

Marxism A current of socialism created by Karl Marx and Friedrich Engels. It stressed the primacy of economics and technology—and, above all, class conflict—in shaping human history. Economic production provided the foundation, the "base" for society, which shaped politics, values, art, and culture (the superstructure). In the modern, industrial era, they believed class conflict boiled down to a two-way struggle between the bourgeoisie (who controlled the means of industrial production) and the proletariat (workers who had only their labor power to sell).

mass consumption Increased purchasing power and appetite for goods in the prosperous and mainly middle-class societies of the early twentieth century, stemming from mass production.

mass culture Distinctive form of popular culture that arose in the wake of World War I. It reflected the tastes of the working and middle classes, who now had more time and money to spend on entertainment, and relied on new technologies, especially film and radio, that could reach an entire nation's population and consolidate their sense of being a single state.

mass production System in which factories were set up to produce huge quantities of identical products, reflecting the early twentieth-century world's demands for greater volume, faster speed, reduced cost, and standardized output.

mastaba Word meaning "bench" in Arabic; it refers to a huge flat structure identical to earlier royal tombs of ancient Egypt.

Mau Mau Uprising (1952–1957) Uprising orchestrated by a Kenyan guerrilla movement; this conflict forced the British to grant independence to the Black majority in Kenya.

Mauryan Empire (321–184 BCE) The first large-scale empire in South Asia, stretching from the Indus in the west to the mouth of the Ganges in the east and nearly to the southern tip of the Indian subcontinent; begun by Chandragupta Maurya, in the aftermath of Alexander's time in India, and expanded to its greatest extent by his grandson Aśoka.

Mawali Non-Arab "clients" to Arab tribes in the early Islamic empire. Because tribal patronage was so much a part of the Arabian cultural system, non-Arabs who converted to Islam affiliated themselves with a tribe and became clients of that tribe.

Maxim gun European weapon that was capable of firing many bullets per second; it was used against Africans in the conquest of the continent.

Maya Civilization that ruled over large stretches of Mesoamerica; it was composed of a series of kingdoms, each built around ritual centers rather than cities. The Maya engaged neighboring peoples in warfare and trade and expanded borders through tributary relationships. They were not defined by a great ruler or one capital city, but by their shared religious beliefs.

McCarthyism Campaign by U.S. Republican senator Joseph McCarthy in the late 1940s and early 1950s to uncover closet communists, particularly in the State Department and in Hollywood.

Meat Inspection Act (1906) Legislation that provided for government supervision of meatpacking operations; it was part of a broader progressive reform movement dedicated to correcting the negative consequences of urbanization and industrialization in the United States.

Mecca Arabian city in which the Prophet Muhammad was born. Mecca was a trading center and pilgrimage destination in the pre-Islamic and Islamic periods. Exiled in 622 CE because of resistance to his message, Muhammad returned to Mecca in 630 CE and claimed the city for Islam.

Medes Rivals of the Neo-Assyrians and the Persians. The Medes inhabited the area from the Zagros Mountains to the modern city of Tehran; known as expert horsemen and archers, they were eventually defeated by the Persians.

megalith Literally, "great stone"; the word *megalith* is used when describing structures such as Stonehenge. These massive structures are the result of cooperative planning and work.

megarons Large buildings found in Troy (level II) that are the predecessors of the classic Greek temple.

Meiji Empire Empire created under the leadership of Mutsuhito, emperor of Japan from 1868 until 1912. During the Meiji period Japan became a world industrial and naval power.

Meiji Restoration (1868–1912) Reign of the Meiji Emperor, which was characterized by a new nationalist identity, economic advances, and political transformation.

Mencius Disciple of Confucius who lived from 372 to 289 BCE.

mercantilism Economic theory that drove European empire builders. In this economic system, the world had a fixed amount of wealth, which meant one country's wealth came at the expense of another's. Mercantilism assumed that colonies existed for the sole purpose of enriching the country that controlled the colony.

Mercosur Free-trade pact between the governments of Argentina, Brazil, Paraguay, and Uruguay.

meritocracy Rule by persons of talent.

Meroitic kingdom Thriving kingdom from the fourth century BCE to 300 CE. A successor to Kush, it was influenced by both Egyptian and Sudanic cultures.

Mestizos Mixed-blood offspring of Spanish settlers and Indigenous people.

Métis Mixed-blood offspring of French settlers and Indigenous people.

Mexican Revolution (1910–1920) Conflict fueled by the unequal distribution of land and by disgruntled workers; it erupted when political elites split over the succession of General Porfirio Díaz after decades of his rule. The fight lasted over ten years and cost 1 million lives, but it resulted in widespread reform and a new constitution.

***Mfecane* movement** African political revolts in the first half of the nineteenth century that were caused by the expansionist methods of King Shaka of the Zulu people.

microsocieties Small-scale, fragmented communities that had little interaction with others. These communities were the norm for peoples living in the Americas and islanders in the Pacific and Aegean from 2000 to 1200 BCE.

Middle Kingdom Period of Egyptian history lasting from about 2055 to 1650 BCE, characterized by a consolidation of power and building activity in Upper Egypt.

migration Long-distance travel for the purpose of resettlement. In the case of early humans, the need to move was usually a response to an environmental shift, such as climate change during the Ice Age.

millenarian Believer (usually religious) in the cataclysmic destruction of a corrupt, fallen society and its replacement by an ideal, utopian future.

millets Minority religious communities of the Ottoman Empire.

minaret Slender tower within a mosque from which Muslims are called to prayer.

minbar Pulpit inside a mosque from which Muslim religious speakers broadcast their message to the faithful.

Ming dynasty Successor to the Mongol Yuan dynasty that reinstituted and reinforced Han Chinese ceremonies and ideals, including rule by an ethnically Han bureaucracy.

Minoans A people who built a large number of elaborate, independent palace centers on Crete, at Knossos, and elsewhere around 2000 BCE. Named after the legendary King Minos, said to have ruled Crete at the time, they sailed throughout the Mediterranean and by 1600 BCE had planted colonies on many Aegean islands, which in turn became trading and mining centers.

mission civilisatrice Term French colonizers used to refer to France's form of "rationalized" colonial rule, which attempted to bring "civilization" to the "uncivilized."

mitochondrial DNA Form of DNA found in mitochondria, structures located outside the nuclei of cells. Examining mitochondrial DNA enables researchers to measure the genetic variation among living organisms, including human beings. Only females pass mitochondrial DNA to their offspring.

Moche A people who extended their power and increased their wealth at the height of the Chimú Empire over several valleys in what is now Peru.

Model T Automobile manufactured by the Ford Motor Company, which was the first to be priced reasonably enough to be sold to the masses.

modernism In the arts, modernism refers to the effort to break with older conventions and seek new ways of seeing and describing the world.

Mohism School of thought in ancient China, named after Mo Di, or Mozi (c. 479–381 BCE). It emphasized one's obligation to society as a whole, not just to one's immediate family or social circle.

monarchy Political system in which one individual holds supreme power and passes that power on to his or her next of kin.

monasticism From the Greek word *monos* (meaning "alone"), the practice of living without the ties of marriage or family, forsaking earthly luxuries for a life of prayer and study. While Christian monasticism originated in Egypt, a variant of ascetic life had long been practiced in Buddhism.

monetization An economic shift from a barter-based economy to one dependent on currency.

Mongols Combination of nomadic forest and steppe peoples who lived by hunting and livestock herding and were expert horsemen. Beginning in 1206, the Mongols launched a series of conquests that brought far-flung parts of the world together under their rule. By incorporating conquered peoples and adapting some of their customs, the Mongols created a unified empire that stretched from the Pacific Ocean to the shores of the eastern Mediterranean and the southern steppes of Eurasia.

monotheism The belief in only one god; to be distinguished from polytheism (the belief in many gods) and henotheism (the belief that there may be many gods but one is superior to the others).

Moors Term employed by Europeans in the medieval period to refer to Muslim occupants of North Africa, the western Sahara, and the Iberian Peninsula.

mosque Place of worship for the people of Islam.

mound people Name for the people of Cahokia, since its landscape was dominated by earthen monuments in the shapes of mounds. The mounds were carefully maintained and were the loci from which Cahokians paid respect to spiritual forces. *See also* Cahokia.

Mu Chinese ruler (956–918 BCE) who put forth a formal bureaucratic system of governance, appointing officials, supervisors, and military captains to whom he was not related. He also instituted a formal legal code.

muckrakers Journalists who aimed to expose political and commercial corruption in late nineteenth- and early twentieth-century America.

Muftis Experts on Muslim religious law.

Mughal Empire One of Islam's greatest regimes. Established in 1526, it was a vigorous, centralized state whose political authority encompassed most of modern-day India. During the sixteenth century, it had a population of between 100 and 150 million.

Muhammad (570–632 CE) Prophet and founder of the Islamic faith. Born in Mecca in Saudi Arabia and orphaned when young, Muhammad lived under the protection of his uncle. His career as a prophet began around 610 CE, with his first experience of spiritual revelation.

Muhammad Ali (r. 1805–1848) Ruler of Egypt who initiated a set of modernizing reforms that sought to make it competitive with the great powers.

mullahs Religious leaders in Iran who in the 1970s led a movement opposing Shah Mohammad Reza Pahlavi and denounced American materialism and secularism.

multinational corporations Corporations based in many different countries that have global investment, trading, and distribution goals.

Muscovy The principality of Moscow. Originally a mixture of Slavs, Finnish tribes, Turkic speakers, and many others, Muscovy used territorial expansion and commercial networks to consolidate a powerful state and expanded to become the Russian Empire, a huge realm that spanned parts of Europe, much of northern Asia, numerous North Pacific islands, and even—for a time—a corner of North America (Alaska).

Muslim Brotherhood Egyptian organization founded in 1928 by Hassan al-Banna. It attacked liberal democracy as a cover for middle-class, business, and landowning interests and fought for a return to a purified Islam.

Muslim League National Muslim party of India.

Mussolini, Benito (1883–1945) Italian dictator and founder of the fascist movement in Italy. During World War II, he allied Italy with Germany and Japan.

Muwahhidin Literally, "unitarians"; followers of the Wahhabi movement that emerged in the Arabian Peninsula in the eighteenth century.

Mycenaeans Mainland competitors of the Minoans who took over Crete around 1400 BCE. Migrating to Greece from central Europe, they brought their Indo-European language, chariots, and metalworking skills, which they used to dominate until 1200 BCE.

Napoleon Bonaparte (1769–1821) General who rose to power in a postrevolutionary coup d'état, eventually proclaiming himself emperor of France. He placed security and order ahead of social reform and created a civil legal code. Napoleon expanded his empire through military action, but after his disastrous Russian campaign, the united European powers defeated Napoleon and forced him into exile. He escaped and reassumed command of his army but was later defeated at the Battle of Waterloo.

Napoleonic Code Legal code drafted by Napoleon in 1804; it distilled different legal traditions to create one uniform law. The code confirmed the abolition of feudal privileges of all kinds and set the conditions for exercising property rights.

National Assembly of France Governing body of France that succeeded the Estates-General in 1789 during the French Revolution. It was composed of, and defined by, the delegates of the Third Estate.

National Association for the Advancement of Colored People (NAACP) A U.S. civil rights organization, founded in 1910, dedicated to ending inequality and segregation for Black Americans.

National Recovery Administration (NRA) U.S. New Deal agency created in 1933 to prepare codes of fair administration and to plan for public works. It was later declared unconstitutional.

nationalism The idea that members of a shared community called a nation should have sovereignty within the borders of their state.

nation-state Form of political organization that derived legitimacy from its inhabitants, often referred to as citizens, who in theory, if not always in practice, shared a common language, common culture, and common history.

native learning Japanese movement to promote nativist intellectual traditions and the celebration of Japanese texts.

native paramountcy British form of "rationalized" colonial rule, which attempted to bring "civilization" to the "uncivilized" by proclaiming that when the interests of European settlers in Africa clashed with those of the African population, the latter should take precedence.

natural rights Belief that emerged in eighteenth-century western Europe and North America that rights fundamental to human nature were discernible to reason and should be affirmed in human-made law.

natural selection Charles Darwin's theory that populations grew faster than the food supply, creating a "struggle for existence" among species. In later work he showed how the passing on of individual traits was also determined by what he called sexual selection—according to which the "best" mates are chosen for their strength, beauty, or talents. The outcome: the "fittest" survived to reproduce, while the less adaptable did not.

Nazis (National Socialist German Workers' Party) German organization dedicated to winning workers over from socialism to nationalism; the first Nazi Party platform combined nationalism with anticapitalism and anti-Semitism.

Neanderthals Members of an early wave of hominins from Africa who settled in western Afro-Eurasia, in an area reaching from present-day Uzbekistan and Iraq to Spain, approximately 150,000 years ago.

Negritos Hunting and gathering inhabitants of the East Asian coastal islands who migrated there around 28,000 BCE but by 2000 BCE had been replaced by new migrants.

Negritude The idea of a Black identity and culture different from, but not inferior to, European cultural forms; shaped by African and African American intellectuals like Senegal's first president, Léopold Sédar Senghor.

Nehemiah Jewish eunuch of the Persian court who was given permission to rebuild the fortification walls around the city of Jerusalem from 440 to 437 BCE.

Neo-Assyrian Empire Afro-Eurasian empire that dominated from 911 to 612 BCE. The Neo-Assyrians extended their control over resources and people beyond their own borders, and their empire lasted for three centuries.

neocolonialism Contemporary geopolitical policy or practice in which a politically, economically, and often militarily superior nation asserts control over a country that remains nominally sovereign.

Nestorian Christians Denomination of Christians whose beliefs about Christ differed from those of the official Byzantine church. Named after Nestorius, former bishop of Constantinople, they emphasized the human aspects of Jesus.

New Deal President Franklin Delano Roosevelt's package of government reforms that were enacted during the 1930s to provide jobs for the unemployed, social welfare programs for the poor, and security to the financial markets.

New Economic Policy Enacted decrees of the Bolsheviks between 1921 and 1927 that grudgingly sanctioned private trade and private property.

New Negro movement *See* Harlem Renaissance.

New World Term applied to the Americas that reflected the Europeans' view that anything previously unknown to them was "new," even if it had existed and supported societies long before European explorers arrived on its shores.

nirvana Literally, "nonexistence"; nirvana is the state of complete liberation from the concerns of worldly life, as in Buddhist thought.

Noble Eightfold Path Buddhist concept of a way of life by which people may rid themselves of individual desire to achieve nirvana. The path consists of wisdom, ethical behavior, and mental discipline.

Noh drama Masked theater favored by Japanese bureaucrats and regional lords during the Tokugawa period.

Nok culture Spectacular culture that arose in present-day Nigeria in the sixth century BCE. Iron smelting occurred there around 600 BCE. Thus the Nok people made the transition from stone to iron materials.

nomads People who move across vast distances without settling permanently in a particular place. Often pastoralists, nomads and transhumant herders introduced new forms of chariot-based warfare that transformed the Afro-Eurasian world.

nongovernmental organizations (NGOs) Term used to refer to private organizations like the Red Cross that play a large role in international affairs. *See also* supranational organizations.

nonviolent resistance Moral and political philosophy of resistance developed by Indian National Congress leader Mohandas Gandhi. Gandhi believed that if Indians pursued self-reliance and self-control in a nonviolent way, the British would eventually have to leave.

North American Free Trade Agreement (NAFTA) Treaty negotiated in the early 1990s to promote free trade between Canada, the United States, and Mexico.

North Atlantic Treaty Organization (NATO) International organization set up in 1949 to provide for the defense of western European countries and the United States from the perceived Soviet threat.

Northern Wei dynasty Regime founded in 386 CE by the Tuoba, a people originally from Inner Mongolia, that lasted one and a half centuries. The rulers of this dynasty adopted many practices of the earlier Chinese Han regime. At the same time, they struggled to consolidate authority over their own nomadic people. Ultimately, several decades of intense internal conflict led to the dynasty's downfall.

Northwest Passage Long-sought marine passageway between the Atlantic and Pacific Oceans along the northern coast of North America.

Oceania Collective name for Australia, New Zealand, and the islands of the southwest Pacific Ocean.

Odyssey An epic tale, composed in the eighth century BCE, of the journey of Odysseus, who traveled the Mediterranean back to his home in Ithaca after the siege of Troy.

oikos The word for "small family unit" in ancient Greece, similar to the *familia* in Rome. Its structure, with men as heads of household over women and children, embodied the fundamental power structure in Greek city-states.

oligarchy Clique of privileged rulers.

Olmecs Mesoamerican people, emerging around 1500 BCE, whose name means "inhabitants in the land of rubber," one of their major trade goods. Living in decentralized agrarian villages, this complex, stratified society shared language and religious ideas that were practiced at sacred ritual centers.

open-door policy Policy proposed by U.S. secretary of state John Hay that would give all foreign nations equal access to trade with China. As European imperial powers carved out spheres of influence in late nineteenth-century China, American leaders worried that the United States would be excluded from trade with China.

Opium Wars (1839–1842, 1856–1860) Wars fought between the British and Qing China over British trade in opium; the result was that China granted to the British the right to trade in five different ports and ceded Hong Kong to the British.

oracle bones Animal bones inscribed, heated, and interpreted by Shang ritual specialists to determine the will of the ancestors.

Organization of the Petroleum Exporting Countries (OPEC) International association established in 1960 to coordinate price and supply policies of oil-producing states.

Orientalism Genre of literature and painting that portrayed the nonwestern peoples of North Africa and Asia as exotic, sensuous, and economically backward with respect to Europeans.

Orientalists Western scholars who specialized in the study of Asia when Orientalism was at its peak.

Orrorin tugenensis Early hominid that first appeared 6 million years ago.

Ottoman Empire A Turkish warrior band that transformed itself into a vast, multicultural, bureaucratic empire that lasted from the early fourteenth century through the early twentieth century and encompassed Anatolia, the Arab world, and large swaths of southern and eastern Europe.

Pacific War (1879–1883) War between Chile and the alliance of Bolivia and Peru.

pagani Pejorative word used by Christians to designate pagans.

palace Official residence of the ruler, his family, and his entourage. The palace was both a social institution and a set of buildings. It first appeared around 2500 BCE, about a millennium later than the Mesopotamian temple, and quickly joined the temple as a defining landmark of city life. Eventually, it became a source of power rivaling the temple, and palace and temple life often blurred, as did the boundary between the sacred and the secular.

Palace of Versailles The palace complex, 11 miles away from the French capital of Paris, built by Louis XIV in the 1670s and 1680s to house and entertain his leading clergymen and nobles, with the hopes of diverting them from plotting against him.

Palmyra Roman trading depot located in modern-day Syria; part of a network of trading cities that connected various regions of Afro-Eurasia.

pan movements Groups that sought to link people across state boundaries in new communities based on ethnicity or, in some cases, religion (for example, pan-Germanism, pan-Islamism, and pan-Slavism).

pandemic An outbreak of disease occurring worldwide or over a great area spanning international boundaries and affecting a large number of people.

Pansophia Ideal republic of inquisitive Christians united in the search for knowledge of nature as a means of loving God.

papacy The institution of the pope, the Catholic spiritual leader in Rome.

papal Of, relating to, or issued by a pope.

Parthians Horse-riding people who pushed southward around the middle of the second century BCE and wiped out the Greek kingdoms in Iran. They then extended their power all the way to the Mediterranean, where they ran up against the Roman Empire in Anatolia and Mesopotamia.

pastoral nomads Pastoral peoples who move with their herds in perpetual motion across large areas, like the steppe lands of Inner Eurasia, and facilitate long-distance trade.

pastoralism A way of life in which humans herd domesticated animals and exploit their products (hides/fur, meat, and milk). Pastoralists include nomadic groups that range across vast distances, as well as transhumant herders who migrate seasonally in a more limited range.

paterfamilias Latin for "father of the family," the foundation of the Roman social order.

patria Latin, meaning "fatherland."

patrons In the Roman system of patronage, men and women of wealth and high social status who protected dependents or "clients" of a lower class.

Pax Mongolica The political and especially the commercial stability that the vast Mongol Empire provided for the travelers and merchants of Eurasia during the thirteenth and fourteenth centuries.

Pax Romana Latin term for "Roman Peace," referring to the period from 25 BCE to 235 CE, when conditions in the Roman Empire were relatively settled and peaceful, allowing trade and the economy to thrive.

Pax Sinica Modern term (paralleling the term *Pax Romana*) for the "Chinese Peace" that lasted from 149 to 87 BCE, a period when agriculture and commerce flourished, fueling the expansion of cities and the growth of the population of Han China.

Peace Preservation Law (1925) Act instituted in Japan that specified up to ten years' hard labor for any member of an organization advocating a basic change in the political system or the abolition of private property.

Pearl Harbor American naval base in Hawaii on which the Japanese launched a surprise attack on December 7, 1941, bringing the United States into World War II.

Peloponnesian War War fought between 431 and 404 BCE between two of Greece's most powerful city-states, Athens and Sparta.

Peninsular War (1808–1813) Conflict in which the Portuguese and Spanish populations, supported by the British, resisted an invasion of the Iberian Peninsula by the French under Napoleon.

Peninsulares Men and women born in Spain or Portugal who resided in the Americas. They regarded themselves as superior to Spaniards or Portuguese born in the colonies (Creoles).

People's Charter Document calling for universal suffrage for adult males, the secret ballot, electoral districts, and annual parliamentary elections. It was signed by over 3 million British between 1839 and 1842.

periplus "Sailing around" manual that preserved firsthand knowledge of navigation strategies and trading advice.

Persepolis Darius I's capital city in the highlands of Fars; a ceremonial center and expression of imperial identity as well as an important administrative hub of the Persian Empire.

Peterloo Massacre (1819) The killing of 11 and wounding of 460 following a peaceful demonstration for political reform by workers in Manchester, England.

Petra Literally, "rock"; city in modern-day Jordan that was the Nabatean capital. It profited greatly by supplying provisions and water to travelers and traders. Many of its houses and shrines were cut into the rocky mountains.

phalanx Military formation used by Philip II of Macedon, whereby heavily armored infantry were closely arrayed in battle.

Philip II of Macedon Father of Alexander the Great, under whose rule Macedonia developed into a large ethnic and territorial state. After unifying Macedonia, Philip went on to conquer neighboring states.

philosophes Enlightenment thinkers who applied scientific reasoning to human interaction and society as opposed to nature.

philosophia Literally, "love of wisdom"; a system of thought that originally included speculation on the nature of the cosmos, the environment, and human existence. It eventually came to include thought about the nature of humans and life in society.

Phoenicians An ethnic group in the Levant known for their ships, trading, and alphabet, and referred to in Hebrew scripture as the Canaanites. The term *Phoenician* (Greek for "purple people") derives from the major trade good they manufactured, a rare and expensive purple dye.

phonemes Primary and distinctive sounds that are characteristic of human language.

piety Strong sense of religious duty and devoutness, often inspiring extraordinary actions.

plant domestication The practice of growing plants, harvesting their seeds, and saving some of the seeds for planting in subsequent growing cycles, resulting in a steady food supply. Plant domestication was practiced as far back as 9000 BCE in the southern Levant and spread from there into the rest of Southwest Asia.

plantation slavery System whereby enslaved labor was used for the cultivation of crops wholly for the sake of producing surplus that was then used for profit; such plantations were a crucial part of the growth of the Mediterranean economy.

Plato (427–347 BCE) Disciple of the great philosopher Socrates; his works are the only record we have of Socrates's teaching. He was also the author of formative philosophical works on ethics and politics.

plebs The "common people" of Rome, whose interests were protected by officials called tribunes.

pochteca Archaic term for merchants of the Mexica.

polities Politically organized communities or states.

polyglot communities Societies composed of diverse linguistic and ethnic groups.

popular culture Affordable and accessible forms of art and entertainment available to people at all levels of society.

popular sovereignty The idea that the power of the state resides in the people.

populists Members of a political movement that supported U.S. farmers in late nineteenth-century America. The term is often used generically to refer to political groups who appeal to the majority of the population.

potassium-argon dating Major dating technique based on the decay of potassium into argon over time. This method makes possible the dating of objects up to a million years old.

potato famine (1840s) Severe famine in Ireland that led to the rise of radical political movements and the migration of large numbers of Irish to the United States.

potter's wheel Fast wheel that enabled people to mass-produce vessels in many different shapes. This advance, invented at the city of Uruk, enabled potters to make significant technical breakthroughs.

pottery Vessels made of mud and, later, clay used for storing and transporting food.

Prague Spring (1968) Program of liberalization by which communist authorities in Czechoslovakia strove to create a democratic and pluralist socialism; crushed by the Soviets, who branded it a "counterrevolutionary" movement.

predestination Belief of many sixteenth- and seventeenth-century Protestant groups that God had foreordained the lives of individuals, including their bad and good deeds.

primitivism Western art movement of the late nineteenth and early twentieth centuries that drew upon the so-called primitive art forms of Africa, Oceania, and pre-Columbian America.

printing press A machine used to print text or pictures from type or plates, dramatically increasing the speed at which information could be copied and disseminated. The spread of printing press technology in the 1450s created a revolution in communication around the world.

progressive reformers Members of the U.S. reform movement in the early twentieth century that aimed to eliminate political corruption, improve working conditions, and regulate the power of large industrial and financial enterprises.

proletarians Industrial wage workers.

prophets Charismatic freelance religious men of power who found themselves in opposition to the formal power of kings, bureaucrats, and priests.

Prophet's Town Indigenous village in present-day Indiana that was burned down by U.S. forces in the early nineteenth century.

Protestant Reformation Religious movement initiated by sixteenth-century monk Martin Luther, who openly criticized the corruption in the Catholic Church and voiced his belief that Christians could speak directly to God. His doctrines gained wide support, and those who followed this new view of Christianity rejected the authority of the papacy and the Catholic clergy, broke away from the Catholic Church, and called themselves "Protestants."

Protestantism Division of Christianity that emerged in western Europe from the Protestant Reformation.

Proto-Indo-European The parent of all the languages in the Indo-European family, which includes, among many others, English, German, Norwegian, Portuguese, French, Russian, Persian, Hindi, and Bengali.

Pullman Strike (1894) American Railway Union strike in response to wage cuts and firings.

Punic Wars Series of three wars fought between Rome and Carthage from 264 to 146 BCE that resulted in the end of Carthaginian hegemony in the western Mediterranean, the growth of Roman military might (army and navy), and the beginning of Rome's aggressive foreign imperialism.

puppet states Governments with little power in the international arena that follow the dictates of their more powerful neighbors or patrons.

Puritans Seventeenth-century reform group of the Church of England; also known as dissenters or nonconformists.

Qadiriyya Sufi order that facilitated the spread of Islam into West Africa.

qadis Judges in the Ottoman Empire.

qanats Underground water channels, vital for irrigation, that were used in Persia. Little evaporation occurred when water was being moved through *qanats*.

Qing dynasty (1644–1911) Minority Manchu rule over China that incorporated new territories, experienced substantial population growth, and sustained significant economic growth.

Questions of King Milinda (Milindapunha) Name of a second-century BCE text espousing the teachings of Buddhism as set forth by Menander, a Yavana king. It featured a discussion between the king and a sophisticated Buddhist sage named Nagasena.

Quetzalcoatl Ancient deity and legendary ruler of Indigenous peoples living in Mexico.

Quran The scripture of the Islamic faith. Originally a verbal recitation, the Quran was eventually compiled into a book with its verses in the order in which we have them today. According to traditional Islamic interpretation, the Quran was revealed to Muhammad by the angel Gabriel over a period of twenty-three years.

radicalism The conviction that real change is possible only by going to the root (in Latin, *radix*) of the problem and promoting complete political and social reform. Tendencies toward radicalism can be found in every culture that develops a complex set of institutions and hierarchies, but have been found most frequently in the west since 1789.

radicals Widely used term in nineteenth-century Europe that referred to those individuals and political organizations that favored the total reconfiguration of Europe's old state system.

radiocarbon dating Dating technique using the isotope C14, contained by all living organisms, which plants acquire directly from the atmosphere and animals acquire indirectly when they consume plants or other animals. When organisms die, the C14 they contain begins to decay into a stable nonradioactive isotope, C12. The rate of decay is regular and measurable, making it possible to ascertain the ages of fossils that leave organic remains up to 40,000 years.

Raj British crown's administration of India following the end of the East India Company's rule after the Rebellion of 1857.

raja "King" in the Kshatriya period in South Asia; could also refer to the head of a family, but indicated the person who had control of land and resources in South Asian city-states.

Ramadan Ninth month of the Muslim year, during which all Muslims must fast during daylight hours.

rape of Nanjing Attack against the Chinese in which the Japanese slaughtered at least 100,000 civilians and raped thousands of women between December 1937 and February 1938.

***Rashtriya Swayamsevak Sangh (RSS)* (1925)** Campaign to organize Hindus as a militant, modern community in India; translated in English as "National Volunteer Organization."

Rebellion of 1857 Indian uprising against the East India Company whose aims were religious purification, an egalitarian society, and local and communal solidarity without the interference of British rule.

rebus Probably originating in Uruk, a representation that transfers meaning from the name of a thing to the sound of that name. For example, a picture of a bee can represent the sound "b." Such pictures opened the door to writing: a technology of symbols that uses marks to represent specific discrete sounds.

Reconquista Spanish reconquest of territories lost to the Islamic empire, beginning with Toledo in 1061.

Red Guards Chinese students who were the shock troopers in the early phases of Mao Zedong's Great Proletarian Cultural Revolution in 1966–1976.

Red Lanterns Female supporters of the Chinese Boxers who dressed in red garments. Most were teenage girls and unmarried women.

Red Turban movement Diverse religious movement in China during the fourteenth century that spread the belief that the world was drawing to an end as Mongol rule was collapsing.

Reds Bolsheviks.

Reich German empire composed of Denmark, Austria, and parts of western France (1933–1945).

Reichstag The German parliament.

Reign of Terror Campaign at the height of the French Revolution in the early 1790s that used violence, including systematic execution of opponents of the revolution, to purge France of its enemies and to extend the revolution beyond its borders; radicals executed as many as 40,000 persons who were judged enemies of the state.

Renaissance Term meaning "rebirth" used by historians to characterize the cultural flourishing of European nations between 1430 and 1550, which emphasized a break from the church-centered medieval world and a new concept of humankind as the center of the world.

republican government Government in which power and rulership rest with representatives of the people, not with a king.

res publica Term (meaning "public thing") used by Romans to describe their Republic, which was advised by a Senate and was governed by popular assemblies of free adult males, who were arranged into voting units, based on wealth and social status, to elect officers and legislate.

Restoration (1815–1848) European movement after the defeat of Napoleon to restore Europe to its pre-French-revolutionary status and to quash radical movements.

Rift Valley Area of northeastern Africa where some of the most important early human archaeological discoveries of fossils were made, especially one of an intact skull that is 1.8 million years old.

river basin Area drained by a river, including all its tributaries. River basins were rich in fertile soil, water for irrigation, and plant and animal life, which made them attractive for human habitation. Cultivators were able to produce surplus agriculture to support the first cities.

Roman army Military force of the Roman Empire. The Romans devised a military draft that could draw from a huge population. In their encounter with Hannibal, they lost up to 80,000 men in three separate encounters and still won the war.

Roman Catholicism Western European Christianity, centered on the papacy in Rome, that emphasizes the atoning power of Jesus's death and aims to expand as far as possible.

Roman law The legal system of Rome, under which disputes were brought to public courts and decisions were made by judges and sometimes by large juries. Rome's legal system featured written law and institutions for settling legal disputes.

roving bandits Large bands of dispossessed and marginalized peasants who vented their anger at tax collectors in the waning years of the Ming dynasty.

Royal Road A 1,600-mile road from Sardis in Anatolia to Susa in Iran; used by messengers, traders, the army, and those taking tribute to the king in the fifth century BCE.

Russification Programs to assimilate people of over 146 dialects into the Russian Empire.

Sack of Constantinople Rampage in 1204 by the Frankish armies on the capital city of Constantinople.

sacred kingships Institutions that marked the centralized politics of West Africa. The inhabitants of these kingships believed that their kings were descendants of the gods.

Sahel The area of sub-Saharan Africa spanning the continent just south of the Sahara Desert.

St. Bartholomew's Day Massacre (1572) Roman Catholic massacre of French Protestants in Paris.

St. Patrick A formerly enslaved man brought to Ireland from Britain who later became a missionary, also called the "Apostle of Ireland." He died in 461 CE.

Salt March (1930) A 240-mile trek to the sea in India, led by Mohandas Gandhi, to gather salt for free, thus breaking the British colonial monopoly on salt.

samurai Japanese warriors who made up the private armies of Japanese daimyos.

Sandinista coalition Left-leaning Nicaraguan coalition of the 1970s and 1980s.

Sanskrit cosmopolis Cultural synthesis based on Hindu spiritual beliefs expressed in the Sanskrit language that unified South Asia in place of a centralized empire.

Santería African-based religion, blended with Christian influences, that was first practiced by enslaved people in Cuba.

Sargon the Great King of Akkad, a city-state located near present-day Baghdad. Reigning from 2334 to 2279 BCE, Sargon helped bring the competitive era of city-states to an end and sponsored monumental works of architecture, art, and literature.

Sasanian Empire Empire that succeeded the Parthians in the mid-220s CE in Inner Eurasia. The Sasanian Empire controlled the trade crossroads of Afro-Eurasia and possessed a strong armored cavalry, which made it a powerful rival to Rome. The Sasanians were also tolerant of Judaism and Christianity, which allowed Christians to flourish.

sati Hindu practice whereby a widow was burned to death on the pyre of her dead husband.

satrap Governor of a province in the Persian Empire. Each satrap was a relative or intimate associate of the king.

satrapy Province in the Persian Empire, ruled over by a governor, called a satrap, who was usually a relative or associate of the king.

satyagraha *See* nonviolent resistance.

scientific method Method of inquiry based on experimentation in nature. Many of its principles were first laid out by the philosopher Sir Francis Bacon (1561–1626), who claimed that real science entailed the formulation of hypotheses that could be tested in carefully controlled experiments.

Scramble for Africa European rush to colonize parts of Africa at the end of the nineteenth century.

scribes Those who mastered writing and used it to document economic transactions, keep lists, and record religious and literary texts; from the very beginning, they were at the top of the social ladder, under the major power brokers.

Scythian ethos Warrior ethos that embodied the extremes of aggressive horse-mounted culture. In part, the Scythian ethos was the result of the constant struggle between settlers, hunters and gatherers, and nomads on the northern frontier of Europe around 1000 BCE.

Sea Peoples Migrants from north of the Mediterranean who invaded cities of Egypt, Asia Minor, and the Levant in the second millennium BCE.

SEATO (Southeast Asia Treaty Organization) Military alliance of pro-American, anticommunist states in Southeast Asia from 1954 to 1977.

Second World Term invented during the Cold War to refer to the communist countries, as opposed to the west (or First World) and the former colonies (or Third World).

second-generation societies First-millennium BCE societies that innovated on their older political, religious, and cultural ideas by incorporating new aspects of cultures they encountered to reshape their way of life.

Seleucus Nikator Successor of Alexander the Great who lived from 358 to 281 BCE. He controlled Mesopotamia, Syria, Persia, and parts of the Punjab.

Self-Strengthening movement A movement of reformist Chinese bureaucrats in the latter half of the nineteenth century that attempted to adopt western elements of learning and technological skill while retaining their core Chinese culture.

Semu Term meaning "outsiders," or non-Chinese people—Mongols, Tanguts, Khitan, Jurchens, Muslims, Tibetans, Persians, Turks, Nestorians, Jews, and Armenians—who became a new ruling elite over a Han majority population in the late thirteenth century.

sepoys Hindu and Muslim recruits of the East India Company's military force.

serfs Peasants who farmed the land and paid fees to be protected and governed by lords under a system of rule called manorialism.

settled agriculture Humans' use of tools, animals, and their own labor to work the same plot of land for more than one growing cycle. It involves switching from a hunting and gathering lifestyle to one based on farming.

Seven Years' War (1756–1763) Also known as the French and Indian War; worldwide war that ended when Prussia defeated Austria, establishing itself as a European power, and when Britain gained control of India and many of France's colonies through the Treaty of Paris.

sexual revolution Increased freedom in sexual behavior, resulting in part from advances in contraception, notably the introduction of oral contraception in 1960, that allowed men and women to limit childbearing and to have sex with less fear of pregnancy.

shah Traditional title of Persian rulers.

shamans Certain humans whose powers supposedly enabled them to commune with the supernatural and to transform themselves wholly or partly into beasts.

shamisen Three-stringed instrument, often played by Japanese geisha.

Shandingdong Man A *Homo sapiens* whose fossil remains and relics can be dated to about 18,000 years ago. His physical characteristics were close to those of modern humans, and he had a similar brain size.

Shang state Dynasty in northeastern China that ruled from 1600 to 1046 BCE. Though not as well defined by borders as the territorial states in the southwest of Asia, it did have a ruling lineage. Four fundamental elements of the Shang state were a metal industry based on copper, pottery making, standardized architectural forms and walled towns, and divination using animal bones.

Shanghai School Late nineteenth-century style of painting characterized by an emphasis on spontaneous brushwork, feeling, and the incorporation of western influences into classical Chinese pieces.

sharecropping System of farming in which tenant farmers rented land and gave over a share of their crops to the land's owners. Sometimes seen as a cheap way for the state to conduct agricultural affairs, sharecropping often resulted in the impoverishment and marginalization of the underclass.

sharia Body of Islamic law that has developed over centuries, based on the Quran, the sayings of Muhammad (*hadith*), and the legal opinions of Muslim scholars (*ulama*).

Sharpeville Massacre (1960) Massacre of sixty-nine Black Africans when police fired upon a rally against the recently passed laws requiring non-White South Africans to carry identity papers.

Shawnees Indigenous tribe that inhabited the Ohio Valley during the eighteenth century.

Shays's Rebellion (1786) Uprising of armed farmers that broke out when the Massachusetts state government refused to offer them economic relief.

Shi Huangdi Title taken by King Zheng in 221 BCE when he claimed the mandate of heaven and consolidated the Qin dynasty. He is known for his tight centralization of power, including standardizing weights, measures, and writing; constructing roads, canals, and the beginnings of the Great Wall; and preparing a massive tomb for himself filled with an army of terra-cotta warriors.

Shiism One of the two main branches of Islam, practiced in the Safavid Empire. Although always a minority sect in the Islamic world, Shiism contains several subsects, each of which has slightly different interpretations of theology and politics.

Shiites Minority tradition within modern Islam that traces political succession through the lineage of Muhammad and breaks with Sunni understandings of succession at the death of Ali (cousin and son-in-law of Muhammad and fourth caliph) in 661 CE.

Shinto Literally, "the way of the gods"; Japan's official religion, which promoted the state and the emperor's divinity.

Shiva The third of three Vedic deities, signifying destruction. *See also* Brahma *and* Vishnu.

shoguns Japanese military commanders. From 1185 to 1333, the Kamakura shoguns served as military "protectors" of the ruler in the city of Heian.

Shotoku (574–622 CE) Prince in the early Japanese Yamoto state who is credited with having introduced Buddhism to Japan.

Shudras Literally, "small ones"; workers and enslaved people from outside the Vedic lineage.

Siddhartha Gautama *See* Buddha.

Sikhism Islamic-inspired religion that calls on its followers to renounce the *varna* (caste) system and to treat all believers as equal before God.

Silicon Valley Valley between the California cities of San Francisco and San Jose, known for its innovative computer and high-technology industries.

silk Luxury textile that became a vastly popular export from China (via the Silk Roads) to the cities of the Roman world.

Silk Roads More than 5,000 miles of trade routes linking China, central Asia, and the Mediterranean. They were named for the silk famously traded along their land and sea routes, although ideas, people, and many other high-value commodities also moved along their lengths.

Silla One of three independent Korean states that may have emerged as early as the third century BCE. These states lasted until 668 CE, when Silla took control over the entire peninsula.

Silver Islands Term used by European merchants in the sixteenth century to refer to Japan because of its substantial trade in silver with China.

Sino-Japanese War (1894–1895) Conflict over the control of Korea in which China was forced to cede the province of Taiwan to Japan.

sipahi Urdu for "soldier."

small seal script Unified script that was used to the exclusion of other scripts under the Qin with the aim of centralizing administration; its use led to a less complicated style of clerical writing than had been in use under the Han.

social contract The idea, drawn from the writings of British philosopher John Locke, that the law should bind both ruler and people.

social Darwinism Belief that Charles Darwin's theory of evolution was applicable to humans and justified the right of the ruling classes or countries to dominate the weak.

social hierarchies Distinctions between the privileged and the less privileged.

Social Security Act (1935) New Deal act that instituted old-age pensions and insurance for the unemployed.

socialism Political ideology that calls for a classless society with collective ownership of all property.

Socrates (469–399 BCE) Philosopher of Athens who encouraged people to reflect on ethics and morality. He stressed the importance of honor and integrity as opposed to wealth and power. Plato was his student.

Sogdians A people who lived in central Asia's commercial centers and maintained the stability and accessibility of the Silk Roads. They were crucial to the interconnectedness of the Afro-Eurasian landmass.

Solidarity The Soviet bloc's first independent trade union, established in Poland at the Gdańsk shipyard.

Song dynasty Chinese dynasty that took over the mandate of heaven for three centuries starting in 960 CE. It ruled in an era of many economic and political successes, but it eventually lost northern China to nomadic tribes.

Song porcelain Type of porcelain perfected during the Song dynasty that was light, durable, and quite beautiful.

South African War (1899–1902) *See* Anglo-Boer War.

Soviet bloc International alliance that included the eastern European countries of the Warsaw Pact as well as the Soviet Union, but also came to include Cuba.

Spanish-American War (1898) War between the United States and Spain in Cuba, Puerto Rico, and the Philippines. It ended with a treaty in which the United States took over the Philippines, Guam, and Puerto Rico; Cuba won partial independence.

speciation The formation of species.

specie Money in coin.

species A group of animals or plants sharing one or more distinctive characteristics.

spiritual ferment Process that occurred after 300 CE in which religion touched more areas of society and culture than before and in different, more demanding ways.

Spring and Autumn period Period between the eighth and fifth centuries BCE during which China was ruled by the feudal system. In this anarchic and turbulent time, there were 148 different tributary states.

SS (Schutzstaffel) Hitler's security police force.

Stalin, Joseph (1878–1953) Leader of the Communist Party and the Soviet Union; sought to create "socialism in one country." The name Stalin means "man of steel."

steel An alloy more malleable and stronger than iron that became essential for industries like shipbuilding and railways.

Stoicism Widespread philosophical movement initiated by Zeno (334–262 BCE). Zeno and his followers sought to understand the role of people in relation to the cosmos. For the Stoics, everything was grounded in nature. Being in love with nature and living a good life required being in control of one's passions and thus indifferent to pleasure or pain.

Strait of Malacca Seagoing gateway to Southeast and East Asia.

Strategic Defense Initiative Master plan, championed by U.S. president Ronald Reagan in the 1980s, that envisioned the deployment of satellites and space missiles to protect the United States from incoming nuclear bombs; nicknamed "Star Wars."

stupa Dome monument marking the burial site of relics of the Buddha.

Suez Canal Channel built in 1869 across the Isthmus of Suez to connect the Mediterranean Sea with the Red Sea in order to lower the costs of international trade.

Sufi brotherhoods Sufi religious orders that were responsible for the expansion of Islam into many regions of the world.

Sufis Islamic mystics who stressed contemplation and ecstasy through poetry, music, and dance.

Sufism Emotional and mystical form of Islam that appealed to the common people.

sultan Islamic political leader. In the Ottoman Empire, the sultan combined a warrior ethos with an unwavering devotion to Islam.

Sumerian King List Text that recounts the making of political dynasties. Recorded around 2000 BCE, it organizes the reigns of kings by dynasty, one city at a time.

Sumerian pantheon The Sumerian gods, each of whom had a home in a particular floodplain city. In the Sumerian belief system, both gods and the natural forces they controlled had to be revered.

Sumerian temples Homes of the gods and symbols of Sumerian imperial identity. Sumerian temples also represented the gods' ability to hoard wealth at sites where people exchanged goods and services. In addition, temples distinguished the urban from the rural world.

Sun Yat-sen (1866–1925) Chinese revolutionary and first provisional president of the Republic of China. Sun played an important role in the overthrow of the Qing dynasty and later founded the Guomindang, the Nationalist Party of China.

Sunnis Majority sect within modern Islam that follows a line of political succession from Muhammad, through the first four caliphs (Abu Bakr, Umar, Uthman, and Ali), to the Umayyads and beyond, with caliphs chosen by election from the *umma* (not from Muhammad's direct lineage).

superior man In the Confucian view, a person of perfected moral character, fit to be a leader.

superpowers Label applied to the United States and the Soviet Union after World War II because of their size, their possession of the atomic bomb, and the fact that each embodied a model of civilization (capitalism and communism, respectively) applicable to the whole world.

supranational organizations Organizations that transcend national boundaries, such as nongovernmental organizations (NGOs), the World Bank, and the International Monetary Fund (IMF). These can be distinguished from international organizations, which are intergovernmental projects in which national governments cooperate for common goals—for example, the United Nations, the World Health Organization, and NATO.

survival of the fittest Charles Darwin's belief that as animal populations grew and resources became scarce, a struggle for existence arose, the outcome of which was that only the "fittest" survived to reproduce.

Suryavansha The second lineage of two (the solar) in Vedic society. *See also* Chandravansha.

Swadeshi movement Voluntary organizations in India that championed the creation of indigenous manufacturing enterprises and schools of nationalist thought in order to gain autonomy from Britain.

syndicalism A political and economic system, elaborated by the French social philosopher Georges Sorel (1847–1922), that sought to replace capitalism with a workplace organization that included unskilled laborers.

tabula rasa Term used by John Locke to describe the human mind before it begins to acquire ideas from experience; Latin for "clean slate."

Taiping Heavenly Kingdom (Heavenly Kingdom of Great Peace) Religious sect established by the Chinese prophet Hong Xiuquan in the mid-nineteenth century. Hong Xiuquan believed that he was Jesus's younger brother. The group struggled to rid the world of evil and "restore" the heavenly kingdom, imagined as a just and egalitarian order.

Taiping Rebellion (1850–1864) Rebellion by followers of Hong Xiuquan and the Taiping Heavenly Kingdom against the Qing government over the economic and social turmoil caused by the Opium Wars. Despite raising an army of 100,000 rebels, the rebellion was crushed.

Taj Mahal Royal palace of the Mughal Empire, built by Shah Jahan in the seventeenth century in homage to his wife, Mumtaz.

Tale of Genji Japanese work written in the early eleventh century by Lady Murasaki that gives vivid accounts of Heian court life; Japan's first novel.

talking cure Psychological practice developed by Sigmund Freud whereby the symptoms of neurotic and traumatized patients would decrease after regular periods of thoughtful discussion.

Talmud Huge volumes of oral commentary on Jewish law eventually compiled in two versions, the Palestinian and the Babylonian, in the fifth and sixth centuries BCE.

Talmud of Jerusalem Codified written volumes of the traditions of Judaism; produced by the rabbis of Galilee around 400 CE.

Tang dynasty (618–907 CE) Regime that promoted a cosmopolitan culture, turning China into the hub of East Asian cultural integration, while expanding the borders of its empire. In order to govern such a diverse empire, the Tang established a political culture and civil service based on Confucian teachings. Candidates for the civil service were required to take examinations, the first of their kind in the world.

Tanzimat Reorganization period of the Ottoman Empire in the mid-nineteenth century; its modernizing reforms affected the military, trade, foreign relations, and civilian life.

tappers Rubber harvesters in Brazil, most of whom were either Indigenous or mixed-blood people.

Tarascans Mesoamerican society of the fifteenth century; rivals to and sometimes subjects of the Aztecs.

tekkes Schools that taught the devotional strategies and religious knowledge needed for students to enter Sufi orders and become masters of the brotherhood.

temple Building where believers worshipped their gods and goddesses and where some peoples believed the deities had their earthly residence.

Tenskwatawa (1775–1836) Shawnee prophet who urged disciples to abstain from alcohol and return to traditional customs, reducing dependence on European trade goods and severing connections to Christian missionaries. His message spread to other tribes, raising the specter of a pan-Indigenous confederacy.

Teotihuacán City-state in a large, mountainous valley in present-day Mexico; the first major community to emerge after the Olmecs.

territorial state A kingdom made up of city-states and hinterlands joined together by a shared identity, controlled through the centralized rule of a charismatic leader, and supported by a large bureaucracy, legal codes, and military expansion.

Third Estate The French people minus the clergy and the aristocracy; this term was popularized in the late eighteenth century and used to exalt the power of the bourgeoisie during the French Revolution.

Third Reich The German state from 1933 to 1945 under Adolf Hitler.

Third World A collective term used for nations of the world, mostly in Asia, Latin America, and Africa, that were not highly industrialized like First World nations or tied to the Soviet bloc (the Second World); it implies a revolutionary challenge to the existing (liberal, capitalist) order. Debate surrounding the best terminology to describe these nations is ongoing.

Thirty Years' War (1618–1648) Conflict begun between Protestants and Catholics in Germany that escalated into a general European war fought against the unity and power of the Holy Roman Empire.

Tiahuanaco Also called Tiwanaku; the first great Andean polity, on the shores of Lake Titicaca.

Tiananmen Square Largest public square in the world and site of the pro-democracy demonstrations in 1989 that ended with the killing of thousands of protesters by the Chinese army.

tiers monde Term meaning "Third World," coined by French intellectuals to describe countries seeking a "third way" between Soviet communism and western capitalism.

Tiglath Pileser III Neo-Assyrian ruler from 745 to 728 BCE who instituted reforms that changed the administrative and social structure of the empire to make it more efficient, and who introduced a standing army.

Tlaxcalans Mesoamerican society of the fifteenth century; these people were enemies of the powerful Aztec Empire.

Tokugawa shogunate Hereditary military administration founded in 1603 that ruled Japan while keeping the emperor as a figurehead; it was toppled in 1868 by reformers who felt that Japan should adopt, not reject, western influences.

Toltecs Mesoamerican peoples who filled the political vacuum left by Teotihuacán's decline; established a temple-filled capital and commercial hub at Tula.

Tomb Culture Warlike group from Northeast Asia who arrived by sea in the middle of the third century CE and imposed their military and social power on southern Japan. These conquerors are known today as the Tomb Culture because of their elevated necropolises near present-day Osaka.

Topkapi Palace Palace complex located in Istanbul that served as both the residence of the sultan, along with his harem and larger household, and the political headquarters of the Ottoman Empire.

total war All-out war involving civilian populations as well as military forces, often used in reference to World War II.

transhumant herders Pastoral peoples who move seasonally from lowlands to highlands, in proximity to city-states, with which they trade the products of their flocks (milk, fur, hides) for urban products (manufactured goods, such as metals).

Trans-Siberian Railroad Railroad built over very difficult terrain between 1891 and 1904 and subsequently expanded; it created an overland bridge for troops, peasant settlers, and commodities to move between Europe and the Pacific.

Treaty of Brest-Litovsk (1918) Separate peace between imperial Germany and the new Bolshevik regime in Russia. The treaty acknowledged the German victory on the Eastern Front and withdrew Russia from the war.

Treaty of Nanjing (1842) Treaty between China and Britain following the Opium Wars; it called for indemnities, the opening of new ports, and the cession of Hong Kong to the British.

Treaty of Tordesillas (1494) Treaty in which the pope decreed that the non-European world would be divided into spheres of trade and missionary responsibility between Spain and Portugal.

trickle trade Method by which a good is passed from one village to another, as in the case of obsidian among farming villages; the practice began around 7000 BCE. Also called "down-the-line trade."

Tripartite Pact (1940) Pact that stated that Germany, Italy, and Japan would act together in all future military ventures.

Triple Entente Alliance developed before World War I that included Britain, France, and Russia.

Troy City founded around 3000 BCE in the far west of Anatolia. Troy is legendary as the site of the war that was launched by the Greeks (the Achaeans) and that was recounted by Homer in the *Iliad*.

Truman Doctrine (1947) Declaration promising U.S. economic and military intervention, whenever and wherever needed, for the sake of preventing communist expansion.

Truth and Reconciliation Commission Quasi-judicial body established after the overthrow of the apartheid system in South Africa and the election of Nelson Mandela as the country's first Black president in 1994. The commission was to gather evidence about crimes committed during the apartheid years. Those who showed remorse for their actions could appeal for clemency. The South African leaders believed that an airing of the grievances from this period would promote racial harmony and reconciliation.

truth commissions Commissions established to inquire into human rights abuses by previous regimes. In Argentina, El Salvador, Guatemala, and South Africa, these commissions were vital for creating a new aura of legitimacy for democracies and for promising to uphold the rights of individuals.

tsar Russian word derived from the Latin *Caesar* to refer to the Russian ruler of Kyiv, and eventually to all rulers in Russia. Also spelled as *czar*.

Tula Toltec capital city; a commercial hub and political and ceremonial center.

Uitlanders Literally, "outsiders"; British populations living in Afrikaner republics, who were denied voting rights and subjected to other forms of discrimination in the late nineteenth century.

ulama Arabic word that means "learned ones" or "scholars"; used for those who devoted themselves to knowledge of Islamic sciences.

Umayyads Family who founded the first dynasty in Islam. They established family rule and dynastic succession to the role of caliph. The first Umayyad caliph established Damascus as his capital and was named Mu'awiya Ibn Abi Sufyan.

umma Arabic word for "community"; used to refer to the Islamic polity or Islamic community.

Universal Declaration of Human Rights (1948) U.N. declaration that laid out the rights to which all human beings are entitled.

universalizing religions Religions that appeal to diverse populations; are adaptable to new cultures and places; promote universal rules and principles; proselytize new believers, often through missionaries; foster community; and, in some cases, do all of this through the support of an empire.

universitas Term used from the end of the twelfth century to denote scholars who came together, first in Paris. The term is borrowed from the merchant communities, where it denoted the equivalent of the modern union.

untouchables People in the Indian *varna* (caste) system whose jobs, usually in the more unsanitary aspects of urban life, rendered them "ritually and spiritually" impure.

Upanishads First-millennium BCE Vedic wisdom literature, in the form of a dialogue between students and teacher; together with the Vedas, they brought a cultural and spiritual unity to much of South Asia.

urban-rural divide Division between those living in cities and those living in rural areas. City dwellers had specialized jobs and mass-produced goods, while those in the countryside cultivated land and herded livestock.

utopian socialism The most visionary of all Restoration-era movements. Utopian socialists like Charles Fourier dreamed of transforming states, workplaces, and human relations and proposed plans to do so.

Vaishyas Householders or lesser clan members in Vedic society who worked the land and tended livestock.

Vardhamana Mahavira Advocate of Jainism who lived from around 540 to 468 BCE; he emphasized interpretation of the Upanishads to govern and guide daily life.

varna Sanskrit for "color"; refers to the four ranked social groups within early Vedic society (priests, warriors, commoners, and laborers). The term *caste*, which derives from the term *casta* ("race/breed" in Spanish and Portuguese) is a later, anachronistic term often used for these divisions.

vassal states Subordinate states that had to pay tribute in luxury goods, raw materials, and manpower as part of a broad confederation of polities under a king's protection.

Vedas Rhymes, hymns, and explanatory texts composed and orally transmitted in Sanskrit by Brahman priests. They shaped the society and religious rituals of Vedic peoples and became central texts in Hinduism.

Vedic peoples Indo-European nomadic group who migrated from the steppes of Inner Asia around 1500 BCE into the Indus basin, on to the Ganges River valley, and then as far south as the Deccan plateau, bringing with them their distinctive religious ideas (Vedas), Sanskrit, and domesticated horses.

veiling Practice of modest dress required of respectable women in the Neo-Assyrian Empire, introduced by Middle Assyrian authorities in the thirteenth century BCE.

Venus figures Representations of the goddess of fertility drawn on the Chauvet Cave in southeastern France. Discovered in 1994, they are probably about 35,000 years old.

Versailles Conference (1919) Peace conference among the victors of World War I; resulted in the Treaty of Versailles, which forced Germany to pay reparations and to give up its colonies to the victors.

Viet Cong Vietnamese communist group committed to overthrowing the government of South Vietnam and reunifying North and South Vietnam.

Viet Minh (League for the Independence of Vietnam) Group founded in 1941 by Ho Chi Minh to oppose the Japanese occupation of Indochina; it later fought the French colonial forces for independence.

Vietnam War (1965–1975) Conflict that resulted from U.S. concern over the spread of communism in Southeast Asia. The United States intervened on the side of South Vietnam in its struggle against peasant-supported Viet Cong guerrilla forces, who wanted to reunite Vietnam under a communist regime. Faced with antiwar opposition at home and ferocious resistance from the Vietnamese, American troops withdrew in 1973; the puppet South Vietnamese government collapsed two years later.

Vikings Warrior group from Scandinavia that used its fighting skills and sophisticated ships to raid and trade deep into eastern Europe, southward into the Mediterranean, and westward to Iceland, Greenland, and North America.

Vishnu The second of three Vedic deities, signifying existence. *See also* Brahma *and* Shiva.

viziers Bureaucrats of the Ottoman Empire.

vodun Mixed religion of African and Christian customs practiced by enslaved and free Blacks in the colony of Saint-Domingue.

Voting Rights Act (1965) Law that granted universal suffrage in the United States.

Wafd Nationalist party that came into existence during a rebellion in Egypt in 1919 and held power sporadically after Egypt was granted limited independence from Britain in 1922.

Wahhabism Early eighteenth-century reform movement organized by Muhammad Ibn Abd al-Wahhab, who preached the absolute oneness of Allah and a return to the pure Islam of Muhammad.

Wang Mang Han minister who usurped the throne in 9 CE because he believed that the Han had lost the mandate of heaven. He ruled until 23 CE.

war ethos Strong social commitment to a continuous state of war. The Roman army constantly drafted men and engaged in annual spring military campaigns. Soldiers were taught to embrace a sense of honor that did not allow them to accept defeat, and those who repeatedly threw themselves into battle were commended.

War of 1812 Conflict between Britain and the United States arising from U.S. grievances over oppressive British maritime practices in the Napoleonic wars.

War on Poverty U.S. president Lyndon Johnson's push for an increased range of social programs and increased spending on social security, health, education, and assistance for the disabled.

Warring States period Period extending from the late fifth century to 221 BCE, when China's regional warring states were unified by the Qin dynasty.

Warsaw Pact (1955–1991) Military alliance between the Soviet Union and other communist states that was established in response to the creation of the North Atlantic Treaty Organization (NATO).

Weimar Republic (1919–1933) Constitutional republic of Germany that was subverted by Hitler soon after he became chancellor.

Western Front Battlefront that stretched from the English Channel through Belgium and France to the Alps during World War I.

White and Blue Niles The two main branches of the Nile, rising out of central Africa and Ethiopia, respectively. They come together at the present-day capital city of Sudan, Khartoum.

White Lotus Rebellion Series of uprisings in northern China (1790–1800s) inspired by mystical beliefs in folk Buddhism and, at times, the idea of restoring the Ming dynasty.

White Wolf Mysterious militia leader, depicted in popular myth as a Chinese Robin Hood whose mission was to rid the country of the injustices of Yuan Shikai's government in the early years of the Chinese republic (1910s).

Whites "Counterrevolutionaries" of the Bolshevik Revolution (1917) who fought the Bolsheviks (the Reds); included former supporters of the tsar, Social Democrats, and large independent peasant armies.

witnessing Dying for one's faith, or becoming a martyr.

wokou Supposedly Japanese pirates, many of whom were actually Chinese subjects of the Ming dynasty.

Works Progress Administration (WPA) New Deal program instituted in 1935 that put nearly 3 million people to work building roads, bridges, airports, and post offices.

World Bank International agency established in 1944 to provide economic assistance to war-torn and poor countries. Its formal title is the International Bank for Reconstruction and Development.

World War I *See* Great War.

World War II (1939–1945) Worldwide war that began in September 1939 in Europe, and even earlier in Asia, and pitted Britain, the United States, and the Soviet Union (the Allies) against Nazi Germany, Japan, and Italy (the Axis).

Wu, Emperor (r. 141–87 BCE) Also known as Emperor Han Wudi, or the "Martial Emperor"; the ruler of the Han dynasty for more than fifty years, during which he expanded the empire through his extensive military campaigns.

Wu Zhao Chinese empress who reigned from 684 to 705 CE. She began as a concubine in the court of Li Shimin and became the mother of his son's child. She eventually gained power equal to that of the emperor, and she named herself regent when she finagled a place for one of her own sons after their father's death.

Xiongnu The most powerful and intrusive of the nomadic peoples of Inner Asia; originally pastoralists from the eastern part of the Asian steppe in what is modern-day Mongolia. They appeared along the frontier with China in the late Zhou dynasty and by the third century BCE had become the most powerful of all the pastoral communities in that area.

Xunzi (310–237 BCE) Confucian moralist whose ideas were influential to Qin rulers. He believed that rational statecraft was more reliable than fickle human nature and that strict laws and severe punishments could create stability in society.

Yalta Accords Results of a meeting between President Roosevelt, Prime Minister Churchill, and Premier Stalin held in the Crimea in 1945 to plan for the post–World War II order.

Yavana kings Sanskrit name for Greek rulers, derived from the Greek name for the area of western Asia Minor called Ionia, a term that was then extended to anyone who spoke Greek or came from the Mediterranean.

yellow press Newspapers that sought mass circulation by featuring sensationalist reporting.

Yellow Turbans Daoist millenarian Chinese religious movement that emerged during the Later (Eastern) Han period. The group was named for the yellow scarves adherents wore around their heads.

Yin City that became the capital of the Shang dynasty in 1350 BCE, ushering in a golden age.

Young Egypt Antiliberal, fascist group that gained a large following in Egypt during the 1930s.

Young Italy Nationalist organization founded in 1832, made up of young students and intellectuals devoted to the unification and renewal of the Italian state.

Yuan dynasty Dynasty established by the Mongols after the defeat of the Song. The Yuan dynasty was strong from 1279 to 1368; its capital was at Dadu, or modern-day Beijing.

Yuan Mongols Mongol rulers of China who were overthrown by the Ming dynasty in 1368.

Yuezhi A Turkic nomadic people who roamed pastoral lands to the west of the Xiongnu territory of central Mongolia. They had friendly relationships with the farming societies in China, but detested the Xiongnu and had frequent armed clashes with them.

zaibatsu Large-scale, family-owned corporations in Japan, consisting of factories, import-export businesses, and banks, that dominated the Japanese economy until 1945.

zamindars Archaic tax system of the Mughal Empire in which decentralized lords collected tribute for the emperor.

Zapatistas Group of Indigenous rebels that rose up against the Mexican government in 1994 and drew inspiration from an earlier Mexican rebel, Emiliano Zapata.

Zheng *See* Shi Huangdi.

Zheng He Ming naval commander who, from 1405 to 1433, led seven massive naval expeditions to impress other peoples with Ming might and to establish tributary relations with Southeast Asia, Indian Ocean ports, the Persian Gulf, and the east coast of Africa.

Zhong Shang Administrative central complex of the Shang.

Zhongguo Term originating in the ancient period and subsequently used to emphasize the central cultural and geographic location of China in the world; means "the middle kingdom."

ziggurat Stepped platform that served as the base of a Sumerian temple, which had evolved from the earlier elevated platform base by the end of the third millennium BCE.

Zionism Political movement advocating the reestablishment of a Jewish homeland in Palestine.

Zoroaster Sometimes known as Zarathustra; thought to have been a teacher around 1000 BCE in eastern Iran and credited with having solidified the region's religious beliefs into a unified system that moved away from animistic nomadic beliefs. The main source for his teachings is a compilation called the Avesta.

Zoroastrianism Dualistic Persian religion, based on the teaching of Zoroaster, in which forces of light and truth battle with those of darkness and falsehood.

Zulus African tribe that, under Shaka, created a ruthless warrior state in southern Africa in the early nineteenth century.

Credits

FRONT MATTER

Pages i, iv–v, 1: Pictures from History/Bridgeman Images; front map pp. ii–iii: ixstudio/Alamy Stock Photo; p. viii: World History Archive/Alamy Stock Photo; pp. ix–xxi, xxiii, xxiv, xxvii: Pictures from History/Bridgeman Images; rear map: Arunas Gabalis/ Alamy Stock Photo.

CHAPTER 10

Photos Page 404: The Picture Art Collection/Alamy Stock Photo; p.406: Godong/Alamy Stock Photo; p.407: Granger; p.409: Lao Ma/Shutterstock; p.412: British Library Board. All Rights Reserved/Bridgeman Images; p.414: (top) Keren Su/China Span/ Alamy Stock Photo; (bottom) Pranay Chandra Singh/Shutterstock; p.415: Rogers Fund 1918 © The Metropolitan Museum of Art; p.418: FLHC 16/Alamy Stock Photo; p.419: (top) akg-images/ Werner Forman; (bottom) Hemis/Alamy Stock Photo; p.421: (top) Granger; (bottom) GL Archive/Alamy Stock Photo; p.423: (top) robertharding/Alamy Stock Photo; (bottom) akg-images/Volker Kreidler; p.424: Bridgeman Images; p.425: © British Library Board/Robana/Art Resource NY; p.428: (top) The Picture Art Collection/Alamy Stock Photo; (bottom) Gavin Hellier/Alamy Stock Photo; p.429: (top) Bridgeman Art Library/Getty Images; (bottom) Rich Mathews/Alamy Stock Photo; p.430: (top) Beren Patterson/Alamy Stock Photo; (bottom) Kevin Schafer/Getty Images; p.433: INTERFOTO/Alamy Stock Photo; p.434: Michael S. Lewiy/Getty Images; p.435: akg-images; p.440: Courtesy of the Brooklyn Museum, Gift of Mr. and Mrs. Alastair B. Martin, the Guennol Collection; p.443: Courtesy of the Brooklyn Museum, Gift of Mr. and Mrs. Carl L. Selden; p.450: Giraudon/ Art Resource NY; p.451: (top) BnF, Dist. RMN-Grand Palais/Art Resource, NY; (bottom) Pictorial Press Ltd/Alamy Stock Photo.

Primary Sources 10.1: Rabban Bar Sāwmā, from *The Monks of Kublai Khan, Emperor of China: Medieval Travels from China through Central Asia to Persia and Beyond*, translated by Sir E.A. Wallis Budge. Originally published by Harrison & Sons, Ltd. in 1928 for the Religious Tract Society. Reprinted by permission of Lutterworth Press. **10.3:** From *Ibn Battuta: Travels in Asia & Africa,1325–1354*, translated by H. A. R. Gibb, pp. 55–57. Copyright © 1929 George Routledge & Sons. Reprinted by permission of Taylor & Francis Books (UK). **10.4:** Al-ʿUmarī, from *Corpus of Early Arabic Sources for West African History*, translated by J.F.P. Hopkins, edited and annotated by N. Levtzion and J.F.P. Hopkins (Cambridge: Cambridge University Press, 1981). © University of Ghana, International Academic Union, Cambridge University Press 1991. Reprinted with the permission of Cambridge University Press.

CHAPTER 11

Photos Page 452: The Picture Art Collection/Alamy Stock Photo; p.455: Sarin Images/Granger; p.458: The Picture Art Collection/ Alamy Stock Photo; p.459: Courtesy of the Brooklyn Museum, Gift of Mr. and Mrs. Alastair B. Martin, the Guennol Collection; p.463: Sonia Halliday Photo Library/Alamy Stock Photo; p.464: Muhammed Enes Yldrm/Anadolu Agency/Getty Images; p.465: Levent Karaoglu/Alamy Stock Photo; p.466: Historic Images/ Alamy Stock Photo; p.467: Historic Collection/Alamy Stock Photo; p.468: Album/Alamy Stock Photo; p.469: World History Archive/Alamy Stock Photo; p.470: volkerpreusser/Alamy Stock Photo; p.473: North Wind Picture Archives/Alamy Stock Photo; p.474: incamerastock/Alamy Stock Photo; p.475: (left) Ian Dagnall/Alamy Stock Photo; (right) Classic Image/Alamy Stock Photo; p.477: Everett Collection Historical/Alamy Stock Photo; p.479: Granger; p.480: The Art Archive/REX/Shutterstock; p.481: © RMN-Grand Palais/Art Resource NY; p.483: (left) The Picture Art Collection/Alamy Stock Photo; (right) Illustration by Greg Harlin, Wood Ronsaville Harlin, Inc.; p.484: © RMN-Grand Palais/Art Resource NY; p.485: Pictures from History/Bridgeman Images; p.489: Courtesy of the Brooklyn Museum, Gift of Mr. and Mrs. Carl L. Selden; p.496: (both) Bridgeman Images; p.497: Granger.

Primary Sources 11.1: Michael Dols, "Ibn al-Wardi's Risalah al-Naba' 'an al-Waba', a Translation of a Major Source for the History of the Black Death in the Middle East" in *Near Eastern Numismatics, Iconography, Epigraphy and History: Studies in Honor of George C. Miles*, ed. Dickran K. Kouymjian (Beirut: American University of Beirut, 1974), 447–454. Reprinted by permission of the American University of Beirut Press. **11.2:** Marchione di Coppo Stefani, Cronaca Fiorentina, edited by Niccolo Rodolico, Vol. 30 of Rerum Italicarum Scriptores (Citta di Castello: S. Lapi, 1903–1913), as translated by Duane Osheim at http://www2.iath.virginia.edu/osheim/marchione.html. Reprinted by permission of Duane Osheim. **11.3:** Ibn Khaldûn, excerpts from *The Muqaddimah: An Introduction to History Vol. 1*, translated by Franz Rosenthal (New York: Pantheon Books, 1958). © 1958 by Bollingen Foundation, Inc. Reprinted by permission of Princeton University Press. **11.4:** al-Maqrizi, "The Guide to the Knowledge of Dynasties and Kings," translated by Hamid Irbouh and excerpted in *The Middle East and Islamic World Reader*, copyright © 2003, Revised edition copyright © 2012 by Marvin Gettleman and Stuart Schaar. Used by permission of Grove/Atlantic, Inc. Any third-party use of this material, outside of this publication, is prohibited.

CHAPTER 12

Photos Page 498: Art Collection 4/Alamy Stock Photo; p.501: Heritage Image Partnership Ltd/Alamy Stock Photo; p.502: Photo Josse/Bridgeman Images; p.503: The Picture Art Collection/Alamy Stock Photo; p.506: DEA/G. DAGLI ORTI/Getty Images; p.508: bpk Bildagentur/Art Resource NY; p.510: Sarin Images/Granger NYC; p.511: (left) Granger NYC; (right) Pictures from History/Granger NYC; p.512: Public Domain via Wikipedia; p.513: (left) Sarin Images/Granger NYC; p.(right) PvE/Alamy Stock Photo; p.514: Courtesy of the Brooklyn Museum, Gift of Mr. and Mrs. Alastair B. Martin, the Guennol Collection; p.516: François Guenet/Art Resource NY; p.518: Pulsar Imagens/Alamy Stock Photo; p.520: Sarin Images/Granger NYC; p.522: akg-images; p.524: INTERFOTO/Alamy Stock Photo; p.525: De Agostini Picture Library/G. Dagli Orti/Bridgeman Images; p.526: akg-images/Cameraphoto; p.528: Reunion des Musees Nationaux/Art Resource, NY; p.531: (top) Courtesy of Indiana University Library; (bottom) The Picture Art Collection/Alamy Stock Photo; p.532: Sarin Images/Granger; p.534: Courtesy of the Brooklyn Museum, Gift of Mr. and Mrs. Alastair B. Martin, the Guennol Collection; p.535: Courtesy of the Brooklyn Museum, Gift of Mr. and Mrs. Carl L. Selden; p.540: (left) Scala/Art Resource, NY; (right) Granger NYC; p.541: RMN-Grand Palais/Art Resource NY.

Primary Sources 12.1: Book Twelve of the Florentine Codex, translated by James Lockhart in *We People Here: Nahuatl accounts of the conquest of Mexico* (Berkeley: University of California Press, 1993), pp. 56–86. Reprinted by permission of the Estate of James Lockhart. **12.4:** T'ien-Tsê Chang, from *Sino-Portuguese Trade From 1514 to 1644: A Synthesis of Portuguese and Chinese Sources* (Leyden: E.J. Brill, 1934), pp. 51–52. Reprinted by permission of Brill Academic Publishers.

CHAPTER 13

Photos Page 542: G. Dagli Orti/© NPL–DeA Picture Library/Bridgeman Images; p.546: (left) Chester Beatty Library/Bridgeman Images; (right) Lordprice Collection/Alamy Stock Photo; p.550: Classic Image/Alamy Stock Photo; p.551: Granger NYC; p.553: (left) Peter Newark American Pictures/Bridgeman Images; (right) North Wind Picture Archives/Alamy Stock Photo; p.554: Universal Images Group North America LLC/Alamy Stock Photo; p.555: Granger; p.557: Stefano Bianchetti/Bridgeman Images; p.560: Courtesy of the Brooklyn Museum, Gift of Mr. and Mrs. Alastair B. Martin, the Guennol Collection; p.561: (left) North Wind Picture Archives/Alamy Stock Photo; (right) The Print Collector/Alamy Stock Photo; p.562: Sarin Images/GRANGER; p.563: Dagli Orti/REX/Shutterstock; p.564: Artokoloro Quint Lox Limited/Alamy Stock Photo; p.566: Granger NYC; p.567: Niday Picture Library/Alamy Stock Photo; p.568: The Picture Art Collection/Alamy Stock Photo; p.569: ART Collection/Alamy Stock Photo; p.570: Courtesy of Rijksmuseum, Amsterdam; p.571: Bridgeman Images; p.572: Album/Alamy Stock Photo; p.573: Dagli Orti/REX/Shutterstock; p.575: G. Dagli Orti/© NPL–DeA Picture Library/Bridgeman Images; p.578: (left) Chris Hellier/Corbis/Getty Images; (right) Granger NYC; p.579: (top) INTERFOTO/Alamy Stock Photo; (bottom) bpk Bildagentur/Museum Boijmans van Beuningen Rotterdam,; p.The Netherlands/Art Resource NY; p.581: Peter Willi/Bridgeman Images; p.582: Bridgeman Images; p.585: Courtesy of the Brooklyn Museum, Gift of Mr. and Mrs. Carl L. Selden; p.590: (left) Courtesy of The Metropolitan Museum of Art; (right) Marylebone Cricket Club/Bridgeman Images; p.591: (left) William Sturgis Bigelow Collection/Bridgeman Images; (right) Courtesy of Metropolitan Museum of Art.

Primary Sources 13.1: Olaudah Equiano, from *Interesting Narrative of the Life of Olaudiah Equiano, or Gustavus Vassa, The African, Written by Himself: A Norton Critical Edition*, edited by Werner Sollors. Copyright © 2001 by W. W. Norton & Company, Inc. Used by permission of W. W. Norton & Company, Inc. **13.4:** Katherine Holt, "Population by Racial Classification, Santiago de Iguape 1835"; "Free and Freed Population by Racial Classification, Iguape 1835"; and "Enslaved Population by Place of Birth, Santiago do Iguape, 1835." From The Bahian History Project, www.mappingbahia.org. Reproduced with permission from Katherine Holt.

CHAPTER 14

Photos Page 592: ART Collection/Alamy Stock Photo; p.594: DeAgostini/Superstock; p.595: Art Resource NY; p.597: Werner Forman/Universal Images Group/Getty Images; p.598: World History Archive/Alamy Stock Photo; p.599: (top) EvrenKalinbacak/Getty Images; (bottom) Art Collection 2/Alamy Stock Pho; p.600: RMN-Grand Palais/Art Resource NY; p.601: (left) Pictures Now/Alamy Stock Photo; (right) ART Collection/Alamy Stock Photo; p.602: Smith Archive/Alamy Stock Photo; p.603: (left) Scala/Art Resource NY; (right)Granger NYC; p.604: Chronicle/Alamy Stock Photo; p.605: (left) Underwood & Underwood/Library of Congress/Corbis/VCG via Getty Images; (right) Library of Congress; p.606: Bridgeman Images; p.607: RMN-Grand Palais/Art Resource NY; p.608: Alan Tobey/Getty Images; p.609: (top) The Trustees of the British Museum/Art Resource NY; (bottom) The Michael C. Rockefeller Memorial Collection Bequest of Nelson A. Rockefeller 1979 © The Metropolitan Museum of Art; p.610: Heritage Images via Getty Images; p.611: RMN-Grand Palais/Art Resource NY; p.612: SPCOLLECTION/Alamy Stock Photo; p.613: Bridgeman Images; p.614: SSPL via Getty Images; p.615: Peter Willi/Superstock; p.616: (top) Archives Charmet/Bridgeman Images; (bottom) Bridgeman Images; p.617: Courtesy of the Brooklyn Museum, Gift of Mr. and Mrs. Alastair B. Martin, the Guennol Collection; p.618: The Getty/Science Source; p.619: The History Collection/Alamy Stock Photo; p.620: Bridgeman Images; p.621: (left) Album/Art Resource, NY; (right) Bridgeman Images; p.622: Album/Alamy Stock Photo; p.623: Courtesy of Le Bulletin de l'Institut Français d'Études Andines; p.624: (left) HIP/Art Resource NY; (right) Sarin Images/Granger NYC; p.628: Courtesy of the Brooklyn Museum, Gift of Mr. and Mrs. Alastair B. Martin, the Guennol Collection; p.629: Courtesy of the Brooklyn Museum, Gift of Mr. and Mrs. Carl L. Selden; p.636: (top row left) Library of Congress; p.(top row middle) British Library Board/ Bridgeman Images; p.(top row right) Art Collection 3/Alamy Stock Photo; p.(bottom left) Christie's Images/Bridgeman Images; p.(bottom right) Bridgeman Images; p.637: (top) Photo 12/Alamy Stock Photo; (bottom left) Art Collection 4/Alamy Stock Photo; (bottom right) WorldPhotos/Alamy Stock Photo.

Primary Sources 14.1: Excerpts from *Montesquieu: The Spirit of the Laws*, Cambridge Texts in the History of Political Thought, translated and edited by Anne M. Cohler, Basia Carolyn Miller, and Harold Samuel Stone (Cambridge: Cambridge University Press, 1989), pp. 338–339. **14.3:** Jean-Jacques Rousseau, from *Rousseau's Political Writings: A Norton Critical Edition*, edited by Alan Ritter and Julia Conaway Bondanella, translated by Julia Conaway Bondanella. Copyright © 1988 by W.W. Norton & Company, Inc. Used by permission of W.W. Norton & Company, Inc. **14.4:** "The Testament of Shimai Soshitsu," from *Sources of Japanese Tradition, Second Edition, Vol. 2: 1600 to 2000*, compiled by Wm. Theodore de Bary, Carol Gluck, and Arthur E. Tiedemann, pp. 310–313. Copyright © 2005 Columbia University Press. Reprinted with permission of the publisher. **14.5:** Excerpts from "Two Edicts from the Ch'ien-Lung Emperor to King George III of England," in J. Mason Gentzler (ed.), *Changing China: Readings in the History of China from the Opium War to the Present*. Copyright © 1977 Praeger Publishers. Reprinted by permission of Cengage Learning.

CHAPTER 15

Photos Page 638: Bridgeman Images; p.440: Antiqua Print Gallery/Alamy Stock Photo; p.641: FALKENSTEINFOTO/Alamy Stock Photo; p.642: Library of Congress; p.646: Granger NYC; p.647: Chronicle/Alamy Stock Photo; p.648: Dagli Orti/REX/Shutterstock; p.649: Bridgeman Images; p.651: Sarin Images/Granger NYC; p.653: (left) Sarin Images/Granger NYC; (right) North Wind Picture Archives/Alamy Stock Photo; p.655: (left) Dagli Orti/REX/Shutterstock; (right) Granger NYC; p.656: Michael Graham-Stewart/Bridgeman Images; p.658: North Wind Picture Archives/Alamy Stock Photo; p.660: Sarin Images/Granger NYC; p.664: Courtesy of the Brooklyn Museum, Gift of Mr. and Mrs. Alastair B. Martin, the Guennol Collection; p.665: Sarin Images/Granger NYC; p.666: Archives Charmet/Bridgeman Images; p.667: Lebrecht Music & Arts/Alamy Stock Photo; p.668: National Army Museum, London/Bridgeman Images; p.670: (top) Granger NYC; (bottom) British Library Board/Bridgeman Images; p.671: The Art Archive/REX/Shutterstock; p.672: (left) British Library Board/Bridgeman Images; (right) Chronicle/Alamy Stock Photo; p.678: Roy Miles Fine Paintings/Bridgeman Images; p.676: Courtesy of the Brooklyn Museum, Gift of Mr. and Mrs. Alastair B. Martin, the Guennol Collection; p.677: Courtesy of the Brooklyn Museum, Gift of Mr. and Mrs. Carl L. Selden; p.684: (left) Erich Lessing/Art Resource, NY; (right) FineArt/Alamy Stock Photo; p.685: (left) Peter Willi/Bridgeman Images; (right) Historic Images/Alamy Stock Photo.

Primary Sources 15.2: Abd al-Rahman al-Jabarti, *Al-Jabarti's Chronicle of the First Seven Months of the French Occupation of Egypt*, translated by S. Moreh (Leiden, E.J. Brill, 1975), 39–40, 42–43, 46–47 © 1975 E.J. Brill, Leiden, Netherlands. Reprinted by permission of the publisher.

CHAPTER 16

Photos Page 686: Pictures from History/Bridgeman Images; p.688: The Picture Art Collection/Alamy Stock Photo; p.693: The History Collection Alamy Stock Photo; p.696: (left) GL Archive/Alamy Stock Photo; (right) Smith Archive/Alamy Stock Photo; p.697: Bonhams London UK/Bridgeman Images; p.699: Pictures from History/Bridgeman Images; p.700: PRISMA ARCHIVO/Alamy Stock Photo; p.703: Granger NYC; p.704: Lebrecht Music and Arts Photo Library/Alamy Stock Photo; p.707: (both) Granger NYC; p.708: Granger NYC; p.710: Witold Skrypczak/Alamy Stock Photo; p.712: Courtesy of the Brooklyn Museum, Gift of Mr. and Mrs. Alastair B. Martin, the Guennol Collection; p.714: Pictorial Press Ltd/Alamy Stock Photo; p.715: (left) Felice Beato/Public Domain; (right) V&A Images London/Art Resource NY; p.716: Artokoloro/Alamy Stock Photo; p.718: Courtesy of the Brooklyn Museum, Gift of Mr. and Mrs. Alastair B. Martin, the Guennol Collection; p.719: Courtesy of the Brooklyn Museum, Gift of Mr. and Mrs. Carl L. Selden; p.728: (left) World History Archive/Alamy Stock Photo; (right) Courtesy of Heidelberg Centre for Transcultural Studies/Universität Heidelberg; p.729: (left) Courtesy of the Bahia Museum of Art; (right) Art Collection 2/Alamy Stock Photo.

Primary Sources 16.2: Nana Asma'u, "Gikku Bello" from Beverly Mack & Jean Boyd (eds.), *One Woman's Jihad: Nana Asma'u, Scholar and Scribe*. Copyright © 2000 by Beverly B. Mack and Jean Boyd. Reprinted with permission of Indiana University Press. **16.4**: From "The Principles of the Heavenly Nature," in *Sources of Chinese Tradition, Second Edition, Vol. 2: From 1600 through the Twentieth Century*, compiled by Wm. Theodore de Bary and Richard Lufrano, pp. 226–30. Copyright © 2000 Columbia University Press. Reprinted with permission of the publisher. **16.5:** Karl Marx and Friedrich Engels, from "Bourgeoisie and Proletariat," in *The Marx–Engels Reader*, Second Edition (New York: W.W. Norton & Company, 1972), pp. 335–345. Edited by Robert C. Tucker.

CHAPTER 17

Photos Page 730: Granger; p.737: (both) Sarin Images/Granger NYC; p.738: Granger NYC; p.740: (left) Artokoloro/Alamy Stock Photo; (right) Magite Historic/Alamy Stock Photo; p.741: Dmitri Kessel/The LIFE Images Collection/Shutterstock; p.742: (left) Topical Press Agency/Getty Images; (right) Richardson/Fox Photos/Getty Images; p.745: Universal History Archive/Shutterstock; p.746: Library of Congress; p.747: (top) Peter Newark American Pictures/Bridgeman Images; (bottom) Hulton Archive/Illustrated London News/Getty Images; p.748: Chris Madden/Alamy Stock Photo; p.749: Private Collection (uncredited photo) from "Through Indian Eyes" by Judith Gutman, Oxford University Press; p.750: Chronicle/Alamy Stock Photo; p.751: (top) Hulton Archive/Getty Images; (bottom) Bridgeman Images; p.752: Dagli Orti/REX/Shutterstock; p.754: Rijksmuseum, Amsterdam, The Netherlands/Bridgeman Images; p.755: (top) Photo 12/Alamy Stock Photo; (bottom) The History Collection/Alamy Stock Photo; p.756: Photo 12/Alamy Stock Photo; p.757: Pictorial Press Ltd/Alamy Stock Photo; p.758: Courtesy of the Brooklyn Museum, Gift of Mr. and Mrs. Alastair B. Martin, the Guennol Collection; p.759: North Wind Picture Archives/Alamy Stock Photo; p.760: (top) Chronicle/Alamy Stock Photo; (bottom) Album/Alamy Stock Photo; p.762: Heritage Image Partnership Ltd/Alamy Stock Photo; p.763: Artokoloro/Alamy Stock Photo; p.765: Granger; p.767: Sovfoto/Universal Images Group/Shutterstock; p.771: Courtesy of the Brooklyn Museum, Gift of Mr. and Mrs. Carl L. Selden; p.778: (left) Kawanabe Kyosai 'School for Spooks' (Bake-bake gakko) no.3 from the series "Drawings for Pleasure by Kyosai" (Kyosai Rakuga) Kawanabe Kyosai Memorial Museum; (right) Granger NYC; p.779: Library of Congress.

CHAPTER 18

Photos Page 780: SuperStock; p.783: (left) Library of Congress; (right) Roger Viollet/Getty Images; p.786: Courtesy of the Brooklyn Museum, Gift of Mr. and Mrs. Alastair B. Martin, the Guennol Collection; p.787: Chronicle/Alamy Stock Photo; p.788: Library of Congress/Corbis/VCG via Getty Images; p.790: ullstein bild/Granger NYC; p.791: akg-images/Alamy Stock Photo; p.793: Pictures from History/Bridgeman Images; p.794: SuperStock; p.795: Science History Images/Alamy Stock Photo; p.796: (left) RBM Vintage Images/Alamy Stock Photo; (right) Hulton-Deutsch/Getty Images; p.797: Public Domain via Wikipedia; p.798: Bettmann/Getty Images; p.799: (left) Dagli Orti/REX/Shutterstock; (right) Sean Sprague/Mexicolore/Bridgeman Images/© 2023 Banco de México Diego Rivera Frida Kahlo Museums Trust, Mexico, D.F./Artists Rights Society (ARS), New York; p.800: Snark/Art Resource NY; p.801: Art Library/Alamy Stock Photo/© 2023 Estate of Pablo Picasso/Artists Rights Society (ARS), New York; p.802: (left) National Gallery London/Art Resource NY; (right) Erich Lessing/Art Resource NY; p.803: The Artchives/Alamy Stock Photo; p.804: (left) Mary Evans Picture Library/SIGMUND FREUD COPYRIGHTS; (right) Historic Collection/Alamy Stock Photo; p.807: Christie's Images/Bridgeman Images; p.808: (left) Courtesy of Porviroscópio/Acervo Iconographia; (right) Museu da Imagem e do Som do Estado do Rio de Janeiro; p.809: Schalkwijk/Art Resource NY./© 2023 Banco de México Diego Rivera Frida Kahlo Museums Trust, Mexico, D.F./Artists Rights Society (ARS), New York; p.811: (left) SZ Photo/Bridgeman Images; (right) Granger; p.812: Art Collection 2/Alamy Stock Photo; p.813: (left) E. O. Hoppe/Getty Images; (right) Dagli Orti/REX/Shutterstock; p.816: Courtesy of the Brooklyn Museum, Gift of Mr. and Mrs. Alastair B. Martin, the Guennol Collection; p.817: Courtesy of the Brooklyn Museum, Gift of Mr. and Mrs. Carl L. Selden; p.824: (left) Art Library/Alamy Stock Photo/© 2023 Estate of Pablo Picasso/Artists Rights Society (ARS), New York; (right) The Picture Art Collection/Alamy Stock Photo; p.825: steeve-x-art/Alamy Stock Photo.

Primary Sources 18.2: Maria Eugenia Echenique: "The Emancipation of Women." Translated by Francisco Manzo Robledo in Paul Brians, et. al., *Reading About the World, Vol. 2.* (1999). Reprinted by permission of Francisco Manzo Robledo. **18.3:** Qui Jin, "An Address to Two Hundred Million Fellow Countrywomen." Reprinted with the permission of Simon & Schuster Publishing Group, a division of Simon & Schuster, Inc., from the Free Press edition of *Chinese Civilization: A Sourcebook*, Second Edition, by Patricia Buckley Ebrey. Copyright © 1993 by Patricia Buckley Ebrey. Copyright © 1981 by The Free Press. All rights reserved. **18.4:** Bahithat al-Badiya "A Lecture in the Club of the Umma Party (1909)" from Margot Badran and Miriam Cooke (eds.), *Opening the Gates: An Anthology of Arab Feminist Writing*, 2nd edition. Copyright © 2004 by Margot Badran and Miriam Cooke. Reprinted with permission of Indiana University Press.

CHAPTER 19

Photos Page 826: Bridgeman Images; p.828: Public Domain; p.831: Heritage Image Partnership Ltd/Alamy Stock Photo; p.834: Courtesy of the Brooklyn Museum, Gift of Mr. and Mrs. Alastair B. Martin, the Guennol Collection; p.835: Three Lions/Getty Images; p.836: (left) Everett Collection Historical/Alamy Stock Photo; (right) ullstein bild via Getty Images; p.840: (left) Album Alamy Stock Photo; (right) Library of Congress; p.841: ullstein bild/Granger NYC; p.842: Chronicle/Alamy Stock Photo; p.843: Hulton Archive/Getty Images; p.844: Granger NYC; p.846: (top) Photo 12/Alamy Stock Photo; (bottom) Library of Congress; p.847: Hulton Archive/Getty Images; p.848: Granger NYC; p.849: Shawshots/Alamy Stock Photo; p.850: Pictorial Press Ltd/Alamy Stock Photo; p.852: (top) Keystone Press/Alamy Stock Photo; (bottom) Photo 12/Alamy Stock Photo; p.854: Heinrich Hoffmann/The LIFE Picture Collection/Shutterstock; p.855: (left) The Art Archive/REX/Shutterstock; (right)Genevieve Naylor/Corbis via Getty Images; p.857: Granger NYC; p.858: (both) Bridgeman Images; p.859: (left) Dinodia Photos/Alamy Stock Photo; (right) ullstein bild via Getty Images; p.860: Sueddeutsche Zeitung Photo/Alamy Stock Photo; p.862: Courtesy of the Brooklyn Museum, Gift of Mr. and Mrs. Alastair B. Martin, the Guennol Collection; p.863: Courtesy of the Brooklyn Museum, Gift of Mr. and Mrs. Carl L. Selden; p.868: Science and Society/SuperStock; p.869: (top) Gift of Edsel B. Ford/Bridgeman Images; (bottom left) Granger Collection; (bottom right) Everett Collection Inc/Alamy.

Primary Sources 19.1: Hannah Arendt, excerpt from *The Origins of Totalitarianism* by Hannah Arendt. Copyright © 1948, 1951, 1966, 1968. Copyright renewed 1976 by Hannah Arendt. Copyright renewed 1994 by Lotte Kohler. Copyright renewed 1979 by Mary McCarthy West. Used by permission of HarperCollins Publishers. And by permission of Penguin Books Ltd. **19.2:** Letter from Anna Kovaleva to Marfa Gudzia in Stephen Kotkin: "Coercion and Identity: Workers' Lives in Stalin's Showcase City," in *Making Workers Soviet: Power, Class, and Identity*, edited by Lewis H. Siegelbaum and Ronald Grigor. Copyright © 1995 by Cornell University. Used by permission of the publisher, Cornell University Press. **19.3:** Victor Klemperer. "1938" from *I Will Bear Witness, Volume 1: A Diary of the Nazi Years: 1933–1941*, translated by Martin Chalmers, translation copyright © 1998 by Martin Chalmers. Used by permission of Random House, an imprint and division of Penguin Random House LLC. All rights reserved. And by permission of The Orion Publishing Group. **19.4:** Excerpt from *Japan in War and Peace*. Copyright © 1993 by John W. Dower. Reprinted by permission of The New Press, www.thenewpress.com, and by permission of Georges Borchardt Inc. for the author.

CHAPTER 20

Photos Page 870: Hulton Deutsch/Getty Images; p.873: (top) Shawshots/Alamy Stock Photo; (bottom) World History Archive/Alamy Stock Photo; p.875: Patrizia Wyss/Alamy Stock Photo; p.876: Courtesy of the Brooklyn Museum, Gift of Mr. and Mrs. Alastair B. Martin, the Guennol Collection; p.879: Three Lions/Getty Images; p.880: Hulton Deutsch/Getty Images; p.881: (top) Everett Collection Historical/Alamy Stock Photo; (bottom) Bettmann/Getty Images; p.884: Granger NYC; p.886: (top) World History Archive/Alamy Stock Photo; (bottom) Bettmann/Getty Images; p.887: Bettmann/Getty Images; p.889: (top) Bettmann/Getty Images; (bottom) SPUTNIK/Alamy Stock Photo; p.890: Heritage Image Partnership Ltd/Alamy Stock Photo; p.891: Hulton Archive/Getty Images; p.892: (top) Stroud/Express/Getty Images; (bottom) FPG/Getty Images; p.893: Hulton Archive/Getty Images; p.894: The Print Collector/Alamy Stock Photo; p.895: (both) Bettmann/Getty Images; p.896: (left) Associated

Press; (right) Granger; (bottom) akg-images; p.897: The Reading Room/Alamy Stock Photo; p.898: Sovfoto/UIG/age rootstock; p.902: (left) Roger-Viollet/TopFoto; p.(right) Bettmann/Getty Images; p.903: (left) World History Archive/Alamy Stock Photo; (right) AP Photo; p.904: Bettmann/Getty Images; p.905: (left) AP Photo/Alvin Quinn; (right) Rolls Press/Popperfoto/Getty Images; p.907: CTK/Alamy Stock Photo; p.909: STR/AFP via Getty Image; p.910: Courtesy of the Brooklyn Museum, Gift of Mr. and Mrs. Alastair B. Martin, the Guennol Collection; p.911: Courtesy of the Brooklyn Museum, Gift of Mr. and Mrs. Carl L. Selden; p.920: (left) Museum Associates/LACMA. Licensed by Art Resource; (right) AF Fotografie/Alamy Stock Photo; p.921: (left) George Rodger/Magnum Photos; (right) Pictures from History/Granger, NY.

Primary Sources 20.1: Mao Zedong, *Selected Works*, in *Sources of Chinese Tradition, Second Edition, Vol. 2: From 1600 through the Twentieth Century*, compiled by Wm. Theodore de Bary and Richard Lufrano, pp. 418–23. Copyright © 2000 Columbia University Press. Reprinted with permission of the publisher. **20.3:** "What Is Negritude?" From a Speech Delivered at Oxford University, England October 26, 1961. Reprinted by permission of the Estate of Léopold Sédar Senghor. **20.4:** Frantz Fanon, "On Violence." From *The Wretched of the Earth*. English translation copyright © 1963 by Présence Africaine. Used by permission of Grove/Atlantic, Inc. Any third-party use of this material, outside of this publication, is prohibited.

CHAPTER 21

Photos Page 922: AP Photo/Anat Givon; p.925: Keystone/Getty Images; p.927: REX/Shutterstock; p.929: Peter Turnley/Corbis/VCG via Getty Images; p.931: david pearson Alamy Stock Photo; p.932: Dana Fradon/CartoonStock; p.934: Courtesy of the Brooklyn Museum, Gift of Mr. and Mrs. Alastair B. Martin, the Guennol Collection; p.938: GEORGE ESIRI/REUTERS; p.939: Uriel Sinai/Getty Images; p.940: © Eros International/ Courtesy: Everett Collection; p.941: (top) Michael Ochs Archives/Getty Images; (bottom left) Nick Laham/Getty Images; (bottom right) Jim McIsaac/Getty Images; p.942: JSK/Alamy Stock Photo; p.943: Serge Attal/Getty Images; p.945: (left) FotoFlirt/Alamy Stock Photo; (right) LEE JAE-WON/REUTERS; p.946: (top left) Gisele Wulfsohn/Panos Pictures; (top right) Chris Johnson/Panos Pictures; (bottom) Vanessa Vick/Redux; p.948: AP Photo/Anat Givon; p.949: (top) Morley Read/Alamy Stock Photo; (bottom) Susan I. Cunningham/Panos Pictures; p.951: (left) AP Photo/Jose Luis Magana; (right) SPUTNIK/Alamy Stock Photo; p.952: Colin McConnell/Toronto Star via Getty Images; p.954: Tom Stoddart Archive/Getty Images; p.955: Peter Turnley/Corbis/VCG via Getty Images; p.956: GABRIEL DUVAL/AFP via Getty Images; p.957: Bettmann/Getty Images; p.958: AP Photo/Jeff Widener; p.959: (top) David Alfaro Siqueiros/Schalkwijk/ Art Resource NY/© 2023 Artists Rights Society (ARS), New York/SOMAAP, Mexico City; (bottom) Clive Shirley/Panos Pictures/Redux; p.960: Courtesy of the Brooklyn Museum, Gift of Mr. and Mrs. Alastair B. Martin, the Guennol Collection; p.961: Courtesy of the Brooklyn Museum, Gift of Mr. and Mrs. Carl L. Selden; p.968: (top left) The Asahi Shimbun via Getty Images; (top right) BOBBY YIP/REUTERS; (bottom left) David South/Alamy Stock Photo; (bottom right) Jim Thompson/Albuquerque Journal/ZUMA Wire/Alamy Live News; p.969: Farshid M. Bina/picture-alliance/dpa/AP Images.

Primary Sources 21.1: Václev Havel, "The Power of the Powerless, in *The Power of the Powerless: Citizens Against the State in Central-Eastern Europe* (M.E. Sharpe, 1985), edited by John Keane. © 1985 Taylor & Francis. Reprinted by permission of Taylor and Francis Books UK. **21.3:** The World Bank**,** From Box 7.2 "Using subsidies to close gender gaps in education," World Bank. 2001. World Development Report 2000/2001: Attacking Poverty. World Development Report. New York: Oxford University Press. © World Bank. https://openknowledge.worldbank.org/handle/10986/11856 License: CC BY 3.0 IGO. **21.4:** Amartya Kumar Sen, "Democracy as a Universal Value." *Journal of Democracy* 10:3 (1999), 6–9. © 1999 National Endowment for Democracy and the Johns Hopkins University Press. Reprinted with permission of Johns Hopkins University Press.

CHAPTER 22

Photos Page 970: SOPA Images Limited/Alamy Stock Photo; p.972: (left) AP Photo/Carmen Taylor; (right) US Navy Photo/Alamy Stock Photo; p.973: (top) PA Images/Alamy Stock Photo; (bottom) EyePress/Newscom; p.975: AP Photo/Jason DeCrow; p.976: (left) Kyle Niemi/U.S. Coast Guard via Getty Images; (right) SAUL LOEB/AFP via Getty Images; p.977: AP Photo/Rich Schultz; p.978: Go Nakamura/Getty Images; p.979: Sipa USA/Alamy Stock Photo; p.980: Jane Campbell/Shutterstock; p.982: Courtesy of the Brooklyn Museum, Gift of Mr. and Mrs. Alastair B. Martin, the Guennol Collection; p.988: (left) AP Photo/Mustafa Quraishi; (right) AP Photo/Andres Kudacki; p.988: MIKE BLAKE/REUTERS; p.992: Nina Liashonok/Ukrinform/Abaca/Sipa USA via AP Images; p.993: (left) ullsteinbild/TopFoto; (right) Timothy O'Rourke/Bloomberg via Getty Images; p.994: AP Photo/Kin Cheung; p.996: AP Photo/Dar Yasin; p.997: (left) Sebastian D'Souza/AFP/Getty Images; (right) AP Photo/Channi Anand; p.1002: AP Photo/Nasser Nasser; p.1004: Alamy Stock Photo; p.1007: (left) Liba Taylor/Corbis Documentary/Getty Images; (right) Herman Wouters/Hollandse Hoogte/Redux; p.1009: (left) Militant video/Site Institute via AP; (right) JASON REED/REUTERS; p.1010: AP Photo/Alexandre Meneghini; p.1010: Xinhua/Alamy Stock Photo; p.1011: (left) Alexander Hassenstein/Getty Images; (right) Kayhan Ozer/Anadolu Agency/Getty Images; p.1012: Michael Nigro/Pacific Press/LightRocket via Getty Images; p.1013: SOPA Images Limited/Alamy Stock Photo; p.1014: Greg Gard/Alamy Stock Photo; p.1017: Courtesy of the Brooklyn Museum, Gift of Mr. and Mrs. Carl L. Selden; p.1024: (left) K M Asad/LightRocket via Getty Images; (right) AP Photo; p.1025: (left) AP Photo/Dolores Ochoa; (right) AP Photo/Nilufer Demir, DHA; p.1026: (left) Ted Soqui/Reuters; (right) AP Photo/Frank Augstein.

Primary Sources 22.1: Excerpted from "Issue Brief: The Paris Agreement on Climate Change," December, 2015, by NRDC, https://nrdc.org/sites/default/files/paris-climate-agreement-IB.pdf. Reprinted with permission. **22.3:** Greta Thunberg, "The World Is Waking Up (UN General Assembly, NYC 9/23/19)" from *No One is Too Small to Make a Difference* by Greta Thunberg, copyright © 2018, 2019 by Greta Thunberg. Used by permission of Penguin Books, an imprint of Penguin Publishing Group, a division of Penguin Random House LLC. All rights reserved. And by permission of Penguin Books Ltd. **22.4:** Excerpts from UNEP (2019). Emissions Gap Report 2019. Executive summary. United Nations Environment Programme, Nairobi. Reprinted with permission.

Index

Italic page references indicate maps, illustrations, or chronology entries.

C

O

Q

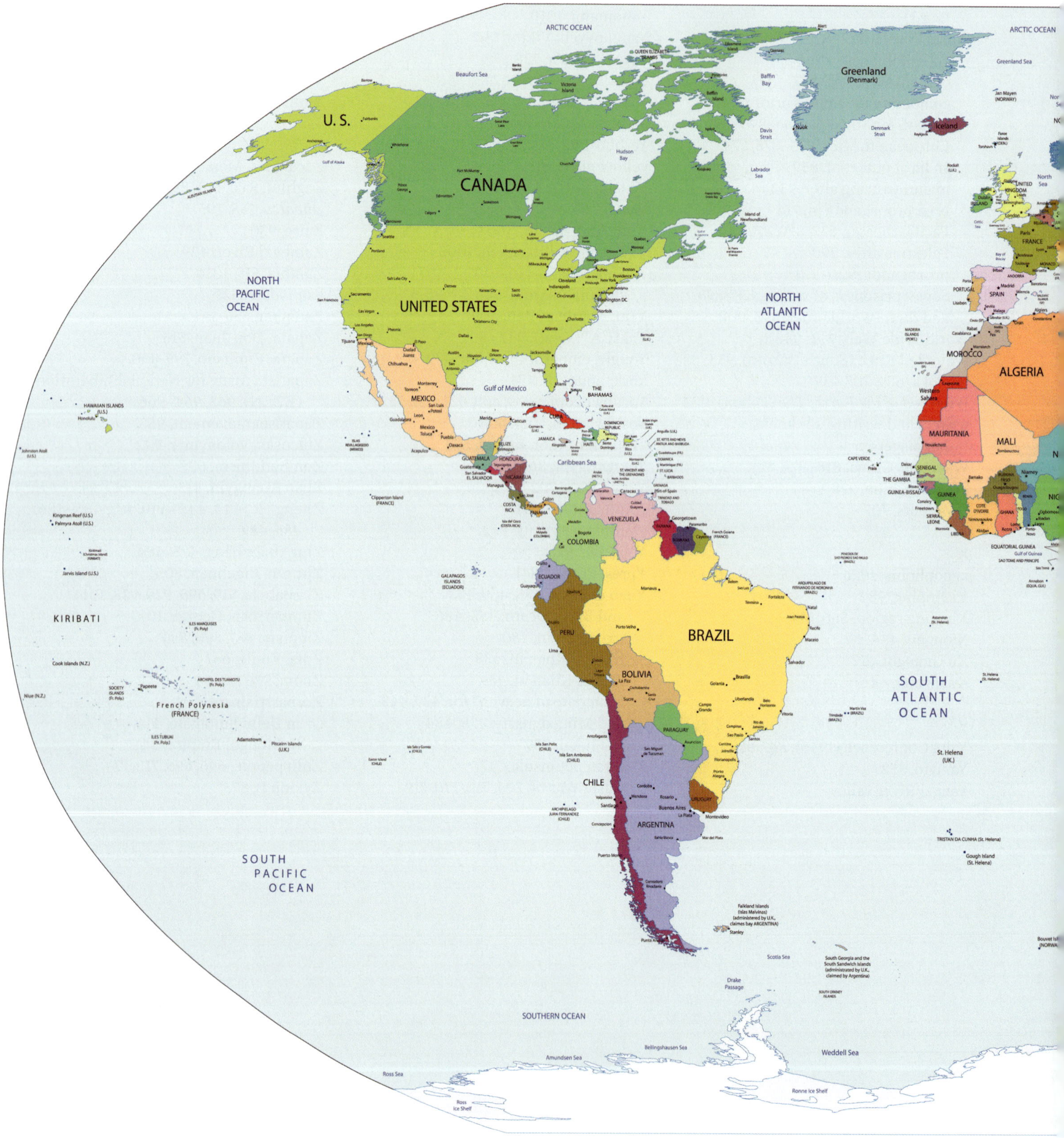

ARCTIC OCEAN
Greenland
(Denmark)
Greenland Sea
Beaufort Sea
Baffin Bay
Iceland
U. S.
CANADA
Hudson Bay
Labrador Sea
Gulf of Alaska
NORTH PACIFIC OCEAN
UNITED STATES
NORTH ATLANTIC OCEAN
Gulf of Mexico
THE BAHAMAS
MEXICO
CUBA
HAITI
JAMAICA
Caribbean Sea
GUATEMALA
HONDURAS
NICARAGUA
COSTA RICA
PANAMA
VENEZUELA
COLOMBIA
ECUADOR
PERU
BRAZIL
BOLIVIA
PARAGUAY
CHILE
ARGENTINA
URUGUAY
HAWAIIAN ISLANDS (U.S.)
KIRIBATI
French Polynesia
(FRANCE)
SOUTH PACIFIC OCEAN
SOUTH ATLANTIC OCEAN
St. Helena (U.K.)
SPAIN
PORTUGAL
FRANCE
MOROCCO
ALGERIA
Western Sahara
MAURITANIA
MALI
CAPE VERDE
SENEGAL
THE GAMBIA
GUINEA-BISSAU
GUINEA
SIERRA LEONE
LIBERIA
GHANA
EQUATORIAL GUINEA
Gulf of Guinea
Scotia Sea
Drake Passage
SOUTHERN OCEAN
Amundsen Sea
Bellingshausen Sea
Weddell Sea
Ross Sea
Ross Ice Shelf
Ronne Ice Shelf

ARCTIC OCEAN
Barents Sea
Kara Sea
Laptev Sea
East Siberian Sea
RUSSIA
SWEDEN
FINLAND
UKRAINE
ROMANIA
POLAND
BELARUS
KAZAKHSTAN
MONGOLIA
Black Sea
TURKEY
UZBEKISTAN
TURKMENISTAN
Sea of Okhotsk
Bering Sea
ALEUTIAN ISLANDS (U.S.)
KURIL ISLANDS
Occupied by SOVIET UNION in 1945, administered by RUSSIA, claimed by JAPAN
NORTH PACIFIC OCEAN
JAPAN
NORTH KOREA
SOUTH KOREA
Sea of Japan
Yellow Sea
East China Sea
CHINA
Mediterranean Sea
SYRIA
IRAQ
IRAN
AFGHANISTAN
PAKISTAN
NEPAL
BHUTAN
BANGLADESH
LIBYA
EGYPT
SAUDI ARABIA
QATAR
OMAN
YEMEN
INDIA
BURMA
LAOS
THAILAND
CAMBODIA
VIETNAM
PHILIPPINES
Philippine Sea
South China Sea
Bay of Bengal
Arabian Sea
CHAD
SUDAN
ERITREA
DJIBOUTI
ETHIOPIA
SOMALIA
CENTRAL AFRICAN REPUBLIC
UGANDA
KENYA
DEMOCRATIC REPUBLIC OF THE CONGO
RWANDA
BURUNDI
TANZANIA
ANGOLA
ZAMBIA
MALAWI
MOZAMBIQUE
ZIMBABWE
NAMIBIA
BOTSWANA
SOUTH AFRICA
SWAZILAND
MADAGASCAR
Mozambique Channel
SEYCHELLES
MALDIVES
SRI LANKA
MAURITIUS
INDIAN OCEAN
MALAYSIA
SINGAPORE
INDONESIA
PALAU
PAPUA NEW GUINEA
SOLOMON ISLANDS
Celebes Sea
Java Sea
Banda Sea
Arafura Sea
Timor Sea
Coral Sea
FEDERATED STATES OF MICRONESIA
MARSHALL ISLANDS
KIRIBATI
TUVALU
SAMOA
VANUATU
FIJI
TONGA
AUSTRALIA
Great Australian Bight
Tasman Sea
NEW ZEALAND
SOUTH PACIFIC OCEAN
French Southern and Antarctic Lands (France)
SOUTHERN OCEAN
Ross Sea
Ross Ice Shelf
tarctica